The Complete Results & Line-ups of the European Champions League 1991-2004

Romeo Ionescu

About the author

Romeo Ionescu was born in Ploiesti, Romania, on 19th December 1962. He fell in love with football statistics the first time he held a sports newspaper in 1970 and since then has collected a great number of sports newspapers, magazines and books, now possessing around 20,000 items. He began to collate statistics when he was a schoolboy and continued as a student in Bucuresti, where he completed his Romanian football statistics, spending hundreds of hours in two national libraries. Romeo began to exchange magazines and footballing material with other enthusiasts overseas in 1985 including his Dutch friend Kees Doeleman. Kees sparked Romeo's interest with European Cup line-ups and provided a lot of match details, which eventually led to production of a book about this competition. After collaborating on several books including *The European Football Yearbook*, *Annuario del Calcio Mondiale*, and a Romanian yearbook, Romeo published his first book, *An Encyclopedia of Romanian Football,* in 2000, followed by books on The European Cup and The European Championship amongst others. By profession a mechanical engineer, he now works as a full-time football statistician and is seeking an appointment with an international agency.

British Library Cataloguing in Publication Data
A catalogue record for this book is available from the British Library

ISBN 1-86223-114-1

Printed by 4edge Ltd. www.4edge.co.uk

FOREWORD

'Hail Wolves v Champions of the World', screamed the headlines one grey December morning in 1954. Wolverhampton Wanderers had recovered from a two-goal deficit to beat Honvéd of Budapest, a significant event maybe, but hardly justifying an outburst of British chauvinism.

Much of the euphoria stemmed from the make-up of the Hungarian team. Puskas, Kocsis and four others had been in national side, which had twice slaughtered England, scoring 13 goals, in the previous 13 months. But Wolves had been favoured by conditions with more incentive than their opponents (who were simply on a European jaunt), and had survived a number of goalmouth escapes earlier in the game. While British eyes viewed the result through rose-tinted spectacles, more objectivity was revealed elsewhere in Europe.

The most far-sighted reaction came from France. In the daily sports paper L'Equipe, the editor Gabriel Hannot decried the overreaction of the English. He wrote: 'We must wait for Wolves to visit Moscow or Budapest before we proclaim their invincibility. There are other clubs of international prowess, notably Milan and Real Madrid to name but two ...'

Hannot's opinion had no emptiness. The next day the paper devoted much space to outline plans for a European tournament, in which patriotic boasts could be put to test. It was not an original thought; there had already been international competitions like the Mitropa Cup before the Second World War, which featured the leading club sides in Austria, Czechoslovakia, Hungary, Yugoslavia and later Switzerland, Italy and Romania. And after the War France, Italy, Spain and Portugal played one another for the Latin Cup. But L'Equipe's plan provided for the whole of Europe, and Gabriel Hannot called for the support of UEFA.

This campaign from France originated an entirely new era in football. Not only did UEFA accept the proposal except for the name (UEFA preferred European Champion Clubs' Cup to Hannot's European Cup, which they wanted to keep for a national sides' competition) but in their acceptance they took a step which certainly cracked and even broke down much of the traditional insularity of top-class club football. Aided by the parallel development of floodlighting, which made practicable the extra fixtures which had to be played in midweek, the European Champion Club's Cup became a tremendous success – though officials might have been a little peeved that their lengthy nomenclature was immediately shortened into the European Cup.

As the European dream became reality, the commercial prospects of international club competition were not lost on the continent's leading participants. Before the end of the decade, the European Cup Winners' Cup had been instituted as a spin-off tournament, while in 1958 the first official contest between national sides, the European Nations Cup, began its life span. Oddly, the actual name European Cup has never been utilised.

The first European Cup tie was played on 4th September 1955, between Sporting Club de Portugal from Lisbon and Partizan of Belgrade; just four days later Real Madrid set out on an astounding run during which they would not lose an aggregate tie for five years!

The first competition commenced in 1955 and comprised 16 entrants, 8 of whom were not actually the reigning champions of their countries at the time. Over the years the number of entrants increased until there were regularly 32 teams competing for the trophy. Between the years of 1955 to 1991 each tie was played on a knock-out basis over two legs and a sister title to this book, *The Complete Results and Line-ups of the European Champion Clubs' Cup 1955-1991 – The Knockout Years*, is also available. This contains full statistics for every game played in the competition during this period.

The 1991-92 season saw the beginning of a new era with the start of the so-called "Champions League". This money-spinning new format saw entrants grouped in Leagues of four teams in certain stages of the competition. Together with a gradual increase in entrants (up to a high of 72 for 2000-2003) this has led to a huge rise in the number of lucrative matches to be played meaning qualification for the Champions League is vitally important for Europe's major teams. This book features every match played since the competition changed to this new League format.

The statistical information contained in this book is a result of 10 years work during which time I have referenced thousands of pages in newspapers and books and I was also helped by many other statisticians. Special thanks are reserved for Kees Doeleman from Almere in Holland for the line-ups, first names of players and photocopies he sent me over a period of many years. Thanks also go to Dirk Karsdorp, Daniel Paquereau, Santiago Velasco, Christian Cusumano and Soccer Books Limited who publish this book. From the many books I have used as a reference, special mention goes to *The European Football Yearbook*, *Annuario del Calcio Mondiale* and *A Statistical History of British Clubs in European Competition.*

I have endeavoured to make the contents of this book as accurate as possible but often, checking two different sources leads to different information for the same match. In cases such as this I have used the most trustworthy information I could find.

Thoughout this book, rather than use English spellings, I have used the correct spelling of Club names and places as used in the country of origin. For example, Rome is Roma, Copenhagen is København etc. If a club's name does not include the name of the town or city from which they originate, this name has been appended. For example, Chelsea and Heart of Midlothian become Chelsea London and Heart of Midlothian Edinburgh accordingly.

Romeo Ionescu

THE EUROPEAN CUP 1991-92

FIRST ROUND

1.FC KAISERSLAUTERN v ETAR VELIKO TÎRNOVO 2-0 (1-0)

Fritz-Walter-Stadion, Kaiserslautern 17.09.1991

Referee: Fortunato Alves de Azevedo (POR) Att: 34,000

1.FC KAISERSLAUTERN: Gerald Ehrmann; Thomas Dooley, Wolfgang Funkel, Oliver Schäfer, Andreas Kröhler, Marco Haber, Demir Hotić, Marcel Witeczek, Markus Kranz, Jürgen Degen, Bernhard Winkler (62 Roger Lutz). Trainer: Karl-Heinz Feldkamp

ETAR: Oleg Morgun; Zvetomir Parvanov, Angel Chervenkov, Rumen Ivanov, Georgi Georgiev (77 Kancho Iordanov), Aleksandar Dimov, Nikolai Gavaliugov, Plamen Petkov, Zanko Zvetanov, Preslav Getov (56 Igor Kislov), Andrian Gaidarski. Trainer: Georgi Vasilev

Goals: Funkel (38 pen, 74)

ETAR VELIKO TÎRNOVO v 1.FC KAISERSLAUTERN 1-1 (1-0)

Ivailo, Veliko Tîrnovo 2.10.1991

Referee: Vadim Zhuk (USSR) Attendance: 12,500

ETAR: Oleg Morgun; Zvetomir Parvanov, Rumen Ivanov, Angel Chervenkov, Georgi Georgiev, Aleksandar Dimov, Plamen Petkov (66 Igor Kislov), Georgi Popivanov (67 Nikolai Gavaliugov), Zanko Zvetanov, Preslav Getov, Petar Vitanov. Trainer: Georgi Vasilev

1.FC KAISERSLAUTERN: Gerald Ehrmann; Wolfgang Funkel, Oliver Schäfer, Reinhard Stumpf, Roger Lutz (88 Uwe Scherr), Bjarne Goldbæk, Demir Hotić, Thomas Dooley, Marcel Witeczek, Bernhard Winkler (74 Jürgen Degen), Thomas Vogel. Trainer: Karl-Heinz Feldkamp

Goals: Chervenkov (45), Degen (90)

CRVENA ZVEZDA BEOGRAD v PORTADOWN FC 4-0 (2-0)

Felsótiszaparti, Szeged 17.09.1991

Referee: Hasan Ceylan (TUR) Attendance: 7,000

CRVENA ZVEZDA: Dragoje Leković; Dusko Radinović, Miroslav Tanjga, Vladimir Jugović, Miodrag Belodedić, Ilija Najdoski, Vlada Stosić, Vladan Lukić, Ilija Ivić (69 Predrag Jovanović), Milorad Ratković, Sinisa Mihajlović. Trainer: Vladimir Popović

PORTADOWN: Michael Keenan; Philip Major, Ian Curliss, Philip Mitchell, Brian Strain, Alfie Stewart, Paul Doolin, Martin Russell, Sandy Fraser, Gregg Davidson, Stevie Cowan. Trainer: Ronnie McFall

Goals: Tanjga (15), Stosić (37), Mihajlović (77, 85)

PORTADOWN FC v CRVENA ZVEZDA BEOGRAD 0-4 (0-2)

Shamrock Park, Portadown 2.10.1991

Referee: Tore Hollung (NOR) Attendance: 5,000

PORTADOWN: Michael Keenan; Philip Major, Kevin McKeever, Philip Mitchell, Brian Strain, Alfie Stewart, Paul Doolin, Martin Russell, Sandy Fraser, Stevie Cowan, Gregg Davidson. Trainer: Ronnie McFall

CRVENA ZVEZDA: Dragoje Leković; Sasa Nedeljković, Miroslav Tanjga, Vladimir Jugović, Miodrag Belodedić, Ilija Najdoski, Vlada Stosić, Vladan Lukić, Darko Pancev, Milorad Ratković, Sinisa Mihajlović (46 Dusko Radinović). Trainer: Vladimir Popović

Goals: Ratković (19, 59), Pancev (38), Radinović (87)

UNION SPORTIVE LUXEMBOURG v OLYMPIQUE de MARSEILLE 0-5 (0-4)

Stade Municipal "Neue Stadion", Luxembourg 18.09.1991

Referee: Michael Caulfield (IRE) Attendance: 9,000

US LUXEMBOURG: John Van Rijswijck; David Borbiconi, Thomas Wolf, Luc Feiereisen, Marc Birsens, Serge Thill, Joël Groff, Gérard Jeitz, Denis Mogenot, Patrick Morocutti, Fabien Mellinger. Trainer: Alex Pecquer

OLYMPIQUE: Pascal Olmeta; Jocelyn Angloma, Basile Boli, Bernard Casoni, Manuel Amoros, Didier Deschamps (72 Patrice Eyraud), Franck Sauzée, Christopher Waddle, Abédi Pelé, Daniel Xuereb (61 Trevor Steven), Jean-Pierre Papin. Trainer: Tomislav Ivić

Goals: Papin (11, 32, 85 pen), Xuereb (15), Sauzée (45)

OLYMPIQUE de MARSEILLE v UNION SPORTIVE LUXEMBOURG 5-0 (1-0)

Vélodrome, Marseille 2.10.1991

Referee: Loizos Loizou (CYP) Attendance: 15,000

OLYMPIQUE: Pascal Olmeta; Jean-Christophe Marquet, Basile Boli (60 Bernard Casoni), José Carlos Mopomuceno Mozer, Manuel Amoros, Jocelyn Angloma, Franck Sauzée (65 Didier Deschamps), Patrice Eyraud, Philippe Durand, Jean-Pierre Papin, Daniel Xuereb. Trainer: Tomislav Ivić

US LUXEMBOURG: John Van Rijswijck; Thomas Wolf, Luc Feiereisen, David Borbiconi, Marc Birsens, Denis Mogenot, Joël Groff (75 Marc Chaussy), Gérard Jeitz, Serge Thill (75 Fernand Heinisch), Patrick Morocutti, Fabien Mellinger. Trainer: Alex Pecquer

Goals: Papin (15, 47), Angloma (56), Eyraud (60), Xuereb (75)

BRØNDBY IF v ZAGLEBIE LUBIN 3-0 (0-0)

Brøndby Stadion, København 18.09.1991

Referee: Wieland Ziller (GER) Attendance: 7,752

BRØNDBY: Mogens Krogh; Brian Jensen, Uche Okechukwu, Erik Rasmussen (83 Friday Elahor), Bjarne Jensen, John Jensen, Henrik Jensen, Kim Christofte, Kim Vilfort, Ronnie Ekelund (74 Ole Bjur), Claus Nielsen. Trainer: Morten Olsen

ZAGLEBIE: Krzysztof Koszarski; Stefan Machaj, Piotr Czachowski, Andrzej Wójcik, Zdzislaw Pietrzykowski, Zbigniew Szewczyk, Bogdan Pisz, Maciej Sliwowski, Miroslaw Prokop (86 Mariusz Olbinski), Aleksandr Gitselov, Leslaw Grech (78 Robert Stachurski). Trainer: Marian Putyra

Goals: Christofte (53 pen), Ekelund (58), Okechukwu (73)

DUNDALK FC v KISPEST HONVÉD BUDAPEST 0-2 (0-2)

Oriel Park, Dundalk 2.10.1991

Referee: Roger Phillippi (LUX) Attendance: 3,500

DUNDALK: Alan O'Neill; David Mackey, Mick Shelley, Ronnie Murphy, James Coll, Peter Hanrahan, Paul Brady, Ricky McEvoy, Terry Eviston, Gino Lawless, Brian Irwin (64 Michael Kavanagh). Trainer: Turlough O'Connor

KISPEST HONVÉD: István Gulyás; József Csábi, András Csepregi, Balázs Bérczy, Attila Plókai, Ervin Kovács, András Cseh, János Marozsán (46 Gábor Halmai), István Vincze, István Pisont, Adrian Negrău. Trainer: György Mezey

Goals: Pisont (24, 29)

ZAGLEBIE LUBIN v BRØNDBY IF 2-1 (0-1)

Zaglebie, Lubin 2.10.1991

Referee: Anders Frisk (SWE) Attendance: 4,000

ZAGLEBIE: Krzysztof Koszarski; Andrzej Wójcik, Zdzislaw Pietrzykowski, Piotr Czachowski, Stefan Machaj, Mariusz Urbaniak, Robert Stachurski (46 Bogdan Pisz), Maciej Sliwowski, Aleksandr Gitselov (46 Leslaw Grech), Mariusz Olbinski, Miroslaw Prokop. Trainer: Marian Putyra

BRØNDBY: Mogens Krogh; Jens Madsen, Brian Jensen, Friday Elahor (18 Jesper Kristensen), Uche Okechukwu, John Jensen, Kim Christofte, Henrik Jensen, Kim Vilfort, Ole Bjur, Ronnie Ekelund (74 Thomas Madsen).
Trainer: Morten Olsen

Goals: Vilfort (28), Czachowski (60), Grech (72)

AC SPARTA PRAHA v GLASGOW RANGERS FC 1-0 (1-0)

Stadión na Letnej, Praha 18.09.1991

Referee: Hubert Forstinger (AUS) Attendance: 11,000

SPARTA: Petr Kouba; Michal Horňák, Jiří Novotný, Jan Sopko, Petr Vrabec, Lumír Mistr, Václav Němeček, Martin Frýdek, Jiří Němec, Horst Siegl (89 Vítězslav Lavička), Pavel Cerný. Trainer: Dušan Uhrín

RANGERS: Andy Goram; Gary Stevens, Richard Gough, Scott Nisbet, David Robertson, Stuart McCall, Ian Ferguson (50 Ian Durrant), Nigel Spackman, Alistair McCoist (88 John Brown), Mark Hateley, Pieter Huistra. Trainer: Walter Smith

Goal: Němec (20)

KISPEST HONVÉD BUDAPEST v DUNDALK FC 1-1 (0-1)

Joysef Bózsik, Budapest 18.09.1991

Referee: Zdravko Jokić (YUG) Attendance: 12,000

KISPEST HONVÉD: István Gulyás; József Csábi (46 Viorel Vancea), András Csepregi, Balázs Bérczy, Attila Plókai, János Marozsán, István Pisont, Ervin Kovács, András Cseh (58 Gábor Halmai), István Vincze, Adrian Negrău.
Trainer: György Mezey

DUNDALK: Alan O'Neill; David Mackey, Ronnie Murphy, James Coll, Mick Shelley, Tom McNulty, Ricky McEvoy, Paul Brady (80 Richard Purdy), Gino Lawless, Terry Eviston, Peter Hanrahan. Trainer: Turlough O'Connor

Goals: McEvoy (30), Negrău (83)

GLASGOW RANGERS FC v AC SPARTA PRAHA 2-1 (0-0, 1-0) (AET)

Ibrox, Glasgow 2.10.1991

Referee: Mario van der Ende (HOL) Attendance: 34,260

RANGERS: Andy Goram; Gary Stevens, Scott Nisbet, Oleg Kuznetsov, David Robertson, Stuart McCall, John Brown (64 Ian Durrant), Nigel Spackman, Aleksei Mikhailichenko, Alistair McCoist (90 John Spencer), Maurice Johnston.
Trainer: Walter Smith

SPARTA: Petr Kouba; Michal Horňák, Jiří Novotný, Jan Sopko, Petr Vrabec, Lumír Mistr, Václav Němeček, Martin Frýdek (96 Vítězslav Lavička), Jiří Němec, Pavel Cerný (117 Rudolf Matta), Horst Siegl. Trainer: Dušan Uhrín

Goals: McCall (47, 93), Nisbet (98 og)

FC BARCELONA v HANSA ROSTOCK 3-0 (1-0)

Camp Nou, Barcelona 18.09.1991

Referee: Alphonse Constantin (BEL) Attendance: 78,000

FC BARCELONA: Andoni ZUBIZARRETA Urreta; Albert FERRER Llopis, Ronald Koeman, JUAN CARLOS Rodríguez Moreno, Josep GUARDIOLA Sala, EUSEBIO Sacristán Mena (46 Aitor BEGUIRISTAIN Mújica), Miguel Ángel NADAL Homar, Richard Witschge, Jon Andoni GOIKOETXEA Lasa, Michael Laudrup, Hristo Stoichkov (68 CRISTÓBAL Parralo Aguilera). Trainer: Johan Cruyff

HANSA: Daniel Hoffmann; František Straka, Heiko März, Gernot Alms, Oldřich Machala, Stefan Böger, Juri Schlünz, Michael Spies (62 Jens Dowe), Stefan Persigehl, Roman Sedláček (81 Harald Krämer), Florian Weichert. Trainer: Uwe Reinders

Goals: Laudrup (24, 46), Goikoetxea (75 og)

HANSA ROSTOCK v FC BARCELONA 1-0 (0-0)

Ostseestadion, Rostock 2.10.1991

Referee: Pierluigi Pairetto (ITA) Attendance: 6,000

HANSA: Daniel Hoffmann; František Straka, Stefan Böger, Gernot Alms, Jens Wahl (66 Harald Krämer), Oldřich Machala, Florian Weichert, Juri Schlünz (46 Stefan Persigehl), Michael Spies, Olaf Bodden, Roman Sedláček. Trainer: Uwe Reinders

FC BARCELONA: Andoni ZUBIZARRETA Urreta; Ronald Koeman, Ricardo Jesús SERNA Orozco, Albert FERRER Llopis, EUSEBIO Sacristán Mena, Josep GUARDIOLA Sala, Michael Laudrup, Aitor BEGUIRISTAIN Mújica, Richard Witschge, JULIO SALINAS Fernández (84 Miguel Ángel NADAL Homar), Hristo Stoichkov (73 José Ramón ALEXANCO Ventosa). Trainer: Johan Cruyff

Goal: Spies (64)

UNIVERSITATEA CRAIOVA v APOLLON LIMASSOL 2-0 (1-0)

Central, Craiova 18.09.1991

Referee: Victor Filipov (USSR) Attendance: 10,000

UNIVERSITATEA: Florian Prunea; Vasile Mănăilă, Emil Săndoi, Adrian Popescu, Nicolae Zamfir; Adrian Pigulea, Gheorghe Barbu (81 Silvian Cristescu), Ion Olaru, Pavel Badea; Eugen Neagoe (57 Roland Agalliu), Gheorghe Craioveanu. Trainer: Sorin Cîrțu

APOLLON: Mihalis Hristofi; Antonis Antrellis Ilia, Giannis Giagkoudakis, Dimitris Ioannou, Haralampos Pittas (88 Andreas Sofokleous); Eugeniusz Ptak, Marios Haralampous, David Kenny, Haralampos Hristofi; Giorgos Iosifidis, Suad Besirevic. Trainer: Diethelm Ferner

Goals: Popescu (22 pen), Agalliu (68)

APOLLON LIMASSOL v UNIVERSITATEA CRAIOVA 3-0 (1-0)

Tsirion, Limassol 2.10.1991

Referee: Dimitar Ivanov Momirov (BUL) Att: 10,000

APOLLON: Mihalis Hristofi; Antonis Antrellis Ilia, Giannis Giagkoudakis, Dimitris Ioannou, Haralampos Pittas; Eugeniusz Ptak, Marios Haralampous, David Kenny, Haralampos Hristofi; Aggelos Tsolakis (22 Giorgos Iosifidis), Suad Besirevic. Trainer: Diethelm Ferner

UNIVERSITATEA: Florian Prunea; Vasile Mănăilă, Adrian Popescu, Emil Săndoi, Nicolae Zamfir; Dănuț Bica, Gheorghe Ciurea (60 Roland Agalliu), Gheorghe Barbu (60 Adrian Pigulea), Silvian Cristescu; Eugen Neagoe, Pavel Badea. Trainer: Sorin Cîrțu

Goals: Ptak (10 pen), Besirevic (56, 79)

IFK GÖTEBORG v FLAMURTARI VLORË 0-0

Ullevi, Göteborg 18.09.1991

Referee: Bragi Bergmann (ICE) Attendance: 4,252

IFK: Thomas Ravelli; Mikael Nilsson, Tore Pedersen, Ola Svensson, Pontus Kåmark; Peter Eriksson, Stefan Rehn, Håkan Mild, Thomas Andersson (82 Kaj Eskelinen); Johnny Ekström, Stefan Lindqvist. Trainer: Roger Gustafsson

FLAMURTARI: Daut Naço; Gjergj Dëma, Kreshnik Çipi, Rrapo Taho, Elidon Lameborshi, Erjon Mëhilli, Eqerem Memushi, Bashkim Shaqiri (88 Ardi Ciruna), Edmond Lutaj, Latif Gjondeda, Viktor Daullja (80 Anesti Vito). Trainer: Edmond Licaj

FLAMURTARI VLORË v IFK GÖTEBORG 1-1 (0-0)

Flamurtari, Vlorë 2.10.1991

Referee: Angelo Amendolia (ITA) Attendance: 7,000

FLAMURTARI: Daut Naço; Gjergj Dëma (74 Viron Daullja), Rrapo Taho, Kreshnik Çipi, Elidon Lameborshi, Erjon Mëhilli, Latif Gjondeda, Eqerem Memushi, Viktor Daullja, Anesti Vito, Sokol Muho (66 Ardi Ciruna). Trainer: Edmond Licaj

IFK: Thomas Ravelli; Ola Svensson, Mikael Nilsson, Thomas Andersson, Stefan Rehn, Tore Pedersen, Håkan Mild, Peter Eriksson, Pontus Kåmark, Johnny Ekström (73 Kaj Eskelinen), Stefan Lindqvist (89 Per-Edmund Mordt). Trainer: Roger Gustafsson

Goals: Viktor Daullja (26), Ekström (68)

SAMPDORIA GENOVA v ROSENBORG BK TRONDHEIM 5-0 (2-0)

Luigi Ferraris, Genova 18.09.1991

Referee: James McCluskey (SCO) Attendance: 25,000

SAMPDORIA: Gianluca Pagliuca; Moreno Mannini, Alessandro Orlando, Fausto Pari, Pietro Vierchowod, Srečko Katanec (46 Marco Lanna), Attilio Lombardo, Antônio Carlos "Toninho" CEREZO, Gianluca Vialli, Giuseppe Dossena (58 Giovanni Invernizzi), Paulo Silas. Trainer: Vujadin Boškov

ROSENBORG: Ola By Rise; øivind Husby, Rune Tangen (58 Bjørn Otto Bragstad), Knut Torbjørn Eggen, Trond Henriksen, Kåre Ingebrigtsen, Hugo Hansen (51 Harald Brattbakk), Bent Skammelsrud, Karl-Petter Løken, Gøran Sørloth, Roar Strand. Trainer: Nils Arne Eggen

Goals: Lombardo (12, 83), Dossena (27, 57), Silas (77)

ROSENBORG BK TRONDHEIM v SAMPDORIA GENOVA 1-2 (0-0)

Lerkendal, Trondheim 2.10.1991

Referee: Sándor Varga (HUN) Attendance: 6,705

ROSENBORG: Ola By Rise; Hugo Hansen, Rune Tangen, Bjørn Otto Bragstad, Trond Henriksen, Kåre Ingebrigtsen, Harald Brattbakk (75 Bjørn Tore Kvarme), Bent Skammelsrud, Karl-Petter Løken, Gøran Sørloth, Roar Strand. Trainer: Nils Arne Eggen

SAMPDORIA: Gianluca Pagliuca; Moreno Mannini, Alessandro Orlando, Fausto Pari, Pietro Vierchowod, Marco Lanna, Attilio Lombardo (46 Gianluca Vialli), Antônio Carlos "Toninho" CEREZO, Renato Buso, Roberto Mancini, Paulo Silas (70 Giovanni Invernizzi). Trainer: Vujadin Boškov

Goals: Strand (83), Vialli (84), Mancini (89 pen)

HAMRUN SPARTANS v SPORT LISBOA E BENFICA 0-6 (0-3)

National, Ta'Qali 18.09.1991

Referee: Alfred Wieser (AUS) Attendance: 6,000

HAMRUN SPARTANS: Ian Leigh; Raymond Vella, John Micallef, Marco Grech, Brian Mundee, Alex Azzopardi, Julian Micallef, Joe Brincat, Michael Degiorgio, Dennis Mizzi (46 Emanuel Brincat), Stefan Sultana. Trainer: Lolly Debattista

BENFICA: Adelino Augusto Barros NENO; JOSÉ CARLOS Martins Ferreira, WILLIAM Amaral de Andrade, PAULO Sérgio Braga MADEIRA, VÍTOR Manuel Araújo PANEIRA, António Augusto da Silva VELOSO (62 Hans Jurgen Stefan SCHWARZ), António Manuel PACHECO Domingos, Jonas Thern (51 PAULO Manuel Carvalho SOUSA), Vasili Kulkov, Sergei Yuran, José RUI Lopes ÁGUAS. Trainer: Sven Göran Eriksson

Goals: Pacheco (30), Yuran (32, 35, 50, 83), Rui Aguas (75)

SPORT LISBOA E BENFICA v HAMRUN SPARTANS 4-0 (0-0)

Estádio da Luz, Lisboa 2.10.1991

Referee: Ernest Kesseler (LUX) Attendance: 10,000

BENFICA: SILVINO Almeida Louro; Pedro VALIDO Franco, PAULO Sérgio Braga MADEIRA, RUI Fernando da Silva BENTO, Hans Jurgen Stefan SCHWARZ, RUI Manuel César COSTA, JOÃO Correia PIRES, CÉSAR Gonçalves BRITO Duarte, Mats Ture Magnusson, Sergei Yuran, ISAÍAS Marques Soares. Trainer: Sven Göran Eriksson

HAMRUN SPARTANS: Ian Leigh; John Micallef, Marco Grech, Brian Mundee, Raymond Vella, Ivan Zammit, Joe Brincat, Michael Degiorgio, Noel Fenech (74 Emanuel Brincat), Dennis Mizzi (84 Alex Azzopardi), Stefan Sultana. Trainer: Lolly Debattista

Goals: Isaías (52), César Brito (70), Yuran (73), Paulo Madeira (75)

ARSENAL FC LONDON v FK AUSTRIA MEMPHIS WIEN 6-1 (1-0)

Highbury, London 18.09.1991

Referee: Rune Larsson (SWE) Attendance: 24,124

ARSENAL: David Seaman; Lee Dixon, Nigel Winterburn, Kevin Campbell, Andrew Linighan, Anthony Adams, Paul Davis, David Rocastle, Alan Smith, Paul Merson, Anders Limpar (82 Perry Groves). Trainer: George Graham

AUSTRIA: Ilia Valov; Attila Sekerlioglu, Anton Pfeffer, Robert Frind, Manfred Zsak, Thomas Flögel (70 Harald Schneider), Andreas Ogris, Arminas Narbekovas, Christian Prosenik, Peter Stöger, Valdas Ivanauskas (81 Ralph Hasenhüttl). Trainer: Herbert Prohaska

Goals: Linighan (38), Smith (50, 52, 65, 66), Ogris (56), Limpar (79)

FK AUSTRIA MEMPHIS WIEN v ARSENAL FC LONDON 1-0 (0-0)

Prater, Wien 2.10.1991

Referee: Aleksei Spirin (USSR) Attendance: 11,000

AUSTRIA: Franz Wohlfahrt; Attila Sekerlioglu, Anton Pfeffer, Manfred Kern, Manfred Zsak, Thomas Flögel, Andreas Ogris, Arminas Narbekovas, Christian Prosenik, Peter Stöger, Valdas Ivanauskas. Trainer: Herbert Prohaska

ARSENAL: David Seaman; Lee Dixon, Nigel Winterburn, Michael Thomas, Andrew Linighan, Anthony Adams, David Rocastle, Kevin Campbell, Alan Smith, Paul Merson (82 Perry Groves), David O'Leary. Trainer: George Graham

Goal: Stöger (77 pen)

HJK HELSINKI v FC DYNAMO KYIV 0-1 (0-1)

Olympiastadion, Helsinki 18.09.1991

Referee: Marek Kowalczyk (POL) Attendance: 3,032

HJK: Juha Karjalainen; Aki Hyryläinen (63 Pasi Rautiainen), Pekka Onttonen, Petri Helin, Jouko Vuorela, Kari Rissanen, Pasi Jaakonsaari, Jari Litmanen, Janne Suokonautio, Ismo Lius, Pasi Tauriainen. Trainer: Jyrki Nieminen

DINAMO: Igor Kutepov; Oleg Luzhnyi, Akhrik Tsveiba, Boris Derkach, Sergei Shmatovalenko, Sergei Zaets, Sergei Kovalets, Andrei Annenkov, Pavel Iakovenko (60 Volodymyr Sharan), Stepan Betsa, Oleg Salenko. Trainer: Anatoly Puzach

Goal: Kovalets (12)

PSV EINDHOVEN v BEŞIKTAŞ JK ISTANBUL 2-1 (1-1)

Philips, Eindhoven 2.10.1991

Referee: Wolf-Günter Wiesel (GER) Attendance: 46,000

PSV: Hans Van Breukelen; Eric Gerets, Stan Valckx, Adri Van Tiggelen, Jan Heintze, Edward Linskens, Gerald Vanenburg, Erwin Koeman, Juul Ellerman, Romário de Souza Faria (70 Twan Scheepers), Kalusha Bwalya. Trainer: Bobby Robson

BEŞIKTAŞ: Jaroslaw Bako; Riza Çalimbay, Recep Çetin, Gökhan Keskin, Hamit Yüksel, Kadir Akbulut, Mehmet Özdilek, Turan Uzun, Ali Gültiken, Feyyaz Uçar, B. Metin Tekin (10 Adam Zejer, 78 Sergen Yalçin).
Trainer: Gordon Milne

Goals: B. Metin (5), Vanenburg (24), Kalusha (58)

FC DYNAMO KYIV v HJK HELSINKI 3-0 (1-0)

Republican, Kyiv 2.10.1991

Referee: Erman Toroglu (TUR) Attendance: 4,300

DINAMO: Igor Kutepov; Oleg Luzhnyi, Andrei Aleksanenkov, Yuri Moroz, Sergei Shmatovalenko, Sergei Kovalets, Pavel Iakovenko, Sergei Zaets, Oleg Salenko, Stepan Betsa (70 Yuri Gritsina), Volodymyr Sharan (45 Viktor Moroz).
Trainer: Anatoly Puzach

HJK: Juha Karjalainen; Aki Hyryläinen, Pekka Onttonen, Petri Helin, Jouko Vuorela, Kari Rissanen, Pasi Jaakonsaari, Antti Heinola (88 Kimmo Tarkkio), Janne Suokonatio, Jari Litmanen, Pasi Tauriainen (18 Ismo Lius).
Trainer: Jyrki Nieminen

Goals: Kovalets (28), Y. Moroz (48), Gritsina (72)

FRAM REYKJAVÍK v PANATHINAIKOS ATHINA 2-2 (0-1)

Laugardalsvöllur, Reykjavík 18.09.1991

Referee: Alan Snoddy (NIR) Attendance: 695

FRAM: Birkir Kristinsson; Jón Sveinsson, Pétur Ormslev, Kristján Jónsson (Cap), Steinar Gudgeirsson, Baldur Bjarnason, Kristinn R.Jonsson, Thorvaldur Örlygsson, Ásgeir Ásgeirsson (60 Pétur Arnthórsson), Jón Erling Ragnarsson, Anton Markússon (77 Haukur Pálmason).
Trainer: Ásgeir Elíasson

PANATHINAIKOS: Jozef Wandzik; Stratos Apostolakis, Hristos Kalatzis, Leonidas Hristodoulou, Giannis Kalitzakis, Kostas Mauridis, Nikos Karageorgiou, Giorgos Donis (65 Kostas Antoniou), Giorgos Athanasiadis, Dimitris Saravakos (Cap), Spiros Maragkos (80 Lissandros Georgamlis).
Trainer: Vasilis Daniil

Goals: Hristodoulou (37, 72), Ragnarsson (58), Arnthórsson (63)

BEŞIKTAŞ JK ISTANBUL v PSV EINDHOVEN 1-1 (0-1)

Inönü, Istanbul 18.09.1991

Referee: Rosario Lo Bello (ITA) Attendance: 32,500

BEŞIKTAŞ: Jaroslaw Bako; Recep Çetin, Gökhan Keskin, Ulvi Güveneroglu (84 Hamit Yüksel), Kadir Akbulut, Riza Çalimbay, Mehmet Özdilek, Turan Uzun, Adam Zejer (46 Ali Gültiken), Feyyaz Uçar, B. Metin Tekin.
Trainer: Gordon Milne

PSV: Hans Van Breukelen; Eric Gerets, Stan Valckx, Jerry De Jong, Jan Heintze, Berry Van Aerle, Gheorghe Popescu, Erwin Koeman, Gerald Vanenburg, Wim Kieft, Juul Ellerman.
Trainer: Bobby Robson

Sent off: Kieft (83)

Goals: Ellerman (27), Mehmet (80 pen)

PANATHINAIKOS ATHINA v FRAM REYKJAVÍK 0-0

Olympiako, Athina 2.10.1991

Referee: Astrit Canaj (ALB) Attendance: 50,000

PANATHINAIKOS: Jozef Wandzik; Stratos Apostolakis, Leonidas Hristodoulou, Kostas Mauridis, Hristos Kalatzis, Nikos Karageorgiou, Paris Georgakopoulos (82 Kostas Antoniou), Giorgos Athanasiadis, Dimitris Saravakos (Cap) (74 Giorgos Donis), Spiros Maragkos, Giannis Kalitzakis.
Trainer: Vasilis Daniil

FRAM: Birkir Kristinsson; Kristján Jónsson (Cap), Jón Sveinsson, Pétur Ormslev, Jón Erling Ragnarsson (78 Pétur Marteinsson), Kristinn R.Jónsson, Pétur Arnthórsson, Thorvaldur Örlygsson, Baldur Bjarnason, Steinar Gudgeirsson, Anton Markússon (14 Ríkhardur Dadason).
Trainer: Ásgeir Elíasson

RSC ANDERLECHT BRUSSEL
v GRASSHOPPER-CLUB ZÜRICH 1-1 (1-0)

Constant Vanden Stock, Brussel 18.09.1991

Referee: Jan Damgaard (DEN) Attendance: 10,000

ANDERLECHT: Filip De Wilde; Bertrand Crasson, Wim Kooiman (67 Jean-François De Sart), Graeme Rutjes, Michel De Wolf, Gert Verheyen, Charles Musonda, Marc Degryse, Danny Boffin, Luis Oliveira, Luc Nilis. Trainer: Aad de Mos

GRASSHOPPER: Martin Brunner; Urs Meier, Georgios Nemtsoudis, Mats Gren, Ramón Vega, Ciriaco Sforza, Steve Guilloud (74 Mario Cantaluppi), Alain Sutter, Peter Közle, Thomas Bickel, André Wiederkehr (74 André Halter). Trainer: Oldřich Svab

Goals: Degryse (43), Nemtsoudis (66)

GRASSHOPPER-CLUB ZÜRICH
v RSC ANDERLECHT BRUSSEL 0-3 (0-2)

Wankdorf, Bern 2.10.1991

Referee: Neil Midgley (ENG) Attendance: 10,800

GRASSHOPPERS: Martin Brunner; Urs Meier, Georgios Nemtsoudis, Mats Gren, Ramón Vega, Ciriaco Sforza, Steve Guilloud, Alain Sutter, Peter Közle (80 Mario Cantaluppi), Thomas Bickel, André Halter (55 André Wiederkehr). Trainer: Oldřich Svab

ANDERLECHT: Filip De Wilde; Jean-Marie Houben, Jean-François De Sart, Graeme Rutjes, Michel De Wolf, Luis Oliveira, Marc Degryse, Johan Walem, Danny Boffin, Luc Nilis (83 Gert Verheyen), John Bosman (61 Wim Kooiman). Trainer: Aad de Mos

Goals: Nilis (8, 24, 82)

SECOND ROUND

PANATHINAIKOS ATHINA
v IFK GÖTEBORG 2-0 (1-0)

Olympiako, Athina 23.10.1991

Referee: Neil Midgley (ENG) Attendance: 55,000

PANATHINAIKOS: Jozef Wandzik; Stratos Apostolakis, Hristos Kalatzis, Leonidas Hristodoulou, Giannis Kalitzakis, Nikos Karageorgiou, Giorgos Athanasiadis (83 Giorgos Donis), Paris Georgakopoulos (67 Kostas Antoniou), Dimitris Saravakos (Cap), Spiros Maragkos, Kostas Mauridis. Trainer: Vasilis Daniil

IFK: Thomas Ravelli; Ola Svensson, Mikael Nilsson, Thomas Andersson (80 Kaj Eskelinen), Per-Edmund Mordt, Tore Pedersen, Håkan Mild, Peter Eriksson, Stefan Rehn, Pontus Kåmark, Johnny Ekström (80 Stefan Lindqvist). Trainer: Roger Gustafsson

Goals: Saravakos (27), Maragkos (49)

IFK GÖTEBORG
v PANATHINAIKOS ATHINA 2-2 (2-0)

Ullevi, Göteborg 6.11.1991

Referee: Ryszard Wójcik (POL) Attendance: 10,684

IFK: Thomas Ravelli; Tore Pedersen, Mikael Nilsson, Ola Svensson; Peter Eriksson, Håkan Mild, Thomas Andersson, Per-Edmund Mordt (75 Fredrik Leksell); Johnny Ekström, Kaj Eskelinen (80 Magnus Johansson), Stefan Lindqvist. Trainer: Roger Gustafsson

PANATHINAIKOS: Jozef Wandzik; Stratos Apostolakis, Kostas Mauridis, Nikos Karageorgiou, Giannis Kalitzakis, Hristos Kalatzis, Leonidas Hristodoulou, Paris Georgakopoulos (55 Kostas Antoniou), Giorgos Athanasiadis (83 Giorgos Donis), Spiros Maragkos, Dimitris Saravakos (Cap). Trainer: Vasilis Daniil

Goals: Svensson (23), Ekström (38), Saravakos (60, 83 pen)

OLYMPIQUE de MARSEILLE
v AC SPARTA PRAHA 3-2 (1-0)

Vélodrome, Marseille 23.10.1991

Referee: Gerhard Kapl (AUS) Attendance: 10,016

OLYMPIQUE: Pascal Olmeta; Jocelyn Angloma, Basile Boli, José Carlos Mopomuceno Mozer, Bernard Casoni, Manuel Amoros, Didier Deschamps, Trevor Steven, Christopher Waddle, Jean-Pierre Papin, Abédi Pelé (84 Daniel Xuereb). Trainer: Tomislav Ivić

SPARTA: Petr Kouba; Michal Horńák, Jiří Novotný, Jan Sopko, Petr Vrabec (74 Vítězslav Lavička), Václav Němeček, Lumír Mistr, Martin Frýdek (67 Roman Kukleta), Jiří Němec, Horst Siegl, Pavel Cerný. Trainer: Dušan Uhrín

Goals: Waddle (33), Papin (56, 59), Vrabec (63 pen), Kukleta (78 pen)

AC SPARTA PRAHA
v OLYMPIQUE de MARSEILLE 2-1 (1-0)

Stadión na Letnej, Praha 6.11.1991

Referee: Allan Gunn (ENG) Attendance: 32,500

SPARTA: Petr Kouba; Michal Horńák, Petr Vrabec, Jiří Novotný, Jiří Němec, Lumír Mistr, Václav Němeček, Martin Frýdek (88 Rudolf Matta), Vítězslav Lavička, Roman Kukleta, Horst Siegl (81 Pavel Cerný). Trainer: Dušan Uhrín

OLYMPIQUE: Pascal Olmeta; Pascal Baills (73 Jocelyn Angloma), Basile Boli, José Carlos Mopomuceno Mozer, Bernard Casoni, Manuel Amoros, Didier Deschamps, Trevor Steven, Abédi Pelé, Jean-Pierre Papin, Christopher Waddle. Trainer: Tomislav Ivić

Goals: Frýdek (38), Siegl (69), Pelé (86)

PSV EINDHOVEN
v RSC ANDERLECHT BRUSSEL 0-0

Philips, Eindhoven 23.10.1991

Referee: Hubert Forstinger (AUS) Attendance: 27,000

PSV: Hans Van Breukelen; Jerry De Jong, Adri Van Tiggelen, Stan Valckx, Jan Heintze, Berry Van Aerle, Gheorghe Popescu, Erwin Koeman, Juul Ellerman, Romário de Souza Faria (35 Twan Scheepers), Kalusha Bwalya. Trainer: Bobby Robson

ANDERLECHT: Filip De Wilde; Jean-Marie Houben, Wim Kooiman, Graeme Rutjes, Michel De Wolf, Johan Walem, Luis Oliveira, Marc Degryse, Danny Boffin, Gert Verheyen (71 John Bosman), Luc Nilis. Trainer: Aad de Mos

SAMPDORIA GENOVA
v KISPEST HONVED BUDAPEST 3-1 (2-0)

Luigi Ferraris, Genova 6.11.1991

Referee: Rune Larsson (SWE) Attendance: 50,000

SAMPDORIA: Gianluca Pagliuca; Moreno Mannini (18 Marco Lanna), Pietro Vierchowod, Fausto Pari, Antônio Carlos "Toninho" CEREZO, Srečko Katanec (63 Giovanni Invernizzi), Attilio Lombardo, Paulo Silas, Gianluca Vialli, Roberto Mancini, Alessandro Orlando. Trainer: Vujadin Boškov

KISPEST HONVÉD: István Gulyás; Balázs Bérczy, József Csábi, András Cseh (77 Donát Cservenkai), Attila Plókai, István Urbányi, István Pisont, Ervin Kovács, Tibor Csehi (46 Gábor Halmai), István Vincze, Adrian Negrău. Trainer: György Mezey

Goals: Lombardo (9), Vialli (26, 46), Pari (65 og)

RSC ANDERLECHT BRUSSEL
v PSV EINDHOVEN 2-0 (1-0)

Constant Vanden Stock, Brussel 6.11.1991

Referee: Bruno Galler (SWI) Attendance: 28,000

ANDERLECHT: Filip De Wilde; Jean-Marie Houben, Jean-François De Sart, Graeme Rutjes, Michel De Wolf, Luis Oliveira (59 John Bosman), Marc Degryse, Johan Walem, Danny Boffin, Gert Verheyen, Luc Nilis (69 Alain Van Baekel). Trainer: Aad de Mos

PSV: Hans Van Breukelen; Eric Gerets, Gheorghe Popescu, Adri Van Tiggelen, Jan Heintze, Berry Van Aerle, Jerry De Jong (33 Stan Valckx), Erwin Koeman, Juul Ellerman (55 Twan Scheepers), Wim Kieft, Kalusha Bwalya.
Trainer: Bobby Robson

Goals: Degryse (11), Boffin (87)

FC DYNAMO KYIV v BRØNDBY IF 1-1 (0-1)

Republican, Kiev 23.10.1991

Referee: John Blankenstein (HOL) Attendance: 20,000

DINAMO: Igor Kutepov; Oleg Luzhnyi, Andrei Aleksanenkov, Yuri Moroz, Sergei Shmatovalenko, Sergei Kovalets, Sergei Zaets, Stepan Betsa (46 Viktor Moroz), Oleg Salenko, Volodymyr Sharan, Yuri Gritsina. Trainer: Anatoly Puzach

BRØNDBY: Mogens Krogh; Bjarne Jensen, Uche Okechukwu, Thomas Madsen, Brian Jensen, John Jensen, Kim Christofte, Henrik Jensen, Kim Vilfort, Ole Bjur (70 Ronnie Ekelund), Claus Nielsen. Trainer: Morten Olsen

Goals: Nielsen (12), Salenko (77 pen)

KISPEST HONVED BUDAPEST
v SAMPDORIA GENOVA 2-1 (0-0)

Jozsef Bózsik, Budapest 23.10.1991

Referee: Jacob Uilenberg (HOL) Attendance: 10,000

KISPEST HONVÉD: István Tarlósi; József Csábi, József Szabados, István Urbányi (74 Gábor Halmai), Tibor Csehi, János Maroszán (46 Donát Cservenkai), Balázs Bérczy, István Pisont, István Vincze, Adrian Negrău, Ervin Kovács. Trainer: György Mezey

SAMPDORIA: Gianluca Pagliuca; Moreno Mannini, Alessandro Orlando, Fausto Pari, Pietro Vierchowod, Marco Lanna, Renato Buso (67 Attilio Lombardo), Antônio Carlos "Toninho" CEREZO, Gianluca Vialli, Roberto Mancini, Srečko Katanec (84 Giovanni Invernizzi). Trainer: Vujadin Boškov

Goals: Pisont (54), Cerezo (58), Cservenkai (72)

BRØNDBY IF v FC DYNAMO KYIV 0-1 (0-1)

Brøndby Stadion, København 6.11.1991

Referee: Leslie John Irvine (NIR) Attendance: 13,712

BRØNDBY: Mogens Krogh; Bjarne Jensen, Uche Okechukwu, Erik Rasmussen, Brian Jensen, John Jensen (72 Jesper Kristensen), Kim Christofte, Henrik Jensen (83 Ronnie Ekelund), Ole Bjur, Claus Nielsen, Kim Vilfort.
Trainer: Morten Olsen

DINAMO: Igor Kutepov; Oleg Luzhnyi, Akhrik Tsveiba, Andrei Aleksanenkov, Sergei Shmatovalenko, Sergei Kovalets (70 Yuri Gritsina), Pavel Iakovenko, Sergei Zaets, Oleg Salenko, Yuri Moroz, Volodymyr Sharan. Trainer: Anatoly Puzach

Sent off: Iakovenko (44)

Goal: Iakovenko (7)

FC BARCELONA
v 1.FC KAISERSLAUTERN 2-0 (1-0)

Camp Nou, Barcelona 23.10.1991

Referee: Gérard Biguet (FRA) Attendance: 80,000

FC BARCELONA: Andoni ZUBIZARRETA Urreta; Ronald Koeman, Albert FERRER Llopis, Josep GUARDIOLA Sala, EUSEBIO Sacristán Mena (62 CRISTÓBAL Parralo Aguilera), Miguel Ángel NADAL Homar, José María BAKERO Escudero, Richard Witschge, Michael Laudrup, Hristo Stoichkov (70 JULIO SALINAS Fernández), Aitor BEGUIRISTAIN Mújica. Trainer: Johan Cruyff

1.FC KAISERSLAUTERN: Gerald Ehrmann; Wolfgang Funkel, Thomas Dooley, Reinhard Stumpf, Marco Haber (77 Jürgen Degen), Uwe Scherr, Guido Hoffmann, Markus Kranz, Stefan Kuntz (60 Bjarne Goldbæk), Marcel Witeczek, Demir Hotić. Trainer: Karl-Heinz Feldkamp

Goals: Beguiristáin (42, 51)

1.FC KAISERSLAUTERN
v FC BARCELONA 3-1 (1-0)

Fritz-Walter-Stadion, Kaiserslautern 6.11.1991

Referee: Erik Fredriksson (SWE) Attendance: 30,200

1.FC KAISERSLAUTERN: Gerald Ehrmann; Wolfgang Funkel, Marco Haber, Oliver Schäfer, Uwe Scherr, Demir Hotić, Bjarne Goldbæk, Guido Hoffmann, Frank Lelle (87 Markus Kranz), Marcel Witeczek, Stefan Kuntz.
Trainer: Karl-Heinz Feldkamp

FC BARCELONA: Andoni ZUBIZARRETA Urreta; Ronald Koeman, CRISTÓBAL Parralo Aguilera, FerNANDO Muñoz, Josep GUARDIOLA Sala (80 Miguel Ángel NADAL Homar), EUSEBIO Sacristán Mena, José María BAKERO Escudero, Richard Witschge, Aitor BEGUIRISTAIN Mújica (66 Ricardo Jesús SERNA Orozco), Michael Laudrup, Hristo Stoichkov.
Trainer: Johan Cruyff

Goals: Hotić (35, 49), Goldbæk (76), Bakero (90)

SPORT LISBOA E BENFICA
v ARSENAL FC LONDON 1-1 (1-1)

Estádio da Luz, Lisboa 23.10.1991

Referee: Tullio Lanese (ITA) Attendance: 80,000

BENFICA: Adelino Augusto Barros NENO; Vasili Kulkov, RUI Fernando da Silva BENTO, PAULO Sérgio Braga MADEIRA, António Augusto da Silva VELOSO (73 António Manuel PACHECO Domingos), Jonas Thern, VÍTOR Manuel Araújo PANEIRA, Hans Jurgen Stefan SCHWARZ, José RUI Lopes ÁGUAS (49 CÉSAR Gonçalves BRITO Duarte), ISAÍAS Marques Soares, Sergei Yuran. Trainer: Sven Göran Eriksson

ARSENAL: David Seaman; Lee Dixon, Nigel Winterburn, Paul Davis, Colin Pates, Anthony Adams, David Rocastle, Anders Limpar (81 Michael Thomas), Alan Smith, Paul Merson, Kevin Campbell (78 Perry Groves).
Trainer: George Graham

Goals: Isaías (15), Campbell (17)

ARSENAL FC LONDON
v SPORT LISBOA E BENFICA 1-3 (1-1, 1-1) (AET)

Highbury, London 6.11.1991

Referee: Aron Schmidhuber (GER) Attendance: 35,815

ARSENAL: David Seaman; Lee Dixon, Nigel Winterburn, Paul Davis, Colin Pates (105 Stephen Bould), Anthony Adams, David Rocastle, Kevin Campbell, Alan Smith, Paul Merson, Anders Limpar (75 Perry Groves). Trainer: George Graham

BENFICA: Adelino Augusto Barros NENO; Vasili Kulkov, PAULO Sérgio Braga MADEIRA, RUI Fernando da Silva BENTO, António Augusto da Silva VELOSO, VÍTOR Manuel Araújo PANEIRA, RUI Manuel César COSTA (81 CÉSAR Gonçalves BRITO Duarte), Jonas Thern, Hans Jurgen Stefan SCHWARZ, ISAÍAS Marques Soares (119 JOSÉ CARLOS Martins Ferreira), Sergei Yuran.
Trainer: Sven Göran Eriksson

Goals: Pates (20), Isaías (36, 107), Kulkov (100)

CRVENA ZVEZDA BEOGRAD
v APOLLON LIMASSOL 3-1 (1-1)

Felsótiszaparti, Szeged 23.10.1991

Referee: Vadim Zhuk (USSR) Attendance: 1,500

CRVENA ZVEZDA: Dragoje Leković; Dusko Radinović, Milorad Ratković, Miodrag Belodedić, Ilija Najdoski, Vladimir Jugović, Vlada Stosić (71 Predrag Jovanović), Dejan Savicević, Sinisa Mihajlović, Darko Pancev (46 Ilija Ivić), Vladan Lukić. Trainer: Vladimir Popović

APOLLON: Mihalis Hristofi; Antonis Ilia Antrellis, Dimitris Ioannou, Haralampos Hristofi, Haralampos Pittas, Hrisostomos Tziouras, Giorgos Iosifidis, Eugeniusz Ptak (90 Andreas Sofokleous), David Kenny, Suad Besirevic, Marios Haralampous. Trainer: Diethelm Ferner

Goals: Pancev (15), Ptak (41), Lukić (71), Savicević (83 pen)

APOLLON LIMASSOL
v CRVENA ZVEZDA BEOGRAD 0-2 (0-0)

Tsirion, Limassol 6.11.1991

Referee: Heinz Holzmann (AUS) Attendance: 10,000

APOLLON: Mihalis Hristofi; Antonis Ilia Antrellis, David Kenny, Dimitris Ioannou, Haralampos Hristofi, Giannis Giagkoudakis, Giorgos Iosifidis, Eugeniusz Ptak, Marios Haralampous (68 Lakis Athanasiou), Aggelos Tsolakis (58 Dimitris Orfanidis), Suad Besirević.
Trainer: Diethelm Ferner

CRVENA ZVEZDA: Zvonko Milojević; Dusko Radinović, Goran Vasilijević, Miodrag Belodedić, Miroslav Tanjga, Vladimir Jugović, Vlada Stosić, Dejan Savicević, Sinisa Mihajlović (77 Dusko Savić), Vladan Lukić, Darko Pancev.
Trainer: Vladimir Popović

Sent off: Besirević (47)

Goals: Savicević (47), Lukić (75 pen)

SEMI-FINAL GROUPS

GROUP A

SAMPDORIA GENOVA
v CRVENA ZVEZDA BEOGRAD 2-0 (1-0)

Luigi Ferraris, Genova 27.11.1991

Referee: Gérard Biguet (FRA) Attendance: 30,000

SAMPDORIA: Gianluca Pagliuca; Moreno Mannini, Srečko Katanec, Fausto Pari, Pietro Vierchowod, Marco Lanna, Antônio Carlos "Toninho" CEREZO (84 Giovanni Invernizzi), Attilio Lombardo, Gianluca Vialli, Roberto Mancini, Ivano Bonetti. Trainer: Vujadin Boškov

CRVENA ZVEZDA: Zvonko Milojević; Dusko Radinović, Goran Vasilijević, Vladimir Jugović, Sasa Nedeljković, Ilija Najdoski, Vlada Stosić, Ilija Ivić (68 Predrag Jovanović), Darko Pancev, Milorad Ratković, Sinisa Mihajlović. Trainer: Vladimir Popović

Goals: Nedeljković (7 og), Vialli (73)

RSC ANDERLECHT BRUSSEL
v PANATHINAIKOS ATHINA 0-0

Constant Vanden Stock, Brussel 27.11.1991

Referee: Brian McGinlay (SCO) Attendance: 24,000

ANDERLECHT: Filip De Wilde; Jean-Marie Houben, Jean-François De Sart, Graeme Rutjes, Michel De Wolf, Luis Oliveira, Johan Walem, Marc Degryse, Danny Boffin, John Bosman (80 Gert Verheyen), Luc Nilis. Trainer: Aad de Mos

PANATHINAIKOS: Jozef Wandzik; Stratos Apostolakis, Kostas Mauridis, Nikos Karageorgiou, Giannis Kalitzakis, Hristos Kalatzis, Leonidas Hristodoulou, Giorgos Athanasiadis (68 Giorgos Donis, 87 Kostas Frantzeskos), Kostas Antoniou, Spiros Maragkos, Dimitris Saravakos (Cap). Trainer: Vasilis Daniil

PANATHINAIKOS ATHINA
v SAMPDORIA GENOVA 0-0

Olympiako, Athina 11.12.1991

Referee: Hubert Forstinger (AUS) Attendance: 51,500

PANATHINAIKOS: Jozef Wandzik; Stratos Apostolakis, Kostas Mauridis, Nikos Karageorgiou, Giannis Kalitzakis, Hristos Kalatzis, Leonidas Hristodoulou, Dimitris Saravakos (Cap), Kostas Antoniou (46 Giorgos Donis), Spiros Maragkos, Kostas Frantzeskos. Trainer: Vasilis Daniil

SAMPDORIA: Gianluca Pagliuca; Moreno Mannini, Srečko Katanec, Fausto Pari, Pietro Vierchowod, Marco Lanna, Antônio Carlos "Toninho" CEREZO, Attilio Lombardo, Gianluca Vialli, Renato Buso, Ivano Bonetti. Trainer: Vujadin Boškov

CRVENA ZVEZDA BEOGRAD
v RSC ANDERLECHT BRUSSEL 3-2 (1-1)

Budapest 12.12.1991

Referee: Leif Sundell (SWE) Attendance: 2,000

CRVENA ZVEZDA: Zvonko Milojević; Dusko Radinović, Miodrag Belodedić, Ilija Najdoski, Goran Vasilijević, Vlada Stosić, Miroslav Tanjga (63 Ilija Ivić), Milorad Ratković, Sinisa Mihajlović, Vladimir Jugović, Darko Pancev. Trainer: Vladimir Popović

ANDERLECHT: Filip De Wilde; Jean-Marie Houben, Jean-François De Sart, Graeme Rutjes, Michel De Wolf, Nii Lamptey (85 Bertrand Crasson), Luis Oliveira (79 Gert Verheyen), Johan Walem, Danny Boffin, John Bosman, Luc Nilis. Trainer: Aad de Mos

Sent off: Najdoski & Bosman (69)

Goals: Ratković (19), Lamptey (33), Nilis (60), Ivić (68), Pancev (87)

RSC ANDERLECHT BRUSSEL
v SAMPDORIA GENOVA 3-2 (0-1)

Constant Vanden Stock, Brussel 4.03.1992

Referee: Aron Schmidhuber (GER) Attendance: 20,000

ANDERLECHT: Peter Maes; Bertrand Crasson, Wim Kooiman, Graeme Rutjes, Michel De Wolf, Johan Walem, Marc Degryse, Danny Boffin (76 Alain Van Baekel), Bruno Versavel, Luis Oliveira (69 Nii Lamptey), Luc Nilis. Trainer: Aad de Mos

SAMPDORIA: Gianluca Pagliuca; Moreno Mannini, Srečko Katanec, Fausto Pari, Pietro Vierchowod, Marco Lanna, Gianluca Vialli, Attilio Lombardo (89 Renato Buso), Antônio Carlos "Toninho" CEREZO, Roberto Mancini, Ivano Bonetti. Trainer: Vujadin Boškov

Goals: Vialli (27, 63), Degryse (54), Nilis (69, 90)

PANATHINAIKOS ATHINA
v CRVENA ZVEZDA BEOGRAD 0-2 (0-0)

Olympiako, Athina 4.03.1992

Referee: Aleksei Spirin (USSR) Attendance: 60,000

PANATHINAIKOS: Jozef Wandzik; Stratos Apostolakis, Kostas Mauridis, Giannis Kalitzakis, Hristos Kalatzis, Nikos Karageorgiou (70 Kostas Frantzeskos), Leonidas Hristodoulou, Kostas Antoniou (58 Giorgos Donis), Spiros Maragkos, Dimitris Saravakos (Cap), Krzysztof Warzycha. Trainer: Vasilis Daniil

CRVENA ZVEZDA: Dragoje Leković (53 Zvonko Milojević); Dusko Radinović, Miodrag Belodedić, Miroslav Tanjga, Elvir Bolić, Goran Vasilijević, Dusko Savić, Vladimir Jugović, Darko Pancev, Ilija Ivić, Sinisa Mihajlović. Trainer: Vladimir Popović

Goals: Pancev (70, 86)

SAMPDORIA GENOVA
v RSC ANDERLECHT BRUSSEL 2-0 (2-0)

Luigi Ferraris, Genova 18.03.1992

Referee: Peter Mikkelsen (DEN) Attendance: 33,874

SAMPDORIA: Gianluca Pagliuca; Moreno Mannini, Marco Lanna, Ivano Bonetti, Srečko Katanec, Fausto Pari, Antônio Carlos "Toninho" CEREZO, Dario Bonetti, Attilio Lombardo, Roberto Mancini (87 Renato Buso), Gianluca Vialli.
Trainer: Vujadin Boškov

ANDERLECHT: Peter Maes; Bertrand Crasson, Wim Kooiman, Graeme Rutjes, Michel De Wolf, Johan Walem, Marc Degryse, Bruno Versavel, Danny Boffin (63 Alain Van Baekel), Luc Nilis, Luis Oliveira (46 Nii Lamptey).
Trainer: Aad de Mos

Goals: Lombardo (35), Mancini (37)

PANATHINAIKOS ATHINA
v RSC ANDERLECHT BRUSSEL 0-0

Olympiako, Athina 1.04.1992

Referee: Joseph Worral (ENG) Attendance: 40,000

PANATHINAIKOS: Jozef Wandzik; Stratos Apostolakis, Nikos Karageorgiou, Leonidas Hristodoulou, Nikos Kourbanas, Kostas Mauridis, Dimitris Saravakos (Cap), Kostas Antoniou, Krzysztof Warzycha, Juan Borelli (80 Giorgos Donis), Lissandros Georgamlis (71 Giorgos Athanasiadis).
Trainer: Vasilis Daniil

ANDERLECHT: Peter Maes; Bertrand Crasson, Graeme Rutjes, Wim Kooiman, Michel De Wolf, Marc Degryse, Johan Walem, Bruno Versavel (68 Alain Van Baekel), Danny Boffin, Luis Oliveira, Luc Nilis (57 Gert Verheyen).
Trainer: Aad de Mos

CRVENA ZVEZDA BEOGRAD
v PANATHINAIKOS ATHINA 1-0 (0-0)

Vasil Levski, Sofia 18.03.1992

Referee: Emilio Soriano Aladren (SPA) Attendance: 23,000

CRVENA ZVEZDA: Zvonko Milojević; Dusko Radinović, Goran Vasilijević, Miroslav Tanjga, Miodrag Belodedić, Milorad Ratković, Ilija Ivić, Vladimir Jugović, Darko Pancev, Dejan Savicević (35 Elvir Bolić), Sinisa Mihajlović.
Trainer: Vladimir Popović

PANATHINAIKOS: Jozef Wandzik; Stratos Apostolakis, Hristos Kalatzis (76 Kostas Frantzeskos), Kostas Mauridis, Giannis Kalitzakis, Kostas Antoniou (78 Giorgos Donis), Nikos Karageorgiou, Leonidas Hristodoulou, Spiros Maragkos, Dimitris Saravakos (Cap), Krzysztof Warzycha.
Trainer: Vasilis Daniil

Sent off: Kalitzakis (83)

Goal: Mihajlović (53 pen)

RSC ANDERLECHT BRUSSEL
v CRVENA ZVEZDA BEOGRAD 3-2 (2-1)

Constant Vanden Stock, Brussel 15.04.1992

Referee: Joël Quiniou (FRA) Attendance: 8,000

ANDERLECHT: Peter Maes; Bertrand Crasson, Wim Kooiman, Graeme Rutjes, Michel De Wolf, Luis Oliveira, Johan Walem, Marc Degryse, Danny Boffin (65 Alain Van Baekel), John Bosman, Nii Lamptey (75 Gert Verheyen).
Trainer: Aad de Mos

CRVENA ZVEZDA: Milić Jovanović; Sasa Nedeljković, Miroslav Tanjga, Dusko Radinović, Mitko Stojkovski, Vladimir Jugović, Elvir Bolić, Milorad Ratković, Sinisa Mihajlović (76 Slavisa Cula), Darko Pancev, Ilija Ivić.
Trainer: Vladimir Popović

Goals: Oliveira (3), Pancev (7), Bosman (44), Cula (80), Degryse (82)

CRVENA ZVEZDA BEOGRAD
v SAMPDORIA GENOVA 1-3 (1-2)

Narodna Armia, Sofia 1.04.1992

Referee: José Rosa dos Santos (POR) Attendance: 35,000

CRVENA ZVEZDA: Zvonko Milojević; Dusko Radinović (75 Ilija Ivić), Milorad Ratković, Miodrag Belodedić, Goran Vasilijević, Sasa Nedeljković, Dejan Savicević (81 Slavisa Cula), Elvir Bolić, Darko Pancev, Sinisa Mihajlović, Vladimir Jugović.
Trainer: Vladimir Popović

SAMPDORIA: Gianluca Pagliuca; Dario Bonetti, Pietro Vierchowod, Marco Lanna, Ivano Bonetti, Attilio Lombardo, Fausto Pari, Srečko Katanec, Antônio Carlos "Toninho" CEREZO (10 Giovanni Invernizzi), Gianluca Vialli, Roberto Mancini. Trainer: Vujadin Boškov

Goals: Mihajlović (19), Katanec (34), Vasilijević (41 og), Mancini (76)

SAMPDORIA GENOVA
v PANATHINAIKOS ATHINA 1-1 (1-1)

Luigi Ferraris, Genova 15.04.1992

Referee: Kurt Rothlisberger (SWI) Attendance: 39,000

SAMPDORIA: Gianluca Pagliuca; Dario Bonetti, Marco Lanna, Moreno Mannini, Fausto Pari, Srečko Katanec, Paulo Silas, Giovanni Invernizzi (78 Renato Buso), Alessandro Orlando, Gianluca Vialli, Roberto Mancini.
Trainer: Vujadin Boškov

PANATHINAIKOS: Jozef Wandzik; Stratos Apostolakis, Nikos Karageorgiou, Leonidas Hristodoulou, Nikos Kourbanas, Kostas Mauridis, Hristos Kalatzis, Spiros Maragkos, Dimitris Saravakos (Cap), Krzysztof Warzycha, Giorgos Donis. Trainer: Vasilis Daniil

Goals: Maragkos (27), Mancini (36)

	P	W	D	L	F	A	Pts
Sampdoria	6	3	2	1	10	5	8
Crvena Zvezda Beograd	6	3	0	3	9	10	6
RSC Anderlecht	6	2	2	2	8	9	6
Panathinaikos	6	0	4	2	1	4	4

AC SPARTA PRAHA v FC DYNAMO KYIV 2-1 (2-0)

Stadión na Letnej, Praha 11.12.1991

Referee: Rosario Lo Bello (ITA) Attendance: 15,000

SPARTA: Petr Kouba; Jiří Novotný, Petr Vrabec, Michal Horňák, Lumír Mistr, Václav Němeček, Martin Frýdek, Jiří Němec, Horst Siegl, Vítězslav Lavička (76 Rudolf Matta), Roman Kukleta. Trainer: Dušan Uhrín

DINAMO: Igor Kutepov; Oleg Luzhnyi, Akhrik Tsveiba, Andrei Aleksanenkov, Sergei Shmatovalenko, Sergei Kovalets, Yuri Moroz, Sergei Zaets, Viktor Moroz, Volodymyr Sharan, Oleg Salenko. Trainer: Anatoly Puzach

Goals: Němeček (13), Vrabec (22), Sharan (55)

GROUP B

FC DYNAMO KYIV v SPORT LISBOA E BENFICA 1-0 (1-0)

Republican, Kiev 27.11.1991

Referee: Keith Stuart Hackett (ENG) Attendance: 47,500

DINAMO: Igor Kutepov; Oleg Luzhnyi, Akhrik Tsveiba, Andrei Aleksanenkov, Sergei Shmatovalenko, Sergei Kovalets, Viktor Moroz, Oleg Salenko, Yuri Moroz, Volodymyr Sharan (77 Stepan Betsa), Sergei Zaets. Trainer: Anatoly Puzach

BENFICA: Adelino Augusto Barros NENO; Vasili Kulkov, PAULO Sérgio Braga MADEIRA, RUI Fernando da Silva BENTO, Jonas Thern, Hans Jurgen Stefan SCHWARZ, António Augusto da Silva VELOSO (66 RUI Manuel César COSTA), VÍTOR Manuel Araújo PANEIRA, José RUI Lopes ÁGUAS, ISAÍAS Marques Soares (75 António Manuel PACHECO Domingos), Sergei Yuran. Trainer: Sven Göran Eriksson

Goal: Salenko (30)

SPORT LISBOA E BENFICA v FC BARCELONA 0-0

Estádio da Luz, Lisboa 11.12.1991

Referee: Bruno Galler (SWI) Attendance: 80,000

BENFICA: Adelino Augusto Barros NENO; VÍTOR Manuel Araújo PANEIRA, PAULO Sérgio Braga MADEIRA, RUI Fernando da Silva BENTO, António Augusto da Silva VELOSO (46 António Manuel PACHECO Domingos), RUI Manuel César COSTA (64 CÉSAR Gonçalves BRITO Duarte), Jonas Thern, Vasili Kulkov, Hans Jurgen Stefan SCHWARZ, ISAÍAS Marques Soares, Sergei Yuran. Trainer: Sven Göran Eriksson

FC BARCELONA: Andoni ZUBIZARRETA Urreta; FerNANDO Muñoz, Ricardo Jesús SERNA Orozco, JUAN CARLOS Rodríguez Moreno, Ronald Koeman; EUSEBIO Sacristán Mena, Josep GUARDIOLA Sala (66 Aitor BEGUIRISTAIN Mújica), Michael Laudrup, Richard Witschge, José María BAKERO Escudero, Hristo Stoichkov (80 JULIO SALINAS Fernández). Trainer: Johan Cruyff

FC BARCELONA v AC SPARTA PRAHA 3-2 (2-1)

Camp Nou, Barcelona 27.11.1991

Referee: Kim Milton Nielsen (DEN) Attendance: 82,000

FC BARCELONA: Andoni ZUBIZARRETA Urreta; FerNANDO Muñoz, Ronald Koeman, Ricardo Jesús SERNA Orozco, Josep GUARDIOLA Sala, José María BAKERO Escudero, Richard Witschge, Guillermo AMOR Martínez, Jon Andoni GOIKOETXEA Lasa (75 Miguel Ángel NADAL Homar), Michael Laudrup, Aitor BEGUIRISTAIN Mújica (64 JUAN CARLOS Rodríguez Moreno). Trainer: Johan Cruyff

SPARTA: Petr Kouba; Michal Horňák, Jiří Novotný, Vítězslav Lavička (81 Rudolf Matta), Petr Vrabec, Jiří Němec, Horst Siegl, Lumír Mistr (70 Pavel Cerný), Václav Němeček, Martin Frýdek, Roman Kukleta. Trainer: Dušan Uhrín

Sent off: Amor (15)

Goals: Amor (15), Vrabec (18), Laudrup (33), Bakero (61), Němeček (64)

FC DYNAMO KYIV v FC BARCELONA 0-2 (0-1)

Republican, Kiev 4.03.1992

Referee: Guy Goethals (BEL) Attendance: 20,000

DINAMO: Igor Kutepov; Oleg Luzhnyi, Akhrik Tsveiba, Anatoli Bessmertniy, Sergei Shmatovalenko, Volodymyr Sharan (76 Sergei Volotek), Yuri Gritsina, Andrei Annenkov, Sergei Zaets, Yuri Moroz, Oleg Salenko. Trainer: Anatoly Puzach

FC BARCELONA: Andoni ZUBIZARRETA Urreta; FerNANDO Muñoz, Ronald Koeman, JUAN CARLOS Rodríguez Moreno, EUSEBIO Sacristán Mena, Josep GUARDIOLA Sala, Miguel Ángel NADAL Homar, José María BAKERO Escudero (64 JULIO SALINAS Fernández), Richard Witschge, Michael Laudrup (55 Aitor BEGUIRISTAIN Mújica), Hristo Stoichkov. Trainer: Johan Cruyff

Goals: Stoichkov (32), Salinas (68)

SPORT LISBOA E BENFICA v AC SPARTA PRAHA 1-1 (0-1)

Estádio da Luz, Lisboa 4.03.1992

Referee: Howard King (WAL) Attendance: 50,000

BENFICA: Adelino Augusto Barros NENO; JOSÉ CARLOS Martins Ferreira, PAULO Sérgio Braga MADEIRA, WILLIAM Amaral de Andrade, António Augusto da Silva VELOSO, Jonas Thern, PAULO Manuel Carvalho SOUSA, RUI Manuel César COSTA, Vasili Kulkov (31 António Manuel PACHECO Domingos), Sergei Yuran, Mats Ture Magnusson. Trainer: Sven Göran Eriksson

SPARTA: Petr Kouba; Jiří Novotný, Jozef Chovanec, Michal Horňák, Petr Vrabec, Lumír Mistr, Jiří Němec, Václav Němeček, Marek Trval (78 Pavel Cerný), Horst Siegl, Martin Frýdek (89 Rudolf Matta). Trainer: Dušan Uhrín

Goals: Novotný (32), Pacheco (53 pen)

FC BARCELONA v FC DYNAMO KYIV 3-0 (0-0)

Camp Nou, Barcelona 18.03.1992

Referee: Karl-Josef Assenmacher (GER) Att: 70,000

FC BARCELONA: Andoni ZUBIZARRETA Urreta; FerNANDO Muñoz, Ronald Koeman, Miguel Ángel NADAL Homar; Jon Andoni GOIKOETXEA Lasa, EUSEBIO Sacristán Mena, Josep GUARDIOLA Sala (73 JULIO SALINAS Fernández), José María BAKERO Escudero (60 Guillermo AMOR Martínez), Richard Witschge, Michael Laudrup, Hristo Stoichkov. Trainer: Johan Cruyff

DINAMO: Valdemaras Martinkenas; Oleg Luzhnyi (81 Sergei Volotek), Akhrik Tsveiba, Sergei Zaets, Sergei Shmatovalenko, Yuri Moroz, Yuri Gritsina, Pavel Iakovenko, Andrei Annenkov, Volodymyr Sharan, Oleg Salenko (76 Gintaras Kvitkauskas). Trainer: Anatoly Puzach

Sent off: Yuri Moroz (58)

Goals: Stoichkov (59, 83), Julio Salinas (87)

AC SPARTA PRAHA v SPORT LISBOA E BENFICA 1-1 (1-1)

Stadión na Letnej, Praha 18.03.1992

Referee: Gérard Biguet (FRA) Attendance: 28,000

SPARTA: Petr Kouba; Michal Horňák, Jan Sopko (63 Rudolf Matta), Jozef Chovanec, Petr Vrabec, Lumír Mistr, Martin Frýdek, Václav Němeček, Jiří Němec, Horst Siegl, Marek Trval (37 Pavel Cerný). Trainer: Dušan Uhrín

BENFICA: Adelino Augusto Barros NENO; JOSÉ CARLOS Martins Ferreira, RUI Fernando da Silva BENTO, WILLIAM Amaral de Andrade, António Augusto da Silva VELOSO, VÍTOR Manuel Araújo PANEIRA, Jonas Thern, Hans Jurgen Stefan SCHWARZ, António Manuel PACHECO Domingos (75 Mats Ture Magnusson), ISAÍAS Marques Soares, CÉSAR Gonçalves BRITO Duarte. Trainer: Sven Göran Eriksson

Goals: Vítor Paneira (30), Chovanec (45)

SPORT LISBOA E BENFICA v FC DYNAMO KYIV 5-0 (1-0)

Estádio da Luz, Lisboa 1.04.1992

Referee: Mario van der Ende (HOL) Attendance: 10,000

BENFICA: Adelino Augusto Barros NENO; JOSÉ CARLOS Martins Ferreira, PAULO Sérgio Braga MADEIRA, WILLIAM Amaral de Andrade, António Augusto da Silva VELOSO, Jonas Thern, VÍTOR Manuel Araújo PANEIRA (75 RUI Manuel César COSTA), Hans Jurgen Stefan SCHWARZ, António Manuel PACHECO Domingos (61 ISAÍAS Marques Soares), Sergei Yuran, CÉSAR Gonçalves BRITO Duarte. Trainer: Sven Göran Eriksson

DINAMO: Valdemaras Martinkenas; Stepan Betsa, Akhrik Tsveiba, Andrei Annenkov, Anatoli Bessmertniy, Yuri Gritsina, Pavel Iakovenko, Sergei Zaets, Oleg Salenko, Gintaras Kvitkauskas (46 Sergei Volotek), Volodymyr Sharan (81 Oleg Matveev). Trainer: Anatoly Puzach

Goals: César Brito (25, 62), Isaías (71), Yuran (83, 87)

AC SPARTA PRAHA v FC BARCELONA 1-0 (0-0)

Stadión na Letnej, Praha 1.04.1992

Referee: Bo Karlsson (SWE) Attendance: 27,374

SPARTA: Petr Kouba; Michal Horňák, Jozef Chovanec, Jiří Novotný, Petr Vrabec (77 Rudolf Matta), Václav Němeček, Lumír Mistr, Martin Frýdek, Roman Vonášek, Pavel Cerný, Horst Siegl (89 Dejan Joksimovič). Trainer: Dušan Uhrín

FC BARCELONA: Andoni ZUBIZARRETA Urreta; FerNANDO Muñoz, Ronald Koeman, Ricardo Jesús SERNA Orozco; Josep GUARDIOLA Sala (74 Miguel Ángel NADAL Homar), EUSEBIO Sacristán Mena, José María BAKERO Escudero, Richard Witschge; JULIO SALINAS Fernández (74 Jon Andoni GOIKOETXEA Lasa), Aitor BEGUIRISTAIN Mújica, Michael Laudrup. Trainer: Johan Cruyff

Goal: Siegl (66)

FC DYNAMO KYIV v AC SPARTA PRAHA 1-0 (0-0)

Republican, Kiev 15.04.1992

Referee: Brian McGinlay (SCO) Attendance: 5,000

DINAMO: Igor Kutepov; Oleg Luzhnyi, Akhrik Tsveiba, Andrei Annenkov, Ervand Sukiasyan (46 Volodymyr Sharan), Oleg Matveev, Pavel Iakovenko (25 Vladislav Ternavski), Sergei Kovalets, Stepan Betsa, Oleg Salenko, Yuri Gritsina. Trainer: Anatoly Puzach

SPARTA: Petr Kouba; Jozef Chovanec, Michal Horňák, Jiří Novotný, Petr Vrabec, Horst Siegl, Václav Němeček, Martin Frýdek, Jiří Němec, Dejan Joksimovič, Pavel Cerný. Trainer: Dušan Uhrín

Sent off: Novotný (90)

Goal: Salenko (83)

FC BARCELONA
v SPORT LISBOA E BENFICA 2-1 (2-1)

Camp Nou, Barcelona 15.04.1992

Referee: Hubert Forstinger (AUS) Attendance: 115,000

FC BARCELONA: Andoni ZUBIZARRETA Urreta; FerNANDO Muñoz, Ronald Koeman, Ricardo Jesús SERNA Orozco, EUSEBIO Sacristán Mena; Josep GUARDIOLA Sala, José María BAKERO Escudero, Guillermo AMOR Martínez (72 Miguel Ángel NADAL Homar), Jon Andoni GOIKOETXEA Lasa, Michael Laudrup (82 José Ramón ALEXANCO Ventosa), Hristo Stoichkov. Trainer: Johan Cruyff

BENFICA: Adelino Augusto Barros NENO; JOSÉ CARLOS Martins Ferreira (63 RUI Manuel César COSTA), PAULO Sérgio Braga MADEIRA, RUI Fernando da Silva BENTO, António Augusto da Silva VELOSO, VÍTOR Manuel Araújo PANEIRA, Hans Jurgen Stefan SCHWARZ, ISAÍAS Marques Soares (78 António Manuel PACHECO Domingos), CÉSAR Gonçalves BRITO Duarte, Sergei Yuran, PAULO Manuel Carvalho SOUSA. Trainer: Sven Göran Eriksson

Goals: Stoichkov (12), Bakero (24), César Brito (28)

	P	W	D	L	F	A	Pts
FC Barcelona	6	4	1	1	10	4	9
AC Sparta Praha	6	2	2	2	7	7	6
Benfica	6	1	3	2	8	5	5
Dynamo Kyiv	6	2	0	4	3	12	4

FINAL

FC BARCELONA
v SAMPDORIA GENOVA 1-0 (0-0)

Wembley, London 20.05.1992

Referee: Aron Schmidhuber (GER) Attendance: 70,827

FC BARCELONA: Andoni ZUBIZARRETA Urreta; FerNANDO Muñoz, Albert FERRER Llopis, Ronald Koeman; JUAN CARLOS Rodríguez Moreno, Josep GUARDIOLA Sala (113 José Ramón ALEXANCO Ventosa), José María BAKERO Escudero, EUSEBIO Sacristán Mena; JULIO SALINAS Fernández (65 Jon Andoni GOIKOETXEA Lasa), Michael Laudrup, Hristo Stoichkov. Trainer: Johan Cruyff

SAMPDORIA: Gianluca Pagliuca; Moreno Mannini, Fausto Pari, Marco Lanna, Pietro Vierchowod, Attilio Lombardo, Antônio Carlos "Toninho" CEREZO, Srečko Katanec, Ivano Bonetti (73 Giovanni Invernizzi), Gianluca Vialli (101 Renato Buso), Roberto Mancini. Trainer: Vujadin Boškov

Goal: R. Koeman (111)

European Cup Goalscorers 1991-92

7 goals: Jean Pierre Papin (Olympique Marseille), Sergei Yuran (Benfica Lisboa)

6 goals: Darko Pancev (Crvena Zvezda), Luc Nilis (Anderlecht), Gianluca Vialli (Sampdoria)

5 goals: Isaías Marques Soares (Benfica)

4 goals: Alan Smith (Arsenal London), Marc Degryse (Anderlecht), Sinisa Mihajlovic (Crvena Zvezda), Attilio Lombardo, Roberto Mancini (Sampdoria), Hristo Stoichkov (Barcelona), César Brito (Benfica)

3 goals: István Pisont (Honvéd Budapest), Milorad Ratkovic (Crvena Zvezda), Saravakos (Panathinaikos), Vrabec (Sparta Praha), José Marías Bakero Escudero, Michael Laudrup (Barcelona), Salenko (Dynamo Kyiv)

2 goals: McCall (Glasgow Rangers), Ekström (IFK Göteborg), Xuereb (Olympique Marseille), Hotić, Funkel (FC Kaiserslautern), Ptak, Besirević (Apollon Limassol), Lukic, Savićević (Crvena Zvezda), Maragkos, Hristodoulou (Panathinaikos), Dossena (Sampdoria), Němeček, Siegl (Sparta Praha), Beguiristáin, Julio Salinas (Barcelona), Pacheco (Benfica), Kovalets (Dynamo Kyiv)

1 goal: Czachowski, Grech (Zaglebie Lubin), McEvoy (Dundalk), Spies (Hansa Rostock), Popescu, Agalliu (Universit.Craiova), Vik. Daullja (Flamurtari), Strand (Rosenborg), Ogris, Stöger (FK Austria Wien), Mehmet, B.Metin (Beşiktaş), Ragnarsson, Arnthórsson (Fram Reykjavík), Nemtsoudis (Grasshopper), Chervenkov (Etar Veliko Trnovo), Svensson (IFK Göteborg), Waddle, Pelé, Sauzée, Angloma, Eyraud (Olympique Marseille), Ellerman, Vanenburg, Kalusha (PSV Eindhoven), Cservenkai, Negrău (Honvéd), Nielsen, Christofte, Ekelund, Okechukwu, Vilfort (Brøndby), Goldbæk, Degen (FC Kaiserslautern), Campbell, Pates, Linighan, Limpar (Arsenal London), Oliveira, Bosman, Lamptey, Boffin (Anderlecht), Cula, Katanec, Ivic, Tanjga, Stosic, Radinovic (Crvena Zvezda), Cerezo, Silas (Sampdoria), Chovanec, Novotný, Kukleta, Frýdek, Němec (Sparta Praha), Amor, R.Koeman (Barcelona), Vítor Paneira, Kulkov, Rui Aguas, Paulo Madeira (Benfica), Sharan, Iakovenko, Y.Moroz, Gritsina (Dynamo Kyiv)

Own goals: Nisbet (Rangers) for Sparta Praha, Straka (Hansa) for Barcelona, Pari (Sampdoria) for Honvéd, Nedeljković, Vasilijević (Crvena Zvezda) for Sampdoria

THE EUROPEAN CUP 1992-93

PRELIMINARY ROUND

SHELBOURNE DUBLIN v TAVRIA SIMFEROPOL 0-0

Tolka Park, Dublin 19.08.1992

Referee: Anders Frisk (SWE) Attendance: 3,200

SHELBOURNE: Jody Byrne; Peter Coyle, Kevin Brady, Michael Neville (Cap), Ken O'Doherty, Garry Haylock, Dessie Gorman, Paul Doolin, Padraig Dully, Gary Howlett, Mark Rutherford. Trainer: Pat Byrne

TAVRIA: Oleg Kolesov; Sergei Shevchenko (78 Vladislav Novikov), Nikolai Turchinenko, Oleksandr Holovko, Igor Volkov (Cap), Sergei Voronezhky, Andrei Oparin, Yuri Gudimenko, Sergei Andreev, Vidmantas Vishniauskas (33 Sefer Alibaev), Sergei Polstianov. Trainer: Anatloi Zaraiev

TAVRIA SIMFEROPOL v SHELBOURNE DUBLIN 2-1 (2-1)

Lokomotiv, Simferopol 2.09.1992

Referee: Gerd Grabher (AUS) Attendance: 10,500

TAVRIA: Oleg Kolesov; Sergei Shevchenko, Nikolai Turchinenko, Oleksandr Holovko, Igor Volkov (Cap), Sergei Voronezhsky, Yuri Gudimenko, Andrei Oparin, Sergei Polstianov, Vidmantas Vishniauskas (61 Vladislav Novikov), Toliat Sheykhametov (74 Sefer Alibaev).
Trainer: Anatloi Zaraiev

SHELBOURNE: Jody Byrne; Peter Coyle, Kevin Brady, Michael Neville (Cap), Ken O'Doherty, Gary Howlett, Dessie Gorman, Paul Doolin, Padraig Dully, Garry Haylock (84 Bobby Browne), Mark Rutherford. Trainer: Jim McCoughlin

Goals: Shevchenko (10), Sheykhametov (15), Dully (42)

VALLETTA FC v MACCABI TEL AVIV 1-2 (0-0)

National, Ta'Qali 19.08.1992

Referee: Ahmet Çakar (TUR) Attendance: 1,500

VALLETTA FC: Charles Cortis; Raymond Briffa (31 William Mackay), Charles Magri, Kristian Laferla (Cap), Osnir Populin, Joe Camilleri, Edmond Lufi (82 Jeremy Agius), Nicky Saliba, Leo Refalo, Joe Zarb, Jesmond Zerafa. Trainer: Joe Caruana

MACCABI: Aleksandr Uvarov; Avi Cohen (Cap), Gadi Brumer, Amir Shelach, Aleksandr Polukarov, Amit Levi, Noam Shoam (79 Yaron Drori), Avi Nimni, Nir Klinger, Itzhak Zohar, Aharon Meir Melika (70 Eli Driks). Trainer: Abraham Grant

Goals: Zerafa (75), Cohen (81), Nimni (88)

MACCABI TEL AVIV v VALLETTA FC 1-0 (1-0)

Ramat-Gan, Tel Aviv 2.09.1992

Referee: Vasilis Nikakis (GRE) Attendance: 5,000

MACCABI: Aleksandr Uvarov; Avi Cohen (Cap), Aleksandr Polukarov, Gadi Brumer, Amir Shelach, Amit Levi, Nir Klinger (59 Arik Shriki), Itzhak Zohar, Avi Nimni, Aharon Meir Melika, Nezah Masuby (56 Eli Driks).
Trainer: Abraham Grant

VALLETTA FC: Charles Cortis; Raymond Briffa, Charles Magri (89 William Mackay), Kristian Laferla (Cap), Osnir Populin, Joe Camilleri, Edmond Lufi, Nicky Saliba, Leo Refalo (88 Jeremy Agius), Joe Zarb, Jesmond Zerafa.
Trainer: Tony Grech

Goal: Melika (23)

KLAKSVIKAR ÍTROTTARFELAG v SKONTO RIGA 1-3 (0-1)

Svangaskard, Toftir 19.08.1992

Referee: Rune Pedersen (NOR) Attendance: 1,500

KÍ: Jakup Mikkelsen; Heini Hansen, Petur Ove Ellingsgaard, John Hansen, Kurt Mørkøre (Cap), Todi Jönsson, Olgar Danielsen, Jan Joensen, Alan Mørkøre, Jan Andreasen, Harley Bertholdsen (46 Sorin Petersen). Trainer: Petur Mohr

SKONTO: Oleg Grishin; Oleg Blagonadezdin, Vitaly Astafjev, Einars Gnedoi, Mikhail Zemlinsky (Cap), Valentin Lobanov (75 Yury Dermentiev), Artur Sketov (34 Aleksei Semjonov), Aleksandr Stradin, Aleksandr Dibrivny, Igor Troitski, Alexander Yeliseyev. Trainer: Mark Zakhodine

Goals: Astafjev (29, 47), Danielsen (46), Semjonov (90)

SKONTO RIGA v KLAKSVIKAR ÍTROTTARFELAG 3-0 (2-0)

Daugava, Riga 2.09.1992

Referee: Ilkka Koho (FIN) Attendance: 3,000

SKONTO: Oleg Grishin; Oleg Blagonadezdin, Vitaly Astafjev, Einars Gnedoi, Mikhail Zemlinsky (Cap), Aleksei Semjonov (65 Valentin Lobanov), Artur Sketov, Aleksandr Stradin, Aleksandr Dibrivny (61 Igor Stepanov), Igor Troitski, Alexander Yeliseyev. Trainer: Mark Zakhodine

KÍ: Jakup Mikkelsen; Heini Hansen, Petur Ove Ellingsgaard, John Hansen, Kurt Mørkøre (Cap), Todi Jönsson, Olgar Danielsen, Jan Joensen (61 Beinur Poulsen), Allan Mørkøre, Fridrin Liskasson, Sorin Petersen (64 Harley Bertholdsen).
Trainer: Petur Mohr

Goals: Yeliseyev (4), Semjonov (38), Astafjev (52)

SCT OLIMPIJA LJUBLJANA v NORMA TALLINN **3-0** (0-0)

Bezigrad Ljubljana 19.08.1992

Referee: Daniel Roduit (SWI) Attendance: 1,587

OLIMPIJA: Marko Simeunović; Nenad Podgajski, Robert Englaro, Samir Zulić, Edin Hadzialagić, Damir Vrabac, Andrej Zelko, Dejan Djuranović, Sandi Valentincić (30 Nenad Protega), Zoran Ubavić (Cap), Nedeljko Topić (82 Igor Benedejcić). Trainer: Lucjo Pertić

NORMA: Tonu Vanakesa (Cap); Leonid Kurilov, Sergei Bragin, Vladimir Uryupin, Eduard Vinogradov, Valentin Komarov, Valeri Chmil (57 Dmitri Tam), Yury Garifulin, Andrey Borisov, Andrey Belokhvostov, Aleksandr Zhurkin. Trainer: Valeri Bondarenko

Goals: Ubavić (48 pen), Topić (50), Vrabac (60)

NORMA TALLINN v OLIMPIJA LJUBLJANA **0-2** (0-1)

Rannavärava, Tallinn 2.09.1992

Referee: Finn Lambek (DEN) Attendance: 1,000

NORMA: Tonu Vanakesa (Cap); Leonid Kurilov, Sergei Bragin, Vladimir Uryupin, Eduard Vinogradov, Valentin Komarov, Valeri Chmil, Igor Reva (54 Yury Volkov), Andrey Borisov, Andrey Belokhvostov, Aleksandr Zhurkin. Trainer: Valeri Bondarenko

OLIMPIJA: Marko Simeunović; Nenad Podgajski, Robert Englaro, Samir Zulić, Edin Hadzialagić, Damir Vrabac, Igor Benedejcić (86 Branko Zibert), Dejan Djuranović, Zoran Ubavić (Cap), Andrej Zelko (75 Nenad Protega), Nedeljko Topić. Trainer: Rado Pisot

Goals: Zulić (27), Djuranović (80)

SCT OLIMPIJA LJUBLJANA v AC MILAN **0-3** (0-1)

Bezigrad, Ljubljana 30.09.1992

Referee: Jiří Ulrich (CZE) Attendance: 13,000

OLIMPIJA: Marko Simeunović; Nenad Podgajski, Robert Englaro, Dejan Djuranović, Edin Hadzialagić, Damir Vrabac, Nenad Protega, Zeljko Milinović, Zoran Ubavić (Cap) (71 Andrej Zelko), Sandi Valentincić, Nedeljko Topić (85 Igor Benedejcić). Trainer: Lucio Pertić

AC MILAN: Sebastiano Rossi; Mauro Tassotti, Franco Baresi (Cap), Stefano Nava, Paolo Maldini, Frank Rijkaard, Alberigo Evani (46 Stefano Eranio), Roberto Donadoni, Zvonimir Boban, Ruud Gullit (61 Marco Simone), Daniele Massaro. Trainer: Fabio Capello

Goals: Massaro (31), Rijkaard (48), Tassotti (85)

LECH POZNAN v SKONTO RIGA **2-0** (2-0)

PKP Lech, Poznan 16.09.1992

Referee: Mitko Mitrev (BUL) Attendance: 18,000

LECH: Kazimierz Sidorczuk; Przemyslaw Bereszynski, Pawel Wojtala, Waldemar Kryger, Marek Rzepka, Kazimierz Moskal (Cap), Dariusz Skrzypczak, Ryszard Remien (75 Igor Korniets), Jerzy Podbrozny, Jaroslaw Araszkiewicz, Miroslaw Trzeciak (66 Dariusz Kofnyt). Trainer: Henryk Apostel

SKONTO: Oleg Grishin; Mikhail Zemlinsky (Cap), Einars Gnedoi, Vitaly Astafjev, Valentin Lobanov, Oleg Blagonadezdin, Artur Sketov (58 Aleksei Semjonov), Igor Stepanov, Aleksandr Dibrivny (46 Sergey Tarasov), Aleksandr Stradin, Alexander Yeliseyev. Trainer: Mark Zakhodine

Goals: Trzeciak (26), Podbrozny (41 pen)

FIRST ROUND

AC MILAN v SCT OLIMPIJA LJUBLJANA **4-0** (2-0)

Giuseppe Meazza, Milano 16.09.1992

Referee: Roman Steindl (AUS) Attendance: 14,324

AC MILAN: Francesco Antonioli; Mauro Tassotti (Cap), Stefano Nava, Alessandro Costacurta, Paolo Maldini, Alberigo Evani, Demetrio Albertini, Ruud Gullit, Gianluigi Lentini (61 Roberto Donadoni), Marco Van Basten (75 Daniele Massaro), Jean-Pierre Papin. Trainer: Fabio Capello

OLIMPIJA: Marko Simeunović; Nenad Podgajski, Samir Zulić, Robert Englaro, Edin Hadzialagić, Damir Vrabec, Igor Benedejcić (67 Branko Zibert), Dejan Djuranović, Zoran Ubavić (Cap), Andrej Zelko (86 Nenad Protega), Nedeljko Topić. Trainer: Rado Pisot

Sent off: Zulic

Goals: Van Basten (5, 50), Albertini (7), Papin (65)

SKONTO RIGA v LECH POZNAN **0-0**

Daugava, Riga 30.09.1992

Referee: Frederick McKnight (NIR) Attendance: 3,500

SKONTO: Oleg Grishin; Mikhail Zemlinsky, Einars Gnedoi, Vitaly Astafjev, Valentin Lobanov, Oleg Blagonadezdin, Artur Sketov (59 Sergey Tarasov), Igor Stepanov (70 Aleksei Semjonov), Igor Troitski, Aleksandr Stradin, Alexander Yeliseyev. Trainer: Mark Zakhodine

LECH: Kazimierz Sidorczuk; Przemyslaw Bereszynski, Pawel Wojtala, Waldemar Kryger, Marek Rzepka, Kazimierz Moskal, Dariusz Skrzypczak, Ryszard Remien (61 Igor Korniets), Jerzy Podbrozny, Jaroslaw Araszkiewicz, Miroslaw Trzeciak. Trainer: Henryk Apostel

PSV EINDHOVEN v ZHALGIRIS VILNIUS 6-0 (2-0)

Philips, Eindhoven 16.09.1992

Referee: James McCluskey (SCO) Attendance: 15,650

PSV: Hans Van Breukelen; Ernest Faber, Adri Van Tiggelen, Gheorghe Popescu, Jan Heintze, Edward Linskens, Erwin Koeman (72 Bwalya Kalusha), Gerald Vanenburg (Cap) (75 Raymond Beerens), Juul Ellerman, Wim Kieft, Arthur Numan. Trainer: Hans Westerhof

ZHALGIRIS: Darius Spetyla; Tomas Ziukas, Tomas Zvirgzdauskas, Virginius Baltusnikas, Ramunas Stonkus (46 Darius Maciulevicius), Andrius Tereskinas, Aurelijus Skarbalius, Viaceslavas Sukristovas (69 Dainius Suliauskas), Aidas Preiksaitis, Ricardas Zdancius (Cap), Eimantas Poderis. Trainer: Vitautas Janciauskas

Goals: E. Koeman (24), Ellerman (36, 60, 64), Kieft (66), Numan (80)

ZHALGIRIS VILNIUS v PSV EINDHOVEN 0-2 (0-2)

Zhalgiris, Vilnius 30.09.1992

Referee: Markus Merk (GER) Attendance: 2,800

ZHALGIRIS: Darius Spetyla; Tomas Zvirgzdauskas, Tomas Ziukas, Virginius Baltusnikas, Dainius Suliauskas, Aurelijus Skarbalius, Ricardas Zdancius (Cap), Grazvydas Mikulenas (46 Vytautas Karvelis), Andrius Tereskinas, Aidas Preiksaitis (66 Ramunas Stonkus), Eimantas Poderis. Trainer: Vitautas Janciauskas

PSV: Hans Van Breukelen; Berry Van Aerle (46 Jerry De Jong), Adri Van Tiggelen, Gheorghe Popescu, Jan Heintze, Edward Linskens, Erwin Koeman (Cap), Juul Ellerman, Arthur Numan, Wim Kieft, Romário de Souza Faria (85 Raymond Beerens). Trainer: Hans Westerhof

Goals: Numan (26), Romário (39)

FC BARCELONA v VIKING STAVANGER 1-0 (0-0)

Nou Camp, Barcelona 16.09.1992

Referee: Lajos Hartmann (HUN) Attendance: 35,000

FC BARCELONA: Andoni Zubizarreta (Cap); Albert Ferrer, Josep GUardiola, Eusebio Sacristán, Richard Witschge (46 Julio Salinas), Miguel Ángel Nadal, Jon Andoni Goikoetxea, Guillermo Amor, Goran Vučević, Michael Laudrup (78 Miguel SOLER Sarasols), Aitor Beguiristain. Trainer: Johannes Cruijff

VIKING: Lars Gaute Bø; Øivind Mellemstrand, Ingve Bøe, Ulf Karlsen (Cap), Roger Nilsen, Erik Pedersen, Sander Solberg, Kenneth Storvik, Egil Fjetland (72 Alf Kåre Tveit), Egil Johan Østenstad (88 Leif Rune Salte), Børre Meinseth. Trainers: Reidar Goa & Berntsen

Goal: Amor (87)

VIKING STAVANGER v FC BARCELONA 0-0

Stavanger Stadium 30.09.1992

Referee: Simo Ruokonen (FIN) Attendance: 12,041

VIKING: Lars Gaute Bø; Øivind Mellemstrand, Ingve Bøe, Ulf Karlsen (Cap), Roger Nilsen, Erik Pedersen, Sander Solberg, Kenneth Storvik (65 Rune Gjerde), Egil Fjetland (76 Børge Rannestad), Egil Johan Østenstad, Børre Meinseth. Trainers: Reidar Goa & Berntsen

FC BARCELONA: Andoni Zubizarreta (Cap); Albert Ferrer, Ronald Koeman, JUAN CARLOS Rodríguez Moreno, Josep GUardiola, Miguel Ángel Nadal, Guillermo Amor, José María Bakero, Michael Laudrup, Hristo Stoichkov (84 Jon Andoni Goikoetxea), Aitor Beguiristain (57 Julio Salinas). Trainer: Johan Cruyff

FC KUUSYSI LAHTI v DINAMO BUCUREŞTI 1-0 (1-0)

Kisapuisto, Lahti 16.09.1992

Referee: Wilfred Wallace (IRE) Attendance: 1,330

KUUSYSI: Jyrki Rovio; Ilkka Remes, Jarmo Saastamoinen (Cap), Kalle Lehtinen, Valery Glusakov, Kimmo Tarkkio, Petri Järvinen, Jari Rinne, Jari Kinnunen, Michael Belfield (84 Harri Munukka), Juha Annunen (88 Sami Vehkakoski). Trainer: Antti Muurinen

DINAMO: Florin Tene; Zoltan Kadar, Tibor Selymes, Gheorghe Mihali (Cap), Adrian Matei, Leo Florian Grozavu, Dorinel Munteanu, Gabor Gerstenmajer, Ioan Sebastian Moga (46 Ovidiu Cornel Hanganu), Daniel Timofte (70 Nelson Mensah), Sulejman Demollari. Trainer: Florin Halagian

Goal: Rinne (16)

DINAMO BUCUREŞTI v KUUSYSI LAHTI 2-0 (0-0, 1-0) (AET)

Dinamo, Bucureşti 30.09.1992

Referee: Stavros Zakestidis (GRE) Attendance: 9,000

DINAMO: Florin Tene; Marian Pană (79 Daniel Timofte), Gheorghe Mihali (Cap), Adrian Matei (46 Nelson Mensah), Tibor Selymes; Zoltan Kadar, Marius Cheregi, Gabor Gerstenmajer, Dorinel Munteanu, Ioan Sebastian Moga, Sulejman Demollari. Trainer: Florin Halagian

KUUSYSI: Jyrki Rovio; Jari Kinnunen, Jarmo Saastamoinen (Cap), Valery Glusakov, Ilkka Remes, Petri Järvinen, Juha Annunen (78 Jari Sulander), Kalle Lehtinen, Jari Rinne (105 Harri Munukka), Kimmo Tarkkio, Michael Belfield. Trainer: Antti Muurinen

Goals: Gerstenmajer (75), Demollari (117)

GLASGOW RANGERS FC v LYNGBY BK 2-0 (1-0)

Ibrox, Glasgow 16.09.1992

Referee: Jacobus Uilenberg (HOL) Attendance: 40,036

RANGERS: Andy Goram; Ian Durrant, David Robertson, Richard Gough (Cap), David McPherson, John Brown, Aleksei Mikhailichenko, Ian Ferguson, Alistair McCoist, Mark Hateley, Pieter Huistra. Manager: Walter Smith

LYNGBY: Kim Brodersen; Svend Erik Larsen, Morten Wieghorst, Michael Gothenborg (Cap), Claus Christiansen, Johnny Vilstrup (87 Anders Nielsen), Henrik Risom, Emeka Ezeugo, Lars Hammer, Morten Nielsen, Henrik Jørgensen (73 Jan Chico Olsen). Trainer: Michael Schäfer

Goals: Hateley (39), Huistra (67)

FERENCVÁROS BUDAPEST v SLOVAN BRATISLAVA 0-0

Üllői út, Budapest 30.09.1992

Referee: Sergei Khusainov (RUS) Attendance: 14,000

FERENCVÁROS: Tamás Balogh; Tibor Simon, András Telek, Mihaly Szűcs, József Keller (Cap), Zsolt Páling, Flórián Albert, Imre Fodor (46 Gábor Balogh), Péter Lipcsei, László Wukovics, Sorin Cigan (80 Péter Deszatnik). Trainer: Tibor Nyilasi

SLOVAN: Alexander Vencel; Tomás Stúpala (Cap), Milos Glonek, Jozef Juriga, Vladimír Kinder, František Klinovsky, Ondrej Kristofík, Peter Dubovský, Stefan Maixner (73 Youssef Haraoui), Jaroslav Timko, Pavol Gostic (60 Stanislav Moravec). Trainer: Dušan Galis

LYNGBY BK v GLASGOW RANGERS FC 0-1 (0-0)

Lyngby Stadium 30.09.1992

Referee: Karl-Josef Assenmacher (GER) Attendance: 4,273

LYNGBY: Kim Brodersen; Svend Erik Larsen, Thomas Rytter (46 Jan Chico Olsen), Michael Gothenborg (Cap), Claus Christiansen; Johnny Vilstrup, Henrik Risom, Morten Wieghorst, Henrik Jørgensen; Morten Nielsen (70 Henrik Lykke), Allan Kuhn. Trainer: Michael Schäfer

RANGERS: Andy Goram; David Robertson, David McPherson, John Brown, Stuart McCall, Trevor Steven, Ian Durrant, Ian Ferguson, Pieter Huistra, Mark Hateley, Alistair McCoist (Cap). Manager: Walter Smith

Goal: Durrant (85)

AUSTRIA WIEN v CSKA SOFIA 3-1 (1-0)

Prater, Wien 16.09.1992

Referee: Ion Crăciunescu (ROM) Attendance: 7,000

AUSTRIA: Franz Wohlfahrt; Manfred Zsak (Cap), Ernst Aigner, Walter Kogler, Christian Prosenik, Peter Stöger, Manfred Schmid, Thomas Flögel (72 Peter Pospisil), Michael Binder, Ralph Hasenhüttl, Robertas Fridrikas. Trainer: Hermann Stessl

CSKA: Georgi Velinov (Cap); Zarko Machev, Stefan Kolev, Krasimir Bezinski, Marius Urukov, Anatoli Nankov (87 Victor Pavlov), Ivailo Kirov, Hristo Koilov, Ivailo Andonov, Vanio Shishkov (89 Boris Khvoinev), Kiril Metkov. Trainer: Asparuh Nikodimov

Goals: Hasenhüttl (16), Shishkov (58), Fridrikas (82), Kogler (90)

SLOVAN BRATISLAVA v FERENCVÁROS BUDAPEST 4-1 (1-0)

Tehelné pole, Bratislava 16.09.1992

Referee: Serge Muhmenthaler (SWI) Attendance: 20,000

SLOVAN: Alexander Vencel; Tomás Stúpala (Cap), Milos Glonek, Vladimír Kinder, František Klinovsky, Jozef Juriga, Ondrej Kristofík, Peter Dubovský, Stefan Maixner (67 Stanislav Moravec), Jaroslav Timko, Pavol Gostic (49 Youssef Haraoui). Trainer: Dušan Galis

FERENCVÁROS: Tamás Balogh; Tibor Simon, András Telek, Tamás Szekeres, Zsolt Páling, Flórián Albert, Mihaly Szűcs, Péter Lipcsei, József Keller (Cap), Gábor Schneider (65 Gábor Balogh), László Wukovics (52 Sándor Szenes). Trainer: Tibor Nyilasi

Sent off: Szenes

Goals: Gostic (20), Dubovský (52, 55), Lipcsei (75), Moravec (82)

CSKA SOFIA v AUSTRIA WIEN 3-2 (1-1)

Narodna Armia, Sofia 30.09.1992

Referee: David Elleray (ENG) Attendance: 10,000

CSKA: Georgi Velinov (Cap); Zarko Machev, Stefan Kolev, Rosen Kirilov, Krasimir Bezinski (46 Hristo Koilov), Anatoli Nankov (69 Anton Dimitrov), Kiril Metkov, Ivailo Kirov, Ivailo Andonov, Stefan Draganov, Boris Khvoinev. Trainer: Asparuh Nikodimov

AUSTRIA: Franz Wohlfahrt; Manfred Zsak (Cap), Ernst Aigner, Walter Kogler, Christian Prosenik, Peter Stöger, Manfred Schmid, Robertas Fridrikas (89 Attila Sekerlioglu), Thomas Flögel, Valdas Ivanauskas (75 Ralph Hasenhüttl), Michael Binder. Trainer: Hermann Stessl

Goals: Metkov (2), Flögel (28), Andonov (60), Ivanauskas (67), Draganov (73 pen)

FC SION v TAVRIA SIMFEROPOL 4-1 (2-0)

Stade de Tourbillon, Sion 16.09.1992

Referee: Léon Schelings (BEL) Attendance: 6,000

FC SION: Stéphane Lehmann; Olivier Biaggi, Dominique Herr, Alain Geiger (Cap), Yvan Quentin, Marc Hottiger, LUIS CARLOS Moreira, Roberto Assis, Reto Gertschen, TÚLIO Humberto Costa, David Orlando. Trainer: Jean-Paul Brigger

TAVRIA: Oleg Kolesov; Nikolai Turchinenko, Vidmantas Vishniauskas, Oleksandr Holovko, Sefer Alibaev (20 Dmitri Gulenkov), Sergei Voronezhsky, Sergei Shevchenko (Cap), Yury Gudimenko, Andrei Oparin, Sergei Polstianov, Toliat Sheyhametov (78 Yury Getikov). Trainer: Anatloi Zaraiev

Sent off: Kolesov (20)

Goals: Hottiger (17), Túlio (35, 73), Assis (77), Shevchenko (85)

TAVRIA SIMFEROPOL v FC SION 1-3 (0-0)

Lokomotiv, Simferopol 30.09.1992

Referee: Christer Fällström (SWE) Attendance: 10,000

TAVRIA: Dmitri Gulenkov; Nikolai Turchinenko, Igor Volkov (Cap), Oleksandr Holovko, Sergei Voronezhsky (86 Vidmantas Vishniauskas), Yury Gudimenko, Sergei Shevchenko, Andrei Oparin, Sergei Polstianov (62 Yury Getikov), Vladislav Novikov, Toliat Sheyhametov. Trainer: Anatloi Zaraiev

FC SION: Stéphane Lehmann; Michel Sauthier, Alain Geiger, Dominique Herr, Yvan Quentin; Marc Hottiger, Blaise Piffaretti (Cap), Roberto Assis (80 Johann Lonfat), LUIS CARLOS Moreira, TÚLIO Humberto Costa, David Orlando (83 Sébastien Fournier). Trainer: Jean-Paul Brigger

Goals: Tulio (67, 77), Shevchenko (69), Herr (89)

UNION SPORTIVE LUXEMBOURG v FC PORTO 1-4 (0-1)

Stade Achille-Hammerel, Luxembourg 16.09.1992

Referee: Patrick Kelly (IRE) Attendance: 3,552

US LUXEMBOURG: John Van Rijswijck; Patrick Feyder, Luc Feiereisen (Cap), Thomas Wolf, David Borbiconi, Yves Picard, Frank Deville, Serge Thill, Christian Joachim (84 Fernand Heinisch), Patrick Morocutti, Denis Mogenot.
Trainer: Heinz Maas

FC PORTO: VÍTOR Manuel Martins BAÍA; JOÃO Domingos Silva PINTO (Cap), ALOÍSIO Pires Alves, FERNANDO Manuel Silva COUTO (79 JORGE Paulo COSTA Almeida), JAIME Fernandes MAGALHÃES, Fernando Óscar BANDEIRINHA Barbosa, RUI FILIPE Tavares Bastos, José Orlando Rocha SEMEDO, JORGE António Pinto COUTO, DOMINGOS José Paciencia Oliveira, Nélson António Gama "TONI".
Trainer: Carlos Alberto Silva

Goals: Semedo (41), Fernando Couto (47), Toni (51), Deville (63), Domingos (90)

FC PORTO v UNION SPORTIVE LUXEMBOURG 5-0 (3-0)

Estádio das Antas, Porto 30.09.1992

Referee: Eyjólfur Ólafsson (ICE) Attendance: 30,000

FC PORTO: VÍTOR Manuel Martins BAÍA (72 Vítor Sérgio Santos VALENTE); JOÃO Domingos Silva PINTO (Cap), JOSÉ CARLOS Nascimento, JORGE Paulo COSTA Almeida, Lubomír Vlk, António dos Santos ANDRÉ (68 João Paulo Santos "PAULINHO SANTOS"), JAIME Fernandes MAGALHÃES, José Orlando Rocha SEMEDO, Manuel Albina Maçãcs "BINO", Emil Kostadinov, Nélson António Gama "TONI".
Trainer: Carlos Alberto Silva

US LUXEMBOURG: John Van Rijswijck; Marc Birsens, Christian Joachim, Thomas Wolf, Patrick Feyder, Serge Thill, David Borbiconi, Luc Feiereisen (Cap), Frank Deville (79 Carlos Geraldo), Patrick Morocutti (39 Yves Picard), Denis Mogenot. Trainer: Roland Schnit

Goals: Kostadinov (16, 35), Toni (26, 61), José Carlos (67)

VÍKINGUR REYKJAVÍK v CSKA MOSKVA 0-1 (0-0)

Víkingsvöllur, Reykjavík 16.09.1992

Referee: Gerald Ashby (ENG) Attendance: 2,900

VÍKINGUR: Gudmundur Hreidarsson; Thorsteinn Thorsteinsson, Janez Zilnik, Helgi Bjarnason, Gudmundur Ingi Magnússon, Adalsteinn Adalsteinsson, Atli Helgason (Cap), Tomislav Bosnjak (29 Helgi Sigurdsson), Hördur Theódórsson, Gudmundur Steinsson (78 Björn Bjartmarz), Atli Einarsson. Trainer: Logi Olafsson

CSKA: Dmitri Kharin (Cap); Aleksei Guschin (70 Yuri Bavykin), Sergei Kolotovkin, Sergei Fokin, Dmitri Bystrov, Vasily Ivanov, Denis Mashkarin, Aleksandr Grishin, Oleg Sergeev, Evgeni Bushmanov (55 Dmitri Korsakov), Ilshat Faizulin. Trainer: Gennadi Kostylev.

Goal: Korsakov (75)

CSKA MOSKVA v VÍKINGUR REYKJAVÍK 4-2 (3-1)

Peschanoe, Moskva 30.09.1992

Referee: Erman Toroglu (TUR) Attendance: 10,000

CSKA: Dmitri Kharin (Cap); Aleksei Guschin (66 Denis Mashkarin), Oleg Malyukov, Dmitri Bystrov, Sergei Fokin, Vasily Ivanov, Valeriy Minko, Aleksandr Grishin, Oleg Sergeev, Dmitri Korsakov, Ilshat Faizulin (60 Mikhail Kolesnikov).
Trainer: Gennadi Kostylev

VÍKINGUR: Gudmundur Hreidarsson; Thorsteinn Thorsteinsson, Janez Zilnik, Helgi Bjarnason, Gudmundur Ingi Magnússon, Adalsteinn Adalsteinsson, Tomislav Bosnjak (72 Gudmundur Steinsson), Atli Helgason (Cap), Hördur Theódórsson (76 Björn Bjartmarz), Helgi Sigurdsson, Atli Einarsson. Trainer: Logi Olafsson

Goals: Sergeev (21), Einarsson (30), Korsakov (34), Grishin (44), Steinsson (73), Kolesnikov (87)

MACCABI TEL AVIV v CLUB BRUGGE KV 0-1 (0-1)

Ramat Gan, Tel Aviv 16.09.1992

Referee: László Vagner (HUN) Attendance: 12,000

MACCABI: Aleksandr Uvarov; Avi Cohen (Cap), Gadi Brumer, Aleksandr Polukarov, Amit Levi, Noam Shoam, Aharon Meir Melika, Avi Nimni, Nir Klinger, Itzhak Zohar, Yaron Drori (70 Eli Driks). Trainer: Abraham Grant

CLUB BRUGGE: Danny Verlinden; Claude Verspaille, Alex Querter (Cap), László Disztl, Rudy Cossey, Dominique Vanmaele, Lorenzo Staelens, Marc Schaessens (75 Pascal Plovie), Stéphane van der Heyden, Gert Verheyen, Tomasz Dziubinski. Trainer: Hugo Broos

Goal: Staelens (35)

CLUB BRUGGE KV v MACCABI TEL AVIV 3-0 (0-0)

Stade Jules George, Liège 30.09.1992

Referee: Rémy Harrel (FRA) Attendance: 7,000

CLUB BRUGGE: Danny Verlinden; Claude Verspaille, László Disztl, Rudy Cossey, Dominique Vanmaele, Franky van der Elst (Cap) (78 Pascal Plovie), Lorenzo Staelens, Marc Schaessens, Stéphane van der Heyden, Foeke Booy, Gert Verheyen. Trainer: Hugo Broos

MACCABI: Aleksandr Uvarov; Avi Cohen (Cap), Gadi Brumer, Alon Brumer, Aleksandr Polukarov, Noam Shoam, Aharon Meir Melika (78 Nezah Masuby), Avi Nimni, Nir Klinger, Itzhak Zohar, Yaron Drori (62 Eli Driks). Trainer: Abraham Grant

Goals: Staelens (56), Verheyen (76, 83)

AEK FC ATHINA v APOEL NICOSIA 1-1 (1-0)

Neas Filadelfeias, Athina 16.09.1992

Referee: Arie Frost (ISR) Attendance: 28,000

AEK: Antonis Minou; Hristos Vasilopoulos (Cap), Vaios Karagiannis, Stelios Manolas, Refik Sabanadzović, Paulos Papaioannou, Alekos Alexandris, Toni Savevski, Stauros Stamatis, Vasilis Dimitriadis, Zoran Slisković (75 Giorgos Agorogiannis). Trainer: Dusko Bajević

APOEL: Andreas Petridis; Kostas Kosta, Kostas Miamiliotis, Dimitris Kleanthous, Lefteris Kouis, Toza Sapurić, Nikos Haralampous, Antros Sotiriou, Sinisa Gogić, Giannis Ioannou (Cap) (61 Costas Fasouliotis), Loukas Hatziloukas (77 Hristodoulos Hristodoulou). Trainer: Jacek Gmoch

Goals: Alexandris (41), Hatziloukas (75)

APOEL NICOSIA v AEK FC ATHINA 2-2 (0-1)

Makarion, Nicosia 30.09.1992

Referee: Charles Agius (MAL) Attendance: 7,200

APOEL: Andreas Petridis; Kostas Kosta, Kostas Miamiliotis, Dimitris Kleanthous (12 Willy Nwakama), Lefteris Kouis, Toza Sapuric, Nikos Haralampous, Antros Sotiriou (69 Kostas Fasouliotis), Sinisa Gogic, Giannis Ioannou (Cap), Loukas Hatziloukas. Trainer: Jacek Gmoch

AEK: Antonis Minou; Hristos Vasilopoulos (Cap), Vaios Karagiannis, Stelios Manolas, Refik Sabanadzovic, Paulos Papaioannou, Alekos Alexandris, Toni Savevski, Vasilis Dimitriadis (66 Anastasios Mitropoulos), Zoran Slisković (82 Giorgos Agorogiannis), Stauros Stamatis.
Trainer: Dusko Bajević

Goals: Sabanadzović (30), Dimitriadis (70), Gogić (77), Fasouliotis (84)

IFK GÖTEBORG v BEŞIKTAŞ JK ISTANBUL 2-0 (0-0)

Nya Ullevi, Göteborg 16.09.1992

Referee: Leslie Irvine (NIR) Attendance: 5,923

IFK: Dick Last; Magnus Johansson, Tore Pedersen, Ola Svensson (Cap) (52 Jonas Ohlsson), Pontus Kåmark, Peter Eriksson, Stefan Rehn, Håkan Mild, Thomas Andersson, Fredrik Leksell (70 Kaj Eskelinen), Johnny Ekström.
Trainer: Roger Gustavsson

BEŞIKTAŞ: Jaroslaw Bako; Recep Çetin, Gökhan Keskin, Ulvi Güveneroglu, Kadir Akbulut (46 Mutlu Topcu), Riza Çalimbay (Cap), Zeki Önatli, Mehmet Özdilek, Yüksel Hamit, Mitar Mrkela (83 Turan Uzun), Feyyaz Uçar.
Trainer: Gordon Milne

Goals: Eskelinen (72), Ekström (82)

BEŞIKTAŞ JK ISTANBUL v IFK GÖTEBORG 2-1 (1-1)

Inönü, Istanbul 30.09.1992

Referee: Angelo Amendolia (ITA) Attendance: 31,462

BEŞIKTAŞ: Jaroslaw Bako; Recep Çetin, Kadir Akbulut, Gökhan Keskin, Ulvi Güveneroglu (60 Turan Uzun), Yüksel Hamit, Feyyaz Uçar, Riza Çalimbay (Cap), Mehmet Özdilek, Mitar Mrkela, Metin Tekin (80 Sergen Yalçin).
Trainer: Gordon Milne

IFK: Dick Last; Tore Pedersen, Ola Svensson, Jonas Ohlsson, Pontus Kåmark, Peter Eriksson, Stefan Rehn, Håkan Mild, Thomas Andersson, Kaj Eskelinen (84 Magnus Johansson), Johnny Ekström (65 Fredrik Leksell).
Trainer: Roger Gustavsson

Goals: Eskelinen (11), Metin (25), Feyyaz (73)

GLENTORAN BELFAST v OLYMPIQUE de MARSEILLE 0-5 (0-4)

The Oval, Belfast 16.09.1992

Referee: Johannes Reygwart (HOL) Attendance: 9,500

GLENTORAN: Alan Paterson; George Neill, Raymond Morrison (72 James McCloskey), John Devine, Duncan Lowry, Robert Bowers (Cap), Andy Mathieson, Gary Hillis (72 John Jameson), Raymond Campbell, Gary McCartney, Eamonn Kavanagh. Trainer: William McCullough

OLYMPIQUE: Pascal Olmeta; Jocelyn Angloma (46 Jean-Jacques Eydelie), Basile Boli, Bernard Casoni (Cap), Manuel Amoros, Franck Sauzée, Jean-Philippe Durand (46 Jean-Marc Ferreri), Didier Deschamps, Rafael Martin Vázquez, Rudi Völler, Abedi Pele. Trainer: Jean Fernández

Goals: Völler (4), Martin Vázquez (21, 30), Sauzée (42), Ferreri (84)

OLYMPIQUE de MARSEILLE v GLENTORAN BELFAST 3-0 (2-0)

Vélodrome, Marseille 30.09.1992

Referee: Fortunato Alves de Azevedo (POR) Att: 10,000

OLYMPIQUE: Fabien Barthez; Manuel Amoros, Basile Boli, Marcel Desailly, Eric Di Meco, Jean-Jacques Eydelie, Jean-Christophe Thomas, Didier Deschamps (Cap) (46 Jean-Christophe Marquet), Rafael Martin Vázquez, Abedi Pele (46 Jean-Philippe Durand), François Omam-Biyik.
Trainer: Jean Fernández

GLENTORAN: Alan Paterson; George Neill, Duncan Lowry, Raymond Morrison, John Devine, Robert Bowers (Cap), Andy Mathieson, Eamonn Kavanagh (59 James McCloskey), John Jameson (78 Justin McBride), Gary McCartney, Gary Hillis.
Trainer: William McCullough

Goals: Omam-Biyik (6), Pele (12), Boli (72)

VfB STUTTGART v LEEDS UNITED 3-0 (0-0)

Neckar, Stuttgart 16.09.1992

Referee: Rune Larsson (SWE) Attendance: 36,000

VfB: Eike Immel; Slobodan Dubajic, Guido Buchwald (Cap), Uwe Schneider, Michael Frontzeck, Andreas Buck, Thomas Strunz (86 Günther Schäfer), Eyjólfur Sverrisson, Ludwig Kögl, Fritz Walter (80 Adrian Knup), Maurizio Gaudino.
Trainer: Christoph Daum

LEEDS UNITED: John Lukic; David Rocastle (46 Steve Hodge), Chris Fairclough, Chris Whyte, Tony Dorigo, Gordon Strachan, David Batty, Gary McAllister (Cap), Gary Speed, Eric Cantona (63 Carl Shutt), Lee Chapman. Manager: Howard Wilkinson

Goals: Walter (63, 68), Buck (81)

LEEDS UNITED v VfB STUTTGART 4-1 (2-1)

Elland Road, Leeds 30.09.1992

Referee: Kim Nilton Nielsen (DEN) Attendance: 20,457

LEEDS UNITED: John Lukic; Scott Sellars, Chris Whyte, Chris Fairclough, Tony Dorigo, David Batty, Gordon Strachan, Gary McAllister (Cap), Gary Speed, Lee Chapman, Eric Cantona. Manager: Howard Wilkinson

VfB: Eike Immel; Günther Schäfer, Slobodan Dubajic, Guido Buchwald (Cap), Michael Frontzeck, Thomas Strunz, Andreas Buck, Eyjólfur Sverrisson, Ludwig Kögl, Maurizio Gaudino (82 Jovica Simanic), Fritz Walter (80 Adrian Knup).
Trainer: Christoph Daum

Goals: Speed (18), Buck (33), McAllister (38 pen), Cantona (66), Chapman (78)

VfB Stuttgart fielded 4 foreign players which was against UEFA rules. UEFA therefore awarded the game to Leeds United with a 3-0 scoreline and a third, deciding match was ordered to be played.

LEEDS UNITED v VfB STUTTGART 2-1 (1-1)

Nou Camp, Barcelona 9.10.1992

Referee: Fabio Baldas (ITA) Attendance: 10,000

LEEDS UNITED: John Lukic; Jon Newsome, Tony Dorigo, David Batty, Chris Fairclough, Chris Whyte, Gordon Strachan, Eric Cantona (76 Carl Shutt), Lee Chapman, Gary McAllister (Cap), Gary Speed. Manager: Howard Wilkinson

VfB: Eike Immel; Günther Schäfer, Slobodan Dubajic, Guido Buchwald (Cap), Michael Frontzeck, Thomas Strunz (25 Alexander Strehmel), Andreas Buck, Eyjólfur Sverisson (79 Adrian Knup), Fritz Walter, André Golke, Ludwig Kögl.
Trainer: Christoph Daum

Goals: Strachan (33), Golke (38), Shutt (77)

SECOND ROUND

IFK GÖTEBORG v LECH POZNAN 1-0 (0-0)

Nya Ullevi, Göteborg 21.10.1992

Referee: Roger Philippi (LUX) Attendance: 8,800

IFK: Thomas Ravelli; Magnus Johansson, Jonas Ohlsson, Ola Svensson (Cap), Pontus Kåmark, Peter Eriksson, Stefan Rehn, Håkan Mild, Patrik Bengtsson, Thomas Andersson (72 Kaj Eskelinen), Johnny Ekström. Trainer: Roger Gustavsson

LECH: Kazimierz Sidorczuk; Jacek Bak, Marek Rzepka, Przemyslaw Bereszynski, Waldemar Kryger, Kazimierz Moskal (Cap), Dariusz Skrzypczak (90 Damian Lukasik), Miroslaw Trzeciak (73 Ryszard Remien), Igor Korniets, Jerzy Podbrozny, Jaroslaw Araszkiewicz. Trainer: Henryk Apostel

Goal: Bengtsson (87)

LECH POZNAN v IFK GÖTEBORG 0-3 (0-1)

PKP Lech, Poznan 4.11.1992

Referee: Patrick Kelly (IRE) Attendance: 28,000

LECH: Kazimierz Sidorczuk; Marek Rzepka, Jacek Bak, Waldemar Kryger (46 Czieslaw Jakolcewicz), Przemyslaw Bereszynski (53 Dariusz Kofynt), Ryszard Remien, Kazimierz Moskal (Cap), Dariusz Skrzypczak, Jerzy Podbrozny, Jaroslaw Araszkiewicz, Miroslaw Trzeciak. Trainer: Henryk Apostel

IFK: Thomas Ravelli; Magnus Johansson, Jonas Ohlsson, Ola Svensson (Cap), Pontus Kåmark (89 Patrik Bengtsson), Peter Eriksson, Stefan Rehn, Håkan Mild, Mikael Nilsson, Thomas Andersson, Johnny Ekström. Trainer: Roger Gustavsson

Goals: Ekström (28), Nilsson (47), Mild (82)

SLOVAN BRATISLAVA v AC MILAN 0-1 (0-0)

Tehelné pole, Bratislava 21.10.1992

Referee: Kim Milton Nielsen (DEN) Attendance: 34,467

SLOVAN: Alexander Vencel; Milos Glonek, Tomás Stúpala (Cap), Vladimír Kinder, Miroslav Chvíla, Ondrej Kristofík, Peter Dubovský, František Klinovsky (70 Youssef Haraoui), Jaroslav Timko, Pavol Gostic (61 Stefan Maixner), Ladislav Pecko. Trainer: Dušan Galis

AC MILAN: Francesco Antonioli; Mauro Tassotti, Alessandro Costacurta, Franco Baresi (Cap), Paolo Maldini, Gianluigi Lentini (81 Marco Simone), Demetrio Albertini, Roberto Donadoni, Zvonimir Boban, Marco Van Basten, Jean-Pierre Papin (46 Enzo Gambaro). Trainer: Fabio Capello

Sent off: Albertini

Goal: Maldini (61)

GLASGOW RANGERS FC v LEEDS UNITED 2-1 (2-1)

Ibrox, Glasgow 21.10.1992

Referee: Alphonse Constantin (BEL) Attendance: 43,251

RANGERS: Andy Goram; David Robertson, Richard Gough (Cap), David McPherson, Stuart McCall, John Brown, Trevor Steven (80 Pieter Huistra), Ian Ferguson, Ian Durrant, Alistair McCoist, Mark Hateley. Manager: Walter Smith

LEEDS UNITED: John Lukic; Jon Newsome, Chris Fairclough, Chris Whyte, Tony Dorigo, Gordon Strachan (88 David Rocastle), David Batty, Gary McAllister (Cap), Gary Speed, Eric Cantona (83 Rod Wallace), Lee Chapman. Manager: Howard Wilkinson

Goals: McAllister (1), Lukic (21 og), McCoist (37)

AC MILAN v SLOVAN BRATISLAVA 4-0 (2-0)

Giuseppe Meazza, Milano 4.11.1992

Referee: Antonio Martin Navarrete (SPA) Att: 30,000

AC MILAN: Francesco Antonioli; Mauro Tassotti (68 Enzo Gambaro), Franco Baresi (Cap), Alessandro Costacurta, Paolo Maldini, Frank Rijkaard, Roberto Donadoni, Zvonimir Boban, Gianluigi Lentini, Daniele Massaro (46 Marco Simone), Jean-Pierre Papin. Trainer: Fabio Capello

SLOVAN: Alexander Vencel; Tomás Stúpala (Cap), Miroslav Chvíla, Ondrej Kristofík, Vladimír Kinder, Marián Zeman, Ladislav Pecko, Youssef Haraoui (62 Stanislav Moravec), Pavol Gostic, Peter Dubovský, Jaroslav Timko (46 Stefan Maixner). Trainer: Dušan Galis

Goals: Boban (28), Rijkaard (29), Simone (49), Papin (71)

LEEDS UNITED v GLASGOW RANGERS FC 1-2 (0-1)

Elland Road, Leeds 4.11.1992

Referee: Aleksei Spirin (RUS) Attendance: 25,118

LEEDS UNITED: John Lukic; Jon Newsome, Tony Dorigo, Chris Fairclough (63 Rod Wallace), Chris Whyte, Gordon Strachan, David Rocastle (63 Steve Hodge), Gary McAllister (Cap), Gary Speed, Eric Cantona, Lee Chapman.
Manager: Howard Wilkinson

RANGERS: Andy Goram; David Robertson, Richard Gough (Cap), David McPherson, John Brown, Dale Gordon (71 Aleksei Mikhailichenko), Ian Ferguson, Stuart McCall, Ian Durrant, Alistair McCoist, Mark Hateley.
Manager: Walter Smith

Goals: Hateley (2), McCoist (59), Cantona (85)

DINAMO BUCUREŞTI v OLYMPIQUE de MARSEILLE 0-0

Naţional, Bucureşti 21.10.1992

Referee: Peter Mikkelsen (DEN) Attendance: 45,000

DINAMO: Florin Tene; Vasile Jercălău, Tibor Selymes, Gheorghe Mihali (Cap), Daniel Timofte, Marius Cheregi, Dorinel Munteanu, Gabor Gerstenmajer, Ovidiu Cornel Hanganu, Zoltan Kadar (65 Constantin Pană), Sulejman Demollari (79 Nelson Mensah).
Trainer: Alexandru Moldovan

OLYMPIQUE: Fabien Barthez; Jocelyn Angloma, Eric Di Meco, Basile Boli, Franck Sauzée, Marcel Desailly, Bernard Casoni (Cap), Jean-Christophe Thomas (46 Jean-Jacques Eydelie), Rudi Völler, Abedi Pele, Didier Deschamps.
Trainer: Jean Fernández

OLYMPIQUE de MARSEILLE v DINAMO BUCUREŞTI 2-0 (1-0)

Vélodrome, Marseille 4.11.1992

Referee: Arcangelo Pezzella (ITA) Attendance: 25,000

OLYMPIQUE: Fabien Barthez; Marcel Desailly, Basile Boli, Bernard Casoni (Cap), Manuel Amoros (66 Jean-Jacques Eydelie), Franck Sauzée, Didier Deschamps, Jean-Philippe Durand, Alen Boksic, Rudi Völler (73 Eric Di Meco), Abedi Pele. Trainer: Jean Fernández

DINAMO: Florin Tene; Vasile Jercălău, Tibor Selymes, Gheorghe Mihali (Cap), Daniel Timofte, Marius Cheregi, Dorinel Munteanu, Gabor Gerstenmajer, Ovidiu Cornel Hanganu (73 Nelson Mensah), Zoltan Kadar, Sulejman Demollari (13 Constantin Pană).
Trainer: Alexandru Moldovan

Goals: Boksic (32, 67)

CLUB BRUGGE KV v AUSTRIA WIEN 2-0 (2-0)

Olympia, Brugge 21.10.1992

Referee: Serge Muhmenthaler (SWI) Attendance: 16,000

CLUB BRUGGE: Danny Verlinden; László Disztl, Claude Verspaille, Rudy Cossey, Stéphane van der Heyden, Marc Schaessens (67 Peter Creve), Lorenzo Staelens, Franky van der Elst (Cap), Tomasz Dziubinski, Foeke Booy (79 Pascal Plovie), Gert Verheyen. Trainer: Hugo Broos

AUSTRIA: Franz Wohlfarth; Christian Prosenik, Manfred Zsak (Cap), Walter Kogler, Anton Pfeffer, Manfred Schmid, Michael Binder, Thomas Flögel, Peter Stöger, Robertas Fridrikas (65 Ralph Hasenhüttl), Valdas Ivanauskas.
Trainer: Hermann Stessl

Goals: Verheyen (22), Booy (41)

AUSTRIA WIEN v CLUB BRUGGE KV 3-1 (0-0)

Gerhard Hanappi, Wien 4.11.1992

Referee: Vasilios Nikakis (GRE) Attendance: 14,000

AUSTRIA: Franz Wohlfahrt; Walter Kogler (60 Robertas Fridrikas), Ernst Aigner, Manfred Zsak (Cap), Anton Pfeffer, Michael Binder, Christian Prosenik, Peter Stöger, Thomas Flögel, Ralph Hasenhüttl, Valdas Ivanauskas.
Trainer: Hermann Stessl

CLUB BRUGGE: Danny Verlinden; Claude Verspaille, Rudy Cossey, László Disztl, Pascal Plovie, Vital Borkelmans, Franky van der Elst (Cap), Lorenzo Staelens, Stéphane van der Heyden, Foeke Booy (86 Peter Creve), Gert Verheyen (71 Tomasz Dziubinski). Trainer: Hugo Broos

Goals: Zsak (49), Van der Heyden (64), Fridrikas (73), Hasenhüttl (90)

FC SION v FC PORTO 2-2 (0-0)

Stade de Tourbillon, Sion 21.10.1992

Referee: John Blankenstein (HOL) Attendance: 14,500

FC SION: Stéphane Lehmann; Alain Geiger, Michel Sauthier, Dominique Herr, Yvan Quentin, Marc Hottiger, Blaise Piffaretti (Cap), Roberto Assis, Márcio Orvela (82 Alexandre Clot), TÚLIO Umberto Costa, David Orlando.
Trainer: Jean-Paul Brigger

FC PORTO: VÍTOR Manuel Martins BAÍA; JOÃO Domingos Silva PINTO (Cap), FERNANDO Manuel Silva COUTO, ALOÍSIO Pires Alves, Fernando Óscar BANDEIRINHA Barbosa, JAIME Fernandes MAGALHÃES, RUI FILIPE Tavares Bastos, António dos Santos ANDRÉ (61 JORGE António Pinto COUTO), José Orlando Rocha SEMEDO, DOMINGOS José Paciencia Oliveira (69 ANTÓNIO CARLOS DOS SANTOS), Emil Kostadinov.
Trainer: Carlos Alberto Silva

Goals: Orlando (55), Assis (60), Semedo (80), F. Couto (83)

FC PORTO v FC SION 4-0 (0-0)

Estádio das Antas, Porto 4.11.1992

Referee: Brian Hill (ENG) Attendance: 35,000

FC PORTO: VÍTOR Manuel Martins BAÍA; JOÃO Domingos Silva PINTO (Cap), JORGE Paulo COSTA Almeida, ALOÍSIO Pires Alves, Fernando Óscar BANDEIRINHA Barbosa, JAIME Fernandes MAGALHÃES, RUI FILIPE Tavares Bastos, José Orlando Rocha SEMEDO (76 JORGE António Pinto COUTO), ANTÓNIO CARLOS DOS SANTOS, DOMINGOS José Paciencia Oliveira, Emil Kostadinov (73 António dos Santos ANDRÉ). Trainer: Carlos Alberto Silva

FC SION: Stéphane Lehmann; Michel Sauthier, Alain Geiger, Dominique Herr, Yvan Quentin (73 Oliver Biaggi), Marc Hottiger, Blaise Piffaretti (Cap), LUIS CARLOS Moreira, Reto Gertschen (62 TÚLIO Umberto Costa), Roberto Assis, David Orlando. Trainer: Jean-Paul Brigger

Goals: Jorge Costa (50), Kostadinov (63), Domingos (85), Magalhães (87)

AEK FC ATHINA v PSV EINDHOVEN 1-0 (0-0)

Neas Filadelfeias, Athina 21.10.1992

Referee: Hubert Forstinger (AUS) Attendance: 31,049

AEK: Antonis Minou; Hristos Vasilopoulos (Cap), Vaios Karagiannis, Stauros Stamatis, Refik Sabanadzović, Paulos Papaioannou, Alekos Alexandris (75 Giorgos Agorogiannis), Vasilis Dimitriadis (86 Anastasios Mitropoulos), Zoran Slisković, Giorgos Koutoulas, Toni Savevski.
Trainer: Dusko Bajević

PSV: Hans Van Breukelen; Berry Van Aerle, Adri Van Tiggelen, Ernest Faber, Jan Heintze, Erwin Koeman, Juul Ellerman, Gerald Vanenburg (Cap) (17 Romário de Souza Faria), Edward Linskens, Wim Kieft, Arthur Numan.
Trainer: Hans Westerhof

Goal: Dimitriadis (53)

PSV EINDHOVEN v AEK FC ATHINA 3-0 (1-0)

Philips, Eindhoven 4.11.1992

Referee: Fabio Baldas (ITA) Attendance: 26,500

PSV: Hans Van Breukelen; Berry Van Aerle, Adri Van Tiggelen, Ernest Faber, Jan Heintze, Edward Linskens, Arthur Numan, Gerald Vanenburg (Cap) (71 Juul Ellerman), Romário de Souza Faria, Wim Kieft, Peter Hoekstra.
Trainer: Hans Westerhof

AEK: Antonis Minou; Giorgos Agorogiannis (60 Anastasios Mitropoulos), Hristos Vasilopoulos (Cap), Stelios Manolas, Manolis Papadopoulos, Vaios Karagiannis, Alekos Alexandris, Paulos Papaioannou, Toni Savevski, Zoran Slisković (36 Dimitris Patikas), Vasilis Dimitriadis.
Trainer: Dusko Bajević

Goals: Romário (5, 51, 84)

CSKA MOSKVA v FC BARCELONA 1-1 (1-0)

Lenin, Moskva 21.10.1992

Referee: Kurt Röthlisberger (SWI) Attendance: 30,000

CSKA: Dmitri Kharin (Cap); Sergei Fokin, Dmitri Bystrov, Sergei Kolotovkin, Vasily Ivanov, Aleksei Guschin, Denis Mashkarin (67 Evgeni Bushmanov), Valeriy Minko, Aleksandr Grishin, Oleg Sergeev, Dmitri Korsakov (62 Ilshat Faizulin).
Trainer: Gennadi Kostylev

FC BARCELONA: Andoni Zubizarreta (Cap); Albert Ferrer, Ronald Koeman, Josep GUardiola (46 Guillermo Amor), Jon Andoni Goikoetxea, Miguel Ángel Nadal, Eusebio Sacristán, Aitor Beguiristain (82 JUAN CARLOS Rodríguez Moreno), Hristo Stoichkov, José María Bakero, Michael Laudrup.
Trainer: Johan Cruyff

Goals: Grishin (18), Beguiristain (59)

FC BARCELONA v CSKA MOSKVA 2-3 (2-1)

Camp Nou, Barcelona 4.11.1992

Referee: Bernd Heynemann (GER) Attendance: 70,000

FC BARCELONA: Andoni Zubizarreta (Cap); Albert Ferrer, Josep GUardiola (46 Eusebio Sacristán), Ronald Koeman, Guillermo Amor, Jon Andoni Goikoetxea, José María Bakero, Miguel Ángel Nadal (66 Julio Salinas), Michael Laudrup, Hristo Stoichkov, Aitor Beguiristain. Trainer: Johan Cruyff

CSKA: Dmitri Kharin (Cap); Aleksei Guschin, Sergei Kolotovkin, Oleg Malyukov, Sergei Fokin, Mikhail Kolesnikov (78 Vasily Ivanov), Denis Mashkarin, Aleksandr Grishin (41 Dmitri Korsakov), Oleg Sergeev, Evgeni Bushmanov, Ilshat Faizulin. Trainer: Gennadi Kostylev

Goals: Nadal (12), Beguiristain (31), Bushmanov (44), Mashkarin (57), Korsakov (61)

CHAMPIONS LEAGUE

GROUP A

CLUB BRUGGE KV v CSKA MOSKVA 1-0 (1-0)

Olympiapark, Brugge 25.11.1992

Referee: Bo Karlsson (SWE) Attendance: 17,000

CLUB BRUGGE: Danny Verlinden; Claude Verspaille (78 Peter Creve), Pascal Plovie, László Disztl (Cap), Rudy Cossey, Vital Borkelmans, Lorenzo Staelens, Franky van der Elst, Gert Verheyen, Daniel Amokachi (88 Alex Querter), Tomasz Dziubinski. Trainer: Hugo Broos

CSKA: Dmitri Kharin (Cap) (46 Aleksandr Guteev); Aleksei Guschin, Dmitri Bystrov, Oleg Malyukov, Sergei Kolotovkin, Evgeni Bushmanov, Denis Mashkarin, Mikhail Kolesnikov, Oleg Sergeev, Aleksandr Grishin (32 Dmitri Korsakov), Ilshat Faizulin. Trainer: Gennadi Kostylev

Goal: Amokachi (16)

GLASGOW RANGERS FC v OLYMPIQUE de MARSEILLE 2-2 (0-1)

Ibrox, Glasgow 25.11.1992

Referee: Sándor Puhl (HUN) Attendance: 41,624

RANGERS: Andy Goram; David McPherson, Richard Gough (Cap) (46 Steven Pressley), John Brown, David Robertson, Neil Murray, Trevor Steven (78 Gary McSwegan), Stuart McCall, Aleksei Mikhailichenko, Ian Durrant, Mark Hateley.
Manager: Walter Smith

OLYMPIQUE: Fabien Barthez; Jocelyn Angloma, Basile Boli, Bernard Casoni (Cap), Marcel Desailly, Eric Di Meco, Didier Deschamps, Franck Sauzée, Abedi Pele, Alen Boksic (84 Jean-Philippe Durand), Rudi Völler (89 Jean-Jacques Eydelie).
Trainer: Jean Fernández

Goals: Boksic (31), Völler (57), McSwegan (79), Hateley (81)

OLYMPIQUE de MARSEILLE v CLUB BRUGGE KV 3-0 (3-0)

Vélodrome, Marseille 9.12.1992

Referee: Aron Schmidhuber (GER) Attendance: 29,000

OLYMPIQUE: Fabien Barthez; Jocelyn Angloma, Bernard Casoni (Cap), Marcel Desailly, Eric Di Meco, Didier Deschamps, Franck Sauzée, Abedi Pele, Jean-Christophe Thomas, Jean-Jacques Eydelie (82 Jean-Philippe Durand), Alen Boksic (86 Jean-Marc Ferreri). Trainer: Jean Fernández

CLUB BRUGGE: Danny Verlinden; László Disztl, Vital Borkelmans, Franky van der Elst (Cap), Gert Verheyen, Stéphane van der Heyden, Lorenzo Staelens, Claude Verspaille, Pascal Plovie, Daniel Amokachi (46 Rudy Cossey), Tomasz Dziubinski. Trainer: Hugo Broos

Goals: Sauzée (4 pen), Boksic (10, 25)

CSKA MOSKVA v GLASGOW RANGERS FC 0-1 (0-1)

Ruhrstadion, Bochum 9.12.1992

Referee: Kim Milton Nielsen (DEN) Attendance: 9,000

CSKA: Aleksandr Guteev; Aleksei Guschin (67 Vasily Ivanov), Sergei Fokin (Cap), Dmitri Bystrov, Oleg Malyukov, Sergei Kolotovkin, Dmitri Korsakov, Valeriy Minko (60 Aleksandr Grishin), Evgeni Bushmanov, Ilshat Faizulin, Oleg Sergeev. Trainer: Gennadi Kostylev

RANGERS: Andy Goram; David McPherson, Trevor Steven, John Brown, Ian Durrant, Stuart McCall, Aleksei Mikhailichenko, Ian Ferguson, David Robertson, Mark Hateley, Alistair McCoist (Cap). Manager: Walter Smith

Goal: Ferguson (13)

OLYMPIQUE de MARSEILLE v CSKA MOSKVA 6-0 (3-0)

Vélodrome, Marseille 17.03.1993

Referee: Serge Muhmenthaler (SWI) Attendance: 30,000

OLYMPIQUE: Fabien Barthez; Marcel Desailly, Basile Boli, Eric Di Meco, Jocelyn Angloma, Franck Sauzée (66 Jean-Jacques Eydelie), Didier Deschamps, Jean-Philippe Durand, Abedi Pele, Rudi Völler (65 Jean-Marc Ferreri), Alen Boksić. Trainer: Raymond Goethals

CSKA: Aleksandr Guteev; Oleg Malyukov, Sergei Kolotovkin, Dmitri Bystrov, Sergei Mamchur, Yuri Antonovich, Valeriy Minko, Denis Mashkarin (40 Dmitri Korsakov), Evgeni Bushmanov (46 Aleksandr Grishin), Oleg Sergeev, Ilshat Faizulin. Trainer: Gennadi Kostylev

Goals: Sauzée (5 pen, 34, 49), Pele (43), Ferreri (71), Desailly (79)

CSKA MOSKVA v OLYMPIQUE de MARSEILLE 1-1 (0-1)

Olympiastadion, Berlin 3.03.1993

Referee: Fabio Baldas (ITA) Attendance: 13,000

CSKA: Evgeni Plotnikov; Sergei Mamchur, Oleg Malyukov, Dmitri Bystrov, Sergei Kolotovkin (Cap), Yuri Antonovich, Valeriy Minko (55 Dmitri Korsakov), Evgeni Bushmanov, Vasily Ivanov (46 Yuri Dudnik), Oleg Sergeev, Ilshat Faizulin. Trainer: Gennadi Kostylev

OLYMPIQUE: Fabien Barthez; Jean-Jacques Eydelie, Jocelyn Angloma, Bernard Casoni (Cap), Marcel Desailly, Eric Di Meco, Franck Sauzée, Didier Deschamps, Igor Dobrovolski (58 Jean-Philippe Durand), Alen Boksic, Abedi Pele. Trainer: Raymond Goethals

Goals: Pele (28), Faizulin (56)

GLASGOW RANGERS FC v CLUB BRUGGE KV 2-1 (1-0)

Ibrox, Glasgow 17.03.1993

Referee: Ryszard Wójcik (POL) Attendance: 42,731

RANGERS: Andy Goram; Scott Nisbet, Richard Gough (Cap), David McPherson, John Brown, Trevor Steven, Neil Murray, Stuart McCall, Ian Durrant (88 David Hagen), Mark Hateley, Alistair McCoist. Manager: Walter Smith

CLUB BRUGGE: Danny Verlinden; Peter Creve, László Disztl, Lorenzo Staelens, Rudy Cossey, Vital Borkelmans, Marc Schaessens (78 Tomasz Dziubinski), Franky van der Elst (Cap), Gert Verheyen, Stéphane van der Heyden, Daniel Amokachi. Trainer: Hugo Broos

Sent off: Hateley

Goals: Durrant (39), Staelens (55), Nisbet (75)

CLUB BRUGGE KV v GLASGOW RANGERS FC 1-1 (1-0)

Olympiapark, Brugge 3.03.1993

Referee: Antonio Martin Navarrete (SPA) Att: 19,000

CLUB BRUGGE: Danny Verlinden; Peter Creve (79 Claude Verspaille), Alex Querter, Lorenzo Staelens, Rudy Cossey, Vital Borkelmans, Gert Verheyen, Franky van der Elst, Tomasz Dziubinski, Foeke Booy, Daniel Amokachi. Trainer: Hugo Broos

RANGERS: Andy Goram; Scott Nisbet (84 Steven Pressley), David McPherson, John Brown, David Robertson, Pieter Huistra, Neil Murray, Stuart McCall, Aleksei Mikhailichenko, Mark Hateley, Alistair McCoist (Cap). Manager: Walter Smith

Goals: Dziubinski (44), Huistra (72)

CSKA MOSKVA v CLUB BRUGGE KV 1-2 (1-1)

Olympiastadion, Berlin 7.04.1993

Referee: Angelo Amendolia (ITA) Attendance: 2,000

CSKA: Evgeni Plotnikov; Aleksei Guschin, Sergei Kolotovkin (Cap), Oleg Malyukov, Dmitri Korsakov (74 Sergei Mamchur), Denis Mashkarin, Valeriy Minko, Evgeni Bushmanov, Vasily Ivanov (30 Yuri Antonovich), Oleg Sergeev, Ilshat Faizulin. Trainer: Gennadi Kostylev

CLUB BRUGGE: Danny Verlinden; Peter Creve, Rudy Cossey, Lorenzo Staelens, Vital Borkelmans, Stéphane van der Heyden, Marc Schaessens, Franky van der Elst (Cap), Tomasz Dziubinski (46 Foeke Booy), Gert Verheyen, Daniel Amokachi (89 Dominique Van Maele). Trainer: Hugo Broos

Goals: Sergeev (18), Schaessens (43), Verheyen (85)

OLYMPIQUE de MARSEILLE v GLASGOW RANGERS FC 1-1 (1-0)

Vélodrome, Marseille 7.04.1993

Referee: Mario van der Ende (HOL) Attendance: 46,000

OLYMPIQUE: Fabien Barthez; Jocelyn Angloma, Eric Di Meco, Basile Boli, Franck Sauzée, Marcel Desailly, Jean-Jacques Eydelie, Alen Boksic, Rudi Völler, Abedi Pele, Didier Deschamps (Cap). Trainer: Raymond Goethals

RANGERS: Andy Goram; Stuart McCall, David Robertson (53 Neil Murray), Richard Gough (Cap), David McPherson, John Brown, Trevor Steven, Ian Ferguson, Alistair McCoist, Ian Durrant, Pieter Huistra (80 Gary McSwegan). Manager: Walter Smith

Goals: Sauzée (16), Durrant (52)

CLUB BRUGGE KV v OLYMPIQUE de MARSEILLE 0-1 (0-1)

Olympiapark, Brugge 21.04.1993

Referee: Ion Crăciunescu (ROM) Attendance: 23,000

CLUB BRUGGE: Danny Verlinden; Peter Creve, László Disztl, Rudy Cossey, Vital Borkelmans, Marc Schaessens, Lorenzo Staelens (78 Alex Querter), Dominique Van Maele (83 Pascal Renier), Tomasz Dziubinski, Gert Verheyen, Daniel Amokachi. Trainer: Hugo Broos

OLYMPIQUE: Fabien Barthez; Jocelyn Angloma, Basile Boli, Marcel Desailly, Jean-Christophe Thomas, Jean-Jacques Eydelie, Jean-Marc Ferreri (46 Franck Sauzée), Didier Deschamps, Abedi Pele, Alen Boksic, Rudi Völler (89 Jean-Philippe Durand). Trainer: Raymond Goethals

Goal: Boksic (2)

GLASGOW RANGERS FC v CSKA MOSKVA 0-0

Ibrox, Glasgow 21.04.1993

Referee: Peter Mikkelsen (DEN) Attendance: 43,142

RANGERS: Andy Goram; Stuart McCall, David Robertson, Richard Gough (Cap), David McPherson, John Brown, Trevor Steven (83 Gary McSwegan), Ian Ferguson, Alistair McCoist, Ian Durrant, Pieter Huistra. Manager: Walter Smith

CSKA: Evgeni Plotnikov; Aleksei Guschin, Sergei Mamchur, Denis Mashkarin, Oleg Malyukov (Cap), Evgeni Bushmanov, Valeriy Minko, Dmitri Korsakov, Yuri Antonovich, Oleg Sergeev, Ilshat Faizulin (62 Yuri Dudnik). Trainer: Gennadi Kostylev

	P	W	D	L	F	A	Pts
Olympique de Marseille	6	3	3	0	14	4	9
Glasgow Rangers FC	6	2	4	0	7	5	8
Club Brugge KV	6	2	1	3	5	8	5
CSKA Moskva	6	0	2	4	2	11	2

GROUP B

FC PORTO v PSV EINDHOVEN 2-2 (1-1)

Estádio das Antas, Porto 25.11.1992

Referee: Antonio Martin Navarrete (SPA) Att: 34,000

FC PORTO: VÍTOR Manuel Martins BAÍA, JOÃO Domingos Silva PINTO (Cap), JOSÉ CARLOS Nascimento, ALOÍSIO Pires Alves, RUI FILIPE Tavares Bastos, JAIME Fernandes MAGALHÃES, José Orlando Rocha SEMEDO (62 ANTÓNIO JOSÉ ALVES RIBEIRO "TOZÉ"), JORGE António Pinto COUTO, António dos Santos ANDRÉ, Emil Kostadinov, DOMINGOS José Paciencia Oliveira. Trainer: Carlos Alberto Silva

PSV: Hans Van Breukelen; Adri Van Tiggelen, Gheorghe Popescu, Jan Heintze (34 Ernest Faber), Edward Linskens, Juul Ellerman, Erwin Koeman (78 Jerry De Jong), Arthur Numan, Gerald Vanenburg (Cap), Wim Kieft, Romário de Souza Faria. Trainer: Hans Westerhof

Sent off: Van Tiggelen (73)

Goals: Jaime Magalhães (35), Romário (43, 60), José Carlos (75)

AC MILAN v IFK GÖTEBORG 4-0 (1-0)

Giuseppe Meazza, Milano 25.11.1992

Referee: Frans van den Wijngaert (BEL) Att: 60,000

AC MILAN: Francesco Antonioli; Mauro Tassotti, Franco Baresi (Cap), Alessandro Costacurta (67 Stefano Nava), Daniele Massaro, Demetrio Albertini, Frank Rijkaard, Gianluigi Lentini (72 Marco Simone), Stefano Eranio, Marco Van Basten, Jean-Pierre Papin. Trainer: Fabio Capello

IFK: Thomas Ravelli; Tore Pedersen, Magnus Johansson, Ola Svensson (Cap), Pontus Kåmark, Peter Eriksson, Stefan Rehn (62 Fredrik Leksell), Håkan Mild, Thomas Andersson, Mikael Nilsson, Johnny Ekström. Trainer: Roger Gustavsson

Goals: Van Basten (33, 52 pen, 61, 63)

IFK GÖTEBORG v FC PORTO 1-0 (0-0)

Nye Ullevi, Göteborg 9.12.1992

Referee: Jozef Marko (CZE) Attendance: 18,000

IFK: Thomas Ravelli; Magnus Johansson, Ola Svensson (Cap), Pontus Kåmark, Mikael Nilsson, Peter Eriksson, Stefan Rehn, Håkan Mild, Patrik Bengtsson (72 Stefan Lindqvist), Thomas Andersson, Johnny Ekström. Trainer: Roger Gustavsson

FC PORTO: VÍTOR Manuel Martins BAÍA, JOÃO Domingos Silva PINTO (Cap), ALOÍSIO Pires Alves, Fernando Óscar BANDEIRINHA Barbosa, FERNANDO Manuel Silva COUTO, ANTÓNIO CARLOS DOS SANTOS (65 ANTÓNIO JOSÉ ALVES RIBEIRO "TOZÉ"), JORGE António Pinto COUTO, José Orlando Rocha SEMEDO, António dos Santos ANDRÉ, Emil Kostadinov, DOMINGOS José Paciencia Oliveira. Trainer: Carlos Alberto Silva

Goal: Eriksson (86)

PSV EINDHOVEN v AC MILAN 1-2 (0-1)

Philips Eindhoven 9.12.1992

Referee: Aleksei Spirin (RUS) Attendance: 27,500

PSV: Hans Van Breukelen; Raymond Beerens, Ernest Faber, Gheorghe Popescu, Jan Heintze, Edward Linskens, Juul Ellerman (40 Peter Hoekstra), Gerald Vanenburg (Cap), Arthur Numan, Wim Kieft, Romário de Souza Faria. Trainer: Hans Westerhof

AC MILAN: Sebastiano Rossi; Mauro Tassotti, Alessandro Costacurta, Franco Baresi (Cap), Paolo Maldini, Frank Rijkaard, Demetrio Albertini, Ruud Gullit (58 Stefano Eranio), Gianluigi Lentini, Marco Van Basten, Marco Simone (88 Daniele Massaro). Trainer: Fabio Capello

Goals: Rijkaard (19), Simone (62), Romário (65)

PSV EINDHOVEN v IFK GÖTEBORG 1-3 (1-3)

Philips Eindhoven 3.03.1993

Referee: Keith Burge (WAL) Attendance: 27,500

PSV: Hans Van Breukelen; Berry Van Aerle, Adri Van Tiggelen (Cap), Gheorghe Popescu, Ernest Faber, Jan Heintze, Edward Linskens (46 Gerald Vanenburg), Arthur Numan, Wim Kieft, Romário de Souza Faria, Peter Hoekstra. Trainer: Hans Westerhof

IFK: Thomas Ravelli; Magnus Johansson, Joachim Björklund, Ola Svensson (Cap), Pontus Kåmark, Peter Eriksson, Stefan Rehn, Håkan Mild, Mikael Nilsson, Mikael Martinsson (67 Thomas Andersson), Johnny Ekström (88 Stefan Lindqvist). Trainer: Roger Gustavsson

Goals: Numan (8), Nilsson (20), Ekström (35, 45)

FC PORTO v AC MILAN 0-1 (0-0)

Estádio das Antas, Porto 3.03.1993

Referee: Aron Schmidhuber (GER) Attendance: 55,000

FC PORTO: VÍTOR Manuel Martins BAÍA, JOÃO Domingos Silva PINTO (Cap), RUI JORGE de Sousa Dias Macedo de Oliveira, ALOÍSIO Pires Alves, FERNANDO Manuel Silva COUTO, Ion Timofte, JORGE Paulo COSTA Almeida, Emil Kostadinov (78 Nélson António Gama "TONI"), JORGE António Pinto COUTO (68 DOMINGOS José Paciencia Oliveira), José Orlando Rocha SEMEDO, João Paulo Santos "PAULINHO SANTOS". Trainer: Carlos Alberto Silva

AC MILAN: Sebastiano Rossi (88 Carlo Cudicini); Mauro Tassotti, Paolo Maldini, Demetrio Albertini, Alessandro Costacurta, Franco Baresi (Cap), Gianluigi Lentini, Zvonimir Boban, Jean-Pierre Papin, Ruud Gullit, Marco Simone (79 Alberigo Evani). Trainer: Fabio Capello

Goal: Papin (72)

IFK GÖTEBORG v PSV EINDHOVEN 3-0 (2-0)

Nya Ullevi, Göteborg 17.03.1993

Referee: Ion Crăciunescu (ROM) Attendance: 35,225

IFK: Thomas Ravelli, Magnus Johansson; Joachim Björklund, Ola Svensson (Cap), Pontus Kåmark, Peter Eriksson (57 Thomas Andersson), Stefan Rehn, Håkan Mild, Mikael Nilsson, Johnny Ekström, Mikael Martinsson. Trainer: Roger Gustavsson

PSV: Hans Van Breukelen; Berry Van Aerle, Adri Van Tiggelen (Cap), Ernest Faber, Jan Heintze, Edward Linskens, Erwin Koeman, Arthur Numan (14 Bwalya Kalusha), Gerald Vanenburg, Romário de Souza Faria, Peter Hoekstra. Trainer: Hans Westerhof

Goals: Nilsson (2), Ekström (45), Martinsson (47)

AC MILAN v FC PORTO 1-0 (1-0)

Giuseppe Meazza, Milano 17.03.1993

Referee: Philip Don (ENG) Attendance: 67,389

AC MILAN: Sebastiano Rossi; Franco Baresi (Cap), Enzo Gambaro, Alessandro Costacurta, Paolo Maldini, Stefano Eranio, Demetrio Albertini, Alberigo Evani, Gianluigi Lentini (65 Daniele Massaro), Jean-Pierre Papin, Marco Simone (77 Dejan Savicević). Trainer: Fabio Capello

FC PORTO: VÍTOR Manuel Martins BAÍA; JOÃO Domingos Silva PINTO (Cap), RUI JORGE de Sousa Dias Macedo de Oliveira, ALOÍSIO Pires Alves, FERNANDO Manuekl Silva COUTO, Ion Timofte (64 DOMINGOS José Paciencia Oliveira), João Paulo Santos "PAULINHO SANTOS", Emil Kostadinov, JORGE António Pinto COUTO, José Orlando Rocha SEMEDO, António dos Santos ANDRÉ (78 Manuel Albino Maçães "BINO"). Trainer: Carlos Alberto Silva

Goal: Eranio (31)

PSV EINDHOVEN v FC PORTO 0-1 (0-0)

Philips, Eindhoven 7.04.1993

Referee: Leslie William Mottram (SCO) Attendance: 27,750

PSV: Hans Van Breukelen; Raymond Beerens, Erwin Koeman (Cap), Ernest Faber, Jan Heintze, Gerald Vanenburg, René Klomp, Edward Linskens, Peter Hoekstra (81 Bwalya Kalusha), Romário de Souza Faria, Wim Kieft (62 Juul Ellerman). Trainer: Hans Westerhof

FC PORTO: VÍTOR Manuel Martins BAÍA; Fernando Óscar BANDEIRINHA Barbosa, JOSÉ CARLOS Nascimento, FERNANDO Manuel Silva COUTO, Lubomír Vlk (65 RUI JORGE de Sousa Dias Macedo de Oliveira), ANTÓNIO JOSÉ ALVES RIBEIRO "TOZÉ" (38 DOMINGOS José Paciencia Oliveira), João Paulo Santos "PAULINHO SANTOS", JORGE Paulo COSTA Almeida, JORGE António Pinto COUTO, Paulo César Vieira Rosa "PAULINHO CÉSAR", Manuel Albino Maçães "BINO". Trainer: Carlos Alberto Silva

Goal: José Carlos (71 pen)

IFK GÖTEBORG v AC MILAN 0-1 (0-0)

Nya Ullevi, Göteborg 7.04.1993

Referee: Karl-Josef Assenmacher (GER) Attendance: 40,323

IFK: Thomas Ravelli; Magnus Johansson, Joachim Björklund, Ola Svensson (Cap), Pontus Kåmark, Peter Eriksson, Stefan Rehn, Håkan Mild, Mikael Nilsson, Mikael Martinsson, Johnny Ekström. Trainer: Roger Gustavsson

AC MILAN: Sebastiano Rossi; Mauro Tassotti (Cap), Stefano Nava, Alberigo Evani, Alessandro Costacurta, Paolo Maldini, Gianluigi Lentini, Frank Rijkaard, Zvonimir Boban, Dejan Savićević, Daniele Massaro (86 Enzo Gambaro). Trainer: Fabio Capello

Goal: Massaro (70)

FC PORTO v IFK GÖTEBORG 2-0 (1-0)

Estádio das Antas, Porto 21.04.1993

Referee: David Elleray (ENG) Attendance: 6,000

FC PORTO: VÍTOR Manuel Martins BAÍA, Fernando Óscar BANDEIRINHA Barbosa, FERNANDO Manuel Silva COUTO, JOSÉ CARLOS Nascimento, RUI JORGE de Sousa Dias Macedo de Oliveira (46 JORGE Paulo COSTA Almeida), António dos Santos ANDRÉ, JAIME Fernandes MAGALHÃES (Cap), José Orlando Rocha SEMEDO, Ion Timofte, DOMINGOS José Paciencia Oliveira, Emil Kostadinov (82 MANUEL ALBINA MAÇÃES "BINO"). Trainer: Carlos Alberto Silva

IFK: Thomas Ravelli; Magnus Johansson, Joachim Björklund (66 Jonas Ohlsson), Pontus Kåmark (Cap), Mikael Nilsson, Stefan Linqvist, Stefan Rehn, Håkan Mild, Patrik Bengtsson, Mikael Martinsson (56 Peter Eriksson), Johnny Ekström. Trainer: Roger Gustavsson

Goals: José Carlos (42), Timofte (56)

AC MILAN v PSV EINDHOVEN 2-0 (2-0)

Giuseppe Meazza, Milano 21.04.1993

Referee: Sándor Puhl (HUN) Attendance: 56,862

AC MILAN: Carlo Cudicini; Stefano Nava, Paolo Maldini, Alessandro Costacurta, Enzo Gambaro, Roberto Donadoni, Fernando De Napoli, Zvonimir Boban, Alberigo Evani (Cap), Dejan Savicević, Marco Simone (32 Daniele Massaro). Trainer: Fabio Capello

PSV: Wim De Ron; Berry Van Aerle (36 Raymond Beerens), Adri Van Tiggelen, Mitchell Van der Gaag, Erwin Koeman, Juul Ellerman, Gerald Vanenburg (Cap), Gheorghe Popescu, Edward Linskens (77 René Klomp), Peter Hoekstra, Romário de Souza Faria. Trainer: Hans Westerhof

Goals: Simone (5, 19)

	P	W	D	L	F	A	Pts
AC Milan	6	6	0	0	11	1	12
IFK Göteborg	6	3	0	3	7	8	6
FC Porto	6	2	1	3	5	5	5
PSV Eindhoven	6	0	1	5	4	13	1

FINAL

OLYMPIQUE de MARSEILLE v AC MILAN 1-0 (1-0)

Olympiastadion, München 26.05.1993

Referee: Kurt Röthlisberger (SWI) Attendance: 72,300

OLYMPIQUE: Fabien Barthez; Jean-Jacques Eydelie, Jocelyn Angloma (62 Jean-Philippe Durand), Basile Boli, Marcel Desailly, Eric Di Meco, Franck Sauzée, Didier Deschamps, Abedi Pele, Alen Boksic, Rudi Völler (79 Jean-Christophe Thomas). Trainer: Raymond Goethals

AC MILAN: Sebastiano Rossi; Mauro Tassotti, Alessandro Costacurta, Franco Baresi (Cap), Paolo Maldini, Demetrio Albertini, Frank Rijkaard, Gianluigi Lentini, Roberto Donadoni (55 Jean-Pierre Papin), Marco Van Basten (85 Stefano Eranio), Daniele Massaro. Trainer: Fabio Capello

Goal: Boli (44)

European Cup Goalscorers 1992-93

7 goals: Romário de Souza Faria (PSV Eindhoven)

6 goals: Alen Boksic, Franck Sauzée (Olympique Marseille), Marco van Basten (Milan)

5 goals: Johnny Ekström (IFK Göteborg)

4 goals: Gert Verheyen (Club Brugge), Marco Simone (Milan), José Carlos (FC Porto), Túlio Humberto Costa (FC Sion)

3 goals: Lorenzo Staelens (Club Brugge), Ian Durrant, Mark Hateley (Rangers Glasgow), Abedi Pele (Olympique Marseille), Jean-Pierre Papin, Frank Rijkaard (Milan), Mikael Nilsson (IFK Göteborg), Juul Ellerman, Arthur Numan (PSV Eindhoven), Emil Kostadinov, Nélson António Gama "Toni" (FC Porto), Dmitri Korsakov (CSKA Moskva), Sergei Shevchenko (Tavria Simferopol), Vitaly Astafjev (Skonto Riga)

2 goals: Walter (VfB Stuttgart), Semjonov (Skonto Riga), Dubovský (Slovan Bratislava), Fridrikas, Hasenhüttl (Austria Wien), Assis (FC Sion), Dimitriadis (AEK Athina), Beguiristain (FC Barcelona), Huistra, McCoist (Glasgow Rangers), Grishin, Sergeev (CSKA Moskva), Boli, Martin Vázquez, Ferreri, Völler (Olympique Marseille), Massaro (AC Milan), Eskelinen (IFK Göteborg), Domingos, Fernando Couto, Jaime Magalhães, Semedo (FC Porto)

1 goal: Dully (Shelbourne), Zerafa (FC Valletta), Danielsen (KI Klaksvik), Ubavić, Topić, Vrabac, Zulić, Djuranović (Olimpija Ljubljana), Rinne (Kuusysi Lahti), Lipcsei (Ferencváros Budapest), Shishkov, Metkov, Andonov, Draganov (CSKA Sofia), Sheykhametov (Tavria Simferopol), Deville (US Luxembourg), Einarsson, Steinsson (Víkingur Reykjavík), Cohen, Nimni, Melika (Macabi Tel Aviv), Hatziloukas, Gogić, Fasouliotis (Apoel Nicosia), Metin, Feyyaz (Beşiktaş Istanbul), Buck, Golke (VfB Stuttgart), Trzeciak, Podbrozny (Lech Poznan), Yeliseyev (Skonto Riga), McAllister, Cantona, Strachan, Shutt (Leeds United), Gostic, Moravec (Slovan Bratislava), Gerstenmajer, Demollari (Dinamo Bucureşti), Zsak, Kogler, Ivanauskas, Flögel (FK Austria Wien), Orlando, Hottiger, Herr (FC Sion), Alexandris, Sabanadzović (AEK Athina), Nadal, Amor (FC Barcelona), Nisbet, Ferguson, McSwegan(Glasgow Rangers), Faizulin, Bushmanov, Mashkarin, Kolesnikov (CSKA Moskva), Schaessens, Dziubinski, Amokachi, Van der Heyden, Booy (Club Brugge), Desailly, Omam-Biyik (Olympique Marseille), Eranio, Maldini, Boban, Albertini, Tassotti (AC Milan), E.Koeman, Kieft (PSV Eindhoven), Martinsson, Eriksson, Bengtsson, Mild (IFK Göteborg), Timofte, Jorge Costa (FC Porto)

Own goal: Lukic (Leeds United) for Glasgow Rangers

THE EUROPEAN CUP 1993-94

PRELIMINARY ROUND

CWMBRAN TOWN v CORK CITY 3-2 (3-0)

Cwmbran stadium, Cwmbran 18.08.1993

Referee: Gylfi Orrasson (ICE) Attendance: 3,582

CWMBRAN TOWN: Patrick O'Hagan; David Burrows, Simon King, Michael Dicks (80 Philip McNeil), James Blackie, Michael Copeman, Norman Parselle (75 Kevin Payne), Wayne Goodridge, Francis Ford, Sean Wharton, John Powell.
Manager: Tony Wilcox

CORK CITY: Phil Harrington; Declan Daly, Stephen Napier, Fergus O'Donoghue, Paul Hague, Declan Roche, Dave Barry (30 Anthony Buckley), Declan Hyde, Tommy Gaynor, Pat Morley, Johnny Glynn (58 John Caulfield).
Manager: Damien Richardson

Goals: King (4 pen), Ford (25, 27), Caulfield (62), Buckley (75)

CORK CITY v CWMBRAN TOWN 2-1 (0-1)

Bishopstown, Cork 1.09.1993

Referee: Johannes P. Th. Reygwart (HOL) Att: 4,000

CORK CITY: Phil Harrington; Declan Daly, Stephen Napier, Fergus O'Donoghue, Paul Hague, Declan Roche (58 Johnny Glynn), Anthony Buckley, Declan Hyde (76 Liam Murphy), Tommy Gaynor, Pat Morley, John Caulfield.
Manager: Damien Richardson

CWMBRAN TOWN: Patrick O'Hagan; David Burrows, Simon King, Philip McNeil, James Blackie, Michael Copeman, Kevin Payne, Wayne Goodridge, Francis Ford, Sean Wharton (76 Mark Smith), Michael Dicks (86 Gary Vaughan).
Manager: Tony Wilcox

Goals: McNeill (7), Morley (75), Glynn (85)

HJK HELSINKI v NORMA TALLIN 1-1 (1-1)

Olzmpic, Helsinki 18.08.1993

Referee: Finn Lambek (DEN) Attendance: 2,000

HJK: Markku Palmroos; Marko Helin (73 Pasi Tauriainen), Aki Hyryläinen, Jari Europaeus, Antti Heinola; Janne Murtomäki, Janne Suokonautio, Sami Ylä-Jussila, Pekka Onttonen; Vesa Tauriainen (63 István Balogh), Jari Vanhala.
Trainer: Jari-Pekka Keurulainen

NORMA: Tõnu Vanakesa; Leonid Kurilov, Eduard Vinogradov, Vladimir Uryupin, Valeri Chmil; Andrei Belokhvostov, Andrei Shapovalov, Aleksandar Zhurkin, Andrei Borisov; Seppo Vilderson (73 Iuri Churilkin), Maksim Rõtshkov. Trainer: Valeri Bondarenko

Goals: Heinola (15), A. Borisov (16)

NORMA TALLIN v HJK HELSINKI 0-1 (0-0)

Rannavärava, Tallin 1.09.1993

Referee: Wojciech Rudy (POL) Attendance: 200

NORMA: Tönu Vanakesa; Leonid Kurilov, Eduard Vinogradov, Vladimir Uryupin, Valeri Chmil; Andrei Belokhvostov, Sergei Bragin, Seppo Vilderson (83 Urmas Liivamaa), Maksim Rõtshkov, Andrei Shapovalov (64 Iuri Churilkin), Aleksandar Zhurkin. Trainer: Valeri Bondarenko

HJK: Antti Niemi; Marko Helin (38 Jouko Vuorela), Aki Hyryläinen, Jari Europaeus, Antti Heinola; Janne Suokonautio (41 Janne Murtomäki), Sami Ylä-Jussila, Pekka Onttonen; Vesa Tauriainen, István Balogh, Jari Vanhala.
Trainer: Jari-Pekka Keurulainen

Goal: Belokhvostov (80 og)

FK EKRANAS PANEVEZYS v FLORIANA FC 0-1 (0-1)

Ekranas, Panevezys 18.08.1993

Referee: Ilkka Koho (FIN) Attendance: 8,000

EKRANAS: Arvydas Skrupskis; Raimondas Petrukaitis, Kestutis Aleksandravicius, Darius Butkus, Albertas Klimavicius, Andrius Staliunas, Vytautas Apanavicius, Linas Niurka (67 Arvydas Mykolaitis), Irmantas Stumbrys, Vaidotas Slekys, Audrius Banevicius (46 Dainius Luksys).
Trainer: Virginijus Liubsys

FLORIANA: David Cluett; Dennis Cauchi, David Galea; Jesmond Delia, Pierre Brincat, John Buttigieg, Kim Wright, James Briscoe (33 Mark Marlow), Mark Miller, Brian Crawley (71 Charles Sciberras), Richard Buhagiar.
Trainer: Mark Miller

Goal: J. Buttigieg (43)

AVENIR BEGGEN v ROSENBORG BK TRONDHEIM 0-2 (0-1)

Stade de Beggen 18.08.1993

Referee: Fernand Meese (BEL) Attendance: 789

AVENIR: Paul Koch; Ralph Ferron, Alex Wilhelm, Jaba Moreira, Jean Vanek, Frank Goergen, Theo Scholten, Luc Holtz, Gabriel Lopes (65 Roby Peters), Armin Krings (79 Serge Jentgen), Markus Krahen. Trainer: Michel Clément

ROSENBORG: Ola By Rise; Ole Einar Martinsen, Bjørn Otto Bragstad, Rune Tangen, Bjørn Tore Kvarme, Kåre Ingebrigtsen, Øyvind Leonhardsen, Bent Skammelsrud, Karl Petter Løken, Tore André Dahlum, Kent Bergersen.
Trainer: Nils Arne Eggen

Goals: Bragstad (19), Løken (54)

FLORIANA FC v EKRANAS PANEREVYS 1-0 (0-0)

Ta' Qali, Valletta 1.09.1993

Referee: Haim Lipkovitz (ISR) Attendance: 2,205

FLORIANA: David Cluett; Dennis Cauchi, David Galea, Jesmond Delia, Pierre Brincat, John Buttigieg, Zoran Popovic (79 Mario Caruana), Kim Wright (26 Albert Busuttil), Mark Miller, Brian Crawley, Richard Buhagiar.
Trainer: Mark Miller

EKRANAS: Arvydas Skrupskis; Raimondas Petrukaitis, Kestutis Aleksandravicius, Darius Butkus (79 Giedrius Juzelenas), Albertas Klimavicius, Andrius Staliunas, Vytautas Apanavicius, Vaidotas Slekys, Irmantas Stumbrys, Linas Niurka (61 Arvydas Mykolaitis), Vidmantas Daveikis.
Trainer: Virginijus Liubsys

Goal: J. Buttigieg (51)

ROSENBORG BK TRONDHEIM v AVENIR BEGGEN 1-0 (0-0)

Lerkendal, Trondheim 1.09.1993

Referee: John Walter Lloyd (WAL) Attendance: 4,481

ROSENBORG: Ola By Rise; Ole Einar Martinsen (79 Trond Henriksen), Rune Tangen, Bjørn Otto Bragstad, Bjørn Tore Kvarme, Kåre Ingebrigtsen, Øyvind Leonhardsen, Bent Skammelsrud, Karl Petter Løken, Tore André Dahlum, Kent Bergersen (70 Vidar Riseth). Trainer: Nils Arne Eggen

AVENIR: Paul Koch; Emmanuel Marchal (87 Ricardo Santos Pinto), Jaba Moreira, Alex Wilhelm, Jean Vanek, Frank Goergen, Theo Scholten, Luc Holtz, Serge Jentgen (83 Patrick Gomes), Roby Peters, Mikhail Zaritski.
Trainer: Michel Clément

Goal: Skammelsrud (69)

SKONTO RIGA v OLIMPIJA LJUBLJANA 0-1 (0-1)

Daugava, Riga 18.08.1993

Referee: Lennart Elofsson (SWE) Attendance: 1,500

SKONTO: Raimond Laizans; Igor Troitsky, Vitali Astafiev, Einars Gnedoy, Mikhail Zemlinsky; Igor Stepanov (76 Vladimir Dragun), Oleg Blagonadezhdin, Sergey Tarasov, Alexandr Dibrivny; Vladimir Babichev (56 Alexey Semenov), Alexandr Eliseyev. Trainer: Alexandr Starkov

OLIMPIJA: Marko Simeunović; Robert Englaro, Milos Hudarin, Zeljko Milinović, Edin Hadjialagić, Damir Vrabac, Dejan Djuranović (.. Miran Pavlin), Igor Benedejcić (.. Marko Gruskovnjak), Nenad Protega; Zoran Ubavić, Nedeljko Topić.
Trainer: Bojan Prasnikar

Goal: Milinović (16)

OLIMPIJA LJUBLJANA
v SKONTO RIGA 0-1 (0-0, 0-0) (AET)

Bezigrad, Ljubljana 1.09.1993

Referee: László Vagner (Ung) Attendance: 2,000

OLIMPIJA: Marko Simeunović; Robert Englaro, Milos Hudarin, Zeljko Milinović, Edin Hadjialagić, Damir Vrabac, Dejan Djuranović (.. Miran Pavlin), Samir Zulić, Nenad Protega, Zoran Ubavić (.. Marko Gruskovnjak), Nedeljko Topić. Trainer: Bojan Prasnikar

SKONTO: Raimond Laizans; Igor Troitsky, Vitali Astafiev, Einars Gnedoy, Mikhail Zemlinsky; Igor Stepanov, Oleg Blagonadezhdin, Alexandr Stradin (70 Vladimir Dragun), Alexandr Dibrivny (58 Alexey Semenov), Vladimir Babichev, Alexandr Eliseyev. Trainer: Alexandr Starkov

Goal: Troitsky (85)

Penalties: 0-1 Zemlinsky, 1-1 Gruskovnjak, 1-2 Troitsky, 2-2 Pavlin, 2-3 Blagonadezdin, 3-3 Protega, 3-4 Semenov, 4-4 Milinović, Eliseyev (miss), 5-5 Zulić, 5-6 Babichev, 6-6 Hudarin, Gnedoy (miss), Vrabac (miss), 6-7 Dragun, 7-7 Englaro, 7-8 Stepanov, 8-8 Simeunović, 8-9 Laizans, 9-9 Topić, 9-10 Zemlinsky, 10-10 Gruskovnjak, 10-11 Igor Troitsky, Pavlin (miss)

OMONOIA NICOSIA v FC AARAU 2-1 (1-0)

Makarion, Nicosia 18.08.1993

Referee: Gheorghe Constantin (ROM) Attendance: 18,000

OMONOIA: Andreas Haritou; Evagoras Hristofi, Giorgos Hristodoulou, Giannis Kalotheou, Andreas Giatrou (46 Sakis Andreou), Andreas Kantilos, Kostas Petsas, Nedim Tutic, Kostas Malekos (71 Athos Hrisanthou), Panikos Xiouroupas, David Kizilashvili. Trainer: Ioncho Arsov

FC AARAU: Andreas Hilfiker; Salvatore Romano, Stefan Marini, Mirko Pavlicevic, Daniel Wyss, René Weiler, Thomas Wyss, Marcel Heldmann, Heinz Hermann, Petar Alexandrov, Ratinho Everson (85 Arne Stiel). Trainer: Rolf Fringer

Goals: Kizilashvili (15, 61), Ratinho (62)

FC AARAU v OMONOIA NICOSIA 2-0 (2-0)

Brügglifeld, Aarau 1.09.1993

Referee: Hermann Albrecht (GER) Attendance: 8356

FC AARAU: Andreas Hilfiker; Stefan Marini, Mirko Pavlicevic, Salvatore Romano, Arne Stiel, Marcel Heldmann, Heinz Hermann, Thomas Wyss, Daniel Wyss, Ratinho Everson (89 René Weiler), Petar Alexandrov. Trainer: Rolf Fringer

OMONOIA: Andreas Haritou; Evagoras Hristofi, Giannis Kalotheou, Kostas Konstantinou, Giorgos Hristodoulou, Kostas Malekos (65 Andreas Kantilos), Athos Hrisanthou, Nedim Tutic (56 Giorgos Savvidis), Kostas Petsas, David Kizilashvili, Panikos Xiouroupas. Trainer: Ioncho Arsov

Goals: Stiel (6), Heldmann (38)

ZIMBRU CHIŞINĂU
v BEITAR JERUSALEM 1-1 (0-1)

Republican, Chişinău 18.08.1993

Referee: Periklis Vasilakis (GRE) Attendance: 16,000

ZIMBRU: Serghei Botnăraş; Boris Cibotaru, Emil Caras, Serghei Nani, Ion Testimiţanu, Radu Rebeja, Alexandru Curtianu, Alexandru Spiridon, Vasile Uzun, Iurie Miterev, Serghei Cleşcenco. Trainer: Sergiu Sârbu

BEITAR: Jacob Asiag; Ilan Elharar, Tommer Azuolai, Sergei Tretyak, Sergei Kolotovkin, Shmuel Levi, Meir Kadosh, Eitan Mizrahi, Vladimir Grechniev (63 Jacob Shwarts), Ronen Harazi (89 Ehod Cahila), Eli Ohana. Trainer: Dror Kashtan

Goals: Harazi (11), Rebeja (83)

BEITAR JERUSALEM
v ZIMBRU CHIŞINĂU 2-0 (1-0)

Teddi Maicha, Jerusalem 1.09.1993

Referee: Lube Spasov (BUL) Attendance: 8,000

BEITAR: Jacob Asiag; Shmuel Levi, Sergei Tretyak, Sergei Kolotovkin, Tommer Azuolai, Ilan Elharar, Meir Kadosh, Vladimir Grechniev, Jacob Shwarts, Ronen Harazi (88 Ronen Shwaig), Eli Ohana (82 Netsach Masuby). Trainer: Dror Kashtan

ZIMBRU: Serghei Botnăraş; Ion Testimiţanu, Serghei Nani, Emil Caras, Radu Rebeja, Boris Cibotaru, Vasile Uzun (46 Vitalie Culibaba), Alexandru Curtianu, Alexandru Spiridon, Iurie Miterev, Serghei Cleşcenco. Trainer: Sergiu Sârbu

Goals: Harazi (4), Grechniev (72 pen)

B 68 TOFTIR v CROATIA ZAGREB 0-5 (0-3)

Svangaskard, Toftir 18.08.1993

Referee: William Crombie (SCO) Attendance: 313

B 68: Olaf Magnussen; Jan Petersen, Jóhannes Danielsen, Oleif Joensen, Eydfinn Olsen; Jákup Djurhuus (61 Jógvan M.Olsen), Súni Fridi Johannesen, Hans Hansen (78 Ingolf Petersen), Össur Hansen; John Petersen, Aksel Höjgaard. Trainer: Jogvan Nordbud

CROATIA: Drazen Ladić; Dzevad Turković, Andrej Panadić, Slavko Istvanić, Damir Lesjak; Sead Halilović, Zeljko Adzić, Jozo Gaspar (30 Zeljko Pakasin), Josko Jelicić; Goran Vlaović, Igor Cvitanović (32 Igor Pamić). Trainer: Miroslav Blazević

Goals: Cvitanović (15), Lesjak (33), Vlaović (43), Turković (86), Adzić (89)

CROATIA ZAGREB v B 68 TOFTIR 6-0 (1-0)

Maksimir, Zagreb 1.09.1993

Referee: Friedrich Kaupe (AUS) Attendance: 8,000

CROATIA: Drazen Ladić; Dzevad Turković, Andrej Panadić, Slavko Istvanić, Damir Lesjak; Zoran Zivković (73 Mario Novaković), Sead Halilović, Zeljko Adzić, Goran Vlaović, Josko Jelicić (41 Mirko Lulić), Igor Cvitanović.
Trainer: Miroslav Blazević

B 68: Olaf Magnussen; Jan Petersen, Jóhannes Danielsen, Eydfinn Olsen; Ingemar Hojgaard, Jógvan Martin Olsen (86 Jákup Djurhuus), Súni Fridi Johannesen, Hans Hansen, Össur Hansen, John Petersen, Aksel Hojgaard (77 Páll Didriksen).
Trainer: Jogvan Nordbud

Goals: Zivković (16), Vlaović (53, 84, 88, 89), S. Halilović (74)

DINAMO TBILISI v LINFIELD BELFAST 2-1 (1-0)

Dinamo, Tbilisi 18.08.1993

Referee: Erman Toroglu (TUR) Attendance: 60,000

DINAMO: Irakli Zoidze; Georgi Nemsadze, Nugzar Lobjanidze, Murtaz Shelia, Gela Inalishvili, Mihail Kavelashvili (81 Georgi Anchabadze), Archil Arveladze, Gocha Jamarauli, Revaz Arveladze, Georgi Kinkladze, Shota Arveladze.
Trainer: Zhvania

LINFIELD: Wesley Lamont; Alan Dornan, John Easton, Lee Doherty, John McConnell, Gary Peebles, Ian McCoosh, Dessie Gorman, Richard Johnston, Garry Haylock (53 Stephen Beatty), Noel Bailie. Manager: Trevor Anderson

Goals: S. Arveladze (7), Johnston (56), Inalishvili (66)

UEFA Awarded the match to Linfield after Dinamo attempted to bribe the referee.

LINFIELD BELFAST v DINAMO TBILISI 1-1 (0-0)

Windsor Park, Belfast 1.09.1993

Referee: Roy Helge Olsen (NOR) Attendance: 5,000

LINFIELD: Wesley Lamont; Alan Dornan, John Easton, Lee Doherty, John McConnell, Stephen Beatty (.. Mark Anderson), Philip Knell (.. Dessie Gorman), Richard Johnston, Garry Haylock, Gary Peebles, Noel Bailie.
Manager: Trevor Anderson

DINAMO: Irakli Zoidze; Georgi Nemsadze, Gocha Chikovani, Murtaz Shelia, Gela Inalishvili, Mihail Kavelashvili, Archil Arveladze, Gocha Jamarauli, Revaz Arveladze, Georgi Kinkladze, Shota Arveladze. Trainer: Zhvania

Goals: S. Arveladze (19), Haylock (71)

PARTIZANI TIRANA v ÍA AKRANES 0-0

Qemal Stafa, Tirana 22.08.1993

Referee: Mateo Beusan (CRO) Attendance: 5,000

PARTIZANI: Avenir Dani; Shahin Berberi, Afrim Myftari, Artan Bano, Ilir Shulku, Ilir Sillo, Nordik Ruhi, Altin Satko, Eduard Dosti, Dritan Hoxha (46 Gentian Liçi), Nikolin Çoçlli (77 Ylli Çekiçi). Trainer: Sulejman Starova

ÍA AKRANES: Kristján Finnbogason; Sturlaugur Haraldsson, Olafur Adolfsson, Luka Lúkas Kostic, Theódór Hervarsson (75 Thórdur Gudjónsson); Olafur Thórdarson, Sigurdur Jónsson, Alexander Högnason, Sigursteinn Gíslason, Haraldur Ingólfsson; Mihajlo Bibercic. Trainer: Gudjón Thórdarson

ÍA AKRANES v PARTIZANI TIRANA 3-0 (0-0)

Akranesvöllur, Akranes 1.09.1993

Referee: Aron Schmidhuber (GER) Attendance: 1,561

ÍA AKRANES: Kristján Finnbogason; Sturlaugur Haraldsson, Olafur Adolfsson, Luka Lúkas Kostic, Sigursteinn Gíslason; Olafur Thórdarson, Sigurdur Jónsson, Alexander Högnason, Haraldur Ingólfsson; Thórdur Gudjónsson, Mihajlo Bibercic.
Trainer: Gudjón Thórdarson

PARTIZANI: Avenir Dani; Artan Bano, Afrim Myftari, Andon Nikolla (75 Shahin Berberi), Ilir Shulku, Ilir Sillo, Nordik Ruhi, Gentian Liçi (75 Dritan Hoxha), Eduard Dosti, Altin Satko, Nikolin Çoçlli. Trainer: Sulejman Starova

Goals: Högnason (70), Gudjónsson (71, 80)

FIRST ROUND

STEAUA BUCUREŞTI v CROATIA ZAGREB 1-2 (1-1)

Steaua, Bucureşti 15.09.1993

Referee: Vadim Zhuk (BLS) Attendance: 16,700

STEAUA: Dumitru Stîngaciu; Tiberiu Csik (27 Sorin Marian Tufan), Daniel Claudiu Prodan, Anton Doboş, Ionel Antonel Pârvu, Iulian Filipescu, Ilie Stan, Basarab Nică Panduru, Ilie Dumitrescu, Adrian Bucur Ilie (70 Viorel Ion), Ion Vlădoiu.
Trainer: Emerich Jenei

CROATIA: Drazen Ladić; Dzevad Turković, Andrej Panadić, Slavko Istvanić, Damir Lesjak; Mario Novaković (46 Zoran Zivković), Jozo Gaspar (69 Zeljko Pakasin), Josko Jelicić, Sead Halilović, Goran Vlaović, Igor Cvitanović.
Trainer: Miroslav Blazević

Goals: Cvitanović (15), Panduru (34), Jelicić (62)

CROATIA ZAGREB v STEAUA BUCUREŞTI 2-3 (1-1)

Olimpija, Ljubljana 28.09.1993

Referee: Vassilios Nikakis (GRE) Attendance: 6,000

CROATIA: Drazen Ladić, Dzevad Turković, Damir Lesjak, Slavko Istvanić, Andrej Panadić, Zeljko Adzić, Zeljko Pakasin (46 Mario Novaković), Josko Jelicić, Sead Halilović, Goran Vlaović, Igor Cvitanović. Trainer: Miroslav Blazević

STEAUA: Dumitru Stîngaciu; Aurel Silviu Panait, Daniel Claudiu Prodan, Anton Doboş, Ionel Antonel Pârvu, Constantin Gâlcă, Basarab Nică Panduru, Ilie Stan, Ilie Dumitrescu, Adrian Bucur Ilie (84 Viorel Ion), Ion Vlădoiu. Trainer: Emerich Jenei

Goals: Vlaović (8), Panduru (40), Vlădoiu (49, 61), Adzić (71)

FC DYNAMO KYIV v FC BARCELONA 3-1 (2-1)

Republikanskiy, Kiev 15.09.1993

Referee: Philip Don (ENG) Attendance: 60,000

DINAMO: Igor Kutepov; Oleh Luzhnyi, Anatoli Bessmertniy, Vitali Ponomarenko, Serhiy Mizin, Serhiy Rebrov, Sergei Kovalets, Sergei Shmatovalenko, Dmytro Topchiev, Viktor Leonenko (77 Volodymyr Sharan), Pavlo Shkapenko. Trainer: Mikhail Fomenko

FC BARCELONA: Andoni Zubizarreta; Alberto Ferrer, Josep Guardiola, Ronald Koeman, Jon Andoni GOIKOETXEA Lasa, IVÁN Iglesias Corteguera, Miguel Ángel Nadal, Guillermo Amor (58 Aitor Beguiristáin), Michael Laudrup, Hristo Stoichkov, Óscar García (66 Julio Salinas). Trainer: Johan Cruijff

Sent off: Mizin (27)

Goals: Shkapenko (6), R. Koeman (27 pen), Leonenko (45 pen, 56)

GALATASARAY ISTANBUL v CORK CITY 2-1 (1-0)

Ali Sami Yen, Istanbul 15.09.1993

Referee: José Maria Garcia-Aranda Encinar (SPA) Attendance: 17,804

GALATASARAY: Hayrettin Demirbaş; Bülent Korkmaz, Reinhard Stumpf, Falko Götz, Yusuf K.Tepekule, Tugay Kerimoğlu, Suat Kaya (86 Erdal Keser), Arif Erdem (76 Mustafa Kocabey), Hamza Hamzaoğlu, Hakan Şükür, Kubilay Türkyılmaz. Trainer: Rainer Hollmann

CORK CITY: Phil Harrington; Cormac Cotter, Declan Daly, Fergus O'Donoghue, Stephen Napier, Anthony Buckley, Dave Barry (81 Declan Roche), Declan Hyde, Liam Murphy, Tommy Gaynor, Pat Morley (89 John Caulfield). Manager: Damien Richardson

Goals: Türkyılmaz (30), Arif (51), Barry (67)

FC BARCELONA v FC DYNAMO KYIV 4-1 (2-1)

Camp Nou, Barcelona 29.09.1993

Referee: Angelo Amendolia (ITA) Attendance: 88,600

FC BARCELONA: Andoni Zubizarreta; Alberto Ferrer, Ronald Koeman, Jon Andoni GOIKOETXEA Lasa, Josep Guardiola, José María Baquero «BAKERO», Miguel Ángel Nadal, Michael Laudrup, Enrique ESTEBARANZ López «QUIQUE» (85 JUAN CARLOS Rodríguez Moreno), ROMÁRIO de Souza Faria, Aitor Beguiristáin (59 Guillermo Amor). Trainer: Johan Cruyff

DINAMO: Igor Kutepov; Oleh Luzhnyi, Anatoli Bessmertniy, Vitali Ponomarenko, Sergei Shmatovalenko, Sergei Kovalets (6 Yuri Gritsina), Andrei Annenkov, Pavlo Shkapenko, Dmytro Topchiev, Serhiy Rebrov, Viktor Leonenko. Trainer: Mikhail Fomenko

Goals: Laudrup (9), Bakero (17, 47), Rebrov (28), R. Koeman (67)

CORK CITY v GALATASARAY ISTANBUL 0-1 (0-0)

Bishopstown, Cork 29.09.1993

Referee: Didier Pauchard (FRA) Attendance: 6,500

CORK CITY: Phil Harrington; Cormac Cotter (80 Johnny Glynn), Fergus O'Donoghue, Declan Daly, Stephen Napier, Anthony Buckley, Dave Barry (83 Declan Roche), Declan Hyde, Liam Murphy, Pat Morley, Tommy Gaynor. Manager: Damien Richardson

GALATASARAY: Hayrettin Demirbaş; Bülent Korkmaz, Falko Götz, Reinhard Stumpf, Erdal Keser (63 Arif Erdem), Yusuf K.Tepekule, Tugay Kerimoğlu, Suat Kaya, Hamza Hamzaoğlu, Hakan Şükür, Kubilay Türkyılmaz (87 Mert Korkmaz). Trainer: Rainer Hollmann

Goal: Türkyılmaz (76)

AS MONACO v AEK FC ATHINA 1-0 (0-0)

Louis II, Monaco 15.09.1993

Referee: Manuel Diaz Vega (SPA) Attendance: 7,000

AS MONACO: Jean-Luc Ettori (Cap); Patrick Valéry, Emmanuel Petit, Franck Dumas, Luc Sonor, Jérôme Gnako, Claude Puel, Youri Djorkaeff, Enzo Scifo (67 Christian Perez), Victor Ikpeba, Amara Simba (86 Patrick Blondeau). Trainer: Arsène Wenger

AEK: Ilias Atmatzidis; Haralampos Kopitsis, Giorgos Koutoulas, Mihalis Vlahos, Vaios Karagiannis (Cap), Refik Sabanadzovic, Toni Savevski, Zoran Slisković (89 Vasilis Tsartas), Alekos Alexandris, Vasilis Dimitriadis (60 Anastasios Mitropoulos), Mihalis Kasapis. Trainer: Dušan Bajević

Goal: Vlahos (80 og)

AEK FC ATHINA v AS MONACO 1-1 (1-1)

Nikos Gkoumas, Athina 29.09.1993

Referee: John Blankenstein (HOL) Attendance: 31,500

AEK: Ilias Atmatzidis; Haralampos Kopitsis, Mihalis Vlahos, Stelios Manolas (Cap), Vaios Karagiannis, Refik Sabanadzović, Alekos Alexandris (68 Anastasios Mitropoulos), Toni Savevski, Mihalis Kasapis (60 Vasilis Tsartas), Zoran Slisković, Vasilis Dimitriadis. Trainer: Dušan Bajević

AS MONACO: Jean-Luc Ettori; Patrick Valéry, Lilian Thuram, Franck Dumas, Emmanuel Petit, Claude Puel, Jérôme Gnako, Youri Djorkaeff, Enzo Scifo (83 Gilles Grimandi), Jürgen Klinsmann (61 Franck Passi), Victor Ikpeba.
Trainer: Arsène Wenger

Goals: Djorkaeff (5), Slisković (12)

GLASGOW RANGERS FC v LEVSKI SOFIA 3-2 (1-0)

Ibrox Stadium, Glasgow 15.09.1993

Referee: Kim Milton Nielsen (DEN) Attendance: 37,013

RANGERS: Ally Maxwell; Gary Stevens, David McPherson, Steven Pressley, David Robertson, Trevor Steven, Stuart McCall, Ian Ferguson, Ian Durrant (74 John Morrow), Mark Hateley, Duncan Ferguson. Manager: Walter Smith

LEVSKI: Oleg Morgun; Emil Kremenliev, Petar Khubchev, Aleksandar Markov, Tsanko Tsvetanov, Zlatko Iankov, Dimitar Trendafilov, Georgi Slavchev, Nikolai Todorov, Daniel Borimirov, Petre Grigoraş (69 Georgi Ivanov).
Trainer: Georgi Vasilev

Goals: McPherson (45), Hateley (58, 78), Borimirov (79), Todorov (83)

KISPEST-HONVÉD FC BUDAPEST v MANCHESTER UNITED FC 2-3 (1-3)

Jozsef Bózsik, Budapest 15.09.1993

Referee: Piero Ceccarini (ITA) Attendance: 9,000

KISPEST-HONVÉD: István Brockhauser; Tibor Csehi, Attila Plókai, János Bánfi, József Szabados, Gábor Halmai, Béla Illés, József Duró (61 Ferenc Orosz), István Vincze, István Stefanov, István Hamar. Trainer: Martti Kuusela

MANCHESTER UNITED: Peter Schmeichel; Dennis Irwin, Steve Bruce, Gary Pallister, Paul Parker, Lee Sharpe, Bryan Robson, Paul Ince, Roy Keane, Eric Cantona, Ryan Giggs (80 Michael Phelan). Manager: Alex Ferguson

Goals: Keane (9, 42), Szabados (41), Cantona (44), Stefanov (69)

LEVSKI SOFIA v GLASGOW RANGERS FC 2-1 (1-1)

Georgi Asparuchov, Sofia 29.09.1993

Referee: Manuel Diaz Vega (SPA) Attendance: 52,500

LEVSKI: Plamen Nikolov; Emil Kremenliev, Petar Khubcev, Tsanko Tsvetanov, Aleksandar Markov, Zlatko Iankov, Daniel Borimirov, Nasko Sirakov, Georgi Slavchev, Nikolai Todorov, Georgi Ivanov (58 Petre Grigoraş). Trainer: Georgi Vasilev

RANGERS: Ally Maxwell; Gary Stevens, Fraser Wishart, Richard Gough, David McPherson, Trevor Steven, Stuart McCall, Ian Ferguson, Ian Durrant, Mark Hateley, David Hagen. Manager: Walter Smith

Goals: Sirakov (36), Durrant (43), Todorov (90)

MANCHESTER UNITED FC v KISPEST-HONVÉD BUDAPEST 2-1 (0-0)

Old Trafford, Manchester 29.09.1993

Referee: Antonio J. López Nieto (SPA) Attendance: 35,718

MANCHESTER UNITED: Peter Schmeichel; Paul Parker, Dennis Irwin (68 Lee Martin), Steve Bruce, Gary Pallister, Lee Sharpe, Bryan Robson, Paul Ince (79 Michael Phelan), Mark Hughes, Eric Cantona, Ryan Giggs. Manager: Alex Ferguson

KISPEST-HONVÉD: István Brockhauser; József Csábi, Attila Plókai, János Bánfi, Tibor Csehi (28 József Duró), Gábor Halmai, Béla Illés, József Szabados, István Sallói, István Vincze, István Hamar (62 Ferenc Orosz). Trainer: Martti Kuusela

Goals: Bruce (55, 64), Sallói (78)

AIK SOLNA v AC SPARTA PRAHA 1-0 (1-0)

Råsunda, Solna 15.09.1993

Referee: Andrei Butenko (RUS) Attendance: 5,854

AIK: Magnus Hedman; Krister Nordin, Peter Larsson, Thomas Lagerlöf, Björn Kindlund, Mattias Johansson, Michael Borgqvist, Dick Lidman, Johan Mjällby, Pascal Simpson, Gary Sundgren. Trainer: Tommy Söderberg

SPARTA: Milan Sova; Lumir Mistr, Jiří Novotný, Aleš Bazant (81 Jozef Kostelnik), Tomas Votava, Zdenek Svoboda, Pavel Nedved (53 Roman Vonasek), Jozef Chovanec, Martin Frýdek, Jozef Kozlej, Horst Siegl. Trainer: Karol Dobias

Goal: Lidman (36)

AC SPARTA PRAHA v AIK SOLNA 2-0 (1-0)

Stadión na Letnej, Praha 29.09.1993

Referee: Jan Damgaard (DEN) Attendance: 16,654

SPARTA: Peter Kouba; Jozef Chovanec, Michal Hornak, Jiří Novotný, Tomas Votava, Jozef Kostelnik, Zdenek Svoboda, Martin Frýdek (87 Peter Gunda), Pavel Nedved, Jozef Kozlej (70 Viktor Dvirnik), Horst Siegl. Trainer: Karol Dobias

AIK: Magnus Hedman; Krister Nordin, Peter Larsson, Johan Mjällby, Björn Kindlund (86 Thomas Lagerlöf), Vadim Evtushenko, Michael Borgqvist, Gary Sundgren, Mattias Johansson, Dick Lidman (67 Kim Bergstrand), Pascal Simpson. Trainer: Tommy Söderberg

Goals: Siegl (15, 81)

ÍA AKRANES v FEYENOORD ROTTERDAM 1-0 (0-0)

Laugardalsvöllur, Reykjavík 15.09.1993

Referee: Sándor Varga (HUN) Attendance: 6,327

ÍA AKRANES: Kristján Finnbogasson, Luka Lúkas Kostic, Sturlaugur Haraldsson, Sigurdur Jónsson, Thórdur Gudjónsson, Alexander Högnason, Olafur Adolfsson, Sigursteinn Gíslason, Mihajlo Bibercic, Olafur Thórdarson, Haraldur Ingólfsson. Trainer: Gudjón Thórdarson

FEYENOORD: Ed De Goey; Errol Refos, John De Wolf, John Metgod, Rob Witschge, Rob Maas, Peter Bosz, Arnold Scholten, Gaston Taument, John Van Loen, Arnar Gunnlaugsson. Trainer: Wim van Hanegem

Goal: Thórdarson (75)

HJK HELSINKI v RSC ANDERLECHT BRUSSEL 0-3 (0-0)

Tammelaan Pallokenttä, Tampere 15.09.1993

Referee: Rune Pedersen (NOR) Attendance: 1,500

HJK: Antti Niemi; Aki Hyryläinen, Jari Europaeus, Marko Helin, Antti Heinola (20 Pasi Tauriainen), Tommi Grönlund, Ari Lehkosuo, Sami Ylä-Jussila, Janne Murtomäki, Vesa Tauriainen (78 Mika Wallden), Jari Vanhala. Trainer: Peltoniemi

ANDERLECHT: Filip De Wilde; Bertrand Crasson, Michel De Wolf, Graeme Rutjes, Danny Boffin (83 Filip Haagdoren), Bruno Versavel, Johan Walem, Pär Zetterberg (78 Charles Musonda), Yaw Preko, Luc Nilis, John Bosman. Trainer: Johan Boskamp

Goals: Bosman (50), Versavel (77), Boffin (84)

FEYNOORD ROTTERDAM v ÍA AKRANES 3-0 (1-0)

Feyenoord, Rotterdam 29.09.1993

Referee: Keith W. Burge (SCO) Attendance: 24,000

FEYENOORD: Ed De Goey; John Metgod, John De Wolf, Errol Refos (71 Henk Fräser), Peter Bosz, Arnold Scholten, Rob Maas, Rob Witschge, Regi Blinker, Gaston Taument, Mike Obiku (66 John Van Loen). Trainer: Wim van Hanegem

ÍA AKRANES: Kristján Finnbogasson; Sturlaugur Haraldsson, Luka Lúkas Kostic, Olafur Adolfsson, Sigursteinn Gíslason, Olafur Thórdarson, Sigurdur Jónsson, Alexander Högnason, Haraldur Ingólfsson, Mihajlo Bibercic (88 Haraldur Hinriksson), Thórdur Gudjónsson. Trainer: Gudjón Thórdarson

Goals: Refos (26), Obiku (61), Blinker (79)

RSC ANDERLECHT BRUSSEL v HJK HELSINKI 3-0 (3-0)

Constant Vandenstock, Brussel 29.09.1993

Referee: Antonio José Almeida Marcal (POR) Att: 11,500

ANDERLECHT: Filip De Wilde; Bertrand Crasson, Graeme Rutjes, Alain van Baekel, Michel De Wolf, Johan Walem, Pär Zetterberg (60 Charles Musonda), John Bosman (78 Filip Haagdoren), Luc Nilis, Bruno Versavel, Danny Boffin. Trainer: Johan Boskamp

HJK: Antti Niemi; Aki Hyryläinen, Pekka Onttonen (68 Ari Lehkosuo), Antti Heinola, Jari Europaeus, Marko Helin, Sami Ylä-Jussila (53 Tommi Grönlund), Mika Wallden, Janne Murtomäki, Vesa Tauriainen, Jari Vanhala. Trainer: Peltoniemi

Goals: Nilis (16, 21, 42)

ROSENBORG BK TRONDHEIM v AUSTRIA WIEN 3-1 (3-1)

Lerkendal, Trondheim 15.09.1993

Referee: Simo Ruokonen (FIN) Attendance: 9,619

ROSENBORG: Ola By Rise; Ole Einar Martinsen, Bjørn Otto Bragstad, Rune Tangen, Bjørn Tore Kvarme, Kåre Ingebrigtsen, Bent Skammelsrud, Øyvind Leonhardsen, Karl Petter Løken, Tore André Dahlum, Kent Bergersen. Trainer: Hansen

AUSTRIA: Franz Wohlfahrt; Manfred Schmid, Manfred Zsak, Walter Kogler, Attila Sekerlioglu; Christian Prosenik, Peter Stöger, Thomas Flögel, Arminas Narbekovas (84 András Keresztúri), Andreas Ogris, Eric Orie (46 Ralph Hasenhüttl). Trainer: Josef Hickersberger

Goals: Tangen (28 pen), Zsak (33 pen), Leonhardsen (35), Løken (42)

AUSTRIA WIEN v ROSENBORG BK TRONDHEIM 4-1 (1-1)

Franz-Horr-stadion, Wien 29.09.1993

Referee: Zbigniew Przesmycki (POL) Attendance: 6,500

AUSTRIA: Franz Wohlfahrt; Walter Kogler, Manfred Zsak, Anton Pfeffer; Manfred Schmid, Christian Prosenik (65 Robertas Fridrikas), Peter Stöger, Arminas Narbekovas, Thomas Flögel, Andreas Ogris, Ralph Hasenhüttl (70 Marcus Pürk). Trainer: Josef Hickersberger

ROSENBORG: Ola By Rise; Ole Einar Martinsen, Bjørn Otto Bragstad, Rune Tangen, Bjørn Tore Kvarme, Vidar Riseth (85 Tor Gunnar Johnsen), Kåre Ingebrigtsen, Bent Skammelsrud, Ronny Støbakk, Tore André Dahlum, Kent Bergersen. Trainer: Hansen

Goals: Narbekovas (12), Dahlum (32), Schmid (50), Zsak (74), Kogler (81)

SKONTO RIGA v SPARTAK MOSKVA 0-5 (0-4)

Daugava, Riga 15.09.1993

Referee: Dimitar Ivanov Momirov (BUL) Attendance: 2,900

SKONTO: Raimond Laizans; Igor Troitsky, Vladimir Dragun, Igor Stepanov, Einars Gnedoy, Mikhail Zemlinsky, Oleg Blagonadezhdin, Alexandr Stradin, Alexandr Dibrivny, Vladimir Babichev (69 Sergey Tarasov), Alexandr Eliseyev (33 Alexey Semenov). Trainer: Alexandr Starkov

SPARTAK: Gintaras Stauče (31 Aleksandr Pomazun); Dmitriy Khlestov, Yuri Nikiforov, Viktor Onopko, Ramiz Mamedov, Ilya Tsymbalar, Valeri Karpin, Sergei Pogodin, Igor Lediakhov, Sergei Rodionov, Vladimir Beschastnikh. Trainer: Oleg Romantsev

Goals: Pogodin (2), Rodionov (7, 40, 43), Beschastnikh (70)

FC PORTO v FLORIANA FC 2-0 (1-0)

Estádio das Antas, Porto 15.09.1993

Referee: Roger Phillipi (LUX) Attendance: 7,000

FC PORTO: VÍTOR Manuel Martins BAÍA; JOÃO Domingos Silva PINTO, FERNANDO Manuel Silva COUTO, ALOÍSIO Pires Alves, RUI JORGE de Sousa Dias Macedo de Oliveira, António dos Santos ANDRÉ, Petar Sotirov MIHTARSHI (68 RUI FILIPE Tavares Bastos), José Orlando Rocha SEMEDO, António José Santos FOLHA (68 JORGE António Pinto COUTO), Emile Lubtchov KOSTADINOV, Nélson António Gama "TONI". Trainer: Tomislav Ivić

FLORIANA: David Cluett, John Buttigieg, Richard Buhagiar (88 Jeffrey Farrugia), Dennis Cauchi, Pierre Brincat, Kim Wright, Albert Busuttil (76 Charles Sciberras), Jesmond Delia, Zoran Popovic, Brian Crawley, Mark Miller. Trainer: Miller

Goals: Kostadinov (8), Semedo (78)

SPARTAK MOSKVA v SKONTO RIGA 4-0 (3-0)

Luzhniki, Moskva 29.09.1993

Referee: Joseph John Timmons (SCO) Attendance: 10,000

SPARTAK: Aleksandr Pomazun; Dmitriy Khlestov, Ramiz Mamedov, Viktor Onopko, Dmitriy Ananko, Ilya Tsymbalar, Nikolai Pisarev (60 Andrei Tikhonov), Valeri Karpin, Andrei Piatnitski, Sergei Rodionov, Vladimir Beschastnikh (60 Igor Lediakhov). Trainer: Oleg Romantsev

SKONTO: Raimond Laizans; Igor Troitsky, Vladimir Dragun, Einars Gnedoy, Igor Stepanov (75 Dzintars Savalnieks), Mikhail Zemlinsky, Oleg Blagonadezhdin, Alexandr Stradin (63 Alexandr Dibrivny), Alexey Semenov, Vladimir Babichev, Alexandr Eliseyev. Trainer: Alexandr Starkov

Goals: Tsimbalar (7, 39), Pisarev (14), Onopko (89)

FLORIANA FC v FC PORTO 0-0

National, Ta'Qali 29.09.1993

Referee: Bujar Pregja (ALB) Attendance: 5,000

FLORIANA: David Cluett, John Buttigieg, Richard Buhagiar, David Galea, Jesmond Delia, Pierre Brincat, Albert Busuttil, Zoran Popovic (87 Charles Sciberras), Mark Miller (88 Mark Marlow), Kim Wright, Brian Crawley. Trainer: Miller

FC PORTO: VÍTOR Manuel Martins BAÍA; JOÃO Domingos Silva PINTO, JOSÉ CARLOS Nascimento, ALOÍSIO Pires Alves, RUI JORGE de Sousa Dias Macedo de Oliveira, João Paulo Santos "PAULINHO SANTOS", RUI FILIPE Tavares Bastos, Carlos Alberto Oliveira SECRETÁRIO, António José Santos FOLHA (46 JORGE António Pinto COUTO), José Orlando Rocha SEMEDO, Emile Lubtchov KOSTADINOV (79 DOMINGOS José Paciencia Oliveira). Trainer: Tomislav Ivić

FC AARAU v AC MILAN 0-1 (0-0)

Zürich 15.09.1993

Referee: Alan Snoddy (NIR) Attendance: 9,400

FC AARAU: Andreas Hilfiker; Ryszard Komornicki, Arne Stiel, Salvatore Romano, Daniel Wyss, René Weiler (86 Dejan Markovic), Heinz Hermann, Thomas Wyss, Marcel Heldmann, Ratinho Everson (84 Stefan Renggli), Petar Alexandrov. Trainer: Rolf Fringer

AC MILAN: Sebastiano Rossi, Mauro Tassotti, Alessandro Costacurta, Franco Baresi, Paolo Maldini (84 Filippo Galli), Brian Laudrup (74 Demetrio Albertini), Stefano Eranio, Zvonimir Boban, Alessandro Orlando, Jean Pierre Papin, Daniele Massaro. Trainer: Fabio Capello

Goal: Papin (54)

AC MILAN v FC AARAU 0-0

Stadio Giuseppe Meazza, Milano 29.09.1993

Referee: Marc Batta (FRA) Attendance: 40,000

AC MILAN: Sebastiano Rossi, Mauro Tassotti, Alessandro Costacurta, Franco Baresi, Alessandro Orlando (82 Filippo Galli), Fernando De Napoli, Zvonimir Boban, Brian Laudrup (76 Daniele Massaro), Roberto Donadoni, Jean Pierre Papin, Marco Simone. Trainer: Fabio Capello

FC AARAU: Andreas Hilfiker; Bernd Kilian, René Weiler, Sascha Stauch (77 Dejan Markovic), Daniel Wyss, Marcel Heldmann (84 Stefan Renggli), Heinz Hermann, Salvatore Romano, Thomas Wyss, Petar Alexandrov, Ratinho Everson. Trainer: Rolf Fringer

WERDER BREMEN v DINAMO MINSK 5-2 (2-0)

Weserstadion, Bremen 16.09.1993

Referee: Serge Muhmenthaler (SWI) Attendance: 10,274

WERDER: Hans-Jürgen Gundelach; Rune Bratseth, Dietmar Beiersdorfer, Ulrich Borowka, Mario Basler (83 Thomas Wolter), Miroslav Votava, Andreas Herzog, Dieter Eilts, Marco Bode (61 Thorsten Legat), Bernd Hobsch, Wynton Rufer. Trainer: Otto Rehhagel

DINAMO: Andrei Satsunkevich; Erik Yakhimovich, Alexander Khatskevich (81 Alexander Taikov), Evgeni Kashentsev, Alexander Lukhvich, Vladimir Zhuravel, Sergei Gerasimets, Valentin Belkevich, Mihail Smirnov, Oleg Chernyavskiy (68 Iuri Shukanov), Valeri Velichko. Trainer: Mihail Vergeyenko

Goals: Hobsch (26, 32, 60), Gerasimets (51), Rufer (55, 90), Velichko (76)

LECH POZNAN v BEITAR JERUSALEM 3-0 (2-0)

Lech, Poznan 15.09.1993

Referee: George Ionescu (ROM) Attendance: 7,000

LECH: Jaroslaw Bako; Marek Rzepka, Jacek Bak, Damian Lukasik, Kazimierz Moskal, Waldemar Kryger, Dariusz Skrzypczak, Ryszard Remien, Jacek Dembinski (69 Dariusz Kofnyt), Jerzy Podbrozny, Miroslaw Trzeciak. Trainer: Roman Jakóbczak

BEITAR: Jacob Asiag; Tommer Azuolai, Sergei Kolotovkin, Ilan Elharar, Sergei Tretyak, Ehod Cahila (46 Netsach Masuby), Shmuel Levi, Meir Kadosh, Jacob Shwarts (71 Ronen Shwaig), Eitan Mizrahi, Ronen Harazi. Trainer: Dror Kashtan

Goals: Moskal (8), Podbrozny (32 pen), Trzeciak (60)

DINAMO MINSK v WERDER BREMEN 1-1 (1-0)

Dinamo, Minsk 29.09.1993

Referee: Sándor Puhl (HUN) Attendance: 7,000

DINAMO: Gennadiy Tumilovich; Erik Yakhimovich, Alexander Taikov, Andrei Ostrovski, Alexander Khatskevich, Sergei Gerasimets, Mihail Smirnov, Valentin Belkevich, Vladimir Zhuravel, Valeri Velichko (86 Oleg Putilo), Iuri Shukanov. Trainer: Mihail Vergeyenko

WERDER: Oliver Reck; Rune Bratseth, Dietmar Beiersdorfer, Thorsten Legat, Mario Basler (65 Andree Wiedener), Miroslav Votava, Andreas Herzog (83 Thomas Schaaf), Dieter Eilts, Marco Bode, Bernd Hobsch, Wynton Rufer. Trainer: Otto Rehhagel

Goals: Belkevich (41), Rufer (81 pen)

BEITAR JERUSALEM v LECH POZNAN 2-4 (1-3)

Teddi Maicha, Jerusalem 29.09.1993

Referee: John Purcell (IRE) Attendance: 5,000

BEITAR: Jacob Asiag; Yahiv Kardi (64 Ronen Shwaig), Meir Kadosh, Sergei Tretyak, Meir Salmi (30 Netsach Masuby), Eitan Mizrahi, Ilan Elharar, Jacob Shwarts, Sergei Kolotovkin, Ronen Harazi, Eli Ohana. Trainer: Dror Kashtan

LECH: Jaroslaw Bako; Marek Rzepka, Pawel Wojtala, Damian Lukasik, Jacek Bak, Waldemar Kryger (72 Dariusz Kofnyt), Dariusz Skrzypczak, Ryszard Remien, Kazimierz Moskal, Jerzy Podbrozny, Miroslaw Trzeciak (68 Jacek Dembinski). Trainer: Roman Jakóbczak

Goals: Lukasik (4), Ohana (12), Trzeciak (24), Podbrozny (31), Dembinski (70), Shwarts (73)

LINFIELD BELFAST v FC KØBENHAVN 3-0 (2-0)

Windsor Park, Belfast 16.09.1993

Referee: Freddy Philippoz (SWI) Attendance: 9,000

LINFIELD: Wesley Lamont; Alan Dornan, John McConnell, John Easton, Noel Bailie, Dessie Gorman (44 Philip Knell), Lee Doherty, Gary Peebles, Stephen Beatty, Richard Johnston, Garry Haylock. Trainer: McKeown

FC KØBENHAVN: Palle Petersen; Henrik Lykke (63 Michael Nielsen), Kenneth Wegner, Diego Tur, Brian Kaus, Lars Højer Nielsen, Morten Falch, Jørgen Juul Jensen, Iørn Uldbjerg, Michael Manniche, Martin Johansen (58 Peter Møller). Trainer: Benny Johansen

Goals: Haylock (38), McConnell (43), Johnston (60)

FC KØBENHAVN
v LINFIELD BELFAST 4-0 (2-0, 3-0) (AET)

Idraetsparken, København 29.09.1993

Referee: Roman Steindl (AUS) Attendance: 4,890

FC KØBENHAVN: Palle Petersen; Christian Lønstrup, Diego Tur (53 Henrik Lykke), Brian Kaus, Lars Höjer Nielsen, Michael Nielsen (86 Kim Mikkelsen), Iørn Uldbjerg, Michael Johansen, Peter Møller, Michael Manniche, Martin Johansen. Trainer: Benny Johansen

LINFIELD: Wesley Lamont; Jeff Spiers, John McConnell, John Easton, Noel Bailie, Lee Doherty, Stephen Beatty, Dessie Gorman, Gary Peebles, Robert Campbell (46 Philip Knell), Garry Haylock. Trainer: McKeown

Goals: Möller (2), Ma.Johansen (26), L.H. Nielsen (90), Mikkelsen (96)

SECOND ROUND

FC PORTO
v FEYENOORD ROTTERDAM 1-0 (0-0)

Estádio das Antas, Porto 20.10.1993

Referee: Remy Harrel (FRA) Attendance: 35,000

FC PORTO: VÍTOR Manuel Martins BAÍA; JOÃO Domingos Silva PINTO, ALOÍSIO Pires Alves, FERNANDO Manuel Silva COUTO, JOSÉ CARLOS Nascimento, RUI JORGE de Sousa Dias Macedo de Oliveira (62 JORGE António Pinto COUTO), JAIME Fernandes MAGALHÃES, Carlos Alberto Oliveira SECRETÁRIO (46 DOMINGOS José Paciencia Oliveira), José Orlando Rocha SEMEDO, João Paulo Santos "PAULINHO SANTOS", Emile Lubtchov KOSTADINOV.
Trainer: Tomislav Ivić

FEYENOORD: Ed De Goey; Ulrich Van Gobbel, John De Wolf, Henk Fräser, Errol Refos, Peter Bosz, Arnold Scholten, Rob Witschge, Gaston Taument, John Van Loen (74 Mike Obiku), Regi Blinker (82 Ruud Heus)
Trainer: Wim van Hanegem

Goal: Domingos (90)

FEYENOORD ROTTERDAM v FC PORTO 0-0

Feyenoord, Rotterdam 3.11.1993

Referee: Kim Milton Nielsen (DEN) Attendance: 42,395

FEYENOORD: Ed De Goey; Errol Refos, John De Wolf, Ulrich Van Gobbel, Henk Fräser (80 Dean Gorré), Arnold Scholten (70 Mike Obiku), Rob Maas, Rob Witschge, Gaston Taument, John Van Loen, Regi Blinker.
Trainer: Wim van Hanegem

FC PORTO: VÍTOR Manuel Martins BAÍA; JOÃO Domingos Silva PINTO, ALOÍSIO Pires Alves, FERNANDO Manuel Silva COUTO, JOSÉ CARLOS Nascimento, José Orlando Rocha SEMEDO, JAIME Fernandes MAGALHÃES (46 RUI FILIPE Tavares Bastos), RUI JORGE de Sousa Dias Macedo de Oliveira, JORGE Paulo COSTA Almeida, Carlos Alberto Oliveira SECRETÁRIO, Emile Lubtchov KOSTADINOV (90 DOMINGOS José Paciencia Oliveira). Trainer: Tomislav Ivić

AS MONACO v STEAUA BUCUREŞTI 4-1 (0-1)

Louis II, Monaco 20.10.1993

Referee: David Elleray (ENG) Attendance: 7,000

AS MONACO: Jean-Luc Ettori; Patrick Valéry, Lilian Thuram, Gilles Grimandi (8 Luc Sonor), Emmanuel Petit, Claude Puel, Youri Djorkaeff, Jérôme Gnako, Enzo Scifo, Jürgen Klinsmann, Victor Ikpeba (86 Franck Passi). Trainer: Arsène Wenger

STEAUA: Dumitru Stîngaciu; Aurel Silviu Panait, Daniel Claudiu Prodan, Anton Doboş, Ionel Antonel Pârvu, Constantin Gâlcă, Ilie Stan, Basarab Nică Panduru (53 Bogdan Bucur), Ilie Dumitrescu, Adrian Bucur Ilie, Ion Vlădoiu.
Trainer: Emerich Jenei

Goals: Dumitrescu (22 pen), Ikpeba (50, 75), Klinsmann (52, 64)

STEAUA BUCUREŞTI v AS MONACO 1-0 (0-0)

Steaua, Bucureşti 3.11.1993

Referee: Serge Muhmenthaler (SWI) Attendance: 21,000

STEAUA: Dumitru Stîngaciu; Aurel Silviu Panait, Bogdan Bucur (78 Adrian Bucur Ilie), Anton Doboş, Ionel Antonel Pârvu, Constantin Gâlcă, Basarab Nică Panduru, Ilie Stan (65 Iulian Filipescu), Ilie Dumitrescu, Marius Mihai Lăcătuş, Ion Vlădoiu. Trainer: Emerich Jenei

AS MONACO: Jean-Luc Ettori; Patrick Valéry, Franck Dumas, Luc Sonor, Emmanuel Petit, Jérôme Gnako, Youri Djorkaeff (57 Franck Passi), Enzo Scifo, Claude Puel, Jürgen Klinsmann, Victor Ikpeba (87 Gilles Grimandi). Trainer: Arsène Wenger

Goal: Dumitrescu (85)

LEVSKI SOFIA v WERDER BREMEN 2-2 (0-0)

Georgi Asparuchov, Sofia 20.10.1993

Referee: Mario van der Ende (HOL) Attendance: 50,000

LEVSKI: Plamen Nikolov; Petar Khubchev, Zlatko Iankov, Aleksandar Markov, Emil Kremenliev, Nikolai Todorov, Gosho Ginchev, Georgi Ivanov (60 Petre Grigoraş), Tsanko Tsvetanov, Daniel Borimirov, Nasko Sirakov. Trainer: Tsvetkov

WERDER: Oliver Reck; Rune Bratseth, Dietmar Beiersdorfer, Ulrich Borowka, Thomas Schaaf, Miroslav Votava, Wynton Rufer, Dieter Eilts, Marco Bode, Bernd Hobsch, Andreas Herzog. Trainer: Otto Rehhagel

Goals: Bode (50), Rufer (52), Iankov (75), Ginchev (90)

WERDER BREMEN v LEVSKI SOFIA 1-0 (0-0)

Weserstadion, Bremen 3.11.1993

Referee: Pierluigi Pairetto (ITA) Attendance: 26,953

WERDER: Hans-Jürgen Gundelach; Miroslav Votava, Dietmar Beiersdorfer, Ulrich Borowka, Mario Basler, Thomas Wolter, Wynton Rufer, Dieter Eilts, Marco Bode, Bernd Hobsch, Andreas Herzog. Trainer: Otto Rehhagel

LEVSKI: Plamen Nikolov; Petar Khubchev, Gosho Ginchev, Aleksandar Markov, Emil Kremenliev, Georgi Slavchev, Zlatko Iankov, Nikolai Todorov, Tsanko Tsvetanov, Daniel Borimirov, Nasko Sirakov. Trainer: Tsvetkov

Goal: Basler (73)

FC KØBENHAVN v AC MILAN 0-6 (0-4)

Idraetsparken, København 20.10.1993

Referee: Guy Goethals (BEL) Attendance: 34,285

FC KØBENHAVN: Palle Petersen; Kenneth Wegner (22 Brian Kaus), Henrik Lykke, Lars Højer Nielsen, Morten Falch, Michael Giolbas, Jørgen Juul Jensen (79 Michael Nielsen), Iørn Uldbjerg, Christian Lønstrup, Michael Manniche, Michael Johansen. Trainer: Benny Johansen

AC MILAN: Sebastiano Rossi, Christian Panucci, Alessandro Costacurta, Franco Baresi (61 Filippo Galli), Paolo Maldini, Demetrio Albertini, Zvonimir Boban, Alessandro Orlando, Brian Laudrup, Jean Pierre Papin, Marco Simone (61 Angelo Carbone). Trainer: Fabio Capello

Goals: Papin (1, 72), Simone (5, 16), B. Laudrup (44), Orlando (61)

RSC ANDERLECHT BRUSSEL v AC SPARTA PRAHA 4-2 (1-1)

Constant Vandenstock, Brussel 3.11.1993

Referee: Antonio Martin Navarrete (SPA) Att: 19,000

ANDERLECHT: Filip De Wilde; Bertrand Crasson, Graeme Rutjes, Michel De Wolf (47 Wim Kooiman), Philippe Albert, Bruno Versavel, Pär Zetterberg, Johan Walem, Danny Boffin, John Bosman, Luc Nilis. Trainer: Johan Boskamp

SPARTA: Peter Kouba; Michal Hornak, Jiří Novotný, Tomas Votava, Roman Vonasek (84 Pavel Nedved), Zdenek Svoboda, Jozef Kostelnik, Jozef Chovanec, Martin Frýdek (58 Jozef Kozlej), Viktor Dvirnik, Horst Siegl. Trainer: Karol Dobias

Goals: Bosman (2), Nilis (47, 73), Versavel (87), Dvirnik (17, 69)

AC MILAN v FC KØBENHAVN 1-0 (1-0)

Giuseppe Meazza, Milano 3.11.1993

Referee: Sándor Puhl (HUN) Attendance: 10,000

AC MILAN: Mario Ielpo, Christian Panucci, Alessandro Costacurta, Filippo Galli, Paolo Maldini (57 Stefano Nava), Demetrio Albertini, Fernando De Napoli, Alessandro Orlando, Brian Laudrup (46 Daniele Massaro), Jean Pierre Papin, Dejan Savicević. Trainer: Fabio Capello

FC KØBENHAVN: Palle Petersen; Christian Lønstrup, Diego Tur, Morten Falch, Brian Kaus, Michael Giolbas, Jørgen Juul Jensen (75 Lars Højer Nielsen), Iørn Uldbjerg, Michael Nielsen, Michael Manniche (80 Peter Møller), Michael Johansen. Trainer: Benny Johansen

Goal: Papin (45)

MANCHESTER UNITED FC v GALATASARAY ISTANBUL 3-3 (2-2)

Old Trafford, Manchester 20.10.1993

Referee: Peter Mikkelsen (DEN) Attendance: 39,396

MANCHESTER UNITED: Peter Schmeichel; Lee Martin, Gary Pallister, Steve Bruce, Lee Sharpe, Bryan Robson (65 Michael Phelan), Roy Keane, Paul Ince, Eric Cantona, Mark Hughes, Ryan Giggs. Manager: Alex Ferguson

GALATASARAY: Hayrettin Demirbaş; Reinhard Stumpf, Bülent Korkmaz, Falko Götz, Arif Erdem, Tugay Kerimoğlu, Uğur Tütüneker, Hakan Şükür, Hamza Hamzaoğlu, Suat Kaya (89 Yusuf B.Altintaş), Kubilay Türkyılmaz (75 Erdal Keser). Trainer: Rainer Hollmann

Goals: B. Robson (3), Hakan (13 og), Arif (16), Türkyılmaz (31, 63), Cantona (81)

AC SPARTA PRAHA v RSC ANDERLECHT BRUSSEL 0-1 (0-0)

Stadión na Letnej, Praha 20.10.1993

Referee: Christer Fallström (SWE) Attendance: 25,621

SPARTA: Peter Kouba; Jozef Kostelnik (82 Pavel Nedved), Michal Hornak, Jiří Novotný, Tomas Votava, Zdenek Svoboda, Roman Vonasek, Jozef Chovanec, Martin Frýdek, Horst Siegl, Jozef Kozlej. Trainer: Karol Dobias

ANDERLECHT: Filip De Wilde; Graeme Rutjes, Michel De Wolf, Philippe Albert, Danny Boffin, Johan Walem, Pär Zetterberg, Bruno Versavel, Alain van Baekel (46 Bertrand Crasson), Luc Nilis, John Bosman (90 Wim Kooiman). Trainer: Johan Boskamp

Goal: Nilis (74)

GALATASARAY ISTANBUL v MANCHESTER UNITED FC 0-0

Ali Sami Yen, Istanbul 3.11.1993

Referee: Kurt Röthlisberger (SWI) Attendance: 30,356

GALATASARAY: Hayrettin Demirbaş; Bülent Korkmaz, Reinhard Stumpf, Falko Götz, Arif Erdem (87 Uğur Tütüneker), Yusuf K.Tepekule, Suat Kaya, Tugay Kerimoğlu, Hamza Hamzaoğlu, Hakan Şükür, Kubilay Türkyılmaz (90 Mert Korkmaz). Trainer: Rainer Hollmann

MANCHESTER UNITED: Peter Schmeichel; Michael Phelan (85 Gary Neville), Paul Parker, Steve Bruce, Dennis Irwin, Roy Keane (72 Dion Dublin), Bryan Robson, Paul Ince, Lee Sharpe, Eric Cantona, Ryan Giggs. Manager: Alex Ferguson

LECH POZNAN v SPARTAK MOSKVA 1-5 (1-3)

Lech, Poznan 20.10.1993

Referee: Karl-Josef Assenmacher (GER) Attendance: 8,762

LECH: Jaroslaw Bako (46 Jacek Przybylski); Pawel Wojtala, Jacek Bak, Damian Lukasik, Marek Rzepka, Waldemar Kryger, Dariusz Skrzypczak, Ryszard Remien (20 Miroslaw Trzeciak), Kazimierz Moskal, Jerzy Podbrozny, Jaroslaw Araszkiewicz. Trainer: Roman Jakóbczak

SPARTAK: Aleksandr Pomazun; Ramiz Mamedov, Viktor Onopko, Yuri Nikiforov, Dmitriy Khlestov, Valeri Karpin, Fiodor Cherenkov (50 Igor Lediakhov), Dmitriy Ananko, Ilya Tsymbalar, Nikolai Pisarev, Vladimir Beschastnikh (75 Andrei Tikhonov). Trainer: Oleg Romantsev

Goals: Pisarev (8, 62), Karpin (10), Onopko (30, 53), Podbrozny (44 pen)

SPARTAK MOSKVA v LECH POZNAN 2-1 (1-1)

Luzhniki, Moskva 3.11.1993

Referee: Gerd Grabher (AUS) Attendance: 10,000

SPARTAK: Aleksandr Pomazun; Ramiz Mamedov, Yuri Nikiforov, Dmitriy Khlestov, Viktor Onopko, Valeri Karpin, Dmitriy Ananko (40 Fiodor Cherenkov), Ilya Tsymbalar, Igor Lediakhov, Vladimir Beschastnikh, Nikolai Pisarev. Trainer: Oleg Romantsev

LECH: Jacek Przybylski; Marek Rzepka, Jacek Bak, Damian Lukasik (72 Pawel Wojtala), Przemyslaw Bereszynski, Waldemar Kryger, Jacek Dembinski, Dariusz Skrzypczak, Kazimierz Moskal, Miroslaw Trzeciak (85 Lukasz Wojciechowski), Jerzy Podbrozny. Trainer: Roman Jakóbczak

Goals: Karpin (7), Dembinski (30), Khlestov (81)

FC BARCELONA v FK AUSTRIA WIEN 3-0 (1-0)

Camp Nou, Barcelona 20.10.1993

Referee: Hellmut Krug (GER) Attendance: 87,600

FC BARCELONA: Andoni Zubizarreta; Alberto Ferrer, Ronald Koeman, Jon Andoni GOIKOETXEA Lasa, Miguel Ángel Nadal, Josep Guardiola, Julio Salinas (62 Guillermo Amor), ROMÁRIO de Souza Faria, Michael Laudrup, Enrique ESTEBARANZ López "QUIQUE", Aitor Beguiristáin (46 Eusebio Sacristán). Trainer: Johan Cruyff

AUSTRIA: Franz Wohlfahrt; Ernst Aigner, Manfred Zsak, Anton Pfeffer, Attila Şekerlioğlu, Walter Kogler; Christian Prosenik, Manfred Schmid, Arminas Narbekovas (66 Eric Orie), Peter Stöger, Ralph Hassenhüttl (59 Robertas Fridrikas). Trainer: Josef Hickersberger

Goals: R. Koeman (33 pen, 67), Quique (89)

FK AUSTRIA WIEN v FC BARCELONA 1-2 (1-1)

Ernst Happel, Wien 3.11.1993

Referee: James McCluskey (SCO) Attendance: 22,000

AUSTRIA: Franz Wohlfahrt; Walter Kogler, Manfred Zsak, Ernst Aigner, Anton Pfeffer; Christian Prosenik, Peter Stöger, Arminas Narbekovas, Thomas Flögel (82 Jürgen Kauz), Andreas Ogris (56 Robertas Fridrikas), Manfred Schmid. Trainer: Josef Hickersberger

FC BARCELONA: Andoni Zubizarreta; Alberto Ferrer, Ronald Koeman, Miguel Ángel Nadal, Eusebio Sacristán, José María Baquero "Bakero" (74 IVÁN Iglesias Corteguera), Guillermo Amor, Jon Andoni GOIKOETXEA Lasa, Hristo Stoichkov, ROMÁRIO de Souza Faria, Aitor Beguiristáin (60 Enrique ESTEBARANZ López "QUIQUE"). Trainer: Johan Cruyff

Goals: Stoichkov (5, 78), Ogris (40)

CHAMPIONS LEAGUE

GROUP A

AS MONACO v SPARTAK MOSKVA 4-1 (2-0)

Louis II, Monaco 24.11.1993

Referee: Fabio Baldas (ITA) Attendance: 18,000

AS MONACO: Jean-Luc Ettori; Patrick Valéry, Emmanuel Petit, Franck Dumas, Luc Sonor, Claude Puel, Lilian Thuram, Youri Djorkaeff (83 Franck Passi), Enzo Scifo, Jürgen Klinsmann, Victor Ikpeba (72 Jérôme Gnako). Trainer: Arsène Wenger

SPARTAK: Aleksandr Pomazun; Ilya Tsymbalar, Andrei Ivanov, Yuri Nikiforov, Dmitriy Khlestov, Ramiz Mamedov, Valeri Karpin, Viktor Onopko, Igor Lediakhov (46 Andrei Piatnitski), Vladimir Beschastnikh (73 Sergei Rodionov), Nikolai Pisarev. Trainer: Oleg Romantsev

Goals: Klinsmann (17), Ikpeba (40), Pisarev (49), Djorkaeff (62 pen), Thuram (90)

GALATASARAY ISTANBUL v FC BARCELONA 0-0

Ali Sami Yen, Istanbul 24.11.1993

Referee: Frans van den Wijgaert (BEL) Attendance: 30,000

GALATASARAY: Hayrettin Demirbaş; Bülent Korkmaz, Falko Götz (28 Yusuf Altintaş), Reinhard Stumpf, Yusuf Tepekule, Uğur Tütüneker (70 Arif Erdem), Tugay Kerimoğlu, Suat Kaya, Hamza Hamzaoğlu, Hakan Şükür, Kubilay Türkyılmaz. Trainer: Rainer Hollmann

FC BARCELONA: Andoni Zubizarreta; Alberto Ferrer, Josep Guardiola, Ronald Koeman, Miguel Ángel Nadal, José María Baquero "BAKERO", JUAN CARLOS Rodríguez Moreno (55 Guillermo Amor), Eusebio Sacristán (82 Enrique ESTEBARANZ López "QUIQUE"), Michael Laudrup, ROMÁRIO de Souza Faria, SERGI Barjuán Esclusa. Trainer: Johan Cruyff

FC BARCELONA v AS MONACO 2-0 (2-0)

Camp Nou, Barcelona 8.12.1993

Referee: Kim Milton Nielsen (DEN) Attendance: 89,000

FC BARCELONA: Andoni Zubizarreta; Alberto Ferrer, Ronald Koeman, SERGI Barjuán Esclusa, Jon Andoni GOIKOETXEA Lasa, Guillermo Amor, Josep Guardiola (80 IVÁN Iglesias Corteguera), José María Baquero "BAKERO", Aitor Beguiristáin (61 Miguel Ángel Nadal), Michael Laudrup, Hristo Stoichkov. Trainer: Johan Cruyff

AS MONACO: Jean-Luc Ettori; Franck Dumas, Patrick Valéry, Lilian Thuram (46 Jérôme Gnako), Emmanuel Petit, Luc Sonor, Youri Djorkaeff (71 Amara Simba), Claude Puel, Enzo Scifo, Jürgen Klinsmann, Victor Ikpeba.
Trainer: Arsène Wenger

Goals: Beguiristáin (15, 26)

AS MONACO v GALATASARAY ISTANBUL 3-0 (2-0)

Louis II, Monaco 2.03.1994

Referee: Hellmut Krug (GER) Attendance: 18,000

AS MONACO: Jean-Luc Ettori; Emmanuel Petit (46 Patrick Valéry), Gilles Grimandi, Lilian Thuram, Patrick Blondeau, Claude Puel, Laurent Viaud (58 Jérôme Gnako), Youri Djorkaeff, Enzo Scifo, Jürgen Klinsmann, Victor Ikpeba.
Trainer: Arsène Wenger

GALATASARAY: Hayrettin Demirbaş; Yusuf K.Tepekule, Mert Korkmaz, Falko Götz, Bülent Korkmaz, Soner Tolungüc (59 Hamza Hamzaoğlu), Tugay Kerimoğlu, Erdal Keser, Uğur Tütüneker, Arif Erdem (85 Okan Buruk), Hakan Şükür.
Trainer: Rainer Hollmann

Goals: Scifo (36), Djorkaeff (41), Klinsmann (55)

SPARTAK MOSKVA v GALATASARAY ISTANBUL 0-0

Luzhniki, Moskva 8.12.1993

Referee: John Blankenstein (HOL) Attendance: 45,000

SPARTAK: Aleksandr Pomazun; Dmitriy Khlestov (33 Andrei Ivanov), Ramiz Mamedov, Ilya Tsymbalar, Nikolai Pisarev, Yuri Nikiforov, Viktor Onopko, Valeri Karpin, Andrei Piatnitski, Igor Lediakhov, Vladimir Beschastnikh (58 Dmitriy Ananko). Trainer: Oleg Romantsev

GALATASARAY: Hayrettin Demirbaş; Mert Korkmaz (85 Erdal Keser), Reinhard Stumpf, Bülent Korkmaz, Yusuf K.Tepekule, Uğur Tütüneker, Tugay Kerimoğlu, Suat Kaya, Hamza Hamzaoğlu, Hakan Şükür, Arif Erdem.
Trainer: Rainer Hollmann

FC BARCELONA v SPARTAK MOSKVA 5-1 (1-1)

Camp Nou, Barcelona 16.03.1994

Referee: Serge Muhmenthaler (SWI) Attendance: 80,000

FC BARCELONA: Andoni Zubizarreta; Alberto Ferrer, Miguel Ángel Nadal, Ronald Koeman (85 Aitor Beguiristáin), SERGI Barjuán Esclusa, Josep Guardiola, Guillermo Amor, José María Baquero "Bakero" (65 Jon Andoni GOIKOETXEA Lasa), IVÁN Iglesias Corteguera, Hristo Stoichkov, ROMÁRIO de Souza Faria. Trainer: Johan Cruyff

SPARTAK: Gintaras Staučе; Andrei Ivanov, Vladislav Ternavski, Dmitriy Khlestov, Yuri Nikiforov, Ilya Tsymbalar, Viktor Onopko, Valeri Karpin, Andrei Piatnitski, Igor Lediakhov (46 Sergei Rodionov), Vladimir Beschastnikh (72 Nikolai Pisarev). Trainer: Oleg Romantsev

Goals: Karpin (3), Stoichkov (33), Amor (75), R. Koeman (77, 80), Romário (86 pen)

SPARTAK MOSKVA v FC BARCELONA 2-2 (0-1)

Luzhniki, Moskva 2.03.1994

Referee: Sándor Puhl (HUN) Attendance: 61,000

SPARTAK: Gintaras Staučе; Vladislav Ternavski, Yuri Nikiforov, Andrei Ivanov, Dmitriy Khlestov, Ilya Tsymbalar, Valeri Karpin, Andrei Piatnitski, Igor Lediakhov, Nikolai Pisarev (46 Sergei Rodionov), Vladimir Beschastnikh.
Trainer: Oleg Romantsev

FC BARCELONA: Andoni Zubizarreta; Alberto Ferrer, Miguel Ángel Nadal, Ronald Koeman, SERGI Barjuán Esclusa, IVÁN Iglesias Corteguera, Guillermo Amor, José María Baquero "Bakero" (72 Jon Andoni GOIKOETXEA Lasa), Aitor Beguiristáin (81 Eusebio Sacristán), Hristo Stoichkov, ROMÁRIO de Souza Faria. Trainer: Johan Cruyff

Goals: Stoichkov (11), Romário (67), Rodionov (77), Karpin (88)

GALATASARAY ISTANBUL v AS MONACO 0-2 (0-0)

Ali Sami Yen, Istanbul 16.03.1994

Referee: Leif Sundell (SWE) Attendance: 32,000

GALATASARAY: Hayrettin Demirbaş; Bülent Korkmaz, Falko Götz, Mert Korkmaz, Yusuf K.Tepekule, Suat Kaya (78 Okan Buruk), Tugay Kerimoğlu (71 Mustafa Kocabey), Uğur Tütüneker, Hamza Hamzaoğlu, Hakan Şükür, Arif Erdem.
Trainer: Rainer Hollmann

AS MONACO: Jean-Luc Ettori; Patrick Valéry, Lilian Thuram, Franck Dumas, Patrick Blondeau, Claude Puel, Laurent Viaud, Youri Djorkaeff, Enzo Scifo (78 Gilles Grimandi), Jürgen Klinsmann, Victor Ikpeba (73 Jérôme Gnako).
Trainer: Arsène Wenger

Goals: Scifo (54), Gnako (88)

SPARTAK MOSKVA v AS MONACO 0-0

Luzhniki, Moskva 30.03.1994

Referee: Piero Ceccarini (ITA) Attendance: 12,000

SPARTAK: Gintaras Stauče; Ramiz Mamedov, Yuri Nikiforov, Vladislav Ternavski (75 Dmitriy Khlestov), Sergei Rodionov (63 Nikolai Pisarev), Ilya Tsymbalar, Valeri Karpin, Igor Lediakhov, Viktor Onopko, Andrei Piatnitski, Vladimir Beschastnikh. Trainer: Oleg Romantsev

AS MONACO: Jean-Luc Ettori; Patrick Blondeau, Lilian Thuram, Franck Dumas, Emmanuel Petit, Laurent Viaud, Claude Puel, Enzo Scifo (83 Christian Perez), Gilles Grimandi, Jürgen Klinsmann, Youri Djorkaeff (70 Wreh). Trainer: Arsène Wenger

FC BARCELONA v GALATASARAY ISTANBUL 3-0 (1-0)

Camp Nou, Barcelona 30.03.1994

Referee: Leslie William Mottram (SCO) Att: 85,000

FC BARCELONA: Andoni Zubizarreta; Alberto Ferrer, Miguel Ángel Nadal, Ronald Koeman, SERGI Barjuán Esclusa, Guillermo Amor, IVÁN Iglesias Corteguera, Enrique ESTEBARANZ López "QUIQUE" (67 Jon Andoni GOIKOETXEA Lasa), Aitor Beguiristáin (57 Eusebio Sacristán), Michael Laudrup, ROMÁRIO de Souza Faria. Trainer: Johan Cruyff

GALATASARAY: Hayrettin Demirbaş; Mert Korkmaz (50 Arif Erdem), Yusuf K.Tepekule, Falko Götz, Bülent Korkmaz, Tugay Kerimoğlu, Uğur Tütüneker, Hamza Hamzaoğlu, Erdal Keser, Hakan Şükür, Suat Kaya (80 Kubilay Türkyılmaz). Trainer: Rainer Hollmann

Goals: Amor (21), R. Koeman (70 pen), Eusebio (77)

GALATASARAY ISTANBUL v SPARTAK MOSKVA 1-2 (0-0)

Ali Sami Yen, Istanbul 13.04.1994

Referee: Gerd Grabher (AUS) Attendance: 22,000

GALATASARAY: Hayrettin Demirbaş; Cihat Arslan, Falko Götz, Mert Korkmaz, Yusuf K.Tepekule, Tugay Kerimoğlu, Suat Kaya, Hamza Hamzaoğlu, Uğur Tütüneker, Kubilay Türkyılmaz (38 Erdal Keser, 46 Reinhard Stumpf), Benhur Babaoglu. Trainer: Rainer Hollmann

SPARTAK: Gintaras Stauče; Ramiz Mamedov, Yuri Nikiforov, Vladislav Ternavski, Ilya Tsymbalar (75 Igor Lediakhov), Valeri Karpin, Viktor Onopko, Andrei Piatnitski, Nikolai Pisarev, Vladimir Beschastnikh, Valeri Masalitin (80 Dmitriy Alenichev). Trainer: Oleg Romantsev

Goals: Onopko (55), Karpin (83), Cihat (86)

AS MONACO v FC BARCELONA 0-1 (0-1)

Louis II, Monaco 13.04.1994

Referee: Ion Crăciunescu (ROM) Attendance: 20,000

AS MONACO: Jean-Luc Ettori; Patrick Blondeau, Lilian Thuram, Franck Dumas, Emmanuel Petit, Claude Puel (76 Christian Pérez), Laurent Viaud, Jérôme Gnako (46 Victor Ikpeba), Enzo Scifo, Youri Djorkaeff, Jürgen Klinsmann. Trainer: Arsène Wenger

FC BARCELONA: Andoni Zubizarreta; Alberto Ferrer, Ronald Koeman, Miguel Ángel Nadal, Josep Guardiola, IVÁN Iglesias Corteguera, SERGI Barjuán Esclusa, Guillermo Amor (73 Eusebio Sacristán), José María Baquero "Bakero" (59 JUAN CARLOS Rodríguez Moreno), ROMÁRIO de Souza Faria, Hristo Stoichkov. Trainer: Johan Cruyff

Goal: Stoichkov (13)

	P	W	D	L	F	A	Pts
FC Barcelona	6	4	2	0	13	3	10
AS Monaco	6	3	1	2	9	4	7
Spartak Moskva	6	1	3	2	6	12	5
Galatasaray Istanbul	6	0	2	4	1	10	2

GROUP B

RSC ANDERLECHT BRUSSEL v AC MILAN 0-0

Constant Vandenstock, Brussel 24.11.1993

Referee: Vadim Zhuk (BLS) Attendance: 28,063

ANDERLECHT: Filip De Wilde; Bertrand Crasson, Graeme Rutjes, Philippe Albert, Michel De Wolf, Bruno Versavel, Pär Zetterberg, Johan Walem, Danny Boffin (90 Alain van Baekel), Filip Haagdoren, John Bosman. Trainer: Johan Boskamp

AC MILAN: Sebastiano Rossi, Christian Panucci, Franco Baresi, Alessandro Costacurta, Paolo Maldini, Brian Laudrup, Demetrio Albertini, Roberto Donadoni, Alessandro Orlando, Jean Pierre Papin, Marco Simone (75 Daniele Massaro). Trainer: Fabio Capello

FC PORTO v WERDER BREMEN 3-2 (2-0)

Estádio das Antas, Porto 24.11.1993

Referee: David Elleray (ENG) Attendance: 30,000

FC PORTO: VÍTOR Manuel Martins BAÍA; JOÃO Domingos Silva PINTO, JOSÉ CARLOS Nascimento, ALOÍSIO Pires Alves, RUI JORGE de Sousa Dias Macedo de Oliveira, JORGE Paulo COSTA Almeida, Carlos Alberto Oliveira SECRETÁRIO, João Paulo Santos "PAULINHO SANTOS" (85 RUI FILIPE Tavares Bastos), José Orlando Rocha SEMEDO, Emile Lubtchov KOSTADINOV (75 JAIME Fernandes MAGALHÃES), DOMINGOS José Paciencia Oliveira. Trainer: Tomislav Ivić

WERDER: Oliver Reck; Mario Basler, Marco Bode (67 Frank Neubarth), Rune Bratseth, Dietmar Beiersdorfer (46 Thomas Wolter), Thorsten Legat, Dieter Eilts, Miroslav Votava, Andreas Herzog, Bernd Hobsch, Wynton Rufer.
Trainer: Otto Rehhagel

Goals: Domingos (6), Rui Jorge (35), José Carlos (81), Hobsch (86), Rufer (87)

AC MILAN v FC PORTO 3-0 (2-0)

Giuseppe Meazza, Milano 1.12.1993

Referee: Leif Sundell (SWE) Attendance: 35,000

AC MILAN: Sebastiano Rossi, Christian Panucci, Paolo Maldini, Demetrio Albertini, Alessandro Costacurta, Franco Baresi, Daniele Massaro, Roberto Donadoni, Jean Pierre Papin (64 Mauro Tassotti), Dejan Savićević, Florin Răducioiu (80 Angelo Carbone). Trainer: Fabio Capello

FC PORTO: VÍTOR Manuel Martins BAÍA; JOÃO Domingos Silva PINTO, PAULO António Prado PEREIRA (46 Alves Nilo Fortes VINHA), ALOÍSIO Pires Alves, FERNANDO Manuel Silva COUTO, JOSÉ CARLOS Nascimento, Carlos Alberto Oliveira SECRETÁRIO, RUI JORGE de Sousa Dias Macedo de Oliveira, DOMINGOS José Paciencia Oliveira, José Orlando Rocha SEMEDO, João Paulo "PAULINHO SANTOS" (46 RUI FILIPE Tavares Bastos). Trainer: Tomislav Ivić

Goals: Răducioiu (16), Panucci (39), Massaro (63)

WERDER BREMEN v RSC ANDERLECHT BRUSSEL 5-3 (0-3)

Weserstadion, Bremen 8.12.1993

Referee: Ion Crăciunescu (ROM) Attendance: 32,000

WERDER: Oliver Reck; Rune Bratseth, Dietmar Beiersdorfer, Ulrich Borowka, Mario Basler (87 Andree Wiedener), Miroslav Votava, Andreas Herzog (46 Thomas Wolter), Dieter Eilts, Marco Bode, Bernd Hobsch, Wynton Rufer.
Trainer: Otto Rehhagel

ANDERLECHT: Filip De Wilde; Marc Emmers, Graeme Rutjes, Philippe Albert, Bertrand Crasson, Pär Zetterbeg (82 Wim Kooiman), Johan Walem, Danny Boffin, Bruno Versavel, Filip Haagdoren, John Bosman (69 Luc Nilis).
Trainer: Johan Boskamp

Goals: Albert (16), Boffin (18, 33), Rufer (66, 89), Bratseth (72), Hobsch (80), Bode (83)

AC MILAN v WERDER BREMEN 2-1 (0-0)

Giuseppe Meazza, Milano 2.03.1994

Referee: Leslie William Mottram (SCO) Attendance: 41,239

AC MILAN: Sebastiano Rossi, Mauro Tassotti, Alessandro Costacurta, Franco Baresi, Paolo Maldini, Stefano Eranio (46 Marco Simone), Marcel Desailly, Roberto Donadoni, Zvonimir Boban, Daniele Massaro, Dejan Savićević (88 Demetrio Albertini). Trainer: Fabio Capello

WERDER: Oliver Reck; Dietmar Beiersdorfer, Thomas Wolter, Frank Neubarth, Thorsten Legat, Mario Basler, Dieter Eilts, Miroslav Votava, Marco Bode (76 Bernd Hobsch), Andreas Herzog, Wynton Rufer. Trainer: Otto Rehhagel

Goals: Maldini (47), Basler (54), Savićević (68)

RSC ANDERLECHT BRUSSEL v FC PORTO 1-0 (0-0)

Constant Vandenstock, Brussel 2.03.1994

Referee: Vassilios Nikakis (GRE) Attendance: 17,000

ANDERLECHT: Filip De Wilde; Olivier Suray (46 Bertrand Crasson), Chidi Nwanu, Philippe Albert, Danny Boffin, Marc Emmers, Johan Walem, Mark Degryse, Bruno Versavel (90 Wim Kooiman), Luc Nilis, John Bosman.
Trainer: Johan Boskamp

FC PORTO: VÍTOR Manuel Martins BAÍA; Fernando Oscar BANDEIRINHA Barbosa, ALOÍSIO Pires Alves, FERNANDO Manuel Silva COUTO, RUI JORGE de Sousa Dias Macedo de Oliveira, Carlos Alberto Oliveira SECRETÁRIO, António dos Santos ANDRÉ (88 António José Santos FOLHA), JORGE Paulo COSTA Almeida, José Orlando Rocha SEMEDO (78 RUI FILIPE Tavares Bastos), Emile Lubtchov KOSTADINOV, Ljubinko Drulović. Trainer: Bobby Robson

Goal: Nilis (88)

WERDER BREMEN v AC MILAN 1-1 (0-0)

Weserstadion, Bremen 16.03.1994

Referee: Kim Milton Nielsen (DEN) Attendance: 31,000

WERDER: Oliver Reck; Dietmar Beiersdorfer, Rune Bratseth, Andree Wiedener, Miroslav Votava, Mario Basler, Frank Neubarth, Marco Bode (88 Lars Unger), Thorsten Legat, Bernd Hobsch, Wynton Rufer. Trainer: Otto Rehhagel

AC MILAN: Sebastiano Rossi, Mauro Tassotti, Alessandro Costacurta, Filippo Galli, Paolo Maldini, Stefano Eranio (56 Marco Simone), Marcel Desailly, Roberto Donadoni, Zvonimir Boban, Dejan Savićević (86 Demetrio Albertini), Daniele Massaro. Trainer: Fabio Capello

Goals: Rufer (52 pen), Savićević (74)

FC PORTO
v RSC ANDERLECHT BRUSSEL 2-0 (1-0)

Estádio das Antas, Porto 16.03.1994

Referee: Václav Krondl (CZE) Attendance: 30,000

FC PORTO: VÍTOR Manuel Martins BAÍA; JOÃO Domingos Silva PINTO, JORGE Paulo COSTA Almeida, ALOÍSIO Pires Alves, RUI JORGE de Sousa Dias Macedo de Oliveira, António dos Santos ANDRÉ, Carlos Alberto Oliveira SECRETÁRIO, José Orlando Rocha SEMEDO, Ion Timofte (72 António José Santos FOLHA), DOMINGOS José Paciencia Oliveira (85 FERNANDO Manuel Silva COUTO), Ljubinko Drulović. Trainer: Bobby Robson

ANDERLECHT: Filip De Wilde; Bertrand Crasson, Chidi Nwanu, Graeme Rutjes, Marc Emmers (70 Filip Haagdoren), Johan Walem, Bruno Versavel (46 John Bosman), Olivier Suray, Luc Nilis, Mark Degryse, Danny Boffin. Trainer: Johan Boskamp

Goals: Drulović (9), Secretário (90)

FC PORTO v AC MILAN 0-0

Estádio das Antas, Porto 13.04.1994

Referee: Sándor Puhl (HUN) Attendance: 48,000

FC PORTO: VÍTOR Manuel Martins BAÍA; JOÃO Domingos Silva PINTO, ALOÍSIO Pires Alves, FERNANDO Manuel Silva COUTO, RUI JORGE de Sousa Dias Macedo de Oliveira, JORGE António Pinto COUTO (75 JAIME Fernandes MAGALHÃES), RUI FILIPE Tavares Bastos, Ion Timofte (68 António José Santos FOLHA), António dos Santos ANDRÉ, DOMINGOS José Paciencia Oliveira, Ljubinko Drulović. Trainer: Bobby Robson

AC MILAN: Sebastiano Rossi, Mauro Tassotti, Alessandro Costacurta, Franco Baresi, Paolo Maldini, Angelo Carbone, Marcel Desailly, Demetrio Albertini, Zvonimir Boban, Dejan Savićević (84 Christian Panucci), Daniele Massaro. Trainer: Fabio Capello

AC MILAN v RSC ANDERLECHT BRUSSEL 0-0

Stadio Giuseppe Meazza, Milano 30.03.1994

Referee: Joël Quiniou (FRA) Attendance: 40,000

AC MILAN: Sebastiano Rossi, Mauro Tassotti, Alessandro Costacurta, Franco Baresi, Paolo Maldini, Marcel Desailly, Demetrio Albertini, Roberto Donadoni, Brian Laudrup (46 Marco Simone), Florin Răducioiu (69 Angelo Carbone), Daniele Massaro. Trainer: Fabio Capello

ANDERLECHT: Filip De Wilde; Bertrand Crasson, Olivier Suray, Chidi Nwanu, Danny Boffin, Marc Emmers, Johan Walem, Filip Haagdoren, Mark Degryse, John Bosman, Luc Nilis. Trainer: Johan Boskamp

RSC ANDERLECHT BRUSSEL
v WERDER BREMEN 1-2 (1-1)

Constant Vandenstock, Brussel 13.04.1994

Referee: Kurt Röthlisberger (SWI) Attendance: 12,000

ANDERLECHT: Filip De Wilde; Bertrand Crasson (46 Michel De Wolf), Guy Marchoul, Chidi Nwanu, Danny Boffin, Johan Walem, Marc Emmers (70 Frédéric Peiremans), Bruno Versavel, Filip Haagdoren, John Bosman, Luc Nilis. Trainer: Johan Boskamp

WERDER: Oliver Reck; Rune Bratseth, Dietmar Beiersdorfer, Miroslav Votava, Frank Neubarth, Ulrich Borowka, Thorsten Legat, Marco Bode, Thomas Schaaf, Mario Basler, Wynton Rufer. Trainer: Otto Rehhagel

Goals: Bode (32, 65), Bosman (44)

WERDER BREMEN v FC PORTO 0-5 (0-2)

Weserstadion, Bremen 30.03.1994

Referee: Manuel Diaz Vega (SPA) Attendance: 32,000

WERDER: Oliver Reck; Thomas Wolter, Rune Bratseth, Andree Wiedener, Mario Basler, Miroslav Votava, Uwe Harttgen (46 Frank Neubarth), Marco Bode, Thorsten Legat, Andreas Herzog, Wynton Rufer (78 Manfred Bockenfeld). Trainer: Otto Rehhagel

FC PORTO: VÍTOR Manuel Martins BAÍA; JORGE Paulo COSTA Almeida, JOÃO Domingos Silva PINTO, FERNANDO Manuel Silva COUTO, RUI JORGE de Sousa Dias Macedo de Oliveira, António dos Santos ANDRÉ, João Paulo Santos "PAULINHO SANTOS" (8 RUI FILIPE Tavares Bastos), Carlos Alberto Oliveira SECRETÁRIO, Ion Timofte, Emile Lubtchov KOSTADINOV (72 DOMINGOS José Paciencia Oliveira), Ljubinko Drulović. Trainer: Bobby Robson

Goals: Rui Filipe (10), Kostadinov (34), Secretário (71), Domingos (74), Timofte (89 pen)

	P	W	D	L	F	A	Pts
AC Milan	6	2	4	0	6	2	8
FC Porto	6	3	1	2	10	6	7
Werder Bremen	6	2	1	3	11	15	5
Anderlecht Brussel	6	1	2	3	5	9	4

SEMI-FINALS

FC BARCELONA v FC PORTO 3-0 (2-0)

Camp Nou, Barcelona 27.04.1994

Referee: Vadim Zhuk (BLS) Attendance: 95,000

FC BARCELONA: Andoni Zubizarreta; Alberto Ferrer, Miguel Ángel Nadal, Ronald Koeman, SERGI Barjuán Esclusa (75 Jon Andoni GOIKOETXEA Lasa), Josep Guardiola, José María Baquero "Bakero", Guillermo Amor, Aitor Beguiristáin (40 IVÁN Iglesias Corteguera), ROMÁRIO de Souza Faria, Hristo Stoichkov. Trainer: Johan Cruyff

FC PORTO: VÍTOR Manuel Martins BAÍA; JOÃO Domingos Silva PINTO, ALOÍSIO Pires Alves, FERNANDO Manuel Silva COUTO, JORGE Paulo COSTA Almeida, António dos Santos Ferreira ANDRÉ (80 João Paulo Maio dos Santos "PAULINHO SANTOS"), Carlos Alberto Oliveira SECRETÁRIO, RUI FILIPE Tavares Bastos, António José Santos FOLHA (66 José Orlando Rocha SEMEDO), Emile Lubtchov KOSTADINOV, Ljubinko Drulović. Trainer: Bobby Robson

Sent off: João Pinto (61)

Goals: Stoichkov (9, 34), R. Koeman (72)

AC MILAN v AS MONACO 3-0 (1-0)

Stadio Giuseppe Meazza, Milano 27.04.1994

Referee: Bernd Heynemann (GER) Attendance: 78,650

AC MILAN: Sebastiano Rossi; Mauro Tassotti, Alessandro Costacurta, Franco Baresi, Christian Panucci, Demetrio Albertini, Roberto Donadoni, Marcel Desailly, Zvonimir Boban, Dejan Savićević (87 Marco Simone), Daniele Massaro (84 Gianluigi Lentini). Trainer: Fabio Capello

AS MONACO: Jean-Luc Ettori; Patrick Blondeau (52 Wreh), Gilles Grimandi, Franck Dumas, Emmanuel Petit, Claude Puel (67 Amara Simba), Jérôme Gnako, Laurent Viaud, Enzo Scifo, Youri Djorkaeff, Jürgen Klinsmann. Trainer: Arsène Wenger

Sent off: Costacurta (40)

Goals: Desailly (14), Albertini (48), Massaro (70)

FINAL

AC MILAN v FC BARCELONA 4-0 (2-0)

Olympiako, Athina 18.05.1994

Referee: Philip Don (ENG) Attendance: 57,000

AC MILAN: Sebastiano Rossi; Mauro Tassotti, Filippo Galli, Paolo Maldini (83 Stefano Nava), Christian Panucci, Roberto Donadoni, Marcel Desailly, Demetrio Albertini, Zvonimir Boban, Dejan Savićević, Daniele Massaro.
Trainer: Fabio Capello.

FC BARCELONA: Andoni Zubizarreta; Alberto Ferrer, Miguel Ángel Nadal, Ronald Koeman, SERGI Barjuán Esclusa (72 Enrique ESTEBARANZ López "QUIQUE"), Josep Guardiola, José Maria Baquero "Bakero", Guillermo Amor, Hristo Stoichkov, ROMÁRIO de Souza Faria, Aitor Beguiristáin (51 Eusebio Sacristán). Trainer: Johan Cruijff

Goals: Massaro (22, 45), Savićević (47), Desailly (59)

European Cup Goalscorers 1993-94:

8 goals: Ronald Koeman (Barcelona); Wynton Rufer (Werder Bremen)

7 goals: Hristo Stoichkov (Barcelona); Luc Nilis (Anderlecht)

6 goals: Goran Vlaovic (Croatia)

5 goals: Valeri Karpin (Spartak Moskva), Bernd Hobsch (Werder Bremen)

4 goals: Kubilay Türkyılmaz (Galatasaray), Viktor Onopko, Nikolai Pisarev, Sergei Rodionov (Spartak Moskva), Marco Bode (Werder Bremen), Jürgen Klinsmann (AS Monaco), Daniele Massaro, Jean-Pierre Papin (AC Milan)

3 goals: Jerzy Podbrozny (Lech Poznan), Danny Boffin, John Bosman (Anderlecht), José Domingos (FC Porto), Youri Djorkaeff, Victor Ikpeba (AS Monaco), Dejan Savićević (AC Milan)

2 goals: Ford (Cwmbran Town), Kizilashvili (Omonoia Nicosia), Adzic, Cvitanovic (Croatia), Leonenko (Dynamo Kyiv), Hateley (Rangers), Gudjónsson (íA Akranes), Løken (Rosenborg), Harazi (Beitar), Dumitrescu, Panduru, Vlădoiu (Steaua Bucureşti), Todorov (Levski), Dvirnik, Siegl (Sparta Praha), Cantona, Keane, Bruce (Manchester United), Trzeciak, Dembinski (Lech Poznan), Zsak (Austria Wien), J.Buttigieg (Floriana), Arif (Galatasaray), Tsimbalar (Spartak Moskva), Versavel (Anderlecht), Basler (Werder Bremen), Kostadinov, Secretário (FC Porto), Scifo (AS Monaco), Bakero, Beguiristáin, Romário, Amor (Fc barcelona), Desailly, Simone (AC Milan)

1 goal: King, McNeill (Cwmbran Town), Borisov (Norma Tallin), Milinovic (Olimpija Ljubljana), Rebeja (Zimbru Chişinău), Lesjak, Turkovic, Zivkovic, S.Halilovic, Jelicic (Croatia), Caulfield, Buckley, Morley, Glynn, Barry (Cork City), Shkapenko, Rebrov (Dynamo Kyiv), Sliskovic (AEK Athina), Szabados, Stefanov, Sallói (Kispest-Honvéd Budapest), McPherson, Durrant (Rangers), Lidman (AIK Solna), Heinola (HJK Helsinki), Högnason, Thordarsson (íA Akranes), Bragstad, Skammelsrud, Tangen, Leonhardsen, Dahlum (Rosenborg), Troitsky (Skonto Riga), Grechniev, Ohana, Shwarts (Beitar), Gerasimets, Velichko, Belkevich (Dinamo Minsk), Haylock, McConnell, Johnston (Linfield), Refos, Obiku, Blinker (Feyenoord), Borimirov, Sirakov, Iankov, Ginchev (Levski), M.Möller, Ma.Johansen, L.H.Nielsen, Mikkelsen (FC København), B.Robson (Manchester United), Moskal, Lukasik (Lech Poznan), Ogris, Narbekovas, Schmid, Kogler (Austria Wien), Ratinho, Stiel, Heldmann (FC Aarau), Cihat (Galatasaray), Khlestov, Pogodin, Beschastnikh (Spartak Moskva), Albert (Anderlecht), Bratseth (Werder), Semedo, Rui Jorge, José Carlos, Drulović, Rui Filipe, Timofte (FC Porto), Thuram, Gnako (AS Monaco), Laudrup, Quique, Eusebio (Barcelona), Laudrup, Orlando, Răducioiu, Panucci, Maldini, Albertini (AC Milan)

Own goals: Belokhvostov (Norma Tallin) for HJK Helsinki, Vlahos (AEK) for AS Monaco, Hakan (Galatasaray) for Manchester United

THE EUROPEAN CUP 1994-95

PRELIMINARY ROUND

STEAUA BUCUREŞTI v SERVETTE GENÈVE 4-1 (3-0)

Steaua, Bucureşti 10.08.1994

Referee: Vasiles Nikakis (GRE) Attendance: 15,000

STEAUA: Dumitru Stîngaciu; Aurel Silviu Panait, Daniel Claudiu Prodan, Anton Doboş, Ionel Antonel Pârvu; Damian Militaru (69 Laurenţiu Dumitru Roşu), Ilie Stan, Basarab Nică Panduru, Constantin Gâlcă; Marius Mihai Lăcătuş (Cap), Adrian Ilie. Trainer: Dumitru Dumitriu

SERVETTE: Marco Pascolo (Cap); Michel Sauthier, Peter Schepull, Jean-Michel Aeby (51 Eddy Barea), René Weiler; Hakan Mild, Sébastien Barberis, Samuel Margarini; José Sinval, Olivier Neuville, Canil Renato (85 Pierre-Alain Prinz) Trainer: Ilija Petković

Goals: Ilie (1), Stan (17 pen), Pârvu (25), Lăcătuş (51), Neuville (72)

SERVETTE GENEVE v STEAUA BUCUREŞTI 1-1 (1-0)

Stade des Charmilles, Genève 24.08.1994

Referee: Markus Merk (GER) Attendance: 5,800

SERVETTE: Marco Pascolo (Cap); Peter Schepull, Boško Djurovski (3 Jean-Michel Aeby), Samuel Margarini; René Weiler, Eddy Barea, Sébastien Barberis, David Sesa; José Sinval, Pierre-Alain Prinz (33 Abatunde Fatusi), Olivier Neuville. Trainer: Ilija Petković

STEAUA: Dumitru Stîngaciu; Aurel Silviu Panait, Daniel Claudiu Prodan, Anton Doboş, Ionel Antonel Pârvu; Ilie Stan, Basarab Nică Panduru, Constantin Gâlcă, Damian Militaru (74 Daniel Iftodi); Marius Mihai Lăcătuş (Cap), Adrian Ilie (69 Marian Popa). Trainer: Dumitru Dumitriu

Goals: Schepull (15), Pîrvu (62)

AC SPARTA PRAHA v IFK GÖTEBORG 1-0 (0-0)

Jablonec 10.08.1994

Referee: Serge Muhmenthaler (SWI) Attendance: 10,000

SPARTA: Petr Kouba, Jiří Novotný, Roman Vonasek, Jan Sopko, Peter Gunda (20 Michal Hornak), Lumir Mistr (59 Zdenek Svoboda), Václav Budka, Pavel Nedved, Horst Siegl (Cap), Josef Němec, Jozef Kozlej. Trainer: Karol Dobias

IFK: Thomas Ravelli, Joachim Björklund, Pontus Kåmark (Cap), Jonas Ohlsson, Mikael Nilsson, Mikael Martinsson (77 Johan Anegrund), Magnus Erlingmark, Stefan Rehn, Stefan Lindqvist, Jesper Blomqvist, Stefan Pettersson. Trainer: Roger Gustafsson

Goal: Budka (89)

IFK GÖTEBORG v AC SPARTA PRAHA 2-0 (1-0)

Ullevi, Göteborg 24.08.1994

Referee: Vadim Zhuk (BLS) Attendance: 13,969

IFK: Thomas Ravelli, Magnus Johansson, Jonas Ohlsson, Joachim Björklund, Mikael Nilsson, Mikael Martinsson (87 Thomas Andersson), Stefan Lindqvist, Stefan Rehn (Cap), Jesper Blomqvist (90 Patrik Bengtsson), Stefan Pettersson, Magnus Erlingmark. Trainer: Roger Gustavsson

SPARTA: Petr Kouba, Jan Sopko (62 Josef Němec), Jozef Chovanec (Cap), Jiří Novotný, Michal Hornak, Peter Gunda, Zdenek Svoboda, Pavel Nedved, Martin Frýdek, Roman Vonasek, Horst Siegl. Trainer: Karol Dobias

Goals: Blomqvist (21), Rehn (62)

AVENIR BEGGEN v GALATASARAY ISTANBUL 1-5 (0-2)

Stade Josy Barthel, Beggen 10.08.1994

Referee: Kenneth Clark (SCO) Attendance: 7,000

AVENIR: Nico Konsbrück, Ralph Ferron, Carlo Weis, Alex Wilhelm, Gabriel Lopes (70 Frank Goergen), Jean Vanek, Patrick Posing, Luc Holtz, Theo Scholten (Cap), Armin Krings (58 Markus Krahen), Mihail Zaritski.
Trainer: Michel Clément

GALATASARAY: Nehizi Baloglu, Sedat Balkanli, Stevisa Kuzmanovski, Bülent Körkmaz, Hamza Hamzaoğlu, Norman Mapeza, Tugay Kerimoğlu (Cap), Yusuf Tepekule (81 Osman Akyol), Kubilay Türkyılmaz, Hakan Şükür, Saffet Sancakli (73 Arif Erdem). Trainer: Reinhard Saftig

Goals: Türkyılmaz (30), Saffet (35), Zaritski (50), Hakan Şükür (69), Arif (76, 89)

GALATASARAY ISTANBUL v AVENIR BEGGEN 4-0 (0-0)

Alsançak, Izmir 24.08.1994

Referee: Dimitar Ivanov Momirov (BUL) Att: 62,000

GALATASARAY: Nezihi Baloglu; Bülent Korkmaz, Tugay Kerimoğlu (Cap), Bekir Gür, Osman Akyol (64 Okan Buruk), Norman Mapeza, Suat Kaya, Hakan Ünsal, Hakan Sükrü, Kubilay Türkyılmaz (60 Saffet Sancakli), Arif Erdem.
Trainer: Reinhard Saftig

AVENIR: Nico Konsbrück, Ralph Ferron (59 Yves Picard), Carlo Weis, Jean Vanek, Alex Wilhelm, Jaba Moreira, Roby Peters, Theo Scholten (Cap), Patrick Posing, Armin Krings, Markus Krahen (44 Mihail Zaritski).
Trainer: Michel Clément

Sent off: Vanek (85)

Goals: Hakan Sükür (52, 64, 83 pen), Saffet (64)

PARIS SAINT GERMAIN v VÁC FC-SAMSUNG 3-0 (1-0)

Parc des Princes, Paris 10.08.1994

Referee: Antonio Jesus Lopez Nieto (SPA) Att: 29637

PSG: Bernard Lama, José Cobos, Alain Roche, Ricardo Gomes, Patrick Colleter, Paul le Guen, Oumar Dieng, Vincent Guérin, Valdo Cândido Filho (77 Daniel Bravo), David Ginola (C), George Weah (85 Jean-Philippe Séchet).
Trainer: Luis Fernández

VAC FC-SAMSUNG: János Koszta, Tibor Nagy (Cap), Zoltán Aczél, Imre Aranyos, Gábor Puglits, István Kasza, János Romanek, József Zvara (78 Elek Nyilas), József Dzurják (80 Zoltán Bánföldi), Tibor Sallai, Antal Füle.
Trainer: János Csank

Sent off: Colleter (70)

Goals: Gomes (30), Weah (48), Roche (82)

CASINO SALZBURG v MACCABI HAIFA 3-1 (0-0)

Lehen, Salzburg 24.08.1994

Referee: Václav Krondl (CZE) Attendance: 9,000

CASINO: Otto Konrad; Leo Lainer (Cap), Christian Fürstaller, Martin Hiden, Thomas Winklhofer, Heimo Pfeifenberger, Mladen Mladenovic, Wolfgang Feiersinger, Franz Aigner (76 Tomislav Kocijan); Nikola Jurcevic, Hermann Stadler (46 Arnold Freissegger). Trainer: Otto Barić

MACCABI: Rafi Cohen, Alon Hazan (Cap), Oleg Kuznetsov, Marco Balbul, Moshe Glam; Alon Harazi, Roni Levi, Eyal Berkovitch, Sergei Kandaurov, Vasili Kardash (58 Haim Revivo), Shay Holzmann (75 Shlomi Amar).
Trainer: Avraham Aboukarat

Goals: Mladenovic (49, 53), Jurcevic (77), Hazan (90)

VÁC FC-SAMSUNG v PARIS SAINT GERMAIN 1-2 (1-1)

Vasas, Budapest 24.10.1994

Referee: Angelo Amendolia (ITA) Attendance: 2,000

VAC FC-SAMSUNG: János Koszta; István Kasza, Zoltán Aczél (71 Zoltán Bánföldi), Tibor Nagy (Cap), Gábor Puglits (30 Tibor Sallai), József Zvara, Elek Nyilas, Imre Aranyos, Antal Füle, István Szedlacsek, János Romanek.
Trainer: János Csank

PSG: Bernard Lama, Oumar Dieng, Alain Roche (Cap), Ricardo Gomes (46 Antoine Kombouaré), Francis Llacer, Vincent Guérin, Jean-Philippe Séchet, Daniel Bravo, Valdo Cândido Filho (60 Paul le Guen), Raí Souza de Oliveira, Patrick M'boma. Trainer: Luis Fernández

Goals: Mboma (19, 66), Füle (30)

AEK FC ATHINA v RANGERS GLASGOW 2-0 (1-0)

Neas Filadelfeia, Athina 10.08.1994

Referee: Peter Mikkelsen (DEN) Attendance: 21,994

AEK: Ilias Atmatzidis; Manolis Papadopoulos, Mihalis Kasapis, Stelios Manolas (Cap), Refik Sabanadzović, Mihalis Vlahos, Dimitris Saravakos, Toni Savevski, Temur Ketsbaia (8 Vasilis Dimitriadis, 85 Giorgos Agorogiannis), Vasilis Tsartas, Hristos Kostis. Trainer: Dušan Bajević

RANGERS: Andy Goram; Gary Stevens, David Robertson, Richard Gough (Cap), Steven Pressley; Stuart McCall, Brian Laudrup, Ian Ferguson, Gordon Durie (78 Ian Durrant), Mark Hateley, Neil Murray. Manager: Walter Smith

Goals: Saravakos (45, 70)

MACCABI HAIFA v CASINO SALZBURG 1-2 (0-0)

Kiriat Eliezer, Haifa 10.08.1994

Referee: Ahmet Cakar (TUR) Attendance: 6,500

MACCABI: Rafi Cohen; Marco Balbul, Oleg Kuznetsov (80 Shay Holzman), Alon Harazi, Moshe Glam; Ztbar Daniel, Roni Levi, Alon Hazan (Cap), Eyal Berkovitch; Haim Revivo (75 Najwan Ghrayiv), Vasili Kardash.
Trainer: Avraham Aboukarat

CASINO: Otto Konrad; Leo Lainer (Cap), Martin Hiden, Christian Fürstaller, Thomas Winklhofer, Peter Artner (56 Heimo Pfeifenberger), Mladen Mladenovic, Arnold Freissegger, Adolf Hütter, Nikola Jurcevic, Ralph Hasenhüttl (76 Tomislav Kocijan). Trainer: Otto Barić

Goals: Revivo (47 pen), A.Hütter (82), Mladenovic (89 pen)

GLASGOW RANGERS FC v AEK FC ATHINA 0-1 (0-1)

Ibrox Park, Glasgow 24.08.1994

Referee: Leif Sundell (SWE) Attendance: 44,789

RANGERS: Andy Goram, David Robertson, Richard Gough (Cap), Basile Boli, Gordon Durie (64 Ian Durrant), Stuart McCall, David McPherson, Ian Ferguson, Brian Laudrup, Duncan Ferguson, Mark Hateley. Manager: Walter Smith

AEK: Ilias Atmatzidis, Manolis Papadopoulos, Stelios Manolas (Cap), Mihalis Vlahos, Giorgos Agorogiannis, Refik Sabanadzović, Mihalis Kasapis, Toni Savevski (77 Stauros Stamatis), Hristos Kostis, Vasilis Tsartas (87 Haralampos Kopitsis), Dimitris Saravakos. Trainer: Dušan Bajević

Goal: Savevski (43)

LEGIA WARSZAWA v HAJDUK SPLIT 0-1 (0-1)

Wojska Polskiego, Warszawa 10.08.1994

Referee: Gerd Grabher (AUS) Attendance: 7,249

LEGIA: Zbigniew Robakiewicz, Piotr Mosor, Juliusz Kruszankin, Krzysztof Ratajczyk, Marek Jozwiak (56 Jacek Zielinski), Marcin Jalocha, Leszek Pisz (Cap), Radoslaw Michalski, Grzegorz Wedzynski, Wojciech Kowalczyk, Jerzy Podbrozny. Trainer: Pawel Janas

HAJDUK: Tonci Gabrić, Karol Prazenica, Darko Butorović, Mirsad Hibić, Igor Stimac, Stipe Andrijasević (Cap), Damir Vuica, Aljosa Asanović, Mario Mestrović (85 Nenad Pralija), Ivica Mornar, Milan Rapaić (78 Robert Vladislavić). Trainer: Ivan Katalinić

Goal: Rapaić (22)

HAJDUK SPLIT v LEGIA WARSZAWA 4-0 (0-0)

Stadion na Poljud, Split 24.08.1994

Referee: David Elleray (ENG) Attendance: 16,183

HAJDUK: Tonci Gabrić, Igor Stimac, Sasa Person, Mirsad Hibić, Darko Butorović, Mario Mestrović, Zoran Vulić (Cap), Stipe Andrijasević (71 Nenad Pralija), Aljosa Asanović, Milan Rapaić, Ivica Mornar (78 Tomislav Erceg). Trainer: Ivan Katalinić

LEGIA: Zbigniew Robakiewicz, Juliusz Kruszankin, Jacek Zielinski, Krzysztof Ratajczyk, Marcin Jalocha (56 Grzegorz Wedzynski), Zbigniew Mandziejewicz, Adam Fedoruk, Radoslaw Michalski (69 Marcin Mieciel), Leszek Pisz (Cap), Jerzy Podbrozny, Wojciech Kowalczyk. Trainer: Pawel Janas

Sent off: Ratajczyk (60)

Goals: Asanović (49, 62), Rapaić (80), Erceg (90)

SILKEBORG IF v FC DYNAMO KYIV 0-0

Silkeborg stadion 10.08.1994

Referee: Eric Blareau (BEL) Attendance: 4,298

SILKEBORG: Einar Rossbach, Peder Knudsen, Morten Bruun (Cap) (63 Michael Hansen), Jacob Laursen, Michael Larsen, Henrik Kastbjerg, Keld Bordinggaard, Peter Sørensen, Søren Frederiksen, Jesper Thygesen, Allan Reese (70 Heine Fernández). Trainer: Bo Nilsson

DINAMO: Olexandr Shovkovskyi, Sergiy Lezhentsev, Vladislav Vashchuk, Andriy Khomin, Volodymyr Sharan, Sergei Kovalets (Cap), Vitaliy Kosovskiy, Serhiy Skachenko, Pavlo Shkapenko, Dmytro Mikhailenko, Serhiy Rebrov. Trainer: Jozsef Szabo

Sent off: Knudsen (60)

FC DYNAMO KYIV v SILKEBORG IF 3-1 (2-0)

Republikansky, Kiev 24.08.1994

Referee: Jacobus Uilenberg (HOL) Attendance: 60,000

DINAMO: Olexandr Shovkovskyi, Sergiy Lezhentsev, Vladislav Vashchuk, Andriy Khomin, Volodymyr Sharan, Sergei Kovalets (Cap), Vitaliy Kosovskiy, Dmytro Mikhailenko, Serhiy Skachenko, Pavlo Shkapenko (80 Alexander Prizetko), Viktor Leonenko (46 Serhiy Rebrov). Trainer: Jozsef Szabo

SILKEBORG: Einar Rossbach, Henrik Kastbjerg (85 Allan Reese), Michael Larsen, Morten Bruun (Cap), Slobodan Marovic, Jacob Laursen, Keld Bordinggaard, Peter Sørensen, Søren Frederiksen, Michael Hansen (35 Jesper Thygesen), Heine Fernández. Trainer: Bo Nilsson

Goals: Skachenko (21), Kovalets (28), Fernández (74), Kosovski (90)

GROUP A

MANCHESTER UNITED FC v IFK GÖTEBORG 4-2 (1-1)

Old Trafford, Manchester 14.09.1994

Referee: Guy Goethals (BEL) Attendance: 33,625

MANCHESTER UNITED: Peter Schmeichel, David May, Steve Bruce (Cap), Gary Pallister, Dennis Irwin; Andrei Kanchelskis, Paul Ince, Nicky Butt, Lee Sharpe; Mark Hughes, Ryan Giggs. Manager: Alex Ferguson

IFK: Thomas Ravelli, Pontus Kåmark (Cap), Joachim Björklund, Mikael Nilsson, Magnus Johansson, Mikael Martinsson, Magnus Erlingmark, Stefan Lindqvist, Jesper Blomqvist, Jonas Ohlsson (44 Stefan Rehn), Stefan Pettersson. Trainer: Roger Gustavsson

Goals: Pettersson (27), Giggs (33, 65), Kanchelskis (48), Rehn (50), Sharpe (70)

FC BARCELONA v GALATASARAY ISTANBUL 2-1 (1-1)

Camp Nou, Barcelona 14.09.1994

Referee: Piero Ceccarini (ITA) Attendance: 80,000

FC BARCELONA: Carlos Busquets, SERGI Barjuán Esclusa, ABELARDO Fernández Artuña, Ronald Koeman (Cap), Josep Guardiola, Eusebio Sacristán, IVÁN Iglesias Corteguera, Guillermo Amor (65 Jordi Cruijff), Aitor Beguiristáin (61 Luis Cembranos), ROMÁRIO de Souza Faria, Hristo Stoichkov. Trainer: Johan Cruijff

GALATASARAY: Gintaras Stauče, Mert Korkmaz, Bülent Korkmaz, Sedat Balkanli, Norman Mapeza, Tugay Kerimoğlu (Cap), Hamza Hamzaoğlu, Saffet Sancakli (70 Arif Erdem), Ergün Pembe (56 Cihat Arslan), Hakan Şükür, Kubilay Türkyılmaz. Trainer: Reinhard Saftig

Goals: Türkyılmaz (14), R. Koeman (30), Amor (50)

GALATASARAY ISTANBUL v MANCHESTER UNITED FC 0-0

Ali Sami Yen, Istanbul 28.09.1994

Referee: Mario van der Ende (HOL) Attendance: 24,385

GALATASARAY: Gintaras Stauče, Mert Korkmaz, Bülent Korkmaz, Sedat Balkanli, Norman Mapeza, Tugay Kerimoğlu (Cap) (46 Arif Erdem), Yusuf Tepekule, Hamza Hamzaoğlu, Saffet Sancakli (75 Osman Akyol), Hakan Şükür, Kubilay Türkyılmaz. Trainer: Reinhard Saftig

MANCHESTER UNITED: Peter Schmeichel, David May, Steve Bruce (Cap), Gary Pallister, Lee Sharpe; Andrei Kanchelskis, Paul Ince, Nicky Butt, Roy Keane; Mark Hughes, Ryan Giggs (65 Paul Parker). Manager: Alex Ferguson

IFK GÖTEBORG v FC BARCELONA 2-1 (0-1)

Gamla Ullevi, Göteborg 28.09.1994

Referee: Bernd Heynemann (GER) Attendance: 33,000

IFK: Thomas Ravelli, Pontus Kåmark, Jonas Ohlsson (65 Magnus Johansson), Joachim Björklund, Mikael Nilsson; Mikael Martinsson (69 Erik Wahlstedt), Stefan Rehn, Stefan Lindqvist, Jesper Blomqvist; Magnus Erlingmark (Cap), Stefan Pettersson. Trainer: Roger Gustavsson

FC BARCELONA: Carlos Busquets, Albert Ferrer, Ronald Koeman, Miguel Ángel Nadal, ABELARDO Fernández Artuña, SERGI Barjuán Esclusa, Gheorghe Hagi (69 IVÁN Iglesias Corteguera), José María Bakero (Cap), Luis Cembranos (81 Guillermo Amor); Jordi Cruijff, Hristo Stoichkov. Trainer: Johan Cruyff

Goals: Stoichkov (10), Erlingmark (74), Blomqvist (89)

IFK GÖTEBORG v GALATASARAY ISTANBUL 1-0 (0-0)

Gamla Ullevi, Göteborg 19.10.1994

Referee: Gerd Grabher (AUS) Attendance: 26,000

IFK: Thomas Ravelli, Pontus Kåmark (Cap), Magnus Johansson, Joachim Björklund, Mikael Nilsson; Mikael Martinsson (74 Erik Wahlstedt), Stefan Lindqvist, Stefan Rehn, Jesper Blomqvist (89 Thomas Andersson); Magnus Erlingmark, Stefan Pettersson. Trainer: Roger Gustavsson

GALATASARAY: Gintaras Stauče, Mert Korkmaz (80 Osman Akyol), Bülent Korkmaz (Cap), Sedat Balkanli, Yusuf Tepekule, Suat Kaya, Norman Mapeza, Hamza Hamzaoğlu, Arif Erdem, Hakan Şükür, Kubilay Türkyılmaz (71 Saffet Sancakli). Trainer: Reinhard Saftig

Goal: Erlingmark (76)

MANCHESTER UNITED FC v FC BARCELONA 2-2 (1-1)

Old Trafford, Manchester 19.10.1994

Referee: Ion Crăciunescu (ROM) Attendance: 40,064

MANCHESTER UNITED: Peter Schmeichel, David May (69 Steve Bruce), Paul Parker, Gary Pallister, Dennis Irwin; Nicky Butt (65 Paul Scholes), Paul Ince (Cap), Roy Keane, Andrei Kanchelskis; Mark Hughes, Lee Sharpe. Manager: Alex Ferguson

FC BARCELONA: Carlos Busquets, Luis Cembranos (46 Eusebio Sacristán), ABELARDO Fernández Artuña, Ronald Koeman, Miguel Ángel Nadal, SERGI Barjuán Esclusa, Josep Guardiola, José María Bakero (Cap), Aitor Beguiristáin (67 Jordi Cruijff); Hristo Stoichkov, ROMÁRIO de Souza Faria. Trainer: Johan Cruyff

Goals: Hughes (19), Romário (34), Bakero (49), Sharpe (80)

GALATASARAY ISTANBUL v IFK GÖTEBORG 0-1 (0-0)

Ali Sami Yen, Istanbul 2.11.1994

Referee: Václav Krondl (CZE) Attendance: 27,300

GALATASARAY: Gintaras Stauče, Mert Korkmaz, Bülent Korkmaz (Cap), Sedat Balkanli, Norman Mapeza, Suat Kaya, Hamza Hamzaoğlu (68 Kubilay Türkyılmaz), Arif Erdem, Yusuf Tepekule (46 Tugay Kerimoğlu); Hakan Şükür, Saffet Sancakli. Trainer: Reinhard Saftig

IFK: Thomas Ravelli, Pontus Kåmark (Cap), Joachim Björklund, Magnus Johansson, Mikael Nilsson; Mikael Martinsson (73 Erik Wahlstedt), Stefan Rehn, Stefan Lindqvist, Jesper Blomqvist (89 Magnus Gustafsson); Magnus Erlingmark, Thomas Andersson. Trainer: Roger Gustavsson

Goal: Erlingmark (86)

FC BARCELONA v MANCHESTER UNITED FC 4-0 (2-0)

Camp Nou, Barcelona 2.11.1994

Referee: Joël Quiniou (FRA) Attendance: 115,000

FC BARCELONA: Carlos Busquets, Albert Ferrer, Ronald Koeman, ABELARDO Fernández Artuña, SERGI Barjuán Esclusa, Josep Guardiola, José María Bakero (Cap) (77 Francisco Javier SANCHEZ JARA), Jordi Cruijff (63 IVÁN Iglesias Corteguera), Guillermo Amor; Hristo Stoichkov, ROMÁRIO de Souza Faria. Trainer: Johan Cruyff

MANCHESTER UNITED: Gary Walsh; Paul Parker, Steve Bruce (Cap), Gary Pallister, Dennis Irwin; Roy Keane, Nicky Butt, Paul Ince, Andrei Kanchelskis; Ryan Giggs (79 Paul Scholes), Mark Hughes. Manager: Alex Ferguson

Goals: Stoichkov (9, 52), Romário (45), Ferrer (88)

IFK GÖTEBORG
v MANCHESTER UNITED FC 3-1 (1-0)

Gamla Ullevi, Göteborg 23.11.1994

Referee: Alfredo Trentalange (ITA) Attendance: 36,385

IFK: Thomas Ravelli, Pontus Kåmark (Cap), Magnus Johansson, Joachim Björklund, Mikael Nilsson; Mikael Martinsson (49 Erik Wahlstedt), Stefan Rehn, Stefan Lindqvist, Jesper Blomqvist; Magnus Erlingmark, Stefan Pettersson (79 Thomas Andersson). Trainer: Roger Gustavsson

MANCHESTER UNITED: Gary Walsh, David May (69 Gary Neville), Steve Bruce (Cap), Gary Pallister, Dennis Irwin; Andrei Kanchelskis, Paul Ince, Brian McClair, Simon Davies (76 Nicky Butt); Eric Cantona, Mark Hughes.
Manager: Alex Ferguson

Sent off: Ince (83)

Goals: Blomqvist (10), Hughes (64), Erlingmark (65), Kåmark (72 pen)

GALATASARAY ISTANBUL
v FC BARCELONA 2-1 (0-1)

Ali Sami Yen, Istanbul 23.11.1994

Referee: Vadim Zhuk (BLS) Attendance: 18,375

GALATASARAY: Gintaras Stauče, Mert Korkmaz, Sedat Balkanli, Bülent Korkmaz (Cap), Yusuf Tepekule (46 Tugay Kerimoğlu), Suat Kaya, Norman Mapeza, Hamza Hamzaoğlu (59 Okan Buruk), Ergün Pembe; Arif Erdem, Hakan Şükür.
Trainer: Reinhard Saftig

FC BARCELONA: Carlos Busquets; Miguel Ángel Nadal, Ronald Koeman, SERGI Barjuán Esclusa, Albert Ferrer; Guillermo Amor, Josep Guardiola (60 ABELARDO Fernández Artuña), José María Bakero (Cap) (70 Aitor Beguiristáin), Eusebio Sacristán; ROMÁRIO de Souza Faria, Hristo Stoichkov. Trainer: Johan Cruyff

Goals: Romário (16), Hakan Şükür (72 pen), Arif (88)

MANCHESTER UNITED FC
v GALATASARAY ISTANBUL 4-0 (2-0)

Old Trafford, Manchester 7.12.1994

Referee: Ryszard Wójcik (POL) Attendance: 39,220

MANCHESTER UNITED: Gary Walsh, Gary Neville, Gary Pallister, Steve Bruce (Cap), Dennis Irwin; Roy Keane, Nicky Butt, Brian McClair, David Beckham; Eric Cantona, Simon Davies. Manager: Alex Ferguson

GALATASARAY: Gintaras Stauče, Ergün Pembe, Sedat Balkanli, Mert Korkmaz, Bülent Korkmaz, Suat Kaya, Tugay Kerimoğlu (Cap) (63 Yusuf Tepekule), Arif Erdem, Hamza Hamzaoğlu (46 Uğur Tütüneker); Hakan Şükür, Kubilay Türkyılmaz. Trainer: Reinhard Saftig

Goals: Davies (2), Beckham (37), Keane (48), Bülent (87 og)

FC BARCELONA v IFK GÖTEBORG 1-1 (0-0)

Camp Nou, Barcelona 7.12.1994

Referee: Frans van den Wijngaert (BEL) Att: 76,000

FC BARCELONA: Carlos Busquets, Miguel Ángel Nadal, Josep Guardiola, Ronald Koeman, SERGI Barjuán Esclusa, José María Bakero (Cap), Eusebio Sacristán, Guillermo Amor (85 Jordi Cruijff), Aitor Beguiristáin (70 ABELARDO Fernández Artuña); Hristo Stoichkov, ROMÁRIO de Souza Faria.
Trainer: Johan Cruyff

IFK: Thomas Ravelli, Pontus Kåmark (C), Magnus Johansson, Joachim Björklund, Mikael Nilsson; Mikael Martinsson (69 Erik Wahlstedt), Magnus Erlingmark, Stefan Lindqvist, Jesper Blomqvist, Stefan Rehn, Stefan Pettersson.
Trainer: Roger Gustavsson

Goals: Bakero (81), Rehn (90)

	P	W	D	L	F	A	Pts
IFK Göteborg	6	4	1	1	10	7	9
FC Barcelona	6	2	2	2	11	8	6
Manchester United	6	2	2	2	11	11	6
Galatasaray Istanbul	6	1	1	4	3	9	3

GROUP B

FC DYNAMO KYIV
v SPARTAK MOSKVA 3-2 (0-2)

Republikansky, Kiev 14.09.1994

Referee: Gerd Grabher (AUS) Attendance: 70,000

DINAMO: Olexandr Shovkovskyi, Oleh Luzhnyi (Cap), Vladislav Vashchuk, Sergi Shmatovalenko (65 Andriy Khomin), Sergei Kovalets, Sergiy Lezhentsev, Dmytro Mikhailenko, Alexander Prizetko, Vitaliy Kosovskiy, Viktor Leonenko, Serhiy Skachenko (54 Serhiy Rebrov).
Trainer: Jozsef Szabo

SPARTAK: Dmitriy Tyapushkin; Ramiz Mamedov, Vladislav Ternavski, Ilya Tsymbalar, Rashid Rakhimov; Sergei Chudin, Oleg Naduda, Dmitriy Alenichev (59 Mukhsin Mukhamadiev), Andrei Piatnitski (Cap); Nikolai Pisarev, Andrei Tikhonov (43 Sergei Rodionov). Trainer: Oleg Romantsev

Goals: Kosovski (12 og), Tikhonov (38), Leonenko (48, 76), Rebrov (86)

PARIS SAINT-GERMAIN v FC BAYERN MÜNCHEN 2-0 (1-0)

Parc des Princes, Paris 14.09.1994

Referee: David Elleray (ENG) Attendance: 37,000

PSG: Bernard Lama, Oumar Dieng, Alain Roche, Ricardo Gomes, Vincent Guérin (88 Francis Llacer), Valdo Cândido Filho (89 Antoine Kombouaré), Daniel Bravo, Paul le Guen, José Cobos; George Weah, David Ginola (Cap). Trainer: Luis Fernández

BAYERN: Oliver Kahn, Jorge de Amorim Campos Jorginho, Oliver Kreuzer, Lothar Matthäus (Cap), Thomas Helmer; Christian Ziege, Markus Schupp, Mehmet Scholl (53 Dietmar Hamann), Christian Nerlinger; Marcel Witeczek (53 Aureliano Mazinho), Alain Sutter. Trainer: Giovanni Trapattoni

Goals: Weah (41), Bravo (83)

FC BAYERN MÜNCHEN v FC DYNAMO KYIV 1-0 (1-0)

Olympiastadion, München 28.09.1994

Referee: Ion Crăciunescu (ROM) Attendance: 26,000

BAYERN: Oliver Kahn, Jorge de Amorim Campos Jorginho, Thomas Helmer, Lothar Matthäus (Cap), Markus Babbel; Markus Schupp, Christian Nerlinger, Mehmet Scholl (64 Dietmar Hamann), Christian Ziege; Marcel Witeczek (46 Jean-Pierre Papin), Alain Sutter. Trainer: Giovanni Trapattoni

DINAMO: Olexandr Shovkovskyi, Sergiy Lezhentsev, Vladislav Vashchuk, Oleh Luzhnyi (Cap), Sergei Kovalets, Sergi Shmatovalenko, Serhiy Mizin, Dmytro Mikhailenko, Vitaliy Kosovskiy; Viktor Leonenko, Alexander Prizetko (68 Serhiy Rebrov). Trainer: Jozsef Szabo

Sent off: Mizin (33)

Goal: Scholl (9)

SPARTAK MOSKVA v PARIS SAINT-GERMAIN 1-2 (1-0)

Luzhniki, Moskva 28.09.1994

Referee: Bo Karlsson (SWE) Attendance: 30,000

SPARTAK: Dmitriy Tyapushkin, Dmitriy Khlestov, Ramiz Mamedov, Yuri Nikiforov, Rashid Rakhimov, Ilya Tsymbalar, Nikolai Pisarev, Viktor Onopko (Cap), Andrei Piatnitski, Andrei Tikhonov, Mukhsin Mukhamadiev (66 Dmitriy Alenichev). Trainer: Oleg Romantsev

PSG: Bernard Lama, José Cobos (81 Francis Llacer), Antoine Kombouaré, Alain Roche, Oumar Dieng; Paul le Guen, Daniel Bravo, Valdo Cândido Filho, Vincent Guérin; George Weah, David Ginola (Cap) (88 Pascal Nouma). Trainer: Luis Fernández

Sent off: Mamedov (57)

Goals: Rakhimov (40), Le Guen (52), Valdo (57)

SPARTAK MOSKVA v FC BAYERN MÜNCHEN 1-1 (0-0)

Luzhniki, Moskva 19.10.1994

Referee: Guy Goethals (BEL) Attendance: 25,000

SPARTAK: Dmitriy Tyapushkin, Yuri Nikiforov (86 Vladislav Ternavski), Dmitriy Ananko, Viktor Onopko (Cap), Rashid Rakhimov; Ilya Tsymbalar, Valeriy Kechinov, Andrei Piatnitski, Nikolai Pisarev, Mukhsin Mukhamadiev (75 Andrei Konovalov), Andrei Tikhonov. Trainer: Oleg Romantsev

BAYERN: Oliver Kahn, Lothar Matthäus (Cap), Markus Babbel, Oliver Kreuzer, Jorge de Amorim Campos JORGINHO, Dieter Frey, Mehmet Scholl, Christian Nerlinger, Alain Sutter (64 Michael Sternkopf), Christian Ziege, Alexander Zickler. Trainer: Giovanni Trapattoni

Goals: Pisarev (77), Babbel (90)

FC DYNAMO KYIV v PARIS SAINT-GERMAIN 1-2 (1-1)

Republikanskiy, Kiev 19.10.1994

Referee: Piero Ceccarini (ITA) Attendance: 70,000

DINAMO: Olexandr Shovkovskyi, Oleh Luzhnyi (Cap), Vladislav Vashchuk, Sergiy Lezhentsev, Sergi Shmatovalenko, Sergei Kovalets, Andriy Khomin, Dmytro Mikhailenko, Vitaliy Kosovskiy (77 Alexander Prizetko), Viktor Leonenko, Serhiy Rebrov (72 Mihail Dzhishkariani). Trainer: Jozsef Szabo

PSG: Bernard Lama, Antoine Kombouaré, Alain Roche (Cap), Oumar Dieng, José Cobos; Paul le Guen, Daniel Bravo, Valdo Cândido Filho, Vincent Guérin; George Weah (88 Patrick Colleter), David Ginola (54 Raí Souza de Oliveira). Trainer: Luis Fernández

Goals: Guérin (26), Leonenko (33 pen), Weah (75)

FC BAYERN MÜNCHEN v SPARTAK MOSKVA 2-2 (2-2)

Olympiastadion, München 2.11.1994

Referee: Mario van der Ende (HOL) Attendance: 31,000

BAYERN: Oliver Kahn, Lothar Matthäus (Cap), Oliver Kreuzer, Samuel Ossei Kuffour, Jorge de Amorim Campos Jorginho, Markus Schupp (63 Dietmar Hamann), Mehmet Scholl (53 Dieter Frey), Christian Nerlinger, Christian Ziege; Alexander Zickler, Marcel Witeczek. Trainer: Giovanni Trapattoni

SPARTAK: Dmitriy Tyapushkin, Dmitriy Ananko, Yuri Nikiforov, Viktor Onopko (Cap), Rashid Rakhimov; Dmitriy Alenichev, Valeriy Kechinov, Dmitriy Khlestov, Andrei Tikhonov; Andrei Piatnitski, Nikolai Pisarev (85 Oleg Naduda). Trainer: Oleg Romantsev

Goals: Tikhonov (4), Nerlinger (28), Alenichev (33), Kuffour (36)

PARIS SAINT-GERMAIN
v FC DYNAMO KYIV 1-0 (0-0)

Parc des Princes, Paris 2.11.1994

Referee: Ahmet Cakar (TUR) Attendance: 33,741

PSG: Bernard Lama, Oumar Dieng, Antoine Kombouaré, Alain Roche (Cap), Patrick Colleter, José Cobos (80 Francis Llacer); Vincent Guérin, Daniel Bravo, Paul le Guen; George Weah, Raí Souza de Oliveira (80 Pascal Nouma). Trainer: Luis Fernández

DINAMO: Olexandr Shovkovskyi, Oleh Luzhnyi (Cap), Sergiy Lezhentsev, Vladislav Vashchuk, Sergi Shmatovalenko, Sergei Kovalets, Dmytro Mikhailenko, Alexander Prizetko, Vitaliy Kosovskiy; Serhiy Rebrov (70 Mihail Dzhishkariani), Serhiy Skachenko. Trainer: Jozsef Szabo

Goal: Weah (68)

FC DYNAMO KYIV
v FC BAYERN MÜNCHEN 1-4 (1-1)

Republikanskiy, Kiev 7.12.1994

Referee: Václav Krondl (CZE) Attendance: 40,000

DINAMO: Olexandr Shovkovskyi, Oleh Luzhnyi (Cap), Sergiy Lezhentsev, Andriy Khomin, Sergei Kovalets, Dmytro Mikhailenko, Serhiy Skachenko, Vitaliy Kosovskiy (64 Alexander Prizetko), Sergei Shevchenko; Viktor Leonenko (62 Serhiy Mizin), Pavlo Shkapenko. Trainer: Jozsef Szabo

BAYERN: Sven Scheuer, Thomas Helmer, Jorge de Amorim Campos JORGINHO, Oliver Kreuzer, Markus Babbel; Christian Ziege, Dietmar Hamann, Lothar Matthäus (Cap) (72 Dieter Frey), Christian Nerlinger; Jean-Pierre Papin, Alain Sutter (77 Mehmet Scholl). Trainer: Giovanni Trapattoni

Goals: Shevchenko (38), Nerlinger (45), Papin (57, 82), Scholl (87)

SPARTAK MOSKVA
v FC DYNAMO KYIV 1-0 (0-0)

Luzhniki, Moskva 23.11.1994

Referee: Rune Pedersen (NOR) Attendance: 30,000

SPARTAK: Dmitriy Tyapushkin, Dmitriy Khlestov, Aleksandr Lipko, Dmitriy Alenichev, Rashid Rakhimov, Yuri Nikiforov, Viktor Onopko, Andrei Tikhonov, Nikolai Pisarev (63 Andrei Konovalov), Andrei Piatnitski (88 Oleg Naduda), Mukhsin Mukhamadiev. Trainer: Oleg Romantsev

DINAMO: Olexandr Shovkovskyi, Oleh Luzhnyi, Vladislav Vashchuk, Andriy Khomin, Volodymyr Sharan, Sergei Kovalets, Sergiy Lezhentsev, Serhiy Rebrov (56 Sergei Shevchenko), Dmytro Mikhailenko (64 Serhiy Mizin), Viktor Leonenko, Pavlo Shkapenko. Trainer: Jozsef Szabo

Sent off: Vashchuk (86)

Goal: Muhamadiev (51)

PARIS SAINT-GERMAIN
v SPARTAK MOSKVA 4-1 (2-0)

Parc des Princes, Paris 7.12.1994

Referee: Atanas Uzunov (BUL) Attendance: 31,461

PSG: Bernard Lama, Oumar Dieng, Alain Roche (Cap), Antoine Kombouaré, Francis Llacer, Daniel Bravo, Raí Souza de Oliveira, Paul le Guen (52 Vincent Guérin), Patrick Colleter; George Weah (67 Bernard Allou), David Ginola. Trainer: Luis Fernández

SPARTAK: Dmitriy Tyapushkin, Dmitriy Khlestov, Yuri Nikiforov, Viktor Onopko (Cap), Aleksandr Lipko; Nikolai Pisarev, Andrei Piatnitski, Valeriy Kechinov (73 Andrei Konovalov), Dmitriy Alenichev; Mukhsin Mukhamadiev (46 Sergei Rodionov), Andrei Tikhonov. Trainer: Oleg Romantsev

Goals: Weah (30, 52), Ginola (42), Raí (59), Rodionov (67)

FC BAYERN MÜNCHEN
v PARIS SAINT-GERMAIN 0-1 (0-0)

Olympiastadion, München 23.11.1994

Referee: Manuel Diaz Vega (SPA) Attendance: 46,000

BAYERN: Oliver Kahn, Thomas Helmer, Lothar Matthäus (Cap), Markus Babbel, Jorge de Amorim Campos Jorginho, Christian Nerlinger, Markus Schupp (63 Dietmar Hamann), Mehmet Scholl, Dieter Frey, Jean-Pierre Papin (69 Alexander Zickler), Alain Sutter. Trainer: Giovanni Trapattoni

PSG: Bernard Lama, Oumar Dieng, Alain Roche (Cap), Patrick Colleter, José Cobos, Daniel Bravo (58 Paul le Guen), Vincent Guérin, Jean-Philippe Séchet, Francis Llacer, Pascal Nouma, David Ginola (65 George Weah). Trainer: Luis Fernández

Goal: Weah (80)

	P	W	D	L	F	A	Pts
Paris Saint-Germain	6	6	0	0	12	3	12
FC Bayern München	6	2	2	2	8	7	6
Spartak Moskva	6	1	2	3	8	12	4
Dynamo Kyiv	6	1	0	5	5	11	2

GROUP C

HAJDUK SPLIT v SPORT LISBOA E BENFICA 0-0

Poljud, Split 14.09.1994

Referee: Serge Muhmenthaler (SWI) Attendance: 26,000

HAJDUK: Tonci Gabrić, Darko Butorović, Sasa Person, Mirsad Hibić, Igor Stimac, Stipe Andrijasević (75 Dean Racunica), Kazimir Vulić (Cap), Milan Rapaić, Ivica Mornar (59 Tomislav Erceg), Aljosa Asanović, Mario Mestrović. Trainer: Ivan Katalinić

BENFICA: Michel Preud'homme; António Augusto da Silva VELOSO (Cap), Paulo César Batista dos Santos "PAULAO", HÉLDER Marino Rodrigues Cristóvao, DIMAS Manuel Marques Teixeira; Manuel António Guimarães "NELO", Vítor Manuel Araújo "VÍTOR PANEIRA" (84 Daniel KENEDY Pimentel Mateus dos Santos), ABEL Luís da Silva Costa XAVIER, Claudio Caniggia (89 CÉSAR Gonçalves BRITO Duarte), José Fernando Gomes TAVARES, ISAÍAS Marques Soares. Trainer: Artur Jorge

Sent off: Stimac (87)

RSC ANDERLECHT BRUSSEL v STEAUA BUCUREŞTI 0-0

Constant vandenstock, Brussel 14.09.1994

Referee: Leslie Mottram (SCO) Attendance: 13,053

ANDERLECHT: Filip De Wilde; Bertrand Crasson, Graeme Rutjes, Marc Emmers, Olivier Doll; Johan Walem, Filip Haagdoren (71 Yaw Preko), Marc Degryse (Cap), Danny Boffin (87 Olivier Suray); John Bosman, Josip Weber. Trainer: Johan Boskamp

STEAUA: Dumitru Stîngaciu; Aurel Silviu Panait, Daniel Claudiu Prodan, Anton Doboş, Tiberiu Csik; Ionel Antonel Pârvu, Basarab Nică Panduru, Ilie Stan, Damian Militaru (88 Laurenţiu Dumitru Roşu); Marius Mihai Lăcătuş (Cap), Adrian Ilie (81 Daniel Iftodi). Trainer: Dumitru Dumitriu

Sent off: Lăcătuş (88)

STEAUA BUCUREŞTI v HAJDUK SPLIT 0-1 (0-0)

Steaua, Bucureşti 28.09.1994

Referee: Václav Krondl (CZE) Attendance: 20,000

STEAUA: Dumitru Stîngaciu; Aurel Silviu Panait, Daniel Claudiu Prodan, Anton Doboş (Cap), Ionel Antonel Pârvu; Damian Militaru (75 Ilie Stan), Basarab Nică Panduru, Tiberiu Csik, Constantin Gâlcă; Laurenţiu Dumitru Roşu, Adrian Ilie (75 Marian Popa). Trainer: Dumitru Dumitriu

HAJDUK: Tonci Gabrić, Darko Butorović, Kazimir Vulić (Cap), Karol Prazenica, Sasa Person, Mirsad Hibić, Nenad Pralija, Aljosa Asanović, Milan Rapaić (90 Hari Vukas), Tomislav Erceg (77 Goran Vučević), Mario Mestrović. Trainer: Ivan Katalinić

Goal: Asanović (89)

SPORT LISBOA E BENFICA v RSC ANDERLECHT BRUSSEL 3-1 (2-0)

Estádio da Luz, Lisboa 28.09.1994

Referee: Vadim Zhuk (BLS) Attendance: 32,000

BENFICA: Michel Preud'homme; ABEL Luís da Silva Costa XAVIER (77 António Augusto da Silva VELOSO), PAULO Sérgio Braga MADEIRA, HÉLDER Marino Rodrigues Cristóvao, DIMAS Manuel Marques Teixeira; José Fernando Gomes TAVARES, Vítor Manuel Araújo "VÍTOR PANEIRA" (Cap), Manuel António Guimarães "NELO", ISAÍAS Marques Soares; JOÃO Manuel Vieira PINTO (88 Daniel KENEDY Pimentel Mateus dos Santos), Claudio Caniggia. Trainer: Artur Jorge

ANDERLECHT: Filip De Wilde; Bertrand Crasson, Graeme Rutjes, Chidi Nwanu, Olivier Doll; Danny Boffin, Johan Walem, Marc Degryse (Cap), Filip Haagdoren; John Bosman, Josip Weber. Trainer: Johan Boskamp

Goals: Caniggia (26, 40), Tavares (72), Paulo Madeira (88 og)

SPORT LISBOA E BENFICA v STEAUA BUCUREŞTI 2-1 (1-0)

Estádio da Luz, Lisboa 19.10.1994

Referee: David Elleray (ENG) Attendance: 35,000

BENFICA: Michel Preud'homme, António Augusto da Silva VELOSO (Cap) (82 CÉSAR Gonçalves BRITO Duarte), José Carlos Nepomuceno MOZER, HÉLDER Marino Rodrigues Cristóvao, DIMAS Manuel Marques Teixeira; José Fernando Gomes TAVARES, Vítor Manuel Araújo "VÍTOR PANEIRA", Manuel António Guimarães "NELO" (82 Daniel KENEDY Pimentel Mateus dos Santos), ISAÍAS Marques Soares; Claudio Caniggia, JOÃO Manuel Vieira PINTO. Trainer: Artur Jorge

STEAUA: Dumitru Stîngaciu, Aurel Silviu Panait, Anton Doboş (Cap), Daniel Claudiu Prodan, Ionel Antonel Pârvu; Ilie Stan, Constantin Gâlcă, Basarab Nică Panduru (84 Daniel Iftodi), Damian Militaru, Iulian Sebastian Filipescu; Laurenţiu Dumitru Roşu (68 Bogdan Vişan Bucur). Trainer: Dumitru Dumitriu

Sent off: Doboş (59).

Goals: Caniggia (44 pen), João Pinto (60), Militaru (89)

HAJDUK SPLIT v RSC ANDERLECHT BRUSSEL 2-1 (1-0)

Poljud, Split 19.10.1994

Referee: Antonio Jesus Lopez Nieto (SPA) Att: 26,000

HAJDUK: Tonci Gabrić, Darko Butorović, Nenad Pralija, Mirsad Hibić, Sasa Person, Stipe Andrijasević, Kazimir Vulić (Cap), Milan Rapaić, Tomislav Erceg (86 Hari Vukas), Aljosa Asanović, Ivica Mornar (57 Goran Vučević). Trainer: Ivan Katalinić

ANDERLECHT: Filip De Wilde, Bertrand Crasson, Graeme Rutjes, Olivier Suray, Chidi Nwanu; Johan Walem, Pär Zetterberg, Frédéric Peiremans, Danny Boffin (Cap); Josip Weber, John Bosman. Trainer: Johan Boskamp

Goals: Pralija (34), Butorović (86), Weber (88)

STEAUA BUCUREŞTI v SPORT LISBOA E BENFICA 1-1 (1-0)

Steaua, Bucureşti 2.11.1994

Referee: Leif Sundell (SWE) Attendance: 17,000

STEAUA: Dumitru Stîngaciu; Aurel Silviu Panait, Daniel Claudiu Prodan, Bogdan Vişan Bucur, Tiberiu Csik; Ilie Stan, Constantin Gâlcă, Daniel Iftodi (71 Viorel Ion), Iulian Sebastian Filipescu; Laurenţiu Dumitru Roşu (80 Marian Popa), Basarab Nică Panduru (Cap).
Trainer: Dumitru Dumitriu

BENFICA: Michel Preud'homme; António Augusto da Silva VELOSO (Cap), José Carlos Nepomuceno MOZER, HÉLDER Marino Rodrigues Cristóvao, DIMAS Manuel Marques Teixeira, ABEL Luís da Silva Costa XAVIER, PAULO Sérgio Braga MADEIRA, Vítor Manuel Araújo "VÍTOR PANEIRA" (86 José Fernando Gomes TAVARES), Manuel António Guimarães "NELO", JOÃO Manuel Vieira PINTO, ISAÍAS Marques Soares.
Trainer: Artur Jorge

Goals: Panduru (27), Hélder (63)

RSC ANDERLECHT BRUSSEL v HAJDUK SPLIT 0-0

Constant vandenstock, Brussel 2.11.1994

Referee: Markus Merk (GER) Attendance: 21,000

ANDERLECHT: Filip De Wilde, Olivier Suray, Graeme Rutjes, Bertrand Crasson, Olivier Doll; Frédéric Peiremans (68 Filip Haagdoren), Pär Zetterberg, Johan Walem, Danny Boffin (Cap); Josip Weber, John Bosman. Trainer: Johan Boskamp

HAJDUK: Tonci Gabrić; Darko Butorović, Igor Stimac, Kazimir Vulić (Cap), Mirsad Hibić, Damir Vuica, Mario Mestrović (80 Stipe Andrijasević), Aljosa Asanović, Nenad Pralija, Ivica Mornar, Milan Rapaić (85 Tomislav Erceg).
Trainer: Ivan Katalinić

SPORT LISBOA E BENFICA v HAJDUK SPLIT 2-1 (1-0)

Stadio da Luz, Lisboa 23.11.1994

Referee: John Blankenstein (HOL) Attendance: 31,000

BENFICA: Michel Preud'homme, PAULO Sérgio Braga MADEIRA, José Carlos Nepomuceno MOZER (C), HÉLDER Marino Rodrigues Cristóvao, DIMAS Manuel Marques Teixeira; ABEL Luís da Silva Costa XAVIER, Manuel António Guimarães "NELO", José Fernando Gomes TAVARES (79 Daniel KENEDY Pimentel Mateus dos Santos), ISAÍAS Marques Soares (63 Vítor Manuel Araújo "VÍTOR PANEIRA"); JOÃO Manuel Vieira PINTO, Claudio Caniggia.
Trainer: Artur Jorge

HAJDUK: Tonci Gabrić; Darko Butorović, Sasa Person (55 Goran Vučević), Kazimir Vulić (Cap), Mirsad Hibić, Damir Vuica, Stipe Andrijasević, Nenad Pralija, Mario Mestrović, Aljosa Asanović, Ivica Mornar (63 Tomislav Erceg).
Trainer: Ivan Katalinić

Goals: Isaías (32), Andrijasević (71), João Pinto (76)

STEAUA BUCUREŞTI v RSC ANDERLECHT BRUSSEL 1-1 (0-1)

Steaua, Bucureşti 23.11.1994

Referee: Ilkka Koho (FIN) Attendance: 10,000

STEAUA: Dumitru Stîngaciu; Aurel Silviu Panait, Daniel Claudiu Prodan, Anton Doboş, Ionel Antonel Pârvu; Ilie Stan, Tiberiu Csik, Basarab Nică Panduru (80 Laurenţiu Dumitru Roşu), Constantin Gâlcă; Marius Mihai Lăcătuş (Cap), Adrian Ilie (76 Marian Popa). Trainer: Dumitru Dumitriu

ANDERLECHT: Filip De Wilde; Olivier Doll, Graeme Rutjes, Bertrand Crasson, Celestine Babayaro; Filip Haagdoren (65 Frédéric Peiremans), Johan Walem, Pär Zetterberg, Danny Boffin; Marc Degryse (Cap), John Bosman.
Trainer: Johan Boskamp

Sent off: Babayaro (37)

Goals: Bosman (43), Doboş (54)

HAJDUK SPLIT v STEAUA BUCUREŞTI 1-4 (0-3)

Poljud, Split 7.12.1994

Referee: James McCluskey (SCO) Attendance: 15,000

HAJDUK: Zoran Slavica, Darko Butorović, Mirsad Hibić, Igor Stimac (46 Dean Racunica), Sasa Person, Stipe Andrijasević, Kazimir Vulić (Cap), Nenad Pralija, Aljosa Asanović, Tomislav Erceg, Goran Vučević (46 Hari Vukas).
Trainer: Ivan Katalinić

STEAUA: Dumitru Stîngaciu (90 Daniel Gherasim); Tiberiu Csik, Anton Doboş, Daniel Claudiu Prodan, Ionel Antonel Pârvu; Damian Militaru, Ilie Stan, Constantin Gâlcă, Laurenţiu Dumitru Roşu; Marius Mihai Lăcătuş (Cap) (88 Viorel Ion), Adrian Ilie (76 Iulian Sebastian Filipescu).
Trainer: Dumitru Dumitriu

Goals: A. Ilie (11, 31), Lăcătuş (23), Andrijasević (48), Gâlcă (90)

RSC ANDERLECHT BRUSSEL v SPORT LISBOA E BENFICA 1-1 (0-0)

Constant van den Stock, Brussel 7.12.1994

Referee: Marc Batta (FRA) Attendance: 20,000

ANDERLECHT: Filip De Wilde; Olivier Doll, Bertrand Crasson, Graeme Rutjes, Danny Boffin, Marc Emmers (66 Filip Haagdoren), Johan Walem, Pär Zetterberg (88 Frédéric Peiremans), Yaw Preko, Marc Degryse (Cap), John Bosman.
Trainer: Johan Boskamp

BENFICA: Michel Preud'homme; António Augusto da Silva VELOSO (Cap), HÉLDER Marino Rodrigues Cristóvao, WILLIAM Amaral de Andrade, DIMAS Manuel Marques Teixeira; Vítor Manuel Araújo "VÍTOR PANEIRA" (66 Daniel KENEDY Pimentel Mateus dos Santos), José Fernando Gomes TAVARES, EDILSON da Silva Ferreira, Manuel António Guimarães "NELO" (66 PAULO Jorge Gomes BENTO); JOÃO Manuel Vieira PINTO, Claudio Caniggia.
Trainer: Artur Jorge

Goals: Rutjes (48), Edilson (82)

	P	W	D	L	F	A	Pts
Sport Lisboa e Benfica	6	3	3	0	9	5	9
Hajduk Split	6	2	2	2	5	7	6
Steaua Bucureşti	6	1	3	2	7	6	5
Anderlecht Brussel	6	0	4	2	4	7	4

GROUP D

CASINO SALZBURG v AEK FC ATHINA 0-0

Ernst Happel, Wien 14.09.1994

Referee: Rémy Harrel (FRA) Attendance: 23,000

CASINO: Otto Konrad; Peter Artner (66 Arnold Freissegger), Leo Lainer (Cap), Heimo Pfeifenberger, Thomas Winklhofer, Wolfgang Feiersinger, Mladen Mladenovic, Adolf Hütter, Franz Aigner, Nikola Jurcevic, Ralph Hasenhüttl (46 Hermann Stadler). Trainer: Otto Barić

AEK: Ilias Atmatzidis, Giorgos Agorogiannis, Stelios Manolas (Cap), Mihalis Vlahos, Vaios Karagiannis, Refik Sabanadzović, Toni Savevski, Vasilis Tsartas, Mihalis Kasapis; Dimitris Saravakos (72 Haralampos Kopitsis), Hristos Kostis. Trainer: Dušan Bajević

AFC AJAX AMSTERDAM v AC MILAN 2-0 (0-0)

Olympisch, Amsterdam 14.09.1994

Referee: Antonio Jesus Lopez Nieto (SPA) Attendance: 35,000

AJAX: Edwin van der Sar, Michael Reiziger, Danny Blind (Cap), Frank De Boer, Ronald de Boer, Frank Rijkaard, Jari Litmanen, Edgar Davids (89 Clarence Seedorf), Finidi George; Patrick Kluivert (75 Peter Van Vossen), Marc Overmars. Trainer: Louis van Gaal

AC MILAN: Sebastiano Rossi, Stefano Nava, Filippo Galli, Franco Baresi (Cap), Paolo Maldini; Roberto Donadoni, Gianluca Sordo (72 Gianluigi Lentini), Zvonimir Boban, Massimo Orlando (67 Giovanni Stroppa); Ruud Gullit, Dejan Savićević. Trainer: Fabio Capello

Goals: R. De Boer (51), Litmanen (65)

AC MILAN v CASINO SALZBURG 3-0 (1-0)

Giuseppe Meazza, Milano 28.09.1994

Referee: Leif Sundell (SWE) Attendance: 23,000

AC MILAN: Sebastiano Rossi, Mauro Tassotti, Franco Baresi (Cap) (22 Filippo Galli), Paolo Maldini, Christian Panucci; Demetrio Albertini, Marcel Desailly, Giovanni Stroppa, Ruud Gullit, Zvonimir Boban, Marco Simone (75 Daniele Massaro). Trainer: Fabio Capello

CASINO: Otto Konrad (60 Herbert Ilsanker); Leo Lainer (Cap), Thomas Winklhofer, Mladen Mladenovic, Peter Artner (60 Martin Hiden), Christian Fürstaller, Franz Aigner, Nikola Jurcevic, Heimo Pfeifenberger, Wolfgang Feiersinger, Tomislav Kocijan (60 Adolf Hütter). Trainer: Otto Barić

Goals: Stroppa (39), Simone (59, 64)

During the first half of the match Konrad was hit by a bottle thrown from the crowd. As a result UEFA deducted 2 points from Milan.

AEK FC ATHINA v AFC AJAX AMSTERDAM 1-2 (1-1)

Nikos Gkoumas, Athina 28.09.1994

Referee: Markus Merk (GER) Attendance: 24,747

AEK: Ilias Atmatzidis, Giorgos Agorogiannis, Mihalis Vlahos, Vaios Karagiannis (74 Nikos Mirtsekis), Stelios Manolas (Cap), Mihalis Kasapis, Dimitris Saravakos, Toni Savevski, Haralampos Kopitsis, Vasilis Tsartas (63 Vasilis Dimitriadis), Hristos Kostis. Trainer: Dušan Bajević

AJAX: Edwin van der Sar, Michael Reiziger, Danny Blind (Cap), Clarence Seedorf, Frank De Boer; Ronald de Boer (76 Michel Kreek), Finidi George, Edgar Davids, Patrick Kluivert, Jari Litmanen, Marc Overmars (64 Peter Van Vossen). Trainer: Louis van Gaal

Goals: Savevski (30), Litmanen (33), Kluivert (63)

AEK FC ATHINA v AC MILAN 0-0

Nikos Gkoumas, Athina 19.10.1994

Referee: Sándor Puhl (HUN) Attendance: 19,699

AEK: Ilias Atmatzidis, Haralampos Kopitsis (77 Giorgos Agorogiannis), Stelios Manolas (Cap), Mihalis Vlahos, Manolis Papadopoulos, Refik Sabanadzović, Toni Savevski, Hristos Kostis (62 Temur Ketsbaia), Vasilis Tsartas, Dimitris Saravakos, Mihalis Kasapis. Trainer: Dušan Bajević

AC MILAN: Sebastiano Rossi; Mauro Tassotti, Alessandro Costacurta, Franco Baresi (Cap), Paolo Maldini (11 Christian Panucci); Ruud Gullit, Roberto Donadoni, Marcel Desailly, Zvonimir Boban, Demetrio Albertini, Daniele Massaro (89 Giovanni Stroppa). Trainer: Fabio Capello

CASINO SALZBURG v AFC AJAX AMSTERDAM 0-0

Ernst Happel, Wien 19.10.1994

Referee: Kurt Röthlisberger (SWI) Attendance: 19,500

CASINO: Otto Konrad, Peter Artner, Leo Lainer, Christian Fürstaller, Martin Hiden, Thomas Winklhofer, Wolfgang Feiersinger, Heimo Pfeifenberger (Cap), Mladen Mladenovic (73 Adolf Hütter), Tomislav Kocijan (78 Ralph Hasenhüttl), Nikola Jurcević. Trainer: Otto Barić

AJAX: Edwin van der Sar; Michael Reiziger, Danny Blind (Cap), Frank Rijkaard, Frank De Boer; Ronald de Boer, Jari Litmanen, Clarence Seedorf, Peter Van Vossen; Patrick Kluivert (67 Nwankwo Kanu), Marc Overmars (46 Michel Kreek). Trainer: Louis van Gaal

AEK FC ATHINA v CASINO SALZBURG 1-3 (1-2)

Nikos Gkoumas, Athina 23.11.1994

Referee: Guy Goethals (BEL) Attendance: 15,000

AEK: Ilias Atmatzidis, Giorgos Agorogiannis (46 Haralampos Kopitsis), Vaios Karagiannis (73 Vasilis Borbokis), Giorgos Koutoulas, Refik Sabanadzović, Mihalis Vlahos (Cap), Dimitris Saravakos, Mihalis Kasapis, Temur Ketsbaia, Hristos Kostis, Vasilis Tsartas. Trainer: Dušan Bajević

CASINO: Otto Konrad, Leo Lainer, Tomislav Kocijan (87 Adolf Hütter), Mladen Mladenovic, Christian Fürstaller, Thomas Winklhofer, Ralph Hasenhüttl (83 Hermann Stadler), Peter Artner, Heimo Pfeifenberger (Cap), Wolfgang Feiersinger, Martin Hiden. Trainer: Otto Barić

Goals: Pfeifenberger (7, 9), Vlahos (28), Hasenhüttl (77)

AC MILAN v AEK FC ATHINA 2-1 (0-1)

Nereo Rocco, Trieste 2.11.1994

Referee: Vadim Zhuk (BLS) Attendance: 17,264

AC MILAN: Sebastiano Rossi, Mauro Tassotti (46 Gianluigi Lentini), Alessandro Costacurta, Franco Baresi (Cap), Paolo Maldini; Demetrio Albertini, Marcel Desailly, Christian Panucci, Roberto Donadoni (73 Giovanni Stroppa); Daniele Massaro, Marco Simone. Trainer: Fabio Capello

AEK: Ilias Atmatzidis, Haralampos Kopitsis (76 Temur Ketsbaia), Vaios Karagiannis, Stelios Manolas (Cap), Refik Sabanadzović, Mihalis Vlahos, Dimitris Saravakos, Toni Savevski, Hristos Kostis, Vasilis Tsartas (74 Giorgos Agorogiannis), Mihalis Kasapis. Trainer: Dušan Bajević

Sent off: Manolas (87)

Goals: Savevski (15), Panucci (68, 73)

AC MILAN v AFC AJAX AMSTERDAM 0-2 (0-1)

Nereo Rocco, Trieste 23.11.1994

Referee: Peter Mikkelsen (DEN) Attendance: 29,764

AC MILAN: Sebastiano Rossi, Christian Panucci, Paolo Maldini, Demetrio Albertini, Alessandro Costacurta, Franco Baresi (Cap), Roberto Donadoni (75 Giovanni Stroppa), Marcel Desailly, Zvonimir Boban (66 Gianluigi Lentini); Marco Simone, Daniele Massaro. Trainer: Fabio Capello

AJAX: Edwin van der Sar, Michael Reiziger, Danny Blind (Cap), Frank Rijkaard, Frank De Boer, Clarence Seedorf, Finidi George, Edgar Davids (80 Marc Overmars), Ronald de Boer, Jari Litmanen, Peter Van Vossen (35 Nwankwo Kanu). Trainer: Louis van Gaal

Goals: Litmanen (2), F. Baresi (66 og)

AFC AJAX AMSTERDAM v CASINO SALZBURG 1-1 (0-0)

Olympisch, Amsterdam 2.11.1994

Referee: Leslie Mottram (SCO) Attendance: 41,000

AJAX: Edwin van der Sar, Michael Reiziger, Frank Rijkaard, Clarence Seedorf, Frank De Boer (Cap); Ronald de Boer, Jari Litmanen, Edgar Davids, Finidi George; Patrick Kluivert (57 Nwankwo Kanu), Marc Overmars (46 Peter Van Vossen). Trainer: Louis van Gaal

CASINO: Otto Konrad, Peter Artner (82 Ralph Hasenhüttl), Wolfgang Feiersinger, Christian Fürstaller, Leo Lainer, Martin Hiden, Thomas Winklhofer, Heimo Pfeifenberger (Cap), Tomislav Kocijan, Mladen Mladenovic (75 Adolf Hütter), Nikola Jurcević. Trainer: Otto Barić

Goals: Kocijan (63), Litmanen (85)

CASINO SALZBURG v AC MILAN 0-1 (0-1)

Ernst Happel, Wien 7.12.1994

Referee: Ion Crăciunescu (ROM) Attendance: 48,000

CASINO: Otto Konrad; Wolfgang Feiersinger, Christian Fürstaller, Martin Hiden (70 Adolf Hütter), Thomas Winklhofer (57 Ralph Hasenhüttl), Peter Artner, Leo Lainer, Heimo Pfeifenberger (Cap), Mladen Mladenovic; Tomislav Kocijan, Nikola Jurcević. Trainer: Otto Barić

AC MILAN: Sebastiano Rossi, Christian Panucci, Filippo Galli, Franco Baresi (Cap), Paolo Maldini; Demetrio Albertini, Marcel Desailly, Dejan Savicević (72 Gianluca Sordo), Roberto Donadoni; Daniele Massaro, Marco Simone (57 Mauro Tassotti). Trainer: Fabio Capello

Goal: Massaro (26)

AFC AJAX AMSTERDAM
v AEK FC ATHINA 2-0 (1-0)

Olympisch, Amsterdam 7.12.1994

Referee: Jorge Monteiro Coroado (POR) Att: 39,138

AJAX: Edwin van der Sar, Michael Reiziger, Danny Blind (Cap), Frank Rijkaard, Frank De Boer; Clarence Seedorf, Jari Litmanen (80 Patrick Kluivert), Tarik Oulida, Finidi George (80 Peter Van Vossen); Ronald de Boer, Marc Overmars. Trainer: Louis van Gaal

AEK: Ilias Atmatzidis, Giorgos Agorogiannis, Giorgos Koutoulas (46 Haralampos Kopitsis), Manolis Papadopoulos, Mihalis Kasapis, Stauros Stamatis (Cap), Mihalis Vlahos, Vasilis Tsartas, Vasilis Borbokis, Dimitris Saravakos, Hristos Kostis (66 Temur Ketsbaia). Trainer: Dušan Bajević

Goals: Oulida (7, 81)

IFK GÖTEBORG
v FC BAYERN MÜNCHEN 2-2 (0-0)

Gamla Ullevi, Göteborg 15.03.1995

Referee: Leslie Mottram (SCO) Attendance: 36,525

IFK: Thomas Ravelli, Pontus Kåmark (Cap), Magnus Johansson, Joachim Björklund, Mikael Nilsson (77 Mats Lilienberg), Mikael Martinsson, Stefan Rehn, Stefan Lindqvist, Jesper Blomqvist, Magnus Erlingmark, Stefan Pettersson (68 Erik Wahlstedt). Trainer: Roger Gustavsson

BAYERN: Sven Scheuer, Markus Babbel, Thomas Helmer (Cap), Oliver Kreuzer, Dieter Frey, Alexander Zickler (81 Samuel Ossei Kuffour), Christian Nerlinger, Mehmet Scholl, Christian Ziege, Marcel Witeczek (62 Markus Schupp), Emil Kostadinov (20 Uwe Gospodarek).
Trainer: Giovanni Trapattoni

Sent off: Scheuer (20)

Goals: Zickler (64), Nerlinger (72), Lilienberg (79), Martinsson (90)

	P	W	D	L	F	A	Pts
AFC Ajax Amsterdam	6	4	2	0	9	2	10
AC Milan	6	3	1	2	6	5	5
Casino Salzburg	6	1	3	2	4	6	5
AEK Athina	6	0	2	4	3	9	2

QUARTER-FINALS

FC BAYERN MÜNCHEN v IFK GÖTEBORG 0-0

Olympiastadion, München 1.03.1995

Referee: Sergei Khusainov (RUS) Attendance: 46,000

BAYERN: Sven Scheuer, Dieter Frey (70 Oliver Kreuzer), Thomas Helmer (Cap), Markus Babbel, Alexander Zickler, Markus Schupp (62 Michael Sternkopf), Mehmet Scholl, Christian Nerlinger, Christian Ziege, Emil Kostadinov, Marcel Witeczek. Trainer: Giovanni Trapattoni

IFK: Thomas Ravelli, Pontus Kåmark (Cap), Magnus Johansson, Jonas Ohlsson, Mikael Nilsson, Mikael Martinsson, Magnus Erlingmark, Stefan Rehn (62 Mats Lilienberg), Stefan Lindqvist, Peter Eriksson, Stefan Pettersson (87 Thomas Andersson). Trainer: Roger Gustavsson

HAJDUK SPLIT v AFC AJAX AMSTERDAM 0-0

Poljud, Split 1.03.1995

Referee: Ryszard Wójcik (POL) Attendance: 34,250

HAJDUK: Tonci Gabrić, Darko Butorović, Igor Stimac, Zoran Vulić (Cap) (46 Damir Vuica), Sasa Person, Nenad Pralija, Stipe Andrijasević, Karol Prazenica, Aljosa Asanović, Ivica Mornar (70 Sead Seferović), Milan Rapaić.
Trainer: Ivan Katalinić

AJAX: Edwin van der Sar, Michael Reiziger, Danny Blind (Cap), Frank De Boer, Frank Rijkaard, Clarence Seedorf, Jari Litmanen, Edgar Davids, Finidi George, Patrick Kluivert (77 Winston Bogarde), Marc Overmars (58 Peter Van Vossen).
Trainer: Louis van Gaal

AFC AJAX AMSTERDAM
v HAJDUK SPLIT 3-0 (2-0)

Olympisch, Amsterdam 15.03.1995

Referee: Ion Crăciunescu (ROM) Attendance: 40,000

AJAX: Edwin van der Sar, Michael Reiziger, Danny Blind (Cap), Frank Rijkaard, Frank De Boer, Ronald de Boer, Jari Litmanen, Clarence Seedorf (79 Winston Bogarde), Finidi George, Nwankwo Kanu (71 Patrick Kluivert), Marc Overmars. Trainer: Louis van Gaal

HAJDUK: Tonci Gabrić, Sasa Person, Igor Stimac (Cap), Mirsad Hibić, Damir Vuica, Karol Prazenica, Mario Mestrović, Aljosa Asanović, Nenad Pralija, Tomislav Erceg (51 Kazimir Vulić), Renato Jurcec (67 Milan Rapaić).
Trainer: Ivan Katalinić

Goals: Kanu (34), F. de Boer (43, 67)

AC MILAN v SPORT LISBOA E BENFICA 2-0 (2-0)

Giuseppe Meazza, Milano 1.03.1995

Referee: Ahmet Cakar (TUR) Attendance: 48,858

AC MILAN: Sebastiano Rossi, Christian Panucci, Filippo Galli, Franco Baresi (Cap), Paolo Maldini, Marcel Desailly, Demetrio Albertini, Zvonimir Boban, Dejan Savićević, Daniele Massaro (46 Giovanni Stroppa), Marco Simone. Trainer: Fabio Capello

BENFICA: Michel Preud'homme, António Augusto da Silva VELOSO (Cap), WILLIAM Amaral de Andrade, José Carlos Nepomuceno MOZER, DIMAS Manuel Marques Teixeira, Vítor Manuel Araújo "VÍTOR PANEIRA", PAULO Jorge Gomes BENTO, ABEL Luís da Silva Costa XAVIER, José Fernando Gomes TAVARES (23 Daniel KENEDY Pimentel Mateus dos Santos, 81 ISAÍAS Marques Soares), JOÃO Manuel Vieira PINTO, Claudio Caniggia. Trainer: Artur Jorge

Goals: Simone (63, 75)

SPORT LISBOA E BENFICA v AC MILAN 0-0

Estádio da Luz, Lisboa 15.03.1995

Referee: Guy Goethals (BEL) Attendance: 52,500

BENFICA: Michel Preud'homme, António Augusto da Silva VELOSO (Cap), WILLIAM Amaral de Andrade (90 HÉLDER Marino Rodrigues Cristóvao), Paulo Pereira, DIMAS Manuel Marques Teixeira, Vítor Manuel Araújo "VÍTOR PANEIRA", PAULO Jorge Gomes BENTO, Manuel António Guimarães "NELO", JOÃO Manuel Vieira PINTO, Claudio Caniggia, EDILSON da Silva Ferreira (59 ISAÍAS Marques Soares). Trainer: Artur Jorge

AC MILAN: Sebastiano Rossi, Christian Panucci, Filippo Galli, Franco Baresi (Cap) (85 Alessandro Costacurta), Paolo Maldini, Stefano Eranio, Marcel Desailly, Zvonimir Boban, Roberto Donadoni, Dejan Savicević, Marco Simone (89 Giovanni Stroppa). Trainer: Fabio Capello

FC BARCELONA v PARIS SAINT-GERMAIN 1-1 (0-0)

Camp Nou, Barcelona 1.03.1995

Referee: Václav Krondl (CZE) Attendance: 115,000

FC BARCELONA: Carlos Busquets, Albert Ferrer, Ronald Koeman, SERGI Barjuán Esclusa, Josep Guardiola (19 Guillermo Amor), José María García "José Mari", José María Bakero (Cap), Aitor Beguiristáin (76 Xabier ESKURZA García), IVÁN Iglesias Corteguera, Igor Korneev, Hristo Stoichkov. Trainer: Johan Cruyff

PSG: Bernard Lama, José Cobos, Antoine Kombouaré, Alain Roche (Cap), Patrick Colleter, Daniel Bravo, Vincent Guérin, Valdo Cândido Filho, Paul le Guen, George Weah, David Ginola (62 Raí Souza de Oliveira). Trainer: Luis Fernández

Goals: Korneev (47 og), Weah (54)

PARIS SAINT-GERMAIN v FC BARCELONA 2-1 (0-0)

Parc des Princes, Paris 15.03.1995

Referee: Gerd Grabher (AUS) Attendance: 45,604

PSG: Bernard Lama, José Cobos, Antoine Kombouaré (Cap), Paul le Guen, Patrick Colleter, Daniel Bravo, Vincent Guérin, Raí Souza de Oliveira, Valdo Cândido Filho, George Weah, David Ginola. Trainer: Luis Fernández

FC BARCELONA: Carlos Busquets, Albert Ferrer, Ronald Koeman, Eusebio Sacristán, SERGI Barjuán Esclusa, Gheorghe Hagi (70 ABELARDO Fernández Artuña), IVÁN Iglesias Corteguera, Miguel Ángel Nadal, José María Bakero (Cap), Aitor Beguiristáin (57 José María García «José Mari»), Hristo Stoichkov. Trainer: Johan Cruyff

Goals: Bakero (50), Raí (72), Guérin (83)

SEMI-FINALS

FC BAYERN MÜNCHEN v AFC AJAX AMSTERDAM 0-0

Olympiastadion, München 5.04.1995

Referee: Ahmet Cakar (TUR) Attendance: 60,000

BAYERN: Uwe Gospodarek, Samuel Ossei Kuffour, Markus Babbel, Thomas Helmer (Cap) (89 Marco Grimm), Christian Ziege, Dietmar Hamann, Markus Schupp, Mehmet Scholl, Christian Nerlinger, Alexander Zickler, Alain Sutter. Trainer: Giovanni Trapattoni

AJAX: Edwin van der Sar, Michael Reiziger, Danny Blind (Cap), Frank De Boer, Ronald de Boer (77 Winston Bogarde), Frank Rijkaard, Jari Litmanen, Clarence Seedorf, Finidi George, Nwankwo Kanu (65 Patrick Kluivert), Marc Overmars. Trainer: Louis van Gaal

AFC AJAX AMSTERDAM v FC BAYERN MÜNCHEN 5-2 (3-1)

Olympisch, Amsterdam 19.04.1995

Referee: Sándor Puhl (HUN) Attendance: 40,000

AJAX: Edwin van der Sar, Michael Reiziger, Danny Blind (Cap), Frank Rijkaard, Winston Bogarde, Ronald de Boer, Finidi George (88 Edgar Davids), Clarence Seedorf, Nwankwo Kanu (67 Patrick Kluivert), Jari Litmanen, Marc Overmars. Trainer: Louis van Gaal

BAYERN: Sven Scheuer, Markus Babbel, Christian Ziege, Samuel Ossei Kuffour, Thomas Helmer (Cap) (42 Oliver Kreuzer), Christian Nerlinger, Dieter Frey, Markus Schupp, Alexander Zickler (73 Alain Sutter), Mehmet Scholl, Marcel Witeczek. Trainer: Giovanni Trapattoni

Goals: Litmanen (11, 47), Witeczek (36), Finidi (41), R. de Boer (45), Scholl (75 pen), Overmars (89)

PARIS SAINT-GERMAIN v AC MILAN 0-1 (0-0)

Parc des Princes, Paris 5.04.1995

Referee: Serge Muhmenthaler (SWI) Attendance: 44,965

PSG: Bernard Lama, Francis Llacer, Ricardo Gomes, Alain Roche (Cap), Paul le Guen, Daniel Bravo, Raí Souza de Oliveira, Vincent Guérin, José Cobos, George Weah, David Ginola. Trainer: Luis Fernández

AC MILAN: Sebastiano Rossi, Christian Panucci, Alessandro Costacurta, Franco Baresi (Cap), Paolo Maldini, Stefano Eranio, Marcel Desailly, Demetrio Albertini, Zvonimir Boban, Dejan Savićević, Marco Simone (84 Daniele Massaro). Trainer: Fabio Capello

Goal: Boban (90)

AC MILAN v PARIS SAINT-GERMAIN 2-0 (1-0)

Giuseppe Meazza, Milano 19.04.1995

Referee: Leslie Mottram (SCO) Attendance: 79,855

AC MILAN: Sebastiano Rossi, Mauro Tassotti (15 Filippo Galli), Paolo Maldini, Franco Baresi (Cap), Christian Panucci, Stefano Eranio, Marcel Desailly, Demetrio Albertini, Zvonimir Boban, Dejan Savićević, Marco Simone (78 Roberto Donadoni). Trainer: Fabio Capello

PSG: Bernard Lama, José Cobos (76 Jean-Philippe Séchet), Ricardo Gomes, Alain Roche (Cap), Vincent Guérin, Daniel Bravo, Valdo Cândido Filho (69 Pascal Nouma), Paul le Guen, Patrick Colleter, George Weah, David Ginola. Trainer: Luis Fernández

Goals: Savicević (20, 67)

FINAL

AFC AJAX AMSTERDAM v AC MILAN 1-0 (0-0)

Ernst Happel, Wien 24.05.1995

Referee: Ion Crăciunescu (ROM) Attendance: 49,700

AJAX: Edwin van der Sar, Michael Reiziger, Danny Blind (Cap), Frank De Boer, Clarence Seedorf (53 Nwankwo Kanu), Frank Rijkaard, Jari Litmanen (69 Patrick Kluivert), Edgar Davids, Finidi George, Ronald de Boer, Marc Overmars. Trainer: Louis van Gaal

AC MILAN: Sebastiano Rossi; Christian Panucci, Alessandro Costacurta, Franco Baresi (Cap), Paolo Maldini, Roberto Donadoni, Demetrio Albertini, Marcel Desailly, Zvonimir Boban (85 Gianluigi Lentini), Daniele Massaro (89 Stefano Eranio), Marco Simone. Trainer: Fabio Capello

Goal: Kluivert (85)

European Cup Goalscorers 1994-95:

8 goals: George Weah (Paris Saint-Germain)

6 goals: Jari Litmanen (Ajax Amsterdam)

5 goals: Hakan Şükür (Galatasaray Istanbul)

4 goals: Marco Simone (Milan), Magnus Erlingmark (IFK Göteborg)

3 goals: Christian Nerlinger, Mehmet Scholl (Bayern München), José María Bakero, Romarío, Hristo Stoichkov (FC Barcelona), Claudio Caniggia (Benfica Lisboa), Viktor Leonenko (Dynamo Kyiv), Adrian Ilie (Steaua Bucureşti), Mladen Mladenovic (Casino Salzburg), Aljosa Asanovic (Hajduk Split), Stefan Rehn, Jesper Blomqvist (IFK Göteborg), Toni Savevski (AEK Athina), Arif Erdem (Galatasaray)

2 goals: Türkyılmaz, Saffet (Galatasaray), Hughes, Giggs, Sharpe (Manchester United), Tikhonov (Spartak Moskva), Pârvu, Lăcătuş (Steaua Bucureşti), Saravakos (AEK Athina), Pfeifenberger (Casino Salzburg), João Pinto (Benfica), Rapaic, Andrijasevic (Hajduk Split), Ronald de Boer, Frank de Boer, Oulida, Kluivert (Ajax), Panucci, Savićević (Milan AC), Raí, Guérin, M'boma (Paris St.Germain), Papin (Bayern München)

1 goal: Schepull, Neuville (Servette Genève), Budka (Sparta Praha), Zaritski (Avenir Beggen), Füle (Vác FC Samsung), Revivo, Hazan (Maccabi Haifa), Fernández (Silkeborg), Davies, Beckham, Keane, Kanchelskis (Manchester United), Shevchenko, Rebrov, Skachenko, Kovalets, Kosovski (Dynamo Kyiv), Rodionov, Muhamadiev, Alenichev, Pisarev, Rakhimov (Spartak Moskva), Stan, Gâlcă, Doboş, Panduru, Militaru (Steaua), Rutjes, Bosman, Weber (Anderlecht), Vlahos (AEK Athina), Hasenhüttl, Kocijan, Jurcevic, A.Hütter (Casino Salzburg), Lilienberg, Martinsson, Kåmark, Pettersson (IFK Göteborg), Edilson, Isaías, Hélder, Tavares (Benfica), Ferrer, R.Koeman, Amor, Korneev (Barcelona), Erceg, Pralija, Butorovic (Hajduk Split), Finidi, Overmars, Kanu (Ajax), Massaro, Stroppa, Boban (Milan), Gomes, Roche, Ginola, Le Guen, Valdo, Bravo (PSG), Witeczek, Zickler, Kuffour, Babbel (Bayern)

Own goals: Bülent (Galatasaray) for Manchester United, Kosovski (Dynamo Kyiv) for Spartak Moskva, Paulo Madeira (Benfica) for Anderlecht, F.Baresi (Milan) for Ajax

THE EUROPEAN CUP 1995-96

PRELIMINARY ROUND

GRASSHOPPER-CLUB ZÜRICH v MACCABI TEL AVIV 1-1 (0-0)

Hardturm, Zürich 9.08.1995

Referee: Juan Ansuategui Roca (SPA) Attendance: 11,100

GRASSHOPPER: Patrick Zuberbühler; Harald Gämperle, Ramón Vega, Mats Gren (Cap), Johann Vogel, Massimo Lombardo, Murat Yakin, Alain Geiger, Alexandre Comisetti (72 Gürkan Sermeter), Ali Ibrahim (61 Joël Magnin), Eric Viscaal. Trainer: Christian Gross

MACCABI: Aleksandr Uvarov; Gadi Brumer, Alon Brumer, Amir Shelach, Yaacov Hilel, Nir Klinger (Cap), Noam Shoam, Victor Moroz (87 Ron Nachman), Itzhak Zohar, Avi Nimni, Evgeni Kashentsev (73 Eli Driks). Trainer: Dror Kashtan

Goals: Yakin (50), Kashentsev (55)

MACCABI TEL AVIV v GRASSHOPPER-CLUB ZÜRICH 0-1 (0-1)

Bloomfield, Tel Aviv 23.08.1995

Referee: Marcello Nicchi (ITA) Attendance: 15,432

MACCABI: Aleksandr Uvarov; Gadi Blumer, Yaacov Hilel (16 Eli Driks), Nir Klinger (Cap), Amit Levi, Amir Shelach, Noam Shoam (67 Meir Melika), Itzhak Zohar (56 Victor Moroz), Alon Blumer, Avi Nimni, Evgeni Kashentsev. Trainer: Dror Kashtan

GRASSHOPPER: Patrick Zuberbühler; Patrick Thüler, Ramón Vega, Mats Gren (Cap), Massimo Lombardo, Harald Gämperle, Alain Geiger, Murat Yakin, Alexandre Comisetti (63 Johann Vogel), Eric Viscaal (46 Ali Ibrahim), Joël Magnin (72 Patrick de Napoli). Trainer: Christian Gross

Goal: Comisetti (4)

GLASGOW RANGERS FC v ANORTHOSIS FAMAGUSTA 1-0 (0-0)

Ibrox stadium, Glasgow 9.08.1995

Referee: Eric Blareau (BEL) Attendance: 43,519

RANGERS: Andy Goram; Stephen Wright, Richard Gough (Cap), Alan McLaren, David Robertson, Brian Reid (46 Gordon Durie), Stuart McCall, Paul Gascoigne, Ian Ferguson (67 Charles Miller), Mark Hateley, Brian Laudrup. Trainer: Walter Smith

ANORTHOSIS: Nikos Panagiotou; Panikos Pounas (82 Vasos Melanarkitis), Sozos Andreou, Spyros Kastanas, Giorgos Panagi, Ilian Kiriakov, Dimitris Assiotis, Kostas Stavrou (Cap), Nikolai Todorov, Sinisa Gogic, Valentin Ignatov (76 Kostas Hristoforou). Trainer: Georgi Vasiliev

Goal: Durie (68)

ANORTHOSIS FAMAGUSTA v GLASGOW RANGERS FC 0-0

Antonis Papadopoulos, Famagusta 23.08.1995

Referee: László Vagner (HUN) Attendance: 9,400

ANORTHOSIS: Nikos Panagiotou; Antros Panagiotou, Sozos Andreou, Spyros Kastanas, Giorgos Panagi, Ilian Kiriakov, Dimitris Assiotis (60 Panikos Pounas), Kostas Stavrou (Cap), Nikolai Todorov, Sinisa Gogic, Valentin Ignatov (75 Marios Thoma). Trainer: Georgi Vasiliev

RANGERS: Andy Goram; Stephen Wright, Alan McLaren, Richard Gough (Cap), David Robertson, Stuart McCall, Gordan Petric, Paul Gascoigne (25 Ian Durrant, 90 Neil Murray), Charles Miller, Mark Hateley, Gordon Durie. Trainer: Walter Smith

LEGIA WARSZAWA v IFK GÖTEBORG 1-0 (0-0)

Wojska Polskiego, Warszawa 9.08.1995

Referee: Jacobus Uilenburg (HOL) Attendance: 15,000

LEGIA: Maciej Szczesny; Zbigniew Mandziejewicz (80 Piotr Mosor), Marek Jozwiak, Jacek Bednarz, Jacek Zielinski, Grzegorz Lewandowski, Leszek Pisz, Radoslaw Michalski, Tomasz Wieszczycki, Jerzy Podbrozny (87 Ryszard Staniek), Cezary Kucharski (77 Andrzej Kubica). Trainer: Pawel Janas

IFK: Thomas Ravelli (43 Dick Last); Pontus Kåmark (Cap), Jonas Ohlsson, Magnus Johansson, Mikael Nilsson, Mikael Martinsson, Magnus Erlingmark, Stefan Landberg, Jesper Blomqvist (57 Peter Eriksson), Mats Lilienberg (81 Erik Wahlstedt), Stefan Pettersson. Trainer: Roger Gustafsson

Goal: Podbrozny (49 pen)

IFK GÖTEBORG v LEGIA WARSZAWA 1-2 (1-0)

Ullevi, Göteborg 23.08.1995

Referee: David Roland Elleray (ENG) Attendance: 11,017

IFK: Dick Last; Pontus Kåmark (Cap), Jonas Ohlsson, Magnus Johansson, Mikael Nilsson, Stefan Landberg (69 Peter Eriksson), Magnus Erlingmark, Stefan Lindqvist, Jesper Blomqvist, Stefan Pettersson, Erik Lilienberg (50 Erik Wahlstedt). Trainer: Roger Gustafsson

LEGIA: Maciej Szczesny; Marek Jozwiak, Jacek Zielinski (Cap), Zbigniew Mandziejewicz, Krzysztof Ratajczyk (38 Leszek Pisz), Grzegorz Lewandowski (87 Adam Fedoruk), Jacek Bednarz, Radoslaw Michalski, Tomasz Wieszczycki, Jerzy Podbrozny, Cezary Kucharski (56 Ryszard Staniek). Trainer: Pawel Janas

Sent off: Ohlsson (29), Erlingmark (76)

Goals: Blomqvist (25), Pisz (73), Bednarz (90)

CASINO SALZBURG v STEAUA BUCUREŞTI 0-0

Lehen, Salzburg 9.08.1995

Referee: Anders Frisk (SWE) Attendance: 11,500

CASINO: Otto Konrad; Mladen Mladenovic, Christian Fürstaller, Leo Lainer; Thomas Winklhofer, Christian Prosenik, Wolfgang Feiersinger, Tibor Jancula (67 Hermann Stadler), Adolf Hütter, Ralph Hasenhüttl, Heimo Pfeifenberger (Cap). Trainer: Otto Barić

STEAUA: Bogdan Stelea; Tiberiu Csik, Anton Doboş, Daniel Claudiu Prodan, Aurel Silviu Panait; Damian Militaru, Bogdan Vişan Bucur, Constantin Gâlcă, Bucurel Adrian Ilie (70 Iulian Sebastian Filipescu), Marius Mihai Lăcătuş (Cap), Ion Vlădoiu (83 Laurenţiu Dumitru Roşu). Trainer: Dumitru Dumitriu

STEAUA BUCUREŞTI v CASINO SALZBURG 1-0 (1-0)

Steaua, Bucureşti 23.08.1995

Referee: Jorge Monteiro Coroado (POR) Att: 18,700

STEAUA: Bogdan Stelea; Aurel Silviu Panait, Anton Doboş, Daniel Claudiu Prodan, Ionel Antonel Pîrvu; Constantin Gâlcă, Damian Militaru (90 Tiberiu Csik), Bogdan Vişan Bucur, Bucurel Adrian Ilie (62 Iulian Sebastian Filipescu), Marius Mihai Lăcătuş (Cap) (60 Laurenţiu Dumitru Roşu), Ion Vlădoiu. Trainer: Dumitru Dumitriu

CASINO: Otto Konrad; Leo Lainer (70 Hermann Stadler), Thomas Winklhofer, Mladen Mladenovic, Christian Fürstaller, Franz Aigner, Ralph Hasenhüttl (57 Dejan Racunica), Christian Prosenik (57 Martin Hiden), Heimo Pfeifenberger (Cap), Wolfgang Feiersinger, Adolf Hütter.
Trainer: Otto Barić

Goal: A. Ilie (34)

FC DYNAMO KYIV v AALBORG BK 1-0 (0-0)

Republikanskiy, Kyiv 9.08.1995

Referee: Jiří Ulrich (CZE) Attendance: 61,000

DINAMO: Olexandr Shovkovskyi; Andriy Khomin, Serhiy Bezhenar, Alexander Holovko, Yuri Maksimov, Yuri Dmitrulin, Yevhen Pokhlebayev, Yuri Kalitvintsev (Cap) (85 Pavlo Shkapenko), Vitaliy Kosovskyi, Serhiy Skachenko (46 Serhiy Rebrov), Andriy Shevchenko. Trainer: Josef Szabo

AALBORG: Thomas Gill; Ib Simonsen (Cap), Torben Boye, Björn Kristensen, Lars Thomsen, Jens Jessen, Henrik Rasmussen, Jan Pedersen, Jens Madsen (84 Thomas Thomasberg), Peter Rasmussen, Erik Bo Andersen (85 Jesper Grönkjaer). Trainer: Sepp Piontek

Goal: Pokhlebaiev (82 pen)

AALBORG BK v FC DYNAMO KYIV 1-3 (0-1)

Aalborg Stadion 23.08.1995

Referee: Atanas Uzunov (BUL) Attendance: 8,700

AALBORG: Thomas Gill; Torben Boye, Ib Simonsen (Cap), Björn Kristensen (46 Calle Facius), Jens Jessen, Lars Thomsen, Henrik Rasmussen, Jan Pedersen (46 Jesper Grönkjaer), Jens Madsen (74 Kristian Thomsen), Peter Rasmussen, Erik Bo Andersen. Trainer: Sepp Piontek

DINAMO: Olexandr Shovkovskyi; Oleg Luzhnyi (81 Andriy Khomin), Alexander Holovko, Yuri Dmitrulin, Serhiy Bezhenar, Yevhen Pokhlebayev, Yuri Maksimov (77 Dmytro Mikhailenko), Yuri Kalitvintsev (Cap), Vitaliy Kosovskyi, Andriy Shevchenko, Serhiy Skachenko (73 Serhiy Rebrov).
Trainer: Josef Szabo

Goals: Kalitvintsev (36), Shevchenko (49, 76), P. Rasmussen (86)

ROSENBORG BK TRONDHEIM v BEŞIKTAŞ JK ISTANBUL 3-0 (2-0)

Lerkendal, Trondheim 9.08.1995

Referee: Hermann Albrecht (GER) Attendance: 14,352

ROSENBORG: Jørn Jamtfall; Björn Tore Kvarme, Björn Otto Bragstad (82 Tom Kåre Staurvik), Erik Hoftun, Ståle Stensaas, Roar Strand, Bent Skammelsrud (Cap), Trond Egil Soltvedt, Karl-Petter Løken, Harald Brattbakk, Jahn Ivat "Mini" Jakobsen. Trainer: Nils Arne Eggen

BEŞIKTAŞ: Raimond Aumann; Ali Günçar, Mutlu Topçu, Ronny Johnsen, Alpay Özalan, Ertugrul Saglam, Sergen Yalçin (78 Oktay Derelioglu), Riza Çalimbay (Cap), Stefan Kuntz, Serdar Topraktepe (57 Mehmet Özdilek), Orhan Kaynak.
Trainer: Christoph Daum

Goals: Hoftun (22), Strand (27), Brattbak (75)

BEŞIKTAŞ JK ISTANBUL v ROSENBORG BK TRONDHEIM 3-1 (1-0)

Inönü, Istanbul 23.08.1995

Referee: Marc Batta (FRA) Attendance: 23,882

BEŞIKTAŞ: Raimond Aumann; Alpay Özalan, Ronny Johnsen, Mutlu Topçu, Recep Çetin, Sergen Yalçin, Riza Çalimbay (Cap), Mehmet Özdilek, Sertan Eser (60 Oktay Derelioglu), Orhan Kaynak, Stefan Kuntz.
Trainer: Christoph Daum

ROSENBORG: Jørn Jamtfall; Björn Tore Kvarme, Björn Otto Bragstad, Ståle Stensaas, Erik Hoftun, Karl-Petter Løken, Roar Strand (89 Tom Kåre Staurvik), Bent Skammelsrud (Cap), Trond Egil Soltvedt (51 Steffen Iversen), Jahn Ivat "Mini" Jakobsen, Harald Brattbakk. Trainer: Nils Arne Eggen

Goals: Kuntz (9, 85 pen), Brattbakk (67), Mehmet (88)

RSC ANDERLECHT BRUSSEL
v FERENCVÁROS BUDAPEST 0-1 (0-0)

Constant Vanden Stock, Brussel 9.08.1995

Referee: Hellmut Krug (GER) Attendance: 15,036

ANDERLECHT: Geert De Vlieger; Bertrand Crasson (52 Filip Haagdoren), Olivier Doll, Georges Grün (Cap), Célestine Babayaro, Yaw Preko, Pär Zetterberg (64 Bruno Versavel), Emmanuel Karagiannis, Johan Walem, Danny Boffin, Gilles De Bilde. Trainer: Herbert Neumann

FERENCVÁROS: Attila Hajdú; Tibor Simon, Zoltán Kecskés, András Telek, Zoran Kuntić (78 Zsolt Nagy), Sergiy Kuznetsov, Flórián Albert (82 Ottó Vincze), Zsolt Páling, Elek Nyilas, Krisztián Lisztes, Goran Kopunović (88 Gábor Zavadszky). Trainer: Dezső Novák

Goals: Kuntić (58)

FERENCVÁROS BUDAPEST
v RSC ANDERLECHT BRUSSEL 1-1 (0-0)

Űllői út, Budapest 23.08.1995

Referee: William Leslie Mottram (SCO) Att: 16,500

FERENCVÁROS: Attila Hajdú; András Telek (Cap), Tibor Simon, Sergiy Kuznetsov, Zsolt Páling, Elek Nyilas, Krisztián Lisztes, Ottó Vincze (73 Gábor Zavadszky), Zoltán Kecskés, Zoran Kuntić, Goran Kopunović (59 Zsolt Nagy). Trainer: Dezső Novák

ANDERLECHT: Filip De Wilde; Olivier Doll, Georges Grün (Cap), Bertrand Crasson (58 Filip Haagdoren), Célestine Babayaro, Bruno Versavel (58 Pär Zetterberg), Johan Walem, Emmanuel Karagiannis (86 John Bosman), Danny Boffin, Yaw Preko, Gilles De Bilde. Trainer: Jean Docks

Goals: Kopunović (50), De Bilde (65)

PANATHINAIKOS ATHINA v HAJDUK SPLIT 0-0

Olympiako, Athina 9.08.1995

Referee: Urs Meier (SWI) Attendance: 42,000

PANATHINAIKOS: Antonis Nikopolidis; Stratos Apostolakis, Marinos Ouzounidis, Giorgos H.Georgiadis, Giannis Kalitzakis (Cap), Giorgos S.Georgiadis, Juan Borelli (75 Leonidas Hristodoulou), Dimitris Markos, Spiros Maragkos, Krzysztof Warzycha, Giorgos Donis (78 Alexandros Alexoudis). Trainer: Juan Ramon Rocha

HAJDUK: Tonci Gabric; Darko Butorović, Darko Jozinović, Mirsad Hibić, Steven Horvat, Igor Stimac (Cap), Kazimir Vulić, Nenad Pralija, Milan Rapaić (82 Mario Mestrović), Aljosa Asanović, Ivica Mornar (74 Mass Sarr). Trainer: Ivan Katalinić

HAJDUK SPLIT
v PANATHINAIKOS ATHINA 1-1 (1-0)

Kantrida, Rijeka 23.08.1995

Referee: Ion Crăciunescu (ROM) Attendance: 10,800

HAJDUK: Tonci Gabrić; Darko Butorović, Darko Jozinović, Igor Stimac, Mirsad Hibić (Cap), Steven Horvat, Kazimir Vulić (14 Mario Mestrović), Nenad Pralija, Aljosa Asanović, Renato Jurcec (68 Mass Sarr), Ivica Mornar. Trainer: Ivan Katalinić

PANATHINAIKOS: Antonis Nikopolidis; Stratos Apostolakis (/Cap), Marinos Ouzounidis, Giorgos H.Georgiadis, Giannis Kalitzakis (Cap), Giorgos S.Georgiadis, Juan Borelli (68 Leonidas Hristodoulou), Dimitris Markos, Spiros Maragkos (52 Alexandros Alexoudis), Giorgos Donis, Krzysztof Warzycha (86 Andreas Lagonikakis). Trainer: Juan Ramon Rocha

Sent off: Stimac (57), Kalitzakis (64)

Goals: Stimac (4), Borelli (53)

CHAMPIONS LEAGUE

GROUP A

FC DYNAMO KYIV
v PANATHINAIKOS ATHINA 1-0 (1-0)

Republicanski, Kyiv 13.09.1995

Referee: Antonio Jesús López Nieto (SPA) Att: 85,000

DINAMO: Alexander Shovkovskyi; Oleg Luzhnyi (71 Serhiy Shmatovalenko), Alexander Holovko, Serhiy Bezhenar, Yuri Dmitrulin, Yuri Kalitvintsev, Vitaliy Kosovskyi, Yuri Maksimov (84 Serhiy Mizin), Yevhen Pokhlebayev, Andriy Shevchenko, Serhiy Rebrov (74 Serhiy Skachenko). Trainer: Josef Szabo

PANATHINAIKOS: Antonis Nikopolidis; Stratos Apostolakis (Cap), Giorgos Kapouranis, Marinos Ouzounidis, Giorgos H.Georgiadis, Dimitris Markos, Juan Borelli (68 Leonidas Hristodoulou), Spiros Maragkos (79 Andreas Lagonikakis), Giorgos Donis, Alexandros Alexoudis, Krzysztof Warzycha. Trainer: Juan Ramon Rocha

Goal: Kosovski (61)

Dynamo Kyiv were ejected from the competition after attempting to bribe the referee López Nieto. Their results were duly cancelled and they were replaced by Aalborg BK.

FC NANTES v FC PORTO 0-0

Le Beaujoire, Nantes 13.09.1995

Referee: Hans-Jürgen Weber (GER) Attendance: 16,873

FC NANTES: David Marraud; Serge Le Dizet, Laurent Guyot, Eric Decroix, Christophe Pignol, Claude Makélélé, Bruno Carotti, Benoît Cauet, Japhet N'Doram (Cap), Roman Kosecki, Franck Renou (63 David Garcion).
Trainer: Jean-Claude Suaudeau

FC PORTO: VÍTOR Manuel Martins BAÍA; JOÃO Domingos Silva PINTO (Cap), ALOÍSIO Pires Alves, JOSÉ CARLOS Nascimento, João Paulo Maio dos Santos «PAULINHO SANTOS», Carlos Alberto Oliveira SECRETÁRIO, EMERSON Moisés Costa (90 Manuel Albino Morim Maçães "BINO"), RUI Gil Soares de BARROS, Russel Latapy, DOMINGOS José Paciencia Oliveira (78 António José Santos FOLHA), Grzegorz Mielcarski. Trainer: Augusto Inacio

PANATHINAIKOS ATHINA v FC NANTES 3-1 (2-0)

Olympiako, Athina 27.09.1995

Referee: Vadim Zhuk (BLS) Attendance: 58,565

PANATHINAIKOS: Jozef Wandzik; Giorgos S.Georgiadis, Marinos Ouzounidis, Giannis Kalitzakis (Cap), Giorgos H.Georgiadis, Dimitris Markos, Spiros Maragkos (86 Thanasis Kolitsidakis), Juan Borelli (80 Nikos Nioplias), Giorgos Donis, Alexandros Alexoudis (68 Giorgos Kapouranis), Krzysztof Warzycha. Trainer: Juan Ramon Rocha

FC NANTES: David Marraud; Serge Le Dizet, Eric Decroix (69 Jean-Marc Chanelet), Laurent Guyot, Christophe Pignol, Claude Makélélé (78 Franck Renou), Bruno Carotti, Benoît Cauet, Japhet N'Doram (Cap), Nicolas Ouédec (69 Laurent Peyrelade), Roman Kosecki. Trainer: Jean-Claude Suaudeau

Goals: Giorgos H. Georgiadis (17), Warzycha (30, 46), N'Doram (88)

FC PORTO v AALBORG BK 2-0 (1-0)

Estádio das Antas, Porto 27.09.1995

Referee: William Leslie Mottram (SCO) Att: 25,000

FC PORTO: VÍTOR Manuel Martins BAÍA, JOÃO Domingos Silva PINTO (Cap) (72 Manuel Albino Morim Maçães "BINO"), João Paulo Maio Santos "PAULINHO SANTOS", JORGE Paulo COSTA Almeida, JOSÉ CARLOS Nascimento, EMERSON Moisés Costa, Carlos Alberto Oliveira SECRETÁRIO, Grzegorz Mielcarski (36 RUI Gil Soares de BARROS), DOMINGOS José Paciencia Oliveira, Russel Latapy, Ljubinko Drulovic (79 António José Santos FOLHA).
Trainer: Augusto Inacio

AALBORG: Thomas Gill; Lars Thomsen (17 Thomas Thomasberg), Torben Boye, Bjørn Kristensen, Jens Jessen, Calle Facius, Ib Simonsen (Cap), Jan Pedersen (63 Jens Madsen), Erik Bo Andersen, Henrik Rasmussen, Peter Rasmussen (79 Jesper Grønkjaer). Trainer: Sepp Piontek

Goals: Rui Barros (41, 62)

FC NANTES v AALBORG BK 3-1 (1-0)

Le Beaujoire, Nantes 18.10.1995

Referee: László Vagner (HUN) Attendance: 29,603

FC NANTES: Dominique Casagrande; Jean-Marc Chanelet, Eric Decroix, Laurent Guyot, Christophe Pignol, Claude Makélélé, Japhet N'Doram (Cap), Reynald Pedros, Benoît Cauet, Nicolas Ouédec (79 Bruno Carotti), Roman Kosecki (89 Frédéric Da Rocha). Trainer: Jean-Claude Suaudeau

AALBORG: Thomas Gill; Torben Boye, Ib Simonsen (Cap), Søren Thorst, Peter Rasmussen, Jens Jessen (88 Jacob Krüger), Calle Facius (81 Thomas Thomasberg), Henrik Rasmussen, Jens Madsen (70 Jesper Grönkjaer), Jan Pedersen, Erik Bo Andersen. Trainer: Sepp Piontek

Goals: Ouédec (5), Andersen (46), Pedros (55), Kosecki (75)

FC PORTO v PANATHINAIKOS ATHINA 0-1 (0-0)

Estádio das Antas, Porto 18.10.1995

Referee: Alfredo Trentalange (ITA) Attendance: 27,500

FC PORTO: VÍTOR Manuel Martins BAÍA; JOÃO Domingos Silva PINTO (Cap) (56 António José Santos FOLHA), JOSÉ CARLOS Nascimento, ALOÍSIO Pires Alves, João Paulo Maio Santos "PAULINHO SANTOS", EMERSON Moisés Costa, Carlos Alberto Oliveira SECRETÁRIO (85 Manuel Albino Morim Maçães "BINO"), Russel Latapy, Ljubinko Drulovic, RUI Gil Soares de BARROS (76 JORGE António Pinto COUTO), DOMINGOS José Paciencia Oliveira.
Trainer: Augusto Inacio

PANATHINAIKOS: Jozef Wandzik; Stratos Apostolakis, Giannis Kalitzakis (Cap), Marinos Ouzounidis, Giorgos H.Georgiadis (90 Andreas Lagonikakis), Dimitris Markos, Giorgos S.Georgiadis, Juan Borelli (66 Giorgos Kapouranis), Giorgos Donis (81 Thanasis Kolitsidakis), Alexandros Alexoudis, Krzysztof Warzycha. Trainer: Juan Ramon Rocha

Sent off: Alexoudis (35)

Goal: Markos (41)

AALBORG BK v PANATHINAIKOS ATHINA 2-1 (1-1)

Aalborg Stadion 25.10.1995

Referee: Hellmut Krug (GER) Attendance: 6,100

AALBORG: Thomas Gill; Torben Boye, Thomas Thomasberg, Jens Jessen, Søren Thorst, Calle Facius, Ib Simonsen (Cap), Jan Pedersen (46 Jens Madsen), Henrik Rasmussen, Erik Bo Andersen, Peter Rasmussen (85 Jesper Grønkjaer).
Trainer: Sepp Piontek

PANATHINAIKOS: Jozef Wandzik; Stratos Apostolakis (/Cap), Marinos Ouzounidis, Giorgos H. Georgiadis, Giannis Kalitzakis (Cap), Dimitris Markos, Juan Borelli (78 Spiros Maragkos), Giorgos Kapouranis, Giorgos S. Georgiadis, Krzysztof Warzycha, Giorgos Donis.
Trainer: Juan Ramon Rocha

Sent off: Kalitzakis (55)

Goals: Andersen (7), Warzycha (41), Madsen (90)

PANATHINAIKOS ATHINA v FC PORTO 0-0

Olympiako, Athina 1.11.1995, H 21,30

Referee: Guy Goethals (BEL) Attendance: 59,336

PANATHINAIKOS: Jozef Wandzik: Giorgos H. Georgiadis, Marinos Ouzounidis, Thanasis Kolitsidakis, Stratos Apostolakis (Cap), Giorgos S. Georgiadis, Dimitris Markos, Juan Borelli (68 Giorgos Kapouranis), Spiros Maragkos, Giorgos Donis, Krzysztof Warzycha (89 Andreas Lagonikakis). Trainer: Juan Ramon Rocha

FC PORTO: VÍTOR Manuel Martins BAÍA; Carlos Alberto Oliveira SECRETÁRIO, RUI JORGE de Sousa Dias Macedo de Oliveira, ALOÍSIO Pires Alves, JORGE Paulo COSTA Almeida, EMERSON Moisés Costa, Pimenta Edmilson, João Paulo Maio Santos "PAULINHO SANTOS", RUI Gil Soares de BARROS (78 Manuel Albino Morim Maçães "BINO"), DOMINGOS José Paciencia Oliveira (Cap), Ljubinko Drulovic (86 António José Santos FOLHA). Trainer: Augusto Inacio

AALBORG BK v FC NANTES 0-2 (0-1)

Aalborg Stadion 1.11.1995

Referee: David Roland Elleray (ENG) Attendance: 6,800

AALBORG: Thomas Gill; Torben Boye, Ib Simonsen (Cap), Sören Thorst, Jens Jessen, Thomas Thomasberg, Jens Madsen (83 Torben Hjermitslev), Calle Facius (71 Kristian Thomsen), Henrik Rasmussen, Peter Rasmussen, Erik Bo Andersen (46 Jesper Grønkjaer). Trainer: Sepp Piontek

FC NANTES: Dominique Casagrande; Bruno Carotti, Eric Decroix, Laurent Guyot, Benoît Cauet (77 Christophe Pignol), Claude Makélélé (58 Jean-Marc Chanelet), Jean-Michel Ferri, Reynald Pedros, Japhet N'Doram (Cap), Nicolas Ouédec (88 Laurent Peyrelade), Roman Kosecki.
Trainer: Jean-Claude Suaudeau

Sent off: Boye (66)

Goals: Guyot (10), Ouédec (68)

PANATHINAIKOS ATHINA v AALBORG BK 2-0 (1-0)

Olympiako, Athina 22.11.1995

Referee: Václav Krondl (CZE) Attendance: 32,532

PANATHINAIKOS: Jozef Wandzik; Stratos Apostolakis (Cap), Marinos Ouzounidis, Giorgos H.Georgiadis, Dimitris Markos, Giorgos S.Georgiadis, Juan Borelli, Spiros Maragkos, Giorgos Donis (88 Andreas Lagonikakis), Alexandros Alexoudis (52 Giorgos Kapouranis), Krzysztof Warzycha.
Trainer: Juan Ramon Rocha

AALBORG: Thomas Gill; Bjørn Kristensen (82 Torben Hjermitslev), Ib Simonsen (Cap), Jacob Krüger, Jens Jessen, Jens Madsen (60 Jesper Grønkjaer), Henrik Rasmussen, Calle Facius, Peter Rasmussen, Erik Bo Andersen, Jan Pedersen.
Trainer: Sepp Piontek

Goals: Alexoudis (1), Giorgos S. Georgiadis (39)

FC PORTO v FC NANTES 2-2 (1-2)

Estádio das Antas, Porto 22.11.1995

Referee: Jacobus Uilenberg (HOL) Attendance: 14,867

FC PORTO: VÍTOR Manuel Martins BAÍA; Carlos Alberto Oliveira SECRETÁRIO, JOSÉ CARLOS Nascimento, JORGE Paulo COSTA Almeida, João Paulo Maio Santos "PAULINHO SANTOS", EMERSON Moisés Costa, RUI Gil Soares de BARROS (60 JORGE António Pinto COUTO), Péter Lipcsei, Pimenta Edmilson (82 António José Santos FOLHA), DOMINGOS José Paciencia Oliveira (Cap), Ljubinko Drulovic (82 Manuel Albino Morim Maçães "BINO").
Trainer: Augusto Inacio

FC NANTES: Dominique Casagrande; Jean-Marc Chanelet, Laurent Guyot, Eric Decroix, Serge Le Dizet, Jean-Michel Ferri (Cap), Claude Makélélé, Bruno Carotti, Benoît Cauet, Reynald Pedros (70 Nicolas Ouédec), Roman Kosecki (76 Franck Renou, 90 Nicolas Savinaud).
Trainer: Jean-Claude Suaudeau

Goals: Pedros (3, 34), Drulovic (10), Jose Carlos (56)

FC NANTES v PANATHINAIKOS ATHINA 0-0

Le Beaujoire, Nantes 6.12.1995

Referee: Leif Sundell (SWE) Attendance: 30,000

FC NANTES: Dominique Casagrande; Jean-Marc Chanelet, Laurent Guyot, Eric Decroix, Serge Le Dizet, Claude Makélélé, Jean-Michel Ferri (Cap), Reynald Pedros, Japhet N'Doram, Roman Kosecki (85 Franck Renou), Nicolas Ouédec.
Trainer: Jean-Claude Suaudeau

PANATHINAIKOS: Jozef Wandzik; Stratos Apostolakis, Giannis Kalitzakis (Cap), Marinos Ouzounidis, Leonidas Hristodoulou, Juan Borelli (90 Giannis Goumas), Dimitris Markos, Giorgos S.Georgiadis, Spiros Maragkos, Giorgos Kapouranis, Andreas Lagonikakis.
Trainer: Juan Ramon Rocha

AALBORG BK v FC PORTO 2-2 (1-0)

Aalborg Stadion 6.12.1995

Referee: Ion Crăciunescu (ROM) Attendance: 3,950

AALBORG: Lars Winde; Jens Jessen, Bjørn Kristensen, Jacob Krüger, Kristian Thomsen, Calle Facius (Cap), Jens Madsen (82 Jari Pedersen), Thomas Thomasberg, Peter Rasmussen (65 Torben Hjermitslev), Erik Bo Andersen, Jesper Grönkjaer (79 Johhny Helledie Nielsen). Trainer: Sepp Piontek

FC PORTO: VÍTOR Manuel Martins BAÍA; JOÃO Domingos Silva PINTO (Cap) (52 RUI Gil Soares de BARROS), RUI JORGE de Sousa Dias Macedo de Oliveira (68 António José Santos FOLHA), ALOÍSIO Pires Alves, JOSÉ CARLOS Nascimento (74 JOÃO MANUEL PINTO Tomé dos Santos); EMERSON Moisés Costa, Carlos Alberto Oliveira SECRETÁRIO, Pimenta Edmilson, João Paulo Maio Santos "PAULINHO SANTOS", Ljubinko Drulovic; DOMINGOS José Paciencia Oliveira. Trainer: Augusto Inacio

Goals: Andersen (11), Emerson (62, 75), Madsen (69)

	P	W	D	L	F	A	Pts
Panathinaikos Athina	6	3	2	1	7	3	11
FC Nantes	6	2	3	1	8	6	9
FC Porto	6	1	4	1	6	5	7
Aalborg BK	6	1	1	4	5	12	4

GROUP B

LEGIA WARSZAWA v ROSENBORG BK TRONDHEIM 3-1 (0-0)

Wojska Polskiego, Warszawa 13.09.1995

Referee: Adrian Porumboiu (ROM) Attendance: 8,184

LEGIA: Maciej Szczesny; Krzysztof Ratajczyk, Zbigniew Mandziejewicz, Jacek Zielinski, Marek Jozwiak, Grzegorz Lewandowski, Tomasz Wieszczycki (80 Radoslaw Michalski), Leszek Pisz (Cap), Jacek Bednarz (83 Adam Fedoruk), Andrzej Kubica (46 Cezary Kucharski), Ryszard Staniek. Trainer: Pawel Janas

ROSENBORG: Jørn Jamtfall; Karl-Petter Løken, Erik Hoftun, Björn Otto Bragstad, Bjørn Tore Kvarme, Ståle Stensaas, Bent Skammelsrud (Cap), Roar Strand, Jahn Ivat "Mini" Jakobsen, Trond Egil Soltvedt (78 Vegard Heggem), Steffen Iversen (89 Tom Kåre Staurvik). Trainer: Nils Arne Eggen

Goals: Jakobsen (64 pen), Pisz (65, 74), Staniek (69)

BLACKBURN ROVERS v SPARTAK MOSKVA 0-1 (0-1)

Edwood Park, Blackburn 13.09.1995

Referee: Michel Piraux (BEL) Attendance: 20,940

BLACKBURN: Tim Flowers; Henning Berg, Ian Pearce, Colin Hendry, Graeme Le Saux, Stuart Ripley (46 Lee Makel), David Batty, Tim Sherwood (Cap), Mark Atkins (73 Chris Sutton), Mike Newell, Alan Shearer. Trainer: Ray Harford

SPARTAK: Stanislav Cherchesov; Ramiz Mamedov, Dmitri Khlestov, Yuri Nikiforov, Andrei Piatnitski, Andrei Tikhonov, Viktor Onopko (Cap), Vasili Kulkov, Ilya Tsymbalar, Sergei Yuran, Valeri Schmarov (88 Valeri Kechinov). Trainer: Oleg Romantsev

Goal: Yuran (42)

SPARTAK MOSKVA v LEGIA WARSZAWA 2-1 (1-0)

Luzhniki, Moskva 27.09.1995

Referee: László Vagner (HUN) Attendance: 18,000

SPARTAK: Stanislav Cherchesov; Ramiz Mamedov, Yuri Nikiforov, Dmitri Khlestov, Andrei Piatnitski, Viktor Onopko (Cap), Vasili Kulkov, Ilya Tsymbalar, Valeri Schmarov, Sergei Yuran, Andrei Tikhonov. Trainer: Oleg Romantsev

LEGIA: Maciej Szczesny; Zbigniew Mandziejewicz, Marek Jozwiak, Jacek Bednarz, Grzegorz Lewandowski (34 Krzysztof Ratajczyk), Jacek Zielinski, Leszek Pisz (Cap), Radoslaw Michalski (71 Adam Fedoruk), Tomasz Wieszczycki, Ryszard Staniek (83 Andrzej Kubica), Cezary Kucharski. Trainer: Pawel Janas

Goals: Nikiforov (13 pen), Yuran (52), Jozwiak (82)

ROSENBORG BK TRONDHEIM v BLACKBURN ROVERS 2-1 (1-0)

Lerkendal, Trondheim 27.09.1995

Referee: Günther Benkö (AUS) Attendance: 12,210

ROSENBORG: Ola By Rise (Cap); Björn Tore Kvarme, Björn Otto Bragstad, Erik Hoftun, Ståle Stensaas, Roar Strand (83 Tom Kåre Staurvik), Bent Skammelsrud, Trond Egil Soltvedt, Karl-Petter Løken (72 Steffen Iversen), Harald Brattbakk (90 Vegard Heggem), Jahn Ivat "Mini" Jakobsen. Trainer: Nils Arne Eggen

BLACKBURN: Tim Flowers; Henning Berg, Ian Pearce, Colin Hendry, Jeff Kenna, David Batty, Mike Newell, Tim Sherwood (Cap) (85 Paul Warhurst), Lee Makel (46 Stuart Ripley), Chris Sutton, Alan Shearer. Trainer: Ray Harford

Goals: Løken (30), Newell (63), Stensaas (86)

LEGIA WARSZAWA v BLACKBURN ROVERS 1-0 (1-0)

Wojska Polskiego, Warszawa 18.10.1995

Referee: Anders Frisk (SWE) Attendance: 15,000

LEGIA: Maciej Szczesny; Jacek Zielinski, Marek Jozwiak, Zbigniew Mandziejewicz, Grzegorz Lewandowski, Radoslaw Michalski, Jacek Bednarz, Ryszard Staniek, Leszek Pisz (Cap), Jerzy Podbrozny, Cezary Kucharski. Trainer: Pawel Janas

BLACKBURN: Tim Flowers; Henning Berg, Colin Hendry, Ian Pearce, Jeff Kenna, Paul Warhurst (81 Mike Newell), David Batty, Tim Sherwood (Cap), Matty Holmes, Alan Shearer, Chris Sutton. Trainer: Ray Harford

Goal: Podbrozny (26)

ROSENBORG BK TRONDHEIM v SPARTAK MOSKVA 2-4 (2-0)

Lerkendal, Trondheim 18.10.1995

Referee: José Maria Garcia Aranda (SPA) Att: 12,216

ROSENBORG: Jørn Jamtfall; Björn Tore Kvarme (46 Vegard Heggem), Björn Otto Bragstad, Erik Hoftun, Ståle Stensaas; Roar Strand (75 Tom Kåre Staurvik), Bent Skammelsrud (Cap), Trond Egil Soltvedt (64 Steffen Iversen), Karl-Petter Løken, Harald Brattbakk, Jahn Ivat «Mini» Jakobsen. Trainer: Nils Arne Eggen

SPARTAK: Stanislav Cherchesov; Ramiz Mamedov, Yuri Nikiforov, Dmitri Khlestov, Andrei Piatnitski (46 Dmitriy Alenichev), Andrei Tikhonov, Viktor Onopko (Cap), Vasili Kulkov, Ilya Tsymbalar, Valeri Schmarov (58 Valeri Kechinov), Sergei Yuran. Trainer: Oleg Romantsev

Goals: Løken (2), Brattbakk (45), Alenichev (59), Nikiforov (65), Kechinov (74, 81)

SPARTAK MOSKVA v ROSENBORG BK TRONDHEIM 4-1 (3-0)

Luzhniki, Moskva 1.11.1995

Referee: Václav Krondl (CZE) Attendance: 42,500

SPARTAK: Stanislav Cherchesov; Dmitri Khlestov, Dmitri Ananko, Viktor Onopko (Cap), Yuri Nikiforov, Ilya Tsymbalar (46 Valeri Kechinov), Vasili Kulkov, Valeri Schmarov, Dmitriy Alenichev (85 Yegor Titov), Sergei Yuran, Andrei Tikhonov. Trainer: Oleg Romantsev

ROSENBORG: Ola By Rise; Karl-Petter Løken, Erik Hoftun, Björn Otto Bragstad, Ståle Stensaas; Roar Strand (63 Vegard Heggem), Bent Skammelsrud (Cap), Harald Brattbakk, Steffen Iversen; Tom Kåre Staurvik, Jahn Ivat "Mini" Jakobsen. Trainer: Nils Arne Eggen

Goals: Schmarov (2), Yuran (9), Tsimbalar (19), Tikhonov (80), Løken (90)

BLACKBURN ROVERS v LEGIA WARSZAWA 0-0

Edwood Park, Blackburn 1.11.1995

Referee: Urs Meier (SWI) Attendance: 20,897

BLACKBURN: Tim Flowers; Henning Berg, Colin Hendry, Ian Pearce, Jeff Kenna, Stuart Ripley, Paul Warhurst (61 Graeme Le Saux), David Batty, Tim Sherwood (Cap), Alan Shearer, Mike Newell (74 Chris Sutton). Trainer: Ray Harford

LEGIA: Maciej Szczesny; Zbigniew Mandziejewicz, Jacek Bednarz, Marcin Jalocha (65 Piotr Mosor), Marek Jozwiak, Grzegorz Lewandowski, Radoslaw Michalski, Ryszard Staniek, Leszek Pisz (Cap), Jerzy Podbrozny (46 Cezary Kucharski), Tomasz Wieszczycki. Trainer: Pawel Janas

SPARTAK MOSKVA v BLACKBURN ROVERS 3-0 (1-0)

Luzhniki, Moskva 22.11.1995

Referee: Pierluigi Pairetto (ITA) Attendance: 25,000

SPARTAK: Stanislav Cherchesov; Dmitri Khlestov, Yuri Nikiforov, Viktor Onopko (Cap), Ramiz Mamedov, Ilya Tsymbalar, Vasili Kulkov, Dmitriy Alenichev, Andrei Tikhonov (87 Mukhsin Mukhamadiev), Sergei Yuran (73 Andrei Piatnitski), Valeri Schmarov (64 Valeri Kechinov). Trainer: Oleg Romantsev

BLACKBURN: Tim Flowers; Henning Berg, Colin Hendry, Paul Warhurst, Graeme Le Saux (57 Matty Holmes), Stuart Ripley (78 Chris Sutton), Tim Sherwood (Cap), David Batty, Jeff Kenna, Alan Shearer, Mike Newell. Trainer: Ray Harford

Goals: Alenichev (28), Nikiforov (47), Mamedov (54)

ROSENBORG BK TRONDHEIM v LEGIA WARSZAWA 4-0 (2-0)

Lerkendal, Trondheim 22.11.1995

Referee: Hans-Jürgen Weber (GER) Attendance: 11,480

ROSENBORG: Ola By Rise (Cap); Björn Tore Kvarme, Tom Kåre Staurvik, Erik Hoftun, Ståle Stensaas, Roar Strand (90 Vegard Heggem), Bent Skammelsrud, Trond Egil Soltvedt, Steffen Iversen, Harald Brattbakk, Jahn Ivat "Mini" Jakobsen. Trainer: Nils Arne Eggen

LEGIA: Maciej Szczesny; Marek Jozwiak, Jacek Zielinski, Zbigniew Mandziejewicz, Grzegorz Lewandowski, Marcin Jalocha, Leszek Pisz (Cap) (17 Cezary Kucharski), Ryszard Staniek, Tomasz Wieszczycki (62 Jacek Bednarz), Jerzy Podbrozny, Radoslaw Michalski. Trainer: Pawel Janas

Goals: Strand (17), Brattbakk (45), Jakobsen (64), Heggem (90)

LEGIA WARSZAWA v SPARTAK MOSKVA 0-1 (0-1)

Wojska Polskiego, Warszawa 6.12.1995

Referee: William Leslie Mottram (SCO) Attendance: 5,972

LEGIA: Maciej Szczesny; Marek Jozwiak, Jacek Zielinski, Zbigniew Mandziejewicz, Grzegorz Lewandowski, Radoslaw Michalski, Leszek Pisz (Cap), Ryszard Staniek (82 Tomasz Wieszczycki), Jacek Bednarz, Jerzy Podbrozny, Cezary Kucharski. Trainer: Pawel Janas

SPARTAK: Stanislav Cherchesov; Ramiz Mamedov, Yuri Nikiforov, Dmitri Khlestov, Dmitriy Alenichev, Andrei Tikhonov, Viktor Onopko (Cap) (82 Dmitri Ananko), Vasili Kulkov, Ilya Tsymbalar, Valeri Schmarov, Valeri Kechinov. Trainer: Oleg Romantsev

Goal: Mamedov (42)

BLACKBURN ROVERS
v ROSENBORG BK TRONDHEIM 4-1 (4-1)

Edwood Park, Blackburn 6.12.1995

Referee: Pauchard (FRA) Attendance: 20,677

BLACKBURN: Tim Flowers; Henning Berg, Paul Warhurst, Nicky Marker, Jeff Kenna, Stuart Ripley, Tim Sherwood (Cap), Matty Holmes (73 Kevin Gallacher), Mike Newell, Alan Shearer, Chris Sutton. Trainer: Ray Harford

ROSENBORG: Ola By Rise (Cap); Björn Tore Kvarme, Björn Otto Bragstad (46 Tom Kåre Staurvik), Erik Hoftun, Ståle Stensaas, Roar Strand (46 Vegard Heggem), Bent Skammelsrud, Trond Egil Soltvedt, Steffen Iversen, Harald Brattbakk, Jahn Ivat "Mini" Jakobsen.
Trainer: Nils Arne Eggen

Goals: Shearer (16 pen), Iversen (30), Newell (31, 38, 40)

STEAUA BUCUREŞTI
v GLASGOW RANGERS FC 1-0 (0-0)

Steaua, Bucureşti 13.09.1995

Referee: Alain Sars (FRA) Attendance: 26,000

STEAUA: Bogdan Stelea; Tiberiu Csik, Daniel Claudiu Prodan, Anton Doboş (Cap), Ionel Antonel Pîrvu; Damian Militaru, Constantin Gâlcă, Narcis Claudiu Răducan, Bogdan Vişan Bucur (46 Iulian Sebastian Filipescu), Bucurel Adrian Ilie (60 Laurenţiu Dumitru Roşu), Ion Vlădoiu (78 Sabin Ilie).
Trainer: Dumitru Dumitriu

RANGERS: Andy Goram; Stephen Wright, Richard Gough (Cap), Alan McLaren, Alex Cleland, Charles Miller (78 Gordon Durie), Paul Gascoigne, Gordan Petric, Brian Laudrup, Alistair McCoist, Ian Durrant (60 Neil Murray).
Trainer: Walter Smith

Sent off: Militaru and McLaren (77)

Goal: Prodan (85)

	P	W	D	L	F	A	Pts
Spartak Moskva	6	6	0	0	15	4	18
Legia Warszawa	6	2	1	3	5	8	7
Rosenborg BK	6	2	0	4	11	16	6
Blackburn Rovers	6	1	1	4	5	8	4

GROUP C

BORUSSIA DORTMUND
v JUVENTUS FC TORINO 1-3 (1-2)

Westfalenstadion, Dortmund 13.09.1995

Referee: Kurt Röthlisberger (SWI) Attendance: 35,800

BORUSSIA: Stefan Klos; Jürgen Kohler, Matthias Sammer, JÚLIO CÉSAR Silva, Stefan Reuter, Steffen Freund, Andreas Möller, Michael Zorc (Cap) (46 Rubén Sosa), Knut Reinhardt, René Tretschok (46 Ibrahim Tanko), Heiko Herrlich (72 Lars Ricken). Trainer: Ottmar Hitzfeld

JUVENTUS: Angelo Peruzzi; Ciro Ferrara, Sergio Porrini, Moreno Torricelli, Gianluca Pessotto, Angelo Di Livio, Antonio Conte (Cap) (86 Giancarlo Marocchi), PAULO Manuel Carvalho de SOUSA, Vladimir Jugović, Michele Padovano, Alessandro del Piero (89 Didier Deschamps).
Trainer: Marcello Lippi

Goals: Möller (1), Padovano (12), Del Piero (37), Conte (69)

GLASGOW RANGERS FC
v BORUSSIA DORTMUND 2-2 (0-1)

Ibrox stadium, Glasgow 27.09.1995

Referee: Jacobus Uilenberg (HOL) Attendance: 33,209

RANGERS: Andy Goram; Stephen Wright, Gordan Petric, Richard Gough (Cap), Alex Cleland, Stuart McCall, Paul Gascoigne, Charles Miller, Brian Laudrup (46 Ian Ferguson), Alistair McCoist, Gordon Durie (74 Ian Durrant).
Trainer: Walter Smith

BORUSSIA: Stefan Klos; Matthias Sammer, Jürgen Kohler, JÚLIO CÉSAR Silva (53 Bodo Schmidt), Stefan Reuter, Steffen Freund, Andreas Möller (84 René Tretschok), Michael Zorc (Cap), Martin Kree, Lars Ricken (79 Patrick Berger), Heiko Herrlich. Trainer: Ottmar Hitzfeld

Goals: Herrlich (19), Gough (63), Kree (69), Ferguson (73)

JUVENTUS FC TORINO
v STEAUA BUCUREŞTI 3-0 (2-0)

Delle Alpi, Torino 27.09.1995

Referee: Dermot Gallagher (ENG) Attendance: 34,500

JUVENTUS: Angelo Peruzzi; Moreno Torricelli, Ciro Ferrara, Alessio Tacchinardi (81 Pietro Vierchowod), Gianluca Pessotto, Angelo Di Livio, PAULO Manuel Carvalho de SOUSA, Didier Deschamps, Fabrizio Ravanelli (67 Antonio Conte), Gianluca Vialli (Cap), Alessandro del Piero (71 Michele Padovano). Trainer: Marcello Lippi

STEAUA: Bogdan Stelea; Tiberiu Csik, Daniel Claudiu Prodan, Anton Doboş, Ionel Antonel Pîrvu; Iulian Sebastian Filipescu (83 Roland Nagy), Constantin Gâlcă, Bucurel Adrian Ilie (77 Aurel Silviu Panait), Narcis Claudiu Răducan, Marius Mihai Lăcătuş (Cap) (53 Laurenţiu Dumitru Roşu), Ion Vlădoiu. Trainer: Dumitru Dumitriu

Goals: Di Livio (34), Del Piero (39), Ravanelli (48)

BORUSSIA DORTMUND v STEAUA BUCUREŞTI 1-0 (0-0)

Westfalenstadion, Dortmund 18.10.1995

Referee: Peter Mikkelsen (DEN) Attendance: 35,200

BORUSSIA: Stefan Klos; Jürgen Kohler, Knut Reinhardt, Steffen Freund, JÚLIO CÉSAR Silva, Matthias Sammer (Cap), Stefan Reuter, Patrick Berger (88 René Tretschok), Ibrahim Tanko (46 Michael Zorc), Lars Ricken (87 Günter Kutowski), Heiko Herrlich. Trainer: Ottmar Hitzfeld

STEAUA: Bogdan Stelea; Aurel Silviu Panait (85 Laurenţiu Dumitru Roşu), Ionel Antonel Pîrvu, Anton Doboş, Constantin Gâlcă, Daniel Claudiu Prodan, Marius Mihai Lăcătuş (Cap), Iulian Sebastian Filipescu (70 Roland Nagy), Ion Vlădoiu, Bucurel Adrian Ilie (63 Narcis Claudiu Răducan), Tiberiu Csik. Trainer: Dumitru Dumitriu

Goal: Ricken (58)

STEAUA BUCUREŞTI v BORUSSIA DORTMUND 0-0

Steaua, Bucureşti 1.11.1995

Referee: Michel Piraux (BEL) Attendance: 14,500

STEAUA: Bogdan Stelea; Tiberiu Csik, Daniel Claudiu Prodan, Anton Doboş, Ionel Antonel Pîrvu; Aurel Silviu Panait, Bogdan Vişan Bucur, Bucurel Adrian Ilie (76 Roland Nagy), Iulian Sebastian Filipescu (65 Narcis Claudiu Răducan), Marius Mihai Lăcătuş (Cap) (59 Laurenţiu Dumitru Roşu), Ion Vlădoiu. Trainer: Dumitru Dumitriu

BORUSSIA: Stefan Klos; Jürgen Kohler, JÚLIO CÉSAR Silva, Matthias Sammer, Martin Kree, Steffen Freund, Michael Zorc (Cap), Andreas Möller, Patrick Berger (86 Knut Reinhardt), Lars Ricken, Rubén Sosa (75 René Tretschok). Trainer: Ottmar Hitzfeld

JUVENTUS FC TORINO v GLASGOW RANGERS FC 4-1 (3-0)

Delle Alpi, Torino 18.10.1995

Referee: Vadim Zhuk (BLS) Attendance: 49,625

JUVENTUS: Angelo Peruzzi; Ciro Ferrara, Sergio Porrini (77 Massimo Carrera), Pietro Vierchowod, Moreno Torricelli, Angelo Di Livio (65 Giancarlo Marocchi), PAULO Manuel Carvalho de SOUSA, Didier Deschamps, Antonio Conte (83 Alessio Tacchinardi), Fabrizio Ravanelli (Cap), Alessandro del Piero. Trainer: Marcello Lippi

RANGERS: Andy Goram; Craig Moore, Stephen Wright (46 John Brown), Richard Gough (Cap), Gordan Petric, David Robertson, Gordon Durie, Stuart McCall (69 Neil Murray), Alex Cleland, Alistair McCoist, Oleg Salenko. Trainer: Walter Smith

Goals: Moore (15 og), Conte (23), Del Piero (30), Ravanelli (74), Gough (77)

GLASGOW RANGERS FC v STEAUA BUCUREŞTI 1-1 (1-0)

Ibrox stadium, Glasgow 22.11.1995

Referee: Nikolai Levnikov (RUS) Attendance: 30,882

RANGERS: Andy Goram; Richard Gough (Cap), Alan McLaren, Gordan Petric, John Brown (75 Gary Bollan), David Robertson, Stuart McCall (46 Neil Murray), Paul Gascoigne, Brian Laudrup, Ian Durrant (86 Charles Miller), Alistair McCoist. Trainer: Walter Smith

STEAUA: Bogdan Stelea; Anton Doboş, Iulian Sebastian Filipescu, Tiberiu Csik, Daniel Claudiu Prodan, Ionel Antonel Pîrvu, Damian Militaru (90 Laurenţiu Dumitru Roşu), Bogdan Vişan Bucur, Bucurel Adrian Ilie (75 Roland Nagy), Marius Mihai Lăcătuş (Cap) (87 Narcis Claudiu Răducan), Ion Vlădoiu. Trainer: Dumitru Dumitriu

Goals: Gascoigne (39), A. Ilie (55)

GLASGOW RANGERS FC v JUVENTUS FC TORINO 0-4 (0-1)

Ibrox stadium, Glasgow 1.11.1995

Referee: Ahmet Cakar (TUR) Attendance: 42,523

RANGERS: Andy Goram (46 William Thomson); Stephen Wright (25 Ian Durrant), Gordan Petric, John Brown, Gary Bollan, Richard Gough (Cap), Stuart McCall, Ian Ferguson, Charles Miller (70 Alistair McCoist), Paul Gascoigne, Oleg Salenko. Trainer: Walter Smith

JUVENTUS: Angelo Peruzzi; Moreno Torricelli, Sergio Porrini (79 Ciro Ferrara), Massimo Carrera, Gianluca Pessotto, Angelo Di Livio, PAULO Manuel Carvalho de SOUSA, Antonio Conte, Alessio Tacchinardi (74 Giancarlo Marocchi), Alessandro del Piero, Gianluca Vialli (Cap) (70 Fabrizio Ravanelli). Trainer: Marcello Lippi

Goals: Del Piero (11), Torricelli (65), Ravanelli (88), Marocchi (90)

JUVENTUS FC TORINO v BORUSSIA DORTMUND 1-2 (0-1)

Delle Alpi, Torino 22.11.1995

Referee: Anders Frisk (SWE) Attendance: 25,621

JUVENTUS: Angelo Peruzzi; Sergio Porrini, Pietro Vierchowod, Massimo Carrera, Gianluca Pessotto, Alessio Tacchinardi (83 Luca Fusi), Angelo Di Livio, Giancarlo Marocchi, Vladimir Jugović (46 Juan Pablo Sorin), Gianluca Vialli (Cap) (65 Alessandro del Piero), Michele Padovano. Trainer: Marcello Lippi

BORUSSIA: Stefan Klos; Martin Kree, Bodo Schmidt, Jürgen Kohler, Steffen Freund, Stefan Reuter, Matthias Sammer, Michael Zorc (Cap), Lars Ricken (68 Patrick Berger), Andreas Möller (89 Rubén Sosa), Heiko Herrlich (76 Karlheinz Riedle). Trainer: Ottmar Hitzfeld

Goals: Zorc (30), Ricken (64), Del Piero (90)

BORUSSIA DORTMUND
v GLASGOW RANGERS FC 2-2 (1-1)

Westfalenstadion, Dortmund 6.12.1995

Referee: Manuel Diaz Vega (SPA) Attendance: 35,800

BORUSSIA: Stefan Klos; Steffen Freund, Thomas Franck, Martin Kree, Carsten Wolters, Michael Zorc (Cap), Andreas Möller, Patrick Berger, Knut Reinhardt (82 Rubén Sosa), Heiko Herrlich, Karlheinz Riedle (66 Günter Kutowski). Trainer: Ottmar Hitzfeld

RANGERS: Andy Goram; Alex Cleland (79 Ian Durrant), Alan McLaren, Richard Gough (Cap), Gary Bollan, David Robertson, Charles Miller (62 Alistair McCoist), Paul Gascoigne, Stuart McCall, Brian Laudrup, Gordon Durie. Trainer: Walter Smith

Goals: Laudrup (11), Möller (17), Riedle (48), Durie (85)

STEAUA BUCUREŞTI
v JUVENTUS FC TORINO 0-0

Steaua, Bucureşti 6.12.1995

Referee: Gerd Grabher (AUS) Attendance: 2,700

STEAUA: Bogdan Stelea; Aurel Silviu Panait, Daniel Claudiu Prodan, Anton Doboş (Cap), Ionel Antonel Pîrvu (46 Laurenţiu Dumitru Roşu), Damian Militaru (86 Sabin Ilie), Tiberiu Csik, Constantin Gâlcă, Roland Nagy, Ion Vlădoiu, Iulian Sebastian Filipescu (64 Narcis Claudiu Răducan). Trainer: Dumitru Dumitriu

JUVENTUS: Michelangelo Rampulla; Sergio Porrini, Ciro Ferrara, Massimo Carrera, Gianluca Pessotto, Moreno Torricelli, Antonio Conte, Vladimir Jugović, Didier Deschamps, Giancarlo Marocchi (Cap) (66 Attilio Lombardo), Fabrizio Ravanelli (46 Alessandro del Piero). Trainer: Marcello Lippi

	P	W	D	L	F	A	Pts
Juventus FC Torino	6	4	1	1	15	4	13
Borussia Dortmund	6	2	3	1	8	8	9
Steaua Bucureşti	6	1	3	2	2	5	6
Glasgow Rangers FC	6	0	3	3	6	14	3

GROUP D

AFC AJAX AMSTERDAM
v REAL MADRID CF 1-0 (1-0)

Olympisch, Amsterdam 13.09.1995

Referee: Piero Ceccarini (ITA) Attendance: 38,000

AJAX: Edwin van der Sar; Michael Reiziger, Winston Bogarde, Frank de Boer (Cap), Ronald de Boer (87 Ignacio Tuhuteru), Martijn Reuser (46 Nordin Wooter), Jari Litmanen, Edgar Davids, Finidi George, Nwankwo Kanu (69 Kiki Musampa), Marc Overmars. Trainer: Louis van Gaal

REAL: Francisco BUYO Sánchez; Miguel Porlan Noguera "CHENDO", Manuel SANCHÍS Hontiyuelo (Cap), Fernando Ruiz HIERRO, Mikel LASA Goikoetxea, LUIS ENRIQUE Martínez García, Fernando Carlos REDONDO Neri, Carlos Alejandro Sierra Fumero "SANDRO" (54 Fredy Eusebio RINCÓN Valencia), José Emilio AMAVISCA Gárate (69 José Miguel González Martín del Campo "MÍCHEL"), RAÚL González Blanco, Iván Luis ZAMORANO Zamora. Trainer: Jorge Alberto Valdano

Goal: Overmars (14)

GRASSHOPPER-CLUB ZÜRICH
v FERENCVÁROS BUDAPEST 0-3 (0-0)

Hardturm, Zürich 13.09.1995

Referee: Rune Pedersen (NOR) Attendance: 15,530

GRASSHOPPER: Patrick Zuberbühler; Johann Vogel, Ramón Vega, Mats Gren, Patrick Thüler (67 Patrick de Napoli), Massimo Lombardo, Marcel Koller (Cap), Alain Geiger, Alexandre Comisetti (57 Ali Ibrahim), Joël Magnin (67 Eric Viscaal), Murat Yakin. Trainer: Christian Gross

FERENCVÁROS: Attila Hajdú; Elek Nyilas, András Telek (Cap), Mihály Szűcs, Dejan Milovanović, Ottó Vincze, Krisztián Lisztes, Tibor Simon, Babatunde Fatusi, Goran Kopunović, Gábor Zavadszky (77 Zsolt Nagy). Trainer: Dezső Novák

Sent off: Gren (33)

Goals: Lisztes (61), Vincze (81, 90)

FERENCVÁROS BUDAPEST
v AFC AJAX AMSTERDAM 1-5 (0-0)

Üllői út, Budapest 27.09.1995

Referee: Vasilis Nikakis (GRE) Attendance: 17,743

FERENCVÁROS: Attila Hajdú; Tibor Simon, András Telek (Cap), Sergiy Kuznetsov (81 József Keller), Zoltán Kecskés, Gábor Zavadszky, Elek Nyilas, Krisztián Lisztes, Ottó Vincze, Zoran Kuntić, Goran Kopunović. Trainer: Dezső Novák

AJAX: Edwin van der Sar; Michael Reiziger, Danny Blind (Cap), Winston Bogarde, Frank de Boer, Ronald de Boer, Jari Litmanen, Edgar Davids, Finidi George, Nwankwo Kanu (59 Patrick Kluivert), Marc Overmars. Trainer: Louis van Gaal

Goals: Litmanen (57, 80 pen, 86), Nyilas (59 pen), Kluivert (67), F.de Boer (85)

REAL MADRID CF
v GRASSHOPPER-CLUB ZÜRICH 2-0 (0-0)

Estadio Santiago Bernabéu, Madrid 27.09.1995

Referee: Zbigniew Przesmycki (POL) Attendance: 62,000

REAL: Francisco BUYO Sánchez; Enrique Sánchez Flores "QUIQUE", Fernando Ruiz HIERRO, Manuel SANCHÍS Hontiyuelo (Cap), Mikel LASA Goikoetxea, Luis MILLA Aspas, Fredy Eusebio RINCÓN Valencia (46 José Miguel González Martín del Campo "MÍCHEL"), Michael LAUDRUP (74 LUIS ENRIQUE Martínez García), José Emilio AMAVISCA Gárate (59 Miguel SOLER Sarasols), RAÚL González Blanco, Iván Luis ZAMORANO Zamora. Trainer: J.A. Valdano

GRASSHOPPER: Patrick Zuberbühler; Georgios Nemtsoudis, Ramón Vega, Alain Geiger, Patrick Thüler; Massimo Lombardo, Marcel Koller (Cap), Alexandre Comisetti (66 Joël Magnin), Murat Yakin, Johann Vogel (76 Eric Viscaal), Duke Udi (58 Patrick de Napoli). Trainer: Christian Gross

Goals: Zamorano (69, 88)

AFC AJAX AMSTERDAM
v GRASSHOPPER-CLUB ZÜRICH 3-0 (1-0)

Olympisch, Amsterdam 18.10.1995

Referee: Adrian Porumboiu (ROM) Attendance: 41,000

AJAX: Edwin van der Sar; Michael Reiziger, Danny Blind (Cap) (73 Arnold Scholten), Frank de Boer, Winston Bogarde, Ronald de Boer (62 Nwankwo Kanu), Jari Litmanen, Edgar Davids, Finidi George, Patrick Kluivert, Marc Overmars. Trainer: Louis van Gaal

GRASSHOPPER: Patrick Zuberbühler; Harald Gämperle, Ramón Vega, Mats Gren, Johann Vogel; Massimo Lombardo, Alain Geiger, Marcel Koller (Cap), Tomasz Rzasa (73 Gürkan Sermeter); Joël Magnin, Eric Viscaal. Trainer: Christian Gross

Goals: Kluivert (10, 68), George (87)

REAL MADRID CF
v FERENCVÁROS BUDAPEST 6-1 (3-0)

Santiago Bernabéu, Madrid 18.10.1995

Referee: Atanas Uzunov (BUL) Attendance: 55,000

REAL: Francisco BUYO Sánchez; Enrique Sánchez Flores "QUIQUE", Manuel SANCHÍS Hontiyuelo (Cap), Fernando Ruiz HIERRO (63 Fernando Muñoz García NANDO), Miguel SOLER Sarasols, José Miguel González Martín del Campo "MÍCHEL", Luis MILLA Aspas, Michael LAUDRUP (58 LUIS ENRIQUE Martínez García), José Emilio AMAVISCA Gárate (58 Juan Eduardo ESNÁIDER), Iván Luis ZAMORANO Zamora, RAÚL González Blanco. Trainer: J.A. Valdano

FERENCVÁROS: Attila Hajdú; András Telek, Mihály Szűcs, József Keller (Cap), Zoltán Kecskés, Krisztián Lisztes, Ottó Vincze (46 Flórián Albert), Elek Nyilas, Dejan Milovanović (56 János Hrutka), Zoran Kuntić (68 Zsolt Nagy), Goran Kopunović. Trainer: Dezső Novák

Goals: Raúl (23, 24, 84), Zamorano (33, 47), Hierro (54), Kopunović (64)

FERENCVÁROS BUDAPEST
v REAL MADRID CF 1-1 (1-0)

Üllői út, Budapest 1.11.1995

Referee: Paul Durkin (ENG) Attendance: 17,117

FERENCVÁROS: Attila Hajdú; András Telek, János Hrutka, Sergiy Kuznetsov, Zsolt Páling, Elek Nyilas, Krisztián Lisztes, József Keller (Cap), Flórián Albert (46 Zsolt Nagy), Goran Kopunović (80 Gábor Zavadszky), Zoran Kuntić (89 Ottó Vincze). Trainer: Dezső Novák

REAL: Francisco BUYO Sánchez; Enrique Sánchez Flores "QUIQUE", Manuel SANCHÍS Hontiyuelo (Cap), Rafael ALKORTA Martínez, Miguel SOLER Sarasols; Michael LAUDRUP, José Miguel González Martín del Campo "MÍCHEL" (62 LUIS ENRIQUE Martínez García), Fernando Carlos REDONDO Neri, RAÚL González Blanco, Juan Eduardo ESNÁIDER, José Emilio AMAVISCA Gárate. Trainer: Jorge Alberto Valdano

Goals: Albert (36), Raúl (74)

GRASSHOPPER-CLUB ZÜRICH
v AFC AJAX AMSTERDAM 0-0

Hardturm, Zürich 1.11.1995

Referee: Nikolai Levnikov (RUS) Attendance: 20,100

GRASSHOPPER: Patrick Foletti; Bernt Haas, Ramón Vega, Mats Gren, Patrick Thüler, Massimo Lombardo, Marcel Koller (Cap), Alain Geiger, Alexandre Comisetti (81 Gürkan Sermeter), Ali Ibrahim (87 Eric Viscaal), Joël Magnin (68 Patrick de Napoli). Trainer: Christian Gross

AJAX: Edwin van der Sar; Michael Reiziger, Danny Blind (Cap), Winston Bogarde, Ronald de Boer, Frank de Boer, Jari Litmanen (60 Nwankwo Kanu), Edgar Davids, Finidi George, Patrick Kluivert, Marc Overmars (74 Martijn Reuser). Trainer: Louis van Gaal

FERENCVÁROS BUDAPEST
v GRASSHOPPER-CLUB ZÜRICH 3-3 (2-1)

Üllői út, Budapest 22.11.1995

Referee: Kim Milton Nielsen (DEN) Attendance: 14,864

FERENCVÁROS: Attila Hajdú; Sergiy Kuznetsov, János Hrutka, József Keller (Cap), Elek Nyilas, Flórián Albert (66 Zsolt Nagy), Mihály Szűcs, Krisztián Lisztes, Zoltán Kecskés (66 Ottó Vincze), Zoran Kuntić, Goran Kopunović (83 Gábor Zavadszky). Trainer: Dezső Novák

GRASSHOPPER: Patrick Foletti; Bernt Haas, Ramón Vega, Mats Gren, Harald Gämperle; Massimo Lombardo, Alain Geiger, Marcel Koller (Cap), Alexandre Comisetti; Nestor Subiat, Ali Ibrahim (88 Joël Magnin). Trainer: Christian Gross

Goals: Albert (20), Subiat (21), Lisztes (24), Comisetti (48), Ali Ibrahim (65), Nyilas (86 pen)

REAL MADRID CF
v AFC AJAX AMSTERDAM 0-2 (0-0)

Santiago Bernabéu, Madrid 22.11.1995

Referee: Hellmut Krug (GER) Attendance: 72,000

REAL: Francisco BUYO Sánchez; Miguel Porlan Noguera "CHENDO" (73 José Miguel González Martín del Campo "MÍCHEL"), Rafael ALKORTA Martínez, Manuel SANCHÍS Hontiyuelo (Cap), Enrique Sánchez Flores "QUIQUE"; Fernando Carlos REDONDO Neri, LUIS ENRIQUE Martínez García, José Emilio AMAVISCA Gárate, Michael LAUDRUP (72 Luis MILLA Aspas), RAÚL González Blanco, Iván Luis ZAMORANO Zamora. Trainer: Jorge Alberto Valdano

AJAX: Edwin van der Sar; Michael Reiziger, Winston Bogarde, Danny Blind (Cap), Kiki Musampa (89 Martijn Reuser), Jari Litmanen, Ronald de Boer, Edgar Davids, Finidi George, Marc Overmars, Patrick Kluivert. Trainer: Louis van Gaal

Goals: Litmanen (64), Kluivert (76)

AFC AJAX AMSTERDAM
v FERENCVÁROS BUDAPEST 4-0 (2-0)

Olympisch, Amsterdam 6.12.1995

Referee: Ilkka Koho (FIN) Attendance: 42,319

AJAX: Edwin van der Sar; Michael Reiziger, Arnold Scholten, Frank de Boer (Cap), Winston Bogarde, Ronald de Boer, Jari Litmanen (76 Nordin Wooter), Edgar Davids (46 Kiki Musampa), Finidi George (76 Martijn Reuser), Patrick Kluivert, Marc Overmars. Trainer: Louis van Gaal

FERENCVÁROS: Attila Hajdú; Zsolt Páling (90 Zsolt Nagy), János Hrutka, Sergiy Kuznetsov, József Keller (Cap), Elek Nyilas, Krisztián Lisztes, Mihály Szűcs, Flórián Albert, Ottó Vincze, Zoran Kuntić (69 Goran Kopunović). Trainer: Dezső Novák

Goals: Overmars (17), R. de Boer (22), Litmanen (62, 66)

GRASSHOPPER-CLUB ZÜRICH
v REAL MADRID CF 0-2 (0-0)

Hardturm, Zürich 6.12.1995

Referee: James McCluskey (SCO) Attendance: 20,100

GRASSHOPPER: Patrick Foletti; Bernt Haas, Ramón Vega, Mats Gren, Harald Gämperle; Massimo Lombardo, Alain Geiger, Marcel Koller, Alexandre Comisetti (76 Gürkan Sermeter), Nestor Subiat (66 Joël Magnin), Ali Ibrahim (82 Patrick de Napoli). Trainer: Christian Gross

REAL: Francisco BUYO Sánchez; Enrique Sánchez Flores «QUIQUE», Manuel SANCHÍS Hontiyuelo, Fernando Ruiz HIERRO (61 Rafael ALKORTA Martínez), Mikel LASA Goikoetxea; LUIS ENRIQUE Martínez García, Michael LAUDRUP (71 Fredy Eusebio RINCóN Valencia), Luis MILLA Aspas, José Emilio AMAVISCA Gárate (61 José Miguel González Martín del Campo «MÍCHEL»), Juan Eduardo ESNÁIDER, RAÚL González Blanco. Trainer: Jorge Alberto Valdano

Goals: Raúl (56), Michel (67)

	P	W	D	L	F	A	Pts
AFC Ajax Amsterdam	6	5	1	0	15	1	16
Real Madrid CF	6	3	1	2	11	5	10
Ferencváros Budapest	6	1	2	3	9	19	5
Grasshopper Zürich	6	0	2	4	3	13	2

QUARTER-FINALS

LEGIA WARSZAWA
v PANATHINAIKOS ATHINA 0-0

Wojska Polskiego, Warszawa 6.03.1996

Referee: Manuel Diaz Vega (SPA) Attendance: 12,000

LEGIA: Maciej Szczesny; Zbigniew Mandziejewicz, Marek Jozwiak, Jacek Bednarz, Jacek Zielinski, Grzegorz Lewandowski (73 Tomasz Wieszczycki), Leszek Pisz (Cap), Radoslaw Michalski, Ryszard Staniek, Cezary Kucharski (65 Tomasz Sokolowski), Jerzy Podbrozny. Trainer: Pawel Janas

PANATHINAIKOS: Jozef Wandzik; Stratos Apostolakis, Giannis Kalitzakis (Cap), Thanasis Kolitsidakis, Dimitris Markos, Giorgos H.Georgiadis, Juan Borelli, Giorgos S.Georgiadis, Spiros Maragkos (80 Giorgos Kapouranis), Krzysztof Warzycha, Alexandros Alexoudis. Trainer: Juan Ramon Rocha

PANATHINAIKOS ATHINA
v LEGIA WARSZAWA 3-0 (1-0)

Olympiako, Athina 20.03.1996

Referee: Sergei Husainov (RUS) Attendance: 74,084

PANATHINAIKOS: Jozef Wandzik; Stratos Apostolakis, Giannis Kalitzakis (Cap), Marinos Ouzounidis, Thanasis Kolitsidakis, Giorgos S.Georgiadis, Juan Borelli (89 Giannis Gkoumas), Spiros Maragkos (82 Nikos Nioplias), Giorgos Kapouranis, Giorgos Donis, Krzysztof Warzycha (89 Andreas Lagonikakis). Trainer: Juan Ramon Rocha

LEGIA: Maciej Szczesny; Radoslaw Michalski, Marcin Jalocha, Jacek Zielinski, Zbigniew Mandziejewicz, Grzegorz Lewandowski, Tomasz Sokolowski (82 Jacek Kacprzak), Tomasz Wieszczycki, Leszek Pisz (Cap), Jerzy Podbrozny, Ryszard Staniek (75 Cezary Kucharski). Trainer: Pawel Janas

Goals: Warzycha (33, 57), Borelli (71)

BORUSSIA DORTMUND v AFC AJAX AMSTERDAM 0-2 (0-1)

Westfalenstadion, Dortmund 6.03.1996

Referee: Dermot Gallagher (ENG) Attendance: 35,800

BORUSSIA: Stefan Klos; Matthias Sammer (Cap), Bodo Schmidt (46 Heiko Herrlich), Jürgen Kohler, JÚLIO CÉSAR Silva, Stefan Reuter, Steffen Freund, Patrick Berger, Knut Reinhardt, Karlheinz Riedle, Lars Ricken (77 Michael Zorc). Trainer: Ottmar Hitzfeld

AJAX: Edwin van der Sar; Michael Reiziger (85 Arnold Scholten), Danny Blind (Cap), Winston Bogarde, Sonny Silooy, Finidi George, Edgar Davids, Nwankwo Kanu, Nordin Wooter (46 Kiki Musampa), Patrick Kluivert, Ronald de Boer. Trainer: Louis van Gaal

Goals: Davids (8), Kluivert (83)

AFC AJAX AMSTERDAM v BORUSSIA DORTMUND 1-0 (0-0)

Olympisch, Amsterdam 20.03.1996

Referee: Václav Krondl (CZE) Attendance: 45,000

AJAX: Edwin van der Sar; Sonny Silooy, Frank de Boer (Cap), Edgar Davids, Winston Bogarde, Arnold Scholten, Jari Litmanen (87 Danny Landzaat), Kiki Musampa, Nordin Wooter, Nwankwo Kanu, Ronald de Boer. Trainer: Louis van Gaal

BORUSSIA: Stefan Klos; Martin Kree, Jürgen Kohler, JÚLIO CÉSAR Silva, René Tretschok (61 Knut Reinhardt), Carsten Wolters (60 Andreas Möller), Lars Ricken, Michael Zorc (Cap), Steffen Freund, Stéphane Chapuisat (79 Rubén Sosa), Karlheinz Riedle. Trainer: Ottmar Hitzfeld

Goal: Musampa (75)

REAL MADRID CF v JUVENTUS FC TORINO 1-0 (1-0)

Santiago Bernabéu, Madrid 6.03.1996

Referee: Kurt Röthlisberger (SWI) Attendance: 86,000

REAL: Francisco BUYO Sánchez (Cap); Miguel Porlan Noguera "CHENDO", Rafael ALKORTA Martínez, José Antonio GARCÍA CALVO; Fernando Ruiz HIERRO, LUIS ENRIQUE Martínez García, Fernando Carlos REDONDO Neri, Miguel SOLER Sarasols (26 Enrique Sánchez Flores "QUIQUE"), Michael LAUDRUP (65 José Miguel González Martín del Campo "MÍCHEL"), Iván Luis ZAMORANO Zamora, RAÚL González Blanco. Trainer: Arsenio Iglesias

JUVENTUS: Angelo Peruzzi; Ciro Ferrara, Pietro Vierchowod, Massimo Carrera (76 Gianluca Pessotto), Moreno Torricelli, PAULO Manuel Carvalho de SOUSA (65 Vladimir Jugović), Attilio Lombardo (46 Michele Padovano), Antonio Conte, Didier Deschamps, Fabrizio Ravanelli (Cap), Alessandro del Piero. Trainer: Marcello Lippi

Goal: Raúl (20)

JUVENTUS FC TORINO v REAL MADRID CF 2-0 (1-0)

Delle Alpi, Torino 20.03.1996

Referee: Mario van der Ende (HOL) Attendance: 62,783

JUVENTUS: Angelo Peruzzi; Moreno Torricelli, Sergio Porrini, Pietro Vierchowod, Gianluca Pessotto, Vladimir Jugović (46 Angelo Di Livio), Didier Deschamps, Antonio Conte, Alessandro del Piero (87 Giancarlo Marocchi), Michele Padovano (73 Attilio Lombardo), Gianluca Vialli (Cap). Trainer: Marcello Lippi

REAL: José Santiago CAÑIZARES Ruiz; Miguel Porlan Noguera "CHENDO", Mikel LASA Goikoetxea, Rafael ALKORTA Martínez, José Antonio GARCÍA CALVO; Luis MILLA Aspas, José Miguel González Martín del Campo "MÍCHEL" (Cap) (65 Juan Eduardo ESNÁIDER), LUIS ENRIQUE Martínez García, Michael LAUDRUP, RAÚL González Blanco, Enrique Sánchez Flores "QUIQUE" (56 Fredy Eusebio RINCÓN Valencia). Trainer: Arsenio Iglesias

Sent off: Alkorta (69), Torricelli (75)

Goals: Del Piero (17), Padovano (53)

FC NANTES v SPARTAK MOSKVA 2-0 (1-0)

Le Beaujoire, Nantes 6.03.1996

Referee: Hellmut Krug (GER) Attendance: 31,500

FC NANTES: Dominique Casagrande; Serge Le Dizet (70 Jean-Marc Chanelet), Laurent Guyot, Eric Decroix, Christophe Pignol, Benoît Cauet, Claude Makélélé, Reynald Pedros, Japhet N'Doram (Cap) (64 Jean-Michel Ferri), Roman Kosecki, Nicolas Ouédec (83 Jocelyn Gourvennec). Trainer: Jean-Claude Suaudeau

SPARTAK: Ruslan Nigmatullin; Dmitri Ananko, Aleksandr Lipko, Yuri Nikiforov, Vadim Yevseyev, Dmitriy Alenichev (71 Artyom Bezrodnyi), Valeri Kechinov, Ramiz Mamedov (34 Sergei Chudin), Ilya Tsymbalar (46 Valeri Schmarov), Andrei Piatnitski (Cap), Andrei Tikhonov. Trainer: Georgi Yartsev

Sent off: Pedros (78)

Goals: N'Doram (28), Ouédec (68)

SPARTAK MOSKVA v FC NANTES 2-2 (2-0)

Lokomotiv, Moskva 20.03.1996

Referee: Serge Muhmenthaler (SWI) Attendance: 28,600

SPARTAK: Ruslan Nigmatullin; Dmitri Ananko, Aleksandr Lipko, Yuri Nikiforov, Vadim Yevseyev, Dmitriy Alenichev, Valeri Kechinov, Ilya Tsymbalar, Andrei Tikhonov, Sergei Nahornyak (75 Artyom Bezrodnyi), Valeri Schmarov (60 Andrei Piatnitski). Trainer: Georgi Yartsev

FC NANTES: Dominique Casagrande; Serge Le Dizet, Eddy Capron, Eric Decroix, Christophe Pignol, Bruno Carotti, Claude Makélélé, Jocelyn Gourvennec (63 Jean-Michel Ferri), Benoît Cauet, Roman Kosecki (84 Jean-Marc Chanelet), Nicolas Ouédec. Trainer: Jean-Claude Suaudeau

Goals: Nikiforov (33, 36), Ouédec (62, 85)

SEMI-FINALS

JUVENTUS FC TORINO v FC NANTES 2-0 (0-0)

Delle Alpi, Torino 3.04.1996

Referee: Dermot Gallagher (ENG) Attendance: 50,425

JUVENTUS: Angelo Peruzzi; Ciro Ferrara, Gianluca Pessotto, Pietro Vierchowod (62 Giancarlo Marocchi), Sergio Porrini, PAULO Manuel Carvalho de SOUSA (82 Massimo Carrera), Angelo Di Livio (75 Attilio Lombardo), Vladimir Jugović, Gianluca Vialli (Cap), Alessandro del Piero, Michele Padovano. Trainer: Marcello Lippi

FC NANTES: Dominique Casagrande; Serge Le Dizet, Eric Decroix, Eddy Capron, Christophe Pignol, Benoît Cauet, Jean-Michel Ferri (Cap), Bruno Carotti, Jocelyn Gourvennec (46 Jean-Marc Chanelet), Roman Kosecki (68 Laurent Guyot), Nicolas Ouédec (86 Laurent Peyrelade). Trainer: Jean-Claude Suaudeau

Goals: Vialli (49), Jugović (65)

FC NANTES v JUVENTUS FC TORINO 3-2 (1-1)

Le Beaujoire, Nantes 17.04.1996

Referee: Sándor Puhl (HUN) Attendance: 34,210

FC NANTES: Dominique Casagrande; Jean-Marc Chanelet, Eddy Capron, Eric Decroix, Christophe Pignol (88 Laurent Peyrelade), Claude Makélélé, Jean-Michel Ferri (Cap), Benoît Cauet, Japhet N'Doram, Roman Kosecki (62 Franck Renou), Nicolas Ouédec (38 Jocelyn Gourvennec). Trainer: Jean-Claude Suaudeau

JUVENTUS: Angelo Peruzzi; Ciro Ferrara, Gianluca Pessotto, Antonio Conte, Pietro Vierchowod, Massimo Carrera, Angelo Di Livio, Didier Deschamps, Gianluca Vialli (Cap) (79 Vladimir Jugović), Alessandro del Piero (46 PAULO Manuel Carvalho de SOUSA), Fabrizio Ravanelli (46 Michele Padovano). Trainer: Marcello Lippi

Goals: Vialli (17), Decroix (43), Paulo Sousa (50), N'Doram (69), Renou (82)

AFC AJAX AMSTERDAM v PANATHINAIKOS ATHINA 0-1 (0-0)

Olympisch, Amsterdam 3.04.1996

Referee: László Vagner (HUN) Attendance: 43,000

AJAX: Edwin van der Sar; Michael Reiziger, Danny Blind (Cap), Frank de Boer, Winston Bogarde, Jari Litmanen (76 Kiki Musampa), Patrick Kluivert, Edgar Davids, Finidi George, Nwankwo Kanu, Ronald de Boer. Trainer: Louis van Gaal

PANATHINAIKOS: Jozef Wandzik; Stratos Apostolakis, Marinos Ouzounidis, Giorgos S.Georgiadis, Giannis Kalitzakis (Cap), Thanasis Kolitsidakis, Juan Borelli (83 Dimitris Markos), Giorgos Kapouranis, Krzysztof Warzycha (90 Nikos Nioplias), Spiros Maragkos (60 Giorgos H.Georgiadis), Giorgos Donis. Trainer: Juan Ramon Rocha

Goal: Warzycha (87)

PANATHINAIKOS ATHINA v AFC AJAX AMSTERDAM 0-3 (0-1)

Olympiako, Athina 17.04.1996

Referee: José Maria Garcia Aranda (SPA) Att: 74084

PANATHINAIKOS: Jozef Wandzik; Stratos Apostolakis, Thanasis Kolitsidakis, Giorgos H.Georgiadis, Giannis Kalitzakis (Cap), Dimitris Markos (85 Andreas Lagonikakis), Juan Borelli, Giorgos Kapouranis, Krzysztof Warzycha, Spiros Maragkos (74 Nikos Nioplias), Giorgos Donis. Trainer: Juan Ramon Rocha

AJAX: Edwin van der Sar; Michael Reiziger, Danny Blind (Cap), Frank de Boer, Sonny Silooy (72 Nordin Wooter), Ronald de Boer, Jari Litmanen, Edgar Davids (86 Arnold Scholten), Finidi George, Nwankwo Kanu, Winston Bogarde. Trainer: Louis van Gaal

Goals: Litmanen (4, 77), Wooter (85)

FINAL

JUVENTUS FC TORINO v AFC AJAX AMSTERDAM 1-1 (1-1, 1-1) (AET)

Stadio Olimpico, Roma 22.05.1996

Referee: Manuel Diaz Vega (SPA) Attendance: 70,000

JUVENTUS: Angelo Peruzzi; Ciro Ferrara, Gianluca Pessotto, Moreno Torricelli, Pietro Vierchowod, PAULO Manuel Carvalho de SOUSA (57 Angelo Di Livio), Didier Deschamps, Antonio Conte (43 Vladimir Jugović), Gianluca Vialli (Cap), Alessandro del Piero, Fabrizio Ravanelli (77 Michele Padovano). Trainer: Marcello Lippi

AJAX: Edwin van der Sar; Sonny Silooy, Danny Blind (Cap), Frank de Boer (69 Arnold Scholten), Winston Bogarde, Ronald de Boer (91 Nordin Wooter), Jari Litmanen, Edgar Davids, Finidi George, Nwankwo Kanu, Kiki Musampa (46 Patrick Kluivert). Trainer: Louis van Gaal

Goals: Ravanelli (12), Litmanen (41)

Penalties: 0-0 Davids (miss), 0-1 Ferrara, 1-1 Litmanen, 1-2 Pessotto, 2-2 Scholten, 2-3 Padovano, 2-3 Silooy (miss), 2-4 Jugović

European Cup Goalscorers 1995-96:

9 goals: Jari Litmanen (Ajax Amsterdam)

6 goals: Alessandro del Piero (Juventus Torino), RAUL González Blanco (Real Madrid), Krzysztof Warzycha (Panathinakos Athina)

5 goals: Patrick Kluivert (Ajax Amsterdam), Yuri Nikiforov (Spartak Moskva), Nicolas Ouédec (FC Nantes)

4 goals: Mike Newell (Blackburn), Fabrizio Ravanelli (Juventus Torino), Iván Luis ZAMORANO Zamora (Real Madrid), Harald Brattbakk (Rosenborg)

3 goals: Erik Bo Andersen (Aalborg), Japhet N'Doram, Reynald Pedros (FC Nantes), Leszek Pisz (Legia Warszawa), Karl-Petter Løken (Rosenborg), Sergei Yuran (Spartak Moskva)

2 goals: Shevchenko (Dynamo Kyiv), Jens Madsen (Aalborg), Möller, Ricken (Borussia Dortmund), Borelli (Panathinakos), Kuntz (Beşiktaş), Gough, Durie (Glasgow Rangers), A.Ilie (Steaua Bucureşti), Albert, Nyilas, Vincze, Lisztes, Kopunović (Ferencváros), Podbrozny (Legia Warszawa), Strand, Jakobsen (Rosenborg), Emerson, Rui Barros (FC Porto), Overmars (Ajax), Mamedov, Alenichev, Kechinov (Spartak Moskva), Padovano, Vialli, Conte (Juventus), Comisetti (Grasshopper)

1 goal: Kashentsev (Maccabi Tel Aviv), Blomqvist (IFK Göteborg), Kalitvintsev, Pokhlebaiev (Dynamo Kyiv), De Bilde (Anderlecht), Stimac (Hajduk Split), Peter Rasmussen (Aalborg BK), Shearer (Blackburn Rovers), Decroix, Renou, Guyot, Kosecki (FC Nantes), Herrlich, Kree, Zorc, Riedle (Borussia Dortmund), Alexoudis, Giorgos S.Georgiadis, Markos, Giorgos H.Georgiadis (Panathinakos), Mehmet (Beşiktaş), Laudrup, Ferguson, Gascoine (Rangers), Prodan (Steaua Bucureşti), Michel, Hierro (Real Madrid), Staniek, Jozwiak, Bednarz (Legia), Heggem, Stensaas, Iversen, Hoftun (Rosenborg), Kuntić (Ferencváros), Drulovic, Jose Carlos (FC Porto), Wooter, Musampa, Davids, R.de Boer, F.de Boer, Finidi (Ajax), Schmarov, Tsimbalar, Tikhonov (Spartak Moskva), Jugović, Paulo Sousa, Di Livio, Torricelli, Marocchi (Juventus), Subiat, Yakin, Ali Ibrahim (Grashopper Zürich)

Own goal: Moore (Rangers) for Juventus Torino

THE EUROPEAN CUP 1996-97

PRELIMINARY ROUND

MACCABI TEL AVIV v FENERBAHÇE ISTANBUL 0-1 (0-1)

Bloomfield, Tel Aviv 7.08.1996

Referee: Günther Benkö (AUS) Attendance: 26,000

MACCABI: Aleksandr Uvarov; Evgeni Kashentsev (75 Miroslaw Trzeciak), Gadi Brumer, Amir Shelach, Yaacov Hilel (81 Boris Matveyev), Noam Shoam, Nir Klinger, Avi Nimni, Alon Brumer, Offer Mizrahi, Eli Driks. Trainer: D. Kashtan

FENERBAHÇE: Rüstü Reçber; Ilker Yagcioglu, Uche Okechukwu, Jes Høgh, Halil Ibrahim Kara, Tayfun Korkut, Kemalettin Sentürk, Bülent Uygun, Augustine Okocha; Elvir Bolic (86 Tarik Dasgün), Emil Kostadinov.
Trainer: Sebastiao Lazaroni

Goal: Kemalettin (42)

FENERBAHÇE ISTANBUL v MACCABI TEL AVIV 1-1 (1-0)

Fenerbahçe, Istanbul 21.08.1996

Referee: László Vagner (HUN) Attendance: 28,437

FENERBAHÇE: Rüstü Reçber; Ilker Yagcioglu, Uche Okechukwu, Jes Høgh, Halil Ibrahim Kara, Bülent Uygun, Kemalettin Sentürk, Augustine Okocha, Tayfun Korkut, Elvir Bolic, Tarik Dasgün (66 Özkan Koçtürk, 87 Tuncay Akgün).
Trainer: Sebastiao Lazaroni

MACCABI: Aleksandr Uvarov; Evgeni Kashentsev, Gadi Brumer, Amir Shelach (84 Nir Sivilia), Yaacov Hilel, Alon Brumer, Nir Klinger, Noam Shoam (64 Haim Hajaj), Avi Nimni, Eli Driks, Offer Mizrahi (68 Boris Matveyev).
Trainer: Dror Kashtan

Goals: Okocha (18), Driks (75)

GLASGOW RANGERS FC v ALANIA VLADIKAVKAZ 3-1 (0-1)

Ibrox Stadium, Glasgow 7.08.1996

Referee: Markus Merk (GER) Attendance: 44,799

RANGERS: Andy Goram; Alex Cleland, Richard Gough, Gordan Petric, Joachim Björklund, Stuart McCall, Jörg Albertz, Ian Ferguson (20 Derek McInnes), Gordon Durie, Alistair McCoist (74 Peter Van Vossen), Brian Laudrup.
Manager: Walter Smith

ALANIA: Dmitriy Kramarenko; Omari Tetradze, Oleg Kornienko, Artur Pagayev, Alan Agayev, Igor Yanovskiy, Inal Dzhioyev, Mirdzhalol Kasymov (65 Vyacheslav Skish), Zaza Revishvili (40 Georgiy Botsiev), Bakhva Tedeyev, Nazim Suleimanov (76 Oleg Sergeev). Trainer: Valeri Gazzayev

Goals: Yanovskiy (30), McInnes (51), McCoist (60), Petric (78)

ALANIA VLADIKAVKAZ v GLASGOW RANGERS FC 2-7 (2-4)

Spartak, Vladikavkaz 21.08.1996

Referee: Urs Meier (SWI) Attendance: 32,000

ALANIA: Zaur Khapov; Artur Pagayev, Omari Tetradze, Oleg Kornienko (79 Vyacheslav Skish), Murtaz Shelia, Zaza Revishvili, Inal Dzhioyev, Igor Yanovskiy, Bakhva Tedeyev (28 Alan Agayev, 57 Oleg Sergeev), Nazim Suleimanov, Anatoliy Kanischev. Trainer: Valeri Gazzayev

RANGERS: Andy Goram; Richard Gough, Gordan Petric, Joachim Björklund, Alex Cleland, Stuart McCall, Derek McInnes (90 Ian Durrant), Jörg Albertz, Brian Laudrup, Alistair McCoist (75 Gordon Durie), Peter Van Vossen (82 Charles Miller). Manager: Walter Smith

Goals: McCoist (1, 13, 17), Yanovskiy (14), Suleimanov (24 pen), Van Vossen (40), Laudrup (55, 83), Miller (87)

PANATHINAIKOS ATHINA v ROSENBORG BK TRONDHEIM 1-0 (1-0)

Olympiako, Athina 7.08.1996

Referee: Michel Piraux (BEL) Attendance: 33,095

PANATHINAIKOS: Jozef Wandzik; Stratos Apostolakis, Giannis Kalitzakis (Cap), Marinos Ouzounidis, Thanasis Kolitsidakis, Giorgos Haralampos Georgiadis, Juan Borelli (71 Nikos Limperopoulos), Dimitris Markos (66 Alexandros Alexoudis), Giorgos Kapouranis, Krzysztof Warzycha, Andreas Lagonikakis (66 Bledar Kola). Trainer: Juan Ramón Rocha

ROSENBORG: Jørn Jamtfall; Karl Petter Løken, Jon Olav Hjelde (29 Karl Oskar Fjørtoft), Erik Hoftun, Ståle Stensaas, Bent Skammelsrud; Roar Strand, Trond Egil Soltvedt, Steffen Iversen, Harald Martin Brattbakk, Jahn Ivar Jakobsen. Trainer: Nils Arne Eggen & Bjørn Hansen

Goal: Warzycha (19)

ROSENBORG BK TRONDHEIM v PANATHINAIKOS ATHINA 3-0 (0-0, 1-0) (AET)

Lerkendal, Trondheim 21.08.1996

Referee: Paul Durkin (ENG) Attendance: 18,625

ROSENBORG: Jørn Jamtfall; Karl Petter Løken (19 Bjørn Tore Kvarme), Bjørn Otto Bragstad (76 Tom Kåre Staurvik), Erik Hoftun, Ståle Stensaas; Roar Strand (88 Vegard Heggem), Bent Skammelsrud, Trond Egil Soltvedt; Jahn Ivar Jakobsen, Steffen Iversen, Harald Martin Brattbakk. Trainer: Nils Arne Eggen

PANATHINAIKOS: Jozef Wandzik; Stratos Apostolakis, Marinos Ouzounidis, Giannis Kalitzakis (Cap), Thanasis Kolitsidakis (76 Louis Hristodoulou), Giorgos Kapouranis, Dimitris Markos, Juan Borelli (97 Spiros Maragkos), Giorgos Haralampos Georgiadis, Krzysztof Warzycha, Alexandros Alexoudis (67 Andreas Lagonikakis). Trainer: Juan Ramon Rocha

Goals: Strand (63), Iversen (94), Heggem (97)

IFK GÖTEBORG v FERENCVÁROS BUDAPEST 3-0 (1-0)

Gamla Ullevi, Göteborg 7.08.1996

Referee: Alain Sars (FRA) Attendance: 5,513

IFK: Thomas Ravelli; Stefan Landberg, Teddy Lucic, Johan Anegrund, Mikael Nilsson, Niclas Alexandersson, Håkan Mild, Stefan Lindqvist, Jesper Blomqvist, Andreas Andersson, Stefan Pettersson (85 Erik Wahlstedt). Trainer: Mats Jingblad

FERENCVÁROS: Attila Hajdú; András Telek, Zsolt Limperger (71 Dejan Milovanović), Norbert Nagy, Mihály Szűcs, Vasile Miriuţă, Zoltán Jagodics, Krisztián Lisztes (74 László Arany), Imre Aranyos; Ferenc Horváth, Igor Nichenko (81 Mezianet Touati). Trainer: Dezső Novák

Goals: Blomqvist (37), Pettersson (50), Andersson (57)

FERENCVÁROS BUDAPEST v IFK GÖTEBORG 1-1 (1-0)

Budapest 21.08.1996

Referee: José María Garcia Aranda (SPA) Att: 5,925

FERENCVÁROS: Ayyila Hajdú (60 József Szeiler); András Telek, Mihály Szűcs (30 Imre Aranyos), Zoltán Jagodics; Zsolt Nagy (81 Zsolt Páling), Vasile Miriuţă, László Arany, Krisztián Lisztes, Norbert Nagy; Ferenc Horváth, Igor Nichenko. Trainer: Dezső Novák

IFK: Thomas Ravelli; Magnus Johansson (75 Stefan Landberg), Teddy Lucic, Jonas Ohlsson, Mikael Nilsson, Niclas Alexandersson, Håkan Mild, Stefan Lindqvist, Jesper Blomqvist, Andreas Andersson, Stefan Pettersson (14 Magnus Erlingmark). Trainer: Mats Jingblad

Goals: Horváth (14), Andersson (87)

WIDZEW LÓDZ v BRØNDBY IF 2-1 (0-0)

Widzew, Lódz 7.08.1996

Referee: Mario van der Ende (HOL) Attendance: 9,500

WIDZEW: Maciej Szczesny; Pawel Wojtala, Tomasz Lapinski (53 Marek Bajor), Radoslaw Michalski, Miroslaw Szymkowiak, Zbigniew Wyciszkiewicz, Ryszard Czerwiec (75 Piotr Szarpak), Rafal Siadaczka, Marek Citko, Marek Koniarek (62 Jacek Dembinski), Slawomir Majak. Trainer: Franciszek Smuda

BRØNDBY: Mogens Krogh; Søren Colding, Lars Olsen, Per Nielsen, Aurelijus Skarbalius, Ole Bjur, Kim Vilfort, Allan Nielsen (85 Kim Daugaard), Allan Ravn, Ruben Bagger (70 Thomas Thøgersen), Peter Møller (77 Ebbe Sand). Trainer: Ebbe Skovdahl

Goals: Dembinski (64), Majak (73), Bjur (75)

BRØNDBY IF v WIDZEW LÓDZ 3-2 (2-0)

Brøndby Stadion, København 21.08.1996

Referee: Ahmet Çakar (TUR) Attendance: 10,438

BRØNDBY: Mogens Krogh; Søren Colding, Per Nielsen, Dan Eggen, Aurelijus Skarbalius, Ole Bjur, Allan Ravn, Allan Nielsen, Kim Vilfort (74 Kim Daugaard), Peter Møller (86 Bo Hansen), Ruben Bagger (68 Ebbe Sand).
Trainer: Ebbe Skovdahl

WIDZEW: Maciej Szczesny; Radoslaw Michalski, Tomasz Lapinski, Pawel Wojtala, Marek Citko, Miroslaw Szymkowiak (63 Marek Bajor), Ryszard Czerwiec, Zbigniew Wyciszkiewicz (46 Jacek Dembinski), Rafal Siadaczka (76 Piotr Szarpak), Slawomir Majak, Andriy Mikhalchuk.
Trainer: Franciszek Smuda

Goals: P. Møller (32), Bjur (44), Vilfort (48), Citko (56), Wojtala (89)

CLUB BRUGGE KV v STEAUA BUCUREŞTI 2-2 (1-1)

Olympiapark, Brugge 7.08.1996

Referee: Rune Pedersen (NOR) Attendance: 10,755

CLUB BRUGGE: Dany Verlinden; Eric Deflandre, Pascal Renier, Lorenzo Staelens, Gert Claessens, Franky van der Elst (Cap), Robert Špehar, Gert Verheyen, Anders Nielsen, Sven Vermant (74 Günther Verjans), Mario Stanić.
Trainer: Hugo Broos

STEAUA: Daniel Gherasim; Denis Şerban, Tiberiu Csik, Bogdan Bucur, Daniel Claudiu Prodan, Iulian Sebastian Filipescu; Damian Militaru, Adrian Ilie (79 Narcis Răducan), Aurel Augustin Călin; Marius Lăcătuş (Cap) (70 Sabin Ilie), Cristian Ciocoiu (58 Roland Nagy).
Trainer: Dumitru Dumitriu

Goals: Nielsen (25), A. Ilie (45, 61), Špehar (54)

GRASSHOPPER-CLUB ZÜRICH v SLAVIA PRAHA 5-0 (2-0)

Hardturm, Zürich 7.08.1996

Referee: Jorge Monteiro Coroado (POR) Attendance: 9,300

GRASSHOPPER: Pascal Zuberbühler; Harald Gämperle, Mats Gren, Boris Smiljanic, Patrick Thüler; Antonio Esposito (78 Marcel Koller), Joël Magnin, Murat Yakin, Alexandre Comisetti (90 Jan Berger); Dinu Viorel Moldovan, Kubilay Türkyılmaz (85 Tomasz Rzasa). Trainer: Christian Gross

SLAVIA: Jan Stejskal; Lubos Kubik, Tomáš Hunal (62 Martin Hysky), Martin Penicka, Sladjan Asanin, Kennedy Chihuri (56 Daniel Smejkal), Edvard Lasota, Pavel Novotný, Ondrej Kristofik (86 Jaromir Jindracek), Robert Vagner, Karel Vacha.
Trainer: František Cipro

Goals: Türkyılmaz (11, 47), Esposito (43), Moldovan (60), Koller (88)

STEAUA BUCUREŞTI v CLUB BRUGGE KV 3-0 (2-0)

Steaua, Bucureşti 21.08.1996

Referee: Pier Luigi Collina (ITA) Attendance: 15,000

STEAUA: Daniel Gherasim; Tiberiu Csik, Marius Achim Baciu, Daniel Claudiu Prodan, Iulian Sebastian Filipescu; Damian Militaru, Bogdan Bucur, Adrian Ilie, Denis Şerban (82 Tudorel Zamfirescu), Marius Lăcătuş (Cap) (31 Roland Nagy), Aurel Augustin Călin (75 Laurenţiu Dumitru Roşu).
Trainer: Dumitru Dumitriu

CLUB BRUGGE: Dany Verlinden; Eric Deflandre (46 Anders Nielsen), Pascal Renier, Dirk Medved, Tjörven de Brul, Günther Verjans (46 Robert Špehar), Gert Claessens, Franky van der Elst (Cap), Gert Verheyen, Sven Vermant, Mario Stanić. Trainer: Hugo Broos

Sent off: Adrian Ilie (56).

Goals: A. Ilie (32, 45), R. Nagy (55)

SLAVIA PRAHA v GRASSHOPPER-CLUB ZÜRICH 0-1 (0-0)

Praha 21.08.1996

Referee: Kim Milton Nielsen (DEN) Attendance: 3,012

SLAVIA: Jaromír Blažek; Martin Penicka, Lubos Kubik, Sladjan Asanin, Jiří Lerch, Edvard Lasota, Pavel Novotný (40 Jaromir Jindracek), Ivo Ulich, Daniel Smejkal (71 Kennedy Chihuri), Jiří Vavra, Karel Vacha (46 Robert Vagner).
Trainer: František Cipro

GRASSHOPPER: Pascal Zuberbühler; Harald Gämperle, Mats Gren, Boris Smiljanic, Patrick Thüler; Joël Magnin (80 Bernt Haas), Murat Yakin, Antonio Esposito, Alexandre Comisetti (68 Tomasz Rzasa); Dinu Viorel Moldovan, Kubilay Türkyılmaz (74 Marcel Koller). Trainer: Christian Gross

Goal: Türkyılmaz (70)

SK RAPID WIEN v FC DYNAMO KYIV 2-0 (1-0)

Wien 7.08.1996

Referee: Anders Frisk (SWE) Attendance: 29,500

RAPID: Michael Konsel; Trifon Ivanov, Thomas Zingler, Andrzej Lesiak; Krzysztof Ratajczyk, Christian Prosenik, Zoran Barisic (46 Roman Pivarnik), Peter Stöger (46 Peter Guggi), Sergei Mandreko, Dietmar Kühbauer, Christian Stumpf. Trainer: Ernst Dokupil

DINAMO: Igor Kutepov; Olexandr Holovko, Serhiy Bezhenar, Mykola Volosyanko, Yuri Dmitrulin, Yevhen Pokhlebayev (69 Vasyl Kardash), Yuri Maksimov, Yuri Kalitvintsev (60 Olexandr Khatskevich), Vitaliy Kosovskyi, Viktor Leonenko, Serhiy Rebrov. Trainer: Jozsef Szabo

Goals: Stumpf (8), Guggi (90)

FC DYNAMO KYIV v SK RAPID WIEN 2-4 (1-3)

Republikanskiy, Kyiv 21.08.1996

Referee: Serge Muhmenthaler (SWI) Attendance: 50,000

DINAMO: Alexander Shovkovskyi; Oleg Luzhnyi, Olexandr Holovko, Olexandr Khatskevich, Mykola Volosyanko (65 Vladislav Vashchuk), Yuri Maksimov, Yuri Kalitvintsev, Dmytro Mikhailenko, Serhiy Rebrov, Vasyl Kardash (46 Yevhen Pokhlebayev), Viktor Leonenko.
Trainer: Jozsef Szabo

RAPID: Michael Konsel; Thomas Zingler, Andrzej Lesiak, Trifon Ivanov, Peter Schöttel, Krzysztof Ratajczyk, Christian Stumpf (75 Marek Penksa), Andreas Heraf, Sergei Mandreko, Dietmar Kühbauer, Christian Prosenik.
Trainer: Ernst Dokupil

Goals: Kalitvintsev (6), Ivanov (23, 42), Kühbauer (32), Holovko (62 og), Maksimov (77)

GLASGOW RANGERS FC v AJ AUXERRE 1-2 (0-0)

Ibrox Stadium, Glasgow 25.09.1996

Referee: Václav Krondl (CZE) Attendance: 37,344

RANGERS: Andy Goram; Craig Moore (78 Erik Bo Andersen), Richard Gough, Joachim Björklund, Alex Cleland, Derek McInnes, Paul Gascoigne, Jörg Albertz, Gordon Durie (64 Ian Ferguson), Peter Van Vossen, Brian Laudrup.
Manager: Walter Smith

AUXERRE: Lionel Charbonnier; Alain Goma, Taribo West, Frédéric Danjou, Franck Rabarivony; Philippe Violeau, Christian Henna, Moussa Saïb; Sabri Lamouchi, Thomas Deniaud (86 Antoine Sibierski), Bernard Diomède.
Trainer: Guy Roux

Goals: Deniaud (55, 69), Gascoigne (71)

CHAMPIONS LEAGUE

GROUP A

AJ AUXERRE v AFC AJAX AMSTERDAM 0-1 (0-1)

Abbé-Deschamps, Auxerre 11.09.1996

Referee: Piero Ceccarini (ITA) Attendance: 18,512

AUXERRE: Lionel Charbonnier; Alain Goma, Taribo West, Nedijeljko Zelić, Franck Rabarivony; Sabri Lamouchi, Moussa Saïb, Christian Henna, Abdelhafid Tasfaout (78 Antoine Sibierski), Lilian Laslandes (81 Steve Marlet), Bernard Diomède. Trainer: Guy Roux

AJAX: Edwin van der Sar; Márcio Santos, Mario Melchiot (81 Menno Willems), Frank De Boer, Winston Bogarde, Mariano Juan, Jari Litmanen (90 Martijn Reuser), Kiki Musampa, Tijjani Babangida, Ronald De Boer, Marc Overmars (63 Rody Turpijn). Trainer: Louis van Gaal

Goal: Litmanen (3)

GRASSHOPPER-CLUB ZÜRICH v GLASGOW RANGERS FC 3-0 (2-0)

Hardturm, Zürich 11.09.1996

Referee: José María Garcia Aranda (SPA) Att: 20,030

GRASSHOPPER: Pascal Zuberbühler; Harald Gämperle, Bernt Haas, Mats Gren, Patrick Thüler; Joël Magnin (73 Massimo Lombardo), Johann Vogel, Antonio Esposito (88 Marcel Koller), Murat Yakin; Dinu Viorel Moldovan, Kubilay Türkyılmaz (86 Tomasz Rzasa). Trainer: Christian Gross

RANGERS: Andy Goram; Joachim Björklund, Richard Gough, Gordan Petric, Alex Cleland (59 Derek McInnes), Paul Gascoigne, Stuart McCall, Gordon Durie (80 Charles Miller), Jörg Albertz, Alistair McCoist (69 Peter Van Vossen), Brian Laudrup. Manager: Walter Smith

Goals: Yakin (18), Türkyılmaz (28, 79)

AFC AJAX AMSTERDAM v GRASSHOPPER-CLUB ZÜRICH 0-1 (0-0)

Amsterdam ArenA, Amsterdam 25.09.1996

Referee: Günther Benkö (AUS) Attendance: 43,134

AJAX: Edwin van der Sar; Márcio Santos, Danny Blind, Frank De Boer, Winston Bogarde, Mariano Juan (68 Mario Melchiot), Jari Litmanen (46 Nordin Wooter), Kiki Musampa, Tijjani Babangida (75 Arnold Scholten), Ronald De Boer, Marc Overmars. Trainer: Louis van Gaal

GRASSHOPPER: Pascal Zuberbühler; Harald Gämperle, Mats Gren, Bernt Haas, Patrick Thüler; Massimo Lombardo (89 Marcel Koller), Murat Yakin, Antonio Esposito, Johann Vogel; Dinu Viorel Moldovan (89 Boris Smiljanic), Joël Magnin (78 Alexandre Comisetti). Trainer: Christian Gross

Goal: Yakin (60)

AFC AJAX AMSTERDAM v GLASGOW RANGERS FC 4-1 (2-0)

Amsterdam ArenA, Amsterdam 16.10.1996

Referee: Hellmut Krug (GER) Attendance: 48,467

AJAX: Edwin van der Sar; John Veldman, Márcio Santos, Frank De Boer, Winston Bogarde, Arnold Scholten, Dani (78 Nordin Wooter), Martijn Reuser (41 Richard Witschge), Tijjani Babangida, Ronald De Boer, Marc Overmars.
Trainer: Louis van Gaal

RANGERS: Theo Snelders; Craig Moore, Richard Gough, Joachim Björklund, Alex Cleland, Stuart McCall, Paul Gascoigne, Derek McInnes (81 Charles Miller), Jörg Albertz, Ian Ferguson (85 Ian Durrant), Brian Laudrup (81 Peter Van Vossen). Manager: Walter Smith

Goals: Dani (25, 41), Babangida (83), Durrant (88), Wooter (89)

AJ AUXERRE v GRASSHOPPER-CLUB ZÜRICH 1-0 (1-0)

Abbé-Deschamps, Auxerre 16.10.1996

Referee: Rune Pedersen (NOR) Attendance: 17,000

AUXERRE: Lionel Charbonnier; Alain Goma, Taribo West, Frédéric Danjou, Franck Rabarivony; Philippe Violeau, Christian Henna, Moussa Saïb; Sabri Lamouchi (82 Antoine Sibierski), Thomas Deniaud, Bernard Diomède.
Trainer: Guy Roux

GRASSHOPPER: Pascal Zuberbühler; Patrick Thüler (80 Joël Magnin), Mats Gren, Boris Smiljanic, Bernt Haas; Alexandre Comisetti (68 Jan Berger), Johann Vogel, Massimo Lombardo, Antonio Esposito (76 Nestor Subiat); Dinu Viorel Moldovan, Kubilay Türkyılmaz. Trainer: Christian Gross

Goal: Deniaud (42)

AFC AJAX AMSTERDAM v AJ AUXERRE 1-2 (1-1)

Amsterdam ArenA, Amsterdam 20.11.1996

Referee: Nikolai Levnikov (RUS) Attendance: 48,700

AJAX: Edwin van der Sar; John Veldman (22 Arno Splinter), Mario Melchiot, Winston Bogarde, Menno Willems, Nordin Wooter (64 Dani), Arnold Scholten, Ronald De Boer, Tijjani Babangida, Patrick Kluivert, Marc Overmars.
Trainer: Louis van Gaal

AUXERRE: Lionel Charbonnier; Taribo West, Franck Silvestre, Frédéric Danjou, Eric Assati (70 Frédéric Jay); Christian Henna, Philippe Violeau, Moussa Saïb; Steve Marlet, Lilian Laslandes (46 Abdelhafid Tasfaout), Bernard Diomède (86 Fabrice Lepaul). Trainer: Guy Roux

Goals: Diomède (11), Babangida (44), Marlet (56)

GLASGOW RANGERS FC v AFC AJAX AMSTERDAM 0-1 (0-1)

Ibrox Stadium, Glasgow 30.10.1996

Referee: Anders Frisk (SWE) Attendance: 42,265

RANGERS: Theo Snelders; Greg Shields, Joachim Björklund, Gordan Petric, Scott Wilson (85 Erik Bo Andersen), David Robertson, Derek McInnes (81 Alistair McCoist), Charles Miller (59 Peter Van Vossen), Jörg Albertz, Ian Durrant, Brian Laudrup. Manager: Walter Smith

AJAX: Edwin van der Sar; John Veldman, Frank De Boer (69 Nordin Wooter), Márcio Santos, Arnold Scholten, Richard Witschge, Mario Melchiot, Ronald De Boer, Tijjani Babangida (71 Dani), Patrick Kluivert, Marc Overmars (78 Rody Turpijn).
Trainer: Louis van Gaal

Goal: Scholten (38)

GLASGOW RANGERS FC v GRASSHOPPER-CLUB ZÜRICH 2-1 (0-0)

Ibrox Stadium, Glasgow 20.11.1996

Referee: László Vagner (HUN) Attendance: 34,192

RANGERS: Andy Goram; Alex Cleland, Richard Gough, Gordan Petric, David Robertson, Charles Miller, Craig Moore, Jörg Albertz, Peter Van Vossen (81 Erik Bo Andersen), Alistair McCoist, Scott Wilson. Manager: Walter Smith

GRASSHOPPER: Pascal Zuberbühler; Bernt Haas, Alain Geiger, Boris Smiljanic, Patrick Thüler; Massimo Lombardo, Antonio Esposito, Johann Vogel (80 Nestor Subiat), Alexandre Comisetti (64 Jan Berger); Joël Magnin, Kubilay Türkyılmaz.
Trainer: Christian Gross

Goals: McCoist (65 pen, 72), Berger (76)

GRASSHOPPER-CLUB ZÜRICH v AJ AUXERRE 3-1 (2-0)

Hardturm, Zürich 30.10.1996

Referee: Vadim Zhuk (BLS) Attendance: 19,200

GRASSHOPPER: Pascal Zuberbühler; Bernt Haas, Mats Gren, Boris Smiljanic, Patrick Thüler; Murat Yakin, Antonio Esposito (85 Joël Magnin), Johann Vogel (78 Alexandre Comisetti), Massimo Lombardo (89 Harald Gämperle); Kubilay Türkyılmaz, Dinu Viorel Moldovan.
Trainer: Christian Gross

AUXERRE: Lionel Charbonnier; Alain Goma, Taribo West, Frédéric Danjou, Eric Assati; Christian Henna, Philippe Violeau, Antoine Sibierski, Moussa Saïb; Steve Marlet, Bernard Diomède (66 Abdelhafid Tasfaout). Trainer: Guy Roux

Goals: Moldovan (17, 29 pen), Gren (48ag, 59)

GRASSHOPPER-CLUB ZÜRICH v AFC AJAX AMSTERDAM 0-1 (0-1)

Hardturm, Zürich 4.12.1996

Referee: Pier Luigi Collina (ITA) Attendance: 20,000

GRASSHOPPER: Pascal Zuberbühler; Georgios Nemtsoudis, Mats Gren, Boris Smiljanic, Patrick Thüler; Massimo Lombardo, Murat Yakin, Antonio Esposito (21 Alexandre Comisetti), Johann Vogel (65 Joël Magnin); Dinu Viorel Moldovan, Nestor Subiat. Trainer: Christian Gross

AJAX: Edwin van der Sar; John Veldman (41 Mario Melchiot), Arno Splinter, Arnold Scholten, Frank De Boer, Ronald De Boer, Martijn Reuser (65 Jari Litmanen), Kiki Musampa, Tijjani Babangida (82 Nordin Wooter), Patrick Kluivert, Marc Overmars. Trainer: Louis van Gaal

Goal: Kluivert (31)

AJ AUXERRE v GLASGOW RANGERS FC 2-1 (2-1)

Abbé-Deschamps, Auxerre 4.12.1996

Referee: Kim Milton Nielsen (DEN) 21,300

AUXERRE: Fabien Cool; Alain Goma, Franck Silvestre, Frédéric Danjou, Franck Rabarivony; Philippe Violeau, Eric Assati, Moussa Saïb; Steve Marlet, Lilian Laslandes, Fabrice Lepaul (76 Antoine Sibierski). Trainer: Guy Roux

RANGERS: Andy Goram; Greg Shields, Richard Gough, Gordan Petric (60 Alistair McCoist), Craig Moore, David Robertson, Ian Ferguson, Trevor Steven, Derek McInnes, Peter Van Vossen (46 Scott Wilson), Erik Bo Andersen. Manager: Walter Smith

Goals: Laslandes (20), Marlet (32), Gough (36)

	P	W	D	L	F	A	Pts
AJ Auxerre	6	4	0	2	8	7	12
AFC Ajax Amsterdam	6	4	0	2	8	4	12
Grasshoppers Zürich	6	3	0	3	8	5	9
Glasgow Rangers FC	6	1	0	5	5	13	3

GROUP B

BORUSSIA DORTMUND v WIDZEW LÓDZ 2-1 (1-0)

Westfalenstadion, Dortmund 11.09.1996

Referee: Karol Ihring (Slvk) Attendance: 39,600

BORUSSIA: Stefan Klos; Jürgen Kohler, Matthias Sammer, JÚLIO CÉSAR Silva, Stefan Reuter, Paul Lambert (24 Wolfgang Feiersinger), Andreas Möller, Michael Zorc, Jörg Heinrich, Heiko Herrlich (77 René Tretschok), Stéphane Chapuisat (90 Vladimir But). Trainer: Ottmar Hitzfeld

WIDZEW: Maciej Szczesny; Pawel Wojtala, Tomasz Lapinski, Andriy Mikhalchuk, Miroslaw Szymkowiak (73 Marek Bajor), Slawomir Majak, Ryszard Czerwiec, Radoslaw Michalski, Rafal Siadaczka (81 Piotr Szarpak), Jacek Dembinski, Marek Citko. Trainer: Franciszek Smuda

Goals: Herrlich (45, 68), Citko (84)

ATLÉTICO MADRID v STEAUA BUCUREŞTI 4-0 (2-0)

Vicente Calderón, Madrid 11.09.1996

Referee: Kim Milton Nielsen (DEN) Attendance: 46,000

ATLÉTICO: José Francisco MOLINA Giménez; Delfí GELI Roura, Antonio Muñoz Gómez "TONI", Roberto SOLOZÁBAL Villanueva (Cap), Santiago Denia Sánchez SANTI; Radek Bejbl, Milinko Pantic, Carlos AGUILERA Martín (65 Juan Manuel LÓPEZ Martínez), Diego Pablo SIMEONE; Francisco Narváez Machón KIKO (62 JUAN CARLOS Gómez), Juan Eduardo ESNÁIDER (83 Leonardo Angel BIAGINI). Trainer: Radomir Antić

STEAUA: Daniel Gherasim; Tiberiu Csik, Marius Achim Baciu, Daniel Claudiu Prodan (Cap), Roland Nagy; Damian Militaru, Bogdan Bucur, Denis Şerban (88 Ioan Leonard Nemţanu), Laurenţiu Dumitru Roşu; Aurel Augustin Călin (67 Tudorel Zamfirescu), Sabin Ilie (52 Cristian Ciocoiu). Trainer: Dumitru Dumitriu **Sent off**: Baciu (27)

Goals: Esnáider (33, 45), Simeone (64, 84)

STEAUA BUCUREŞTI v BORUSSIA DORTMUND 0-3 (0-2)

Steaua, Bucureşti 25.09.1996

Referee: Paul Durkin (ENG) Attendance: 15,000

STEAUA: Daniel Gherasim (46 Bogdan Stelea); Iulian Sebastian Filipescu, Tiberiu Csik, Daniel Claudiu Prodan, Roland Nagy; Damian Militaru, Bogdan Bucur (46 Tudorel Zamfirescu), Denis Şerban, Sabin Ilie (62 Laurenţiu Dumitru Roşu); Marius Mihai Lăcătuş (Cap), Aurel Augustin Călin. Trainer: Dumitru Dumitriu

BORUSSIA: Stefan Klos; Wolfgang Feiersinger, Stefan Reuter, Jürgen Kohler, JÚLIO CÉSAR Silva, Michael Zorc (Cap), Paul Lambert, Andreas Möller (86 Vladimir But), Jörg Heinrich (83 René Tretschok), Heiko Herrlich, Lars Ricken (75 Stéphane Chapuisat). Trainer: Ottmar Hitzfeld

Goals: Ricken (7), Heinrich (37), Chapuisat (77)

WIDZEW LÓDZ v ATLÉTICO MADRID 1-4 (1-2)

Widzew, Lódz 25.09.1996

Referee: Anders Frisk (SWE) Attendance: 10,000

WIDZEW: Maciej Szczesny; Pawel Wojtala, Miroslaw Szymkowiak (76 Marcin Zajac), Radoslaw Michalski, Andriy Mikhalchuk, Piotr Szarpak (12 Zbigniew Wyciszkiewicz, 62 Pawel Miaszkiewicz), Slawomir Majak, Marek Bajor, Daniel Bogusz, Jacek Dembinski, Marek Citko. Trainer: Franciszek Smuda

ATLÉTICO: José Francisco MOLINA Giménez; Delfí GELI Roura, Santiago Denia Sánchez SANTI, Roberto SOLOZÁBAL Villanueva, Antonio Muñoz Gómez «TONI»; Carlos AGUILERA Martín (68 Juan Manuel LÓPEZ Martínez), Radek Bejbl, Milinko Pantic, Diego Pablo SIMEONE (78 PABLO Alfaro Armengot); Francisco Narváez Machón KIKO (82 ROBERTO Fresnedoso Prieto), Juan Eduardo ESNÁIDER. Trainer: Radomir Antić

Goals: Pantic (25), Simeone (32, 58), Citko (45), Kiko (60)

STEAUA BUCUREŞTI v WIDZEW LÓDZ 1-0 (0-0)

Steaua, Bucureşti 16.10.1996

Referee: Giorgos Bikas (GRE) Attendance: 10,000

STEAUA: Bogdan Stelea; Iulian Sebastian Filipescu, Marius Achim Baciu, Tiberiu Csik, Roland Nagy, Tudorel Zamfirescu; Aurel Augustin Călin (46 Laurenţiu Dumitru Roşu), Denis Şerban, Damian Militaru; Sabin Ilie (46 Cristian Ciocoiu, 89 Ilie Iulian Miu), Marius Mihai Lăcătuş (Cap). Trainer: Dumitru Dumitriu

WIDZEW: Maciej Szczesny; Marek Bajor, Pawel Wojtala, Tomasz Lapinski (Cap), Daniel Bogusz, Miroslaw Szymkowiak, Radoslaw Michalski, Pawel Miaszkiewicz (84 Marcin Zajac), Slawomir Majak, Marek Citko, Jacek Dembinski. Trainer: Franciszek Smuda

Goal: Bogusz (83 og)

ATLÉTICO MADRID v BORUSSIA DORTMUND 0-1 (0-0)

Vicente Calderón, Madrid 16.10.1996

Referee: Michel Piraux (BEL) Attendance: 50,000

ATLÉTICO: José Francisco MOLINA Giménez; Delfí GELI Roura, Santiago Denia Sánchez SANTI, Roberto SOLOZÁBAL Villanueva, Antonio Muñoz Gómez «TONI»; Radek Bejbl (75 JUAN CARLOS Gómez), Carlos AGUILERA Martín (78 Juan Manuel LÓPEZ Martínez), Milinko Pantic, Diego Pablo SIMEONE; Francisco Narváez Machón KIKO, Juan Eduardo ESNÁIDER. Trainer: Radomir Antić

BORUSSIA: Stefan Klos; Jürgen Kohler, JÚLIO CÉSAR Silva (67 Martin Kree), Wolfgang Feiersinger, Stefan Reuter, Lars Ricken (70 Jovan Kirovski), Michael Zorc, Paul Lambert, Jörg Heinrich, René Tretschok (85 Heiko Herrlich), Stéphane Chapuisat. Trainer: Ottmar Hitzfeld

Goal: Reuter (51)

WIDZEW LÓDZ v STEAUA BUCUREŞTI 2-0 (1-0)

Widzew, Lódz 30.10.1996

Referee: Graziano Cesari (ITA) Attendance: 8,000

WIDZEW: Maciej Szczesny; Pawel Wojtala, Tomasz Lapinski (Cap), Daniel Bogusz, Miroslaw Szymkowiak, Radoslaw Michalski, Ryszard Czerwiec, Slawomir Majak, Andriy Mikhalchuk, Marek Citko, Jacek Dembinski (87 Zbigniew Wyciszkiewicz). Trainer: Franciszek Smuda

STEAUA: Bogdan Stelea; Tudorel Zamfirescu, Daniel Claudiu Prodan, Tiberiu Csik, Ilie Iulian Miu, Roland Nagy, Damian Militaru, Adrian Ilie, Denis Şerban (65 Laurenţiu Dumitru Roşu), Marius Mihai Lăcătuş (Cap) (75 Cristian Ciocoiu), Aurel Augustin Călin (57 Sabin Ilie). Trainer: Dumitru Dumitriu

Goals: Majak (40), Czerwiec (48)

BORUSSIA DORTMUND v ATLÉTICO MADRID 1-2 (1-2)

Westfalenstadion, Dortmund 30.10.1996

Referee: László Vagner (HUN) Attendance: 45,000

BORUSSIA: Stefan Klos; Steinar Pedersen (82 Jovan Kirovski), Stefan Reuter, JÚLIO CÉSAR Silva, Michael Zorc, Paul Lambert, Andreas Möller, Knut Reinhardt, Heiko Herrlich, Stéphane Chapuisat, René Tretschok (68 Lars Ricken). Trainer: Ottmar Hitzfeld

ATLÉTICO: José Francisco MOLINA Giménez; Delfí GELI Roura (60 Juan Manuel LÓPEZ Martínez), Santiago Denia Sánchez SANTI, Roberto SOLOZÁBAL Villanueva, Antonio Muñoz Gómez «TONI»; ROBERTO Fresnedoso Prieto, Juan VIZCAÍNO Morcillo, Milinko Pantic (83 Carlos AGUILERA Martín), Radek Bejbl; Francisco Narváez Machón KIKO, Juan Eduardo ESNÁIDER (79 PABLO Alfaro Armengot). Trainer: Radomir Antić

Goals: Herrlich (17), Roberto (37), Pantic (42)

WIDZEW LÓDZ v BORUSSIA DORTMUND 2-2 (2-1)

Widzew, Lódz 20.11.1996

Referee: Rune Pedersen (NOR) Attendance: 18,000

WIDZEW: Maciej Szczesny; Pawel Wojtala, Tomasz Lapinski, Daniel Bogusz, Miroslaw Szymkowiak (56 Zbigniew Wyciszkiewicz), Radoslaw Michalski, Ryszard Czerwiec, Slawomir Majak, Andriy Mikhalchuk, Marek Citko, Jacek Dembinski. Trainer: Franciszek Smuda

BORUSSIA: Stefan Klos; Jürgen Kohler, Matthias Sammer, Jörg Heinrich, René Tretschok (22 Stéphane Chapuisat), Stefan Reuter, Paul Lambert, Andreas Möller, Lars Ricken (82 Ibrahim Tanko), Knut Reinhardt (90 Martin Kree), Heiko Herrlich. Trainer: Ottmar Hitzfeld

Goals: Lambert (14), Dembinski (15, 20), Kohler (65)

STEAUA BUCUREŞTI v ATLÉTICO MADRID 1-1 (0-1)

Steaua, Bucureşti 20.11.1996

Referee: Urs Meier (SWI) Attendance: 18,000

STEAUA: Bogdan Stelea; Roland Nagy, Daniel Claudiu Prodan, Marius Achim Baciu, Ilie Iulian Miu; Damian Militaru (72 Laurenţiu Dumitru Roşu), Bogdan Bucur (71 Ioan Leonard Nemţanu), Aurel Augustin Călin (27 Cristian Ciocoiu), Denis Şerban; Marius Mihai Lăcătuş (Cap), Sabin Ilie. Trainer: Dumitru Dumitriu

ATLÉTICO: José Francisco MOLINA Giménez; Delfí GELI Roura, Roberto SOLOZÁBAL Villanueva (Cap), Juan Manuel LÓPEZ Martínez, PABLO Alfaro Armengot; José Luis Pérez CAMINERO, Radek Bejbl, Milinko Pantic (72 Juan VIZCAÍNO Morcillo), Diego Pablo SIMEONE (89 Carlos AGUILERA Martín); Francisco Narváez Machón KIKO, Juan Eduardo ESNÁIDER (83 JUAN CARLOS Gómez). Trainer: R. Antić

Goals: Pantic (25), S. Ilie (46)

BORUSSIA DORTMUND v STEAUA BUCUREŞTI 5-3 (3-1)

Westfallenstadion, Dortmund 4.12.1996

Referee: Hugh Dallas (SCO) Attendance: 37,000

BORUSSIA: Stefan Klos; Matthias Sammer, Jürgen Kohler, Martin Kree, Jörg Heinrich (67 Steinar Pedersen), Paul Lambert, Michael Zorc (Cap), Knut Reinhardt, René Tretschok, Stéphane Chapuisat, Karlheinz Riedle (64 Ibrahim Tanko). Trainer: Ottmar Hitzfeld

STEAUA: Bogdan Stelea (Cap); Ilie Iulian Miu, Tiberiu Csik, Bogdan Bucur, Marius Achim Baciu; Damian Militaru, Roland Nagy, Denis Şerban (65 Ioan Leonard Nemţanu), Laurenţiu Dumitru Roşu (46 Cristian Ciocoiu); Sabin Ilie, Aurel Augustin Călin. Trainer: Dumitru Dumitriu

Goals: Chapuisat (13, 22), S. Ilie (17 pen), Tretschok (43), Baciu (52), Riedle (63), Zorc (65), Călin (79)

ATLÉTICO MADRID v WIDZEW LÓDZ 1-0 (0-0)

Vicente Calderón, Madrid 4.12.1996

Referee: Václav Krondl (CZE) Attendance: 23,000

ATLÉTICO: José Francisco MOLINA Giménez; Delfí GELI Roura, Santiago Denia Sánchez SANTI, PABLO Alfaro Armengot, Antonio Muñoz Gómez "TONI"; José Luis Pérez CAMINERO (46 Carlos AGUILERA Martín), Juan VIZCAÍNO Morcillo (46 Radek Bejbl), Milinko Pantic, Diego Pablo SIMEONE (86 Juan Manuel LÓPEZ Martínez); Francisco Narváez Machón KIKO, Juan Eduardo ESNÁIDER. Trainer: Radomir Antić

WIDZEW: Maciej Szczesny; Tomasz Lapinski, Radoslaw Michalski, Daniel Bogusz, Pawel Wojtala, Miroslaw Szymkowiak (88 Pawel Miaszkiewicz), Slawomir Majak, Ryszard Czerwiec, Andriy Mikhalchuk (78 Zbigniew Wyciszkiewicz), Jacek Dembinski, Marek Citko. Trainer: Franciszek Smuda

Goal: Pantić (83)

	P	W	D	L	F	A	Pts
Atlético Madrid	6	4	1	1	12	4	13
Borussia Dortmund	6	4	1	1	14	8	13
Widzew Lódz	6	1	1	4	6	10	4
Steaua Bucureşti	6	1	1	4	5	15	4

GROUP C

JUVENTUS FC TORINO v MANCHESTER UNITED FC 1-0 (1-0)

Stadio delle Alpi, Torino 11.09.1996

Referee: Markus Merk (GER) Attendance: 50,000

JUVENTUS: Angelo Peruzzi; Ciro Ferrara, Paolo Montero (90 Mark Juliano), Sergio Porrini, Gianluca Pessotto; Antonio Conte, Didier Deschamps, Zinedine Zidane (77 Angelo Di Livio); Alessandro del Piero, Christian Vieri (73 Nicola Amoruso), Alen Boksic. Trainer: Marcello Lippi

MANCHESTER UNITED: Peter Schmeichel; Gary Neville, Dennis Irwin, Ronny Johnsen, Gary Pallister, Nicky Butt, David Beckham, Ryan Giggs (46 Brian McClair), Eric Cantona, Karel Poborsky (76 Ole Gunnar Solskjaer), Jordi Cruijff (76 Andy Cole). Manager: Alex Ferguson

Goal: Boksić (33)

SK RAPID WIEN v FENERBAHÇE ISTANBUL 1-1 (0-1)

Wien 11.09.1996

Referee: Michel Piraux (BEL) Attendance: 41,500

RAPID: Michael Konsel; Peter Guggi (59 Patrick Jovanovic), Trifon Ivanov, Peter Schöttel, René Wagner (57 Peter Stöger), Andreas Heraf, Dietmar Kühbauer, Christian Prosenik, Andrzej Lesiak, Thomas Zingler, Marek Penksa (57 Christian Stumpf). Trainer: Ernst Dokupil

FENERBAHÇE: Rüstü Reçber; Ilker Yagcioglu, Uche Okechukwu, Jes Høgh, Tayfun Korkut, Halil Ibrahim Kara, Tarik Dasgün (79 Tuncay Akgün), Augustine Okocha, Kemalettin Sentürk, Bülent Uygun, Elvir Bolić. Trainer: Sebastiao Lazaroni

Goals: Bolic (31), Stumpf (70)

FENERBAHÇE ISTANBUL v JUVENTUS FC TORINO 0-1 (0-1)

Fenerbahçe, Istanbul 25.09.1996

Referee: Serge Muhmenthaler (SWI) Attendance: 29,000

FENERBAHÇE: Rüstü Reçber; Ilker Yagcioglu, Jes Høgh, Uche Okechukwu, Halil Ibrahim Kara, Bülent Uygun, Augustine Okocha, Kemalettin Sentürk, Tuncay Akgün (81 Erol Bulut), Tarik Dasgün (87 Benhur Babaoglu), Elvir Bolić. Trainer: Sebastiao Lazaroni

JUVENTUS: Michelangelo Rampulla; Ciro Ferrara, Paolo Montero, Sergio Porrini, Gianluca Pessotto; Antonio Conte, Didier Deschamps, Zinedine Zidane (69 Angelo Di Livio); Christian Vieri (59 Michele Padovano), Alen Boksic, Alessandro del Piero (82 Alessio Tacchinardi). Trainer: Marcello Lippi

Goal: Boksić (22)

MANCHESTER UNITED FC
v SK RAPID WIEN **2-0** (2-0)

Old Trafford, Manchester 25.09.1996

Referee: Rémy Harrel (FRA) Attendance: 51,831

MANCHESTER UNITED: Peter Schmeichel; Gary Neville, Gary Pallister, Ronny Johnsen (18 David May), Dennis Irwin, Roy Keane, David Beckham, Eric Cantona, Ryan Giggs, Karel Poborsky (79 Nicky Butt), Ole Gunnar Solskjaer (74 Andy Cole). Manager: Alex Ferguson

RAPID: Michael Konsel; Peter Schöttel, Trifon Ivanov, Andrzej Lesiak, Christian Prosenik, Andreas Heraf, Dietmar Kühbauer, Thomas Zingler (71 Patrick Jovanovic), Peter Stöger (63 Zoran Barisic), Krzysztof Ratajczyk, René Wagner (63 Christian Stumpf). Trainer: Ernst Dokupil

Goals: Solskjaer (19), Beckham (27)

MANCHESTER UNITED FC
v FENERBAHÇE ISTANBUL **0-1** (0-0)

Old Trafford, Manchester 30.10.1996

Referee: Mario van der Ende (HOL) Attendance: 53,297

MANCHESTER UNITED: Peter Schmeichel; Gary Neville (82 Philip Neville), David May, Ronny Johnsen, Dennis Irwin, Karel Poborsky (67 Paul Scholes), David Beckham, Roy Keane, Nicky Butt, Jordi Cruijff (67 Ole Gunnar Solskjaer), Eric Cantona. Manager: Alex Ferguson

FENERBAHÇE: Rüstü Reçber; Ilker Yagcioglu, Jes Høgh (79 Bülent Uygun), Uche Okechukwu, Kemalettin Sentürk, Tuncay Akgün (73 Mustafa Dogan), Saffet Akbas, Erol Bulut, Augustine Okocha, Emil Kostadinov, Elvir Bolić (82 Tarik Dasgün). Trainer: Sebastiao Lazaroni

Goal: Bolic (78)

FENERBAHÇE ISTANBUL
v MANCHESTER UNITED FC **0-2** (0-0)

Fenerbahçe, Istanbul 16.10.1996

Referee: Manuel Diaz Vega (SPA) Attendance: 26,000

FENERBAHÇE: Rüstü Reçber; Ilker Yagcioglu, Jes Høgh, Uche Okechukwu, Bülent Uygun (64 Erol Bulut), Tuncay Akgün (84 Tarik Dasgün), Kemalettin Sentürk, Augustine Okocha, Halil Ibrahim Kara; Emil Kostadinov (84 Aygün Taskiran), Elvir Bolić. Trainer: Sebastiao Lazaroni

MANCHESTER UNITED: Peter Schmeichel; Gary Neville, David May, Gary Pallister, Dennis Irwin, David Beckham, Eric Cantona, Ronny Johnsen, Nicky Butt, Ole Gunnar Solskjaer, Jordi Cruijff (73 Karel Poborsky). Manager: Alex Ferguson

Goals: Beckham (55), Cantona (60)

JUVENTUS FC TORINO
v SK RAPID WIEN **5-0** (3-0)

Stadio delle Alpi, Torino 30.10.1996

Referee: Hugh Dallas (SCO) Attendance: 26,143

JUVENTUS: Angelo Peruzzi; Moreno Torricelli, Ciro Ferrara, Paolo Montero, Gianluca Pessotto (71 Sergio Porrini); Didier Deschamps, Vladimir Jugović, Angelo Di Livio (64 Attilio Lombardo); Zinedine Zidane, Alessandro del Piero, Alen Boksic (65 Michele Padovano). Trainer: Marcello Lippi

RAPID: Michael Konsel; Thomas Zingler, Trifon Ivanov, Peter Schöttel, Christian Prosenik, Andreas Heraf, Dietmar Kühbauer, Peter Stöger (65 Roman Pivarnik), Marek Penksa (46 Krzysztof Ratajczyk), Sergei Mandreko, Christian Stumpf (46 Patrick Jovanovic). Trainer: Ernst Dokupil

Goals: Boksic (5, 59), Montero (27), Del Piero (29, 75)

SK RAPID WIEN
v JUVENTUS FC TORINO **1-1** (1-1)

Wien 16.10.1996

Referee: Kim Milton Nielsen (DEN) Attendance: 46,500

RAPID: Michael Konsel; Thomas Zingler, Trifon Ivanov, Peter Schöttel, Christian Prosenik, Dietmar Kühbauer, Andreas Heraf, Peter Stöger, Andrzej Lesiak, Christian Stumpf, René Wagner (69 Sergei Mandreko). Trainer: Ernst Dokupil

JUVENTUS: Michelangelo Rampulla; Sergio Porrini, Ciro Ferrara, Paolo Montero, Moreno Torricelli; Angelo Di Livio, Didier Deschamps (84 Gianluca Pessotto), Alessio Tacchinardi (71 Attilio Lombardo), Vladimir Jugović; Alen Boksic, Christian Vieri (63 Michele Padovano). Trainer: Marcello Lippi

Goals: Vieri (9), Lesiak (20)

MANCHESTER UNITED FC
v JUVENTUS FC TORINO **0-1** (0-1)

Old Trafford, Manchester 20.11.1996

Referee: José María Garcia Aranda (SPA) Att: 53,529

MANCHESTER UNITED: Peter Schmeichel; Gary Neville, David May, Ronny Johnsen, Philip Neville (12 Brian McClair), Roy Keane, Nicky Butt, David Beckham, Ryan Giggs, Eric Cantona, Ole Gunnar Solskjaer (82 Jordi Cruijff). Manager: Alex Ferguson

JUVENTUS: Angelo Peruzzi; Sergio Porrini, Ciro Ferrara, Paolo Montero, Moreno Torricelli (83 Mark Juliano); Didier Deschamps, Angelo Di Livio (81 Alessio Tacchinardi), Vladimir Jugović, Zinedine Zidane; Alen Boksic, Alessandro del Piero. Trainer: Marcello Lippi

Goal: Del Piero (37 pen)

FENERBAHÇE ISTANBUL v SK RAPID WIEN 1-0 (0-0)

Fenerbahçe, Istanbul 20.11.1996

Referee: Sándor Puhl (HUN) Attendance: 25,000

FENERBAHÇE: Rüstü Reçber; Ilker Yagcioglu, Jes Høgh, Uche Okechukwu, Kemalettin Sentürk, Tuncay Akgün (52 Mustafa Dogan), Augustine Okocha, Saffet Akbas, Erol Bulut; Emil Kostadinov (89 Tarik Dasgün), Elvir Bolić. Trainer: Sebastiao Lazaroni

RAPID: Michael Konsel; Andrzej Lesiak, Trifon Ivanov, Peter Schöttel, Andreas Heraf, Peter Stöger, Dietmar Kühbauer, Krzysztof Ratajczyk (84 Patrick Jovanovic), Christian Prosenik (78 Peter Guggi), René Wagner, Marek Penksa (78 Christian Stumpf). Trainer: Ernst Dokupil

Goal: Høgh (75)

JUVENTUS FC TORINO v FENERBAHÇE ISTANBUL 2-0 (1-0)

Stadio delle Alpi, Torino 4.12.1996

Referee: Bernd Heynemann (GER) Attendance: 13,000

JUVENTUS: Angelo Peruzzi; Moreno Torricelli, Sergio Porrini, Paolo Montero, Mark Juliano; Angelo Di Livio, Alessio Tacchinardi, Zinedine Zidane (77 Ciro Ferrara), Attilio Lombardo; Michele Padovano (85 Ivano Trotta), Alessandro del Piero (46 Nicola Amoruso). Trainer: Marcello Lippi

FENERBAHÇE: Rüstü Reçber; Ilker Yagcioglu (83 Mustafa Dogan), Uche Okechukwu, Saffet Akbas, Erol Bulut, Kemalettin Sentürk, Jes Høgh (87 Aygün Taskiran), Augustine Okocha, Tuncay Akgün (72 Tarik Dasgün); Elvir Bolić, Emil Kostadinov. Trainer: Sebastiao Lazaroni

Goals: Padovano (41), Amoruso (84)

SK RAPID WIEN v MANCHESTER UNITED FC 0-2 (0-1)

Wien 4.12.1996

Referee: Leif Sundell (SWE) Attendance: 45,000

RAPID: Michael Konsel; Peter Schöttel, Trifon Ivanov, Thomas Zingler, Christian Prosenik, Andreas Heraf, Dietmar Kühbauer, Peter Stöger (66 Sergei Mandreko), Krzysztof Ratajczyk, Christian Stumpf (63 Marek Penksa), René Wagner. Trainer: Ernst Dokupil

MANCHESTER UNITED: Peter Schmeichel; Gary Neville (90 Chris Casper), David May, Gary Pallister, Dennis Irwin, David Beckham, Nicky Butt (82 Karel Poborsky), Roy Keane (77 Brian McClair), Ryan Giggs, Eric Cantona, Ole Gunnar Solskjaer. Manager: Alex Ferguson

Goals: Giggs (24), Cantona (72)

	P	W	D	L	F	A	Pts
Juventus FC Torino	6	5	1	0	11	1	16
Manchester United	6	3	0	3	6	3	9
Fenerbahçe Istanbul	6	2	1	3	3	6	7
Rapid Wien	6	0	2	4	2	12	2

GROUP D

AC MILAN v FC PORTO 2-3 (1-0)

Giuseppe Meazza, Milano 11.09.1996

Referee: Mario Van de Ende (HOL) Attendance: 33,000

AC MILAN: Sebastiano Rossi; Michael Reiziger (40 Mauro Tassotti), Filippo Galli, Paolo Maldini, Christian Panucci; Demetrio Albertini, Marcel Desailly, Zvonimir Boban (70 Stefano Eranio); Marco Simone, Roberto Baggio, George Weah (71 Edgar Davids). Trainer: Oscar Washington Tabarez

FC PORTO: Andrezej Wozniak; Luís Bonfim Marcos "LULA", JORGE Paulo COSTA Almeida, ALOÍSIO Pires Alves (73 Ljubinko Drulovic), João Paulo Maio dos Santos "PAULINHO SANTOS", SÉRGIO Paulo Marceneiro CONCEIÇÃO, FERNANDO Manuel Antunes MENDES, Zlatko Zahovic, José Alberto da Mota BARROSO (62 Mário JARDEL Almeida Ribeiro), EDMILSON Gonçalves Pimenta, ARTUR Duarte de Oliveira (86 RUI Gil Soares de BARROS). Trainer: António Oliveira

Goals: Simone (14), Artur (52), Weah (69), Jardel (75, 83)

IFK GÖTEBORG v ROSENBORG BK TRONDHEIM 2-3 (1-1)

Gamla Ullevi, Göteborg 11.09.1996

Referee: Atanas Uzunov (BUL) Attendance: 23,682

IFK: Thomas Ravelli; Magnus Johansson, Jonas Ohlsson (73 Erik Wahlstedt), Teddy Lucic, Mikael Nilsson, Stefan Landberg, Niclas Alexandersson (83 Mikael Martinsson), Jesper Blomqvist, Stefan Lindqvist, Andreas Andersson, Magnus Erlingmark. Trainer: Mats Jingblad

ROSENBORG: Jørn Jamtfall; Karl Petter Løken, Erik Hoftun, Bjørn Otto Bragstad (74 Tom Kåre Staurvik), Ståle Stensaas; Roar Strand (84 Vegard Heggem), Bent Skammelsrud, Trond Egil Soltvedt; Jahn Ivar Jakobsen, Steffen Iversen, Harald Martin Brattbakk. Trainer: Nils Arne Eggen

Goals: Jakobsen (32), Erlingmark (38, 49), Iversen (52), Brattbakk (64)

ROSENBORG BK TRONDHEIM v AC MILAN 1-4 (1-3)

Lerkendal, Trondheim 25.09.1996

Referee: David Roland Elleray (ENG) Attendance: 20,849

ROSENBORG: Jørn Jamtfall; Karl Petter Løken, Bjørn Otto Bragstad (34 Tom Kåre Staurvik), Erik Hoftun, Ståle Stensaas; Roar Strand (81 Vegard Heggem), Bent Skammelsrud, Trond Egil Soltvedt, Jahn Ivar Jakobsen (77 Bjørn Tore Kvarme), Steffen Iversen; Harald Martin Brattbakk.
Trainer: Nils Arne Eggen

AC MILAN: Sebastiano Rossi; Alessandro Costacurta, Marcel Desailly, Paolo Maldini, Christian Panucci; Massimo Ambrosini, Demetrio Albertini, Edgar Davids, Dejan Savićević (46 Stefano Eranio); George Weah, Marco Simone (73 Roberto Baggio). Trainer: Oscar Washington Tabarez

Goals: Simone (6, 21, 24), Soltvedt (15), Weah (55)

FC PORTO v IFK GÖTEBORG 2-1 (1-0)

Estádio das Antas, Porto 25.09.1996

Referee: Ahmet Çakar (TUR) Attendance: 30,000

FC PORTO: Andrezej Wozniak; SÉRGIO Paulo Marceneiro CONCEIÇÃO, JORGE Paulo COSTA Almeida, ALOÍSIO Pires Alves, Luís Bonfim Marcos "LULA", RUI JORGE de Sousa Dias Macedo de Oliveira, FERNANDO Manuel Antunes MENDES, João Paulo Maio dos Santos "PAULINHO SANTOS", EDMILSON Gonçalves Pimenta (66 António José dos Santos FOLHA), Mário JARDEL Almeida Ribeiro (83 Ljubinko Drulovic), ARTUR Duarte de Oliveira.
Trainer: António Oliveira

IFK: Thomas Ravelli; Stefan Landberg, Jonas Ohlsson, Teddy Lucic, Mikael Nilsson, Niclas Alexandersson, Magnus Erlingmark, Stefan Lindqvist, Jesper Blomqvist, Stefan Pettersson (83 Mikael Martinsson), Andreas Andersson.
Trainer: Mats Jingblad

Goals: Artur (27, 51), Jorge Costa (71 og)

IFK GÖTEBORG v AC MILAN 2-1 (0-0)

Gamla Ullevi, Göteborg 16.10.1996

Referee: Ryszard Wójcik (POL) Attendance: 42,450

IFK: Thomas Ravelli; Mikael Nilsson, Teddy Lucic, Stefan Landberg (78 Magnus Johansson), Jonas Ohlsson, Niclas Alexandersson, Stefan Lindqvist, Magnus Erlingmark, Jesper Blomqvist, Stefan Pettersson (74 Erik Wahlstedt), Andreas Andersson. Trainer: Mats Jingblad

AC MILAN: Sebastiano Rossi; Christian Panucci, Alessandro Costacurta, Marcel Desailly, Paolo Maldini; Tomas Locatelli (70 Michael Reiziger), Demetrio Albertini, Massimo Ambrosini, Zvonimir Boban; George Weah, Marco Simone (78 Christophe Dugarry). Trainer: Oscar Washington Tabarez

Goals: Weah (52), Wahlstedt (75), Alexandersson (84)

ROSENBORG BK TRONDHEIM v FC PORTO 0-1 (0-0)

Lerkendal, Trondheim 16.10.1996

Referee: Charles Agius (MAL) Attendance: 20,412

ROSENBORG: Jørn Jamtfall; Vegard Heggem, Bjørn Tore Kvarme, Erik Hoftun, Ståle Stensaas (85 Tom Kåre Staurvik); Jahn Ivar Jakobsen, Roar Strand, Bent Skammelsrud, Trond Egil Soltvedt, Harald Martin Brattbakk; Steffen Iversen.
Trainer: Nils Arne Eggen

FC PORTO: Henrique HILÁRIO Sampaio; SÉRGIO Paulo Marceneiro CONCEIÇÃO (79 RUI Gil Soares de BARROS), JORGE Paulo COSTA Almeida, ALOÍSIO Pires Alves, FERNANDO Manuel Antunes MENDES, José Alberto da Mota BARROSO, Zlatko Zahovic, EDMILSON Gonçalves Pimenta, João Paulo Maio dos Santos «PAULINHO SANTOS», ARTUR Duarte de Oliveira, Ljubinko Drulovic (69 Mário JARDEL Almeida Ribeiro). Trainer: António Oliveira

Goal: Jardel (90)

AC MILAN v IFK GÖTEBORG 4-2 (3-2)

Giuseppe Meazza, Milano 30.10.1996

Referee: Marc Batta (FRA) Attendance: 29,803

AC MILAN: Sebastiano Rossi; Christian Panucci, Alessandro Costacurta, Marcel Desailly, Paolo Maldini; Demetrio Albertini, Edgar Davids (84 Francesco Coco), Tomas Locatelli (46 Stefano Eranio), Zvonimir Boban; George Weah, Marco Simone (63 Roberto Baggio).
Trainer: Oscar Washington Tabarez

IFK: Thomas Ravelli; Stefan Landberg, Jonas Ohlsson, Teddy Lucic, Mikael Nilsson, Niclas Alexandersson (74 Peter Eriksson), Magnus Erlingmark, Stefan Lindqvist, Jesper Blomqvist, Andreas Andersson (81 Mikael Martinsson), Stefan Pettersson. Trainer: Mats Jingblad

Goals: Boban (4), Albertini (14 pen), Blomqvist (27), Andersson (32), Locatelli (44), Baggio (90)

FC PORTO v ROSENBORG BK TRONDHEIM 3-0 (2-0)

Estádio das Antas, Porto 30.10.1996

Referee: Bernd Heynemann (GER) Attendance: 15,000

FC PORTO: Henrique HILÁRIO Sampaio; JOÃO Domingos Silva PINTO, JORGE Paulo COSTA Almeida, ALOÍSIO Pires Alves, FERNANDO Manuel Antunes MENDES, João Paulo Maio dos Santos "PAULINHO SANTOS", RUI Gil Soares de BARROS (56 SÉRGIO Paulo Marceneiro CONCEIÇÃO), EDMILSON Gonçalves Pimenta (72 José Alberto da Mota BARROSO), Zlatko Zahovic, ARTUR Duarte de Oliveira (62 Mário JARDEL Almeida Ribeiro), Ljubinko Drulović.
Trainer: António Oliveira

ROSENBORG: Jørn Jamtfall; Bjørn Tore Kvarme, Bjørn Otto Bragstad (46 Kristian Sørli), Erik Hoftun, Ståle Stensaas; Vegard Heggem, Roar Strand (78 Karl Oskar Fjørtoft), Bent Skammelsrud, Trond Egil Soltvedt, Harald Martin Brattbakk; Steffen Iversen. Trainer: Nils Arne Eggen

Goals: Zahović (32), Drulović (41), Artur (60)

FC PORTO v AC MILAN 1-1 (0-0)

Estádio das Antas, Porto 20.11.1996

Referee: Gerd Grabher (AUS) Attendance: 50,000

FC PORTO: Henrique HILÁRIO Sampaio; SÉRGIO Paulo Marceneiro CONCEIÇÃO, JORGE Paulo COSTA Almeida, ALOÍSIO Pires Alves, FERNANDO Manuel Antunes MENDES, José Alberto da Mota BARROSO, Manuel Albino Morim Maçaes "BINO" (66 António José dos Santos FOLHA), EDMILSON Gonçalves Pimenta, Zlatko Zahovic, ARTUR Duarte de Oliveira (83 JOÃO MANUEL PINTO Tomé dos Santos), Ljubinko Drulovic (54 Mário JARDEL Almeida Ribeiro). Trainer: António Oliveira

AC MILAN: Sebastiano Rossi; Christian Panucci, Alessandro Costacurta, Franco Baresi, Paolo Maldini; Stefano Eranio (89 Christophe Dugarry), Zvonimir Boban, Marcel Desailly (81 Massimo Ambrosini), Edgar Davids; Roberto Baggio (79 Marco Simone), George Weah.
Trainer: Oscar Washington Tabarez

Goals: Davids (56), Edmilson (71)

IFK GÖTEBORG v FC PORTO 0-2 (0-0)

Gamla Ullevi, Göteborg 4.12.1996

Referee: Dick Jol (HOL) Attendance: 19,448

IFK: Thomas Ravelli; Jonas Ohlsson, Teddy Lucic, Stefan Landberg (18 Magnus Johansson, 83 Erik Wahlstedt), Mikael Nilsson, Peter Eriksson (75 Mats Lilienberg), Magnus Erlingmark, Stefan Lindqvist, Jesper Blomqvist, Stefan Pettersson, Andreas Andersson. Trainer: Mats Jingblad

FC PORTO: Henrique HILÁRIO Sampaio; ALOÍSIO Pires Alves, FERNANDO Manuel Antunes MENDES (46 ARTUR Duarte de Oliveira), SÉRGIO Paulo Marceneiro CONCEIÇÃO, Ljubinko Drulovic (88 António José dos Santos FOLHA), Mário JARDEL Almeida Ribeiro (79 RUI Gil Soares de BARROS), José Alberto da Mota BARROSO, JOÃO MANUEL PINTO Tomé dos Santos, João Paulo Maio dos Santos "PAULINHO SANTOS", EDMILSON Gonçalves Pimenta, Zlatko Zahović. Trainer: António Oliveira

Goals: Jardel (64), Edmilson (89)

ROSENBORG BK TRONDHEIM v IFK GÖTEBORG 1-0 (0-0)

Lerkendal, Trondheim 20.11.1996

Referee: Eric Blareau (BEL) Attendance: 19,849

ROSENBORG: Jørn Jamtfall; Bjørn Tore Kvarme, Erik Hoftun, Jon Olav Hjelde, Ståle Stensaas; Vegard Heggem, Roar Strand (88 Karl Oskar Fjørtoft), Bent Skammelsrud, Trond Egil Soltvedt; Harald Martin Brattbakk, Steffen Iversen. Trainer: Nils Arne Eggen

IFK: Thomas Ravelli; Stefan Landberg, Teddy Lucic, Jonas Ohlsson, Mikael Nilsson, Niclas Alexandersson, Magnus Erlingmark, Stefan Lindqvist (87 Mikael Martinsson), Peter Eriksson, Stefan Pettersson (87 Erik Wahlstedt), Andreas Andersson. Trainer: Mats Jingblad

Goal: Skammelsrud (66 pen)

	P	W	D	L	F	A	Pts
FC Porto	6	5	1	0	12	4	16
Rosenborg BK	6	3	0	3	7	11	9
AC Milan	6	2	1	3	13	11	7
IFK Göteborg	6	1	0	5	7	13	3

AC MILAN v ROSENBORG BK TRONDHEIM 1-2 (1-1)

Giuseppe Meazza, Milano 4.12.1996

Referee: Giorgos Bikas (GRE) Attendance: 28,695

AC MILAN: Sebastiano Rossi; Michael Reiziger (65 Tomas Locatelli), Alessandro Costacurta, Franco Baresi, Paolo Maldini; Demetrio Albertini, Zvonimir Boban, Massimo Ambrosini (46 Christian Panucci), Dejan Savićević; Roberto Baggio (46 Marco Simone), Christophe Dugarry. Trainer: Oscar Washington Tabarez

ROSENBORG: Jørn Jamtfall; Bjørn Tore Kvarme, Jon Olav Hjelde, Erik Hoftun, Ståle Stensaas; Roar Strand (89 Jahn Ivar Jakobsen), Bent Skammelsrud, Trond Egil Soltvedt; Vegard Heggem, Steffen Iversen, Harald Martin Brattbakk. Trainer: Nils Arne Eggen

Goals: Brattbakk (29), Dugarry (45), Heggem (72)

QUARTER-FINALS

BORUSSIA DORTMUND v AJ AUXERRE 3-1 (1-0)

Westfalenstadion, Dortmund 5.03.1997

Referee: José María Garcia Aranda (SPA) Att: 47,500

BORUSSIA: Stefan Klos; Wolfgang Feiersinger (38 René Schneider), Stefan Reuter, Martin Kree, Lars Ricken (90 René Tretschok), PAULO Manuel Carvalho de SOUSA, Andreas Möller, Paul Lambert, Jörg Heinrich, Karlheinz Riedle, Stéphane Chapuisat (81 Ibrahim Tanko).
Trainer: Ottmar Hitzfeld

AUXERRE: Lionel Charbonnier; Taribo West, Franck Silvestre, Frédéric Danjou, Alain Goma; Sabri Lamouchi, Philippe Violeau, Christian Henna (46 Antoine Sibierski), Moussa Saïb; Lilian Laslandes, Bernard Diomède.
Trainer: Guy Roux

Goals: Riedle (13), Schneider (54), Lamouchi (75), Möller (83)

AJ AUXERRE v BORUSSIA DORTMUND 0-1 (0-0)

Abbé-Deschamps, Auxerre 19.03.1997

Referee: Günther Benkö (AUS) Attendance: 21,500

AUXERRE: Lionel Charbonnier; Taribo West (85 Nedijeljko Zelic), Franck Silvestre, Frédéric Danjou, Alain Goma; Philippe Violeau, Moussa Saïb, Sabri Lamouchi; Antoine Sibierski (80 Fabrice Lepaul), Lilian Laslandes, Bernard Diomède. Trainer: Guy Roux

BORUSSIA: Stefan Klos; Matthias Sammer, Jörg Heinrich, Jürgen Kohler, Martin Kree, Lars Ricken (80 Wolfgang Feiersinger), Andreas Möller, PAULO Manuel Carvalho de SOUSA (87 Heiko Herrlich), Paul Lambert, Karlheinz Riedle, Stéphane Chapuisat (80 Michael Zorc). Trainer: Ottmar Hitzfeld

Goal: Ricken (60)

MANCHESTER UNITED FC v FC PORTO 4-0 (2-0)

Old Trafford, Manchester 5.03.1997

Referee: Anders Frisk (SWE) Attendance: 53,415

MANCHESTER UNITED: Peter Schmeichel; Gary Neville, Gary Pallister, David May, Dennis Irwin, David Beckham, Ronny Johnsen, Eric Cantona, Ryan Giggs, Ole Gunnar Solskjaer, Andy Cole. Manager: Alex Ferguson

FC PORTO: Henrique HILÁRIO Sampaio; SÉRGIO Paulo Marceneiro CONCEIÇÃO, ALOÍSIO Pires Alves, JORGE Paulo COSTA Almeida, João Paulo Maio dos Santos "PAULINHO SANTOS", José Alberto da Mota BARROSO, Zlatko Zahovic, João Carlos Rodrigues da COSTA (24 Mário JARDEL Almeida Ribeiro), Ljubinko Drulovic, EDMILSON Gonçalves Pimenta, ARTUR Duarte de Oliveira (46 RUI Gil Soares de BARROS). Trainer: António Oliveira

Goals: May (22), Cantona (34), Giggs (61), Cole (80)

FC PORTO v MANCHESTER UNITED FC 0-0

Estádio das Antas, Porto 19.03.1997

Referee: Kim Milton Nielsen (DEN) Attendance: 38,000

FC PORTO: Andrezej Wozniak; JOÃO Domingos Silva PINTO (37 Zlatko Zahovic), JOÃO MANUEL PINTO Tomé dos Santos, JORGE Paulo COSTA Almeida, FERNANDO Manuel Antunes MENDES (50 Grzegorz Mielcarski), João Paulo Maio dos Santos "PAULINHO SANTOS", José Alberto da Mota BARROSO (47 Arnold Wetl), RUI JORGE de Sousa Dias Macedo de Oliveira, Ljubinko Drulovic, EDMILSON Gonçalves Pimenta, Mário JARDEL Almeida Ribeiro. Trainer: António Oliveira

MANCHESTER UNITED: Peter Schmeichel; Gary Neville, David May, Gary Pallister, Dennis Irwin (80 Philip Neville), David Beckham (80 Karel Poborsky), Nicky Butt, Roy Keane, Ronny Johnsen, Eric Cantona, Ole Gunnar Solskjaer (70 Paul Scholes). Manager: Alex Ferguson

AFC AJAX AMSTERDAM v ATLÉTICO MADRID 1-1 (0-1)

Amsterdam ArenA, Amsterdam 5.03.1997

Referee: Markus Merk (GER) Attendance: 51,000

AJAX: Edwin van der Sar; Mario Melchiot (83 John Veldman), Danny Blind, Richard Witschge, Frank De Boer, Ronald De Boer, Jari Litmanen, Kiki Musampa (46 Arnold Scholten), Tijjani Babangida (70 Nordin Wooter), Patrick Kluivert, Marc Overmars. Trainer: Louis van Gaal

ATLÉTICO: José Francisco MOLINA Giménez; Delfí GELI Roura (87 Juan VIZCAÍNO Morcillo), Santiago Denia Sánchez SANTI, Roberto SOLOZÁBAL Villanueva, Antonio Muñoz Gómez "TONI"; Radek Bejbl, Carlos AGUILERA Martín, Milinko Pantic (75 Veljko Paunovic), Diego Pablo SIMEONE, José Luis Pérez CAMINERO; Juan Eduardo ESNÁIDER. Trainer: Radomir Antić

Goals: Esnáider (8), Kluivert (53)

ATLÉTICO MADRID v AFC AJAX AMSTERDAM 2-3 (1-0, 1-1) (AET)

Vicente Calderón, Madrid 19.03.1996

Referee: Serge Muhmenthaler (SWI) Attendance: 50,018

ATLÉTICO: José Francisco MOLINA Giménez; Carlos AGUILERA Martín, Santiago Denia Sánchez SANTI, Roberto SOLOZÁBAL Villanueva, Delfí GELI Roura; Radek Bejbl, Milinko Pantic, Diego Pablo SIMEONE (115 Juan Manuel LÓPEZ Martínez), José Luis Pérez CAMINERO; Francisco Narváez Machón KIKO, Juan Eduardo ESNÁIDER (89 Leonardo Angel BIAGINI). Trainer: Radomir Antić

AJAX: Edwin van der Sar; Mario Melchiot, Danny Blind (46 John Veldman), Frank De Boer, Arnold Scholten, Richard Witschge, Jari Litmanen (79 Dani), Kiki Musampa (85 Nordin Wooter), Tijjani Babangida, Ronald De Boer, Marc Overmars. Trainer: Louis van Gaal

Goals: Kiko (29), R.de Boer (49), Dani (100), Pantic (105 pen), Babangida (119)

ROSENBORG BK TRONDHEIM v JUVENTUS FC TORINO 1-1 (0-0)

Lerkendal, Trondheim 5.03.1997

Referee: Marc Batta (FRA) Attendance: 20,246

ROSENBORG: Jørn Jamtfall; André Bergdølmo (80 Bjørn Otto Bragstad), Jon Olav Hjelde, Erik Hoftun, Ståle Stensaas; Roar Strand, Bent Skammelsrud, Trond Egil Soltvedt; Vegard Heggem, Sigurd Rushfeldt (67 Harald Martin Brattbakk), Jahn Ivar Jakobsen. Trainer: Nils Arne Eggen

JUVENTUS: Angelo Peruzzi; Moreno Torricelli, Ciro Ferrara, Paolo Montero, Mark Juliano; Didier Deschamps (81 Alessio Tacchinardi), Vladimir Jugović, Angelo Di Livio, Zinedine Zidane; Michele Padovano (60 Nicola Amoruso), Christian Vieri. Trainer: Marcello Lippi

Goals: Soltvedt (51), Vieri (53)

JUVENTUS FC TORINO
v ROSENBORG BK TRONDHEIM 2-0 (1-0)

Stadio delle Alpi, Torino 19.03.1996

Referee: Vitor Melo Pereira (POR) Attendance: 35,371

JUVENTUS: Angelo Peruzzi; Ciro Ferrara, Paolo Montero, Sergio Porrini, Mark Juliano; Angelo Di Livio (76 Attilio Lombardo), Didier Deschamps, Vladimir Jugović, Zinedine Zidane (83 Alessio Tacchinardi), Christian Vieri (44 Alen Boksic), Nicola Amoruso. Trainer: Marcello Lippi

ROSENBORG: Jørn Jamtfall; Erik Hoftun, Ståle Stensaas; Roar Strand (59 Harald Martin Brattbakk), Bent Skammelsrud, Jahn Ivar Jakobsen (66 Karl Oskar Fjørtoft), Vegard Heggem, Jon Olav Hjelde, Trond Egil Soltvedt, André Bergdølmo; Sigurd Rushfeldt. Trainer: Nils Arne Eggen

Goals: Zidane (29), Amoruso (89 pen)

SEMI-FINALS

BORUSSIA DORTMUND
v MANCHESTER UNITED FC 1-0 (0-0)

Westfalenstadion, Dortmund 9.04.1997

Referee: Nikolai Levnikov (RUS) Attendance: 48,500

BORUSSIA: Stefan Klos; Stefan Reuter, Wolfgang Feiersinger, Martin Kree, Lars Ricken (90 Steffen Freund), Paul Lambert, Andreas Möller, PAULO Manuel Carvalho de SOUSA, Jörg Heinrich, Heiko Herrlich (90 Michael Zorc), René Tretschok (85 Knut Reinhardt). Trainer: Ottmar Hitzfeld

MANCHESTER UNITED: Raymond Van der Gouw; Gary Neville, Ronny Johnsen, Gary Pallister, Dennis Irwin, David Beckham, Nicky Butt, Roy Keane, Ryan Giggs (83 Paul Scholes), Eric Cantona, Ole Gunnar Solskjaer (74 Andy Cole). Manager: Alex Ferguson

Goal: Tretschok (78)

MANCHESTER UNITED FC
v BORUSSIA DORTMUND 0-1 (0-1)

Old Trafford, Manchester 23.04.1997

Referee: Urs Meier (SWI) Attendance: 53,600

MANCHESTER UNITED: Peter Schmeichel; Gary Neville, David May (86 Paul Scholes), Gary Pallister, Philip Neville, Ronny Johnsen, Nicky Butt, David Beckham, Eric Cantona, Ole Gunnar Solskjaer (58 Ryan Giggs), Andy Cole. Manager: Alex Ferguson

BORUSSIA: Stefan Klos; Stefan Reuter (25 René Tretschok), Wolfgang Feiersinger, Jürgen Kohler, Martin Kree, Jörg Heinrich, Paul Lambert, Andreas Möller, Lars Ricken (61 Michael Zorc), Karlheinz Riedle (73 Heiko Herrlich), Stéphane Chapuisat. Trainer: Ottmar Hitzfeld

Goal: Ricken (8)

AFC AJAX AMSTERDAM
v JUVENTUS FC TORINO 1-2 (0-2)

Amsterdam ArenA, Amsterdam 9.04.1997

Referee: Antonio Jesús Lopez Nieto (SPA) Att: 51,200

AJAX: Edwin van der Sar; Mario Melchiot, Danny Blind, Frank De Boer, Arnold Scholten (77 Nordin Wooter), Richard Witschge (71 Dani), Kiki Musampa (28 Winston Bogarde), Jari Litmanen, Tijjani Babangida, Ronald De Boer, Marc Overmars. Trainer: Louis van Gaal

JUVENTUS: Angelo Peruzzi; Sergio Porrini, Ciro Ferrara, Paolo Montero, Gianluca Pessotto; Angelo Di Livio (70 Alessio Tacchinardi), Didier Deschamps, Vladimir Jugović (85 Attilio Lombardo), Zinedine Zidane; Christian Vieri, Nicola Amoruso. Trainer: Marcello Lippi

Goals: Amoruso (14), Vieri (41), Litmanen (68)

JUVENTUS FC TORINO
v AFC AJAX AMSTERDAM 4-1 (2-0)

Stadio delle Alpi, Torino 23.04.1997

Referee: Kim Milton Nielsen (DEN) Attendance: 62,377

JUVENTUS: Angelo Peruzzi; Ciro Ferrara, Paolo Montero, Mark Juliano, Angelo Di Livio; Alessio Tacchinardi, Didier Deschamps, Zinedine Zidane (83 Antonio Conte), Attilio Lombardo; Alen Boksic, Christian Vieri (68 Nicola Amoruso). Trainer: Marcello Lippi

AJAX: Edwin van der Sar; Mario Melchiot, Danny Blind, Frank De Boer, Arnold Scholten (56 Kiki Musampa), Richard Witschge (83 Mariano Juan), Jari Litmanen, Winston Bogarde, Tijjani Babangida, Ronald De Boer, Marc Overmars. Trainer: Louis van Gaal

Goals: Lombardo (35), Vieri (36), Melchiot (74), Amoruso (78), Zidane (81)

FINAL

BORUSSIA DORTMUND
v JUVENTUS FC TORINO 3-1 (2-0)

Olympiastadion, München 28.05.1997

Referee: Sándor Puhl (HUN) Attendance: 59,000

BORUSSIA: Stefan Klos; Jürgen Kohler, Matthias Sammer, Martin Kree, Stefan Reuter, Paul Lambert, PAULO Manuel Carvalho de SOUSA, Jörg Heinrich, Andreas Möller (89 Michael Zorc), Karlheinz Riedle (67 Heiko Herrlich), Stéphane Chapuisat (70 Lars Ricken). Trainer: Ottmar Hitzfeld

JUVENTUS: Angelo Peruzzi; Sergio Porrini (46 Alessandro del Piero), Ciro Ferrara, Paolo Montero, Mark Juliano; Angelo Di Livio, Didier Deschamps, Zinedine Zidane, Vladimir Jugović; Christian Vieri (73 Nicola Amoruso), Alen Boksic (89 Alessio Tacchinardi). Trainer: Marcello Lippi

Goals: Riedle (29, 34), Del Piero (64), Ricken (70)

European Cup Goalscorers 1996-97:

6 goals: Alistair McCoist (Rangers)

5 goals: Milinko Pantic (Atlético Madrid), Kubilay Türkyılmaz (Grasshopper)

4 goals: Nicola Amoruso, Alen Boksic, Alessandro del Piero, Christian Vieri (Juventus Torino), Artur Duarte de Oliveira, Mário Jardel Almeida Ribeiro (FC Porto), Diego Simeone (Atlético Madrid), Lars Ricken, Karlheinz Riedle (Borussia Dortmund), Marco Simone (AC Milan), Adrian Ilie (Steaua)

3 goals: Eric Cantona (Manchester United), Andersson (IFK Göteborg), Citko, Dembinski (Widzew), Moldovan (Grasshopper), Deniaud (Auxerre), Weah (Milan), Esnáider (Atlético), Dani, Babangida (Ajax), Chapuisat, Herrlich (Borussia)

2 goals: Bolić (Fenerbahçe), Yanovskiy (Alania), Laudrup (Rangers), Brattbakk, Heggem, Iversen, Soltvedt (Rosenborg), Blomqvist, Erlingmark (IFK Göteborg), Bjur (Brøndby IF), Majak (Widzew), Yakin (Grasshopper), S.Ilie (Steaua), Ivanov, Stumpf (Rapid Wien), Marlet (Auxerre), Edmilson (FC Porto), Kiko (Atlético Madrid), Beckham, Giggs (Manchester United), Kluivert, Litmanen (Ajax), Zidane (Juventus), Tretschok (Borussia)

1 goal: Driks (Maccabi Tel Aviv), Kemalettin, Okocha, Høgh (Fenerbahçe), Suleimanov (Alania), McInnes, Petric, Van Vossen, Miller, Gascoigne, Durrant, Gough (Rangers), Warzycha (Panathinakos), Strand, Jakobsen, Skammelsrud (Rosenborg), Horváth (Ferencváros), Pettersson, Wahlstedt, Alexandersson (IFK Göteborg), P.Møller, Vilfort (Brøndby), Wojtala, Czerwiec (Widzew), Esposito, Koller, Gren, Berger (Grasshopper), Nielsen, Špehar (Brugge), Baciu, R.Nagy, Călin (Steaua), Kalitvintsev, Maksimov (Dynamo Kyiv), Guggi, Kühbauer, Lesiak (Rapid Wien), Diomède, Laslandes, Lamouchi (Auxerre), Dugarry, Davids, Boban, Albertini, Locatelli, Baggio (Milan), Zahovic, Drulovic (FC Porto), Roberto (Atlético), May, Cole, Solskjaer (Manchester United), Wooter, Scholten, R.de Boer, Melchiot (Ajax), Lombardo, Padovano, Montero (Juventus), Schneider, Möller, Zorc, Lambert, Kohler, Reuter, Heinrich (Borussia)

Own goals: Jorge Costa (FC Porto) for Rosenborg, Gren (Grasshopper) for Auxerre, Bogusz (Widzew) for Steaua, Holovko (Dynamo Kyiv) for Rapid Wien

THE EUROPEAN CUP 1997-98

PRELIMINARY ROUND

DERRY CITY LONDONDERRY v MARIBOR TEATANIC 0-2 (0-0)

Brandywell, Derry 23.07.1997

Referee: Hans-Jürgen Weber (GER) Attendance: 3,120

DERRY CITY: Declan Devine; Eamonn Doherty, Paul Curran, Gavin Dykes, Kevin Brady (60 Ryan Coyle), Tom Mohan, Peter Hutton, Paul Hegarty, Sean Hargan, Liam Coyle, Gary Beckett. Manager: Felix Healy

TEATANIC: Marko Simeunović; Matjaz Kek, Marinko Sarkezi, Spasoje Bulajić, Milan Sterbal, Alojz Fricelj, Franc Fridl (84 Nastja Ceh), Damjan Gajser (90 Stanković), Gregor Zidan, Viktor Paço, Oskar Drobne (66 Ismet Munishi). Trainer: Bojan Prasnikar

Goals: Zidan (59), Gajser (79)

MARIBOR TEATANIC v DERRY CITY LONDONDERRY 1-0 (0-0)

Ljudski vrt, Maribor 30.07.1997

Referee: Karl-Erik Nilsson (SWE) Attendance: 5,463

TEATANIC: Marko Simeunović; Matjaz Kek, Marinko Sarkezi, Spasoje Bulajić (59 Ismet Munishi), Milan Sterbal, Alojz Fricelj, Franc Fridl, Damjan Gajser (79 Nastja Ceh), Gregor Zidan (79 Zikica Vuksanović), Viktor Paço, Oskar Drobne. Trainer: Bojan Prasnikar

DERRY CITY: Tony O'Dowd; Eamonn Doherty, Kevin Brady (66 Sean Gallagher), Peter Hutton, Paul Curran, Gavin Dykes, Tom Mohan, Paul Hegarty, Liam Coyle (67 Ryan Semple), Ryan Coyle, Sean Hargan. Manager: Felix Healy

Goal: Drobne (48)

1.FC KOŠICE v ÍA AKRANES 3-0 (1-0)

Vsesportovy areal, Košice 23.07.1997

Referee: Aron Huzu (ROM) Attendance: 5,747

FC KOŠICE: Ladislav Molnar; András Telek, Ivan Kozak, Peter Dzurik; Miroslav Sovic, Marek Spilar, Vladislav Zvara, Dušan Toth, Ruslan Lyubarskyi (80 Ivan Lapsansky), Robert Semenik (74 Lubomir Faktor), Jozef Kozlej (66 Vladimir Janocko). Trainer: Jan Kozak

ÍA: Thórdur Thórdarson; Sturlaugur Haraldsson, Gunnlaugur Jónsson, Steinar Adolfsson, Pálmi Haraldsson; Olafur Thórdarsson, Alexander Högnason, Jóhannes Hardarson, Kári Steinn Reynisson, Unnar Örn Valgeirsson, Haraldur Hinriksson. Trainer: Ivan Golac

Goals: Semenik (30), Toth (48), Sovic (64)

ÍA AKRANES v 1.FC KOŠICE 0-1 (0-0)

Akranesvöllur, Akranes 30.07.1997

Referee: Alan Snoddy (NIR) Attendance: 2,000

ÍA: Thórdur Thórdarson; Olafur Adolfsson, Gunnlaugur Jónsson, Steinar Adolfsson, Aleksandar Linta, Pálmi Haraldsson (66 Unnar Örn Valgeirsson), Alexander Högnasson, Olafur Thórdarsson, Jóhannes Hardarson (68 Sturlaugur Haraldsson), Haraldur Ingólfsson, Kári Steinn Reynisson (80 Haraldur Hinriksson). Trainer: Ivan Golac

FC KOŠICE: Ladislav Molnar; András Telek, Ivan Kozak, Peter Dzurik, Dušan Toth, Miroslav Sovic, Vladislav Zvara (46 Lubomir Faktor), Marek Spilar, Ruslan Lyubarskyi (75 Ivan Lapsansky), Robert Semenik (56 Marian Bochnovic), Jozef Kozlej. Trainer: Jan Kozak

Goal: Faktor (66)

VALLETTA FC v SKONTO RIGA 1-0 (1-0)

National Ta'Qali 23.07.1997

Referee: Naoum Mintiouris (GRE) Attendance: 3,535

VALLETTA FC: Sean Sullivan; Drasko Braunovic, Jeffrey Chetcuti, Kristian Laferla, Darren Debono, Ivan Zammit (83 Stefan Giglio), Gilbert Agius, Nicholas Saliba, Boško Tatar, Lino Galea, Ferenc Lovász (55 Ivan Woods). Trainer: Edward Aquilina

SKONTO: Alexander Kolinko; Igor Stepanov, Levan Silagadze, Mikhail Zemlinsky, Oleg Blagonadezhdin, Valery Ivanov, Marian Pakhar (61 Andrei Shtolcers), Vladimir Babichev, David Chaladze, Mikhail Mikholap (70 Vladimir Kolesnichenko), Vitaly Astafyev (78 Igor Slesarchuk). Trainer: Alexander Starkov

Goal: Galea (15)

PARTIZAN BEOGRAD v CROATIA ZAGREB 1-0 (0-0)

Partizan, Beograd 23.07.1997

Referee: Ryszard Wójcik (POL) Attendance: 30,000

PARTIZAN: Ivica Kralj; Djordje Svetlicić, Drazen Bolić, Ivan Tomić, Mladen Krstajić, Predrag Pazin, Dejan Vukicević, Goran Trobok (46 Sasa Ilić), Goran Obradović (69 Milan Stojanoski), Ljubisa Ranković, Dragan Stojisavljević (63 Dragan Isailović). Trainer: Ljubisa Tumbaković

CROATIA: Drazen Ladić; Damir Krznar, Silvio Marić (87 Danijel Stefulj), Goran Jurić, Mark Viduka (85 Zoran Brlenić), Dario Simić, Danijel Sarić, Robert Prosinecki, Stjepan Tomas, Igor Cvitanović, Krunoslav Jurcić. Trainer: Marijan Vlak

Goal: Isailović (86)

SKONTO RIGA v VALLETTA FC 2-0 (2-0)

Daugava, Riga 30.07.1997

Referee: Lars Gerner (DEN) Attendance: 5,500

SKONTO: Alexander Kolinko; Igor Stepanov, Levan Silagadze, Mikhail Zemlinsky, Yury Shevlyakov (68 Oleg Blagonadezhdin), Valery Ivanov, Marian Pakhar (73 Andrei Shtolcers), Vladimir Babichev, David Chaladze (27 Alexander Rekhviashvili), Mikhail Mikholap, Vitaly Astafyev. Trainer: Alexander Starkov

VALLETTA FC: Sean Sullivan; Jeffrey Chetcuti, Kristian Laferla, Darren Debono, Gilbert Agius, Nicholas Saliba, Boško Tatar (71 Jeremy Agius), Joseph Zarb, Lino Galea (54 Drasko Braunovic), Joseph Camilleri, Ivan Woods (46 Ivan Zammit). Trainer: Edward Aquilina

Goals: Astafyev (14), Mikholap (26)

CROATIA ZAGREB v PARTIZAN BEOGRAD 5-0 (4-0)

Maksimir, Zagreb 30.07.1997

Referee: Gilles Veissière (FRA) Attendance: 33,000

CROATIA: Drazen Ladić; Damir Krznar, Silvio Marić (68 Vladimir Petrović), Goran Jurić, Dario Simić, Danijel Sarić, Robert Prosinecki, Edin Mujcin (72 Zoran Brlenić), Krunoslav Jurcić, Igor Cvitanović, Mark Viduka (76 Stjepan Tomas). Trainer: Marijan Vlak

PARTIZAN: Ivica Kralj; Drazen Bolić, Zoltan Sabo, Igor Tasevski, Djordje Svetlicić, Mladen Krstajić, Ivan Tomić, Goran Trobok, Goran Obradović (46 Dragan Isailović), Dejan Vukicević (46 Sasa Ilić), Dragan Stojisavljević (66 Zoran Cirić). Trainer: Ljubisa Tumbakovic

Goals: Marić (13, 42), Cvitanović (15, 69), Viduka (24)

FC PYUNIK EREVAN v MTK BUDAPEST 0-2 (0-0)

Hrazdan, Erevan 23.07.1997

Referee: René Temmink (HOL) Attendance: 5,000

PYUNIK: Armen Avagyan; Artur Mkrchyan, Sarkis Hovsepyan, Haik Gevorgyan, Vardan Minasyan, Suren Shakhalyan (49 Gegham Hovhannisyan), Armen Sanamyan, Seyran Poghosyan (76 Romik Khachatryan), Hamlet Mkhitaryan, Armen Shahgeldyan, Arsen Avetisyan (46 Varazdat Avetisyan).

MTK: Gábor Babos; Zoltán Molnár, Attila Kuttor, Tamás Szekeres, László Farkashazy, Gábor Halmai, Béla Illés, Tamás Szamosi, Gábor Egressy (75 Tamás Zimmermann), Krisztián Kenesei (88 Sándor Preisinger), Ferenc Orosz (62 Csaba Madar). Trainer: József Garami

Goals: Illés (83), Preisinger (89)

MTK BUDAPEST v PYUNIK EREVAN 4-3 (2-0)

Hungária út, Budapest 30.07.1997

Referee: Gary Stephen Willard (ENG) Attendance: 1,787

MTK: Gábor Babos (75 Balázs Rabóczki); Gábor Korolovszky, Attila Kuttor, Tamás Szekeres, László Farkashazy, Béla Illés, Gábor Halmai, Tamás Szamosi (65 Tamás Zimmermann), Gábor Egressy, Krisztián Kenesei, Sándor Preisinger (54 Csaba Madar). Trainer: József Garami

PYUNIK: Armen Avagyan; Artur Mkrchyan, Sarkis Hovsepyan, Seyran Poghosyan, Vardan Minasyan, Aramais Tonoyan (46 Hamlet Mkhitaryan), Varazdat Avetisyan (73 Suren Shakhalyan), Armen Sanamyan, Romik Khachatryan (60 Gegham Hovhannisyan), Haik Gevorgyan, Armen Shahgeldyan.

Goals: Illés (18, 41), Preisinger (46), Kuttor (74), Sanamyan (81, 88), Shahgeldyan (87)

FC CRUSADERS BELFAST v DINAMO TBILISI 1-3 (0-1)

Seaview, Belfast 23.07.1997

Referee: Vitor Manuel Melo Pereira (POR) Att: 1,500

CRUSADERS: Damian Grant; Alan Dornan (65 Mick Deegan), Gary McCartney (79 Chris Morgan), Glenn Dunlop, Robert Lawlor, Stuart Mellon, Paul Dwyer (55 Trevor McMullan), Donal O'Brien, Gavin Arthur, Stephen Baxter, Glenn Hunter. Manager: Roy Walker

DINAMO: Irakli Zoidze; Kakhi Kaladze, Givi Didava, Mamuka Machavariani, Gia Chkhaidze, Kakhi Gogichaishvili (90 Rati Aleksidze), Giorgi Kiknadze, Levan Tskitishvili, David MuJiří (90 Levan Khomeriki), Aleksandre Iashvili (79 David Kizilashvili), Georgi Anchabadze. Trainer: David Kipiani

Goals: Kiknadze (31), Gogichaishvili (50), MuJiří (65), Baxter (71)

DINAMO TBILISI v FC CRUSADERS BELFAST 5-1 (3-0)

Boris Paichadze, Tbilisi 30.07.1997

Referee: Ahmet Cakar (TUR) Attendance: 12,000

DINAMO: Irakli Zoidze; Kakhi Kaladze, Givi Didava, Mamuka Machavariani (7 Rati Aleksidze), Kakhi Gogichaishvili (77 Levan Khomeriki), Giorgi Kiknadze, Georgi Anchabadze, Gia Chkhaidze, Levan Tskitishvili, Aleksandre Iashvili, David MuJiří (77 Givi Kvaratskhelia). Trainer: David Kipiani

CRUSADERS: Damian Grant; Trevor McMullan, Glenn Dunlop, Aaron Callaghan, Robert Lawlor (46 Paul Dwyer), Glenn Hunter, Donal O'Brien (72 Kirk Hunter), Mick Deegan, Gavin Arthur (72 Chris Morgan), Roy Walker, Stephen Baxter. Manager: Roy Walker

Goals: Iashvili (21, 36), MuJiří (44, 60), G. Hunter (61), Khomeriki (82)

SILEKS KRATOVO v BEITAR JERUSALEM 1-0 (0-0)

Kratovo 23.07.1997

Referee: Eric Romain (BEL) Attendance: 2,000

SILEKS: Kiro Trajcev; Marjan Nikolov, Vladimir Kolev, Igor Djuzelov, Dragan Veselinoski, Ljubodrag Milosevic, Vlatko Gosev (81 Borce Ivanov), Rade Karanfilovski, Miroslav Dzokic (81 Mite Nacevski), Srdjan Zaharievski, Vlatko Stojcevski (65 Vlatko Novakov). Trainer: Zoran Smileski

BEITAR: Itzhak David Korenfain; David Perets (62 Nir Avraham Sivilia), Sergiy Tretyak, Ehud Eliyahu Cahila, Tomer Azoulay, Jan Telesnikov, Eitan Mizrahi, István Pisont, István Hamar, István Sallói, Eliahu Ohana. Trainer: Dror Kashtan

Sent off: Nikolov (64)

Goal: Karanfilovski (54 pen)

BEITAR JERUSALEM v SILEKS KRATOVO 3-0 (2-0)

Teddi Malcha, Jerusalem 30.07.1997

Referee: Alain Sars (FRA) Attendance: 8,000

BEITAR: Itzhak David Korenfain; Eitan Mizrahi, Sergiy Tretyak, Tomer Azoulay, Ehud Eliyahu Cahila; Jan Telesnikov, Raanan Deree, István Pisont, István Hamar, István Sallói; Eliahu Ohana. Trainer: Dror Kashtan

SILEKS: Kiro Trajcev; Vlatko Novakov (72 Goranco Georgiev), Vladimir Kolev (58 Borce Ivanov), Igor Djuzelov, Dragan Veselinoski, Ljubodrag Milosevic, Vlatko Gosev, Rade Karanfilovski, Miroslav Dzokic, Srdjan Zaharievski, Vlatko Stojcevski (65 Mite Nacevski). Trainer: Zoran Smileski

Goals: Sallói (5), Ohana (34), Hamar (76)

STEAUA BUCUREŞTI v CSKA SOFIA 3-3 (1-0)

Steaua, Bucureşti 23.07.1997

Referee: Hellmut Krug (GER) Attendance: 14,000

STEAUA: Zoltan Ritli; Laurenţiu Reghecampf, Adrian Matei, Valeriu Răchită, Marius Achim Baciu; Denis Şerban, Iosif Rotariu, Roland Nagy (58 Laurenţiu Dumitru Roşu), Damian Militaru; Marius Mihai Lăcătuş (Cap), Cristian Ciocoiu (68 Cătălin Munteanu). Trainer: Mihai Stoichiţă

CSKA: Petko Petkov; Emil Kremenliev, Ivo Slavchev, Filip Filipov (64 Risto Milosavov), Dobromir Mitov, Stefan Lulchev, Anatoli Nankov (Cap), Georgi Iordanov (70 Bozo Djurkovic), Milen Petkov, Petar Zhabov (86 Metodi Deianov), Ivailo Andonov. Trainer: Georgi Vasilev

Sent off: Matei (56), Nankov (80)

Goals: Rotariu (8), Andonov (47), Nankov (49, 68), Lăcătuş (72), Munteanu (83)

CSKA SOFIA v STEAUA BUCUREŞTI 0-2 (0-1)

Narodna Armia, Sofia 30.07.1997

Referee: Graziano Cesari (ITA) Attendance: 20,000

CSKA: Ilia Vasilev; Emil Kremenliev, Filip Filipov, Stefan Lulchev, Dobromir Mitov (Cap), Ivo Slavchev, Georgi Iordanov (57 Metodi Deianov), Ivailo Andonov, Bozo Djurkovic (44 Petar Zhabov), Milen Petkov, Galin Ivanov (50 Dimitar Ivanov). Trainer: Georgi Vasilev

STEAUA: Zoltan Ritli; Laurenţiu Reghecampf, Tiberiu Csik, Valeriu Răchită, Marius Achim Baciu, Iulian Ilie Miu (78 Cătălin Munteanu), Denis Georgian Şerban, Iosif Rotariu, Damian Militaru (59 Roland Nagy), Marius Mihai Lăcătuş (88 Cristian Ciocoiu), Laurenţiu Dumitru Roşu.
Trainer: Mihai Stoichiţă

Goals: Şerban (35), Reghecampf (51)

FC LANTANA TALLINN v FC JAZZ PORI 0-2 (0-1)

Maarjamäe, Tallinn 23.07.1997

Referee: Tom Henning Øvrebø (NOR) Attendance: 2,000

LANTANA: Sergei Ussoltsev, Andrei Krasnopjorov, Urmas Hepner, Aleksandr Lebedev, Sergei Bragin, Andrei Borisov, Konstantin Karin, Vitalijus Danilicevas (61 Oleg Gorjatsov), Stanislav Svetogor (66 Dmitri Kulikov), Andrei Mitjunov (46 Vitali Leitan), Oleg Kolotsei. Trainer: Anatoli Belov

JAZZ: Ilkka Siitonen; Rami Nieminen, Ari-Pekka Roiko, Pasi Sulonen, Janne Hietanen, Janne Puputti, Juha Riippa, Rami Hakanpää (70 Jani Suikkanen), Pedro Massacessi, Harri Puhakainen, Antonio Pogioli MARCO. Trainer: Jari Pyykölä

Goals: Nieminen (4, 76)

CONSTRUCTORUL CHIŞINĂU v FC MPKC MOZYR 1-1 (1-1)

Republican, Chişinău 23.07.1997

Referee: Hartmut Strampe (GER) Attendance: 6,000

CONSTRUCTORUL: Serghei Dinov; Igor Filip, Ivan Tabanov, Vasile Apachiţei, Eric Ococo, Oleg Şişchin, Iulian Bursuc, Mihai Alexa (53 Igor Cuciuc), Iuri Bezuglâi (73 Victor Colomeeţ), Victor Comlionoc, Aurel Druţă (83 Alexandru Scrupschi). Trainer: Felix Veranean

MPKC: Vladimir Gayev; Andrei Lukashevich, Oleg Sisoyev, Valeriy Apanas, Sergei Polyakov, Evgeniy Lovchev, Yuri Maleyev (46 Kakhaber Esaiashvili, 82 Alexei Khodykin), Levan Berishvili, Boris Gorovoi, Vasiliy Kushnir, Dmitriy Denisyuk (90 Igor Osipenko). Trainer: Aleksandr Bubnov

Goals: Apachiţei (18), Berishvili (23 pen)

FC JAZZ PORI v FC LANTANA TALLINN 1-0 (0-0)

Porin, Pori 30.07.1997

Referee: Vladimir Hrinak (SVK) Attendance: 3,760

JAZZ: Ilkka Siitonen; Rami Nieminen, Ari-Pekka Roiko, Pasi Sulonen, Vesa Rantanen; Janne Puputti, Juha Riippa, Rami Hakanpää (80 Jarno Heinikangas), Pedro Massacessi (56 Saku Laaksonen), Harri Puhakainen (83 Jani Suikkanen), Antonio Pogioli MARCO. Trainer: Jari Pyykölä

LANTANA: Sergei Ussoltsev; Andrei Krasnopjorov, Urmas Hepner, Aleksandr Lebedev, Oleg Kolotsei, Sergei Bragin, Nikolai Toshtshev (71 Andrei Tjunin), Konstantin Karin, Vitalijus Danilicevas, Stanislav Svetogor (51 Andrei Mitjunov), Vitali Leitan (46 Dmitri Kulikov). Trainer: Anatloi Belov

Goal: Marco (65)

FC MPKC MOZYR v CONSTRUCTORUL CHIŞINĂU 3-2 (1-1)

Yunost, Mozyr 30.07.1997

Referee: Alain Hamer (LUX) Attendance: 6,900

MPKC: Vladimir Gayev; Andrei Lukashevich, Oleg Sisoyev, Valeriy Apanas, Sergei Polyakov, Evgeniy Lovchev, Boris Gorovoi, Alexei Khodykin (39 Vasiliy Kushnir), Yuri Maleyev (46 Kakhaber Esaiashvili, 70 Vyacheslav Banul), Dmitriy Denisyuk, Levan Berishvili. Trainer: Aleksandr Bubnov

CONSTRUCTORUL: Serghei Dinov; Igor Filip, Ivan Tabanov, Iurie Platon, Vasile Apachiţei (54 Veaceslav Bugniac), Oleg Şişchin (66 Eugen Boicenco), Iulian Bursuc, Mihai Alexa, Iuri Bezuglâi (54 Aurel Druţă), Victor Colomeeţ, Victor Comlionoc. Trainer: Felix Veranean, Aleksandr Maţiura

Goals: Denisyuk (7), Alexa (32), Berishvili (53), Comlionoc (67), Kushnir (69)

GOTU ITROTTARFELAG v GLASGOW RANGERS FC 0-5 (0-2)

Svangaskard, Toftir 23.07.1997

Referee: Miko Vuorela (FIN) Attendance: 2,500

GI: Jens Martin Knudsen; Janus Rasmussen, Henning Jarnskor, Samal Joensen, Øssur Hansen, Hagnar Højgaard, Magni Jarnskor (81 Heini Heinasson), Pauli Jarnskor (69 Erland Tvorfoss), Tummas Magnussen (59 Magni Jacobsen), Simun Petur Justinussen, Runi Justinussen.
Trainer: Pall Gudlaugsson

RANGERS: Antti Niemi; Alex Cleland, Joachim Björklund, Craig Moore (77 Stephen Wright), Tony Vidmar, Jonas Thern, Jörg Albertz, Marco Negri, Ian Ferguson, Gordon Durie, Brian Laudrup (38 Alistair McCoist). Manager: Walter Smith

Goals: Negri (19), Durie (25, 80), McCoist (65, 90)

GLASGOW RANGERS FC v GOTU ITROTTARFELAG 6-0 (2-0)

Ibrox Stadium, Glasgow 30.07.1997

Referee: Romans Lajuks (LAT) Attendance: 44,433

RANGERS: Antti Niemi; Craig Moore, Joachim Björklund, Sergio Porrini (83 Alex Cleland), Gordon Durie (77 Ian Durrant), Paul Gascoigne (46 Jörg Albertz), Jonas Thern, Ian Ferguson, Marco Negri, Alistair McCoist, Tony Vidmar. Manager: Walter Smith

GI: Jens Martin Knudsen; Janus Rasmussen, Henning Jarnskor, Samal Joensen, Øssur Hansen, Hagnar Højgaard, Magni Jarnskor, Simun Petur Justinussen, Runi Justinussen, Joan Petur Olsen, Erland Tvorfoss (72 Pauli Jarnskor). Trainer: Pall Gudlaugsson

Goals: Durie (22), Negri (42, 90), McCoist (58), Albertz (58), Ferguson (84)

FC DYNAMO KYIV v BARRY TOWN 2-0 (1-0)

Olympiyskyi, Kyiv 23.07.1997

Referee: Sarvan Oguz (TUR) Attendance: 12,000

DYNAMO: Olexandr Shovkovskyi; Olexandr Radchenko, Vladislav Vashchuk, Olexandr Holovko, Yuri Dmitrulin, Olexandr Khatskevich (66 Dmytro Mikhailenko), Andriy Gusin, Pavlo Shkapenko (66 Yuri Maksimov), Yuri Kalitvintsev, Valentin Belkevich, Serhiy Rebrov. Trainer: Valeriy Lobanovskyi

BARRY: Mark Ovendale; Terry Evans, Gareth Knott, Gary Lloyd, Andrew York, Colin Loss, Phil Johnson, Dean Huggins, Craig Evans (74 David O'Gorman), Anthony Bird, Darren Ryan. Manager: Gary Barnett

Goals: Rebrov (31), Maksimov (83)

NEFTCHI BAKU v WIDZEW LÓDZ 0-2 (0-2)

Tofig Bakhramov, Baku 23.07.1997

Referee: Dermot Gallagher (ENG) Attendance: 5,000

NEFTCHI: Elhan Hasanov; Vugar Ismaylov, Mekhman Yunusov, Vidadi Rzayev (81 Tarlan Makhmudov), Adagim Niftaliev (74 Ruslan Musayev), Kamal Kuliyev, Yunis Huseynov, Zaur Ismaylov, Ilgham Yadullayev (74 Djeykhun Sultanov), Kurban Kurbanov, Khagani Mamedov. Trainer: Ruslan Abdullajev

WIDZEW: Slawomir Olszewski; Dariusz Gesior, Miroslaw Szymkowiak, Rafal Siadaczka, Andriy Mikhalchuk, Zbigniew Wyciszkiewicz (46 Daniel Bogusz), Maciej Terlecki, Alexandru Curtianu (46 Pawel Miaszkiewicz), Piotr Szarpak, Jacek Dembinski (68 Marek Bajor), Andrzej Kobylanski. Trainer: Franciszek Smuda

Goals. Terlecki (23), Dembinski (43)

BARRY TOWN v FC DYNAMO KYIV 0-4 (0-0)

Jenner Park, Barry 30.07.1997

Referee: Gylfi Thor Orrasson (ICE) Attendance: 2,380

BARRY: Mark Ovendale; Terry Evans, Gary Lloyd, Andrew York, Richard Jones, Gary Barnett (57 Craig Evans), Anthony Bird, Chris Pike (46 Colin Loss), Darren Ryan, Dean Huggins (89 Phil Johnson), David O'Gorman. Manager: Gary Barnett

DYNAMO: Olexandr Shovkovskyi; Olexandr Holovko, Vladislav Vashchuk, Yuri Dmitrulin, Yuri Kalitvintsev, Andriy Gusin, Olexandr Khatskevich (68 Olexandr Radchenko), Pavlo Shkapenko (46 Yuri Maksimov), Valentin Belkevich (77 Dmytro Mikhailenko), Serhiy Rebrov, Oleh Luzhnyi. Trainer: Valeriy Lobanovskyi

Sent off: Ryan (44)

Goals: Belkevich (53), Maksimov (67, 78), Vashchuk (80)

WIDZEW LÓDZ v NEFTCHI BAKU 8-0 (5-0)

Widzew, Lódz 30.07.1997

Referee: Atanas Uzunov (BUL) Attendance: 4,769

WIDZEW: Arkadiusz Onyszko; Marek Bajor, Miroslaw Szymkowiak, Rafal Siadaczka (46 Daniel Bogusz), Marcin Zajac, Radoslaw Michalski, Pawel Miaszkiewicz (46 Alexandru Curtianu), Maciej Terlecki, Piotr Szarpak, Andrzej Kobylanski (46 Zbigniew Wyciszkiewicz), Jacek Dembinski. Trainer: Franciszek Smuda

NEFTCHI: Elhan Hasanov; Arif Asadov, Makhman Yunusov, Adagim Niftaliev (27 Ilgham Yadullaev), Vugar Ismaylov, Vidadi Rzayev, Yunis Huseynov, Ruslan Musayev (85 Khagani Mamedov), Djeykhun Sultanov, Kurban Kurbanov, Makhmud Kurbanov. Trainer: Ruslan Abdullajev

Goals: Szarpak (3, 70 pen, 76), Kobylanski (8), Zajac (14), Dembinski (25, 30), Curtianu (68)

FC SION v JEUNESSE d'ESCH 4-0 (3-0)

Stade de Tourbillon, Sion 23.07.1997

Referee: Amit Klein (ISR) Attendance: 7,000

FC SION: Fabrice Borer; David Murray; Stefan Wolf, Yvan Quentin; Sébastien Lipawski (48 James Derivaz), Jean-Jacques Eydelie, Johan Lonfat (68 Marc Hodel), Gerardo Seoane, Martin Lengen; Ahmed Ouattara (80 Stéphane Grichting), Marco Grassi. Trainer: Alberto Bigon

JEUNESSE: Philippe Felgen; Johny Thill, Marc Lamborelle, Jean Wagner, Patrick Meyers (77 Carlo Pace), Dany Theis, Denis Scuto, Yves Divoy, Claude Meylender, Patrick Morocutti (86 Vito Marchione), Paolo Amodio. Trainer: Alex Pecquer

Goals: Lipawski (5, 45), Seoane (15), Derivaz (61)

JEUNESSE d'ESCH v FC SION 0-1 (0-0)

Stade de la Frontière, Esch-sur-Alzette 30.07.1997

Referee: Pavlin Jirku (CZE) Attendance: 1,600

JEUNESSE: Philippe Felgen; Roland Schaack (77 Patrick Meyers), Marc Lamborelle, Jean Wagner, Claude Ganser, Dany Theis, Denis Scuto, Yves Divoy, Claude Meylender, Patrick Morocutti (77 Carlo Pace), Paolo Amodio (87 Vito Marchione). Trainer: Alex Pecquer

FC SION: Abiodun Baruwa; Luiz Milton; Alexandre Quennoz (74 Stefan Wolf), Stéphane Grichting, Sébastien Zambaz, Marc Hodel, Gerardo Seoane, Jean-Jacques Eydelie, Martin Lengen; Ahmed Ouattara (78 Marco Grassi), Frédéric Chassot (67 James Derivaz). Trainer: Alberto Bigon

Goal: Zambaz (89)

ANORTHOSIS FAMAGUSTA v KAREDA SIAULIAI 3-0 (1-0)

Antonis Papadopoulos, Larnaca 23.07.1997

Referee: Charles Agius (MAL) Attendance: 5,457

ANORTHOSIS: Nikos Panagiotou; Stavros Foukaris, Zaharias Haralampous (77 Paris Ilia), Dimitris Ioannou, Kostas Stavrou, Panikos Pounas, Panikos Neocleous (65 Hristos Kotsonis), Vladan Tomic, Giannakis Okas, Pambis Andreou (59 Vesko Mihajlovic), Slobodan Krcmarevic. Trainer: Dušan Mitosevic

KAREDA: Vaidotas Zutautas; Tomas Kancelskis, Zilvinas Zudys (72 Saulius Atmanavicius), Egidijus Zukauskas, Stasys Baranauskas, Deimantas Bicka, Vidas Dancenka, Audrius Zuta (15 Rolandas Vaineikis), Saulius Mikalajunas, Igoris Stukalinas, Arturas Fomenka (78 Mindaugas Ciapas). Trainer: Algimantas Liubinskas

Goals: Krcmarević (20), Okas (47, 81)

KAREDA SIAULIAI v ANORTHOSIS FAMAGUSTA 1-1 (1-1)

Šiauliai stadion 30.07.1997

Referee: Graham Poll (ENG) Attendance: 5,000

KAREDA: Vaidotas Zutautas (Cap); Tomas Kancelskis, Zilvinas Zudys, Egidijus Zukauskas, Vidas Dancenka, Audrius Zuta (38 Remigijus Pocius), Saulius Mikalajunas, Igoris Stukalinas, Rolandas Vaineikis, Deimantas Bicka (46 Mindaugas Ciapas, 62 Saulius Atmanavicius), Arturas Fomenka. Trainer: Algimantas Liubinskas

ANORTHOSIS: Nikos Panagiotou; Stavros Foukaris (30 Hristos Kotsonis), Zaharias Haralampous (75 Dimitris Assiotis), Dimitris Ioannou, Sozos Andreou, Kostas Stavrou, Panikos Pounas, Vladan Tomic, Giannakis Okas, Vasos Melanarkitis, Vesko Mihajlovic (71 Pambis Andreou). Trainer: Dušan Mitosević

Goals: Mihajlović (10), Mikalajunas (24)

QUALIFYING ROUND

1.FC KOŠICE v SPARTAK MOSKVA 2-1 (2-1)

Vsesportovy areal, Košice 13.08.1997

Referee: Charles Agius (MAL) Attendance: 9,270

FC KOŠICE: Ladislav Molnar; Ivan Kozak, András Telek, Peter Dzurik, Dušan Toth, Miroslav Sovic, Vladislav Zvara (65 Robert Semenik), Marek Spilar, Vladimir Janocko, Ruslan Lyubarskiy (70 Albert Rusnak), Jozef Kozlej (81 Radoslav Kráľ). Trainer: Jan Kozak

SPARTAK: Aleksandr Filimonov; Ramiz Mamedov (70 Vadim Yevseyev), Sergei Gorlukovich, Dmitriy Ananko, Dmitriy Khlestov, Aleksei Bakharev (44 Aleksei Melyoshin), Dmitriy Alenichev, Yegor Titov, Andrei Tikhonov, Ilya Tsymbalar, Sergei Dmitriev (81 ROBSON Luís Pereira da Silva). Trainer: Oleg Romantsev

Goals: Kozlej (16), Dmitriev (37), Kozak (43 pen)

SPARTAK MOSKVA v 1.FC KOŠICE 0-0

Lokomotiv, Moskva 27.08.1997

Referee: Michel Piraux (BEL) Attendance: 26,000

SPARTAK: Aleksandr Filimonov; Sergei Gorlukovich, Dmitriy Khlestov, Ilya Tsymbalar, Dmitriy Ananko (46 Konstantin Golovskoi), Dmitriy Alenichev, Yegor Titov, Andrei Tikhonov, Vadim Yevseyev, Sergei Dmitriev (33 Valeriy Kechinov), ROBSON Luís Pereira da Silva (76 Sergei Lutovinov). Trainer: Oleg Romantsev

FC KOŠICE: Ladislav Molnar; Marek Spilar, András Telek, Ivan Kozak, Peter Dzurik, Ruslan Lyubarskyi (77 Albert Rusnak), Dušan Toth (46 Vladimir Janocko), Jozef Kozlej (66 Lubomir Faktor), Vladislav Zvara, Miroslav Sovic, Radoslav Kráľ. Trainer: Jan Kozak

BEŞIKTAŞ JK ISTANBUL v MARIBOR TEATANIC 0-0

Inönü, Istanbul 13.08.1997

Referee: Gilles Veissière (FRA) Attendance: 15,000

BEŞIKTAŞ: Marijan Mrmic; Recep Çetin, Rahim Zafer (72 Yusuf Tokuç), Alpay Özalan, Erkan Avseren (58 Oktay Derelioglu), Mehmet Özdilek, Zlatko Iankov, Tayfur Havutçu, Serdar Topraktepe (54 Mutlu Topçu), Daniel Amokachi, Iordan Lechkov. Trainer: John Toshack

TEATANIC: Marko Simeunović; Milan Sterbal, Franc Fridl, Spasoje Bulajić, Matjaz Kek, Marinko Sarkezi, Alojz Fricelj (90 Ismet Munishi), Gregor Zidan, Viktor Paço (68 Zvjezdan Ljubobratović), Damjan Gajser, Oskar Drobne (75 Zeljko Milinović). Trainer: Bojan Prasnikar

MARIBOR TEATANIC v BEŞIKTAŞ JK ISTANBUL 1-3 (0-1)

Ljudski vrt, Maribor 27.08.1997

Referee: Pier Luigi Collina (ITA) Attendance: 7,000

TEATANIC: Marko Simeunović; Milan Sterbal, Spasoje Bulajić (71 Zeljko Milinović), Matjaz Kek, Marinko Sarkezi, Franc Fridl (53 Nastja Ceh), Oskar Drobne, Gregor Zidan, Viktor Paço (55 Slavisa Nikolić), Alojz Fricelj, Damjan Gajser. Trainer: Bojan Prasnikar

BEŞIKTAŞ: Marijan Mrmic; Recep Çetin, Rahim Zafer, Alpay Özalan, Erkan Avseren, Tayfur Havutçu, Zlatko Iankov, Iordan Lechkov (72 Yusuf Tokuç), Serdar Topraktepe, Daniel Amokachi (76 Oktay Derelioglu), Mehmet Özdilek (83 Hikmet Çapanoglu). Trainer: John Toshack

Goals: Mehmet (44), Amokachi (61), Tayfur (82), Zidan (86)

OLYMPIAKOS PEIRAIAS v FC MPKC MOZYR 5-0 (0-0)

Spiros Louis, Athina 13.08.1997

Referee: Rune Pedersen (NOR) Attendance: 27,470

OLYMPIAKOS: Dimitris Eleftheropoulos; Mirsad Varesanović (46 Bozidar Pantović), Kiriakos Karataidis (Cap), Giorgos Anatolakis, Grigoris Georgatos, Petros Passalis, Predrag Djordjević, Alekos Alexandris, Vasilis Karapialis (46 Andreas Niniadis), Sinisa Gogić, Peter Ofori-Quaye (62 Stelios Giannakopoulos). Trainer: Dušan Bajević

MPKC MOZYR: Vladimir Gayev; Andrei Lukashevich, Oleg Sisoyev, Valeriy Apanas, Sergei Polyakov, Evgeniy Lovchev, Levan Berishvili, Boris Gorovoi, Vasiliy Kushnir (46 Yuri Maleyev), Dmitriy Denisyuk, Viktor Kukar (32 Vankhaz Voskanov, 61 Vyacheslav Banul). Trainer: Aleksandr Bubnov

Goals: Niniadis (59), Gogic (63, 67), Georgatos (77), Alexandris (83)

FC SION v GALATASARAY ISTANBUL 1-4 (1-2)

Stade de Tourbillon, Sion 13.08.1997

Referee: Nikolai Levnikov (RUS) Attendance: 12,500

FC SION: Fabrice Borer; Stefan Wolf, Luiz Milton, Alain Gaspoz (46 Martin Lengen), Yvan Quentin, Johan Lonfat, Jean-Jacques Eydelie, Sébastien Zambaz, Daniel Camadini (59 Gerardo Seoane); Didier Tholot, Marco Grassi (76 James Derivaz). Trainer: Alberto Bigon

GALATASARAY: Volkan Kilimci; Fatih Akyel, Bülent Korkmaz, Gheorghe Popescu, Vedat Inceefe (83 Feti Okuroglu), Tugay Kerimoğlu, Ergün Pembe, Gheorghe Hagi (73 Osman Coskun), Arif Erdem (67 Suat Kaya), Adrian Ilie, Hakan Ünsal. Trainer: Fatih Terim

Goals: Milton (4 og), Arif (9), Lonfat (32), Ilie (60), Suat (85)

MPKC MOZYR v OLYMPIAKOS PEIRAIAS 2-2 (2-1)

Yunost, Mozyr 27.08.1997

Referee: Hermann Albrecht (GER) Attendance: 4,300

MPKC MOZYR: Vladimir Gayev; Andrei Lukashevich, Oleg Sisoyev, Valeriy Apanas, Sergei Polyakov, Evgeniy Lovchev, Yuri Maleyev (60 Mikhail Vavilov), Boris Gorovoi, Vasiliy Kushnir, Dmitriy Denisyuk (60 Kakhaber Esaiashvili), Levan Berishvili. Trainer: Aleksandr Bubnov

OLYMPIAKOS: Dimitris Eleftheropoulos; Giorgos Anatolakis, Kiriakos Karataidis (Cap), Bozidar Pantović, Nikos Dabizas (74 Peter Ofori-Quaye), Refik Sabanadzović, Predrag Djordjević, Stelios Giannakopoulos (60 Sinisa Gogić), Andreas Niniadis, Alekos Alexandris, Ilija Ivić (62 Grigoris Georgatos). Trainer: Dušan Bajević

Goals: Berishvili (5), Anatolakis (9), Kushnir (19), Niniadis (54)

GALATASARAY ISTANBUL v FC SION 4-1 (0-0)

Ali Sami Yen, Istanbul 27.08.1997

Referee: Mario van der Ende (HOL) Attendance: 25,000

GALATASARAY: Volkan Kilimci; Fatih Akyel, Gheorghe Popescu, Bülent Korkmaz (61 Vedat Inceefe), Iulian Filipescu (77 Suat Kaya), Hakan Ünsal, Tugay Kerimoğlu, Gheorghe Hagi, Ergün Pembe (70 Arif Erdem), Adrian Ilie, Hakan Sükür. Trainer: Fatih Terim

FC SION: Fabrice Borer; Stéphane Grichting, Luiz Milton, Stefan Wolf, Martin Lengen, Johan Lonfat (46 David Murray), Marc Hodel, Sébastien Zambaz (72 Alexandre Quennoz), Daniel Camadini; Didier Tholot (46 Sébastien Lipawski), Ahmed Ouattara. Trainer: Alberto Bigon

Goals: Ilie (40, 52, 56), Fatih (62), Ouattara (70)

SV SALZBURG v AC SPARTA PRAHA 0-0

Lehen, Salzburg 13.08.1997

Referee: Manuel Diaz Vega (SPA) Attendance: 6300

SV: Szabolcs Sáfár; Walter Kogler, Thomas Winklhofer, Andrzej Lesiak, Richard Kitzbichler, Heiko Lässig, Walter Hörmann (46 René Aufhauser), Valdas Ivanauskas (46 Nikola Jurcevic), Martin Amerhauser; Eduard Glieder, László Klausz. Trainer: Heribert Weber

SPARTA: Tomáš Poštulka; Zdenek Svoboda, Michal Hornak, Jiří Novotný, Ivan Hasek, Miroslav Baranek (88 Lumir Mistr), Václav Němeček, Martin Hasek (83 Szilard Nemeth), Martin Cizek, Vratislav Lokvenc, Josef Obajdin (64 Michal Bilek). Trainer: Jozef Chovanec

AC SPARTA PRAHA v SV SALZBURG 3-0 (2-0)

Stadión na Letnej, Praha 27.08.1997

Referee: László Vagner (HUN) Attendance: 15,620

SPARTA: Tomáš Poštulka; Zdenek Svoboda, Tomáš Repka, Jiří Novotný, Martin Hasek (82 Michal Bilek), Michal Hornak (79 Vladimir Cifranic), Miroslav Baranek, Václav Němeček, Martin Cizek, Vratislav Lokvenc, Horst Siegl (72 Josef Obajdin). Trainer: Jozef Chovanec

SV: Szabolcs Sáfár; Roman Szewczyk, Franz Aigner, Walter Kogler, Thomas Winklhofer, Heiko Lässig, Gernot Plassnegger, René Aufhauser (46 Eduard Glieder), Martin Amerhauser, Richard Kitzbichler (46 Valdas Ivanauskas), Nikola Jurcevic. Trainer: Heribert Weber

Goals: Baranek (28), Lokvenc (43), Svoboda (66)

IFK GÖTEBORG v GLASGOW RANGERS FC 3-0 (0-0)

Nya Ullevi, Göteborg 13.08.1997

Referee: Vítor Manuel Melo Perreira (POR) Att: 23,126

IFK: Thomas Ravelli; Magnus Johansson, Magnus Erlingmark, Teddy Lucic, Olof Magnusson, Niclas Alexandersson, Stefan Pettersson, Stefan Lindqvist, Pär Karlsson, Andreas Andersson (87 Peter Eriksson), Robert Andersson (87 Johnny Ekström). Trainer: Mats Jingblad

RANGERS: Andy Goram; Sergio Porrini, Joachim Björklund, Alex Cleland, Tony Vidmar, Jonas Thern, Paul Gascoigne, Ståle Stensaas, Jörg Albertz (69 Ian Ferguson), Marco Negri (69 Alistair McCoist), Gordon Durie. Manager: Walter Smith

Goals: Pettersson (56), Karlsson (58), Eriksson (88)

GLASGOW RANGERS FC v IFK GÖTEBORG 1-1 (1-0)

Ibrox Stadium, Glasgow 27.08.1997

Referee: Bernd Heynemann (GER) Attendance: 45,585

RANGERS: Andy Goram; Craig Moore, Sergio Porrini, Joachim Björklund, Charles Miller (79 Jörg Albertz), Ian Ferguson (54 Brian Laudrup), Jonas Thern, Paul Gascoigne, Ståle Stensaas, Marco Negri, Alistair McCoist (64 Gordon Durie). Manager: Walter Smith

IFK: Thomas Ravelli, Olof Magnusson, Teddy Lucic, Magnus Erlingmark, Mikael Nilsson, Niclas Alexandersson, Stefan Pettersson, Stefan Lindqvist, Peter Eriksson, Robert Andersson (74 Emmanuel Tetteh), Andreas Andersson (84 Johnny Ekström). Trainer: Mats Jingblad

Goals: Miller (24), R. Andersson (49)

FC BARCELONA v SKONTO RIGA 3-2 (1-1)

Camp Nou, Barcelona 13.08.1997

Referee: Fernand Meese (BEL) Attendance: 50,000

FC BARCELONA: Rudolfus Hubertus HESP; Michael Reiziger, ABELARDO Fernández Antuña, FERNANDO Manuel Silva COUTO (53 Albert FERRER Llopis), SERGI Barjuan Esclusa, LUIS ENRIQUE Martínez García, Josep GUARDIOLA Sala, Dragan Cirić (63 Juan Antonio PIZZI Torroja), Luis Filipe Madeira Caeiro "FIGO"; GIOVANNI Silva de Oliveira, Emmanuel Amunike (65 Hristo Stoichkov). Trainer: Louis van Gaal

SKONTO: Alexander Kolinko; Yury Shevlyakov, Igor Stepanov, Levan Silagadze, Valery Ivanov, Alexander Rekhviashvili (83 Andrei Shtolcers), Vitaly Astafyev, Imants Bleidelis, Mikhail Zemlinsky, Vladimir Babichev (73 Oleg Blagonadezhdin), Mikhail Mikholap (71 Marian Pakhar). Trainer: Alexander Starkov

Goals: Babichev (25), Giovanni (26, 70), Abelardo (46 og), Stoichkov (90 pen)

SKONTO RIGA v FC BARCELONA 0-1 (0-1)

Daugava, Riga 27.08.1997

Referee: Terje Hauge (NOR) Attendance: 12,000

SKONTO: Alexander Kolinko; Igor Stepanov, Levan Silagadze, Mikhail Zemlinsky, Yury Shevlyakov, Valery Ivanov (78 Oleg Blagonadezhdin), Imants Bleidelis (59 Marian Pakhar), Vladimir Babichev, Mikhail Mikholap, Alexander Rekhviashvili, Vitaly Astafyev (59 David Chaladze). Trainer: Alexander Starkov

FC BARCELONA: Rudolfus Hubertus HESP; Michael Reiziger, Miquel Ángel NADAL Homar, Josep GUARDIOLA Sala (57 Albert FERRER Llopis), SERGI Barjuan Esclusa, Luis Filipe Madeira Caeiro "FIGO", GIOVANNI Silva de Oliveira, Guillermo AMOR Martínez, Emmanuel Amunike (78 Christophe Dugarry), Dragan Cirić (67 Hristo Stoichkov), Sonny ANDERSON da Silva. Trainer: Louis van Gaal

Goal: S. Anderson (52)

BRØNDBY IF v FC DYNAMO KYIV 2-4 (1-2)

Brøndby Stadion, København 13.08.1997

Referee: Armand Ancion (BEL) Attendance: 10,318

BRØNDBY: Mogens Krogh; Søren Colding, Dan Eggen, Per Nielsen, Jens Risager, Ole Bjur, John Jensen, Thomas Thøgersen (46 Kim Daugaard), Ruben Bagger (85 Allan Ravn), Ebbe Sand (80 Søren Krogh), Bo Hansen. Trainer: Ebbe Skovdahl

DYNAMO: Olexandr Shovkovskyi;, Oleh Luzhnyi (86 Mykola Volosyanko), Olexandr Holovko, Vladislav Vashchuk, Yuri Dmitrulin, Yuri Kalitvintsev, Andriy Gusin, Olexandr Khatskevich, Yuri Maksimov (74 Olexandr Radchenko), Andriy Shevchenko, Serhiy Rebrov. Trainer: Valeriy Lobanovskyi

Goals: Gusin (8), Bagger (22), Shevchenko (35), Rebrov (74), Holovko (81), Daugaard (90 pen)

FC DYNAMO KYIV v BRØNDBY IF 0-1 (0-1)

Olympiyskyi, Kyiv 27.08.1997

Referee: Stefano Braschi (ITA) Attendance: 17,000

DYNAMO: Olexandr Shovkovskyi; Oleh Luzhnyi (89 Mykola Volosyanko), Olexandr Holovko, Vladislav Vashchuk, Andriy Gusin, Olexandr Khatskevich (74 Valentin Belkevich), Vitaliy Kosovskyi, Yuri Kalitvintsev (82 Olexandr Radchenko), Yuri Maksimov, Serhiy Rebrov, Andriy Shevchenko. Trainer: Valeriy Lobanovskyi

BRØNDBY: Mogens Krogh; Ole Bjur, Per Nielsen, Jens Risager, Søren Colding, Allan Ravn, John Jensen (68 Peter Madsen), Kim Daugaard (84 Søren Krog), Thomas Thøgersen, Ruben Bagger (88 Kenneth Rasmussen), Dan Eggen. Trainer: Ebbe Skovdahl

Goal: Colding (19)

FEYENOORD ROTTERDAM v FC JAZZ PORI 6-2 (3-1)

Feyenoord, Rotterdam 13.08.1997

Referee: Alfredo Trentalange (ITA) Attendance: 24,330

FEYENOORD: Jerzy Dudek; George Boateng, Henk Fräser, Fernando Picun, Patricio Graff (85 Paul Bosvelt), Kees Van Wonderen, Jean-Paul Van Gastel, Pablo Sánchez, Giovanni Van Bronckhorst, Julio Ricardo Cruz, Henk Vos. Trainer: Arie Haan

JAZZ: Ilkka Siitonen; Ari-Pekka Roiko, Pasi Sulonen, Rami Nieminen, Vesa Rantanen (50 Rami Hakanpää), Saku Laaksonen, Juha Riippa, Janne Puputti, Janne Mäkelä (73 Janne Hietanen), Fabio Orsi (46 Harri Puhakainen), Antonio Pogioli MARCO. Trainer: Jari Pyykölä

Goals: Van Gastel (14 pen, 65 pen), Vos (22, 39), Marco (28, 70), Sánchez (58), Van Bronckhorst (85)

NEWCASTLE UNITED v CROATIA ZAGREB 2-1 (1-0)

St. James' Park, Newcastle 13.08.1997

Referee: Václav Krondl (CZE) Attendance: 34,365

NEWCASTLE UNITED: Shay Given; Steve Watson, Alessandro Pistone, Philippe Albert (67 Steve Howey), Stuart Pearce, Robert Lee, David Batty, John Beresford, Temur Ketsbaia, Jon Dahl Tomasson (.Keith Gillespie), Faustino Asprilla. Manager: Kenny Dalglish

CROATIA: Drazen Ladić; Damir Krznar, Silvio Marić (89 Edin Mujcin), Goran Jurić, Srdjan Mladinić, Dario Simić, Robert Prosinecki, Danijel Sarić (82 Stjepan Tomas), Krunoslav Jurcić, Igor Cvitanović, Mark Viduka. Trainer: Marijan Vlak

Goals: Beresford (21, 71), Cvitanović (51)

FC JAZZ PORI v FEYENOORD ROTTERDAM 1-2 (1-1)

Porin, Pori 27.08.1997

Referee: Aron Huzu (ROM) Attendance: 2,720

JAZZ: Ilkka Siitonen; Janne Mäkelä (64 Ari-Pekka Roiko), Pasi Sulonen (59 Janne Puputti), Rami Nieminen, Janne Hietanen, Jarno Heinikangas, Saku Laaksonen, Juha Riippa, Fabio Orsi (79 Pedro Massacessi), Rami Hakanpää, Antonio Pogioli MARCO. Trainer: Jari Pyykölä

FEYENOORD: Jerzy Dudek; George Boateng, Henk Fräser, Fernando Picun, Patricio Graff, Paul Bosvelt, Jean-Paul Van Gastel, Pablo Sánchez, Giovanni Van Bronckhorst (83 Igor Korneev), Glaúcio Jesus (76 David Connolly), Julio Ricardo Cruz. Trainer: Arie Haan

Goals: Boateng (21), Laaksonen (37), Van Gastel (90)

CROATIA ZAGREB v NEWCASTLE UNITED 2-2 (0-1)

Maksimir, Zagreb 27.08.1997

Referee: Urs Meier (SWI) Attendance: 36,000

CROATIA: Drazen Ladić; Danijel Sarić (78 Josip Simić, 97 Stjepan Tomas), Dario Simić, Goran Jurić, Srdjan Mladinić, Edin Mujcin, Silvio Marić, Robert Prosinecki, Krunoslav Jurcić, Igor Cvitanović, Mark Viduka (73 Vladimir Petrović). Trainer: Marijan Vlak

NEWCASTLE UNITED: Shay Given; Stuart Pearce (30 Steve Howey), Philippe Albert, Alessandro Pistone, Steve Watson, John Beresford (83 Keith Gillespie), Robert Lee, David Batty, Warren Barton, Jon Dahl Tomasson (101 Temur Ketsbaia), Faustino Asprilla. Manager: Kenny Dalglish

Goals: Asprilla (44 pen), Simić (59), Cvitanović (90), Ketsbaia (120)

BAYER 04 LEVERKUSEN v DINAMO TBILISI 6-1 (2-0)

Ulrich-Haberland-Stadion, Leverkusen 13.08.1997

Referee: Peter Mikkelsen (DEN) Attendance: 20,500

BAYER: Dirk Heinen; Christian Wörns, Jens Nowotny, Markus Happe, Hans-Peter Lehnhoff (77 René Rydlewicz), Nico Kovac (50 Frederico da Rosa EMERSON), Carsten Ramelow, Stefan Beinlich, Jan Heintze, Ulf Kirsten, Erik Meijer (65 Paulo Roberto Rink). Trainer: Christoph Daum

DINAMO: Irakli Zoidze; Nugzar Lobjanidze, Kakhi Kaladze (27 Zviad Jeladze), Valter Guchua, Givi Didava, Gia Chkhaidze, Giorgi Kiknadze, Kakhi Gogichaishvili, Levan Tskitishvili (50 Aleksandre Gogoberishvili), David MuJiří (65 Levan Khomeriki), Aleksandre Iashvili. Trainer: David Kipiani

Goals: Lehnhoff (4), Ramelow (44), Meijer (47, 62), Iashvili (58), Kirsten (56), Rink (85)

DINAMO TBILISI
v BAYER 04 LEVERKUSEN 1-0 (1-0)

Boris Paichadze, Tbilisi 27.08.1997

Referee: Paul Durkin (ENG) Attendance: 10,000

DINAMO: Irakli Zoidze (Cap); Levan Tskitishvili, Zviad Jeladze, Nugzar Lobjanidze, Givi Didava, Valter Guchua, Giorgi Kiknadze, Aleksandre Gogoberishvili (66 Rati Aleksidze), Gia Chkhaidze, David MuJiří (89 Givi Kvaratskhelia), Aleksandre Iashvili. Trainer: David Kipiani

BAYER: Dirk Heinen; Jens Nowotny, Christian Wörns, Markus Happe, Hans-Peter Lehnhoff (77 Frederico da Rosa EMERSON), Nico Kovac, Carsten Ramelow, Stefan Beinlich, Jan Heintze, Ulf Kirsten (70 Markus Feldhoff), Erik Meijer (70 Paulo Roberto Rink). Trainer: Christoph Daum

Goal: MuJiří (11)

WIDZEW LÓDZ v AC PARMA 1-3 (0-1)

Widzew, Lódz 13.08.1997

Referee: Marc Batta (FRA) Attendance: 12,453

WIDZEW: Arkadiusz Onyszko; Miroslaw Szymkowiak, Tomasz Lapinski, Dariusz Gesior, Radoslaw Michalski, Andriy Mikhalchuk (81 Marek Szemonski), Maciej Terlecki (60 Alexandru Curtianu), Piotr Szarpak, Rafal Siadaczka, Jacek Dembinski, Andrzej Kobylanski (46 Marcin Zajac). Trainer: Franciszek Smuda

PARMA: Gian Luigi Buffon; Roberto Mussi, Lilian Thuram, Fabio Cannavaro, Antonio Benarrivo, Massimo Crippa, Néstor Sensini, Dino Baggio, Reynald Pedros (60 Pietro Strada), Hernán Crespo (61 Filippo Maniero), Enrico Chiesa (80 Stefano Fiore). Trainer: Carlo Ancelotti

Goals: Chiesa (27, 46, 48), Mikhalchuk (52)

STEAUA BUCUREŞTI
v PARIS SAINT GERMAIN 3-2 (0-1)

Steaua Bucureşti 13.08.1997

Referee: José Maria Garcia-Aranda Encinar (SPA)
Attendance: 20,000

STEAUA: Zoltan Ritli; Laurenţiu Reghecampf, Tiberiu Csik, Valeriu Răchită, Marius Achim Baciu, Roland Nagy; Denis Georgian Şerban, Iosif Rotariu, Damian Militaru (62 Cătălin Munteanu), Marius Mihai Lăcătuş (80 Ion Lavi Hrib), Laurenţiu Dumitru Roşu (84 Cristian Ciocoiu). Trainer: Mihai Stoichiţă

PSG: Christophe Revault; Laurent Fournier, Paul le Guen, Alain Roche, Jimmy Algérino; Vincent Guérin, Bruno Ngotty, RAÍ Souza Vieira, Franck Gava; Marco Simone (80 Patrice Loko), Florian Maurice. Trainer: Ricardo Gomes

Goals: Guérin (19), Rotariu (54 pen), Maurice (65), Şerban (71), Lăcătuş (78)

The match was awarded 3-0 to Steaua Bucureşti after Paris Saint-Germain fielded an ineligible player.

AC PARMA v WIDZEW LÓDZ 4-0 (2-0)

Ennio Tardini, Parma 27.08.1997

Referee: Hugh Dallas (SCO) Attendance: 25,000

PARMA: Gian Luigi Buffon; ZÉ MARIA Ferreira, Lilian Thuram, Fabio Cannavaro, Antonio Benarrivo, Reynald Pedros, Néstor Sensini (73 Mauro Milanese), Dino Baggio, Massimo Crippa (67 Pierluigi Orlandini), Hernán Crespo, Enrico Chiesa (67 ADAILTON Martins).
Trainer: Carlo Ancelotti

WIDZEW: Arkadiusz Onyszko; Miroslaw Szymkowiak, Radoslaw Michalski, Daniel Bogusz, Rafal Siadaczka, Alexandru Curtianu, Bleriot Heuyot Tobit, Piotr Szarpak, Maciej Terlecki, Andrzej Kobylanski (77 Marek Szemonski), Marcin Zajac. Trainer: Franciszek Smuda

Goals: Pedros (37), Sensini (41, 52), Adailton (78)

PARIS SAINT GERMAIN
v STEAUA BUCUREŞTI 5-0 (4-0)

Parc des Princes, Paris 27.08.1997

Referee: Dick Jol (HOL) Attendance: 42,585

PSG: Christophe Revault; Bruno Ngotty, Alain Roche, Paul le Guen; Jimmy Algérino, LEONARDO Nascimento, Franck Gava, Didier Domi; Florian Maurice (76 Jérôme Leroy), RAÍ Souza Vieira (Cap), Marco Simone. Trainer: Ricardo Gomes

STEAUA: Zoltan Ritli; Laurenţiu Reghecampf, Tiberiu Csik, Valeriu Răchită, Iulian Ilie Miu, Roland Nagy (35 Ion Lavi Hrib); Denis Georgian Şerban (80 Cătălin Munteanu), Iosif Rotariu, Marius Achim Baciu (67 Cristian Ciocoiu), Damian Militaru, Laurenţiu Dumitru Roşu. Trainer: Mihai Stoichiţă

Goals: Raí (3 pen, 23 pen, 56), Simone (31), Maurice (41)

BEITAR JERUSALEM
v SPORTING CLUBE DE PORTUGAL LISBOA 0-0

Teddi Malcha, Jerusalem 13.08.1997

Referee: Günther Benkö (AUS) Attendance: 7,400

BEITAR: Itzhak David Korenfain; Raanan Deree, Sergiy Tretyak, Tomer Azoulay, David Amsalem; Yossi Abuksis (85 Jan Telesnikov), Alon Harazi, István Pisont, István Hamar; István Sallói (79 Nir Avraham Sivilia), Eliahu Ohana.
Trainer: Dror Kashtan

SPORTING: Filip De Wilde; Abdelilah SABER, MARCO AURELIO Cunha dos Santos, Roberto Luís Gaspar Deus Severo "BETO", Luis Miguel Pedrosa, OCEANO Andrade da Cruz, Didier Lang, PEDRO Alexandre dos Santos BARBOSA (74 César RAMIREZ Caje), Carlos Miguel (63 José Luís da Cruz VIDIGAL), Mustapha Hadji, LEANDRO Machado (63 Ivailo Stoimenov Iordanov). Trainer: Octávio Machado

SPORTING CLUBE DE PORTUGAL LISBOA v BEITAR JERUSALEM 3-0 (1-0)

José Alvalade, Lisboa 27.08.1997

Referee: Leif Sundell (SWE) Attendance: 50,000

SPORTING: Filip De Wilde; Abdelilah SABER, Roberto Luís Gaspar Deus Severo "BETO", MARCO AURELIO Cunha dos Santos, Luis Miguel Pedrosa (79 VINICIUS Conceição e Silva), OCEANO Andrade da Cruz (Cap), Didier Lang, Mustapha Hadji (73 Pedro Martins), PEDRO Alexandre dos Santos BARBOSA (70 Carlos Miguel), Ivailo Stoimenov Iordanov, LEANDRO Machado. Trainer: Octávio Machado

BEITAR: Itzhak David Korenfain; Ehud Eliyahu Cahila (59 Eitan Mizrahi), Sergiy Tretyak, Tomer Azoulay, Raanan Deree (25 Shmul Levi), Yossi Abuksis, David Amsalem, Alon Harazi, István Pisont, István Sallói, Eliahu Ohana (40 Nir Avraham Sivilia). Trainer: Dror Kashtan

Goals: Iordanov (5), Leandro (55, 68)

ANORTHOSIS FAMAGUSTA v LIERSE SK 2-0 (1-0)

Antonis Papadopoulos, Larnaca 13.08.1997

Referee: Alain Sars (FRA) Attendance: 7,456

ANORTHOSIS: Nikos Panagiotou; Stavros Foukaris, Sozos Andreou, Dimitris Ioannou, Zaharias Haralampous (89 Histos Kotsonis), Panikos Pounas, Vladan Tomic, Vesko Mihajlovic, Slobodan Krcmarevic (79 Pambis Andreou), Vasos Melanarkitis, Giannakis Okas (65 Panagiotis Egkomitis). Trainer: Dušan Mitosević

LIERSE: Philippe Vande Walle; David Brocken, Eric Van Meir, Claus Eftevaag, Nico Van Kerckhoven, Frank Leen, Yves Serneels, Pascal Bovri (81 Frédéric Wilkin), Pieter Huistra, Filip Haagdoren, Ralph Hasenhütl. Trainer: Jos Daerden

Goals: Okkas (42), Mihajlovic (90)

LIERSE SK v ANORTHOSIS FAMAGUSTA 3-0 (1-0)

Herman Vanderpoorten, Lier 27.08.1997

Referee: Lubos Michel (SVK) Attendance: 6,600

LIERSE: Philippe Vande Walle; David Brocken, Eric Van Meir, Claus Eftevaag, Yves Serneels, Frank Leen, Thomas Zdebel, Nico Van Kerckhoven, Filip Haagdoren (87 Daniel Scavone), Ralph Hasenhüttl (65 Robby Van de Weyer), Pieter Huistra (80 Andrew Uwuigbe). Trainer: Jos Daerden

ANORTHOSIS: Nikos Panagiotou; Stavros Foukaris, Zaharias Haralampous (87 Hristos Kotsonis), Dimitris Ioannou, Sozos Andreou (51 Kostas Stavrou), Slobodan Krcmarevic, Panikos Pounas, Vladan Tomic, Giannakis Okas (70 Panagiotis Egkomitis), Vasos Melanarkitis, Vesko Mihajlovic. Trainer: Dušan Mitosević

Sent off: Ioannou (69)

Goals: Van Meir (22 pen), Hasenhüttl (47), Tomic (84 og)

MTK BUDAPEST v ROSENBORG BK TRONDHEIM 3-2 (2-2)

The match was abandoned due to floodlight failure and a full replay was ordered.

MTK BUDAPEST v ROSENBORG BK TRONDHEIM 0-1 (0-0)

Hungáriá úti, Budapest 14.08.1997

Referee: Ahmet Cakar (TUR) Attendance: 5,000

MTK: Gábor Babos; József Csábi, Attila Kuttor, Tamás Szamosi, László Farkashazi, Tamás Zimmermann, Gábor Halmai, Béla Illés, Ferenc Orosz, Gábor Egressy, Krisztián Kenesei (63 Aurél Csertoi, 84 Csaba Madar). Trainer: József Garami

ROSENBORG: Jørn Jamtfall; Vegard Heggem, Bjørn Otto Bragstad, Erik Hoftun, André Bergdølmo, Harald Brattbakk (90 Andreas Mayer), Roar Strand, Bent Skammelsrud, Runar Berg, Jahn Ivar Jakobsen (85 Tore André Dahlum), Sigurd Rushfeldt. Trainer: Nils Arne Eggen

Goal: Rushfeldt (88)

ROSENBORG BK TRONDHEIM v MTK BUDAPEST 3-1 (2-0)

Lerkendal, Trondheim 27.08.1997

Referee: Serge Muhmenthaler (SWI) Attendance: 15,014

ROSENBORG: Jørn Jamtfall; André Bergdølmo, Erik Hoftun, Bjørn Otto Bragstad, Vegard Heggem, Roar Strand (86 Andreas Mayer), Runar Berg, Bent Skammelsrud; Sigurd Rushfeldt (90 Tore André Dahlum), Harald Brattbakk, Jahn Ivar Jakobsen. Trainer: Nils Arne Eggen

MTK: Gábor Babos; Zoltán Molnár, Attila Kuttor, László Farkashazi, Ferenc Orosz (61 Sándor Preisinger), Béla Illés, Gábor Egressy (75 Csaba Madar), Gábor Halmai, Tamás Szamosi, Krisztián Kenesei, József Csábi. Trainer: József Garami

Goals: Jakobsen (14 pen, 16), Kuttor (77), Brattbakk (84)

CHAMPIONS LEAGUE

GROUP A

AC SPARTA PRAHA v AC PARMA 0-0

Stadión na Letnej, Praha 17.09.1997

Referee: Dick Jol (HOL) Attendance: 17,846

SPARTA: Tomáš Poštulka, Tomáš Repka, Zdenek Svoboda, Martin Cizek (46 Petr Gabriel), Jiří Novotný, Vratislav Lokvenc, Horst Siegl (86 Josef Obajdin), Martin Hasek, Lumir Mistr (71 Marian Lalik), Miroslav Baranek, Václav Němeček. Trainer: Jozef Chovanec

PARMA: Gian Luigi Buffon; ZÉ MARIA Ferreira, Antonio Benarrivo, Néstor Sensini, Dino Baggio, Massimo Crippa, Pietro Strada, Hernán Crespo (80 Filippo Maniero), Fabio Cannavaro, Enrico Chiesa, Lilian Thuram. Trainer: Carlo Ancelotti

GALATASARAY ISTANBUL v BORUSSIA DORTMUND 0-1 (0-0)

Ali Sami Yen, Istanbul 17.09.1997

Referee: José Maria Garcia-Aranda Encinar (SPA) Attendance: 30,000

GALATASARAY: Volkan Kilimci; Hakan Ünsal, Fatih Akyel, Bülent Korkmaz, Gheorghe Popescu, Ümit Davala (67 Arif Erdem), Tugay Kerimoğlu, Gheorghe Hagi, Ergün Pembe, Adrian Ilie, Hakan Sükür. Trainer: Fatih Terim

BORUSSIA: Stefan Klos; Knut Reinhardt, Wolfgang Feiersinger, Jürgen Kohler (46 Martin Kree), JÚLIO CÉSAR Silva, Paul Lambert, Steffen Freund (46 Vladimir But), Michael Zorc, Jörg Heinrich, Heiko Herrlich, Stéphane Chapuisat. Trainer: Nevio Scala

Goal: Chapuisat (73)

BORUSSIA DORTMUND v AC SPARTA PRAHA 4-1 (1-0)

Bökelberg, Dortmund 1.10.1997

Referee: Vítor Manuel Melo Pereira (POR) Att: 42,000

BORUSSIA: Stefan Klos; Stefan Reuter, Matthias Sammer, Wolfgang Feiersinger (76 Michael Zorc), Jürgen Kohler, Knut Reinhardt, Paulo Manuel Sousa (81 Paul Lambert), Andreas Möller, Jörg Heinrich, Heiko Herrlich (85 Scott Booth), Stéphane Chapuisat. Trainer: Nevio Scala

SPARTA: Tomáš Poštulka, Tomáš Repka, Zdenek Svoboda, Jiří Novotný, Michal Hornak (30 Josef Obajdin), Martin Hasek (54 Petr Gabriel), Václav Němeček, Ivan Hasek, Martin Cizek, Vratislav Lokvenc (70 Szilard Nemeth), Horst Siegl. Trainer: Jozef Chovanec

Goals: Herrlich (20), Chapuisat (59,75), Heinrich (69), Siegl (76)

AC PARMA v GALATASARAY ISTANBUL 2-0 (2-0)

Ennio Tardini, Parma 1.10.1997

Referee: Serge Muhmenthaler (SWI) Attendance: 15,922

PARMA: Gian Luigi Buffon; ZÉ MARIA Ferreira (76 Roberto Mussi), Lilian Thuram, Fabio Cannavaro, Mauro Milanese, Massimo Crippa, Néstor Sensini, Dino Baggio, Pietro Strada (67 Stefano Fiore), Enrico Chiesa (87 Filippo Maniero), Hernán Crespo. Trainer: Carlo Ancelotti

GALATASARAY: Volkan Kilimci; Iulian Filipescu, Fatih Akyel, Bülent Korkmaz, Hakan Ünsal, Ergün Pembe (46 Adrian Ilie), Gheorghe Popescu, Tugay Kerimoğlu, Ümit Davala (78 Mehmet Gönülagar), Hakan Sükür, Arif Erdem (62 Okan Buruk). Trainer: Fatih Terim

Goals: Sensini (24), Crespo (39)

AC PARMA v BORUSSIA DORTMUND 1-0 (0-0)

Ennio Tardini, Parma 22.10.1997

Referee: Gilles Veissière (FRA) Attendance: 13,449

PARMA: Gian Luigi Buffon; ZÉ MARIA Ferreira (76 Roberto Mussi), Fabio Cannavaro, Lilian Thuram, Antonio Benarrivo, Massimo Crippa, Néstor Sensini, Dino Baggio, Pietro Strada (76 Mario Stanić), Hernán Crespo, Enrico Chiesa (88 Stefano Fiore). Trainer: Carlo Ancelotti

BORUSSIA: Stefan Klos; Stefan Reuter, Wolfgang Feiersinger (87 Michael Zorc), JÚLIO CÉSAR Silva, Jürgen Kohler, Jörg Heinrich, Steffen Freund (79 Heiko Herrlich), PAULO Manuel Carvalho de SOUSA, Andreas Möller, Vladimir But, Stéphane Chapuisat. Trainer: Nevio Scala

Goal: Crespo (62)

AC SPARTA PRAHA v GALATASARAY ISTANBUL 3-0 (1-0)

Stadión na Letnej, Praha 22.10.1997

Referee: David Roland Elleray (ENG) Attendance: 11,108

SPARTA: Tomáš Poštulka, Tomáš Repka, Michal Hornak (90 Szilard Nemeth), Zdenek Svoboda, Jiří Novotný, Petr Gabriel (85 Vladimir Cifranic), Horst Siegl, Václav Němeček, Miroslav Baranek (77 Josef Obajdin), Martin Hasek, Vratislav Lokvenc. Trainer: Jozef Chovanec

GALATASARAY: Volkan Kilimci; Fatih Akyel, Vedat Inceefe, Gheorghe Popescu, Iulian Filipescu, Hakan Ünsal, Tugay Kerimoğlu, Gheorghe Hagi (46 Ergün Pembe), Ümit Davala, Arif Erdem (46 Hakan Sükür), Adrian Ilie (69 Bülent Korkmaz). Trainer: Fatih Terim

Sent off: Vedat (35) and Hakan Ünsal (67)

Goals: Siegl (34), Gabriel (66), Obajdin (87)

BORUSSIA DORTMUND v AC PARMA 2-0 (0-0)

Bökelberg, Dortmund 5.11.1997

Referee: Kim Milton Nielsen (DEN) Attendance: 40,000

BORUSSIA: Stefan Klos; Stefan Reuter, JÚLIO CÉSAR Silva, Wolfgang Feiersinger, Jörg Heinrich, Christian Timm (46 Jovan Kirovski), PAULO Manuel Carvalho de SOUSA (79 Steffen Freund), Paul Lambert, Andreas Möller, Vladimir But, Stéphane Chapuisat (50 Scott Booth). Trainer: Nevio Scala

PARMA: Gian Luigi Buffon; Roberto Mussi, Fabio Cannavaro, Lilian Thuram, Antonio Benarrivo, Mario Stanić (70 Filippo Maniero), Dino Baggio, Néstor Sensini, Pietro Strada (30 Massimo Crippa), Hernán Crespo, Enrico Chiesa (78 Stefano Fiore). Trainer: Carlo Ancelotti

Goals: Möller (50, 75)

GALATASARAY ISTANBUL v AC SPARTA PRAHA 2-0 (0-0)

Ali Sami Yen, Istanbul 5.11.1997

Referee: Michel Piraux (BEL) Attendance: 16,000

GALATASARAY: Volkan Kilimci; Fatih Akyel, Gheorghe Popescu, Bülent Korkmaz, Osman Coskun, Ümit Davala (75 Arif Erdem), Tugay Kerimoğlu, Gheorghe Hagi (89 Emre Belözoglu), Ergün Pembe, Hakan Sükür (82 Adnan Ilgin), Adrian Ilie. Trainer: Fatih Terim

SPARTA: Tomáš Poštulka; Tomáš Repka, Tomáš Votava (65 Petr Gabriel), Michal Hornak, Zdenek Svoboda, Martin Cizek, Martin Hasek, Miroslav Baranek (21 Josef Obajdin), Jiří Novotný, Vratislav Lokvenc, Horst Siegl (65 Václav Němeček). Trainer: Jozef Chovanec

Goals: Tugay (58, 85)

AC PARMA v AC SPARTA PRAHA 2-2 (1-0)

Ennio Tardini, Parma 26.11.1997

Referee: Leif Sundell (SWE) Attendance: 16,200

PARMA: Gian Luigi Buffon; ZÉ MARIA Ferreira, Lilian Thuram, Fabio Cannavaro, Mauro Milanese, Stefano Fiore, Dino Baggio, Federico Giunti, Mario Stanić (84 Pierluigi Orlandini), Hernán Crespo (84 Filippo Maniero), Enrico Chiesa. Trainer: Carlo Ancelotti

SPARTA: Tomáš Poštulka, Tomáš Repka, Tomáš Votava, Michal Hornak, Zdenek Svoboda, Martin Cizek, Jiří Novotný, Horst Siegl, Petr Gabriel (70 Václav Němeček), Lumir Mistr (50 Vratislav Lokvenc), Miroslav Baranek (62 Josef Obajdin). Trainer: Jozef Chovanec

Goals: Chiesa (21, 90 pen), Novotný (88), Obajdin (89)

BORUSSIA DORTMUND v GALATASARAY ISTANBUL 4-1 (2-0)

Bökelberg, Dortmund 26.11.1997

Referee: Rune Pedersen (NOR) Attendance: 45,000

BORUSSIA: Stefan Klos; Stefan Reuter, Wolfgang Feiersinger, JÚLIO CÉSAR Silva, Steffen Freund, PAULO Manuel Carvalho de SOUSA (78 Christian Timm), Vladimir But (46 Jovan Kirovski), Andreas Möller (46 Michael Zorc), Jörg Heinrich, Heiko Herrlich, Stéphane Chapuisat. Trainer: Nevio Scala

GALATASARAY: Volkan Kilimci; Iulian Filipescu, Arif Erdem, Gheorghe Popescu, Bülent Korkmaz, Fatih Akyel, Ümit Davala (46 Okan Buruk), Tugay Kerimoğlu, Ergün Pembe, Emre Belözoglu (36 Osman Coskun), Hakan Sükür. Trainer: Fatih Terim

Goals: But (22), Herrlich (33), Zorc (47, 86 pen), Ergun (87)

AC SPARTA PRAHA v BORUSSIA DORTMUND 0-3 (0-1)

Stadión na Letnej, Praha 10.12.1997

Referee: Hugh Dallas (SCO) Attendance: 10,925

SPARTA: Tomáš Poštulka; Tomáš Votava, Zdenek Svoboda, Jiří Novotný (52 Miroslav Baranek), Josef Obajdin (67 Lumir Mistr), Václav Němeček, Martin Hasek, Martin Cizek, Petr Gabriel, Horst Siegl (77 Pospisil), Vratislav Lokvenc. Trainer: Jozef Chovanec

BORUSSIA: Stefan Klos; Stefan Reuter, Wolfgang Feiersinger, Martin Kree, Steffen Freund, Lars Ricken (68 Björn Mehnert), Andreas Möller (64 Scott Booth), Vladimir But (80 Christian Timm), Knut Reinhardt, Heiko Herrlich, Jovan Kirovski. Trainer: Nevio Scala

Goals: Möller (30), Kirovski (47), Booth (71)

GALATASARAY ISTANBUL v AC PARMA 1-1 (0-0)

Ali Sami Yen, Istanbul 10.12.1997

Referee: László Vagner (HUN) Attendance: 14,000

GALATASARAY: Volkan Kilimci; Bülent Korkmaz, Fatih Akyel, Iulian Filipescu (84 Osman Coskun), Ergün Pembe, Tugay Kerimoğlu, Gheorghe Popescu, Gheorghe Hagi, Ümit Davala (68 Arif Erdem), Hakan Sükür, Adrian Ilie. Trainer: Fatih Terim

PARMA: Gian Luigi Buffon; ZÉ MARIA Ferreira (72 Roberto Mussi), Lilian Thuram, Luigi Apolloni, Mauro Milanese (72 ADAILTON Martins), Mario Stanić, Stefano Fiore, Dino Baggio, Massimo Crippa; Enrico Chiesa, Filippo Maniero (83 Hernán Cespo). Trainer: Carlo Ancelotti

Goals: Chiesa (46), Ilie (51)

	P	W	D	L	F	A	Pts
Borussia Dortmund	6	5	0	1	14	3	15
AC Parma	6	2	3	1	6	5	9
AC Sparta Praha	6	1	2	3	6	11	5
Galatasaray Istanbul	6	1	1	4	4	11	4

GROUP B

FC KOŠICE v MANCHESTER UNITED FC 0-3 (0-1)

Vsesportovy areal, Košice 17.09.1997

Referee: Leif Sundell (SWE) Attendance: 10,000

FC KOŠICE: Ladislav Molnar; Marek Spilar, András Telek, Ivan Kozak, Vladimir Janocko, Ruslan Lyubarskyi (46 Albert Rusnak), Jozef Kozlej (77 Lubomir Faktor), Robert Semenik, Vladislav Zvara, Miroslav Sovic, Radoslav Kráľ. Trainer: Jan Kozak

MANCHESTER UNITED: Peter Schmeichel; Gary Neville, Dennis Irwin, Gary Pallister, David Beckham (75 Brian McClair), Nicky Butt, Andy Cole, Karel Poborsky, Roy Keane, Paul Scholes, Henning Berg. Manager: Alex Ferguson

Goals: Irwin (30), Berg (61), Cole (88)

JUVENTUS FC TORINO v FEYENOORD ROTTERDAM 5-1 (3-0)

Delle Alpi, Torino 17.09.1997

Referee: Bernd Heynemann (GER) Attendance: 24,000

JUVENTUS: Angelo Peruzzi; Alessandro Birindelli, Ciro Ferrara, Paolo Montero, Manuel DIMAS Marques Teixeira, Antonio Conte, Didier Deschamps, Zinedine Zidane (71 Gianluca Pessotto), Angelo Di Livio, Filippo Inzaghi (81 Daniel Fonseca), Alessandro del Piero (59 Alessio Tacchinardi). Trainer: Marcello Lippi

FEYENOORD: Jerzy Dudek; Ulrich Van Gobbel, Henk Fräser, Fernando Picun (68 David Connolly), Patricio Graff, Jean-Paul Van Gastel, Pablo Sánchez, Giovanni Van Bronckhorst, Julio Ricardo Cruz, Paul Bosvelt, Igor Korneev (46 George Boateng). Trainer: Arie Haan

Sent off: Di Livio (57)

Goals: Del Piero (3, 11 pen), Inzaghi (34), Van Gastel (57), Zidane (63), Birindelli (80)

FEYENOORD ROTTERDAM v FC KOŠICE 2-0 (2-0)

Feyenoord, Rotterdam 1.10.1997

Referee: Alain Sars (FRA) Attendance: 31,500

FEYENOORD: Jerzy Dudek; Ulrich Van Gobbel (61 George Boateng), Henk Fräser, Fernando Picun, Patricio Graff, Paul Bosvelt (89 David Connolly), Jean-Paul Van Gastel, Pablo Sánchez (80 Kees Van Wonderen), Giovanni Van Bronckhorst, Igor Korneev, Julio Ricardo Cruz. Trainer: Arie Haan

FC KOŠICE: Ladislav Molnar; Marek Spilar, Ivan Kozak, Peter Dzurik, András Telek, Miroslav Sovic (85 Ruslan Lyubarskyi), Vladimir Janocko, Robert Semenik (72 Albert Rusnak), Radoslav Kráľ (68 Lubomir Faktor), Jozef Kozlej, Vladislav Zvara. Trainer: Jan Kozak

Goals: Van Gastel (26 pen), Cruz (34)

MANCHESTER UNITED FC v JUVENTUS FC TORINO 3-2 (1-1)

Old Trafford, Manchester 1.10.1997

Referee: Antonio Jesus Lopez Nieto (SPA) Att: 53,428

MANCHESTER UNITED: Peter Schmeichel; Gary Neville, Ronny Johnsen, Henning Berg, Gary Pallister, Dennis Irwin, David Beckham, Nicky Butt (38 Paul Scholes), Ryan Giggs, Ole Gunnar Solskjaer (49 Philip Neville), Teddy Sheringham. Manager: Alex Ferguson

JUVENTUS: Angelo Peruzzi; Alessandro Birindelli, Ciro Ferrara, Paolo Montero, Manuel DIMAS Marques Teixeira, Fabio Pecchia (69 Mark Iuliano), Zinedine Zidane, Didier Deschamps, Alessio Tacchinardi (19 Gianluca Pessotto), Alessandro del Piero (78 Nicola Amoruso), Filippo Inzaghi. Trainer: Marcello Lippi

Sent off: Deschamps (65)

Goals: Del Piero (1), Sheringham (38), Scholes (69), Giggs (89), Zidane (90)

MANCHESTER UNITED FC v FEYENOORD ROTTERDAM 2-1 (1-0)

Old Trafford, Manchester 22.10.1997

Referee: Serge Muhmenthaler (SWI) Attendance: 53,188

MANCHESTER UNITED: Peter Schmeichel; Gary Neville, Gary Pallister, Philip Neville, Dennis Irwin, David Beckham, Nicky Butt, Paul Scholes, Ryan Giggs, Teddy Sheringham, Andy Cole (81 Ole Gunnar Solskjaer). Manager: Alex Ferguson

FEYENOORD: Jerzy Dudek; Ulrich Van Gobbel, Fernando Picun, Bernard Schuiteman, Patricio Graff, Kees Van Wonderen, Paul Bosvelt, Jean-Paul Van Gastel, Giovanni Van Bronckhorst (38 Igor Korneev), Pablo Sánchez (76 George Boateng), David Connolly (73 Henk Vos). Trainer: Arie Haan

Goals: Scholes (32), Irwin (72 pen), Vos (82)

1.FC KOŠICE v JUVENTUS FC TORINO 0-1 (0-1)

Vsesportovy areal, Košice 22.10.1997

Referee: Edgar Steinborn (GER) Attendance: 10,021

FC KOŠICE: Ladislav Molnar; Ivan Kozak, András Telek, Peter Dzurik, Marek Spilar, Miroslav Sovic (25 Ruslan Lyubarski), Vladislav Zvara, Vladimir Janocko, Dušan Toth (86 Marian Bochnovic), Robert Semenik (78 Albert Rusnak), Jozef Kozlej. Trainer: Jan Kozak

JUVENTUS: Angelo Peruzzi (37 Michelangelo Rampulla); Gianluca Pessotto, Alessandro Birindelli, Mark Iuliano, Manuel DIMAS Marques Teixeira; Angelo Di Livio (32 Fabio Pecchia), Alessio Tacchinardi, Antonio Conte, Zinedine Zidane; Filippo Inzaghi, Alessandro del Piero. Trainer: Marcello Lippi

Goal: Del Piero (34)

FEYENOORD ROTTERDAM v MANCHESTER UNITED FC 1-3 (0-2)

Feyenoord, Rotterdam 5.11.1997

Referee: Sándor Puhl (HUN) Attendance: 42,500

FEYENOORD: Jerzy Dudek; Ulrich Van Gobbel, George Boateng, Bernard Schuiteman, Patricio Graff (34 Geoffrey Claeys), Kees Van Wonderen, Jean-Paul Van Gastel, Paul Bosvelt (81 Clemens Zwijnenberg), Giovanni Van Bronckhorst, Igor Korneev, Julio Ricardo Cruz (75 Henk Vos). Trainer: Geert Meijer

MANCHESTER UNITED: Peter Schmeichel; Gary Neville, Gary Pallister, Henning Berg, Dennis Irwin (82 Philip Neville), David Beckham, Nicky Butt, Paul Scholes (76 Karel Poborsky), Ryan Giggs, Teddy Sheringham, Andy Cole (76 Ole Gunnar Solskjaer). Manager: Alex Ferguson

Goals: Cole (31, 44, 74), Korneev (86)

MANCHESTER UNITED FC v FC KOŠICE 3-0 (1-0)

Old Trafford, Manchester 27.11.1997

Referee: Cakar Ahmet (TUR) Attendance: 52,535

MANCHESTER UNITED: Peter Schmeichel; Gary Neville, Ronny Johnsen, Gary Pallister, Philip Neville (75 Henning Berg), David Beckham, Nicky Butt (55 Ole Gunnar Solskjaer), Paul Scholes, Ryan Giggs (75 Karel Poborsky), Andy Cole, Teddy Sheringham. Manager: Alex Ferguson

FC KOŠICE: Ladislav Molnar; Robert Semenik, Ivan Kozak, Marek Spilar, Dušan Toth, Miroslav Sovic, Peter Dzurik, Vladislav Zvara (80 Lubomir Faktor), Vladimir Janocko (31 Albert Rusnak); Ruslan Lyubarskyi, Jozef Kozlej (83 Marian Bochnovic). Trainer: Jan Kozak

Goals: Cole (41), Faktor (85 og), Sheringham (90)

JUVENTUS FC TORINO v FC KOŠICE 3-2 (1-0)

Delle Alpi, Torino 5.11.1997

Referee: Juan Ansuategui Roca (SPA) Attendance: 3,500

JUVENTUS: Angelo Peruzzi; Alessandro Birindelli, Ciro Ferrara, Alessio Tacchinardi, Mark Iuliano; Antonio Conte, Didier Deschamps, Zinedine Zidane (57 Nicola Amoruso), Fabio Pecchia (69 Moreno Torricelli); Filippo Inzaghi (57 Daniel Fonseca), Alessandro del Piero.
Trainer: Marcello Lippi

FC KOŠICE: Ladislav Molnar; Robert Semenik, Ivan Kozak, András Telek, Dušan Toth, Radoslav Kráľ (69 Lubomir Faktor), Miroslav Sovic, Vladislav Zvara, Ruslan Lyubarskyi (75 Albert Rusnak), Vladimir Janocko (81 Marian Bochnovic), Jozef Kozlej. Trainer: Jan Kozak

Goals: Del Piero (42), Amoruso (58), Fonseca (61), Lyubarskyi (66), Toth (71)

FC KOŠICE v FEYENOORD ROTTERDAM 0-1 (0-0)

Vsesportovy areal, Košice 10.12.1997

Referee: Jorge Monteiro Coroado (POR) Attendance: 2,662

FC KOŠICE: Ladislav Molnar; Ivan Kozak, Robert Semenik, Marek Spilar, Peter Dzurik, Miroslav Sovic, Vladislav Zvara (80 Lubomir Faktor), Vladimir Janocko (31 Albert Rusnak), Dušan Toth, Jozef Kozlej (83 Marian Bochnovic), Ruslan Lyubarskyi. Trainer: Jan Kozak

FEYENOORD: Jerzy Dudek; George Boateng, Ulrich Van Gobbel, Kees Van Wonderen, Clemens Zwijnenberg, Paul Bosvelt, Jean-Paul Van Gastel, Pablo Sánchez (67 Igor Korneev), Giovanni Van Bronckhorst, Henk Vos, David Connollly (46 Robin Nelisse, 85 Bernard Schuiteman).
Trainer: Leo Beenhakker

Goal: Van Bronckhorst (81)

FEYENOORD ROTTERDAM v JUVENTUS FC TORINO 2-0 (0-0)

Feyenoord, Rotterdam 26.11.1997

Referee: Nikolai Levnikov (RUS) Attendance: 35,000

FEYENOORD: Jerzy Dudek; Clemens Zwijnenberg, Kees Van Wonderen, Ulrich Van Gobbel, Geoffrey Claeys, George Boateng, Jean-Paul Van Gastel, Pablo Sánchez (67 Paul Bosvelt), Giovanni Van Bronckhorst, Julio Ricardo Cruz, Henk Vos. Trainer: Leo Beenhakker

JUVENTUS: Angelo Peruzzi; Alessandro Birindelli, Ciro Ferrara, Mark Iuliano (73 Manuel DIMAS Marques Teixeira), Gianluca Pessotto, Angelo Di Livio, Didier Deschamps (42 Moreno Torricelli), Zinedine Zidane, Alessio Tacchinardi, Nicola Amoruso, Alessandro del Piero (68 Daniel Fonseca).
Trainer: Marcello Lippi

Goals: Cruz (66, 88)

JUVENTUS FC TORINO v MANCHESTER UNITED FC 1-0 (0-0)

Delle Alpi, Torino 10.12.1997

Referee: Gilles Veissière (FRA) Attendance: 47,766

JUVENTUS: Angelo Peruzzi; Alessandro Birindelli (75 Manuel DIMAS Marques Teixeira), Ciro Ferrara, Mark Iuliano, Moreno Torricelli; Angelo Di Livio, Zinedine Zidane, Antonio Conte (65 Paolo Montero), Alessio Tacchinardi (46 Fabio Pecchia), Filippo Inzaghi, Daniel Fonseca.
Trainer: Marcello Lippi

MANCHESTER UNITED: Peter Schmeichel; Gary Neville, Gary Pallister, Henning Berg, Philip Neville, David Beckham, Ronny Johnsen, Teddy Sheringham, Ryan Giggs, Karel Poborsky (81 Brian McClair), Ole Gunnar Solskjaer (74 Andy Cole). Manager: Alex Ferguson

Goal: Inzaghi (84)

	P	W	D	L	F	A	Pts
Manchester United FC	6	5	0	1	14	5	15
Juventus FC Torino	6	4	0	2	12	8	12
Feyenoord Rotterdam	6	3	0	3	8	10	9
FC Košice	6	0	0	6	2	13	0

GROUP C

PSV EINDHOVEN v FC DYNAMO KYIV 1-3 (1-1)

Philips, Eindhoven 17.09.1997

Referee: Rune Pedersen (NOR) Attendance: 30,000

PSV: Ronald Waterreus; Chris Van der Weerden (72 Tomasz Iwan), Jaap Stam, Stan Valckx, Arthur Numan, Zeljko Petrovic, Wim Jonk, Marc Degryse (53 Luc Nilis), Philip Cocu, Gilles De Bilde (77 Peter Møller), Boudewijn Zenden. Trainer: Dick Advocaat

DYNAMO: Olexandr Shovkovskyi; Vladislav Vashchuk, Olexandr Holovko, Olexandr Khatskevich (55 Valentin Belkevich), Vitaliy Kosovskyi, Yuri Dmitrulin, Yuri Kalitvintsev, Yuri Maksimov (77 Dmytro Mikhailenko), Andriy Gusin (72 Serhiy Bezhenar), Andriy Shevchenko, Serhiy Rebrov. Trainer: Valeriy Lobanovskyi

Goals: Maksimov (33), Jonk (40), Rebrov (47), Shevchenko (90)

NEWCASTLE UNITED v FC BARCELONA 3-2 (2-0)

St.James' Park, Newcastle 17.09.1997

Referee: Pier Luigi Collina (ITA) Attendance: 36,600

NEWCASTLE UNITED: Shay Given; Steve Watson, Philippe Albert, Warren Barton, John Beresford, David Batty, Robert Lee (Cap), John Barnes (81 Temur Ketsbaia), Jon Dahl Tomasson (77 Darren Peacock), Keith Gillespie, Faustino Asprilla. Manager: Kenny Dalglish

FC BARCELONA: Rudolfus Hubertus HESP; Albert CELADES López, Michael Reiziger, Miquel Ángel NADAL Homar, SERGI Barjuan Esclusa, Ivan DE LA PEÑA López, Emmanuel Amunike (46 Dragan Ćirić), Luis Filipe Madeira Caeiro "FIGO" (Cap), Vitor Barbosa Ferreira "RIVALDO", LUIS ENRIQUE Martínez García, Sonny ANDERSON Da Silva (56 Christophe Dugarry). Trainer: Louis van Gaal

Goals: Asprilla (22 pen, 31, 49), Luis Enrique (73), Figo (89)

FC BARCELONA v PSV EINDHOVEN 2-2 (0-0)

Camp Nou, Barcelona 1.10.1997

Referee: Hellmut Krug (GER) Attendance: 80,000

FC BARCELONA: Rudolfus Hubertus HESP; Albert CELADES López, Miquel Ángel NADAL Homar (58 Josep GUARDIOLA Sala), SERGI Barjuan Esclusa, Michael Reiziger, Ivan DE LA PEÑA López, Luis Filipe Madeira Caeiro «FIGO» (Cap), Vitor Barbosa Ferreira «RIVALDO», LUIS ENRIQUE Martínez García, Dragan Ćirić (72 Juan Antonio PIZZI Torroja), Sonny ANDERSON Da Silva (15 Christophe Dugarry). Trainer: Louis van Gaal

PSV: Ronald Waterreus; Ernest Faber, Jaap Stam, Arthur Numan (Cap), Zeljko Petrovic, Wim Jonk (83 Peter Møller), Chris Van der Weerden, Philip Cocu, Boudewijn Zenden (67 Luc Nilis), Tomasz Iwan (39 Marcos Batista Vampeta), Gilles De Bilde. Trainer: Dick Advocaat

Sent off: Van der Weerden (34)

Goals: Luis Enrique (60, 73), Cocu (70), P. Møller (86)

FC DYNAMO KYIV v NEWCASTLE UNITED 2-2 (2-0)

Olympiyskyi, Kyiv 1.10.1997

Referee: Peter Mikkelsen (DEN) Attendance: 100,000

DYNAMO: Olexandr Shovkovskyi; Oleh Luzhnyi (41 Serhiy Bezhenar), Olexandr Holovko, Vladislav Vashchuk, Yuri Dmitrulin, Vitaliy Kosovskyi, Andriy Shevchenko, Serhiy Rebrov, Andriy Gusin, Olexandr Khatskevich (74 Olexandr Radchenko), Valentin Belkevich (68 Dmytro Mikhailenko). Trainer: Valeriy Lobanovskyi

UNITED: Shay Given; Warren Barton, Darren Peacock, Philippe Albert, John Beresford, Keith Gillespie, David Batty, John Barnes, Steve Watson, Faustino Asprilla (28 Jon Dahl Tomasson), Robert Lee (46 Temur Ketsbaia). Manager: Kenny Dalglish

Goals: Rebrov (4), Shevchenko (28), Beresford (78), Holovko (85 og)

FC DYNAMO KYIV v FC BARCELONA 3-0 (2-0)

Olympiyskyi, Kyiv 22.10.1997

Referee: Markus Merk (GER) Attendance: 100,000

DYNAMO: Olexandr Shovkovskyi; Oleh Luzhnyi (57 Mykola Volosyanko), Olexandr Holovko, Yuri Dmitrulin, Yuri Maksimov (84 Dmytro Mikhailenko), Andriy Gusin, Vladislav Vashchuk, Yuri Kalitvintsev, Andriy Shevchenko, Vitaliy Kosovskyi, Serhiy Rebrov. Trainer: Valeriy Lobanovskyi

FC BARCELONA: Rudolfus Hubertus HESP; Albert FERRER Llopis, FERNANDO Manuel Silva COUTO, SERGI Barjuan Esclusa, Luis Filipe Madeira Caeiro "FIGO" (81 Dragan Ćirić), LUIS ENRIQUE Martínez García, Michael Reiziger, Vitor Barbosa Ferreira "RIVALDO", ROGER García Junyant, Christophe Dugarry (80 Juan Antonio PIZZI Torroja), ÓSCAR García Junyent (62 Carlos BUSQUETS Barroso). Trainer: Louis van Gaal **Sent off**: Hesp (60)

Goals: Rebrov (5), Maksimov (32), Kalitvintsev (66)

PSV EINDHOVEN v NEWCASTLE UNITED 1-0 (1-0)

Philips, Eindhoven 22.10.1997

Referee: Stefano Braschi (ITA) Attendance: 29,200

PSV: Ronald Waterreus; Marcos Batista Vampeta, Jaap Stam, Ernest Faber, Arthur Numan, Zeljko Petrovic (80 Peter Møller), Wim Jonk, Tomasz Iwan (63 Ovidiu Stîngă), Philip Cocu, Luc Nilis (80 Arnold Bruggink), Gilles De Bilde. Trainer: Dick Advocaat

NEWCASTLE UNITED: Shay Given; Warren Barton (80 Philippe Albert), Darren Peacock, Steve Howey, John Beresford (66 Temur Ketsbaia), Keith Gillespie, Robert Lee, David Batty, Steve Watson, Ian Rush, Jon Dahl Tomasson. Manager: Kenny Dalglish

Goal: Jonk (37)

FC BARCELONA v NEWCASTLE UNITED 1-0 (1-0)

Camp Nou, Barcelona 26.11.1997

Referee: Marc Batta (FRA) Attendance: 25,000

FC BARCELONA: Rudolfus Hubertus HESP; Albert FERRER Llopis, ABELARDO Fernández Antuña, FERNANDO Manuel Silva COUTO, Albert CELADES López, GIOVANNI Silva de Oliveira (80 Miquel Ángel NADAL Homar), Josep GUARDIOLA Sala (65 Guillermo AMOR Martínez), Michael Reiziger, Vitor Barbosa Ferreira «RIVALDO», Dragan Cirić, Sonny ANDERSON Da Silva (55 Juan Antonio PIZZI Torroja). Trainer: Louis van Gaal

NEWCASTLE UNITED: Shaka Hislop; Steve Watson, Philippe Albert (46 Aaron Hughes), Darren Peacock (30 Stuart Pearce), John Beresford, Alessandro Pistone, David Batty, John Barnes, Des Hamilton, Temur Ketsbaia, Jon Dahl Tomasson. Manager: Kenny Dalglish

Goal: Giovanni (17)

FC BARCELONA v FC DYNAMO KYIV 0-4 (0-3)

Camp Nou, Barcelona 5.11.1997

Referee: Hugh Dallas (SCO) Attendance: 52,500

FC BARCELONA: VÍTOR Manuel Martins BAÍA; Albert FERRER Llopis, FERNANDO Manuel Silva COUTO, Albert CELADES López, SERGI Barjuan Esclusa, Luis Filipe Madeira Caeiro "FIGO", Dragan Cirić, Michael Reiziger, Vitor Barbosa Ferreira "RIVALDO", GIOVANNI Silva de Oliveira (53 Guillermo AMOR Martínez), ÓSCAR García Junyent (70 Miquel Ángel NADAL Homar). Trainer: Louis van Gaal

DYNAMO: Olexandr Shovkovskyi; Oleh Luzhnyi (59 Mykola Volosyanko), Olexandr Holovko, Vladislav Vashchuk, Yuri Dmitrulin, Vitaliy Kosovskyi, Yuri Kalitvintsev (46 Yuri Maksimov), Andriy Gusin (60 Dmytro Mikhailenko), Olexandr Khatskevich, Andriy Shevchenko, Serhiy Rebrov. Trainer: Valeriy Lobanovskyi

Sent off: Sergi (46)

Goals: Shevchenko (9, 32, 44 pen), Rebrov (77)

FC DYNAMO KYIV v PSV EINDHOVEN 1-1 (1-0)

Olympiyskyi, Kyiv 27.11.1997

Referee: Piero Ceccarini (ITA) Attendance: 80,000

DYNAMO: Olexandr Shovkovskyi; Oleh Luzhnyi (88 Mykola Volosyanko), Vladislav Vashchuk, Yuri Dmitrulin, Olexandr Khatskevich, Olexandr Holovko, Yuri Maksimov (85 Serhiy Bezhenar), Yuri Kalitvintsev, Vitaliy Kosovskyi, Serhiy Rebrov, Andriy Shevchenko. Trainer: Valeriy Lobanovskyi

PSV: Ronald Waterreus; Marcos Batista Vampeta, Jaap Stam, Ernest Faber, Arthur Numan, Ovidiu Stîngă, Wim Jonk, Philip Cocu, Tomasz Iwan (38 Stan Valckx), Luc Nilis, Gilles De Bilde (85 Marc Degryse). Trainer: Dick Advocaat

Goals: Rebrov (17), De Bilde (68)

NEWCASTLE UNITED v PSV EINDHOVEN 0-2 (0-1)

St.James' Park, Newcastle 5.11.1997

Referee: Günther Benkö (AUS) Attendance: 35,214

NEWCASTLE UNITED: Shay Given; Warren Barton, Philippe Albert, Des Hamilton, Alessandro Pistone, Steve Watson, Keith Gillespie, John Barnes, John Beresford, Temur Ketsbaia, Jon Dahl Tomasson. Manager: Kenny Dalglish

PSV: Ronald Waterreus; Marcos Batista Vampeta, Jaap Stam, Stan Valckx, Arthur Numan, Zeljko Petrovic, Wim Jonk, Philip Cocu, Tomasz Iwan, Luc Nilis, Gilles De Bilde. Trainer: Dick Advocaat

Goals: Nilis (33), De Bilde (90)

PSV EINDHOVEN v FC BARCELONA 2-2 (0-1)

Philips, Eindhoven 10.12.1997

Referee: Anders Frisk (SWE) Attendance: 30,000

PSV: Ronald Waterreus; Ovidiu Stîngă, Stan Valckx, Ernest Faber, Arthur Numan, Tomasz Iwan (46 Peter Møller), Wim Jonk (90 Jan-Willem Van Ede), Philip Cocu, Boudewijn Zenden, Arnold Bruggink, Gilles De Bilde. Trainer: Dick Advocaat

FC BARCELONA: Rudolfus Hubertus HESP; Michael Reiziger, ABELARDO Fernández Antuña, Albert FERRER Llopis, Luis Filipe Madeira Caeiro "FIGO", Albert CELADES López (90 Guillermo AMOR Martínez), Josep GUARDIOLA Sala (48 FERNANDO Manuel Silva COUTO), Vitor Barbosa Ferreira "RIVALDO", ROGER García Junyent, Sonny ANDERSON Da Silva, GIOVANNI Silva de Oliveira (76 Dragan Cirić). Trainer: Louis van Gaal

Goals: Abelardo (31), Jonk (54), De Bilde (56), Giovanni (67)

NEWCASTLE UNITED v FC DYNAMO KYIV 2-0 (2-0)

St.James' Park, Newcastle 10.12.1997

Referee: Hellmut Krug (GER) Attendance: 33,694

NEWCASTLE UNITED: Shaka Hislop; Steve Watson, Philippe Albert, Darren Peacock, Stuart Pearce, Keith Gillespie, Robert Lee, David Batty, John Barnes, Alessandro Pistone (46 Aaron Hughes), Faustino Asprilla (57 Temur Ketsbaia). Manager: Kenny Dalglish

DYNAMO: Olexandr Shovkovskyi; Oleh Luzhnyi, Serhiy Bezhenar, Yuri Dmitrulin, Mykola Volosyanko (79 Olexandr Radchenko), Andriy Gusin, Yuri Kalitvintsev, Vitaliy Kosovskyi, Dmytro Mikhailenko (79 Oleh Venhlynskyi), Andriy Shevchenko, Serhiy Rebrov. Trainer: Valeriy Lobanovskyi

Goals: Barnes (10), Pearce (21)

	P	W	D	L	F	A	Pts
Dynamo Kyiv	6	3	2	1	13	6	11
PSV Eindhoven	6	2	3	1	9	8	9
Newcastle United	6	2	1	3	7	8	7
FC Barcelona	6	1	2	3	7	14	5

GROUP D

REAL MADRID CF v ROSENBORG BK TRONDHEIM 4-1 (3-1)

Santiago Bernabéu, Madrid 17.09.1997

Referee: Gilles Veissière (FRA) Attendance: 53,000

REAL: José Santiago CAÑIZARES Ruiz; ROBERTO CARLOS da Silva, Aitor KARANKA De la Hoz, Fernando Ruiz HIERRO, Christian Panucci, Manuel SANCHÍS Hontiyuelo (Cap), José ZÉ ROBERTO da Silva (74 VICTOR Sánchez del Amo), Clarence Seedorf, RAÚL González Blanco, Predrag Mijatović (58 Fernando Carlos REDONDO Neri), Davor Suker (58 Fernando MORIENTES Sánchez). Trainer: Jupp Heynckes

ROSENBORG: Jørn Jamtfall; André Bergdølmo, Erik Hoftun, Bjørn Otto Bragstad, Vegard Heggem, Runar Berg, Bent Skammelsrud (Cap), Roar Strand, Jahn Ivar Jakobsen (74 Andreas Mayer), Sigurd Rushfeldt (58 Robert Boateng), Harald Brattbakk. Trainer: Nils Arne Eggen

Goals: Panucci (7), Jakobsen (22), Zé Roberto (38), Raúl (43), Morientes (83)

OLYMPIAKOS PEIRAIAS v FC PORTO 1-0 (1-0)

Olympiako, Athina 17.09.1997

Referee: Sándor Puhl (HUN) Attendance: 75,000

OLYMPIAKOS: Kiriakos Tohouroglou; Mirsad Varesanović, Kiriakos Karataidis (Cap), Giorgos Anatolakis, Stelios Giannakopoulos, Andreas Niniadis, Alekos Alexandris (60 Nikos Dabizas), Ilija Ivić (90 Refik Sabanadzović), Predrag Djordjević, Petros Passalis, Grigoris Georgatos (81 Sinisa Gogić). Trainer: Dušan Bajević

FC PORTO: RUI Manuel da Silva CORREIA; João Paulo Maio dos Santos "PAULINHO SANTOS", ALOÍSIO Pires Alves, FERNANDO Manuel Antunes MENDES, SERGIO Marceneiro CONCEIÇÃO, RUI Gil Soares de BARROS (51 Nuno Gonçalves da Rocha CAPUCHO), António José dos Santos FOLHA (60 ARTUR Duarte de Oliveira), Ljubinko Drulovic, Mário JARDEL Almeida Ribeiro, JOÃO MANUEL PINTO Tomé dos Santos (33 José Alberto Mata BARROSO), Zlatko Zahovic. Trainer: António Oliveira

Goal: Giannakopoulos (6)

FC PORTO v REAL MADRID CF 0-2 (0-1)

Estádio das Antas, Porto 1.10.1997

Referee: Piero Ceccarini (ITA) Attendance: 40,000

FC PORTO: RUI Manuel da Silva CORREIA; JOÃO MANUEL PINTO Tomé dos Santos, ALOÍSIO Pires Alves (Cap), Joaquim da Silva NEVES (40 Ljubinko Drulovic), Daniel KENEDY Pimental Mateus dos Santos, José Alberto Mata BARROSO (59 António José dos Santos FOLHA), SERGIO Marceneiro CONCEIÇÃO, RUI Gil Soares de BARROS (46 ARTUR Duarte de Oliveira), João Paulo Maio dos Santos "PAULINHO SANTOS", Zlatko Zahovic, Mário JARDEL Almeida Ribeiro. Trainer: António Oliveira

REAL: José Santiago CAÑIZARES Ruiz; Christian Panucci, Manuel SANCHÍS Hontiyuelo (Cap), Fernando Ruiz HIERRO, ROBERTO CARLOS da Silva, Clarence Seedorf (83 VÍCTOR Sánchez del Amo), Fernando Carlos REDONDO Neri, RAÚL González Blanco, José Emilio AMAVISCA Gárate, Predrag Mijatović (82 Fernando MORIENTES Sánchez), Davor Suker (60 JAIME Sánchez Fernández). Trainer: Jupp Heynckes

Goals: Hierro (14), Raúl (78)

ROSENBORG BK TRONDHEIM v OLYMPIAKOS PEIRAIAS 5-1 (3-0)

Lerkendal, Trondheim 1.10.1997

Referee: Hugh Dallas (SCO) Attendance: 16,038

ROSENBORG: Jørn Jamtfall; Vegard Heggem, Christian Steen, Erik Hoftun, André Bergdølmo, Roar Strand, Bent Skammelsrud, Runar Berg, Jahn Ivar Jakobsen, Sigurd Rushfeldt, Harald Brattbakk. Trainer: Nils Arne Eggen

OLYMPIAKOS: Kiriakos Tohouroglou; Mirsad Varesanović, Kiriakos Karataidis (Cap), Giorgos Anatolakis, Grigoris Georgatos (60 Peter Ofori-Quaye), Predrag Djordjević, Stelios Giannakopoulos (54 Andreas Niniadis), Petros Passalis, Ilija Ivić (74 Sinisa Gogić), Alekos Alexandris, Ilias Poursanidis. Trainer: Dušan Bajević

Goals: Brattbakk (14, 79), Strand (33, 43), Rushfeldt (56), Ofori-Quaye (69)

ROSENBORG BK TRONDHEIM v FC PORTO 2-0 (2-0)

Lerkendal, Trondheim 22.10.1997

Referee: Nikolai Levnikov (RUS) Attendance: 17,214

ROSENBORG: Jørn Jamtfall; Vegard Heggem, Bjørn Otto Bragstad, Erik Hoftun, André Bergdølmo, Roar Strand (58 Fredrik Winsnes), Bent Skammelsrud, Runar Berg, Jahn Ivar Jakobsen (58 Tore André Dahlum), Harald Brattbakk, Sigurd Rushfeldt. Trainer: Nils Arne Eggen

FC PORTO: RUI Manuel da Silva CORREIA; João Paulo Maio dos Santos "PAULINHO SANTOS", Luis Marcos LULA, ALOÍSIO Pires Alves, FERNANDO Manuel Antunes MENDES, RUI Gil Soares de BARROS (46 Zlatko Zahovic), João Carlos COSTA (40 Ljubinko Drulovic), José Alberto Mata BARROSO, ARTUR Duarte de Oliveira, Youssef Chippo, Mário JARDEL Almeida Ribeiro (46 Nuno Gonçalves da Rocha CAPUCHO). Trainer: António Oliveira

Goals: Rushfeldt (10), Brattbakk (37)

REAL MADRID CF v OLYMPIAKOS PEIRAIAS 5-1 (2-1)

Santiago Bernabéu, Madrid 22.10.1997

Referee: Pier Luigi Collina (ITA) Attendance: 48,000

REAL: José Santiago CAÑIZARES Ruiz; Aitor KARANKA De la Hoz, Fernando Ruiz HIERRO, ROBERTO CARLOS da Silva, Clarence Seedorf (80 VÍCTOR Sánchez del Amo), JAIME Sánchez Fernández, Fernando Carlos REDONDO Neri, RAÚL González Blanco, José ZÉ ROBERTO da Silva (69 José Emilio AMAVISCA Gárate), Fernando MORIENTES Sánchez (76 Manuel SANCHÍS Hontiyuelo), Davor Suker. Trainer: Jupp Heynckes

OLYMPIAKOS: Kiriakos Tohouroglou; Bozidar Pantović, Giorgos Anatolakis, Ilias Poursanidis (85 Grigoris Georgatos), Kiriakos Karataidis (Cap), Predrag Djordjević, Petros Passalis, Nikos Dabizas, Vasilis Karapialis (70 Sinisa Gogić), Dimitris Mavrogenidis (70 Andreas Niniadis), Peter Ofori-Quaye. Trainer: Dušan Bajević

Goals: Dabizas (18), Suker (31 pen, 65 pen), Morientes (44), Víctor (85), Roberto Carlos (89)

FC PORTO v ROSENBORG BK TRONDHEIM 1-1 (1-0)

Estádio das Antas, Porto 5.11.1997

Referee: Dermot Gallagher (ENG) Attendance: 11,000

FC PORTO: RUI Manuel da Silva CORREIA; João Paulo Maio dos Santos "PAULINHO SANTOS", RUI JORGE de Sousa, JOÃO MANUEL PINTO Tomé dos Santos, ALOÍSIO Pires Alves, João Carlos COSTA (33 José Alberto Mata BARROSO), RUI Gil Soares de BARROS, Zlatko Zahovic, SERGIO Marceneiro CONCEIÇÃO (23 Nuno Gonçalves da Rocha CAPUCHO, 80 ARTUR Duarte de Oliveira), Ljubinko Drulovic, Mário JARDEL Almeida Ribeiro. Trainer: António Oliveira

ROSENBORG: Jørn Jamtfall; André Bergdølmo, Erik Hoftun, Bjørn Otto Bragstad, Vegard Heggem, Roar Strand (89 Fredrik Winsnes), Runar Berg, Bent Skammelsrud, Harald Brattbakk, Sigurd Rushfeldt, Tore André Dahlum (65 Børge Hernes). Trainer: Nils Arne Eggen

Goals: Jardel (7), Strand (88)

OLYMPIAKOS PEIRAIAS v REAL MADRID CF 0-0

Olympiako, Athina 5.11.1997

Referee: Hellmut Krug (GER) Attendance: 50,000

OLYMPIAKOS: Kiriakos Tohouroglou; Bozidar Pantović, Kiriakos Karataidis (Cap), Ilias Poursanidis, Giorgos Anatolakis, Giorgos Amanatidis (76 Nikos Dabizas), Petros Passalis, Grigoris Georgatos, Stelios Giannakopoulos (73 Dimitris Mavrogenidis), Ilija Ivić (89 Alekos Alexandris), Peter Ofori-Quaye. Trainer: Dušan Bajević

REAL: José Santiago CAÑIZARES Ruiz; Christian Panucci, Aitor KARANKA De la Hoz, Fernando Ruiz HIERRO, Manuel SANCHÍS Hontiyuelo, Clarence Seedorf (62 JAIME Sánchez Fernández), Fernando Carlos REDONDO Neri, José ZÉ ROBERTO da Silva, RAÚL González Blanco, Davor Suker (62 VÍCTOR Sánchez del Amo), Predrag Mijatović. Trainer: Jupp Heynckes

ROSENBORG BK TRONDHEIM v REAL MADRID CF 2-0 (1-0)

Lerkendal, Trondheim 27.11.1997

Referee: Paul Durkin (ENG) Attendance: 19,147

ROSENBORG: Jørn Jamtfall; André Bergdølmo, Erik Hoftun, Bjørn Otto Bragstad, Vegard Heggem, Roar Strand, Runar Berg, Bent Skammelsrud, Sigurd Rushfeldt, Harald Brattbakk, Jahn Ivar Jakobsen. Trainer: Nils Arne Eggen

REAL: José Santiago CAÑIZARES Ruiz; Miguel Porlan Noguera "CHENDO", Fernando Ruiz HIERRO, Manuel SANCHÍS Hontiyuelo, Aitor KARANKA De la Hoz, Fernando Carlos REDONDO Neri, Clarence Seedorf (78 VÍCTOR Sánchez del Amo), RAÚL González Blanco, José ZÉ ROBERTO da Silva (46 JAIME Sánchez Fernández), Fernando MORIENTES Sánchez (78 DANIel García), Predrag Mijatović. Trainer: Jupp Heynckes

Goals: Strand (44), Brattbakk (52)

FC PORTO v OLYMPIAKOS PEIRAIAS 2-1 (1-1)

Estádio das Antas, Porto 27.11.1997

Referee: Michel Piraux (BEL) Attendance: 8,000

FC PORTO: RUI Manuel da Silva CORREIA; Darko Butorovic, JOÃO MANUEL PINTO Tomé dos Santos, Luis Marcos LULA, RUI JORGE de Sousa, João Paulo Maio dos Santos "PAULINHO SANTOS", Daniel KENEDY Pimental Mateus dos Santos (46 João Carlos COSTA), SERGIO Marceneiro CONCEIÇÃO (19 RUI Gil Soares de BARROS), Nuno Gonçalves da Rocha CAPUCHO (46 ARTUR Duarte de Oliveira), Ljubinko Drulovic, Mário JARDEL Almeida Ribeiro. Trainer: António Oliveira

OLYMPIAKOS: Kiriakos Tohouroglou; Giorgos Amanatidis (76 Vasilis Karapialis), Kiriakos Karataidis (Cap), Giorgos Anatolakis, Grigoris Georgatos, Nikos Dabizas, Petros Passalis, Dimitris Mavrogenidis, Alekos Alexandris (55 Peter Ofori-Quaye), Ilija Ivić (86 Stelios Giannakopoulos), Predrag Djordjević. Trainer: Dušan Bajević

Goals: Yorgatos (24), Jardel (28, 53)

REAL MADRID CF v FC PORTO 4-0 (2-0)

Santiago Bernabéu, Madrid 10.12.1997

Referee: Pierluigi Pairetto (ITA) Attendance: 65,000

REAL: José Santiago CAÑIZARES Ruiz; JAIME Sánchez Fernández, Manuel SANCHÍS Hontiyuelo (80 Aitor KARANKA De la Hoz), Fernando Ruiz HIERRO, ROBERTO CARLOS da Silva, Clarence Seedorf, Fernando Carlos REDONDO Neri, RAÚL González Blanco (60 José María GUTIérrez Hernández), José Emilio AMAVISCA Gárate, Fernando MORIENTES Sánchez (69 VÍCTOR Sánchez del Amo), Davor Suker. Trainer: Jupp Heynckes

FC PORTO: RUI Manuel da Silva CORREIA; JOÃO MANUEL PINTO Tomé dos Santos (32 José Silva GASPAR), ALOÍSIO Pires Alves, FERNANDO Manuel Antunes MENDES (60 Grzegorz Mielcarski), João Paulo Maio dos Santos "PAULINHO SANTOS", José Alberto Mata BARROSO, RUI Gil Soares de BARROS, Joaquim da Silva NEVES, António José dos Santos FOLHA (32 Nuno Gonçalves da Rocha CAPUCHO), Zlatko Zahovic, Ljubinko Drulovic. Trainer: António Oliveira

Goals: Hierro (6), Suker (29, 73 pen), Roberto Carlos (48)

OLYMPIAKOS PEIRAIAS v ROSENBORG BK TRONDHEIM 2-2 (0-0)

Olympiako, Athina 10.12.1997

Referee: Günther Benkö (AUS) Attendance: 21,000

OLYMPIAKOS: Kiriakos Tohouroglou; Kiriakos Karataidis (Cap), Nikos Dabizas, Giorgos Anatolakis (73 Alekos Alexandris), Ilias Poursanidis (86 Anastasios Mitropoulos), Dimitris Mavrogenidis, Petros Passalis, Grigoris Georgatos (73 Stelios Giannakopoulos), Bozidar Pantović, Ilija Ivić, Predrag Djordjević. Trainer: Dušan Bajević

ROSENBORG: Jørn Jamtfall; André Bergdølmo, Erik Hoftun, Bjørn Otto Bragstad, Vegard Heggem; Roar Strand, Runar Berg, Bent Skammelsrud; Jahn Ivar Jakobsen, Sigurd Rushfeldt, Harald Brattbakk. Trainer: Nils Arne Eggen.

Goals: Mavrogenidis (48), Rushfeldt (49, 69), Djordjevic (89)

	P	W	D	L	F	A	Pts
Real Madrid CF	6	4	1	1	15	4	13
Rosenborg BK	6	3	2	1	13	8	11
Olympiakos Peiraias	6	1	2	3	6	14	5
FC Porto	6	1	1	4	3	11	4

GROUP E

FC BAYERN MÜNCHEN v BEŞIKTAŞ JK ISTANBUL 2-0 (1-0)

Olympiastadion, München 17.09.1997

Referee: Kim Milton Nielsen (DEN) Attendance: 38,000

BAYERN: Oliver Kahn; Lothar Matthäus, Thomas Helmer, Markus Babbel, Mario Basler (87 Bixente Lizarazu), Dietmar Hamann, Thomas Strunz, Mehmet Scholl, Michael Tarnat, Giovane Elber (81 Carsten Jancker), Ruggiero Rizzitelli (52 Thorsten Fink). Trainer: Giovanni Trapattoni

BEŞIKTAŞ: Fevzi Tuncay; Rahim Zafer, Alpay Özalan, Recep Çetin, Erkan Avseren, Tayfur Havutçu, Zlatko Iankov, Mehmet Özdilek (72 Iordan Lechkov), Serdar Topraktepe (78 Emre Eren), Oktay Derelioglu, Daniel Amokachi (80 Mustafa Öztürk). Trainer: John Toshack

Goals: Helmer (3), Basler (70)

PARIS SAINT GERMAIN v IFK GÖTEBORG 3-0 (1-0)

Parc des Princes, Paris 17.09.1997

Referee: Paul Durkin (ENG) Attendance: 28,189

PSG: Christophe Revault; Laurent Fournier (78 Vincent Guérin), Alain Roche, Paul le Guen, Didier Domi; Jérôme Leroy (70 Jimmy Algérino), Bruno Ngotty, RAÍ Souza Vieira (85 Édouard Cissé), Franck Gava, Florian Maurice, Marco Simone. Trainer: Ricardo Gomes

IFK: Thomas Ravelli; Olof Magnusson, Magnus Erlingmark, Teddy Lucic, Mikael Nilsson, Stefan Landberg (57 Emmanuel Tetteh), Niclas Alexandersson, Stefan Pettersson, Peter Eriksson, Johnny Ekström (57 Pär Karlsson), Robert Andersson. Trainer: Mats Jingblad

Goals: Ngotty (28), Lucic (51 og), Raí (81 pen)

IFK GÖTEBORG
v FC BAYERN MÜNCHEN 1-3 (0-2)

Gamla Ullevi, Göteborg 1.10.1997

Referee: Mario van der Ende (HOL) Attendance: 26,503

IFK: Thomas Ravelli; Magnus Johansson, Teddy Lucic, Magnus Erlingmark, Mikael Nilsson; Niclas Alexandersson, Stefan Lindqvist, Pär Karlsson, Stefan Pettersson, Robert Andersson (57 Peter Eriksson), Emmanuel Tetteh (85 Mikael Martinsson). Trainer: Mats Jingblad

BAYERN: Oliver Kahn; Markus Babbel, Thomas Helmer, Samuel Osei Kuffour, Thomas Strunz (38 Thorsten Fink), Dietmar Hamann, Christian Nerlinger, Mehmet Scholl (77 Mario Basler), Michael Tarnat, Carsten Jancker, Giovane Elber. Trainer: Giovanni Trapattoni

Goals: Jancker (2), Hamann (35), Lucic (85), Elber (90)

FC BAYERN MÜNCHEN
v PARIS SAINT GERMAIN 5-1 (2-0)

Olympiastadion, München 22.10.1997

Referee: Manuel Diaz Vega (SPA) Attendance: 45,000

BAYERN: Oliver Kahn; Markus Babbel, Thomas Helmer, Samuel Osei Kuffour, Dietmar Hamann (72 Thorsten Fink), Mario Basler (75 Alexander Zickler), Christian Nerlinger, Mehmet Scholl, Michael Tarnat, Giovane Elber, Carsten Jancker (76 Ruggiero Rizzitelli). Trainer: Giovanni Trapattoni

PSG: Christophe Revault; Laurent Fournier (70 Jimmy Algérino), Alain Roche, Paul le Guen, Didier Domi (46 Francis Llacer), Jérôme Leroy, Bruno Ngotty (55 Eric Rabesandratana), RAÍ Souza Vieira, Franck Gava, Florian Maurice, Marco Simone. Trainer: Ricardo Gomes

Goals: Elber (4, 71), Jancker (20, 47), Simone (48), Helmer (51)

BEŞIKTAŞ JK ISTANBUL
v PARIS SAINT GERMAIN 3-1 (2-0)

Inönü, Istanbul 1.10.1997

Referee: Günther Benkö (AUS) Attendance: 22,000

BEŞIKTAŞ: Fevzi Tuncay; Rahim Zafer, Alpay Özalan, Recep Çetin, Erkan Avseren, Tayfur Havutçu, Zlatko Iankov, Mehmet Özdilek, Serdar Topraktepe (72 Mutlu Topçu), Oktay Derelioglu (75 Ertugrul Saglam), Daniel Amokachi (86 Iordan Lechkov). Trainer: John Toshack

PSG: Christophe Revault; Laurent Fournier, Alain Roche, Paul le Guen (64 Vincent Guérin), Didier Domi, EDMILSON Gonçalves (46 Jimmy Algérino), Bruno Ngotty, RAÍ Souza Vieira, Franck Gava (61 Jérôme Leroy); Marco Simone, Florian Maurice. Trainer: Ricardo Gomes

Goals: Oktay (6, 42), Simone (65), Ertugrul (84)

IFK GÖTEBORG
v BEŞIKTAŞ JK ISTANBUL 2-1 (2-1)

Gamla Ullevi, Göteborg 5.11.1997

Referee: Armand Ancion (BEL) Attendance: 14,073

IFK: Thomas Ravelli; Magnus Johansson, Teddy Lucic, Mikael Nilsson, Olof Magnusson; Niclas Alexandersson, Stefan Lindqvist, Pär Karlsson (85 Emmanuel Tetteh), Johnny Ekström (75 Sören Järelöw), Robert Andersson (73 Peter Eriksson), Stefan Pettersson. Trainer: Mats Jingblad

BEŞIKTAŞ: Marijan Mrmic; Alpay Özalan, Rahim Zafer (58 Salih Akkaya), Serdar Topraktepe, Tayfur Havutçu, Zlatko Iankov, Mehmet Özdilek (55 Yusuf Tokuç), Iordan Lechkov, Recep Çetin (69 Fevzi Tuncay), Ertugrul Saglam, Oktay Derelioglu. Trainer: John Toshack

Sent off. Mrmic (68) and Ravelli (74)

Goals: Pettersson (17 pen), R. Andersson (23), Oktay (44)

BEŞIKTAŞ JK ISTANBUL
v IFK GÖTEBORG 1-0 (1-0)

Inönü, Istanbul 22.10.1997

Referee: László Vagner (HUN) Attendance: 35,000

BEŞIKTAŞ: Marijan Mrmic; Recep Çetin, Rahim Zafer, Erkan Avseren, Ertugrul Saglam, Zlatko Iankov, Tayfur Havutçu, Serdar Topraktepe, Mehmet Özdilek, Daniel Amokachi (84 Iordan Lechkov), Oktay Derelioglu. Trainer: John Toshack

IFK: Thomas Ravelli; Teddy Lucic, Magnus Erlingmark, Magnus Johansson, Mikael Nilsson, Peter Eriksson (80 Johnny Ekström), Stefan Lidqvist, Mikael Martinsson (63 Pär Karlsson), Stefan Pettersson, Niclas Alexandersson, Robert Andersson (70 Emmanuel Tetteh). Trainer: Mats Jingblad

Goal: Oktay (6)

PARIS SAINT GERMAIN
v FC BAYERN MÜNCHEN 3-1 (1-1)

Parc des Princes, Paris 5.11.1997

Referee: Piero Ceccarini (ITA) Attendance: 32,274

PSG: Christophe Revault; Jimmy Algérino, Paul le Guen, Eric Rabesandratana, Francis Llacer (68 Jérôme Leroy), Laurent Fournier, Édouard Cissé, Vincent Guérin, Franck Gava, Florian Maurice (82 Pierre Ducrocq), RAÍ Souza Vieira. Trainer: Ricardo Gomes

BAYERN: Oliver Kahn; Samuel Osei Kuffour, Thomas Helmer, Markus Babbel, Mehmet Scholl (86 Alexander Zickler), Dietmar Hamann, Thorsten Fink, Christian Nerlinger, Michael Tarnat, Carsten Jancker, Giovane Elber (71 Mario Basler). Trainer: Giovanni Trapattoni

Goals: Gava (17), Babbel (28), Maurice (72), Leroy (75)

BEŞIKTAŞ JK ISTANBUL
v FC BAYERN MÜNCHEN 0-2 (0-2)

Inönü, Istanbul 26.11.1997

Referee: Urs Meier (SWI) Attendance: 26,000

BEŞIKTAŞ: Fevzi Tuncay; Erkan Avseren, Recep Çetin (60 Emre Eren), Alpay Özalan, Serdar Topraktepe (80 Osman Ustünel), Ertugrul Saglam, Zlatko Iankov, Iordan Lechkov, Hikmet Çapanoglu (63 Daniel Amokachi), Tayfur Havutçu, Oktay Derelioglu. Trainer: John Toshack

BAYERN: Oliver Kahn; Samuel Osei Kuffour, Lothar Matthäus, Thomas Helmer, Mehmet Scholl (83 Alexander Zickler), Dietmar Hamann, Thorsten Fink (88 Markus Babbel), Christian Nerlinger, Michael Tarnat, Carsten Jancker (75 Ruggiero Rizzitelli), Giovane Elber.
Trainer: Giovanni Trapattoni

Goals: Jancker (5), Helmer (32)

IFK GÖTEBORG
v PARIS SAINT GERMAIN 0-1 (0-0)

Gamla Ullevi, Göteborg 26.11.1997

Referee: Giorgos Bikas (GRE) Attendance: 19,323

IFK: Sören Järelöw; Olof Magnusson, Magnus Erlingmark, Teddy Lucic, Mikael Nilsson, Niclas Alexandersson, Stefan Pettersson, Stefan Lindqvist (64 Peter Eriksson), Pär Karlsson, Johnny Ekström (88 Mikael Martinsson), Robert Andersson. Trainer: Mats Jingblad

PSG: Christophe Revault; Alain Roche (61 Jimmy Algérino), Paul le Guen, Eric Rabesandratana, Laurent Fournier (75 EDMILSON Gonçalves), Jérôme Leroy, Bruno Ngotty, Franck Gava, Didier Domi, RAÍ Souza Vieira, Florian Maurice (89 Francis Llacer). Trainer: Ricardo Gomes

Sent off: Algérino (75)

Goal: Rabesandratana (87)

FC BAYERN MÜNCHEN
v IFK GÖTEBORG 0-1 (0-0)

Olympiastadion, München 10.12.1997

Referee: Stefano Braschi (ITA) Attendance: 27,000

BAYERN: Oliver Kahn; Markus Babbel, Lothar Matthäus, Thomas Helmer (21 Christian Nerlinger), Alexander Zickler (57 Frank Gerster), Dietmar Hamann, Thorsten Fink, Mehmet Scholl, Michael Tarnat, Carsten Jancker, Ruggiero Rizzitelli (57 Giovane Elber). Trainer: Giovanni Trapattoni

IFK: Thomas Ravelli; Olof Magnusson, Teddy Lucic, Magnus Erlingmark, Mikael Nilsson, Peter Eriksson, Magnus Johansson, Pär Karlsson, Mikael Martinsson (90 Jimmy Svensson), Johnny Ekström (72 Christian Lundström), Robert Andersson (82 Emmanuel Tetteh). Trainer: Mats Jingblad

Goal: Babbel (54 og)

PARIS SAINT GERMAIN
v BEŞIKTAŞ JK ISTANBUL 2-1 (1-1)

Parc des Princes, Paris 10.12.1997

Referee: Antonio Jesus López Nieto (SPA) Att: 34,038

PSG: Christophe Revault; Fabrice Kelban, Paul le Guen, Pierre Ducrocq, Francis Llacer, EDMILSON Gonçalves (70 Édouard Cissé), Jérôme Leroy, RAÍ Souza Vieira, Franck Gava; Marco Simone, Florian Maurice. Trainer: Ricardo Gomes

BEŞIKTAŞ: Marijan Mrmic; Serdar Topraktepe (67 Iordan Lechkov), Alpay Özalan, Rahim Zafer, Erkan Avseren, Tayfur Havutçu, Recep Çetin, Zlatko Iankov, Mehmet Özdilek, Daniel Amokachi (78 Osman Ustünel), Oktay Derelioglu (72 Ertugrul Saglam). Trainer: John Toshack

Goals: Gava (24), Mehmet (38), Simone (59)

	P	W	D	L	F	A	Pts
FC Bayern München	6	4	0	2	13	6	12
Paris Saint Germain	6	4	0	2	11	10	12
Beşiktaş Istanbul	6	2	0	4	6	9	6
IFK Göteborg	6	2	0	4	4	9	6

GROUP F

SPORTING CLUBE DE PORTUGAL LISBOA
v AS MONACO 3-0 (2-0)

José Alvalade, Lisboa 17.09.1997

Referee: Urs Meier (SWI) Attendance: 27,000

SPORTING: Filip De Wilde; Abdelilah SABER, MARCO AURELIO Cunha dos Santos, Roberto Luís Gaspar Deus Severo «BETO», VINICIUS Conceição e Silva, OCEANO Andrade da Cruz, Didier Lang (84 César RAMIREZ Caje), Pedro Martins, Mustapha Hadji (88 QUIM BERTO Ferreira), PEDRO Alexandre dos Santos BARBOSA (74 Afonso Martins), LEANDRO Machado. Trainer: Octávio Machado

AS MONACO: Fabien Barthez; Salif Diao, Franck Dumas, Philippe Léonard, Christophe Pignol (46 Muhamed Konjic), Francisco Da Costa (46 Victor Ikpeba), Sylvain Legwinski, John Collins, Ali Benarbia; Robert Špehar, David Trezeguet. Trainer: Jean Tigana

Goals: Oceano (3), Hadji (7), Leandro (64)

BAYER 04 LEVERKUSEN v SK LIERSE 1-0 (1-0)

Ulrich-Haberland-Stadion, Leverkusen 17.09.1997

Referee: Stefano Braschi (ITA) Attendance: 22,500

BAYER: Dirk Heinen; Markus Happe, Christian Wörns, Jens Nowotny (90 Frederico da Rosa EMERSON), Nico Kovac (86 Robert Kovac), Ulf Kirsten (74 Paulo Roberto Rink), Erik Meijer, Carsten Ramelow, Hans-Peter Lehnhoff, Jan Heintze, Stefan Beinlich. Trainer: Christoph Daum

LIERSE: Philippe Vande Walle; Yves Serneels, Eric Van Meir, Pieter Huistra (80 Daniel Scavone), Frank Leen, Filip Haagdoren, Ralph Hasenhüttl, Nico Van Kerckhoven, Thomas Zdebel, Carl Hoefkens (69 Robby Van de Weyer), Claus Eftevaag. Trainer: Jos Daerden

Sent off: Beinlich (75)

Goal: Beinlich (29 pen)

AS MONACO v SK LIERSE 5-1 (1-0)

Louis II, Monaco 22.10.1997

Referee: Terje Hauge (NOR) Attendance: 7,000

AS MONACO: Fabien Barthez (Cap); Willy Sagnol, Muhamed Konjic, Franck Dumas (46 Bruno Irles), Christophe Pignol, Sylvain Legwinski, Martin Djetou, Ali Benarbia, John Collins (78 Japhet N'Doram), Thierry Henry, Victor Ikpeba (78 David Trezeguet). Trainer: Jean Tigana

LIERSE: Philippe Vande Walle; David Brocken, Claus Eftevaag, Eric Van Meir, Daniel Scavone (73 Robby Van de Weyer), Frank Leen, Thomas Zdebel, Filip Haagdoren (73 Yves Serneels), Nico Van Kerckhoven, Pieter Huistra, Ralph Hasenhüttl (80 Andrew Uwuigbe). Trainer: Jos Daerden

Goals: Henry (31), Collins (51), Van Meir (60), Ikpeba (66), Trezeguet (87, 90)

LIERSE SK v SPORTING CLUBE DE PORTUGAL LISBOA 1-1 (0-0)

Herman Vanderpoorten, Lier 1.10.1997

Referee: Sándor Piller (HUN) Attendance: 10,000

LIERSE: Philippe Vande Walle; David Brocken, Pascal Bovri, Eric Van Meir, Daniel Scavone, Filip Haagdoren, Frank Leen, Thomas Zdebel, Claus Eftevaag, Pieter Huistra (90 Carl Hoefkens), Ralph Hasenhüttl. Trainer: Jos Daerden

SPORTING: Filip De Wilde; VINICIUS Conceição e Silva, Roberto Luís Gaspar Deus Severo "BETO", MARCO AURELIO Cunha dos Santos, Pedro Martins, Mustapha Hadji, OCEANO Andrade da Cruz, QUIM BERTO Ferreira, Didier Lang, LEANDRO Machado, PEDRO Alexandre dos Santos BARBOSA (65 SIMÃO Pedro Fonseca Sabrosa). Trainer: Octávio Machado

Goals: Leandro (86), Huistra (88)

SPORTING CLUBE DE PORTUGAL LISBOA v BAYER 04 LEVERKUSEN 0-2 (0-0)

José Alvalade, Lisboa 22.10.1997

Referee: Serguei Khusainov (RUS) Attendance: 22,000

SPORTING: Filip De Wilde; QUIM BERTO Ferreira, Roberto Luís Gaspar Deus Severo "BETO" (76 César RAMIREZ Caje), MARCO AURELIO Cunha dos Santos, VINICIUS Conceição e Silva, SIMÃO Pedro Fonseca Sabrosa, José Luís da Cruz VIDIGAL, Mustapha Hadji (35 Bruno Giménez), Didier Lang, LEANDRO Machado, Pedro Martins (55 NENE Fabio Camillo). Trainer: Octávio Machado

BAYER: Dirk Heinen; Dirk Lottner, Christian Wörns, Markus Happe, Hans-Peter Lehnhoff, Frederico da Rosa EMERSON (86 Boris Zivkovic), Carsten Ramelow, Stefan Beinlich, Jan Heintze, Erik Meijer, Ulf Kirsten (86 Martin Frýdek). Trainer: Christoph Daum

Goals: Beinlich (68), Emerson (81)

AS MONACO v BAYER 04 LEVERKUSEN 4-0 (1-0)

Louis II, Monaco 1.10.1997

Referee: David Roland Elleray (ENG) Attendance: 7,000

AS MONACO: Fabien Barthez; Martin Djetou, Franck Dumas, Muhamed Konjic (46 Bruno Irles), Sylvain Legwinski (55 Philippe Christanval), Japhet N'Doram (72 Ali Benarbia), John Collins, Christophe Pignol, Victor Ikpeba, David Trezeguet, Thierry Henry. Trainer: Jean Tigana

BAYER: Dirk Heinen; Robert Kovac, Dirk Lottner, Markus Happe, Jan Heintze, Hans-Peter Lehnhoff (61 René Rydlewicz), Boris Zivkovic (61 Paulo Roberto Rink), Frederico da Rosa EMERSON, Nico Kovac, Markus Feldhoff (85 Martin Frýdek), Erik Meijer. Trainer: Christoph Daum

Sent off: R. Kovac (69)

Goals: Henry (30, 84), Ikpeba (74, 90)

LIERSE SK v AS MONACO 0-1 (0-0)

Herman Vanderpoorten, Lier 5.11.1997

Referee: Leif Sundell (SWE) Attendance: 7,000

LIERSE: Philippe Vande Walle; Yves Seernels, Claus Eftevaag, Eric Van Meir (70 Carl Hoefkens), David Brocken (79 Robby Van de Weyer), Frank Leen, Filip Haagdoren (83 Jurgen Cavens), Thomas Zdebel, Nico Van Kerckhoven, Ralph Hasenhüttl, Pieter Huistra. Trainer: Jos Daerden

AS MONACO: Fabien Barthez; Willy Sagnol, Muhamed Konjic, Bruno Irles, Philippe Léonard (80 Salif Diao), Sylvain Legwinski, Ali Benarbia (72 Stéphane Carnot), Martin Djetou, John Collins, Thierry Henry (65 David Trezeguet), Victor Ikpeba. Trainer: Jean Tigana

Goal: Ikpeba (75)

BAYER 04 LEVERKUSEN v SPORTING CLUBE DE PORTUGAL LISBOA 4-1 (1-1)

Ulrich-Haberland-Stadion, Leverkusen 5.11.1997

Referee: Cakar Ahmet (TUR) Attendance: 22,500

BAYER: Dirk Heinen; Robert Kovac, Christian Wörns, Markus Happe, Hans-Peter Lehnhoff, Frederico da Rosa EMERSON, Carsten Ramelow, Nico Kovac (57 Martin Frýdek), Jan Heintze, Ulf Kirsten (46 Paulo Roberto Rink), Erik Meijer (87 Markus Feldhoff). Trainer: Christoph Daum

SPORTING: Filip De Wilde; QUIM BERTO Ferreira, NENE Fabio Camillo, MARCO AURELIO Cunha dos Santos, VINICIUS Conceição e Silva (40 Abdelilah SABER), Pedro Martins (89 LUIS MIGUEL Fonseca), OCEANO Andrade da Cruz, José Luís da Cruz VIDIGAL, Mustapha Hadji, PEDRO Alexandre dos Santos BARBOSA, LEANDRO Machado (76 Bruno Gimenez). Trainer: Francisco Vital

Sent off: Vidigal (22) and Pedro Barbosa (82)

Goals: Emerson (15, 73), Hadji (44), Rink (84), Frýdek (90)

AS MONACO v SPORTING CLUBE DE PORTUGAL LISBOA 3-2 (0-2)

Louis II, Monaco 26.11.1997

Ref: José Maria Garcia-Aranda Encinar (SPA) Att: 9,287

AS MONACO: Fabien Barthez; Willy Sagnol, Bruno Irles, Franck Dumas, Christophe Pignol, Sylvain Legwinski, Ali Benarbia (73 Stéphane Carnot), Martin Djetou (19 Thierry Henry), John Collins, David Trezeguet, Victor Ikpeba. Trainer: Jean Tigana

SPORTING: Filip De Wilde (23 TIAGO Alexandre Baptista Ferreira); Abdelilah SABER, MARCO AURELIO Cunha dos Santos, NENE Fabio Camillo, QUIM BERTO Ferreira (73 VINICIUS Conceição e Silva), Didier Lang, Mustapha Hadji, OCEANO Andrade da Cruz (78 Afonso Martins), Pedro Martins, LUIS MIGUEL Fonseca, LEANDRO Machado. Trainer: Francisco Vital

Goals: Luis Miguel (31), Oceano (37 pen), Trezeguet (65), Henry (75, 90)

LIERSE SK v BAYER 04 LEVERKUSEN 0-2 (0-0)

Herman Vanderpoorten, Lier 26.11.1997

Referee: Graham Poll (ENG) Attendance: 8,000

LIERSE: Philippe Vande Walle; David Brocken (78 Andrew Uwuigbe), Yves Serneels, Claus Eftevaag (69 Jurgen Cavens), Daniel Scavone, Filip Haagdoren, Frank Leen, Thomas Zdebel, Carl Hoefkens, Ralph Hasenhüttl (70 Tim De Keyser), Robby Van de Weyer. Trainer: Jos Daerden

BAYER: Dirk Heinen; Robert Kovac, Christian Wörns, Markus Happe, Hans-Peter Lehnhoff (82 Boris Zivkovic), Frederico da Rosa EMERSON, Carsten Ramelow, Stefan Beinlich, Jan Heintze, Erik Meijer (42 Paulo Roberto Rink), Ulf Kirsten (89 Nico Kovac). Trainer: Christoph Daum

Sent off: Happe (70)

Goals: Emerson (54), Kirsten (66)

SPORTING CLUBE DE PORTUGAL LISBOA v LIERSE SK 2-1 (0-1)

José Alvalade, Lisboa 10.12.1997

Referee: Leslie John Irvine (NIR) Attendance: 10,000

SPORTING: Filip De Wilde; QUIM BERTO Ferreira, MARCO AURÉLIO Cunha dos Santos, José Luís da Cruz VIDIGAL, VINICIUS Conceição e Silva, Afonso Martins (46 Bruno Gimenez), Pedro Martins (46 Carlos Miguel), Roberto Luís Gaspar Deus Severo "BETO", Didier Lang, César RAMIREZ Caje, LEANDRO Machado (89 Ivailo Stoimenov Iordanov). Trainer: Vicente Cantatore

LIERSE: Patrick Deman; David Brocken, Daniel Scavone, Eric Van Meir, Yves Serneels, Thomas Zdebel, Carl Hoefkens (84 Andrew Uwuigbe), Frank Leen (70 Pascal Bovri), Robby Van de Weyer, Filip Haagdoren, Pieter Huistra (74 Jurgen Cavens). Trainer: Jos Daerden

Goals: Haagdoren (27), César Ramírez (46), Bruno Gimenez (67)

BAYER 04 LEVERKUSEN v AS MONACO 2-2 (1-0)

Ulrich-Haberland-Stadion, Leverkusen 10.12.1997

Referee: Pier Luigi Collina (ITA) Attendance: 22,500

BAYER: Dirk Heinen; Robert Kovac, Jens Nowotny, Christian Wörns, Nico Kovac (61 Boris Zivkovic), Hans-Peter Lehnhoff, Carsten Ramelow, Stefan Beinlich, Jan Heintze, Erik Meijer, Ulf Kirsten (86 Paulo Roberto Rink). Trainer: Christoph Daum

AS MONACO: Fabien Barthez; Willy Sagnol, Bruno Irles, Franck Dumas, Christophe Pignol, Sylvain Legwinski, Ali Benarbia (63 Stéphane Carnot), Martin Djetou (9 Salif Diao), John Collins (59 Thierry Henry), David Trezeguet, Victor Ikpeba. Trainer: Jean Tigana

Goals: Beinlich (29), Meijer (59), Pignol (63), Henry (81)

	P	W	D	L	F	A	Pts
AS Monaco	6	4	1	1	15	8	13
Bayer 04 Leverkusen	6	4	1	1	11	7	13
Sporting Lisboa	6	2	1	3	9	11	7
Lierse SK	6	0	1	5	3	12	1

QUARTER-FINALS

BAYER 04 LEVERKUSEN v REAL MADRID CF 1-1 (1-0)

Ulrich-Haberland-Stadion, Leverkusen 4.03.1998

Referee: Kim Milton Nielsen (DEN) Attendance: 22,000

BAYER: Dirk Heinen; Jens Nowotny, Christian Wörns, Boris Zivkovic, Hans-Peter Lehnhoff (71 Markus Feldhoff), Frederico da Rosa EMERSON (87 Dirk Lottner), Carsten Ramelow, Stefan Beinlich, Jan Heintze; Ulf Kirsten, Paulo Roberto Rink. Trainer: Christoph Daum

REAL: Bodo Illgner; Christian Panucci, Fernando Ruiz HIERRO, Manuel SANCHÍS Hontiyuelo (Cap), ROBERTO CARLOS da Silva; Christian Karembeu, Fernando Carlos REDONDO Neri, Clarence Seedorf, SAVIO Bortolini Pimental (87 José Emilio AMAVISCA Gárate); RAÚL González Blanco (71 Fernando MORIENTES Sánchez), Predrag Mijatović. Trainer: Jupp Heynckes

Goals: Beinlich (17), Karembeu (73)

REAL MADRID CF v BAYER 04 LEVERKUSEN 3-0 (0-0)

Santiago Bernabéu, Madrid 18.03.1998

Referee: Nikolai Levnikov (RUS) Attendance: 85,000

REAL: Bodo Illgner; Christian Panucci, Manuel SANCHÍS Hontiyuelo, Fernando Ruiz HIERRO, ROBERTO CARLOS da Silva (88 José Emilio AMAVISCA Gárate), Christian Karembeu, Clarence Seedorf, Fernando Carlos REDONDO Neri, SAVIO Bortolini Pimental (36 Fernando MORIENTES Sánchez); RAÚL González Blanco, Predrag Mijatović (82 JAIME Sánchez Fernández). Trainer: Jupp Heynckes

BAYER: Dirk Heinen; Christian Wörns, Jens Nowotny, Markus Happe, Hans-Peter Lehnhoff (51 Paulo Roberto Rink), Carsten Ramelow, Boris Zivkovic, Frederico da Rosa EMERSON, Jan Heintze; Stefan Beinlich (82 Erik Meijer), Ulf Kirsten. Trainer: Christoph Daum

Goals: Karembeu (49), Morientes (57), Hierro (89 pen)

JUVENTUS FC TORINO v FC DYNAMO KYIV 1-1 (0-0)

Delle Alpi, Torino 4.03.1998

Referee: Paul Durkin (ENG) Attendance: 40,723

JUVENTUS: Angelo Peruzzi; Mark Iuliano, Paolo Montero, Moreno Torricelli (63 Manuel DIMAS Marques Teixeira), Alessandro Birindelli (67 Antonio Conte), Angelo Di Livio (81 Daniel Fonseca), Didier Deschamps, Zinedine Zidane, Edgar Davids; Alessandro del Piero, Filippo Inzaghi. Trainer: Marcello Lippi

DYNAMO: Olexandr Shovkovskyi; Serhiy Bezhenar, Olexandr Holovko, Oleh Luzhnyi (70 Olexandr Radchenko), Yuri Dmitrulin (46 Mykola Volosyanko), Vitaliy Kosovskyi, Yuri Kalitvintsev, Andriy Gusin, Aleksei Gerasimenko (70 Dmytro Mikhailenko); Andriy Shevchenko, Serhiy Rebrov. Trainer: Valeriy Lobanovskyi

Goals: Gusin (57), Inzaghi (70)

FC DYNAMO KYIV v JUVENTUS FC TORINO 1-4 (0-1)

Olympiyskyi, Kyiv 18.03.1998

Referee: Marc Batta (FRA) Attendance: 100,000

DYNAMO: Olexandr Shovkovskyi; Serhiy Bezhenar, Olexandr Holovko, Olexandr Khatskevich (63 Olexandr Radchenko), Vitaliy Kosovskyi, Andriy Gusin, Yuri Kalitvintsev (37 Vasyl Kardash), Aleksei Gerasimenko, Yuri Dmitrulin; Andriy Shevchenko, Serhiy Rebrov. Trainer: Valeriy Lobanovskyi

JUVENTUS: Angelo Peruzzi; Alessandro Birindelli (7 Manuel DIMAS Marques Teixeira), Mark Iuliano, Paolo Montero, Gianluca Pessotto; Antonio Conte, Didier Deschamps, Edgar Davids, Zinedine Zidane; Alessandro del Piero, Filippo Inzaghi (79 Alessio Tacchinardi). Trainer: Marcello Lippi

Goals: Inzaghi (29, 65, 73), Rebrov (54), Del Piero (89)

FC BAYERN MÜNCHEN v BORUSSIA DORTMUND 0-0

Olympiastadion, München 4.03.1998

Referee: Pier Luigi Collina (ITA) Attendance: 60,000

BAYERN: Oliver Kahn; Markus Babbel, Lothar Matthäus (75 Thorsten Fink), Thomas Helmer; Mario Basler, Dietmar Hamann, Christian Nerlinger, Mehmet Scholl (71 Thomas Strunz), Michael Tarnat, Giovane Elber, Carsten Jancker. Trainer: Giovanni Trapattoni

BORUSSIA: Stefan Klos; Jürgen Kohler, Wolfgang Feiersinger, JÚLIO CÉSAR Silva; Vladimir But, Steffen Freund, Lars Ricken, Andreas Möller, Jörg Heinrich, Harry Decheiver (64 Heiko Herrlich), Stéphane Chapuisat (88 Michael Zorc). Trainer: Nevio Scala

BORUSSIA DORTMUND v FC BAYERN MÜNCHEN 1-0 (0-0, 0-0) (AET)

Bökelberg, Dortmund 18.03.1998

Referee: László Vagner (HUN) Attendance: 48,500

BORUSSIA: Stefan Klos; Jürgen Kohler, Wolfgang Feiersinger, JÚLIO CÉSAR Silva, Stefan Reuter (105 Michael Zorc), Steffen Freund (79 Lars Ricken), Vladimir But, Andreas Möller, Jörg Heinrich; Harry Decheiver (120 René Schneider), Stéphane Chapuisat. Trainer: Nevio Scala

BAYERN: Oliver Kahn; Markus Babbel, Lothar Matthäus (111 Thomas Strunz), Samuel Osei Kuffour; Mehmet Scholl, Dietmar Hamann, Thorsten Fink, Christian Nerlinger (110 Bixente Lizarazu), Michael Tarnat; Giovane Elber (110 Alexander Zickler), Carsten Jancker. Trainer: Giovanni Trapattoni

Goal: Chapuisat (109)

AS MONACO v MANCHESTER UNITED FC 0-0

Louis II, Monaco 4.03.1998

Referee: Manuel Diaz Vega (SPA) Attendance: 18,000

AS MONACO: Fabien Barthez; Willy Sagnol, Franck Dumas, Muhamed Konjic, Philippe Léonard; Sylvain Legwinski, Martin Djetou, Ali Benarbia (75 Stéphane Carnot), John Collins, Victor Ikpeba (61 Robert Špehar), Thierry Henry (79 Fabien Lefèvre). Trainer: Jean Tigana

MANCHESTER UNITED: Peter Schmeichel; Gary Neville, Ronny Johnsen, Henning Berg, Dennis Irwin (66 Brian McClair); David Beckham, Paul Scholes, Nicky Butt, Philip Neville; Teddy Sheringham, Andy Cole.
Manager: Alex Ferguson

MANCHESTER UNITED FC v AS MONACO 1-1 (0-1)

Old Trafford, Manchester 18.03.1998

Referee: Hellmut Krug (GER) Attendance: 53,683

MANCHESTER UNITED: Raimond Van der Gouw; Philip Neville, Gary Neville (33 Henning Berg), Ronny Johnsen, Dennis Irwin; David Beckham, Paul Scholes (46 Michael Clegg), Nicky Butt, Ole Gunnar Solskjaer; Andy Cole, Teddy Sheringham. Manager: Alex Ferguson

AS MONACO: Fabien Barthez; Willy Sagnol, Muhamed Konjic (74 Francisco Da Costa), Franck Dumas, Philippe Léonard; Ali Benarbia (67 Stéphane Carnot), Djibril Diawara, Martin Djetou, John Collins; David Trezeguet, Victor Ikpeba (59 Thierry Henry). Trainer: Jean Tigana

Goals: Trezeguet (5), Solskjaer (53)

AS MONACO v JUVENTUS FC TORINO 3-2 (1-1)

Louis II, Monaco 15.04.1998

Referee: Urs Meier (SWI) Attendance: 15,000

AS MONACO: Fabien Barthez; Lilian Martin, Philippe Christanval, Djibril Diawara, Philippe Léonard (64 Willy Sagnol), Martin Djetou, Ali Benarbia, John Collins; Victor Ikpeba (79 Robert Špehar), David Trezeguet, Thierry Henry.
Trainer: Jean Tigana

JUVENTUS: Angelo Peruzzi; Moreno Torricelli, Alessandro Birindelli, Mark Iuliano, Manuel DIMAS Marques Teixeira; Antonio Conte, Alessio Tacchinardi, Zinedine Zidane (60 Fabio Pecchia), Gianluca Pessotto; Alessandro del Piero, Filippo Inzaghi (6 Nicola Amoruso, 72 Edgar Davids).
Trainer: Marcello Lippi

Goals: Amoruso (14), Léonard (38), Henry (50), Del Piero (74), Špehar (83)

REAL MADRID CF v BORUSSIA DORTMUND 2-0 (1-0)

Santiago Bernabéu, Madrid 1.04.1998

Referee: Mario van der Ende (HOL) Attendance: 85,000

REAL: Bodo Illgner; ROBERTO CARLOS da Silva, Fernando SANZ Durán, Manuel SANCHÍS Hontiyuelo, Christian Panucci; Fernando Carlos REDONDO Neri, Christian Karembeu, RAÚL González Blanco, Clarence Seedorf; Fernando MORIENTES Sánchez (87 JAIME Sánchez Fernández), Predrag Mijatović (52 Davor Suker).
Trainer: Jupp Heynckes

BORUSSIA: Stefan Klos; Knut Reinhardt, JÚLIO CÉSAR Silva, Manfred Binz, Martin Kree, Stefan Reuter, Vladimir But, Lars Ricken (81 Michael Zorc), Steffen Freund, Heiko Herrlich (46 Harry Decheiver), Stéphane Chapuisat.
Trainer: Nevio Scala

Goals: Morientes (25), Karembeu (67)

SEMI-FINALS

JUVENTUS FC TORINO v AS MONACO 4-1 (2-0)

Delle Alpi, Torino 1.04.1998

Referee: Nikolai Levnikov (RUS) Attendance: 56,550

JUVENTUS: Angelo Peruzzi; Moreno Torricelli (58 Antonio Conte), Mark Iuliano, Paolo Montero, Gianluca Pessotto (46 Alessandro Birindelli); Angelo Di Livio (66 Alessio Tacchinardi), Didier Deschamps, Zinedine Zidane, Edgar Davids; Filippo Inzaghi, Alessandro del Piero.
Trainer: Marcello Lippi

AS MONACO: Fabien Barthez; Willy Sagnol, Muhamed Konjic, Philippe Cristanval, Lilian Martin (67 Thierry Henry), Djibril Diawara, Martin Djetou, Christophe Pignol (40 Francisco Da Costa), Ali Benarbia (74 Stéphane Carnot); David Trezeguet, Victor Ikpeba. Trainer: Jean Tigana

Goals: Del Piero (34, 45 pen, 62 pen), Da Costa (66), Zidane (88)

BORUSSIA DORTMUND v REAL MADRID CF 0-0

Bökelberg, Dortmund 15.04.1998

Referee: Paul Durkin (ENG) Attendance: 48,500

BORUSSIA: Stefan Klos; Manfred Binz, Stefan Reuter, Wolfgang Feiersinger, Martin Kree (12 Michael Zorc), Ibrahim Tanko (70 Harry Decheiver), Jörg Heinrich, Vladimir But, Andreas Möller, Lars Ricken (75 Christian Timm), Stéphane Chapuisat. Trainer: Nevio Scala

REAL: Bodo Illgner; ROBERTO CARLOS da Silva, Fernando Ruiz HIERRO, Fernando SANZ Durán, Christian Panucci; Fernando Carlos REDONDO Neri, Christian Karembeu, José Emilio AMAVISCA Gárate, Clarence Seedorf (87 José María GUTIDrrez Hernández); RAÚL González Blanco (73 JAIME Sánchez Fernández), Fernando MORIENTES Sánchez (89 VÍCTOR Sánchez del Amo). Trainer: Jupp Heynckes

FINAL

REAL MADRID CF
v JUVENTUS FC TORINO 1-0 (0-0)

Amsterdam Arena 20.05.1998

Referee: Hellmut Krug (GER) Attendance: 47,500

REAL: Bodo Illgner; ROBERTO CARLOS da Silva, Manuel SANCHÍS Hontiyuelo, Fernando Ruiz HIERRO, Christian Panucci; Fernando Carlos REDONDO Neri, Clarence Seedorf, Christian Karembeu, RAÚL González Blanco (90 José Emilio AMAVISCA Gárate); Predrag Mijatović (89 Davor Suker), Fernando MORIENTES Sánchez (81 JAIME Sánchez Fernández). Trainer: Jupp Heynckes

JUVENTUS: Angelo Peruzzi; Gianluca Pessotto (71 Daniel Fonseca), Mark Iuliano, Paolo Montero, Moreno Torricelli, Angelo Di Livio (46 Alessio Tacchinardi); Edgar Davids, Didier Deschamps (78 Antonio Conte), Zinedine Zidane; Alessandro del Piero, Filippo Inzaghi.
Trainer: Marcello Lippi

Goal: Mijatović (66)

European Cup Goalscorers 1997-98:

10 goals: Alessandro del Piero (Juventus Torino)

8 goals: Serhiy Rebrov (Dynamo Kyiv)

7 goals: Thierry Henry (AS Monaco)

6 goals: Enrico Chiesa (Parma), Filippo Inzaghi (Juventus Torino), Andriy Shevchenko (Dynamo Kyiv)

5 goals: Adrian Ilie (Galatasaray), Jean-Paul Van Gastel (Feyenoord), Andy Cole (Manchester United), Yuri Maksimov (Dynamo Kyiv), Harald Brattbakk, Sigurd Rushfeldt (Rosenborg)

4 goals: Igor Cvitanovic (Croatia Zagreb), David MuJiří (Dinamo Tbilisi), Stéphane Chapuisat (Borussia Dortmund), Faustino Asprilla (Newcastle United), GIOVANNI Silva de Oliveira (Barcelona), Fernando Morientes, Davor Suker (Real Madrid), Roar Strand (Rosenborg), Carsten Jancker (Bayern), RAÍ Souza Vieira, Marco Simone (Paris St.Germain), Oktay Derelioglu (Beşiktaş Istanbul), Leandro Machado (Sporting Lisboa), Stefan Beinlich, Frederico da Rosa EMERSON (Bayer Leverkusen), Victor Ikpeba, David Trezeguet (AS Monaco)

3 goals: Levan Berishvili (MPKC Mozyr), Gordon Durie, Alistair McCoist, Marco Negri (Glasgow Rangers), Marco (Jazz Pori), Aleksandre Iashvili (Dinamo Tbilisi), Jacek Dembinski, Piotr Szarpak (Widzew Lódz), Giannakis Okas (Anorthosis Famagusta), Béla Illés (MTK Budapest), Néstor Sensini (Parma), Andreas Möller (Borussia Dortmund), Julio Ricardo Cruz, Henk Vos (Feyenoord), Zinedine Zidane (Juventus), John Beresford (Newcastle United), Luis Enrique (Barcelona), Gilles De Bilde, Wim Jonk (PSV Eindhoven), Fernando Ruiz Hierro, Christian Karembeu (Real Madrid), Jahn Ivar Jakobsen (Rosenborg), Mário Jardel (FC Porto), Giovane Elber, Thomas Helmer (Bayern), Erik Meijer (Bayer Leverkusen)

2 goals: Sanamyan (Pyunik Erevan), Nankov (CSKA Sofia), Zidan (Maribor Teatanic), Lipawski (FC Sion), Kushnir (MPKC Mozyr), Maric (Croatia), Nieminen (Jazz Pori), Mihajlovic (Anorthosis Famagusta), Kuttor, Preisinger (MTK Budapest), Crespo (Parma), Obajdin, Siegl (Sparta Praha), Tugay (Galatasaray), Herrlich, Zorc (Borussia Dortmund), Van Bronckhorst (Feyenoord), Toth (FC Košice), Irwin, Scholes, Sheringham (Manchester United), Amoruso (Juventus), Gusin (Dynamo Kyiv), Roberto Carlos, Raúl (Real Madrid), Gogić, Niniadis, Georgatos (Olympiakos Peiraias), Pettersson, R.Andersson (IFK Göteborg), Gava, Maurice (Paris St.Germain), Mehmet (Beşiktaş), Hadji, Oceano (Sporting Lisboa), Van Meir (Lierse SK), Kirsten, Rink (Bayer Leverkusen)

1 goal: Isailovic (Partizan Beograd), Galea (Valletta FC), Shahgeldyan (Pyunik Erevan), Baxter, G.Hunter (Crusaders Belfast), Karanfilovski (Sileks Kratovo), Andonov (CSKA Sofia), Apachiței, Alexa, Comlionoc (Constructorul Chişinău), Mikalajunas (Kareda Siauliai), Dmitriev (Spartak Moskva), Gajser, Drobne (Maribor Teatanic), Ouattara, Lonfat, Seoane, Derivaz, Zambaz (FC Sion), Denisyuk (MPKC Mozyr), Miller, Albertz, Ferguson (Glasgow Rangers), Babichev, Astafyev, Mikholap (Skonto Riga), Bagger, Daugaard, Colding (Brøndby IF), Simic, Viduka (Croatia Zagreb), Laaksonen (Jazz Pori), Kiknadze, Gogichaishvili, Khomeriki (Dinamo Tbilisi), Rotariu, Lăcătuş, Munteanu, Şerban, Reghecampf (Steaua), Mikhalchuk, Terlecki, Kobylanski, Zajac, Curtianu (Widzew Lódz), Sallói, Ohana, Hamar (Beitar Jerusalem), Krcmarevic (Anorthosis Famagusta), Pedros, Adailton (Parma), Novotný, Gabriel, Baranek, Lokvenc, Svoboda (Sparta Praha), Ergun, Arif, Suat, Fatih (Galatasaray), But, Kirovski, Booth, Heinrich (Borussia Dortmund), Korneev, Sánchez, Boateng (Feyenoord), Lyubarskyi, Kozlej, Kozak, Semenik, Sovic, Faktor (FC Košice), Giggs, Berg, Solskjaer (Manchester United), Fonseca, Birindelli (Juventus), Barnes, Pearce, Ketsbaia (Newcastle United), Abelardo, Figo, Stoichkov, S.Anderson (Barcelona), Nilis, Cocu, P.Møller (PSV Eindhoven), Kalitvintsev, Holovko, Belkevich, Vashchuk (Dynamo Kyiv), Víctor, Panucci, Zé Roberto, Mijatović (Real Madrid), Mavrogenidis, Djordjević, Dabizas, Ofori-Quaye, Anatolakis, Giannakopoulos, Alexandris (Olympiakos Peiraias), Babbel, Hamann, Basler (Bayern), Lucic, Karlsson, Eriksson (IFK Göteborg), Rabesandratana, Leroy, Ngotty (Paris St.Germain), Ertugrul, Amokachi, Tayfur (Beşiktaş Istanbul), César Ramírez, Bruno Gimenez, Luis Miguel, Iordanov (Sporting Lisboa), Haagdoren, Huistra, Hasenhüttl (Lierse SK), Frýdek, Lehnhoff, Ramelow (Bayer Leverkusen), Collins, Pignol, Da Costa, Léonard, Špehar (AS Monaco)

Own goals: Milton (FC Sion) for Galatasaray, Abelardo (Barcelona) for Skonto Riga, Faktor (FC Košice) for Manchester United, Holovko (Dynamo Kyiv) for Newcastle, Babbel (Bayern) for IFK Göteborg, Lucic (IFK Göteborg) for Paris St.Germain, Tomic (Anorthosis) for Lierse SK

THE EUROPEAN CUP 1998-99

FIRST QUALIFYING ROUND

CELTIC FC GLASGOW v ST. PATRICK'S ATHLETIC DUBLIN 0-0

Celtic, Glasgow 22.07.1998

Referee: Bohdan Benedik (SVK) Attendance: 56,865

CELTIC: Jonathan Gould; Jackie McNamara (67 Simon Donnelly), Stéphane Mahé, Marc Rieper (83 Enrico Annoni), Tom Boyd, Craig Burley, Paul Lambert, Alan Stubbs, Regi Blinker, Henrik Larsson, Harald Brattbakk (46 Darren Jackson). Trainer: Jozef Venglos

ST. PATRICK'S: Trevor Wood; Jeff Clarke, Paul Campbell, Patrick Lynch, Colin Hawkins, Paul Osam, Eddie Gormley, Martin Russell, Trevor Molloy (72 Martin Reilly), Leon Braithwaite (82 Trevor Croly), Ian Gilzean.
Trainer: Liam Buckley

ST. PATRICK'S ATHLETIC DUBLIN v CELTIC FC GLASGOW 0-2 (0-1)

Tolka Park, Dublin 29.07.1998

Referee: Mikko Vuorela (FIN) Attendance: 8,929

ST. PATRICK'S: Trevor Wood; Jeff Clarke, Paul Campbell (46 Keith Doyle), Patrick Lynch, Colin Hawkins, Paul Osam, Eddie Gormley, Thomas Morgan (46 Martin Russell), Leon Braithwaite, Ian Gilzean (75 Martin Reilly), Trevor Molloy.
Trainer: Liam Buckley

CELTIC: Jonathan Gould; Jackie McNamara, Alan Stubbs, Malky Mackay, Tom Boyd, Craig Burley, Darren Jackson (68 Simon Donnelly), Paul Lambert, Regi Blinker (75 Tosh McKinlay), Henrik Larsson, Harald Brattbakk.
Trainer: Jozef Venglos

Goals: Brattbakk (12), Larsson (72)

FC OBILIC BEOGRAD v ÍB VESTMANNAEYJAR 2-0 (1-0)

Obilić, Beograd 22.07.1998

Referee: Peter Jones (ENG) Attendance: 1,500

OBILIC: Nenad Lukić; Kuzman Babeu, Miroslav Savić (46 Sasa Zorić), Zivojin Juksić, Igor Manojlović (60 Aco Vasiljević), Nenad Grozdić, Goran Serafimović, Dragan Sarac, Sasa Kovacević, Marjan Zivković (81 Predrag Filipović), Darko Vargec. Trainer: Dragan Okuka

ÍBV: Gunnar Sigurdsson; Ivar Ingimarsson, Ingi Sigurdsson, Zoran Miljkovic, Hlynur Stefánsson, Kristinn Lárusson, Steingrímur Jóhanesson (82 Kristján Georgsson), Kjartan Antonsson (75 Hjalti Jóhanesson), Ivar Bjarklind, Gudni Rúnar Helgason, Kristinn Halfidason (74 Jens Paeslack).
Trainer: Bjarni Jóhansson

Goals: Juksić (18), Grozdić (65)

ÍB VESTMANNAEYJAR v FC OBILIC BEOGRAD 1-2 (1-0)

Hásteinsvöllur, Vestmannaeyjar 29.07.1998

Referee: John Rowbotham (SCO) Attendance: 654

ÍBV: Gunnar Sigurdsson; Ivar Ingimarsson, Ingi Sigurdsson, Zoran Miljkovic, Hlynur Stefánsson, Kristinn Lárusson (84 Sindri Grétarsson), Steingrímur Jóhanesson, Kjartan Antonsson (77 Hjalti Jóhanesson), Ivar Bjarklind (73 Jens Paeslack), Rúnar Helgason, Kristinn Halfidason.
Trainer: Bjarni Jóhansson

OBILIC: Nenad Lukić; Kuzman Babeu, Miroslav Savić (46 Sasa Zorić), Zivojin Juksić, Igor Manojlović (59 Aco Vasiljević), Nenad Grozdić, Goran Serafimović, Dragan Sarac, Sasa Kovacević, Predrag Filipović (71 Marjan Zivković), Darko Vargec. Trainer: Dragan Okuka

Goals: Halfidason (22), Vasiljević (65), Grozdić (89)

HJK HELSINKI v FK EREVAN 2-0 (0-0)

Olympiastadion, Helsinki 22.07.1998

Referee: Roland Beck (LIE) Attendance: 2,317

HJK: Tommi Koivistoinen; Aarno Turpeinen, Ville Nylund, Jari Ilola, Jari Jäväjä (70 Shefki Kuqi), Vesa Vasara (78 Mikael Forssell), Erkka Lehtola (42 Peter Kopteff), Jarkko Juhani Wiss, Markku Kanerva, Mika Antero Kottila, Mika Lehkosuo.
Trainer: Antti Muurinen

FK: Harutyun Abrahamyan; Vardan Khachatryan (73 Karen Grigoryan), Aramais Tonoyan, Artur Mkrchyan, Levon Stepanyan, Armen Shakhalyan (66 Armen Sahakyan), Araik Nigoyan, Tigran Yesayan (78 Armen Markosyan), Guglielmo Cecutti, Regis Christian Garault, Philippe Barraud.
Trainer: Samuel Darbinian

Goals: Wiss (50), Kuqi (85)

FK EREVAN v HJK HELSINKI 0-3 (0-2)

Hrazdan Erevan 29.07.1998

Referee: Hans-Jürgen Weber (GER) Attendance: 1,500

FK: Harutyun Abrahamyan; Vardan Khachatryan, Aramais Tonoyan, Artur Mkrchyan (40 Karen Grigoryan), Levon Stepanyan, Armen Shakhalyan (34 Armen Markosyan), Araik Nigoyan, Tigran Yesayan, Guglielmo Cecutti, Regis Christian Garault, Philippe Barraud (56 Armen Karapetyan).
Trainer: Samuel Darbinian

HJK: Tommi Koivistoinen; Aarno Turpeinen, Ville Nylund, Jarmo Saastamoinen, Jari Jäväjä (78 Gustavo Manduca), Vesa Vasara (73 Peter Kopteff), Jarkko Juhani Wiss, Markku Kanerva, Aki Riihilahti, Mika Antero Kottila (46 Shefki Kuqi), Mika Lehkosuo. Trainer: Antti Muurinen

Goals: Lehkosuo (1, 81 pen), Jäväjä (28)

LITEKS LOVECH v HALMSTADS BK 2-0 (1-0)

Neftochimik, Burgas 22.07.1998

Referee: Miroslav Liba (CZE) Attendance: 16,000

LITEKS: Stoian Stavrev; Rosen Kirilov, Stefan Kolev, Marian Todorov, Stoicho Stoilov, Dimcho Beliakov (58 Luís Motta, 79 Stefan Iurukov), Alban Bushi, Dragoljub Simonovic, Zlatomir Zagorcic, Altin Haxhi, Radostin Kishishev.
Trainer: Ferario Spasov

HALMSTADS: Björn Nordberg; Mikael Gustavsson, Tommy Jönsson, Jesper Mattsson, Mats Lilienberg, Fredrik Ljungberg, Artim Sakiri (73 Jeffrey Aubynn), Fredrik Andersson, Peter Vougt, Björn Carlsson, Michael Svensson.
Trainer: Tom Prahl

Goals: Bushi (7), Iurukov (89)

HALMSTADS BK v LITEKS LOVECH 2-1 (2-0)

Örjans Vall, Halmstad 29.07.1998

Referee: Attila Juhos (HUN) Attendance: 3,438

HALMSTADS: Björn Nordberg; Mikael Gustavsson, Torbjörn Arvidsson, Tommy Jönsson (85 Michael Svensson), Jesper Mattsson, Mats Lilienberg, Fredrik Ljungberg, Artim Sakiri, Fredrik Andersson (71 Henrik Rolfsson), Peter Vougt, Björn Carlsson (87 Stefan Selakovic). Trainer: Tom Prahl

LITEKS: Stoian Stavrev; Rosen Kirilov, Stefan Kolev, Stoicho Stoilov, Dimcho Beliakov (69 Stefan Iurukov), Nikolai Dimitrov (64 Rosen Emilov), Alban Bushi, Dragoljub Simonovic (88 Marian Todorov), Zlatomir Zagorcic, Altin Haxhi, Radostin Kishishev. Trainer: Ferario Spasov

Goals: Sakiri (38), Arvidsson (42), Iurukov (76)

STEAUA BUCUREŞTI v FLORA TALLIN 4-1 (2-1)

Steaua Bucureşti 22.07.1998

Referee: Oguz Sarvan (TUR) Attendance: 10,000

STEAUA: Zoltan Ritli; Adrian Matei, Valeriu Răchită, Miodrag Belodedici; Laurenţiu Aurelian Reghecampf (84 Marius Achim Baciu), Damian Militaru, Denis Georgian Şerban, Laurenţiu Dumitru Roşu; Marius Mihai Lăcătuş (Cap) (74 Marius Sebastian Luca), Cristian Ciocoiu (78 Ion Lavi Hrib), Ionel Daniel Dănciulescu. Trainer: Mihai Stoichiţă

FLORA: Toomas Tohver; Marko Kristal, Viktor Alonen, Marek Lemsalu (60 Andres Oper), Sergei Hohlov-Simson, Janek Meet; Tomas Razanauskas, Martin Reim, Sergei Terehhov; Kristen Viikmäe (46 Pål Christian Alsaker), Indrek Zelinski (85 Maksim Smirnov). Trainer: Teitur Thórdarson

Goals: Ciocoiu (12, 40), Terehhov (41), Şerban (77 pen), Dănciulescu (89)

FLORA TALLIN v STEAUA BUCUREŞTI 3-1 (1-0)

Maarjamäe, Tallin 29.07.1998

Referee: John Ferry (NIR) Attendance: 1,500

FLORA: Toomas Tohver; Urmas Kirs, Sergei Hohlov-Simson, Martin Reim (Cap), Viktor Alonen; Pål Christian Alsaker, Tomas Razanauskas, Maksim Smirnov, Sergei Terehhov (65 Andres Oper); Indrek Zelinski (82 Kristen Viikmäe), Marko Kristal. Trainer: Teitur Thórdarson

STEAUA: Zoltan Ritli; Miodrag Belodedici, Valeriu Răchită, Adrian Matei; Laurenţiu Aurelian Reghecampf, Denis Georgian Şerban, Erik Augustin Lincar, Iulian Ilie Miu; Marius Mihai Lăcătuş (Cap) (80 Marius Sebastian Luca), Cristian Ciocoiu (76 Laurenţiu Dumitru Roşu), Ionel Daniel Dănciulescu. Trainer: Mihai Stoichiţă

Sent off: Reghecampf (89)

Goals: Smirnov (41), Zelinski (47), Dănciulescu (71), Oper (81)

LKS LÓDZ v KAPAZ GANJA 4-1 (1-0)

LKS, Lódz 22.07.1998

Referee: Amit Klein (ISR) Attendance: 2,500

LKS: Boguslaw Wyparlo; Tomasz Kos (58 Jacek Pluciennik), Witold Bendkowski, Tomasz Lenart, Rafal Pawlak, Rafal Niznik, Miroslaw Trzeciak, Omondiagbe Darlington (46 Ariel Jakubowski), Zbigniew Wyciszkiewicz, Tomasz Cebula (74 Jacek Paszulewicz), Tomasz Wieszczycki.
Trainer: Marek Dziuba

KAPAZ: Huseyn Magomedov; Fizuli Allakhverdiev, Faik Jabbarov, Makhmud Kurbanov, Khalig Mardanov, Dmitri Smirnov (58 Fazil Parvarov), Badri Kvaratskhelia (58 Imamiar Suleymanov), Vyacheslav Lychkin, Yunis Huseynov, Vidadi Rzayev, Aslan Kerimov. Trainer: Mehman Allahverdiev

Goals: Cebula (12), Trzeciak (50 pen, 76 pen), Wieszczycki (73), Suleymanov (83)

KAPAZ GANJA v LKS LÓDZ 1-3 (0-1)

Ganja 29.07.1998

Referee: Konrad Plautz (AUS) Attendance: 8,000

KAPAZ: Huseyn Magomedov; Fizuli Allakhverdiev, Faik Jabbarov, Makhmud Kurbanov (67 Jeykhun Tanriverdiyev), Khalig Mardanov, Dmitri Smirnov, Ramiz Mamedov, Badri Kvaratskhelia (61 Roin Kerdzevadze), Yunis Huseynov, Vidadi Rzayev, Aslan Kerimov. Trainer: Mehman Allahverdiev

LKS: Boguslaw Wyparlo; Tomasz Kos, Witold Bendkowski, Tomasz Lenart (33 Ariel Jakubowski), Rafal Pawlak (65 Jacek Paszulewicz), Rafal Niznik, Miroslaw Trzeciak, Omondiagbe Darlington (72 Jacek Pluciennik), Zbigniew Wyciszkiewicz, Tomasz Cebula, Tomasz Wieszczycki.
Trainer: Marek Dziuba

Goals: Trzeciak (45, 49), Smirnov (53), Wieszczycki (81)

KAREDA SIAULIAI
v MARIBOR TEATANIC 0-3 (0-1)

Siauliai 22.07.1998

Referee: Brian Lawlor (WAL) Attendance: 3,500

KAREDA: Marius Poskus; Tadas Graziunas, Zilvinas Zudys, Gytis Gelgota, Tomas Kancelskis (46 Nerijus Barasa), Igoris Stukalinas, Arturas Fomenka (46 Vidas Dancenka), Audrius Zuta, Deimantas Bicka, Kestutis Rudzionis (61 Remigijus Pocius), Maksim Razumov. Trainer: Aleksandr Piskarev

TEATANIC: Tomaz Murko; Milan Sterbal, Muamer Vugdalić (59 Franc Fridl), Matjaz Kek, Marinko Sarkezi, Marko Kmetec (70 Gregor Zidan), Nastja Ceh, Dalibor Filipović (78 Peter Breznik), Damjan Gajser, Stipe Balajić, Dejan Djuranović. Trainer: Bojan Prasnikar

Goals: Gajser (42, 87), Filipović (70)

VLLAZNIA SHKODËR
v DINAMO TBILISI 3-1 (1-0)

Loro Boriçi, Shkodër 29.07.1998

Referee: Alfred Micallef (MAL) Attendance: 1,155

VLLAZNIA: Armir Grima; Luan Zmijani, Suad Lici (63 Brihen Bizi), Astrit Premçi, Ilir Shkabari (54 Luan Jahja), Alban Noga, Altin Xhahysa, Vjoresin Sinani, Armando Cungu, Salvador Kaçaj, Auron Miloti. Trainer: Vasil Bici

DINAMO: Ramaz Sogolashvili; Zviad Jeladze, Givi Didava, Archil Sakhvadze, Rati Aleksidze, Levan Kobiashvili, Levan Tskitishvili, Levan Khomeriki (69 Mikhail Ashvetia), Valter Guchua, David MuJiří (75 Levan Melkadze), Givi Kvaratskhelia (84 Revaz Kemoklidze). Trainer: Murtaz Khurtsilava

Goals: Cungu (12), Miloti (87), Ashvetia (89), Noga (90 pen)

MARIBOR TEATANIC
v KAREDA SIAULIAI 1-0 (0-0)

Ljudski vrt, Maribor 29.07.1998

Referee: Jørn West Larsen (DEN) Attendance: 2,405

TEATANIC: Tomaz Murko; Gregor Zidan (68 Peter Breznik), Stipe Balajić, Muamer Vugdalić, Matjaz Kek, Marinko Sarkezi, Damjan Gajser (55 Besnik Kollari), Dejan Djuranović, Dalibor Filipović, Nastja Ceh, Marko Kmetec (84 Damir Pekić). Trainer: Bojan Prasnikar

KAREDA: Marius Poskus; Tadas Graziunas, Zilvinas Zudys, Gytis Gelgota, Nerijus Barasa, Darius Maciulevicius (62 Arturas Fomenka), Igoris Stukalinas, Deimantas Bicka, Egidijus Juska, Vidas Dancenka, Maksim Razumov (83 Kestutis Rudzionis). Trainer: Aleksandr Piskarev

Goal: Balajić (76)

VALLETTA FC
v ANORTHOSIS FAMAGUSTA 0-2 (0-0)

National, Ta'Qali 22.07.1998

Referee: Joaquim Bento Marques (POR) Attendance: 1,706

VALLETTA FC: Reginald Cini; Drasko Braunovic (66 Joe Zarb), Jeffrey Chetcuti, Kristian Laferla, Darren Debono, Joe Camilleri, Gilbert Agius, Nicky Saliba, Alexander Ivanov (73 Nenad Veselji), Stefan Giglio, Karl Bonnici. Trainer: Krasimir Manolov

ANORTHOSIS: Nikos Panagiotou; Vasos Melanarkitis, Dimitris Ioannou, Stavros Foukaris (46 Paris Ilia), Panagiotis Egkomitis, Vladan Tomic, Vesko Mihajlovic, Slobodan Krcmarevic (46 Zoran Cirić), Lambros Lambrou, Themis Agathokleous, Antros Sotiriou (65 Giannakis Okas). Trainer: Dušan Mitosević

Goals: Ilia (52), Okkas (80)

DINAMO TBILISI
v VLLAZNIA SHKODËR 1-0 (0-0)

Boris Paichadze, Tbilisi 22.07.1998

Referee: Carlo Bertolini (SWI) Attendance: 7,800

DINAMO: Ramaz Sogolashvili; Zviad Jeladze, Givi Didava, Rati Aleksidze, Levan Kobiashvili, Levan Tskitishvili, Levan Khomeriki, Revaz Kemoklidze (79 Archil Sakhvadze), Valter Guchua, David MuJiří (51 Mikhail Ashvetia), Givi Kvaratskhelia. Trainer: Murtaz Khurtsilava

VLLAZNIA: Armir Grima; Luan Zmijani (83 Luan Jahja), Suad Lici, Astrit Premçi, Ilir Shkabari, Alban Noga, Altin Xhahysa (62 Armando Shllaku), Vjoresin Sinani, Armando Cungu, Salvador Kaçaj, Auron Miloti (90 Brihen Bizi). Trainer: Vasil Bici

Goal: Khomeriki (53)

The match was awarded 3-0 to Dinamo Tbilisi.

ANORTHOSIS FAMAGUSTA
v VALLETTA FC 6-0 (3-0)

Antonis Papadopoulos, Larnaca 29.07.1998

Referee: Ladislav Gadosi (SVK) Attendance: 5,000

ANORTHOSIS: Nikos Panagiotou; Vasos Melanarkitis, Zaharias Haralampous (58 Lambros Lambrou), Stavros Foukaris, Vladan Tomic, Giannakis Okas, Vesko Mihajlovic (46 Antros Sotiriou), Panikos Pounas, Paris Ilia, Pambis Andreou, Zoran Cirić (40 Panagiotis Egkomitis). Trainer: Dušan Mitosević

VALLETTA FC: Reginald Cini; Drasko Braunovic, Jeffrey Chetcuti, Kristian Laferla, Darren Debono, Joe Camilleri, Gilbert Agius, Stefan Giglio (46 Nenad Veselji), Alexander Ivanov, Joe Zarb, Karl Bonnici (34 Jeremy Agius, 78 Ivan Woods). Trainer: Krasimir Manolov

Goals: Cirić (16), Haralampous (18), Andreou (45 pen), Sotiriou (51, 90), Okkas (75)

ZIMBRU CHIŞINĂU v ÚJPESTI BUDAPEST **1-0** (1-0)

Republican, Chişinău 22.07.1998

Referee: Tomasz Mikulski (POL) Attendance: 7,000

ZIMBRU: Vasili Coşelev; Oleg Fistican, Constantin Kulik, Ion Testimiţanu, Andrei Telesnenco, Valeriu Catînsus, Radu Rebeja (69 Serghei Zgura), Igor Oprea, Iurie Miterev (69 Boris Cebotari), Sergiu Epureanu, Victor Berco (72 Vladislav Gavriliuc). Trainer: Semion Altman

ÚJPESTI: Szabolcs Bíró; Csaba Fehér, Vilmos Sebök, Zoltán Tamási, Zoltán Kovács, Krisztián Kvasz, Balázs Kiskapusi (60 Goran Kopunović), Norbert Tóth, Vasile Miriuţă, Attila Korsós, Tamás Petö. Trainer: Peter Varhidi

Sent off: Fistican (27)

Goal: Kulik (11 pen)

JEUNESSE d'ESCH v GRASSHOPPER-CLUB ZÜRICH **0-2** (0-2)

Stade de la Frontière, Esch sur Alzette 29.07.1998

Referee: John McDermott (IRE) Attendance: 612

JEUNESSE: Philippe Felgen; Johny Thill (73 David Borbiconi), Roland Schaack, Claude Meylender, Marc Lamborelle, Denis Scuto, Paolo Amodio, Patrick Morocutti (89 Claude Ganser), Dany Theis, Carlo Pace (57 Yves Divoy), Manuel Cardoni. Trainer: Maurice Spitoni

GRASSHOPPER: Philipp Bernt Haas, Giuseppe Mazzarelli, Antonio Esposito, Kubilay Türkyılmaz, Blaise N'Kufo (46 Mikheil Kavelashvili), Ricardo Cabanas, Boris Smiljanic, Joël Magnin (46 Reto Zanni), Bruno Berner, Nenad Savic (72 Felix Magro). Trainer: Rolf Fringer

Goals: Esposito (37 pen), Türkyılmaz (43)

ÚJPESTI BUDAPEST v ZIMBRU CHIŞINĂU **3-1** (1-1)

Megyeri úti, Budapest 29.07.1998

Referee: Giorgos Psihomanis (GRE) Attendance: 8,000

ÚJPESTI: Szabolcs Bíró; Sándor Jenei, Csaba Fehér, Vilmos Sebök, Zoltán Tamási, Zoltán Kovacs, Miklós Herczeg, Norbert Tóth (71 Balázs Kiskapusi), Vasile Miriuţă, Attila Korsós (57 Goran Kopunović), Tamás Petö. Trainer: Peter Varhidi

ZIMBRU: Vasili Coşelev; Constantin Kulik, Ion Testimiţanu, Andrei Telesnenko, Valeriu Catînsus, Radu Rebeja, Igor Oprea, Iurie Miterev, Sergiu Epureanu (90 Vladislav Robu), Boris Cebotari, Victor Berco (87 Vladislav Gavriliuc). Trainer: Semion Altman

Sent off: Peto (74), Miterev (84) and Shebek (90)

Goals: Miriuţă (17), Kulik (28), Z. Kovács (73, 90)

FC DYNAMO KYIV v BARRY TOWN FC **8-0** (4-0)

Dynamo, Kyiv 22.07.1998

Referee: Andreas Georgiou (CYP) Attendance: 11,800

DYNAMO: Olexandr Shovkovskyi; Olexandr Holovko, Vladislav Vashchuk, Yuri Dmitrulin, Kakhi Kaladze, Yuri Kalitvintsev (46 Aleksei Gerasimenko), Vitaliy Kosovskyi (69 Oleh Venhlynskyi), Andriy Shevchenko, Andriy Gusin (56 Valentin Belkevich), Serhiy Rebrov, Olexandr Khatskevich. Trainer: Valeriy Lobanovskyi

BARRY: David Nurse; Gary Lloyd, Richard Jones, Andrew York, Lee Barrow, Gary Barnett, Danny Carter, Eifion Williams (59 Craig Evans), Mark Dempsey, Mike Thorpe, Terry Evans. Trainer: Gary Barnett

Goals: Rebrov (9, 16, 37, 82), Shevchenko (34, 60), Gerasimenko (18), Belkevich (65)

GRASSHOPPER-CLUB ZÜRICH v JEUNESSE d'ESCH **6-0** (3-0)

Hardturm, Zürich 22.07.1998

Referee: Sergei Gusev (RUS) Attendance: 4,800

GRASSHOPPER: Philipp Bernt Haas, Giuseppe Mazzarelli, Boris Smiljanic, Sven Christ; Avi Tikva (68 Reto Zanni), Mihai Tararache, Ricardo Cabanas, Mikheil Kavelashvili (65 Felix Magro); Joël Magnin, Blaise N'Kufo (71 Bruno Berner). Trainer: Rolf Fringer

JEUNESSE: Philippe Felgen; Johny Thill, Marc Lamborelle, Roland Schaack, Claude Meylender, Claude Ganser (27 Yves Divoy), Dany Theis (71 Carlo Pace), Denis Scuto, Manuel Cardoni, Paolo Amodio, Patrick Morocutti (46 Manuel Schauls). Trainer: Maurice Spitoni

Goals: N'Kufo (6, 51), Kavelashvili (29), Cabanas (41), Tikva (65 pen), Tararache (90)

BARRY TOWN FC v FC DYNAMO KYIV **1-2** (1-1)

Jenner Park, Barry 29.07.1998

Referee: Bujar Pregja (ALB) Attendance: 890

BARRY: Pat Mountain; Terry Evans, Gary Lloyd, Richard Jones, Andrew York, Lee Barrow, Gary Barnett, Danny Carter, Craig Evans, Eifion Williams, Mark Dempsey. Trainer: Gary Barnett

DYNAMO: Vyacheslav Kernozenko; Oleh Luzhnyi, Olexandr Khatskevich, Kakhi Kaladze, Vladislav Vashchuk, Serhiy Fedorov, Dmytro Mikhailenko, Serhiy Konovalov (46 Serhiy Rebrov), Oleh Venhlynskyi, Andriy Shevchenko (70 Aleksei Gerasimenko), Valentin Belkevich (76 Vitaliy Kosovskyi). Trainer: Valeriy Lobanovskyi

Goals: Mykhailenko (11), Williams (30), Venhlynskyi (50)

SILEKS KRATOVO v CLUB BRUGGE KV 0-0

Sileks, Kratovo 22.07.1998

Referee: Juan Manuel Brito Arceo (SPA) Attendance: 2,400

SILEKS: Kire Trajcev; Nikolçe Tanusev, Dragan Veselinoski, Igor Duzelov, Vlatko Gosev (89 Aleksandar Konjanovski), Trajkovski (67 Vladimir Kolev), Srdjan Zaharievski, Vlatko Novakov, Risto Bozinov, Ljupco Spinovski (77 Vlatko Stojcevski), Pance Stojanov. Trainer: Djokica Hadzievski

CLUB BRUGGE: Dany Verlinden; Eric Deflandre, Aleksandar Ilic, Vital Borkelmans, Franky van der Elst, Khalilou Fadiga (81 Ebou Sillah), Darco Anic, Gert Claessens (70 Sven Vermant), Tjörven de Brul, Eric Addo, Edgaras Jankauskas (82 Koen Schockaert). Trainer: Eric Gerets

CLUB BRUGGE v SILEKS KRATOVO 2-1 (2-0)

Jan Breydel, Brugge 29.07.1998

Referee: Sergei Shmolik (BLS) Attendance: 3,317

CLUB BRUGGE: Dany Verlinden; Eric Deflandre, Aleksandar Ilic (40 Vital Borkelmans), Milan Lesnjak, Franky van der Elst, Darco Anic (46 Ebou Sillah), Gert Claessens, Tjörven de Brul, Sven Vermant, Eric Addo, Edgaras Jankauskas (78 Elonga Elos Ekakia). Trainer: Eric Gerets

SILEKS: Kire Trajcev; Nikolçe Tanusev (65 Stefan Petkovski), Dragan Veselinoski, Igor Duzelov, Vlatko Gosev (70 Goranco Georgiev), Trajkovski (65 Vladimir Kolev), Srdjan Zaharievski, Vlatko Novakov, Risto Bozinov, Ljupco Spinovski, Pance Stojanov. Trainer: Djokica Hadzievski

Goals: Vermant (3), Claessens (30), Bozinov (76)

BEITAR JERUSALEM v B 36 TÓRSHAVN 4-1 (3-0)

Teddi Malcha, Jerusalem 22.07.1998

Referee: Spiridon Papadakos (GRE) Attendance: 7,000

BEITAR: Itzhak Korenfain; Jan Telesnikov, Serhiy Tretyak, Eitan Mizrahi (46 Nir Sivilia), Yossi Abuksis, István Sallói, Raanan Deree, István Hamar (75 Nir Reichman), Offer Shitrit, Ilan Bakhar, Asi Domb. Trainer: Dror Kashtan

B 36: Egin Høgnesen; Ninoslav Milanković, Mikkjal Thomassen, Rogvi Larsen (84 Bjarni Prior), Ronnie Samuelsen, Pol Thorsteinsson, Tomislav Sivic (83 Aki Mørk), Jens Kristian Hansen, Jakup a Borg (46 Jan Guttesen), John Petersen, Arnbjørn Danielsen. Trainer: Tomislav Sivić

Goals: Shitrit (2), Sallói (9, 45, 78), Petersen (73 pen)

B 36 TÓRSHAVN v BEITAR JERUSALEM 0-1 (0-0)

Svangaskard, Toftir 27.07.1998

Referee: Algirdas Dubinskas (Lit) Attendance: 600

B 36: Egin Høgnesen; Ninoslav Milanković, Mikkjal Thomassen (82 Jakup Martin Joensen), Ronnie Samuelsen (74 Aki Mørk), Pol Thorsteinsson, Tomislav Sivic (87 Rogvi Larsen), Jens Kristian Hansen, Jakup a Borg, John Petersen, Arnbjørn Danielsen, Jan Guttesen. Trainer: Tomislav Sivić

BEITAR: Itzhak Korenfain; Shmuel Levi, Jan Telesnikov, Serhiy Tretyak, Yossi Abuksis, Nir Sivilia (67 Eli Ohana), Raanan Deree, István Hamar, Offer Shitrit, Ilan Bakhar, Asi Domb. Trainer: Dror Kashtan

Goal: Hamar (68)

CLIFTONVILLE FC BELFAST v 1.FC KOŠICE 1-5 (1-3)

Solitude, Belfast 22.07.1998

Referee: Gylfi Orrasson (ICE) Attendance: 4,500

CLIFTONVILLE: Paul Reece; Stephen Small, Gerry Flynn (51 Joe Kerr), Martin Tabb, Thomas McCallion, Gary Sliney (73 Larry McMahon), Tim McCann, Michael Collins (81 Jim McDonagh), Jody Tolan, Marty McCann, Michael Donnelly. Manager: Marty Quinn

FC KOŠICE: Miroslav Seman; Dušan Toth (69 Milan Jambor), Ivan Kozak, Peter Dzurik (78 Radoslav Kráľ), Marek Spilar, Miroslav Sovic, Szilard Nemeth, Robert Semenik, Vladislav Zvara (52 Jan Kozak), Martin Prohaszka, Ruslan Lyubarskyi. Trainer: Jan Kozak

Goals: Zvara (22, 29), Nemeth (35), Flynn (45), Lyubarskyi (65), Prohaszka (78)

1.FC KOŠICE v CLIFTONVILLE FC BELFAST 8-0 (3-0)

Vsesportovy areal, Košice 29.07.1998

Referee: Milan Mitrović (SVN) Attendance: 1,948

FC KOŠICE: Miroslav Seman; Tomas Gerich, Ivan Kozak (46 Dušan Toth), Miroslav Sovic (58 Ruslan Lyubarskyi), Szilard Nemeth (46 Martin Prohaszka), Jozef Kozlej, Robert Semenik, Milan Jambor, Radoslav Kráľ, Jan Kozak, Vladimir Janocko. Trainer: Jan Kozak

CLIFTONVILLE: Paul Reece; Stephen Small, Gerry Flynn, Martin Tabb, Thomas McCallion, Gary Sliney (72 Larry McMahon), Tim McCann, Michael Collins (72 Damien Davey), Jody Tolan, Marty McCann (72 Jim McDonagh), Michael Donnelly. Manager: Marty Quinn

Goals: J. Kozak (3), Janocko (14, 53), Nemeth (31), Prohaszka (57, 72), Lyubarskyi (66), Kozlej (83)

SKONTO RIGA v DINAMO MINSK 0-0

Daugava, Riga 22.07.1998

Referee: Robert Sedlacek (AUS) Attendance: 3,000

SKONTO: Oleg Karavayev; Igor Stepanov, Levan Silagadze, Mikhail Zemlinsky, Valentin Lobanyov, Marian Pakhar, Vladimir Babichev, Mikhail Mikholap (73 Vitas Rimkus), Yury Laizans (46 Imants Bleidelis), Vitaly Astafyev, Andreyus Tereshkinas (72 Ilya Novikov). Trainer: Alexander Starkov

DINAMO: Andrei Satsunkevich; Dmitriy Makarenko, Vitaliy Volodenkov, Pavel Rodnenok (46 Alexandr Mishchishin), Vladimir Ostrikov, Oleg Chernyavskiy, Andrei Shilo, Alexandr Vyazhevich, Alexandr Osipovich, Alexandr Khrapkovskiy, Sergei Ermolenko. Trainer: Vladimir Kurnev

DINAMO MINSK v SKONTO RIGA 1-2 (1-1)

Dinamo, Minsk 29.07.1998

Referee: Constantin Zotta (ROM) Attendance: 5,700

DINAMO: Andrei Satsunkevich; Dmitriy Makarenko, Vitaliy Volodenkov, Alexandr Mishchishin, Vladimir Ostrikov (53 Andrei Lobanov), Oleg Chernyavskiy (58 Pavel Rodnenok), Andrei Shilo, Alexandr Vyazhevich (87 Yuri Lagodich), Alexandr Osipovich, Alexandr Khrapkovskiy, Sergei Ermolenko. Trainer: Vladimir Kurnev

SKONTO: Oleg Karavayev; Igor Stepanov, Levan Silagadze, Mikhail Zemlinsky, Valentin Lobanyov, Marian Pakhar, Vladimir Babichev (82 Alexander Pindeyev), Mikhail Mikholap (65 Imants Bleidelis), Yury Laizans, Vitas Rimkus (50 Ilya Novikov), Vitaly Astafyev.
Trainer: Alexander Starkov

Goals: Osipovich (26), Astafyev (45), Novikov (72)

SECOND QUALIFYING ROUND

ROSENBORG BK TRONDHEIM v CLUB BRUGGE 2-0 (0-0)

Lerkendal, Trondheim 12.08.1998

Referee: Hugh Dallas (SCO) Attendance: 12,919

ROSENBORG: Jørn Jamtfall; André Bergdølmo, Bjørn Otto Bragstad, Ole Christer Basma, Børge Hernes (81 Andreas Mayer), Erik Hoftun, Roar Strand, Bent Skammelsrud, Runar Berg, Sigurd Rushfeldt, Jan Derek Sørensen (68 Tore André Dahlum). Trainer: Trond Sollied

CLUB BRUGGE: Dany Verlinden; Eric Deflandre, Tjörven de Brul, Aleksandar Ilic, Vital Borkelmans, Gunther Verjans (62 Koen Schockaert), Franky van der Elst, Eric Addo (70 Edgaras Jankauskas), Sven Vermant, Elonga Elos Ekakia, Gert Claessens (83 Ebou Sillah). Trainer: Eric Gerets

Goals: Rushfeldt (61), Skammelsrud (81)

CLUB BRUGGE v ROSENBORG BK TRONDHEIM 4-2 (1-1)

Jan Breydel, Brugge 26.08.1998

Referee: Urs Meier (SWI) Attendance: 10,000

CLUB BRUGGE: Dany Verlinden; Eric Deflandre, Tjörven de Brul, Milan Lesnjak, Vital Borkelmans, Eric Addo (59 Sven Vermant), Franky van der Elst, Khalilou Fadiga, Gert Claessens, Elonga Elos Ekakia (70 Gunther Verjans), Edgaras Jankauskas (59 Koen Schockaert). Trainer: Eric Gerets

ROSENBORG: Jørn Jamtfall; Ole Christer Basma, Bjørn Otto Bragstad, Erik Hoftun, André Bergdølmo, Roar Strand (90 Fredrik Winsnes), Bent Skammelsrud, Runar Berg (82 Andreas Mayer); Børge Hernes, Sigurd Rushfeldt, Jahn Ivar Jakobsen (89 Jan Derek Sørensen). Trainer: Trond Sollied

Goals: Fadiga (23), Rushfeldt (41, 71), Claessens (46, 84), Schockaert (77)

MANCHESTER UNITED FC v LKS LÓDZ 2-0 (1-0)

Old Trafford, Manchester 12.08.1998

Referee: Atanas Uzunov (BUL) Attendance: 50,906

MANCHESTER UNITED: Peter Schmeichel; Gary Neville, Dennis Irwin, Ronny Johnsen, Jaap Stam, David Beckham, Nicky Butt, Andy Cole, Ryan Giggs, Roy Keane, Paul Scholes (81 Ole Gunnar Solskjaer). Manager: Alex Ferguson

LKS: Boguslaw Wyparlo; Rafal Pawlak, Witold Bendkowski, Grzegorz Krysiak, Tomasz Kos, Tomasz Wieszczycki, Rafal Niznik (53 Rodrigo Carbone), Omondiagbe Darlington (79 Ariel Jakubowski), Zbigniew Wyciszkiewicz, Tomasz Cebula, Zdzislaw Zuberek (68 Jacek Paszulewicz).
Trainer: Marek Dziuba

Goals: Giggs (16), Cole (81)

LKS LÓDZ v MANCHESTER UNITED FC 0-0

LKS, Lódz 26.08.1998

Referee: Graziano Cesari (ITA) Attendance: 8,000

LKS: Boguslaw Wyparlo; Witold Bendkowski, Grzegorz Krysiak, Rafal Pawlak, Tomasz Lenart (81 Jacek Plucinennik), Ariel Jakubowski (84 Artur Bugaj), Tomasz Kos, Rafal Niznik, Zbigniew Wyciszkiewicz, Tomasz Wieszczycki, Zdzislaw Zuberek (51 Piotr Matys). Trainer: Marek Dziuba

MANCHESTER UNITED: Peter Schmeichel; Philip Neville, Dennis Irwin, Jaap Stam, Ronny Johnsen, Nicky Butt, Roy Keane, David Beckham, Ryan Giggs (64 Ole Gunnar Solskjaer), Paul Scholes, Teddy Sheringham.
Manager: Alex Ferguson

LITEKS LOVECH v SPARTAK MOSKVA 0-5 (0-0)

Neftochimik, Burgas 12.08.1998

Referee: Alain Sars (FRA) Attendance: 15,000

LITEKS: Stoian Stavrev; Dimitar Balabanov (46 Stefan Iurukov), Rosen Emilov, Marian Todorov, Stoicho Stoilov, Nikolai Dimitrov, Alban Bushi, Dragoljub Simonovic, Zlatomir Zagorcic, Luís Motta (55 Veselin Sarbakov), Radostin Kishishev. Trainer: Ferario Spasov

SPARTAK: Aleksandr Filimonov; Dmitriy Khlestov, Ilya Tsymbalar, Evgeniy Bushmanov, Dmitriy Ananko, Vasiliy Baranov, Yegor Titov, Andrei Tikhonov, Dmytro Parfyonov, Aleksandr Shirko (62 Leandro SAMARONI da Rosa Fernandes), Nikolai Pisarev. Trainer: Oleg Romantsev

Goals: Pisarev (55, 86), Titov (65), Samaroni (77), Tsymbalar (90)

GRASSHOPPER-CLUB ZÜRICH v GALATASARAY ISTANBUL 2-3 (1-2)

Hardturm, Zürich 26.08.1998

Referee: Vítor Manuel Melo Pereira (POR) Att: 8,000

GRASSHOPPER: Pascal Zuberbühler; Bernt Haas, Mats Gren, Boris Smiljanic, Sven Christ; Avi Tikva, Antonio Esposito (75 Patrick de Napoli), Johann Vogel, Ricardo Cabanas (65 Joël Magnin); Mikheil Kavelashvili (46 Blaise N'Kufo), Kubilay Türkyılmaz. Trainer: Rolf Fringer

GALATASARAY: Claudio Taffarel; Iulian Filipescu, Gheorghe Popescu, Vedat Inceefe, Hakan Ünsal (85 Tolunay Kafkas), Okan Buruk, Tugay Kerimoğlu (46 Ergün Pembe), Suat Kaya, Gheorghe Hagi (81 Bülent Korkmaz), Hakan Şükür, Hasan Sas Gökhan. Trainer: Fatih Terim

Goals: Hakan Şükür (17, 45), Türkyılmaz (45), Hagi (65 pen), Vogel (70 pen)

SPARTAK MOSKVA v LITEKS LOVECH 6-2 (3-1)

Lokomotiv, Moskva 26.08.1998

Referee: Lubos Michel (SVK) Attendance: 15,000

SPARTAK: Aleksandr Filimonov; Sergei Gorlukovich, Ilya Tsymbalar, Evgeniy Bushmanov, Dmitriy Ananko, Vasiliy Baranov, Yegor Titov, Andrei Tikhonov, Dmytro Parfyonov, Aleksandr Shirko (53 Luís ROBSON Pereira da Silva), Nikolai Pisarev (58 Leandro SAMARONI da Rosa Fernandes). Trainer: Oleg Romantsev

LITEKS: Vitomir Vutov; Stefan Kolev, Rosen Emilov, Marian Todorov, Stoicho Stoilov (61 Vasil Kirov), Dimcho Beliakov (83 Luís Motta), Nikolai Dimitrov, Dimitar Kardaliev, Igor Bogdanovic (46 Alban Bushi), Veselin Ignatov, Altin Haxhi. Trainer: Ferario Spasov

Goals: Tikhonov (7, 32), Beliakov (28), Titov (37), Tsymbalar (48), Bushi (71), Robson (54, 90)

CELTIC FC GLASGOW v CROATIA ZAGREB 1-0 (0-0)

Celtic Park, Glasgow 12.08.1998

Referee: José María Garcia Aranda Encinar (SPA) Attendance: 51397

CELTIC: Jonathan Gould; Marc Rieper, Alan Stubbs, Tom Boyd, Jackie McNamara, Craig Burley, Henrik Larsson, Paul Lambert, Regi Blinker, Simon Donnelly, Harald Brattbakk (46 Darren Jackson). Trainer: Jozef Venglos

CROATIA: Drazen Ladić; Dario Simić, Goran Jurić, Mario Tokić, Mario Cvitanović, Tomislav Rukavina, Silvio Marić (81 Josip Simić), Krunoslav Jurcić, Robert Prosinecki, Josko Jelicić (75 Edin Mujcin), Mark Viduka. Trainer: Zlatko Kranjcar

Goal: Jackson (50)

GALATASARAY ISTANBUL v GRASSHOPPER-CLUB ZÜRICH 2-1 (0-0)

Ali Sami Yen, Istanbul 12.08.1998

Referee: Marc Batta (FRA) Attendance: 21,043

GALATASARAY: Claudio Taffarel; Iulian Filipescu, Gheorghe Popescu, Vedat Inceefe (84 Fatih Akyel), Ergün Pembe, Hasan Sas Gökhan, Tugay Kerimoğlu, Suat Kaya, Emre Belözoglu (46 Okan Buruk), Hakan Şükür, Gheorghe Hagi. Trainer: Fatih Terim

GRASSHOPPER: Pascal Zuberbüler; Bernt Haas, Mats Gren, Boris Smiljanic, Sven Christ; Johann Vogel, Joël Magnin, Antonio Esposito (77 Avi Tikva), Ricardo Cabanas (68 Mihai Tararache); Blaise N'Kufo (68 Mikheil Kavelashvili), Kubilay Türkyılmaz. Trainer: Rolf Fringer

Goals: Hagi (59 pen), Hakan Şükür (65), Vogel (87)

CROATIA ZAGREB v CELTIC FC GLASGOW 3-0 (2-0)

Maksimir, Zagreb 26.08.1998

Referee: Pierluigi Collina (ITA) Attendance: 27,000

CROATIA: Drazen Ladić; Mario Tokić, Silvio Marić (84 Danijel Sarić), Goran Jurić, Robert Prosinecki, Mark Viduka (73 Tomislav Sokota), Tomislav Rukavina, Dario Simić, Mario Cvitanović, Josko Jelicić (60 Edin Mujcin), Krunoslav Jurcić. Trainer: Zlatko Kranjcar

CELTIC: Jonathan Gould; Tom Boyd, Stéphane Mahé, Jackie McNamara, Marc Rieper; Alan Stubbs, Henrik Larsson, Craig Burley, Paul Lambert, Darren Jackson (76 Simon Donnelly), Regi Blinker (63 Harald Brattbakk). Trainer: Jozef Venglos

Goals: Marić (23), Prosinecki (44 pen, 68)

MARIBOR TEATANIC v PSV EINDHOVEN 2-1 (1-0)

Ljudski vrt, Maribor 12.08.1998

Referee: Anders Frisk (SWE) Attendance: 5,000

TEATANIC: Luka Gresak; Gregor Zidan, Stipe Balajić, Muamer Vugdalić, Matjaz Kek, Marinko Sarkezi, Damjan Gajser (61 Milan Sterbal), Dejan Djuranović, Dalibor Filipović, Nastja Ceh (72 Besnik Kollari), Marko Kmetec (82 Peter Breznik). Trainer: Bojan Prasnikar

PSV: Patrick Lodewijks; André Ooijer (75 Björn Van der Doelen), Yuri Nikiforov, Davy Oyen, Abel Luis Xavier Silva Costa, Ruud Van Nistelrooij, Gilles De Bilde, Joonas Kolkka, Dmitri Khokhlov (81 Jorge Henrique Amaral de Castro "JORGINHO"), Joaquim MARCOS Dos Santos, Tomek Iwan (72 Dennis Rommedahl). Trainer: Bobby Robson

Goals: Filipović (14), Marcos (60), Breznik (85)

PSV EINDHOVEN v MARIBOR TEATANIC 4-1 (1-1,2-1)

Philips, Eindhoven 26.08.1998

Referee: Brian Lawlor (WAL) Attendance: 11,500

PSV: Patrick Lodewijks; Theo Lucius, Joaquim MARCOS Dos Santos (70 Dennis Rommedahl), Abel Luis Xavier Silva Costa, Jorge Henrique Amaral de Castro "JORGINHO" (46 Arnold Bruggink), Tomek Iwan, Dmitri Khokhlov, André Ooijer, Joonas Kolkka (111 Björn Van der Doelen), Gilles De Bilde, Ruud Van Nistelrooij. Trainer: Bobby Robson

TEATANIC: Goran Stanković; Gregor Zidan, Matjaz Kek, Marinko Sarkezi, Muamer Vugdalić, Nastja Ceh (81 Peter Breznik), Damjan Gajser (66 Milan Sterbal), Stipe Balajić, Dejan Djuranović, Dalibor Filipović, Marko Kmetec (37 Franc Fridl). Trainer: Bojan Prasnikar

Goals: Filipović (5), Van Nistelrooij (8), Bruggink (70), Rommedahl (100), De Bilde (103)

FC DYNAMO KYIV v AC SPARTA PRAHA 0-1 (0-1)

Olympiyskyi, Kyiv 12.08.1998

Referee: Bernd Heynemann (GER) Attendance: 15,000

DYNAMO: Olexandr Shovkovskyi; Vladislav Vashchuk, Oleh Luzhnyi, Olexandr Holovko, Vitaliy Kosovskyi (57 Serhiy Konovalov), Olexandr Khatskevich, Yuri Kalitvintsev (46 Aleksei Gerasimenko), Andriy Gusin, Kakhi Kaladze (79 Valentin Belkevich), Serhiy Rebrov, Andriy Shevchenko. Trainer: Valeriy Lobanovskyi

SPARTA: Tomáš Poštulka; Tomáš Votava, Michal Hornak, Jiří Novotný, Vlastimil Svoboda, Miroslav Baranek, Martin Hasek, Martin Cizek (77 Antonin Mlejnsky), Pavel Novotný, Horst Siegl, Vratislav Lokvenc. Trainer: Zdenek Scasny

Goal: Baranek (5)

AC SPARTA PRAHA v FC DYNAMO KYIV 0-1 (0-0, 0-1) (AET)

Stadión na Letnej, Praha 26.08.1998

Referee: Gilles Veissière (FRA) Attendance: 17,998

SPARTA: Tomáš Poštulka; Tomáš Votava, Martin Hasek, Michal Hornak, Martin Cizek, Jiří Novotný, Vratislav Lokvenc, Horst Siegl, Antonin Mlejnsky (93 Ludek Straceny), Pavel Novotný (88 Petr Gabriel), Miroslav Baranek. Trainer: Zdenek Scasny

DYNAMO: Olexandr Shovkovskyi; Oleh Luzhnyi, Aleksei Gerasimenko (85 Vladimir Makovskiy), Olexandr Holovko, Vladislav Vashchuk (67 Serhiy Konovalov), Yuri Dmitrulin, Kakhi Kaladze, Vitaliy Kosovskyi (70 Valentin Belkevich), Andriy Shevchenko, Serhiy Rebrov, Andriy Gusin. Trainer: Valeriy Lobanovskyi

Goal: Votava (88 og)

Penalties: 0-1 Rebrov, 1-1 Cizek, 1-2 Kaladze, Votava (miss), Shevchenko (miss), Straceny (miss), Konovalov (miss), Baranek (miss), 1-3 Dmitrulin

1.FC KOŠICE v BRØNDBY IF 0-2 (0-0)

Vsesportovy areal, Košice 12.08.1998

Referee: Manuel Diaz Vega (SPA) Attendance: 4,725

FC KOŠICE: Ladislav Molnar; Robert Semenik, Ivan Kozak, Peter Dzurik, Marek Spilar, Miroslav Sovic, Vladislav Zvara, Ruslan Lyubarskyi (68 Jozef Kozlej), Dušan Toth, Szilard Nemeth (68 Vladimir Janocko), Martin Prohaszka. Trainer: Jan Kozak

BRØNDBY: Emeka Andersen; Kenneth Rasmussen, Per Nielsen, Søren Colding, Brian Jensen, Ole Bjur (81 Jesper Thygesen), Kim Daugaard, John Jensen, Thomas Lindrup (69 Ruben Bagger), Ebbe Sand, Bo Hansen (88 Mikkel Jensen). Trainer: Ebbe Skovdahl

Goals: Daugaard (54), Thygesen (85)

BRØNDBY IF v 1.FC KOŠICE 0-1 (0-1)

Idraetsparken, København 26.08.1998

Referee: Michel Piraux (BEL) Attendance: 16,962

BRØNDBY: Emeka Andersen; Søren Colding, Per Nielsen, Kenneth Rasmussen, Anders Bjerregaard, Ole Bjur, John Jensen, Kim Daugaard, Jesper Thygesen (64 Ruben Bagger, 78 Thomas Lindrup), Ebbe Sand, Bo Hansen (83 Allan Ravn). Trainer: Ebbe Skovdahl

FC KOŠICE: Ladislav Molnar; Robert Semenik, Radoslav Kráľ, Peter Dzurik, Ivan Lapsansky (66 Vladimir Janocko), Miroslav Sovic, Vladislav Zvara, Dušan Toth, Ruslan Lyubarskyi, Jozef Kozlej, Martin Prohaszka (55 Szilard Nemeth). Trainer: Jan Kozak

Goal: Lapsansky (39)

FC INTERNAZIONALE MILANO
v SKONTO RIGA 4-0 (3-0)

Giuseppe Meazza, Milano 12.08.1998

Referee: Fritz Stuchlik (AUS) Attendance: 16,000

INTER: Gianluca Pagliuca; Francesco Colonnese, Giuseppe Bergomi (60 Salvatore Fresi), Fabio Galante, Benoit Cauet, José Moedin ZÉ ELIAS (46 Javier Zanetti), Diego Simeone, Mauro Milanese, Nicola Ventola, Ivan Zamorano, Roberto Baggio (66 Andrea Pirlo). Trainer: Luigi Simoni

SKONTO: Oleg Karavayev; Yury Laizans, Igor Stepanov, Levan Silagadze, Vsevolod Lidaks, Imants Bleidelis, Alexander Rekhviashvili, Vladimir Babichev (80 Vladimir Melnik), Vitaly Astafyev (5 Vitas Rimkus, 58 Ilya Novikov), Marian Pakhar, Mikhail Mikholap. Trainer: Alexander Starkov

Goals: Zamorano (4), Simeone (10), Ventola (21), Baggio (59)

SKONTO RIGA
v FC INTERNAZIONALE MILANO 1-3 (1-1)

Daugava, Riga 26.08.1998

Referee: Giorgos Bikas (GRE) Attendance: 6,500

SKONTO: Oleg Karavayev; Levan Silagadze, Igor Stepanov, Valentin Lobanyov, Imants Bleidelis, Mikhail Zemlinsky, Vladimir Babichev, Alexander Rekhviashvili, Vladimir Melnik (46 Ilya Novikov), Marian Pakhar (85 Andrei Rubins), Mikhail Mikholap (85 Vitas Rimkus). Trainer: Alexander Starkov

INTER: Gianluca Pagliuca; Giuseppe Bergomi, Salvatore Fresi, Fabio Galante, Javier Zanetti, Aron Winter (74 Cristiano Zanetti), Benoit Cauet, Mauro Milanese, Youri Djorkaeff (71 Andrea Pirlo), Ivan Zamorano, Roberto Baggio (71 Alvaro Recoba). Trainer: Luigi Simoni

Goals: Zamorano (8), Mikholap (23), Galante (54), Djorkaeff (71)

OLYMPIAKOS PEIRAIAS
v ANORTHOSIS FAMAGUSTA 2-1 (2-0)

Olympiako, Athina 12.08.1998

Referee: René Temmink (HOL) Attendance: 28,047

OLYMPIAKOS: Dimitris Eleftheropoulos; Kiriakos Karataidis (Cap), Grigoris Georgatos (63 Stilianos Sfakianakis), Peter Ofori-Quaye, LUCIANO Nunes de Souza, Ilija Ivić (68 Felix Aboague), Petros Passalis (46 Geeorgios Anatolakis), Ilias Poursanidis, Predrag Djordjević, Stelios Giannakopoulos, Dimitris Mavrogenidis.
Trainer: Dušan Bajević

ANORTHOSIS: Nikos Panagiotou; Vasos Melanarkitis, Zaharias Haralampous (73 Lambros Lambrou), Dimitris Ioannou, Panagiotis Egkomitis, Loukas Louka (46 Stavros Foukaris), Vladan Tomic, Vesko Mihajlovic (81 Pambis Andreou), Slobodan Krcmarevic, Panikos Pounas, Paris Ilia.
Trainer: Dušan Mitosević

Goals: Giannakopoulos (12), Luciano (32), Mihajlović (64)

ANORTHOSIS FAMAGUSTA
v OLYMPIAKOS PEIRAIAS 2-4 (1-0)

Antonis Papadopoulos, Larnaca 26.08.1998

Referee: Miroslav Radoman (YUG) Attendance: 10,000

ANORTHOSIS: Nikos Panagiotou; Lambros Lambrou (60 Pambis Andreou), Zaharias Haralampous (74 Loukas Louka), Stavros Foukaris, Panagiotis Egkomitis (82 Zoran Cirić), Vasos Melanarkitis, Giannakis Okas, Vesko Mihajlovic, Slobodan Krcmarevic, Panikos Pounas, Paris Ilia.
Trainer: Dušan Mitosević

OLYMPIAKOS: Dimitris Eleftheropoulos; Kiriakos Karataidis (Cap), Grigoris Georgatos, Peter Ofori-Quaye, Giorgos Anatolakis (46 Vasilis Karapialis), LUCIANO Nunes de Souza (89 Sinisa Gogić), Ilija Ivić (68 Stelios Giannakopoulos), Ilias Poursanidis, Predrag Djordjević, Dimitris Mavrogenidis, Giorgos Amanatidis.
Trainer: Dušan Bajević

Goals: Mihajlovic (36), Georgatos (47), Djordjević (57, 86), Krcmarević (80), Gogić (90)

SPORT LISBOA E BENFICA
v BEITAR JERUSALEM 6-0 (2-0)

Estádio Da Luz, Lisboa 12.08.1998

Referee: Edgar Steinborn (GER) Attendance: 55,000

BENFICA: Michel Ghislain Preud'homme; José Carlos Leite SOUSA, PAULO Sérgio Braga MADEIRA, RONALDO Guiaro, Scott Christopher Minto, Karel Poborsky (69 Hugo Cardoso PORFÍRIO), José António CALADO da Silva, Michael Thomas, Mark Pembridge, Brian Deane (76 Nuno Miguel Soares Ribeiro "NUNO GOMES"), Martin Ulf Pringle (56 JOÃO Manuel VIEIRA PINTO). Trainer: Graeme Souness

BEITAR: Itzhak Korenfain; Shmuel Levi, Serhiy Tretyak, Asi Domb, Amir Shelach, István Hamar, Jan Telesnikov, Yossi Abuksis, István Sallói, Ilan Bakhar, Offer Shitrit (65 Eli Ohana). Trainer: Dror Kashtan

Goals: Pembridge (25, 80), Deane (29), Calado (64 pen), Shelach (79 og), Nuno Gomes (85 pen)

BEITAR JERUSALEM
v SPORT LISBOA E BENFICA 4-2 (2-1)

Teddi Malcha, Jerusalem 26.08.1998

Referee: Ryszard Wójcik (POL) Attendance: 1,300

BEITAR: Itzhak Korenfain; Raanan Deree, Asi Domb, Amir Shelach, Jan Telesnikov, Ilan Bakhar, István Sallói, Yossi Abuksis, István Hamar, Nir Reichman (83 Eitan Mizrahi), Offer Shitrit (68 Eli Ohana). Trainer: Dror Kashtan

BENFICA: Michel Ghislain Preud'homme; José Carlos Leite SOUSA, PAULO Sérgio Braga MADEIRA, RONALDO Guiaro, Scott Christopher Minto, Sergei Kandaurov (53 Karel Poborsky), Michael Thomas, José António CALADO da Silva (74 Tahar El Khalej), Mark Pembridge, JOÃO Manuel VIEIRA PINTO, Nuno Miguel Soares Ribeiro "NUNO GOMES" (54 Martin Ulf Pringle). Trainer: Graeme Souness

Goals: Nuno Gomes (17 pen), Hamar (25), Sallói (28), Shitrit (51), Abuksis (80), João Pinto (90)

DINAMO TBILISI v ATHLETIC BILBAO 2-1 (2-0)

Boris Paichadze, Tbilisi 12.08.1998

Referee: Rune Pedersen (NOR) Attendance: 12,500

DINAMO: David Gvaramadze; Ivane Makharadze, Zviad Jeladze, Valter Guchua, Givi Didava, Rati Aleksidze, David MuJiří (87 Levan Melkadze), Giorgi Kiknadze, Levan Tskitishvili, Levan Khomeriki (89 Giorgi Shengelia), Mikhail Ashvetia. Trainer: Murtaz Khurtsilava

ATHLETIC: Imanol ETXEBERRIA Egaña; CÉSAR Fernández de las Heras Caneda, Carlos GARCÍA, Francisco "Patxi" FERREIRA Colmenero, Aitor LARRAZÁBAL Bilbao; Andoni IMAZ Garmendia, Josu URRUTIA Telleria (66 Domingo NAGORE Arbizu), JAVIer Gómez GONZÁLEZ (82 Julen GUERRERO López), Bittor ALKIZA Fernández, Santiago EZQUERRO Marín, Ismael URZAIZ Aranda (62 Joseba ETXEBERRIA Lizardi). Trainer: Luis Fernández

Goals: Khomeriki (15), Tskitishvili (30), Imaz (47)

ATHLETIC BILBAO v DINAMO TBILISI 1-0 (0-0)

San Mamés, Bilbao 26.08.1998

Referee: László Vagner (HUN) Attendance: 34,600

ATHLETIC: Imanol ETXEBERRIA Egaña; Jesús María LACRUZ Gómez, Carlos GARCÍA, Rafael ALKORTA Martínez, Aitor LARRAZÁBAL Bilbao; Andoni IMAZ Garmendia, Julen GUERRERO López, Bittor ALKIZA Fernández (86 JOSÉ MARIa García Lafuente), Joseba ETXEBERRIA Lizardi (86 JAVIer Gómez GONZÁLEZ); Ismael URZAIZ Aranda (86 JORGE PÉREZ Sáenz), Santiago EZQUERRO Marín. Trainer: Luis Fernández

DINAMO: David Gvaramadze; Ivane Makharadze, Givi Didava, Zviad Jeladze, Levan Kobiashvili, David MuJiří, Valter Guchua, Giorgi Kiknadze, Levan Tskitishvili, Levan Khomeriki, Mikhail Ashvetia (53 Levan Melkadze). Trainer: Murtaz Khurtsilava

Goal: J. Etxeberria (53)

HJK HELSINKI v FC METZ 1-0 (0-0)

Olympiastadion, Helsinki 12.08.1998

Referee: Roelof Luinge (HOL) Attendance: 8,287

HJK: Tommi Koivistoinen; Aarno Turpeinen, Jari Ilola, Jarmo Saastamoinen, Ville Nylund, Aki Riihilahti, Jarkko Juhani Wiss, Mika Lehkosuo, Marcelo Goncalves De Oliveira Piracaía (86 Jari Jäväjä), Mika Antero Kottila (88 Hannu Tihinen), Shefki Kuqi (66 Luiz António). Trainer: Antti Muurinen

METZ: Lionel Letizi; David Régis, Sylvain Kastendeuch, Jeff Strasser, Pascal Pierre; Franck Rizzetto (73 Christophe Le Grix), Grégory Proment, Frédéric Meyrieu, Danny Boffin (86 Youns Diani), Franck Histilloles, Vladan Lukić. Trainer: Joël Muller

Goal: Riihilahti (72)

FC METZ v HJK HELSINKI 1-1 (0-0)

Saint-Symphorien, Metz 26.08.1998

Referee: William Smith Young (SCO) Attendance: 10,000

METZ: Lionel Letizi; David Régis (70 Ludovic Asuar), Sylvain Kastendeuch, Jeff Strasser, Pascal Pierre; Grégory Proment, Franck Rizzetto, Frédéric Meyrieu, Danny Boffin, Louis Saha, Vladan Lukic. Trainer: Joël Muller

HJK: Tommi Koivistoinen; Aarno Turpeinen, Jari Ilola, Jarmo Saastamoinen, Mika Lehkosuo, Ville Nylund, Jarkko Juhani Wiss, Shefki Kuqi (90 Hannu Tihinen), Marcelo Goncalves De Oliveira Piracaía (66 Vesa Vasara), Aki Riihilahti, Mika Antero Kottila (76 Markku Kanerva). Trainer: Antti Muurinen

Goals: Vaasara (69), Meyrieu (79 pen)

FC BAYERN MÜNCHEN v FC OBILIC BEOGRAD 4-0 (0-0)

Olympiastadion, München 12.08.1998

Referee: Terje Hauge (NOR) Attendance: 37,000

BAYERN: Oliver Kahn; Markus Babbel, Lothar Matthäus, Thomas Linke, Thomas Strunz, Stefan Effenberg (77 Bixente Lizarazu), Thorsten Fink, Michael Tarnat (57 Carsten Jancker), Mario Basler (57 Alexander Zickler), Giovane De Souza Elber, Hasan Salihamidzic. Trainer: Ottmar Hitzfeld

OBILIC: Nenad Lukić; Kuzman Babeu, Miroslav Savić, Marjan Zivković (66 Predrag Filipović), Dragan Sarac, Sasa Zorić, Zivojin Juksić, Nenad Grozdić, Darko Vargec, Sasa Kovacević (62 Igor Manojlović), Zoran Ranković (72 Sasa Viciknez). Trainer: Dragan Okuka

Goals: Effenberg (59), Elber (63), Zickler (66), Fink (76)

FC OBILIC BEOGRAD v FC BAYERN MÜNCHEN 1-1 (0-0)

FK Obilić, Beograd 26.08.1998

Referee: Antonio Jesus Lopez Nieto (SPA) Att: 8,500

OBILIC: Nenad Lukić; Kuzman Babeu, Miroslav Savić (72 Predrag Ocokoljić), Sasa Mrkić, Goran Serafimović, Marjan Zivković, Sasa Zorić, Nenad Grozdić, Dragan Sarac, Aco Vasiljević (64 Sasa Viciknez), Zoran Ranković (52 Sasa Kovacević). Trainer: Dragan Okuka

BAYERN: Oliver Kahn; Thomas Helmer, Lothar Matthäus, Thomas Linke, Thomas Strunz, Hasan Salihamidzic, Stefan Effenberg (83 Thorsten Fink), Jens Jeremies, Michael Tarnat, Giovane De Souza Elber (65 Ali Daei), Carsten Jancker (65 Alexander Zickler). Trainer: Ottmar Hitzfeld

Goals: Sarac (67), Matthäus (90)

SK STURM GRAZ v ÚJPEST BUDAPEST 4-0 (2-0)

Arnold Schwarzenegger, Graz 12.08.1998

Referee: Robert Antony Boggi (ITA) Attendance: 10,323

STURM: Kazimierz Sidorczuk; Markus Schupp, Darko Milanic, Mario Posch, Markus Schopp, Roman Mählich, Hannes Reinmayr (73 Georg Bardel), Didier Angibeaud, Günther Neukirchner (83 Jan-Pieter Martens); Ivica Vastic, Mario Haas. Trainer: Ivica Osim

ÚJPESTI: Szabolcs Biró; Csaba Fehér, Zoltán Tamási, Balázs Kiskapusi, Sándor Jenei, Goran Kopunović, Attila Korsós (88 Krisztián Kvasz), Norbert Tóth (65 Balázs Bérczy), Zoltán Szlezák, Miklós Herczeg (80 Dénes Eszenyi), Zoltán Kovács. Trainer: Peter Varhidi

Goals: Vastic (7, 70), Neukirchner (82), Haas (89)

ÚJPEST BUDAPEST v SK STURM GRAZ 2-3 (1-1)

Megyeri úti, Budapest 26.08.1998

Referee: Arturo Dauden Ibañez (SPA) Attendance: 2,350

ÚJPESTI: Szabolcs Biró; Sándor Jenei, Csaba Fehér, Zoltán Szlezák, Vilmos Sebök, József Mogyorósi, Zoltán Kovács, Miklós Herczeg (80 Dénes Eszenyi), Balázs Kiskapusi (60 Balázs Bérczy), Norbert Tóth, Attila Korsós (64 Krisztián Kvasz). Trainer: Peter Varhidi

STURM: Kazimierz Sidorczuk; Günther Neukirchner, Roman Mählich (83 Georg Bardel), Markus Schupp, Hannes Reinmayr, Mario Posch, Didier Angibeaud (76 Mehrdad Minavand), Markus Schopp (76 Franco Foda), Ranko Popovic; Ivica Vastic, Mario Haas. Trainer: Ivica Osim

Goals: Haas (8), Z. Kovács (36), Reinmayr (50, 56), Jenei (72)

STEAUA BUCUREŞTI v PANATHINAIKOS ATHINA 2-2 (1-1)

Steaua, Bucureşti 12.08.1998

Referee: Piero Ceccarini (ITA) Attendance: 15,000

STEAUA: Gabriel Rotaru; Miodrag Belodedici, Valeriu Răchită, Adrian Matei; Iulian Ilie Miu (71 Marius Sebastian Luca), Denis Georgian Şerban (89 Ion Lavi Hrib), Erik Augustin Lincar, Mihăiţă Gabriel Szekely, Laurenţiu Dumitru Roşu; Marius Mihai Lăcătuş, Ionel Daniel Dănciulescu. Trainer: Mihai Stoichiţă

PANATHINAIKOS: Jozef Wandzik; Giorgos Alexopoulos, Vladan Milojević, Giannis Gkoumas; Andreas Lagonikakis, Stratos Apostolakis (81 Konstandinos Konstantinidis), Erik Mykland, Aljosa Asanović, Aggelos Basinas; Nikos Limperopoulos (84 Bledar Kola), Krzysztof Warzycha (Cap). Trainer: Vasilis Daniil

Goals: Asanović (5), Şerban (9), Limperopoulos (67), Szekely (75)

PANATHINAIKOS ATHINA v STEAUA BUCUREŞTI 6-3 (3-2)

Olympiako, Athina 26.08.1998

Referee: Mario van der Ende (HOL) Attendance: 60,000

PANATHINAIKOS: Jozef Wandzik; Stratos Apostolakis, Giorgos Alexopoulos, Vladan Milojević, Giannis Gkoumas, Aggelos Basinas (77 Bledar Kola); Andreas Lagonikakis (56 Konstandinos Konstantinidis), Erik Mykland, Aljosa Asanović; Krzysztof Warzycha, Nikos Limperopoulos (85 Frank Strandli). Trainer: Vasilis Daniil

STEAUA: Gabriel Rotaru; Laurenţiu Aurelian Reghecampf, Adrian Matei, Valeriu Răchită, Miodrag Belodedici; Iulian Ilie Miu, Denis Georgian Şerban, Erik Augustin Lincar, Laurenţiu Dumitru Roşu (72 Damian Militaru); Marius Mihai Lăcătuş (83 Marius Sebastian Luca), Ionel Daniel Dănciulescu. Trainer: Mihai Stoichiţă

Goals: Milojević (8 pen), Răchită (13, 17), Lincar (29 og), Limperopoulos (36), Warzycha (59, 67), Belodedici (61), Asanović (88 pen)

CHAMPIONS LEAGUE

GROUP A

FC PORTO v OLYMPIAKOS PEIRAIAS 2-2 (0-0)

Estádio das Antas, Porto 16.09.1998

Referee: Gilles Veissière (FRA) Attendance: 35,000

FC PORTO: Ivica Kralj, Carlos Alberto de Oliveira SECRETÁRIO, JORGE Paulo COSTA Almeida, ALOÍSIO Pires Alves, FERNANDO Manuel Antunes MENDES, Dorival Guidoni Júnior «DORIVA», João Paulo Maio dos Santos PAULINHO SANTOS, Zlatko Zahovic (70 Youssef Chippo), Ljubinko Drulovic (58 ARTUR Duarte de Oliveira), Nuno Fernando Gonçalves da Rocha «CAPUCHO», Mario JARDEL Almeida Ribeiro (90 Nică Basarab Panduru). Trainer: Fernando Manuel Costa Santos

OLYMPIAKOS: Dimitris Eleftheropoulos; Dimitris Mavrogenidis, Kiriakos Karataidis (Cap), Giorgos Anatolakis, Grigoris Georgatos, Luciano Nunes De Souza (87 Sinisa Gogić), Ilias Poursanidis, Giorgos Amanatidis (82 Vasilis Karapialis), Predrag Djordjević, Ilija Ivic (78 Stilianos Giannakopoulos), Peter Ofori-Quaye. Trainer: Dušan Bajević

Goals: Zahović (65), Jardel (82), Giannakopoulos (87), Gogić (90)

CROATIA ZAGREB v AFC AJAX AMSTERDAM 0-0

Maksimir, Zagreb 16.09.1998

Referee: Kim Milton Nielsen (DEN) Attendance: 33,000

CROATIA: Drazen Ladić, Mario Tokić, Goran Jurić, Dario Simić, Mario Cvitanović, Tomislav Rukavina (57 Danijel Sarić), Robert Prosinecki, Edin Mujcin, Josko Jelicić (79 Tomislav Sokota), Mark Viduka (68 Mihael Mikić), Silvio Marić. Trainer: Zlatko Kranjcar.

AJAX: Edwin van der Sar; Ole Tobiasen, Danny Blind, Frank de Boer, DANIel Da Cruz Carvalho (63 Ronald de Boer), Sunday Oliseh, Jari Litmanen, Richard Witschge, Tijjani Babangida (77 Giorgi Kinkladze), Benedict McCarthy, Peter Hoekstra (71 Jesper Grønkjaer). Trainer: Morten Olsen

OLYMPIAKOS PEIRAIAS v CROATIA ZAGREB 2-0 (1-0)

Olympiako, Athina 30.09.1998

Referee: David Roland Elleray (ENG) Attendance: 60,000

OLYMPIAKOS: Dimitris Eleftheropoulos; Kiriakos Karataidis (Cap), Giorgos Amanatidis (75 Paraskevas Antzas), Ilias Poursanidis, Stilianos Giannakopoulos, Dimitris Mavrogenidis, Vasilis Karapialis (72 Andreas Niniadis), Giorgos Anatolakis, Predrag Djordjević, Alekos Alexandris (90 Luciano Nunes De Souza), Sinisa Gogić.
Trainer: Dušan Bajević

CROATIA: Drazen Ladić, Mario Tokić, Goran Jurić, Josko Jelicić (74 Tomislav Sokota), Mario Cvitanović, Edin Mujcin (46 Nermin Sabić), Dario Simić, Silvio Marić, Krunoslav Jurcić, Tomislav Rukavina, Mark Viduka (81 Josip Simić).
Trainer: Zlatko Kranjcar

Goals: Alexandris (21), Gogic (80)

AFC AJAX AMSTERDAM v FC PORTO 2-1 (0-0)

Amsterdam ArenA 30.09.1998

Referee: Piero Ceccarini (ITA) Attendance: 40,000

AJAX: Edwin van der Sar; Ole Tobiasen, Andrzej Rudy, Frank de Boer, Ronald de Boer, Sunday Oliseh, Jari Litmanen, Richard Witschge (65 Daniel Da Cruz Carvalho "DANI"), Tijjani Babangida (90 Jesper Grønkjaer), Shota Arveladze (79 Gerald Sibon), Peter Hoekstra. Trainer: Morten Olsen

FC PORTO: RUI Manuel Da Silva CORREIA; Carlos Alberto De Oliveira SECRETÁRIO, ALOÍSIO Pires Alves, FERNANDO Manuel Antunes MENDES (46 Youssef Chippo), Dorival Guidoni Junior "DORIVA", Nuno Fernando Gonçalves da Rocha "CAPUCHO" (68 ARTUR Duarte De Oliveira), Zlatko Zahovic, João Paulo Maio dos Santos PAULINHO SANTOS, Mario JARDEL Almeida Ribeiro, JORGE Paulo Almeida COSTA, Ljubinko Drulovic (83 RUI Gil Soares BARROS).
Trainer: Fernando Manuel Costa Santos

Goals: Rudy (57), Zahovic (68), Litmanen (86 pen)

OLYMPIAKOS PEIRAIAS v AFC AJAX AMSTERDAM 1-0 (1-0)

Olympiako, Athina 21.10.1998

Referee: José Manuel Diaz Vega (SPA) Attendance: 73,250

OLYMPIAKOS: Dimitris Eleftheropoulos; Kiriakos Karataidis (Cap), Grigoris Georgatos, Giorgos Anatolakis, Ilias Poursanidis, Predrag Djordjević, Stilianos Giannakopoulos, Giorgos Amanatidis, Sinisa Gogić (74 Peter Ofori-Quaye), Vasilis Karapialis (85 Andreas Niniadis), Alekos Alexandris (68 Petros Passalis). Trainer: Dušan Bajević

AJAX: Edwin van der Sar; Ole Tobiasen, Andrzej Rudy, Sunday Oliseh, Frank de Boer, Ronald de Boer, Jari Litmanen, Richard Witschge, Wamberto Sousa Campos (46 Daniel Da Cruz Carvalho « DANI »), Shota Arveladze (79 Benedict McCarthy), Jesper Grønkjaer (46 Giorgi Kinkladze).
Trainer: Morten Olsen

Goal: Alexandris (38)

FC PORTO v CROATIA ZAGREB 3-0 (2-0)

Estádio das Antas, Porto 21.10.1998

Referee: Günter Benkö (AUS) Attendance: 25,000

FC PORTO: Ivica Kralj; Carlos Alberto de Oliveira SECRETÁRIO, JORGE Paulo COSTA Almeida, ALOÍSIO Pires Alves, FERNANDO Manuel Antunes MENDES, João Paulo Maio dos Santos PAULINHO SANTOS, Dorival Guidoni Júnior "DORIVA", Zlatko Zahovic (90 Youssef Chippo), Nuno Fernando Gonçalves da Rocha "CAPUCHO" (81 RUI Gil Soares BARROS), Ljubinko Drulovic (64 ARTUR Duarte de Oliveira), Mário JARDEL Almeida Ribeiro.
Trainer: Fernando Manuel Costa Santos

CROATIA: Drazen Ladić; Goran Jurić, Dario Simić, Mario Tokić, Tomislav Rukavina, Josko Jelicić (46 Edin Mujcin), Krunoslav Jurcić, Danijel Sarić (46 Nermin Sabić), Damir Krznar, Silvio Marić (58 Mark Viduka), Tomislav Sokota.
Trainer: Zlatko Kranjcar

Goals: Drulovic (33), Zahovic (43, 76)

AFC AJAX AMSTERDAM v OLYMPIAKOS PEIRAIAS 2-0 (1-0)

Amsterdam ArenA 4.11.1998

Referee: Stefano Braschi (ITA) Attendance: 45,000

AJAX: Edwin van der Sar; Ole Tobiasen (36 Daniel Da Cruz Carvalho "DANI"), Sunday Oliseh, Frank de Boer, Tom Sier, Ronald de Boer, Richard Witschge, Jari Litmanen (40 Dean Gorré), Wamberto Sousa Campos, Shota Arveladze (27 Benedict McCarthy), Peter Hoekstra. Trainer: Morten Olsen

OLYMPIAKOS: Dimitris Eleftheropoulos; Kiriakos Karataidis (Cap), Grigoris Georgatos, Giorgos Anatolakis, Petros Passalis, Predrag Djordjević (67 Andreas Niniadis), Stilianos Giannakopoulos, Dimitris Mavrogenidis, Sinisa Gogić (75 Ilija Ivić), Vasilis Karapialis, Alekos Alexandris (54 Peter Ofori-Quaye). Trainer: Dušan Bajević

Goals: Witschge (32), Gorré (88)

CROATIA ZAGREB v FC PORTO 3-1 (2-1)

Maksimir, Zagreb 4.11.1998

Referee: Markus Merk (GER) Attendance: 10,000

CROATIA: Drazen Ladić; Goran Jurić, Dario Simić, Mario Tokić, Danijel Sarić (75 Mario Cvitanović), Josko Jelicić, Tomislav Rukavina, Edin Mujcin, Damir Krznar (46 Igor Biscan), Silvio Marić (56 Josip Simić), Mihael Mikić.
Trainer: Zlatko Kranjcar

FC PORTO: Ivica Kralj; Carlos Alberto de Oliveira SECRETÁRIO, JOÃO MANUEL PINTO Tomé dos Santos, ALOÍSIO Pires Alves (75 Grzegorz Mielcarski), FERNANDO Manuel Antunes MENDES (75 Youssef Chippo), João Paulo Maio dos Santos PAULINHO SANTOS, Dorival Guidoni Júnior "DORIVA", Zlatko Zahovic, Ljubinko Drulovic, Nuno Fernando Gonçalves da Rocha "CAPUCHO", RUI Gil Soares BARROS (27 Mário JARDEL Almeida Ribeiro).
Trainer: Fernando Manuel Costa Santos

Goals: Mikić (7), Rukavina (37), Jardel (39), Mujcin (67)

AFC AJAX AMSTERDAM v CROATIA ZAGREB 0-1 (0-0)

Amsterdam ArenA 25.11.1998

Referee: Marc Batta (FRA) Attendance: 46,000

AJAX: Edwin van der Sar; Kofi Mensah, Danny Blind (Cap), Frank de Boer, Tom Sier (42 Mario Melchiot), Ronald de Boer, Daniel Da Cruz Carvalho "DANI", Richard Witschge, Wamberto Sousa Campos (72 Tijjani Babangida), Brutil Hose (64 Benedict McCarthy), Peter Hoekstra. Trainer: M. Olsen

CROATIA: Drazen Ladić; Goran Jurić, Dario Simić, Mario Tokić, Danijel Sarić (53 Josip Simić), Tomislav Rukavina (80 Nermin Sabić), Igor Biscan, Josko Jelicić, Damir Krznar (46 Krunoslav Jurcić), Silvio Marić, Mario Cvitanović.
Trainer: Velimir Zajec

Goal: J. Simić (68)

OLYMPIAKOS PEIRAIAS v FC PORTO 2-1 (1-0)

Olympiako, Athina 25.11.1998

Referee: Hugh Dallas (SCO) Attendance: 75,000

OLYMPIAKOS: Dimitris Eleftheropoulos; Kiriakos Karataidis (Cap), Ilias Poursanidis, Stilianos Giannakopoulos (53 Petros Passalis), Dimitris Mavrogenidis, Predrag Djordjević, Vasilis Karapialis (69 Paraskevas Antzas), Grigoris Georgatos (82 LUCIANO Nunes de Souza), Giorgos Anatolakis, Sinisa Gogić, Alekos Alexandris.
Trainer: Dušan Bajević **Sent off**: Antzas (83)

FC PORTO: RUI Manuel da Silva CORREIA; Carlos Alberto de Oliveira SECRETÁRIO, ALOÍSIO Pires Alves, FERNANDO Manuel Antunes MENDES (90 JOÃO MANUEL PINTO Tomé dos Santos), JORGE Paulo COSTA Almeida, Dorival Guidoni Júnior "DORIVA", Carlos Narciso CHAÍNHO (56 RUI Gil Soares BARROS), Nuno Fernando Gonçalves da Rocha "CAPUCHO" (66 Miklos Fehér), Zlatko Zahović, Ljubinko Drulović, Mário JARDEL Almeida Ribeiro.
Trainer: Fernando Manuel Costa Santos

Goals: Gogić (18), Djordjević (55), Zahović (80)

CROATIA ZAGREB v OLYMPIAKOS PEIRAIAS 1-1 (1-0)

Maksimir, Zagreb 9.12.1998

Referee: Rune Pedersen (NOR) Attendance: 16,546

CROATIA: Drazen Ladić; Goran Jurić, Danijel Sarić, Edin Mujcin, Igor Biscan (69 Josip Simić), Dario Simić, Mario Tokić, Tomislav Rukavina, Josko Jelicić (87 Krunoslav Jurcić), Mihael Mikić (72 Domagoj Abramović), Silvio Marić.
Trainer: Velimir Zajec

OLYMPIAKOS: Dimitris Eleftheropoulos; Kiriakos Karataidis (Cap), Grigoris Georgatos, Giorgos Anatolakis, Ilias Poursanidis, Predrag Djordjevic (61 LUCIANO Nunes de Souza), Stilianos Giannakopoulos (79 Alekos Alexandris), Dimitris Mavrogenidis, Giorgos Amanatidis, Sinisa Gogić (84 Peter Ofori-Quaye), Andreas Niniadis.
Trainer: Dušan Bajević

Goals: Jelicić (35), Giannakopoulos (64)

FC PORTO v AFC AJAX AMSTERDAM 3-0 (0-0)

Estádio das Antas, Porto 9.12.1998

Referee: Pierluigi Collina (ITA) Attendance: 15,000

FC PORTO: RUI Manuel da Silva CORREIA; JOÃO MANUEL PINTO Tomé dos Santos, JORGE Paulo COSTA Almeida, ALOÍSIO Pires Alves, João Paulo Maio dos Santos PAULINHO SANTOS, Dorival Guidoni Júnior "DORIVA", Carlos Narciso CHAÍNHO, Nică Basarab Panduru (50 Youssef Chippo), Zlatko Zahovic (82 RUI Gil Soares BARROS), Ljubinko Drulovic (87 Grzegorz Mielcarski), Mário JARDEL Almeida Ribeiro.
Trainer: Fernando Manuel Costa Santos

AJAX: Edwin van der Sar; Kofi Mensah, Danny Blind, Sunday Oliseh, Frank de Boer, Andrzej Rudy (74 Benedict McCarthy), Dean Gorré (46 DANIel Da Cruz Carvalho), Peter Hoekstra, Wamberto Sousa Campos, Ronald de Boer, Jesper Grønkjaer (76 Tijjani Babangida). Trainer: Morten Olsen

Goals: Zahović (53, 71), Drulović (79)

	P	W	D	L	F	A	Pts
Olympiakos Peiraias	6	3	2	1	8	6	11
Croatia Zagreb	6	2	2	2	5	7	8
FC Porto	6	2	1	3	11	9	7
AFC Ajax Amsterdam	6	2	1	3	4	6	7

GROUP B

ATHLETIC BILBAO v ROSENBORG BK TRONDHEIM 1-1 (1-0)

San Mamés, Bilbao 16.09.1998

Referee: Vasyl Melnichuk (UKR) Attendance: 35,000

ATHLETIC: Imanol ETXEBERRIA Egaña; Andoni IMAZ Garmendia, Roberto RÍOS Patus (46 Jesús María LACRUZ Gómez), Rafael ALKORTA Martínez, Aitor LARRAZÁBAL Bilbao, Carlos GARCÍA, JOSÉ MARIa García Lafuente (74 Josu URRUTIA Telleria), JAVIer Gómez GONZÁLEZ, Julen GUERRERO López (68 Ismael URZAIZ Aranda), Santiago EZQUERRO Marin, Joseba ETXEBERRIA Lizardi. Trainer: Luis Fernández

ROSENBORG: Jørn Jamtfall; Ole Christer Basma, Erik Hoftun, Bjørn Otto Bragstad, André Bergdølmo, Roar Strand, Bent Skammelsrud, Runar Berg, Børge Hernes (80 Jan Derek Sørensen), Sigurd Rushfeldt, Jahn Ivar Jakobsen (90 Tore André Dahlum). Trainer: Trond Sollied

Goals: J. Etxeberria (6), Strand (65)

JUVENTUS FC TORINO v GALATASARAY ISTANBUL 2-2 (1-1)

Stadio delle Alpi, Torino 16.09.1998

Referee: Markus Merk (GER) Attendance: 37,192

JUVENTUS: Angelo Peruzzi, Alessandro Birindelli, Igor Tudor, Alessio Tacchinardi, Gianluca Pessotto (68 Jocelyn Blanchard), Angelo Di Livio, Didier Deschamps, Edgar Davids, Daniel Fonseca (33 Michelangelo Rampulla), Filippo Inzaghi (62 Zinedine Zidane), Alessandro del Piero. Trainer: Marcello Lippi **Sent off**: Peruzzi (32)

GALATASARAY: Claudio Taffarel, Iulian Filipescu, Vedat Inceefe, Gheorghe Popescu, Hakan Ünsal, Gheorghe Hagi, Ümit Davala, Tugay Kerimoğlu (79 Arif Erdem), Okan Buruk, Hasan Sas Gökhan (82 Ergün Pembe), Hakan Şükür. Trainer: Fatih Terim

Goals: Inzaghi (16), Hakan Şükür (44), Umit (63), Birindelli (68)

GALATASARAY ISTANBUL v ATHLETIC BILBAO 2-1 (1-1)

Ali Sami Yen, Istanbul 30.09.1998

Referee: Grahan Poll (ENG) Attendance: 24,000

GALATASARAY: Claudio Taffarel; Iulian Filipescu (32 Fatih Akyel), Gheorghe Popescu, Vedat Inceefe (75 Bülent Korkmaz), Ümit Davala (69 Arif Erdem), Okan Buruk, Tugay Kerimoğlu, Hasan Sas Gökhan, Gheorghe Hagi, Hakan Ünsal, Hakan Şükür. Trainer: Fatih Terim

ATHLETIC: Imanol ETXEBERRIA Egaña; Carlos GARCÍA, Roberto RÍOS Patus, Rafael ALKORTA Martínez, Aitor LARRAZÁBAL Bilbao, Andoni IMAZ Garmendia, Josu URRUTIA Telleria (85 Julen GUERRERO López), Bittor ALKIZA Fernández, Joseba ETXEBERRIA Lizardi (70 JAVIer Gómez GONZÁLEZ), Ismael URZAIZ Aranda (79 Jesús María LACRUZ Gómez), Santiago EZQUERRO Marin.

Goals: Okan (15), Urzaiz (16), Hagi (90)

ROSENBORG BK TRONDHEIM v JUVENTUS FC TORINO 1-1 (0-1)

Lerkendal, Trondheim 30.09.1998

Referee: Armand Ancion (BEL) Attendance: 15,385

ROSENBORG: Jørn Jamtfall; Andre Bergdølmo, Ole Christer Basma, Bjørn Otto Bragstad, Erik Hoftun, Runar Berg, Bent Skammelsrud, Roar Strand (83 Fredrik Winsnes), Jan Derek Sørensen (54 Børge Hernes), Sigurd Rushfeldt (61 Tore Andre Dahlum), Jahn Ivar Jakobsen. Trainer: Trond Sollied

JUVENTUS: Michelangelo Rampulla; Alessandro Birindelli, Igor Tudor, Paolo Montero, Zoran Mirkovic (77 Gianluca Pessotto), Alessio Tacchinardi, Zinedine Zidane (78 Marcelo Danubio Zalayeta), Didier Deschamps, Edgar Davids, Filippo Inzaghi (60 Daniel Fonseca), Alessandro del Piero. Trainer: Marcello Lippi

Goals: Inzaghi (27), Skammelsrud (69 pen)

ROSENBORG BK TRONDHEIM v GALATASARAY ISTANBUL 3-0 (0-0)

Lerkendal, Trondheim 21.10.1998

Referee: Nikolai Levnikov (RUS) Attendance: 15,000

ROSENBORG: Arni Gautur Arason; Ole Christer Basma, Bjørn Otto Bragstad, Erik Hoftun, Andre Bergdølmo; Roar Strand, Bent Skammelsrud, Fredrik Winsnes (77 Andreas Mayer); Jan Derek Sørensen (77 Tore André Dahlum), Sigurd Rushfeldt, Jahn Ivar Jakobsen (56 Børge Hernes). Trainer: Trond Sollied

GALATASARAY: Claudio Taffarel; Fatih Akyel, Gheorghe Popescu, Vedat Inceefe, Okan Buruk (87 Emre Belözoglu), Ümit Davala (76 Tolunay Kafkas), Ergün Pembe, Hakan Ünsal, Gheorghe Hagi, Hasan Sas Gökhan (87 Arif Erdem), Hakan Şükür. Trainer: Fatih Terim

Sent off: Vedat (79)

Goals: Rushfeldt (69, 86, 90)

ATHELTIC BILBAO v JUVENTUS FC TORINO 0-0

San Mamés, Bilbao 21.10.1998

Referee: Kim Milton Nielsen (DEN) Attendance: 39,000

ATHLETIC: Imanol ETXEBERRIA Egaña; Jesús María LACRUZ Gómez, Rafael ALKORTA Martínez (4 Roberto RÍOS Patus), Carlos GARCÍA García, Aitor LARRAZÁBAL Bilbao; Andoni IMAZ Garmendia, Josu URRUTIA Telleria (85 JORGE PÉREZ Sáenz), Bittor ALKIZA Fernández, Julen GUERRERO López (57 Santiago EZQUERRO Marín); Joseba ETXEBERRIA Lizardi, Ismael URZAIZ Aranda. Trainer: Luis Fernández

JUVENTUS: Angelo Peruzzi; Alessandro Birindelli, Igor Tudor, Paolo Montero; Angelo Di Livio, Didier Deschamps, Edgar Davids (77 Alessio Tacchinardi), Gianluca Pessotto (29 Mark Iuliano); Zinedine Zidane, Filippo Inzaghi, Alessandro del Piero (81 Daniel Fonseca). Trainer: Marcello Lippi

JUVENTUS FC TORINO
v ATHLETIC BILBAO 1-1 (0-1)

Stadio delle Alpi, Torino 4.11.1998

Referee: Hugh Dallas (SCO) Attendance: 44,584

JUVENTUS: Angelo Peruzzi; Igor Tudor (46 Jocelyn Blanchard), Mark Iuliano, Paolo Montero, Angelo Di Livio (84 Simone Perrotta), Edgar Davids, Alessio Tacchinardi, Zinedine Zidane, Gianluca Pessotto (55 Nicola Amoruso), Alessandro del Piero, Filippo Inzaghi. Trainer: Marcello Lippi

ATHLETIC: Imanol ETXEBERRIA Egaña; Carlos GARCÍA, Francisco "Patxi" FERREIRA Colmenero, Aitor LARRAZÁBAL Bilbao, Andoni IMAZ Garmendia (57 Jesús María LACRUZ Gómez), Roberto RÍOS Patus, Bittor ALKIZA Fernández, Mikel LASA Goikoetxea (73 JORGE PÉREZ Sáenz), Julen GUERRERO López, Joseba ETXEBERRIA Lizardi, Santiago EZQUERRO Marín (66 Ismael URZAIZ Aranda). Trainer: Luis Fernández

Sent off: Lacruz (82)

Goals: Guerreo (45), Lasa (68 og)

GALATASARAY ISTANBUL
v ROSENBORG BK TRONDHEIM 3-0 (0-0)

Ali Sami Yen, Istanbul 4.11.1998

Referee: Heinz Hellmut Krug (GER) Attendance: 20,000

GALATASARAY: Claudio Taffarel; Fatih Akyel, Gheorghe Popescu, Iulian Filipescu, Okan Buruk (84 Ufuk Talay), Gheorghe Hagi (78 Ümit Davala), Tugay Kerimoğlu, Ergün Pembe (46 Arif Erdem), Hakan Ünsal, Hasan Sas Gökhan, Hakan Şükür. Trainer: Fatih Terim

ROSENBORG: Arni Gautur Arason; Ole Christer Basma, André Bergdølmo, Erik Hoftun, Bent Inge Johnsen; Roar Strand, Bent Skammelsrud, Runar Berg; Tore André Dahlum (65 Børge Hernes), Sigurd Rushfeldt, Jahn Ivar Jakobsen (61 Jan Derek Sørensen). Trainer: Trond Sollied

Goals: Hakan Şükür (55, 74), Arif (66)

ROSENBORG BK TRONDHEIM
v ATHLETIC BILBAO 2-1 (1-0)

Lerkendal, Trondheim 25.11.1998

Referee: Bernd Heynemann (GER) Attendance: 15,454

ROSENBORG: Jørn Jamtfall; André Bergdølmo, Erik Hoftun, Bjørn Otto Bragstad, Morten Pedersen; Roar Strand (79 Fredrik Winsnes), Bent Skammelsrud, Runar Berg (90 Andreas Mayer); Jan Derek Sørensen (84 Tore André Dahlum), Sigurd Rushfeldt, Jahn Ivar Jakobsen. Trainer: Trond Sollied

ATHLETIC: Imanol ETXEBERRIA Egaña; FELIPE Guréndez Aldanondo, Josu URRUTIA Telleria (46 Ismael URZAIZ Aranda), Roberto RÍOS Patus, Francisco "Patxi" FERREIRA Colmenero, Andoni IMAZ Garmendia, Aitor LARRAZÁBAL Bilbao (46 Carlos GARCÍA), Julen GUERRERO López (60 JORGE PÉREZ Sáenz), Bittor ALKIZA Fernández; Santiago EZQUERRO Marín, Joseba ETXEBERRIA Lizardi. Trainer: Luis Fernández

Goals: Sørensen (2, 50), Pérez (90)

GALATASARAY ISTANBUL
v JUVENTUS FC TORINO 1-1 (0-0)

Ali Sami Yen, Istanbul 2.12.1998

Referee: Gilles Veissière (FRA) Attendance: 22,920

GALATASARAY: Claudio Taffarel; Fatih Akyel, Gheorghe Popescu, Iulian Filipescu, Okan Buruk, Gheorghe Hagi, Tolunay Kafkas (76 Arif Erdem), Ümit Davala, Hakan Ünsal (88 Vedat Inceefe), Hakan Şükür, Hasan Sas Gökhan (76 Suat Kaya). Trainer: Fatih Terim

JUVENTUS: Angelo Peruzzi (59 Michelangelo Rampulla); Alessandro Birindelli, Ciro Ferrara, Paolo Montero, Mark Iuliano; Jocelyn Blanchard, Zinedine Zidane, Antonio Conte, Didier Deschamps, Gianluca Pessotto (66 Nicola Amoruso), Filippo Inzaghi (81 Igor Tudor). Trainer: Marcello Lippi

Goals: Amoruso (77), Suat (90)

JUVENTUS FC TORINO
v ROSENBORG BK TRONDHEIM 2-0 (2-0)

Stadio delle Alpi, Torino 9.12.1998

Referee: Mario van der Ende (HOL) Attendance: 7,174

JUVENTUS: Angelo Peruzzi; Alessandro Birindelli, Igor Tudor, Paolo Montero, Gianluca Pessotto (63 Edgar Davids), Antonio Conte (87 Angelo Di Livio), Didier Deschamps, Alessio Tacchinardi; Zinedine Zidane, Filippo Inzaghi, Nicola Amoruso (68 Mark Iuliano). Trainer: Marcello Lippi

ROSENBORG: Jørn Jamtfall; André Bergdølmo, Bjørn Otto Bragstad, Erik Hoftun, Morten Pedersen (66 Børge Hernes); Roar Strand, Bent Inge Johnsen (56 Fredrik Winsnes), Runar Berg, Jahn Ivar Jakobsen; Jan Derek Sørensen (46 Tore André Dahlum), Sigurd Rushfeldt. Trainer: Trond Sollied

Goals: Inzaghi (16), Amoruso (36)

ATHLETIC BILBAO
v GALATASARAY ISTANBUL 1-0 (1-0)

San Mamés, Bilbao 9.12.1998

Referee: Urs Meier (SWI) Attendance: 16,000

ATHLETIC: Imanol ETXEBERRIA Egaña; Iñigo LARRAÍNZAR Santamaría, Carlos GARCÍA, Francisco "Patxi" FERREIRA Colmenero, Aitor LARRAZÁBAL Bilbao; FELIPE Gueréndez Aldanondo, Domingo NAGORE Arbizu (83 CÉSAR Fernández de las Heras Caneda), JAVIer Gómez GONZÁLEZ (76 Joseba ETXEBERRIA Lizardi), Julen GUERRERO López; JORGE PÉREZ Sáenz (74 Mikel LASA Goikoetxea), Santiago EZQUERRO Marín. Trainer: Luis Fernández

GALATASARAY: Claudio Taffarel; Gheorghe Popescu, Iulian Filipescu, Fatih Akyel, Okan Buruk, Gheorghe Hagi, Ümit Davala, Tolunay Kafkas (65 Burak Akdis), Suat Kaya (65 Vedat Inceefe), Arif Erdem, Hasan Sas Gökhan (88 Emre Belözoglu). Trainer: Fatih Terim

Goal: Guerrero (43)

	P	W	D	L	F	A	Pts
Juventus FC Torino	6	1	5	0	7	5	8
Galatasaray Istanbul	6	2	2	2	8	8	8
Rosenborg BK	6	2	2	2	7	8	8
Athletic Bilbao	6	1	3	2	5	6	6

GROUP C

REAL MADRID CF v FC INTERNAZIONALE MILANO 2-0 (0-0)

Ramón Sánchez Pizjuán, Sevilla 16.09.1998

Referee: Hugh Dallas (SCO) Attendance: 40,000

REAL: Bodo Illgner; Christian Panucci, Fernando Ruiz HIERRO, Manuel SANCHÍS Hontiyuelo, ROBERTO CARLOS Da Silva, RAÚL González Blanco, Fernando Carlos REDONDO Neri, Clarence Seedorf, SÁVIO Bortolini Pimental (89 Christian Karembeu); Fernando MORIENTES Sánchez (86 Robert Jarni), Predrag Mijatović. Trainer: Guus Hiddinck

INTER: Gianluca Pagliuca; Giuseppe Bergomi, Salvatore Fresi, Fabio Galante, Mauro Milanese, Javier Zanetti, Benoit Cauet (46 Mickael Silvestre), Aron Winter (80 Nicola Ventola), Diego Simeone, RONALDO Luiz Nazario Da Lima (72 Andrea Pirlo), Ivan Zamorano. Trainer: Luigi Simoni

Sent off: Fresi (42)

Goals: Hierro (79 pen), Seedorf (90)

SK STURM GRAZ v SPARTAK MOSKVA 0-2 (0-0)

Arnold Schwarzenegger, Graz 16.09.1998

Referee: Atanas Uzunov (BUL) Attendance: 11,000

STURM: Kazimierz Sidorczuk; Günther Neukirchner, Darko Milanic, Ranko Popovic, Markus Schopp, Roman Mählich, Hannes Reinmayr (61 Didier Angibeaud), Markus Schupp, Mario Posch; Ivica Vastic, Mario Haas. Trainer: Ivica Osim

SPARTAK: Aleksandr Filimonov; Dmitriy Ananko, Evgeniy Bushmanov, Dmytro Parfyonov, Vasiliy Baranov, Yegor Titov, Dmitriy Khlestov, Ilya Tsymbalar, Andrei Tikhonov, Nikolai Pisarev (77 Leandro SAMARONI da Rosa Fernandes), Aleksandr Shirko (46 Anatoliy Kanischev).
Trainer: Oleg Romantsev

Goals: Titov (60), Tsymbalar (63)

SPARTAK MOSKVA v REAL MADRID CF 2-1 (0-0)

Luzhniki, Moskva 30.09.1998

Referee: Bernd Heynemann (GER) Attendance: 60,000

SPARTAK: Aleksandr Filimonov; Vasiliy Baranov, Dmitriy Ananko, Evgeniy Bushmanov, Dmitriy Khlestov, Andrei Tikhonov, Dmytro Parfyonov, Yegor Titov, Ilya Tsymbalar, Luís ROBSON Pereira da Silva (85 Maxim Buznikin), Nikolai Pisarev (67 Anatoliy Kanischev). Trainer: Oleg Romantsev

REAL: Bodo Illgner; Christian Panucci, Fernando Ruiz HIERRO, Manuel SANCHÍS Hontiyuelo, ROBERTO CARLOS Da Silva; Christian Karembeu (79 Fernando MORIENTES Sánchez), Clarence Seedorf, Fernando Carlos REDONDO Neri; SÁVIO Bortolini Pimental, Predrag Mijatović, RAÚL González Blanco. Trainer: Guus Hiddinck

Goals: Raúl (64), Tsymbalar (71), Titov (77)

FC INTERNAZIONALE MILANO v SK STURM GRAZ 1-0 (0-0)

Stadio Giuseppe Meazza, Milano 30.09.1998

Referee: Rune Pedersen (NOR) Attendance: 24,791

INTER: Gianluca Pagliuca; Mickael Silvestre, Giuseppe Bergomi, Fabio Galante, Javier Zanetti, Francesco Moriero (72 Andrea Pirlo), Aron Winter, Youri Djorkaeff, Diego Simeone, Benoit Cauet (64 Ivan Zamorano), Nicola Ventola.
Trainer: Luigi Simoni

STURM: Kazimierz Sidorczuk; Mario Posch, Darko Milanic (79 Didier Angibeaud), Franco Foda, Günther Neukirchner, Roman Mählich, Hannes Reinmayr (90 Mehrdad Minavand), Markus Schopp (58 Ranko Popovic), Markus Schupp; Ivica Vastic, Mario Haas. Trainer: Ivica Osim

Goal: Djorkaeff (90)

FC INTERNAZIONALE MILANO v SPARTAK MOSKVA 2-1 (1-0)

Giuseppe Meazza, Milano 21.10.1998

Referee: Marc Batta (FRA) Attendance: 44,199

INTER: Gianluca Pagliuca; Diego Simeone, Taribo West, Fabio Galante, Mickael Silvestre; Benoit Cauet, PAULO Manuel SOUSA Carvalho, Aron Winter, Youri Djorkaeff (34 Andrea Pirlo); RONALDO Luiz Nazario Da Lima (73 José Moedin ZÉ ELIAS), Nicola Ventola (83 Ivan Zamorano).
Trainer: Luigi Simoni

SPARTAK: Aleksandr Filimonov; Dmytro Parfyonov, Dmitriy Khlestov, Ilya Tsymbalar, Evgeniy Bushmanov, Dmitriy Ananko, Vasiliy Baranov (80 Aleksei Melyoshin), Miroslav Romaschenko, Luís ROBSON Pereira da Silva, Nikolai Pisarev (66 Anatoliy Kanischev), Andrei Tikhonov.
Trainer: Oleg Romantsev

Goals: Ventola (32), Ronaldo (58), Tsymbalar (65)

REAL MADRID CF v SK STURM GRAZ 6-1 (2-1)

Estadio Santiago Bernabéu, Madrid 21.10.1998

Referee: Graham Barber (ENG) Attendance: 30,000

REAL: Bodo Illgner; Christian Panucci, Manuel SANCHÍS Hontiyuelo, Fernando Ruiz HIERRO, ROBERTO CARLOS Da Silva; Clarence Seedorf, Christian Karembeu (46 JAIME Sánchez Fernández), Robert Jarni, SÁVIO Bortolini Pimental; RAÚL González Blanco (80 José María GUTIérrez Hernández), Predrag Mijatović (74 Davor Suker).
Trainer: Guus Hiddinck

STURM: Kazimierz Sidorczuk; Franco Foda; Günther Neukirchner (68 Tomislav Kocijan), Ranko Popovic; Markus Schopp, Mario Posch, Markus Schupp (89 Jan-Pieter Martens), Roman Mählich, Hannes Reinmayr; Ivica Vastic, Mario Haas.
Trainer: Ivica Osim

Goals: Vastic (8), Sávio (13, 90), Raúl (22), Jarni (61, 78), Popovic (67 og)

SPARTAK MOSKVA
v FC INTERNAZIONALE MILANO 1-1 (0-0)

Luzhniki, Moskva 4.11.1998

Referee: Urs Meier (SWI) Attendance: 77,000

SPARTAK: Aleksandr Filimonov; Dmitriy Ananko, Evgeniy Bushmanov, Maxim Buznikin (46 Nikolai Pisarev), Miroslav Romaschenko, Vasiliy Baranov (63 Aleksei Melyoshin), Yegor Titov, Andrei Tikhonov, Ilya Tsymbalar, Luís ROBSON Pereira da Silva, Dmytro Parfyonov. Trainer: Oleg Romantsev

INTER: Gianluca Pagliuca; Giuseppe Bergomi (75 Andrea Pirlo), Fabio Galante, Francesco Colonnese, Javier Zanetti, Benoit Cauet, PAULO Manuel SOUSA Carvalho, Diego Simeone, Francesco Moriero (90 Mickael Silvestre), RONALDO Luiz Nazario Da Lima (67 Nicola Ventola), Ivan Zamorano. Trainer: Luigi Simoni

Goals: Tikhonov (68), Simeone (88)

SK STURM GRAZ v REAL MADRID CF 1-5 (1-2)

Arnold Schwarzenegger, Graz 5.11.1998

Referee: Karl Erik Nilsson (SWE) Attendance: 13,851

STURM: Kazimierz Sidorczuk; Mario Posch, Ranko Popovic (71 Ajibade Babalade), Darko Milanic, Franco Foda, Günther Neukirchner, Hannes Reinmayr (71 Tomislav Kocijan), Mehrdad Minavand, Markus Schupp; Ivica Vastic, Mario Haas (75 Jan-Pieter Martens). Trainer: Ivica Osim

REAL: Bodo Illgner, Christian Panucci (77 Christian Karembeu), Fernando Ruiz HIERRO, Manuel SANCHÍS Hontiyuelo, ROBERTO CARLOS Da Silva, Clarence Seedorf (71 José María GUTIérrez Hernández), Fernando Carlos REDONDO Neri, RAÚL González Blanco, Robert Jarni, Predrag Mijatović, SÁVIO Bortolini Pimental (62 Davor Suker). Trainer: Guus Hiddinck

Goals: Haas (4), Panucci (7, 61), Mijatović (35), Seedorf (57), Suker (74)

FC INTERNAZIONALE MILANO
v REAL MADRID CF 3-1 (0-0)

Giuseppe Meazza, Milano 25.11.1998

Referee: Markus Merk (GER) Attendance: 78,829

INTER: Gianluca Pagliuca; Giuseppe Bergomi, Francesco Colonnese, Fabio Galante, Taribo West, Francesco Moriero (57 Javier Zanetti), Aron Winter, PAULO Manuel SOUSA Carvalho (74 Benoit Cauet), Diego Simeone, RONALDO Luiz Nazario Da Lima, Ivan Zamorano (68 Roberto Baggio).
Trainer: Luigi Simoni

REAL: Bodo Illgner; IVÁN CAMPO Ramos, Manuel SANCHÍS Hontiyuelo (88 Davor Suker), Fernando SANZ Durán, ROBERTO CARLOS Da Silva (80 Robert Jarni), Clarence Seedorf, Fernando Carlos REDONDO Neri, JAIME Sánchez Fernández, RAÚL González Blanco, Predrag Mijatović, SÁVIO Bortolini Pimental.
Trainer: Guus Hiddinck

Goals: Zamorano (51), Seedorf (59), Baggio (86, 90)

SPARTAK MOSKVA v SK STURM GRAZ 0-0

Luzhniki, Moskva 25.11.1998

Referee: Michel Piraux (BEL) Attendance: 30,000

SPARTAK: Aleksandr Filimonov; Sergei Gorlukovich, Evgeniy Bushmanov, Dmitriy Khlestov, Ilya Tsymbalar, Vasiliy Baranov, Dmitriy Ananko, Yegor Titov, Andrei Tikhonov, Aleksandr Shirko (68 Maxim Buznikin), Luís ROBSON Pereira da Silva (57 Anatoliy Kanischev).
Trainer: Oleg Romantsev

STURM: Kazimierz Sidorczuk; Markus Schopp, Darko Milanic, Ranko Popovic, Mario Posch, Tomislav Kocijan (57 Jan-Pieter Martens), Roman Mählich, Markus Schupp, Gilbert Prilasnig; Ivica Vastic, Mario Haas (90 Ajibade Babalade).
Trainer: Ivica Osim

SK STURM GRAZ
v FC INTERNAZIONALE MILANO 0-2 (0-0)

Arnold Schwarzenegger, Graz 9.12.1998

Referee: Jacek Granat (POL) Attendance: 12,685

STURM: Kazimierz Sidorczuk; Franco Foda; Darko Milanic (46 Jan-Pieter Martens), Ranko Popovic; Markus Schopp, Markus Schupp, Tomislav Kocijan (84 Roman Wallner), Günther Neukirchner (77 Gilbert Prilasnig), Mario Posch; Mario Haas, Hannes Reinmayr. Trainer: Ivica Osim

INTER: Gianluca Pagliuca; Francesco Colonnese, Giuseppe Bergomi, Fabio Galante, Javier Zanetti, Aron Winter, José Moedin ZÉ ELIAS (82 Alvaro Recoba), Diego Simeone, Mickael Silvestre, RONALDO Luiz Nazario Da Lima (61 Ivan Zamorano), Youri Djorkaeff (70 Roberto Baggio).
Trainer: Mircea Lucescu

Goals: J. Zanetti (63), Baggio (80)

REAL MADRID CF v SPARTAK MOSKVA 2-1 (1-0)

Estadio Santiago Bernabéu, Madrid 9.12.1998

Referee: László Vagner (HUN) Attendance: 60,000

REAL: Bodo Illgner; IVÁN CAMPO Ramos, Fernando Ruiz HIERRO, Fernando SANZ Durán; Christian Panucci (59 JAIME Sánchez Fernández), Clarence Seedorf, Fernando Carlos REDONDO Neri, ROBERTO CARLOS da Silva; RAÚL González Blanco, Predrag Mijatović, SÁVIO Bortolini Pimental. Trainer: Guus Hiddinck

SPARTAK: Aleksandr Filimonov; Dmytro Parfyonov, Dmitriy Khlestov, Ilya Tsymbalar, Evgeniy Bushmanov, Dmitriy Ananko, Vasiliy Baranov, Luís ROBSON Pereira da Silva (75 Anatoliy Kanischev), Yegor Titov, Aleksandr Shirko, Andrei Tikhonov. Trainer: Oleg Romantsev

Goals: Raúl (34), Sávio (66), Khlestov (89)

	P	W	D	L	F	A	Pts
Internazionale Milano	6	4	1	1	9	5	13
Real Madrid CF	6	4	0	2	17	8	12
Spartak Moskva	6	2	2	2	7	6	8
SK Sturm Graz	6	0	1	5	2	16	1

GROUP D

BRØNDBY IF v FC BAYERN MÜNCHEN 2-1 (0-0)

Brøndby Stadion, København 16.09.1998

Referee: László Vágner (HUN) Attendance: 30,378

BRØNDBY: Mogens Krogh; Søren Colding, Kenneth Rasmussen, Per Nielsen, Brian Jensen, Ole Bjur, John Jensen, Kim Daugaard (73 Mikkel Jensen), Allan Ravn, Thomas Lindrup (76 Søren Krogh), Ebbe Sand (56 Bo Hansen). Trainer: Ebbe Skovdahl

BAYERN: Oliver Kahn; Markus Babbel, Lothar Matthäus, Thomas Helmer, Thomas Strunz (73 Jens Jeremies), Stefan Effenberg, Thorsten Fink, Mario Basler (73 Alexander Zickler), Bixente Lizarazu, Giovane De Souza Elber, Carsten Jancker (77 Hasan Salihamidzic). Trainer: Ottmar Hitzfeld

Goals: Babbel (77), Helmer (87 og), Ravn (90)

MANCHESTER UNITED FC v FC BARCELONA 3-3 (2-0)

Old Trafford, Manchester 16.09.1998

Referee: Stefano Braschi (ITA) Attendance: 53,601

MANCHESTER UNITED: Peter Schmeichel; Gary Neville, Jaap Stam, Henning Berg, Dennis Irwin (79 Philip Neville), David Beckham, Roy Keane, Paul Scholes, Ryan Giggs (84 Jesper Blomqvist), Ole Gunnar Solskjaer (55 Nicky Butt), Dwight Yorke. Manager: Alex Ferguson

FC BARCELONA: Rudolfus Hubertus Hesp; Michael Reiziger, LUIS ENRIQUE Martínez García, ABELARDO Fernández Antuña, SERGI Barjuan Esclusa; Philip Cocu, GIOVANNI Silva de Oliveira (68 XAVIer Hernández Creus), Luis Filipe Madeira Caeiro "FIGO", Vitor Barbosa Ferreira "RIVALDO"; Boudewijn Zenden, Sonny ANDERSON da Silva. Trainer: Louis van Gaal

Sent off: Butt (80)

Goals: Giggs (17), Scholes (24), Anderson (46), Giovanni (58 pen), Beckham (63), Luis Enrique (70 pen)

FC BARCELONA v BRØNDBY IF 2-0 (1-0)

Camp Nou, Barcelona 30.09.1998

Referee: Gerd Grabher (AUS) Attendance: 70,000

FC BARCELONA: Rudolfus Hubertus Hesp; Samuel Gbenga Okunowo (76 Boudewijn Zenden), ABELARDO Fernández Antuña, ROGER García Junyent, SERGI Barjuan Esclusa, Luis Filipe Madeira Caeiro "FIGO", GIOVANNI Silva de Oliveira (46 XAVIer Hernández Creus), Philip Cocu (65 Michael Reiziger), Vitor Barbosa Ferreira "RIVALDO", LUIS ENRIQUE Martínez García, Sonny ANDERSON da Silva. Trainer: Louis van Gaal

BRØNDBY: Mogens Krogh; Aurelius Skarbalius, Kenneth Rasmussen, Per Nielsen, Brian Jensen, Ole Bjur (76 Søren Krogh), Allan Ravn (12 Mikkel Jensen), John Jensen, Kim Daugaard, Thomas Lindrup (64 Bo Hansen), Ebbe Sand. Trainer: Ebbe Skovdahl

Goals: Anderson (42, 85)

FC BAYERN MÜNCHEN v MANCHESTER UNITED FC 2-2 (1-1)

Olympiastadion, München 30.09.1998

Referee: Marc Batta (FRA) Attendance: 53,000

BAYERN: Oliver Kahn; Markus Babbel, Lothar Matthäus, Thomas Linke, Thomas Strunz, Stefan Effenberg, Jens Jeremies (62 Thorsten Fink), Hasan Salihamidzic (63 Berkant Göktan), Bixente Lizarazu, Giovane De Souza Elber, Carsten Jancker (63 Ali Daei). Trainer: Ottmar Hitzfeld

MANCHESTER UNITED: Peter Schmeichel; Philip Neville, Jaap Stam, Gary Neville, Dennis Irwin, David Beckham, Paul Scholes, Roy Keane, Jesper Blomqvist (69 Jordi Cruijff), Dwight Yorke, Teddy Sheringham. Manager: Alex Ferguson

Goals: Elber (11, 90), Yorke (30), Scholes (49)

FC BAYERN MÜNCHEN
v FC BARCELONA 1-0 (1-0)

Olympiastadion, München 21.10.1998

Referee: Anders Frisk (SWE) Attendance: 55,000

BAYERN: Oliver Kahn; Jens Jeremies, Markus Babbel (80 Thomas Linke), Samuel Osei Kuffour, Bixente Lizarazu, Thorsten Fink, Stefan Effenberg, Michael Tarnat, Mario Basler, Giovane De Souza Elber (89 Carsten Jancker), Hasan Salihamidzic (80 Alexander Zickler).
Trainer: Ottmar Hitzfeld

FC BARCELONA: Rudolfus Hubertus Hesp; Samuel Gbenga Okunowo, ABELARDO Fernández Antuña, Michael Reiziger; Philip Cocu, XAVIer Hernández Creus (87 ÓSCAR García Junyent), LUIS ENRIQUE Martínez García (77 Boudewijn Zenden), GIOVANNI Silva de Oliveira; Luis Filipe Madeira Caeiro "FIGO", Sonny ANDERSON da Silva, Vitor Barbosa Ferreira "RIVALDO". Trainer: Louis van Gaal

Goal: Effenberg (45)

MANCHESTER UNITED FC
v BRØNDBY IF 5-0 (4-0)

Old Trafford, Manchester 4.11.1998

Referee: Lubos Michel (SVK) Attendance: 53,250

MANCHESTER UNITED: Peter Schmeichel; Philip Neville (31 Wesley Brown), Gary Neville, Jaap Stam, Dennis Irwin, David Beckham, Paul Scholes, Roy Keane, Jesper Blomqvist (46 Jordi Cruijff), Andy Cole (55 Ole Gunnar Solskjaer), Dwight Yorke. Manager: Alex Ferguson

BRØNDBY: Emeka Andersen; Ole Bjur (74 Søren Krogh), Per Nielsen, Søren Colding, Allan Ravn, John Jensen, Kim Daugaard, Aurelius Skarbalius, Kenneth Rasmussen, Ruben Bagger (68 Jesper Thygesen), Ebbe Sand (77 Bo Hansen).
Trainer: Ebbe Skovdahl

Goals: Beckham (6), Cole (13), P.Neville (15), Yorke (27), Scholes (63)

BRØNDBY IF
v MANCHESTER UNITED FC 2-6 (1-3)

Brøndby Stadion, København 21.10.1998

Referee: Vitor Manuel Melo Pereira (POR) Att: 40,315

BRØNDBY: Mogens Krogh; Søren Colding, Kenneth Rasmussen, Per Nielsen (31 Mikkel Jensen), Brian Jensen (27 Vragel Da Silva), Ole Bjur, Allan Ravn, Kim Daugaard, Thomas Lindrup, Ebbe Sand, Bo Hansen (67 Ruben Bagger).
Trainer: Ebbe Skovdahl

MANCHESTER UNITED: Peter Schmeichel; Wesley Brown, Philip Neville, Gary Neville, Jaap Stam, Roy Keane, Paul Scholes, Jesper Blomqvist, Andy Cole (60 Ole Gunnar Solskjaer), Dwight Yorke (65 Mark Wilson), Ryan Giggs (60 Jordi Cruijff). Manager: Alex Ferguson

Goals: Giggs (2, 21), Cole (28), Daugaard (35), Keane (55), Yorke (59), Solskjaer (62), Sand (90)

FC BAYERN MÜNCHEN v BRØNDBY IF 2-0 (1-0)

Olympiastadion, München 25.11.1998

Referee: Ogüz Sarvan (TUR) Attendance: 34,000

BAYERN: Oliver Kahn; Markus Babbel, Lothar Matthäus, Samuel Osei Kuffour, Bixente Lizarazu, Thomas Strunz, Mario Basler, Jens Jeremies (70 Thorsten Fink), Michael Tarnat, Alexander Zickler (46 Carsten Jancker), Giovane De Souza Elber (84 Hasan Salihamidzic). Trainer: Ottmar Hitzfeld

BRØNDBY: Emeka Andersen; Søren Colding, Kenneth Rasmussen, Per Nielsen (68 Vragel Da Silva), Aurelius Skarbalius, Ole Bjur, John Jensen, Kim Daugaard, Ruben Bagger (65 Thomas Lindrup), Bo Hansen (70 Bent Christensen), Ebbe Sand. Trainer: Ebbe Skovdahl

Goals: Jancker (51), Basler (57)

FC BARCELONA
v FC BAYERN MÜNCHEN 1-2 (1-0)

Camp Nou, Barcelona 4.11.1998

Referee: Pierluigi Collina (ITA) Attendance: 85,000

FC BARCELONA: Rudolfus Hubertus Hesp; Samuel Gbenga Okunowo, ABELARDO Fernández Antuña, Albert CELADES López, SERGI Barjuan Esclusa; GIOVANNI Silva de Oliveira, XAVIer Hernández Creus, Philip Cocu; Luis Filipe Madeira Caeiro «FIGO», Sonny ANDERSON da Silva, Vitor Barbosa Ferreira «RIVALDO». Trainer: Louis van Gaal

BAYERN: Oliver Kahn; Markus Babbel, Lothar Matthäus, Samuel Osei Kuffour, Mario Basler (64 Hasan Salihamidzic), Thorsten Fink, Stefan Effenberg, Michael Tarnat (76 Thomas Strunz), Bixente Lizarazu, Giovane De Souza Elber, Alexander Zickler (64 Ali Daei). Trainer: Ottmar Hitzfeld

Goals: Giovanni (29 pen), Zickler (47), Salihamidzic (87)

FC BARCELONA
v MANCHESTER UNITED FC 3-3 (1-1)

Camp Nou, Barcelona 25.11.1998

Referee: Günter Benkö (AUS) Attendance: 67,650

FC BARCELONA: Rudolfus Hubertus Hesp; Samuel Gbenga Okunowo, Albert CELADES López, Michael Reiziger, SERGI Barjuan Esclusa; GIOVANNI Silva de Oliveira, XAVIer Hernández Creus, Vitor Barbosa Ferreira "RIVALDO", Luis Filipe Madeira Caeiro "FIGO"; Sonny ANDERSON da Silva, Boudewijn Zenden. Trainer: Louis van Gaal

MANCHESTER UNITED: Peter Schmeichel; Wesley Brown, Gary Neville, Jaap Stam, Dennis Irwin, David Beckham (80 Nicky Butt), Roy Keane, Paul Scholes, Jesper Blomqvist, Dwight Yorke, Andy Cole. Manager: Alex Ferguson

Goals: Anderson (1), Yorke (25, 68), Cole (53), Rivaldo (56, 72)

BRØNDBY IF v FC BARCELONA 0-2 (0-2)

Brøndby Stadion, København 9.12.1998

Referee: Nikolai Levnikov (RUS) Attendance: 40,892

BRØNDBY: Mogens Krogh; Søren Colding, Kenneth Rasmussen, Per Nielsen, Aurelius Skarbalius, Ole Bjur, John Jensen (80 Jesper Thygesen), Kim Daugaard (70 Bent Christensen), Ebbe Sand, Ruben Bagger (74 Thomas Lindrup), Bo Hansen. Trainer: Ebbe Skovdahl

FC BARCELONA: Rudolfus Hubertus Hesp; Michael Reiziger, Albert CELADES López, Samuel Gbenga Okunowo; XAVIer Hernández Creus, Josep GUARDIOLA Sala, Vitor Barbosa Ferreira "RIVALDO" (64 ROGER García Junyent), SERGI Barjuan Esclusa; Luis Filipe Madeira Caeiro "FIGO", Sonny ANDERSON da Silva (46 GIOVANNI Silva de Oliveira), Philip Cocu (88 Iban Javier CUADRADO Alonso). Trainer: Louis van Gaal

Goals: Figo (5), Rivaldo (35)

MANCHESTER UNITED FC v FC BAYERN MÜNCHEN 1-1 (1-1)

Old Trafford, Manchester 9.12.1998

Referee: Dick Jol (HOL) Attendance: 54,434

MANCHESTER UNITED: Peter Schmeichel; Gary Neville, Dennis Irwin (46 Ronny Johnsen), Jaap Stam, David Beckham, Andy Cole, Ryan Giggs, Roy Keane, Paul Scholes, Dwight Yorke (64 Nicky Butt), Wesley Brown. Manager: Alex Ferguson

BAYERN: Oliver Kahn; Markus Babbel, Lothar Matthäus (61 Thomas Linke), Samuel Osei Kuffour, Thomas Strunz, Jens Jeremies, Stefan Effenberg, Bixente Lizarazu, Alexander Zickler (82 Mario Basler), Giovane De Souza Elber (81 Carsten Jancker), Hasan Salihamidzić. Trainer: Ottmar Hitzfeld

Goals: Keane (43), Salihamidzic (56)

	P	W	D	L	F	A	Pts
FC Bayern München	6	3	2	1	9	6	11
Manchester United	6	2	4	0	20	11	10
FC Barcelona	6	2	2	2	11	9	8
Brøndby IF	6	1	0	5	4	18	3

GROUP E

RC LENS v ARSENAL FC LONDON 1-1 (0-0)

Félix-Bollaert, Lens 16.09.1998

Referee: Heinz Hellmut Krug (GER) Attendance: 33,371

RC LENS: Guillaume Warmuz; Eric Sikora, Ernest Etchi Oben (81 Aboubacar Sankhare), Frédéric Déhu, Xavier Méride (76 Cyril Rool), Alex Nyarko, Mickaël Debève, Stéphane Dalmat, Pascal Nouma (70 Daniel Moreira), Vladimir Smicer, Tony Vairelles. Trainer: Daniel Leclercq

ARSENAL: David Seaman; Lee Dixon, Anthony Adams, Martin Keown, Nigel Winterburn, Ray Parlour, Patrick Vieira, Emmanuel Petit (73 Stephen Hughes), Marc Overmars, Dennis Bergkamp (90 Rémi Garde), Nicolas Anelka. Manager: Arsène Wenger

Goals: Overmars (51), Vairelles (90)

PANATHINAIKOS ATHINA v FC DYNAMO KYIV 2-1 (0-1)

OlympiakoSpyros Louis, Athina 16.09.1998

Referee: Vitor Manuel Melo Pereira (POR) Att: 25,000

PANATHINAIKOS: Jozef Wandzik; Konstandinos Konstantinidis, Konstandinos Kiassos, Vladan Milojević, Leonidas Vokolos (67 Bledar Kola), Giannis Gkoumas, Stratos Apostolakis, Aljosa Asanović, Erik Mykland, Nikos Limperopoulos (90 Giorgos Alexopoulos), Krzysztof Warzycha (Cap) (86 Frank Strandli). Trainer: Vasilis Daniil

DYNAMO: Olexandr Shovkovskyi; Olexandr Holovko, Yuri Dmitrulin, Oleh Luzhnyi, Aleksei Gerasimenko (77 Yuri Kalitvintsev), Vladislav Vashchuk, Kakhi Kaladze, Andriy Gusin, Valentin Belkevich (74 Serhiy Konovalov), Serhiy Rebrov, Andriy Shevchenko. Trainer: Valeriy Lobanovskyi

Goals: Rebrov (31), Mykland (57), Limperopoulos (68)

FC DYNAMO KYIV v RC LENS 1-1 (0-0)

Olympiyskyi, Kyiv 30.09.1998

Referee: Günter Benkö (AUS) Attendance: 50,000

DYNAMO: Olexandr Shovkovskyi; Oleg Luzhnyi, Vladislav Vashchuk, Olexandr Holovko, Yuri Dmitrulin (83 Olexandr Kiryukhin), Kakhi Kaladze, Andriy Gusin, Vitaliy Kosovskyi, Aleksei Gerasimenko (78 Yuri Kalitvintsev), Andriy Shevchenko, Serhiy Rebrov. Trainer: Valeriy Lobanovskyi

RC LENS: Guillaume Warmuz; Cyrille Magnier, Xavier Méride, Ernest Etchi Oben, Cyril Rool, Mickaël Debève (73 Daniel Moreira), Stéphane Dalmat, Frédéric Déhu, Alex Nyarko, Vladimir Smicer (81 Wagneau Eloi), Anthony Vairelles (66 Pascal Nouma). Trainer: Daniel Leclercq

Goals: Shevchenko (61), Vairelles (62)

ARSENAL FC LONDON v PANATHINAIKOS ATHINA 2-1 (0-0)

Wembley, London 30.09.1998

Referee: Antonio Jesús López Nieto (SPA) Att: 73,454

ARSENAL: David Seaman; Lee Dixon, Martin Keown, Anthony Adams, Nigel Winterburn, Rémi Garde (79 Nélson David Vivas), Patrick Vieira, Emmanuel Petit, Marc Overmars, Dennis Bergkamp, Nicolas Anelka.
Manager: Arsène Wenger.

PANATHINAIKOS: Jozef Wandzik; Stratos Apostolakis (Cap), Vladan Milojević, Konstandinos Kiassos (71 Bledar Kola), Konstandinos Konstantinidis, Giannis Gkoumas, Aljosa Asanović, Frank Strandli (83 Igor Sypniewski), Erik Mykland, Andreas Lagonikakis, Nikos Limperopoulos (83 Mauro Carlos Pereira da Silva). Trainer: Vasilis Daniil

Goals: Adams (65), Keown (73), da Silva (88)

FC DYNAMO KYIV v ARSENAL FC LONDON 3-1 (1-0)

Olympiyskyi, Kyiv 4.11.1998

Referee: Piero Ceccarini (ITA) Attendance: 76,600

DYNAMO: Olexandr Shovkovskyi; Oleh Luzhnyi, Vladislav Vashchuk, Olexandr Holovko, Yuri Dmitrulin, Andriy Gusin, Vitaliy Kosovskyi, Vasyl Kardash, Valentin Belkevich (89 Yuri Kalitvintsev), Andriy Shevchenko, Serhiy Rebrov.
Trainer: Valeriy Lobanovskyi

ARSENAL: David Seaman; Lee Dixon, Martin Keown, Steve Bould (44 Gilles Grimandi), Nigel Winterburn, Patrick Vieira, Nélson Vivas (84 Rémi Garde), Emmanuel Petit, Ray Parlour, Luís Boa Morte (67 Stephen Hughes), Christopher Wreh.
Manager: Arsène Wenger

Goals: Rebrov (27 pen), Holovko (62), Shevchenko (72), Hughes (83)

ARSENAL FC LONDON v FC DYNAMO KYIV 1-1 (0-0)

Wembley, London 21.10.1998

Referee: Ryszard Wójcik (POL) Attendance: 73,256

ARSENAL: David Seaman; Lee Dixon, Nigel Winterburn, Anthony Adams, Nicolas Anelka (84 Nélson David Vivas), Dennis Bergkamp, Marc Overmars, Martin Keown, Ray Parlour, Stephen Hughes, Rémi Garde.
Manager: Arsène Wenger

DYNAMO: Olexandr Shovkovskyi; Oleh Luzhnyi, Kakhi Kaladze, Olexandr Holovko, Vladislav Vashchuk, Yuri Dmitrulin, Andriy Gusin (82 Vasyl Kardash), Valentin Belkevich, Vitaliy Kosovskyi, Andriy Shevchenko, Serhiy Rebrov. Trainer: Valeriy Lobanovskyi

Goals: Bergkamp (73), Rebrov (90)

PANATHINAIKOS ATHINA v RC LENS 1-0 (0-0)

Olympiako, Athina 4.11.1998

Referee: José Maria García-Aranda Encinar (SPA)
Attendance: 55,031

PANATHINAIKOS: Jozef Wandzik; Stratos Apostolakis, Vladan Milojević, Aggelos Basinas, Andreas Lagonikakis, Giannis Gkoumas, Konstandinos Konstantinidis, Leonidas Vokolos, Aljosa Asanović (82 Konstandinos Kiassos), Krzysztof Warzycha (Cap) (87 Mauro da Silva), Nikos Limperopoulos. Trainer: Vasilis Daniil

RC LENS: Guillaume Warmuz; Eric Sikora, Cyrille Magnier, Frédéric Déhu, Xavier Méride, Mickaël Debève (59 Vladimir Smicer), Alex Nyarko, Stéphane Dalmat, Cyril Rool, Pascal Nouma (70 Wagneau Eloi), Tony Vairelles.
Trainer: Daniel Leclercq

Goal: Vokolos (53)

RC LENS v PANATHINAIKOS ATHINA 1-0 (0-0)

Félix-Bollaert, Lens 21.10.1998

Referee: Dick Jol (HOL) Attendance: 32,757

RC LENS: Guillaume Warmuz; Eric Sikora, Frédéric Déhu, Xavier Méride; Mickaël Debève, Stéphane Dalmat (65 Wagneau Eloi), Alex Nyarko, Cyril Rool; Vladimir Smicer (72 Daniel Moreira), Pascal Nouma, Tony Vairelles.
Trainer: Daniel Leclercq

PANATHINAIKOS: Jozef Wandzik; Konstandinos Konstantinidis, Stratos Apostolakis (Cap), Aljosa Asanović, Giannis Gkoumas, Andreas Lagonikakis (82 Erik Mykland), Nikos Limperopoulos, Bledar Kola, Leonidas Vokolos, Konstandinos Kiassos (46 Aggelos Basinas), Mauro da Silva (58 Alexandros Alexoudis). Trainer: Vasilis Daniil

Goal: Eloi (81)

ARSENAL FC LONDON v RC LENS 0-1 (0-0)

Wembley, London 25.11.1998

Referee: Anders Frisk (SWE) Attendance: 73,707

ARSENAL: David Seaman; Lee Dixon, Anthony Adams (46 Steve Bould), Martin Keown, Nigel Winterburn, Marc Overmars, Rémi Garde (69 Nélson Vivas), Stephen Hughes, Ray Parlour, Nicolas Anelka, Christopher Wreh (69 Luís Boa Morte). Manager: Arsène Wenger

RC LENS: Guillaume Warmuz; Eric Sikora, Cyrille Magnier, Frédéric Déhu, Yoann Lachor, Mickaël Debève, Alex Nyarko, Cyril Rool, Vladimir Smicer (81 Daniel Moreira), Pascal Nouma (61 Wagneau Eloi), Tony Vairelles.
Trainer: Daniel Leclercq

Sent off: Parlour and Vairelles (90)

Goal: Debève (72)

FC DYNAMO KYIV v PANATHINAIKOS ATHINA 2-1 (0-1)

Olympiyskyi, Kyiv 25.11.1998

Referee: Hellmut Krug (GER) Attendance: 45,000

DYNAMO: Olexandr Shovkovskyi; Oleh Luzhnyi, Olexandr Holovko, Serhiy Fedorov, Yuri Dmitrulin, Vasyl Kardash (77 Dmytro Mikhailenko), Olexandr Khatskevich, Andriy Gusin, Vitaliy Kosovskyi (46 Valentin Belkevich), Andriy Shevchenko, Serhiy Rebrov. Trainer: Valeriy Lobanovskyi

PANATHINAIKOS: Jozef Wandzik; Leonidas Vokolos, Giorgos Alexopoulos, Konstandinos Kiassos (83 Mauro da Silva), Andreas Lagonikakis, Stratos Apostolakis (77 Bledar Kola), Aggelos Basinas, Konstandinos Konstantinidis, Aljosa Asanović, Krzysztof Warzycha (Cap), Nikos Limperopoulos. Trainer: Vasilis Daniil

Goals: Lagonikakis (36), Rebrov (72), Basinas (80 og)

PANATHINAIKOS ATHINA v ARSENAL FC LONDON 1-3 (0-0)

Olympiako, Athina 9.12.1998

Referee: Stefano Braschi (ITA) Attendance: 41,105

PANATHINAIKOS: Jozef Wandzik; Konstandinos Konstantinidis (69 Frank Strandli), Stratos Apostolakis, Vladan Milojević, Aljosa Asanović, Giannis Gkoumas, Andreas Lagonikakis, Nikos Limperopoulos, Bledar Kola (56 Igor Sypniewski), Krzysztof Warzycha (Cap), Aggelos Basinas (78 Leonidas Vokolos). Trainer: Vasilis Daniil

ARSENAL: David Seaman; Nélson Vivas, Paolo Vernazza, Steve Bould, Matthew Upson, Alberto Mendez (78 Michael Black), David Grondin, Gilles Grimandi, Luís Boa Morte, Nicolas Anelka, Christopher Wreh. Manager: Arsène Wenger

Goals: Mendez (66), Sypniewski (74), Anelka (78), Boa Morte (85)

RC LENS v FC DYNAMO KYIV 1-3 (0-0)

Félix-Bollaert, Lens 9.12.1998

Referee: Lubos Michel (SVK) Attendance: 39,423

RC LENS: Guillaume Warmuz; Yoann Lachor, Cyrille Magnier, Frédéric Déhu, Xavier Méride (81 Philippe Brunel); Alex Nyarko, Mickaël Debève, Stéphane Dalmat (88 Daniel Moreira), Vladimir Smicer; Pascal Nouma, Wagneau Eloi (64 Marc-Vivien Foé). Trainer: Daniel Leclercq

DYNAMO: Olexandr Shovkovskyi; Oleh Luzhnyi, Olexandr Khatskevich, Olexandr Holovko, Vladislav Vashchuk, Yuri Dmitrulin (46 Vitaliy Kosovskyi), Kakhi Kaladze (67 Olexandr Kiryukhin), Andriy Gusin, Vasyl Kardash (51 Valentin Belkevich), Andriy Shevchenko, Serhiy Rebrov. Trainer: Valeriy Lobanovskyi

Goals: Kaladze (60), Vashchuk (76), Smicer (77), Shevchenko (85)

	P	W	D	L	F	A	Pts
Dynamo Kyiv	6	3	2	1	11	7	11
RC Lens	6	2	2	2	5	6	8
Arsenal FC London	6	2	2	2	8	8	8
Panathinaikos Athina	6	2	0	4	6	9	6

GROUP F

PSV EINDHOVEN v HJK HELSINKI 2-1 (0-1)

Philips, Eindhoven 16.09.1998

Referee: Lubos Michel (SVK) Attendance: 14,460

PSV: Ronald Waterreus; Theo Lucius, Abel Luis Xavier Silva Costa, Joaquim MARCOS Dos Santos, Davy Oyen, Tomek Iwan (60 Dennis Rommedahl), Yuri Nikiforov (54 Arnold Bruggink), Dmitri Khokhlov, André Ooijer, Joonas Kolkka, Gilles De Bilde (87 Claudio de Oliveira Pereira). Trainer: Bobby Robson

HJK: Tommi Koivistoinen; Jari Ilola, Ville Nylund, Jarmo Saastamoinen, Hannu Tihinen, Aki Riihilahti, Vesa Vasara (68 Peter Kopteff), Mika Lehkosuo, Shefki Kuqi (85 Markku Kanerva), Mika Antero Kottila (68 Jari Jäväjä), Marcelo Goncalves De Oliveira Piracaía. Trainer: Antti Muurinen

Goals: Kottila (31), Ooijer (57), Bruggink (90)

1.FC KAISERSLAUTERN v SPORT LISBOA E BENFICA 1-0 (1-0)

Fritz-Walter-Stadion, Kaiserslautern 16.09.1998

Referee: Pierluigi Collina (ITA) Attendance: 31,112

1.FC KAISERSLAUTERN: Andreas Reinke; Harry Koch, Hany Ramzy, Michael Schjønberg, Andreas Buck, Everson Rodrigues Ratinho (88 Thomas Riedl), Ciriaco Sforza, Martin Wagner, Axel Roos (72 Marco Reich), Olaf Marschall, Marian Hristov. Trainer: Otto Rehhagel

BENFICA: Michel Ghislain Preud'homme; Tahar El Khalej, RONALDO Guiaro, PAULO Sérgio Braga MADEIRA, BRUNO Miguel Leite BASTO, JOÃO Manuel VIEIRA PINTO (65 Karel Poborsky), Michael Thomas, José António CALADO da Silva, Mark Pembridge, Martin Ulf Pringle, Brian Deane (76 HUGO Miguel Ribeiro LEAL, 89 José Carlos Leite SOUSA). Trainer: Graeme Souness

Sent off: Tahar (89)

Goal: Wagner (41)

SPORT LISBOA E BENFICA v PSV EINDHOVEN 2-1 (0-0)

Estádio Da Luz, Lisboa 30.09.1998

Referee: Nikolai Levnikov (RUS) Attendance: 45,000

BENFICA: Michel Ghislain Preud'homme; José Carlos Leite SOUSA, Luís Filipe ANDRADE Oliveira, RONALDO Guiaro, BRUNO Miguel Leite BASTO, Karel Poborsky (77 Brian Deane), Michael Thomas (60 Sergei Kandaurov), HUGO Miguel Ribeiro LEAL, Mark Pembridge, JOÃO Manuel VIEIRA PINTO, Nuno Miguel Soares Ribeiro «NUNO GOMES» (77 Martin Ulf Pringle). Trainer: Graeme Souness

PSV: Ronald Waterreus; Theo Lucius, Abel Luis Xavier Silva Costa, Ernest Faber, Dmitri Khokhlov, Joonas Kolkka, Tomek Iwan (63 Dennis Rommedahl), Björn Van der Doelen (80 Arnold Bruggink), Joaquim MARCOS Dos Santos, Gilles De Bilde (63 Luc Nilis), Ruud Van Nistelrooij.
Trainer: Bobby Robson

Goals: Nuno Gomes (47), Rommedahl (70), João Pinto (77)

HJK HELSINKI v 1.FC KAISERSLAUTERN 0-0

Olympia, Helsinki 30.09.1998

Referee: Leslie Irvine (NIR) Attendance: 21,217

HJK: Jani Viander; Hannu Tihinen, Jari Ilola (83 Erkka Lehtola), Ville Nylund, Jarmo Saastamoinen, Jarkko Juhani Wiss, Markku Kanerva, Aki Riihilahti, Marcelo Goncalves De Oliveira Piracaía (69 Vesa Vasara), Mika Lehkosuo, Shefki Kuqi (75 Luiz António Moraes). Trainer: Antti Muurinen

1.FC KAISERSLAUTERN: Andreas Reinke; Hany Ramzy, Samir Kamouna Ibrahim, Andreas Buck (65 Jürgen Rische), Marco Reich (70 Uwe Rösler), Pascal Ojigwe, Ciriaco Sforza, Thomas Riedl (85 Harry Koch), Martin Wagner, Olaf Marschall, Marian Hristov. Trainer: Otto Rehhagel

HJK HELSINKI v SPORT LISBOA E BENFICA 2-0 (1-0)

Olympia, Helsinki 21.10.1998

Referee: Václav Krondl (CZE) Attendance: 25,126

HJK: Jani Viander; Ville Nylund, Markku Kanerva, Jarmo Saastamoinen, Hannu Tihinen; Mika Lehkosuo, Jari Ilola, Shefki Kuqi (63 Luiz António), Vesa Vasara (30 Aki Riihilahti); Marcelo Goncalves De Oliveira Piracaía, Mika Antero Kottila (79 Peter Kopteff). Trainer: Antti Muurinen

BENFICA: Michel Ghislain Preud'homme; José Carlos Leite SOUSA, PAULO Sérgio Braga MADEIRA, RONALDO Guiaro, Scott Christopher Minto, HUGO Miguel Ribeiro LEAL, Michael Thomas, Sergei Kandaurov (79 José António CALADO da Silva), Mark Pembridge, Martin Ulf Pringle (74 Hugo Cardoso PORFíRIO), Nuno Miguel Soares Ribeiro "NUNO GOMES" (60 Karel Poborsky).
Trainer: Graeme Souness

Goals: Lehkosuo (20 pen), Kottila (70)

PSV EINDHOVEN v 1.FC KAISERSLAUTERN 1-2 (0-0)

Philips, Eindhoven 21.10.1998

Referee: Alain Sars (FRA) Attendance: 22,500

PSV: Ronald Waterreus; Theo Lucius, Andrius Skerla, Yuri Nikiforov (73 Arnold Bruggink), Chris Van der Weerden, Dennis Rommedahl, Dmitri Khokhlov, Björn Van der Doelen (80 Tomek Iwan), Luc Nilis, Ruud Van Nistelrooij, Joonas Kolkka (73 Gilles De Bilde). Trainer: Bobby Robson

1.FC KAISERSLAUTERN: Andreas Reinke; Hany Ramzy, Samir Kamouna Ibrahim, Harry Koch, Axel Roos, Michael Ballack (59 Thomas Riedl), Ciriaco Sforza, Pascal Ojigwe, Marco Reich (59 Janos Hrutka), Uwe Rösler (75 Jürgen Rische), Marian Hristov. Trainer: Otto Rehhagel

Goals: Riedl (67), Khokhlov (78), Rische (80)

SPORT LISBOA E BENFICA v HJK HELSINKI 2-2 (0-1)

Estádio Da Luz, Lisboa 4.11.1998

Referee: László Vágner (HUN) Attendance: 25,000

BENFICA: Michel Ghislain Preud'homme; Luís Filipe ANDRADE Oliveira (46 Hugo Cardoso PORFÍRIO), PAULO Sérgio Braga MADEIRA, RONALDO Guiaro, Scott Christopher Minto, José António CALADO da Silva, Karel Poborsky (81 Martin Ulf Pringle), HUGO Miguel Ribeiro LEAL, Mark Pembridge, JOÃO Manuel VIEIRA PINTO, Nuno Miguel Soares Ribeiro "NUNO GOMES". Trainer: G. Souness

HJK: Tommi Koivistoinen; Hannu Tihinen, Jarmo Saastamoinen, Markku Kanerva, Ville Nylund; Jari Ilola, Shefki Kuqi (88 Peter Kopteff), Mika Lehkosuo, Marcelo Goncalves De Oliveira Piracaía (60 Mikael Forssell), Aki Riihilahti, Mika Antero Kottila (81 Luiz António). Trainer: Antti Muurinen

Goals: Minto (4 og), Nuno Gomes (77), Calado (80), Luiz António (85)

1.FC KAISERSLAUTERN v PSV EINDHOVEN 3-1 (0-1)

Fritz-Walter-Stadion, Kaiserslautern 4.11.1998

Referee: David Elleray (ENG) Attendance: 31,444

1.FC KAISERSLAUTERN: Andreas Reinke; Samir Kamouna Ibrahim, Ciriaco Sforza, Harry Koch (34 Marco Reich), Axel Roos, Michael Ballack, Thomas Riedl, Andreas Buck (67 José Carlos Jesus JÚNIOR), Olaf Marschall, Marian Hristov, Uwe Rösler (46 Jürgen Rische). Trainer: Otto Rehhagel

PSV: Patrick Lodewijks; Abel Luis Xavier Silva Costa, Yuri Nikiforov, Andrius Skerla, Davy Oyen, Chris Van der Weerden (59 Joaquim MARCOS Dos Santos), Björn Van der Doelen (75 Dennis Rommedahl), Dmitri Khokhlov, Tomek Iwan, Ruud Van Nistelrooij, Luc Nilis (27 Wilbert Need).
Trainer: Bobby Robson

Sent off: Lodewijks (27)

Goals: Van Nistelrooij (18), Rische (68), M. Reich (77), Hristov (90)

HJK HELSINKI v PSV EINDHOVEN 1-3 (0-1)

Olympia, Helsinki 25.11.1998

Referee: José Maria García-Aranda Encinar (SPA) Attendance: 33,000

HJK: Tommi Koivistoinen; Hannu Tihinen (83 Mikael Forssell), Markku Kanerva (46 Luiz António), Jarmo Saastamoinen, Ville Nylund, Shefki Kuqi (72 Peter Kopteff), Aarno Turpeinen, Mika Lehkosuo, Marcelo Goncalves De Oliveira Piracaía, Aki Riihilahti, Mika Antero Kottila. Trainer: Antti Muurinen

PSV: Ronald Waterreus; Abel Luis Xavier Silva Costa, Yuri Nikiforov, Dmitri Khokhlov, Davy Oyen, Tomek Iwan, Chris Van der Weerden, Björn Van der Doelen, Joonas Kolkka (75 Theo Lucius), Luc Nilis (85 Arnold Bruggink), Ruud Van Nistelrooij. Trainer: Bobby Robson

Goals: Van Nistelrooij (30, 67, 82 pen), Lehkosuo (70 pen)

1.FC KAISERSLAUTERN v HJK HELSINKI 5-2 (1-1)

Fritz-Walter-Stadion, Kaiserslautern 9.12.1998

Referee: Kim Milton Nielsen (DEN) Attendance: 27,310

1.FC KAISERSLAUTERN: Andreas Reinke; Ciriaco Sforza (Cap) (85 Thomas Riedl), Samir Kamouna Ibrahim, Janos Hrutka, Andreas Buck, Hany Ramzy, Michael Ballack (46 Jürgen Rische), Harry Koch (38 Uwe Rösler), Marco Reich, Olaf Marschall, Marian Hristov. Trainer: Otto Rehhagel

HJK: Jani Viander; Hannu Tihinen, Jarmo Saastamoinen, Ville Nylund, Aarno Turpeinen; Mika Lehkosuo, Aki Riihilahti, Jari Ilola, Marcelo Goncalves De Oliveira Piracaía (66 Peter Kopteff); Mika Antero Kottila (83 Mikael Forssell), Shefki Kuqi (59 Luiz António). Trainer: Antti Muurinen

Goals: Ilola (29), Rösler (43, 61, 80), Marschall (49), Luiz António (68), Rische (85)

SPORT LISBOA E BENFICA v 1.FC KAISERSLAUTERN 2-1 (1-0)

Estádio Da Luz, Lisboa 25.11.1998

Referee: Graham Barber (ENG) Attendance: 25,000

BENFICA: Sergei Ivanovich Ovchinnikov; Tahar El Khalej, PAULO Sérgio Braga MADEIRA, RONALDO Guiaro, Scott Christopher Minto, Karel Poborsky, José António CALADO da Silva, HUGO Miguel Ribeiro LEAL, Mark Pembridge, JOÃO Manuel VIEIRA PINTO, Nuno Miguel Soares Ribeiro "NUNO GOMES". Trainer: Graeme Souness

1.FC KAISERSLAUTERN: Andreas Reinke; Samir Kamouna Ibrahim, Hany Ramzy, Axel Roos (46 Harry Koch), Andreas Buck (46 José Carlos Jesus JúNIOR), Thomas Riedl, Michael Ballack, Pascal Ojigwe (56 Jürgen Rische), Marco Reich, Olaf Marschall, Marian Hristov. Trainer: Otto Rehhagel

Goals: Nuno Gomes (39), João Pinto (70), Rische (90)

	P	W	D	L	F	A	Pts
1.FC Kaiserslautern	6	4	1	1	12	6	13
Sport Lisboa e Benfica	6	2	2	2	8	9	8
PSV Eindhoven	6	2	1	3	10	11	8
HJK Helsinki	6	1	2	3	8	12	5

PSV EINDHOVEN v SPORT LISBOA E BENFICA 2-2 (1-0)

Philips, Eindhoven 9.12.1998

Referee: Karl-Erik Nilsson (SWE) Attendance: 17,900

PSV: Ronald Waterreus; Theo Lucius, Andrius Skerla, Abel Luis Xavier Silva Costa, Chris Van der Weerden, Tomek Iwan (72 Dennis Rommedahl), Dmitri Khokhlov, Björn Van der Doelen (82 Arnold Bruggink), Joonas Kolkka (72 Georgi Gakhoidze), Ruud Van Nistelrooij, Luc Nilis. Trainer: Bobby Robson

BENFICA: Sergei Ivanovich Ovchinnikov; Luís Filipe ANDRADE Oliveira, RONALDO Guiaro, Tahar El Khalej, Scott Christopher Minto, Michael Thomas (69 José António CALADO da Silva), Karel Poborsky (82 Martin Ulf Pringle), Mark Pembridge (88 BRUNO Miguel Leite BASTO), HUGO Miguel Ribeiro LEAL, JOÃO Manuel VIEIRA PINTO, Nuno Miguel Soares Ribeiro "NUNO GOMES". Trainer: Graeme Souness

Goals: Khokhlov (41), Nuno Gomes (47 pen, 63), Van Nistelrooij (89)

QUARTER-FINALS

REAL MADRID CF v FC DYNAMO KYIV 1-1 (0-0)

Estadio Santiago Bernabéu, Madrid 3.03.1999

Referee: Stefano Braschi (ITA) Attendance: 35,183

REAL: Bodo Illgner; Christian Panucci, Fernando Ruiz HIERRO, Manuel SANCHÍS Hontiyuelo (57 IVÁN CAMPO Ramos), ROBERTO CARLOS Da Silva, Clarence Seedorf (57 SÁVIO Bortolini Pimental), Fernando Carlos REDONDO Neri, José María GUTIérrez Hernández, RAÚL González Blanco, Predrag Mijatović, Fernando MORIENTES Sánchez (76 Davor Suker). Trainer: John Benjamin Toshack

DYNAMO: Olexandr Shovkovskyi; Oleh Luzhnyi (89 Olexandr Kiryukhin), Vladislav Vashchuk, Olexandr Holovko, Kakhi Kaladze, Olexandr Khatskevich, Andriy Gusin, Valentin Belkevich (80 Vasyl Kardash), Vitaliy Kosovskyi (83 Serhiy Kormiltsev), Serhiy Rebrov, Andriy Shevchenko. Trainer: Valeriy Lobanovskyi

Goals: Shevchenko (54), Mijatović (66)

FC DYNAMO KYIV v REAL MADRID CF 2-0 (0-0)

Olympiyskyi, Kyiv 17.03.1999

Referee: Anders Frisk (SWE) Attendance: 81,500

DYNAMO: Olexandr Shovkovskyi; Oleh Luzhnyi, Olexandr Holovko, Vladislav Vashchuk, Kakhi Kaladze, Olexandr Khatskevich, Andriy Gusin, Vasyl Kardash (46 Valentin Belkevich), Vitaliy Kosovskyi (85 Artem Yashkin), Serhiy Rebrov, Andriy Shevchenko. Trainer: Valeriy Lobanovskyi

REAL: Bodo Illgner; Christian Panucci, IVÁN CAMPO Ramos, Fernando Ruiz HIERRO, ROBERTO CARLOS Da Silva; Clarence Seedorf (67 Davor Suker), Manuel SANCHÍS Hontiyuelo (71 José María GUTIérrez Hernández), Fernando Carlos REDONDO Neri, Robert Jarni (82 Christian Karembeu), RAÚL González Blanco, Fernando MORIENTES Sánchez. Trainer: John Benjamin Toshack

Goals: Shevchenko (62, 79)

MANCHESTER UNITED FC v FC INTERNAZIONALE MILANO 2-0 (2-0)

Old Trafford, Manchester 3.03.1999

Referee: Hellmut Krug (GER) Attendance: 54,682

MANCHESTER UNITED: Peter Schmeichel; Gary Neville, Jaap Stam, Ronny Johnsen (46 Henning Berg), Dennis Irwin, David Beckham, Paul Scholes (69 Nicky Butt), Roy Keane, Ryan Giggs, Andy Cole, Dwight Yorke.
Manager: Alex Ferguson

INTER: Gianluca Pagliuca; Francesco Colonnese, Giuseppe Bergomi, Fabio Galante, Javier Zanetti, Youri Djorkaeff, Benoit Cauet, Diego Simeone, Áron Winter, Ivan Zamorano (68 Nicola Ventola), Roberto Baggio (79 Andrea Pirlo).
Trainer: Mircea Lucescu

Goals: Yorke (6, 45)

FC INTERNAZIONALE MILANO v MANCHESTER UNITED FC 1-1 (0-0)

Giuseppe Meazza, Milano 17.03.1999

Referee: Gilles Veissière (FRA) Attendance: 79,528

INTER: Gianluca Pagliuca; Francesco Colonnese, Giuseppe Bergomi (69 Francesco Moriero), Taribo West, Mickael Silvestre, Javier Zanetti, Benoit Cauet, Roberto Baggio, Diego Simeone (77 José Moedin ZÉ ELIAS), Ivan Zamorano, RONALDO Luiz Nazario Da Lima (59 Nicola Ventola).
Trainer: Mircea Lucescu

MANCHESTER UNITED: Peter Schmeichel; Gary Neville, Henning Berg, Jaap Stam, Dennis Irwin, David Beckham, Roy Keane, Ronny Johnsen (76 Paul Scholes), Ryan Giggs (81 Philip Neville), Dwight Yorke, Andy Cole.
Manager: Alex Ferguson

Goals: Ventola (63), Scholes (88)

JUVENTUS FC TORINO v OLYMPIAKOS PEIRAIAS 2-1 (1-0)

Stadio delle Alpi, Torino 3.03.1999

Referee: José Maria García-Aranda Encinar (SPA)
Attendance: 33,671

JUVENTUS: Angelo Peruzzi; Zoran Mirkovic, Mark Iuliano, Paolo Montero, Angelo Di Livio (90 Alessio Tacchinardi), Antonio Conte, Didier Deschamps, Zinedine Zidane, Edgar Davids, Daniel Fonseca (82 Alessandro Birindelli), Filippo Inzaghi. Trainer: Carlo Ancelotti

OLYMPIAKOS: Dimitris Eleftheropoulos; Giorgos Amanatidis, Giorgos Anatolakis, Kiriakos Karataidis (Cap), Grigoris Georgatos (88 Andreas Niniadis), Dimitris Mavrogenidis, Ilias Poursanidis, Vasilis Karapialis (73 Alekos Alexandris), Stilianos Giannakopoulos (73 Ilija Ivić), Predrag Djordjević, Sinisa Gogić. Trainer: Dušan Bajević

Goals: Inzaghi (38), Conte (79), Niniadis (90 pen)

OLYMPIAKOS PEIRAIAS v JUVENTUS FC TORINO 1-1 (1-0)

Olympiako, Athina 17.03.1999

Referee: Markus Merk (GER) Attendance: 71,022

OLYMPIAKOS: Dimitris Eleftheropoulos; Kiriakos Karataidis (Cap), Giorgos Amanatidis (86 Alekos Alexandris), Giorgos Anatolakis, Grigoris Georgatos (86 LUCIANO Nunes de Souza), Stilianos Giannakopoulos, Dimitris Mavrogenidis, Ilias Poursanidis, Predrag Djordjević, Vasilis Karapialis (78 Kofi Amponsah), Sinisa Gogić. Trainer: Dušan Bajević

JUVENTUS: Michelangelo Rampulla; Zoran Mirkovic (82 Alessandro Birindelli), Mark Iuliano, Paolo Montero, Angelo Di Livio, Antonio Conte, Zinedine Zidane (89 Alessio Tacchinardi), Didier Deschamps, Edgar Davids, Filippo Inzaghi, Juan Eduardo Esnaider (69 Nicola Amoruso).
Trainer: Carlo Ancelotti

Goals: Gogić (12), Conte (85)

FC BAYERN MÜNCHEN v 1.FC KAISERSLAUTERN 2-0 (2-0)

Olympiastadion, München 3.03.1999

Referee: Nikolai Levnikov (RUS) Attendance: 54,000

BAYERN: Oliver Kahn; Markus Babbel, Thomas Linke, Lothar Matthäus (46 Michael Tarnat), Bixente Lizarazu, Mario Basler (83 Hasan Salihamidzic), Jens Jeremies, Stefan Effenberg, Thomas Strunz (76 Alexander Zickler), Giovane De Souza Elber, Carsten Jancker. Trainer: Ottmar Hitzfeld

1.FC KAISERSLAUTERN: Andreas Reinke; Michael Ballack, Hany Ramzy, Thomas Riedl, Marco Reich, Janos Hrutka (69 Harry Koch), Andreas Buck (56 Everson Rodrigues Ratinho), Ciriaco Sforza, Jürgen Rische (73 Samir Kamouna Ibrahim), Martin Wagner, Uwe Rösler. Trainer: Otto Rehhagel

Sent off: Ramzy (71)

Goals: Elber (30), Effenberg (34)

1.FC KAISERSLAUTERN v FC BAYERN MÜNCHEN 0-4 (0-3)

Fritz-Walter-Stadion, Kaiserslautern 17.03.1999

Referee: Urs Meier (SWI) Attendance: 31,500

1.FC KAISERSLAUTERN: Andreas Reinke; Harry Koch, Janos Hrutka, Ciriaco Sforza, Michael Ballack, Marco Reich, Thomas Riedl (60 José Carlos Jesus JúNIOR), Everson Rodrigues Ratinho (46 Axel Roos), Martin Wagner, Uwe Rösler (76 Pascal Ojigwe), Jürgen Rische.
Trainer: Otto Rehhagel

BAYERN: Oliver Kahn; Markus Babbel, Lothar Matthäus, Thomas Linke, Samuel Osei Kuffour, Bixente Lizarazu, Mario Basler (73 Hasan Salihamidzic), Stefan Effenberg (46 Mehmet Scholl), Jens Jeremies (46 Thorsten Fink), Carsten Jancker, Alexander Zickler. Trainer: Ottmar Hitzfeld

Sent off: Hrutka (8)

Goals: Effenberg (9 pen), Jancker (22, 39), Basler (56)

FC DYNAMO KYIV v FC BAYERN MÜNCHEN 3-3 (2-1)

Olympiyskyi, Kyiv 7.04.1999

Referee: Kim Milton Nielsen (DEN) Attendance: 75,000

DYNAMO: Olexandr Shovkovskyi; Oleh Luzhnyi, Olexandr Holovko, Vladislav Vashchuk, Kakhi Kaladze, Andriy Gusin, Olexandr Khatskevich (80 Olexandr Kiryukhin), Valentin Belkevich, Vitaliy Kosovskyi, Andriy Shevchenko, Serhiy Rebrov. Trainer: Valeriy Lobanovskyi

BAYERN: Oliver Kahn; Markus Babbel, Thomas Strunz, Lothar Matthäus, Samuel Osei Kuffour, Michael Tarnat, Jens Jeremies, Stefan Effenberg, Hasan Salihamidzic, Carsten Jancker (90 Ali Daei), Mehmet Scholl (71 Alexander Zickler).
Trainer: Ottmar Hitzfeld

Goals: Shevchenko (15, 43), Tarnat (45), Kosovskyi (49), Effenberg (78), Jancker (90)

SEMI-FINALS

MANCHESTER UNITED FC v JUVENTUS FC TORINO 1-1 (0-0)

Old Trafford, Manchester 7.04.1999

Referee: Manuel Diaz Vega (SPA) Attendance: 54,487

MANCHESTER UNITED: Peter Schmeichel; Gary Neville, Henning Berg (46 Ronny Johnsen), Jaap Stam, Dennis Irwin, David Beckham, Roy Keane, Paul Scholes, Ryan Giggs, Dwight Yorke (79 Teddy Sheringham), Andy Cole.
Manager: Alex Ferguson

JUVENTUS: Angelo Peruzzi; Zoran Mirkovic, Paolo Montero (68 Ciro Ferrara), Mark Iuliano, Gianluca Pessotto, Angelo Di Livio (78 Alessio Tacchinardi), Edgar Davids, Didier Deschamps, Antonio Conte, Zinedine Zidane, Filippo Inzaghi (88 Juan Eduardo ESNÁIDER). Trainer: Carlo Ancelotti

Goals: Conte (25), Giggs (90)

JUVENTUS FC TORINO v MANCHESTER UNITED FC 2-3 (2-2)

Stadio Delle Alpi, Torino 21.04.1999

Referee: Urs Meier (SWI) Attendance: 60,806

JUVENTUS: Angelo Peruzzi; Alessandro Birindelli (46 Nicola Amoruso), Ciro Ferrara, Mark Iuliano (46 Paolo Montero), Gianluca Pessotto, Antonio Conte, Didier Deschamps, Zinedine Zidane, Edgar Davids, Angelo Di Livio (79 Daniel Fonseca), Filippo Inzaghi. Trainer: Carlo Ancelotti

MANCHESTER UNITED: Peter Schmeichel; Gary Neville, Ronny Johnsen, Jaap Stam, Dennis Irwin, David Beckham, Roy Keane, Nicky Butt, Jesper Blomqvist (68 Paul Scholes), Dwight Yorke, Andy Cole. Manager: Alex Ferguson

Goals: Inzaghi (6, 11), Keane (24), Yorke (34), Cole (84)

FC BAYERN MÜNCHEN v FC DYNAMO KYIV 1-0 (1-0)

Olympiastadion, München 21.04.1999

Referee: Vitor Manuel Melo Pereira (POR) Att: 60,000

BAYERN: Oliver Kahn; Markus Babbel, Thomas Linke, Lothar Matthäus, Samuel Osei Kuffour, Mario Basler, Jens Jeremies, Stefan Effenberg, Michael Tarnat (84 Thorsten Fink), Carsten Jancker (76 Ali Daei), Alexander Zickler (76 Hasan Salihamidzić). Trainer: Ottmar Hitzfeld

DYNAMO: Olexandr Shovkovskyi; Oleh Luzhnyi, Olexandr Holovko, Vladislav Vashchuk, Kakhi Kaladze, Andriy Gusin (81 Vasyl Kardash), Olexandr Khatskevich, Valentin Belkevich, Vitaliy Kosovskyi, Andriy Shevchenko, Serhiy Rebrov.
Trainer: Valeriy Lobanovskyi

Goal: Basler (35)

FINAL

MANCHESTER UNITED FC v FC BAYERN MÜNCHEN 2-1 (0-1)

Nou Camp, Barcelona 26.05.1999

Referee: Pierluigi Collina (ITA) Attendance: 90,245

MANCHESTER UNITED: Peter Schmeichel; Gary Neville, Dennis Irwin, Ronny Johnsen, Jaap Stam, David Beckham, Nicky Butt, Andy Cole (82 Ole Gunnar Solskjaer), Ryan Giggs, Jesper Blomqvist (65 Teddy Sheringham), Dwight Yorke.
Manager: Alex Ferguson

BAYERN: Oliver Kahn; Markus Babbel, Samuel Osei Kuffour, Lothar Matthäus (80 Thorsten Fink), Stefan Effenberg, Mario Basler (88 Hasan Salihamidzic), Jens Jeremies, Michael Tarnat, Carsten Jancker, Alexander Zickler (70 Mehmet Scholl), Thomas Linke. Trainer: Ottmar Hitzfeld

Goals: Basler (6), Sheringham (89), Solskajer (90)

European Cup Goalscorers 1998-99:

10 goals: Andriy Shevchenko (Dynamo Kyiv),

8 goals: Dwight Yorke (Manchester United), Serhiy Rebrov (Dynamo Kyiv),

7 goals: Zlatko Zahovic (FC Porto), Nuno Gomes (Benfica Lisboa),

6 goals: Filippo Inzaghi (Juventus Torino), Sigurd Rushfeldt (Rosenborg Trondheim), Hakan Şükür (Galatasaray Istanbul), Ruud Van Nistelrooy (PSV Eindhoven), Andy Cole, Ryan Giggs (Manchester United)

5 goals: Ilya Tsymbalar (Spartak Moskva), Sinisa Gogic (Olympiakos Peiraias), Stefan Effenberg (Bayern München)

4 goals: Paul Scholes (Manchester United), Mario Basler, Giovane Elber, Carsten Jancker (Bayern München), István Sallói (Beitar Jerusalem), Yegor Titov (Spartak Moskva), Sonny Anderson (FC Barcelona), Mika Lehkosuo (HJK Helsinki), Roberto Baggio (Inter Milano), Jürgen Rische (FC Kaiserslautern)

3 goals: Claessens (Club Brugge), Filipovic (Maribor Teatanic), Prohaszka (FC Košice), Z.Kovács (Újpesti Budapest), Hagi (Galatasaray), Haas, Vastic (Sturm Graz), Tikhonov (Spartak Moskva), Rivaldo (FC Barcelona), Limperopoulos (Panathinakos Athina), João Pinto (Benfica), Raúl , Sávio, Seedorf (Real Madrid), Ventola, Zamorano (Inter Milano), Yannakopoulos (Olympiakos Peiraias), Rösler (FC Kaiserslautern), Conte (Juventus Torino), Keane (Manchester United)

2 goals: Kulik (Zimbru Chişinău), Jak, Trzeciak, Wieszczycki (LKS Lódz), Bushi, Iurukov (Liteks Lovech), N'Kufo, Türkyılmaz, Vogel (Grasshopper Zürich), Gajser (Maribor Teatanic), Janocko, Lyubarskyi, Nemeth , Zvara (FC Košice), Mihajlovic, Okkas, Sotiriou (Anorthosis Famagusta), Hamar, Shitrit (Beitar Jerusalem), Grozdic (Obilic Beograd), Ciocoiu, Dănciulescu, Răchită, Şerban (Steaua Bucureşti), Prosinecki (Croatia Zagreb), Drulovic, Jardel (FC Porto), Sørensen, Skammelsrud (Rosenborg Trondheim), Guerrero, J.Etxeberria (Athletic Bilbao), Reinmayr (Sturm Graz), Pisarev, Robson (Spartak Moskva), Daugaard (Brøndby IF), Giovanni (FC Barcelona), Warzycha, Asanovic (Panathinakos Athina), Vairelles (Lens), Kottila , Luiz António (HJK Helsinki), Bruggink, Khokhlov, Rommedahl (PSV Eindhoven), Calado, Pembridge (Benfica), Panucci, Jarni, Mijatović (Real Madrid), Djorkaeff , Simeone (Inter Milano), Alexandris, Jurcevic (Olympiakos Peiraias), Amoruso (Juventus Torino), Solskjaer (Manchester United), Salihamidzic, Zickler (Bayern München)

1 goal: Halfidason (ÍB Vestmannaeyjar), Sakiri, Arvidsson (Halmstads BK), Terehhov, Smirnov, Zelinski, Oper (Flora Tallinn), Suleymanov , Smirnov (Kapaz Ganja), Cungu, Miloti, Noga (Vllaznia Shkodër), Williams (Barry Town), Bozinov (Sileks Kratovo), Petersen (B36 Tórshavn), Flynn (FC Cliftonville Belfast), Osipovich (Dinamo Minsk), Fadiga, Schockaert, Vermant (Club Brugge), Cebula (LKS Lódz), Beliakov (Liteks Lovech), Kavelashvili, Cabanas, Tikva, Tararache, Esposito (Grasshopper Zürich), Jackson, Brattbakk, Larsson (Celtic Glasgow), Breznik, Balajic (Maribor Teatanic), Baranek (Sparta Praha), Lapsansky, J.Kozak, Kozlej (FC Košice), Mikholap, Astafyev, Novikov (Skonto Riga), Krcmarevic, Ilia, Cirić, Haralampous, Andreou (Anorthosis Famagusta), Abuksis (Beitar Jerusalem), Khomeriki, Tskitishvili , Ashvetia (Dinamo Tbilisi), Meyrieu (FC Metz), Sarac, Juksic, Vasiljevic (Obilic Beograd), Jenei, Miriuţă (Újpesti Budapest), Szekely, Belodedici (Steaua Bucureşti), Jelicic, J.Simic, Mikic, Rukavina, Mujcin, Maric (Croatia Zagreb), Witschge, Gorré, Rudy, Litmanen (Ajax Amsterdam), Strand (Rosenborg), Pérez, Urzaiz, Imaz (Athletic Bilbao), Arif, Okan, Umit (Galatasaray Istanbul), Neukirchner (Sturm Graz), Khlestov, Samaroni (Spartak Moskva), Sand, Ravn, Thygesen (Brøndby IF), Figo, Luis Enrique (FC Barcelona), Sypniewski, Lagonikakis, Vokolos, Mauro, Mykland, Milojevic (Panathinakos Athina), Mendez, Anelka, Boa Morte, Hughes, Bergkamp, Adams, Keown, Overmars (Arsenal London), Smicer, Debève, Eloi (Lens), Ilola, Vaasara, Riihilahti, Wiss, Kuqi, Jäväjä (HJK Helsinki), Ooijer, Marcos, De Bilde (PSV Eindhoven), Deane (Benfica), Hierro, Suker (Real Madrid), J.Zanetti, Ronaldo, Galante (Inter Milano), Niniadis, Djordjevic, Luciano, Yorgatos (Olympiakos Peiraias), Marschall, M.Reich, Hristov, Riedl, Wagner (FC Kaiserslautern), Suat, Birindelli (Juventus Torino), Kosovskyi, Kaladze, Vashchuk, Holovko, Gerasimenko, Belkevich, Mykhailenko, Venhlynskyi (Dynamo Kyiv), Sheringham, Beckham, P.Neville, Beckham (Manchester United), Tarnat, Babbel, Fink, Matthäus (Bayern München)

Own goals: Votava (Sparta Praha) for Dynamo Kyiv, Shelach (Beitar) for Benfica, Lincar (Steaua Bucureşti) for Panathinakos, Lasa (Athletic Bilbao) for Juventus Torino, Popovic (Sturm Graz) for Real Madrid, Helmer (Bayern) for Brøndby, Basinas (Panathinakos) for Dynamo Kyiv, Minto (Benfica) for HJK Helsinki

THE EUROPEAN CUP 1999-2000

FIRST QUALIFYING ROUND

ÍBV-ÍTHRÓTTAFÉLAG VESTMANNAEYJAR v SK TIRANA 1-0 (1-0)

Hásteinsvöllur, Vestmannaeyjar 13.07.1999

Referee: Richard O'Hanlon (IRE) Attendance: 790

ÍBV: Birkir Kristinsson; Ívar Bjarklind, Kjartan Antonsson, Zoran Miljkovic, Hlynur Stefánsson, Ingi Sigurdsson; Ívar Ingimarsson, Gudni Helgason (79 Jóhann Möller), Baldur Bragason, Allan Mørkøre (62 Goran Aleksic); Steingrímur Jóhannesson. Trainer: Bjarni Jóhansson

SK TIRANA: Blendi Nallbani; Elvis Sina, Saimir Malko, Thamas Nevil Dede, Krenar Alimehmeti; Ardian Mema, Alban Tafaj, Sokol Bulku, Sokol Prenga; Sokol Ishka (75 Ervin Bulku), Nikolin Çoçlli (65 Nordik Ruhi). Trainer: Shkëlkim Muça

Goal: S. Jóhannesson (45)

SK TIRANA v ÍBV-ÍTHRÓTTAFÉLAG VESTMANNAEYJAR 1-2 (0-2)

Qemal Stafa, Tirana 21.07.1999

Referee: Robert Anthony Boggi (ITA) Attendance: 5,000

SK TIRANA: Blendi Nallbani; Elvis Sina, Saimir Malko (46 Nordik Ruhi), Thamas Nevil Dede, Krenar Alimehmeti, Alban Tafaj, Alpin Gallo (46 Sokol Bulku); Ardian Mema, Sokol Prenga, Nikolin Çoçlli (73 Ervin Demneri); Sokol Ishka. Trainer: Shkëlkim Muça

ÍBV: Birkir Kristinsson; Zoran Miljkovic, Hlynur Stefánsson, Ingi Sigurdsson (73 Bjarni Vidarsson), Hjalti Jóhannesson; Ívar Ingimarsson, Gudni Helgason, Baldur Bragason, Goran Aleksic (25 Ívar Bjarklind), Allan Mørkøre (80 Sindri Grétarsson); Steingrímur Jóhannesson. Trainer: Bjarni Jóhansson

Goals: Jóhannesson (32), Sigurdsson (45), Bulku (80)

SLOGA JUGOMAGNAT SKOPJE v KAPAZ GANJA 1-0 (0-0)

Cair, Skopje 14.07.1999

Referee: Attila Juhos (HUN) Attendance: 1,000

SLOGA: Gogo Jovcev; Esad Colaković, Saso Zdravevski, Arsim Abazi; Masar Omeragić, Nedzmedin Memedi, Feim Beganović, Nebi Mustafi (73 Bruno Presilski), Refik Arif (58 Gasi Fetai), Ardzend Beciri; Saso Blazevski (58 Zoran Miserdovski). Trainer: Gjore Jovanovski

KAPAZ: Huseyn Magomedov; Elhan Shakhniyarov, Vasif Veliyev, Emin Kuliyev, Ramiz Mamedov; Makhmud Kurbanov, Azer Jabbarov, Vidadi Rzayev, Roin Kerdzevadze (71 Adil Sukurov); Rovshan Akhmedov, Yunis Huseynov (76 Imamyar Suleymanov). Trainer: Mehman Allahverdiev

Goal: Memedi (66)

KAPAZ GANJA v SLOGA JUGOMAGNAT SKOPJE 2-1 (1-1)

Tofig Bakhramov, Baku 21.07.1999

Referee: Gennady Yakubovsky (BLS) Attendance: 6,000

KAPAZ: Huseyn Magomedov; Elhan Shakhniyarov, Vasif Veliyev (46 Imamyar Suleymanov), Emin Kuliyev, Ramiz Mamedov; Makhmud Kurbanov, Azer Jabbarov (72 Fazil Parvarov), Vidadi Rzayev, Roin Kerdzevadze (68 Fizuli Allakhverdiev); Rovshan Akhmedov, Yunis Huseynov. Trainer: Mehman Allahverdiev

SLOGA: Gogo Jovcev; Esad Colaković, Saso Zdravevski, Arsim Abazi; Masar Omeragić, Nedzmedin Memedi, Feim Beganović, Nebi Mustafi (80 Bruno Presilski), Refik Arif, Ardzend Beciri (46 Zoran Miserdovski); Saso Blazevski (85 Gasi Fetai). Trainer: Gjore Jovanovski

Goals: Mamedov (20), Memedi (35), Rzayev (90)

PARTIZAN BEOGRAD v FLORA TALLINN 6-0 (3-0)

Partizan, Beograd 14.07.1999

Referee: Philippe Leuba (SWI) Attendance: 9,000

PARTIZAN: Radisa Ilić; Vuk Rasović, Aleksandar Stanojević (21 Igor Duljaj), Milan Stojanoski, Mladen Krstajić (40 Nenad Misković); Goran Trobok, Djordje Tomić, Vladimir Ivić (86 Ivica Ilijev), Sasa Ilić; Mateja Kezman, Milorad Peković. Trainer: Miodrag Jesić

FLORA: Toomas Tohver; Marek Lemsalu, Raio Piiroja, Sergei Hohlov- Simson, Erko Saviauk (65 Martin Lepa); Viktor Alonen (76 Aivar Anniste), Kert Haavistu (57 Marko Kristal), Tomas Razanauskas, Sergei Terehhov; Indrek Zelinski, Kristen Viikmäe. Trainer: Teitur Thórdarson

Goals: S. Ilić (12), Peković (25, 71), Ivić (36, 75), Kezman (56)

FLORA TALLINN v PARTIZAN BEOGRAD 1-4 (0-2)

Maarjamäe, Tallinn 21.07.1999

Referee: Tom Henning Øvrebø (NOR) Attendance: 400

FLORA: Toomas Tohver; Raio Piiroja, Sergei Hohlov-Simson, Viktor Alonen, Erko Saviauk (68 Martin Lepa); Aivar Anniste, Kert Haavistu, Tomas Razanauskas, Sergei Terehhov (41 Priit Reiska); Indrek Zelinski (35 Marko Kristal), Kristen Viikmäe. Trainer: Teitur Thórdarson

PARTIZAN: Radisa Ilić; Vuk Rasović, Igor Duljaj, Mateja Kezman (75 Goran Obradović), Milorad Peković; Aleksandar Stanojević, Goran Trobok, Vladimir Ivić (84 Nenad Misković), Sasa Ilić; Milan Stojanoski (43 Branko Savić), Djordje Tomić. Trainer: Miodrag Jesić

Goals: Kezman (10, 69), S. Ilić (20), Viikmäe (52), Tomić (82)

BARRY TOWN FC v VALLETTA FC 0-0

Jenner Park, Barry 14.07.1999

Referee: Charles Schaack (LUX) Attendance: 2,400

BARRY TOWN: Dave Wells; Terry Evans, Darren Davies, Richard Jones, Andrew York; Lee Barrow, Gary Barnett, Danny Carter, Paul Mitchell; Chris Sloan, James Ince (63 Justin Perry). Trainer: Gary Barnett

VALLETTA FC: Reginald Cini; Stefan Giglio, Jeffrey Chetcuti, Sinisa Radak, Darren Debono; John Buttigieg, Gilbert Agius (90 Edward Azzopardi), Nicky Saliba, Nenad Veselji (75 Joe Camilleri); Alexander Ivanov, Daniel Thewma. Trainer: Krasimir Manolov

GLENTORAN BELFAST v LITEKS LOVECH 0-2 (0-0)

The Oval, Belfast 21.07.1999

Referee: Dick van Egmond (HOL) Attendance: 2,005

GLENTORAN: Alan Gough; Colin Nixon (34 Stephen Livingstone), John Kennedy, Chris Walker, Michael Ferguson, Paul Leeman (87 Darren Finlay); Timothy McCann, Peter Batey, Scott Young; Rory Hamill (74 David Rainey), Stuart Elliot. Trainer: Roy Coyle

LITEKS: Vitomir Vutov; Said Ibraimov (79 Ivan Rusev), Jivko Jelev, Stefan Kolev, Nikolai Dimitrov, Zlatomir Zagorcic; Alban Bushi, Svetoslav Todorov (71 Velizar Dimitrov), Altin Haxhi; Ibe Johnson, Marin Petrov (75 Rosen Emilov). Trainer: Alexandar Zheliazkov

Goals: Haxhi (64), Bushi (89)

FC VALLETTA v BARRY TOWN FC 3-2 (2-1)

National Ta' Qali 20.07.1999

Referee: Bruno Derrien (FRA) Attendance: 2,996

VALLETTA FC: Reginald Cini; Stefan Giglio, Jeffrey Chetcuti, Sinisa Radak, Darren Debono; John Buttigieg, Nicky Saliba (85 Edward Azzopardi), Nenad Veselji (69 Kristian Laferla), Alexander Ivanov (59 Joe Camilleri); Gilbert Agius, Daniel Thewma. Trainer: Krasimir Manolov

BARRY TOWN: Dave Wells; Terry Evans, Darren Davies, Richard Jones, Andrew York, Lee Barrow, Paul Mitchell; Gary Barnett (85 Jodie Jenkins), Danny Carter, James Ince (46 Chris Sloan); Justin Perry. Trainer: Gary Barnett

Sent off: Evans (67)

Goals: G. Agius (42, 45), Sloan (44, 56), Chetcuti (55)

HB TÓRSHAVN v FC HAKA VALKEAKOSKI 1-1 (0-0)

Gundadalur, Tórshavn 14.07.1999

Referee: Miroslaw Ryszka (POL) Attendance: 1,600

HB: Bardur Johannesen; Bjarki Mohr, Hans á Lag, Jóhannes Joensen, Hans Frodi Hansen; Jens Erik Rasmussen (74 Eydun Højgaard), Rúni Nolsøe, Hallur Danielsen (70 Rói Árting); Súni Fridi Johannesen, Magnus á Lakjuni, John Heri Dam (65 Andrew av Fløtum). Trainer: Ion Geolgău

HAKA: András Vilnrotter; Tero Penttilä, Lasse Karjalainen, Janne Salli, Jouni Räsänen (78 Tommi Torkkeli); Oleg Ivanov (57 Kai Nyyssönen), Janne Hyökyvaara, David Wilson, Jari Niemi (87 Martin Reynders); Jukka Ruhanen, Valeriy Popovich. Trainer: Keith Armstrong

Goals: á Lakjuni (47), Popovich (64)

LITEKS LOVECH v GLENTORAN BELFAST 3-0 (2-0)

Lovech stadion 14.07.1999

Referee: Zoran Arsić (YUG) Attendance: 4,000

LITEKS: Vitomir Vutov; Said Ibraimov, Stefan Kolev, Nikolai Dimitrov, Zlatomir Zagorcic; Ibe Johnson, Rosen Emilov (46 Ivan Rusev), Alban Bushi (78 Luis Carlos Motta), Altin Haxhi; Marin Petrov, Svetoslav Todorov (70 Velizar Dimitrov). Trainer: Alexandar Zheliazkov

GLENTORAN: Alan Gough; Colin Nixon, John Kennedy, Chris Walker, Michael Ferguson; Paul Leeman, Timothy McCann (46 Scott Young), Rory Hamill, Stuart Elliot (85 Darren Finlay); Peter Batey, Justin McBride (73 David Rainey). Trainer: Roy Coyle

Goals: Haxhi (12), Bushi (34 pen), Petrov (81)

FC HAKA VALKEAKOSKI v HB TÓRSHAVN 6-0 (2-0)

Tehtaakenttä, Valkeakoski 21.07.1999

Referee: Algirdas Dubinskas (LIT) Attendance: 2,241

HAKA: Andras Vilnrotter; Jouni Räsänen, Janne Savolainen; Tero Penttilä, Lasse Karjalainen, Janne Salli (54 Janne Hyökyvaara), David Wilson, Jari Niemi; Martin Reynders (71 Oleg Ivanov), Kai Nyyssönen (61 Tommi Torkkeli), Valeriy Popovich. Trainer: Keith Armstrong

HB: Bardur Johannesen; Bjarki Mohr, Jakup Eli Olsen (12 Jan Dam), Hans á Lag, Jóhannes Joensen, Hans Frodi Hansen; Jens Erik Rasmussen, Rúni Nolsøe; Andrew av Fløtum, Magnus á Lakjuni (49 Bárdur Mortansson), John Heri Dam (46 Súni Fridi Johannesen). Trainer: Ion Geolgău

Goals: Salli (26), Reynders (44), Nyyssönen (47), Wilson (62), Popovich (80), Torkkeli (90)

JEUNESSE D'ESCH v SKONTO RIGA 0-2 (0-0)

Stade de la Frontière, Esch 14.07.1999

Referee: Lawrence Sammut (MAL) Attendance: 1,000

JEUNESSE: John van Rijswijck; Roland Schaack, Claude Meylender (79 Jean Wagner), Marc Lamborelle, Manuel Schauls; Yves Divoy (74 Carlo Pace), Manuel Cardoni, Claude Kurtz, David Borbiconi; Paolo Amodio, Patrick Morocutti (56 Gordon Braun). Trainer: Eric Brusco

SKONTO: Alexander Kolinko; Mikhail Zemlinsky, Yury Laizans, Andreyus Tereskinas, David Chaladze (79 Vladimir Kolesnichenko); Oleg Blagonadezhdin (82 Victor Olshansky), Alexander Rekhviashvili, Imants Bleidelis, Vitaly Astafyev; Andrei Rubins (79 Levan Korgalidze), Mikhail Mikholap. Trainer: Alexander Starkov

Goals: Astafyev (66), Mikholap (73)

SKONTO RIGA v JEUNESSE ESCH 8-0 (2-0)

Daugava, Riga 21.07.1999

Referee: Jan Hald (DEN) Attendance: 1,100

SKONTO: Alexander Kolinko; Levan Silagadze (46 Andreyus Tereskinas), Mikhail Zemlinsky, Yury Laizans; Oleg Blagonadezhdin (64 Igor Stepanov), Alexander Rekhviashvili (72 Vladimir Melnik), Imants Bleidelis, Andrei Rubins, Vitaly Astafyev; Mikhail Mikholap, Vladimir Kolesnichenko. Trainer: Alexander Starkov

JEUNESSE: Philippe Felgen; Johny Thill, Roland Schaack, Marc Lamborelle, Manuel Schauls (24 Ludovic Laruell), Jean Wagner; Yves Divoy (55 Ernad Sabotic), Manuel Cardoni, Claude Kurtz (63 Carlo Pace); Paolo Amodio, Gordon Braun. Trainer: Eric Brusco

Goals: Bleidelis (38, 50), Mikholap (40, 54, 61, 84 pen, 90 pen), Kolesnichenko (77)

ST. PATRICK'S ATHLETIC v ZIMBRU CHIŞINĂU 0-5 (0-3)

Richmond Park, Dublin 14.07.1999

Referee: Lucílio Cardoso Cortez Batista (POR) Att: 3,300

ST. PATRICK'S ATHLETIC: Trevor Wood; William Burke, Paul Campbell, Stephen McGuinness, Colin Hawkins; Eddie Gormley, Paul Osam (61 Shane Harte), Trevor Croly, Martin Russell (46 Marcus Hallows); Trevor Molloy, Ian Gilzean (83 Robbie Devereux). Trainer: Liam Buckley

ZIMBRU: Denis Romanenco; Constantin Kulik, Andrei Telesnenco, Sergiu Dodul (90 Sergiu Butelschi), Vadim Boreţ; Valeriu Catînsus, Ruslan Ghilazev, Igor Oprea, Boris Tropaneţ; Sergiu Epureanu, Victor Berco (77 Kiril Rîbacov). Trainer: Semion Altman

Goals: Berco (29, 41), Epureanu (35, 83), Boreţ (70)

ZIMBRU CHIŞINĂU v ST. PATRICK'S ATHLETIC 5-0 (3-0)

Republican, Chişinău 21.07.1999

Referee: Giorgos Borovilos (GRE) Attendance: 4,000

ZIMBRU: Denis Romanenco; Constantin Kulik, Andrei Telesnenco, Sergiu Dodul, Boris Tropaneţ (72 Sergiu Butelschi); Valeriu Catînsus, Ruslan Ghilazev, Igor Oprea, Sergiu Epureanu (82 Vladislav Gavriliuc), Vadim Boreţ; Victor Berco (57 Iuri Miterev). Trainer: Semion Altman

ST. PATRICK'S ATHLETIC: Trevor Wood; Stephen McGuinness, Martin Russell (46 Paul Osam), Colin Hawkins, Thomas Morgan; Desmond Byrne (46 Paul Campbell), Eddie Gormley, Shane Harte, Robbie Devereux, Trevor Croly; Trevor Molloy. Trainer: Liam Buckley

Goals: Tropaneţ (22, 40), Boreţ (30, 75), Oprea (85 pen)

ZALGIRIS VILNIUS v TSEMENT ARARAT 2-0 (1-0)

Zalgiris, Vilnius 14.07.1999

Referee: Sten Johanzon (SWE) Attendance: 1,000

ZALGIRIS: Audrius Dilys; Andrejus Sorokinas, Nerijus Radzius (68 Zydrunas Grudzinskas), Vladimiras Buzmakovas, Sergejus Novikovas; Igoris Stesko, Andrius Joksas (78 Giedrius Barevicius), Arturas Stesko; Robertas Poskus, Dainius Saulenas (70 Rolandas Karcemarskas), Nerijus Vasiliauskas. Trainer: Kestutis Latoza

TSEMENT: Ashot Dadamyan; Aram Ayrapetyan, Karen Simonyan, Tigran Hovhannisyan (46 Norik Hokhoyan), Araik Voskanyan; Rafik Nazaryan, Haik Harutyunyan, Romik Khachatryan, Artak Minasyan (66 Eghish Melikyan), Karen Asatryan; Ara Akopyan (55 Hayk Akopyan). Trainer: Varujan Sukiasyan

Goals: I. Stesko (45), A. Stesko (87)

TSEMENT ARARAT v ZALGIRIS VILNIUS 0-3 (0-2)

Tsement, Ararat 21.07.1999

Referee: Ihor Horozhankin (UKR) Attendance: 504

TSEMENT: Armen Avagyan; Aram Ayrapetyan, Karen Simonyan, Araik Voskanyan (36 Vahan Arzumanyan); Rafik Nazaryan, Razmik Grigoryan, Romik Khachatryan (32 Karen Asatryan), Artak Minasyan (56 Norik Hokhoyan), Aram Akopyan; Ara Hakobyan, Hayk Akopyan. Trainer: Varujan Sukiasyan

ZALGIRIS: Audrius Dilys; Andrejus Sorokinas, Nerijus Radzius, Zydrunas Grudzinskas, Andrius Joksas (72 Andrius Puotkalis), Vladimiras Buzmakovas, Sergejus Novikovas; Igoris Stesko, Arturas Stesko; Robertas Poskus (68 Giedrius Barevicius), Nerijus Vasiliaukas (77 Egidijus Juska). Trainer: Kestutis Latoza

Goals: Novikovas (7), Joksas (30), Vasiliaukas (65)

SECOND QUALIFYING ROUND

SK RAPID WIEN v VALLETTA FC 3-0 (0-0)

Gerhard-Hanappi, Wien 28.07.1999

Referee: Miroslav Vitkovic (CRO) Attendance: 14,500

RAPID: Ladislav Maier; Oliver Freund, Günter Schießwald, Peter Schöttel, Jens Dowe; Dejan Savicević, Andreas Lagonikakis (68 Marek Penksa), Michael Hatz (46 Otto Szabo), Arnold Wetl; René Wagner (81 Angelo Vier), Gerd Wimmer. Trainer: Heribert Weber

VALLETTA FC: Reginald Cini; Stefan Giglio, Jeffrey Chetcuti, Sinisa Radak, Darren Debono; John Buttigieg (25 Kristian Laferla), Gilbert Agius, Nicky Saliba (88 Jeremy Agius), Nenad Veselji (70 Joe Camilleri), Alexander Ivanov; Daniel Thewma. Trainer: Krasimir Manolov

Goals: Dowe (54), Savićević (74), Penksa (86)

VALLETTA FC v SK RAPID WIEN 0-2 (0-0)

National, Ta' Qali 4.08.1999

Referee: Orhan Erdemir (TUR) Attendance: 1,525

VALLETTA FC: Reginald Cini (71 Sean Sullivan); Stefan Giglio (78 Darren Debono), Jeffrey Chetcuti, Edward Azzopardi, Sinisa Radak; Gilbert Agius, Nicky Saliba, Nenad Veselji, Joe Camilleri; Alexander Ivanov (41 Kristian Laferla), Daniel Thewma. Trainer: Krasimir Manolov

RAPID: Ladislav Maier; Gerd Wimmer, Günter Schießwald, Peter Schöttel, Michael Hatz; Andreas Heraf (65 Arnold Wetl,), Oliver Freund (80 Thomas Zingler), Jens Dowe, Andreas Lagonikakis; René Wagner, Marek Penksa (73 Florian Schwarz). Trainer: Heribert Weber

Sent off: Azzopardi (48)

Goals: Dowe (71), Lagonikasis (88)

ANORTHOSIS FAMAGUSTA v SLOVAN BRATISLAVA 2-1 (1-0)

Antonis Papadopoulos, Larnaca 28.07.1999

Referee: Claus Bo Larsen (DEN) Attendance: 4,711

ANORTHOSIS: Nikos Panagiotou; Vasos Melanarkitis, Stavros Foukaris, Loukas Louka; Zaharias Haralampous (84 Zoran Cirić), Sasa Jovanovic (67 Hristos Kotsonis), Zoran Milinkovic, Marios Neofytou (61 Giorgos Iosifides), Panagotis Egkomitis; Giannakis Okas, Mike Obiku.
Trainer: Dušan Mitosević

SLOVAN: Miroslav König; Ladislav Pecko, Stanislav Varga, Milan Timko, Zsolt Hornyak; Norbert Hrncar, Robert Tomaschek, Roman Skrtel, Marek Fabula; Tibor Jancula (88 Miroslav Kriss), Jozef Majoros (75 Lubomir Meszaros).
Trainer: Stanislav Griga

Goals: Obiku (26, 88 pen), Hrncar (51)

SLOVAN BRATISLAVA v ANORTHOSIS FAMAGUSTA 1-1 (0-0)

Tehelné pole, Bratislava 4.08.1999

Referee: Franck De Bleeckere (BEL) Attendance: 10,770

SLOVAN: Miroslav König; Ladislav Pecko, Stanislav Varga, Milan Timko, Milos Sobona; Norbert Hrncar, Robert Tomaschek, Roman Skrtel (46 Marek Fabula), Miroslav Kriss (46 Pavol Sedlák); Tibor Jancula, Jozef Majoros (74 Lubomir Meszaros). Trainer: Stanislav Griga

ANORTHOSIS: Nikos Panagiotou; Vasos Melanarkitis, Loukas Louka, Stavros Foukaris, Zaharias Haralampous (48 Hristos Kotsonis); Panagotis Egkomitis, Zoran Milinkovic, Sasa Jovanovic, Panikos Pounas; Giannakis Okas (77 Giorgos Iosifides), Mike Obiku (84 Andreas Melanarkitis).
Trainer: Dušan Mitosević

Sent off: Milinkovic (27)

Goals: Obiku (58), Timko (60)

PARTIZAN BEOGRAD v NK RIJEKA 3-1 (2-0)

Partizan, Beograd 28.07.1999

Referee: Alain Hamer (LUX) Attendance: 21,746

PARTIZAN: Nikola Damjanac; Aleksandar Stanojević, Igor Duljaj, Vuk Rasović, Mladen Krstajić (90 Nenad Misković); Goran Trobok, Djordje Tomić, Sasa Ilić (77 Aleksandar Vuković), Vladimir Ivić (67 Ivica Ilijev); Mateja Kezman, Milorad Peković. Trainer: Miodrag Jesić

NK RIJEKA: Džoni Tafra; Mauro Tomišić, Nenad Matković, Damir Milinović, Bozidar Cacić; Goran Brajković, Admir Hasancić, Jasmin Agić, Dalibor Višković (46 Boris Pavić); Boško Balaban (70 Sérgio de Oliveira), Barnabás Sztipánovics. Trainer: Nenad Gracan

Goals: S. Ilić (10), Krstajić (22, 88), Sztipánovics (56)

NK RIJEKA v PARTIZAN BEOGRAD 0-3 (0-2)

Kantrida, Rijeka 4.08.1999

Referee: Günter Benkö (AUS) Attendance: 10,500

NK RIJEKA: Džoni Tafra; Nenad Matković (46 Josip Modrić), Damir Milinović, Bozidar Cacić, Mauro Tomišić; Goran Brajković, Admir Hasancić, Jasmin Agić (69 Damir Matulović), Dalibor Višković; Boško Balaban (80 Vedran Peteh), Barnabás Sztipánovics. Trainer: Nenad Gracan

PARTIZAN: Nikola Damjanac; Aleksandar Stanojević, Igor Duljaj (70 Branko Savić), Vuk Rasović, Mladen Krstajić; Goran Trobok, Djordje Tomić, Sasa Ilić, Vladimir Ivić; Mateja Kezman (82 Aleksander Vuković), Milorad Peković (77 Ivica Ilijev). Trainer: Miodrag Jesić

Goals: Kezman (7, 82), Ivić (19)

CSKA MOSKVA v MOLDE FK 2-0 (1-0)

Peschanoe, Moskva 28.07.1999

Referee: Manuel Enrique Mejuto González (SPA)
Attendance: 15,000

CSKA: Dmitriy Goncharov; Valeriy Minko, Evgeniy Varlamov, Maksim Bokov, Sergei Semak; Oleg Kornaukhov, Dmitriy Khomukha, Oleg Şişchin, Marek Holly (83 Andrei Tsaplin); Vladimir Kulik, Sergei Filippenkov (62 Goran Gutalj). Trainer: Oleg Dolmatov

MOLDE FK: Morten Bakke; Trond Strande (90 Petter Christian Singsaas), Trond Andersen, Jo Tessem, Knut Anders Fostervold; Odd Inge Olsen, Karl Oskar Fjørtoft, Daniel Berg Hestad, Ole Bjørn Sundgot (80 Freddy dos Santos); Andreas Lund, Thomas Mork. Trainer: Erik Brakstad

Goals: Şişchin (7), Khomukha (85)

MOLDE FK v CSKA MOSKVA 4-0 (0-0)

Nye Molde 4.08.1999

Referee: Gary Willard (ENG) Attendance: 5,203

MOLDE FK: Morten Bakke; Trond Strande (81 Freddy dos Santos), Trond Andersen, Pål Lydersen, Knut Anders Fostervold; Odd Inge Olsen (46 Magne Hoseth), Karl Oskar Fjørtoft, Daniel Berg Hestad, Jo Tessem; Andreas Lund, Thomas Mork (76 Ole Bjørn Sundgot).
Trainer: Erik Brakstad

CSKA: Dmitriy Goncharov; Valeriy Minko, Evgeniy Varlamov, Maksim Bokov, Sergei Semak; Oleg Kornaukhov, Dmitriy Khomukha (80 Goran Gutalj), Oleg Şişchin (46 Sergei Filippenkov), Igor Aksyonov; Marek Holly, Vladimir Kulik.
Trainer: Oleg Dolmatov

Sent off: Holly (55)

Goals: Tessem (47), Berg Hestad (65), Hoseth (67, 81)

LITEKS LOVECH v WIDZEW LÓDZ 4-1 (1-0)

Lovech stadion 28.07.1999

Referee: Bernd Heynemann (GER) Attendance: 3,500

LITEKS: Vitomir Vutov; Marin Petrov (62 Marjan Zivkovic), Stefan Kolev, Zlatomir Zagorcic, Said Ibraimov (46 Ivan Rusev); Nikolai Dimitrov, Ibe Johnson, Nebojsa Jelenkovic, Altin Haxhi (65 Svetlan Kondev); Alban Bushi, Svetoslav Todorov. Trainer: Alexandar Zheliazkov

WIDZEW: Slawomir Olszewski; Rafal Pawlak, Tomasz Lapinski, Daniel Bogusz (84 Maciej Terlecki), Maciej Stolarczyk; Slawomir Gula, Dariusz Gesior, Radoslaw Michalski, Tomasz Kielbowicz; Marek Citko (68 Marcin Zajac), Artur Wichniarek. Trainer: Marek Dziuba

Goals: Todorov (40, 78), Zivkovic (82 pen), Wichniarek (88 pen), Kondev (90)

WIDZEW LÓDZ v LITEX LOVECH 4-1 (1-1, 4-1) (AET)

Widzew, Lódz 4.08.1999

Referee: Stéphane Bré (FRA) Attendance: 4,800

WIDZEW: Slawomir Olszewski; Daniel Bogusz, Tomasz Lapinski, Maciej Stolarczyk, Rafal Pawlak (59 Marcin Zajac); Dariusz Gesior, Rafal Kaczmarczyk (84 Slawomir Gula), Radoslaw Michalski, Tomasz Kielbowicz; Marek Citko (57 Maciej Terlecki), Artur Wichniarek. Trainer: Marek Dziuba

LITEKS: Vitomir Vutov; Jivko Jelev, Zlatomir Zagorcic, Stefan Kolev, Nikolai Dimitrov (66 Radostin Kishishev, 104 Svetlan Kondev); Marjan Zivkovic, Ibe Johnson, Nebojsa Jelenkovic, Altin Haxhi; Svetoslav Todorov (66 Louis Motta), Alban Bushi.
Trainer: Alexandar Zheliazkov

Sent off: Bogusz (96)

Goals: Gesior (14), Todorov (30), Wichniarek (52, 60), Michalski (75)

Penalties: 1-0 Michalski, 1-1 Kolev, 2-1 Wichniarek, 2-2 Zagorcic, Gesior (miss), Zivkovic (miss), Stolarczyk (miss), Kondev (miss), 3-2 Terlecki, Bushi (miss)

FC HAKA VALKEAKOSKI v GLASGOW RANGERS FC 1-4 (0-3)

Tehtaakenttä, Valkeakoski 28.07.1999

Referee: Vladimir Hrinak (SVK) Attendance: 3,341

HAKA: Andras Vilnrotter; Tero Penttilä, Lasse Karjalainen, Jouni Räsänen, Oleg Ivanov (57 Tommi Torkkeli); Janne Hyökyvaara (83 Jarkko Okkonen), Martin Reynders, Valeriy Popovich, Janne Savolainen; David Wilson, Jari Niemi (73 Kai Nyyssönen). Trainer: Keith Armstrong

RANGERS: Stefan Klos; Dariusz Adamczuk, Craig Moore, Lorenzo Amoruso, Arthur Numan; Barry Ferguson, Claudio Reyna (34 Barry Nicholson), Giovanni van Bronckhorst (69 Jörg Albertz), Neil McCann; Michael Mols, Rodney Wallace (69 Jonatan Johansson). Trainer: Dick Advocaat

Goals: Amoruso (18), Mols (27, 42), Niemi (51), Johansson (86)

GLASGOW RANGERS FC v FC HAKA VALKEAKOSKI 3-0 (2-0)

Ibrox, Glasgow 4.08.1999

Referee: Lubomir Pucek (CZE) Attendance: 46,443

RANGERS: Stefan Klos; Dariusz Adamczuk, Craig Moore, Lorenzo Amoruso, Arthur Numan (40 Tony Vidmar); Barry Ferguson (71 Barry Nicholson), Jonatan Johansson, Giovanni van Bronckhorst, Jörg Albertz; Michael Mols (46 Gabriel Omar Amato), Rodney Wallace. Trainer: Dick Advocaat

HAKA: Andras Vilnrotter; Tero Penttilä, Lasse Karjalainen, Jouni Räsänen (61 Janne Savolainen), Oleg Ivanov (55 Kai Nyyssönen); Martin Reynders, Valeriy Popovich, Jukka Rantala, David Wilson; Jarkko Okkonen, Jari Niemi (71 Tommi Torkkeli). Trainer: Keith Armstrong

Goals: Wallace (15), Johansson (28), Amato (66)

DINAMO TBILISI v ZIMBRU CHIŞINĂU 2-1 (0-0)

Boris Paichadze, Tbilisi 28.07.1999

Referee: Dietmar Drabek (AUS) Attendance: 5,000

DINAMO: Danny D'Hondt; David Chichveishvili, Givi Didava, Vaso Gigiadze, Giorgi Shashiashvili; Archil Sakhvadze (72 Levan Khomeriki), Giorgi Kiknadze, Rati Aleksidze, Tengiz Sichinava; Mikhail Ashvetia, Andre de Sousa (72 Klimenti Tsitaishvili). Trainer: Johan Boskamp

ZIMBRU: Denis Romanenco; Constantin Kulik, Andrei Telesnenco, Sergiu Dodul, Vadim Boreţ; Valeriu Catînsus, Ruslan Ghilazev, Igor Oprea, Sergiu Epureanu (85 Kiril Rîbacov), Boris Tropaneţ (74 Sergiu Butelschi); Victor Berco. Trainer: Semion Altman

Goals: Berco (67), Tsitaishvili (81), Khomeriki (90)

ZIMBRU CHIŞINĂU v DINAMO TBILISI 2-0 (1-0)

Stadionul Speia 4.08.1999

Referee: Luc Huyghe (BEL) Attendance: 10,000

ZIMBRU: Denis Romanenco; Sergiu Dodul (46 Vladislav Robu), Constantin Kulik, Vadim Boreţ, Andrei Telesnenco; Valeriu Catînsus, Ruslan Ghilazev, Igor Oprea, Sergiu Epureanu; Boris Tropaneţ, Victor Berco (88 Kiril Rîbacov). Trainer: Semion Altman

DINAMO: Danny D'Hondt; Otar Khizaneishvili, David Chichveishvili, Givi Didava, Giorgi Kiknadze; Rati Aleksidze, Mikhail Ashvetiya (69 Klimenti Tsitaishvili), Tengiz Sichinava, Levan Khomeriki; Vaso Gigiadze (52 Georgi Shengelia), Andre de Sousa. Trainer: Johan Boskamp

Goals: Dodul (23), Epureanu (90)

DNEPR-TRANSHASH MOGILEV v AIK SOLNA 0-1 (0-0)

Spartak, Mogilev 28.07.1999

Referee: Alan Snoddy (NIR) Attendance: 4,300

DNEPR: Sergei Astapchik; Vladimir Shuneiko, Vladimir Klimovich, Alexandr Baranov; Dmitriy Kalachev (89 Kiril Bykov), Yuri Lukashov, Yaroslav Sverdlov, Dmitriy Likhtarovich, Vitaliy Lanko; Dmirtiy Ogorodnik (73 Evgeniy Kozlov), Vladimir Solodukhin (71 Evgeniy Kapov). Trainer: Valeriy Streltsov

AIK: Mattias Asper; Michael Brundin, Tomas Gustafsson, Mike Kjølø, Pontus Kåmark; Krister Nordin (82 David Ljung), Ola Andersson (64 Karl Corneliusson), Thomas Lagerlöf; Nebojsa Novakovic, Daniel Tjernström, Martin Åslund. Trainer: Stuart Baxter

Goal: Tjernström (89)

AIK SOLNA v DNEPR-TRANSMASH MOGILEV 2-0 (0-0)

Råsunda, Solna 4.08.1999

Referee: Stuart Dougal (SCO) Attendance: 11,857

AIK: Mattias Asper; Karl Corneliusson (75 Ola Andersson), Michael Brundin, Tomas Gustafsson, Mike Kjølø, Pontus Kåmark; Krister Nordin, Daniel Tjernström, Thomas Lagerlöf; Nebojsa Novakovic (85 David Ljung), Martin Åslund (46 Christer Mattiasson). Trainer: Stuart Baxter

DNEPR: Sergei Astapchik; Vladimir Shuneiko, Vladimir Klimovich, Alexandr Baranov; Dmitriy Kalachev, Ihor Chumachenko, Yuri Lukashov, Yaroslav Sverdlov, Dmitriy Likhtarovich, Vitaliy Lanko (75 Evgeniy Kozlov); Vladimir Solodukhin (64 Dmitriy Ogorodnik). Trainer: Valeriy Streltsov

Goals: Corneliusson (55), Gustafsson (77)

SLOGA JUGOMAGNAT SKOPJE v BRØNDBY IF 0-1 (0-1)

Cair, Skopje 28.07.1999

Referee: Jack van Hulten (HOL) Attendance: 5,000

SLOGA: Gogo Jovcev; Esad Colaković, Saso Zdravevski, Arsim Abazi, Masar Omeragić; Nedzmedin Memedi, Feim Beganović (75 Bruno Presilski), Nebi Mustafi (62 Saso Blazevski), Refik Arif, Ardzend Beciri; Zoran Miserdovski (62 Gasi Fetai). Trainer: Gjore Jovanovski

BRØNDBY: Mogens Krogh; Per Lundgren Nielsen, Vragel da Silva, Martin Smith, Søren Colding; Ole Bjur, Allan Ravn (77 Mads Olsen), Kim Daugaard, Mikkel Jensen; Bent Christensen (62 Peter Madsen), Ruben Bagger (81 Søren Krogh). Trainer: Tom Køhlert

Goal: Daugaard (15)

BRØNDBY IF v SLOGA JUGOMAGNAT SKOPJE 1-0 (1-0)

Brøndby Stadion, København 4.08.1999

Referee: Vasily Melnichuk (UKR) Attendance: 8,538

BRØNDBY: Mogens Krogh; Per Lundgren Nielsen, Vragel da Silva, Martin Smith, Søren Colding; Ole Bjur, Allan Ravn, Kim Daugaard, Mikkel Jensen (85 Mads Olsen); Ruben Bagger (75 Thomas Lindrup), Peter Madsen (80 Bent Christensen). Trainer: Tom Køhlert

SLOGA: Gogo Jovcev; Esad Colaković, Saso Zdravevski, Arsim Abazi, Masar Omeragić, Zoran Miserdovski, Nedzmedin Memedi, Feim Beganović (70 Bruno Presilski), Nebi Mustafi (60 Saso Blazevski), Refik Arif (62 Gasi Fetai), Ardzend Beciri. Trainer: Gjore Jovanovski

Goal: Daugaard (3 pen)

RAPID BUCUREŞTI v SKONTO RIGA 3-3 (1-2)

Rapid, Bucureşti 28.07.1999

Referee: Oguz Sarvan (TUR) Attendance: 4,150

RAPID: Bogdan Lobonţ; Nicolae Stanciu, Mircea Rednic, Adrian Iencsi; Cristian Bolohan (46 Dorel Mutică), Dănuţ Lupu, Claudiu Narcis Răducan, Marius Măldărăşanu, Constantin Schumacher; Constantin Barbu (63 Mihai Valentin Dăscălescu), Bogdan Andone (34 Zeno Bundea). Trainer: Mircea Lucescu

SKONTO: Alexander Kolinko; Mikhail Zemlinsky, Andreyus Tereskinas (75 Zurab Mentesashvili), Yury Laizans; Oleg Blagonadezhdin, Alexander Rekhviashvili, Imants Bleidelis, Andrei Rubins, Vitaly Astafyev, David Chaladze (56 Levan Silagadze); Mikhail Mikholap. Trainer: Alexander Starkov

Goals: Chaladze (4, 33), Barbu (14), Schumacher (53), Astafyev (61), Mutică (73)

SKONTO RIGA v RAPID BUCUREŞTI 2-1 (0-1)

Daugava, Riga 4.08.1999

Referee: Kenneth Clark (SCO) Attendance: 2,850

SKONTO: Alexander Kolinko; Levan Silagadze, Mikhail Zemlinsky, Yury Laizans; Oleg Blagonadezhdin (69 Zurab Menteshashvili), Alexander Rekhviashvili, Imants Bleidelis, Andrei Rubins, Vitaly Astafyev; Mikhail Mikholap, David Chaladze (78 Andreyus Tereskinas). Trainer: Alexander Starkov

RAPID: Bogdan Lobonţ; Nicolae Stanciu, Mircea Rednic, Adrian Iencsi; Ioan Sabău (76 Cristian Bolohan), Claudiu Răducan, Marius Măldărăşanu (78 Constantin Schumacher), Dorel Mutică; Constantin Barbu, Dănuţ Lupu, Sergiu Radu. Trainer: Mircea Lucescu

Sent off: Răducan (81)

Goals: Răducan (33), Laizans (77), Rubins (87)

BEŞIKTAŞ JK ISTANBUL v HAPOEL HAIFA 1-1 (0-0)

BJK Inönü, Istanbul 28.07.1999

Referee: Paul Anthony Durkin (ENG) Attendance: 12,000

BEŞIKTAŞ: Ike Shorunmu; Ali Eren Beserler (41 Jamal Sellami), Oliver Schäfer, Tayfur Havutçu, Rahim Zafer, Mutlu Topçu; Mehmet Özdilek (72 Attila Birlik), Ayhan Akman, Yasin Sülün; Nihat Kahveci (61 Ahmet Dursun), Ertugrul Saglam. Trainer: Karlheinz Feldkamp

HAPOEL: Dudu Auat; Alon Halfon, Offer Talker, Ran Ben Shimon, Amir Shelach; Goran Milanko (87 Meir Ben-Margi), Dmitri Ulianov, Giovanni Rosso, David Amsalem, Oren Zitoni; Nir Sivilia (60 Amir Torjman). Trainer: Eli Gutman

Goals: Rosso (76), Ayhan (90)

HAPOEL HAIFA v BEŞIKTAŞ JK ISTANBUL 0-0

Kiriat Eliezer, Haifa 4.08.1999

Referee: Lutz-Michael Fröhlich (GER) Attendance: 12,000

HAPOEL: Dudu Auat; Alon Halfon, Offer Talker, Ran Ben Shimon, Amir Shelach; Dmitri Ulianov, Giovanni Rosso, Oren Zitoni (75 Meir Ben-Margi), David Amsalem, Goran Milanko; Nir Sivilia (58 Amir Torjman, 89 Oren Nissim). Trainer: Eli Gutman

BEŞIKTAŞ: Ike Shorunmu; Tayfur Havutçu, Ali Eren Beserler (46 Ertugrul Saglam), Rahim Zafer, Mutlu Topçu (70 Ersen Martin); Attila Birlik, Ayhan Akman, Jamal Sellami, Yasin Sülün; Ahmet Dursun, Nihat Kahveci (46 Mehmet Özdilek). Trainer: Karlheinz Feldkamp

FC DYNAMO KYIV v ZALGIRIS VILNIUS 2-0 (1-0)

Olympyiskyi, Kyiv 28.07.1999

Referee: Graham Poll (ENG) Attendance: 14,600

DYNAMO: Olexandr Shovkovskyi; Olexandr Borysovych Holovko, Vladislav Vashchuk, Yuri Dmitrulin, Kakhi Kaladze; Aleksei Gerasimenko, Andriy Gusin, Artem Yashkin, Serhiy Kormiltsev (56 Serhiy Serebryannikov); Serhiy Rebrov, Maxim Shatskykh. Trainer: Valeriy Lobanovskiy

ZALGIRIS: Audrius Dilys; Andrejus Sorokinas, Nerijus Radzius (82 Egidijus Juska), Zydrunas Grudzinskas, Andrius Joksas (76 Dainius Saulenas), Vladimiras Buzmakovas, Sergejus Novikovas; Igoris Stesko, Arturas Stesko; Robertas Poskus, Nerijus Vasiliaukas (68 Giedrius Barevicius). Trainer: Kestutis Latoza

Goals: Shatskykh (38, 78)

ZALGIRIS VILNIUS v FC DYNAMO KYIV 0-1 (0-1)

Zalgiris, Vilnius 4.08.1999

Referee: Georg Dardenne (GER) Attendance: 4,000

ZALGIRIS: Audrius Dilys; Andrejus Sorokinas, Darius Sanajevas, Andrius Joksas (46 Dainius Saulenas), Vladimiras Buzmakovas, Sergejus Novikovas; Igoris Stesko, Arturas Stesko; Arturas Sobolis, Robertas Poskus, Nerijus Vasiliaukas (77 Andrius Puotkalis). Trainer: Kestutis Latoza

DYNAMO: Olexandr Shovkovskyi; Olexandr Kiryukhin (59 Serhiy Fedorov), Olexandr Borysovych Holovko, Vladislav Vashchuk, Yuri Dmitrulin, Kakhi Kaladze; Aleksei Gerasimenko, Andriy Gusin, Artem Yashkin (79 Serhiy Kormiltsev); Serhiy Rebrov, Maxim Shatskykh (66 Serhiy Serebryannikov). Trainer: Valeriy Lobanovskiy

Goal: Rebrov (35)

ÍBV-ÍTHRÓTTAFÉLAG VESTMANNAEYJAR v MTK BUDAPEST 0-2 (0-1)

Hásteinsvöllur, Vestmannaeyjar 28.07.1999

Referee: Terje Hauge (NOR) Attendance: 827

ÍBV: Birkir Kristinsson; Ívar Ingimarsson, Ívar Bjarklind, Hjalti Jóhannesson, Goran Aleksic; Zoran Miljkovic, Hlynur Stefánsson, Ingi Sigurdsson, Allan Mørkøre; Baldur Bragason, Steingrímur Jóhannesson (60 Gudni Helgason). Trainer: Bjarni Jóhansson

MTK: Gábor Babos; Csaba Fehér, Attila Kuttor, Csaba Madar, Ádám Komlósi; Károly Erös (46 Iván Balaskó), Béla Illés (65 Sándor Preisinger), Tamás Szamosi, Krisztián Kenesei (75 Ákos Buzsáky); Nicolae Ilea, Gábor Halmai. Trainer: Henk ten Cate

Goals: Halmai (18), Preisinger (72)

MTK BUDAPEST v ÍBV-ÍTHRÓTTAFÉLAG VESTMANNAEYJAR 3-1 (3-0)

Hungária úti, Budapest 4.08.1999

Referee: Miroslav Radoman (YUG) Attendance: 2,000

MTK: Gábor Babos; Csaba Fehér (36 Iván Balaskó), Attila Kuttor, Csaba Madar, Ádám Komlósi; Károly Erös, Béla Illés, Tamás Szamosi, Krisztián Kenesei; Nicolae Ilea (63 Sándor Preisinger), Gábor Halmai (75 Norbert Elek). Trainer: Henk ten Cate

ÍBV: Birkir Kristinsson; Ívar Ingimarsson (58 Kjartan Antonsson), Ívar Bjarklind, Hjalti Jóhannesson, Goran Aleksic; Zoran Miljkovic, Hlynur Stefánsson, Steingrímur Jóhannesson (68 Jóhann Möller), Allan Mørkøre; Gudni Helgason, Baldur Bragason (74 Bjarni Vidarsson). Trainer: Bjarni Jóhansson

Goals: Ilea (4), Kuttor (25), Illés (41), Bjarklind (90)

NK MARIBOR v KRC GENK 5-1 (1-1)

Ljudski vrt, Maribor 28.07.1999

Referee: Fiorenzo Treossi (ITA) Attendance: 3,958

NK MARIBOR: Marko Simeunović; Marinko Sarkezi, Marinko Galić, Geri Çipi; Gregor Zidan (90 Martin Pregelj), Dejan Djuranović, Stipe Balajić, Simon Seslar, Amir Karić (81 Muamer Vugdalić); Kliton Bozgo, Dalibor Filipović (53 Ante Simundza). Trainer: Bojan Prasnikar

KRC GENK: István Brockhauser; Daniel Kimoni, Domenico Olivieri, Chris van Geem (81 Bjarni Gudjónsson), Jesper Jansson; Wilfried Delbroek, Thórdur Gudjónsson (65 Ilir Caushllari), Besnik Hasi, Marc Hendrickx; Branko Strupar, Zoran Ban (74 Ferenc Horváth). Trainer: Jos Heyligen

Goals: Balajić (24), Strupar (37), Galić (62), Karić (69 pen), Simundza (76), Djuranović (90)

KRC GENK v NK MARIBOR 3-0 (1-0)

Sclessin, Liège 4.08.1999

Referee: Juan Ansuategui Roca (SPA) Attendance: 6,779

KRC GENK: István Brockhauser; Marc Hendrickx (60 Ferenc Horváth), Daniel Kimoni, Domenico Olivieri, Chris van Geem (46 Ngoy N'Sumbu); Benjamin Rogério de Oliveira (79 Fabio Pereira), Wilfried Delbroek, Besnik Hasi; Souleymane Oulare, Branko Strupar, Thórdur Gudjónsson. Trainer: Jos Heyligen

NK MARIBOR: Marko Simeunović; Simon Seslar (53 Muamer Vugdalić), Gregor Zidan, Amir Karić, Ante Simundza (81 Martin Pregelj); Geri Çipi, Stipe Balajić (65 Dalibor Filipović), Dejan Djuranović, Marinko Galić; Kliton Bozgo, Marinko Sarkezi. Trainer: Bojan Prasnikar

Sent off: Karic (67), Olivieri (90)

Goals: Th. Gudjónsson (45, 61), Horváth (64)

THIRD QUALIFYING ROUND

OLYMPIQUE LYON v NK MARIBOR 0-1 (0-0)

Stade Gerland, Lyon 11.08.1999

Referee: Sergei Khussainov (RUS) Attendance: 25,365

OLYMPIQUE: Grégory Coupet; Jacek Bak, Hubert Fournier, Jean-Christophe Devaux; Steed Malbranque, Philippe Violeau, Vikash Dhorasoo, David Linarès (68 Frédéric Kanouté); Sonny Anderson, Alain Caveglia, Tony Vairelles. Trainer: Bernard Lacombe

NK MARIBOR: Marko Simeunović; Marinko Sarkezi, Marinko Galić, Muamer Vugdalić; Gregor Zidan, Stipe Balajić (80 Martin Pregelj), Dejan Djuranović, Simon Seslar, Suad Fileković; Ante Simundza (66 Dalibor Filipović), Kliton Bozgo. Trainer: Bojan Prasnikar

Goal: Filipović (89)

NK MARIBOR v OLYMPIQUE LYON 2-0 (2-0)

Ljudski vrt, Maribor 25.08.1999

Referee: Oguz Sarvan (TUR) Attendance: 7,021

NK MARIBOR: Marko Simeunović; Geri Çipi, Marinko Galić, Marinko Sarkezi; Gregor Zidan, Muamer Vugdalić (73 Suad Fileković), Dejan Djuranović, Simon Seslar, Stipe Balajić (50 Amir Karić); Ante Simundza (89 Dalibor Filipović), Kliton Bozgo. Trainer: Bojan Prasnikar

OLYMPIQUE: Grégory Coupet; Patrice Carteron, Hubert Fournier, Jacek Bak, Serge Blanc (51 Christophe Delmotte); Philippe Violeau, Steed Malbranque (56 Frédéric Kanouté), Vikash Dhorasoo; Tony Vairelles, Alain Caveglia (35 Pierre Laigle), Sonny Anderson.

Goals: Simundza (24), Balajić (45)

ZIMBRU CHIŞINĂU v PSV EINDHOVEN 0-0

Speia 11.08.1999

Referee: Giorgos Bikas (GRE) Attendance: 8,500

ZIMBRU: Denis Romanenco; Sergiu Dodul (73 Iuri Miterev), Constantin Kulik, Andrei Telesnenco, Valeriu Catînsus; Vadim Boreţ, Ruslan Ghilazev, Igor Oprea (88 Oleg Fistican), Sergiu Epureanu, Boris Tropaneţ (81 Vladislav Robu); Victor Berco. Trainer: Semion Altman

PSV: Ronald Waterreus; André Ooijer, Jürgen Dirkx, Ernest Faber, Jan Heintze; Ovidiu Stîngă, Johann Vogel (85 Björn van der Doelen), Dmitriy Khokhlov; Arnold Bruggink (81 Wilfred Bouma), Luc Nilis (87 Dennis Rommedahl), Ruud van Nistelrooy. Trainer: Eric Gerets

PARTIZAN BEOGRAD v SPARTAK MOSKVA 1-3 (0-1)

Partizan, Beograd 25.08.1999

Referee: Antonio Jesus López Nieto (SPA) Att: 18216

PARTIZAN: Nikola Damjanac; Vuk Rasović, Igor Duljaj, Mladen Krstajić, Aleksandar Stanojević; Goran Trobok, Vladimir Ivić (65 Marjan Gerasimovski), Sasa Ilić, Djordje Tomić; Mateja Kezman, Milorad Peković (71 Ivica Iliev). Trainer: Miodrag Jesić

SPARTAK: Aleksandr Filimonov; Yuri Kovtun, Dmitriy Khlestov, Evgeniy Bushmanov, Dmytro Parfyonov; Vasiliy Baranov, Viktor Bulatov, Yegor Titov, Andrei Tikhonov (23 Artyom Bezrodnyi); Aleksandr Shirko (86 Ilya Tsymbalar), Luís ROBSON Pereira. Trainer: Oleg Romantsev

Goals: Shirko (19, 46), Kezman (72), Titov (83 pen)

PSV EINDHOVEN v ZIMBRU CHIŞINĂU 2-0 (0-0)

Philips, Eindhoven 25.08.1999

Referee: Günter Benkö (AUS) Attendance: 20,000

PSV: Ronald Waterreus; André Ooijer, Jan Heintze, Jürgen Dirkx, Ernest Faber; Ovidiu Stîngă (46 Dennis Rommedahl), Mark van Bommel, Johann Vogel, Wilfred Bouma (67 Joonas Kolkka); Ruud van Nistelrooy, Arnold Bruggink (56 Luc Nilis). Trainer: Eric Gerets

ZIMBRU: Denis Romanenco; Sergiu Dodul (68 Vladislav Robu), Vadim Boreţ, Andrei Telesnenco, Valeriu Catînsus, Igor Oprea; Constantin Kulik, Ruslan Ghilazev (86 Kiril Rîbacov), Boris Tropaneţ, Sergiu Epureanu; Victor Berco (46 Iurie Miterev). Trainer: Semion Altman

Goals: Nilis (80), Ooijer (88)

CHELSEA FC LONDON v SKONTO RIGA 3-0 (0-0)

Stamford Bridge, London 11.08.1999

Referee: Urs Meier (SWI) Attendance: 22,043

CHELSEA: Ed de Goey; Albert Ferrer, Frank Leboeuf, Marcel Desailly, Graeme Le Saux; Dan Petrescu (77 Bjarne Goldbæk), Didier Deschamps (65 Célestine Babayaro), Gustavo Poyet, Dennis Wise; Gianfranco Zola (65 Tore André Flo), Chris Sutton. Manager: Gianluca Vialli

SKONTO: Alexander Kolinko; Yury Laizans, Mikhail Zemlinsky, Levan Silagadze, Andreyus Tereskinas; Imants Bleidelis, Alexander Rekhviashvili, Vitaly Astafyev, Andrei Rubins; Mikhail Mikholap (76 Zurab Menteshashvili), David Chaladze (40 Oleg Blagonadezhdin). Trainer: Alexander Starkov

Sent off: Tereskinas (33)

Goals: Babayaro (76), Poyet (77), Sutton (84)

SPARTAK MOSKVA v PARTIZAN BEOGRAD 2-0 (1-0)

Luzhniki, Moskva 11.08.1999

Referee: Bernd Heynemann (GER) Attendance: 45,000

SPARTAK: Aleksandr Filimonov; Yuri Kovtun, Dmitriy Khlestov, Evgeniy Bushmanov, Viktor Bulatov; Dmytro Parfyonov, Valeriy Kechinov, Luís ROBSON Pereira, Andrei Tikhonov; Yegor Titov, Aleksandr Shirko. Trainer: Oleg Romantsev

PARTIZAN: Nikola Damjanac; Vuk Rasović, Mladen Krstajić, Igor Duljaj, Aleksandar Stanojević (88 Zoltan Sabo); Goran Trobok (65 Marjan Gerasimovski), Vladimir Ivić (71 Ivica Ilijev), Sasa Ilić, Djordje Tomić; Mateja Kezman, Milorad Peković. Trainer: Miodrag Jesić

Goals: Shirko (39), Tikhonov (73)

SKONTO RIGA v CHELSEA FC LONDON 0-0

Daugava, Riga 25.08.1999

Referee: Gilles Veissière (FRA) Attendance: 5,600

SKONTO: Alexander Kolinko; Levan Silagadze, Mikhail Zemlinsky, Yury Laizans (87 Vladimir Kolesnichenko); Alexander Rekhviashvili, Imants Bleidelis (75 Zurab Menteshashvili), Andrei Rubins, Vitaly Astafyev; Oleg Blagonadezhdin, Mikhail Mikholap, David Chaladze (63 Vladimir Babichev). Trainer: Alexander Starkov

CHELSEA: Ed de Goey (79 Carlo Cudicini); Dan Petrescu, Célestine Babayaro, Jes Høgh, Marcel Desailly; Gustavo Poyet (64 Mark Nicholls), Dennis Wise, Bjarne Goldbæk (83 John Harley); Tore André Flo, Jody Morris, Mikael Forssell. Manager: Gianluca Vialli

SK RAPID WIEN v GALATASARAY ISTANBUL 0-3 (0-2)

Gerhard-Hanappi, Wien 11.08.1999

Referee: Kim Milton Nielsen (DEN) Attendance: 30,200

RAPID: Ladislav Maier; Gerd Wimmer, Günter Schießwald, Peter Schöttel, Michael Hatz (75 Arnold Wetl); Thomas Zingler (46 Otto Szabo), Oliver Freund, Jens Dowe, Andreas Lagonikakis; Marek Penksa, René Wagner. Trainer: Heribert Weber

GALATASARAY: Cláudio Taffarel; Fatih Akyel, Carlos Capone, Gheorghe Popescu, Hakan Ünsal; Okan Buruk (75 Ergün Pembe), Ümit Davala, Suat Kaya, Emre Belözoglu (82 Ahmet Yildirim); Gheorghe Hagi, Hakan Şükür (79 Arif Erdem). Trainer: Fatih Terim

Goals: Hakan Ünsal (34), Fatih (38), Hagi (90)

GALATASARAY ISTANBUL v SK RAPID WIEN 1-0 (0-0)

Ali Sami Yen, Istanbul 25.08.1999

Referee: Pierluigi Collina (ITA) Attendance: 15,000

GALATASARAY: Cláudio Taffarel; Fatih Akyel, Carlos Capone, Gheorghe Popescu, Hakan Ünsal; Ümit Davala (63 Tugay Kerimoğlu), Suat Kaya, Emre Belözoglu (79 Saffet Akyüz), Gheorghe Hagi; Okan Buruk, Hakan Şükür (29 Arif Erdem). Trainer: Fatih Terim

RAPID: Ladislav Maier; Gerd Wimmer, Günter Schießwald, Thomas Zingler, Michael Hatz (71 Peter Schöttel,); Marek Penksa, Andreas Heraf (46 Dejan Savicević), Jens Dowe, Arnold Wetl (27 Oliver Freund); Florian Schwarz, Andreas Lagonikakis. Trainer: Heribert Weber

Sent off: Thomas Zingler (90)

Goal: Okan Buruk (52)

FIORENTINA FIRENZE v WIDZEW LÓDZ 3-1 (1-0)

Artemio Franchi, Firenze 11.08.1999

Referee: David Elleray (ENG) Attendance: 30,601

FIORENTINA: Francesco Toldo; Tomáš Repka, Pasquale Padalino, Daniele Adani, Angelo di Livio (52 Mauro Bressan); Sandro Cois, Rui Costa, Jörg Heinrich; Enrico Chiesa, Gabriel Batistuta (7 Abel Balbo), Predrag Mijatović. Trainer: Giovanni Trapattoni

WIDZEW: Slawomir Olszewski; Rafal Pawlak, Radoslaw Michalski, Tomasz Lapinski, Maciej Stolarczyk; Maciej Terlecki (60 Slawomir Gula), Dariusz Gesior, Tomasz Kielbowicz (87 Dariusz Dudek), Rafal Kaczmarczyk; Marek Citko (70 Marcin Zajac), Artur Wichniarek. Trainer: Marek Dziuba

Goals: Adani (17), Cois (57), Adani (73 og), Rui Costa (90)

WIDZEW LÓDZ v FIORENTINA FIRENZE 0-2 (0-1)

Widzew, Lódz 25.08.1999

Referee: Alain Sars (FRA) Attendance: 6,500

WIDZEW: Marek Matuszek; Daniel Bogusz, Maciej Terlecki, Rafal Pawlak; Slawomir Gula (62 Miroslaw Szymkowiak), Radoslaw Michalski, Dariusz Gesior (79 Dariusz Dudek), Rafal Kaczmarczyk, Tomasz Kielbowicz; Marek Citko, Artur Wichniarek (76 Marcin Zajac). Trainer: Marek Dziuba

FIORENTINA: Francesco Toldo; Tomáš Repka, Pasquale Padalino, Alessandro Pierini; Angelo di Livio, Sandro Cois (70 Paul Okon), Christian Amoroso, Jörg Heinrich, Rui Costa (85 Aldo Firicano); Enrico Chiesa (73 Abel Balbo), Predrag Mijatović. Trainer: Giovanni Trapattoni

Goals: Chiesa (40), Cois (68)

AALBORG B v FC DYNAMO KYIV 1-2 (0-2)

Aalborg, stadion 11.08.1999

Referee: Atanas Ouzounov (BUL) Attendance: 8,492

AaB: Jimmy Nielsen; Jens Jessen, Thomas Bælum, Jozo Matovac, Brian Priske; Allan Gaarde, Lars Harbo Thomsen (78 Søren Frederiksen), Anders Andersson, Thomas Gaardsøe (66 Henrik Rasmussen), Andres Oper; Frank Strandli. Trainer: Hans Backe

DYNAMO: Olexandr Shovkovskyi; Aleksei Gerasimenko, Olexandr Holovko, Vladislav Vashchuk; Yuri Dmitrulin, Artem Yashkin, Andriy Gusin, Vasyl Kardash (61 Sergei Konovalov), Kakhi Kaladze; Serhiy Rebrov, Maxim Shatskykh. Trainer: Valeriy Lobanovskiy

Goals: Rebrov (13), Shatskykh (39), Strandli (55)

FC DYNAMO KYIV v AALBORG B 2-2 (0-1)

Olympyiskyi, Kyiv 25.08.1999

Referee: Michel Piraux (BEL) Attendance: 15,000

DYNAMO: Olexandr Shovkovskyi; Aleksei Gerasimenko (59 Serhiy Kormiltsev), Olexandr Holovko, Vladislav Vashchuk; Yuri Dmitrulin, Kakhi Kaladze, Vitaliy Kosovskyi, Serhiy Rebrov, Andriy Gusin; Artem Yashkin, Maxim Shatskykh. Trainer: Valeriy Lobanovskiy

AaB: Jimmy Nielsen; Brian Priske, Thomas Bælum, Jozo Matovac, Jens Jessen; Thomas Gaardsøe, Anders Andersson, Lars Harbo Thomsen, Allan Gaarde; Frank Strandli, Andres Oper. Trainer: Hans Backe

Goals: Oper (9), Gaarde (47), Gusin (74), Shatskykh (90)

GLASGOW RANGERS FC v PARMA 2-0 (1-0)

Ibrox, Glasgow 11.08.1999

Referee: José Maria García Aranda (SPA) Att: 49,263

RANGERS: Stefan Klos; Sergio Porrini, Craig Moore, Lorenzo Amoruso, Tony Vidmar (56 Jörg Albertz); Barry Ferguson, Claudio Reyna, Giovanni van Bronckhorst, Neil McCann; Rodney Wallace, Michael Mols. Trainer: Dick Advocaat

PARMA: Gianluigi Buffon; Luigi Sartor, Lilian Thuram, Fabio Cannavaro; Michele Serena, Dino Baggio (61 Diego Fuser), Johan Walem, Alain Boghossian, Paolo Vanoli; Ariel Ortega (83 Stefano Torrisi), Marco Di Vaio (85 Mario Stanić). Trainer: Alberto Malesani

Sent off: Cannavaro (27)

Goals: Vidmar (33), Reyna (76)

PARMA v GLASGOW RANGERS FC 1-0 (0-0)

Ennio Tardini,, Parma 25.08.1999

Referee: Karl-Erik Nilsson (SWE) Attendance: 24,087

PARMA: Gianluigi Buffon; Saliou Lassissi, Stefano Torrisi, Lilian Thuram; Diego Fuser, Dino Baggio, Alain Boghossian (64 Johan Walem), Paolo Vanoli (78 Michele Serena), Ariel Ortega; Hernán Crespo, Marco Di Vaio (64 Mario Stanić). Trainer: Alberto Malesani

RANGERS: Lionel Charbonnier; Sergio Porrini, Craig Moore, Lorenzo Amoruso; Dariusz Adamczuk (83 Colin Hendry), Claudio Reyna, Barry Ferguson (73 Jörg Albertz), Giovanni van Bronckhorst, Tony Vidmar; Rodney Wallace (60 Neil McCann), Michael Mols. Trainer: Dick Advocaat

Goal: Walem (68)

BRØNDBY IF v BOAVISTA FC PORTO 1-2 (0-1)

Brøndby Stadion, København 11.08.1999

Referee: Nikolai Levnikov (RUS) Attendance: 9,060

BRØNDBY: Mogens Krogh; Søren Colding, Vragel da Silva, Per Lundgren Nielsen, Martin D. Smith; Allan Ravn (79 Mads Olsen), Kim Daugaard (74 Mikkel Jensen), Peter Madsen (46 Aurelius Skarbalius); Ole Bjur, Bent Christensen, Ruben Bagger. Trainer: Tom Køhlert

BOAVISTA: Bassey WILLIAM Andem; PAULO Jorge Ferreira de SOUSA, Carlos Magalhães "LITOS", PEDRO EMANUEL Silva, MÁRIO Magalhães da SILVA (63 Almani Samori da Silva MOREIRA); RUI Fernando Pereira BENTO, LUÍS MANUEL Rodrigues Viana (46 EMANUEL Faria Braga), Ion Timofte; JORGE António Pinto do COUTO, Augustine Ahinful (74 GILMAR Estevan), William QUEVEDO. Trainer: Jaime Pacheco

Sent off: da Silva (13)

Goals: Mário Silva (25), Smith (65), Moreira (73)

BOAVISTA FC PORTO v BRØNDBY IF 4-2 (1-0, 1-2) (AET)

Estádio do Bessa, Porto 25.08.1999

Referee: Pascal Garibian (FRA) Attendance: 9,000

BOAVISTA: Bassey WILLIAM Andem; PAULO Jorge Ferreira de SOUSA, Carlos Magalhães "LITOS", PEDRO EMANUEL Silva, MÁRIO Magalhães da SILVA; RUI Fernando Pereira BENTO, LUÍS MANUEL Rodrigues Viana, Ion Timofte (70 Luís JORGE Pinto da SILVA); Augustine Ahinful, Almani Samori da Silva MOREIRA (55 JORGE António Pinto do COUTO), GILMAR Estevan (82 WHELLITON Augusto Silva). Trainer: Jaime Pacheco

BRØNDBY IF: Mogens Krogh; Søren Colding, Per Lundgren Nielsen, Dan Anton Johansen, Martin Smith; Ole Bjur, Kim Daugaard, Allan Ravn, Ruben Bagger; Bent Christensen (84 Søren Krogh), Peter Graulund (71 Peter Madsen). Trainer: Tom Køhlert

Goals: Litos (13), Christensen (47), Bjur (90), Ahinful (99, 110), Rui Bento (117)

AEK FC ATHINA v AIK SOLNA 0-0

Nikos Gkoumas, Athina 11.09.1999

Referee: Juan Antonio Fernández Marín (SPA) Att: 24,000

AEK: Ilias Atmatzidis; Goran Petric, Haralampos Kopitsis (79 Vladimir Matijasevic), Mihalis Kapsis; Dimitris Markos (66 Hristos Maladenis), Toni Savevski, Dragan Cirić, Andreas Zikos, Vasilis Lakis; Nenad Bjeković (76 Sotiris Konstantinidis), Themistoklis Nikolaidis. Trainer: Ljubisa Tumbaković

AIK: Mattias Asper; Michael Brundin, Tomas Gustafsson, Mike Kjølø (69 David Ljung), Pontus Kåmark; Krister Nordin, Ola Andersson, Daniel Tjernström, Thomas Lagerlöf; Nebojsa Novakovic (89 Daniel Hoch), Andreas Andersson (62 Martin Åslund). Trainer: Stuart Baxter

AIK SOLNA v AEK FC ATHINA 1-0 (0-0)

Råsunda, Solna 25.08.1999

Referee: Graziano Cesari (ITA) Attendance: 31,115

AIK: Mattias Asper; Krister Nordin, Karl Corneliusson (50 Christer Mattiasson), Michael Brundin, Tomas Gustafsson; Nebojsa Novakovic (79 Ola Andersson), Daniel Tjernström, Andreas Andersson, Thomas Lagerlöf; Mike Kjølø (88 David Ljung), Pontus Kåmark. Trainer: Stuart Baxter

AEK: Ilias Atmatzidis; Mihalis Kasapis, Vasilis Lakis, Goran Petric, Traianos Dellas; Dimitris Markos (76 Vladimir Matijasevic), Andreas Zikos, Dragan Cirić, Toni Savevski (65 Sotiris Konstantinidis); Themistoklis Nikolaidis, Hristos Maladenis. Trainer: Ljubisa Tumbaković

Goal: Novakovic (58)

HAPOEL HAIFA v VALENCIA CF 0-2 (0-0)

Kiriat Eliezer, Haifa 11.08.1999

Referee: Markus Merk (GER) Attendance: 14,500

HAPOEL: Dudu Auat; Offer Talker, Ran Ben Shimon, Amir Shelach, Alon Halfon; Oren Zitoni, Goran Milanko (71 Oren Nissim), Dmitri Ulianov, Giovanni Rosso, David Amsalem; Nir Sivilia (71 Amir Torjman). Trainer: Eli Gutman

VALENCIA: Santiago CAÑIZARES Ruiz; Jocelyn Angloma, Joachim Björklund, Miroslav Djukić, Daniel Fagiani; Miguel Ángel ANGULO, David ALBELDA Aliques, Gaizka MENDIETA Zabala, Francisco FARINÓS Zapata (80 GERARD López Segú); Adrian Ilie (65 JUAN Ginés SÁNCHEZ Moreno), CLAUDIO Javier LÓPEZ. Trainer: Héctor Raúl Cuper

Goals: López (68), Farinós (74)

ANORTHOSIS FAMAGUSTA v HERTHA BSC BERLIN 0-0

Antonis Papadopoulos, Larnaca 25.08.1999

Referee: Eric Romain (BEL) Attendance: 8,000

ANORTHOSIS: Nikos Panagiotou; Vasos Melanarkitis, Loukas Louka, Andreas Melanarkitis; Panagotis Egkomitis (89 Giorgos Iosifides), Marios Neofytou (71 Sasa Jovanovic), Zoran Milinkovic, Zaharias Haralampous (65 Zoran Cirić), Stavros Foukaris; Mike Obiku, Giannakis Okas. Trainer: Dušan Mitosević

HERTHA: Gábor Király; Hendrik Herzog, Kostas Konstantinidis, Eyjólfur Sverrisson; Sebastian Deisler, Pál Dárdai, René Tretschok, Michael Hartmann, Dariusz Wosz (70 Anthony Sanneh); Ali Daei (70 Sixten Veit), Ilija Aracic (90 Andreas Schmidt). Trainer: Jürgen Röber

VALENCIA CF v HAPOEL HAIFA 2-0 (0-0)

Mestalla, Valencia 25.08.1999

Referee: Anders Frisk (SWE) Attendance: 23,157

VALENCIA: Santiago CAÑIZARES Ruiz; Jocelyn Angloma, Joachim Björklund, Miroslav Djukić, Daniel Fagiani; David ALBELDA Aliques, Francisco FARINÓS Zapata (69 GERARD López Segú), Gaizka MENDIETA Zabala, Miguel Ángel ANGULO; CLAUDIO Javier LÓPEZ (83 Christian Alberto "KILY" GONZÁLEZ Peret), JUAN Ginés SÁNCHEZ Moreno. Trainer: Héctor Raúl Cuper

HAPOEL: Dudu Auat; Offer Talker, Ami Azoulay (66 Meir Ben-Margi); Amir Shelach, Alon Halfon, David Amsalem, Goran Milanko, Dmitri Ulianov, Giovanni Rosso; Nir Sivilia (56 Oren Nissim), Amir Torjman (73 Kfir Leibovitz). Trainer: Eli Gutman

Goals: Sánchez (59, 66)

SK STURM GRAZ v SERVETTE GENÈVE 2-1 (2-1)

Arnold Schwarzenegger, Graz 11.08.1999

Referee: Lucílio Cardoso Cortez Batista (POR) Att: 10,688

STURM: Josef Schicklgruber; Franco Foda, Darko Milanic (80 Giorgos Koutsoupias), Ranko Popovic; György Korsós, Hannes Reinmayr, Markus Schupp, Gilbert Prilasnig (89 Mehrdad Minavand), Jan Pieter Martens; Ivica Vastic, Gerald Strafner (63 Tomislav Kocijan). Trainer: Ivica Osim

SERVETTE: Eric Pédat (40 Fabien Margairaz); Stefan Wolf, Sébastien Jeanneret, JUAREZ de Souza; Lanjame Ouadja (73 Carlos Varela), Franck Durix, Johann Lonfat, Edwin Vurens, Patrick Bühlmann; Alexandre Rey (53 Léonard Thurre), Martin Petrov. Trainer: Gérard Castella

Goals: Vastic (35), Martens (45), Lonfat (45)

HERTHA BSC BERLIN v ANORTHOSIS FAMAGUSTA 2-0 (1-0)

Olympiastadion, Berlin 11.08.1999

Referee: Hugh Dallas (SCO) Attendance: 42,500

HERTHA: Gábor Király; Hendrik Herzog, Kjetil Rekdal (67 Andreas Schmidt), Eyjólfur Sverrisson; Kostas Konstantinidis, Andreas Thom, René Tretschok, Michael Hartmann, Dariusz Wosz (78 Pál Dárdai); Michael Preetz, Ali Daei (84 Ilija Aracic). Trainer: Jürgen Röber

ANORTHOSIS: Nikos Panagiotou; Vasos Melanarkitis, Stavros Foukaris (67 Giorgos Iosifides), Loukas Louka; Panagotis Egkomitis, Andreas Melanarkitis, Panikos Pounas, Zaharias Haralampous, Sasa Jovanovic (71 Marios Neofytou); Mike Obiku (82 Zoran Cirić), Giannakis Okas. Trainer: Dušan Mitosević

Goals: Daei (2), Preetz (58)

SERVETTE GENÈVE v SK STURM GRAZ 2-2 (0-0)

Stade des Charmilles, Genève 25.08.1999

Referee: Graham Barber (ENG) Attendance: 8,829

SERVETTE: Eric Pédat; Stefan Wolf, Sébastien Jeanneret (76 Lanjame Ouadja), JUAREZ da Souza; Franck Durix, Faouzi El Brazi, Edwin Vurens (67 Martin Petrov), Patrick Bühlmann; Carlos Varela (85 Elvir Melunovic), Alexandre Rey, Léonard Thurre. Trainer: Gérard Castella

STURM: Josef Schicklgruber; Franco Foda, Darko Milanic, Ranko Popovic (46 Roman Mählich), Günther Neukirchner; Markus Schopp (66 György Korsós), Gilbert Prilasnig (85 Hannes Reinmayr), Markus Schupp, Jan Pieter Martens; Ivica Vastic, Tomislav Kocijan. Trainer: Ivica Osim

Goals: Juarez (50), Kocijan (54), Vastic (78), Thurre (89)

MOLDE FK v RCD MALLORCA 0-0

Nye Molde 11.08.1999

Referee: Mario van der Ende (HOL) Attendance: 8,573

MOLDE FK: Morten Bakke; Trond Strande, Jo Tessem, Pål Lydersen (46 Freddy dos Santos), Knut Anders Fostervold, Daniel Berg Hestad; Magne Hoseth, Odd Inge Olsen, Karl Oskar Fjørtoft, Thomas Mork (61 Ole Bjørn Sundgot); Andreas Lund. Trainer: Erik Brakstad

RCD MALLORCA: Germán Adrián BURGOS; Javier OLAIZOLA Rodríguez, FERNANDO NIÑO, Gustavo Lionel SIVIERO, Miguel SOLER Sarasols; LAUREN Bisan-Etame Mayer, Vicente ENGONGA Maté, Ariel Miguel Santiago IBAGAZA (84 Juan José SERRIZUELA), Jovan Stanković; Gustavo Domingo QUINTEROS (66 Iván César Gabrich), CARLOS Domínguez Dominguez (79 Ardijan Djokaj). Trainer: Mario Carlos Gomez

RCD MALLORCA v MOLDE FK 1-1 (1-0)

San Moix, Palma de Mallorca 25.08.1999

Referee: Stefano Braschi (ITA) Attendance: 23,000

RCD MALLORCA: LEOnardo FRANCO; Javier OLAIZOLA Rodríguez, FERNANDO NIÑO, Gustavo Lionel SIVIERO, Miguel SOLER Sarasols; LAUREN Bisan-Etame Mayer, Vicente ENGONGA Maté (86 DIEGO TRISTÁN Herrera), Ariel Miguel Santiago IBAGAZA, Gustavo Domingo QUINTEROS (60 Iván César Gabrich); Jovan Stanković, CARLOS Domínguez Dominguez (77 Francisco SOLER Atencia). Trainer: Mario Carlos Gomez

MOLDE FK: Morten Bakke; Freddy Dos Santos, Jo Tessem, Pål Lydersen, Knut Anders Fostervold; Karl Oskar Fjørtoft, Daniel Berg Hestad, Magne Hoseth (85 Petter Christian Singsaas), Thomas Mork (70 Ole Bjørn Sundgot); Odd Inge Olsen, Andreas Lund. Trainer: Erik Brakstad

Sent off: Fernando Niño (84)

Goals: Stankovic (22 pen), Lund (85 pen)

CROATIA ZAGREB v MTK BUDAPEST 0-0

Maksimir, Zagreb 11.08.1999

Referee: Graham Poll (ENG) Attendance: 15,000

CROATIA: Drazen Ladić; Goran Jurić, Igor Biščan, Stjepan Tomas, Tomislav Rukavina (69 Danijel Šarić); Edin Mujcin, Robert Prosinecki, Krunoslav Jurcić, Mario Cvitanović (78 Ardian Kozniku); Mihael Mikić (40 Zoran Pavlović), Josip Simić. Trainer: Osvaldo Ardiles

MTK: Gábor Babos; Emil Lörincz, Csaba Fehér (55 Krisztián Kenesei), Ádám Komlósi, Attila Kuttor; Tamás Szamosi, Károly Erös, Gábor Halmai, Béla Illés; Gábor Egressy (46 Glenn Helder), Nicolae Ilea (62 Sándor Preisinger). Trainer: Henk ten Cate

Sent off: Mujcin (17), Halmai (67)

MTK BUDAPEST v CROATIA ZAGREB 0-2 (0-0)

Hungária úti, Budapest 25.08.1999

Referee: Jan Wegereef (HOL) Attendance: 6,000

MTK: Gábor Babos; Emil Lörincz, Csaba Fehér (83 Henrik Kovács), Ádám Komlósi, Attila Kuttor; Tamás Szamosi, Károly Erös, Csaba Madar, Béla Illés; Glenn Helder (77 Sándor Preisinger), Nicolae Ilea (46 Gábor Egressy). Trainer: Henk ten Cate

CROATIA: Drazen Ladić; Goran Jurić, Igor Biščan, Stjepan Tomas, Tomislav Rukavina; Mario Tokić, Robert Prosinecki (82 Josko Jelicić), Krunoslav Jurcić, Mario Cvitanović; Ardian Kozniku (46 Mihael Mikić), Josip Simić (87 Tomislav Šokota). Trainer: Osvaldo Ardiles

Sent off: Komlósi (84)

Goals: Simić (60, 83)

FK TEPLICE v BORUSSIA DORTMUND 0-1 (0-0)

Stadion Na Stínadlech, Teplice 11.08.1999

Referee: Dermot Gallagher (ENG) Attendance: 15,000

FK TEPLICE: Libor Machácek; Petr Brabec, Miroslav Rada, Marián Rizek; Petr Fousek, Michal Bílek, Zdenko Frtala (74 Aleš Pikl), Dušan Tesarik; Michal Kolomaznik (70 Radek Divecký), Martin Frýdek (70 Jaromír Jindrácek), Pavel Verbír. Trainer: Josef Pesice

BORUSSIA: Jens Lehmann; Jürgen Kohler, Stefan Reuter, Christian Wörns; Dédé, Christian Nerlinger, Miroslav Stevic, Lars Ricken (90 Alfred Nijhuis); Andreas Möller, Fredi Bobic (89 Sergei Barbarez), Viktor Ikpeba (77 Heiko Herrlich). Trainer: Michael Skibbe

Goal: Nerlinger (66)

BORUSSIA DORTMUND v FK TEPLICE 1-0 (0-0)

Westfalenstadion, Dortmund 25.08.1999

Referee: Alfredo Trentalange (ITA) Attendance: 48,000

BORUSSIA: Jens Lehmann; Christian Wörns, Wolfgang Feiersinger, Jürgen Kohler (82 Alfred Nijhuis); Miroslav Stevic, Christian Nerlinger, Dédé, Giuseppe Reina (86 Lars Ricken), Andreas Möller; Heiko Herrlich, Viktor Ikpeba (90 Fredi Bobic). Trainer: Michael Skibbe

FK TEPLICE: Libor Machácek; Marián Rizek, Miroslav Rada, Petr Brabec; Petr Fousek, Zdenko Frtala (73 Martin Frýdek), Michal Bílek, Dušan Tesarik, Michal Kolomaznik; Pavel Verbír (75 Štepán Vachoušek), Radek Divecký (82 Jaromír Jindrácek). Trainer: Josef Pesice

Goal: Herrlich (90)

CHAMPIONS LEAGUE

FIRST STAGE – GROUP A

BAYER 04 LEVERKUSEN v SS LAZIO ROMA 1-1 (1-1)

Ulrich-Haberland-Stadion, Leverkusen 14.09.1999

Referee: Graham Poll (ENG) Attendance: 22,500

BAYER: Adam Matysek; Robert Kovac, Jens Nowotny, Frankie Hejduk, Vratislav Gresko (67 Stefan Beinlich); Zé Roberto, Émerson Ferreira da Rosa, Bernd Schneider, Carsten Ramelow; Thomas Reichenberger (82 Róbson Ponte), Oliver Neuville (73 Thomas Brdaric). Trainer: Christoph Daum

LAZIO: Luca Marchegiani; Paolo Negro, Sinisa Mihajlovic, Alessandro Nesta, Giuseppe Pancaro; Roberto Mancini (76 Pavel Nedved), Attilio Lombardo, Dejan Stankovic, Juan Sebastián Verón (50 Diego Simeone), Matías Almeyda; Alen Boksic (80 Marcelo Salas). Trainer: Sven Göran Eriksson

Goals: Neuville (14), Mihajlović (18)

FC DYNAMO KYIV v NK MARIBOR 0-1 (0-0)

Olympyiskyi, Kyiv 14.09.1999

Referee: Leslie Irvine (NIR) Attendance: 35,000

DYNAMO: Olexandr Shovkovskyi; Aleksei Gerasimenko (70 Sergei Konovalov), Olexandr Borysovych Holovko, Vladislav Vashchuk; Yuri Dmitrulin, Kakhi Kaladze, Vitaliy Kosovskyi, Andriy Gusin, Serhiy Kormiltsev (60 Serhiy Fedorov); Serhiy Rebrov, Maxim Shatskykh (66 Oleh Venhlynskyi). Trainer: Valeriy Lobanovskiy

NK MARIBOR: Marko Simeunović; Geri Çipi, Marinko Galić, Marinko Sarkezi; Simon Seslar, Gregor Zidan, Amir Karić, Stipe Balajić (64 Muamer Vugdalić), Dejan Djuranović; Ante Simundza (82 Dalibor Filipović), Kliton Bozgo (90 Martin Pregelj). Trainer: Bojan Prasnikar

Goal: Simundza (73)

SS LAZIO ROMA v FC DYNAMO KYIV 2-1 (0-0)

Stadio Olimpico, Roma 22.09.1999

Referee: Manuel Diaz Vega (SPA) Attendance: 37,348

LAZIO: Marco Ballotta; Paolo Negro, Alessandro Nesta, Sinisa Mihajlovic, Giuseppe Favalli; Dejan Stankovic (52 Marcelo Salas), Matías Almeyda, Juan Sebastián Verón (81 Attilio Lombardo), Pavel Nedved; Alen Boksic, Roberto Mancini (75 Diego Simeone). Trainer: Sven Göran Eriksson

DYNAMO: Olexandr Shovkovskyi; Vladislav Vashchuk, Aleksei Gerasimenko (46 Sergei Konovalov), Serhiy Fedorov, Olexandr Holovko, Yuri Dmitrulin; Andriy Gusin, Kakhi Kaladze, Serhiy Kormiltsev (46 Vitaliy Kosovskyi); Maxim Shatskykh (83 Oleh Venhlynskyi), Serhiy Rebrov. Trainer: Valeriy Lobanovskiy

Goals: Rebrov (68 pen), Negro (70), Salas (72)

NK MARIBOR v BAYER 04 LEVERKUSEN 0-2 (0-0)

Ljudski vrt, Maribor 22.09.1999

Referee: Jan Wegereef (HOL) Attendance: 10,090

NK MARIBOR: Marko Simeunović; Marinko Galić, Muamer Vugdalić, Geri Çipi; Gregor Zidan, Dejan Djuranović, Stipe Balajić (85 Mehmet Dragusha), Simon Seslar, Suad Fileković (52 Martin Pregelj); Kliton Bozgo, Ante Simundza. Trainer: Bojan Prasnikar

BAYER: Adam Matysek; Boris Zivkovic, Jens Nowotny (70 Róbson Ponte), Robert Kovac; Bernd Schneider, Carsten Ramelow, Émerson Ferreira da Rosa, Vratislav Gresko; Stefan Beinlich, Oliver Neuville (82 Thomas Brdaric), Ulf Kirsten. Trainer: Christoph Daum

Goals: Zivkovic (82), Kirsten (90)

SS LAZIO ROMA v NK MARIBOR 4-0 (0-0)

Olimpico, Roma 29.09.1999

Referee: Lucílio Cardoso Cortez Batista (POR) Att: 29,571

LAZIO: Luca Marchegiani; Paolo Negro, Sinisa Mihajlovic (72 Matías Almeyda), Alessandro Nesta, Giuseppe Pancaro; Néstor Sensini, Sérgio Conceição, Attilio Lombardo (67 Juan Sebastián Verón), Dejan Stankovic (46 Marcelo Salas); Roberto Mancini, Simone Inzaghi. Trainer: Sven Göran Eriksson

NK MARIBOR: Marko Simeunović; Muamer Vugdalić, Geri Çipi, Marinko Galić; Simon Seslar, Gregor Zidan (81 Martin Pregelj), Amir Karić, Dejan Djuranović; Ante Simundza (46 Marinko Sarkezi), Stipe Balajić, Kliton Bozgo (68 Dalibor Filipović). Trainer: Bojan Prasnikar

Sent off: Çipi (20)

Goals: Inzaghi (60), Sérgio Conceição (62), Salas (71, 76)

BAYER 04 LEVERKUSEN v FC DYNAMO KYIV 1-1 (0-0)

Ulrich-Haberland-Stadion, Leverkusen 29.09.1999

Referee: Claude Colombo (FRA) Attendance: 22,500

BAYER: Adam Matysek; Jörg Reeb, Jens Nowotny, Robert Kovac, Stefan Beinlich; Bernd Schneider, Émerson Ferreira da Rosa, Carsten Ramelow; Róbson Ponte (85 Thomas Reichenberger), Ulf Kirsten, Oliver Neuville (46 Frankie Hejduk). Trainer: Christoph Daum

DYNAMO: Olexandr Shovkovskyi; Ramiz Mamedov (81 Serhiy Fedorov), Olexandr Borysovych Holovko, Vladislav Vashchuk, Yuri Dmitrulin (74 Serhiy Kormiltsev); Sergei Konovalov (59 Aleksei Gerasimenko), Andriy Gusin, Kakhi Kaladze, Vitaliy Kosovskyi; Maxim Shatskykh, Serhiy Rebrov. Trainer: Valeriy Lobanovskiy

Goals: Kirsten (52), Gusin (71)

NK MARIBOR v SS LAZIO ROMA 0-4 (0-1)

Ljudski vrt, Maribor 19.10.1999

Referee: Terje Hauge (NOR) Attendance: 9,156

NK MARIBOR: Marko Simeunović; Muamer Vugdalić, Marinko Galić, Marinko Sarkezi; Gregor Zidan, Dejan Djuranović, Simon Seslar (84 Mehmet Dragusha), Amir Karić, Stipe Balajić; Kliton Bozgo (61 Dalibor Filipović), Ante Simundza (78 Martin Pregelj). Trainer: Bojan Prasnikar

LAZIO: Marco Ballotta; Giuseppe Pancaro, Alessandro Nesta (18 Fernando Couto), Sinisa Mihajlovic, Giuseppe Favalli; Sérgio Conceição (75 Dario Marcolin), Dejan Stankovic, Diego Simeone, Néstor Sensini, Pavel Nedved (70 Guerino Gottardi); Simone Inzaghi. Trainer: Sven Göran Eriksson

Goals: Mihajlovic (36), Inzaghi (50, 73), Stankovic (63)

FC DYNAMO KYIV v BAYER 04 LEVERKUSEN 4-2 (2-1)

Olympyiskyi, Kyiv 19.10.1999

Referee: Karl-Erik Nilsson (SWE) Attendance: 47,000

DYNAMO: Olexandr Shovkovskyi; Ramiz Mamedov, Olexandr Borysovych Holovko, Vladislav Vashchuk, Yuri Dmitrulin (58 Artem Yashkin); Aleksei Gerasimenko (46 Valentin Belkevich), Andriy Gusin, Kakhi Kaladze, Vitaliy Kosovskyi; Maxim Shatskykh, Serhiy Rebrov.
Trainer: Valeriy Lobanovskiy

BAYER: Adam Matysek; Jörg Reeb, Jens Nowotny, Boris Zivkovic; Frankie Hejduk (77 Róbson Ponte), Carsten Ramelow, Émerson Ferreira da Rosa, Stefan Beinlich; Oliver Neuville, Ulf Kirsten, Bernd Schneider.
Trainer: Christoph Daum

Goals: Kosovskyi (4), Kirsten (12), Shatskykh (36), Neuville (49), Holovko (61), Vashchuk (89)

NK MARIBOR v FC DYNAMO KYIV 1-2 (0-1)

Ljudski vrt, Maribor 27.10.1999

Referee: Juan Antonio Fernández Marín (SPA) Att: 9,600

NK MARIBOR: Luka Gresak; Geri Çipi, Gregor Zidan, Muamer Vugdalić, Marinko Sarkezi (87 Suad Fileković), Amir Karić; Dejan Djuranović, Simon Seslar, Stipe Balajić (61 Kliton Bozgo); Ante Simundza, Dalibor Filipović (69 Martin Pregelj).
Trainer: Bojan Prasnikar

DYNAMO: Olexandr Shovkovskyi; Ramiz Mamedov, Olexandr Borysovych Holovko, Vladislav Vashchuk, Yuri Dmitrulin; Kakhi Kaladze, Andriy Gusin, Artem Yashkin (6 Valentin Belkevich), Vitaliy Kosovskyi; Maxim Shatskykh, Serhiy Rebrov. Trainer: Valeriy Lobanovskiy

Goals: Rebrov (37, 84 pen), Balajić (50)

SS LAZIO ROMA v BAYER 04 LEVERKUSEN 1-1 (1-1)

Stadio Olimpico, Roma 27.10.1999

Referee: Hugh Dallas (SCO) Attendance: 30,627

LAZIO: Luca Marchegiani; Giuseppe Pancaro, Fernando Couto, Sinisa Mihajlovic, Giuseppe Favalli; Sérgio Conceição (76 Dejan Stankovic), Juan Sebastián Verón (89 Diego Simeone), Matías Almeyda, Pavel Nedved; Marcelo Salas, Alen Boksic (59 Simone Inzaghi). Trainer: Sven Göran Eriksson

BAYER: Adam Matysek; Jörg Reeb (67 Frankie Hejduk), Jens Nowotny, Boris Zivkovic; Bernd Schneider, Émerson Ferreira da Rosa, Carsten Ramelow, Stefan Beinlich, Vratislav Gresko (25 Markus Happe); Oliver Neuville, Ulf Kirsten (88 Zoran Mamic). Trainer: Christoph Daum

Goals: Nedved (1), Kirsten (44)

FC DYNAMO KYIV v SS LAZIO ROMA 0-1 (0-1)

Olympyiskyi, Kyiv 2.11.1999

Referee: Paul Anthony Durkin (ENG) Attendance: 67,800

DYNAMO: Olexandr Shovkovskyi; Olexandr Holovko, Vladislav Vashchuk, Yuri Dmitrulin; Ramiz Mamedov, Andriy Gusin, Serhiy Fedorov (46 Maxim Shatskykh), Kakhi Kaladze, Vitaliy Kosovskyi; Serhiy Rebrov, Valentin Belkevich.
Trainer: Valeriy Lobanovskiy

LAZIO: Marco Ballotta; Guerino Gottardi, Fernando Couto, Paolo Negro, Giuseppe Pancaro; Dejan Stankovic (64 Gian Piero Pinzi), Diego Simeone, Néstor Sensini, Dario Marcolin; Simone Inzaghi, Roberto Mancini.
Trainer: Sven Göran Eriksson

Goal: Mamedov (17 og)

BAYER 04 LEVERKUSEN v NK MARIBOR 0-0

Ulrich-Haberland-Stadion, Leverkusen 2.11.1999

Referee: David Elleray (ENG) Attendance: 22,500

BAYER: Adam Matysek; Jens Nowotny, Jörg Reeb (46 Thomas Brdaric), Boris Zivkovic; Bernd Schneider (76 Torben Hoffmann), Émerson Ferreira da Rosa, Carsten Ramelow, Frankie Hejduk, Stefan Beinlich; Thomas Reichenberger (46 Róbson Ponte), Oliver Neuville. Trainer: Christoph Daum

NK MARIBOR: Luka Gresak; Muamer Vugdalić, Marinko Galić, Marinko Sarkezi; Gregor Zidan, Dejan Djuranović, Stipe Balajić (90 Mehmet Dragusha), Simon Seslar, Amir Karić; Dalibor Filipović (90 Suad Fileković), Ante Simundza (56 Kliton Bozgo). Trainer: Bojan Prasnikar

	P	W	D	L	F	A	Pts
SS Lazio Roma	6	4	2	0	13	3	14
Dynamo Kyiv	6	2	1	3	8	8	7
Bayer 04 Leverkusen	6	1	4	1	7	7	7
NK Maribor	6	1	1	4	2	12	4

FIRST STAGE – GROUP B

FIORENTINA FIRENZE v ARSENAL FC LONDON 0-0

Artemio Franchi, Firenze 14.09.1999

Referee: Hellmut Krug (GER) Attendance: 33,903

FIORENTINA: Francesco Toldo; Tomáš Repka, Pasquale Padalino, Alessandro Pierini (84 Daniele Adani); Rui Costa, Sandro Cois, Angelo di Livio, Jörg Heinrich; Predrag Mijatović, Gabriel Batistuta, Enrico Chiesa.
Trainer: Giovanni Trapattoni

ARSENAL: Alex Manninger; Nigel Winterburn, Patrick Vieira, Martin Keown, Tony Adams, Oleg Luzhny; Fredrik Ljungberg, Marc Overmars, Gilles Grimandi; Davor Suker (61 Nwankwo Kanu), Dennis Bergkamp (82 Thierry Henry).
Manager: Arsène Wenger

AIK SOLNA v FC BARCELONA 1-2 (0-0)

Råsunda, Solna 14.09.1999

Referee: Alain Sars (FRA) Attendance: 30,543

AIK: Mattias Asper; Krister Nordin, Ola Andersson, Michael Brundin, Pontus Kåmark (86 Karl Corneliusson); Nebojsa Novakovic (86 Christer Mattiasson), Daniel Tjernström (74 Hans Bergh), Thomas Lagerlöf, David Ljung; Andreas Andersson, Mike Kjølø. Trainer: Stuart Baxter

FC BARCELONA: Rodolfus Hubuertus "Ruud" Hesp; SERGI Barjuán Esclusa, Winston Bogarde (17 ABELARDO Fernández Artuńa), Frank de Boer, XAVIer Hernández Creus (79 GABRIel García De la Torre); Ronald de Boer, Luis Filipe Madeira Caeiro "FIGO", Philip John William Cocu, Jari Litmanen; Patrick Kluivert (74 DANIel García Lara), Vítor Borba Ferreira "RIVALDO". Trainer: Louis van Gaal

Goals: Novakovic (72), Abelardo (86), Dani (90)

ARSENAL FC LONDON v AIK SOLNA 3-1 (1-0)

Arsenal,, London 22.09.1999

Referee: Vítor Manuel Melo Pereira (POR) Att: 71,227

ARSENAL: Alex Manninger; Lee Dixon, Nigel Winterburn, Martin Keown, Tony Adams; Patrick Vieira, Fredrik Ljungberg (69 Thierry Henry), Gilles Grimandi (56 Silvinho); Davor Suker, Dennis Bergkamp, Marc Overmars (69 Nwankwo Kanu). Manager: Arsène Wenger

AIK: Mattias Asper; Krister Nordin, Ola Andersson 88, Michael Brundin, Thomas Lagerlöf, Pontus Kåmark (46 Mike Kjølø); Tomas Gustafsson, Nebojsa Novakovic (82 Martin Åslund), Andreas Andersson (88 Karl Corneliusson); Daniel Tjernström, David Ljung. Trainer: Stuart Baxter

Goals: Ljungberg (28), Nordin (53), Henry (89), Suker (90)

FC BARCELONA v FIORENTINA FIRENZE 4-2 (2-0)

Camp Nou, Barcelona 22.09.1999

Referee: Kim Milton Nielsen (DEN) Attendance: 69,486

FC BARCELONA: Rodolfus Hubuertus "Ruud" Hesp; Michael Reiziger, Ronald de Boer, SERGI Barjuán Esclusa, Winston Bogarde; Josep GUARDIOLA Sala (79 XAVIer Hernández Creus), Philip John William Cocu (76 Boudewijn Zenden), LUIS ENRIQUE Martínez García; Luis Filipe Madeira Caeiro "FIGO", Patrick Kluivert (60 DANIel García Lara), Vítor Borba Ferreira "RIVALDO". Trainer: Louis van Gaal

FIORENTINA: Francesco Toldo; Tomáš Repka, Daniele Adani, Pasquale Padalino; Rui Costa, Sandro Cois, Angelo di Livio, Jörg Heinrich, Christian Amoroso (56 Enrico Chiesa); Predrag Mijatović (86 Abel Balbo), Gabriel Batistuta (77 Guillermo Amor). Trainer: Giovanni Trapattoni

Goals: Figo (7), Luis Enrique (10), Batistuta (50), Rivaldo (68 pen, 70), Chiesa (79)

FC BARCELONA v ARSENAL FC LONDON 1-1 (1-0)

Camp Nou, Barcelona 29.09.1999

Referee: Markus Merk (GER) Attendance: 87,574

FC BARCELONA: Rodolfus Hubuertus "Ruud" Hesp; Michael Reiziger (70 Ronald de Boer), Frank de Boer, Winston Bogarde, SERGI Barjuán Esclusa; Josep GUARDIOLA Sala, LUIS ENRIQUE Martínez García (77 Jari Litmanen), Philip John William Cocu; Luis Filipe Madeira Caeiro "FIGO", DANIel García Lara, Vítor Borba Ferreira "RIVALDO".
Trainer: Louis van Gaal

ARSENAL: Alex Manninger; Lee Dixon, Nigel Winterburn, Martin Keown, Tony Adams; Patrick Vieira, Ray Parlour (74 Thierry Henry), Gilles Grimandi; Marc Overmars (80 Fredrik Ljungberg), Dennis Bergkamp (74 Davor Suker), Nwankwo Kanu. Manager: Arsène Wenger

Sent off: Grimandi (80)

Goals: Luis Enrique (16), Kanu (81)

AIK SOLNA v FIORENTINA FIRENZE 0-0

Råsunda, Solna 29.09.1999

Referee: Günter Benkö (AUS) Attendance: 30,195

AIK: Mattias Asper; Mike Kjølø, David Ljung, Michael Brundin, Tomas Gustafsson; Daniel Tjernström, Ola Andersson (55 Karl Corneliusson), Krister Nordin, Thomas Lagerlöf; Andreas Andersson, Nebojsa Novakovic.
Trainer: Stuart Baxter

FIORENTINA: Francesco Toldo; Tomáš Repka, Pasquale Padalino, Alessandro Pierini; Angelo di Livio (61 Mauro Bressan), Sandro Cois (90 Fabio Rossitto), Rui Costa, Jörg Heinrich; Enrico Chiesa, Gabriel Batistuta, Predrag Mijatović (72 Abel Balbo). Trainer: Giovanni Trapattoni

ARSENAL FC LONDON v FC BARCELONA 2-4 (1-2)

Arsenal, London 19.10.1999

Referee: Urs Meier (SWI) Attendance: 73,091

ARSENAL: David Seaman; Lee Dixon, Nigel Winterburn, Martin Keown (73 Matthew Upson), Tony Adams; Ray Parlour, Patrick Vieira, Fredrik Ljungberg (76 Thierry Henry); Marc Overmars, Dennis Bergkamp, Nwankwo Kanu (76 Davor Suker). Manager: Arsène Wenger

FC BARCELONA: Francesco ARNAU Grabalosa; Michael Reiziger, SERGI Barjuán Esclusa, Winston Bogarde, ABELARDO Fernández Artuña; Josep GUARDIOLA Sala (90 Frédéric Déhu), LUIS ENRIQUE Martínez García (71 GABRIel García De la Torre), Philip John William Cocu (90 Boudewijn Zenden); Luis Filipe Madeira Caeiro "FIGO", Patrick Kluivert, Vítor Borba Ferreira "RIVALDO". Trainer: Louis van Gaal

Goals: Rivaldo (15 pen), Luis Enrique (16), Bergkamp (44), Figo (56), Cocu (70), Overmars (85)

FIORENTINA FIRENZE v AIK SOLNA 3-0 (2-0)

Artemio Franchi, Firenze 19.10.1999

Referee: Jan Wegereef (HOL) Attendance: 15,280

FIORENTINA: Francesco Toldo; Tomáš Repka, Aldo Firicano, Alessandro Pierini; Sandro Cois (70 Paul Okon), Angelo di Livio, Rui Costa, Jörg Heinrich; Enrico Chiesa (81 Abel Balbo), Predrag Mijatović (52 Christian Amoroso), Gabriel Batistuta. Trainer: Giovanni Trapattoni

AIK: Mattias Asper; Mike Kjølø, David Ljung, Michael Brundin, Tomas Gustafsson, Ola Andersson; Krister Nordin, Daniel Tjernström, Thomas Lagerlöf (57 Karl Corneliusson); Nebojsa Novakovic (46 Daniel Hoch), Christer Mattiasson (72 Andreas Johansson). Trainer: Stuart Baxter

Goals: Batistuta (5), Chiesa (36), Abel Balbo (86)

ARSENAL FC LONDON v FIORENTINA FIRENZE 0-1 (0-0)

Arsenal, London 27.10.1999

Referee: Lubos Michel (SVK) Attendance: 73,256

ARSENAL: David Seaman; Lee Dixon (74 Davor Suker), Martin Keown, Tony Adams, Nigel Winterburn; Ray Parlour (57 Fredrik Ljungberg), Patrick Vieira, Emmanuel Petit (60 Nelson Vivas); Marc Overmars, Dennis Bergkamp, Nwankwo Kanu. Manager: Arsène Wenger

FIORENTINA: Francesco Toldo; Alessandro Pierini, Aldo Firicano, Tomáš Repka; Angelo di Livio, Fabio Rossitto, Sandro Cois (46 Daniele Adani), Jörg Heinrich; Rui Costa, Gabriel Batistuta, Enrico Chiesa. Trainer: Giovanni Trapattoni

Goal: Batistuta (75)

FC BARCELONA v AIK SOLNA 5-0 (3-0)

Camp Nou, Barcelona 27.10.1999

Referee: Leslie Irvine (NIR) Attendance: 40,050

FC BARCELONA: Francesco ARNAU Grabalosa; Carlos Puyol (46 Fernando Macedo "NANO"), Frédéric Déhu, ABELARDO Fernández Artuña (81 Michael Reiziger), GABRIel García De la Torre; Ronald de Boer, XAVIer Hernández Creus, Jari Litmanen (60 MARIO Alberto Rosas Montero); SIMÃO Pedro Fonseca Sabrosa, Patrick Kluivert, Boudewijn Zenden. Trainer: Louis van Gaal

AIK: Mattias Asper; Mike Kjølø, David Ljung, Pontus Kåmark, Tomas Gustafsson, Michael Brundin; Karl Corneliusson, Daniel Tjernström (75 Thomas Lagerlöf), Krister Nordin (46 Andreas Andersson), Daniel Hoch (46 Christer Mattiasson); Nebojsa Novakovic. Trainer: S. Baxter

Goals: Kluivert (14, 33), Zenden (43), Gabri (53), Déhu (56)

AIK SOLNA v ARSENAL FC LONDON 2-3 (1-1)

Råsunda, Solna 2.11.1999

Referee: Hartmut Strampe (GER) Attendance: 33,005

AIK: Mattias Asper (72 Lee Baxter); Thomas Lagerlöf, Mike Kjølø, Pontus Kåmark, Tomas Gustafsson; Karl Corneliusson (72 Martin Åslund), Krister Nordin, Ola Andersson, Daniel Tjernström; Nebojsa Novakovic, Andreas Andersson. Trainer: Stuart Baxter

ARSENAL: Alex Manninger; Lee Dixon, Matthew Upson, Oleg Luzhny (78 Nelson Vivas), Nigel Winterburn; Fredrik Ljungberg, Patrick Vieira, Emmanuel Petit (78 Stefan Malz); Marc Overmars, Nwankwo Kanu, Davor Suker (78 Stephen Hughes). Manager: Arsène Wenger

Goals: Overmars (17, 52), A. Andersson (41, 68), Suker (56)

FIORENTINA FIRENZE v FC BARCELONA 3-3 (1-2)

Artemio Franchi, Firenze 2.11.1999

Referee: Hugh Dallas (SCO) Attendance: 23,588

FIORENTINA: Francesco Toldo; Jörg Heinrich, Aldo Firicano, Alessandro Pierini, Daniele Adani; Mauro Bressan, Angelo di Livio, Fabio Rossitto (90 Guillermo Amor), Rui Costa; Abel Balbo, Enrico Chiesa (34 Paul Okon). Trainer: Giovanni Trapattoni

FC BARCELONA: Francesco ARNAU Grabalosa; Ronald de Boer (46 Carlos Puyol), Frédéric Déhu, Winston Bogarde, Boudewijn Zenden; LUIS ENRIQUE Martínez García, Josep GUARDIOLA Sala (46 XAVIer Hernández Creus), Philip John William Cocu; Luis Filipe Madeira Caeiro "FIGO", Patrick Kluivert, Vítor Borba Ferreira "RIVALDO".

Goals: Bressan (14), Figo (20), Rivaldo (43, 74), Balbo (56, 69)

	P	W	D	L	F	A	Pts
FC Barcelona	6	4	2	0	19	9	14
Fiorentina Firenze	6	2	3	1	9	7	9
Arsenal FC London	6	2	2	2	9	9	8
AIK Solna	6	0	1	5	4	16	1

FIRST STAGE – GROUP C

BOAVISTA FC PORTO v ROSENBORG BK TRONDHEIM 0-3 (0-2)

Estádio do Bessa, Porto 14.09.1999

Referee: Graziano Cesari (ITA) Attendance: 8,000

BOAVISTA: Bassey WILLIAM Andem; PAULO Jorge Ferreira de SOUSA, PEDRO EMANUEL Silva, Carlos Magalhães "LITOS", MÁRIO Magalhães da SILVA; RUI Fernando Pereira BENTO, Ion Timofte (9 António José Faria FORMOSO), LUÍS MANUEL Rodrigues Viana (46 EMANUEL Faria Braga), JORGE António Pinto do COUTO; GILMAR Estevan (54 WHELLITON Augusto Silva), Augustine Ahinful. Trainer: Jaime Pacheco

ROSENBORG: Jørn Jamtfall; André Bergdølmo, Erik Hoftun, Bjørn Otto Bragstad, Bent Inge Johnsen; Roar Strand (89 Fredrik Winsnes), Ørjan Berg, Bent Skammelsrud, Jan Derek Sørensen (82 Tore André Dahlum); Jahn Ivar "Mini" Jakobsen, John Carew. Trainer: Nils Arne Eggen

Goals: Sørensen (10), Ø. Berg (43), R. Strand (73)

FEYENOORD ROTTERDAM v BORUSSIA DORTMUND 1-1 (0-0)

Feyenoord, Rotterdam 14.09.1999

Referee: José Maria García-Aranda (SPA) Att: 34,500

FEYENOORD: Jerzy Dudek; Paul Bosvelt, Bert Konterman, Kees van Wonderen, Tomasz Rzasa (46 Jan de Visser); Jean-Paul van Gastel, Jon Dahl Tomasson, Patrick Paauwe; Bonaventure Kalou, Julio Ricardo Cruz, Peter van Vossen (82 Radoslav Samardzic). Trainer: Leo Beenhakker

BORUSSIA: Jens Lehmann; Evanilson, Stefan Reuter, Alfred Nijhuis (77 Sergei Barbarez), Dédé; Giuseppe Reina, Christian Nerlinger, Miroslav Stevic (66 Wolfgang Feiersinger), Lars Ricken, Andreas Möller; Fredi Bobic (90 Heiko Herrlich). Trainer: Michael Skibbe

Goals: van Wonderen (67), Bobic (71)

ROSENBORG BK TRONDHEIM v FEYENOORD ROTTERDAM 2-2 (2-2)

Lerkendal, Trondheim 22.09.1999

Referee: Miroslav Radoman (YUG) Attendance: 14,149

ROSENBORG: Jørn Jamtfall; André Bergdølmo, Erik Hoftun, Bjørn Otto Bragstad, Bent Inge Johnsen (65 Fredrik Winsnes); Roar Strand, Ørjan Berg, Bent Skammelsrud; Jan Derek Sørensen, John Carew, Jahn Ivar "Mini" Jakobsen (59 Tore André Dahlum). Trainer: Nils Arne Eggen

FEYENOORD: Jerzy Dudek; Kees van Wonderen, Bert Konterman, Jan de Visser, Ulrich van Gobbel; Jean-Paul van Gastel, Paul Bosvelt, Jon Dahl Tomasson, Patrick Paauwe; Bonaventure Kalou, Julio Ricardo Cruz. Trainer: Leo Beenhakker

Goals: Tomasson (12), Carew (21, 24), Kalou (22)

BORUSSIA DORTMUND v BOAVISTA FC PORTO 3-1 (1-1)

Westfalenstadion, Dortmund 22.09.1999

Referee: Atanas Ouzounov (BUL) Attendance: 38,000

BORUSSIA: Jens Lehmann; Jürgen Kohler, Stefan Reuter, Evanilson; Christian Nerlinger, Dédé, Lars Ricken, Otto Addo (79 Miroslav Stevic); Andreas Möller, Giuseppe Reina (88 Alfred Nijhuis), Fredi Bobic (73 Heiko Herrlich). Trainer: Michael Skibbe

BOAVISTA: Bassey WILLIAM Andem; PAULO Jorge Ferreira de SOUSA, RUI Fernando Pereira BENTO, PEDRO EMANUEL Silva, Carlos Magalhães "LITOS", MÁRIO Magalhães da SILVA; LUÍS MANUEL Rodrigues Viana (45 António José Faria FORMOSO), CÉSAR de Loma Atienza, Luís JORGE Pinto da SILVA; José ROGÉRIO de Melo (64 Joaquim Silva "MARTELINHO"), Augustine Ahinful (71 GILMAR Estevan). Trainer: Jaime Pacheco

Goals: Möller (40), Rui Bento (44), Bobic (53, 65)

BOAVISTA FC PORTO v FEYENOORD ROTTERDAM 1-1 (0-0)

Estádio do Bessa, Porto 29.09.1999

Referee: Graham Poll (ENG) Attendance: 5,397

BOAVISTA: Bassey WILLIAM Andem; PAULO Jorge Ferreira de SOUSA, Carlos Magalhães "LITOS", PEDRO EMANUEL Silva, MÁRIO Magalhães da SILVA; RUI Fernando Pereira BENTO, Luís JORGE Pinto da SILVA, EMANUEL Faria Braga (79 António José Faria FORMOSO), JORGE António Pinto do COUTO; Augustine Ahinful (68 DOUALA M'Bela Rudolph), CÉSAR de Loma Atienza (46 GILMAR Estevan). Trainer: Jaime Pacheco

FEYENOORD: Jerzy Dudek; Ulrich van Gobbel, Kees van Wonderen, Bert Konterman, Jan de Visser; Paul Bosvelt, Jean-Paul van Gastel, Jon Dahl Tomasson, Patrick Paauwe; Julio Ricardo Cruz (58 Peter van Vossen), Bonaventure Kalou. Trainer: Leo Beenhakker

Sent off: Andem (90)

Goals: Bosvelt (62), Mário Silva (87)

ROSENBORG BK TRONDHEIM v BORUSSIA DORTMUND 2-2 (1-2)

Lerkendal, Trondheim 29.09.1999

Referee: Paul Anthony Durkin (ENG) Attendance: 14,086

ROSENBORG: Jørn Jamtfall; André Bergdølmo, Erik Hoftun, Bjørn Otto Bragstad, Christer Basma (25 Fredrik Winsnes); Roar Strand, Ørjan Berg, Bent Skammelsrud; Jahn Ivar "Mini" Jakobsen (64 Tore André Dahlum), Jan Derek Sørensen, John Carew. Trainer: Nils Arne Eggen

BORUSSIA: Jens Lehmann; Stefan Reuter, Evanilson (46 Karsten Baumann), Jürgen Kohler, Dédé; Miroslav Stevic (74 Alfred Nijhuis), Lars Ricken, Christian Nerlinger; Giuseppe Reina, Sergei Barbarez, Heiko Herrlich (70 Otto Addo). Trainer: Michael Skibbe

Goals: Barbarez (11), Kohler (22), Sørensen (35), Carew (68)

BORUSSIA DORTMUND
v ROSENBORG BK TRONDHEIM 0-3 (0-1)

Westfalenstadion, Dortmund 19.10.1999

Referee: Antonio Jesus López Nieto (SPA) Att: 40,000

BORUSSIA: Jens Lehmann; Stefan Reuter, Christian Wörns (46 Fredi Bobic), Jürgen Kohler, Dédé; Evanilson (83 Sead Kapetanovic), Lars Ricken, Christian Nerlinger (61 Otto Addo); Giuseppe Reina, Sergei Barbarez, Andreas Möller. Trainer: Michael Skibbe

ROSENBORG: Jørn Jamtfall; Roar Strand, Bjørn Otto Bragstad, Erik Hoftun, André Bergdølmo; Fredrik Winsnes, Bent Skammelsrud, Ørjan Berg; Jan Derek Sørensen, John Carew, Jahn Ivar "Mini" Jakobsen. Trainer: Nils Arne Eggen

Sent off: Ricken (69)

Goals: Sørensen (17, 58), F. Winsnes (70)

BORUSSIA DORTMUND
v FEYENOORD ROTTERDAM 1-1 (1-0)

Westfalenstadion, Dortmund 27.10.1999

Referee: Claude Colombo (FRA) Attendance: 39,000

BORUSSIA: Jens Lehmann; Stefan Reuter, Evanilson, Jürgen Kohler, Dédé; Miroslav Stevic, Andreas Möller, Christian Nerlinger; Giuseppe Reina, Fredi Bobic (74 Sergei Barbarez), Otto Addo. Trainer: Michael Skibbe

FEYENOORD: Jerzy Dudek; Ulrich van Gobbel (78 Igor Korneev), Bert Konterman, Ferry de Haan, Tomasz Rzasa; Paul Bosvelt, Patrick Paauwe (58 Peter van Vossen), Jan de Visser; Bonaventure Kalou, Jon Dahl Tomasson, Somalia (58 Ellery Caïro). Trainer: Leo Beenhakker

Goals: Addo (45), van Vossen (72)

FEYENOORD ROTTERDAM
v BOAVISTA FC PORTO 1-1 (0-0)

Feyenoord, Rotterdam 19.10.1999

Referee: Alfredo Trentalange (ITA) Attendance: 35,800

FEYENOORD: Jerzy Dudek; Jean-Paul van Gastel, Bert Konterman, Jan de Visser, Ulrich van Gobbel; Paul Bosvelt, Patrick Paauwe (69 Somalia); Bonaventure Kalou, Julio Ricardo Cruz, Jon Dahl Tomasson, Peter van Vossen (46 Radoslav Samardzić). Trainer: Leo Beenhakker

BOAVISTA: RICARDO Alexandre Pereira; PAULO Jorge Ferreira de SOUSA, Carlos Magalhães "LITOS", Luís JORGE Pinto da SILVA, PEDRO EMANUEL Silva; RUI Fernando Pereira BENTO, LUÍS MANUEL Rodrigues Viana (74 Sérgio Carvalho), EMANUEL Faria Braga, Ion Timofte (88 José ROGÉRIO de Melo); Augustine Ahinful (80 Joaquim Silva "MARTELINHO"), JORGE António Pinto do COUTO. Trainer: Jaime Pacheco

Goals: Tomasson (76), Timofte (83 pen)

FEYENOORD ROTTERDAM
v ROSENBORG BK TRONDHEIM 1-0 (0-0)

Feyenoord, Rotterdam 2.11.1999

Referee: Manuel Diaz Vega (SPA) Attendance: 36,776

FEYENOORD: Jerzy Dudek; Tomasz Rzasa, Ulrich van Gobbel, Ferry de Haan, Bert Konterman; Kees van Wonderen (72 Patrick Paauwe), Jan de Visser, Igor Korneev (75 Somalia), Radoslav Samardzic (86 Peter van Vossen); Jon Dahl Tomasson, Bonaventure Kalou. Trainer: Leo Beenhakker

ROSENBORG: Jørn Jamtfall; Roar Strand, Bjørn Otto Bragstad, Erik Hoftun, André Bergdølmo; Fredrik Winsnes, Bent Skammelsrud, Ørjan Berg, Jahn Ivar "Mini" Jakobsen (62 Tore André Dahlum); Jan Derek Sørensen, John Carew. Trainer: Nils Arne Eggen

Goal: Somalia (86)

ROSENBORG BK TRONDHEIM
v BOAVISTA FC PORTO 2-0 (0-0)

Lerkendal, Trondheim 27.10.1999

Referee: Michel Piraux (BEL) Attendance: 14,167

ROSENBORG: Jørn Jamtfall; Roar Strand, Bjørn Otto Bragstad, Erik Hoftun, André Bergdølmo; Fredrik Winsnes, Bent Skammelsrud, Ørjan Berg (89 Bent Inge Johnsen); Jan Derek Sørensen, John Carew, Jahn Ivar "Mini" Jakobsen (58 Tore André Dahlum). Trainer: Nils Arne Eggen

BOAVISTA: RICARDO Alexandre Pereira; Carlos Magalhães "LITOS", PAULO Jorge Ferreira de SOUSA, RUI Fernando Pereira BENTO, PEDRO EMANUEL Silva; LUÍS MANUEL Rodrigues Viana (71 Augustine Ahinful), Luís JORGE Pinto da SILVA, Ion Timofte, NÍLTON Rogério Fernandes; WHELLITON Augusto Silva (84 GILMAR Estevan), JORGE António Pinto do COUTO. Trainer: Jaime Pacheco

Goals: Ø. Berg (61), Dahlum (66)

BOAVISTA FC PORTO
v BORUSSIA DORTMUND 1-0 (1-0)

Estádio do Bessa, Porto 2.11.1999

Referee: Lubos Michel (SVK) Attendance: 4,289

BOAVISTA: RICARDO Alexandre Pereira; PAULO Jorge Ferreira de SOUSA, Carlos Magalhães "LITOS", Sérgio Carvalho, PEDRO EMANUEL Silva; NÍLTON Rogério Fernandes, LUÍS MANUEL Rodrigues Viana (90 CARLOS ALBERTO Ribeiro Pereira), Luís JORGE Pinto da SILVA, EMANUEL Faria Braga; WHELLITON Augusto Silva (62 José ROGÉRIO de Melo), DOUALA M'Bela Rudolph (69 RICARDO Jorge Fernandes SILVA). Trainer: Jaime Pacheco

BORUSSIA: Jens Lehmann; Stefan Reuter, Jürgen Kohler; Christian Wörns (76 Sergei Barbarez), Miroslav Stevic, Lars Ricken, Christian Nerlinger (46 Heiko Herrlich), Dédé; Giuseppe Reina (62 Evanilson), Fredi Bobic, Otto Addo. Trainer: Michael Skibbe

Sent off: Nilton (65)

Goal: Pedro Emanuel (16)

	P	W	D	L	F	A	Pts
Rosenborg BK	6	3	2	1	12	5	11
Feyenoord Rotterdam	6	1	5	0	7	6	8
Borussia Dortmund	6	1	3	2	7	9	6
Boavista FC Porto	6	1	2	3	4	10	5

FIRST STAGE – GROUP D

MANCHESTER UNITED FC
v CROATIA ZAGREB 0-0

Old Trafford, Manchester 14.09.1999

Referee: Nikolai Levnikov (RUS) Attendance: 53,250

MANCHESTER UNITED: Raimond van der Gouw; Jaap Stam, Phillip Neville, Henning Berg; David Beckham, Paul Scholes, Michael Clegg (76 Quinton Fortune), Mark Wilson (61 Teddy Sheringham); Andy Cole, Ryan Giggs, Dwight Yorke. Manager: Sir Alex Ferguson

CROATIA: Drazen Ladić; Mario Tokić, Goran Jurić, Tomislav Rukavina (89 Tomislav Šokota), Danijel Šarić, Stjepan Tomas; Edin Mujcin (70 Milijenko Mumlek), Mario Cvitanović, Krunoslav Jurcić; Josip Simić (67 Mihael Mikić), Igor Bišcan. Trainer: Osvaldo Ardiles

OLYMPIQUE de MARSEILLE
v SK STURM GRAZ 2-0 (2-0)

Vélodrome, Marseille 14.09.1999

Referee: Oguz Sarvan (TUR) Attendance: 25,000

OLYMPIQUE: Stéphane Porato; Patrick Blondeau, Sébastien Pérez, Eduardo Berizzo, William Gallas; Robert Pires, Stéphane Dalmat (76 Djamel Belmadi), Peter Luccin; Frédéric Brando, Florian Maurice (83 Kaba Diawara), Fabrizio Ravanelli (88 Seydou Keita). Trainer: Rolland Courbis

STURM: Josef Schicklgruber; Günther Neukirchner (82 Giorgos Koutsoupias), Franco Foda, Gilbert Prilasnig; Roman Mählich, Markus Schupp, Hannes Reinmayr (46 György Korsós), Jan Pieter Martens (46 Marko Pantelic), Ferdinand Feldhofer; Ivica Vastic, Tomislav Kocijan.
Trainer: Ivica Osim

Goals: Pires (9), Ravanelli (33)

CROATIA ZAGREB
v OLYMPIQUE de MARSEILLE 1-2 (0-1)

Maksimir, Zagreb 22.09.1999

Referee: Stefano Braschi (ITA) Attendance: 25,000

CROATIA: Drazen Ladić; Mario Tokić (46 Tomislav Šokota), Goran Jurić, Stjepan Tomas, Josip Simić; Danijel Šarić, Krunoslav Jurcić, Mario Cvitanović (46 Milijenko Mumlek); Igor Bišcan, Tomislav Rukavina (76 Josko Jelicić), Edin Mujcin. Trainer: Osvaldo Ardiles

OLYMPIQUE: Stéphane Porato; Sébastien Pérez, William Gallas, Eduardo Berizzo, Patrick Blondeau (58 Frédéric Brando); Pierre Issa, Seydou Keita (67 Fabrizio Ravanelli), Robert Pires, Peter Luccin; Stéphane Dalmat, Ibrahima Bakayoko (86 Kaba Diawara). Trainer: Rolland Courbis

Goals: Bakayoko (5), Šokota (64), Pérez (77)

SK STURM GRAZ
v MANCHESTER UNITED FC 0-3 (0-3)

Arnold Schwarzenegger-Stadion, Graz 22.09.1999

Referee: Alfredo Trentalange (ITA) Attendance: 16,480

STURM: Kazimierz Sidorczuk; Franco Foda, Gilbert Prilasnig (71 Giorgos Koutsoupias), Ferdinand Feldhofer (72 György Korsós); Günther Neukirchner, Roman Mählich (75 Hannes Reinmayr), Markus Schupp, Ivica Vastic, Jan Pieter Martens; Gerald Strafner, Tomislav Kocijan. Trainer: Ivica Osim

MANCHESTER UNITED: Raimond van der Gouw; Dennis Irwin, Henning Berg, Jaap Stam, Phillip Neville; David Beckham, Roy Keane (62 Mark Wilson), Paul Scholes, Jordi Cruijff (68 Teddy Sheringham); Andy Cole (76 Ole Gunnar Solskjær), Dwight Yorke. Manager: Alex Ferguson

Goals: Keane (16), Yorke (31), Cole (33)

MANCHESTER UNITED FC
v OLYMPIQUE de MARSEILLE 2-1 (0-1)

Old Trafford, Manchester 29.09.1999

Referee: José Maria García-Aranda (SPA) Att: 53993

MANCHESTER UNITED: Raimond van der Gouw; Dennis Irwin, Henning Berg (77 Teddy Sheringham), Jaap Stam, Phillip Neville; David Beckham, Nicky Butt, Paul Scholes; Ole Gunnar Solskjær (72 Quinton Fortune), Andy Cole (86 Michael Clegg), Dwight Yorke. Manager: Alex Ferguson

OLYMPIQUE: Stéphane Porato; Sébastien Pérez, William Gallas, Yannick Fischer, Patrick Blondeau; Peter Luccin (77 Iván de la Peña), Frédéric Brando, Pierre Issa (82 Djamel Belmadi), Stéphane Dalmat; Ibrahima Bakayoko, Fabrizio Ravanelli (62 Robert Pires). Trainer: Rolland Courbis

Goals: Bakayoko (41), Cole (79), Scholes (83)

CROATIA ZAGREB v SK STURM GRAZ 3-0 (2-0)

Maksimir, Zagreb 29.09.1999

Referee: Antonio Jesus López Nieto (SPA) Att: 21,158

CROATIA: Drazen Ladić; Goran Jurić, Stjepan Tomas, Igor Bišcan; Danijel Šarić, Mario Cvitanović, Tomislav Rukavina (74 Mario Tokić), Krunoslav Jurcić, Edin Mujcin (66 Robert Prosinecki); Josip Simić, Tomislav Šokota (79 Mihael Mikić). Trainer: Osvaldo Ardiles

STURM: Josef Schicklgruber; Franco Foda, Darko Milanic (66 Ferdinand Feldhofer), Günther Neukirchner; Markus Schopp (50 György Korsós), Roman Mählich (73 Marko Pantelic), Gilbert Prilasnig, Jan Pieter Martens, Tomislav Kocijan; Ivica Vastic, Gerald Strafner. Trainer: Ivica Osim

Goals: Rukavina (28), Šokota (34, 58 pen)

SK STURM GRAZ v CROATIA ZAGREB 1-0 (1-0)

Arnold Schwarzenegger-Stadion, Graz 19.10.1999

Referee: Alain Hamer (LUX) Attendance: 12,000

STURM: Josef Schicklgruber; Günther Neukirchner, Gilbert Prilasnig, Ferdinand Feldhofer, Markus Schopp; Roman Mählich, Markus Schupp, György Korsós, Jan Pieter Martens (90 Gerald Strafner); Ivica Vastic, Tomislav Kocijan (81 Hannes Reinmayr). Trainer: Ivica Osim

CROATIA: Drazen Ladić (12 Tomislav Butina); Goran Jurić, Igor Bišcan, Stjepan Tomas (46 Mario Cvitanović); Danijel Šarić, Edin Mujcin, Krunoslav Jurcić, Robert Prosinecki, Tomislav Rukavina; Tomislav Šokota, Josip Simić (46 Mihael Mikić). Trainer: Osvaldo Ardiles

Goal: Kocijan (40) or Mujcin og

OLYMPIQUE de MARSEILLE v MANCHESTER UNITED FC 1-0 (0-0)

Vélodrome, Marseille 19.10.1999

Referee: Hellmut Krug (GER) Attendance: 56,879

OLYMPIQUE: Stéphane Porato; Sébastien Pérez, William Gallas, Eduardo Berizzo, Patrick Blondeau; Pierre Issa, Frédéric Brando (64 Iván de la Peña), Robert Pires, Peter Luccin, Stéphane Dalmat (88 Loris Reina); Fabrizio Ravanelli (74 Florian Maurice). Trainer: Rolland Courbis

MANCHESTER UNITED: Mark Bosnich; Dennis Irwin, Henning Berg (83 Ole Gunnar Solskjær), Jaap Stam, Phillip Neville; David Beckham, Roy Keane, Paul Scholes; Ryan Giggs, Dwight Yorke, Andy Cole. Manager: Alex Ferguson

Goal: Gallas (69)

CROATIA ZAGREB v MANCHESTER UNITED FC 1-2 (0-1)

Maksimir, Zagreb 27.10.1999

Referee: Dick Jol (HOL) Attendance: 27,500

CROATIA: Tomislav Butina; Goran Jurić (36 Robert Prosinecki), Stjepan Tomas, Goce Sedloski, Danijel Šarić; Mario Tokić, Tomislav Rukavina, Edin Mujcin, Mario Cvitanović (69 Milijenko Mumlek); Tomislav Šokota, Mihael Mikić (54 Josip Simić). Trainer: Osvaldo Ardiles

MANCHESTER UNITED: Mark Bosnich; Dennis Irwin, Jaap Stam, Henning Berg, Phillip Neville; David Beckham, Roy Keane, Paul Scholes (68 Jonathan Greening); Ryan Giggs, Andy Cole (79 Jordi Cruijff), Dwight Yorke (59 Ole Gunnar Solskjær). Manager: Alex Ferguson

Goals: Beckham (32), Keane (49), Prosinecki (90)

SK STURM GRAZ v OLYMPIQUE de MARSEILLE 3-2 (1-0)

Arnold Schwarzenegger-Stadion, Graz 27.10.1999

Referee: Atanas Uzunov (BUL) Attendance: 14,850

STURM: Josef Schicklgruber; Ferdinand Feldhofer (39 Gerald Strafner), Günther Neukirchner, Gilbert Prilasnig, Markus Schopp (81 Hannes Reinmayr); Roman Mählich, Markus Schupp, Jan Pieter Martens; Ivica Vastic, Tomislav Kocijan, Mehrdad Minavand (76 Georg Bardel). Trainer: Ivica Osim

OLYMPIQUE: Stéphane Porato; Sébastien Pérez, William Gallas, Eduardo Berizzo, Patrick Blondeau 68; Pierre Issa (46 Iván de la Peña, 51 Christophe Dugarry), Peter Luccin, Robert Pires, Stéphane Dalmat; Florian Maurice (70 Loris Reina), Fabrizio Ravanelli. Trainer: Rolland Courbis

Sent off: Blondeau (68)

Goals: Mählich (18), Dugarry (53, 78), Kocijan (61, 84)

MANCHESTER UNITED FC v SK STURM GRAZ 2-1 (0-0)

Old Trafford, Manchester 2.11.1999

Referee: Rune Pedersen (NOR) Attendance: 53,745

MANCHESTER UNITED: Mark Bosnich; Gary Neville, Henning Berg, David May, Dennis Irwin (76 Danny Higginbotham); Jonathan Greening (65 Jordi Cruijff), Roy Keane, Mark Wilson (54 Phillip Neville), Ryan Giggs; Ole Gunnar Solskjær, Andy Cole. Manager: Alex Ferguson

STURM: Josef Schicklgruber; Gerald Strafner, Günther Neukirchner, Gilbert Prilasnig, Markus Schopp; Roman Mählich, Didier Angibeaud (71 Georg Bardel), Mehrdad Minavand, Jan Pieter Martens (71 Hannes Reinmayr); Ivica Vastić, Tomislav Kocijan (74 Michael Bochtler). Trainer: Ivica Osim

Goals: Solskjær (56), Keane (69), Vastić (88 pen)

OLYMPIQUE de MARSEILLE v CROATIA ZAGREB 2-2 (0-1)

Vélodrome, Marseille 2.11.1999

Referee: Pierluigi Collina (ITA) Attendance: 33,800

OLYMPIQUE: Stéphane Porato; Sébastien Pérez, Peter Luccin, Eduardo Berizzo, Loris Reina; Djamel Belmadi, Frédéric Brando, Daniel Gastón Montenegro (59 Stéphane Dalmat), Christophe Dugarry (66 Robert Pires); Kaba Diawara, Ibrahima Bakayoko (78 Fabrizio Ravanelli). Trainer: Rolland Courbis

CROATIA: Tomislav Butina; Mario Tokić, Tomislav Rukavina, Stjepan Tomas; Danijel Šarić, Krunoslav Jurcić, Mario Cvitanović, Robert Prosinecki (70 Josko Jelicić), Edin Mujcin (68 Milijenko Mumlek); Josip Simić, Tomislav Šokota (62 Mihael Mikić). Trainer: Osvaldo Ardiles

Goals: Mujcin (42), Bakayoko (53), Mikić (84), Diawara (89)

	P	W	D	L	F	A	Pts
Manchester United	6	4	1	1	9	4	13
Olympique de Marseille	6	3	1	2	10	8	10
SK Sturm Graz	6	2	0	4	5	12	6
Croatia Zagreb	6	1	2	3	7	7	5

FIRST STAGE – GROUP E

OLYMPIAKOS PEIRAIAS v REAL MADRID CF 3-3 (1-2)

OAKA Spiros Louis, Athina 15.09.1999

Referee: Mario van der Ende (HOL) Attendance: 70,800

OLYMPIAKOS: Dimitris Eleftheropoulos; Kiriakos Karataidis, Giorgos Amanatidis, Ilias Poursandis; Stelios Giannakopoulos (60 Sinisa Gogić), Predrag Djordjević, Zlatko Zahović (86 Andreas Niniadis); GIOVANNI da Silva Oliveira, Dimitris Mavrogenidis (46 Kofi Amponsah), Peter Ofori-Quaye, Giorgos Anatolakis. Trainer: Dušan Bajević

REAL: Iker Casillas; Miguel Ángel Salgado Fernández "MÍCHEL SALGADO", ROBERTO CARLOS Da Silva, Fernándo Ruíz Hierro (60 IVÁN HELGUERA Bujía), FERNANDO Carlos REDONDO Neri (73 Jose Maria GUTIérrez Hernández); RAÚL González Blanco, Steve McManaman, GEREMI Nijtap Fotso, JÚLIO CÉSAR Santos Correa; Fernando MORIENTES Sánchez (54 Nicolas Anelka), SÁVIO Bortolini Pimentel. Trainer: John Benjamin Toshack

Goals: Giovanni (11, 64), Sávio (24), Roberto Carlos (32), Zahovic (67), Raúl (80)

MOLDE FK v FC PORTO 0-1 (0-0)

Nye Molde 15.09.1999

Referee: Alain Hamer (LUX) Attendance: 8,739

MOLDE FK: Morten Bakke; Knut Anders Fostervold, Daniel Berg Hestad, Jo Tessem, Freddy dos Santos; Karl Oskar Fjørtoft (88 Ole Bjørn Sundgot), Andreas Lund, Odd Inge Olsen; Thomas Mork (46 André Schei Lindbaek), Magne Hoseth, Trond Strande. Trainer: Erik Brakstad

FC PORTO: VÍTOR Manuel Martins BAÍA; JORGE Paulo COSTA Almeida, ARGÉLico Fuks, Carlos Alberto SECRETÁRIO, José Marcelo "ESQUERDINHA"; Emílio Manuel Delgado PEIXE (82 João Paulo Maio dos Santos "PAULINHO SANTOS"), Ljubinko Drulovic (90 ALOÍSIO Pires Alves), Carlos Narciso CHAINHO, Nuno F.G. Rocha "CAPUCHO" (54 ALESSANDRO Andrade de Oliveira); Mário JARDEL Almeida Ribeiro, Anderson Luís de Sousa "DECO". Trainer: F. Santos

Goal: Deco (89)

REAL MADRID CF v MOLDE FK 4-1 (1-0)

Santiago Bernabéu, Madrid 21.09.1999

Referee: Hartmut Strampe (GER) Attendance: 15,000

REAL: Iker Casillas; Miguel Ángel Salgado Fernández "MÍCHEL SALGADO", ROBERTO CARLOS Da Silva, IVÁN CAMPO Ramos, JÚLIO CÉSAR Santos Correa; FERNANDO Carlos REDONDO Neri, Steve McManaman (64 Elvir Baljic), SÁVIO Bortolini Pimentel (74 Samuel ETO'O Fils), IVÁN HELGUERA Bujía; Fernando MORIENTES Sánchez, Nicolas Anelka (56 Jose María GUTIérrez Hernández). Trainer: John Benjamin Toshack

MOLDE FK: Morten Bakke; Pål Lydersen (85 Petter Christian Singsaas), Knut Anders Fostervold, Jo Tessem, Trond Strande; Daniel Berg Hestad, Karl Oskar Fjørtoft, Odd Inge Olsen, Andre Schei Lindbaek (89 Ole Bjørn Sundgot); Andreas Lund, Magne Hoseth (66 Thomas Mork).

Goals: Morientes (27), Sávio (60, 70 pen), Lindbaek (80), Guti (81)

FC PORTO v OLYMPIAKOS PEIRAIAS 2-0 (1-0)

Estádio das Antas, Porto 21.09.1999

Referee: David Roland Elleray (ENG) Attendance: 21,500

FC PORTO: VÍTOR Manuel Martins BAÍA; JORGE Paulo COSTA Almeida, ARGÉLico Fuks, Carlos Narciso CHAINHO (76 RUI Gil Soares BARROS), Anderson Luís de Sousa "DECO" (90 ALOÍSIO Pires Alves); Emílio Manuel Delgado PEIXE, Carlos Alberto SECRETÁRIO, Nuno F.G. Rocha "CAPUCHO" (62 ALESSANDRO Andrade de Oliveira), José Marcelo "ESQUERDINHA"; Ljubinko Drulovic, Mário JARDEL Almeida Ribeiro. Trainer: Fernando Santos

OLYMPIAKOS: Dimitris Eleftheropoulos; Kiriakos Karataidis, Andreas Niniadis, Giorgos Amanatidis, Ilias Poursandis, Giorgos Anatolakis; Predrag Djordjević (90 Alekos Alexandris), Kofi Amponsah (59 Sinisa Gogić), Zlatko Zahović (75 Luciano Nunes de Souza); GIOVANNI da Silva Oliveira, Peter Ofori-Quaye. Trainer: Dušan Bajević

Goals: Esquerdinha (6), Jardel (47)

REAL MADRID CF v FC PORTO 3-1 (2-1)

Santiago Bernabéu, Madrid 28.09.1999

Referee: Pierluigi Collina (ITA) Attendance: 41,000

REAL: Albano Bizarri; Miguel Ángel Salgado Fernández "MÍCHEL SALGADO", ROBERTO CARLOS Da Silva, Fernándo Ruíz Hierro, JÚLIO CÉSAR Santos Correa; FERNANDO Carlos REDONDO Neri, Steve McManaman (56 Clarence Seedorf), IVÁN HELGUERA Bujía (83 Manuel SANCHÍS Hontiyuelo), SÁVIO Bortolini Pimentel (89 Samuel ETO'O Fils); RAÚL González Blanco, Fernando MORIENTES Sánchez. Trainer: John Benjamin Toshack

FC PORTO: VÍTOR Manuel Martins BAÍA; Carlos Alberto SECRETÁRIO, JORGE Paulo COSTA Almeida, ARGÉLico Fuks, José Marcelo "ESQUERDINHA"; Emílio Manuel Delgado PEIXE, Carlos Narciso CHAINHO (56 RUBENS Rodrigues dos Santos JÚNIOR), Nuno F.G. Rocha "CAPUCHO" (50 ALESSANDRO Andrade de Oliveira, 87 Miklós Fehér), Anderson Luís de Sousa "DECO"; Ljubinko Drulovic, Mário JARDEL Almeida Ribeiro. Trainer: Fernando Santos

Goals: Morientes (23), Jardel (28), Helguera (37), Hierro (68 pen)

OLYMPIAKOS PEIRAIAS v MOLDE FK 3-1 (1-0)

OAKA Spiros Louis, Athina 28.09.1999

Referee: Lubos Michel (SVK) Attendance: 40,299

OLYMPIAKOS: Dimitris Eleftheropoulos; Kiriakos Karataidis, Giorgos Amanatidis, Ilias Poursanidis; GIOVANNI da Silva Oliveira, Predrag Djordjević, Petros Passalis, Vasilis Karapialis (62 Sinisa Gogić); Peter Ofori-Quaye (67 Luciano Nunes de Souza, 79 Paraskevas Antzas), Zlatko Zahović, Giorgos Anatolakis. Trainer: Dušan Bajević

MOLDE FK: Morten Bakke; Pål Lydersen, Knut Anders Fostervold, Daniel Berg Hestad, Jo Tessem; Karl Oskar Fjørtoft, Andreas Lund, Odd Inge Olsen; Thomas Mork (54 André Schei Lindbaek), Trond Strande (72 Freddy dos Santos), Ole Bjørn Sundgot (74 Magne Hoseth). Trainer: Erik Brakstad

Goals: Giovanni (16, 70), Lund (58), Luciano (77)

FC PORTO v REAL MADRID CF 2-1 (2-0)

Estádio das Antas, Porto 20.10.1999

Referee: Bernd Heynemann (GER) Attendance: 36,550

FC PORTO: VÍTOR Manuel Martins BAÍA; Carlos Alberto SECRETÁRIO, JORGE Paulo COSTA Almeida, ARGÉLico Fuks (74 ALOÍSIO Pires Alves), José Marcelo "ESQUERDINHA"; Emílio Manuel Delgado PEIXE, Carlos Narciso CHAINHO; Nuno F.G. Rocha "CAPUCHO" (72 João Paulo Maio dos Santos "PAULINHO SANTOS"), Anderson Luís de Sousa "DECO", RUBENS Rodrigues dos Santos JÚNIOR (36 Ljubinko Drulovic), Mário JARDEL Almeida Ribeiro. Trainer: Fernando Santos

REAL: Bodo Illgner; Miguel Ángel Salgado Fernández "MÍCHEL SALGADO", Fernándo Ruíz Hierro, IVÁN CAMPO Ramos, ROBERTO CARLOS Da Silva; GEREMI Nijtap Fotso (66 Jose María GUTIérrez Hernández), FERNANDO Carlos REDONDO Neri; RAÚL González Blanco, Nicolas Anelka (47 Clarence Seedorf), SÁVIO Bortolini Pimentel, Fernando MORIENTES Sánchez. Trainer: John Benjamin Toshack

Goals: Jardel (13, 35), Peixe (68 og)

MOLDE FK v OLYMPIAKOS PEIRAIAS 3-2 (0-2)

Nye Molde 20.10.1999

Referee: Ryszard Wójcik (POL) Attendance: 10,230

MOLDE FK: Morten Bakke; Trond Strande (Freddy dos Santos), Pål Lydersen, Knut Anders Fostervold; Odd Inge Olsen, Karl Oskar Fjørtoft, Daniel Berg Hestad; Ole Bjørn Sundgot (74 Magne Hoseth), Jo Tessem, Andreas Lund, Thomas Mork (54 André Schei Lindbaek). Trainer: Erik Brakstad

OLYMPIAKOS: Dimitris Eleftheropoulos; Giorgos Amanatidis, Giorgos Anatolakis, Kiriakos Karataidis (58 Paraskevas Antzas), Predrag Djordjević; Dimitris Mavrogenidis, Petros Passalis (77 Stelios Giannakopoulos), Ilias Poursandis, Vasilis Karapialis (46 Peter Ofori-Quaye); Zlatko Zahović, GIOVANNI da Silva Oliveira. Trainer: Dušan Bajević

Goals: Mavrogenidis (36), Zahovic (40), Lund (54, 59), Berg Hestad (72)

REAL MADRID CF v OLYMPIAKOS PEIRAIAS 3-0 (1-0)

Estadio Santiago Bernabéu 26.10.1999

Referee: Markus Merk (GER) Attendance: 23,000

REAL: Albano Bizarri; GEREMI Nijtap Fotso (62 Miguel Ángel Salgado Fernández "MÍCHEL SALGADO"), Fernándo Ruíz Hierro (41 IVÁN CAMPO Ramos), JÚLIO CÉSAR Santos Correa, ROBERTO CARLOS Da Silva; Clarence Seedorf, IVÁN HELGUERA Bujía, FERNANDO Carlos REDONDO Neri, Jose María GUTIérrez Hernández (71 Steve McManaman); RAÚL González Blanco, Fernando MORIENTES Sánchez. Trainer: John Benjamin Toshack

OLYMPIAKOS: Dimitris Eleftheropoulos; Kofi Amponsah (62 Stelios Giannakopoulos), Giorgos Anatolakis, Petros Passalis, Kiriakos Karataidis, Giorgos Amanatidis; Ilias Poursandis, Predrag Djordjević, Dimitris Mavrogenidis (76 Andreas Niniadis); Zlatko Zahović, Sinisa Gogić. Trainer: Dušan Bajević

Goals: Raúl (21), Morientes (64), Roberto Carlos (83)

FC PORTO v MOLDE FK **3-1** (2-0)

Estádio das Antas, Porto 26.10.1999

Referee: Graham Barber (ENG) Attendance: 26,100

FC PORTO: VÍTOR Manuel Martins BAÍA; Carlos Alberto SECRETÁRIO, JORGE Paulo COSTA Almeida, ALOÍSIO Pires Alves, José Marcelo "ESQUERDINHA"; Carlos Narciso CHAINHO (69 RICARDO André Pinho de SOUSA), Emílio Manuel Delgado PEIXE, Anderson Luís de Sousa "DECO" (29 ALESSANDRO Andrade de Oliveira), Nuno F.G. Rocha "CAPUCHO"; Ljubinko Drulovic, Mário JARDEL Almeida Ribeiro (76 DOMINGOS Paciência de Oliveira). Trainer: Fernando Santos

MOLDE FK: Morten Bakke; Freddy dos Santos, Petter Christian Singsaas, Trond Strande; Odd Inge Olsen (84 Ole Bjørn Sundgot), Karl Oskar Fjørtoft, Daniel Berg Hestad, Pål Lydersen; Jo Tessem (61 Andre Lindbaek), Andreas Lund, Magne Hoseth (86 Thomas Mork). Trainer: Erik Brakstad

Goals: Deco (1, 28), Jardel (58), Berg Hestad (82)

MOLDE FK v REAL MADRID CF **0-1** (0-1)

Nye Molde 3.11.1999

Referee: Gilles Veissière (FRA) Attendance: 10,785

MOLDE FK: Morten Bakke; Trond Strande, Petter Christian Singsaas, Pål Lydersen, Knut Anders Fostervold (46 Freddy dos Santos); Odd Inge Olsen, Karl Oskar Fjørtoft, Daniel Berg Hestad, Jo Tessem (87 Thomas Mork); Andreas Lund, Magne Hoseth (61 André Schei Lindbaek). Trainer: Erik Brakstad

REAL: Albano Bizarri; Miguel Ángel Salgado Fernández "MÍCHEL SALGADO", JÚLIO CÉSAR Santos Correa, Aitor KARANKA de la Hoz, ROBERTO CARLOS Da Silva; IVÁN CAMPO Ramos, Christian Karembeu, Manuel SANCHÍS Hontiyuelo, IVÁN HELGUERA Bujía, Clarence Seedorf; Carlos Reina ARANDA (55 Samuel ETO'O Fils).
Trainer: John Benjamin Toshack

Goal: Karembeu (43)

OLYMPIAKOS PEIRAIAS v FC PORTO **1-0** (0-0)

OAKA Spiros Louis, Athina 3.11.1999

Referee: Kim Milton Nielsen (DEN) Attendance: 24,131

OLYMPIAKOS: Dimitris Eleftheropoulos; Dimitris Mavrogenidis, Giorgos Amanatidis (46 Sinisa Gogić), Paraskevas Antzas (79 Kofi Amponsah), Kiriakos Karataidis; Petros Passalis, Predrag Djordjević, Stelios Giannakopoulos, Zlatko Zahović; GIOVANNI da Silva Oliveira, Peter Ofori-Quaye (46 Vasilis Karapialis). Trainer: Dušan Bajević

FC PORTO: Henrique HILÁRIO Sampaio; RUBENS Rodrigues dos Santos JÚNIOR, ALOÍSIO Pires Alves, Carlos Alberto SECRETÁRIO, RICARDO André Pinho de SOUSA (64 Miklós Fehér); Ljubinko Drulovic, RODOLFO Luís Costa Correia (64 Carlos Narciso CHAINHO), ALESSANDRO Andrade de Oliveira, João Paulo Maio dos Santos "PAULINHO SANTOS"; ROMEU António Soares Almeida (72 Carlos Eduardo Ventura "DUDA"), RICARDO Emidio Pinho de SOUSA. Trainer: Fernando Santos

Goal: Giannakopoulos (56)

	P	W	D	L	F	A	Pts
Real Madrid CF	6	4	1	1	15	7	13
FC Porto	6	4	0	2	9	6	12
Olympiakos Peiraias	6	2	1	3	9	12	7
Molde FK	6	1	0	5	6	14	3

FIRST STAGE – GROUP F

FC BAYERN MÜNCHEN v PSV EINDHOVEN **2-1** (1-0)

Olympiastadion, München 15.09.1999

Referee: Gilles Veissière (FRA) Attendance: 30,000

BAYERN: Oliver Kahn; Bixente Lizarazu, Samuel Kuffour, Patrik Andersson, Lothar Matthäus; Mehmet Scholl (87 Hasan Salihamidzic), Thomas Strunz, Stefan Effenberg, Jens Jeremies; Paulo Sérgio (79 Alexander Zickler), Roque Santa Cruz (68 Carsten Jancker). Trainer: Ottmar Hitzfeld

PSV: Ronald Waterreus; Jürgen Dirkx (77 Arnold Bruggink), Ernest Faber, Jan Heintze, Johann Vogel; Mark van Bommel 90, Dmitri Khokhlov, Yuri Nikiforov (82 Wilfred Bouma), Tomek Iwan; Ruud van Nistelrooy, Luc Nilis.
Trainer: Eric Gerets

Sent off: van Bommel (90)

Goals: Paulo Sérgio (11, 69), Khokhlov (59)

VALENCIA CF v GLASGOW RANGERS FC **2-0** (0-0)

Mestalla, Valencia 15.09.1999

Referee: Lubos Michel (SVK) Attendance: 31,524

VALENCIA: Santiago CAÑIZARES Ruiz; Mauricio Pellegrino, Joachim Björklund, Amedeo Carboni, Jocelyn Angloma; Gaizka MENDIETA Zabala, GERARD López Segú, Christian Alberto "KILY" GONZÁLEZ Peret, David ALBELDA Aliques; CLAUDIO Javier LÓPEZ (71 Adrian Ilie), JUAN Ginés SÁNCHEZ Moreno (80 Miguel Ángel ANGULO).
Trainer: Héctor Raúl Cuper

RANGERS: Lionel Charbonnier; Sergio Porrini (72 Andrei Kanchelskis), Craig Moore, Lorenzo Amoruso, Tony Vidmar; Barry Ferguson, Giovanni van Bronckhorst (85 Jonatan Johansson), Claudio Reyna; Michael Mols, Gabriel Omar Amato, Neil McCann (46 Jörg Albertz).
Trainer: Dick Advocaat

Goals: Moore (57 og), Kily González (74)

GLASGOW RANGERS FC v FC BAYERN MÜNCHEN 1-1 (1-0)

Ibrox, Glasgow 21.09.1999

Referee: Ryszard Wójcik (POL) Attendance: 49,960

RANGERS: Lionel Charbonnier; Sergio Porrini, Craig Moore, Lorenzo Amoruso, Arthur Numan; Barry Ferguson, Giovanni van Bronckhorst, Jörg Albertz, Claudio Reyna; Michael Mols (84 Colin Hendry), Jonatan Johansson (90 Neil McCann). Trainer: Dick Advocaat

BAYERN: Stefan Wessels; Samuel Kuffour, Lothar Matthäus (81 Alexander Zickler), Thomas Linke; Bixente Lizarazu (46 Carsten Jancker), Stefan Effenberg, Jens Jeremies, Michael Tarnat; Mehmet Scholl, Giovane Élber (73 Roque Santa Cruz), Hasan Salihamidzić. Trainer: Ottmar Hitzfeld

Goals: Albertz (22), Tarnat (90)

FC BAYERN MÜNCHEN v VALENCIA CF 1-1 (1-0)

Olympiastadion, München 28.09.1999

Referee: Graziano Cesari (ITA) Attendance: 31,000

BAYERN: Oliver Kahn; Thomas Linke, Lothar Matthäus, Samuel Kuffour; Hasan Salihamidzic, Jens Jeremies, Stefan Effenberg, Michael Tarnat; Alexander Zickler (46 Roque Santa Cruz), Giovane Élber (62 Carsten Jancker), Mehmet Scholl. Trainer: Ottmar Hitzfeld

VALENCIA: Andrés PALOP Cervera; Jocelyn Angloma, Mauricio Pellegrino, Joachim Björklund, Amedeo Carboni; Christian Alberto "KILY" GONZÁLEZ Peret (84 Francisco FARINÓS Zapata), Gaizka MENDIETA Zabala (87 Miguel Ángel ANGULO), GERARD López Segú, David ALBELDA Aliques; JUAN Ginés SÁNCHEZ Moreno (62 Adrian Ilie), CLAUDIO Javier LÓPEZ. Trainer: Héctor Raúl Cuper

Goals: Élber (6), Gerard (80)

PSV EINDHOVEN v VALENCIA CF 1-1 (0-1)

Philips, Eindhoven 21.09.1999

Referee: Rune Pedersen (NOR) Attendance: 26,500

PSV: Ronald Waterreus; Jürgen Dirkx, Ernest Faber (56 Rob Wielaert), Jan Heintze, Yuri Nikiforov; Dmitri Khokhlov, Johann Vogel, Dennis Rommedahl (74 Joonas Kolkka), Ovidiu Stîngă (69 Wilfred Bouma); Ruud van Nistelrooy, Arnold Bruggink. Trainer: Eric Gerets

VALENCIA: Santiago CAÑIZARES Ruiz (64 Andrés PALOP Cervera); Mauricio Pellegrino, Joachim Björklund, Amedeo Carboni, Jocelyn Angloma; Gaizka MENDIETA Zabala, GERARD López Segú, Christian Alberto "KILY" GONZÁLEZ Peret, David ALBELDA Aliques; CLAUDIO Javier LÓPEZ (90 ÓSCAR García Junyent), JUAN Ginés SÁNCHEZ Moreno (74 Miguel Ángel ANGULO). Trainer: Héctor Raúl Cuper

Goals: López (4), van Nistelrooy (72 pen)

GLASGOW RANGERS FC v PSV EINDHOVEN 4-1 (2-1)

Ibrox, Glasgow 20.10.1999

Referee: Pierluigi Collina (ITA) Attendance: 50,023

RANGERS: Stefan Klos; Sergio Porrini, Craig Moore, Lorenzo Amoruso, Barry Ferguson; Giovanni van Bronckhorst, Tony Vidmar, Neil McCann (70 Jörg Albertz), Derek McInnes; Michael Mols (80 Jonatan Johansson), Rodney Wallace (87 Andrei Kanchelskis). Trainer: Dick Advocaat

PSV: Ivica Kralj; Ernest Faber, Jan Heintze, Yuri Nikiforov, Ovidiu Stingă (73 Dennis Rommedahl), Rob Wielaert (31 Joonas Kolkka); Mark van Bommel, Dmitri Khokhlov, Johann Vogel; Ruud van Nistelrooy, Luc Nilis (85 Arnold Bruggink). Trainer: Eric Gerets

Goals: Amoruso (19), Mols (34, 80), van Nistelrooy (45 pen), McCann (56)

PSV EINDHOVEN v GLASGOW RANGERS FC 0-1 (0-0)

Philips, Eindhoven 28.09.1999

Referee: Anders Frisk (SWE) Attendance: 28,000

PSV: Ronald Waterreus; Jürgen Dirkx, Jan Heintze, Yuri Nikiforov, Rob Wielaert; Dmitri Khokhlov, Björn van der Doelen (80 Arnold Bruggink), Dennis Rommedahl (63 Joonas Kolkka), Ovidiu Stîngă (68 Wilfred Bouma); Ruud van Nistelrooy, Luc Nilis. Trainer: Eric Gerets

RANGERS: Lionel Charbonnier; Sergio Porrini, Craig Moore, Lorenzo Amoruso, Arthur Numan; Barry Ferguson, Giovanni van Bronckhorst, Claudio Reyna (24 Jörg Albertz), Neil McCann; Michael Mols, Rodney Wallace. Trainer: Dick Advocaat

Goal: Albertz (85)

VALENCIA CF v FC BAYERN MÜNCHEN 1-1 (1-1)

Mestalla, Valencia 20.10.1999

Referee: Anders Frisk (SWE) Attendance: 44,000

VALENCIA: Andrés PALOP Cervera; Miguel Ángel ANGULO, Joachim Björklund (20 Miroslav Djukić), Mauricio Pellegrino, Amedeo Carboni; Gaizka MENDIETA Zabala (65 Francisco FARINÓS Zapata), David ALBELDA Aliques, GERARD López Segú, Christian Alberto "KILY" GONZÁLEZ Peret (85 ÓSCAR García Junyent); CLAUDIO Javier LÓPEZ, Adrian Ilie. Trainer: Héctor Raúl Cuper

BAYERN: Oliver Kahn; Samuel Kuffour, Lothar Matthäus, Thomas Linke; Markus Babbel, Jens Jeremies, Stefan Effenberg, Bixente Lizarazu; Alexander Zickler (75 Hasan Salihamidzic), Giovane Élber (81 Carsten Jancker), Paulo Sérgio (90 Roque Santa Cruz). Trainer: Ottmar Hitzfeld

Goals: Ilie (11), Effenberg (18 pen)

PSV EINDHOVEN v FC BAYERN MÜNCHEN 2-1 (1-0)

Philips, Eindhoven 26.10.1999

Referee: Paul Anthony Durkin (ENG) Attendance: 29,003

PSV: Ronald Waterreus; Ernest Faber, Jürgen Dirkx, Eric Addo, Jan Heintze; Ovidiu Stîngă, Mark van Bommel, Johann Vogel, Joonas Kolkka (88 Tomek Iwan); Luc Nilis (72 Arnold Bruggink), Ruud van Nistelrooy. Trainer: Eric Gerets

BAYERN: Stefan Wessels; Patrik Andersson, Lothar Matthäus, Thomas Linke; Markus Babbel (68 Hasan Salihamidzic), Stefan Effenberg, Jens Jeremies, Bixente Lizarazu; Paulo Sérgio (26 Roque Santa Cruz), Giovane Élber, Alexander Zickler (75 Carsten Jancker).
Trainer: Ottmar Hitzfeld

Sent off: Jeremies (90)

Goals: van Nistelrooy (40), Santa Cruz (51), Nilis (57)

VALENCIA CF v PSV EINDHOVEN 1-0 (0-0)

Mestalla, Valencia 3.11.1999

Referee: Graham Barber (ENG) Attendance: 26,266

VALENCIA: Andrés PALOP Cervera; Miguel Ángel ANGULO, Miroslav Djukić, Mauricio Pellegrino, Amedeo Carboni; Francisco FARINÓS Zapata, Gaizka MENDIETA Zabala, GERARD López Segú, Christian Alberto "KILY" GONZÁLEZ Peret; JUAN Ginés SÁNCHEZ Moreno (77 ÓSCAR García Junyent), CLAUDIO Javier LÓPEZ.
Trainer: Héctor Raúl Cuper

PSV: Ronald Waterreus; Ernest Faber (59 Jürgen Dirkx), Jan Heintze, Yuri Nikiforov, Eric Addo; Ovidiu Stîngă, Mark van Bommel, Joonas Kolkka, Dmitri Khokhlov; Luc Nilis (71 Dennis Rommedahl), Ruud van Nistelrooy.
Trainer: Eric Gerets

Goal: López (70)

GLASGOW RANGERS FC v VALENCIA CF 1-2 (0-2)

Ibrox, Glasgow 26.10.1999

Referee: Günter Benkö (AUS) Attendance: 50,063

RANGERS: Stefan Klos; Sergio Porrini, Lorenzo Amoruso, Craig Moore, Tony Vidmar (61 Jörg Albertz); Derek McInnes (38 Andrei Kanchelskis), Barry Ferguson, Giovanni van Bronckhorst, Neil McCann; Michael Mols, Rodney Wallace (75 Jonatan Johansson). Trainer: Dick Advocaat

VALENCIA: Andrés PALOP Cervera; Miguel Ángel ANGULO, Mauricio Pellegrino, Miroslav Djukić, Amedeo Carboni; Gaizka MENDIETA Zabala (80 Miguel Ángel Soria), David ALBELDA Aliques, Christian Alberto "KILY" GONZÁLEZ Peret (67 Francisco FARINÓS Zapata), Adrian Ilie (61 JUAN Ginés SÁNCHEZ Moreno); GERARD López Segú, CLAUDIO Javier LÓPEZ. Trainer: Héctor Raúl Cuper

Goals: Mendieta (35), López (45), Moore (60)

	P	W	D	L	F	A	Pts
Valencia CF	6	3	3	0	8	4	12
FC Bayern München	6	2	3	1	7	6	9
Glasgow Rangers FC	6	2	1	3	7	7	7
PSV Eindhoven	6	1	1	4	5	10	4

FC BAYERN MÜNCHEN v GLASGOW RANGERS FC 1-0 (1-0)

Olympiastadion, München 3.11.1999

Referee: Vítor Manuel Melo Pereira (POR) Att: 54,000

BAYERN: Oliver Kahn; Markus Babbel, Lothar Matthäus, Thomas Linke; Thomas Strunz, Thorsten Fink, Stefan Effenberg (74 Michael Tarnat), Bixente Lizarazu; Mehmet Scholl (66 Hasan Salihamidzic), Giovane Élber, Roque Santa Cruz (66 Paulo Sérgio). Trainer: Ottmar Hitzfeld

RANGERS: Stefan Klos; Sergio Porrini, Craig Moore, Lorenzo Amoruso, Arthur Numan (72 Neil McCann); Barry Ferguson, Giovanni van Bronckhorst, Claudio Reyna, Jörg Albertz; Michael Mols (30 Jonatan Johansson), Rodney Wallace (80 Gabriel Omar Amato). Trainer: Dick Advocaat

Goal: Strunz (33 pen)

FIRST STAGE – GROUP G

AC SPARTA PRAHA v GIRONDINS de BORDEAUX 0-0

Stadión na Letnej, Praha 15.09.1999

Referee: Terje Hauge (NOR) Attendance: 14,928

SPARTA: Tomáš Poštulka; Petr Gabriel, Jiří Novotný, Milan Fukal; Vladimír Labant, Martin Hašek, Zdenek Svoboda(90 Pavel Novotný), Miroslav Baranek, Tomáš Rosický (84 Martin Prohászka); Vratislav Lokvenc, Horst Siegl (58 Libor Sionko).
Trainer: Ivan Hašek

GIRONDINS: Ulrich Ramé; Nisa Saveljic, François Grenet, Kodjo Afanou, Hervé Alicarte; Jean-Christophe Rouvière, Johan Micoud, Corentin Martins (90 Laurent Batlles), Lassina Diabaté; Lilian Laslandes, Sylvain Wiltord.
Trainer: Elie Baup

WILLEM II TILBURG v SPARTAK MOSKVA 1-3 (0-2)

Willem II, Tilburg 15.09.1999

Referee: Juan Antonio Fernández Marín (SPA) Att: 14,000

WILLEM II: Kris Mampaey; Geoffrey Prommayon, Delano Hill, Raymond Victoria, Marcel Valk (62 Ousmane Sanou); Arno Arts, Tomás Galasek, Kew Jaliens; Jattoo Ceesay, Mariano Bombarda, Dmitriy Shukov (90 Mark Schenning). Trainer: Co Adriaanse

SPARTAK: Aleksandr Filimonov; Yuri Kovtun, Dmitriy Khlestov, Dmytro Parfyonov; Evgeniy Bushmanov, Vasiliy Baranov, Artyom Bezrodnyi, Luís ROBSON Pereira; Yegor Titov (71 Vadim Yevseyev), Valeriy Kechinov (46 Ilya Tsymbalar), Andrei Tikhonov. Trainer: Oleg Romantsev

Goals: Tikhonov (27 pen, 37, 53 pen), Arts (56)

AC SPARTA PRAHA v WILLEM II TILBURG 4-0 (3-0)

Stadión na Letnej, Praha 28.09.1999

Referee: Bernd Heynemann (GER) Attendance: 10,581

SPARTA: Tomáš Poštulka; Petr Gabriel, Vladimír Labant, Jiří Novotný, Milan Fukal; Martin Hašek, Michal Horňák, Miroslav Baranek (82 Josef Obajdin), Tomáš Rosický; Libor Sionko (84 Horst Siegl), Martin Prohászka (36 Jiří Jarošik). Trainer: Ivan Hašek

WILLEM II: Kris Mampaey; Geoffrey Prommayon, Delano Hill, Marco Gentile (46 Mariano Bombarda), Raymond Victoria; Arno Arts, Tomás Galasek, Kew Jaliens; Jattoo Ceesay, Yassine Abdellaoui (81 Ousmane Sanou), Dmitri Shukov. Trainer: Co Adriaanse

Goals: J. Novotný (26), Prohászka (29 pen), Rosický (40), Jarošik (58)

GIRONDINS de BORDEAUX v WILLEM II TILBURG 3-2 (2-1)

Parc Lescure, Bordeaux 21.09.1999

Referee: Graham Barber (ENG) Attendance: 13,231

GIRONDINS: Ulrich Ramé; Nisa Saveljic, Jérôme Bonnissel, François Grenet, Kodjo Afanou; Jean-Christophe Rouvière, Johan Micoud, Corentin Martins (63 Laurent Batlles), Lassina Diabaté; Lilian Laslandes, Sylvain Wiltord (73 Pascal Feindouno). Trainer: Elie Baup

WILLEM II: Kris Mampaey; Delano Hill, Raymond Victoria, Kew Jaliens; Marcel Valk, Arno Arts, Tomás Galasek, Yassine Abdellaoui (58 Ousmane Sanou), Jattoo Ceesay, Mariano Bombarda (74 Mark Schenning), Dmitriy Shukov. Trainer: Co Adriaanse

Goals: Victoria (17, o.g.), Laslandes (22), Abdellaoui (40), Sanou (70), Feindouno (82)

GIRONDINS de BORDEAUX v SPARTAK MOSKVA 2-1 (1-0)

Parc Lescure, Bordeaux 28.09.1999

Referee: Urs Meier (SWI) Attendance: 18,676

GIRONDINS: Ulrich Ramé; François Grenet, Kodjo Afanou, Nisa Saveljic, Jérôme Bonnissel; Corentin Martins (72 Laurent Batlles), Michel Pavon, Lassina Diabaté, Johan Micoud; Sylvain Wiltord (87 Pascal Feindouno), Lilian Laslandes. Trainer: Elie Baup

SPARTAK: Aleksandr Filimonov; Dmytro Parfyonov, Evgeniy Bushmanov, Dmitriy Khlestov, Vadim Yevseyev, Vasiliy Baranov (55 Valeriy Kechinov), Viktor Bulatov (46 Ilya Tsymbalar), Yegor Titov, Andrei Tikhonov; Aleksandr Shirko, Artyom Bezrodnyi. Trainer: Oleg Romantsev

Goals: Wiltord (9), Micoud (56), Bezrodnyi (64)

SPARTAK MOSKVA v AC SPARTA PRAHA 1-1 (0-1)

Luzhniki, Moskva 21.09.1999

Referee: Karl-Erik Nilsson (SWE) Attendance: 43,000

SPARTAK: Aleksandr Filimonov; Yuri Kovtun, Dmitriy Khlestov, Evgeniy Bushmanov, Dmytro Parfyonov; Ilya Tsymbalar (56 Aleksandr Shirko), Vasiliy Baranov (63 Valeriy Kechinov), Viktor Bulatov (70 Artyom Bezrodnyi), Yegor Titov; Andrei Tikhonov, Luís ROBSON Pereira. Trainer: Oleg Romantsev

SPARTA: Tomáš Poštulka; Petr Gabriel, Michal Horňák, Jiří Novotný, Milan Fukal; Vladimír Labant, Martin Hašek, Libor Sionko, Tomáš Rosický (76 Josef Obajdin); Vratislav Lokvenc, Miroslav Baranek (86 Martin Prohászka). Trainer: Ivan Hašek

Sent off: Kovtun (68), Robson (82)

Goals: Lokvenc (17), Bezrodnyi (73)

WILLEM II TILBURG v AC SPARTA PRAHA 3-4 (2-1)

Willem, Tilburg 20.10.1999

Referee: Oguz Sarvan (TUR) Attendance: 13,419

WILLEM II: Kris Mampaey (64 Jimmy van Fessem); Geoffrey Prommayon, Mark Schenning, Delano Hill, Kew Jaliens; Tomás Galasek, Raymond Victoria, Denny Landzaat; Jattoo Ceesay, Mariano Bombarda (59 Marcel Valk), Dmitri Shukov (76 Ousmane Sanou). Trainer: Co Adriaanse

SPARTA: Tomáš Poštulka; Milan Fukal, Jiří Novotný, Petr Gabriel, Vladimír Labant; Zdenek Svoboda, Miroslav Baranek (86 Josef Obajdin), Martin Hašek; Tomáš Rosický (61 Horst Siegl), Libor Sionko, Vratislav Lokvenc (79 Jiří Jarošik). Trainer: Ivan Hašek

Sent off: Galásek (53)

Goals: Bombarda (1), Shukov (6), J. Novotný (17), Schenning (50), Labant (54 pen, 90 pen), Baranek (62)

SPARTAK MOSKVA v GIRONDINS de BORDEAUX 1-2 (0-1)

Luzhniki, Moskva 20.10.1999

Referee: Graham Poll (ENG) Attendance: 46,300

SPARTAK: Aleksandr Filimonov; Dmytro Parfyonov, Dmitriy Khlestov, Evgeniy Bushmanov, Yuri Kovtun; Vasiliy Baranov (55 Valeriy Kechinov), Yegor Titov, Viktor Bulatov, Andrei Tikhonov; Artyom Bezrodnyi, Aleksandr Shirko. Trainer: Oleg Romantsev

GIRONDINS: Ulrich Ramé; François Grenet, Kodjo Afanou, Hervé Alicarte, Jérôme Bonnissel; Corentin Martins (76 Jean-Christophe Rouvière), Lassina Diabaté, Michel Pavon, Johan Micoud; Sylvain Wiltord (87 Laurent Batlles), Lilian Laslandes. Trainer: Elie Baup

Goals: Micoud (21), Tikhonov (55 pen), Wiltord (76)

GIRONDINS de BORDEAUX v AC SPARTA PRAHA 0-0

Parc Lescure, Bordeaux 26.10.1999

Referee: Manuel Diaz Vega (SPA) Attendance: 22,138

GIRONDINS: Ulrich Ramé; David Jemmali, Nisa Saveljic, Hervé Alicarte, Jérôme Bonnissel; Corentin Martins (76 Johan Micoud), Jean-Christophe Rouvière, Michel Pavon, Lassina Diabaté (66 Laurent Batlles); Sylvain Wiltord (90 Marc Zanotti), Lilian Laslandes. Trainer: Elie Baup

SPARTA: Tomáš Poštulka; Michal Horňák, Milan Fukal, Jiří Novotný, Petr Gabriel, Vladimír Labant; Miroslav Baranek (89 Zdenek Svoboda), Martin Hašek, Tomáš Rosický (90 Jiří Jarošik); Vratislav Lokvenc (81 Horst Siegl), Libor Sionko. Trainer: Ivan Hašek

SPARTAK MOSKVA v WILLEM II TILBURG 1-1 (1-0)

Luzhniki, Moskva 26.10.1999

Referee: Lucílio Cardoso Cortez Batista (POR) Att: 16,700

SPARTAK: Aleksandr Filimonov; Yuri Kovtun 90, Dmitriy Khlestov, Evgeniy Bushmanov, Dmytro Parfyonov; Vasiliy Baranov (46 Vadim Yevseyev), Viktor Bulatov (58 Valeriy Kechinov), Yegor Titov, Andrei Tikhonov; Artyom Bezrodnyi, Aleksandr Shirko. Trainer: Oleg Romantsev

WILLEM II: Jimmy van Fessem, Geoffrey Prommayon, Marco Gentile, Delano Hill, Mark Schenning; Raymond Victoria, Jos van Nieuwstadt, Denny Landzaat (84 Marcel Valk); Ousmane Sanou (86 Dennis Schulp), Jattoo Ceesay, Dmitri Shukov (76 Erwin Hermes). Trainer: Co Adriaanse

Sent off: Kovtun (90)

Goals: Bezrodnyi (25), Sanou (63)

WILLEM II TILBURG v GIRONDINS de BORDEAUX 0-0

Willem II, Tilburg 3.11.1999

Referee: Miroslav Radoman (YUG) Attendance: 13,000

WILLEM II: Jimmy van Fessem; Geoffrey Prommayon, Tomás Galasek, Marco Gentile, Mark Schenning (90 Delano Hill); Kew Jaliens, Raymond Victoria (87 Marcel Valk), Denny Landzaat (76 Adil Ramzi); Jattoo Ceesay, Ousmane Sanou, Dmitri Shukov. Trainer: Co Adriaanse

GIRONDINS: Teddy Richert; David Jemmali, Hervé Alicarte, Kodjo Afanou, Jérôme Bonnissel; Laurent Batlles (68 Pascal Feindouno), Lassina Diabaté, Jean-Christophe Rouvière, Johan Micoud; Corentin Martins (83 François Grenet), Sylvain Wiltord. Trainer: Elie Baup

AC SPARTA PRAHA v SPARTAK MOSKVA 5-2 (2-2)

Stadión na Letnej, Praha 3.11.1999

Referee: Michel Piraux (BEL) Attendance: 12,106

SPARTA: Tomáš Poštulka; Milan Fukal, Jiří Novotný, Petr Gabriel; Michal Horňák, Josef Obajdin (75 Jiří Jarošik), Martin Hašek, Tomáš Rosický (69 Zdenek Svoboda), Vladimír Labant; Libor Sionko (85 Horst Siegl), Vratislav Lokvenc. Trainer: Ivan Hašek

SPARTAK: Aleksandr Filimonov; Dmytro Parfyonov, Evgeniy Bushmanov, Dmitriy Khlestov, Dmitriy Ananko; Viktor Bulatov, Yegor Titov, Artyom Bezrodnyi, Andrei Tikhonov; Luís ROBSON Pereira (53 Vasiliy Baranov), Aleksandr Shirko (73 Aleksei Melyoshin). Trainer: Oleg Romantsev

Sent off: Tikhonov (62),

Goals: Lokvenc (1, 65), Rosický (11), Bulatov (34), Bezrodnyi (45), Fukal (49), Labant (63 pen)

	P	W	D	L	F	A	Pts
AC Sparta Praha	6	3	3	0	14	6	12
Girondins de Bordeaux	6	3	3	0	7	4	12
Spartak Moskva	6	1	2	3	9	12	5
Willem II Tilburg	6	0	2	4	7	15	2

FIRST STAGE – GROUP H

CHELSEA FC LONDON v AC MILAN 0-0

Stamford Bridge, London 15.09.1999

Referee: Anders Frisk (SWE) Attendance: 33,873

CHELSEA: Ed de Goey; Dan Petrescu, Célestine Babayaro, Frank Leboeuf (81 Jes Høgh), Albert Ferrer; Marcel Desailly, Didier Deschamps, Gustavo Poyet (80 Graeme Le Saux), Dennis Wise; Tore André Flo (85 Chris Sutton), Gianfranco Zola. Manager: Gianluca Vialli

AC MILAN: Christian Abbiati; Thomas Helveg, Paolo Maldini, Alessandro Costacurta, Roberto Ayala; Demetrio Albertini, Gennaro Gattuso, Andrés Guglielminpietro; Andriy Shevchenko, LEONARDO Nascimento de Araújo (83 Federico Giunti), Oliver Bierhoff. Trainer: Alberto Zaccheroni

GALATASARAY ISTANBUL v HERTHA BSC BERLIN **2-2** (1-2)

Ali Sami Yen, Istanbul 15.09.1999

Referee: Urs Meier (SWI) Attendance: 25,000

GALATASARAY: Cláudio Taffarel; Bruno Everton Quadros (46 Tugay Kerimoğlu), Gheorghe Popescu, Hakan Ünsal, Carlos Capone; Okan Buruk (46 Fatih Akyel), Suat Kaya, Gheorghe Hagi, Ümit Davala; Arif Erdem (67 Márcio dos Santos), Hakan Şükür. Trainer: Fatih Terim

HERTHA: Gábor Király; Hendrik Herzog, Andreas Schmidt, Thomas Helmer (17 Sixten Veit, 46 Andreas Neuendorf); Kostas Konstantinidis 84, Pál Dárdai, Michael Hartmann; Dariusz Wosz (50 Andreas Thom), Ali Daei, Michael Preetz, Sebastian Deisler. Trainer: Jürgen Röber

Sent off: Konstantinidis (84)

Goals: Preetz (12), Wosz (13), Hakan Şükür (24), Hagi (86 pen)

AC MILAN v GALATASARAY ISTANBUL **2-1** (2-0)

Giuseppe Meazza, Milano 21.09.1999

Referee: Hugh Dallas (SCO) Attendance: 37,822

AC MILAN: Christian Abbiati; Paolo Maldini, Alessandro Costacurta (83 Bruno N'Gotty), Roberto Ayala; Thomas Helveg, Demetrio Albertini, Gennaro Gattuso, SERGINHO Claúdio dos Santos; Andriy Shevchenko (88 Maurizio Ganz), LEONARDO Nascimento de Araújo (69 Federico Giunti), Oliver Bierhoff. Trainer: Alberto Zaccheroni

GALATASARAY: Cláudio Taffarel; Bruno Everton Quadros (46 Okan Buruk), Gheorghe Popescu, Fatih Akyel (49 Ergün Pembe), Carlos Capone; Suat Kaya, Gheorghe Hagi (46 Arif Erdem), Ahmet Yildirim, Ümit Davala, Hakan Ünsal; Hakan Şükür. Trainer: Fatih Terim

Goals: Leonardo (44), Shevchenko (45), Ümit (50)

HERTHA BSC BERLIN v CHELSEA FC LONDON **2-1** (1-0)

Olympiastadion, Berlin 21.09.1999

Referee: Michel Piraux (BEL) Attendance: 51,541

HERTHA: Gábor Király; Hendrik Herzog, Dick van Burik, Anthony Sanneh (66 Sixten Veit), Andreas Schmidt; Dariusz Wosz, Pál Dárdai (80 Thomas Helmer), René Tretschok (12 Kai Michalke), Sebastian Deisler; Michael Preetz, Ali Daei. Trainer: Jürgen Röber

CHELSEA: Ed de Goey; Dan Petrescu, Frank Leboeuf, Marcel Desailly, Albert Ferrer (64 Gabriele Ambrosetti); Célestine Babayaro, Didier Deschamps, Dennis Wise, Graeme Le Saux (71 Jody Morris); Tore André Flo (64 Chris Sutton), Gianfranco Zola. Manager: Gianluca Vialli

Goals: Ali Daei (3, 70), Leboeuf (86 pen)

AC MILAN v HERTHA BSC BERLIN **1-1** (0-0)

Giuseppe Meazza, Milano 28.09.1999

Referee: Gilles Veissière (FRA) Attendance: 40,941

AC MILAN: Christian Abbiati; Alessandro Costacurta, Roberto Ayala, Paolo Maldini; Thomas Helveg (57 Andrés Guglielminpietro), Demetrio Albertini (75 Federico Giunti), Gennaro Gattuso, SERGINHO Claúdio dos Santos; LEONARDO Nascimento de Araújo, Oliver Bierhoff, Andriy Shevchenko. Trainer: Alberto Zaccheroni

HERTHA: Gábor Király; Thomas Helmer, Hendrik Herzog, Dick van Burik, Andreas Schmidt; Sebastian Deisler, Pál Dárdai, Dariusz Wosz (82 Andreas Neuendorf), Kai Michalke; Ali Daei, Michael Preetz. Trainer: Jürgen Röber

Goals: Daei (69), Bierhoff (74)

CHELSEA FC LONDON v GALATASARAY ISTANBUL **1-0** (0-0)

Stamford Bridge 28.09.1999

Referee: Dick Jol (HOL) Attendance: 33,426

CHELSEA: Ed de Goey; Célestine Babayaro, Frank Leboeuf, Marcel Desailly (63 Jes Høgh), Albert Ferrer; Dan Petrescu, Dennis Wise, Gabriele Ambrosetti (53 Gustavo Poyet), Jody Morris; Chris Sutton (85 Tore André Flo), Gianfranco Zola. Manager: Gianluca Vialli

GALATASARAY: Cláudio Taffarel; Gheorghe Popescu, Fatih Akyel, Hakan Ünsal, Carlos Capone; Okan Buruk (72 Emre Belözoglu), Gheorghe Hagi (73 Hasan Sas Gökhan), Ümit Davala, Ergün Pembe; Arif Erdem (34 Mehmet Bölükbasi), Hakan Şükür. Trainer: Fatih Terim

Sent off: Taffarel (33)

Goal: Petrescu (55)

HERTHA BSC BERLIN v AC MILAN **1-0** (1-0)

Olympiastadion, Berlin 20.10.1999

Referee: José Maria García-Aranda (SPA) Att: 60530

HERTHA: Gábor Király; Kjetil Rekdal, Eyjólfur Sverrisson, Thomas Helmer, Dick van Burik; Sebastian Deisler, Pál Dárdai (87 Anthony Sanneh), Dariusz Wosz, Kai Michalke; Ali Daei (70 Ilija Aracic), Michael Preetz. Trainer: Jürgen Röber

AC MILAN: Christian Abbiati; Luigi Sala, Alessandro Costacurta (46 Roberto Ayala), Paolo Maldini; Andrés Guglielminpietro, Demetrio Albertini, Massimo Ambrosini (64 Federico Giunti), SERGINHO Claúdio dos Santos (75 Pierluigi Orlandini); LEONARDO Nascimento de Araújo, Andriy Shevchenko, Oliver Bierhoff. Trainer: Alberto Zaccheroni

Goal: Wosz (41)

GALATASARAY ISTANBUL v CHELSEA FC LONDON 0-5 (0-1)

Ali Sami Yen, Istanbul 20.10.1999

Referee: Vítor Manuel Melo Pereira (POR) Att: 20600

GALATASARAY: Mehmet Bölükbasi; Fatih Akyel (46 Ümit Davala), Carlos Capone, Gheorghe Popescu, Emre Belözoglu; Arif Erdem, Okan Buruk, Hakan Ünsal, Gheorghe Hagi (46 Hasan Sas Gökhan); Hakan Şükür (65 Saffet Akyüz), Tugay Kerimoğlu. Trainer: Fatih Terim

CHELSEA: Ed de Goey; Célestine Babayaro, Frank Leboeuf, Marcel Desailly, Graeme Le Saux; Didier Deschamps (67 Dan Petrescu), Gustavo Poyet (67 Dennis Wise), Albert Ferrer, Jody Morris; Tore André Flo, Gianfranco Zola (76 Gabriele Ambrosetti). Manager: Gianluca Vialli

Goals: Flo (32, 49), Zola (54), Wise (79), Ambrosetti (88)

GALATASARAY ISTANBUL v AC MILAN 3-2 (1-1)

Ali Sami Yen, Istanbul 3.11.1999

Referee: Antonio Jesus López Nieto (SPA) Att: 17,361

GALATASARAY: Cláudio Taffarel; Ümit Davala, Carlos Capone, Gheorghe Popescu (70 Ergün Pembe), Hakan Ünsal; Okan Buruk, Emre Belözoglu, Gheorghe Hagi (66 Hasan Şaş Gökhan), Ahmet Yildirim; Hakan Şükür, Arif Erdem (72 Márcio dos Santos). Trainer: Fatih Terim

AC MILAN: Christian Abbiati; Bruno N'Gotty, Roberto Ayala, Paolo Maldini; Thomas Helveg, Demetrio Albertini, Gennaro Gattuso, Andrés Guglielminpietro (57 SERGINHO Claúdio dos Santos), Federico Giunti (88 Oliver Bierhoff); Andriy Shevchenko, George Weah (83 Zvonimir Boban). Trainer: Alberto Zaccheroni

Goals: Weah (20), Capone (27), Giunti (51), Hakan Şükür (87), Ümit (90 pen)

HERTHA BSC BERLIN v GALATASARAY ISTANBUL 1-4 (1-0)

Olympiastadion, Berlin 26.10.1999

Referee: Kim Milton Nielsen (DEN) Attendance: 71,520

HERTHA: Gábor Király; Kjetil Rekdal (81 Andreas Neuendorf), Dick van Burik, Thomas Helmer (14 Hendrik Herzog), Eyjólfur Sverrisson; Sebastian Deisler, Andreas Schmidt, Dariusz Wosz, Kai Michalke; Ali Daei, Michael Preetz (74 Ilija Aracic). Trainer: Jürgen Röber

GALATASARAY: Cláudio Taffarel; Fatih Akyel (46 Ergün Pembe), Carlos Capone, Gheorghe Popescu, Ahmet Yildirim; Okan Buruk, Suat Kaya, Emre Belözoglu, Hasan Sas Gökhan (71 Tugay Kerimoğlu), Arif Erdem (87 Emrah Eren); Hakan Şükür. Trainer: Fatih Terim

Goals: Rekdal (35 pen), Hakan Şükür (48, 66), Tugay (81), Okan (90)

CHELSEA FC LONDON v HERTHA BSC BERLIN 2-0 (2-0)

Stamford Bridge 3.11.1999

Referee: Karl-Erik Nilsson (SWE) Attendance: 33,623

CHELSEA: Ed de Goey; Albert Ferrer, Marcel Desailly (86 Bernard Lambourde), Jes Høgh (66 Frank Leboeuf), Célestine Babayaro, Dennis Wise; Dan Petrescu, Didier Deschamps; Gianfranco Zola (64 Gustavo Poyet), Chris Sutton, Tore André Flo. Manager: Gianluca Vialli

HERTHA: Gábor Király; Dick van Burik, Thomas Helmer (58 Andreas Schmidt), Eyjólfur Sverrisson, Kjetil Rekdal; Anthony Sanneh, Sebastian Deisler, Dariusz Wosz (46 Kostas Konstantinidis), Kai Michalke; Michael Preetz, Ali Daei (46 Ilija Aracic). Trainer: Jürgen Röber

Sent off: Sutton (90)

Goals: Deschamps (11), Ferrer (44)

AC MILAN v CHELSEA FC LONDON 1-1 (0-0)

Giuseppe Meazza 26.10.1999

Referee: Nikolai Levnikov (RUS) Attendance: 74,855

AC MILAN: Christian Abbiati; Alessandro Costacurta, Roberto Ayala, Paolo Maldini; Andrés Guglielminpietro, Massimo Ambrosini, Gennaro Gattuso, SERGINHO Claúdio dos Santos (86 Pierluigi Orlandini), LEONARDO Nascimento de Araújo (57 Zvonimir Boban); Oliver Bierhoff, Andriy Shevchenko. Trainer: Alberto Zaccheroni

CHELSEA: Ed de Goey; Albert Ferrer, Frank Leboeuf, Marcel Desailly, Célestine Babayaro; Dan Petrescu (46 Jody Morris), Didier Deschamps, Dennis Wise, Gustavo Poyet (75 Roberto di Matteo); Tore André Flo, Gianfranco Zola (84 Gabriele Ambrosetti). Manager: Gianluca Vialli

Goals: Bierhoff (74), Wise (77)

	P	W	D	L	F	A	Pts
Chelsea FC London	6	3	2	1	10	3	11
Hertha BSC Berlin	6	2	2	2	7	10	8
Galatasaray Istanbul	6	2	1	3	10	13	7
AC Milan	6	1	3	2	6	7	6

SECOND STAGE – GROUP A

HERTHA BSC BERLIN v FC BARCELONA 1-1 (1-1)

Olympiastadion, Berlin 23.11.1999

Referee: Nikolai Levnikov (RUS) Attendance: 60,500

HERTHA: Gábor Király; Marko Rehmer (72 Sixten Veit), Dick van Burik, Eyjólfur Sverrisson; Andreas Thom, Andreas Schmidt, Kostas Konstantinidis, Kai Michalke (87 Hendrik Herzog), Dariusz Wosz; Ali Daei, Michael Preetz.

FC BARCELONA: Rodolfus Hubuertus "Ruud" Hesp; Michael Reiziger, Frank de Boer, Frédéric Déhu, Boudewijn Zenden; Ronald de Boer (69 SIMÃO Pedro Fonseca Sabrosa), LUIS ENRIQUE Martínez García, Josep GUARDIOLA Sala, Philip John William Cocu; Luis Filipe Madeira Caeiro "FIGO", Patrick Kluivert (72 DANIel García Lara). Trainer: Louis van Gaal

Goals: Luis Enrique (14), Michalke (33)

AC SPARTA PRAHA v FC PORTO 0-2 (0-0)

Stadión na Letnej, Praha 23.11.1999

Referee: Gilles Veissière (FRA) Attendance: 14,625

SPARTA: Tomáš Poštulka; Milan Fukal, Jiří Novotný, Petr Gabriel, Michal Horňák; Josef Obajdin (70 Jiří Jarošik), Miroslav Baranek, Martin Hašek, Tomáš Rosický (88 Zdenek Svoboda); Libor Sionko (71 Horst Siegl), Vratislav Lokvenc.

FC PORTO: VÍTOR Manuel Martins BAÍA; Carlos Alberto SECRETÁRIO, JORGE Paulo COSTA Almeida, ALOÍSIO Pires Alves, José Marcelo "ESQUERDINHA"; Anderson Luís de Sousa "DECO", João Paulo Maio dos Santos "PAULINHO SANTOS", Carlos Narciso CHAINHO (90 DOMINGOS Paciência de Oliveira), RUBENS Rodrigues dos Santos JÚNIOR (73 Ljubinko Drulovic); Nuno F.G. Rocha "CAPUCHO", Mário JARDEL Almeida Ribeiro (87 ARGÉLico Fuks). Trainer: Fernando Santos

Goals: Drulović (77), Jardel (84)

FC PORTO v HERTHA BSC BERLIN 1-0 (0-0)

Estádio das Antas, Porto 8.12.1999

Referee: Ryszard Wójcik (POL) Attendance: 24,200

FC PORTO: VÍTOR Manuel Martins BAÍA (75 Henrique HILÁRIO Sampaio); Carlos Alberto SECRETÁRIO, JORGE Paulo COSTA Almeida, ALOÍSIO Pires Alves, José Marcelo "ESQUERDINHA"; João Paulo Maio dos Santos "PAULINHO SANTOS", Anderson Luís de Sousa "DECO", Carlos Narciso CHAINHO, RUBENS Rodrigues dos Santos JÚNIOR (56 Ljubinko Drulovic); Nuno F.G. Rocha "CAPUCHO", Mário JARDEL Almeida Ribeiro (90 RICARDO Emidio Pinho de SOUSA). Trainer: Fernando Santos

HERTHA: Gábor Király; Kostas Konstantinidis (82 Ali Daei), Hendrik Herzog, Dick van Burik, Eyjólfur Sverrisson; Marko Rehmer (46 Michael Hartmann), Andreas Schmidt, Kai Michalke, Andreas Neuendorf (64 Andreas Thom); Dariusz Wosz, Michael Preetz. Trainer: Jürgen Röber

Sent off: Paulinho Santos (90)

Goal: Drulovic (79)

FC BARCELONA v AC SPARTA PRAHA 5-0 (2-0)

Camp Nou, Barcelona 8.12.1999

Referee: Pierluigi Collina (ITA) Attendance: 54,303

FC BARCELONA: Francesco ARNAU Grabalosa; Michael Reiziger (84 XAVIer Hernández Creus), Frank de Boer, Frédéric Déhu, Boudewijn Zenden; LUIS ENRIQUE Martínez García (76 Ronald de Boer), Josep GUARDIOLA Sala, Philip John William Cocu; Luis Filipe Madeira Caeiro "FIGO" (76 SIMÃO Pedro Fonseca Sabrosa), Patrick Kluivert, Vítor Borba Ferreira "RIVALDO". Trainer: Louis van Gaal

SPARTA: Tomáš Poštulka; Petr Gabriel, Jiří Novotný, Milan Fukal, Michal Horňák; Martin Hašek 38, Tomáš Rosický, Vlastimil Svoboda (17 René Bolf), Miroslav Baranek; Libor Sionko (70 Jiří Jarošik), Vratislav Lokvenc.
Trainer: Ivan Hašek

Sent off: Martin Hašek (38)

Goals: Kluivert (44, 70), Luis Enrique (45, 76), Guardiola (60)

FC BARCELONA v FC PORTO 4-2 (3-1)

Camp Nou, Barcelona 1.03.2000

Referee: Paul Anthony Durkin (ENG) Attendance: 71,500

FC BARCELONA: Rodolfus Hubuertus "Ruud" Hesp; Carlos Puyol (46 Michael Reiziger), Frank de Boer, ABELARDO Fernández Artuńa, Boudewijn Zenden (52 Frédéric Déhu); Josep GUARDIOLA Sala, LUIS ENRIQUE Martínez García, Philip John William Cocu, Luis Filipe Madeira Caeiro "FIGO" (86 Ronald de Boer); Patrick Kluivert, Vítor Borba Ferreira "RIVALDO". Trainer: Louis van Gaal

FC PORTO: Henrique HILÁRIO Sampaio; Carlos Alberto SECRETÁRIO, JORGE Paulo COSTA Almeida, ALOÍSIO Pires Alves, José Marcelo "ESQUERDINHA"; Emílio Manuel Delgado PEIXE (75 ALESSANDRO Andrade de Oliveira), Carlos Narciso CHAINHO, Nuno F.G. Rocha "CAPUCHO" (75 CLAYTON Ferreira Cruz), RUI Gil Soares BARROS (39 DOMINGOS Pacięncia de Oliveira); Ljubinko Drulovic, Mário JARDEL Almeida Ribeiro. Trainer: Fernando Santos

Goals: Jardel (5, 79), Rivaldo (16, 87), F. de Boer (23), Kluivert (45)

HERTHA BSC BERLIN v AC SPARTA PRAHA 1-1 (1-0)

Olympiastadion, Berlin 1.03.2000

Referee: Claude Colombo (FRA) Attendance: 30,337

HERTHA: Christian Fiedler; Hendrik Herzog, Dick van Burik, Eyjólfur Sverrisson; Sebastian Deisler, Andreas Schmidt, Sixten Veit, Michael Hartmann, Dariusz Wosz (88 Bryan Roy); Michael Preetz, Ali Daei. Trainer: Jürgen Röber

SPARTA: Jaromír Blažek; Milan Fukal, Jiří Novotný, René Bolf, Petr Gabriel; Libor Sionko, Tomáš Rosický, Jiří Jarošik, Miroslav Baranek; Josef Obajdin (75 Pavel Hapal), Vratislav Lokvenc (68 Horst Siegl). Trainer: Ivan Hašek

Goals: Veit (45), Siegl (84)

FC PORTO v FC BARCELONA 0-2 (0-1)

Estádio das Antas, Porto 7.03.2000

Referee: Stefano Braschi (ITA) Attendance: 45,492

FC PORTO: Henrique HILÁRIO Sampaio; Carlos Alberto SECRETÁRIO, RICARDO Emidio Pinho de SOUSA, ALOÍSIO Pires Alves, Nuno F.G. Rocha "CAPUCHO"; José Marcelo "ESQUERDINHA", Emílio Manuel Delgado PEIXE (46 Carlos Narciso CHAINHO), RUBENS Rodrigues dos Santos JÚNIOR (45 DOMINGOS Paciência de Oliveira), João Paulo Maio dos Santos "PAULINHO SANTOS" (64 CLAYTON Ferreira Cruz); Ljubinko Drulovic, Mário JARDEL Almeida Ribeiro. Trainer: Fernando Santos

FC BARCELONA: Rodolfus Hubuertus "Ruud" Hesp; Carlos Puyol, ABELARDO Fernández Artuña, Frank de Boer, Winston Bogarde; Ronald de Boer, Josep GUARDIOLA Sala, Philip John William Cocu (46 GABRIel García De la Torre); Luis Filipe Madeira Caeiro "FIGO" (90 XAVIer Hernández Creus), Patrick Kluivert, Vítor Borba Ferreira "RIVALDO" (75 DANIel García Lara). Trainer: Louis van Gaal

Goals: Abelardo (37), Rivaldo (59)

AC SPARTA PRAHA v HERTHA BSC BERLIN 1-0 (0-0)

Stadión na Letnej, Praha 7.03.2000

Referee: Anders Frisk (SWE) Attendance: 9,101

SPARTA: Jaromír Blažek; Milan Fukal, Jiří Novotný, René Bolf; Petr Gabriel, Jiří Jarošik, Miroslav Baranek, Pavel Hapal (65 Horst Siegl), Tomáš Rosický; Vratislav Lokvenc, Libor Sionko (74 Vlastimil Svoboda). Trainer: Ivan Hašek

HERTHA: Christian Fiedler; Kostas Konstantinidis, Kjetil Rekdal (90 Anthony Sanneh), Hendrik Herzog; Marko Rehmer, Andreas Schmidt, Bryan Roy (79 Michael Preetz), Kai Michalke (21 Sixten Veit), Michael Hartmann; Ali Daei, Alex Alves. Trainer: Jürgen Röber

Goal: Fukal (90)

FC BARCELONA v HERTHA BSC BERLIN 3-1 (1-1)

Camp Nou, Barcelona 15.03.2000

Referee: Michel Piraux (BEL) Attendance: 48,000

FC BARCELONA: Rodolfus Hubuertus "Ruud" Hesp; Carlos Puyol, ABELARDO Fernández Artuña (53 Frédéric Déhu), Frank de Boer, Winston Bogarde; Ronald de Boer (71 Jari Litmanen), XAVIer Hernández Creus, GABRIel García De la Torre; Luis Filipe Madeira Caeiro "FIGO" (46 SIMÃO Pedro Fonseca Sabrosa), Patrick Kluivert, Vítor Borba Ferreira "RIVALDO". Trainer: Louis van Gaal

HERTHA: Gábor Király; Hendrik Herzog, Eyjólfur Sverrisson, Dick van Burik (56 Dariusz Wosz); Kai Michalke, Marko Rehmer (59 Andreas Neuendorf), Andreas Schmidt (78 Anthony Sanneh), Michael Hartmann, Ante Covic; Michael Preetz, Alex Alves. Trainer: Jürgen Röber

Goals: Alves (7), Xavi (11), Gabri (49), Kluivert (83)

FC PORTO v AC SPARTA PRAHA 2-2 (1-0)

Estádio das Antas, Porto 15.03.2000

Referee: Günter Benkö (AUS) Attendance: 27,400

FC PORTO: VÍTOR Manuel Martins BAÍA; JORGE Paulo COSTA Almeida, Carlos Alberto SECRETÁRIO, RICARDO Emidio Pinho de SOUSA, José Marcelo "ESQUERDINHA"; DOMINGOS Paciência de Oliveira (89 João Paulo Maio dos Santos "PAULINHO SANTOS"), Carlos Narciso CHAINHO (53 Emílio Manuel Delgado PEIXE), Anderson Luís de Sousa "DECO"; Nuno F.G. Rocha "CAPUCHO" (82 RUI Gil Soares BARROS), Mário JARDEL Almeida Ribeiro, Ljubinko Drulović. Trainer: Fernando Santos

SPARTA: Jaromír Blažek; Jiří Novotný, Milan Fukal, René Bolf (81 Michal Horňák), Petr Gabriel; Miroslav Baranek, Tomáš Rosický, Zdenek Svoboda (85 Horst Siegl), Jiří Jarošik; Vratislav Lokvenc, Libor Sionko (54 Josef Obajdin). Trainer: Ivan Hašek

Goals: Jorge Costa (16), Capucho (64), Lokvenc (64), Fukal (90)

HERTHA BSC BERLIN v FC PORTO 0-1 (0-0)

Olympiastadion, Berlin 21.03.2000

Referee: Pierluigi Collina (ITA) Attendance: 30,506

HERTHA: Gábor Király; Eyjólfur Sverrisson, Dick van Burik (46 Kostas Konstantinidis), Hendrik Herzog, Anthony Sanneh; Bryan Roy, Kai Michalke, Sebastian Deisler (46 Pal Dárdai), Ante Covic; Ali Daei, Alex Alves (56 Ilija Aracic). Trainer: Jürgen Röber

FC PORTO: VÍTOR Manuel Martins BAÍA; Carlos Alberto SECRETÁRIO, JORGE Paulo COSTA Almeida, ALOÍSIO Pires Alves, José Marcelo "ESQUERDINHA"; Carlos Narciso CHAINHO, Anderson Luís de Sousa "DECO" (90 Emílio Manuel Delgado PEIXE), João Paulo Maio dos Santos "PAULINHO SANTOS"; Nuno F.G. Rocha "CAPUCHO" (76 ALESSANDRO Andrade de Oliveira), Mário JARDEL Almeida Ribeiro, Ljubinko Drulovic (67 CLAYTON Ferreira Cruz). Trainer: Fernando Santos

Goal: Clayton (70)

AC SPARTA PRAHA v FC BARCELONA 1-2 (1-0)

Stadión na Letnej, Praha 21.03.2000

Referee: Rune Pedersen (NOR) Attendance: 20,224

SPARTA: Jaromír Blažek; René Bolf, Jiří Novotný, Petr Gabriel; Milan Fukal, Libor Sionko, Jiří Jarošik, Tomáš Rosický, Zdenek Svoboda (59 Pavel Hapal); Vratislav Lokvenc, Josef Obajdin (71 Jan Flachbart). Trainer: Ivan Hašek

FC BARCELONA: Rodolfus Hubuertus "Ruud" Hesp; Michael Reiziger, Frédéric Déhu, Frank de Boer, Winston Bogarde; Philip John William Cocu (75 Jari Litmanen), Josep GUARDIOLA Sala (60 XAVIer Hernández Creus), GABRIel García De la Torre; SIMÃO Pedro Fonseca Sabrosa, DANIel García Lara, Vítor Borba Ferreira "RIVALDO" (46 Ronald de Boer). Trainer: Louis van Gaal

Goals: Z. Svoboda (18), Gabri (52, 89)

	P	W	D	L	F	A	Pts
FC Barcelona	6	5	1	0	17	5	16
FC Porto	6	3	1	2	8	8	10
Sparta Praha	6	1	2	3	5	12	5
Hertha BSC Berlin	6	0	2	4	3	8	2

GIRONDINS de BORDEAUX
v FIORENTINA FIRENZE 0-0

Parc Lescure, Bordeaux 8.12.1999

Referee: Karl-Erik Nilsson (SWE) Attendance: 21,987

GIRONDINS: Ulrich Ramé; François Grenet, Nisa Saveljic, Kodjo Afanou, Hervé Alicarte; Corentin Martins (85 Jean-Christophe Rouvière), Lassina Diabaté, Michel Pavon, Johan Micoud; Sylvain Wiltord, Lilian Laslandes.
Trainer: Elie Baup

FIORENTINA: Francesco Toldo; Tomáš Repka, Aldo Firicano, Alessandro Pierini; Moreno Torricelli, Angelo di Livio, Christian Amoroso (70 Fabio Rossitto), Jörg Heinrich, Rui Costa; Enrico Chiesa (70 Mauro Bressan), Abel Balbo.
Trainer: Giovanni Trapattoni

SECOND STAGE – GROUP B

FIORENTINA FIRENZE
v MANCHESTER UNITED FC 2-0 (1-0)

Artemio Franchi, Firenze 23.11.1999

Referee: Bernd Heynemann (GER) Attendance: 36,002

FIORENTINA: Francesco Toldo; Tomáš Repka, Aldo Firicano, Alessandro Pierini (79 Daniele Adani), Moreno Torricelli; Angelo di Livio (67 Fabio Rossitto), Sandro Cois, Rui Costa, Jörg Heinrich; Abel Balbo (79 Mauro Bressan), Gabriel Batistuta. Trainer: Giovanni Trapattoni

MANCHESTER UNITED: Mark Bosnich; Gary Neville, Henning Berg (63 Phillip Neville), Jaap Stam, Dennis Irwin; David Beckham, Paul Scholes, Roy Keane; Ryan Giggs, Andy Cole (63 Teddy Sheringham), Dwight Yorke (63 Ole Gunnar Solskjær). Manager: Alex Ferguson

Goals: Batistuta (24), Balbo (52)

MANCHESTER UNITED FC
v VALENCIA CF 3-0 (1-0)

Old Trafford, Manchester 8.12.1999

Referee: Kim Milton Nielsen (DEN) Attendance: 54,606

MANCHESTER UNITED: Raimond van der Gouw; Gary Neville, Jaap Stam, Dennis Irwin, Phillip Neville; David Beckham, Paul Scholes (72 Nicky Butt), Roy Keane, Ryan Giggs; Ole Gunnar Solskjær, Andy Cole (72 Dwight Yorke).
Manager: Alex Ferguson

VALENCIA: Andrés PALOP Cervera; Jocelyn Angloma, Miroslav Djukić, Joachim Björklund, Mauricio Pellegrino; Amedeo Carboni, Gaizka MENDIETA Zabala, Francisco FARINÓS Zapata, Luis MILLA Aspas; CLAUDIO Javier LÓPEZ (85 Goran Vlaovic), ÓSCAR García Junyent (69 JUAN Ginés SÁNCHEZ Moreno). Trainer: Héctor Raúl Cuper

Goals: Keane (38), Solskjær (47), Scholes (70)

VALENCIA CF
v GIRONDINS de BORDEAUX 3-0 (0-0)

Mestalla, Valencia 23.11.1999

Referee: Dick Jol (HOL) Attendance: 24,492

VALENCIA: Andrés PALOP Cervera; Jocelyn Angloma, Miroslav Djukić, Mauricio Pellegrino, Amedeo Carboni; Francisco FARINÓS Zapata (80 Miguel Ángel ANGULO), Gaizka MENDIETA Zabala, GERARD López Segú, Christian Alberto "KILY" GONZÁLEZ Peret; CLAUDIO Javier LÓPEZ (90 JUAN Ginés SÁNCHEZ Moreno), Adrian Ilie (75 David ALBELDA Aliques). Trainer: Héctor Raúl Cuper

GIRONDINS: Ulrich Ramé; François Grenet, Nisa Saveljic, Kodjo Afanou, Hervé Alicarte; Corentin Martins (58 Stéphane Ziani), Michel Pavon, Lassina Diabaté (86 Jean-Christophe Rouvière), Johan Micoud; Lilian Laslandes, Sylvain Wiltord.
Trainer: Elie Baup

Goals: Farinós (60), Ilie (68), Kily González (90)

MANCHESTER UNITED FC
v GIRONDINS de BORDEAUX 2-0 (1-0)

Old Trafford, Manchester 1.03.2000

Referee: Hartmut Strampe (GER) Attendance: 59,786

MANCHESTER UNITED: Raimond van der Gouw; Gary Neville, Dennis Irwin, Jaap Stam, Michaël Silvestre; David Beckham, Nicky Butt, Ryan Giggs (88 Ole Gunnar Solskjær), Roy Keane (88 Quinton Fortune); Andy Cole (81 Phillip Neville), Teddy Sheringham. Manager: Alex Ferguson

GIRONDINS: Ulrich Ramé; Jérôme Bonnissel, François Grenet, Kodjo Afanou, Hervé Alicarte; Michel Pavon, Johan Micoud, Corentin Martins (65 Stéphane Ziani), Lassina Diabaté; Lilian Laslandes, Sylvain Wiltord.
Trainer: Elie Baup

Goals: Giggs (42), Sheringham (84)

FIORENTINA FIRENZE v VALENCIA CF 1-0 (1-0)

Artemio Franchi, Firenze 1.03.2000

Referee: Markus Merk (GER) Attendance: 25,676

FIORENTINA: Francesco Toldo; Tomáš Repka, Moreno Torricelli, Daniele Adani, Alessandro Pierini (80 Andrea Tarozzi); Rui Costa, Sandro Cois (83 Christian Amoroso), Angelo di Livio (73 Fabio Rossitto), Jörg Heinrich; Predrag Mijatović, Gabriel Batistuta. Trainer: Giovanni Trapattoni

VALENCIA: Santiago CAÑIZARES Ruiz; Mauricio Pellegrino, Miroslav Djukić, Amedeo Carboni, Jocelyn Angloma; Francisco FARINÓS Zapata, GERARD López Segú, Christian Alberto "KILY" GONZÁLEZ Peret, Luis MILLA Aspas (26 Miguel Ángel ANGULO); CLAUDIO Javier LÓPEZ, Adrian Ilie (80 JUAN Ginés SÁNCHEZ Moreno). Trainer: Héctor Raúl Cuper

Goal: Mijatović (20 pen)

GIRONDINS de BORDEAUX v MANCHESTER UNITED FC 1-2 (1-1)

Parc Lescure, Bordeaux 7.03.2000

Referee: Jan Wegereef (HOL) Attendance: 30,130

GIRONDINS: Ulrich Ramé; François Grenet, Nisa Saveljic, Kodjo Afanou, Jérôme Bonnissel; Stéphane Ziani (60 Jean-Christophe Rouvière), Laurent Batlles (9 Lassina Diabaté), Michel Pavon, Johan Micoud; Sylvain Wiltord (82 Pascal Feindouno), Lilian Laslandes. Trainer: Elie Baup

MANCHESTER UNITED: Raimond van der Gouw; Gary Neville, Jaap Stam, Michaël Silvestre, Dennis Irwin (83 Ole Gunnar Solskjær); David Beckham, Roy Keane, Nicky Butt, Ryan Giggs; Teddy Sheringham (77 Dwight Yorke), Andy Cole (86 Henning Berg). Manager: Alex Ferguson

Sent off: Laslandes (23)

Goals: Pavon (9), Keane (33), Solskjær (84)

VALENCIA CF v FIORENTINA FIRENZE 2-0 (1-0)

Mestalla, Valencia 7.03.2000

Referee: Hellmut Krug (GER) Attendance: 32,871

VALENCIA: Santiago CAÑIZARES Ruiz; Mauricio Pellegrino, Miroslav Djukić, Gaizka MENDIETA Zabala, Amedeo Carboni, Jocelyn Angloma; CLAUDIO Javier LÓPEZ, Francisco FARINÓS Zapata, GERARD López Segú, Christian Alberto "KILY" GONZÁLEZ Peret (90 Miguel Ángel ANGULO); Adrian Ilie (77 ÓSCAR García Junyent). Trainer: Héctor Raúl Cuper

FIORENTINA: Giuseppe Taglialatela; Moreno Torricelli (77 Andrea Tarozzi), Tomáš Repka, Daniele Adani, Alessandro Pierini; Jörg Heinrich (53 Christian Amoroso), Sandro Cois, Angelo di Livio, Rui Costa; Predrag Mijatović (57 Abel Balbo), Gabriel Batistuta. Trainer: Giovanni Trapattoni

Goals: Ilie (35), Mendieta (90 pen)

MANCHESTER UNITED FC v FIORENTINA FIRENZE 3-1 (2-1)

Old Trafford, Manchester 15.03.2000

Referee: Ryszard Wójcik (POL) Attendance: 59,926

MANCHESTER UNITED: Mark Bosnich; Gary Neville, Henning Berg, Jaap Stam, Dennis Irwin; David Beckham, Roy Keane, Paul Scholes, Ryan Giggs; Dwight Yorke, Andy Cole. Manager: Alex Ferguson

FIORENTINA: Francesco Toldo; Tomáš Repka, Daniele Adani, Alessandro Pierini, Moreno Torricelli (76 Andrea Tarozzi); Angelo di Livio (76 Christian Amoroso), Fabio Rossitto, Rui Costa, Jörg Heinrich; Gabriel Batistuta, Predrag Mijatović (63 Enrico Chiesa). Trainer: Giovanni Trapattoni

Sent off: Rossitto (62)

Goals: Batistuta (16), Cole (20), Keane (33), Yorke (70)

GIRONDINS de BORDEAUX v VALENCIA CF 1-4 (0-1)

Parc Lescure, Bordeaux 15.03.2000

Referee: Fritz Stuchlik (AUS) Attendance: 21,472

GIRONDINS: Ulrich Ramé; François Grenet, Hervé Alicarte, Nisa Saveljic, Jérôme Bonnissel; Stéphane Ziani, Lassina Diabaté (50 Kodjo Afanou), Michel Pavon, Johan Micoud (77 Jean-Christophe Rouvière); Pascal Feindouno (62 Giuseppe Colucci). Sylvain Wiltord. Trainer: Elie Baup

VALENCIA: Santiago CAÑIZARES Ruiz; Jocelyn Angloma, Miroslav Djukić, Mauricio Pellegrino, Amedeo Carboni; Gaizka MENDIETA Zabala (56 Joachim Björklund), Francisco FARINÓS Zapata, GERARD López Segú, Christian Alberto "KILY" GONZÁLEZ Peret (86 ÓSCAR García Junyent); Adrian Ilie (73 Miguel Ángel ANGULO), JUAN Ginés SÁNCHEZ Moreno. Trainer: Héctor Raúl Cuper

Sent off: Saveljic (47)

Goals: Djukić (41), Mendieta (48 pen), Wiltord (54), Kily González (72), Sánchez (90)

FIORENTINA FIRENZE v GIRONDINS de BORDEAUX 3-3 (0-1)

Artemio Franchi, Firenze 21.03.2000

Referee: Dieter Schoch (SWI) Attendance: 14,239

FIORENTINA: Francesco Toldo; Tomáš Repka, Aldo Firicano, Alessandro Pierini; Moreno Torricelli, Rui Costa, Sandro Cois (73 Paul Okon), Angelo di Livio, Mauro Bressan (83 Christian Amoroso); Gabriel Batistuta (80 Abel Balbo), Enrico Chiesa. Trainer: Giovanni Trapattoni

GIRONDINS: Ulrich Ramé; Jérôme Bonnissel, Lassina Diabaté, Laurent Batlles, Hervé Alicarte 46; Jean-Christophe Rouvière (73 Giuseppe Colucci), Michel Pavon, Johan Micoud (80 Marc Zanotti), Stéphane Ziani (59 Nicolas Sahnoun); Sylvain Wiltord, Lilian Laslandes. Trainer: Elie Baup

Sent off: Alicarte (46)

Goals: Wiltord (5), Chiesa (47 pen), Batistuta (61), Rui Costa (64), Zanotti (87), Batlles (90)

VALENCIA CF v MANCHESTER UNITED FC 0-0

Mestalla, Valencia 21.03.2000

Referee: Lubos Michel (SVK) Attendance: 40,419

VALENCIA: Santiago CAÑIZARES Ruiz; Jocelyn Angloma, Miroslav Djukić, Mauricio Pellegrino, Amedeo Carboni; Miguel Ángel ANGULO, Francisco FARINÓS Zapata, GERARD López Segú, Christian Alberto "KILY" GONZÁLEZ Peret; JUAN Ginés SÁNCHEZ Moreno (70 Adrian Ilie), CLAUDIO Javier LÓPEZ. Trainer: Héctor Raúl Cuper

MANCHESTER UNITED: Mark Bosnich; Gary Neville, Henning Berg, Jaap Stam, Dennis Irwin; Paul Scholes, Roy Keane, Nicky Butt, Quinton Fortune; Ole Gunnar Solskjær (67 Jordi Cruijff), Teddy Sheringham. Manager: Alex Ferguson

	P	W	D	L	F	A	Pts
Manchester United	6	4	1	1	10	4	13
Valencia CF	6	3	1	2	9	5	10
Fiorentina Firenze	6	2	2	2	7	8	8
Girondins de Bordeaux	6	0	2	4	5	14	2

SECOND STAGE – GROUP C

FC DYNAMO KYIV v REAL MADRID CF 1-2 (0-1)

Olympyiskyi, Kyiv 24.11.1999

Referee: David Elleray (ENG) Attendance: 17,500

DYNAMO: Olexandr Shovkovskyi; Ramiz Mamedov, Vladislav Vashchuk, Olexandr Holovko, Yuri Dmitrulin; Artem Yashkin, Andriy Gusin, Sergei Konovalov (46 Maxim Shatskykh), Olexandr Khatskevitch; Valentin Belkevich, Serhiy Rebrov. Trainer: Valeriy Lobanovskiy

REAL: Albano Bizarri; Miguel Ángel Salgado Fernández "MÍCHEL SALGADO" (27 IVÁN CAMPO Ramos), Christian Karembeu, JÚLIO CÉSAR Santos Correa, ROBERTO CARLOS Da Silva; Clarence Seedorf (90 Aitor KARANKA de la Hoz), IVÁN HELGUERA Bujía, Jose María GUTIérrez Hernández, SÁVIO Bortolini Pimentel (69 Manuel SANCHÍS Hontiyuelo); RAÚL González Blanco, Fernando MORIENTES Sánchez. Trainer: Vicente del Bosque

Goals: Morientes (17), Raúl (48), Rebrov (86 pen)

ROSENBORG BK TRONDHEIM v FC BAYERN MÜNCHEN 1-1 (0-1)

Lerkendal, Trondheim 24.11.1999

Referee: Stefano Braschi (ITA) Attendance: 14,167

ROSENBORG: Jørn Jamtfall; André Bergdølmo, Erik Hoftun, Bjørn Otto Bragstad, Christer Basma; Fredrik Winsnes (71 Tore André Dahlum), Bent Skammelsrud, Ørjan Berg; Jan Derek Sørensen, John Carew, Roar Strand. Trainer: Nils Arne Eggen

BAYERN: Oliver Kahn; Markus Babbel, Patrik Andersson, Samuel Kuffour, Michael Tarnat; Thorsten Fink, Stefan Effenberg, Mehmet Scholl (82 Alexander Zickler); Paulo Sérgio (79 Roque Santa Cruz), Carsten Jancker, Hasan Salihamidzić. Trainer: Ottmar Hitzfeld

Goals: Jancker (10), Skammelsrud (47)

FC BAYERN MÜNCHEN v FC DYNAMO KYIV 2-1 (1-0)

Olympiastadion, München 7.12.1999

Referee: Hugh Dallas (SCO) Attendance: 18,000

BAYERN: Oliver Kahn; Lothar Matthäus, Samuel Kuffour, Thomas Linke; Markus Babbel, Thorsten Fink, Michael Tarnat, Hasan Salihamidzic; Paulo Sérgio (90 Michael Wiesinger), Carsten Jancker, Roque Santa Cruz (75 Alexander Zickler). Trainer: Ottmar Hitzfeld

DYNAMO: Olexandr Shovkovskyi; Vasyl Kardash, Olexandr Borysovych Holovko, Vladislav Vashchuk, Yuri Dmitrulin; Olexandr Khatskevitch (48 Aleksei Gerasimenko), Andriy Gusin, Kakhi Kaladze, Artem Yashkin (46 Oleh Venhlynskyi); Valentin Belkevich, Serhiy Rebrov. Trainer: Valeriy Lobanovskiy

Goals: Jancker (6), Rebrov (50), Paulo Sérgio (80)

REAL MADRID CF v ROSENBORG BK TRONDHEIM 3-1 (1-0)

Santiago Bernabéu, Madrid 7.12.1999

Referee: Michel Piraux (BEL) Attendance: 16,500

REAL: Iker Casillas; Christian Karembeu, Fernándo Ruíz Hierro, Aitor KARANKA de la Hoz, ROBERTO CARLOS Da Silva; IVÁN HELGUERA Bujía, FERNANDO Carlos REDONDO Neri, Jose María GUTIérrez Hernández (65 Clarence Seedorf, 90 Nicolas Anelka), SÁVIO Bortolini Pimentel; RAÚL González Blanco, Fernando MORIENTES Sánchez (89 JÚLIO CÉSAR Santos Correa). Trainer: Vicente del Bosque

ROSENBORG: Jørn Jamtfall; Christer Basma, Bent Inge Johnsen, Erik Hoftun, André Bergdølmo; Roar Strand (90 Thorn Hogne Aarøy), Bent Skammelsrud, Ørjan Berg; Jan Derek Sørensen, John Carew, Jahn Ivar "Mini" Jakobsen (52 Fredrik Winsnes). Trainer: Nils Arne Eggen

Goals: Raúl (18), Carew (48), Sávio (85), Roberto Carlos (90)

REAL MADRID CF v FC BAYERN MÜNCHEN 2-4 (1-3)

Santiago Bernabéu, Madrid 29.02.2000

Referee: Kim Milton Nielsen (DEN) Attendance: 60,000

REAL: Iker Casillas; Miguel Ángel Salgado Fernández "MÍCHEL SALGADO", Fernándo Ruíz Hierro, Aitor KARANKA de la Hoz, ROBERTO CARLOS Da Silva; GEREMI Nijtap Fotso, FERNANDO Carlos REDONDO Neri, Jose María GUTIérrez Hernández (62 Steve McManaman); Fernando MORIENTES Sánchez (79 Perica Ognjenovic), RAÚL González Blanco, Nicolas Anelka.
Trainer: Vicente del Bosque

BAYERN: Oliver Kahn; Markus Babbel (62 Thomas Linke), Lothar Matthäus, Samuel Kuffour, Bixente Lizarazu; Hasan Salihamidzic, Thorsten Fink, Stefan Effenberg; Paulo Sérgio, Giovane Élber (86 Roque Santa Cruz), Mehmet Scholl (86 Michael Tarnat). Trainer: Ottmar Hitzfeld

Goals: Scholl (21), Effenberg (24), Morientes (25), Fink (39), Raúl (48), Paulo Sérgio (66)

FC DYNAMO KYIV v ROSENBORG BK TRONDHEIM 2-1 (2-0)

Olympyiskyi, Kyiv 29.02.2000

Referee: Lubos Michel (SVK) Attendance: 36,000

DYNAMO: Olexandr Shovkovskyi; Aleksei Gerasimenko, Ramiz Mamedov (86 Serhiy Fedorov), Andrei Nesmachnyi, Andriy Gusin, Olexandr Borysovych Holovko; Olexandr Khatskevich, Valentin Belkevich, Kakhi Kaladze; Georgi Demetradze (87 Maxim Shatskykh), Serhiy Rebrov.
Trainer: Valeriy Lobanovskiy

ROSENBORG: Arni Gautur Arason; Christer Basma, Bjørn Otto Bragstad, Erik Hoftun, André Bergdølmo; Roar Strand (46 Øyvind Storflor, 90 Bent Inge Johnsen), Bent Skammelsrud, Ørjan Berg; Fredrik Winsnes, John Carew, Jahn Ivar "Mini" Jakobsen. Trainer: Nils Arne Eggen

Goals: Khatskevich (9), Rebrov (29), Jakobsen (48)

FC BAYERN MÜNCHEN v REAL MADRID CF 4-1 (2-0)

Olympiastadion, München 8.03.2000

Referee: Dick Jol (HOL) Attendance: 59,000

BAYERN: Oliver Kahn; Samuel Kuffour, Lothar Matthäus (90 Patrik Andersson), Thomas Linke; Hasan Salihamidzic, Stefan Effenberg, Thorsten Fink, Bixente Lizarazu; Paulo Sérgio, Giovane Élber (74 Alexander Zickler), Mehmet Scholl (88 Michael Wiesinger). Trainer: Ottmar Hitzfeld

REAL: Iker Casillas; Miguel Ángel Salgado Fernández "MÍCHEL SALGADO", Fernándo Ruíz Hierro, Aitor KARANKA de la Hoz (69 Nicolas Anelka), ROBERTO CARLOS Da Silva; GEREMI Nijtap Fotso (63 Steve McManaman), FERNANDO Carlos REDONDO Neri, Jose María GUTIérrez Hernández, IVÁN HELGUERA Bujía; RAÚL González Blanco, Fernando MORIENTES Sánchez (84 IVÁN CAMPO Ramos). Trainer: Vicente del Bosque

Goals: Scholl (2), Élber (30), Helguera (69), Zickler (79, 90)

ROSENBORG BK TRONDHEIM v FC DYNAMO KYIV 1-2 (1-1)

Lerkendal, Trondheim 8.03.2000

Referee: Alain Hamer (LUX) Attendance: 13,067

ROSENBORG: Arni Gautur Arason; Bjørn Otto Bragstad, Erik Hoftun, Christer Basma, Bent Inge Johnsen; Roar Strand (78 Kenneth Storvik), Bent Skammelsrud, Ørjan Berg; Jan Derek Sørensen, John Carew, Jahn Ivar "Mini" Jakobsen (78 Morten Knutsen). Trainer: Nils Arne Eggen

DYNAMO: Olexandr Shovkovskyi; Aleksei Gerasimenko, Andrei Nesmachnyi (67 Serhiy Kormiltsev), Serhiy Fedorov, Ramiz Mamedov; Olexandr Khatskevich, Valentin Belkevich, Kakhi Kaladze, Andriy Gusin; Maxim Shatskykh (46 Georgi Demetradze), Serhiy Rebrov. Trainer: Valeriy Lobanovskiy

Goals: Rebrov (32, 67), Ø. Berg (38)

REAL MADRID CF v FC DYNAMO KYIV 2-2 (1-1)

Santiago Bernabéu 14.03.2000

Referee: Alain Sars (FRA) Attendance: 38,000

REAL: Iker Casillas; Miguel Ángel Salgado Fernández "MÍCHEL SALGADO", Fernándo Ruíz Hierro, Aitor KARANKA de la Hoz, ROBERTO CARLOS Da Silva; GEREMI Nijtap Fotso (80 IVÁN HELGUERA Bujía), FERNANDO Carlos REDONDO Neri, Jose María GUTIérrez Hernández, Steve McManaman (61 José Manuel MECA); RAÚL González Blanco, Fernando MORIENTES Sánchez.
Trainer: Vicente del Bosque

DYNAMO: Olexandr Shovkovskyi; Ramiz Mamedov, Aleksei Gerasimenko, Andrei Nesmachnyi, Olexandr Holovko; Valentin Belkevich, Olexandr Khatskevich, Andriy Gusin, Maxim Shatskykh (46 Vasyl Kardash); Georgi Demetradze, Serhiy Rebrov (78 Igor Kostyuk).
Trainer: Valeriy Lobanovskiy

Goals: Raúl (14 pen), Khatskevich (42), Hierro (56 og), Roberto Carlos (72)

FC BAYERN MÜNCHEN v ROSENBORG BK TRONDHEIM 2-1 (2-0)

Olympiastadion, München 14.03.2000

Referee: Alfredo Trentalange (ITA) Attendance: 20,000

BAYERN: Oliver Kahn; Markus Babbel, Patrik Andersson, Samuel Kuffour; Thorsten Fink, Jens Jeremies, Michael Tarnat, Mehmet Scholl (75 Hasan Salihamidzic); Alexander Zickler, Carsten Jancker (75 Giovane Élber), Paulo Sérgio (84 Roque Santa Cruz). Trainer: Ottmar Hitzfeld

ROSENBORG: Arni Gautur Arason; André Bergdølmo, Bjørn Otto Bragstad, Bent Inge Johnsen, Christer Basma; Roar Strand (82 Fredrik Winsnes), Bent Skammelsrud, Ørjan Berg; Jan Derek Sørensen, John Carew, Morten Knutsen (73 Jahn Ivar "Mini" Jakobsen). Trainer: Nils Arne Eggen

Sent off: Bragstad (90)

Goals: Scholl (11), Paulo Sérgio (39 pen), Carew (64)

FC DYNAMO KYIV
v FC BAYERN MÜNCHEN 2-0 (1-0)

Olympyiskyi, Kyiv 22.03.2000

Referee: Gilles Veissière (FRA) Attendance: 70,000

DYNAMO: Olexandr Shovkovskyi; Ramiz Mamedov, Aleksei Gerasimenko, Andrei Nesmachnyi (36 Artem Yashkin), Olexandr Holovko; Andriy Gusin, Olexandr Khatskevich (85 Vasyl Kardash), Valentin Belkevich, Kakhi Kaladze; Georgi Demetradze, Serhiy Rebrov (85 Maxim Shatskykh). Trainer: Valeriy Lobanovskiy

BAYERN: Stefan Wessels; Hasan Salihamidzic, Thomas Linke (77 Nils-Eric Johansson), Patrik Andersson, Samuel Kuffour; Michael Wiesinger, Thorsten Fink, Michael Tarnat; Roque Santa Cruz (77 David Jarolim), Alexander Zickler (35 Antonio di Salvo), Slawomir Wojciechowski. Trainer: Ottmar Hitzfeld

Goals: Kaladze (34), Demetradze (72)

ROSENBORG BK TRONDHEIM
v REAL MADRID CF 0-1 (0-1)

Lerkendal, Trondheim 22.03.2000

Referee: Nikolai Levnikov (RUS) Attendance: 13,000

ROSENBORG: Arni Gautur Arason; Erik Hoftun, Bent Inge Johnsen, André Bergdølmo, Christer Basma; Roar Strand, Bent Skammelsrud, Ørjan Berg; Jan Derek Sørensen, John Carew, Jahn Ivar "Mini" Jakobsen (70 Morten Knutsen). Trainer: Nils Arne Eggen

REAL: Iker Casillas; Miguel Ángel Salgado Fernández "MÍCHEL SALGADO", Fernándo Ruíz Hierro (46 Aitor KARANKA de la Hoz), IVÁN CAMPO Ramos, ROBERTO CARLOS Da Silva; FERNANDO Carlos REDONDO Neri, Jose María GUTIérrez Hernández, IVÁN HELGUERA Bujía, Steve McManaman; RAÚL González Blanco, David Aganzo (57 Elvir Baljic, 85 Christian Karembeu). Trainer: Vicente del Bosque

Sent off: Guti (54)

Goal: Raúl (3)

	P	W	D	L	F	A	Pts
FC Bayern München	6	4	1	1	13	8	13
Real Madrid CF	6	3	1	2	11	12	10
Dynamo Kyiv	6	3	1	2	10	8	10
Rosenborg BK	6	0	1	5	5	11	1

SECOND STAGE – GROUP D

OLYMPIQUE de MARSEILLE
v SS LAZIO ROMA 0-2 (0-0)

Vélodrome, Marseille 24.11.1999

Referee: Manuel Diaz Vega (SPA) Attendance: 42,261

OLYMPIQUE: Stéphane Porato; Sébastien Pérez (67 Florian Maurice), William Gallas, Eduardo Berizzo, Yannick Fischer; Frédéric Brando, Peter Luccin, Stéphane Dalmat, Robert Pires; Christophe Dugarry, Kaba Diawara (58 Fabrizio Ravanelli). Trainer: Rolland Courbis

LAZIO: Luca Marchegiani; Giuseppe Favalli, Alessandro Nesta, Sinisa Mihajlovic, Giuseppe Pancaro; Sérgio Conceição, Dejan Stankovic, Néstor Sensini, Pavel Nedved (81 Matías Almeyda); Roberto Mancini (74 Juan Sebastián Verón), Marcelo Salas (79 Alen Boksic). Trainer: Sven Göran Eriksson

Goals: Stankovic (64), Sérgio Conceição (77)

CHELSEA FC LONDON
v FEYENOORD ROTTERDAM 3-1 (1-0)

Stamford Bridge, London 24.11.1999

Referee: José Maria Garcia-Aranda (SPA) Att: 29,704

CHELSEA: Ed de Goey; Albert Ferrer, Marcel Desailly, Frank Leboeuf, Célestine Babayaro; Dan Petrescu, Didier Deschamps (86 Samuele Dalla Bona), Dennis Wise, Gustavo Poyet (86 Roberto di Matteo); Tore André Flo, Gianfranco Zola. Manager: Gianluca Vialli

FEYENOORD: Jerzy Dudek; Ulrich van Gobbel, Jan de Visser, Bert Konterman, Kees van Wonderen; Paul Bosvelt, Jean-Paul van Gastel, Jon Dahl Tomasson (58 Julio Ricardo Cruz); Peter van Vossen (60 Radoslav Samardzic), Bonaventure Kalou, Somalia. Trainer: Leo Beenhakker

Goals: Babayaro (45), Flo (67, 85), Cruz (90)

FEYENOORD ROTTERDAM
v OLYMPIQUE de MARSEILLE 3-0 (0-0)

Feyenoord, Rotterdam 7.12.1999

Referee: Vítor Manuel Melo Pereira (POR) Att: 42,000

FEYENOORD: Jerzy Dudek; Christian Gyan, Bert Konterman, Kees van Wonderen, Tomasz Rzasa; Paul Bosvelt, Jean-Paul van Gastel, Patrick Paauwe; Bonaventure Kalou, Julio Ricardo Cruz, Peter van Vossen (37 Jan de Visser). Trainer: Leo Beenhakker

OLYMPIQUE: Stéphane Porato; Sébastien Perez 79, William Gallas, Eduardo Berizzo (46 Pierre Issa), Yannick Fischer 62; Robert Pires (68 Lilian Martin), Frédéric Brando, Peter Luccin, Stéphane Dalmat; Florian Maurice (81 Ibrahima Bakayoko), Christophe Dugarry. Trainer: Rolland Courbis

Sent off: van Wonderen (7), Fischer (62), Pérez (79)

Goals: Cruz (72, 90), Bosvelt (83)

SS LAZIO ROMA v CHELSEA FC LONDON 0-0

Stadio Olimpico, Roma 7.12.1999

Referee: Hellmut Krug (GER) Attendance: 38,662

LAZIO: Luca Marchegiani; Guerino Gottardi, Fernando Couto, Alessandro Nesta, Giuseppe Favalli; Attilio Lombardo (69 Alen Boksic), Diego Simeone, Juan Sebastián Verón, Pavel Nedved, Roberto Mancini (79 Sérgio Conceição); Simone Inzaghi (46 Marcelo Salas). Trainer: Sven Göran Eriksson

CHELSEA: Ed de Goey; Albert Ferrer, Marcel Desailly, Frank Leboeuf, Célestine Babayaro; Dan Petrescu, Didier Deschamps (75 Roberto di Matteo), Gustavo Poyet, Dennis Wise; Gianfranco Zola, Tore André Flo. Manager: Gianluca Vialli

FEYENOORD ROTTERDAM v SS LAZIO ROMA 0-0

Feyenoord, Rotterdam 8.03.2000

Referee: Günter Benkö (AUS) Attendance: 45,356

FEYENOORD: Jerzy Dudek; Ulrich van Gobbel, Kees van Wonderen, Bert Konterman, Tomasz Rzasa; Paul Bosvelt, Jean-Paul van Gastel, Patrick Paauwe (66 Bonaventure Kalou), Jan de Visser; Julio Ricardo Cruz, Jon Dahl Tomasson. Trainer: Leo Beenhakker

LAZIO: Luca Marchegiani; Paolo Negro, Sinisa Mihajlovic, Alessandro Nesta, Giuseppe Pancaro; Sérgio Conceição, Juan Sebastián Verón, Néstor Sensini, Pavel Nedved; Marcelo Salas, Roberto Mancini (66 Simone Inzaghi). Trainer: Sven Göran Eriksson

SS LAZIO ROMA v FEYENOORD ROTTERDAM 1-2 (1-0)

Olimpico, Roma 29.02.2000

Referee: Antonio Jesus López Nieto (SPA) Att: 17,883

LAZIO: Luca Marchegiani; Attilio Lombardo, Fernando Couto, Sinisa Mihajlovic (40 Paolo Negro), Guerino Gottardi; Diego Simeone, Néstor Sensini, Juan Sebastián Verón (69 Pavel Nedved), Roberto Mancini; Alen Boksic, Simone Inzaghi (60 Dejan Stankovic). Trainer: Sven Göran Eriksson

FEYENOORD: Jerzy Dudek; Ulrich van Gobbel, Bert Konterman, Ferry de Haan, Tomasz Rzasa; Paul Bosvelt, Jean-Paul van Gastel (82 Christian Gyan), Patrick Paauwe, Jan de Visser (75 Radoslav Samardzic); Bonaventure Kalou (46 Jon Dahl Tomasson), Julio Ricardo Cruz. Trainer: Leo Beenhakker

Goals: Verón (37), Tomasson (78, 84)

CHELSEA FC LONDON v OLYMPIQUE de MARSEILLE 1-0 (1-0)

Stamford Bridge, London 8.03.2000

Referee: Juan Antonio Fernández Marín (SPA) Att: 33,206

CHELSEA: Ed de Goey; Albert Ferrer, Marcel Desailly, Frank Leboeuf, Célestine Babayaro; Dennis Wise, Didier Deschamps (79 Roberto di Matteo), Jody Morris; Gianfranco Zola (79 John Harley), Gustavo Poyet, Tore André Flo. Manager: Gianluca Vialli

OLYMPIQUE: Stéphane Trévisan; Sébastien Pérez (38 Yannick Fischer), Jean-Pierre Cyprien (66 Iván de la Peña), Peter Luccin, Jacques Abardonado, Stéphane Dalmat; Frédéric Brando, Robert Pires, Jérôme Leroy; Ibrahima Bakayoko, Cyrille Pouget. Trainer: Rolland Courbis

Goal: Wise (27)

OLYMPIQUE de MARSEILLE v CHELSEA FC LONDON 1-0 (1-0)

Vélodrome, Marseille 29.02.2000

Referee: Rune Pedersen (NOR) Attendance: 24,700

OLYMPIQUE: Stéphane Trévisan; Patrick Blondeau, Jean-Pierre Cyprien, Peter Luccin, Jacques Abardonado, Stéphane Dalmat; Robert Pires, Frédéric Brando, Jérôme Leroy; Ibrahima Bakayoko (90 Artur Moses), Cyrille Pouget (72 Iván de la Peña). Trainer: Rolland Courbis

CHELSEA: Ed de Goey; Albert Ferrer (81 Jody Morris), Frank Leboeuf, Marcel Desailly, John Harley; Dan Petrescu, Didier Deschamps (62 Roberto di Matteo), Dennis Wise, Gustavo Poyet; Gianfranco Zola, Tore André Flo (81 Chris Sutton). Manager: Gianluca Vialli

Goal: Pires (16)

SS LAZIO ROMA v OLYMPIQUE de MARSEILLE 5-1 (3-0)

Olimpico, Roma 14.03.2000

Referee: Anders Frisk (SWE) Attendance: 28,875

LAZIO: Luca Marchegiani; Paolo Negro, Alessandro Nesta, Sinisa Mihajlovic (60 Fernando Couto), Giuseppe Pancaro (74 Guerino Gottardi); Sérgio Conceição, Dejan Stankovic (68 Néstor Sensini), Diego Simeone, Pavel Nedved; Simone Inzaghi, Alen Boksic. Trainer: Sven Göran Eriksson

OLYMPIQUE: Stéphane Porato; Yannick Fischer (46 Richard Martini), Peter Luccin, Jacques Abardonado; Lilian Martin (46 Ibrahima Bakayoko), Frédéric Brando, Iván de la Peña, Stéphane Dalmat, Jérôme Leroy; Robert Pires, Cyrille Pouget (61 Artur Moses). Trainer: Rolland Courbis

Goals: Inzaghi (17, 37, 38, 71), Leroy (50), Boksic (82)

FEYENOORD ROTTERDAM
v CHELSEA FC LONDON 1-3 (0-1)

Feyenoord, Rotterdam 14.03.2000

Referee: Knud Erik Fisker (DEN) Attendance: 44,000

FEYENOORD: Jerzy Dudek; Ulrich van Gobbel, Bert Konterman, Kees van Wonderen, Tomasz Rzasa; Paul Bosvelt, Jean-Paul van Gastel, Patrick Paauwe (46 Bonaventure Kalou), Jan de Visser (69 Radoslav Samardzic); Julio Ricardo Cruz, Jon Dahl Tomasson. Trainer: Leo Beenhakker

CHELSEA: Ed de Goey; Dan Petrescu, Frank Leboeuf, Marcel Desailly, Célestine Babayaro; Roberto di Matteo, Didier Deschamps, Dennis Wise, Gustavo Poyet (77 Jody Morris); Tore André Flo, Gianfranco Zola (90 Gabriele Ambrosetti). Manager: Gianluca Vialli

Goals: Zola (39), Kalou (59), Wise (64), Flo (69)

OLYMPIQUE de MARSEILLE
v FEYENOORD ROTTERDAM 0-0

Vélodrome, Marseille 22.03.2000

Referee: Arturo Daudén Ibañez (SPA) Attendance: 10,000

OLYMPIQUE: Stéphane Porato; Richard Martini, Peter Luccin, Jacques Abardonado; Jérôme Leroy, Frédéric Brando, Seydou Keita (90 Benjamin Gavanon), Yannick Fischer, Loris Reina; Ibrahima Bakayoko (62 Artur Moses), Iván de la Peña. Trainer: Rolland Courbis

FEYENOORD: Jerzy Dudek; Ulrich van Gobbel (80 Igor Korneev), Bert Konterman, Kees van Wonderen, Tomasz Rzasa; Paul Bosvelt, Jean-Paul van Gastel (75 Somalia), Jon Dahl Tomasson, Jan de Visser (65 Peter van Vossen); Bonaventure Kalou, Julio Ricardo Cruz. Trainer: Leo Beenhakker

Sent off: Martini (75)

CHELSEA FC LONDON
v SS LAZIO ROMA 1-2 (1-0)

Stamford Bridge, London 22.03.2000

Referee: Vítor Manuel Melo Pereira (POR) Att: 34,260

CHELSEA: Ed de Goey; Albert Ferrer, Frank Leboeuf (62 Jes Høgh), Marcel Desailly, Célestine Babayaro (74 John Harley); Roberto di Matteo (74 Jody Morris), Didier Deschamps, Dan Petrescu, Gustavo Poyet; Tore André Flo, Gianfranco Zola. Manager: Gianluca Vialli

LAZIO: Luca Marchegiani; Paolo Negro, Fernando Couto 83, Sinisa Mihajlovic, Giuseppe Pancaro; Dejan Stankovic (46 Alen Boksic), Diego Simeone, Matías Almeyda, Pavel Nedved; Juan Sebastián Verón, Simone Inzaghi (68 Marcelo Salas, 87 Guerino Gottardi). Trainer: Sven Göran Eriksson

Sent off: Fernando Couto (83)

Goals: Poyet (45), Inzaghi (54), Mihajlović (66)

	P	W	D	L	F	A	Pts
SS Lazio Roma	6	3	2	1	10	4	11
Chelsea FC London	6	3	1	2	8	5	10
Feyenoord	6	2	2	2	7	7	8
Olympique de Marseille	6	1	1	4	2	11	4

QUARTER-FINALS

REAL MADRID CF
v MANCHESTER UNITED FC 0-0

Santiago Bernabéu, Madrid 4.04.2000

Referee: Gilles Veissière (FRA) Attendance: 64,119

REAL: Iker Casillas; Miguel Ángel Salgado Fernández "MÍCHEL SALGADO", IVÁN CAMPO Ramos, Aitor KARANKA de la Hoz, ROBERTO CARLOS Da Silva; IVÁN HELGUERA Bujía, FERNANDO Carlos REDONDO Neri, Steve McManaman, SÁVIO Bortolini Pimentel (76 Elvir Baljic); Fernando MORIENTES Sánchez (86 Perica Ognjenovic), RAÚL González Blanco. Trainer: Vicente del Bosque

MANCHESTER UNITED: Mark Bosnich; Gary Neville, Jaap Stam, Henning Berg, Dennis Irwin (87 Michaël Silvestre); David Beckham, Roy Keane, Paul Scholes (81 Nicky Butt), Ryan Giggs; Andy Cole, Dwight Yorke (76 Teddy Sheringham). Manager: Alex Ferguson

MANCHESTER UNITED FC
v REAL MADRID CF 2-3 (0-1)

Old Trafford, Manchester 19.04.2000

Referee: Pierluigi Collina (ITA) Attendance: 59,178

MANCHESTER UNITED: Raimond van der Gouw; Gary Neville, Jaap Stam, Henning Berg (62 Teddy Sheringham), Dennis Irwin (46 Michaël Silvestre); David Beckham, Roy Keane, Paul Scholes, Ryan Giggs; Dwight Yorke, Andy Cole (62 Ole Gunnar Solskjær). Manager: Alex Ferguson

REAL: Iker Casillas; Miguel Ángel Salgado Fernández "MÍCHEL SALGADO", Aitor KARANKA de la Hoz, IVÁN CAMPO Ramos, ROBERTO CARLOS Da Silva; Steve McManaman (89 JÚLIO CÉSAR Santos Correa), FERNANDO Carlos REDONDO Neri, IVÁN HELGUERA Bujía, SÁVIO Bortolini Pimentel (65 GEREMI Nijtap Fotso); RAÚL González Blanco, Fernando MORIENTES Sánchez (72 Nicolas Anelka). Trainer: Vicente del Bosque

Goals: Keane (21 og), Raúl (50, 52), Beckham (64), Scholes (88 pen)

FC PORTO v FC BAYERN MÜNCHEN 1-1 (0-0)

Estádio das Antas, Porto 4.04.2000

Referee: Nikolai Levnikov (RUS) Attendance: 20,125

FC PORTO: Henrique HILÁRIO Sampaio; Fernando NÉLSON Jesus Vieira Alves, JORGE Paulo COSTA Almeida, ALOÍSIO Pires Alves, José Marcelo "ESQUERDINHA"; João Paulo Maio dos Santos "PAULINHO SANTOS", Anderson Luís de Sousa "DECO", Carlos Narciso CHAINHO (84 DOMINGOS Paciência de Oliveira); Nuno F.G. Rocha "CAPUCHO" (73 CLAYTON Ferreira Cruz), Mário JARDEL Almeida Ribeiro, Ljubinko Drulović. Trainer: Fernando Santos

BAYERN: Oliver Kahn; Markus Babbel, Samuel Kuffour, Patrik Andersson, Bixente Lizarazu; Hasan Salihamidzic (80 Roque Santa Cruz), Stefan Effenberg, Jens Jeremies; Paulo Sérgio, Giovane Élber (73 Carsten Jancker), Mehmet Scholl (87 Thorsten Fink). Trainer: Ottmar Hitzfeld

Goals: Jardel (47), Paulo Sérgio (80)

FC BAYERN MÜNCHEN v FC PORTO 2-1 (1-0)

Olympiastadion, München 19.04.2000

Referee: Hugh Dallas (SCO) Attendance: 45,000

BAYERN: Oliver Kahn; Markus Babbel, Thomas Linke, Patrik Andersson, Michael Tarnat (81 Samuel Kuffour); Thorsten Fink, Jens Jeremies, Mehmet Scholl; Paulo Sérgio, Giovane Élber (90 Carsten Jancker), Roque Santa Cruz (68 Hasan Salihamidzić). Trainer: Ottmar Hitzfeld

FC PORTO: Henrique HILÁRIO Sampaio; Fernando NÉLSON Jesus Vieira Alves, JORGE Paulo COSTA Almeida, ALOÍSIO Pires Alves, José Marcelo "ESQUERDINHA"; João Paulo Maio dos Santos "PAULINHO SANTOS", Anderson Luís de Sousa "DECO" (60 CLAYTON Ferreira Cruz), Carlos Narciso CHAINHO (44 RUI Gil Soares BARROS, 77 DOMINGOS Paciência de Oliveira); Nuno F.G. Rocha "CAPUCHO", Mário JARDEL Almeida Ribeiro, Ljubinko Drulović. Trainer: Fernando Santos

Goals: Paulo Sérgio (15), Jardel (89), Linke (90)

CHELSEA FC LONDON v FC BARCELONA 3-1 (3-0)

Stamford Bridge, London 5.04.2000

Referee: Markus Merk (GER) Attendance: 35,641

CHELSEA: Ed de Goey; Albert Ferrer, Emerson Thome, Marcel Desailly, Célestine Babayaro; Dan Petrescu (71 Roberto di Matteo), Didier Deschamps, Dennis Wise, Jody Morris; Tore André Flo (87 Chris Sutton), Gianfranco Zola. Manager: Gianluca Vialli

FC BARCELONA: Rodolfus Hubuertus "Ruud" Hesp; Carlos Puyol (46 Jari Litmanen), ABELARDO Fernández Artuña, Frank de Boer, Winston Bogarde; GABRIel García De la Torre, XAVIer Hernández Creus, Philip John William Cocu; Luis Filipe Madeira Caeiro "FIGO", Patrick Kluivert (71 DANIel García Lara), Vítor Borba Ferreira "RIVALDO". Trainer: Louis van Gaal

Goals: Zola (30), Flo (34, 38), Figo (64)

FC BARCELONA v CHELSEA FC LONDON 5-1 (2-0, 3-1) (AET)

Camp Nou, Barcelona 18.04.2000

Referee: Anders Frisk (SWE) Attendance: 96,249

FC BARCELONA: Rodolfus Hubuertus "Ruud" Hesp; Carlos Puyol (86 ABELARDO Fernández Artuña), Michael Reiziger (105 SERGI Barjuán Esclusa), Frank de Boer, Boudewijn Zenden (72 DANIel García Lara); GABRIel García De la Torre, Josep GUARDIOLA Sala, Philip John William Cocu; Luis Filipe Madeira Caeiro "FIGO", Patrick Kluivert, Vítor Borba Ferreira "RIVALDO". Trainer: Louis van Gaal

CHELSEA: Ed de Goey; Albert Ferrer (46 Bernard Lambourde), Frank Leboeuf, Marcel Desailly, Célestine Babayaro; Roberto di Matteo, Didier Deschamps (102 Dan Petrescu), Dennis Wise, Jody Morris; Tore André Flo, Gianfranco Zola (106 Gustavo Poyet). Manager: Gianluca Vialli

Sent off: Babayaro (98)

Goals: Rivaldo (24, 97 pen), Figo (45), Flo (60), Dani (83), Kluivert (104)

VALENCIA CF v SS LAZIO ROMA 5-2 (3-1)

Mestalla, Valencia 5.04.2000

Referee: Kim Milton Nielsen (DEN) Attendance: 41,800

VALENCIA: Santiago CAÑIZARES Ruiz; Jocelyn Angloma, Miroslav Djukić, Mauricio Pellegrino, Amedeo Carboni; Miguel Ángel ANGULO, Francisco FARINÓS Zapata, GERARD López Segú, Christian Alberto "KILY" GONZÁLEZ Peret; JUAN Ginés SÁNCHEZ Moreno (82 ÓSCAR García Junyent), CLAUDIO Javier LÓPEZ. Trainer: Héctor Raúl Cuper

LAZIO: Marco Ballotta; Guerino Gottardi, Paolo Negro, Sinisa Mihajlovic, Giuseppe Pancaro; Dejan Stankovic (62 Sérgio Conceição), Diego Simeone (76 Marcelo Salas), Matías Almeyda, Pavel Nedved; Simone Inzaghi (68 Alen Boksic), Juan Sebastián Verón. Trainer: Sven Göran Eriksson

Goals: Angulo (2), Gerard (4, 40, 79), Inzaghi (28), Salas (87), López (90)

SS LAZIO ROMA v VALENCIA CF 1-0 (0-0)

Olimpico, Roma 18.04.2000

Referee: Dick Jol (HOL) Attendance: 53,135

LAZIO: Luca Marchegiani; Paolo Negro, Alessandro Nesta, Sinisa Mihajlovic, Giuseppe Pancaro (76 Roberto Mancini); Sérgio Conceição, Matías Almeyda (84 Diego Simeone), Juan Sebastián Verón, Pavel Nedved (46 Simone Inzaghi); Marcelo Salas, Alen Boksić. Trainer: Sven Göran Eriksson

VALENCIA: Santiago CAÑIZARES Ruiz; Jocelyn Angloma, Miroslav Djukić, Mauricio Pellegrino, Joachim Björklund; Gaizka MENDIETA Zabala (61 David ALBELDA Aliques), Francisco FARINÓS Zapata, GERARD López Segú, Christian Alberto "KILY" GONZÁLEZ Peret; CLAUDIO Javier LÓPEZ, Miguel Ángel ANGULO (82 ÓSCAR García Junyent). Trainer: Héctor Raúl Cuper

Goal: Verón (52)

VALENCIA CF v FC BARCELONA 4-1 (3-1)

Mestalla, Valencia 2.05.2000

Referee: Urs Meier (SWI) Attendance: 55,124

VALENCIA: Santiago CAÑIZARES Ruiz; Jocelyn Angloma, Miroslav Djukić, Mauricio Pellegrino, Amedeo Carboni; Gaizka MENDIETA Zabala, Francisco FARINÓS Zapata, GERARD López Segú (83 JUAN Ginés SÁNCHEZ Moreno), Christian Alberto "KILY" GONZÁLEZ Peret; Miguel Ángel ANGULO (78 David ALBELDA Aliques), CLAUDIO Javier LÓPEZ (90 Adrian Ilie). Trainer: Héctor Raúl Cuper

FC BARCELONA: Rodolfus Hubuertus "Ruud" Hesp; Carlos Puyol (46 Winston Bogarde), Frank de Boer, Josep GUARDIOLA Sala, Michael Reiziger; GABRIel García De la Torre, Vítor Borba Ferreira "RIVALDO", Philip John William Cocu; DANIel García Lara (61 Jari Litmanen), Patrick Kluivert, Boudewijn Zenden (75 SIMÃO Pedro Fonseca Sabrosa). Trainer: Louis van Gaal

Goals: Angulo (10, 43), Pellegrino (27 og), Mendieta (45 pen), López (90)

REAL MADRID CF v FC BAYERN MÜNCHEN 2-0 (2-0)

Santiago Bernabéu, Madrid 3.05.2000

Referee: Anders Frisk (SWE) Attendance: 74,871

REAL: Iker Casillas; Miguel Ángel Salgado Fernández "MÍCHEL SALGADO", IVÁN CAMPO Ramos, Aitor KARANKA de la Hoz, ROBERTO CARLOS Da Silva, IVÁN HELGUERA Bujía; Steve McManaman, FERNANDO Carlos REDONDO Neri, RAÚL González Blanco; Nicolas Anelka (80 Elvir Baljic), Fernando MORIENTES Sánchez (61 SÁVIO Bortolini Pimentel). Trainer: Vicente del Bosque

BAYERN: Oliver Kahn; Markus Babbel, Thomas Linke, Jens Jeremies; Bixente Lizarazu, Hasan Salihamidzic (78 Roque Santa Cruz), Thorsten Fink, Michael Tarnat (46 Michael Wiesinger); Paulo Sérgio, Giovane Élber (78 Carsten Jancker), Mehmet Scholl. Trainer: Ottmar Hitzfeld

Goals: Anelka (4), Jeremies (33 og)

FC BARCELONA v VALENCIA CF 2-1 (0-0)

Camp Nou, Barcelona 10.05.2000

Referee: Vítor Manuel Melo Pereira (POR) Att: 85,377

FC BARCELONA: Rodolfus Hubuertus "Ruud" Hesp; Michael Reiziger, Frank de Boer, ABELARDO Fernández Artuña (76 Jari Litmanen); XAVIer Hernández Creus, Josep GUARDIOLA Sala (69 SERGI Barjuán Esclusa), Philip John William Cocu, Vítor Borba Ferreira "RIVALDO"; Luís Filipe Madeira Caeiro "FIGO", Patrick Kluivert, Boudewijn Zenden (63 SIMÃO Pedro Fonseca Sabrosa). Trainer: Louis van Gaal

VALENCIA: Santiago CAÑIZARES Ruiz; Jocelyn Angloma (86 GERARDO García), Miroslav Djukić, Mauricio Pellegrino, Amedeo Carboni; Gaizka MENDIETA Zabala, Francisco FARINÓS Zapata (90 JUAN Ginés SÁNCHEZ Moreno), GERARD López Segú, Christian Alberto "KILY" GONZÁLEZ Peret (74 David ALBELDA Aliques); Miguel Ángel ANGULO, CLAUDIO Javier LÓPEZ. Trainer: Héctor Raúl Cuper

Goals: Mendieta (69), F. de Boer (78), Cocu (90)

FC BAYERN MÜNCHEN v REAL MADRID CF 2-1 (1-1)

Olympiastadion, München 9.05.2000

Referee: Graham Poll (ENG) Attendance: 60,234

BAYERN: Oliver Kahn; Markus Babbel (60 Hasan Salihamidzic), Patrik Andersson, Samuel Kuffour, Bixente Lizarazu; Paulo Sérgio, Jens Jeremies (59 Thorsten Fink), Stefan Effenberg, Mehmet Scholl, Giovane Élber, Carsten Jancker (79 Roque Santa Cruz). Trainer: Ottmar Hitzfeld

REAL: Iker Casillas; GEREMI Nijtap Fotso, IVÁN CAMPO Ramos, IVÁN HELGUERA Bujía, JÚLIO CÉSAR Santos Correa, ROBERTO CARLOS Da Silva; Steve McManaman (90 Elvir Baljic), FERNANDO Carlos REDONDO Neri, SÁVIO Bortolini Pimentel (81 Christian Karembeu); RAÚL González Blanco, Nicolas Anelka (89 Manuel SANCHÍS Hontiyuelo). Trainer: Vicente del Bosque

Goals: Jancker (12), Anelka (31), Élber (54)

FINAL

REAL MADRID CF v VALENCIA CF 3-0 (1-0)

Saint-Denis, Paris 24.05.2000

Referee: Stefano Braschi (ITA) Attendance: 78,759

REAL: Iker Casillas; Miguel Ángel Salgado Fernández "MÍCHEL SALGADO" (85 Fernándo Ruíz Hierro), Aitor KARANKA de la Hoz, IVÁN HELGUERA Bujía, IVÁN CAMPO Ramos, ROBERTO CARLOS Da Silva; Steve McManaman, FERNANDO Carlos REDONDO Neri, RAÚL González Blanco; Nicolas Anelka (80 Manuel SANCHÍS Hontiyuelo), Fernando MORIENTES Sánchez (72 SÁVIO Bortolini Pimentel). Trainer: Vicente del Bosque

VALENCIA: Santiago CAÑIZARES Ruiz; Jocelyn Angloma, Miroslav Djukić, Mauricio Pellegrino, GERARDO García (69 Adrian Ilie); Gaizka MENDIETA Zabala, Francisco FARINÓS Zapata, GERARD López Segú, Christian Alberto "KILY" GONZÁLEZ Peret; Miguel Ángel ANGULO, CLAUDIO Javier LÓPEZ. Trainer: Héctor Raúl Cuper

Goals: Morientes (39), McManaman (67), Raúl (75)

Qualifying Round Goalscorers 1999-2000:

6 goals: Kezman (Partizan Beograd), Mikholap (Skonto Riga)

4 goals: Maxim Shatskykh (Dynamo Kyiv)

3 goals: Todorov (Liteks Lovech), Berco, Boreţ, Epureanu (Zimbru Chişinău), S. Ilić, Ivić (Partizan Beograd), Shirko (Spartak Moskva), Obiku (Anorthosis Famagusta), Wichniarek (Widzew Lódz)

2 goals: Sloan (Barry Town), G. Agius (FC Valletta), Haxhi, Bushi (Liteks Lovech), Popovich (Haka Valkeakoski), Memedi (Sloga Jugomagnat Skopje), S.Jóhannesson (IB Vestmannaeyjar), Th. Gudjónsson (RC Genk), Simundza, Balajić (NK Maribor), Tropaneţ (Zimbru Chişinău), Peković, Krstajić (Partizan Beograd), Astafyev, Bleidelis, Chaladze (Skonto Riga), Dowe (Rapid Wien), Cois (Fiorentina), Rebrov (Dynamo Kyiv), Mols (Glasgow Rangers), Daugaard (Brøndby IF), Ahinful (Boavista Porto), Sánchez (Valencia CF), Vastic (Sturm Graz), Hoseth (Molde FK), Simić (Croatia Zagreb)

1 goal: Bulku (SK Tirana), Mamedov, Rzayev (Kapaz Ganja), Viikmäe (Flora Tallinn), á Lakjuni (HB Tórshavn), Chetcuti (FC Valletta), Hrncar, Timko (Slovan Bratislava), Sztipánovics (NK Rijeka), Şişchin, Khomukha (CSKA Moskva), Zivkovic, Kondev, Petrov (Liteks Lovech), Niemi, Salli, Reynders, Nyyssönen, Wilson, Torkkeli (Haka Valkeakoski), Tsitaishvili, Khomeriki (Dinamo Tbilisi), Răducan, Barbu, Schumacher, Mutică (Rapid Bucureşti), Ayhan (Beşiktaş Istanbul), Novikovas, Joksas, Vasiliaukas, I. Stesko, A. Stesko (Zalgiris Vilnius), Sigurdsson, Bjarklind (IB Vestmannaeyjar), Horváth, Strupar (RC Genk), Filipović, Galić, Karić, Djuranović (NK Maribor), Nilis, Ooijer (PSV Eindhoven), Dodul, Oprea (Zimbru Chişinău), Tomić (Partizan Beograd), Titov, Tikhonov (Spartak Moskva), Babayaro, Poyet, Sutton (Chelsea London), Laizans, Rubins, Kolesnichenko (Skonto Riga), Hakan Ünsal, Fatih, Hagi, Okan Buruk (Galatasaray Istanbul), Lagonikasis, Savićević, Penksa (Rapid Wien), Chiesa, Adani, Rui Costa (Fiorentina), Strandli, Oper, Gaarde (Aalborg), Gusin (Dynamo Kyiv), Vidmar, Reyna, Wallace, Johansson, Amato, Amoruso, Moore (Glasgow Rangers), Walem (Parma), Christensen, Bjur, Smith (Brøndby IF), Mário Silva, Moreira, Litos, Rui Bento (Boavista Porto), Corneliusson, Novakovic, Gustafsson, Tjernström (AIK Solna), Rosso (Hapoel Haifa), López, Farinós (Valencia CF), Daei, Preetz (Hertha Berlin), Kocijan, Martens (Sturm Graz), Juarez, Thurre, Lonfat (Servette Genève), Stankovic (RCD Mallorca), Lund, Tessem, Berg Hestad (Molde FK), Halmai, Preisinger, Ilea, Kuttor, Illés (MTK Budapest), Herrlich, Nerlinger (Borussia Dortmund), Gesior, Michalski (Widzew Lódz)

Own goal: Adani (Fiorentina) for Widzew Lódz

Champions League Goalscorers 1999-2000:

10 goals: Mário Jardel (FC Porto), Vítor Borba Ferreira "RIVALDO" (FC Barcelona)

9 goals: Simone Inzaghi (Lazio Roma), RAÚL González Blanco (Real Madrid)

8 goals: Serhiy Rebrov (Dynamo Kyiv), Tore André Flo (Chelsea London),

7 goals: Patrick Kluivert (FC Barcelona), Paulo Sergio (Bayern München)

6 goals: Gabriel Batistuta (Fiorentina Firenze), Roy Keane (Manchester United), Luis Enrique (FC Barcelona), Fernando Morientes (Real Madrid)

5 goals: John Carew (Rosenborg Trondheim), Luis Filipe Madeira Caeiro "FIGO" (FC Barcelona), Claudio Lopez, Gaizka Mendieta (Valencia CF)

4 goals: Kirsten (Bayer Leverkusen), Giovanni (Olympiakos Peiraias), Bezrodnyi, Tikhonov (Spartak Moskva), Lokvenc (Sparta Praha), Balbo (Fiorentina Firenze), Wiltord (Girondins de Bordeaux), Sørensen (Rosenborg Trondheim), Hakan Şükür (Galatasaray Istanbul), Wise (Chelsea London), Salas (Lazio Roma), Tomasson (Feyenoord Rotterdam), Gabri (FC Barcelona), Gerard (Valencia CF), Sávio (Real Madrid),

3 goals: Overmars (Arsenal London), Bobic (Borussia Dortmund), Kocijan (Sturm Graz), Šokota (Croatia Zagreb), Lund (Molde FK), van Nistelrooy (PSV Eindhoven), Ali Daei (Hertha Berlin), Fukal, Labant (Sparta Praha), Chiesa (Fiorentina Firenze), Ø. Berg (Rosenborg Trondheim), Bakayoko (Olympique Marseille), Cole, Scholes, Solskjær (Manchester United), Deco (FC Porto), Zola (Chelsea London), Mihajlović (Lazio Roma), Cruz (Feyenoord Rotterdam), Élber, Jancker, Scholl (Bayern München), Angulo (Valencia CF), Roberto Carlos (Real Madrid)

2 goals: Neuville (Bayer Leverkusen), Zivkovic (Bayer Leverkusen), A. Andersson (AIK Solna), Suker (Arsenal London), Zahovic (Olympiakos Peiraias), Berg Hestad (Molde FK), Albertz, Mols (Glasgow Rangers), Sanou (Willem II Tilburg), Bierhoff (AC Milan), Wosz (Hertha Berlin), J. Novotný, Rosický (Sparta Praha), Micoud (Girondins de Bordeaux), Khatskevich (Dynamo Kyiv), Dugarry, Pires (Olympique Marseille), Ümit (Galatasaray Istanbul), Beckham, Yorke (Manchester United), Drulovic (FC Porto), Sérgio Conceição, Stanković, Verón (Lazio Roma), Bosvelt, Kalou (Feyenoord Rotterdam), Abelardo, Cocu, Dani, F. de Boer, (FC Barcelona), Effenberg, Zickler (Bayern München), Ilie, Kily González (Valencia CF), Anelka, Helguera (Real Madrid)

1 goal: Balajić, Simundza (NK Maribor), Nordin, Novakovic (AIK Solna), Bergkamp, Kanu, Ljungberg, Henry (Arsenal London), Timofte, Barbarez, Kohler, Möller (Borussia Dortmund), Pedro Emanuel, Mário Silva, Rui Bento (Boavista Porto), Vastić, Mählich (Sturm Graz), Mikić, Mujcin, Prosinecki, Rukavina (Croatia Zagreb), Giannakopoulos, Mavrogenidis, Luciano (Olympiakos Peiraias), Lindbaek (Molde FK), Nilis, Khokhlov (PSV Eindhoven), Moore, Amoruso, McCann (Glasgow Rangers), Schenning, Bombarda, Shukov, Abdellaoui, Arts (Willem II Tilburg), Bulatov (Spartak Moskva), Giunti, Weah, Leonardo, Shevchenko (AC Milan), Alves, Veit, Michalke, Rekdal, Preetz (Hertha BSC Berlin), Z.Svoboda, Siegl, Baranek, Proházka, Jarošik (Sparta Praha), Rui Costa, Mijatović, Bressan (Fiorentina Firenze), Zanotti, Batlles, Pavon, Laslandes, Feindouno (Girondins de Bordeaux), Kaladze, Demetradze, Raúl, Roberto Carlos, Kosovskyi, Shatskykh, Holovko, Vashchuk, Gusin (Dynamo Kyiv), Skammelsrud, Dahlum, F.Winsnes, R. Strand (Rosenborg), Diawara, Gallas, Leroy, Pérez, Ravanelli (Olympique Marseille), Capone, Tugay, Okan, Hagi (Galatasaray Istanbul), Giggs, Sheringham (Manchester United), Clayton, Jorge Costa, Capucho, Esquerdinha (FC Porto), Babayaro, Poyet, Deschamps, Ferrer, Ambrosetti, Petrescu, Leboeuf (Chelsea London), Boksić, Nedved, Negro (Lazio Roma), Somalia, van Vossen, Addo, van Wonderen (Feyenoord), Xavi, Guardiola, Zenden, Déhu (FC Barcelona), Linke, Jakobsen, Fink, Strunz, Santa Cruz, Tarnat (Bayern München), Djukić, Sánchez (Valencia CF), McManaman, Karembeu, Hierro, Guti (Real Madrid)

Own goals: Mamedov (Dynamo Kyiv) for Lazio, Peixe (FC Porto) for Real Madrid, Moore (Glasgow Rangers) for Valencia CF, Victoria (Willem II) for Girondins de Bordeaux, Hierro (Real Madrid) for Dynamo Kyiv, Keane (Manchester United) for Real Madrid, Pellegrino (Valencia CF) for FC Barcelona, Jeremies (Bayern München) for Real Madrid

CHAMPIONS LEAGUE 2000-2001

FIRST QUALIFYING ROUND

BIRKIRKARA FC v KR REYKJAVÍK 1-2 (1-0)

National, Ta' Qali 12.07.2000

Referee: Giorgos Douros (GRE) Attendance: 848

BIRKIRKARA: Robert Savic (12 Charles Sciberras); Drasko Braunović, Graham Bencini, Michael Spiteri (72 Hubert Suda), Ivan Zammit (Cap), Michael Cutajar, Joe Brincat, Michael Galea, Chucks Kajetan Nwoko, Adrian Popescu, Jonathan Magri Overend (85 Simon Sammut).
Trainer: Georgev Atanas Marinov

KR: Kristján Finnbogason; Bjarni Thorsteinsson, Sigursteinn Gíslason, Thormódur Egilson (Cap), Sigurdur Örn Jonsson, Sigthor Juliusson, Andri Sigthorsson (90 Magnús Már Lúdvíksson), Gudmundur Benediktsson (75 Ivar Bjarklind), Gunnar Einarsson, Arnar Jon Sigurgeirsson (82 Egill Atlason), Thórhallur Hinriksson. Trainer: Pétur Pétursson

Goals: Nwoko (45), Sigthorsson (47), Juliusson (72)

KR REYKJAVÍK v BIRKIRKARA 4-1 (2-0)

KR v Völlur, Reykjavík 19.07.2000

Referee: Simon Jones (WAL) Attendance: 1,844

KR: Kristján Finnbogason (Cap) (66 Bjarki Gudmundsson); Bjarni Thorsteinsson, Sigursteinn Gíslason (46 Ivar Bjarklind), David Winnie, Sigurdur Örn Jonsson (46 Arnar Jon Sigurgeirsson), Sigthor Juliusson, Einar Thór Daníelsson, Andri Sigthorsson, Gudmundur Benediktsson, Gunnar Einarsson, Thórhallur Hinriksson. Trainer: Pétur Pétursson

BIRKIRKARA: Charles Sciberras; Drasko Braunovic, Graham Bencini, Michael Spiteri (80 Alan Tabone), Kenneth Scicluna, Ivan Zammit (Cap), Michael Cutajar, Joe Brincat, Chucks Kajetan Nwoko (76 Simon Sammut), Adrian Popescu (52 Michael Galea), Jonathan Magri Overend.
Trainer: Georgev Atanas Marinov

Sent off: Braunovic (58)

Goals: Winnie (16), Benediktsson (45), Spiteri (52), Sigthorsson (58, 63)

F91 DUDELANGE v LEVSKI SOFIA 0-4 (0-2)

Josy Barthel, Luxembourg 12.07.2000

Referee: Herbert Fandel (GER) Attendance: 1,121

F91: Paul Koch; Roger Lutz, Jean-Pierre Vanek, Christophe Boulard, Nicolas Funck; Marco Morgante (Cap), Romain Provenier (72 Telmo Matos), David Cangini; Stefano Fanelli (58 Gordon Braun), Evariste Kabongo, Florim Alijaj (64 Marco Delazzer). Trainer: Carlo Weis

LEVSKI: Dimitar Ivankov (Cap); Martin Stankov (64 Oleksandr Koval), Biser Ivanov (46 Zaharin Sirakov), Georgi Markov, Ilian Stoianov, Predrag Pazin; Aleksandar Aleksandrov, Elin Topuzakov, Eduard Tsykhmeistruk; Georgi Ivanov, LEONIDAS Ferreira de Pau (71 Dimitar Telkiyski). Trainer: Georgi Todorov

Goals: Ivanov (11, 87), Ivankov (16 pen), Tsykhmeistruk (68)

LEVSKI SOFIA v F91 DUDELANGE 2-0 (1-0)

Georgi Asparuhov, Sofia 19.07.2000

Referee: Paul Allaerts (BEL) Attendance: 5,284

LEVSKI: Dimitar Ivankov (Cap); Georgi Markov, Ilian Stoianov, Dalibor Dragic (46 Martin Stankov), Predrag Pazin; Aleksandar Aleksandrov, Eduard Tsykhmeistruk, Elin Topuzakov (28 Oleksandr Koval), Dimitar Telkiyski; Georgi Ivanov (54 Tchavdar Petrov Atanassov), Ferreira de Pau Leônidas. Trainer: Georgi Todorov

F91: Paul Koch; Roger Lutz, Jean-Pierre Vanek, Christophe Boulard (75 José Barreto Pereira), Nicolas Funck; Romain Provenier, David Cangini; Mino Barnabo, Stefano Fanelli (Cap) (62 Florim Alijaj), Marco Delazzer (87 Gordon Braun), Evariste Kabongo. Trainer: Carlo Weis

Goals: Ivanov (35), Ivankov (52 pen)

HAKA VALKEAKOSKI v LINFIELD BELFAST 1-0 (0-0)

Tehtaankenttä, Valkeakoski 12.07.2000

Referee: Nikolai Ivanov (RUS) Attendance: 1,799

HAKA: András Vilnrotter; Janne Salli (Cap), Jaakko Pasanen (71 Janne Hyökyvaara), Jarkko Okkonen; Oleg Ivanov, Jukka Ruhanen (78 Dragan Bajic), David Wilson, Jukka Koskinen; Martin Reynders, Kai Nyyssönen (65 Tommi Torkkeli), Péter Kovács. Trainer: Keith Armstrong

LINFIELD: Paul Mathers; Stephen Collier, John Easton, Patrick McShane (83 Ian Young), William Murphy, Gavin Arthur; Noel Bailie (Cap), Norman Kelly, Stephen Beatty; Anthony Gorman, David Larmour (63 Glenn Ferguson). Trainer: David Jeffrey

Goal: Wilson (56)

LINFIELD BELFAST v FC HAKA VALKEAKOSKI 2-1 (1-0)

Windsor Park, Belfast 19.07.2000

Referee: Egill Mar Markusson (ICE) Attendance: 3,587

LINFIELD: Paul Mathers, Stephen Collier, John Easton (85 Craig McCracken), Jamie Henry Marks, William Murphy, Stephen Beatty, Christopher Morgan, Anthony Gorman, Glenn Ferguson (81 Patrick McShane), Norman Kelly, Noel Bailie (Cap). Trainer: David Jeffrey

HAKA: Andras Vilnrotter, Lasse Karjalainen, Janne Salli (Cap), Kai Nyyssönen (86 Marco Antonio Pogioli), Jukka Ruhanen, Tommi Torkkeli (77 Martin Reynders), Peter Kovacs, David Wilson, Jarkko Okkonen, Juuso Kangaskorpi, Jukka Koskinen (76 Janne Antero Savolainen). Trainer: Keith Armstrong

Goals: Ferguson (22 pen, 72), Kovacs (85 pen)

KÍ KLAKSVIK v FK CRVENA ZVEZDA BEOGRAD 0-3 (0-1)

Toftír Stadium 12.07.2000

Referee: Kjell G. Alseth (NOR) Attendance: 950

KÍ: Zoltan Kujundzić; Andrzei Pacek, Niclas Niclasen, Marek Wierzbicki; Jan Andreasen, Harley Bertholdsen, Jan Joensen (Cap), Rogvi Jakobsen (78 Símun Joensen); Arnold Joensen (63 Kristian a Lakjuni), Hedin A Lakjuni, Ove Nysted (65 Srecko Milicević). Trainer: Tomislav Sivić

CRVENA ZVEZDA: Aleksander Kocić; Marjan Marković, Stevo Glogovac, Dejan Ilić, Nenad Lalatović; Ivan Gvozdenović, Srdan Bajcetić (Cap); Goran Drulić (70 Vladislav Mirković), Branko Bosković (78 Jovan Markoski), Leo Lerinc (81 Blaze Georgijevski), Dragan Stevanović. Trainer: Slavoljub Muslin

Goals: Ilić (44), Stevanović (68), Mirković (90)

CRVENA ZVEZDA BEOGRAD v KÍ KLAKSVIK 2-0 (2-0)

Crvena Zvezda, Beograd 19.07.2000

Referee: Zsolt Szabo (HUN) Attendance: 8,000

CRVENA ZVEZDA: Aleksandar Kocić, Marjan Marković, Ivan Gvozdenović, Dejan Ilić (67 Blaze Georgijevski), Goran Drulić, Branko Bosković (69 Jovan Markoski), Milivoje Vitakić, Nenad Lalatović, Srdan Bajcetić (Cap), Leo Lerinc, Dragan Stevanović (72 Vladislav Mirković). Trainer: Slavoljub Muslin

KÍ: Zoltan Kujundzić, Kristian a Lakjuni, Jan Andreasen, Harley Bertholdsen, Arnold Joensen (46 Srecko Milicević), Jan Joensen (Cap) (86 Allan Joensen), Rogvi Jacobsen, Niclas Niclasen, Hedin a Lakjuni (71 Hjalgrim Elttør), Ove Nysted, Marek Wierzbicki. Trainer: Tomislav Sivić

Goals: Bosković (10 pen), Drulić (17)

TOTAL NETWORK SOLUTIONS LLANSANTFFRAID v FC LEVADIA MAARDU 2-2 (0-0)

Racecourse Ground, Wrexham 12.07.2000

Referee: Joseph Attard (MAL) Attendance: 1,432

TNS LLANSANTFFRAID: Lee Williams; Dewi Parry, Lee Coathup, Steven Evans, Timothy Richard Edwards (Cap); Timothy Alexander, Mark Roberts, John Toner, Gary Powell (58 Michael Paul Maloney); Anthony Wright (78 Nicholas John Ward), Christopher Edge (83 Colin Joseph Lee Webster). Trainer: Andy Cale

FC LEVADIA: Sergei Pareiko; Dalius Staleljunas, Igor Prins (Cap), Eduard Vinogradov, Andrei Krasnopjorov; Konstantin Kolbasenko, Maksim Rõtškov, Vitali Leitan (70 Vladimir Tselnokov), Sergei Bragin; Indro Olumets, Iouri Fenin (63 Toomas Krõm). Trainer: Sergei Ratnikov

Goals: Bragin (50), Wright (62), Krasnopjorov (88), Toner (89)

FC LEVADIA MAARDU v TNS LLANSANTFFRAID 4-0 (0-0)

Kadriorg, Tallinn 19.07.2000

Referee: Jørn West Larsen (DEN) Attendance: 2,000

FC LEVADIA: Sergei Pareiko; Juri Leitan, Dalius Staleljunas, Igor Prins (Cap), Andrei Krasnopjorov; Konstantin Kolbasenko (76 Dmitri Kirilov), Maksim Rõtškov, Sergei Bragin, Toomas Krom (57 Vladimir Tselnokov); Indro Olumets (65 Vitali Leitan), Iouri Fenin. Trainer: Sergei Ratnikov

TNS LLANSANTFFRAID: Lee Williams; Dewi Parry, Lee Coathup (46 Nicholas John Ward), Steven Evans (68 Kenneth Michael McKenna), Timothy Richard Edwards (Cap), Timothy Alexander, Mark Roberts, John Toner, Michael Paul Maloney; Anthony Wright, Christopher Edge (68 Gary Roger Evans). Trainer: Andy Cale

Goals: Krom (49), Fenin (58), Tselnokov (60), Edwards (64 og)

SHIRAK GYUMRI v FC BATE BORISOV 1-1 (1-1)

City, Gyumri 12.07.2000

Referee: Michal Benes (CZE) Attendance: 1,500

SHIRAK: Raimond Zaduryan; Gagik Margaryan, Hovhannis Demirtshian, Felix Khodoyan, Artur Petrosyan (Cap), Hovhannes Tahmazyan, Kolya Yepranosyan (62 Aram Tumasyan), Tigran Davtyan, Mher Avanesyan, Arsen Avetisyan, Ararat Harutyunyan. Trainer: Andranik Adamyan

BATE: Aleksandr Fedorovich (Cap); Oleg Korol, Vitaliy Rogozhkin, Andrei Divakov, Vitaliy Panasiuk, Vitaliy Kutuzov (77 Artem Goncharyk), Evgeni Loshankov, Yuri Doroshkevich (60 Vyacheslav Hryharau), Leonid Lagun, Alexei Baga (46 Vadim Skripchenko), Gennadi Mardas. Trainer: Yuri Puntus

Goals: Kutusau (24), Tahmazyan (30)

FC BATE BORISOV v SHIRAK GYUMRI 2-1 (1-0)

City, Borisov 19.07.2000

Referee: Ante Kulusić (CRO) Attendance: 2,138

BATE: Aleksandr Fedorovich (Cap); Oleg Korol, Vitaliy Rogozhkin, Andrei Divakov, Vitaliy Panasiuk, Vitaliy Kutuzov, Evgeni Loshankov, Alexei Baga (55 Alexandr Ermakovich), Vladimir Nevinskiy (88 Artem Goncharyk), Gennadi Mardas, Vadim Skripchenko (71 Leonid Lagun). Trainer: Yuri Puntus

SHIRAK: Artur Hovhannisyan; Aram Tumasyan, Gagik Margaryan, Hovhannis Demirtshian, Felix Khodoyan, Artur Petrosyan (Cap), Hovhannes Tahmazyan, Kolya Yepranosyan, Tigran Davtyan, Mher Avanesyan, Ararat Harutyunyan (62 Hakob Artoyan). Trainer: Andranik Adamyan

Goals: Rahozhkin (17), Loshankov (58), Tahmazyan (74)

FC SKONTO RIGA v FK SHAMKIR 2-1 (0-0)

Daugava, Riga 12.07.2000

Referee: Douglas McDonald (SCO) Attendance: 3,200

FC SKONTO: Alexander Kolinko, Igor N.Stepanov, Jurijs Laizans (45 Valentins Lobanyov), Oleg Blagonadezhdin, Aleksandr Rekhviashvili (Cap), Orestas Buitkus, Andrejs Rubins, Vladimir Kolesnichenko, Zurab Menteshashvili (70 Levan Korgalidze), Jevgeny Buda (46 Mikhail Mikholap), Mantas Samusevas. Trainer: Alexander Starkovs

FK SHAMKIR: Rauf Mekhdiev, Mubariz Orudjev, Mekhman Yunusov (Cap), Azer Mamedov, Faig Jabbarov, Ali Abushev, Makhmud Kurbanov, Khalig Mardanov, Ismagil Mamedov, Khagani Mamedov (45 Viktor Kulikov), Badri Kvaratschkheliya (90 Arif Mamedov). Trainer: Agasalim Mirjavadov

Goals: Kolesnichenko (47, 90 pen), Kulikov (82)

FK SHAMKIR v FC SKONTO RIGA 4-1 (1-1, 2-1) (AET)

Tofik Bakhramov, Baku 19.07.2000

Referee: Miroslaw Ryszka (POL) Attendance: 10,500

FK SHAMKIR: Rauf Mekhdiev, Mubariz Orudjev (62 Agil Mamedov), Mekhman Yunusov (Cap), Nizami Odjaguevdiev, Faig Jabbarov, Ali Abushev (78 Khagani Mamedov), Makhmud Kurbanov, Khalig Mardanov, Ismagil Mamedov (73 Etimad Kurbanov), Viktor Kulikov, Badri Kvaratschkheliya. Trainer: Agasalim Mirjavadov

FC SKONTO: Alexander Kolinko, Igor N.Stepanov, Mikhail Zemlinsky, V.Lobanyov, Oleg Blagonadezhdin (102 Jurijs Laizans), Aleksandr Rekhviashvili (Cap), Orestas Buitkus, Andrejs Rubins, Vladimir Kolesnichenko (71 Mikhail Mikholap), Andrejus Tereshkinas (92 Levan Korgalidze), Mantas Samusevas. Trainer: Alexander Starkovs

Goals: Kvaratschkheliya (3, 90, 100), Samusevas (31), Kulikov (110)

SLOGA JUGOMAGNAT SKOPJE v SHELBOURNE DUBLIN **0-1** (0-0)

Gradski, Skopje 12.07.2000

Referee: Wolfgang Sowa (AUS) Attendance: 6,000

SLOGA JUGOMAGNAT: Jane Nikoloski; Goran Jovanovski, Zoran Sterjovski, Saso Zdravevski, Zoran Jovanovski; Nebi Mustafi, Goran Maznov, Oldzaj Bajram (46 Goran Janevski), Argend Beciri (Cap), Bruno Presilski (46 Arben Nuhiji); Zekirija Ramadan (75 Gasi Ramadani). Trainer: Gjorgji Jovanovski

SHELBOURNE: Steven Williams; Owen Heary, Tony McCarthy; Paul Doolin (46 Garry Haylock), Robbie Raeside (46 Pat Scully), Pat Fenlon, Mark Hutchison, James Keddy; Desmond Baker, Stephen Geoghegan (Cap) (77 Richard Foran), Richard Baker. Trainer: Dermot Keely

Goal: R. Baker (85)

ZIMBRU CHIŞINĂU v SK TIRANË **3-2** (2-2)

Speia 19.07.2000

Referee: Giorgos Kiprianides (CYP) Attendance: 4,000

ZIMBRU: Denis Romanenco; Victor Berco, Constantin Kulik, Vadim Boreţ, Viaceslav Rusnac, Valeriu Catînsus, Ruslan Ghilazev, Igor Oprea (Cap) (56 Dumitru Guşilă), Iuri miterev (90 Alexandru Grab), Sergiu Epureanu (80 Lado Akhalaia), Boris Cebotari. Trainer: Alexandru Spiridon

SK TIRANË: Isli Hidi; Elvis Sina, Rezart Dabulla, Johan Driza, Krenar Alimehmeti (Cap), Sokol Bulku, Gentian Hajdari, Ervin Bulku (65 Erion Rizvanolli), Zoltán Kenesei (69 Enkli Memishi), Indrit Fortuzi, Mahir Halili (80 Anesti Vito). Trainer: Shkëlkim Muça

Goals: Oprea (10, 34), Dabulla (12), Kenesei (26), Boreţ (84)

SHELBOURNE DUBLIN v SLOGA JUGOMAGNAT SKOPJE **1-1** (0-0)

Tolka Park, Dublin 19.07.2000

Referee: Bruno Derrien (FRA) Attendance: 6,511

SHELBOURNE: Steven Williams, Owen Heary, Tony McCarthy, Pat Scully (Cap), Desmond L.Baker, Paul Doolin (88 Jonathan Prizeman), Garry Haylock (69 Richard Foran), Richard Baker, Pat Fenlon, Mark Hutchison, James Keddy. Trainer: Dermot Keely

SLOGA JUGOMAGNAT: Jane Nikoloski, Goran Jovanovski, Zoran Sterjovski, Saso Zdravevski, Zoran Jovanovski, Zekirija Ramadan (78 Oldzaj Bajram), Nebi Mustafi (79 Gasi Ramadani), Goran Maznov, Argend Beciri (Cap), Goran Janevski (58 Bruno Presilski), Arben Nuhiji. Trainer: Gjorgji Jovanovski

Goals: Haylock (67), Nuhiji (81 pen)

FBK KAUNAS v NK BROTNJO CITLUK **4-0** (3-0)

S Darius & S Girenas SC, Kaunas 12.07.2000

Referee: Jack C.D. van Hulten (HOL) Attendance: 950

FBK: Marius Poskus, Nerijus Barasa, Tomas Kancelskis, Yuri Gritsina, Gintaras Juodeikis, Marius Bezykornovas (70 Darius Regelskis), Audrius Zuta (77 Andrius Puotkalis), Audrius Ksanavicius (Cap) (89 Gytis Gelgota), Vadimas Petrenka, Ignas Dedura, Irmantas Zelmikas. Trainer: Senderis Girsovicius

NK BROTNJO: Nenad Dzidić, Miro Klajić, Sinisa Jozić, Ivica Simunović (77 Darko Cvijanović), Andrei Zivković, Sinisa Polak (37 Sladanko Marić), Miroslav Laus (40 Mijo Katić), Dragan Blatnak, Nikola Juricić (Cap), Danijel Bajkusa, Dalibor Silić. Trainer: Ivo Istuk

Goals: Ksanavicius (11, 36), Zuta (17), Puotkalis (85)

SK TIRANË v ZIMBRU CHIŞINĂU **2-3** (2-2)

Qemal Stafa, Tirana 12.07.2000

Referee: Phillipe Leuba (SWI) Attendance: 4,200

SK TIRANË: Blendi Nallbani; Elvis Sina, Thamas Nevil Thamas Dede, Krenar Alimehmeti (Cap), Alban Tafaj (50 Gentian Hajdari); Ardian Mema, Bledar Devolli, Indrit Fortuzi; Rezart Dabulla, Zoltán Kenesei (59 Enkli Memishi), Mahir Halili (64 Erion Ritzvanolli). Trainer: Shkëlkim Muça

ZIMBRU: Denis Romanenco; Constantin Kulik (69 Alexsandru Grab), Vadim Boreţ, Viacheslav Rusnac; Valeriu Catînsus, Ruslan Ghilazev, Igor Oprea (Cap) (82 Levan Gvazava), Sergiu Epureanu, Boris Cebotari; Iuri miterev (59 Dumitru Guşilă), Victor Berco. Trainer: Alexandru Spiridon

Goals: Dede (14), Fortuzi (16), Berco (29, 50), Boreţ (45)

NK BROTNJO CITLUK v FBK KAUNAS **3-0** (3-0)

Bare, Citluk 19.07.2000

Referee: Jozef Kacenga (SVK) Attendance: 4,325

NK BROTNJO: Nenad Dzidić, Miro Klajić, Robert Milos (86 Sinisa Polak), Ivica Simunović, Andrei Zivković, Mijo Katić, Miroslav Laus, Dragan Blatnak (71 Darko Cvijanović), Nikola Juricić (Cap), Danijel Bajkusa, Dalibor Silić. Trainer: Ivo Istuk

FBK: Marius Poskus, Nerijus Barasa, Tomas Kancelskis, Yuri Gritsina, Gintaras Juodeikis (74 Arunas Mika), Audrius Zuta (61 Marius Bezykornovas), Darius Regelskis, Audrius Ksanavicius (Cap), Vadimas Petrenka, Ignas Dedura, Irmantas Zelmikas (90 Gytis Gelgota). Trainer: Senderis Girsovicius

Sent off: Laus (88)

Goals: Katić (32, 40 pen), Juricić (37)

SECOND QUALIFYING ROUND

RSC ANDERLECHT BRUSSEL v ANORTHOSIS FAMAGUSTA 4-2 (3-1)

Constant vanden Stock, Brussel 26.07.2000

Referee: Knud Stadsgaard (DEN) Attendance: 21,746

ANDERLECHT: Filip de Wilde; Glen de Boeck, Lorenzo Staelens (Cap), Didier Dheedene, Patrick van Diemen; Yves Vanderhaeghe, Alin Stoica (79 Giannis Anastasiou), Walter Baseggio, Bart Goor; Tomasz Radzinski (90 Aruna Dindane), Jan Koller. Trainer: Aimé Anthuenis

ANORTHOSIS: Nikos Panagiotou (Cap); Stavros Foukaris (63 Giorgos Iosifidis), Vasos Melanarkitis, Dimitris Ioannou, Zaharias Haralampous (85 Marios Neofytou); Zoran Milinkovic, Nikodimos Papavasileiou, Resid Pepic (46 Panikos Pounas), Hristos Kotsonis; Dejan Pavlović, Slobodan Krcmarević. Trainer: Dušan Mitosević

Goals: Baseggio (4), Pavlovic (9), Koller (15, 28, 59), Papavasileiou (90)

ANORTHOSIS FAMAGUSTA v RSC ANDERLECHT BRUSSEL 0-0

GSP, Nicosia 2.08.2000

Referee: Hermann Albrecht (GER) Attendance: 5,652

ANORTHOSIS: Nikos Panagiotou (Cap); Vasos Melanarkitis, Dimitris Ioannou, Marios Neofytou (75 Loukas Louka), Giorgos Iosifidis; Panikos Pounas, Zoran Milinković, Nikodimos Papavasileiou, Hristos Kotsonis (46 Zaharias Haralampous); Dejan Pavlović (60 Stelios Hristou), Slobodan Krcmarevic. Trainer: Dušan Mitosević

ANDERLECHT: Filip de Wilde; Bertrand Crasson, Lorenzo Staelens (Cap), Glen de Boeck, Patrick van Diemen, Yves Vanderhaeghe; Alin Stoica, Walter Baseggio (88 Didier Dheedene), Bart Goor; Jan Koller, Tomasz Radzinski (90 Oleg Yashchuk). Trainer: Aimé Antheunis

Sent off: Haralampous (71)

BEŞIKTAŞ JK ISTANBUL v LEVSKI SOFIA 1-0 (0-0)

Inonü, Istanbul 26.07.2000

Referee: Fiorenzo Treossi (ITA) Attendance: 20,800

BEŞIKTAŞ: Ike Ibrahim Shorunmu; Miroslav Karhan, Tayfur Havutçu, Sead Halilagic (60 Erman Güraçar), Ümit Bozkurt; Nihat Kahveci, Mehmet Özdilek (Cap) (71 Ibrahim Üzülmez), Markus Münch, Ayhan Akman; Ahmet Dursun, Pascal Olivier Nouma. Trainer: Nevio Scala

LEVSKI: Dimitar Ivankov (Cap); Biser Ivanov, Georgi Markov, Konstantin Kainov (46 Ferreira de Pau Leônidas), Ilian Stoianov, Predrag Pazin; Aleksandar Aleksandrov (46 Martin Stankov), Eduard Tsykhmeistruk, Elin Topuzakov, Oleksandr Koval; Georgi Ivanov. Trainer: Georgi Todorov

Goal: Nouma (81)

LEVSKI SOFIA v BEŞIKTAŞ JK ISTANBUL 1-1 (0-1)

Georgi Asparuhov, Sofia 2.08.2000

Referee: Morgan Norman (SWE) Attendance: 20,865

LEVSKI: Dimitar Ivankov; Martin Stankov, Biser Ivanov, Georgi Markov, Ilian Stoianov, Predrag Pazin; Stanimir Stoilov (Cap) (46 Georgi Georgiev), Aleksandar Aleksandrov (71 Zahari Sirakov), Eduard Tsykhmeistruk (57 Konstantin Kainov), Elin Topuzakov; Georgi Ivanov.
Trainer: Georgi Todorov

BEŞIKTAŞ: Ike Ibrahim Shorunmu; Miroslav Karhan (86 Rahim Zafer), Sead Halilagic, Ümit Bozkurt, Dmitri Khlestov (46 Erman Güraçar); Tayfur Havutçu, Nihat Kahveci, Mehmet Özdilek (Cap) (55 Ayhan Akman), Markus Münch; Ahmet Dursun, Pascal Nouma. Trainer: Nevio Scala

Goals: Tayfur (35), Markov (64)

BRØNDBY IF v KR REYKJAVÍK 3-1 (1-1)

Brøndby Stadion, København 26.07.2000

Referee: John McDermott (IRE) Attendance: 8,567

BRØNDBY IF: Søren Krogh (Cap); Per Nielsen, Dan Anton Johansen, Søren Colding; Ruben Bagger, Aurelijus Skarbalius, Mikkel Jensen, Thomas Lindrup (86 Allan Ravn); Peter Madsen, Peter Graulund (46 Magnus Svensson), Mattias Jonson (74 Ole Bjur). Trainer: Åge Hareide

KR: Kristján Finnbogason; Bjarni Thorsteinsson, Sigursteinn Gíslason, Thormodur Egilsson (Cap), Einar Danielsson (74 Ivar Bjarklind), Gunnar Einarsson; Sigurdur Örn Jonsson, Sigthor Juliusson, Thorhallur Hinriksson; Thorstein Jónsson, Andri Sigþorsson. Trainer: Pétur Pétursson

Goals: Bagger (14), Danielsson (18), Lindrup (50), Madsen (84)

KR REYKJAVÍK v BRØNDBY IF 0-0

Laugardalsvöllur, Reykjavík 2.08.2000

Referee: Dejan Delević (YUG) Attendance: 3,077

KR: Kristján Finnbogason; Bjarni Thorsteinsson, Thormodur Egilsson (Cap), Gunnar Einarsson (60 Ivar Bjarklind); Sigursteinn Gíslason, Sigurdur Örn Jónsson, Gudmundur Benediktsson, Thorhallur Hinriksson (70 Thorstein Jónsson); Sigthor Júlíusson, Einar Danielsson (46 Johann Thorhallsson), Andri Sigþorsson. Trainer: Pétur Pétursson

BRØNDBY IF: Mogens Krogh (Cap); Per Nielsen, Dan Anton Johansen, Søren Colding, Aurelijus Skarbalius; Ole Bjur, Allan Ravn, Magnus Svensson, Mikkel Jensen, Thomas Lindrup (68 Peter Madsen); Ruben Bagger. Trainer: Åge Hareide

DINAMO BUCUREŞTI v POLONIA WARSZAWA 3-4 (2-2)

Naţional, Bucureşti 26.07.2000

Referee: Víctor José Esquinas Torres (SPA) Att: 18,500

DINAMO: Ştefan Gabriel Preda; Giani Stelian Kiriţă, Daniel Florea, Gheorghe Mihali, Cristian Mugur Bolohan; Florentin Petre (71 Claudiu Drăgan), Cătălin Hâldan (Cap), Florin Cernat (46 Iulian Tameş), Dănuţ Lupu; Adrian Dumitru Mihalcea (80 Ion Mara), Marius Niculae.
Trainer: Cornel Dinu

POLONIA: Maciej Szczesny (Cap); Tomas Zvirgzdauskas, Arkadiusz Kaliszan, Mariusz Pawlak, Tomasz Kielbowicz, Tomasz Ciesielski (46 Zbigniew Wyciszkiewicz); Tomasz Wieszczycki (80 Emanuel Ekwuene), Arkadiusz Bak; Maciej Bykowski (88 Maciej Scherfchen), Igor Golaszewski, Emmanuel Olisadebe. Trainer: Dariusz Wdowczyk

Goals: Lupu (7 pen), Wieszczycki (23), Olisadebe (35), Mihalcea (45), Wieszczycki (58), Niculae (63), Golaszewski (88)

POLONIA WARSZAWA v DINAMO BUCUREŞTI 3-1 (0-1)

Petro, Plock 2.08.2000

Referee: Jorge Emanuel Monteiro Coroado (POR)
Attendance: 3,560

POLONIA: Maciej Szczesny (Cap); Tomas Zvirgzdauskas, Arkadiusz Kaliszan (84 Maciej Scherfchen), Mariusz Pawlak, Tomasz Kielbowicz; Tomasz Wieszczycki, Zbigniew Wyciszkiewicz, Arkadiusz Bak; Maciej Bykowski (6 Pawel Kaczorowski), Igor Golaszewski (79 Emanuel Ekwuene), Emmanuel Olisadebe. Trainer: Dariusz Wdowczyk

DINAMO: Ştefan Preda; Valentin Năstase, Daniel Florea (59 Giani Kiriţă), Gheorghe Mihali, Cristian Bolohan; Florentin Petre, Cătălin Hâldan (Cap), Dănuţ Lupu, Iulian Tameş; Adrian Dumitru Mihalcea, Marius Niculae (46 Claudiu Drăgan).
Trainer: Cornel Dinu

Goals: Tameş (43), Olisadebe (59, 61), Golaszewski (65)

GLASGOW RANGERS FC v FBK KAUNAS 4-1 (1-1)

Ibrox, Glasgow 26.07.2000

Referee: Emanuel Zammit (MAL) Attendance: 45,974

RANGERS: Stefan Klos; Fernando Ricksen, Craig Moore (Cap), Scott Wilson (46 Neil McCann), Tony Vidmar (72 Kenny Miller); Barry Ferguson, Allan Johnston, Claudio Reyna, Jörg Albertz; Jonatan Johansson (46 Billy Dodds), Rodney Wallace. Trainer: Dick Advocaat

FBK: Marius Poskus; Nerijus Barasa, Tomas Kancelskis, Darius Regelskis, Vadimas Petrenka, Ignas Dedura; Gintaras Juodeikis, Marius Bezykornovas, Audrius Zuta, Irmantas Zelmikas; Audrius Ksanavicius (Cap).
Trainer: Senderis Girsovicius

Sent off: Petrenka (40) and Barasa (65)

Goals: Johnston (15), Zuta (27), Albertz (62 pen), Dodds (89, 90)

FBK KAUNAS v GLASGOW RANGERS FC 0-0

S Darius & S Girenas SC Kaunas 2.08.2000

Referee: Frank de Bleeckere (BEL) Attendance: 4,000

FBK: Gytis Padimanskas, Tomas Kancelskis, Vitalijus Danilicevas (62 Andrius Velicka), Gintaras Juodeikis, Marius Bezykornovas (82 Andrius Puotkalis), Audrius Zuta, Arunas Mika, Darius Regelskis (46 Gytis Gelgota), Audrius Ksanavicius (Cap), Ignas Dedura, Irmantas Zelmikas.
Trainer: Senderis Girsovicius

RANGERS: Stefan Klos, Fernando Ricksen (75 Andrei Kanchelskis), Bert Konterman, Lorenzo Amoruso (Cap), Tony Vidmar (46 Sergio Porrini), Barry Ferguson, Claudio Reyna, Giovanni van Bronckhorst, Willaim Dodds, Rodney Wallace (70 Allan Johnston), TUGAY Kerimoglu.
Trainer: Dick Advocaat

FC HAKA VALKEAKOSKI v INTER BRATISLAVA 0-0

Tehtaankenttä, Valkeakoski 26.07.2000

Referee: Laurent Duhamel (FRA) Attendance: 1,785

FC HAKA: András Vilnrotter; Janne Salli (Cap), Jaakko Pasanen, Jarkko Okkonen (71 Dragan Bajic), Jukka Koskinen; Lasse Karjalainen, Oleg Ivanov, Tommi Torkkeli (78 Kai Nyyssönen), David Wilson (80 Jukka Ruhanen); Martin Reynders, Péter Kovács. Trainer: Keith Armstrong

INTER: Miroslav Hyll (Cap); Marián Suchancok, Tomáš Gerich, Peter Dzurik, Zsolt Hornyak; Jan Chrenko, Attila Pinte, Martin Sevela, Marian Lalik; Peter Babnic (87 Radovan Kocurek), Szilárd Németh (83 Marek Krejci).
Trainer: Jozef Bubenko

INTER BRATISLAVA v FC HAKA VALKEAKOSKI 1-0 (0-0, 0-0) (AET)

ASK Inter Slovnaft, Bratislava 2.08.2000

Referee: Helmut Fleischer (GER) Attendance: 2,570

INTER: Miroslav Hyll (Cap); Marián Suchancok, Tomáš Gerich (94 Martin Sevela), Roman Kratochvíl, Zsolt Hornyak; Peter Dzurik, Jan Chrenko, Attila Pinte (118 Marian Cisovsky), Marian Lalik; Peter Babnic (70 Radovan Kocurek), Szilárd Németh. Trainer: Jozef Bubenko

FC HAKA: András Vilnrotter; Dragan Bajic, Janne Salli (Cap), Jukka Koskinen (91 Jouni Räsänen); Lasse Karjalainen, Oleg Ivanov (76 Kai Nyyssönen), Janne Hyökyvaara (73 Tommi Torkkeli), David Wilson; Martin Reynders, Jukka Ruhanen, Péter Kovács. Trainer: Keith Armstrong

Goal: S. Németh (108)

HELSINGBORGS IF v FC BATE BORISOV 0-0

Olympia, Helsingborg 26.07.2000

Referee: Igorj Ishchenko (UKR) Attendance: 4,417

HELSINGBORGS IF: Sven Andersson; Ola Nilsson, Roland Nilsson, Jozo Matovac, Nicklas Persson, Christoffer Andersson; Bjørn Johansen, Ulrik Jansson (Cap) (84 Niklas Sandberg), Rade Prica (73 Michael Hansson); ALVARO Marcio Santos, Stig Johansen (76 Erik Wahlstedt).
Trainer: Nanne Bergstrand

BATE: Alexandre Fedarovich (Cap); Oleg Korol, Gennadi Mardas, Vadim Skripchenko; Vitaliy Rogozkin, Alexandar Ermakovich, Yevgeni Loshankov, Alexei Baga (69 Vitali Panasiuk), Vladimir Nevinskiy (60 Leanid Lagun); Andrei Divakov, Vitali Kutuzov (86 Dmitriy Akulich).
Trainer: Yuri Puntus

FC BATE BORISOV v HELSINGBORGS IF 0-3 (0-2)

Dinamo, Minsk 2.08.2000

Referee: Meir Levi (ISR) Attendance: 7,540

BATE: Alexandre Fedorovich (Cap), Oleg Korol, Vitaliy Rogozhkin, Vitali Panasiuk (46 Leanid Lagun), Alexandar Ermakovich, Vitali Kutuzov (78 Dmitriy Akulich), Yevgeni Loshankov, Alexei Baga, Vladimir Nevinskiy (61 Vyacheslav Hryharau), Gennadi Mardas, Vadim Skripchenko.
Trainer: Yuri Puntus

HELSINGBORGS IF: Sven Andersson, Ola Nilsson, Roland Nilsson, Jozo Matovac, Bjørn Johansen, Ulrik Jansson (Cap), ALVARO Marcio Santos (73 Erik Wahlstedt), Nicklas Persson, Michael Hansson (84 Lars Bakkerud), Rade Prica (57 Stig Johansen), Christoffer Andersson.
Trainer: Nanne Bergstrand

Goals: Alvaro (11), C. Andersson (24), Wahlstedt (85)

CRVENA ZVEZDA BEOGRAD v TORPEDO KUTAISI 4-0 (3-0)

Crvena Zvezda, Beograd 26.07.2000

Referee: Dietmar Drabek (AUS) Attendance: 14,636

CRVENA ZVEZDA: Aleksander Kocić; Marjan Marković (67 Goran Bunjevcevic), Stevo Glogovac, Dejan Ilić, Nenad Lalatović; Ivan Gvozdenović, Branko Bosković, Srdan Bajcetić (Cap); Goran Drulić, Mihailo Pjanović (73 Dragan Stevanovic), Leo Lerinc (38 Saša Zorić).
Trainer: Slavoljub Muslin

TORPEDO: Irakli Zoidze; Mikheil Makhviladze, Walter Guchua, Badri Akhvlediani, Vakhtang Khvadagiani; Zurab Ionanidze (76 Mikheil Bobokhidze), Zurab Archvadze, Tengiz Sichinava, Kakhaber Chkhetiani; David Janashia (Cap) (46 Kakha Kvetenadze), George Megreladze (46 Gia Imedadze).
Trainer: David Kipiani

Goals: Drulić (24, 90), Bosković (37), Pjanović (39)

TORPEDO KUTAISI v CRVENA ZVEZDA BEOGRAD 2-0 (1-0)

David Kiladze, Kutaisi 2.08.2000

Referee: Uriah Rennie (ENG) Attendance: 3,200

TORPEDO: Irakli Zoidze; Mikheil Makhviladze, Walter Guchua, Badri Akhvlediani (67 Vakhtang Turmanidze), Vakhtang Khvadagiani; Zurab Ionanidze (80 Malkhaz Asatiani), Zurab Archvadze, Gia Chkhaidze, Tengiz Sichinava; David Janashia (Cap), Gia Imedadze (64 George Megreladze).
Trainer: David Kipiani

CRVENA ZVEZDA: Aleksander Kocić; Stevo Glogovac, Goran Bunjevcević (Cap), Dejan Ilić (43 Marjan Marković), Milivoje Vitakić, Saša Zorić; Ivan Gvozdenović (88 Milenko Acimović), Branko Bosković (73 Blaze Georgijevski), Srdan Bajcetić; Goran Drulić, Dragan Stevanović.
Trainer: Slavoljub Muslin

Goals: Imedadze (41), Janashia (90)

SHAKHTAR DONETSK v FC LEVADIA MAARDU 4-1 (2-0)

Shakhtyor, Donetsk 26.07.2000

Referee: Milan Mitrovic (SVN) Attendance: 25,000

SHAKHTAR: Yuri Virt; Dainius Gleveckas, Anatoliy Tymoshchuk, Serhiy Popov (Cap), Vyacheslav Shevchuk (75 Isaac Okoronkwo); Aleksei Bakharev, Hennadiy Zubov, Valeriy Kriventsov (46 Marian Aliuţă), Vitali Abramov; Serhiy Atelkin, Andriy Vorobei (58 Oleksii Bielik).
Trainer: Viktor Prokopenko

FC LEVADIA: Sergei Pareiko; Juri Leitan, Dalius Staleljunas, Igor Prins (Cap), Andrei Kalimullin; Konstantin Kolbasenko, Maksim Rõtškov, Iouri Fenin (43 Vladimir Tselnokov, 71 Toomas Krõm), Sergei Bragin (87 Vitali Leitan), Andrei Krasnoperov; Indro Olumets. Trainer: Sergei Ratnikov

Goals: Atelkin (4, 16, 57), Bielik (71), Rõtškov (80)

FC LEVADIA MAARDU v SHAKHTAR DONETSK 1-5 (0-2)

Kadriorg, Tallinn 2.08.2000

Referee: Martin Ingvarsson (SWE) Attendance: 1,500

FC LEVADIA: Sergei Pareiko; Dalius Staleljunas, Igor Prins (Cap), Eduard Vinogradov (29 Juri Leitan), Andrei Krasnoperov; Konstantin Kolbasenko, Maksim Rõtškov (62 Vitali Leitan), Indro Olumets, Iouri Fenin, Sergei Bragin; Vladimir Tselnokov (79 Toomas Krõm).
Trainer: Sergei Ratnikov

SHAKHTAR: Yuri Virt; Mikhailo Starostyak (55 Aleksandr Shmarko), Dainius Gleveckas, Anatoliy Tymoshchuk, Serhiy Popov (Cap) (46 Serhiy Kovalev), Vyacheslav Shevchuk; Aleksei Bakharev (60 Marian Aliuţă), Hennadiy Zubov, Vitali Abramov; Serhiy Atelkin, Andriy Vorobei.
Trainer: Viktor Prokopenko

Goals: Vorobei (26, 31, 79 pen), Bragin (48), Atelkin (90), Zubov (90+)

SLAVIA PRAHA v FK SHAMKIR 1-0 (0-0)

Strahov, Praha 26.07.2000

Referee: Emil Božinovski (MAC) Attendance: 2,819

SLAVIA: Radek Černý; Luboš Kozel, Lukáš Došek, Adam Petrouš, Karel Rada (Cap); Ivo Ulich (46 Lumir Sedlácek), Richard Dostalek, Radim Necas, Tomáš Kuchar (65 Robert Vágner); Ludek Zelenka, Petr Švancara.
Trainer: František Cipro

FK SHAMKIR: Rauf Mekhdiev; Agil Mamedov (66 Mubqriz Orudjev), Mekhman Yunusov (Cap), Nizami Odjagverdiev (46 Azer Mamedov), Faig Jabbarov; Ali Abushev, Makhmud Kurbanov, Khalig Mardanov, Ismagil Mamedov (79 Etimad Kurbanov); Viktor Kulikov, Badri Kvaratskheliya.
Trainer: Agasalim Mirjavadov

Goal: Zelenka (38)

ROSENBORG BK TRONDHEIM v SHELBOURNE FC 1-1 (0-0)

Lerkendal, Trondheim 2.08.2000

Referee: Massimo Busacca (SWI) Attendance: 5,470

ROSENBORG: Arni Gautur Arason; Erik Hoftun, Christer Basma, Bent Inge Johnsen, Ståle Stensaas; Roar Strand (88 Øyvind Svenning), Ørjan Berg, Bent Skammelsrud, Morten Knutsen (64 Børge Hernes), Fredrik Winsnes; Frode Johnsen (78 Petter Belsvik). Trainer: Nils Arne Eggen

SHELBOURNE: Steven Williams; Owen Heary, Tony McCarthy, Pat Scully (Cap); Richie Baker, Pat Fenlon, Mark Hutchison, James Keddy, David Byrne (65 Paul Doolin); Desmond Baker, Stephen Geoghegan (62 Richard Foran).
Trainer: Dermot Keely

Goals: Foran (64), Berg (80)

FK SHAMKIR v SLAVIA PRAHA 1-4 (0-1)

Tofik Bakhramov, Baku 2.08.2000

Referee: Roy Helge Olsen (NOR) Attendance: 12,000

FK SHAMKIR: Rauf Mekhdiev; Mubariz Orudjev, Mekhman Yunusov (Cap), Azer Mamedov, Faig Jabbarov, Ali Abushev, Makhmud Kurbanov, Khalig Mardanov (46 Agil Mamedov), Ismagil Mamedov, Viktor Kulikov (59 Khagani Mamedov), Badri Kvaratskheliya (74 Etimad Kurbanov).
Trainer: Agasalim Mirjavadov

SLAVIA: Radek Černý; Luboš Kozel, Lukáš Došek, Tomáš Došek (67 Petr Svancara), Adam Petrouš, Karel Rada (Cap); Ivo Ulich, Richard Dostálek, Radim Necas (72 Jiří Lerch); Ludek Zelenka, Jiří Skála (50 Tomáš Kuchar).
Trainer: František Cipro

Goals: Dostálek (38), Kvaratskheliya (49), T. Došek (57, 60), Švancara (69)

SK STURM GRAZ v HAPOEL TEL AVIV 3-0 (1-0)

Arnold Schwarzenegger, Graz 26.07.2000

Referee: Metin Tokat (TUR) Attendance: 10,298

STURM: Josef Schicklgruber; Günther Neukirchner, Franco Foda, Gerald Strafner, Andrés Fleurquin; Markus Schupp (83 Ramiz Mamedov), Hannes Reinmayr, Markus Schopp, Mehrdad Minavand; Ivica Vastic (Cap), Tomislav Kocijan (63 Sergei Yuran). Trainer: Ivica Osim

HAPOEL: Shavit Elimelech; Igal Antebi, Shimon Gershon (Cap), Ilan Bakhar, Eyal Ben Ami; Milan Osterc (71 David Dahan), István Pisont, Denis Onischenko, Avraham Tikva (84 Omri Afek), Salim Toema (71 Pini Balali); Asaf Domb.
Trainer: Dror Kashtan

Sent off: Domb (67)

Goals: Vastic (14), Reinmayr (74), Neukirchner (90)

SHELBOURNE FC v ROSENBORG BK TRONDHEIM 1-3 (0-2)

Tolka Park, Dublin 26.07.2000

Referee: Ivan Dobrinov (BUL) Attendance: 8,642

SHELBOURNE: Steven Williams; Owen Heary, Tony McCarthy, Pat Scully (Cap); Richie Baker, Patrick Fenlon, Mark Hutchison, James Keddy; Desmond Baker (77 Ian Gilzean), Garry Haylock (46 David Byrne), Stephen Geoghegan (46 Richard Foran). Trainer: Dermot Keely

ROSENBORG: Arni Gautur Arason; Erik Hoftun, Christer Basma, Bent Inge Johnsen, Ståle Stensaas; Roar Strand (80 Børge Hernes), Ørjan Berg, Bent Skammelsrud, Fredrik Winsnes; Jan Derek Sørensen (90 Morten Knutsen), Frode Johnsen (71 Petter Belsvik). Trainer: Nils Arne Eggen

Goals: Berg (2), Winsnes (14), Foran (61), Belsvik (90)

HAPOEL TEL AVIV v SK STRUM GRAZ 1-2 (0-0)

Bloomfield, Tel Aviv 2.08.2000

Referee: Sorin Corpodean (ROM) Attendance: 5,000

HAPOEL: Shavit Elimelech; Yaacov Hilel, Shimon Gershon (Cap) (80 Dean Racunica), Igal Antebi, Ilan Bakhar; Milan Osterc, István Pisont, Denis Onischenko (68 Avraham Tikva), Salim Toema, Omri Afek; Pini Balali. Trainer: Dror Kashtan

STURM: Josef Schicklgruber; Günther Neukirchner (68 Gilbert Prilasnig), Franco Foda, Gerald Strafner, György Korsós, Ramiz Mamedov; Markus Schupp, Ranko Popovic, Sergei Yuran (71 Imre Szabics); Ivica Vastic (Cap) (46 Ferdinand Feldhofer), Tomislav Kocijan. Trainer: Ivica Osim

Sent off: Feldhofer (66)

Goals: Korsós (71), Balali (80), Kocijan (85)

ZIMBRU CHIŞINĂU v NK MARIBOR 2-0 (0-0)

Speia 26.07.2000

Referee: Alan Snoddy (NIR) Attendance: 3,000

ZIMBRU: Denis Romanenco; Boris Cebotari, Andrei Telesnenco, Victor Berco (88 Ljubisa Ristić); Constantin Kulik, Vadim Boreţ, Valeriu Catînsus, Ruslan Ghilazev, Igor Oprea (Cap); Iuri miterev (62 Lado Akhalaia), Sergiu Epureanu (75 Boris Tropaneţ). Trainer: Alexandru Spiridon

NK MARIBOR: Marko Simeunović (Cap); Vladimir Kokol, Muamer Vugdalić, Marinko Sarkezi (33 Suad Fileković); Ales Krizan (70 Simon Dvorsak), Simon Seslar, Amir Karić, Nasta Ceh, Stipe Balajić; Ante Simundza, Klodian Arberi (53 Andrej Kvas). Trainer: Matjaz Kek

Goals: Kulik (48 pen), Epureanu (66)

NK MARIBOR v ZIMBRU CHIŞINĂU 1-0 (1-0)

Ljudski vrt, Maribor 2.08.2000

Referee: Mikko Vuorela (FIN) Attendance: 6,000

NK MARIBOR: Marko Simeunović (Cap); Muamer Vugdalić, Vladimir Kokol (55 Gregor Zidan), Marinko Sarkezi; Ales Krizan, Simon Seslar, Amir Karić, Nasta Ceh (80 Simon Dvorsak), Stipe Balajić, Fabijan Cipot (46 Ismet Ekmecić); Ante Simundza. Trainer: Matjaz Kek

ZIMBRU: Denis Romanenco; Constantin Kulik (72 Dumitru Guşilă), Boris Cebotari, Andrei Telesnenco; Vadim Boreţ, Valeriu Catinsus, Ruslan Ghilazev, Igor Oprea (Cap), Sergiu Epureanu; Iuri miterev (76 Lado Akhalaia), Victor Berco. Trainer: Alexandru Spiridon

Sent off: Oprea (61) and Miterev (90)

Goal: Ceh (3)

HAJDUK SPLIT v DUNAFERR SE 0-2 (0-0)

Poljud, Split 26.07.2000

Referee: Cosimo Bolognino (ITA) Attendance: 16,000

HAJDUK: Stipe Pletikosa; Igor Duzelov, Tony Grdić, Slaven Bilić (Cap), Ante Jazić, Josip Bulat; Igor Musa, Ivan Leko (61 Vik Lalić), Ante Miše (67 Tonci Pirija); Stanko Bubalo (48 Ivan Bošnjak), Mate Bilić. Trainer: Petar Nadoveza

DUNAFERR: Balázs Rabóczki; Zoltan Molnar, Miklós Salamon (Cap), György Kiss, Tibor Pomper; László Éger, Henrik Rósa, Gabor Bagoly; Ferenc Orosz, Attila Tököli (88 Igor Nichenko), Gábor Zavadszky (83 Ferenc Lengyel). Trainer: Sándor Egervári

Goals: Tököli (57), Éger (90)

DUNAFERR SE v HAJDUK SPLIT 2-2 (1-2)

ETO Stadion, Győr 2.08.2000

Referee: Dermot Gallagher (ENG) Attendance: 10,750

DUNAFERR: Balázs Rabóczki; Zoltan Molnar, Miklós Salamon (Cap), György Kiss, Tibor Pomper, László Éger; Attila Tököli (90 Igor Nichenko), Henrik Rósa (88 Ferenc Kóczián), Gabor Bagoly; Ferenc Orosz (76 Ferenc Lengyel), Gábor Zavadszky. Trainer: Sándor Egervári

HAJDUK: Stipe Pletikosa; Dalibor Božac, Goran Sablić, Slaven Bilić (Cap), Ante Jazić, Vik Lalić, Darko Miladin; Igor Musa (79 Stanko Bubalo), Ivan Leko (66 Srdan Andrić), Mate Bilić; Ivan Bošnjak. Trainer: Petar Nadoveza

Sent off: Božac (83)

Goals: M. Bilić (9, 28), Zavadszky (20), Tököli (87)

THIRD QUALIFYING ROUND

INTER BRATISLAVA v OLYMPIQUE LYON 1-2 (0-0)

ASK Inter Slovnaft, Bratislava 7.08.2000

Referee: Tomasz Mikulski (POL) Attendance: 3,540

INTER: Miroslav Hyll; Marián Suchancok, Roman Kratochvíl, Zsolt Hornyak, Radovan Kocurek; Peter Dzurik, Jan Chrenko, Juraj Czinege, Attila Pinte; Peter Babnic, Szilárd Németh. Trainer: Jozef Bubenko

OLYMPIQUE: Grégory Coupet; Eric Deflandre, Florent Laville, Jérémie Bréchet; Philippe Violeau, Pierre Laigle (72 Christophe Delmotte), Vikash Dhorasoo, Marc-Vivien Foé, Patrick Müller; Sonny ANDERSON da Silva (84 Steve Marlet), Tony Vairelles (73 Jacek Bak). Trainer: Jacques Santini

Sent off: Laville (90)

Goals: Ânderson (50), S. Németh (75), Delmotte (90)

OLYMPIQUE LYON v INTER BRATISLAVA 2-1 (0-1)

Stade Municipal de Gerland, Lyon 23.08.2000

Referee: Roelof Luinge (HOL) Attendance: 20,318

OLYMPIQUE: Grégory Coupet; Eric Deflandre, Jacek Bak (30 Jean-Marc Chanelet), Jérémie Bréchet; Philippe Violeau, Vikash Dhorasoo, Marc-Vivien Foé, Patrick Müller, David Linarès (88 Steed Malbranque); Steve Marlet (82 Christophe Delmotte), Sonny ANDERSON da Silva. Trainer: Jacques Santini

INTER: Miroslav Hyll; Marian Cisovsky, Marián Suchancok, Tomáš Gerich (65 Marek Krejci), Roman Kratochvíl, Zsolt Hornyak, Martin Sevela (58 Radovan Kocurek); Peter Dzurik, Attila Pinte, Marian Lalik (86 Peter Babnic); Szilárd Németh. Trainer: Jozef Bubenko

Goals: Pinte (36), Marlet (55), Malbranque (89)

BRØNDBY IF v HAMBURGER SV 0-2 (0-0)

Brøndby Stadion, København 8.08.2000

Referee: Thomas Michael McCurry (SCO) Att: 11,682

BRØNDBY IF: Mogens Krogh; Ole Bjur, Per Nielsen, Dan Anton Johansen, Søren Colding; Allan Ravn (64 Mattias Jonson), Magnus Svensson, Aurelijus Skarbalius, Mikkel Jensen; Peter Graulund (71 Thomas Lindrup), Ruben Bagger. Trainer: Åge Hareide

HAMBURGER SV: Hans-Jörg Butt; Andrei Panadic, Ingo Hertzsch, Nico-Jan Hoogma; Martin Groth, Nico Kovac (83 Jan Sandmann), Sergei Barbarez, Bernd Hollerbach; Mehdi Mahdavikia (88 Thomas Doll), Anthony Yeboah, Marcel Ketelaer (70 Marek Heinz). Trainer: Frank Pagelsdorf

Goals: Barbarez (83), Mahdavikia (85)

HAMBURGER SV v BRØNDBY IF 0-0

AOL Arena, Hamburg 22.08.2000

Referee: Zeljko Sirić (CRO) Attendance: 44,351

HAMBURGER SV: Hans-Jörg Butt; Andrei Panadic, Ingo Hertzsch, Nico-Jan Hoogma; Martin Groth, Nico Kovac, Bernd Hollerbach (72 Jan Sandmann), Rodolfo Esteban CARDOSO (85 Stig Tøfting); Marek Heinz, Anthony Yeboah, Roy Präger (68 Mehdi Mahdavikia). Trainer: Frank Pagelsdorf

BRØNDBY IF: Mogens Krogh; Per Nielsen, Dan Anton Johansen, Søren Colding; Ole Bjur, Allan Ravn (60 Mattias Jonson), Magnus Svensson, Aurelijus Skarbalius, Mikkel Jensen (60 Thomas Lindrup); Peter Graulund, Ruben Bagger (83 Peter Foldgast). Trainer: Åge Hareide

Sent off: Johansen (82)

BEŞIKTAŞ JK ISTANBUL v LOKOMOTIV MOSKVA 3-0 (1-0)

Inönü, Istanbul 8.08.2000

Referee: Alfredo Trentalange (ITA) Attendance: 14,000

BEŞIKTAŞ: Ike Ibrahim Shorunmu; Miroslav Karhan, Sead Halilagic, Ümit Bozkurt (46 Rahim Zafer), Dmitri Khlestov (37 Erman Güraçar); Tayfur Havutçu, Nihat Kahveci, Mehmet Özdilek, Markus Münch; Ahmet Dursun (60 Murat Alaçayir), Pascal Nouma. Trainer: Nevio Scala

LOKOMOTIV: Ruslan Nigmatullin; Gennadiy Nizhegorodov, Vadim Yevseyev, Oleg Pashinin, Igor Chugainov, Andrei Lavrik; Yuri Drozdov, Dmitri Loskov, Evgeni Kharlachev (54 Andrei Solomatin); Dmitriy Bulykin (83 Albert Sarkisyan), Zaza Janashia (65 Ruslan Pimenov). Trainer: Yuri Semin

Goals: Nihat (10), Nouma (80), Karhan (90)

LOKOMOTIV MOSKVA v BEŞIKTAŞ JK ISTANBUL 1-3 (0-1)

Luzhniki, Moskva 23.08.2000

Referee: Lutz-Michael Fröhlich (GER) Attendance: 10,200

LOKOMOTIV: Ruslan Nigmatullin; Igor Cherevchenko, Andrei Lavrik, Gennadiy Nizhegorodov, Igor Chugainov; Yuri Drozdov (71 Vadim Yevseyev), Albert Sarkisyan, Dmitri Loskov, Evgeni Kharlachev (46 Filipe Vaz de Azevedo).; Ruslan Pimenov, Zaza Janashia (69 Dmitriy Bulykin). Trainer: Yuri Semin

BEŞIKTAŞ: Ike Ibrahim Shorunmu; Miroslav Karhan (80 Yasin Sülün), Sead Halilagic (84 Rahim Zafer), Ümit Bozkurt; Tayfur Havutçu, Nihat Kahveci, Markus Münch, Erman Güraçar, Ibrahim Üzülmez; Ahmet Dursun, Pascal Nouma (63 Dmitri Khlestov). Trainer: Nevio Scala

Goals: Nouma (28), Cherevchenko (50), Nihat (73), Tayfur (87)

SK STURM GRAZ v FEYENOORD ROTTERDAM 2-1 (1-1)

Arnold Schwarzenegger, Graz 8.08.2000

Referee: Terje Hauge (NOR) Attendance: 15,100

STURM: Josef Schicklgruber; Günther Neukirchner, Franco Foda (62 Ramiz Mamedov), Andrés Fleurquin; Markus Schupp (78 György Korsós), Hannes Reinmayr (71 Imre Szabics), Markus Schopp, Mehrdad Minavand, Tomislav Kocijan; Gerald Strafner, Sergei Yuran. Trainer: Ivica Osim

FEYENOORD: Jerzy Dudek; Christian Gyan, Tomasz Rzasa, Kees van Wonderen, Ferry de Haan; Paul Bosvelt (79 Arco Jochemsen), Jon Dahl Tomasson, Peter van Vossen (58 Jan de Visser), Patrick Paauwe; Bonaventure Kalou, Igor Korneev (81 Julio Ricardo Cruz). Trainer: Bert van Marwijk

Sent off: Strafner (90), Julio Ricardo Cruz (90)

Goals: Korneev (7), Schopp (23 pen, 90 pen)

FEYENOORD ROTTERDAM v SK STURM GRAZ 1-1 (0-0)

Feyenoord, Rotterdam 23.08.2000

Referee: Víctor José Esquinas Torres (SPA) Att: 34,000

FEYENOORD: Jerzy Dudek; Christian Gyan (46 Brett Emerton), Ferry de Haan, Kees van Wonderen, Tomasz Rzasa; Paul Bosvelt, Patrick Paauwe, LEONARDO Victor Santiago, Bonaventure Kalou; Jon Dahl Tomasson (62 SOMALIA Wanderson de Paula Sabino), Igor Korneev (73 Arco Jochemsen). Trainer: Bert van Marwijk

STURM: Josef Schicklgruber; Günther Neukirchner, Franco Foda, Andrés Fleurquin; Markus Schupp, Ramiz Mamedov, Markus Schopp, Mehrdad Minavand (46 Gilbert Prilasnig); Hannes Reinmayr (64 Roman Mählich), Tomislav Kocijan, Sergei Yuran (76 Imre Szabics). Trainer: Ivica Osim

Goals: Reinmayr (54), Jochemsen (87)

ZIMBRU CHIŞINĂU v AC SPARTA PRAHA 0-1 (0-0)

Speia 8.08.2000

Referee: Jacek Granat (POL) Attendance: 3,300

ZIMBRU: Denis Romanenco; Viaceslav Rusnac (90 Boris Tropaneţ), Boris Cebotari, Andrei Telesnenco; Vadim Boret, Valeriu Catînsus (43 Ghenadie Olexici), Ruslan Ghilazev, Sergiu Epureanu; Dumitru Guşilă, Lado Akhalaia (18 Iulian Arhire), Victor Berco. Trainer: Alexandru Spiridon

SPARTA: Tomáš Poštulka; Zdenek Grygera, Jiří Novotný, René Bolf, Milan Fukal (7 Michal Hornák); Zdenek Svoboda, Libor Sionko, Jiří Jarošik, Tomáš Rosický (87 Martin Hašek); Marek Kincl (90 Horst Siegl), Josef Obajdin. Trainer: Ivan Hasek

Goal: Obajdin (61)

AC SPARTA PRAHA v ZIMBRU CHIŞINĂU 1-0 (0-0)

Stadión na Letnej, Praha 23.08.2000

Referee: Vasily Melnichuk (UKR) Attendance: 8,588

SPARTA: Tomáš Poštulka; Jiří Novotný, René Bolf, Milan Fukal; Zdenek Svoboda, Libor Sionko (75 Petr Papoušek), Pavel Novotný, Jiří Jarošik, Tomáš Rosický; Marek Kincl (62 Horst Siegl), Josef Obajdin (87 Jan Flachbart). Trainer: Ivan Hasek

ZIMBRU: Denis Romanenco; Constantin Kulik, Vadim Boreţ, Boris Cebotari, Andrei Telesnenco; Valeriu Catînsus, Ruslan Ghilazev, Sergiu Epureanu, Iulian Arhire (59 Dumitru Guşilă); Iuri Miterev (65 Lado Akhalaia), Victor Berco (46 Ghenadie Olexici). Trainer: Alexandru Spiridon

Sent off: Cebotari (40)

Goal: Obajdin (57)

AC MILAN v DINAMO ZAGREB 3-1 (1-1)

Giuseppe Meazza 9.08.2000

Referee: Alain Hamer (LUX) Attendance: 37,323

AC MILAN: Christian Abbiati; Paolo Maldini (Cap), Demetrio Albertini, Alessandro Costacurta, José Chamot, Sergio Claudio dos Santos "SERGINHO"; Gennaro Gattuso, José María Romero Poyón "JOSÉ MARI" (77 Gianni Comandini), Massimo Ambrosini (49 Andrés Guglielminpietro); Andrei Shevchenko, LEONARDO Nascimento de Araújo (87 Francesco Coco). Trainer: Alberto Zaccheroni

DINAMO: Tomislav Butina; Goce Sedloski, Zoran Pavlović, Boško Balaban, Igor Bišcan (Cap); Kristijan Polovanec (46 Dino Drpić), Nermin Sabić (76 Mario Bazina), Jasmin Agić, Mihael Mikić; Edin Mujcin, Renato Pilipović (65 Tomislav Šokota). Trainer: Marijan Vlak

Goals: Pilipović (19), Shevchenko (21, 59), Comandini (90)

DINAMO ZAGREB v AC MILAN 0-3 (0-2)

Maksimir, Zagreb 22.08.2000

Referee: Juan Ansuátegui Roca (SPA) Attendance: 26,500

DINAMO: Tomislav Butina; Mario Tokić (61 Renato Pilipović), Goce Sedloski, Nermin Sabić; Jasmin Agić, Mihael Mikić, Edin Mujcin (52 Mario Bazina), Zoran Pavlović; Boško Balaban (68 Tomislav Šokota), Igor Cvitanović, Igor Bišcan (Cap). Trainer: Marijan Vlak

AC MILAN: Christian Abbiati; Paolo Maldini (Cap), Alessandro Costacurta (69 José Victor ROQUE JUNIOR), José Chamot, Francesco Coco; Demetrio Albertini, Gennaro Gattuso, Andrés Guglielminpietro (79 Sergio Claudio dos Santos "SERGINHO"); Andrei Shevchenko, Gianni Comandini, José María Romero Poyón "JOSÉ MARI" (58 Massimo Ambrosini). Trainer: Alberto Zaccheroni

Sent off: Agić (43)

Goals: Shevchenko (23, 42), José Marí (55)

SHAKHTAR DONETSK v SLAVIA PRAHA 0-1 (0-0)

Shakhtyor, Donetsk 9.08.2000

Referee: Pascal Garibian (FRA) Attendance: 31,547

SHAKHTAR: Yuri Virt; Mikhailo Starostyak, Dainius Gleveckas, Anatoliy Tymoshchuk, Serhiy Popov (67 Oleksii Bielik); Aleksei Bakharev, Serhiy Kovalev (80 Valeriy Kriventsov), Hennadiy Zubov, Vitali Abramov; Serhiy Atelkin, Andriy Vorobei. Trainer: Viktor Prokopenko

SLAVIA: Radek Černý; Luboš Kozel, Lukáš Došek, Adam Petrouš, Karel Rada, Libor Koller; Ivo Ulich, Richard Dostalek, Tomáš Kuchar (89 Jiří Lerch); Tomáš Došek (90 Lumir Sedlácek), Ludek Zelenka (80 Robert Vágner). Trainer: František Cipro

Goal: Ullch (89)

SLAVIA PRAHA v SHAKHTAR DONETSK 0-2 (0-0, 0-1) (AET)

Strahov, Praha 22.08.2000

Referee: Leslie Irvine (NIR) Attendance: 8,578

SLAVIA: Radek Černý; Luboš Kozel, Lukáš Došek, Adam Petrouš, Karel Rada, Libor Koller; Jiří Lerch, Ivo Ulich, Richard Dostalek (98 Petr Švancara); Tomáš Došek (46 Robert Vágner, 70 Tomáš Kuchar), Ludek Zelenka. Trainer: František Cipro

SHAKHTAR: Yuri Virt; Mikhailo Starostyak (80 Valeriy Kriventsov), Dainius Gleveckas, Anatoliy Tymoshchuk, Serhiy Popov, Vyacheslav Shevchuk; Aleksei Bakharev, Hennadiy Zubov, Vitali Abramov (72 Oleksii Bielik); Serhiy Atelkin (117 Aleksandr Shmarko), Andriy Vorobei. Trainer: Viktor Prokopenko

Goals: Vorobei (90), Atelkin (97)

FC ST. GALLEN v GALATASARAY ISTANBUL 1-2 (1-1)

Hardturm, Zürich 9.08.2000

Ref: Manuel Enrique Mejuto González (SPA) Att: 16,066

FC ST. GALLEN: Jörg Stiel (Cap); Marco Zwyssig, Marc Zellweger, Ivan dal Santo, Giuseppe Mazzarelli; Guido Alves Pereira Neto (46 Daniel Imhof), Sascha Müller, Luis Filho JAIRO; Jerron Nixon (63 Sergio Colacino), Terinio Ionel Gane, Charles Baye Amoah (76 Sebastiao Pereira do Nascimento DIDI). Trainer: Marcel Koller **Sent off**: Mazzarelli (89)

GALATASARAY: Claudio André Taffarel; Bülent Korkmaz (Cap) (85 Emre Asik), Gheorghe Popescu; Emre Belözoglu, Okan Buruk (79 Ümit Davala), Suat Kaya, Hakan Ünsal (46 Faruk Atalay), Ergün Penbe; Mário JARDEL Almeida Ribeiro, Carlos Alberto de Oliveira "CAPONE", Mandingo dos Santos MARCIO. Trainer: Mircea Lucescu

Goals: Amoah (14), Jardel (39, 78)

GALATASARAY ISTANBUL v FC ST. GALLEN 2-2 (2-1)

Ali Sami Yen 22.08.2000

Referee: Knud Erik Fisker (DEN) Attendance: 16,337

GALATASARAY: Claudio André Taffarel; Bülent Korkmaz, Gheorghe Popescu, Fatih Akyel; Emre Belözoglu, Okan Buruk, Suat Kaya, Hakan Ünsal (55 Faruk Atalay), Ergün Penbe; Mário JARDEL Almeida Ribeiro (82 Ümit Davala), Mandingo dos Santos MARCIO (46 Serkan Aykut). Trainer: M. Lucescu

FC ST. GALLEN: Jörg Stiel; Marco Zwyssig, Marc Zellweger, Ivan dal Santo; Guido Alves Pereira Neto (65 Jan Berger), Sascha Müller, Daniel Imhof, Luis Filho JAIRO; Jerron Nixon (67 Sergio Colacino), Tersinio Ionel Gane (56 Sebastiao Pereira do Nascimento DIDI), Charles Baye Amoah. Trainer: Marcel Koller

Goals: Zellweger (22, og), Jardel (29 pen), Gane (30), Amoah (85)

POLONIA WARSZAWA v PANATHINAIKOS ATHINA 2-2 (1-2)

Petro, Plock 9.08.2000

Referee: Joaquim Paulo Paraty da Silva (POR) Att: 7,700

POLONIA: Maciej Szczesny; Tomas Zvirgzdauskas, Mariusz Pawlak (28 Mariusz Malinowski), Arkadiusz Kaliszan, Tomasz Wieszczycki (77 Emanuel Ekwuene); Arkadiusz Bak, Tomasz Kielbowicz, Zbigniew Wyciszkiewicz, Tomasz Reginis; Emmanuel Olisadebe, Igor Golaszewski (64 Pawel Kaczorowski). Trainer: Dariusz Wdowczyk

PANATHINAIKOS: Antonis Nikopolidis; PERCY Celso OLIVARES Polanco, Panagiotis Fissas, René Henriksen, Leonidas Vokolos; PAULO Manuel SOUSA Carvalho, Aggelos Basinas (82 Evaggelos Koutsoures), Bledar Kola (65 Igor Sypniewski), Giorgos Karagounis; Nikos Limperopoulos, Krzysztof Warzycha (62 Giorgos Nasiopoulos). Trainer: Aggelos Anastasiadis

Goals: Warzycha (11), Fissas (37), Kielbowicz (45), Kaliszan (68)

PANATHINAIKOS ATHINA v POLONIA WARSZAWA 2-1 (1-0)

OAKA Spiros Louis, Athina 23.08.2000

Referee: Edgar Steinborn (GER) Attendance: 41,156

PANATHINAIKOS: Antonis Nikopolidis; PERCY Celso OLIVARES Polanco (51 Karlheinz Pflipsen), Panagiotis Fissas, René Henriksen, Leonidas Vokolos; Aggelos Basinas (64 Giannis Goumas), PAULO Manuel SOUSA Carva, Bledar Kola; Krzysztof Warzycha (73 Goran Vlaović), Giorgos Karagounis, Nikos Limperopoulos. Trainer: Aggelos Anastasiadis

POLONIA: Maciej Szczesny; Mariusz Pawlak (64 Tomasz Ciesielski), Tomas Zvirgzdauskas, Tomasz Wieszczycki (62 Tomasz Reginis), Piotr Dziewicki; Arkadiusz Kaliszan, Zbigniew Wyciszkiewicz 62, Arkadiusz Bak, Igor Golaszewski (72 Pawel Kaczorowski); Tomasz Kielbowicz, Emmanuel Olisadebe. Trainer: Dariusz Wdowczyk

Sent off: Kaliszan (45)

Goals: Limperopoulos (30), Pflipsen (61 pen), Bak (86)

FC TIROL INNSBRUCK v VALENCIA CF 0-0

Tivoli, Innsbruck 9.08.2000

Referee: Mike Riley (ENG) Attendance: 6,615

FC TIROL: Stanislav Cherchesov; Walter Kogler, Robert Wazinger, Aleksander Knavs; Roland Kirchler, Markus Anfang, Michael Baur, Jerzy Brzeczek, Stefan Marasek (84 Wolfgang Mair), Jürgen Panis; Radoslav Gilewicz. Trainer: Kurt Jara

VALENCIA: José Santiago CAÑIZARES Ruíz; Mauricio Pellegrino, Joachim Björklund, Amedeo Carboni, Jocelyn Angloma; Gaizka MENDIETA Zabala, VICENTE Rodríguez Guillén, David ALBELDA Aliques; DIEGO Martín ALONSO Lopez, Miguel Angel ANGULO Valderrey, Adrian Ilie (74 Zlatko Zahovic). Trainer: Héctor Raúl Cuper

VALENCIA CF v FC TIROL INNSBRUCK 4-1 (2-0)

Mestalla, Valencia 23.08.2000

Referee: Domenico Messina (ITA) Attendance: 43,700

VALENCIA: José Santiago CAÑIZARES Ruíz; Mauricio Pellegrino, Joachim Björklund, Didier Deschamps, Amedeo Carboni, Jocelyn Angloma (44 David ALBELDA Aliques); Gaizka MENDIETA Zabala, Cristian Alberto "KILY" GONZÁLEZ, Rubén BARAJA Vegas; Zlatko Zahovic (73 Juan Gines SÁNCHEZ Moreno), DIEGO Martín ALONSO Lopez (79 John Carew). Trainer: Héctor Raúl Cuper

FC TIROL: Stanislav Cherchesov; Walter Kogler, Oliver Prudlo, Jürgen Panis; Roland Kirchler, Markus Anfang (79 Andreas Schiener), Michael Baur, Stefan Marasek; Radoslav Gilewicz, Alfred Hörtnagl (46 Jerzy Brzeczek), Eduard Glieder (71 Markus Scharrer). Trainer: Kurt Jara

Sent off: Marasek (68)

Goals: Mendieta (23, 52 pen), Diego Alonso (44, 62), Gilewicz (66)

FC DYNAMO KYIV v CRVENA ZVEZDA BEOGRAD 0-0

Olympiyskyi, Kyiv 9.08.2000

Referee: Dermot Gallagher (ENG) Attendance: 17,000

DYNAMO: Vyacheslav Kernozenko; Oleksandr Khatskevich, Olexander Holovko, Vladislav Vashchuk, Yuri Dmitrulin, Andrei Nesmachnyi; Andriy Gusin, Artem Yashkin, Hennadiy Moroz (63 Valentin Belkevich); Maxim Shatskykh, Georgi Demetradze (72 Serhiy Serebryannikov).
Trainer: Valeriy Lobanovskyi

CRVENA ZVEZDA: Aleksander Kocić; Marjan Marković, Stevo Glogovac, Goran Bunjevcević, Nenad Lalatović; Ivan Gvozdenović, Branko Bosković, Srdan Bajcetić; Goran Drulić (80 Boban Stojanović), Mihailo Pjanović, Leo Lerinc (83 Saša Zorić). Trainer: Slavoljub Muslin

TSV 1860 MÜNCHEN v LEEDS UNITED 0-1 (0-0)

Olympiastadion, München 23.08.2000

Referee: Claus Bo Larsen (DEN) Attendance: 56,000

TSV 1860: Michael Hofmann; Stephan Paßlack (63 Bernhard Winkler), Marco Kurz, Martin Stranzl; Thomas Häßler, Harald Cerny, Erik Mykland, Daniel Borimirov (76 Markus Beierle), Daniel Bierofka (73 Roman Tyce); Martin Max, Paul Agostino.
Trainer: Werner Lorant

LEEDS UNITED: Nigel Martyn; Gary Kelly, Ian Harte, Lucas Radebe, Jonathan Woodgate, Danny Mills; Lee Bowyer, Matthew Jones (73 Gareth Evans), Michael Duberry; Mark Viduka, Alan Smith. Manager: David Anthony O'Leary

Goal: Smith (46)

CRVENA ZVEZDA BEOGRAD v FC DYNAMO KYIV 1-1 (1-1)

Crvena Zvezda, Beograd 23.08.2000

Referee: Kyros Vassaras (GRE) Attendance: 52,000

CRVENA ZVEZDA: Aleksander Kocić; Marjan Marković, Stevo Glogovac, Goran Bunjevcević, Nenad Lalatović (70 Milenko Acimovic); Ivan Gvozdenović, Branko Bosković (60 Dejan Ilić), Srdan Bajcetić; Goran Drulić (85 Dragan Stevanović), Mihailo Pjanović, Leo Lerinc.
Trainer: Slavoljub Muslin

DYNAMO: Vyacheslav Kernozenko; Oleksandr Khatskevich, Olexander Holovko, Vladislav Vashchuk, Yuri Dmitrulin, Kakhi Kaladze, Andrei Nesmachnyi; Valentin Belkevich, Andriy Gusin, Artem Yashkin (82 Hennadiy Moroz); Maxim Shatskykh (77 Georgi Demetradze).
Trainer: Valeriy Lobanovskyi

Goals: Bosković (22), Belkevich (33)

HERFØLGE BK v GLASGOW RANGERS FC 0-3 (0-2)

Herfølge Stadium 9.08.2000

Referee: Lubomir Pucek (CZE) Attendance: 3,523

HERFØLGE BK: Jákup Mikkelsen; Steven Lustü, Henrik Lykke; Lars Jakobsen, Kenneth Jensen (37 Jesper Jacobsen), Thomas Høyer, Kenneth Kastrup, Michael Thomsen, Tommy Schram (81 Jesper Heyde); Jesper Falck, Chris Hermansen (65 Thomas Knudsen). Trainer: John "Faxe" Jensen

RANGERS: Stefan Klos; Sergio Porrini, Bert Konterman, Lorenzo Amoruso, Claudio Reyna; Barry Ferguson, Neil McCann (59 Allan Johnston), Giovanni van Bronckhorst, Jörg Albertz; Billy Dodds (70 Andrei Kanchelskis), Rodney Wallace (63 Kenny Miller). Trainer: Dick Advocaat

Goals: Albertz (27), Wallace (31), Amoruso (60)

LEEDS UNITED v TSV 1860 MÜNCHEN 2-1 (1-0)

Elland Road, Leeds 9.08.2000

Referee: Kostas Kapitanis (CYP) Attendance: 33,769

LEEDS UNITED: Nigel Martyn; Gary Kelly, Ian Harte, Olivier Dacourt, Lucas Radebe (Cap); Michael Bridges (78 Danny Mills), Lee Bowyer, Eirik Bakke, Michael Duberry; Mark Viduka, Alan Smith. Manager: David Anthony O'Leary

TSV 1860: Michael Hofmann; Ned Zelic, Marco Kurz (Cap), Tomáš Votava, Martin Stranzl (81 Bernhard Winkler); Thomas Häßler, Harald Cerny, Erik Mykland, Daniel Bierofka (46 Stephan Paßlack); Martin Max, Paul Agostino.
Trainer: Werner Lorant

Sent off: Zelic (42), Dacourt (74) and Bakke (83)

Goals: Smith (39), Harte (71 pen), Agostino (90)

GLASGOW RANGERS FC v HERFØLGE BK 3-0 (0-0)

Ibrox, Glasgow 23.08.2000

Referee: Dani Koren (ISR) Attendance: 36,141

RANGERS: Stefan Klos; Fernando Ricksen (46 Andrei Kanchelskis), Bert Konterman, Lorenzo Amoruso; Claudio Reyna, Barry Ferguson, Neil McCann, Giovanni van Bronckhorst, Jörg Albertz (74 Allan Johnston); Billy Dodds (74 Tony Vidmar), Rodney Wallace. Trainer: Dick Advocaat

HERFØLGE BK: Jákup Mikkelsen; Steven Lustü, Henrik Lykke, Dan Lübbers; Lars Jakobsen (62 Thomas Knudsen), Thomas Høyer, Kenneth Kastrup, Tommy Schram (80 John "Faxe" Jensen), Jesper Heyde; Jesper Falck, Jesper Jacobsen (71 Chris Hermansen). Trainer: John "Faxe" Jensen

Goals: Wallace (47), Johnston (79), Kanchelskis (90)

HELSINGBORGS IF
v FC INTERNAZIONALE MILANO 1-0 (0-0)

Olympia, Helsingborg 9.08.2000

Referee: Zoran Arsić (YUG) Attendance: 12,617

HELSINGBORGS IF: Sven Andersson; Ola Nilsson, Roland Nilsson, Jozo Matovac, Nicklas Persson, Christoffer Andersson; Bjørn Johansen, Ulrik Jansson, Michael Hansson; ÁLVARO Marcio Santos, Erik Wahlstedt (73 Stig Johansen). Trainer: Nanne Bergstrand

INTERNAZIONALE: Sebastien Frey; Iván CORDOBA Sepulveda, Laurent Blanc, Cyrille Domoraud (46 Fabio Macellari), Matteo Ferrari; Vladimir Jugović, Benoit Cauet, Cristian Brocchi; Robbie Keane, Andrea Pirlo (75 Clarence Seedorf), Hakan Sükür (69 Iván Zamorano). Trainer: Marcelo Lippi

Goal: Hansson (81)

FC INTERNAZIONALE MILANO
v HELSINGBORGS IF 0-0

Giuseppe Meazza, Milano 23.08.2000

Referee: Vladimir Hrinak (SVK) Attendance: 49,949

INTERNAZIONALE: Sebastien Frey; Dario Simic, Laurent Blanc, Iván CORDOBA Sepulveda, Fabio Macellari; Benoit Cauet (70 Luigi Di Biagio), Clarence Seedorf, Vladimir Jugovic, Andrea Pirlo (46 Alvaro Recoba); Iván Zamorano (46 Robbie Keane), Hakan Sükür. Trainer: Marcelo Lippi

HELSINGBORGS IF: Sven Andersson; Roland Nilsson, Ola Nilsson, Jozo Matovac, Nicklas Persson; Christoffer Andersson, Stig Johansen (88 Mattias Lindström), Erik Wahlstedt (59 Lars Bakkerud), Michael Hansson (70 Rade Prica); Ulrik Jansson, ALVARO Marcio Santos. Trainer: Nanne Bergstrand

RSC ANDERLECHT BRUSSEL
v FC PORTO 1-0 (1-0)

Constant vanden Stock, Brussel 9.08.2000

Referee: Tom Henning Øvrebø (NOR) Attendance: 14,263

ANDERLECHT: Filip de Wilde; Glen de Boeck (7 Didier Dheedene), Lorenzo Staelens, Patrick van Diemen, Bertrand Crasson; Yves Vanderhaeghe, Bart Goor, Walter Baseggio, Alin Stoica (78 Oleg Yashchuk); Jan Koller, Tomasz Radzinski (88 Aruna Dindane). Trainer: Aimé Antheunis

FC PORTO: Sergei Ovchinnikov, JORGE Paulo COSTA Almeida, Fernando NÉLSON Jesus Vieira Alves, ALOÍSIO Pires Alves, CARLOS Humberto PAREDES Monges (57 Carlos Narciso CHAINHO), Ljubinko Drulović, Dmitri Alenichev (67 Miran Pavlin), João Paulo Maio Santos PAULINHO SANTOS, RUBENS Rodrigues dos Santos JÚNIOR, Silvio Maric (23 DOMINGOS José Paciencia Oliveira), CLAYTON Ferreira Cruz.
Trainer: FERNANDO Manuel Fernandes da Costa SANTOS

Goal: Koller (38)

FC PORTO v RSC ANDERLECHT BRUSSEL 0-0

Estádio das Antas, Porto 23.08.2000

Referee: Cosimo Bolognino (ITA) Attendance: 34,908

FC PORTO: Sergei Ovchinnikov; Fernando NÉLSON Jesus Vieira Alves, RICARDO Emidio Ramalho SILVA, JORGE Paulo COSTA Almeida, RUBENS Rodrigues dos Santos JÚNIOR (66 DOMINGOS José Paciencia Oliveira); Dmitri Alenichev, João Paulo Maio Santos "PAULINHO SANTOS", Carlos Narciso CHAINHO (46 Miran PAVLIN); Nuno Gonçalves Rocha "CAPUCHO", Ljubinko DRULOVIĆ, Juan Antonio PIZZI Torroija (66 ROMEU Antonio Soares Almeda). Trainer: FERNANDO Manuel Fernandes da Costa SANTOS

ANDERLECHT: Filip de Wilde; Bertrand Crasson, Lorenzo Staelens, Didier Dheedene, Yves Vanderhaeghe; Walter Baseggio (77 Aleksandar Ilic), Besnik Hasi, Patrick van Diemen, Bart Goor (87 Davy Oyen); Tomasz Radzinski (75 Oleg Yashchuk), Jan Koller. Trainer: Aimé Antheunis

DUNAFERR SE
v ROSENBORG BK TRONDHEIM 2-2 (0-0)

ETO, Györ 9.08.2000

Referee: Atanas Uzunov (BUL) Attendance: 14,000

DUNAFERR: Balázs Rabóczki; Zoltan Molnar, Miklós Salamon, György Kiss (84 Tamás Nagy), Tibor Pomper, László Éger; Ferenc Orosz (46 Igor Nichenko), Henrik Rósa, Gabor Bagoly (57 Ferenc Lengyel); Attila Tököli, Gábor Zavadszky. Trainer: Sándor Egervári

ROSENBORG: Arni Gautur Arason; Erik Hoftun, Christer Basma, Bent Inge Johnsen, Ståle Stensaas; Roar Strand (74 Morten Knutsen), Ørjan Berg, Bent Skammelsrud, Fredrik Winsnes; Jan Derek Sørensen (81 Petter Belsvik), Frode Johnsen. Trainer: Nils Arne Eggen

Goals: Strand (51), Lengyel (80), Knutsen (86), Tököli (87)

ROSENBORG BK TRONDHEIM
v DUNAFERR SE 2-1 (1-1)

Lerkendal, Trondheim 23.08.2000

Referee: Miroslav Liba (CES) Attendance: 9,424

ROSENBORG: Arni Gautur Arason; Erik Hoftun, Christer Basma (25 Petter Belsvik), Bent Inge Johnsen, Ståle Stensaas; Roar Strand, Ørjan Berg, Bent Skammelsrud, Morten Knutsen, Fredrik Winsnes; Frode Johnsen. Trainer: Nils Arne Eggen

DUNAFERR: Balázs Rabóczki; Zoltan Molnar, Miklós Salamon, Tibor Pomper, László Éger; Henrik Rósa, Ferenc Kóczián (77 Tamás Nagy), Gabor Bagoly (46 Ferenc Lengyel); Ferenc Orosz, Attila Tököli, Gábor Zavadszky.
Trainer: Sándor Egervári

Goals: Berg (4), Tököli (17), Belsvik (48)

FIRST STAGE – GROUP A

SPARTAK MOSKVA v BAYER 04 LEVERKUSEN 2-0 (0-0)

Luzhniki, Moskva 12.09.2000

Referee: Paul Anthony Durkin (ENG) Attendance: 64,000

SPARTAK: Aleksandr Filimonov; Yuri Kovtun, Dmitriy Ananko, Dmytro Parfyonov, Viktor Bulatov; Andrejs Štolcers (46 Vasiliy Baranov), Yegor Titov, Andrei Tikhonov, Artyom Bezrodnyi; Aleksandr Shirko (74 Marcos Antonio Aparecido Cipriano "MARCÃO"), Luis ROBSON Pereira da Silva (75 Maxim Kalinichenko). Trainer: Oleg Romantsev

BAYER: Pascal Zuberbühler; Robert Kovac, Jens Nowotny, Boris Zivković; "ZE ROBERTO" da Silva (61 Thomas Brdaric), Paulo Roberto Rink, Michael Ballack, Jurica Vranješ, Pascal Ojigwe (62 Bernd Schneider); Oliver Neuville, Carsten Ramelow. Trainer: Christoph Daum

Goals: Titov (51), Bezrodnyi (89)

SPORTING CLUBE DE PORTUGAL LISBOA v REAL MADRID CF 2-2 (2-0)

Estadio José Alvalade, Lisboa 12.09.2000

Referee: Alfredo Trentalange (ITA) Attendance: 42,000

SPORTING: Peter Schmeichel; César Prates, Roberto L.G. Deus Severo "BETO", RUI JORGE de Oliveira, André Cruz; Ricardo Manuel da Silva SÁ PINTO (80 Maurício EDMILSON Gonçalves Pimenta), Pavel Horváth, Hugo (73 BRUNO Eduardo M.de CAIRES), Manuel Albino Morim Morçães "BINO"; Alberto Acosta, JOÃO Manuel Vieira PINTO (85 Antonio J.G. Gonzalez "TOÑITO"). Trainer: Augusto Inácio

REAL: Iker CASILLAS Fernandez; MICHEL SALGADO Fernandez, ROBERTO CARLOS da Silva, Iván HELGUERA Bujia, IVÁN CAMPO Ramos; Luis Filipe Madeira Caeiro "FIGO", SÁVIO Bortolini Pimentel, FLÁVIO de CONCEIÇÃO (60 José María Gutiérrez Hernandez "GUTI"), Claude Makélélé (60 Albert CELADES Lopez); RAÚL González Blanco, Pedro MUNITIS Alvarez (90 JULIO CESAR Santos Correa). Trainer: Vicente del Bosque

Goals: Sá Pinto (39), Cruz (42), Roberto Carlos (50), Rui Jorge (76 og)

BAYER 04 LEVERKUSEN v SPORTING CLUBE DE PORTUGAL LISBOA 3-2 (0-1)

BayArena, Leverkusen 20.09.2000

Referee: Knud Erik Fisker (DEN) Attendance: 22,500

BAYER: Pascal Zuberbühler; Boris Zivkovic, Jens Nowotny, Robert Kovac; Pascal Ojigwe (46 Thomas Brdaric), Carsten Ramelow, Vratislav Gresko (68 Andreas Neuendorf), Bernd Schneider (90 Jurica Vranješ); Michael Ballack, Paulo Roberto Rink, Oliver Neuville. Trainer: Christoph Daum

SPORTING: Peter Schmeichel; César Prates, Roberto L.G. Deus Severo "BETO", André Cruz, RUI JORGE de Oliveira (75 Antonio J.G. Gonzalez "TOÑITO"), Pavel Horvath (61 Phil Babb), Hugo, Manuel Albino Morim Morçães "BINO", JOÃO Manuel Vieira PINTO, Alberto Acosta (74 Mbo Mpenza), Ricardo Manuel da Silva SÁ PINTO. Trainer: Augusto Inácio

Sent off: João Pinto II (41)

Goals: Cruz (12), Ramelow (65), Brdaric (73), Neuville (77), Sá Pinto (79 pen)

REAL MADRID CF v SPARTAK MOSKVA 1-0 (0-0)

Santiago Bernabeu, Madrid 20.09.2000

Referee: Leslie Irvine (NIR) Attendance: 32,000

REAL: Iker CASILLAS Fernandez; MICHEL SALGADO Fernandez, Iván HELGUERA Bujia, Aitor KARANKA de la Hoz, ROBERTO CARLOS da Silva; Albert CELADES Lopez (81 Fernando Ruíz HIERRO), Claude Makélélé, Luis Filipe Madeira Caeiro "FIGO", SÁVIO Bortolini Pimentel (65 Steve McManaman); José María Gutiérrez Hernandez "GUTI", Pedro MUNITIS Alvarez (89 Jorge López Marco "TOTE"). Trainer: Vicente del Bosque

SPARTAK: Aleksandr Filimonov; Jerrt Christian Tchuisse (58 Aleksandr Shirko), Dmytro Parfyonov, Dmitriy Ananko, Viktor Bulatov, Yuri Kovtun; Andrei Tikhonov, Yegor Titov, Andrejs Štolcers (65 Artyom Bezrodnyi); Maxim Kalinichenko, Luis ROBSON Pereira da Silva (75 Marcos Antonio Aparecido Cipriano "MARCÃO"). Trainer: Oleg Romantsev

Goal: Helguera (51)

SPARTAK MOSKVA v SPORTING CLUBE DE PORTUGAL LISBOA 3-1 (1-1)

Luzhniki, Moskva 27.09.2000

Referee: Alain Hamer (LUX) Attendance: 56,000

SPARTAK: Aleksandr Filimonov; Jerry Christian Tchuisse, Dmitriy Ananko, Dmytro Parfyonov, Yuri Kovtun; Andrejs Štolcers (46 Vasiliy Baranov), Yegor Titov, Viktor Bulatov, Artyom Bezrodnyi; Aleksandr Shirko (46 Marcos Antonio Aparecido Cipriano "MARCÃO"), Luis ROBSON Pereira da Silva. Trainer: Oleg Romantsev

SPORTING: Peter Schmeichel; César Prates, Roberto L.G. Deus Severo "BETO", André Cruz, RUI JORGE de Oliveira (70 Antonio J.G. Gonzalez "TOÑITO"); Manuel Dimas, Manuel Albino Morim Morçães "BINO", Hugo (70 Alberto Acosta), Pavel Horváth; Ricardo Manuel da Silva SÁ PINTO, Mbo Mpenza (82 RODRIGO Fabri). Trainer: Augusto Inácio

Goals: Sá Pinto (24), Robson (44), Marcão (68, 82)

BAYER 04 LEVERKUSEN
v REAL MADRID CF 2-3 (2-1)

BayArena, Leverkusen 27.09.2000

Referee: Karl-Erik Nilsson (SWE) Attendance: 22,500

BAYER: Pascal Zuberbühler; Robert Kovac, Jens Nowotny, Boris Zivkovic; Jörg Reeb, "ZÉ ROBERTO" da Silva (79 Vratislav Gresko), Michael Ballack, Bernd Schneider (79 Thomas Brdaric), Carsten Ramelow; Paulo Roberto Rink, Oliver Neuville. Trainer: Christoph Daum

REAL: Iker CASILLAS Fernandez; MICHEL SALGADO Fernandez, ROBERTO CARLOS da Silva, Fernando Ruíz HIERRO, Aitor KARANKA de la Hoz; Iván HELGUERA Bujia, Luis Filipe Madeira Caeiro "FIGO", FLÁVIO de CONCEIÇÃO (90 IVÁN CAMPO Ramos), Santiago Solari (51 RAÚL González Blanco); José María Gutiérrez Hernandez "GUTI", Pedro MUNITIS Alvarez (87 Manuel SANCHÍS Hontiyuelo). Trainer: Vicente del Bosque

Goals: Schneider (27), Roberto Carlos (32, 75), Ballack (44), Guti (69)

SPORTING CLUBE DE PORTUGAL LISBOA
v SPARTAK MOSKVA 0-3 (0-1)

Estadio José Alvalade, Lisboa 17.10.2000

Referee: Graham Barber (ENG) Attendance: 30,000

SPORTING: Peter Schmeichel; Manuel Dimas, César Prates, RUI JORGE de Oliveira (38 RODRIGO Fabri), Roberto L.G. Deus Severo "BETO", André Cruz; Pavel Horváth (57 Pedro Barbosa), Manuel Albino Morim Morçães "BINO"; JOÃO Manuel Vieira PINTO (57 Mbo Mpenza), Ricardo Manuel da Silva SÁ PINTO, Alberto Acosta.
Trainer: Augusto Inácio

SPARTAK: Aleksandr Filimonov; Yuri Kovtun, Dmitriy Ananko, Dmytro Parfyonov; Vasiliy Baranov, Viktor Bulatov, Yegor Titov, Jerry Christian Tchuisse, Artyom Bezrodnyi; Marcos Antonio Aparecido Cipriano "MARCÃO" (62 Maxim Kalinichenko), Luis ROBSON Pereira da Silva (85 Nikolai Pisarev). Trainer: Oleg Romantsev

Goals: Manuel Dimas (16 og), Titov (52, 68)

REAL MADRID CF
v BAYER 04 LEVERKUSEN 5-3 (2-1)

Santiago Bernabeu, Madrid 17.10.2000

Referee: Domenico Messina (ITA) Attendance: 60,000

REAL: Luis CÉSAR Sánchez Domínguez; GEREMI Sorele Fotso Ndjitap, Fernando Ruíz HIERRO (16 Albert CELADES Lopez), IVÁN CAMPO Ramos, ROBERTO CARLOS da Silva; Iván HELGUERA Bujia, Claude Makélélé, SÁVIO Bortolini Pimentel (71 Santiago Solari); Luis Filipe Madeira Caeiro "FIGO" (89 Pedro MUNITIS Alvarez), RAÚL González Blanco, José María Gutiérrez Hernandez "GUTI".
Trainer: Vicente del Bosque

BAYER: Pascal Zuberbühler; Boris Zivković, Jens Nowotny, Robert Kovac; Jörg Reeb, Michael Ballack, Carsten Ramelow (70 Paulo Roberto Rink), "ZÉ ROBERTO" da Silva; Oliver Neuville (70 ROBSON Ponté), Ulf Kirsten, Thomas Brdaric (87 Bernd Schneider). Trainer: Christoph Daum

Goals: Guti (4, 64), Brdaric (20), Helguera (24), Kirsten (55), Raúl (75), Rink (77), Figo (87 pen)

REAL MADRID CF v SPORTING CLUBE DE PORTUGAL LISBOA 4-0 (2-0)

Santiago Bernabeu, Madrid 25.10.2000

Referee: Urs Meier (SWI) Attendance: 55,029

REAL: Luis CÉSAR Sánchez Domínguez, GEREMI Sorele Fotso Ndjitap, IVÁN CAMPO Ramos, Iván HELGUERA Bujia, ROBERTO CARLOS da Silva (69 Santiago Solari); Luis Filipe Madeira Caeiro "FIGO" (52 Steve McManaman), Albert CELADES Lopez, Claude Makélélé, SÁVIO Bortolini Pimentel; José María Gutiérrez Hernandez "GUTI", Pedro MUNITIS Alvarez (61 Fernando MORIENTES Sánchez).
Trainer: Vicente del Bosque

SPORTING: Nélson; César Prates, Roberto L.G. Deus Severo "BETO", André Cruz, Manuel Dimas; Mbo Mpenza, Hugo (71 Pedro Barbosa), DELFIM José Rola Teixeira (46 Manuel Albino Morim Morçães "BINO"), Alan Mahon (46 Alberto Acosta); JOÃO Manuel Vieira PINTO, Ricardo Manuel da Silva SÁ PINTO. Trainer: Augusto Inácio

Goals: Guti (12), Sávio (42), Morientes (62, 70)

BAYER 04 LEVERKUSEN
v SPARTAK MOSKVA 1-0 (0-0)

BayArena, Leverkusen 25.10.2000

Referee: Ryszard Wójcik (POL) Attendance: 22,500

BAYER: Adam Matysek; Torben Hoffmann, Jens Nowotny, Boris Zivkovic; Jörg Reeb, Carsten Ramelow, Michael Ballack (76 Thomas Brdaric), Oliver Neuville, "ZÉ ROBERTO" da Silva (81 Jurica Vranješ); Ulf Kirsten, Paulo Roberto Rink (46 Pascal Ojigwe). Trainer: Christoph Daum

SPARTAK: Aleksandr Filimonov; Dmitriy Ananko, Jerry Christian Tchuisse, Dmytro Parfyonov, Yuri Kovtun; Viktor Bulatov, Vasiliy Baranov, Artyom Bezrodnyi, Yegor Titov; Marcos Antonio Aparecido Cipriano "MARCÃO" (58 Maxim Kalinichenko), Luis ROBSON Pereira da Silva.
Trainer: Oleg Romantsev

Goal: Ballack (52)

SPARTAK MOSKVA v REAL MADRID CF 1-0 (0-0)

Luzhniki, Moskva 7.11.2000

Referee: Stéphane Bré (FRA) Attendance: 80,000

SPARTAK: Aleksandr Filimonov; Maxim Kalinichenko, Jerry Christian Tchuisse, Dmitriy Ananko, Yuri Kovtun; Vasiliy Baranov, Viktor Bulatov, Yegor Titov, Artyom Bezrodnyi; Marcos Antonio Aparecido Cipriano "MARCÃO" (64 Aleksandr Shirko), Luis ROBSON Pereira da Silva. Trainer: Oleg Romantsev

REAL: Luis CÉSAR Sánchez Domínguez; MICHEL SALGADO Fernandez, Aitor KARANKA de la Hoz, GEREMI Sorele Fotso Ndjitap, Santiago Solari; Steve McManaman, Claude Makélélé, Manuel SANCHÍS Hontiyuelo (86 Francisco PAVON Barahona), Pedro MUNITIS Alvarez (74 Jorge López Marco "TOTE"); Alberto RIVERA Pizarro, Fernando MORIENTES Sánchez. Trainer: Vicente del Bosque

Goal: Gérémi (47 og)

SPORTING CLUBE DE PORTUGAL LISBOA v BAYER 04 LEVERKUSEN 0-0

Estadio José Alvalade, Lisboa 7.11.2000

Referee: Oguz Sarvan (TUR) Attendance: 8,000

SPORTING: Nélson; César Prates, Phil Babb, André Cruz, Manuel Dimas; DELFIM José Rola Teixeira, Hugo (46 Maurício EDMILSON Gonçalves Pimenta), Manuel Albino Morim Morçães "BINO", JOÃO Manuel Vieira PINTO (81 RODRIGO Fabri); Alberto Acosta, Pedro Barbosa. Trainer: Augusto Inácio

BAYER: Pascal Zuberbühler; Boris Zivkovic, Jurica Vranješ, Robert Kovac; Frankie Hejduk (72 Thomas Brdaric), Bernd Schneider (75 Andreas Neuendorf), Pascal Ojigwe, Torben Hoffmann, "ZÉ ROBERTO" da Silva; Robson Ponte (71 Oliver Neuville), Paulo Roberto Rink. Trainer: Christoph Daum

	P	W	D	L	F	A	Pts
Real Madrid CF	6	4	1	1	15	8	13
Spartak Moskva	6	4	0	2	9	3	12
Bayer 04 Leverkusen	6	2	1	3	9	12	7
Sporting Lisboa	6	0	2	4	5	15	2

FIRST STAGE – GROUP B

SHAKHTAR DONETSK v SS LAZIO ROMA 0-3 (0-1)

Shakhtyor, Donetsk 12.09.2000

Referee: Michel Piraux (BEL) Attendance: 31,511

SHAKHTAR: Yuri Virt; Dainius Gleveckas, Vyacheslav Shevchuk, Anatoliy Tymoshchuk, Serhiy Popov; Hennadiy Zubov, Aleksei Bakharev, Vitali Abramov (77 Oleksii Bielik), Aleksandr Shmarko; Serhiy Atelkin, Andriy Vorobei. Trainer: Viktor Prokopenko

LAZIO: Angelo Peruzzi; Giuseppe Pancaro, Alessandro Nesta, Siniša Mihajlovic (53 Manuel FERNANDO Silva COUTO), Giuseppe Favalli; Dejan Stankovic (81 Attilio Lombardo), Juan Verón, Diego Simeone (83 Roberto Sensini), Pavel Nedved; CLAUDIO Javier LÓPEZ, Simone Inzaghi. Trainer: Sven-Göran Eriksson

Goals: Inzaghi (27), Nedved (68), López (78)

AC SPARTA PRAHA v ARSENAL FC LONDON 0-1 (0-1)

Stadión na Letnej, Praha 12.09.2000

Referee: Gilles Veissière (FRA) Attendance: 17,666

SPARTA: Tomáš Poštulka; Zdenek Grygera, Jiří Novotný, René Bolf, Radek Mynár (86 Jan Flachbart), Petr Papoušek (79 Martin Prohászka); Zdenek Svoboda, Pavel Novotný, Tomáš Rosický; Marek Kincl (61 Horst Siegl), Josef Obajdin. Trainer: Ivan Hasek

ARSENAL: David Seaman; Lee Dixon, Martin Keown, Silvio Mendes "SILVINHO", Oleg Luzhny; Robert Pires, Fredrik Ljungberg (80 Nelson Vivas), Patrick Vieira, Gilles Grimandi; Nwankwo Kanu, Thierry Henry (77 Sylvain Wiltord). Manager: Arsène Wenger

Goal: Silvinho (33)

SS LAZIO ROMA v AC SPARTA PRAHA 3-0 (1-0)

Stadio Olimpico, Roma 20.09.2000

Referee: Kyros Vassaras (GRE) Attendance: 45,100

LAZIO: Luca Marchegiani; Giuseppe Pancaro, Alessandro Nesta, Manuel FERNANDO Silva COUTO, Giuseppe Favalli (80 Francesco Colonnese); Dejan Stankovic, Juan Verón, Diego Simeone, Pavel Nedved (80 Roberto Sensini); J. Marcelo SALAS Melinão, Simone Inzaghi (73 Attilio Lombardo). Trainer: Sven-Göran Eriksson

SPARTA: Tomáš Poštulka; Michal Hornák, Jiří Novotný, René Bolf, Zdenek Grygera; Radek Mynár (46 Vladimír Labant), Zdenek Svoboda (78 Václav Koloušek), Jiří Jarošik, Tomáš Rosický; Marek Kincl (82 Horst Siegl), Josef Obajdin. Trainer: Ivan Hasek

Goal: Inzaghi (35,70), Simeone (58)

ARSENAL FC LONDON
v SHAKHTAR DONETSK 3-2 (1-2)

Arsenal, Highbury, London 20.09.2000

Referee: Hartmut Strampe (GER) Attendance: 33,922

ARSENAL: David Seaman; Silvio Mendes "SILVINHO", Martin Keown, Oleg Luzhny, Lee Dixon; Gilles Grimandi, Fredrik Ljungberg (66 Dennis Bergkamp), Patrick Vieira, Robert Pires (34 Sylvain Wiltord); Thierry Henry, Nwankwo Kanu. Manager: Arséne Wenger

SHAKHTAR: Yuri Virt; Mikhailo Starostyak, Dainius Gleveckas, Serhiy Popov, Aleksei Bakharev (70 Oleksii Bielik); Anatoliy Tymoshchuk, Vyacheslav Shevchuk, Vitali Abramov (58 Valeriy Kriventsov), Serhiy Atelkin (77 Serhiy Kovalev); Hennadiy Zubov, Andriy Vorobei.

Sent off: Popov (45)

Goals: Bakharev (26), Vorobei (29), Wiltord (45), Keown (85, 90)

SHAKHTAR DONETSK
v AC SPARTA PRAHA 2-1 (1-1)

Shakhtyor, Donetsk 17.10.2000

Referee: Atanas Uzunov (BUL) Attendance: 20,000

SHAKHTAR: Yuri Virt; Mikhailo Starostyak (67 Oleksii Bielik), Dainius Gleveckas, Serhiy Popov, Isaac Okoronkwo; Aleksei Bakharev, Hennadiy Zubov, Vitali Abramov (58 Valeriy Kriventsov), Anatoliy Tymoshchuk; Serhiy Atelkin, Andriy Vorobei (90 Serhiy Kovalev). Trainer: Viktor Prokopenko

SPARTA: Tomáš Poštulka; Zdenek Grygera, Vladimír Labant, René Bolf (90 Marek Kincl), Michal Hornák, Jiří Novotný; Martin Hašek (90 Pavel Novotný), Libor Sionko, Jiří Jarošik, Tomáš Rosický; Josef Obajdin (80 Václav Koloušek). Trainer: Ivan Hasek

Sent off: Grygera (87)

Goals: Jarošik (16), Gleveckas (35), Zubov (87 pen)

AC SPARTA PRAHA
v SHAKHTAR DONETSK 3-2 (0-0)

Stadión na Letnej, Praha 27.09.2000

Referee: Konrad Plautz (AUS) Attendance: 7,391

SPARTA: Tomáš Poštulka; Zdenek Grygera, René Bolf, Jiří Novotný, Vladimír Labant; Michal Hornák, Zdenek Svoboda (87 Václav Koloušek), Jiří Jarošik, Tomáš Rosický; Libor Sionko (90 Petr Papoušek), Josef Obajdin (76 Martin Prohászka). Trainer: Ivan Hasek

SHAKHTAR: Yuri Virt; Mikhailo Starostyak, Dainius Gleveckas, Anatoliy Tymoshchuk, Vyacheslav Shevchuk; Hennadiy Zubov, Serhiy Kovalev (78 Vitali Abramov), Marian Aliuţă, Aleksei Bakharev; Serhiy Atelkin (79 Oleksii Bielik), Andriy Vorobei. Trainer: Viktor Prokopenko

Goals: Rosický (54), Zubov (56), Hornák (73), Jarošik (82), Hornák (84 og)

SS LAZIO ROMA
v ARSENAL FC LONDON 1-1 (1-0)

Stadio Olimpico, Roma 17.10.2000

Referee: Hellmut Krug (GER) Attendance: 40,151

LAZIO: Angelo Peruzzi; Paolo Negro, Alessandro Nesta, Siniša Mihajlovic, Giuseppe Pancaro; Pavel Nedved, Diego Simeone, Juan Verón, Dejan Stankovic (46 CLAUDIO Javier LÓPEZ); Simone Inzaghi (69 Hernán Crespo), Marcelo SALAS Melinão. Trainer: Sven-Göran Eriksson

ARSENAL: John Lukic; Silvio Mendes "SILVINHO", Martin Keown, Lee Dixon, Oleg Luzhny, Gilles Grimandi (69 LAUREN Bisan Etame-Mayer); Ray Parlour (60 Robert Pires), Patrick Vieira, Fredrik Ljungberg (74 Sylvain Wiltord); Nwankwo Kanu, Thierry Henry. Manager: Arséne Wenger

Goals: Nedved (24), Pires (88)

ARSENAL FC LONDON
v SS LAZIO ROMA 2-0 (1-0)

Arsenal Stadium Highbury, London 27.09.2000

Referee: José María García-Aranda Encinar (SPA) Attendance: 34,521

ARSENAL: David Seaman; Patrick Vieira, Martin Keown, Tony Adams, Silvio Mendes "SILVINHO"; Dennis Bergkamp (79 Nelson Vivas), Ray Parlour, Oleg Luzhny, Fredrik Ljungberg; Thierry Henry (84 Sylvain Wiltord), Nwankwo Kanu. Manager: Arséne Wenger

LAZIO: Luca Marchegiani; Paolo Negro, Alessandro Nesta, Siniša Mihajlovic, Giuseppe Pancaro; Pavel Nedved, Diego Simeone, Juan Verón, Dejan Stanković (46 Attilio Lombardo, 74 Fabrizio Ravanelli); CLAUDIO Javier LÓPEZ, Simone Inzaghi (57 Marcelo SALAS Melinão). Trainer: Sven-Göran Eriksson

Goals: Ljungberg (43, 56)

SS LAZIO ROMA
v SHAKHTAR DONETSK 5-1 (0-1)

Stadio Olimpico, Roma 25.10.2000

Referee: Alain Sars (FRA) Attendance: 14,746

LAZIO: Angelo Peruzzi; Giuseppe Pancaro, Alessandro Nesta, Manuel FERNANDO Silva COUTO, Giuseppe Favalli; Attilio Lombardo (71 Roberto Sensini), Roberto Baronio (46 Dejan Stankovic), Juan Verón, Pavel Nedved; Simone Inzaghi (46 Hernán Crespo), CLAUDIO Javier LÓPEZ. Trainer: Sven-Göran Eriksson

SHAKHTAR: Yuri Virt; Anatoliy Tymoshchuk, Isaac Okoronkwo, Dainius Gleveckas, Hennadiy Zubov; Serhiy Kovalev (84 Mikhailo Starostyak), Marian Aliuţă (71 Oleksii Bielik), Serhiy Popov (75 Aleksandr Shmarko), Aleksei Bakharev; Andriy Vorobei, Serhiy Atelkin. Trainer: Viktor Prokopenko

Goals: Vorobei (41), López (48, 68, 90), Favalli (54), Verón (57)

ARSENAL FC LONDON
v AC SPARTA PRAHA 4-2 (3-1)

Arsenal Stadium Highbury, London 25.10.2000

Referee: Alain Hamer (LUX) Attendance: 34,497

ARSENAL: David Seaman; Nelson Vivas, Oleg Luzhny, Lee Dixon, Silvio Mendes «SILVINHO» (46 Ashley Cole); LAUREN Bisan Etame-Mayer, Robert Pires (63 Dennis Bergkamp), Patrick Vieira, Ray Parlour; Nwankwo Kanu, Thierry Henry (70 Sylvain Wiltord). Manager: Arséne Wenger

SPARTA: Tomáš Poštulka; René Bolf, Michal Hornák, Jiří Novotný, Vladimír Labant; Libor Sionko (85 Petr Papoušek), Martin Hašek, Jiří Jarošik, Tomáš Rosický; Tomáš Jun (46 Radek Mynár), Marek Kincl. Trainer: Ivan Hasek

Goals: Parlour (5), Lauren Etamé (8), Dixon (35), Labant (40 pen), Kanu (51), Rosický (90)

SHAKHTAR DONETSK
v ARSENAL FC LONDON 3-0 (1-0)

Shakhtyor, Donetsk 7.11.2000

Referee: Knud Erik Fisker (DEN) Attendance: 30,000

SHAKHTAR: Yuri Virt; Mikhailo Starostyak, Dainius Gleveckas, Serhiy Popov, Isaac Okoronkwo; Aleksei Bakharev, Hennadiy Zubov, Vitali Abramov (77 Marian Aliuță), Anatoliy Tymoshchuk; Serhiy Atelkin (52 Oleksii Bielik), Andriy Vorobei (86 Marian Savu). Trainer: Viktor Prokopenko

ARSENAL: Stuart Taylor; Lee Dixon, Martin Keown, Matthew Upson, Nelson Vivas, Ashley Cole; LAUREN Bisan Etame-Mayer, Ray Parlour (72 Paolo Vernazza); Thierry Henry (62 Fredrik Ljungberg), Nwankwo Kanu, Sylvain Wiltord. Manager: Arséne Wenger

Goals: Atelkin (34), Vorobei (57), Bielik (66)

AC SPARTA PRAHA v SS LAZIO ROMA 0-1 (0-1)

Stadión na Letnej, Praha 7.11.2000

Referee: Arturo Daudén Ibáñez (SPA) Attendance: 19,414

SPARTA: Jaromír Blažek; Martin Hašek (86 Radek Mynár), Zdenek Grygera, Jiří Novotný, René Bolf, Vladimír Labant; Petr Papoušek, Zdenek Svoboda (61 Martin Prohászka), Jiří Jarošik, Tomáš Rosický; Horst Siegl (81 Marek Kincl). Trainer: Ivan Hasek

LAZIO: Luca Marchegiani; Guerino Gottardi, Manuel FERNANDO Silva COUTO, Francesco Colonnese, Emanuele Pesaresi; Attilio Lombardo, Dejan Stankovic, Roberto Baronio, Fabrizio Ravanelli; Simone Inzaghi (85 Daniele Ruggiu), José Marcelo SALAS Melinão (46 Emanuele Berrettoni, 90 Andrea Luciani). Trainer: Sven-Göran Eriksson

Goal: Ravanelli (43)

	P	W	D	L	F	A	Pts
Arsenal FC London	6	4	1	1	11	8	13
SS Lazio Roma	6	4	1	1	13	4	13
Shakhtar Donetsk	6	2	0	4	10	15	6
AC Sparta Praha	6	1	0	5	6	13	3

FIRST STAGE – GROUP C

OLYMPIQUE LYON v SC HEERENVEEN 3-1 (2-1)

Gerland, Lyon 12.09.2000

Referee: Stuart Dougal (SCO) Attendance: 22,687

OLYMPIQUE: Grégory Coupet; Eric Deflandre, Florent Laville (60 Patrick Müller), EDMILSON José Gomes De Moraes, Jérémie Bréchet; Marc-Vivien Foé, David Linarès, Pierre Laigle, Vikash Dhorasoo; Sonny ANDERSON da Silva (76 Steed Malbranque), Steve Marlet (90 Sidney Govou). Trainer: Jacques Santini

SC HEERENVEEN: Hans Vonk; Max Houttuin, Ronnie Venema, Johan Hansma, Gérard de Nooijer; Jeffrey Talan (83 Arjan Ebbinge), Arek Radomski, Sander van Gessel (72 Harris Huizingh); Daniël Jensen (39 Ignacio Tuhuteru), Anthony Lurling, Mika Nurmela. Trainer: Foppe de Haan

Goals: Ânderson (2), Houttuin (10 og), Talan (35), Marlet (58)

VALENCIA CF
v OLYMPIAKOS PEIRAIAS 2-1 (2-0)

Mestalla, Valencia 12.09.2000

Referee: Anders Frisk (SWE) Attendance: 30,722

VALENCIA: José Santiago CAÑIZARES Ruíz; Jocelyn Angloma, Mauricio Pellegrino, Miroslav Djukic, Amedeo Carboni; Gaizka MENDIETA Zabala, Rubén BARAJA Vegas, Didier Deschamps, Cristian Alberto «KILY» GONZÁLEZ; Zlatko Zahović (66 Juan Gines SÁNCHEZ Moreno), DIEGO Martín ALONSO Lopez (86 John Carew). Trainer: Héctor Raúl Cuper

OLYMPIAKOS: Dimitrios Eleftheropoulos; Dimitrios Mavrogenidis (73 Peter Ofori-Quaye), Giorgos Amanatidis, Hristos Patsatzoglou, Hristos Kontis; Ilias Poursanidis (85 Stelios Giannakopoulos), José Elías Junior Moedim «ZÉ ELIAS», Pär Zetterberg, LUCIANO Nunes de Souza (90 Lampros Houtos); Predrag Djordjevic, GIOVANNI Silva de Oliveira. Trainer: Giannis Mazourakis

Goals: Baraja (36), Diego Alonso (45), Djordjević (74)

OLYMPIAKOS PEIRAIAS v OLYMPIQUE LYON 2-1 (2-0)

OAKA Spiros Louis, Athina 20.09.2000

Referee: Graham Poll (ENG) Attendance: 69,048

OLYMPIAKOS: Dimitrios Eleftheropoulos; Hristos Patsatzoglou, Giorgos Amanatidis, Paraskevas Antzas, Grigoris Georgatos; LUCIANO Nunes de Souza (74 Stelios Giannakopoulos), José Elías Junior Moedim «ZÉ ELIAS» (72 Ilias Poursanidis), Predrag Djordjevic, Pär Zetterberg; GIOVANNI Silva de Oliveira, Peter Ofori-Quaye (82 Dimitrios Mavrogenidis). Trainer: Giannis Mazourakis

OLYMPIQUE: Grégory Coupet; Eric Deflandre, EDMILSON José Gomes De Moraes, Florent Laville, Jérémie Bréchet; Marc-Vivien Foé, Philippe Violeau (65 Pierre Laigle), David Linarès (65 Steed Malbranque), Vikash Dhorasoo (65 Patrick Müller); Sonny ANDERSON da Silva, Steve Marlet. Trainer: Jacques Santini

Goals: Ofori-Quaye (19), Giovanni (34), Foé (88)

SC HEERENVEEN v VALENCIA CF 0-1 (0-1)

Abe Lenstra, Heerenveen 20.09.2000

Referee: Valentin Ivanov (RUS) Attendance: 14,300

SC HEERENVEEN: Hans Vonk; Arjan Ebbinge, Ronnie Venema, Johan Hansma, Gérard de Nooijer; Arek Radomski, Daniël Jensen (82 Romano Denneboom), Harris Huizingh; Mika Nurmela, Jeffrey Talan, Anthony Lurling. Trainer: Foppe de Haan

VALENCIA: José Santiago CAÑIZARES Ruíz; Jocelyn Angloma, Mauricio Pellegrino, Miroslav Djukic, Amedeo Carboni; Gaizka MENDIETA Zabala, Didier Deschamps (10 Luis Milla), Rubén BARAJA Vegas, Cristian Alberto « KILY" GONZÁLEZ (46 VICENTE Rodríguez Guillén); Juan Gines SÁNCHEZ Moreno, DIEGO Martín ALONSO Lopez (80 John Carew). Trainer: Héctor Raúl Cuper

Goal: "Kily" González (38)

VALENCIA CF v OLYMPIQUE LYON 1-0 (0-0)

Mestalla, Valencia 27.09.2000

Referee: Stefano Braschi (ITA) Attendance: 30,529

VALENCIA: José Santiago CAÑIZARES Ruíz; Mauricio Pellegrino, Miroslav Djukic, Jocelyn Angloma, Amedeo Carboni; Gaizka MENDIETA Zabala, Rubén BARAJA Vegas, Luís MILLA Aspas (71 Zlatko Zahovic), Cristian Alberto "KILY" GONZÁLEZ (80 VICENTE Rodríguez Guillén); DIEGO Martín ALONSO Lopez (62 John Carew), Juan Gines SÁNCHEZ Moreno. Trainer: Héctor Raúl Cuper

OLYMPIQUE: Grégory Coupet; EDMILSON José Gomes De Moraes, Florent Laville, Marc-Vivien Foé, Jérémie Bréchet; David Linarès (82 Sidney Govou), Patrick Müller, Jean-Marc Chanelet, Steed Malbranque; Sonny ANDERSON da Silva, Steve Marlet. Trainer: Jacques Santini

Goal: Zahović (78)

OLYMPIAKOS PEIRAIAS v SC HEERENVEEN 2-0 (0-0)

OAKA Spiros Louis, Athina 27.09.2000

Referee: Claus Bo Larsen (DEN) Attendance: 52,000

OLYMPIAKOS: Dimitrios Eleftheropoulos; Hristos Patsatzoglou, Giorgos Amanatidis, Grigoris Georgatos, Paraskevas Antzas; LUCIANO Nunes de Souza (83 Stelios Giannakopoulos), Predrag Djordjevic, José Elías Junior Moedim «ZÉ ELIAS», Pär Zetterberg (86 Ilias Poursanidis); Peter Ofori-Quaye (89 Andreas Niniadis), GIOVANNI Silva de Oliveira. Trainer: Giannis Mazourakis

SC HEERENVEEN: Hans Vonk; Ronnie Venema, Johan Hansma, Gérard de Nooijer, Arjan Ebbinge; Arek Radomski, Daniël Jensen, Jeffrey Talan (44 Max Houttuin); Mika Nurmela, Harris Huizingh (81 Romano Denneboom), Anthony Lurling (83 Ignacio Tuhuteru). Trainer: Foppe de Haan

Goals: Giovanni (52, 69)

OLYMPIQUE LYON v VALENCIA CF 1-2 (0-1)

Municipal de Gerland, Lyon 17.10.2000

Referee: Paul Anthony Durkin (ENG) Attendance: 38,959

OLYMPIQUE: Grégory Coupet; Eric Deflandre, Florent Laville, Jérémie Bréchet, EDMILSON José Gomes De Moraes; Marc-Vivien Foé, Pierre Laigle (67 Philippe Violeau), Christophe Delmotte (46 Tony Vairelles), Steed Malbranque (67 David Linarès); Sonny ANDERSON da Sil, Steve Marlet. Trainer: Jacques Santini

VALENCIA: José Santiago CAÑIZARES Ruíz; Jocelyn Angloma, Mauricio Pellegrino, Miroslav Djukić, Amedeo Carboni; Rubén BARAJA Vegas, Zlatko Zahovic (71 David ALBELDA Aliques), Gaizka MENDIETA Zabala (61 Miguel Angel ANGULO Valderrey), Cristian Alberto «KILY» GONZÁLEZ; John Carew (81 DIEGO Martín ALONSO Lopez), Juan Gines SÁNCHEZ Moreno. Trainer: Héctor Raúl Cuper

Sent off: Foé (62)

Goals: Sánchez (45), Baraja (86), Marlet (90)

SC HEERENVEEN v OLYMPIAKOS PEIRAIAS 1-0 (0-0)

Abe Lenstra, Heerenveen 17.10.2000

Referee: Hartmut Strampe (GER) Attendance: 13,500

SC HEERENVEEN: Hans Vonk; Ronnie Venema, Godfrey Nwankpa (31 Sander van Gessel), Tieme Klompe, Gérard de Nooijer; Jeffrey Talan, Daniël Jensen, Arek Radomski; Mika Nurmela, Harris Huizingh, Anthony Lurling. Trainer: Foppe de Haan

OLYMPIAKOS: Dimitrios Eleftheropoulos; Hristos Patsatzoglou, Giorgos Amanatidis, Hristos Kontis, Grigoris Georgatos (83 Lampros Khoutos); Predrag Djordjevic, Pär Zetterberg, José Elías Junior Moedim «ZÉ ELIAS», LUCIANO Nunes de Souza (75 Giorgos Anatolakis); GIOVANNI Silva de Oliveira, Peter Ofori-Quaye. Trainer: Giannis Mazourakis

Goal: Jensen (83)

SC HEERENVEEN v OLYMPIQUE LYON 0-2 (0-0)

Abe Lenstra, Heerenveen 25.10.2000

Referee: Lucílio Cardoso Cortez Baptista (POR) Att: 14,025

SC HEERENVEEN: Hans Vonk; Ronnie Venema, Tieme Klompe, Johan Hansma, Gérard de Nooijer; Mika Nurmela, Arek Radomski (25 Sander van Gessel, 71 Romano Denneboom), Daniël Jensen, Anthony Lurling; Jeffrey Talan (68 Santi Kolk), Harris Huizingh. Trainer: Foppe de Haan

OLYMPIQUE: Grégory Coupet; Eric Deflandre, EDMILSON José Gomes De Moraes, Florent Laville, Philippe Violeau; Steve Marlet, David Linarès, Jérémie Bréchet, Tony Vairelles (83 Patrick Müller); Christophe Delmotte (60 Vikash Dhorasoo), Sonny ANDERSON da Silva (33 Steed Malbranque). Trainer: Jacques Santini

Goals: Malbranque (68), Marlet (78)

OLYMPIAKOS PEIRAIAS v VALENCIA CF 1-0 (0-0)

OAKA Spiros Louis, Athina 25.10.2000

Referee: Alfredo Trentalange (ITA) Attendance: 50,359

OLYMPIAKOS: Dimitrios Eleftheropoulos; Hristos Patsatzoglou, Hristos Kontis, Giorgos Amanatidis, Grigoris Georgatos (59 Alekos Alexandris); Predrag Djordjević, José Elías Junior Moedim «ZÉ ELIAS», Pär Zetterberg, LUCIANO Nunes de Souza (59 Stelios Giannakopoulos); GIOVANNI Silva de Oliveira, Lampros Houtos (74 Giorgos Anatolakis). Trainer: Giannis Mazourakis

VALENCIA: José Santiago CAÑIZARES Ruíz; GERARDO García León, Mauricio Pellegrino, Miroslav Djukic, Amedeo Carboni; Líbero PARRI (80 Jocelyn Angloma), Didier Deschamps, David ALBELDA Aliques (49 Luís MILLA Aspas), VICENTE Rodríguez Guillén; DIEGO Martín ALONSO Lopez (66 John Carew), Miguel Angel ANGULO Valderrey. Trainer: Héctor Raúl Cuper

Goal: Djordjević (65 pen)

OLYMPIQUE LYON v OLYMPIAKOS PEIRAIAS 1-0 (1-0)

Municipal de Gerland, Lyon 7.11.2000

Referee: Günter Benkö (AUS) Attendance: 37,908

OLYMPIQUE: Grégory Coupet; Eric Deflandre, EDMILSON José Gomes De Moraes, Florent Laville (71 Serge Blanc), Jérémie Bréchet; Marc-Vivien Foé, Philippe Violeau, Pierre Laigle, Sonny ANDERSON da Silva (85 Sidney Govou); Steve Marlet, Tony Vairelles (59 David Linarès). Trainer: Jacques Santini

OLYMPIAKOS: Dimitrios Eleftheropoulos; Giorgos Amanatidis, Paraskevas Antzas, Hristos Kontis, Hristos Patsatzoglou (75 Stelios Giannakopoulos); José Elías Junior Moedim «ZÉ ELIAS», Ilias Poursanidis (54 Dimitrios Mavrogenidis), Pär Zetterberg, Jorge Gabriel ALVEZ Fernández, GIOVANNI Silva de Oliveira (54 Peter Ofori-Quaye); Predrag Djordjević. Trainer: Giannis Mazourakis

Goal: Laigle (2)

VALENCIA CF v SC HEERENVEEN 1-1 (1-1)

Mestalla, Valencia 7.11.2000

Referee: Michel Piraux (BEL) Attendance: 19,079

VALENCIA: Andrés PALOP; Líbero PARRI (46 Juan Gines SÁNCHEZ Moreno), Joachim Björklund, Miroslav Djukic, Mauricio Pellegrino; VICENTE Rodríguez Guillén, David ALBELDA Aliques (78 John Carew), Rubén BARAJA Vegas; Miguel Angel ANGULO Valderrey, Zlatko Zahović, DIEGO Martín ALONSO Lopez. Trainer: Héctor Raúl Cuper

SC HEERENVEEN: Hans Vonk; Ronnie Venema, Johan Hansma, Arjan Ebbinge, Gérard de Nooijer; Sander van Gessel, Daniël Jensen (63 Thomas Holm), Jeffrey Talan (72 Harvey Wijngaarde); Mika Nurmela, Harris Huizingh, Anthony Lurling. Trainer: Foppe de Haan

Sent off: Ebbinge (60)

Goals: Diego Alonso (10), Venema (37)

	P	W	D	L	F	A	Pts
Valencia CF	6	4	1	1	7	4	13
Olympique Lyon	6	3	0	3	8	6	9
Olympiakos Peiraias	6	3	0	3	6	5	9
SC Heerenveen	6	1	1	4	3	9	4

FIRST STAGE – GROUP D

GLASGOW RANGERS FC v SK STURM GRAZ 5-0 (3-0)

Ibrox Park, Glasgow 12.09.2000

Referee: Lucílio Cardoso Cortez Baptista (POR) Att: 49,317

RANGERS: Stefan Klos; Claudio Reyna, Bert Konterman, Lorenzo Amoruso, Arthur Numan; Ronald de Boer (72 Neil McCann), Barry Ferguson, Jörg Albertz, Giovanni van Bronckhorst; Allan Johnston (77 Andrei Kanchelskis), Michael Mols (59 Billy Dodds). Trainer: Dick Advocaat

STURM: Josef Schicklgruber; Ramiz Mamedov, Franco Foda, Gerald Strafner, Markus Schopp; Markus Schupp, György Korsós, Andrés Fleurquin, Gilbert Prilasnig; Hannes Reinmayr (80 Imre Szabics), Sergei Yuran (80 Roman Mählich). Trainer: Ivica Osim

Goals: Mols (9), Ronald de Boer (19), Albertz (29), van Bronckhorst (72), Dodds (85)

GALATASARAY ISTANBUL v AS MONACO 3-2 (2-0)

Ali Sami Yen, Istanbul 12.09.2000

Referee: Arturo Daudén Ibáñez (SPA) Attendance: 17,905

GALATASARAY: Claudio André Taffarel; Bülent Korkmaz, Gheorghe Popescu, Carlos Alberto de Oliveira "CAPONE"; Emre Belözoglu, Okan Buruk (18 Bülent Akin), Suat Kaya, Gheorghe Hagi, Hakan Ünsal; Ümit Aydin Davala (66 Gökhan Hasan Sas), Mário JARDEL Almeida Ribeiro (90 Mandingo dos Santos MARCIO). Trainer: Mircea Lucescu

AS MONACO: Stéphane Porato; Bruno Irles, Philippe Christanval, Rafael Márquez Alvarez, Philippe Léonard (11 John Riise); Ludovic Giuly, Martin Djétou, Ousmane Dabo, Nicolas Bonnal (90 Pontus Farnerud); Shabani Nonda (78 Dado Prso), Marco Simone. Trainer: Claude Puel

Sent off: Hagi (69) and Dabo (72)

Goals: Jardel (16), Hagi (29), Nonda (50), Simone (62 pen), Capone (80)

AS MONACO v GLASGOW RANGERS FC 0-1 (0-1)

Louis II, Monaco 20.09.2000

Referee: Atanas Uzunov (BUL) Attendance: 12,000

AS MONACO: Stéphane Porato; Bruno Irles, Julien Rodríguez, Rafael Márquez Alvarez, Eric Abidal; Martin Djétou, Nicolas Bonnal (69 Xavier Gravelaine), Ludovic Giuly, John Riise (46 Dado Prso); Marco Simone, Shabani Nonda (84 Uliano Courville). Trainer: Claude Puel

RANGERS: Stefan Klos; Claudio Reyna (87 Tony Vidmar), Bert Konterman, Lorenzo Amoruso, Arthur Numan; Barry Ferguson, Tugay Kerimoglu, Ronald de Boer, Giovanni van Bronckhorst; Allan Johnston, Michael Mols (58 Neil McCann). Trainer: Dick Advocaat

Goal: van Bronckhorst (8)

SK STURM GRAZ v GALATASARAY ISTANBUL 3-0 (1-0)

Arnold Schwarzenegger, Graz 20.09.2000

Referee: René Temmink (HOL) Attendance: 15,400

STURM: Josef Schicklgruber; Günther Neukirchner, Ranko Popovic, Gilbert Prilasnig; Markus Schopp, Markus Schupp, Andrés Fleurquin, Hannes Reinmayr (71 Gerald Strafner), Mehrdad Minavand; Tomislav Kocijan (46 Ramiz Mamedov), Sergei Yuran (83 György Korsós). Trainer: Ivica Osim

GALATASARAY: Claudio André Taffarel; Carlos Alberto de Oliveira "CAPONE", Bülent Korkmaz, Gheorghe Popescu, Hakan Ünsal; Bülent Akin, Suat Kaya, Ahmet Yildirim (46 Mandingo dos Santos MARCIO), Gökhan Hasan Sas (46 Ergün Penbe); Ümit Davala (70 Faruk Atalay), Mário JARDEL Almeida Ribeiro. Trainer: Mircea Lucescu

Sent off: Suat Kaya (69)

Goals: Yuran (32), Schopp (64), Schupp (81)

GALATASARAY ISTANBUL v GLASGOW RANGERS FC 3-2 (0-0)

Ali Sami Yen, Istanbul 27.09.2000

Referee: Pierluigi Collina (ITA) Attendance: 22,030

GALATASARAY: Claudio André Taffarel; Fatih Akyel, Gheorghe Popescu, Bülent Korkmaz, Hakan Ünsal; Ümit Davala, Emre Belözoglu (76 Faruk Atalay), Gökhan Hasan Sas (90 Ahmet Yildirim), Bülent Akin, Ergün Penbe; Mário JARDEL Almeida Ribeiro. Trainer: Mircea Lucescu

RANGERS: Stefan Klos; Claudio Reyna, Bert Konterman, Lorenzo Amoruso, Arthur Numan; Barry Ferguson, Tugay Kerimoglu, Giovanni van Bronckhorst; Ronald de Boer, Michael Mols (67 Billy Dodds), Allan Johnston (59 Andrei Kanchelskis). Trainer: Dick Advocaat

Goals: Bülent Akin (51), Hakan Ünsal (57), Jardel (70), Kanchelskis (72), van Bronckhorst (90)

AS MONACO v SK STURM GRAZ 5-0 (3-0)

Louis II, Monaco 27.09.2000

Referee: Eric Romain (BEL) Attendance: 7,380

AS MONACO: Stéphane Porato; Franck Jurietti, Bruno Irles, Rafael Márquez Alvarez, David di Tommaso; Martin Djétou (74 Pontus Farnerud), Philippe Christanval, Ludovic Giuly (46 Nicolas Bonnal), Xavier Gravelaine; Shabani Nonda, Marco Simone (56 Dado Prso). Trainer: Claude Puel

STURM: Josef Schicklgruber; Franco Foda (46 Gerald Strafner), Ranko Popovic (69 Imre Szabics), Ramiz Mamedov (46 Ferdinand Feldhofer); Andrés Fleurquin, Gilbert Prilasnig, Mehrdad Minavand, Markus Schopp, György Korsós; Hannes Reinmayr, Sergei Yuran. Trainer: Ivica Osim

Goals: Simone (13, 38, 41), Farnerud (77), Nonda (84)

GLASGOW RANGERS FC v GALATASARAY ISTANBUL 0-0

Ibrox Park, Glasgow 17.10.2000

Referee: Markus Merk (GER) Attendance: 49,603

RANGERS: Stefan Klos; Bert Konterman, Sergio Porrini, Tony Vidmar (72 Scott Wilson); Jörg Albertz, Ronald de Boer, Claudio Reyna, Tugay Kerimoglu, Barry Ferguson; Andrei Kanchelskis, Peter Løvenkrands (56 Neil McCann). Trainer: Dick Advocaat

GALATASARAY: Claudio André Taffarel; Bülent Korkmaz, Gheorghe Popescu, Ümit Davala, Fatih Akyel, Hakan Ünsal; Bülent Akin, Gökhan Hasan Sas, Ergün Penbe; Mário JARDEL Almeida Ribeiro (87 Mandingo dos Santos MARCIO)., Gheorghe Hagi (72 Okan Buruk). Trainer: Mircea Lucescu

SK STURM GRAZ v AS MONACO 2-0 (1-0)

Arnold Schwarzenegger, Graz 17.10.2000

Referee: Graziano Cesari (ITA) Attendance: 15,000

STURM: Kazimierz Sidorczuk (82 Josef Schicklgruber); Günther Neukirchner, Ranko Popovic (59 Gilbert Prilasnig), Ramiz Mamedov, Markus Schopp; György Korsós, Andrés Fleurquin, Markus Schupp, Tomislav Kocijan; Hannes Reinmayr (70 Gerald Strafner), Ivica Vastic.
Trainer: Ivica Osim

AS MONACO: Stéphane Porato; Pablo Contreras, Philippe Christanval, Bruno Irles, Franck Jurietti; Martin Djétou, Marcelo Gallardo, Ludovic Giuly, Ousmane Dabo (46 Nicolas Bonnal); Marco Simone, Dado Prso (83 Wagneau Éloi).
Trainer: Claude Puel

Goals: Schopp (39, 88)

GLASGOW RANGERS FC v AS MONACO 2-2 (1-1)

Ibrox Park, Glasgow 7.11.2000

Referee: L'uboš Michel (SVK) Attendance: 50,228

RANGERS: Jesper Christiansen; Fernando Ricksen, Lorenzo Amoruso, Scott Wilson, Arthur Numan, Tony Vidmar; Barry Ferguson, Ronald de Boer (78 Rodney Wallace), Jörg Albertz (86 Neil McCan); Michael Mols (56 Tugay Kerimoglu), Kenny Miller. Trainer: Dick Advocaat

AS MONACO: Stéphane Porato; F. da Costa "COSTINHA", Pablo Contreras, Bruno Irles, Philippe Christanval; Ousmane Dabo, Nicolas Bonnal, Ludovic Giuly (69 Wagneau Éloi), Marcelo Gallardo (26 Xavier Gravelaine); Marco Simone, Shabani Nonda (57 Dado Prso). Trainer: Claude Puel

Goals: Miller (3), Costinha (39), Mols (52), Simone (78)

SK STURM GRAZ v GLASGOW RANGERS FC 2-0 (1-0)

Arnold Schwarzenegger, Graz 25.10.2000

Referee: Antonio López Nieto (SPA) Attendance: 15,400

STURM: Josef Schicklgruber; Günther Neukirchner, Ramiz Mamedov (83 Ferdinand Feldhofer), Ranko Popovic, György Korsós; Markus Schupp, Hannes Reinmayr (46 Mehrdad Minavand), Tomislav Kocijan, Gilbert Prilasnig; Sergei Yuran (65 Gerald Strafner), Andrés Fleurquin. Trainer: Ivica Osim

RANGERS: Jesper Christiansen; Lorenzo Amoruso, Bert Konterman, Sergio Porrini (78 Marco Negri), Arthur Numan; Tugay Kerimoglu, Barry Ferguson, Ronald de Boer, Giovanni van Bronckhorst (55 Neil McCann); Andrei Kanchelskis, Rodney Wallace (73 Billy Dodds). Trainer: Dick Advocaat

Sent off: Numan (85)

Goals: Yuran (20), Prilasnig (90)

AS MONACO v GALATASARAY ISTANBUL 4-2 (4-1)

Louis II, Monaco 25.10.2000

Referee: Rune Pedersen (NOR) Attendance: 10,690

AS MONACO: Stéphane Porato; Pablo Contreras, Franck Jurietti, Rafael Márquez Alvarez (42 Bruno Irles), Nicolas Bonnal; Martin Djétou, Philippe Christanval, Ludovic Giuly (63 Ousmane Dabo), Marcelo Gallardo; Shabani Nonda (66 Philippe Léonard), Marco Simone. Trainer: Claude Puel

GALATASARAY: Kerem Inan; Ümit Davala (61 Gökhan Hasan Sas), Gheorghe Popescu, Bülent Korkmaz; Hakan Ünsal, Okan Buruk, Suat Kaya (85 Mandingo dos Santos MARCIO), Carlos Alberto de Oliveira «CAPONE», Ergün Penbe; Gheorghe Hagi (42 Bülent Akin), Mário JARDEL Almeida Ribeiro. Trainer: Mircea Lucescu

Sent off: Jurietti (60), Djétou (64)

Goals: Contreras (6), Bonnal (19), Simone (22), Hakan Ünsal (24), Nonda (26), Bülent Korkmaz (63)

GALATASARAY ISTANBUL v SK STURM GRAZ 2-2 (1-0)

Ali Sami Yen, Istanbul 7.11.2000

Referee: Karl-Erik Nilsson (SWE) Attendance: 20,354

GALATASARAY: Kerem Inan; Fatih Akyel, Gheorghe Popescu, Bülent Korkmaz, Hakan Ünsal; Okan Buruk, Ergün Penbe, Emre Belözoglu, Gökhan Hasan Sas (86 Faruk Atalay); Gheorghe Hagi (67 Serkan Aykut), Mário JARDEL Almeida Ribeiro (90 Mandingo dos Santos MARCIO).
Trainer: Mircea Lucescu

STURM: Kazimierz Sidorczuk; Günther Neukirchner, Gilbert Prilasnig, Ramiz Mamedov; Markus Schopp, Markus Schupp (61 György Korsós), Hannes Reinmayr (46 Sergei Yuran), Andrés Fleurquin, Mehrdad Minavand (87 Gerald Strafner); Tomislav Kocijan, Ivica Vastic. Trainer: Ivica Osim

Sent off: Emre Belözoglu (79)

Goals: Ergün (30 pen), Yuran (64), Jardel (75), Hakan Ünsal (80 og)

	P	W	D	L	F	A	Pts
SK Sturm Graz	6	3	1	2	9	12	10
Galatasaray Istanbul	6	2	2	2	10	13	8
Glasgow Rangers FC	6	2	2	2	10	7	8
AS Monaco	6	2	1	3	13	10	7

FIRST STAGE – GROUP E

PANATHINAIKOS ATHINA
v RC DEPORTIVO LA CORUÑA 1-1 (1-0)

OAKA Spiros Louis, Athina 13.09.2000

Referee: Hugh Dallas (SCO) Attendance: 48,050

PANATHINAIKOS: Antonis Nikopolidis; PERCY Celsio OLIVARES Polanco, Leonidas Vokolos, René Henriksen, Panagiotis Fissas; Aggelos Basinas, PAULO Manuel SOUSA Carvalho (56 Karlheinz Pflipsen), Giorgos Karagounis, Bledar Kola (77 Igor Sypniewski); Nikos Limperopoulos, Krzysztof Warzycha (69 Evaggelos Koutsoures).
Trainer: Aggelos Anastasiadis

DEPORTIVO: José Francisco MOLINA Gimenez; MANUEL PABLO García Díaz, Noureddine Naybet, Enrique Fernández ROMERO, DONATO Gama da Silva; EMERSON Moisés Costa (72 Juan Carlos VALERÓN Santana), VÍCTOR Sánchez del Amo (81 Lionel Sebastián SCALONI), MAURO da SILVA Gomes, Francisco Javier González Pérez "FRAN", Walter Gerardo PANDIANI; DIEGO TRISTÁN Herrera (86 CÉSAR SAMPAIO Campos). Trainer: Javier IRURETA

Goals: Warzycha (29), Naybet (84)

HAMBURGER SV
v JUVENTUS FC TORINO 4-4 (1-2)

AOL Arena, Hamburg 13.09.2000

Referee: Vitor Manuel Melo Pereira (POR) Att: 48,500

HAMBURGER SV: Hans-Jörg Butt; Andrei Panadic, Nico-Jan Hoogma, Ingo Hertzsch, Nico Kovac; Martin Groth (27 Stig Tøfting), Bernd Hollerbach (46 Marcel Ketelaer), Rodolfo Cardoso (67 Roy Präger), Mehdi Mahdavikia, Sergei Barbarez; Anthony Yeboah. Trainer: Frank Pagelsdorf

JUVENTUS: Edwin van der Sar; Ciro Ferrara, Igor Tudor, Mark Iuliano (59 Alessandro Birindelli); Fabián O'Neill (73 Jonathan Bachini), Alessio Tacchinardi, Edgar Davids, Gianluca Pessotto, Zinedine Zidane; Filippo Inzaghi, Alessandro Del Piero (59 Darko Kovacević).
Trainer: Carlo Ancelotti

Goals: Tudor (6), Yeboah (17), Inzaghi (36, 52, 88 pen), Mahdavikia (65), Butt (72 pen), Kovac (82)

JUVENTUS FC TORINO
v PANATHINAIKOS ATHINA 2-1 (1-1)

Delle Alpi, Torino 19.09.2000

Referee: Rune Pedersen (NOR) Attendance: 35,422

JUVENTUS: Edwin van der Sar; Michele Paramatti, Igor Tudor, Ciro Ferrara, Gianluca Pessotto (46 Jonathan Bachini); Antonio Conte (60 Alessandro Birindelli), Alessio Tacchinardi, Zinedine Zidane, Edgar Davids; Filippo Inzaghi, Alessandro Del Piero (62 David Trézéguet). Trainer: Carlo Ancelotti

PANATHINAIKOS: Antonis Nikopolidis; René Henriksen, Giannis Goumas, Leonidas Vokolos, Panagiotis Fissas (87 Igor Sypniewski); PERCY Celsio OLIVARES Polanco, Giorgos Karagounis (82 Karlheinz Pflipsen), Aggelos Basinas, Bledar Kola; Krzysztof Warzycha (77 Giorgos Nasiopoulos), Nikos Limperopoulos. Trainer: Aggelos Anastasiadis

Goals: Tacchinardi (35), Goumas (45), Trézéguet (83)

RC DEPORTIVO LA CORUÑA
v HAMBURGER SV 2-1 (1-0)

Estadio Riazor, La Coruña 19.09.2000

Referee: Dick Jol (HOL) Attendance: 20,045

DEPORTIVO: José Francisco MOLINA Gimenez; MANUEL PABLO García Díaz, DONATO Gama da Silva, Noureddine Naybet, Enrique Fernández ROMERO; VÍCTOR Sánchez del Amo (82 Lionel Sebastián SCALONI), MAURO da SILVA Gomes, EMERSON Moisés Costa (63 Juan Carlos VALERÓN Santana), Francisco Javier González Pérez "FRAN"; Walter Gerardo PANDIANI, DIEGO TRISTÁN Herrera (66 José Óscar "TURU" Flores). Trainer: Javier IRURETA

HAMBURGER SV: Hans-Jörg Butt; Andrei Panadić, Nico-Jan Hoogma, Ingo Hertzsch; Stig Tøfting, Nico Kovac, Bernd Hollerbach, Sergei Barbarez (87 Andreas Fischer); Mehdi Mahdavikia, Anthony Yeboah (46 Rodolfo Cardoso), Marcel Ketelaer (46 Roy Präger). Trainer: Frank Pagelsdorf

Goals: Pandiani (44), Barbarez (53), Scaloni (90)

HAMBURGER SV
v PANATHINAIKOS ATHINA 0-1 (0-1)

AOL Arena, Hamburg 26.09.2000

Referee: Dermot Gallagher (ENG) Attendance: 44,363

HAMBURGER SV: Hans-Jörg Butt; Andrei Panadic, Nico-Jan Hoogma, Jochen Kientz (46 Marcel Ketelaer); Stig Tøfting, Nico Kovac, Rodolfo Cardoso (4 Roy Präger), Bernd Hollerbach; Mehdi Mahdavikia, Sergei Barbarez, Marek Heinz (64 Anthony Yeboah). Trainer: Frank Pagelsdorf

PANATHINAIKOS: Konstantinos Chalkias; PERCY Celsio OLIVARES Polanco, Leonidas Vokolos, René Henriksen, Panagiotis Fissas; Aggelos Basinas (86 Evaggelos Koutsoures), Giannis Goumas, Giorgos Karagounis, Fernando Galetto (73 Bledar Kola); Nikos Limperopoulos, Giorgos Nasiopoulos (58 Danijel Šaric). Trainer: Aggelos Anastasiadis

Goal: Nasiopoulos (36)

JUVENTUS FC TORINO v RC DEPORTIVO LA CORUÑA 0-0

Delle Alpi, Torino 26.09.2000

Referee: Urs Meier (SWI) Attendance: 35,733

JUVENTUS: Edwin van der Sar; Igor Tudor, Ciro Ferrara, Mark Iuliano, Alessandro Birindelli (73 Michele Paramatti); Alessio Tacchinardi (60 Antonio Conte), Edgar Davids, Gianluca Pessotto, Zinedine Zidane; Filippo Inzaghi (65 Alessandro Del Piero), David Trézéguet.
Trainer: Carlo Ancelotti

DEPORTIVO: José Francisco MOLINA Gimenez; MANUEL PABLO García Díaz, DONATO Gama da Silva, Noureddine Naybet, Enrique Fernández ROMERO; Lionel Sebastián SCALONI (80 Juan Carlos VALERÓN Santana), MAURO da SILVA Gomes, CÉSAR SAMPAIO Campos, Francisco Javier González Pérez «FRAN» (69 FERNANDO Sánchez Ciprita); Walter Gerardo PANDIANI, José Óscar «TURU» Flores (57 EMERSON Moisés Costa). Trainer: Javier IRURETA

Sent off: Zidane (68)

PANATHINAIKOS ATHINA v HAMBURGER SV 0-0

OAKA Spiros Louis, Athina 18.10.2000

Referee: Leslie Irvine (NIR) Attendance: 37,680

PANATHINAIKOS: Konstantinos Chalkias; René Henriksen, Giannis Goumas, Leonidas Vokolos, Aggelos Basinas; Fernando Galetto (71 Krzysztof Warzycha), Panagiotis Fissas, PERCY Celsio OLIVARES Polanco (61 Karlheinz Pflipsen), Giorgos Karagounis; Goran Vlaovic (81 Giorgos Nasiopoulos), Nikos Limperopoulos. Trainer: Aggelos Anastasiadis

HAMBURGER SV: Hans-Jörg Butt; Ingo Hertzsch, Nico-Jan Hoogma, Andrei Panadic; Martin Groth (62 Roy Präger), Stig Tøfting, Nico Kovac, Bernd Hollerbach (71 Marcel Ketelaer); Sergei Barbarez, Anthony Yeboah (78 Marinus Bester), Marek Heinz. Trainer: Frank Pagelsdorf

RC DEPORTIVO LA CORUÑA v JUVENTUS FC TORINO 1-1 (1-1)

Estadio Riazor, La Coruña 18.10.2000

Referee: Gilles Veissière (FRA) Attendance: 25,789

DEPORTIVO: José Francisco MOLINA Gimenez; MANUEL PABLO García Díaz, Noureddine Naybet, DONATO Gama da Silva, Enrique Fernández ROMERO; CÉSAR SAMPAIO Campos, EMERSON Moisés Costa, VÍCTOR Sánchez del Amo (87 Lionel Sebastián SCALONI), Djalma Feitosa Dias 'DJALMINHA', José Óscar «TURU» Flores (66 FERNANDO Sánchez Ciprita); Walter Gerardo PANDIANI (76 DIEGO TRISTÁN Herrera). Trainer: Javier IRURETA

JUVENTUS: Edwin van der Sar; Igor Tudor, Ciro Ferrara, Mark Iuliano; Antonio Conte, Alessio Tacchinardi (89 Alessandro Birindelli), Edgar Davids, Gianluca Pessotto; Alessandro Del Piero, Filippo Inzaghi (71 David Trézéguet), Darko Kovacevic (62 Jonathan Bachini).
Trainer: Carlo Ancelotti

Goals: Inzaghi (10), Víctor (12)

RC DEPORTIVO LA CORUÑA v PANATHINAIKOS ATHINA 1-0 (0-0)

Estadio Riazor, La Coruña 24.10.2000

Referee: Kim Milton Nielsen (DEN) Attendance: 22,326

DEPORTIVO: José Francisco MOLINA Gimenez; MANUEL PABLO García Díaz, Enrique Fernández ROMERO, Noureddine Naybet, DONATO Gama da Silva; Djalma Feitosa Dias 'DJALMINHA' (82 DIEGO TRISTÁN Herrera), EMERSON Moisés Costa, CÉSAR SAMPAIO Campos, VÍCTOR Sánchez del Amo (62 Lionel Sebastián SCALONI); José Óscar «TURU» Flores (61 FERNANDO Sánchez Ciprita), Walter Gerardo PANDIANI. Trainer: Javier IRURETA

PANATHINAIKOS: Konstantinos Chalkias (65 Antonis Nikopolidis); René Henriksen, Giannis Goumas, Leonidas Vokolos, Danijel Šaric; Fernando Galetto (46 PAULO Manuel SOUSA Carvalho), Krzysztof Warzycha, Aggelos Basinas, Panagiotis Fissas; Nikos Limperopoulos, Giorgos Karagounis (61 Bledar Kola). Trainer: Aggelos Anastasiadis

Goal: Pandiani (82)

JUVENTUS FC v HAMBURGER SV 1-3 (0-1)

Delle Alpi, Torino 24.10.2000

Referee: Stuart Dougal (SCO) Attendance: 35,209

JUVENTUS: Edwin van der Sar; Ciro Ferrara (55 Marco Zanchi), Igor Tudor, Mark Iuliano; Michele Paramatti, Gianluca Pessotto, Antonio Conte, Zinedine Zidane, Edgar Davids; Filippo Inzaghi (55 Alessandro Del Piero), David Trézéguet (55 Darko Kovacević). Trainer: Carlo Ancelotti

HAMBURGER SV: Hans-Jörg Butt; Jochen Kientz (50 Mehdi Mahdavikia), Andrei Panadic, Ingo Hertzsch, Nico-Jan Hoogma; Nico Kovac (17 Ronald Maul), Stig Tøfting, Sergei Barbarez, Anthony Yeboah; Roy Präger, Marcel Ketelaer (74 Marek Heinz). Trainer: Frank Pagelsdorf

Sent off: Zidane (29), Davids (33)

Goals: Präger (24), Yeboah (48), Kovacević (56), Panadic (62)

PANATHINAIKOS ATHINA v JUVENTUS FC TORINO 3-1 (1-1)

OAKA Spiros Louis, Athina 8.11.2000

Referee: Dick Jol (HOL) Attendance: 67,000

PANATHINAIKOS: Antonis Nikopolidis; René Henriksen, Giannis Goumas, Leonidas Vokolos; Danijel Šaric, Aggelos Basinas, PAULO Manuel SOUSA Carvalho (46 Fernando Galetto), Giorgos Karagounis (81 Igor Sypniewski), Panagiotis Fissas; Nikos Limperopoulos, Krzysztof Warzycha (75 Goran Vlaović). Trainer: Aggelos Anastasiadis

JUVENTUS: Edwin van der Sar; Ciro Ferrara, Marco Zanchi (57 Michelangelo Rampulla), Mark Iuliano; Antonio Conte, Alessio Tacchinardi, Fabián O'Neill (60 Alessandro Birindelli), Gianluca Pessotto; Alessandro Del Piero, Darko Kovacević, Filippo Inzaghi (63 David Trézéguet).
Trainer: Carlo Ancelotti

Sent off: van der Sar (56), Kovacević (68)

Goals: Paulo Sousa (7), Inzaghi (24), Basinas (58 pen), Warzycha (65)

HAMBURGER SV
v RC DEPORTIVO LA CORUÑA 1-1 (1-0)

AOL Arena, Hamburg 8.11.2000

Referee: Anders Frisk (SWE) Attendance: 48,500

HAMBURGER SV: Hans-Jörg Butt; Jochen Kientz (66 Marcel Ketelaer), Andrei Panadić, Nico-Jan Hoogma, Nico Kovac (17 Ingo Hertzsch); Stig Tøfting, Bernd Hollerbach, Sergei Barbarez, Mehdi Mahdavikia; Roy Präger, Anthony Yeboah (55 Marinus Bester). Trainer: Frank Pagelsdorf

DEPORTIVO: José Francisco MOLINA Gimenez; MANUEL PABLO García Díaz, CÉSAR Martín Villar, HÉLDER Marino Rodrigues Cristovão, Joan CAPDEVILA Méndez; EMERSON Moisés Costa (76 Luís Miguel RAMIS Monfort), DONATO Gama da Silva (46 CÉSAR SAMPAIO Campos), Lionel Sebastián SCALONI, FERNANDO Sánchez Ciprita; Juan Carlos VALERÓN Santana, Walter Gerardo PANDIANI (46 Roy Makaay). Trainer: Javier IRURETA

Goals: Mahdavikia (10), Makaay (58)

	P	W	D	L	F	A	Pts
Deportivo La Coruña	6	2	4	0	6	4	10
Panathinaikos Athina	6	2	2	2	6	5	8
Hamburger SV	6	1	3	2	9	9	6
Juventus FC Torino	6	1	3	2	9	12	6

FIRST STAGE – GROUP F

HELSINGBORGS IF
v FC BAYERN MÜNCHEN 1-3 (0-1)

Olympia, Helsingborg 13.09.2000

Referee: Graham Barber (ENG) Attendance: 12,623

HELSINGBORGS IF: Sven Andersson; Roland Nilsson, Ola Nilsson, Jozo Matovac, Nicklas Persson; Bjørn Johansen, Ulrik Jansson (77 Jesper Jansson), Stig Johansen (61 Hans Eklund), Christoffer Andersson (73 Rade Prica), Michael Hansson; ÁLVARO Marcio Santos. Trainer: Nanne Bergstrand

BAYERN: Oliver Kahn (67 Stefan Wessels); Willy Sagnol, Patrick Andersson, Samuel Kuffour, Bixente Lizarazu; Thorsten Fink, Michael Wiesinger, Ciriaco Sforza, Hasan Salihamidzic (83 Owen Hargreaves); Mehmet Scholl (65 Thomas Strunz), Carsten Jancker. Trainer: Ottmar Hitzfeld

Sent off: Kuffour (38)

Goals: Scholl (7), Salihamidzić (48), Jancker (55), Bjørn Johansen (90)

ROSENBORG BK TRONDHEIM
v PARIS SAINT-GERMAIN 3-1 (1-1)

Lerkendal, Trondheim 13.09.2000

Referee: Oguz Sarvan (TUR) Attendance: 13,721

ROSENBORG: Arni Gautur Arason; Christer Basma, Bent Inge Johnsen, Ståle Stensaas; Jan Derek Sørensen, Fredrik Winsnes, Bent Skammelsrud, Ørjan Berg, Roar Strand (78 Morten Knutsen); Frode Johnsen, Erik Hoftun. Trainer: Nils Arne Eggen

PSG: Lionel Letizi; Talal el-Karkouri, Jimmy Algerino, Frédéric Déhu, Sylvain Distin; Edouard Cissé, Laurent Robert (67 Augustine Okocha), Peter Luccin, Stéphane Dalmat; Correa Dionisio CHRISTIAN (82 Laurent Leroy), Nicolas Anelka. Trainer: Philippe Bergeroo

Goals: Christian (7), Ørjan Berg (18), Frode Johnsen (62), Skammelsrud (90 pen)

PARIS SAINT-GERMAIN
v HELSINGBORGS IF 4-1 (1-1)

Parc des Princes, Paris 19.09.2000

Referee: Hugh Dallas (SCO) Attendance: 28,303

PSG: Lionel Letizi; Jimmy Algerino, Talal el-Karkouri, Eric Rabesandratana, Bernard Mendy; Peter Luccin, Stéphane Dalmat (82 Igor Yanovski), Ali Benarbia (75 Edouard Cissé), Laurent Robert; Correa Dionisio CHRISTIAN (89 Laurent Leroy), Nicolas Anelka. Trainer: Philippe Bergeroo

HELSINGBORGS IF: Sven Andersson; Ola Nilsson, Roland Nilsson, Jozo Matovac, Nicklas Persson; Stig Johansen (82 Rade Prica), Jesper Jansson, Ulrik Jansson, Bjørn Johansen (82 Hans Eklund), Christoffer Andersson (72 Michael Hansson); ALVARO Marcio Santos. Trainer: Nanne Bergstrand

Goals: Anelka (25), Bjørn Johansen (45), Robert (63), Christian (81), El-Karkouri (90)

FC BAYERN MÜNCHEN
v ROSENBORG BK TRONDHEIM 3-1 (0-1)

Olympiastadion, München 19.09.2000

Referee: Juan Antonio Fernández Marín (SPA) Att: 20,000

BAYERN: Oliver Kahn; Willy Sagnol, Thomas Linke, Bixente Lizarazu (44 Michael Tarnat); Michael Wiesinger, Thorsten Fink, Ciriaco Sforza; Patrick Andersson (46 Roque Santa Cruz, 73 Giovane Élber), Mehmet Scholl, Carsten Jancker, Hasan Salihamidzić. Trainer: Ottmar Hitzfeld

ROSENBORG: Jørn Jamtfall; Christer Basma, Bent Inge Johnsen, Erik Hoftun, Ståle Stensaas; Fredrik Winsnes, Bent Skammelsrud, Ørjan Berg; Jan Derek Sørensen, Frode Johnsen, Roar Strand (81 Morten Knutsen). Trainer: Nils Arne Eggen

Goals: Sørensen (38), Jancker (73), Élber (77), Linke (80)

ROSENBORG BK TRONDHEIM
v HELSINGBORGS IF 6-1 (2-0)

Lerkendal, Trondheim 26.09.2000

Referee: Jan Wegereef (HOL) Attendance: 13,700

ROSENBORG: Jørn Jamtfall; Christer Basma (82 Petter Belsvik), Bent Inge Johnsen, Erik Hoftun, Ståle Stensaas; Fredrik Winsnes (87 Kenneth Storvik), Bent Skammelsrud, Ørjan Berg; Jan Derek Sørensen, Frode Johnsen, Roar Strand (75 Morten Knutsen). Trainer: Nils Arne Eggen

HELSINGBORGS IF: Sven Andersson; Marcus Lindberg (59 Christoffer Andersson), Ola Nilsson, Jozo Matovac, Nicklas Persson; Bjørn Johansen, Ulrik Jansson (36 Stig Johansen), Jesper Jansson, Hans Eklund, Michael Hansson; ALVARO Marcio Santos (70 Rade Prica). Trainer: Nanne Bergstrand

Goals: Frode Johnsen (21, 29, 79), Strand (51, 52), Stig Johansen (65 og), Prica (90)

PARIS SAINT-GERMAIN
v FC BAYERN MÜNCHEN 1-0 (0-0)

Parc des Princes, Paris 26.09.2000

Referee: Domenico Messina (ITA) Attendance: 42,009

PSG: Lionel Letizi; Jimmy Algerino, Frédéric Déhu, Eric Rabesandratana, Bernard Mendy; Stéphane Dalmat, Peter Luccin, Ali Benarbia (69 Pierre Ducrocq), Laurent Robert; Correa Dionisio CHRISTIAN (79 Laurent Leroy), Nicolas Anelka. Trainer: Philippe Bergeroo

BAYERN: Oliver Kahn; Willy Sagnol (77 Thomas Strunz), Patrick Andersson, Thomas Linke, Michael Tarnat; Michael Wiesinger (77 Roque Santa Cruz), Ciriaco Sforza, Thorsten Fink, Mehmet Scholl; Carsten Jancker (83 Giovane ÉLBER), Hasan Salihamidzić. Trainer: Ottmar Hitzfeld

Goal: Leroy (90)

HELSINGBORGS IF
v ROSENBORG BK TRONDHEIM 2-0 (1-0)

Olympia, Helsingborg 18.10.2000

Referee: Valentin Ivanov (RUS) Attendance: 12,587

HELSINGBORGS IF: Sven Andersson; Roland Nilsson, Ola Nilsson, Jozo Matovac, Nicklas Persson; Stig Johansen, Jesper Jansson, Ulrik Jansson (74 Erik Wahlstedt), Bjørn Johansen, Rade Prica (84 Christoffer Andersson); Hans Eklund (60 ALVARO Marcio Santos). Trainer: Nanne Bergstrand

ROSENBORG: Jørn Jamtfall; Christer Basma, Bent Inge Johnsen, Erik Hoftun, Ståle Stensaas; Fredrik Winsnes (88 Kenneth Storvik), Bent Skammelsrud, Ørjan Berg; Jan Derek Sørensen, Frode Johnsen (60 Petter Belsvik), Roar Strand. Trainer: Nils Arne Eggen

Sent off: Hoftun (72)

Goals: Jesper Jansson (32), Álvaro (77)

FC BAYERN MÜNCHEN
v PARIS SAINT-GERMAIN 2-0 (1-0)

Olympiastadion, München 18.10.2000

Referee: Vitor Manuel Melo Pereira (POR) Att: 33,000

BAYERN: Oliver Kahn; Willy Sagnol, Patrick Andersson, Thomas Linke (29 Jens Jeremies), Michael Tarnat; Ciriaco Sforza, Thorsten Fink, Hasan Salihamidzić, Mehmet Scholl; Roque Santa Cruz (76 PAULO SÉRGIO Silvestre do Nascimento), Carsten Jancker (58 Giovane Élber). Trainer: Ottmar Hitzfeld

PSG: Lionel Letizi; Jimmy Algerino, Eric Rabesandratana, Sylvain Distin, Bernard Mendy (71 Augustine Okocha); Frédéric Déhu, Peter Luccin (84 Edouard Cissé), Stéphane Dalmat, Laurent Robert; Correa Dionisio CHRISTIAN, Nicolas Anelka. Trainer: Philippe Bergeroo

Goals: Salihamidzić (3), Paulo Sérgio (89)

FC BAYERN MÜNCHEN v HELSINGBORGS IF 0-0

Olympiastadion, München 24.10.2000

Referee: Kyros Vassaras (GRE) Attendance: 19,000

BAYERN: Oliver Kahn; Willy Sagnol, Thomas Linke, Ciriaco Sforza, Michael Tarnat; Hasan Salihamidzic, Jens Jeremies (84 Alexander Zickler), Thorsten Fink; Carsten Jancker (67 Giovane ÉLBER), Mehmet Scholl, Roque Santa Cruz (67 PAULO SÉRGIO Silvestre do Nascimento). Trainer: Ottmar Hitzfeld

HELSINGBORGS IF: Sven Andersson; Ola Nilsson, Roland Nilsson, Jozo Matovac, Nicklas Persson (72 Rade Prica); Bjørn Johansen, Ulrik Jansson, Jesper Jansson, Stig Johansen (81 Michael Hansson), Christoffer Andersson; ÁLVARO Marcio Santos (81 Hans Eklund). Trainer: Nanne Bergstrand

PARIS SAINT-GERMAIN
v ROSENBORG BK TRONDHEIM 7-2 (4-2)

Parc des Princes, Paris 24.10.2000

Referee: José María García-Aranda Encinar (SPA) Attendance: 39,536

PSG: Lionel Letizi; Eric Rabesandratana, Jimmy Algerino, Sylvain Distin, Bernard Mendy; Peter Luccin (60 Pierre Ducrocq), Laurent Robert, Stéphane Dalmat, Frédéric Déhu; Correa Dionisio CHRISTIAN (73 Laurent Leroy), Nicolas Anelka. Trainer: Philippe Bergeroo

ROSENBORG: Jørn Jamtfall; Christer Basma, Roar Strand (71 Tor Trondsen), Bent Inge Johnsen, Ståle Stensaas (85 Robert Boateng); Ørjan Berg, Bent Skammelsrud, Fredrik Winsnes (55 Petter Belsvik); Jan Derek Sørensen, Frode Johnsen, Christer George. Trainer: Nils Arne Eggen

Goals: Déhu (16), Christian (25), Anelka (35, 90), George (36, 38), Luccin (45), Leroy (76), Robert (87 pen)

HELSINGBORGS IF v PARIS SAINT-GERMAIN 1-1 (0-1)

Olympia, Helsingborg 8.11.2000

Referee: Graham Poll (ENG) Attendance: 12,583

HELSINGBORGS IF: Sven Andersson; Roland Nilsson, Ola Nilsson, Jozo Matovac, Nicklas Persson; Stig Johansen, Jesper Jansson, Michael Hansson (66 Erik Wahlstedt), Rade Prica, Ulrik Jansson (46 Hans Eklund); ALVARO Marcio Santos (76 Mattias Lindström). Trainer: Nanne Bergstrand

PSG: Lionel Letizi; Alliou Cissé, Eric Rabesandratana, Sylvain Distin, Frédéric Déhu; Pierre Ducrocq, Augustine Okocha, Edouard Cissé, Laurent Robert (75 Igor Yanovski); Nicolas Anelka (85 Talal el-Karkouri), Laurent Leroy. Trainer: Philippe Bergeroo

Goals: Anelka (34), Persson (71)

ROSENBORG BK TRONDHEIM v FC BAYERN MÜNCHEN 1-1 (1-0)

Lerkendal, Trondheim 8.11.2000

Referee: René Temmink (HOL) Attendance: 13,965

ROSENBORG: Arni Gautur Arason; Christer Basma (86 Petter Belsvik), Bent Inge Johnsen, Erik Hoftun, Ståle Stensaas; Fredrik Winsnes, Bent Skammelsrud, Christer George (82 Roar Strand); Jan Derek Sørensen, Morten Knutsen, Frode Johnsen. Trainer: Nils Arne Eggen

BAYERN: Stefan Wessels; Willy Sagnol, Samuel Kuffour, Ciriaco Sforza, Michael Tarnat; Thorsten Fink, Stefan Effenberg (63 Jens Jeremies), Hasan Salihamidzic (63 Mehmet Scholl); Michael Wiesinger (74 Giovane ÉLBER), Alexander Zickler, Carsten Jancker. Trainer: Ottmar Hitzfeld

Goals: Frode Johnsen (27), Jeremies (88)

	P	W	D	L	F	A	Pts
FC Bayern Münich	6	3	2	1	9	4	11
Paris Saint Germain	6	3	1	2	14	9	10
Rosenborg BK	6	2	1	3	13	15	7
Helsingborgs IF	6	1	2	3	6	14	5

FIRST STAGE – GROUP G

MANCHESTER UNITED FC v RSC ANDERLECHT BRUSSEL 5-1 (3-0)

Old Trafford, Manchester 13.09.2000

Referee: Terje Hauge (NOR) Attendance: 62,749

MANCHESTER UNITED: Fabien Barthez; Gary Neville, Denis Irwin (69 Phillip Neville), Ronny Johnsen, Michaël Silvestre; David Beckham, Ryan Giggs (59 Ole Gunnar Solskjær), Roy Keane, Paul Scholes; Andy Cole (74 Dwight Yorke), Teddy Sheringham. Manager: Alex Ferguson

ANDERLECHT: Filip de Wilde; Yves Vanderhaeghe, Glen de Boeck, Lorenzo Staelens, Didier Dheedene; Bart Goor (58 Aleksandar Ilic), Walter Baseggio, Patrick van Diemen (46 Davy Oyen), Bertrand Crasson; Jan Koller, Tomasz Radzinski (59 Souleymane Youla). Trainer: Aimé Antheunis

Goals: Cole (15, 50, 72), Irwin (32 pen), Sheringham (42), Koller (55)

PSV EINDHOVEN v FC DYNAMO KYIV 2-1 (1-1)

Philips, Eindhoven 13.09.2000

Referee: Graziano Cesari (ITA) Attendance: 27,500

PSV: Ronald Waterreus; Chris van der Weerden, Yuri Nikiforov, Kevin Hofland (82 André Ooijer), Jan Heintze; CLAUDIO de Oliveira Pereira (37 Theo Lucius), Johann Vogel, Mark van Bommel, Wilfred Bouma; Arnold Bruggink (85 John de Jong), Mateja Kezman. Trainer: Eric Gerets

DYNAMO: Oleksandr Shovkovskyi; Yuri Dmitrulin, Olexander Holovko, Vladislav Vashchuk, Andriy Gusin (82 Hennadiy Moroz), Andrei Nesmachnyi; Valentin Belkevich, Oleksandr Khatskevich (74 Vladimir Kuzmichev), Kakhi Kaladze; Maxim Shatskykh (74 Serhiy Serebryannikov), Georgi Demetradze. Trainer: Valeriy Lobanovskyi

Goals: Shatskykh (6), Lucius (39), Bruggink (53)

FC DYNAMO KYIV v MANCHESTER UNITED FC 0-0

Olympiyskyi, Kyiv 19.09.2000

Referee: Kim Milton Nielsen (DEN) Attendance: 60,000

DYNAMO: Oleksandr Shovkovskyi; Andrei Nesmachnyi, Olexandr Holovko, Vladislav Vashchuk, Kakhi Kaladze; Andriy Gusin (87 Serhiy Fedorov), Oleksandr Khatskevich, Valentin Belkevich, Yuri Dmitrulin (83 László Bodnár); Maxim Shatskykh, Georgi Demetradze (68 Vladimir Kuzmichev). Trainer: Valeriy Lobanovskyi

MANCHESTER UNITED: Raimond van der Gouw; Gary Neville, Michaël Silvestre, Ronny Johnsen, Denis Irwin; David Beckham, Roy Keane, Nicky Butt; Ryan Giggs, Andy Cole (78 Ole Gunnar Solskjær), Dwight Yorke (67 Teddy Sheringham). Manager: Alex Ferguson

RSC ANDERLECHT BRUSSEL
v PSV EINDHOVEN 1-0 (0-0)

Constant van den Stock 19.09.2000

Referee: Antonio López Nieto (SPA) Attendance: 22,500

ANDERLECHT: Filip de Wilde; Bertrand Crasson, Lorenzo Staelens, Glen de Boeck, Didier Dheedene; Bart Goor, Walter Baseggio, Oleg Yashchuk (58 Alin Stoica), Yves Vanderhaeghe; Tomasz Radzinski (73 Aruna Dindane), Jan Koller.
Trainer: Aimé Antheunis

PSV: Ronald Waterreus; Jan Heintze, André Ooijer, Yuri Nikiforov, Chris van der Weerden; Dennis Rommedahl (63 Theo Lucius), Johann Vogel, Mark van Bommel; Wilfred Bouma (78 Joonas Kolkka), Arnold Bruggink (72 John de Jong), Mateja Kezman. Trainer: Eric Gerets

Goal: Dheedene (80)

FC DYNAMO KYIV
v RSC ANDERLECHT BRUSSEL 4-0 (0-0)

Olympiyskyi, Kyiv 26.09.2000

Referee: Alain Sars (FRA) Attendance: 41,000

DYNAMO: Oleksandr Shovkovsky; Andrei Nesmachnyi, Olexander Holovko, Vladislav Vashchuk, Yuri Dmitrulin; Valentin Belkevich, Kakhi Kaladze (66 Vladimir Kuzmichev), Andriy Gusin, Serhiy Fedorov (46 László Bodnár); Maxim Shatskykh, Georgi Demetradze.
Trainer: Valeriy Lobanovskyi

ANDERLECHT: Filip de Wilde; Bertrand Crasson (63 Oleg Yashchuk), Glen de Boeck (59 Alin Stoica), Lorenzo Staelens, Didier Dheedene; Yves Vanderhaeghe, Bart Goor (81 Souleymane Youla), Walter Baseggio, Patrick van Diemen; Tomasz Radzinski, Jan Koller. Trainer: Aimé Antheunis

Goals: Gusin (52), Shatskykh (82), Demetradze (89, 90)

PSV EINDHOVEN
v MANCHESTER UNITED FC 3-1 (2-1)

Philips, Eindhoven 26.09.2000

Referee: Markus Merk (GER) Attendance: 28,500

PSV: Ronald Waterreus; Jan Heintze, Yuri Nikiforov, Kevin Hofland, Chris van der Weerden; Mark van Bommel, Johann Vogel, Björn van der Doelen (77 Theo Lucius); Mateja Kezman (84 Joonas Kolkka), Arnold Bruggink, Wilfred Bouma (80 Dennis Rommedahl). Trainer: Eric Gerets

MANCHESTER UNITED: Raimond van der Gouw; Gary Neville, Michaël Silvestre (70 Ronnie Wallwork), Wesley Brown, Phillip Neville; Nicky Butt, Roy Keane, Paul Scholes (70 David Beckham); Jonathan Greening (70 Ryan Giggs), Dwight Yorke, Ole Gunnar Solskjær.
Manager: Alex Ferguson

Goals: Scholes (3 pen), Bouma (17), van Bommel (38), Kezman (64)

RSC ANDERLECHT BRUSSEL
v FC DYNAMO KYIV 4-2 (4-1)

Constant van den Stock, Brussel 18.10.2000

Referee: Herbert Fandel (GER) Attendance: 22,089

ANDERLECHT: Filip de Wilde; Bertrand Crasson, Lorenzo Staelens, Glen de Boeck, Didier Dheedene; Alin Stoica (87 Aruna Dindane), Yves Vanderhaeghe, Walter Baseggio, Bart Goor; Tomasz Radzinski, Jan Koller.
Trainer: Aimé Antheunis

DYNAMO: Oleksandr Shovkovsky; Oleksandr Khatskevich, Olexander Holovko, Vladislav Vashchuk (56 Aleksei Gerasimenko), Kakhi Kaladze; Artyom Yashkin (51 Vladimir Kuzmichev), Andriy Gusin, Valentin Belkevich, Andrei Nesmachnyi; László Bodnár, Georgi Demetradze (77 Serhiy Serebryannikov). Trainer: Valeriy Lobanovskyi

Goals: Kaladze (1), Vashchuk (10 og), Radzinski (38, 41), Stoica (45), Belkevich (87)

MANCHESTER UNITED FC
v PSV EINDHOVEN 3-1 (1-0)

Old Trafford, Manchester 18.10.2000

Referee: Juan Antonio Fernández Marín (SPA) Att: 66,313

MANCHESTER UNITED: Fabien Barthez; Gary Neville, Denis Irwin (80 Wesley Brown), Ronny Johnsen, Michaël Silvestre; David Beckham (88 Nicky Butt), Roy Keane, Paul Scholes; Ryan Giggs, Andy Cole, Teddy Sheringham (74 Dwight Yorke). Manager: Alex Ferguson

PSV: Ronald Waterreus; Jan Heintze, Chris van der Weerden, Yuri Nikiforov, Kevin Hofland; Mark van Bommel, Johann Vogel, Björn van der Doelen (73 John de Jong); Adil Ramzi (65 Joonas Kolkka), Mateja Kezman, Arnold Bruggink (29 Theo Lucius). Trainer: Eric Gerets

Goals: Sheringham (8), van Bommel (76), Scholes (82), Yorke (87)

RSC ANDERLECHT BRUSSEL
v MANCHESTER UNITED FC 2-1 (2-1)

Constant van den Stock, Brussel 24.10.2000

Referee: Stefano Braschi (ITA) Attendance: 22,506

ANDERLECHT: Filip de Wilde; Yves Vanderhaeghe, Glen de Boeck, Lorenzo Staelens, Bart Goor; Didier Dheedene, Walter Baseggio, Alin Stoica (81 Davy Oyen), Bertrand Crasson; Jan Koller, Tomasz Radzinski (90 A.Dindane).
Trainer: Aimé Antheunis

MANCHESTER UNITED: Fabien Barthez; Gary Neville, Denis Irwin (78 Ole Gunnar Solskjær), Ronny Johnsen, Michaël Silvestre (63 Wesley Brown); David Beckham, Nicky Butt, Paul Scholes; Andy Cole, Ryan Giggs, Dwight Yorke.
Manager: Alex Ferguson

Goals: Radzinski (15, 34), Irwin (36 pen)

FC DYNAMO KYIV v PSV EINDHOVEN 0-1 (0-1)

Olympiyskyi, Kyiv 24.10.2000

Referee: Konrad Plautz (AUS) Attendance: 40,000

DYNAMO: Oleksandr Shovkovsky; Oleksandr Khatskevich, Olexander Holovko, Yuri Dmitrulin, Maxim Shatskykh, Vladislav Vashchuk (19 Serhiy Fedorov); Valentin Belkevich, Andrei Nesmachnyi, Kakhi Kaladze (54 Vladimir Kuzmichev); Georgi Demetradze (74 Artyom Yashkin), Andriy Gusin. Trainer: Valeriy Lobanovskyi

PSV: Ronald Waterreus; Chris van der Weerden, Yuri Nikiforov, André Ooijer, Jan Heintze; Theo Lucius (73 Dennis Rommedahl), Mark van Bommel, Johann Vogel, Adil Ramzi; John de Jong (85 Tomasz Iwan), Mateja Kezman (90 Joonas Kolkka). Trainer: Eric Gerets

Goal: Ooijer (45)

	P	W	D	L	F	A	Pts
Anderlecht Brussel	6	4	0	2	11	14	12
Manchester United	6	3	1	2	11	7	10
PSV Eindhoven	6	3	0	3	9	9	9
Dynamo Kyiv	6	1	1	4	7	8	4

MANCHESTER UNITED FC v FC DYNAMO KYIV 1-0 (1-0)

Old Trafford, Manchester 8.11.2000

Referee: Claude Colombo (FRA) Attendance: 66,776

MANCHESTER UNITED: Fabien Barthez; Phillip Neville, Gary Neville, Wesley Brown, Denis Irwin; David Beckham, Roy Keane, Nicky Butt; Ryan Giggs (34 Quinton Fortune, 88 Michaël Silvestre), Andy Cole, Teddy Sheringham (74 Dwight Yorke). Manager: Alex Ferguson

DYNAMO: Oleksandr Shovkovsky; Andrei Nesmachnyi, Olexander Holovko (76 Serhiy Fedorov), Vladislav Vashchuk, Kakhi Kaladze; László Bodnár, Oleksandr Khatskevich, Valentin Belkevich, Aleksei Gerasimenko (62 Vladimir Kuzmichev), Vitali Lysytsky; Maxim Shatskykh (67 Georgi Demetradze). Trainer: Valeriy Lobanovskyi

Goal: Sheringham (18)

PSV EINDHOVEN v RSC ANDERLECHT BRUSSEL 2-3 (1-2)

Philips, Eindhoven 8.11.2000

Referee: Pierlugi Collina (ITA) Attendance: 33,500

PSV: Ronald Waterreus; André Ooijer, Jan Heintze, Yuri Nikiforov, Kevin Hofland; Mark van Bommel, Johann Vogel; John de Jong (38 Arnold Bruggink), Dennis Rommedahl (42 Mateja Kezman), Joonas Kolkka, Adil Ramzi (84 CLAUDIO de Oliveira Pereira). Trainer: Eric Gerets

ANDERLECHT: Filip de Wilde; Didier Dheedene, Glen de Boeck, Lorenzo Staelens, Bertrand Crasson; Bart Goor, Walter Baseggio, Alin Stoica (55 Besnik Hasi), Yves Vanderhaeghe; Tomasz Radzinski (84 Souleymane Youla), Jan Koller. Trainer: Aimé Antheunis

Sent off: Hofland (89)

Goals: Crasson (9), Koller (37), Adil Ramzi (45, 47), Youla (90)

FIRST STAGE – GROUP H

AC MILAN v BEŞIKTAŞ JK ISTANBUL 4-1 (3-1)

Giuseppe Meazza, Milano 13.09.2000

Referee: Ryszard Wójcik (POL) Attendance: 53,436

AC MILAN: Nelson de Jesus Silva "DIDA"; José Chamot, Alessandro Costacurta, Paolo Maldini; Thomas Helveg, Demetrio Albertini, Federico Giunti (85 Drazen Brncic), Francesco Coco (76 Sergio Claudio dos Santos "SERGINHO"); Luca Saudati (62 Andrés Guglielminpietro "GULY"), Oliver Bierhoff, Andrei Shevchenko. Trainer: Alberto Zaccheroni

BEŞIKTAŞ: Ike Shorunmu; Yasin Sülün (61 Mehmet Özdilek), Sead Halilagic (70 Dmitri Khlestov), Ümit Bozkurt, Erman Güraçar; Tayfur Havutçu, Miroslav Karhan, Ibrahim Üzülmez (76 Bayram Kadir Bektas), Markus Münch; Ahmet Dursun, Pascal Nouma. Trainer: Nevio Scala

Goals: Tayfur (20 pen), Coco (36), Bierhoff (44), Shevchenko (45 pen, 77)

FC BARCELONA v LEEDS UNITED 4-0 (2-0)

Camp Nou, Barcelona 13.09.2000

Referee: Markus Merk (GER) Attendance: 90,838

FC BARCELONA: Richard Dutruel; Frank de Boer, ABELARDO Fernández Antuna, SERGI Barjuán Esclusa; Phillip Cocu (54 Emmanuel Petit), RIVALDO Vitor Borbosa Ferreira (73 ALFONSO Pérez Muñoz), Marc Overmars, GERARD López Segú, SIMÃO Pedro Fonseca Sabrosa; Patrick Kluivert, Daniel García Lara "DANI" (65 Iván DE LA PEÑA). Trainer: Llorenç Serra Ferrer

LEEDS UNITED: Nigel Martyn; Gary Kelly, Ian Harte, Danny Mills, Michael Duberry; Olivier Dacourt, Lucas Radebe (90 Daniel John Hay), Lee Bowyer, Stephen McPhail (73 Anthony Hackworth); Michael Bridges, Alan Smith. Manager: David Anthony O'Leary

Goals: Rivaldo (10), Frank de Boer (20), Kluivert (75, 84)

LEEDS UNITED v AC MILAN 1-0 (0-0)

Elland Road, Leeds 19.09.2000

Referee: Günter Benkö (AUS) Attendance: 35,329

LEEDS UNITED: Nigel Martyn; Gary Kelly, Michael Duberry, Danny Mills, Ian Harte; Lee Bowyer, Dominic Matteo, Olivier Dacourt, Eirik Bakke; Michael Bridges, Alan Smith. Manager: David Anthony O'Leary

AC MILAN: Nelson de Jesus Silva "DIDA"; José Chamot, Alessandro Costacurta, Paolo Maldini; Thomas Helveg, Demetrio Albertini, Federico Giunti (90 Luca Saudati), Andrés Guglielminpietro (59 Diego De Ascentis), Francesco Coco; Andrei Shevchenko, Oliver Bierhoff.
Trainer: Alberto Zaccheroni

Goal: Bowyer (89)

BEŞIKTAŞ JK ISTANBUL v FC BARCELONA 3-0 (1-0)

Inönü, Istanbul 19.09.2000

Referee: Claude Colombo (FRA) Attendance: 20,000

BEŞIKTAŞ: Ike Shorunmu; Erman Güraçar (90 Rahim Zafer), Ümit Bozkurt, Tayfur Havutçu; Miroslav Karhan, Ahmet Dursun (81 Yasin Sülün), Nihat Kahveci, Markus Münch, Dmitri Khlestov; Ibrahim Üzülmez, Pascal Nouma (88 Fazli Ulusal). Trainer: Nevio Scala

FC BARCELONA: Richard Dutruel; Frank de Boer, ABELARDO Fernández Antuna, SERGI Barjuán Esclusa (65 ALFONSO Pérez Muñoz); Iván DE LA PEÑA, GERARD López Segú, Emmanuel Petit; SIMÃO Pedro Fonseca Sabrosa (77 Boudewijn Zenden), RIVALDO Vitor Borbosa Ferreira, Marc Overmars, Patrick Kluivert (74 Daniel García Lara "DANI").
Trainer: Llorenç Serra Ferrer

Goals: Ahmet Dursun (38, 75), Nouma (87)

FC BARCELONA v AC MILAN 0-2 (0-1)

Camp Nou, Barcelona 26.09.2000

Referee: Hellmut Krug (GER) Attendance: 98,000

FC BARCELONA: Richard Dutruel; Michael Reiziger, ABELARDO Fernández Antuna (80 Daniel García Lara «DANI»), Frank de Boer, SERGI Barjuán Esclusa; Iván DE LA PEÑA (46 LUIS ENRIQUE Martínez), Phillip Cocu, GERARD López Segú (64 Marc Overmars), SIMÃO Pedro Fonseca Sabrosa; RIVALDO Vitor Borbosa Ferreira, Patrick Kluivert.
Trainer: Llorenç Serra Ferrer

AC MILAN: Nelson de Jesus Silva "DIDA"; José Chamot, Alessandro Costacurta, Paolo Maldini, Gennaro Gattuso (90 Andrés Guglielminpietro); Federico Giunti, Massimo Ambrosini (85 Thomas Helveg), Demetrio Albertini, Francesco Coco; Andrei Shevchenko, Oliver Bierhoff (76 Gianni Comandini). Trainer: Alberto Zaccheroni

Goals: Coco (45), Bierhoff (71)

LEEDS UNITED v BEŞIKTAŞ JK ISTANBUL 6-0 (3-0)

Elland Road, Leeds 26.09.2000

Referee: V. M. Melo Pereira (POR) Attendance: 34,485

LEEDS UNITED: Nigel Martyn; Gary Kelly, Lucas Radebe, Danny Mills, Ian Harte, Dominic Matteo; Eirik Bakke, Olivier Dacourt (75 Stephen McPhail), Lee Bowyer; Alan Smith (80 Darren Huckerby), Mark Viduka.
Manager: David Anthony O'Leary

BEŞIKTAŞ: Ike Shorunmu; Miroslav Karhan, Tayfur Havutçu, Ahmet Dursun, Dmitri Khlestov; Ümit Bozkurt, Nihat Kahveci; Erman Güraçar (82 Rahim Zafer), Pascal Nouma (72 Fazli Ulusal), Markus Münch, Ibrahim Üzülmez (72 Mehmet Özdilek). Trainer: Nevio Scala

Goals: Bowyer (7, 90+), Viduka (12), Matteo (22), Bakke (65), Huckerby (90)

BEŞIKTAŞ JK ISTANBUL v LEEDS UNITED 0-0

Inönü, Istanbul 18.10.2000

Referee: Jan Wegereef (HOL) Attendance: 16,021

BEŞIKTAŞ: Ike Shorunmu; Miroslav Karhan, Tayfur Havutçu, Ali Eren Beserler (63 Murat Alaçayir), Ahmet Dursun (81 Ayhan Akman); Dmitri Khlestov, Mehmet Özdilek (81 Ibrahim Üzülmez), Markus Münch, Ümit Bozkurt; Nihat Kahveci, Yasin Sülün. Trainer: Nevio Scala

LEEDS UNITED: Paul Robinson; Gary Kelly, Ian Harte, Jonathan Woodgate, Danny Mills, Dominic Matteo; Eirik Bakke, Lee Bowyer, Jacob Burns; Mark Viduka, Michael Bridges (28 Darren Huckerby, 86 Stephen McPhail).
Manager: David Anthony O'Leary

AC MILAN v FC BARCELONA 3-3 (3-2)

Giuseppe Meazza, Milano 18.10.2000

Referee: Hugh Dallas (SCO) Attendance: 79,945

AC MILAN: Christian Abbiati; José Vitor ROQUE JUNIOR, Alessandro Costacurta, Paolo Maldini; Gennaro Gattuso, Demetrio Albertini, Massimo Ambrosini, Francesco Coco; José María Romero Poyón 'JOSÉ MARÍ' (69 Zvonimir Boban), Oliver Bierhoff, Andrei Shevchenko.
Trainer: Alberto Zaccheroni

FC BARCELONA: Richard Dutruel; Carlos PUYOL Saforcada, ABELARDO Fernández Antuna, Emmanuel Petit (29 Michael Reiziger); XAVI Hernández Creus, LUIS ENRIQUE Martínez, Phillip Cocu (46 Frank de Boer), SERGI Barjuán Esclusa, SIMÃO Pedro Fonseca Sabrosa; ALFONSO Pérez Muñoz (62 Daniel García Lara "DANI"), RIVALDO Vitor Borbosa Ferreira. Trainer: Llorenç Serra Ferrer

Goals: Albertini (14, 39), Rivaldo (19, 43, 68), José Marí (45)

BEŞIKTAŞ JK ISTANBUL v AC MILAN 0-2 (0-2)

Inönü, Istanbul 24.10.2000

Referee: Hartmut Strampe (GER) Attendance: 18,000

BEŞIKTAŞ: Ike Shorunmu; Ali Eren Beserler (46 Erman Güraçar), Ümit Bozkurt, Tayfur Havutçu, Dmitri Khlestov; Miroslav Karhan (46 Ibrahim Üzülmez), Yasin Sülün, Markus Münch, Mehmet Özdilek (72 Ayhan Akman); Nihat Kahveci, Ahmet Dursun. Trainer: Nevio Scala

AC MILAN: Nelson de Jesus Silva "DIDA"; José Vitor ROQUE JUNIOR, Alessandro Costacurta, Paolo Maldini, Gennaro Gattuso (84 Thomas Helveg); Demetrio Albertini, Massimo Ambrosini, Francesco Coco, José María Romero Poyón 'JOSÉ MARÍ' (88 Sergio Claudio dos Santos "SERGINHO"); Oliver Bierhoff (72 Zvonimir Boban), Andrei Shevchenko. Trainer: Alberto Zaccheroni

Goals: Shevchenko (38), José Marí (43)

FC BARCELONA v BEŞIKTAŞ JK ISTANBUL 5-0 (2-0)

Camp Nou, Barcelona 8.11.2000

Referee: Urs Meier (SWI) Attendance: 65,000

FC BARCELONA: Francesc ARNAU Grabalosa; Charles PUYOL Saforcada, ABELARDO Fernández Antuna, Emmanuel Petit, Xavier Hernández Creus 'XAVI' (83 Gabriel García de la Torre 'GABRI'); Phillip Cocu, SIMÃO Pedro Fonseca Sabrosa (64 GERARD López Segú), LUIS ENRIQUE Martínez Garcia, SERGI Barjuán Esclusa; RIVALDO Vitor Borbosa Ferreira, Daniel García Lara «DANI» (64 Patrick Kluivert). Trainer: Llorenç Serra Ferrer

BEŞIKTAŞ: Fevzi Tuncay; Ümit Bozkurt, Tayfur Havutçu, Ali Eren Beserler (21 Erman Güraçar); Nihat Kahveci, Yasin Sülün, Mehmet Özdilek (85 Ilhan Sahin), Ibrahim Üzülmez (78 Bayram Kadir Bektas), Markus Münch; Ayhan Akman, Ahmet Dursun. Trainer: Nevio Scala

Goals: Cocu (11), Luis Enrique (17, 49), Rivaldo (81 pen), Gabri (88)

LEEDS UNITED v FC BARCELONA 1-1 (1-0)

Elland Road, Leeds 24.10.2000

Referee: Terje Hauge (NOR) Attendance: 36,729

LEEDS UNITED: Paul Robinson; Gary Kelly, Ian Harte, Jonathan Woodgate, Danny Mills; Olivier Dacourt (75 Jacob Burns), Lee Bowyer, Eirik Bakke, Dominic Matteo; Mark Viduka, Alan Smith. Manager: David Anthony O'Leary

FC BARCELONA: Richard Dutruel; Michael Reiziger (66 GERARD López Segú), ABELARDO Fernández Antuna, Carlos PUYOL Saforcada; Phillip Cocu, SERGI Barjuán Esclusa, Xavier Hernández Creus 'XAVI', SIMÃO Pedro Fonseca Sabrosa, LUIS ENRIQUE Martínez Garcia (66 Daniel García Lara "DANI"); ALFONSO Pérez Muñoz, RIVALDO Vitor Borbosa Ferreira. Trainer: Llorenç Serra Ferrer

Goals: Bowyer (5), Rivaldo (90)

	P	W	D	L	F	A	Pts
AC Milan	6	3	2	1	12	6	11
Leeds United FC	6	2	3	1	9	6	9
FC Barcelona	6	2	2	2	13	9	8
Beşiktaş Istanbul	6	1	1	4	4	17	4

AC MILAN v LEEDS UNITED FC 1-1 (0-1)

Giuseppe Meazza, Milano 8.11.2000

Referee: Kim Milton Nielsen (DEN) Attendance: 52,289

AC MILAN: Nelson de Jesus Silva "DIDA"; José Chamot, José Vitor ROQUE JUNIOR, Paolo Maldini; Thomas Helveg, Demetrio Albertini, Gennaro Gattuso, Sergio Claudio dos Santos "SERGINHO"; LEONARDO Nascimento de Araújo (54 Zvonimir Boban), Oliver Bierhoff, Andrei Shevchenko. Trainer: Alberto Zaccheroni

LEEDS UNITED: Paul Robinson; Gary Kelly, Lucas Radebe, Danny Mills, Ian Harte; Lee Bowyer, Eirik Bakke, Olivier Dacourt, Dominic Matteo; Mark Viduka, Alan Smith. Manager: David Anthony O'Leary

Goals: Matteo (45), Serginho (68)

SECOND STAGE – GROUP A

VALENCIA CF v SK STURM GRAZ 2-0 (1-0)

Mestalla, Valencia 21.11.2000

Referee: Kim Milton Nielsen (DEN) Attendance: 26,142

VALENCIA: José Santiago CAÑIZARES Ruíz; Mauricio Pellegrino, Joachim Björklund (59 Roberto AMARILLA Nescano), Miroslav Djukić, Rubén BARAJA Vegas (90 Luís MILLA Aspas); Gaizka MENDIETA Zabala, Cristian Alberto "KILY" GONZÁLEZ (82 VICENTE Rodríguez Guillén), Jocelyn Angloma, David ALBELDA Aliques; John Carew, Juan Gines SÁNCHEZ Moreno. Trainer: Héctor Raúl Cuper

STURM: Kazimierz Sidorczuk; Günther Neukirchner, Gilbert Prilasnig, Tomislav Kocijan; Markus Schupp, Hannes Reinmayr (84 Imre Szabics), Ramiz Mamedov, Markus Schopp (78 Ferdinand Feldhofer), Mehrdad Minavand; Ivica Vastic, György Korsós. Trainer: Ivica Osim

Goals: Carew (45), Sánchez (47)

MANCHESTER UNITED FC v PANATHINAIKOS ATHINA 3-1 (0-0)

Old Trafford, Manchester 21.11.2000

Referee: Domenico Messina (ITA) Attendance: 65,024

MANCHESTER UNITED: Fabien Barthez; Gary Neville, Phillip Neville, Wesley Brown, Michaël Silvestre; David Beckham, Nicky Butt, Roy Keane, Paul Scholes; Teddy Sheringham, Dwight Yorke. Manager: Alex Ferguson

PANATHINAIKOS: Antonis Nikopolidis; René Henriksen, Fernando Galetto, Leonidas Vokolos, Panagiotis Fissas; Giannis Goumas, Krzysztof Warzycha (75 Kostas Kiassos), Igor Sypniewski (79 PERCY Celso OLIVARES Polanco), Aggelos Basinas, Giorgos Karagounis (67 Goran Vlaović); Nikos Limperopoulos. Trainer: Aggelos Anastasiadis

Goals: Sheringham (48), Karagounis (64), Scholes (81, 90)

VALENCIA CF v MANCHESTER UNITED FC 0-0

Mestalla, Valencia 14.02.2001

Referee: Dick Jol (HOL) Attendance: 45,700

VALENCIA: José Santiago CAÑIZARES Ruíz, Jocelyn Angloma, Roberto Fabián AYALA, Mauricio Pellegrino, Amedeo Carboni, Miguel Angel ANGULO Valderrey, Gaizka MENDIETA Zabala, Rubén BARAJA Vegas, Cristian Alberto "KILY" GONZÁLEZ, John Carew (75 DIEGO Martín ALONSO Lopez), Pablo César AIMAR. Trainer: Héctor Raúl Cuper

MANCHESTER UNITED: Fabien Barthez; Gary Neville, Jaap Stam., Wesley Brown, Michaël Silvestre, David Beckham (75 Nicky Butt), Roy Keane, Paul Scholes, Teddy Sheringham, Andy Cole (85 Ole Gunnar Solskjaer), Ryan Giggs. Manager: Alex Ferguson

SK STURM GRAZ v MANCHESTER UNITED FC 0-2 (0-1)

Arnold Schwarzenegger, Graz 6.12.2000

Referee: Anders Frisk (SWE) Attendance: 16,500

STURM: Kazimierz Sidorczuk; Günther Neukirchner (82 Gerald Strafner), Gilbert Prilasnig, Ramiz Mamedov (85 Roman Mählich), Ranko Popović; György Korsós (70 Hannes Reinmayr), Markus Schopp, Mehrdad Minavand, Andrés Fleurquin; Ivica Vastić, Tomislav Kocijan.
Trainer: Ivica Osim

MANCHESTER UNITED: Fabien Barthez; Gary Neville, Wesley Brown, Michaël Silvestre, Denis Irwin (89 Phillip Neville); David Beckham, Nicky Butt (80 Ryan Giggs), Roy Keane, Paul Scholes; Teddy Sheringham, Dwight Yorke (89 Ole Gunnar Solskjær). Manager: Alex Ferguson

Goals: Scholes (18), Giggs (89)

SK STURM GRAZ v PANATHINAIKOS ATHINA 2-0 (0-0)

Arnold Schwarzenegger, Graz 14.02.2001

Referee: Ryszard Wójcik (POL) Attendance: 16,500

STURM: Kazimierz Sidorczuk; Günther Neukirchner, Markus Schupp, György Korsós, Markus Schopp (79 Robert Ibersberger), Andrés Fleurquin, Gilbert Prilasnig, Mehrdad Minavand, Sergei Yuran (56 Mario Haas), Ivica Vastic, Tomislav Kocijan (90 Imre Szabics). Trainer: Ivica Osim

PANATHINAIKOS: Antonis Nikopolidis; Aggelos Basinas, Giannis Goumas (77 Giorgos Nasiopoulos), René Henriksen, Leonidas Vokolos, PERCY Celso OLIVARES Polanco (53 Derek Boateng), Danijel Šaric, Giorgos Karagounis (66 PAULO Manuel SOUSA Carvalho), Evaggelos Koutsoures, Krzysztof Warzycha, Nikos Limperopoulos.
Trainer: Aggelos Anastasiadis

Goals: Haas (60), Kocijan (85)

PANATHINAIKOS ATHINA v VALENCIA CF 0-0

OAKA Spiros Louis, Athina 6.12.2000

Referee: Markus Merk (GER) Attendance: 42,068

PANATHINAIKOS: Antonis Nikopolidis; René Henriksen, Leonidas Vokolos, Evaggelos Koutsoures (74 Igor Sypniewski), Panagiotis Fissas (64 PERCY Celso OLIVARES Polanco); Giannis Goumas, Danijel Šarić, Giorgos Karagounis, Aggelos Basinas; Krzysztof Warzycha (70 Goran Vlaović), Nikos Limperopoulos. Trainer: Aggelos Anastasiadis

VALENCIA: José Santiago CAÑIZARES Ruíz; Mauricio Pellegrino, Miroslav Djukic, Amedeo Carboni, Rubén BARAJA Vegas; Gaizka MENDIETA Zabala, Cristian Alberto "KILY" GONZÁLEZ (74 VICENTE Rodríguez Guillén), Jocelyn Angloma, David ALBELDA Aliques; Miguel Angel ANGULO Valderrey (75 Adrian Ilie), John Carew (86 DIEGO Martín ALONSO Lopez). Trainer: Héctor Raúl Cuper

PANATHINAIKOS ATHINA v SK STURM GRAZ 1-2 (0-2)

OAKA Spirs Louis, Athina 20.02.2001

Referee: Alain Sars (FRA) Attendance: 14,413

PANATHINAIKOS: Antonis Nikopolidis; René Henriksen, PERCY Celso OLIVARES Polanco, Leonidas Vokolos (54 Derek Boateng), Panagiotis Fissas (46 Danijel Šaric), Giannis Goumas, Giorgos Nasiopoulos, Aggelos Basinas, Giorgos Karagounis, Krzysztof Warzycha (70 Goran Vlaović), Nikos Limperopoulos. Trainer: Aggelos Anastasiadis

STURM: Kazimierz Sidorczuk; Günther Neukirchner, Markus Schupp, György Korsós, Markus Schopp, Gilbert Prilasnig, Mehrdad Minavand (84 Robert Ibertsberger), Andrés Fleurquin, Mario Haas (70 Imre Szabics), Ivica Vastić, Tomislav Kocijan (90 Peter Hlinka). Trainer: Ivica Osim

Goals: Schopp (25), Haas (42), Goumas (73)

MANCHESTER UNITED FC
v VALENCIA CF 1-1 (1-0)

Old Trafford, Manchester 20.02.2001

Referee: Helmut Krug (GER) Attendance: 66,715

MANCHESTER UNITED: Fabien Barthez, Gary Neville, Wesley Brown, Jaap Stam, Mikael S.Silvestre, David Beckham, Roy Keane, Paul Scholes, Ryan Giggs (18 Nicky Butt), Andy Cole, Teddy Sheringham (63 Ole Gunnar Solskjær). Manager: Alex Ferguson

VALENCIA: José Santiago CAÑIZARES Ruíz, Jocelyn Angloma, Roberto Fabián AYALA, Mauricio Pellegrino, Amedeo Carboni, Miguel Angel ANGULO Valderrey (65 Juan Gines SÁNCHEZ Moreno), Gaizka MENDIETA Zabala, Rubén BARAJA Vegas, Cristian Alberto "KILY" GONZÁLEZ (76 VICENTE Rodríguez Guillén), John Carew, Pablo César AIMAR (89 David ALBELDA Aliques). Trainer: Héctor Raúl Cuper

Goals: Cole (12), Brown (87 og)

PANATHINAIKOS FC ATHINA
v MANCHESTER UNITED FC 1-1 (1-0)

OAKA Spiros Louis, Athina 7.03.2001

Referee: K-E. Nilsson (SWE) Attendance: 27,300

PANATHINAIKOS: Antonis Nikopolidis, Giorgos Seitaridis, René Henriksen, Panagiotis Fissas, PERCY Celso OLIVARES Polanco, Giorgos Karagounis, Giannis Goumas, Derek Boateng, Aggelos Basinas (85 Karl-Heinz Pflipsen), Goran Vlaović (59 Fernando Galetto), Nikos Limperopoulos (66 Krzysztof Warzycha). Trainer: Aggelos Anastasiadis

MANCHESTER UNITED: Fabien Barthez, Gary Neville, Wesley Brown, Jaap Stam, Mikael S.Silvestre (64 Luke Chadwick), David Beckham, Roy Keane, Paul Scholes, Phillip Neville (78 Teddy Sheringham), Andy Cole (78 Ole Gunnar Solskjær), Dwight Yorke. Manager: Alex Ferguson

Goals: Seitaridis (25), Scholes (90)

SK STURM GRAZ v VALENCIA CF 0-5 (0-1)

Arnold Schwarzenegger, Graz 7.03.2001

Referee: Stefano Braschi (ITA) Attendance: 16,200

STURM: Kazimierz Sidorczuk; Gerald Strafner, Gilbert Prilasnig, György Korsós, Markus Schupp, Mehrdad Minavand (75 Jan Pieter Martens, Tomislav Kocijan (62 Imre Szabics), Robert Ibertsberger, Andrés Fleurquin (62 Ferdinand Feldhofer), Ivica Vastic, Mario Haas. Trainer: Ivica Osim

VALENCIA: José Santiago CAÑIZARES Ruíz, Jocelyn Angloma, Miroslav Djukić, Mauricio Pellegrino, Roberto Fabián AYALA, Juan Gines SÁNCHEZ Moreno, Gaizka MENDIETA Zabala (82 David ALBELDA Aliques), Didier Deschamps, Cristian Alberto "KILY" GONZÁLEZ (76 VICENTE Rodríguez Guillén), John Carew (79 DIEGO Martín ALONSO Lopez), Pablo César AIMAR. Trainer: Héctor Raúl Cuper

Sent off: Prilasnig (35)

Goals: Ayala (5), Carew (50), Kily González (52), Alonso (88, 90)

MANCHESTER UNITED FC
v SK STURM GRAZ 3-0 (2-0)

Old Trafford, Manchester 13.03.2001

Referee: Valentin Ivanov (BLS) Attendance: 66,404

MANCHESTER UNITED: Fabien Barthez ; Gary Neville, Denis Irwin, Jaap Stam, Michaël Silvestre, Nicky Butt, Roy Keane, Paul Scholes (74 Jonathan Greening), Luke Chadwick, Ole Gunnar Solskjaer, Teddy Sheringham. Manager: Alex Ferguson

STURM: Kazimierz Sidorczuk ; Günther Neukirchner, Roman Mählich (46 Peter Hlinka), Markus Schupp (65 Jan Pieter Martens), György Korsos, Markus Schopp, Mehrdad Minavand (46 Imre Szabics), Robert Ibertsberger, Andrés Fleurquin, Ivica Vastic, Mario Haas. Trainer: Ivica Osim

Goals: Butt (5), Sheringham (20), Keane (86)

VALENCIA CF
v PANATHINAIKOS FC ATHINA 2-1 (1-1)

Mestalla, Valencia 13.03.2001

Referee: Knud Erik Fisker (DEN) Attendance: 40,000

VALENCIA: José Santiago CAÑIZARES Ruíz, Jocelyn Angloma, Roberto Fabián AYALA, Miroslav Djukić, David ALBELDA Aliques (66 Pablo César AIMAR), Rubén BARAJA Vegas, Didier Deschamps (28 Joachim Björklund), Juan Gines SÁNCHEZ Moreno, VICENTE Rodríguez Guillén, Zlatko Zahović, DIEGO Martín ALONSO Lopez (70 John Carew). Trainer: Héctor Raúl Cuper

PANATHINAIKOS: Konstantinos Chalkias, Giorgos Seitaridis, Leonidas Vokolos, Panagiotis Fissas, PERCY Celso OLIVARES Polanco, Giorgos Karagounis, Giannis Goumas, Giorgos Nasiopoulos (46 Evaggelos Koutsoures), Aggelos Basinas, Goran Vlaović (57 Krzysztof Warzycha), Nikos Limperopoulos (72 Helgi Sigurdsson). Trainer: Aggelos Anastasiadis

Goals: Basinas (28 pen), Sánchez (39), Angloma (75)

	P	W	D	L	F	A	Pts
Valencia CF	6	3	3	0	10	2	12
Manchester United FC	6	3	3	0	10	3	12
SK Sturm Graz	6	2	0	4	4	13	6
Panathinaikos Athina	6	0	2	4	4	10	2

SECOND STAGE – GROUP B

PARIS SAINT-GERMAIN v RC DEPORTIVO LA CORUÑA 1-3 (1-0)

Parc des Princes, Paris 21.11.2001

Referee: Hellmut Krug (GER) Attendance: 31,890

PSG: Lionel Letizi; Peter Luccin, Correa Dionisio CHRISTIAN, Frédéric Déhu (74 Godwin Okpara), Sylvain Distin; Augustine Okocha, Laurent Robert, Jimmy Algerino, Pierre Ducrocq (74 Edouard Cissé); Laurent Leroy, Bernard Mendy (90 Grégory Paisley). Trainer: Philippe Bergeroo

DEPORTIVO: José Francisco MOLINA Gimenez; MANUEL PABLO García Díaz, Noureddine Naybet, Joan CAPDEVILA Méndez, DONATO Gama da Silva (89 HÉLDER Marino Rodrigues Cristovão); MAURO da SILVA Gomes, DIEGO TRISTÁN Herrera (62 Roy Makaay), EMERSON Moisés Costa, VÍCTOR Sánchez del Amo; José Óscar "TURU" Flores, Juan Carlos VALERÓN Santana (81 Lionel Sebastián SCALONI). Trainer: Javier IRURETA

Goals: Algerino (37), Naybet (64), Turu Flores (70), Makaay (90)

AC MILAN v GALATASARAY ISTANBUL 2-2 (0-2)

Giuseppe Meazza, Milano 21.11.2000

Referee: Urs Meier (SWI) Attendance: 46,324

AC MILAN: Christian Abbiati; Paolo Maldini, José Chamot (51 Luigi Sala), José Vitor ROQUE JUNIOR; Gennaro Gattuso, José María Romero Poyón "JOSÉ MARI", Federico Giunti, Massimo Ambrosini, Sergio Claudio dos Santos "SERGINHO"; Andrei Shevchenko, Oliver Bierhoff. Trainer: A. Zaccheroni

GALATASARAY: Kerem Inan; Vedat Inceefe, Bülent Korkmaz, Gheorghe Popescu (69 Carlos Alberto de Oliveira "CAPONE"), Fatih Akyel (77 Emre Asik); Okan Buruk, Suat Kaya (80 Ümit Davala), Gheorghe Hagi, Gökhan Hasan Sas; Mário JARDEL Almeida Ribeiro, Ergün Penbe. Trainer: Mircea Lucescu

Goals: Jardel (39), Hasan Sas (41), José Marí (47), Shevchenko (73 pen)

GALATASARAY ISTANBUL v PARIS SAINT-GERMAIN FC 1-0 (0-0)

Ali Sami Yen, Istanbul 6.12.2000

Referee: Ryszard Wójcik (POL) Attendance: 19,021

GALATASARAY: Claudio André Taffarel; Bülent Korkmaz, Emre Belözoglu (34 Ümit Davala), Fatih Akyel, Carlos Alberto de Oliveira "CAPONE"; Okan Buruk, Suat Kaya (80 Faruk Atalay), Hakan Ünsal (73 Vedat Inceefe), Ergün Penbe; Mário JARDEL Almeida Ribeiro, Gökhan Hasan Sas. Trainer: Mircea Lucescu

PSG: Lionel Letizi; Talal el-Karkouri, Peter Luccin, Eric Rabesandratana, Sylvain Distin (85 Jimmy Algerino); Laurent Robert, Stéphane Dalmat (71 Nicolas Anelka), Edouard Cissé, Pierre Ducrocq; Laurent Leroy (76 Correa Dionisio CHRISTIAN), Igor Yanovski. Trainer: Philippe Bergeroo

Goal: Ümit (51 pen)

RC DEPORTIVO LA CORUÑA v AC MILAN 0-1 (0-1)

Estadio Riazor, La Coruña 6.12.2000

Referee: Graham Poll (ENG) Attendance: 34,776

DEPORTIVO: José Francisco MOLINA Gimenez; MANUEL PABLO García Díaz, Enrique Fernández ROMERO, Noureddine Naybet, DONATO Gama da Silva; MAURO da SILVA Gomes, Djalma Feitosa Dias "DJALMINHA », EMERSON Moisés Costa (80 Lionel Sebastián SCALONI), VÍCTOR Sánchez del Amo (69 FERNANDO Sánchez Ciprita); DIEGO TRISTÁN Herrera, José Óscar "TURU" Flores (55 Roy Makaay). Trainer: Javier IRURETA

AC MILAN: Christian Abbiati; Paolo Maldini, Alessandro Costacurta, José Vitor ROQUE JUNIOR; Gennaro Gattuso, Thomas Helveg (90 Andrés Guglielminpietro), José María Romero Poyón "JOSÉ MARI" (81 Sergio Claudio dos Santos "SERGINHO"), Massimo Ambrosini, Francesco Coco; Zvonimir Boban (67 Federico Giunti), Andrei Shevchenko. Trainer: Alberto Zaccheroni

Goal: Helveg (45)

AC MILAN v PARIS SAINT-GERMAIN 1-1 (1-1)

Giuseppe Meazza, Milano 14.02.2001

Referee: Anders Frisk (SWE) Attendance: 50,043

AC MILAN: Christian Abbiati, Luigi Sala, José Vitor ROQUE JUNIOR, Paolo Maldini, Thomas Helveg, Demetrio Albertini, Federico Giunti, Sergio Claudio dos Santos "SERGINHO", Andrei Shevchenko, Oliver Bierhoff (46 I.Ba), LEONARDO de Nascimento de Araujo (77 Gianni Comandini). Trainer: Alberto Zaccheroni **Sent off**: Roque Júnior (42)

PSG: Lionel Letizi, Bernard Mendy, Alliou Cissé, Sylvain Distin, Didier Domi, Pierre Ducrocq, Frédéric Déhu, Edouard Cissé (90 Laurent Leroy), Mikel ARTETA Amatriain (69 Augustine Okocha), Ali Benarbia (57 Laurent Robert), Nicolas Anelka. Trainer: Philippe Bergeroo

Goals: Leonardo (27), Anelka (30)

GALATASARAY SK ISTANBUL v RC DEPORTIVO LA CORUÑA 1-0 (1-0)

Ali Sami Yen, Istanbul 14.02.2001

Referee: Kim Milton Nielsen (DEN) Attendance: 20,158

GALATASARAY: Claudio André TAFFAREL, HAKAN Ünsal (26 ERGÜN Penbe), BÜLENT Korkmaz, Gheorghe Popescu, FATIH Akyel, ÜMIT Davala (64 OKAN Buruk), SUAT Kaya (82 ARIF Erdem), Gheorghe Hagi, EMRE Belözoglu, HASAN Gökhan Sas, Mário JARDEL Almeida Ribeiro.

DEPORTIVO: José Francisco MOLINA Gimenez, MANUEL PABLO García Díaz, Noureddine Naybet, DONATO Gama da Silva, Enrique Fernández ROMERO, Lionel Sebastián SCALONI (55 VÍCTOR Sánchez del Amo), MAURO da SILVA Gomes, Juan Carlos VALERÓN Santana, Djalma Feitosa Dias "DJALMINHA" (78 Walter Gerardo PANDIANI), Francisco J.González Pérez "FRAN", DIEGO TRISTÁN Herrera (59 Roy Makaay). Trainer: Javier IRURETA

Goal: SUAT Kaya (11)

RC DEPORTIVO LA CORUÑA v GALATASARAY SK ISTANBUL 2-0 (1-0)

Estadio Riazor, La Coruña 20.02.2001

Referee: Hartmut Strampe (GER) Attendance: 24,055

DEPORTIVO: Jacques Songo'o, MANUEL PABLO García Díaz, Noureddine Naybet, DONATO Gama da Silva, Enrique Fernández ROMERO, VÍCTOR Sánchez del Amo (82 Lionel Sebastián SCALONI), MAURO da SILVA Gomes, Juan Carlos VALERÓN Santana, Djalma Feitosa Dias «DJALMINHA» (74 Walter Gerardo PANDIANI), Francisco J.González Pérez «FRAN» (61 Roy Makaay), DIEGO TRISTÁN Herrera.

GALATASARAY: Claudio André TAFFAREL, VEDAT Inceefe, Gheorghe Popescu, Carlos Alberto de Oliveira «CAPONE», FATIH Akyel, ERGÜN Penbe, SUAT Kaya (46 AHMET Yildirim), OKAN Buruk, Gheorghe Hagi (80 ARIF Erdem), Bülent Akin, Mário JARDEL Almeida Ribeiro (80 SERKAN Aykut). Trainer: Mircea Lucescu

Sent off: Vedat (58)

Goals: Víctor (40), Djalminha (73 pen)

PARIS SAINT-GERMAIN v AC MILAN 1-1 (0-0)

Parc des Princes, Paris 20.02.2001

Referee: Jan W. Wegereef (HOL) Attendance: 41,450

PSG: Lionel Letizi, Mikel ARTETA Amatriain, Alliou Cissé (60 Pierre Ducrocq), Sylvain Distin, Didier Domi, Laurent Leroy (86 Eric Rabesandratana), Frédéric Déhu, Edouard Cissé, Ali Benarbia (70 Peter Luccin), Nicolas Anelka, Laurent Robert. Trainer: Philippe Bergeroo

AC MILAN: Christian Abbiati, Thomas Helveg, Luigi Sala, Paolo Maldini, Gennaro Gattuso, Demetrio Albertini, Francesco Coco, Sergio Claudio dos Santos "SERGINHO" (77 José María Romero Poyón "JOSÉ MARI"), I.Ba (70 José A.Chamot), Andrei Shevchenko, LEONARDO de Nascimento de Araujo (82 Zvonimir Boban). Trainer: A. Zaccheroni

Goals: Robert (75), José Mari (90)

RC DEPORTIVO LA CORUÑA v PARIS SAINT-GERMAIN FC 4-3 (0-2)

Estadio Riazor, La Coruña 7.03.2001

Referee: Urs Meier (SWI) Attendance: 35,000

DEPORTIVO: José Francisco MOLINA Gimenez, MANUEL PABLO García Díaz, Noureddine Naybet, DONATO Gama da Silva, Enrique Fernández ROMERO, VÍCTOR Sánchez del Amo, MAURO da SILVA Gomes, Djalma Feitosa Dias «DJALMINHA», EMERSON Moisés Costa (46 Walter Gerardo PANDIANI), Francisco J.González Pérez «FRAN» (59 DIEGO TRISTÁN Herrera), Roy Makaay (85 Lionel Sebastián SCALONI). Trainer: Javier IRURETA

PSG: Lionel Letizi, Alliou Cissé, Frédéric Déhu, Sylvain Distin, Bernard Mendy, Jimmy Algerino, Mikel ARTETA Amatriain (56 Peter Luccin), Pierre Ducrocq, Augustine Okocha (74 Igor Yanovski), Ali Benarbia (62 Eric Rabesandratana), Laurent Leroy. Trainer: Philippe Bergeroo

Goals: Okocha (29), Leroy (43, 55), Pandiani (57, 76, 84), Diego Tristán (60)

GALATASARAY SK ISTANBUL v AC MILAN 2-0 (1-0)

Ali Sami Yen, Istanbul 7.03.2001

Referee: Helmut Krug (GER) Attendance: 20,000

GALATASARAY: Claudio André TAFFAREL, Carlos Alberto de Oliveira "CAPONE", BÜLENT Korkmaz (76 EMRE Asik), Gheorghe Popescu, AHMET Yildirim, OKAN Buruk, Gheorghe Hagi, ÜMIT Davala (85 ARIF Erdem), EMRE Belözoglu, HASAN Gökhan Sas, Mário JARDEL Almeida Ribeiro (88 FARUK Atalay). Trainer: Mircea Lucescu

AC MILAN: Nelson de Jesus Silva "DIDA", Luigi Sala, José A.Chamot, Paolo Maldini, I.Ba (79 José María Romero Poyón "JOSÉ MARI"), Zvonimir Boban (69 Sergio Claudio dos Santos "SERGINHO"), Federico Giunti, Pablo GARCÍA Pérez, Francesco Coco, LEONARDO de Nascimento de Araujo (54 Oliver Bierhoff), Andrei Shevchenko. Trainer: A. Zaccheroni

Goals: Hagi (20), Jardel (86)

AC MILAN v DEPORTIVO LA CORUÑA 1-1 (0-0)

Giuseppe Meazza, Milano 13.03.2001

Referee: Hugh Dallas (SCO) Attendance: 70,103

AC MILAN: Sebastiano Rossi, José Vitor ROQUE JUNIOR, Alessandro Costacurta (60 I.Ba), Paolo Maldini, Thomas Helveg, Demetrio Albertini, Zvonimir Boban (60 Oliver Bierhoff), Gennaro Ivan Gattuso, Francesco Coco (70 Sergio Claudio dos Santos "SERGINHO"), Andrei Shevchenko, José María Romero Poyón "JOSÉ MARI".
Trainer: Alberto Zaccheroni

DEPORTIVO: José Francisco MOLINA Gimenez, MANUEL PABLO García Díaz, Noureddine Naybet, DONATO Gama da Silva, Enrique Fernández ROMERO, VÍCTOR Sánchez del Amo, MAURO da SILVA Gomes (23 HÉLDER Marino Rodrigues Cristovão), Djalma Feitosa Dias "DJALMINHA", EMERSON Moisés Costa, Francisco J.González Pérez "FRAN" (64 Joan CAPDEVILA Méndez), Roy Makaay (81 Walter Gerardo PANDIANI). Trainer: Javier IRURETA

Goals: Djalminha (74 pen), Shevchenko (86 pen)

PARIS SAINT-GERMAIN FC v GALATASARAY SK ISTANBUL 2-0 (2-0)

Parc des Princes, Paris 13.03.2001

Referee: Vitor Manuel MELO PEREIRA (POR) Att: 31,254

PSG: Lionel Letizi, Jimmy Algerino, Frédéric Déhu, Sylvain Distin, Eric Rabesandratana, Pierre Ducrocq, Mikel ARTETA Amatriain (36 Ali Benarbia), Peter Luccin, Edouard Cissé, Laurent Leroy (89 Sélim Benachour), Correa Dionisio CHRISTIAN (72 Michaël Madar). **Sent off**: Ducrocq (89)
Trainer: Philippe Bergeroo

GALATASARAY: Claudio André TAFFAREL, Carlos Alberto de Oliveira "CAPONE", Gheorghe Popescu (58 FATIH Akyel), ERGÜN Penbe, AHMET Yildirim (46 FARUK Atalay), SUAT Kaya (46 Bülent Akin), ÜMIT Davala, EMRE Belözoglu, SERKAN Aykut, EMRE Asik, Mário JARDEL Almeida Ribeiro.
Trainer: Mircea Lucescu

Goals: Christian (3, 27)

	P	W	D	L	F	A	Pts
Deportivo La Coruña	6	3	1	2	10	7	10
Galatasaray Istanbul	6	3	1	2	6	6	10
AC Milan	6	1	4	1	6	7	7
Paris Saint Germain	6	1	2	3	8	10	5

SECOND STAGE – GROUP C

FC BAYERN MÜNCHEN v OLYMPIQUE LYON 1-0 (0-0)

Olympiastadion, München 22.11.2000

Referee: José María García-Aranda Encinar (SPA)
Attendance: 18,000

BAYERN: Oliver Kahn; Samuel Kuffour, Thomas Linke, Ciriaco Sforza, Michael Tarnat (75 Bixente Lizarazu); Jens Jeremies, Thorsten Fink, Stefan Effenberg, Alexander Zickler; PAULO SÉRGIO Silvestre do Nascimento, Giovane Élber (85 Carsten Jancker). Trainer: Ottmar Hitzfeld

OLYMPIQUE: Grégory Coupet; Eric Deflandre, EDMÍLSON José Gomes De Moraes, Jérémie Bréchet, David Linarès (74 Tony Vairelles); Patrick Müller, Marc-Vivien Foé, Pierre Laigle, Philippe Violeau (74 Steed Malbranque); Sonny ANDERSON da Silva, Steve Marlet (81 Sidney Govou).
Trainer: Jacques Santini

Goal: Jeremies (55)

SPARTAK MOSKVA v ARSENAL FC LONDON 4-1 (1-1)

Luzhniki, Moskva 22.11.2000

Referee: Pierluigi Collina (ITA) Attendance: 70,000

SPARTAK: Aleksandr Filimonov; Jerry Christian Tchuisse, Dmitriy Ananko (88 Evgeni Bushmanov), Yuri Kovtun; Viktor Bulatov, Yegor Titov, Dmytro Parfyonov, Artyom Bezrodnyi, Vasiliy Baranov; Luis ROBSON Pereira da Silva, Marcos Antonio Aparecido Cipriano "MARCÃO".
Trainer: Oleg Romantsev

ARSENAL: Alex Manninger; Tony Adams, Martin Keown, Nelson Vivas; Nwankwo Kanu (66 Sylvain Wiltord), Ray Parlour, Fredrik Ljungberg, Silvio Mendes "SILVINHO", Oleg Luzhny; Thierry Henry, Robert Pires (70 LAUREN Bisan Etame-Mayer). Manager: Arséne Wenger

Goals: Silvinho (2), Marcão (29, 51), Titov (77), Robson (82)

OLYMPIQUE LYON v SPARTAK MOSKVA 3-0 (3-0)

Municipal de Gerland, Lyon 5.12.2000

Referee: Juan Antonio Fernández Marín (SPA) Att: 38404

OLYMPIQUE: Grégory Coupet; Eric Deflandre, EDMILSON José Gomes De Moraes, David Linarès, Jérémie Bréchet; Philippe Violeau, Pierre Laigle, Vikash Dhorasoo (82 Steed Malbranque), Patrick Müller; Steve Marlet (89 Tony Vairelles), Sonny ANDERSON da Silva (72 Jacek Bak).
Trainer: Jacques Santini

SPARTAK: Aleksandr Filimonov; Yuri Kovtun, Jerry Christian Tchuisse, Evgeni Bushmanov (46 Aleksandr Schyogolev); Vasiliy Baranov, Viktor Bulatov, Yegor Titov, Dmytro Parfyonov, Artyom Bezrodnyi; Marcos Antonio Aparecido Cipriano «MARCÃO», Luis ROBSON Pereira da Silva (46 Maxim Kalinichenko). Trainer: Oleg Romantsev

Goals: Marlet (2), Ânderson (31, 42)

ARSENAL FC LONDON v FC BAYERN MÜNCHEN 2-2 (1-0)

Arsenal Stadium, Highbury, London 5.12.2000

Referee: Stefano Braschi (ITA) Attendance: 35,318

ARSENAL: Alex Manninger; Martin Keown, Tony Adams, Oleg Luzhny (82 LAUREN Bisan Etame-Mayer), Ashley Cole; Patrick Vieira, Fredrik Ljungberg, Gilles Grimandi; Robert Pires (77 Sylvain Wiltord), Thierry Henry, Nwankwo Kanu.
Manager: Arséne Wenger

BAYERN: Oliver Kahn; Willy Sagnol (46 PAULO SÉRGIO Silvestre do Nascimento), Samuel Kuffour, Ciriaco Sforza, Michael Tarnat, Thomas Linke; Mehmet Scholl (83 Alexander Zickler), Stefan Effenberg, Jens Jeremies; Giovane Élber, Hasan Salihamidzic. Trainer: Ottmar Hitzfeld

Goals: Henry (4), Kanu (55), Tarnat (56), Scholl (66)

FC BAYERN MÜNCHEN v SPARTAK MOSKVA 1-0 (0-0)

Olympiastadion, München 13.02.2001

Referee: Knud Erik Fisker (DEN) Attendance: 31,000

BAYERN: Oliver Kahn, Samuel Kuffour, Jens Jeremies, Thomas Linke, Mehmet Scholl (84 Willy Sagnol), Thorsten Fink, Stefan Effenberg (90 Michael Tarnat), Bixente Lizarazu, PAULO SÉRGIO Silvestre do Nascimento (65 Carsten Jancker), Giovane ÉLBER, Hasan Salihamidzić.
Trainer: Ottmar Hitzfeld

SPARTAK: Aleksandr Filimonov, Jerry Christian Tchuisse, Dmitriy Ananko, Igor Mitreski, Yuri Kovtun, Vasiliy Baranov, Yegor Titov, Viktor Bulatov, Jafar Irismetov, Luis ROBSON Pereira da Silva , Marcos Antonio Aparecido Cipriano "MARCÃO" (72 Artyom Bezrodnyi).
Trainer: Oleg Romantsev

Goal: Élber (79)

OLYMPIQUE LYONNAIS
v ARSENAL FC LONDON 0-1 (0-0)

Municipal de Gerland, Lyon 13.02.2001

Referee: Urs Meier (SWI) Attendance: 39,514

OLYMPIQUE: Grégory Coupet, Eric Deflandre, EDMILSON José Gomes De Moraes, Patrick Müller, Jérémie Brechet, Philippe Violeau (75 Steed Malbranque), Vikash Dhorasoo (75 Sidney Govou), Marc-Vivien Foé, Pierre Laigle (83 Christophe Delmotte), Steve Marlet, Sonny ANDERSON da Silva.
Trainer: Jacques Santini

ARSENAL: David Seaman, Lee Dixon, Tony Adams, Gilles Grimandi, Ashley Cole, LAUREN Bisan Etame-Mayer, Patrick Vieira, Ray Parlour, Robert Pires (69 Fredrik Ljungberg), Nwankwo Kanu (90 Nelson D.Vivas), Thierry Henry.
Manager: Arséne Wenger

Goal: Henry (59)

ARSENAL FC LONDON
v SPARTAK MOSKVA 1-0 (0-0)

Arsenal, Highbury, London 6.03.2001

Referee: Rune Pedersen (NOR) Attendance: 35,196

ARSENAL: David Seaman, Lee Dixon, Tony Adams, Gilles Grimandi, Ashley Cole, Robert Pires (71 Sylvain Wiltord), Patrick Vieira, LAUREN Bisan Etame-Mayer, Fredrik Ljungberg, Dennis Bergkamp (71 Nwankwo Kanu), Thierry Henry (90 Nelson Vivas). Manager: Arséne Wenger

SPARTAK: Aleksandr Filimonov, Yuri Kovtun, Jerry Christian Tchuisse, Igor Mitreski, Dmitri.Parfyonov, Vasiliy Baranov, Yegor Titov (54 Nikolai Pisarev), Viktor Bulatov, Jafar Irismetov, Luis ROBSON Pereira da Silva , Maxim Kalynychenko. Trainer: Oleg Romantsev

Goal: Henry (82)

ARSENAL FC LONDON
v OLYMPIQUE LYONNAIS 1-1 (1-0)

Arsenal Stadium, Highbury, London 21.02.2001

Referee: Ľuboš Michel (SVK) Attendance: 34,303

ARSENAL: David Seaman, Lee Dixon, Gilles Grimandi, Oleg Luzhnyi, Ashley Cole, Fredrik Ljungberg, Patrick Vieira, Ray Parlour, Robert Pires (80 LAUREN Bisan Etame-Mayer), Dennis Bergkamp (71 Sylvain Wiltord), Thierry Henry (83 Nwankwo Kanu). Manager: Arséne Wenger

OLYMPIQUE: Grégory Coupet, Eric Deflandre, EDMILSON José Gomes De Moraes, Patrick Müller, Jérémie Brechet, Philippe Violeau, Marc-Vivien Foé (67 David Linares), Sidney Govou (79 Patrice Loko), Pierre Laigle (67 Vikash Dhorasoo), Steve Marlet, Sonny ANDERSON da Silva.
Trainer: Jacques Santini

Goals: Bergkamp (33), Edmilson (90)

OLYMPIQUE LYONNAIS
v FC BAYERN MÜNCHEN 3-0 (2-0)

Municipal de Gerland, Lyon 6.03.2001

Referee: Dick Z.G. Jol (HOL) Attendance: 39,460

OLYMPIQUE: Grégory Coupet, Eric Deflandre, Christophe Delmotte, Claudio Roberto da Silva CAÇAPA, Jérémie Brechet, Philippe Violeau, Vikash Dhorasoo (87 Steed Malbranque), David Linares, Pierre Laigle, Sonny ANDERSON da Silva (76 Jean-Marc Chanelet), Sidney Govou (83 Patrice Loko).
Trainer: Jacques Santini

BAYERN: Oliver Kahn, Samuel Kuffour (46 Carsten Jancker), Patrick Andersson, Thomas Linke, Willy Sagnol, Jens Jeremies, Stefan Effenberg, Michael Tarnat, PAULO SÉRGIO Silvestre do Nascimento, Giovane ÉLBER, Hasan Salihamidzić (71 Mehmet Scholl). Trainer: Ottmar Hitzfeld

Goals: Govou (13, 20), Laigle (71)

SPARTAK MOSKVA
v FC BAYERN MÜNCHEN 0-3 (0-1)

Luzhniki, Moskva 21.02.2001

Referee: Antonio Jesus López Nieto (SPA) Att: 65,000

SPARTAK: Aleksandr Filimonov, Jerry Christian Tchuisse, Dmitriy Ananko, Igor Mitreski, Dmytro Parfyonov, Vasiliy Baranov (80 Artyom Bezrodnyi), Yegor Titov, Viktor Bulatov, Jafar Irismetov (69 Marcos Antonio Aparecido Cipriano "MARCÃO"), Luis ROBSON Pereira da Silva, Maxim Kalynychenko. Trainer: Oleg Romantsev

BAYERN: Oliver Kahn, Thomas Linke, Patrick Andersson, Samuel Kuffour, Willy Sagnol, Thorsten Fink (90 Owen Hargreaves), Stefan Effenberg, Bixente Lizarazu, Mehmet Scholl (82 PAULO SÉRGIO Silvestre do Nascimento), Giovane ÉLBER (82 Carsten Jancker), Hasan Salihamidzić.
Trainer: Ottmar Hitzfeld

Goals: Scholl (17, 75 pen), Paulo Sergio (87)

FC BAYERN MÜNCHEN
v ARSENAL FC LONDON 1-0 (1-0)

Olympiastadion, München 14.03.2001

Referee: Anders Frisk (SWE) Attendance: 58,000

BAYERN: Oliver Kahn, Thomas Linke, Samuel Kuffour, Patrick Andersson, Bixente Lizarazu, Hasan Salihamidzić, Thorsten Fink, Jens Jeremies, Mehmet Scholl (90 Michael Wiesinger), Giovane ÉLBER (90 Michael Tarnat), Carsten Jancker. Trainer: Ottmar Hitzfeld

ARSENAL: David Seaman, Lee Dixon, Tony Adams, Gilles Grimandi, Ashley Cole, Robert Pires (76 Silvio Mendes "SILVINHO"), Patrick Vieira, LAUREN Bisan Etame-Mayer, Fredrik Ljungberg (61 Ray Parlour), Nwankwo Kanu (61 Sylvain Wiltord), Thierry Henry. Manager: Arséne Wenger

Goal: Élber (10)

SPARTAK MOSKVA v OLYMPIQUE LYONNAIS 1-1 (1-0)

Luzhniki, Moskva 14.03.2001

Referee: Kyros Vassaras (GRE) Attendance: 10,000

SPARTAK: Aleksandr Filimonov, Yuri Kovtun, Jerry Christian Tchuisse, Igor Mitreski, Dmytro Parfyonov (53 Artyom Bezrodnyi), Vasiliy Baranov, Yegor Titov, Viktor Bulatov, Maxim Kalynychenko, Luis ROBSON Pereira da Silva (83 Jafar Irismetov), Marcos Antonio Aparecido Cipriano "MARCÃO" (75 German Lovchev). Trainer: Oleg Romantsev

OLYMPIQUE: Grégory Coupet, Christophe Delmotte (57 Sidney Govou), EDMILSON José Gomes De Moraes, Claudio Roberto da Silva CAÇAPA, Jean-Marc Chanelet, Philippe Violeau (85 Jérémie Brechet), Vikash Dhorasoo, Patrick Müller, Pierre Laigle, Steve Marlet (83 Patrice Loko), Sonny ANDERSON da Silva. Trainer: Jacques Santini

Goals: Parfyonov (4 pen), Anderson (68 pen)

RSC ANDERLECHT BRUSSEL v SS LAZIO ROMA 1-0 (0-0)

Constant van den Stock 22.11.2000

Referee: L'uboš Michel (SVK) Attendance: 21,631

ANDERLECHT: Filip de Wilde; Bertrand Crasson, Aleksandar Ilic, Olivier Doll; Alin Stoica, Didier Dheedene, Walter Baseggio, Bart Goor, Besnik Hasi; Tomasz Radzinski (90 Patrick van Diemen), Jan Koller.
Trainer: Aimé Antheunis

LAZIO: Angelo Peruzzi; Giuseppe Pancaro, Alessandro Nesta, Siniša Mihajlovic, Giuseppe Favalli; Diego Simeone, Dejan Stanković, Attilio Lombardo (62 Fabrizio Ravanelli), Pavel Nedved; José Marcelo SALAS Melinão (78 Simone Inzaghi), Hernán Crespo (62 Roberto Baronio).
Trainer: Sven-Göran Eriksson

Sent off: Stankovic (89)

Goal: Radzinski (83)

	P	W	D	L	F	A	Pts
FC Bayern München	6	4	1	1	8	5	13
Arsenal FC London	6	2	2	2	6	8	8
Olympique Lyonnais	6	2	2	2	8	4	8
Spartak Moskva	6	1	1	4	5	10	4

SECOND STAGE GROUP D

LEEDS UNITED v REAL MADRID CF 0-2 (0-0)

Elland Road, Leeds 22.11.2000

Referee: Dick Jol (HOL) Attendance: 36,794

LEEDS UNITED: Paul Robinson; Gary Kelly, Danny Mills, Jonathan Woodgate, Ian Harte, Lucas Radebe; Lee Bowyer, Jacob Burns (60 Jason Wilcox), Dominic Matteo; Alan Smith, Mark Viduka. Manager: David Anthony O'Leary

REAL: Iker CASILLAS Fernandez; ROBERTO CARLOS da Silva, GEREMI Sorele Fotso Ndjitap, Fernando Ruíz HIERRO, IVÁN CAMPO Ramos; Iván HELGUERA Bujia, Steve McManaman, Claude Makélélé, José María Gutiérrez Hernandez "GUTI" (89 Pedro MUNITIS Alvarez); Luis Filipe Madeira Caeiro "FIGO" (84 SÁVIO Bortolini Pimentel), RAÚL González Blanco. Trainer: Vicente del Bosque

Goals: Hierro (66), Raúl (68)

REAL MADRID CF v RSC ANDERLECHT BRUSSEL 4-1 (3-0)

Estadio Santiago Bernabeu, Madrid 5.12.2000

Referee: Hugh Dallas (SCO) Attendance: 54,713

REAL: Iker CASILLAS Fernandez; ROBERTO CARLOS da Silva, Fernando Ruíz HIERRO (65 FLÁVIO de CONCEIÇÃO), GEREMI Sorele Fotso Ndjitap, Aitor KARANKA de la Hoz; Iván HELGUERA Bujia, Steve McManaman, Claude Makélélé (78 Albert CELADES Lopez); Fernando MORIENTES Sánchez, Luis Filipe Madeira Caeiro "FIGO", RAÚL González Blanco (56 SÁVIO Bortolini Pimentel). Trainer: Vicente del Bosque

ANDERLECHT: Filip de Wilde; Glen de Boeck, Didier Dheedene, Bertrand Crasson, Olivier Doll; Yves Vanderhaeghe (59 Alin Stoica), Bart Goor, Patrick van Diemen, Besnik Hasi (62 Aleksandar Ilic); Jan Koller, Tomasz Radzinski.
Trainer: Aimé Antheunis

Goals: Morientes (12), Figo (23 pen), Helguera (44), Roberto Carlos (73), Stoica (89)

SS LAZIO ROMA v LEEDS UNITED 0-1 (0-0)

Stadio Olimpico, Roma 5.12.2000

Referee: Claude Colombo (FRA) Attendance: 26,502

LAZIO: Angelo Peruzzi; Giuseppe Pancaro, Alessandro Nesta, Manuel FERNANDO Silva COUTO, Giuseppe Favalli; Diego Simeone, Pavel Nedved, Juan Verón (71 Fabrizio Ravanelli), Attilio Lombardo (83 Guerino Gottardi); José Marcelo SALAS Melinão, Hernán Crespo. Trainer: Sven-Göran Eriksson

LEEDS UNITED: Paul Robinson; Gary Kelly, Lucas Radebe, Olivier Dacourt, Jonathan Woodgate; Lee Bowyer, Jason Wilcox (76 Harry Kewell), Eirik Bakke, Dominic Matteo; Mark Viduka, Alan Smith. Manager: David Anthony O'Leary

Goal: Smith (80)

LEEDS UNITED
v RSC ANDERLECHT BRUSSEL 2-1 (0-0)

Elland Road, Leeds 13.02.2001

Referee: Karl-Erik Nilsson (SWE) Attendance: 36,064

LEEDS UNITED: Nigel Martyn; Lucas Radebe, Danny Mills, Rio Ferdinand, Ian Harte, Olivier Dacourt (73 Eirik Bakke), Lee Bowyer, David Batty, Dominic Matteo (54 Harry Kewell), Alan Smith, Mark Viduka. Manager: David Anthony O'Leary

ANDERLECHT: Zvonko Milojevic; Bertrand Crasson, Glen de Boeck, Aleksandar Ilic, Didier Dheedene, Alin Stoica, Yves Vandenhaeghe, Walter Baseggio, Bart Goor, Tomasz Radzinski, Jan Koller. Trainer: Aimé Antheunis

Goals: Stoica (65), Harte (74), Bowyer (87)

REAL MADRID CF
v SS LAZIO ROMA 3-2 (1-1)

Santiago Bernabéu, Madrid 13.02.2001

Referee: Gilles Veissière (FRA) Attendance: 72,500

REAL: Iker CASILLAS Fernandez, MICHEL SALGADO Fernandez, Fernando Ruíz HIERRO, Aitor KARANKA de la Hoz, ROBERTO CARLOS da Silva, Luis Filipe Madeira Caeiro "FIGO", Claude Makélélé, Iván HELGUERA Bujia (90 Santiago H.Solari), Steve McManaman (76 José María Gutiérrez Hernandez "GUTI"), RAÚL González Blanco, Fernando MORIENTES Sánchez (66 Pedro MUNITIS Alvarez).
Trainer: Vicente del Bosque

LAZIO: Angelo Peruzzi, Paolo Negro, Manuel FERNANDO Silva COUTO, Alessandro Nesta, Giuseppe Pancaro, Lucas Castroman (60 Guerino Gottardi), Juan S.Veron (79 Roberto Baronio), Diego P. Simeone (90 Siniša Mihajlovic), Pavel Nedved, Hernán J. Crespo, José Marcelo SALAS Melinão.
Trainer: Sven-Göran Eriksson

Goals: Crespo (4), Morientes (32), Helguera (82), Gottardi (84), Figo (89 pen)

SS LAZIO ROMA v REAL MADRID CF 2-2 (1-1)

Stadio Olimpico, Roma 21.02.2001

Referee: Vitor Manuel MELO PEREIRA (POR) Att: 50,223

LAZIO: Angelo Peruzzi, Paolo Negro, Manuel FERNANDO Silva COUTO, Giuseppe Pancaro, Giuseppe Favalli, Lucas Castroman, Siniša Mihajlović (81 Roberto Baronio), Diego P.Simeone, Pavel Nedved, Hernán J.Crespo, José Marcelo SALAS Melinão (74 Simone Inzaghi).
Trainer: Sven-Göran Eriksson

REAL: Luis CÉSAR Sánchez Domínguez, MICHEL SALGADO Fernandez, Fernando Ruíz HIERRO, GEREMI Sorele Fotso Ndjitap, ROBERTO CARLOS da Silva, Luis Filipe Madeira Caeiro "FIGO" (90 Aitor KARANKA de la Hoz), Claude Makélélé, Iván HELGUERA Bujia (64 Albert CELADES Lopez), Santiago Hernán Solari, RAÚL González Blanco, José María Gutiérrez Hernandez "GUTI" (69 Pedro MUNITIS Alvarez). Trainer: Vicente del Bosque

Goals: Nedved (4), Solari (32), Crespo (53), Raúl (73)

RSC ANDERLECHT BRUSSEL
v LEEDS UNITED 1-4 (0-3)

Constant vanden Stock, Brussel 21.02.2001

Referee: Rune Pedersen (NOR) Attendance: 22,600

ANDERLECHT: Zvonko Milojevic; Aleksandar Ilic (39 Aruna Dindane), Didier Dheedene, Glen de Boeck, Bertrand Crasson, Bart Goor, Walter Baseggio, Alin Stoica, Yves Vandenhaeghe, Tomasz Radzinski, Jan Koller.
Trainer: Aimé Antheunis

LEEDS UNITED: Nigel Martyn; Ian Harte, Rio Ferdinand, Lucas Radebe, Danny Mills, Dominic Matteo, Olivier Dacourt, David Batty, Eirik Bakke, Alan Smith, Mark Viduka (83 Harry Kewell). Manager: David Anthony O'Leary

Goals: Smith (13, 38), Viduka (34), Koller (76), Harte (81 pen)

REAL MADRID CF v LEEDS UNITED 3-2 (2-1)

Santiago Bernabeu, Madrid 6.03.2001

Referee: Ryszard Wojcik (POL) Attendance: 45,000

REAL: Luis CÉSAR Sánchez Domínguez, GEREMI Sorele Fotso Ndjitap, Fernando Ruíz HIERRO, Aitor KARANKA de la Hoz, Santiago Hernán Solari, Luis Filipe Madeira Caeiro "FIGO" (90 Alberto RIVERA Pizarro), Albert CELADES Lopez, Claude Makélélé (87 SÁVIO Bortolini Pimentel), Steve McManaman, RAÚL González Blanco, Fernando MORIENTES Sánchez (76 Pedro MUNITIS Alvarez).
Trainer: Vicente del Bosque

LEEDS UNITED: Nigel Martyn, Rio Ferdinand, Lucas Radebe (65 Gary Kelly), Ian Harte, Harry Kewell, David Batty, Eirik Bakke (86 Jason Wilcox), Olivier Dacourt, Dominic Matteo, Alan Smith, Mark Viduka.
Manager: David Anthony O'Leary

Goals: Smith (6), Raúl (7, 60), Figo (41), Viduka (54)

SS LAZIO ROMA
v RSC ANDERLECHT BRUSSEL 2-1 (1-0)

Stadio Olimpico, Roma 6.03.2001

Referee: Juan Antonio Fernandez Marín (SPA) Att: 8,368

LAZIO: Luca Marchegiani; Paolo Negro, Siniša Mihajlović, Giuseppe Pancaro, Francesco Colonnese, CLAUDIO Javier LÓPEZ (78 Andrea Luciani), Roberto Baronio, Emanuele Pesaresi, Dejan Stankovic, Simone Inzaghi, Fabrizio Ravanelli.
Trainer: Sven-Göran Eriksson

ANDERLECHT: Zvonko Milojevic, Aleksandar Ilic, Yves Vanderhaeghe, Glen de Boeck, Olivier Doll, Bertrand Crasson (82 Patrick van Diemen), Bart Goor, Didier Dheedene, Besnik Hasi (80 Aruna Dindane), Jan Koller (45 Alin Stoica), Tomasz Radzinski. Trainer: Aimé Antheunis

Goals: López (40), Stoica (50), Baronio (77)

RSC ANDERLECHT BRUSSEL v REAL MADRID CF 2-0 (0-0)

Constant vanden Stock, Brussel 14.03.2001

Referee: Alain Sars (FRA) Attendance: 22,000

ANDERLECHT: Zvonko Milojevic, Aleksandar Ilic, Glen de Boeck, Olivier Doll, Bart Goor, Alin Stoica (83 Aruna Dindane), Walter Baseggio, Patrick van Diemen, Besnik Hasi (75 Yves Vanderhaeghe), Souleymane Youla (70 Jan Koller), Tomasz Radzinski. Trainer: Aimé Antheunis

REAL: Iker CASILLAS Fernandez, MICHEL SALGADO Fernandez, GEREMI Sorele Fotso Ndjitap, Iván HELGUERA Bujia, ROBERTO CARLOS da Silva (70 Santiago H.Solari), Alberto RIVERA Pizarro, Manuel SANCHÍS Hontiyuelo (88 RUBÉN González Rocha), Albert CELADES Lopez, SÁVIO Bortolini Pimentel , Pedro MUNITIS Alvarez, Fernando MORIENTES Sánchez (62 Jorge López Marco "TOTE"). Trainer: Vicente del Bosque

Goals: Dindane (85), Goor (90)

LEEDS UNITED v SS LAZIO ROMA 3-3 (2-2)

Elland Road, Leeds 14.03.2001

Referee: Konrad Plautz (AUS) Attendance: 36,741

LEEDS UNITED: Paul Robinson, Gary Kelly, Alan Maybury (90 David Batty), Ian Harte, Lee Bowyer, Danny Mills, Jason Wilcox, Jacob Burns, Dominic Matteo, Harry Kewell, Mark Viduka (64 Anthony Hackworth). Manager: David Anthony O'Leary

LAZIO: Luca Marchegiani, Francesco Colonnese, Manuel FERNANDO Silva COUTO, Sinisa Mihajlović, Emanuele Pesaresi, Lucas Castroman (89 Daniele Ruggiu), Roberto Baronio, Dejan Stanković, Pavel Nedved, CLAUDIO Javier LÓPEZ (73 I.Marcelo SALAS Melinão), Fabrizio Ravanelli Trainer: Sven-Göran Eriksson

Goals: Ravanelli (21), Bowyer (28), Mihajlović (29 pen, 90), Wilcox (43), Viduka (62)

	P	W	D	L	F	A	Pts
Real Madrid CF	6	4	1	1	14	9	13
Leeds United FC	6	3	1	2	12	10	10
RSC Anderlecht Brussel	6	2	0	4	7	12	6
SS Lazio Roma	6	1	2	3	9	11	5

QUARTER-FINALS

MANCHESTER UNITED FC v FC BAYERN MÜNCHEN 0-1 (0-0)

Old Trafford, Manchester 3.04.2001

Referee: Antonio Jesus López Nieto (SPA) Att: 66,584

MANCHESTER UNITED: Fabien Barthez, Gary Neville, Wesley Brown, Jaap Stam, Mikael S.Silvestre, David Beckham (86 Dwight Yorke), Roy Keane, Paul Scholes, Ryan Giggs, Andy Cole, Ole Gunnar Solskjær. Manager: Alex Ferguson

BAYERN: Oliver Kahn, Thomas Linke, Patrick Andersson, Samuel Kuffour, Hasan Salihamidzić, Stefan Effenberg, Jens Jeremies, Mehmet Scholl (77 PAULO SÉRGIO Silvestre do Nascimento), Bixente Lizarazu, Giovane ÉLBER, Carsten Jancker (69 Alexander Zickler). Trainer: Ottmar Hitzfeld

Goal: Paulo Sergio (86)

FC BAYERN MÜNCHEN v MANCHESTER UNITED FC 2-1 (2-0)

Olympiastadion, München 18.04.2001

Referee: Vitor Manuel Melo Pereira (POR) Att: 60,000

BAYERN: Oliver Kahn, Thomas Linke, Patrick Andersson, Samuel Kuffour, Willy Sagnol, Jens Jeremies, Stefan Effenberg, Michael Tarnat, Giovane ÉLBER (64 Roque Santa Cruz), Carsten Jancker (35 Alexander Zickler), Mehmet Scholl (88 PAULO SÉRGIO Silvestre do Nascimento). Trainer: Ottmar Hitzfeld

MANCHESTER UNITED: Fabien Barthez, Gary Neville, Jaap Stam, Wesley Brown (85 Luke Chadwick), Mikael S.Silvestre, Paul Scholes, Roy Keane, Nicky Butt (78 Ole Gunnar Solskjær), Ryan Giggs, Andy Cole, Dwight Yorke (66 Teddy Sheringham). Manager: Alex Ferguson

Goals: Élber (5), Scholl (40), Giggs (49)

GALATASARAY SK ISTANBUL v REAL MADRID CF 3-2 (0-2)

Ali Sami Yen, Istanbul 3.04.2001

Referee: Pierluigi Collina (ITA) Attendance: 21,000

GALATASARAY: Claudio André TAFFAREL , Carlos Alberto de Oliveira "CAPONE" (46 FATIH Akyel), BÜLENT Korkmaz, Gheorghe Popescu, ERGÜN Penbe, OKAN Buruk, SUAT Kaya (46 Bülent Akin), Gheorghe Hagi, ÜMIT Davala, HASAN Gökhan Sas, Mário JARDEL Almeida Ribeiro. Trainer: Mircea Lucescu

REAL: Iker CASILLAS Fernandez, MICHEL SALGADO Fernandez, Fernando Ruíz HIERRO, Aitor KARANKA de la Hoz, ROBERTO CARLOS da Silva, Luis Filipe Madeira Caeiro "FIGO", Claude Makélélé (62 Albert CELADES Lopez), Iván HELGUERA Bujia, Steve McManaman (89 Santiago Hernán Solari), RAÚL González Blanco, Fernando MORIENTES Sánchez (69 José María Gutiérrez Hernandez "GUTI"). Trainer: Vicente del Bosque

Goals: Helguera (33), Makélélé (43), Ümit (47 pen), Hasan Şaş (66), Jardel (75)

REAL MADRID CF v GALATASARAY SK ISTANBUL 3-0 (3-0)

Santiago Bernabéu, Madrid 18.04.2001

Referee: Anders Frisk (SWE) Attendance: 81,000

REAL: Iker CASILLAS Fernandez, MICHEL SALGADO Fernandez, Fernando Ruíz HIERRO, Aitor KARANKA de la Hoz, ROBERTO CARLOS da Silva (90 Santiago Hernán Solari), Luis Filipe Madeira Caeiro "FIGO" (86 SÁVIO Bortolini Pimentel), Claude Makélélé, Iván HELGUERA Bujia, Steve McManaman, RAÚL González Blanco, José María Gutiérrez Hernandez "GUTI" (75 FLÁVIO de CONCEIÇÃO). Trainer: Vicente del Bosque

GALATASARAY: Claudio André TAFFAREL, ÜMIT Davala, BÜLENT Korkmaz, FATIH Akyel, EMRE Asik, OKAN Buruk, SUAT Kaya (46 Bülent Akin), Gheorghe Hagi, EMRE Belözoglu, HASAN Gökhan Sas (67 ARIF Erdem), Mário JARDEL Almeida Ribeiro. Trainer: Mircea Lucescu

Goals: Raúl (15, 37), Helguera (28)

LEEDS UNITED FC v RC DEPORTIVO LA CORUÑA 3-0 (1-0)

Elland Road, Leeds 4.04.2001

Referee: Gilles Veissière (FRA) Attendance: 35,508

LEEDS UNITED: Nigel Martyn, Danny Mills, Dominic Matteo, Rio Ferdinand, Ian Harte, Lee Bowyer, David Batty, Olivier Dacourt, Harry Kewell (84 Jason Wilcox), Alan Smith, Mark Viduka. Manager: David Anthony O'Leary

DEPORTIVO: José Francisco MOLINA Gimenez, MANUEL PABLO García Díaz, Noureddine Naybet, CÉSAR Martín Villar, Enrique Fernández ROMERO, Lionel Sebastián SCALONI (71 DIEGO TRISTÁN Herrera), Djalma Feitosa Dias "DJALMINHA", EMERSON Moisés Costa, Aldo Pedro DUSCHER (54 Juan Carlos VALERÓN Santana), Francisco J.González Pérez "FRAN" (71 Walter Gerardo PANDIANI), Roy Makaay. Trainer: Javier IRURETA

Goals: Harte (26), Smith (51), Ferdinand (66)

RC DEPORTIVO LA CORUÑA v LEEDS UNITED FC 2-0 (1-0)

Estadio Riazor, La Coruña 17.04.2001

Referee: Stefano Braschi (ITA) Attendance: 35,600

DEPORTIVO: José Francisco MOLINA Gimenez, MANUEL PABLO García Díaz, Noureddine Naybet, DONATO Gama da Silva, Enrique Fernández ROMERO, VÍCTOR Sánchez del Amo (62 DIEGO TRISTÁN Herrera), MAURO da SILVA Gomes, Djalma Feitosa Dias «DJALMINHA» (69 Juan Carlos VALERÓN Santana), Francisco J.González Pérez «FRAN», Roy Makaay, Walter Gerardo PANDIANI (79 José Óscar «TURU» Flores). Trainer: Javier IRURETA

LEEDS UNITED: Nigel Martyn, Danny Mills, Dominic Matteo, Rio Ferdinand, Ian Harte, Lee Bowyer, David Batty, Olivier Dacourt, Harry Kewell (78 Eirik Bakke), Alan Smith, Mark Viduka. Manager: David Anthony O'Leary

Goals: Djalminha (9 pen), Diego Tristán (73)

ARSENAL FC LONDON v VALENCIA CF 2-1 (0-1)

Arsenal, Highbury London 4.04.2001

Referee: Dick Z.G.Jol (HOL) Attendance: 35,104

ARSENAL: David Seaman, Lee Dixon, Martin Keown, Tony Adams, Ashley Cole, Fredrik Ljungberg (46 Sylvain Wiltord), Patrick Vieira, Ray Parlour, Robert Pires, Nwankwo Kanu (84 LAUREN Bisan Etame-Mayer), Thierry Henry. Manager: Arséne Wenger

VALENCIA: José Santiago CAÑIZARES Ruíz, Jocelyn Angloma, Roberto Fabián AYALA, Mauricio Pellegrino, Amedeo Carboni, Gaizka MENDIETA Zabala (89 VICENTE Rodríguez Guillén), Rubén BARAJA Vegas, Pablo César AIMAR (68 Miguel Angel ANGULO Valderrey), Cristian Alberto "KILY" GONZÁLEZ, Juan Gines SÁNCHEZ Moreno, John Carew. Trainer: Héctor Raúl Cuper

Goals: Ayala (41), Henry (58), Parlour (60)

VALENCIA CF v ARSENAL FC LONDON 1-0 (0-0)

Mestalla, Valencia 17.04.2001

Referee: Kim Milton Nielsen (DEN) Attendance: 41,441

VALENCIA: José Santiago CAÑIZARES Ruíz, Jocelyn Angloma, Roberto Fabián AYALA (50 Miroslav Djukić), Mauricio Pellegrino, Amedeo Carboni, Miguel Angel ANGULO Valderrey (67 Pablo César AIMAR (ARG)), Gaizka MENDIETA Zabala, Rubén BARAJA Vegas, VICENTE Rodríguez Guillén, Juan Gines SÁNCHEZ Moreno (72 Zlatko Zahović), John Carew. Trainer: Héctor Raúl Cuper

ARSENAL: David Seaman, Lee Dixon, Martin Keown, Tony Adams, Ashley Cole, LAUREN Bisan Etame-Mayer, Patrick Vieira, Ray Parlour (46 Fredrik Ljungberg), Robert Pires (77 Nwankwo Kanu), Sylvain Wiltord, Thierry Henry. Manager: Arséne Wenger

Goal: Carew (76)

SEMI-FINALS

REAL MADRID CF v FC BAYERN MÜNCHEN 0-1 (0-0)

Santiago Bernabéu, Madrid 1.05.2001

Referee: Anders Frisk (SWE) Attendance: 75,600

REAL: Iker CASILLAS Fernandez, MICHEL SALGADO Fernandez (77 Pedro MUNITIS Alvarez), Fernando Ruíz HIERRO, Aitor KARANKA de la Hoz, ROBERTO CARLOS da Silva, Luis Filipe Madeira Caeiro "FIGO", Claude Makélélé, Iván HELGUERA Bujia, Steve McManaman, RAÚL González Blanco, José María Gutiérrez Hernandez "GUTI" (55 SÁVIO Bortolini Pimentel). Trainer: Vicente del Bosque

BAYERN: Oliver Kahn, Samuel Kuffour, Patrick Andersson, Thomas Linke, Willy Sagnol, Jens Jeremies, Stefan Effenberg, Bixente Lizarazu, Hasan Salihamidzić, Mehmet Scholl (72 PAULO SÉRGIO Silvestre do Nascimento), Giovane ÉLBER (74 Carsten Jancker). Trainer: Ottmar Hitzfeld

Goal: Élber (55)

FC BAYERN MÜNCHEN v REAL MADRID CF 2-1 (2-1)

Olympiastadion, München 9.05.2001

Referee: Kim Milton Nielsen (DEN) Attendance: 60,000

BAYERN: Oliver Kahn, Samuel Kuffour, Patrick Andersson, Thomas Linke, Willy Sagnol, Jens Jeremies (70 Ciriaco Sforza), Owen Hargreaves, Bixente Lizarazu, Hasan Salihamidzić, Giovane ÉLBER (86 Alexander Zickler), Mehmet Scholl (59 Roque Santa Cruz). Trainer: Ottmar Hitzfeld

REAL: Iker CASILLAS Fernandez, MICHEL SALGADO Fernandez, Fernando Ruíz HIERRO, Aitor KARANKA de la Hoz (66 Fernando MORIENTES Sánchez), ROBERTO CARLOS da Silva, Luis Filipe Madeira Caeiro "FIGO", Claude Makélélé, Iván HELGUERA Bujia, Steve McManaman (61 SÁVIO Bortolini Pimentel), RAÚL González Blanco, José María Gutiérrez Hernandez "GUTI".
Trainer: Vicente del Bosque

Goals: Élber (8), Figo (18), Jeremies (34)

LEEDS UNITED FC v VALENCIA CF 0-0

Elland Road, Leeds 2.05.2001

Referee: Pierluigi Collina (ITA) Attendance: 36,437

LEEDS UNITED: Nigel Martyn, Danny Mills, Rio Ferdinand, Dominic Matteo, Ian Harte, Lee Bowyer, David Batty, Olivier Dacourt, Harry Kewell, Alan Smith, Mark Viduka. Manager: David Anthony O'Leary

VALENCIA: José Santiago CAÑIZARES Ruíz, Jocelyn Angloma, Roberto Fabián AYALA, Mauricio Pellegrino, Amedeo Carboni, Gaizka MENDIETA Zabala, David ALBELDA Aliques, Rubén BARAJA Vegas, Cristian Alberto "KILY" GONZÁLEZ (90 VICENTE Rodríguez Guillén), Juan Gines SÁNCHEZ Moreno (67 Zlatko Zahović), John Carew.
Trainer: Héctor Raúl Cuper

VALENCIA CF v LEEDS UNITED FC 3-0 (1-0)

Mestalla, Valencia 8.05.2001

Referee: Urs Meier (SWI) Attendance: 53,200

VALENCIA: José Santiago CAÑIZARES Ruíz, Jocelyn Angloma, Roberto Fabián AYALA, Mauricio Pellegrino, FABIO AURELIO Rodríguez, Gaizka MENDIETA Zabala (73 Miguel Angel ANGULO Valderrey), David ALBELDA Aliques, Pablo César AIMAR (70 Didier Deschamps), Cristian Alberto "KILY" GONZÁLEZ (65 VICENTE Rodríguez Guillén), Juan Gines SÁNCHEZ Moreno, John Carew.
Trainer: Héctor Raúl Cuper

LEEDS UNITED: Nigel Martyn, Danny Mills, Rio Ferdinand, Dominic Matteo, Ian Harte, Eirik Bakke, David Batty, Olivier Dacourt, Harry Kewell, Alan Smith, Mark Viduka. Manager: David Anthony O'Leary

Sent off: Smith (90)

Goals: Sánchez (16, 47), Mendieta (52)

FINAL

FC BAYERN MÜNCHEN v VALENCIA CF 1-1 (0-1, 1-1) (AET)

Stadio Giuseppe Meazza, Milano 23.05.2001

Referee: Dick Z.G. Jol (HOL) Attendance: 74,000

BAYERN: Oliver Kahn, Samuel Kuffour, Patrick Andersson, Thomas Linke, Willy Sagnol (46 Carsten Jancker), Stefan Effenberg, Owen Hargreaves, Bixente Lizarazu, Hasan Salihamidzić, Mehmet Scholl (118 PAULO SÉRGIO Silvestre do Nascimento), Giovane ÉLBER (100 Alexander Zickler). Trainer: Ottmar Hitzfeld

VALENCIA: José Santiago CAÑIZARES Ruíz, Jocelyn Angloma, Roberto Fabián AYALA (90 Miroslav Djukić), Mauricio Pellegrino, Amedeo Carboni, Gaizka MENDIETA Zabala, Rubén BARAJA Vegas, Pablo César AIMAR (46 David ALBELDA Aliques), Cristian Alberto "KILY" GONZÁLEZ, Juan Gines SÁNCHEZ Moreno (66 Zlatko Zahović), John Carew. Trainer: Héctor Raúl Cuper

Goals: Mendieta (3 pen), Effenberg (50 pen)

Penalties: 0-0 Paulo Sérgio, 0-1 Mendieta, 1-1 Salihamidzić, 1-2 Carew, 2-2 Zickler, Zahović (miss), Andersson (miss), Carboni (miss), 3-2 Effenberg, 3-3 Baraja, 4-3 Lizarazu, 4-4 "KILY" GONZÁLEZ, 5-4 Linke, Pellegrino (miss)

Qualifying Round Goalscorers 2000-2001:

5 goals: Serhiy Atelkin (Shakhtar Donetsk),

4 goals: Badri Kvaratskheliya (FK Shamkir),), Andrei Shevchenko (Milan AC), Andriy Vorobei (Shakhtar Donetsk), Jan Koller (Anderlecht Brussel), Attila Tököli (Dunaferr SE)

3 goals: Georgi Ivanov (Levski Sofia), Sigthorsson (KR Reykjavik), Nouma (Beşiktaş Istanbul), Jardel (Galatasaray Istanbul), Olisadebe (Polonia Warszawa), Bosković, Drulić (Crvena Zvezda Beograd), Berg (Rosenborg Trondheim), Schopp (Sturm Graz),

2 goals: Ferguson (Linfield Belfast), Tahmazyan (Shirak Gyumri), Kolesnichenko (Skonto Riga), Katić (NK Brotnjo Citluk), Ivankov (Levski Sofia), Ksanavicius, Zuta (FBK Kaunas), Bragin (Levadia Maardu), Kulikov (FK Shamkir), Foran (Shelbourne), M.Bilić (Hajduk Split), S.Németh (Inter Bratislava), Nihat, Tayfur (Beşiktaş Istanbul), Haas, Kocijan, Reinmayr (Sturm Graz), Oprea, Berco, Boreț (Zimbru Chişinău), Obajdin (Sparta Praha), T.Došek (Slavia Praha), Amoah (FC St Gallen), Wieszczycki, Golaszewski (Polonia Warszawa), Mendieta, Diego Alonso (Valencia CF), Smith (Leeds United), Albertz, Dodds, Johnston, Wallace (Glasgow Rangers), Belsvik (Rosenborg Trondheim), Basinas, Goumas, Warzycha (Panathinaikos Athina),

1 goal: Nwoko, Spiteri (Birkirkara FC), Wright (62), Toner (TNS Llasantffreid), Samusevas (Skonto Riga), Nuhiji (Sloga Jugomagnat Skopje), Dede, Fortuzi, Dabulla, Kenesei (SK Tiranë), Juricić (NK Brotnjo Citluk), Pavlović, Papavasileiou (Anorthosis Famagusta), Markov, Tsykhmeistruk (Levski Sofia), Danielsson, Juliusson, Winnie, Benediktsson (KR Reykjavik), Lupu, Mihalcea, Niculae, Tameş (Dinamo Bucureşti), Puotkalis (FBK Kaunas), Kovacs, Wilson (Haka Valkeakoski), Kutusau, Rahozhkin, Loshankov (FC BATE Borisov), Imedadze, Janashia (Torpedo Kutaisi), Rõtškov, Krasnopjorov, Krom, Fenin, Tselnokov (Levadia Maardu), Pinte (Inter Bratislava), Baker, Haylock (Shelbourne), Balali (Hapoel Tel Aviv), Ceh (NK Maribor), Marlet, Malbranque, Ânderson, Delmotte (Olympique Lyon), Barbarez, Mahdavikia (Hamburger SV), Bagger, Lindrup, Madsen (Brøndby IF), Cherevchenko (Lokomotiv Moskva), Karhan (Beşiktaş Istanbul), Korneev, Jochemsen (Feyenoord Rotterdam), Korsós, Vastic, Neukirchner (Sturm Graz), Kulik, Epureanu (Zimbru Chişinău), Pilipović (Dinamo Zagreb), Comandini, José Marí (Milan AC), Bielik, Zubov (Shakhtar Donetsk), Ulich, Dostálek, Švancara, Zelenka (Slavia Praha), Gane (FC St Gallen), Warzycha, Fissas, Limperopoulos, Pflipsen (Panathinaikos Athina), Kielbowicz, Kaliszan, Bak (Polonia Warszawa), Gilewicz (FC Tirol Innsbruck), Ilić, Pjanović, Stevanović, Mirković (Crvena Zvezda Beograd), Belkevich (Dynamo Kyiv), Agostino (TSV 1860 München), Harte (Leeds United), Amoruso, Kanchelskis (Glasgow Rangers), Hansson, Alvaro, C.Andersson, Wahlstedt (Helsingborgs IF), Baseggio (Anderlecht Brussel), Lengyel, Zavadszky, Éger (Dunaferr SE), Strand, Knutsen, Winsnes (Rosenborg Trondheim)

Own goals: Edwards (TNS Llasanrffraid) for Levadia Maardu, Zellweger (FC St Gallen) for Galatasaray

Champions League Goalscorers 2000-2001:

7 goals: RAUL González (Real Madrid)

6 goals: Mário JARDEL (Galatasaray), Marco Simone (AS Monaco), RIVALDO (FC Barcelona), Lee Bowyer (Leeds United), Iván Helguera (Real Madrid), Paul Scholes (Manchester United), Giovane Élber (Bayern München),

5 goals: Filippo Inzaghi (Juventus Torino), Frode Johnsen (Rosenborg Trondheim), Andriy Shevchenko (Milan AC), Nicolas Anelka, Correa Dionisio CHRISTIAN (Paris Saint Germain), Tomasz Radzinski (Anderlecht Brussel), Teddy Sheringham (Manchester United), Walter Pandiani (RC Deportivo La Coruña), Alan Smith (Leeds United), Luís Figo (Real Madrid), Claudio Lopez (Lazio Roma), Mehmet Scholl (Bayern München), Juan Sanchez (Valencia CF)

4 goals: José Marí (Milan AC), Leroy (Paris St Germain), Marcos Antonio Aparecido Cipriano «MARCÃO», Yegor Titov (Spartak Moskva), Ânderson, Marlet (Olympique Lyon), Alin Stoica (Anderlecht Brussel), Mark Viduka (Leeds United), Diego Alonso (Valencia CF), Andy Cole (Manchester United), Thierry Henry (Arsenal), José María Gutiérrez Hernandez "GUTI", Fernando Morientes, Roberto Carlos (Real Madrid)

3 goals: Sá Pinto (Sporting Lisboa), Vorobei (Shakhtar Donetsk), Giovanni (Olympiakos Peiraias), Schopp, Yuran (Sturm Graz), Nonda (AS Monaco), van Bronckhorst (Glasgow Rangers), Robert (Paris St Germain), Koller (Anderlecht), Djalminha (Deportivo La Coruña), Harte (Leeds United), Carew (Valencia CF), Jeremies, Paulo Sérgio (Bayern München), Inzaghi, Nedved (Lazio Roma)

2 goals: Cruz (Sporting Lisboa), Brdaric, Ballack (Bayer Leverkusen), Zubov (Shakhtar Donetsk), Jarošik, Rosický (Sparta Praha), Djordjević (Olympiakos Peiraias), Mols (Glasgow Rangers), Mahdavikia, Yeboah (Hamburger SV), Bjørn Johansen (Helsingborgs IF), George, Strand (Rosenborg Trondheim), Shatskykh, Demetradze (Dynamo Kyiv), Adil Ramzi, van Bommel (PSV Eindhoven), Ahmet Dursun (Beşiktaş Istanbul), Kluivert, Luis Enrique (FC Barcelona), Albertini, Coco, Bierhoff (Milan AC), Robson (Spartak Moskva), Govou, Laigle (Olympique Lyon), Diego Tristán, Makaay, Víctor, Naybet (Deportivo La Coruña), Ayala, Baraja, Kily González, Mendieta (Valencia CF), Giggs, Irwin (Manchester United), Hagi, Hakan Ünsal, Hasan Şaş, Ümit (Galatasaray Istanbul), Jancker, Salihamidzić (Bayern München), Kanu, Keown, Ljungberg, Silvinho, Parlour (Arsenal London), Matteo (Leeds United), Crespo, Mihajlović, Ravanelli (Lazio Roma),

1 goal: Rink, Kirsten, Schneider, Ramelow, Neuville (Bayer Leverkusen), Atelkin, Bielik, Gleveckas, Bakharev (Shakhtar Donetsk), Labant, Hornák (Sparta Praha), Venema, Jensen, Talan (SC Heerenveen), Ofori-Quaye (Olympiakos), Prilasnig, Schupp (Sturm Graz), Farnerud, Costinha, Contreras, Bonnal (AS Monaco), Miller, Kanchelskis, Ronald de Boer, Johnston, Dodds (Glasgow Rangers), Kovacević, Tacchinardi, Trézéguet, Tudor (Juventus Torino), Präger, Panadic, Barbarez, Butt, Kovac (Hamburger SV), Persson, Jesper Jansson, Álvaro, Prica (Helsingborgs IF), Sørensen, Ørjan Berg, Skammelsrud (Rosenborg Trondheim), Belkevich, Gusin (Dynamo Kyiv), Nouma, Tayfur (Beşiktaş), Cocu, Gabri, Frank de Boer (FC Barcelona), Seitaridis, Karagounis, Paulo Sousa, Nasiopoulos (Panathinaikos), Helveg, Leonardo, Serginho (Milan AC), Okocha, Algerino, Déhu, Luccin, El-Karkouri (Paris St Germain), Parfyonov, Bezrodnyi (Spartak Moskva), Edmilson, Malbranque, Foé (Olympique Lyon), Ooijer, Bouma, Kezman, Lucius, Bruggink (PSV Eindhoven), Turu Flores, Scaloni (Deportivo La Coruña), Dindane, Goor, Crasson, Youla, Kaladz, Dheedene (Anderlecht), Angloma, Zahović (Valencia CF), Butt, Keane, Yorke (Man. United), Suat Kaya, Ergün, Bülent Korkmaz, Bülent Akin, Capone (Galatasaray), Effenberg, Tarnat, Linke (Bayern München), Bergkamp, Lauren Etamé, Dixon, Pires, Wiltord (Arsenal London), Makélélé, Solari, Hierro, Sávio (Real Madrid), Ferdinand, Wilcox, Bakke, Huckerby (Leeds United), Baronio, Gottardi, Favalli, Verón, Simeone (Lazio Roma)

Own goals: Rui Jorge (Sporting Lisboa) for Real Madrid, Manuel Dimas (Sporting Lisboa) for Spartak Moskva, Gérémi (Real Madrid) for Spartak Moskva, Hornák (Sparta Praha) for Shakhtar Donetsk, Houttuin (SC Heerenveen) for Olympique Lyon, Hakan Ünsal (Galatasaray) for Sturm Graz, Stig Johansen (Helsingborgs IF) for Rosenborg, Vashchuk (Dynamo Kyiv) for Anderlecht Brussel, Brown (Manchester United) for Valencia CF

CHAMPIONS LEAGUE 2001-2002

FIRST QUALIFYING ROUND

FC ARAKS ARARAT v FC SHERIFF TIRASPOL 0-1 (0-0)

Republican, Erevan 11.07.2001

Referee: Athanasios Briakos (GRE) Attendance: 8,500

FC ARAKS: Harutyun Abrahamyan, Marius Skideris, Eduard Sukiasyan, Arkadi Dokhoyan, Hovhannes Demirtshyan, Hayk Gevorgyan (65 Hayk Hakobyan), Artur Voskanyan, Feliks Khojoyan, Razmik Grigoryan (Cap) (53 Romeo Jenebyan), Artak Minasyan, Ara Hakobyan (36 Aram Hakobyan). Trainer: Varuzhan Sukiasyan

FC SHERIFF: Oleksandr Bokarev, Odia Chidi, Ruslan BARBUROŞ (89 Dmitry Parhomenco), Yuri Bukel, Vazha Tarhnishvili (Cap), Vladimir Tanurcov (74 Alexandr Lapac), Victor Comlionoc, Veaceslav Bugneac (71 Serghei Dadu), Victor Barîşev, Vadim Boreţ, Evgheny Patula. Trainer: Vladimir Zemlianoi

Goal: Barburoş (62)

FC SHERIFF TIRASPOL v FC ARAKS ARARAT 2-0 (1-0)

Tiraspol Stadion 18.07.2001

Referee: Nikolai Ivanov (RUS) Attendance: 4,800

FC SHERIFF: Oleksandr Bokarev, Odia Chidi, Igor Kharkovchenko, Yuri Bukel, Vazha Tarhnishvili (Cap), Victor Barîşev (56 Veaceslav Bugneac), Vadim Boreţ, Evgheny Patula (73 Andriy Nesteruc), Ruslan Barburoş, Victor Comlionoc (78 Alexandr Lapac), Serghei Dadu. Trainer: Valeri Vasiliev

FC ARAKS: Harutyun Abrahamyan (Cap), Arkadi Dokhoyan, Marius Skideris, Hayk Gevorgyan, Hovhannes Demirtshyan (55 Romeo Jenebyan), Karen Simonyan (27 Norik Hokhoyan), Feliks Khojoyan, Ashot Grigoryan (69 Artak Minasyan), Artur Voskanyan, Aram Hakobyan, Hayk Hakobyan. Trainer: Varuzhan Sukiasyan **Sent off**: A. Hakobyan (87)

Goals: Comlionoc (12), Dadu (90)

LINFIELD FC BELFAST v FC TORPEDO KUTAISI 0-0

Windsor Park, Belfast 11.07.2001

Referee: Jouni Hyytiä (FIN) Attendance: 2,699

LINFIELD: Robert Robinson, Stephen Collier (87 Norman Kelly), William Murphy, Mark Picking, Darren Murphy, Russell Kelly, David Larmour, Anthony Gorman (82 Garth Scates), Glenn Ferguson, Justin McBride (10 Jamie Henry Marks), Noel Bailie (Cap). Trainer: David Jeffrey

FC TORPEDO: David Gvaramadze, Mikheil Makhviladze (32 Shalva Isiani), Givi Didava (Cap), Sevasti Todua, Revaz Kemoklidze, Zviad Kutateladze (46 Roman Akhalkatsi), Mikheil Ashvetia (82 Boris Goncharov), Valeri Abramidze, Malkhaz Asatiani, Vakhtang Akopyan, Vakhtang Khvadagani. Trainer: Revaz Dzodzuashvili

FC TORPEDO KUTAISI v LINFIELD FC BELFAST 1-0 (0-0)

David Kiladze, Kutaisi 18.07.2001

Referee: Jack C.D. van Hulten (HOL) Attendance: 7,130

FC TORPEDO: David Gvaramadze, Givi Didava (Cap), Sevasti Todua, Revaz Kemoklidze, Zviad Kutateladze (72 Mikheil Makhviladze), Mikheil Ashvetia (83 Boris Goncharov), Valeri Abramidze, Roman Akhalkatsi (46 Dimitri Paramonovi), Malkhaz Asatiani, Vakhtang Akopyan, Vakhtang Khvadagani. Trainer: Revaz Dzodzuashvili

LINFIELD: Robert Robinson, Stephen Collier, Patrick McShane, Mark Picking, William Murphy, Russell Kelly (75 David Larmour), Jamie Henry Marks (65 Garth Scates), Anthony Gorman, Glenn Ferguson, Norman Kelly (65 Darren Murphy), Noel Bailie (Cap). Trainer: David Jeffrey

Sent off: Khvadagani (81) and Bailie (84)

Goal: Ashvetia (68)

FC LEVSKI SOFIA v FK ZELJEZNICAR SARAJEVO 4-0 (3-0)

Georgi Asparuhov, Sofia 11.07.2001

Referee: Douglas McDonald (SCO) Attendance: 16,121

LEVSKI: Georgi Petkov, Martin Stankov, Ivo Trenchev, Biser Ivanov, Georgi Markov, Ilian Stoianov, Rogerio GAUCHO Botelho (76 Stanislav Angelov), Iordan Terziev, Georgi Ivanov (Cap), Konstantin Golovskoi (63 Stanimir Stoilov), Miodrag Pantelic (56 Asen Nikolov). Trainer: Ljubo Petrovic

ZELJEZNICAR: Miroslav Kruzik, Adin Mulaosmanović, Admir Adzem, Edis Mulalić, Nihad Alić, Denis Karić, Almir Gredić, Senad Zerić (46 Nermin Fatić), Hadis Zubanović (76 Arsim Prepoli), Dzelaludin Muharemović (Cap), Sead Seferović. Trainer: Amar Osim

Goals: Terziev (7), G. Ivanov (20, 73 pen), Markov (28)

FK ZELJEZNICAR SARAJEVO v LEVSKI SOFIA 0-0

Olimpijski, Sarajevo 18.07.2001

Referee: Bruno Derrien (FRA) Attendance: 3,000

ZELJEZNICAR: Miroslav Kruzik, Bulend Biscević, Admir Adzem, Edis Mulalić, Adin Mulaosmanović (Cap) (46 Senad Zerić), Almir Gredić, Nihad Alić, Hadis Zubanović, Dzelaludin Muharemovic, Denis Karić (87 Nermin Fatić), Sead Seferović (76 Sahmir Garcević). Trainer: Amar Osim

LEVSKI: Georgi Petkov, Dalibor Dragic, Stanimir Stoilov (Cap), Biser Ivanov, Ivo Trenchev, Iordan Terziev (60 Stanislav Angelov), Svetoslav Barkanichkov (83 Asen Nikolov), Ilian Stoianov, Georgi Chilikov (69 Rogério GAUCHO Botelho), Konstantin Golovskoi, Miodrag Pantelic. Trainer: Ljubo Petrovic

FK SLOGA JUGOMAGNAT SKOPJE v FBK KAUNAS 0-0

City, Skopje 11.07.2001

Referee: Franz Xaver Wack (GER) Attendance: 2,538

FK SLOGA JUGOMAGNAT: Jane Nikoloski, Goran Jovanovski, Refik Arif (Cap) (80 Ertan Demiri), Zoran Jovanovski, Goran Stankovski, Nebi Mustafi, Bruno Presilski, Arben Nuhiji, Toni Banduliev, Husein Beganovic, Zekirija Ramadan. Trainer: Ekrem Maglajlija

FBK KAUNAS: Eduardas Kurskis, Darius Sanajevas (73 Irmantas Zelmikas), Darius Gvildys, Tomas Kancelskis (Cap), Vitalijus Danilicevas (87 Andrius Puotkalis), Gintaras Juodeikis, Marius Bezykornovas, Vadimas Petrenka, Remigijus Pocius (69 Audrius Slekys), Darius Regelskis, Tadas Papeckys. Trainer: Saulius Širmelis

FBK KAUNAS v FK SLOGA JUGOMAGNAT SKOPJE 1-1 (0-0)

S Darius & S Girenas SC, Kaunas 18.07.2001

Referee: Eric Blareau (BEL) Attendance: 660

FBK KAUNAS: Eduardas Kurskis, Darius Sanajevas, Darius Gvildys, Tomas Kancelskis (Cap), Vitalijus Danilicevas (72 Audrius Slekys), Gintaras Juodeikis, Marius Bezykornovas, Vadim Petrenka (54 Andrius Puotkalis), Remigijus Pocius (46 Andrius Velicka), Darius Regelskis, Tadas Papeckys. Trainer: Saulius Širmelis

FK SLOGA JUGOMAGNAT: Gogo Jovcev, Goran Jovanovski, Toni Banduliev, Nebi Mustafi, Bruno Presilski (70 Ertan Demiri), Arben Nuhiji, Ardzend Beciri (90 Todor Ivanoski), Husein Beganovic, Zekirija Ramadan, Refik Arif (Cap), Oldzaj Bajram. Trainer: Ekrem Maglajlija

Goals: Arben Nuhiji (52), Papeckys (65)

F91 DUDELANGE v FC SKONTO RIGA 1-6 (1-1)

Josy Barthel, Luxembourg 11.07.2001

Referee: Marian Salomir (ROM) Attendance: 1,068

F91 DUDELANGE: Paul Koch (Cap), Roger Lutz, Jean-Philippe Facques, Christophe Boulard, Sébstien Remy, Frédéric Cicchirillo, Marco Delazzer (74 José Llamas), Evariste Kabongo, Romain Provenier, David Cangini (82 Ludovic Biancalani), Lehit Zeghdane (67 Johan Bellini). Trainer: Carlo Weis

FC SKONTO: Andrey Piedels, Arturs Zakrishevskis, Mikhail Zemlinsky, Oleg Blagonadezhdin, Alexandre Rekhviashvili (Cap) (74 Valentin Lobanyov), Orestas Buitkus, Maris Verpakovskis, Vladimir Kolesnichenko, Andrius Tereskinas, Zurab Menteshashvili (53 Levan Korgalidze), Andriy Chernov (56 Mikhail Mikholap). Trainer: Alexander Starkovs

Sent off: Facques (64)

Goals: Verpakovskis (2), Cicchirillo (43), Mikholap (60, 75), Kolesnichenko (65, 85), Zemlinsky (71 pen)

FC SKONTO RIGA v F91 DUDELANGE 0-1 (0-0)

Skonto, Riga 18.07.2001

Referee: Jon Skjervold (NOR) Attendance: 1,500

FC SKONTO: Andrey Piedels, Arturs Zakrishevskis, Valentin Lobanyov (61 Aleksandr Jelisjevs), Alexander Rekhviashvili (Cap), Orestas Buitkus, Maris Verpakovskis, Vladimir Kolesnichenko, Mikhail Mikholap (46 Zurab Menteshashvili), Andrius Tereskinas, Andriy Chernov, Mantas Samusevas (40 Mikhail Zemlinsky). Trainer: Alexander Starkovs

F91 DUDELANGE: Paul Koch (Cap), Roger Lutz, Sébastien Remy (89 José Pereira Barreto), Frédéric Cicchirillo, Joaquim Machado Evariste Kabongo, Romain Provenier, David Cangini, Lehit Zeghdane (81 José Llamas), Johan Bellini, Rudy Marchal (77 Telmo Matos). Trainer: Carlo Weis

Goal: Cicchirillo (77)

VALLETTA FC v HAKA VALKEAKOSKEN 0-0

National, Ta'Qali 11.07.2001

Referee: Paul McKeon (IRE) Attendance: 1,726

VALLETTA FC: Emil Mitkov Dimitrov, Daniel Theuma, Christian Laferla (Cap), Darren Debono, Ivan Zammit, Gilbert Agius, Nicky Saliba, David Carabott (76 René Forace), Chris Oretan, Pavel Mraz, Kamil Dvorak. Trainer: Krasimir Manolov

HAKA: András Vilnrotter, Dragan Bajić, Lasse Karjalainen (Cap), Jarmo Saastamoinen, Liro Aalto, Kai Nysssönen, Tommi Torkkeli (80 Jaakko Pasanen), Péter Kovács, David Wilson, Jarkko Okkonen, Juuso Totte Kangaskorpi. Trainer: Keith Armstrong

HAKA VALKEAKOSKEN v VALLETTA FC 5-0 (4-0)

Tehtaankenttä, Valkeakosken 18.07.2001

Referee: Miroslav Liba (CZE) Attendance: 2,423

HAKA: András Vilnrotter, Dragen Bajić (70 MARCO António Pogioli), Lasse Karjalainen (Cap), Jarmo Saastamoinen, Oleg Ivanov, Ville Väisänen, Tommi Torkkeli, Péter Kovács (68 Kai Nysssönen), David Wilson, Jarkko Okkonen, Juuso Totte Kangaskorpi (63 Jaakko Pasanen). Trainer: Keith Armstrong

VALLETTA FC: Emil Mitkov Dimitrov (28 Sean Sullivan), Daniel Theuma (71 Karl Bonnici), Christian Laferla (Cap), Darren Debono, Ivan Zammit, Gilbert Agius, Nicky Saliba, Chris Oretan, Pavel Mraz, René Forace, Kamil Dvorak (57 David Carabott). Trainer: Krasimir Manolov

Sent off: Mraz (60)

Goals: Torkkeli (4), P. Kovács (15, 22, 28), Marco (90)

VB VÁGUR v FC SLAVIYA MOZYR 0-0

Tórsvøllur, Tórshavn 11.07.2001

Referee: David Malcolm (NIR) Attendance: 480

VB VÁGUR: Bjarni Johansen, Eydun Jacobsen (Cap), Magni Jacobsen, Palli Augustinussen, Tórdur Holm (88 Michael i Lagabø), Jon M. Gaerdbø (90 Gisli D. Sveinbjørnsson), Predrag Zivković (57 Marner Richardt), Marek Wierzbicki, Robert Cieslewicz, Birgir Jørgensen, Jón Pauli Olsen. Trainer: Krzysztof Popczynski

FC SLAVIYA: Vitaly Varyvonchik, Vladimir Sorochynskiy, Fedor Lukachenko, Artur Matveichik (55 Alexandr Gruber), Oleg Samatov (Cap), Nebojsa Jovovic (46 Kiril Rybakov), Valeriy Stripeikis, Juvorad Djordjevic, Ruslan Danilyuk, Radojica Vasić, Alexander Pantic. Trainer: Vladimir Petrovic

FC SLAVIYA MOZYR v VB VÁGUR 5-0 (5-0)

Yunost, Mozyr 18.07.2001

Referee: John McDermott (IRE) Attendance: 2,150

FC SLAVIYA: Vitaly Varyvonchyk, Vladimir Sorochynskiy (17 Ruslan Danilyuk), Fedor Lukachenko, Artur Matveychik, Denis Pervushin, Oleg Samatov (Cap), Valeriy Stripeykis, Igor Rakovski (42 Vladzimir Korytsko), Radojica Vasić, Aleksander Pantić (46 Alexandr Gruber), Kiril Rybakov. Trainer: Vladimir Petrovic

VB VÁGUR: Bjarni Johansen, Eydun Jacobsen (Cap), Magni Jacobsen, Palli Augustinussen, Tórdur Holm, Jon M. Gaerdbø (65 Michael i Lagabø), Predrag Zivković, Marek Wierzbicki, Robert Cieslewicz, Birgir Jørgensen (43 Dan Djurhuus), Jón Pauli Olsen (65 Marner Richardt). Trainer: Krzysztof Popczynski

Goals: Jacobsen (4 og), Stripeykis (12, 27 pen, 31), Rybakov (23)

BARRY TOWN FC v FC SHAMKIR 2-0 (0-0)

Jenner Park, Barry 11.07.2001

Referee: Darko Ceferin (SVN) Attendance: 1,992

BARRY TOWN: Tim Clarke, Terry Evans, Gary Gilbert Lloyd, Scott Morgan, Andrew David York (Cap), Lee Phillips, Kenneth James Brown (60 James Jenkins), Jonathan Charles French, Jamie David Moralee (85 Matthew Howard Davies), Mike Flynn, Luke Roy Staton. Trainer: Peter Nicholas

FC SHAMKIR: Huseyn Magomedov, Aslan Kerimov, Mehman Yunusov (Cap), Azer Mamedov, Etimad Kurbanov (73 Mirbagir Isayev), Makhmud Kurbanov, Khalig Mardanov, Ismagil Mamedov, Khagani Mamedov (70 Badri Kvaratskhelia), Ilham Yadullayev (70 Viktor Kulikov), Vidadi Rzayev. Trainer: Aghahalim Miravadov

Goals: York (63), French (68)

FC SHAMKIR v BARRY TOWN FC 0-1 (0-0)

Tofig Bakhramov, Baku 18.07.2001

Referee: Dietmar Drabek (AUS) Attendance: 7,000

FC SHAMKIR: Huseyn Magomedov, Aslan Kerimov, Mehman Yunusov (Cap), Azer Mamedov, Makhmud Kurbanov, Khalig Mardanov, Ismagil Mamedov, Badri Kvaratskhelia, Mirbagir Isayev (46 Etimad Kurbanov), Viktor Kulikov (77 Agil Mamedov), Vidadi Rzayev (70 Khagani Mamedov). Trainer: Aghahalim Miravadov

BARRY TOWN: Tim Clarke, Terry Evans, Gary Gilbert Lloyd, James Jenkins, Andrew David York (Cap), Lee Phillips (82 Neil Anthony Sharp), Kenneth James Brown (76 Richard Joseph Kennedy), Jonathan Charles French, Jamie David Moralee (79 Matthew Howard Davies), Mike Flynn, Luke Roy Staton. Trainer: Peter Nicholas

Sent off: Kvaratskhelia (8)

Goal: Phillips (58)

BOHEMIANS FC DUBLIN v FC LEVADIA MAARDU 3-0 (2-0)

Dalymount Park, Dublin 11.07.2001

Referee: Dieter Schoch (SWI) Attendance: 3,832

BOHEMIANS: Wayne Russell, Brian Shelley (88 Anthony O'Connor), Simon Webb, Kevin Hunt (Cap), Shaun Maher, Avery John, Paul Byrne, Stephen Caffrey, Alex Nesovic (82 Fergal Harkin), Glen Crowe (84 Gary O'Neill), Mark Rutherford. Trainer: Pete Mahon

FC LEVADIA: Ernest Martinsons, Juri Leitan (74 Oleg Lepik), Oleksandr Tatarinov, Dmitri Kulikov, Maksim Rõtshkov, Juri Fenin (87 Indro Olumets), Sergei Bragin (Cap), Andrei Krasnopjorov, Andrei Kalimullin, Toomas Krõm (58 Vitali Leitan), Vladimir Tselnokov. Trainer: Valeri Bondarenko

Goals: Maher (2), Crowe (10, 56 pen)

FC LEVADIA MAARDU v BOHEMIANS FC DUBLIN 0-0

Lilleküla, Tallinn 18.07.2001

Referee: Knud Stadsgaard (DEN) Attendance: 1,034

FC LEVADIA: Ernest Martinsons, Oleksandr Tatarinov, Andrei Krasnopjorov, Andrei Kalimullin, Sergei Bragin (Cap), Maksim Rõtshkov, Dmitri Kulikov, Juri Fenin, Vitali Leitan (77 Indro Olumets), Vladimir Tselnokov, Toomas Krõm. Trainer: Valeri Bondarenko

BOHEMIANS: Wayne Russell, Brian Shelley, Simon Webb, Kevin Hunt (Cap), Shaun Maher, Avery John, Paul Byrne, Stephen Caffrey, Alex Nesovic (75 Fergal Harkin), Glen Crowe (85 Gary O'Neill), Mark Rutherford. Trainer: Pete Mahon

KR REYKJAVIK
v KS VLLAZNIA SHKODËR 2-1 (0-1)

Laugardalsvöllur, Reykajvik 11.07.2001

Referee: Bernhard Brugger (AUS) Attendance: 1,373

KR REYKJAVIK: Bjarki Gudmundsson, Sigurdur Öm Jónsson, Tryggvi Bjarnason, Gunnar Einarsson, Sigursteinn Gíslason (Cap), Einar Thór Daníelsson, Sigthór Júlíusson (59 Sigurvin Olafsson), Thórhallur Hinriksson, Andrew Roddie, Sergio Ommel (46 Moussa Dagnogo), Gudmundur Benediktsson (82 Thormódur Egilsson).
Trainer: David Peter Winnie **Sent off**: E.T. Danielsson (80)

VLLAZNIA: Arjon Mustafa, Suad Lici, Astrit Premçi (67 Ilir Dibra), Safet Osja, Oltjon Osmani, Vioresin Sinani (Cap) (90 Albert Kaçi), Amarildo Belisha, Edmond Dalipaj (64 Eldorado Merkoci), Elvin Beqiri, Klodian Duro, Saimir Patushi.
Trainer: Dervish Haxhiosmanovic

Goals: K.Duro (17), Benediktsson (63), Olafsson (78)

KS VLLAZNIA SHKODËR
v KR REYKAJVIK 1-0 (0-0)

Qemal Stafa, Tirana 18.07.2001

Referee: Alon Yefet (ISR) Attendance: 5,000

KS VLLAZNIA: Arjon Mustafa, Suad Lici, Ilir Dibra, Safet Osja, Oltjon Osmani, Vioresin Sinani (Cap), Edi Martini (49 Eldorado Merkoci), Edmond Dalipaj, Elvin Beqiri, Klodian Duro, Saimir Patushi (20 Amarildo Belisha).
Trainer: Dervish Haxhiosmanovic

KR REYKJAVIK: Kristján Finnbogason, Thormódur Egilsson, Gunnar Einarsson, Tryggvi Bjarnason, Sigurdur Örn Jónsson (73 Sigthór Júlíusson), Sigurvin Olafsson (65 Arnar Jón Sigurgeirsson), Thórhallur Hinriksson, Sigursteinn Gíslason (Cap), Andrew Roddie, Gudmundur Benediktsson (56 Sergio Ommel), Moussa Dagnogo.
Trainer: David Peter Winnie

Goal: Duro (62)

SECOND QUALIFYING ROUND

FC HAKA VALKEAKOSKEN
v MACCABI HAIFA FC 0-1 (0-1)

Tehtaankenttä, Valkeakosken 24.07.2001

Referee: Dermot Gallagher (ENG) Attendance: 3,350

FC HAKA: András Vilnrotter, Dragan Bajić (77 Jaakko Pasanen), Lasse Karjalainen (Cap), Oleg Ivanov (64 Valeriy Popovich), Liro Aalto, Ville Väisänen, Tommi Torkkeli, Péter Kovács (72 Kai Nysssönen), David Wilson, Jarkko Okkonen, Juuso Totte Kangaskorpi. Trainer: Keith Armstrong

MACCABI: Dudu Awat, Raimondas Zutautas, Alon Harazi, Arik Benado (Cap), Adoram Keissy, Giovanni Rosso, Andrei Ostrovski, Avishay Zano, Yakubu Ayegbeni (80 Nir Sivilia), Yaniv Katan (87 Reuven Atar), Nenad Pralija.
Trainer: Avraham Grant

Sent off: Nyssönen (85)

Goal: Zano (28 pen)

MACCABI HAIFA FC
v FC HAKA VALKEAKOSKEN 4-0 (1-0)

Kiriat Eliezer, Haifa 1.08.2001

Referee: Zoran Arsić (YUG) Attendance: 8,000

MACCABI: Dudu Awat, Raimondas Zutautas, Alon Harazi, Arik Benado (Cap), Adoram Keissy, Giovanni Rosso, Walid Badir (70 Yakubu Ayegbeni), Andrei Ostrovski, Avishay Zano (80 Yossi Benayoun), Yaniv Katan, Nenad Pralija (79 Reuven Atar). Trainer: Avraham Grant

FC HAKA: András Vilnrotter, Dragan Bajic (78 Oleg Ivanov), Lasse Karjalainen (Cap), Janne Mäkelä, Liro Aalto (78 Juuso Totte Kangaskorpi), Ville Väisänen, Jukka Ruhanen (46 Jaakko Pasanen), Tommi Torkkeli, Péter Kovács, David Wilson, Jarkko Okkonen. Trainer: Keith Armstrong

Goals: Rosso (39), Katan (57, 78, 90)

Maccabi Haifa FC fielded a suspended player (Walid Badir) so the game was awarded 3-0 to FC Haka by UEFA.

FC SLAVIYA MOZYR
v AŠK INTER SLOVNAFT BRATISLAVA 0-1 (0-1)

Yunost, Mozyr 25.07.2001

Referee: Stephen Dunn (ENG) Attendance: 2,420

FC SLAVIYA: Vitaly Varyvonchyk, Fedor Lukachenko, Artur Matveychik (79 Alexandr Gruber), Denis Pervushin, Oleg Samatov (Cap), Jafar Irismetov, Valeriy Stripeykis, Juvorad Djordjević, Andrey Lukashevich (46 Ruslan Danilyuk), Radojica Vasić, Aleksander Pantić (90 Nebojsa Jovović).
Trainer: Vladimir Petrović

INTER: Miroslav Hyll, Marian Cisovsky, Marián Suchancok (Cap), Tomas Gerich, Peter Dzurik, Radoslav Kunzo, Roman Kratochvíl, Juraj Czinege, Alias Lembakoali (72 Saša Micovic), Miroslav Drobnak (62 Martin Sevela), Marian Lalik (90 Peter Petras). Trainer: Jozef Bubenko

Goal: Kunzo (43)

AŠK INTER SLOVNAFT BRATISLAVA
v FC SLAVIYA MOZYR 1-0 (0-0)

ASK Inter Slovnaft, Bratislava 1.08.2001

Referee: Edo Trivković (CRO) Attendance: 2,500

INTER: Miroslav Hyll, Marian Cisovsky, Marián Suchancok (Cap), Tomas Gerich, Peter Dzurik, Radoslav Kunzo, Roman Kratochvíl, Juraj Czinege, Alias Lembakoali (79 Saša Micovic), Miroslav Drobnak (59 Martin Sevela), Marian Lalik (83 Peter Petras). Trainer: Jozef Bubenko

FC SLAVIYA: Sergey Sinitsyn, Artur Matveychik (57 Igor Rakovsky), Denis Pervushin, Oleg Samatov (Cap), Jafar Irismetov, Valeriy Stripeykis, Igor Balin, Juvorad Djordjević, Radojica Vasić, Dmitry Chaley (64 Alexandr Gruber), Aleksander Pantić. Trainer: Vladimir Petrovic

Goal: Lembakoali (73)

SK SKONTO RIGA
v TS WISLA KRAKÓW 1-2 (0-0)

Daugava, Riga 25.07.2001

Referee: Leif Sundell (SWE) Attendance: 2,000

FC SKONTO: Andrey Piedels, Arturs Zakrishevskis, Mikhail Zemlinsky, Oleg Blagonadezhdin, Alexandre Rekhviashvili (Cap), Orestas Buitkus, Maris Verpakovskis, Vladimir Kolesnichenko, Andrius Tereskinas (77 Valentin Lobanyov), Zurab Menteshashvili (73 Levan Korgalidze), Andriy Chernov (63 Mikhail Mikholap). Trainer: Alexander Starkovs

WISLA: Artur Sarnat, Miroslaw Szymkowiak, Bogdan Zajac, Kamil Kosowski, Arkadiusz Glowacki, Kazimierz Moskal (Cap), Grzegorz Pater (73 Sunday Ibrahim), Maciej Zurawski, Ryszard Czerwiec, Marek Zajac, Tomasz Frankowski (84 Tomasz Kulawik). Trainer: Franciszek Smuda

Goals: Glowacki (48), Korgalidze (78), Zurawski (79 pen)

TS WISLA KRAKÓW
v FC SKONTO RIGA 1-0 (0-0)

Wisła,, Kraków 1.08.2001

Referee: Nicolai Vollquartz (DEN) Attendance: 4,500

WISLA: Artur Sarnat, Marek Zając, Bogdan Zając, Kazimierz Moskal (Cap), Arkadiusz Głowacki, Grzegorz Pater (60 Tomasz Frankowski), Olgierd Moskalewicz, Ryszard Czerwiec (75 Tomasz Kulawik), Kamil Kosowski, Maciej Żurawski, Grzegorz Niciński (78 Marcin Baszczyński). Trainer: Franciszek Smuda

SKONTO: Andrey Piedels, Arturs Zakrishevskis, Mikhail Zemlinsky, Valentin Lobanyov, Oleg Blagonadezhdin, Alexandre Rekhviashvili (Cap), Orestas Buitkus (79 Audrius Ksanavicius), Maris Verpakovskis, Vladimir Kolesnichenko (61 Mikhail Mikholap), Zurab Menteshashvili, Andriy Chernov (63 Levan Korgalidze). Trainer: Alexander Starkovs

Goal: Żurawski (85)

FC TORPEDO KUTAISI
v FC KØBENHAVN 1-1 (0-1)

David Kiladze, Kutaisi 25.07.2001

Referee: Frank de Bleeckere (BEL) Attendance: 11,500

TORPEDO: David Gvaramadze, Zurab Ionanidze, Mikheil Makhviladze (84 Zviad Kutateladze), Givi Didava (Cap), Sevasti Todua, Revaz Kemoklidze, Mikheil Ashvetia, Valeri Abramidze, Roman Akhalkatsi (50 Shota Babunashvili), Malkhaz Asatiani, Dimitri Paramonovi (50 George Shengelia). Trainer: Revaz Dzodzuashvili

FC KØBENHAVN: Magnus Kihlstedt, Thomas Rytter, Kim Madsen, Christian Bager Poulsen, Niclas Jensen, Thomas Røll Larsen, Sibusiso Zuma (77 Morten Bisgaard), Thomas Thorninger (68 Peter Christiansen), Jacob Laursen, Michael "Mio" Nielsen (Cap), Christian Lønstrup. Trainer: Kent Karlsson

Goals: Zuma (43), M. Ashvetia (77)

FC KØBENHAVN
v FC TORPEDO KUTAISI 3-1 (1-0)

Parken, København 1.08.2001

Referee: Pascal Garibian (FRA) Attendance: 14,345

FC KØBENHAVN: Magnus Kihlstedt, Thomas Rytter, Kim Madsen, Christian Bager Poulsen, Niclas Jensen, Thomas Røll Larsen, Sibusiso Zuma (70 Carsten Fredgaard), Heine Fernandez, Thomas Thorninger (82 Peter Christiansen), Jacob Laursen, Christian Lønstrup (Cap) (61 Morten Bisgaard). Trainer: Kent Karlsson

TORPEDO: David Gvaramadze, Zurab Ionanidze (Cap), Mikheil Makhviladze, Sevasti Todua, Revaz Kemoklidze, Mikheil Ashvetia, Valeri Abramidze, Roman Akhalkatsi (58 Zviad Kutateladze), Malkhaz Asatiani (36 Boris Goncharov), Vakhtang Akopyan, Dimitri Paramonovi (68 Paata Gvirjishvili). Trainer: Revaz Dzodzuashvili

Goals: Zuma (45), Lønstrup (59), Fernandez (74), Kutateladze (90)

FC SHAKHTAR DONETSK
v FC LUGANO 3-0 (1-0)

Shakhtyor, Donetsk 25.07.2001

Referee: Roy Helge Olsen (NOR) Attendance: 31,714

SHAKHTAR: Yuri Virt, Mykhailo Starostyak, Anatoliy Tymoshchuk, Marian Aliuţă, Aleksei Bakharev (72 Igor Duzelov), Hennadiy Zubov (Cap) (79 Serhiy Atelkin), Andriy Vorobei, Assane Ndiaye, Julius Aghahowa, Isaak Okoronkwo, Andriy Konyushenko (30 Serhiy Popov). Trainer: Viktor Prokopenko

FC LUGANO: Stefano Razzetti, Mamady Kaba, Olivier Biaggi, Markus Brunner, Joël Magnin (72 Ludovic Magnin), Dario Rota (Cap), Sergio Bastida (79 Goran Grubesic), Alain Gaspoz, AIRTON Graciliano Dos Santos, Julio Hernán Rossi, André Muff (62 Fabrizio Bullo). Trainer: Roberto Morinini

Goals: Bakharev (21), Tymoshchuk (57), Vorobei (65)

FC LUGANO
v FC SHAKHTAR DONETSK 2-1 (0-1)

Comunale di Cornaredo, Lugano 31.07.2001

Referee: Juan ANSUATEGUI ROCA (SPA) Att: 3,300

FC LUGANO: Stefano Razzetti, Mamady Kaba (46 Régis Rothenbühler), Zlatomir Zagorcic, Olivier Biaggi, Alain Gaspoz, Dario Rota (Cap), Sergio Bastida, Ludovic Magnin (75 Fabrizio Bullo), AIRTON Graciliano Dos Santos (87 Bruno Sutter), Joël Magnin, Julio Hernán Rossi. Trainer: Roberto Morinini

SHAKHTAR: Yuri Virt, Mykhailo Starostyak, Anatoliy Tymoshchuk, Serhiy Popov (Cap), Marian Aliuţă, Aleksei Bakharev (64 Andriy Konyushenko), Hennadiy Zubov (84 Mariusz Lewandowski), Andriy Vorobei (53 Serhiy Atelkin), Assane Ndiaye, Julius Aghahowa, Isaak Okoronkwo. Trainer: Viktor Prokopenko

Sent off: Ndiaye (90), Rota (90)

Goals: Aghahowa (13), Gaspoz (53), Rossi (66)

OMONOIA FC NICOSIA v FK CRVENA ZVEZDA BEOGRAD 1-1 (0-1)

GSP, Nicosia 25.07.2001

Referee: Eduardo ITURRALDE GONZALEZ (SPA)
Attendance: 16,756

OMONOIA: Antros Hristofi, Giorgos Theodotou, Nikolas Georgiou (46 Gunter Thiebaut), Hristos Panagiotou, Petros Konnafis, Kyriakos Mitsingas, Kostas Kaiafas, Haris Nikolaou, Vesko Mihajlović, Rainer Rauffmann (Cap), Lefteris Kontolefteros. Trainer: Henk Houwaart

CRVENA ZVEZDA: Ivan Randjelovic, Marjan Marković, Nemanja Vidić (70 Goran Djukić), Vladimir Matijasević, Ivan Vukomanović, Leo Lerinc (70 Branko Bosković), Ivan Gvozdenović (Cap), Dejan Ilić (77 Saša Kocić), Darko Spalević, Milenko Acimović, Mihajlo Pjanović.
Trainer: Slavoljub Muslin

Goals: Pjanovic (30), Thiebaut (70)

FK CRVENA ZVEZDA BEOGRAD v OMONOIA FC NICOSIA 2-1 (0-0)

FK Crvena Zvezda, Beograd 1.08.2001

Referee: Lutz Michael Fröhlich (GER) Attendance: 18,145

CRVENA ZVEZDA: Vladimir Disljenković, Marjan Marković (61 Stevo Glogovac), Nenad Lalatović (Cap), Vladimir Matijasević, Ivan Vukomanović, Leo Lerinc, Ivan Gvozdenović, Branko Bosković (89 Nemanja Vidić), Darko Spalević (64 Branko Jelić), Milenko Acimović, Mihajlo Pjanović.
Trainer: Slavoljub Muslin

OMONOIA: Antros Hristofi, Giorgos Theodotou, Ioakim Ioakim, Hristos Panagiotou, Haris Nikolaou (67 Alexis Pittas), Rainer Rauffmann (Cap), Vesko Mihajlović, Kostas Kaiafas, Kyriakos Mitsingas (57 Nikolas Georgiou), Gunter Thiebaut (57 Lefteris Kontolefteros), Petros Konnafis.
Trainer: Henk Houwaart

Goals: Lerinc (53), Kaiafas (71), Acimović (79)

FC LEVSKI SOFIA v SK BRANN BERGEN 0-0

Georgi Asparuhov, Sofia 25.07.2001

Referee: Stefano Farina (ITA) Attendance: 13,780

LEVSKI: Georgi Petkov, Martin Stankov, Stanmir Stoilov (Cap), Dalibor Dragic, Georgi Markov, Ilian Stoianov (66 Dimitar Telkiyski), Miodrag Pantelic (68 Todor Kolev), Konstantin Golovskoi, Georgi Ivanov, Asen Nikolov (78 Iordan Terziev), Elin Topuzakov. Trainer: Ljubo Petrović

BRANN: Ivar Rønningen, Geirmund Brendesaeter, Roy Wassberg, Egil Ulfstein, Erlend Hanstveit, Alex Marcel Valencia (80 Azar Karadas), Joachim Walltin, Svante Lennart Samuelsson (Cap), Raymond Kvisvik, Thorstein Helstad (90 Tommy Knarvik), Petter Furuseth Olsen.
Trainer: Teitur Thordarson

SK BRANN BERGEN v FC LEVSKI SOFIA 1-1 (1-1)

Brann, Bergen 1.08.2001

Referee: Jacek Granat (POL) Attendance: 10,902

BRANN: Ivar Rønningen, Geirmund Brendesaeter, Roy Wassberg, Egil Ulfstein, Erlend Hanstveit, Alex Marcel Valencia, Joachim Walltin, Svante Lennart Samuelsson (Cap), Raymond Kvisvik (69 Thorstein Helstad), Azar Karadas (77 Tommy Knarvik), Petter Furuseth Olsen.
Trainer: Teitur Thordarson

FC LEVSKI: Georgi Petkov (28 Iordan Gospodinov), Martin Stankov, Georgi Markov, Dalibor Dragic, Ivo Trenchev, Ilian Stoianov, Konstantin Golovskoi (89 Stanislav Angelov), Rogério GAUCHO Botelho, Georgi Ivanov (Cap), Elin Topuzakov, Miodrag Pantelic (64 Stanimir Stoilov).
Trainer: Ljubo Petrovic

Goals: G. Ivanov (5), Walltin (16)

GALATASARAY SK ISTANBUL v KS VLLAZNIA SHKODËR 2-0 (1-0)

Ali Sami Yen, Istanbul 25.07.2001

Referee: Joaquim Paulo Paraty Da Silva (POR) Att: 14,804

GALATASARAY: Kerem Inan, Bülent Korkmaz (Cap), Gheorghe Popescu, Arif Erdem (46 Berkant Göktan), Suat Kaya, Ümit Karan (78 Serkan Aykut), HASAN Gökhan ŞAŞ, Ümit Davala, Carlos Alberto de Oliveira "CAPONE" (56 Sébastien Perez), Hakan Ünsal, Ergün Penbe.
Trainer: Mircea Lucescu

KS VLLAZNIA: Arjon Mustafa, Suad Lici, Safet Osja, Oltjon Osmani, Amarildo Belisha, Vioresin Sinani (Cap), Eldorado Merkoci (86 Albert Kaçi), Edmond Dalipaj (81 Edmond Doçi), Ilir Dibra, Elvin Beqiri, Klodian Duro.
Trainer: Dervish Haxhiosmanović

Goals: Ümit Karan (18), Suat (90)

KS VLLAZNIA SHKODËR v GALATASARAY SK ISTANBUL 1-4 (1-1)

Qemal Stafa, Tirana 1.08.2001

Referee: Michael Riley (ENG) Attendance: 4,600

KS VLLAZNIA: Arjon Mustafa, Suad Lici, Safet Osja, Oltjon Osmani (56 Astrit Premçi), Vioresin Sinani (Cap) (82 Edmond Doçi), Amarildo Belisha, Edmond Dalipaj, Elvin Beqiri, Klodian Duro, Ilir Dibra, Eldorado Merkoci (65 Albert Kaçi).
Trainer: Dervish Haxhiosmanovic

GALATASARAY: Ali Faryd Camilo Mondragón, Bülent Korkmaz (Cap), Gheorghe Popescu, Arif Erdem, Suat Kaya, Ümit Karan (65 Serkan Aykut), HASAN Gökhan ŞAŞ, Ümit Davala, Carlos Alberto de Oliveira "CAPONE" (65 Sébastien Perez), Hakan Ünsal, Ergün Penbe (71 Bülent Akin).
Trainer: Mircea Lucescu

Sent off: Dibra (40)

Goals: Sinani (33), Ümit Karan (38), Hasan Şaş (48), Arif (67), Serkan (80)

RSC ANDERLECHT BRUSSEL v FC SHERIFF TIRASPOL 4-0 (2-0)

Constant Vanden Stock, Brussel 25.07.2001

Referee: Tomasz Mikulski (POL) Attendance: 21,055

ANDERLECHT: Filip de Wilde, Bertrand Crasson, Olivier Doll, Glen de Boeck (Cap), Aleksandar Ilic, Besnik Hasi, Yves Vanderhaeghe, Walter Baseggio (58 Tarek El Said), Alin Stoica (67 Gilles de Bilde), Oleg Yashchuk, Aruna Dindane (78 Ivica Mornar). Trainer: Aime Antheunis

FC SHERIFF: Oleksandr Bokarev, Odia Chidi, Yuri Bukel, Serghei Dadu, Igor Kharkovchenko, Vazha Tarhnishvili (Cap), Victor Barîşev, Vadim Boreţ, Iacov Zalevschi (46 Veaceslav Bugneac), Ruslan Barburoş (55 Evgheny Patula), Victor Comlionoc. Trainer: Valeri Vasiliev

Goals: Crasson (18, 81), de Boeck (41, 65)

SLOGA JUGOMAGNAT SKOPJE v STEAUA BUCUREŞTI 1-2 (0-2)

City, Skopje 1.08.2001

Referee: Kristinn Jakobsson (ICE) Attendance: 462

FK SLOGA JUGOMAGNAT: Gogo Jovcev, Goran Jovanovski, Vladimir Sekulovski, Refik Arif, Zoran Jovanovski, Nebi Mustafi, Bruno Presilski (57 Ilco Georgioski), Arben Nuhiji, Ardzend Beciri (Cap) (70 Ardijan Nuhiji), Oldzaj Barjam (57 Ertan Demiri), Husein Beganovic. Trainer: Ekrem Maglajija

STEAUA: Martin Tudor, Florentin Dumitru (46 Daniel Bălan), Mirel Rădoi, Ilie Miu (Cap), Dumitru Mitriţă (65 Valeriu Bordeanu); Sorin Paraschiv, Erik Augustin Lincar, N'Gassam Falemi, Pompiliu Stoica; Claudiu Răducanu (75 Alexandru Piţurcă), Adrian Neaga. Trainer: Victor Piţurcă

Goals: Falemi (17), Răducanu (41), Arben Nuhiji (87)

FC SHERIFF TIRASPOL v RSC ANDERLECHT 1-2 (1-1)

Tiraspol Stadion 1.08.2001

Referee: Martin Hansson (SWE) Attendance: 4,498

FC SHERIFF: Oleksandr Bokarev, Odia Chidi, Vazha Tarhnishvili (Cap), Yuri Bukel, Igor Kharkovchenko, Veaceslav Bugneac (55 Vladimir Tanurcov), Vadim Boreţ, Victor Barîşev, Victor Comlionoc (67 Chiedu Chukwueke), Evgheny Patula (63 Ruslan Barburoş), Serghei Dadu. Trainer: Valeri Vasiliev

ANDERLECHT: Filip de Wilde, Aleksandar Ilic, Yves Vanderhaeghe, Glen de Boeck (Cap), Walter Baseggio (29 Tarek El Said), Olivier Doll, Besnik Hasi, Bertrand Crasson (77 Emmanuel Pirard), Ivica Mornar (73 Gilles de Bilde), Oleg Yashchuk, Aruna Dindane. Trainer: Aime Antheunis

Goals: Boreţ (4), Yashchuk (28 pen), de Boeck (59)

FERENCVÁROSI TC BUDAPEST v HNK HAJDUK SPLIT 0-0

Üllői út, Budapest 25.07.2001

Referee: Mikko Vuorela (FIN) Attendance: 9,259

FERENCVÁROS: Lajos Szűcs, Attila Dragóner, János Hrutka, Norbert Nagy (57 Gábor Gyepes), Marius Cheregi, Attila Kriston (65 Alex Monken Arruda), Péter Lipcsei (Cap), Tibor Szabó, Igor Szkukalek, Attila Pinte, Zoltán Gera. Trainer: János Csank

HAJDUK: Stipe Pletikosa, Darko Butorovic, Krunoslav Rendulic, Igor Stimac (Cap), Goran Sablic, Vlatko Dolonga, Igor Musa, Mario Carevic (71 Ante Mise), Ivan Bosnjak (81 Srdan Andrić), Zvonimir Deranja, Mate Bilić. Trainer: Nenad Gracan

STEAUA BUCUREŞTI v SLOGA JUGOMAGNAT SKOPJE 3-0 (2-0)

Steaua, Bucureşti 25.07.2001

Referee: Pasquale Rodomonti (ITA) Attendance: 9,200

STEAUA: Martin Tudor; Florentin Dumitru, Marius Baciu (Cap), Mirel Rădoi, Dumitru Mitriţă; Cătălin Liţă (46 Sorin Paraschiv), Erik Augustin Lincar, Eugen Trică, Pompiliu Stoica; Claudiu Răducanu (65 Adrian Neaga), Ion Dănciulescu (81 Nana N'Gassam Falemi). Trainer: Victor Piţurcă

FK SLOGA JUGOMAGNAT: Gogo Jovcev, Goran Jovanovski, Toni Banduliev, Zoran Jovanovski, Nebi Mustafi, Arben Nuhiji, Ardzend Beciri, Husein Beganovic, Zekirija Ramadan, Refik Arif (Cap), Oldzaj Barjam (54 Ilco Georgioski). Trainer: Ekrem Maglajija

Goals: Răducanu (1, 19), Trică (83)

HNK HAJDUK SPLIT v FERENCVÁROSI TC BUDAPEST 0-0 (AET)

Poljud, Split 1.08.2001

Referee: Orhan Erdemir (TUR) Attendance: 26,400

HAJDUK: Stipe Pletikosa, Igor Stimac (Cap), Goran Sablić, Vlatko Dolonga (104 Hrvoje Vejić), Darko Butorović (65 Dario Srna), Igor Musa, Mario Carević, Krunoslav Rendulić, Ivan Bosnjak, Mate Bilić (75 Aljosa Asanović), Zvonimir Deranja. Trainer: Nenad Gracan

FERENCVÁROS: Lajos Szűcs, Attila Dragóner, Igor Szkukalek, Attila Pinte, János Hrutka (59 Gábor Gyepes), Zoltán Balog, Marius Cheregi (110 Alex Monken Arruda), Tibor Szabó (98 Gábor Vén), Péter Lipcsei (Cap), Attila Kriston, Zoltán Gera. Trainer: János Csank

Penalties: Arruda (miss), 1-0 Asanović, 1-1 Pinte, Srna (miss), 1-2 Szkukalek, 2-2 Carevic, 2-3 Lipcsei, 3-3 Deranja, 3-4 Vén, 4-4 Stimac, Dragóner (miss), 5-4 Musa

NK MARIBOR v GLASGOW RANGERS FC 0-3 (0-1)

Ljudski vrt, Maribor 25.07.2001

Referee: Mario van der Ende (HOL) Attendance: 6,100

NK MARIBOR: Marko Simeunovic (Cap), Samir Duro, Ales Krizan, Simon Sešlar (58 Miha Golob), Simon Dvorsak, Barnabás Sztipánovics, Suad Filekovic, Stipe Balajic (88 Bostjan Znuderl), Marinko Sarkezi, Fabijan Cipot (73 Andrej Kvas), Matej Snofl. Trainer: Ivan Susak

RANGERS: Stefan Klos, Fernando Jacob Ricksen, Craig Moore, Lorenzo Amoruso (46 Barry Ferguson), Arthur Numan (Cap), Claudio Paul Caniggia (69 Michael Mols), Christian Nerlinger (64 Neil Doherty McCann), Tore André Flo, Claudio Reyna, Bert Konterman, Russell Latapy. Trainer: Dick Advocaat

Goals: Flo (38, 73 pen), Nerlinger (56)

GLASGOW RANGERS FC v NK MARIBOR 3-1 (0-1)

Ibrox, Glasgow 1.08.2001

Referee: Jorge Emanuel MONTEIRO COROADO (POR) Attendance: 50,000

RANGERS: Stefan Klos, Fernando Jacob Ricksen, Craig Moore, Bert Konterman, Anthony Vidmar, Barry Ferguson (Cap), Claudio Paul Caniggia (73 Billy Dodds), Christian Nerlinger (38 Neil Doherty McCann), Tore André Flo, Russell Latapy (50 Scott Wilson), Stephen Hughes. Trainer: Dick Advocaat

NK MARIBOR: Marko Simeunovic (Cap) (73 Tomaz Murko), Samir Duro, Ales Krizan, Simon Sešlar, Andrej Kvas (60 Miha Golob), Suad Filekovic, Bostjan Znuderl, Stipe Balajic, Vanja Starcevic (77 Faruk Ihtijarevic), Matej Snofl, Zikica Buksanovic. Trainer: Ivan Susak

Goals: Starcevic (16), Flo (55), Caniggia (58, 71)

BOHEMIANS FC DUBLIN v HALMSTADS BK 1-2 (1-1)

Dalymount Park, Dublin 25.07.2001

Referee: Erol Ersoy (TUR) Attendance: 4,225

BOHEMIANS: Wayne Russell, Brian Shelley, Simon Webb, Kevin Hunt (Cap), Shaun Maher, Avery John, Paul Byrne (62 Fergal Harkin), Stephen Caffrey, Alex Nesovic (62 David Morrison), Glen Crowe (81 Gary O'Neill), Mark Rutherford. Trainer: Pete Mahon

HALMSTADS BK: Håkan Svensson, Torbjörn Arvidsson, Tommy Jönsson, Stefan Vennberg, Mikael Nilsson, Petter Hansson (Cap) (46 Fredrik Gustafsson), Fredrik Andersson (57 Emil Jensen), Samuel Wowoah, Stefan Selakovic (88 Björn Carlsson), Robert Andersson, Michael Svensson. Trainer: Tom Prahl

Goals: Crowe (23), Jönsson (31 pen), Selakovic (55)

HALMSTADS BK v BOHEMIANS FC DUBLIN 2-0 (0-0)

Örjans Vall, Halmstad 1.08.2001

Referee: Ivan Dobrinov (BUL) Attendance: 3,643

HALMSTADS BK: Håkan Svensson, Torbjörn Arvidsson (88 Mattias Ekstrom), Tommy Jönsson, Mikael Nilsson, Petter Hansson (Cap), Fredrik Andersson, Samuel Wowoah (84 Björn Carlsson), Stefan Selakovic, Robert Andersson (74 Henrik Bertilsson), Michael Svensson, Emil Jensen. Trainer: Tom Prahl

BOHEMIANS: Wayne Russell, Brian Shelley, Simon Webb, Kevin Hunt (Cap), Shaun Maher (64 Gary O'Neill), Avery John, Paul Byrne (70 David Morrison), Stephen Caffrey, Trevor Molloy (76 David Hill), Glen Crowe, Mark Rutherford. Trainer: Pete Mahon

Goals: Jönsson (57), Selakovic (68)

FC PORTO v BARRY TOWN FC 8-0 (5-0)

Estádio das Antas 25.07.2001

Referee: Giorgos Kasnaferis (GRE) Attendance: 43,050

FC PORTO: Sergei Ovchinnikov, JORGE Paulo COSTA Almeida (Cap), Carlos Humberto PAREDES Monges, Carlos Alberto Oliveira SECRETÁRIO (69 RICARDO Alberto Silveira CARVALHO), Anderson Luis de Sousa "DECO" (73 Dimitri Alenichev), JORGE Almeida Gomes de ANDRADE, Sven Fredrick Olof SÖDERSTRÖM, Nuno Fernando Gonçalves da Rocha "CAPUCHO" (61 CÃNDIDO Alves Moreira da COSTA), CLAYTON Ferreira CRUZ, MARIO Magalhães da SILVA, Renivaldo Pereira des Jesus "PENA". Trainer: Octavio Coelho Machado

BARRY TOWN: Tim Clarke, Terry Evans (50 Richard Joseph Kennedy), Gary Gilbert Lloyd, James Jenkins (50 Scott Morgan), Andrew David York (Cap), Lee Phillips, Kenneth James Brown (65 Matthew Howard Davies), Jonathan Charles French, Jamie David Moralee, Mike Flynn, Luke Roy Staton. Trainer: Peter Nicholas

Goals: Pena (12, 51, 52, 72), Deco (22 pen, 23 pen, 43), Söderström (41)

BARRY TOWN FC v FC PORTO 3-1 (2-1)

Jenner Park, Barry 1.08.2001

Referee: Dani Koren (ISR) Attendance: 2,377

BARRY TOWN: Tim Clarke, Terry Evans, Gary Gilbert Lloyd, Richard Joseph Kennedy, Andrew David York (Cap), Lee Phillips (82 Neil Anthony Sharp), Kenneth James Brown, Jonathan Charles French, Jamie David Moralee, Michael Flynn (51 James Jenkins), Luke Roy Staton (67 Matthew Howard Davies). Trainer: Peter Nicholas

FC PORTO: PEDRO Manuel ESPINHA Ferreira, JORGE Paulo COSTA Almeida (Cap), RICARDO Alberto Silveira CARVALHO, Francisco José Rodrigues da Costa "COSTINHA", RUBENS dos Santos JÚNIOR, Alessandro ANDRADE OLIVEIRA, Hugo Benjamin IBARRA (54 HELDER Manuel Marques POSTIGA), RAFAEL Gustavo DIAS (61 Dmitri Alenichev), Victor QUINTANA (70 João Paulo Maio dos Santos "PAULINHO SANTOS"), CANDIDO Alveira Moreira da COSTA, RICARDO Emidio Ramalho da SILVA. Trainer: Octavio Coelho Machado

Goals: Rafael Dias (17), Phillips (37), Flynn (39), Lloyd (89 pen)

THIRD QUALIFYING ROUND

LOKOMOTIV MOSKVA v FC TIROL INNSBRUCK 3-1 (2-1)

Saturn, Ramenskoye 7.08.2001

Referee: Kim Milton Nielsen (DEN) Attendance: 12,500

LOKOMOTIV: Ruslan Nigmatullin, Gennadiy Nizhegorodov, Jacob Lekcetho, Igor Chugainov (Cap), Marat Izmailov, Vladimir Maminov, James Chibuzor Obiorah (73 Maxim Buznikin), Dmitriy Loskov (75 Sergei Ignashevich), Dmitry Sennikov, Milan Obradovic, Ruslan Pimenov (61 Zaza Janashia). Trainer: Yuri Semin

FC TIROL: Marc Ziegler, Walter Kogler, Robert Wazinger, Marco Zwyssig, Roland Kirchler (Cap), Radoslaw Gilewicz, Jerzy Brzeczek, Alfred Hörtnagl, Robert Ibertsberger, Patrik Jezek (74 Markus Scharrer), Jürgen Panis (34 Olivier Prudlo). Trainer: Kurt Jara

Goals: Lekcetho (2), Kirchler (19), Izmailov (37), Ignashevich (79)

FC TIROL INNSBRUCK v LOKOMOTIV MOSKVA 0-1 (0-0)

Tivoli, Innsbruck 22.08.2001

Referee: Mario van der Ende (HOL)

FC TIROL: Marc Ziegler, Walter Kogler, Marco Zwyssig, Roland Kirchler, Michael Baur, Radoslaw Gilewicz, Jerzy Brzeczek (72 Eduard Glieder), Robert Ibertsberger, Stefan Marasek, Markus Scharrer (46 Wolfgang Mair), Patrik Jezek. Trainer: Kurt Jara

LOKOMOTIV: Ruslan Nigmatullin, Gennadiy Nizhegorodov, Jacob Lekcetho, Sergei Ignashevich, Igor Chugainov, Marat Izmailov (46 Vladimir Maminov), James Chibuzor Obiorah, Dmitriy Loskov, Dmitry Sennikov, Milan Obradovic, Ruslan Pimenov (76 Yuri Drozdov). Trainer: Yuri Semin

Goal: Maminov (51)

The result of this game was cancelled by UEFA. The referee erroneously booked Vladimir Maminov instead of Ruslan Pimenov. Ruslan Pimenov had already been booked and therefore would have been sent off. A replay was ordered on 9th September 2001.

FC TIROL INNSBRUCK v LOKOMOTIV MOSKVA 1-0 (1-0)

Tivoli, Innsbruck 8.09.2001

Referee: Vitor Manuel MELO PEREIRA (POR) Att: 15,500

FC TIROL: Marc Ziegler, Walter Kogler, Marco Zwyssig, Roland Kirchler, Michael Baur, Radoslaw Gilewicz, Jerzy Brzeczek, Alexander Hörtnagl, Robert Ibertsberger (61 Eduard Glieder), Stefan Marasek (76 Ibrahim Sidi Be), Patrik Jezek. Trainer: Kurt Jara

LOKOMOTIV: Ruslan Nigmatullin, Gennadiy Nizhegorodov, Jacob Lekcetho, Sergei Ignashevich, Igor Chugainov, Marat Izmailov, Vladimir Maminov, James Chibuzor Obiorah (56 Zaza Janashia), Dmitriy Loskov, Dmitry Sennikov, Milan Obradovic. Trainer: Yuri Semin

Sent off: Hörtnagl (63)

Goal: Brzeczek (30)

FC SHAKHTAR DONETSK v BV BORUSSIA DORTMUND 0-2 (0-1)

Shakhtyor, Donetsk 7.08.2001

Referee: Knud Erik Fisker (DEN) Attendance: 31,714

SHAKHTAR: Yuri Virt, Mykhailo Starostyak (79 Mariusz Lewandowski), Anatoliy Tymoshchuk, Serhiy Popov (Cap), Marian Aliuță (75 Serhiy Atelkin), Aleksei Bakharev, Hennadiy Zubov, Andriy Vorobei, Julius Aghahowa, Isaak Okoronkwo, Daniel Florea. Trainer: Viktor Prokopenko

BORUSSIA: Jens Lehmann, EVANILSON Aparecido Ferreira, Jürgen Kohler (Cap), Jörg Heinrich, Jan Koller, Tomáš Rosicky (64 Márcio AMOROSO Dos Santos), Giuseppe Reina (74 Miroslav Stević), Sunday Oliseh, Leonardo de Deus Santos "DEDÉ", Lars Ricken (81 Fredi Bobic), Christoph Metzelder. Trainer: Matthias Sammer

Goals: Ricken (35), Oliseh (73)

BV BORUSSIA DORTMUND v FC SHAKHTAR DONETSK 3-1 (0-1)

Westfalenstadion, Dortmund 22.08.2001

Referee: Karl-Erik Nilsson (SWE) Attendance: 47,000

BORUSSIA: Jens Lehmann, Christian Wörns, EVANILSON Aparecido Ferreira, Jürgen Kohler, Stefan Reuter, Jan Koller (79 Fredi BOBIC), Tomáš Rosicky, Sunday Oliseh, Leonardo de Deus Santos "DEDÉ", Lars Ricken (77 Miroslav Stević), Márcio AMOROSO Dos Santos (88 Ahmed Reda Madouni). Trainer: Matthias Sammer

SHAKHTAR: Yuri Virt, Mykhailo Starostyak, Anatoliy Tymoshchuk, Serhiy Popov, Marian Aliuță, Aleksei Bakharev (70 Olexiy Belik), Hennadiy Zubov, Andriy Vorobei, Julius Aghahowa, Isaak Okoronkwo, Daniel Florea. Trainer: Viktor Prokopenko

Goals: Aghahowa (7), Koller (50, 68), Amoroso (64)

WISŁA KRAKÓW v FC BARCELONA 3-4 (3-2)

Wisła, Kraków 8.08.2001

Referee: Rune Pedersen (NOR) Attendance: 7,506

WISLA: Artur Sarnat, Miroslaw Szymkowiak (79 Marek Zajac), Bogdan Zajac (79 Sunday Ibrahim), Marcin Baszczynski, Kamil Kosowski, Arkadiusz Glowacki, Kazimierz Moskal, Grzegorz Pater, Maciej Zurawski, Tomasz Frankowski (69 Ryszard Czerwiec), Olgierd Moskalewicz. Trainer: Franciszek Smuda

FC BARCELONA: Roberto Óscar BONANO, Patrik Andersson, Xavier Hernández Creus "XAVI", Patrick Kluivert, Reinaldo Vítor Borba Ferreira "RIVALDO", Marc Overmars (60 Philip Cocu), SERGI Barjuán Esclusa, Fábio Rochemback (81 Michael Reiziger), Philippe Christanval, Gabriel García de la Torre "GABRI", LUIS ENRIQUE Martínez Garcia (87 Roberto TRASHORRAS GAYOSO). Trainer: Carlos REXACH Cerda

Goals: Pater (22, 32), Frankowski (38), Rivaldo (31 pen, 34, 73), Kluivert (56)

FC BARCELONA v TS WISLA KRAKÓW 1-0 (0-0)

Camp Nou, Barcelona 21.08.2001

Referee: Gilles Veissière (FRA) Attendance: 58,233

FC BARCELONA: Roberto Óscar BONANO, Patrik Andersson, Xavier Hernández Creus "XAVI", Javier Pedro SAVIOLA (78 GEOVANNI Deiberson Mauricio), Philip Cocu (84 Gabriel García de la Torre "GABRI"), Patrick Kluivert, Reinaldo Vítor Borba Ferreira "RIVALDO", SERGI Barjuán Esclusa, Philippe Christanval, Carles PUYOL Saforcada, Fábio Rochemback (56 LUIS ENRIQUE Martínez Garcia). Trainer: Carlos REXACH Cerda

WISLA: Artur Sarnat, Miroslaw Szymkowiak, Marcin Baszczynski, Kamil Kosowski (76 Grzegorz Nicinski), Arkadiusz Glowacki, Kazimierz Moskal, Grzegorz Pater (70 Marek Zajac), Maciej Zurawski, Ryszard Czerwiec (82 Tomasz Kulawik), Olgierd Moskalewicz, Sunday Ibrahim. Trainer: Franciszek Smuda

Goal: Luis Enrique (72)

FC KØBENHAVN v SS LAZIO ROMA 2-1 (0-0)

Parken, København 8.08.2001

Referee: Nikolai Levnikov (RUS) Attendance: 37,516

FC KØBENHAVN: Magnus Kihlstedt, Thomas Rytter, Kim Madsen, Christian Bager Poulsen, Niclas Jensen, Thomas Røll Larsen, Sibusiso Zuma, Heine Fernandez, Thomas Thorninger, Jacob Laursen, Christian Lønstrup (Cap). Trainer: Kent Karlsson

LAZIO: Angelo Peruzzi, Dino Baggio, Karel Poborsky, Claudio Javier López, Hernán Jorge Crespo, Sinisa Mihajlovic, Alessandro Nesta (Cap), Diego Pablo Simeone, Giuseppe Pancaro, Paolo Negro, Stefano Fiore. Trainer: Dino Zoff

Goals: Crespo (56), Laursen (73 pen), Fernandez (85)

SS LAZIO ROMA v FC KØBENHAVN 4-1 (0-0)

Stadio Olimpico, Roma 21.08.2001

Referee: Hellmut Krug (GER) Attendance: 37,133

LAZIO: Angelo Peruzzi, Karel Poborsky (53 Lucas Castroman), Claudio Javier López, Hernán Jorge Crespo, Sinisa Mihajlović (60 Francesco Colonnese), Alessandro Nesta, Diego Pablo Simeone, Giuseppe Pancaro, Paolo Negro (35 Giuseppe Favalli), Stefano Fiore, Gaizka MENDIETA Zabala. Trainer: Dino Zoff

FC KØBENHAVN: Magnus Kihlstedt, Thomas Rytter, Kim Madsen (73 Carsten Fredgaard), Christian Bager Poulsen, Niclas Jensen, Thomas Røll Larsen, Sibusiso Zuma, Todi Jónsson (67 Heine Fernandez), Thomas Thorninger (66 Morten Bisgaard), Jacob Laursen, Christian Lønstrup. Trainer: Kent Karlsson

Goals: Crespo (48, 63), López (64), Zuma (81), Fiore (90)

GALATASARAY SK ISTANBUL v LEVSKI SOFIA 2-1 (1-0)

Ali Sami Yen, Istanbul 8.08.2001

Referee: Herbert Fandel (GER) Attendance: 16,051

GALATASARAY: Ali Faryd Camilo MONDRAGÓN, Carlos Alberto de Oliveira "CAPONE" (57 Sébstien PEREZ), Bülent Korkmaz (Cap), Gheorghe Popescu, Ergün Penbe, Ümit Davala, HASAN Gökhan ŞAŞ, Suat Kaya (73 Ali Riza Sergen Yalçin), Bülent Akin, Arif Erdem (61 Berkant Göktan), Ümit Karan. Trainer: Mircea Lucescu

LEVSKI: Georgi Petkov, Martin Stankov, Stanimir Stoilov (Cap), Georgi Markov (46 Dimitar Telkiyski), Dalibor Dragic, Ilian Stoianov, Stanislav Genchev, Rogério GAUCHO Botelho (63 Stanislav Angelov), Georgi Ivanov, Elin Topuzakov, Miodrag Pantelic (90 Svetoslav Barkanichkov). Trainer: Ljubo Petrovic

Goals: Ümit Karan (9), Ümit Davala (74), G.Ivanov (78)

LEVSKI SOFIA v GALATASARAY SK ISTANBUL 1-1 (0-0)

Georgi Asparuhov, Sofia 22.08.2001

Referee: Claude Colombo (FRA) Attendance: 25,500

LEVSKI: Georgi Petkov, Martin Stankov, Stanimir Stoilov, Biser Ivanov (64 Dimitar Telkiyski), Georgi Markov, Stanislav Genchev, Konstantin Golovskoi, Ilian Stoianov (46 Rogério GAUCHO Botelho, 70 Todor Kolev), Georgi Ivanov, Miodrag Pantelic, Elin Topuzakov. Trainer: Ljubo Petrovic

GALATASARAY: Ali Faryd Camilo MONDRAGÓN, Bülent Korkmaz, Emre Asik, Suat Kaya, Arif Erdem (65 Berkant Göktan), HASAN Gökhan ŞAŞ, Bülent Akin, Ümit Davala, Carlos Alberto de Oliveira "CAPONE", Serkan Aykut (84 Vedat Inceefe), Ergün Penbe. Trainer: Mircea Lucescu

Goals: Serkan (50), Pantelic (78)

INTER SLOVNAFT BRATISLAVA v ROSENBORG BK TRONDHEIM 3-3 (0-1)

ASK Inter Slovnaft, Bratislava 8.08.2001

Referee: Lucilio Cardoso CORTEZ BATISTA (POR) Attendance: 5,150

INTER: Miroslav Hyll, Marian Cisovsky, Marián Suchancok (Cap), Tomas Gerich, Peter Dzurik, Radoslav Kunzo, Roman Kratochvíl, Juraj Czinege (45 Miroslav Drobnak), Alias Lembakoali (85 Martin Sevela), Peter Petras (28 Marian Lalik), Saša Micovic. Trainer: Jozef Bubenko

ROSENBORG: Arni Gautur Arason, Erik Hoftun (Cap), Christer Basma, Roar Strand (79 Fredrik Winsnes), Ørjan Berg, Bent Inge Johnsen, Bent Andre Skammelsrud, Janne Saarinen, Frode Johnsen, Harald Martin Brattbakk (90 Christer George), Sigurd Rushfeldt. Trainer: Nils Arne Eggen

Goals: Brattbakk (10), Lembakoali (50, 62), Drobnak (67), Skammelsrud (76 pen), Kunzo (88 og)

ROSENBORG BK TRONDHEIM v ASK INTER SLOVNAFT BRATISLAVA 4-0 (3-0)

Lerkendal, Trondheim 22.08.2001

Referee: Hartmut Strampe (GER) Attendance: 15,212

ROSENBORG: Arni Gautur Arason, Erik Hoftun, Christer Basma, Roar Strand (88 Christer George), Ørjan Berg (71 Fredrik Winsnes), Bent Inge Johnsen, Bent Andre Skammelsrud, Janne Saarinen, Frode Johnsen, Harald Martin Brattbakk (86 Dagfinn Enerly), Sigurd Rushfeldt. Trainer: Nils Arne Eggen

INTER: Miroslav Hyll, Marian Cisovsky, Marián Suchancok, Tomas Gerich, Peter Dzurik, Radoslav Kunzo, Roman Kratochvíl, Juraj Czinege, Alias Lembakoali (66 Peter Petras), Saša Micovic (35 Miroslav Drobnak), Marian Lalik. Trainer: Jozef Bubenko

Goals: Frode Johnsen (10), Rushfeldt (15), Skammelsrud (43), Strand (86)

HALMSTADS BK v RSC ANDERLECHT BRUSSEL 2-3 (1-0)

Örjans Vall, Halmstad 8.08.2001

Referee: Ryszard Wojcik (POL) Attendance: 3,876

HALMSTADS BK: Håkan Svensson, Torbjörn Arvidsson, Tommy Jönsson, Mikael Nilsson, Petter Hansson (Cap), Fredrik Andersson, Samuel Wowoah, Stefan Selakovic, Robert Andersson (81 Björn Carlsson), Michael Svensson, Emil Jensen. Trainer: Tom Prahl

ANDERLECHT: Filip de Wilde, Aleksandar Ilic, Yves Vanderhaeghe, Glen de Boeck (Cap), Tarek El Said (46 Oleg Yashchuk), Marc Hendrikx, Besnik Hasi, Bertrand Crasson, Ki-Hyeon Seol (80 Ivica Mornar), Emmanuel Pirard, Aruna Dindane (90 Gilles de Bilde). Trainer: Aime Antheunis

Goals: M.Svensson (13), Seol (56), Hasi (66), Selakovic (76), Mornar (87)

RSC ANDERLECHT BRUSSEL v HALMSTADS BK 1-1 (0-1)

Constant Vanden Stock, Brussel 22.08.2001

Referee: Kyros Vasaras (GRE) Attendance: 16,850

ANDERLECHT: Filip de Wilde, Aleksandar Ilic, Yves Vanderhaeghe, Glen de Boeck, Marc Hendrikx (46 Tarek El Said), Besnik Hasi, Bertrand Crasson, Ki-Hyeon Seol (46 Ivica Mornar), Emmanuel Pirard, Aruna Dindane, Gilles de Bilde (89 Oleg Yashchuk). Trainer: Aime Antheunis

HALMSTADS BK: Håkan Svensson, Torbjörn Arvidsson, Tommy Jönsson, Joel Borgstrand (83 Henrik Bertilsson), Mikael Nilsson, Petter Hansson, Fredrik Andersson, Samuel Wowoah, Stefan Selakovic, Robert Andersson, Michael Svensson (32 Mattias Ekstrom). Trainer: Tom Prahl

Goals: Jönsson (12), de Boeck (83)

SK SLAVIA PRAHA v PANATHINAIKOS FC ATHINA 1-2 (0-1)

Strahov, Praha 8.08.2001

Referee: Alain Hamer (LUX) Attendance: 14,707

SLAVIA: Radek Černý, Lukáš Došek (76 Lumir Sedlácek), Patrick Gedeon, Ludek Zelenka (61 Tomáš Došek), Richard Dostálek, Darko Suskavcevic, Adam Petrouš, Jiri Skála (46 Tomáš Kuchar), Pavel Kuka (Cap), Ivo Svoboda, Martin Müller. Trainer: Josef Pesice

PANATHINAIKOS: Antonis Nikopolidis, Giorgos Seitaridis, Panagiotis Fissas, Sotiris Kyrgiakos, René Henriksen, Aggelos Basinas, Jan Michaelsen, Joonas Einari Kolkka (87 Daniel Sarić), Mihalis Konstantinou (68 Emmanuel Olisadebe), Giorgos Karagounis (83 Fernando Edgar Galetto), Nikos Liberopoulos (Cap). Trainer: Giannis Kirastas

Sent off: Černý (86)

Goals: Liberopoulos (25), Karagounis (57), Kuka (68)

PANATHINAIKOS FC ATHINA v SK SLAVIA PRAHA 1-0 (1-0)

Apostolos Nikolaidis, Athina 22.08.2001

Referee: Anders Frisk (SWE) Attendance: 14,718

PANATHINAIKOS: Antonis Nikopolidis, Giorgos Seitaridis, Panagiotis Fissas, Sotiris Kyrgiakos, René Henriksen, Aggelos Basinas, Jan Michaelsen, Joonas Einari Kolkka, Mihalis Konstantinou (82 Leonidas Vokolos), Giorgos Karagounis (63 PAULO Manuel SOUSA Carvalho), Nikos Liberopoulos (35 Goran Vlaović). Trainer: Giannis Kirastas

SLAVIA: Michal Václavik, Tomáš Došek, Ľuboš Kozel, Patrick Gedeon, Pavel Novotny, Richard Dostálek (69 Lukáš Došek), Lumir Sedlácek (55 Ivo Svoboda), Adam Petrouš, Pavel Kuka, Martin Müller, Tomáš Kuchar. Trainer: Josef Pesice

Goal: Basinas (27 pen)

HAKA VALKEAKOSKEN v LIVERPOOL FC 0-5 (0-1)

Olympic, Helsinki 8.08.2001

Referee: Arturo DAUDÉN IBÁÑEZ (SPA) Att: 33,217

HAKA: András Vilnrotter, Lasse Karjalainen (Cap) (83 Oleg Ivanov), Janne Mäkelä. Liro Aalto, Ville Väisänen, Valeriy Popovich (70 Jukka Ruhanen), Tommi Torkkeli (72 Jaakko Pasanen), Péter Kovács, David Wilson, Jarkko Okkonen, Juuso Totte Kangaskorpi. Trainer: Keith Armstrong

LIVERPOOL: Pegguy Arphexad, Stéphane Henchoz, Sami Tuomas Hyypiä (Cap), Markus Babbel, Emile William Wanhoe Heskey (72 Robert Bernard Fowler), Michael James Owen, Patrik Berger, Dietmar Hamann, Steven George Gerrard (64 Danny Ben Murphy), Jamie Carragher, Jari Litmanen (58 Gary McAllister). Trainer: Gérard Houllier

Goals: Heskey (32), Owen (55, 64, 87), Hyypiä (86)

LIVERPOOL FC v HAKA VALKEAKOSKEN 4-1 (1-1)

Anfield, Liverpool 21.08.2001

Referee: Terje Hauge (NOR) Attendance: 31,602

LIVERPOOL: Pegguy Arphexad, Sami Tuomas Hyypiä (66 Markus Babbel), Emile William Wanhoe Heskey (60 Jari Litmanen), Robert Bernard Fowler, Jamie Redknapp (72 Steven George Gerrard), Nick Barmby, Bernard Diomède, Igor Biŝcan, Grégory Vignal, Stephen Wright, Djimi Traoré. Trainer: Gérard Houllier

HAKA: András Vilnrotter, Dragan Bajić (81 Marko Koivuranta), Lasse Karjalainen, Liro Aalto, Jukka Ruhanen (66 Mikko Innanen), Tommi Torkkeli, Péter Kovács, David Wilson, Jarkko Okkonen, Juuso Totte Kangaskorpi, MARCO António Pogioli (78 Oleg Ivanov). Trainer: Keith Armstrong

Goals: Fowler (37), P.Kovács (45), Redknapp (50), Heskey (57), Wilson (83 og)

STEAUA BUCUREŞTI v DINAMO KYIV 2-4 (1-3)

Steaua, Bucureşti 8.08.2001

Referee: Konrad Plautz (AUS) Attendance: 15,000

STEAUA: Martin Gheorghe Tudor, Florentin Dumitru, Mirel Matei Rădoi, Marius Achim Baciu (Cap), Dumitru Mitriţă, Sorin Ion Paraschiv (38 Ionel Daniel Dănciulescu), Nana Falemi N'Gassam (45 Erik Augustin Lincar), Pompiliu Sorin Stoica, Eugen Trică, Adrian Constantin Neaga (77 Daniel Bălan), Claudiu Nicu Răducanu. Trainer: Victor Piţurcă

DINAMO: Aleksandr Filimonov, Alexandr Khatskevich, Olexandr Borysovych Holovko (Cap), Vladyslav Vashchuk, Olexandr Melashchenko (83 Florin Lucian Cernat), Valentin Belkevich, Serhiy Fedorov, Isi "LUCKY" Idahor, Andriy Nesmachnyi, Serhiy Serebrennikov (67 Georgi Ivanov Peev), Goran Gavrancic (59 László Bodnár). Trainer: Valeryi Lobanovskyi

Goal: Belkevich (9 pen, 26), Trică (30, 53), Idahor (43), Melaschenko (63)

DINAMO KYIV v STEAUA BUCUREŞTI 1-1 (0-1)

Olympiyskyi, Kyiv 21.08.2001

Referee: Graham Barber (ENG) Attendance: 22,000

DINAMO: Aleksandr Filimonov, Alexandr Khatskevich, Olexandr Borysovych Holovko, Vladyslav Vashchuk, Olexandr Melashchenko (79 Serhiy Serebrennikov), Valentin Belkevich, Tiberiu Ghioane, Isi "LUCKY" IDAHOR (68 Georgi Ivanov Peev), László Bodnár, Andriy Nesmachnyi, Goran Gavrancic. Trainer: Valeryi Lobanovskyi

STEAUA: Tiberiu Adrian Lung, Florentin Dumitru, Ilie Iulian Miu, Marius Achim Baciu, Erik Augustin Lincar, Pompiliu Sorin Stoica, Adrian Constantin Neaga (82 Marius Vintilă), Eugen Trică (60 Nana Falemi N'Gassam), Daniel Bălan, Ionel Daniel Dănciulescu (71 Victorio Alexandru Piţurcă), Dumitru Mitriţă. Trainer: Victor Piţurcă **Sent off**: Baciu (52)

Goals: Neaga (30), Melashchenko (46)

HNK HAJDUK SPLIT v RCD MALLORCA 1-0 (1-0)

Poljud, Split 8.08.2001

Referee: Alain Sars (FRA) Attendance: 26,922

HAJDUK: Stipe Pletikosa, Darko Butorović (80 Dario Srna), Krunoslav Rendulić, Hrvoje Vuković (86 Hrvoje Vejić), Igor Stimac (Cap), Vlatko Dolonga, Srdjan Andrić, Igor Musa, Mario Carević, Zvonimir Deranja (68 Ante Mise), Mate Bilić. Trainer: Nenad Gracan

RCD MALLORCA: Leonardo "LEO" FRANCO, Fatih Akyel (79 Alberto RIERA Ortega), Fernando NIÑO Bejarano, Samuel ETO'O Fils, Ariel Miguel Santiago IBAGAZA, Javíer OLAIZOLA Rodríguez (Cap), Alvaro NOVO Ramírez, MARCOS Martín de la Fuente, Alberto LUQUE Martos, Miguel Angel NADAL Homar, Vicente ENGONGA Maté (58 CARLOS Dominguez Dominguez). Trainer: Bernd Krauss

Sent off: Rendulic (46), Carevic (87)

Goal: Bilić (29)

RCD MALLORCA v HNK HAJDUK SPLIT 2-0 (1-0, 1-0) (AET)

Son Moix, Palma de Mallorca 21.08.2001

Referee: Hugh Dallas (SCO) Attendance: 23,500

RCD MALLORCA: Leonardo "LEO" FRANCO, MIQUEL SOLER Sarasols, Fernando NIÑO Bejarano, Samuel ETO'O Fils, Ariel Miguel Santiago IBAGAZA (77 Alberto RIERA Ortega), Javíer OLAIZOLA Rodríguez, Alvaro NOVO Ramírez (71 CARLOS Dominguez Dominguez), MARCOS Martín de la Fuente, Alberto LUQUE Martos, Miguel Angel NADAL Homar, Vicente ENGONGA Maté (91 Leonardo Angel BIAGINI Bruzzese). Trainer: Bernd Krauss

HAJDUK: Stipe Pletikosa, Ante Mise, Goran Sablić, Hrvoje Vuković, Dario Srna, Vlatko Dolonga, Igor Musa (95 Vedran Celiscak), Hrvoje Vejić, Srdjan Andrić (68 Tonci Pirija), Ivan Bosnjak (75 Zvonimir Deranja), Mate Bilic. Trainer: Nenad Gracan

Goals: Eto'o (25), Luque (92)

FK CRVENA ZVEZDA BEOGRAD
v BAYER 04 LEVERKUSEN 0-0

FK Crvena Zvezda, Beograd 8.08.2001

Referee: Jan W. Wegereef (HOL) Attendance: 37,169

FK CRVENA ZVEZDA: Vladimir Disljenković, Marjan Marković, Ivan Vukomanović, Vladimir Matijasević, Nenad Lalatović (Cap), Dejan Ilić (59 Vidak Bratić), Leo Lerinc, Milenko Acimović (80 Branko Bosković), Ivan Gvozdenović, Mihajlo Pjanović (85 Darko Spalević), Branko Jelić. Trainer: Slavoljub Muslin

BAYER: Hans-Jörg Butt, Jens Nowotny (Cap), Boris Zivković (73 Jurica Vranjes), Ulf Kirsten (70 Thomas Brdarić), Yildiray Bastürk, Lucimar Ferreira da Silva "LUCIO", Bernd Schneider, Zoltan Sebescen, Oliver Neuville, Carsten Ramelow, Diego Rodolfo Placente. Trainer: Klaus Toppmöller

BAYER 04 LEVERKUSEN
v FK CRVENA ZVEZDA BEOGRAD 3-0 (2-0)

BayArena, Leverkusen 21.08.2001

Referee: Domenico Messina (ITA) Attendance: 22,500

BAYER: Hans-Jörg Butt, Jens Nowotny, Ulf Kirsten (67 Pascal Ojigwe), Yildiray Bastürk, Michael Ballack, Lucimar Ferreira da Silva "LUCIO", Bernd Schneider (84 Jurica Vranjes), Zoltan Sebescen (79 Boris Zivković), Oliver Neuville, Carsten Ramelow, Diego Rodolfo Placente. Trainer: Klaus Toppmöller

FK CRVENA ZVEZDA: Vladimir Disljenković, Marjan Marković, Ivan Vukomanović, Vladimir Matijasević, Nenad Lalatović, Leo Lerinc (79 Stevo Glogovac), Ivan Gvozdenović, Dejan Ilić (67 Saša Kocić), Darko Spalević, Milenko Acimović (56 Vidak Bratić), Branko Bosković. Trainer: Slavoljub Muslin

Goals: Neuville (13, 59), Kirsten (31)

AFC AJAX AMSTERDAM
v CELTIC FC GLASGOW 1-3 (1-2)

Amsterdam, ArenA 8.08.2001

Referee: Antonio Jesus LÓPEZ NIETO (SPA) Att: 51,859

AJAX: Fred Grim (Cap), Hatem Trabelsi, Petri Pasanen, Abubakari Yakubu (74 Andy van der Meyde), Cristian Chivu, Daniel Cruz, Rafael van der Vaart, Pius Ikedia (46 Zlatan Ibrahimović), Nikos Machlas, Shota Arveladze, Ahmed Hossam. Trainer: Co Adriaanse

CELTIC: Robert Douglas, Johan Mjällby, Tom Boyd (Cap), Joos Valgaeren, Didier Agathe, Paul Lambert, Neil Francis Lennon, Jackie McNamara, Bobby Alfred Manuel PETTA (87 Stephen Andrew Guppy), Henrik Larsson (84 John Hartson), Christopher Roy Sutton. Trainer: Martin O'Neill

Goals: Petta (7), Agathe (19), S. Arveladze (40), Sutton (55)

CELTIC FC GLASGOW
v AFC AJAX AMSTERDAM 0-1 (0-1)

Celtic Park, Glasgow 22.08.2001

Referee: Stefano Braschi (ITA) Attendance: 60,000

CELTIC: Robert Douglas, Tom Boyd, Jackie McNamara (63 Lubomir Moravcik), Joos Valgaeren, Henrik Larsson, Christopher Roy Sutton, Paul Lambert, Didier Agathe, Neil Francis Lennon, Stephen Andrew Guppy, Johan Mjällby. Trainer: Martin O'Neill

AJAX: Fred Grim, Ferdi Vierklau (63 Richard Knopper), André Bergdølmo (76 Ahmed Hossam), Cristian Chivu, Hatem Trabelsi, MAXWELL Scherrer Cabelino Andrade, Shota Arveladze, WAMBERTO de Jesus Sousa Campos, Nikos Machlas (55 Zlatan Ibrahimović), Abubakari Yakubu, Rafael van der Vaart. Trainer: Co Adriaanse

Goal: Wamberto (30)

GLASGOW RANGERS FC
v FENERBAHÇE SK ISTANBUL 0-0

Ibrox, Glasgow 8.08.2001

Referee: Urs Meier (SWI) Attendance: 49,472

RANGERS: Stefan Klos, Anthony Vidmar, Craig Moore, Scott Wilson, Arthur Numan (Cap), Fernando Jacob Ricksen, Stephen Hughes, Bert Konterman, Neil Doherty McCann, Claudio Paul Caniggia (46 Michael Mols), Tore André Flo. Trainer: Dick Advocaat

FENERBAHÇE: Rüştü Reçber, Mert Meric, Ogün Temizkanoglu (Cap), Mustafa Dogan (77 Niyazi SERHAT Akin), Zoran Mirkovic, Milan Rapajc, Haim Michael Revivo (86 Bernt Kennet Andersson), Ümit Özat, Nikola Lazetic, Abdullah Ercan, Samuel Johnson. Trainer: Mustafa Denizli

Sent off: Mols (56)

FENERBAHÇE SK ISTANBUL
v GLASGOW RANGERS FC 2-1 (1-0)

Sükrü Saraçoglu, Istanbul 22.08.2001

Referee: Pierluigi Collina (ITA) Attendance: 30,000

FENERBAHÇE: Rüstü Reçber, Mert Meric, Ogün Temizkanoglu, Mustafa Dogan, Zoran Mirkovic, Milan Rapajc (76 Bernt Kennet Andersson), Haim Michael Revivo (71 Niyazi SERHAT Akin), Ümit Özat, Nikola Lazetic (90 Deniz Uygar), Abdullah Ercan, Samuel Johnson. Trainer: Mustafa Denizli

RANGERS: Stefan Klos, Fernando Jacob Ricksen, Lorenzo Amoruso, Arthur Numan, Tore André Flo, Claudio Reyna (80 Stephen Hughes), Ronald de Boer, Bert Konterman, Andrei Kanchelskis (71 Claudio Paul Caniggia), Scott Wilson, Anthony Vidmar (46 Maurice Ross). Trainer: Dick Advocaat

Goals: Revivo (4), Serhat (72), Ricksen (75)

PARMA AC v LILLE OLYMPIQUE SC 0-2 (0-0)

Ennio Tardini, Parma 8.08.2001

Ref: Juan Antonio FERNANDEZ MARIN (SPA) Att: 14,974

PARMA: Sebastien Frey, Roberto Néstor Sensini, Sabri Lamouchi (70 Stephen Appiah), Savo Milosević (83 Henri Patrick M'Boma), Hidetoshi Nakata, JUNIOR de Souza Jenilson Angelo, Fabio Cannavaro (Cap), Marco di Vaio, Matias Jesus Almeyda, Jonathan Bachini (68 Marco Marchionni), Martin Djetou. Trainer: Renzo Ulivieri

OLYMPIQUE: Grégory Wimbee, Pascal Cygan (Cap), Abdelilah Fahmi, Dagui Orphie Bakari (85 Mikkel Beck), Salaheddine Bassir (69 Bruno Cheyrou), Stéphane Pichot (86 Benoît Cheyrou), Grégory Tafforeau, Johnny Ecker, Christophe Landrin, Sylvain N'Diaye, Fernando Osvaldo D'Amico. Trainer: Vahid Halilhodzić

Goals: Bassir (47), Ecker (80)

LILLE OLYMPIQUE SC v PARMA AC 0-1 (0-1)

Grimonprez Jooris, Lille 22.08.2001

Referee: Graham Poll (ENG) Attendance: 14,358

OLYMPIQUE: Grégory Wimbee, Pascal Cygan, Abdelilah Fahmi, Dagui Orphie Bakari, Djezon Boutoille (71 Salaheddine Bassir), Stéphane Pichot, Grégory Tafforeau, Johnny Ecker, Sylvain N'Diaye, Fernando Osvaldo D'Amico, Bruno Cheyrou (83 Benoît Cheyrou). Trainer: Vahid Halilhodzić

PARMA: Sebastien Frey, Roberto Néstor Sensini, Luigi Sartor (56 Savo Milosević), Hidetoshi Nakata, Alain Boghossian (67 Sabri Lamouchi), Sergei Gurenko (46 JUNIOR de Souza Jenilson Angelo), Fabio Cannavaro, Marco di Vaio, Matias Jesus Almeyda, Marco Marchionni, Martin Djetou. Trainer: Renzo Ulivieri

Goal: Sensini (28)

FC PORTO v GRASSHOPPER-CLUB ZÜRICH 2-2 (1-0)

Estádio das Antas, Porto 8.08.2001

Referee: L'uboš Michel (SVK) Attendance: 46,142

FC PORTO: Sergei Ovchinnikov, JORGE Paulo COSTA Almeida (Cap), Carlos Humberto PAREDES Monges (86 Francisco José Rodrigues da Costa "COSTINHA"), Anderson Luis de Sousa "DECO" (15 RAFAEL Gustavo Dias), JORGE Almeida Gomes de ANDRADE, Sven Fredrik Olof SÖDERSTRÖM, Hugo Benjamin IBARRA, Nuno Fernando Gonçalves da Rocha "CAPUCHO", CLAYTON Ferreira Cruz (55 HELDER Manuel Marques POSTIGA), MARIO Magalhães da SILVA, Renivaldo Pereira des Jesus "PENA". Trainer: Octavio Coelho Machado

GRASSHOPPER: Peter Jehle, Bruno Berner, Boris Smiljanic (Cap), Mihai Tararache, Papa Bouba Diop, Roland Schwegler, Pascal Castillo, Christoph Spycher, Mladen Petric (77 Benjamin Mwaruwari), Ariel Morales (65 Andreas Gerber), Richard Nuñez (90 Luca Ippoliti). Trainer: Hans-Peter Zaugg

Goals: Paredes (6), Nuñez (50), Petric (57), H. Postiga (59)

GRASSHOPPER-CLUB ZÜRICH v FC PORTO 2-3 (0-2)

Hardturm, Zürich 22.08.2001

Referee: Stuart Dougal (CZE) Attendance: 16,066

GRASSHOPPER: Peter Jehle, Bruno Berner, Boris Smiljanic (65 Stéphane Chapuisat), Mihai Tararache (90 Ricardo Cabañas), Papa Bouba Diop, Roland Schwegler, Pascal Castillo, Christoph Spycher, Mladen Petric, Ariel Morales (46 Benjamin Mwaruwari), Richard Nuñez. Trainer: Hans-Peter Zaugg

FC PORTO: Sergei Ovchinnikov, JORGE Paulo COSTA Almeida, Carlos Humberto PAREDES Monges (36 Francisco José Rodrigues da Costa "COSTINHA"), Anderson Luis de Sousa "DECO", JORGE Almeida Gomes de ANDRADE, Sven Fredrik Olof SÖDERSTRÖM (46 RICARDO Emidio Ramalho da SILVA), Hugo Benjamin IBARRA, Nuno Fernando Gonçalves da Rocha "CAPUCHO", CLAYTON Ferreira Cruz, MARIO Magalhães da SILVA (82 RUBENS dos Santos JUNIOR), Renivaldo Pereira des Jesus "PENA". Trainer: Octavio Coelho Machado

Sent off: Diop (66)

Goals: Clayton (14), Capucho (43), Petric (78), Deco (80), Chapuisat (87)

FIRST STAGE – GROUP A

FC LOKOMOTIV MOSKVA v RSC ANDERLECHT BRUSSEL 1-1 (1-1)

Dinamo, Moskva 11.09.2001

Referee: Vladimir Hrinak (SVK) Attendance: 12,000

LOKOMOTIV: Ruslan Nigmatullin, Milan Obradovic, Yuri Drozdov, Dmitry Sennikov, Jacob Lekcetho, Igor Chugainov, Marat Izmailov, Vladimir Maminov, Sergei Ignashevich, Maxim Buznikin (66 Nemanja Vucicevic), Ruslan Pimenov (75 Zaza Janashia). Trainer: Yuri Semin

ANDERLECHT: Filip de Wilde, Emmanuel Pirard, Glen de Boeck, Bertrand Crasson, Aleksandar Ilic, Aruna Dindane (88 Ki-Hyeon Seol), Besnik Hasi, Yves Vanderhaeghe, Marc Hendrikx, Gilles de Bilde (77 Alin Stoica), Ivica Mornar (90 Joris van Hout). Trainer: Aime Antheunis

Goals: Hendrikx (15), Maminov (18)

AS ROMA v REAL MADRID CF 1-2 (0-0)

Stadio Olimpico, Roma 11.09.2001

Referee: Graham Poll (ENG) Attendance: 71,878

AS ROMA: Ivan Pelizzoli, Jonathan Zebina, António Carlos Zago, Walter Adriano Samuel, Marcos Evangelista de Moraes "CAFU" (82 Abel Eduardo Balbo), Francesco Totti, Marcos ASSUNÇÃO Dos Santos (61 Antonio Cassano), EMERSON Ferreira da Rosa, Vincent Candela, Gabriel Omar Batistuta, Vincenzo Montella (46 Francisco Govinho LIMA). Trainer: Fabio Capello

REAL: Iker CASILLAS Fernández, Miguel Angel "MICHEL" SALGADO, Fernando Ruíz HIERRO, Aitor KARANKA De la Hoz, ROBERTO CARLOS da Silva, Luis Filipe Madeira FIGO, FLÁVIO de CONCEIÇÃO, Claude Makelele, Steve McManaman, RAÚL González Blanco, José María Gutiérrez "GUTI" (87 IVÁN CAMPO Ramos). Trainer: Vicente Del BOSQUE Gonzalez

Goals: Figo (50), Guti (63), Totti (73 pen)

RSC ANDERLECHT BRUSSEL v AS ROMA 0-0

Constant Vanden Stock, Brussel 19.09.2001

Referee: Karl-Erik Nilsson (SWE) Attendance: 21,436

ANDERLECHT: Filip de Wilde, Bertrand Crasson, Glen de Boeck, Joris van Hout, Marc Hendrikx, Aruna Dindane, Besnik Hasi, Walter Baseggio (86 Tarek El Said), Yves Vanderhaeghe, Alin Stoica (78 Ode Ochinabo Thompson), Ivica Mornar (67 Gilles de Bilde). Trainer: Aime Antheunis

AS ROMA: Francesco Antonioli, Jonathan Zebina, António Carlos Zago, Walter Adriano Samuel, Marcos Evangelista de Moraes "CAFU", Damiano Tommasi, Francisco Govinho LIMA, EMERSON Ferreira da Rosa, Vincent Candela, Gabriel Omar Batistuta (82 Vincenzo Montella), Francesco Totti. Trainer: Fabio Capello

REAL MADRID CF
v FC LOKOMOTIV MOSKVA 4-0 (1-0)

Santiago Bernabéu, Madrid 19.09.2001

Referee: Stéphane Bré (FRA) Attendance: 45,045

REAL: Iker CASILLAS Fernández, Miguel Angel "MICHEL" SALGADO, Fernando Ruíz HIERRO, Aitor KARANKA De la Hoz, ROBERTO CARLOS da Silva (83 Santiago Hernán SOLARI), Luis Filipe Madeira FIGO (88 Steve McManaman), FLÁVIO de CONCEIÇÃO (76 Albert CELADES López), Claude Makelele, Pedro MUNITIS Alvarez, RAÚL González Blanco, SÁVIO Bortolini Pimentel. Trainer: Vicente Del BOSQUE Gonzalez

LOKOMOTIV: Ruslan Nigmatullin, Yuri Drozdov, Jacob Lekcetho, Igor Chugainov, Milan Obradovic, Dmitriy Loskov, Marat Izmailov, Vladimir Maminov, James Chibuzor Obiorah (60 Maxim Buznikin), Igor Cherevchenko, Ruslan Pimenov (74 Nemanja Vucicevic). Trainer: Yuri Semin

Goals: Munitis (39), Figo (64 pen), Roberto Carlos (81), Sávio (87)

REAL MADRID CF
v RSC ANDERLECHT BRUSSEL 4-1 (0-1)

Santiago Bernabéu, Madrid 26.09.2001

Referee: Terje Hauge (NOR) Attendance: 53,500

REAL: Iker CASILLAS Fernández, Miguel Angel "MICHEL" SALGADO (69 GEREMI Sorele Fotso Ndjitap), Fernando Ruíz HIERRO, Aitor KARANKA De la Hoz, ROBERTO CARLOS da Silva, Luis Filipe Madeira FIGO, Albert CELADES López, Claude Makelele (81 Elvir Baljić), Santiago Hernán SOLARI, RAÚL González Blanco, Pedro MUNITIS Alvarez (72 Fernando MORIENTES Sánchez). Trainer: Vicente Del BOSQUE Gonzalez

ANDERLECHT: Filip de Wilde, Bertrand Crasson, Glen de Boeck, Joris van Hout, Aleksandar Ilic, Besnik Hasi (59 Gilles de Bilde), Walter Baseggio (66 Tarek El Said), Alin Stoica (71 Ode Ochinabo Thompson), Yves Vanderhaeghe, Marc Hendrikx, Aruna Dindane. Trainer: Aime Antheunis

Goals: Dindane (33), Celades (49), Raúl (51, 68), Solari (79)

AS ROMA v LOKOMOTIV MOSKVA 2-1 (0-0)

Stadio Olimpico, Roma 26.09.2001

Referee: Hartmut Strampe (GER) Attendance: 38,472

AS ROMA: Francesco Antonioli, Jonathan Zebina, António Carlos Zago, Walter Adriano Samuel, Marcos Evangelista de Moraes "CAFU" (63 Gianni GUIGOU Martínez), Damiano Tommasi (62 Marcos ASSUNÇAO Dos Santos), Francesco Totti, Francisco Govinho LIMA, Vincent Candela, Marco Delvecchio, Vincenzo Montella (46 Gabriel Omar Batistuta). Trainer: Fabio Capello

LOKOMOTIV: Ruslan Nigmatullin, Yuri Drozdov, Milan Obradovic, Igor Chugainov, Sergey Ignashevich, Jacob Lekcetho, Marat Izmailov, Vladimir Maminov, Dmitriy Loskov, Igor Cherevchenko, Ruslan Pimenov (74 Maxim Buznikin). Trainer: Yuri Semin

Goals: Obradovic (59), Chugainov (69 og), Totti (79)

RSC ANDERLECHT BRUSSEL
v REAL MADRID CF 0-2 (0-2)

Constant Vanden Stock, Brussel 16.10.2001

Referee: Knud Erik Fisker (DEN) Attendance: 21,922

ANDERLECHT: Filip de Wilde, Bertrand Crasson, Aleksandar Ilic, Lamine Traore, Marc Hendrikx, Aruna Dindane, Walter Baseggio (46 Tarek El Said), Yves Vanderhaeghe, Besnik Hasi, Oleg Yashchuk (79 Ode Ochinabo Thompson), Ivica Mornar. Trainer: Aime Antheunis

REAL: CÉSAR Sánchez Domínguez, Miguel Angel "MICHEL" SALGADO, Fernando Ruíz HIERRO (60 RUBÉN González Rocha), Francisco PAVÓN Barahona, ROBERTO CARLOS da Silva, Luis Filipe Madeira FIGO, Albert CELADES López, Claude Makelele, Steve McManaman (70 SÁVIO Bortolini Pimentel), RAÚL González Blanco, José María Gutiérrez "GUTI" (77 Fernando MORIENTES Sánchez). Trainer: Vicente Del BOSQUE Gonzalez

Goals: Raúl (19), McManaman (35)

LOKOMOTIV MOSKVA v AS ROMA 0-1 (0-0)

Dinamo, Moskva 16.10.2001

Referee: Dick Z.G. Jol (HOL) Attendance: 16,000

LOKOMOTIV: Ruslan Nigmatullin, James Chibuzor Obiorah, Milan Obradovic, Igor Chugainov, Sergey Ignashevich, Jacob Lekcetho, Marat Izmailov, Vladimir Maminov, Dmitriy Loskov, Igor Cherevchenko, Ruslan Pimenov. Trainer: Yuri Semin

AS ROMA: Francesco Antonioli, Jonathan Zebina, António Carlos Zago, Walter Adriano Samuel, Marcos Evangelista de Moraes "CAFU" (89 Diego Fuser), Damiano Tommasi (83 Marcos ASSUNÇAO Dos Santos), Francisco Govinho LIMA, EMERSON Ferreira da Rosa, Gianni GUIGOU Martínez, Gabriel Omar Batistuta, Francesco Totti.
Trainer: Fabio Capello

Goal: Cafu (78)

RSC ANDERLECHT BRUSSEL v LOKOMOTIV MOSKVA 1-5 (1-2)

Constant Vanden Stock, Brussel 24.10.2001

Referee: Thomas Michael McCurry (SCO) Att: 25,502

ANDERLECHT: Filip de Wilde, Bertrand Crasson, Glen de Boeck, Aleksandar Ilic, Marc Hendrikx, Oleg Yashchuk (52 Yasin Karaca), Besnik Hasi, Yves Vanderhaeghe, Tarek El Said (46 Giles de Bilde), Aruna Dindane (64 Nenad Jestrovic), Ivica Mornar. Trainer: Aime Antheunis

LOKOMOTIV: Ruslan Nigmatullin, Jacob Lekcetho (84 Gennady Nizhegorodov), Igor Chugainov, Dmitriy Sennikov, Sergey Ignashevich, Ruslan Pimenov (76 Yuri Drozdov), Vladimir Maminov, Igor Cherevchenko, Marat Izmailov, James Chibuzor Obiorah (55 Maxim Buznikin), Dmitriy Loskov.
Trainer: Yuri Semin

Goals: Ilic (2), Izmailov (13), Sennikov (28), Pimenov (58), Buznikin (63, 69)

REAL MADRID CF v AS ROMA 1-1 (0-1)

Santiago Bernabéu, Madrid 24.10.2001

Referee: Hellmut Krug (GER) Attendance: 63,000

REAL: CÉSAR Sánchez Domínguez, Miguel Angel "MICHEL" SALGADO, Fernando Ruíz HIERRO (46 Iván HELGUERA Bujía), Francisco PAVÓN Barahona, ROBERTO CARLOS da Silva (46 Santiago Hernán SOLARI), Luis Filipe Madeira FIGO, Albert CELADES López, Claude Makelele, Zinedine Zidane, RAÚL González Blanco, Fernando MORIENTES Sánchez (77 Pedro MUNITIS Alvarez).
Trainer: Vicente Del BOSQUE Gonzalez

AS ROMA: Francesco Antonioli, Marcos Evangelista de Moraes "CAFU", Jonathan Zebina, António Carlos Zago (46 ALDAIR Nascimento dos Santos), Walter Adriano Samuel, Vincent Candela, Damiano Tommasi (65 Marcos ASSUNÇAO Dos Santos), EMERSON Ferreira da Rosa, Francisco Govinho LIMA, Gabriel Omar Batistuta, Francesco Totti (88 Marco Delvecchio). Trainer: Fabio Capello

Goals: Totti (35), Figo (75 pen)

LOKOMOTIV MOSKVA v REAL MADRID CF 2-0 (1-0)

Dinamo, Moskva 30.10.2001

Referee: Michael Riley (ENG) Attendance: 18,000

LOKOMOTIV: Ruslan Nigmatullin, Dmitriy Sennikov, Sergey Ignashevich, Igor Cherevchenko (78 Yuri Drozdov), Igor Chugainov (24 Milan Obradović), Jacob Lekcetho, Marat Izmailov, Vladimir Maminov, Dmitriy Loskov, Maxim Buznikin (75 James Chibuzor Obiorah), Ruslan Pimenov.
Trainer: Yuri Semin

REAL: CÉSAR Sánchez Domínguez, Oscar MIÑAMBRES Pascual, Iván HELGUERA Bujía, Francisco PAVÓN Barahona, Raúl BRAVO Sanfélix, Santiago Hernán SOLARI, Albert ÇELADES López, Claude Makelele (72 RUBÉN González Rocha), Steve McManaman (61 Lopéz Rocha Valmiro "VALDO"), Pedro MUNITIS Alvarez, Fernando MORIENTES Sánchez (61 Carlos Reina ARANDA).
Trainer: Vicente Del BOSQUE Gonzalez

Goals: Buznikin (30), Cherevchenko (50)

AS ROMA v RSC ANDERLECHT BRUSSEL 1-1 (0-1)

Stadio Olimpico, Roma 30.10.2001

Referee: Eric Poulat (FRA) Attendance: 28,157

AS ROMA: Ivan Pelizzoli, Sebastiano Siviglia, ALDAIR Nascimento dos Santos, Walter Adriano Samuel, Marcos Evangelista de Moraes "CAFU", Ivan Tomic (71 Daniele de Rossi), Marcos ASSUNÇAO Dos Santos, EMERSON Ferreira da Rosa, Gianni GUIGOU Martínez, Marco Delvecchio, Antonio Cassano (76 Abel Eduardo Balbo).
Trainer: Fabio Capello

ANDERLECHT: Filip de Wilde, Bertrand Crasson (46 Joris van Hout), Glen de Boeck, Lamine Traore, Aleksandar Ilic, Alin Stoica, Walter Baseggio, Yves Vanderhaeghe, Marc Hendrikx (46 Davy Oyen), Oleg Yashchuk, Ivica Mornar (78 Nenad Jestrovic). Trainer: Aime Antheunis

Goals: Mornar (11), Delvecchio (52)

	P	W	D	L	F	A	Pts
Real Madrid CF	6	4	1	1	13	5	13
AS Roma	6	2	3	1	6	5	9
Lokomotiv Moskva	6	2	1	3	9	9	7
RSC Anderlecht Brussel	6	0	3	3	4	13	3

FIRST STAGE – GROUP B

FC DINAMO KYIV v BV BORUSSIA DORTMUND 2-2 (2-0)

Olimpiyskyi, Kyiv 11.09.2001

Referee: Ľuboš Michel (SVK) Attendance: 60,000

DINAMO: Aleksandr Filimonov, Goran Gavrancic, Olexandr Borysovych Holovko (25 Serhiy Fedorov), Vladyslav Vashchuk, Andriy Nesmachnyi, Tiberiu Ghioane, Valentin Belkevich , Serhiy Serebrennikov (46 Florin Lucian Cernat), Alexandr Khatskevich (64 László Bodnár), Isi "LUCKY" IDAHOR, Olexandr Melashchenko. Trainer: Valeryi Lobanovskyi

BORUSSIA: Jens Lehmann, EVANILSON Aparecido Ferreira, Jürgen Kohler, Christian Wörns, Leonardo de Deus Santos "DEDÉ", Stefan Reuter, Sunday Oliseh (53 Miroslav Stević), Lars Ricken, Tomáš Rosicky (84 Jan Derek Sørensen), Márcio AMOROSO Dos Santos (89 Fredi Bobić), Jan Koller. Trainer: Matthias Sammer

Goals: Melashchenko (15), Idahor (46), Koller (56), Amoroso (74)

LIVERPOOL FC v BOAVISTA FC PORTO 1-1 (1-1)

Anfield, Liverpool 11.09.2001

Referee: Kyros Vasaras (GRE) Attendance: 30,015

LIVERPOOL: Jerzy Dudek, Grégory Vignal, Sami Tuomas Hyypiä, Stéphane Henchoz, Jamie Carragher, Steven George Gerrard, Gary McAllister, Dietmar Hamann, Danny Ben Murphy (71 John Arne Riise), Michael James Owen, Emile William Wanhoe Heskey. Trainer: Gérard Houllier

BOAVISTA: RICARDO Alexandre Pereira, Nuno Miguel FRECHAUT Barreto, PEDRO EMANUEL dos Santos Silva, PAULO Cesar TURRA, ERIVAN Nascimento de Lima, Armando Gonçalves Teixeira "PETIT", GLAUBER Gomes da Farias, Erwin SÁNCHEZ Freking (59 PEDRO J. Santos dos SANTOS), ALEXANDRE Luiz GOULART, Elpidio Pereira da SILVA Filho (79 Elisérgio da Silva "SERGINHO"), Carlos Eduardo Ventura "DUDA" (84 José da Silva BOSINGWA). Trainer: Jaime Moreira PACHECO

Goals: Silva (3), Owen (29)

BOAVISTA FC PORTO v FC DINAMO KYIV 3-1 (3-1)

Estádio do Bessa, Porto 19.09.2001

Referee: Alfredo Trentalange (ITA) Attendance: 6,800

BOAVISTA: RICARDO Alexandre Pereira, Nuno Miguel FRECHAUT Barreto, PEDRO EMANUEL dos Santos Silva, PAULO Cesar TURRA, ERIVAN Nascimento de Lima, Armando Gonçalves Teixeira "PETIT", GLAUBER Gomes da Farias, Erwin SÁNCHEZ Freking, Carlos Eduardo Ventura "DUDA" (81 José da Silva BOSINGWA), ALEXANDRE Luiz GOULART (76 PEDRO J. Santos dos SANTOS), Elpidio Pereira da SILVA Filho (87 MARCIO Mandinga dos SANTOS). Trainer: Jaime Moreira PACHECO

DINAMO: Aleksandr Filimonov, Goran Gavrancic, Olexandr Borysovych Holovko, Vladyslav Vashchuk, Andriy Nesmachnyi, Tiberiu Ghioane, Valentin Belkevich, Serhiy Fedorov, Alexandr Khatskevich (57 Isi "Lucky" Idahor), Florin Lucian Cernat, Olexandr Melashchenko.
Trainer: Valeryi Lobanovskyi

Goals: Sánchez (4), Ghioane (5), Silva (11), Duda (30)

BV BORUSSIA DORTMUND v LIVERPOOL FC 0-0

Westfalenstadion, Dortmund 19.09.2001

Referee: Iordan Ivanov (BUL) Attendance: 46,000

BORUSSIA: Jens Lehmann, EVANILSON Aparecido Ferreira, Jürgen Kohler, Christian Wörns, Leonardo de Deus Santos "DEDÉ", Jan Derek Sørensen (87 Fredi Bobić), Stefan Reuter, Miroslav Stević, Tomáš Rosicky, Márcio AMOROSO Dos Santos (87 Lars Ricken), Jan Koller.
Trainer: Matthias Sammer

LIVERPOOL: Jerzy Dudek, Grégory Vignal, Sami Tuomas Hyypiä, Stéphane Henchoz, John Arne Riise (75 Gary McAllister), Danny Ben Murphy, Dietmar Hamann, Steven George Gerrard, Jamie Carragher, Michael James Owen, Emile William Wanhoe Heskey. Trainer: Gérard Houllier

BOAVISTA FC PORTO v BV BORUSSIA DORTMUND 2-1 (2-0)

Estádio do Bessa, Porto 26.09.2001

Referee: Rune Pedersen (NOR) Attendance: 7,600

BOAVISTA: RICARDO Alexandre Pereira, Nuno Miguel FRECHAUT Barreto, PEDRO EMANUEL dos Santos Silva, PAULO Cesar TURRA, ERIVAN Nascimento de Lima, Armando Gonçalves Teixeira "PETIT", GLAUBER Gomes da Farias (76 António Filipe de Sousa GOUVEIA), Erwin SÁNCHEZ Freking, Carlos Eduardo Ventura "DUDA", ALEXANDRE Luiz GOULART (81 José da Silva BOSINGWA), Elpidio Pereira da SILVA Filho (76 Elisérgio da Silva "SERGINHO"). Trainer: Jaime Moreira PACHECO

BORUSSIA: Jens Lehmann, Stefan Reuter, Christian Wörns, Jürgen Kohler (63 Lars Ricken), Jan Derek Sørensen (46 Fredi Bobić), Miroslav Stević (83 Heiko Herrlich), EVANILSON Aparecido Ferreira, Tomáš Rosicky, Leonardo de Deus Santos "DEDÉ", Márcio AMOROSO Dos Santos, Jan Koller.
Trainer: Matthias Sammer

Sent off: Amoroso (90)

Goals: Silva (23), Sánchez (39), Amoroso (76)

LIVERPOOL FC v DINAMO KYIV 1-0 (1-0)

Anfield, Liverpool 26.09.2001

Referee: Pierluigi Collina (ITA) Attendance: 33,513

LIVERPOOL: Jerzy Dudek, Grégory Vignal, Sami Tuomas Hyypiä, Stéphane Henchoz, Jamie Carragher, Steven George Gerrard, Nick Barmby (62 Danny Ben Murphy), Dietmar Hamann, John Arne Riise (79 Gary McAllister), Jari Litmanen (64 Robert Bernard Fowler), Emile William Wanhoe Heskey. Trainer: Gérard Houllier

DINAMO: Aleksandr Filimonov, Goran Gavrancic, Olexandr Borysovych Holovko, Vladyslav Vashchuk, Andriy Nesmachnyi, Tiberiu Ghioane, Valentin Belkevich (81 Serhiy Serebrennikov), Serhiy Fedorov, Isi "Lucky" Idahor, Florin Lucian Cernat (69 Georgi Ivanov Peev), Olexandr Melashchenko. Trainer: Valeryi Lobanovskyi

Goal: Litmanen (23)

BV BORUSSIA DORTMUND v BOAVISTA FC PORTO 2-1 (0-1)

Westfalenstadion, Dortmund 16.10.2001

Referee: Stefano Braschi (ITA) Attendance: 41,247

BORUSSIA: Jens Lehmann, EVANILSON Aparecido Ferreira, Christian Wörns, Christoph Metzelder, Leonardo de Deus Santos "DEDÉ", Stefan Reuter, Lars Ricken (90 Ahmed Reda Madouni), Miroslav Stević, Tomáš Rosicky (90 Jürgen Kohler), Jan Derek Sørensen (76 Sunday Oliseh), Jan Koller. Trainer: Matthias Sammer

BOAVISTA: RICARDO Alexandre Pereira, RUI ÓSCAR Neves de Sousa, PEDRO EMANUEL dos Santos Silva, PAULO Cesar TURRA, ERIVAN Nascimento de Lima, Nuno Miguel FRECHAUT Barreto, José da Silva BOSINGWA (46 Armando Gonçalves Teixeira "PETIT"), Erwin SÁNCHEZ Freking, ALEXANDRE Luiz GOULART (70 Elpidio Pereira da SILVA Filho), MARCIO Mandinga dos SANTOS (59 Joaquim Pereira da Silva "MARTELINHO"), Carlos Eduardo Ventura "DUDA". Trainer: Jaime Moreira PACHECO

Goals: Goulart (33), Ricken (50), Koller (68)

FC DINAMO KYIV v LIVERPOOL FC 1-2 (0-1)

Olimpiyskyi, Kyiv 16.10.2001

Referee: Claude Colombo (FRA) Attendance: 50,000

DINAMO: Vitaly Reva, Goran Gavrancic, Olexandr Borysovych Holovko, Vladyslav Vashchuk, Andriy Nesmachnyi, Tiberiu Ghioane, Alexandr Khatskevich, Valentin Belkevich, László Bodnár (56 Andriy Gusin), Florin Lucian Cernat, Olexandr Melashchenko (79 Isi "Lucky" Idahor). Trainer: Valeryi Lobanovskyi

LIVERPOOL: Jerzy Dudek, Jamie Carragher, Sami Tuomas Hyypiä, Stéphane Henchoz, John Arne Riise, Vladimir Smicer (79 Jamie Redknapp), Gary McAllister, Steven George Gerrard, Danny Ben Murphy, Nick Barmby (62 Patrik Berger), Emile William Wanhoe Heskey. Trainer: Gérard Houllier

Goals: Murphy (43), Ghioane (59), Gerrard (67)

BOAVISTA FC PORTO v LIVERPOOL FC 1-1 (0-1)

Estádio do Bessa, Porto 24.10.2001

Referee: Karl-Eric Nilsson (SWE) Attendance: 9,800

BOAVISTA: RICARDO Alexandre Pereira, RUI ÓSCAR Neves de Sousa (26 Joaquim Pereira da Silva "MARTELINHO"), PEDRO EMANUEL dos Santos Silva, PAULO Cesar TURRA, ERIVAN Nascimento de Lima, Nuno Miguel FRECHAUT Barreto, Armando Gonçalves Teixeira "PETIT", Erwin SÁNCHEZ Freking, Carlos Eduardo Ventura "DUDA" (56 José da Silva BOSINGWA), Elpidio Pereira da SILVA Filho, ALEXANDRE Luiz GOULART (56 MARCIO Mandinga dos SANTOS). Trainer: Jaime Moreira PACHECO

LIVERPOOL: Jerzy Dudek, Jamie Carragher, Sami Tuomas Hyypiä (6 Stephen Wright), Stéphane Henchoz, John Arne Riise, Dietmar Hamann, Gary McAllister (76 Patrik Berger), Danny Ben Murphy, Vladimir Smicer, Robbie Fowler, Emile William Wanhoe Heskey. Trainer: Gérard Houllier

Goals: Murphy (16), Silva (59)

BV BORUSSIA DORTMUND v FC DINAMO KYIV 1-0 (1-0)

Westfalenstadion, Dortmund 24.10.2001

Referee: Kyros Vassaras (GRE) Attendance: 41,500

BORUSSIA: Jens Lehmann, EVANILSON Aparecido Ferreira, Christian Wörns, Christoph Metzelder, Leonardo de Deus Santos "DEDÉ", Stefan Reuter, Tomáš Rosicky, Sunday Oliseh, Jan Derek Sørensen (84 Francis Bugri), Jan Koller, Lars Ricken (90 Ahmed Reda Madouni). Trainer: Matthias Sammer

DINAMO: Vitaly Reva, Tiberiu Ghioane, Vladyslav Vashchuk, Serhiy Fedorov, Andriy Nesmachnyi, Goran Gavrancić (62 László Bodnár), Andriy Gusin, Valentin Belkevich, Alexandr Khatskevich, Isi "Lucky" Idahor (53 Florin Lucian Cernat), Olexandr Melashchenko. Trainer: Valeryi Lobanovskyi

Goal: Rosicky (34)

FC DINAMO KYIV v BOAVISTA FC PORTO 1-0 (0-0)

Olimpiyskyi, Kyiv 30.10.2001

Referee: Fritz Stuchlik (AUS) Attendance: 18,000

DINAMO: Vitaly Reva, Tiberiu Ghioane, Vladyslav Vashchuk, Serhiy Fedorov (60 Goran Gavrancic), Andriy Nesmachnyi, Georgi Ivanov Peev (76 Florin Lucian Cernat), Andriy Gusin, Valentin Belkevich, Alexandr Khatskevich, Maksim Shatskikh (90 Serhiy Serebrennikov), Olexandr Melashchenko. Trainer: Valeryi Lobanovskyi

BOAVISTA: RICARDO Alexandre Pereira, Nuno Miguel FRECHAUT Barreto, PEDRO EMANUEL dos Santos Silva (81 Elisérgio da Silva "SERGINHO"), MÁRIO Jorge Amoro LOJA, ERIVAN Nascimento de Lima, José da Silva BOSINGWA, Armando Gonçalves Teixeira "PETIT", Erwin SÁNCHEZ Freking, Carlos Eduardo Ventura "DUDA", Elpidio Pereira da SILVA Filho (54 MARCIO Mandinga dos SANTOS), ALEXANDRE Luiz GOULART (54 Joaquim Pereira da Silva "MARTELINHO"). Trainer: Jaime Moreira PACHECO

Goal: Melashchenko (49)

LIVERPOOL FC
v BV BORUSSIA DORTMUND 2-0 (1-0)

Anfield, Liverpool 30.10.2001

Referee: Kim Milton Nielsen (DEN) Attendance: 41,507

LIVERPOOL: Jerzy Dudek, Stephen Wright, Jamie Carragher, Stéphane Henchoz, John Arne Riise, Vladimir Smicer (65 Patrik Berger), Dietmar Hamann, Steven George Gerrard (85 Jamie Redknapp), Danny Ben Murphy, Michael James Owen (76 Robbie Fowler), Emile William Wanhoe Heskey. Trainer: Phillip Brian Thompson

BORUSSIA: Jens Lehmann, EVANILSON Aparecido Ferreira, Stefan Reuter, Christian Wörns, Christoph Metzelder, Leonardo de Deus Santos "DEDÉ", Lars Ricken, Sunday Oliseh (68 Fredi Bobić), Tomáš Rosicky, Jan Derek Sørensen, Jan Koller. Trainer: Matthias Sammer

Goals: Smicer (15), Wright (82)

	P	W	D	L	F	A	Pts
Liverpool FC	6	3	3	0	7	3	12
Boavista FC Porto	6	2	2	2	8	7	8
Borussia Dortmund	6	2	2	2	6	7	8
Dynamo Kyiv	6	1	1	4	5	9	4

FIRST STAGE – GROUP C

RCD MALLORCA
v ARSENAL FC LONDON 1-0 (1-0)

Son Moix, Palma de Mallorca 11.09.2001

Referee: Knud Erik Fisker (DEN) Attendance: 19,019

RCD MALLORCA: Leonardo "LEO" FRANCO, Javíer OLAIZOLA Rodríguez, Fernando NIÑO Bejarano, Miguel Angel NADAL Homar, MIQUEL SOLER Sarasols, Alejandro CAMPANO Hernando, Vicente ENGONGA Maté (67 VICENTE Fernández Pujante), MARCOS Martín de la Fuente, Ariel Miguel Santiago IBAGAZA (46 Alvaro NOVO Ramírez), Alberto LUQUE Martos (76 Veljko PAUNOVIC), Samuel ETO'O Fils. Trainer: Bernd Krauss

ARSENAL: David Seaman, LAUREN Bisan Etame-Mayer, Sol Campbell, Martin Keown, Ashley Cole, Robert Pires (79 Ray Parlour), Patrick Vieira, Giovanni Van Bronckhorst, Fredrik Ljungberg (71 Francis Jeffers), Sylvain Wiltord (72 Nwankwo Kanu), Thierry Henry. Trainer: Arsène Wenger

Sent off: Cole (11)

Goal: Engonga (12 pen)

SCHALKE 04 GELSENKIRCHEN
v PANATHINAIKOS FC ATHINA 0-2 (0-0)

Parkstadion, Gelsenkirchen 11.09.2001

Referee: Stefano Braschi (ITA) Attendance: 52,333

SCHALKE 04: Oliver Reck, Tomasz Hajto, Marco van Hoogdalem (78 Kristijan Djordjević), Tomasz Waldoch, Nico van Kerckhoven, Jiří Nemec, Niels Oude Kamphuis, Andreas Möller (59 Marc Wilmots), Jörg Böhme (68 Gerald Kwabena Asamoah), Victor Agali, Emile Mpenza. Trainer: Hubertus Joseph Stevens

PANATHINAIKOS: Antonis Nikopolidis, Giorgos Seitaridis, René Henriksen, Panagiotis Fissas, Jan Michaelsen (76 Leonidas Vokolos), PAULO Manuel SOUSA Carvalho, Aggelos Basinas, Giorgos Karagounis, Joonas Einari Kolkka (68 Goran Vlaović), Mihalis Konstantinou (89 Daniel Sarić), Sotiris Kyrgiakos. Trainer: Giannis Kirastas

Goals: Vlaovic (75), Basinas (80)

ARSENAL FC LONDON
v SCHALKE 04 GELSENKIRCHEN 3-2 (2-1)

Highbury, London 19.09.2001

Referee: Claude Colombo (FRA) Attendance: 35,361

ARSENAL: David Seaman, LAUREN Bisan Etame-Mayer, Martin Keown, Gilles Grimandi, Giovanni van Bronckhorst, Fredrik Ljungberg, Patrick Vieira, Ray Parlour, Robert Pires (76 Junichi Inamoto), Sylvain Wiltord (72 Dennis Bergkamp), Thierry Henry (90 Matthew Upson). Trainer: A. Wenger

SCHALKE 04: Oliver Reck, Tomasz Hajto, Tomasz Waldoch, Nico van Kerckhoven, Sven Vermant (54 Gerald Kwabena Asamoah), Marco van Hoogdalem, Niels Oude Kamphuis, Andreas Möller (72 Kristijan Djordjević), Jörg Böhme (82 Youri Mulder), Victor Agali, Emile Mpenza. Trainer: Hubertus Joseph Stevens

Goals: Ljungberg (33), Henry (36, 47), van Hoogdalem (43), Mpenza (59)

PANATHINAIKOS FC ATHINA
v RCD MALLORCA 2-0 (2-0)

OAKA Spiros Louis, Athina 19.09.2001

Referee: Konrad Plautz (AUS) Attendance: 15,003

PANATHINAIKOS: Antonis Nikopolidis, Giorgos Seitaridis, René Henriksen, Panagiotis Fissas, Jan Michaelsen, PAULO Manuel SOUSA Carvalho, Aggelos Basinas, Giorgos Karagounis (80 Joonas Einari Kolkka), Sotiris Kyrgiakos, Goran Vlaovic (84 Leonidas Vokolos), Mihalis Konstantinou (80 Emmanuel Olisadebe). Trainer: Giannis Kirastas

RCD MALLORCA: Leonardo "LEO" FRANCO, FATIH Akyel, Fernando NIÑO Bejarano, Miguel Angel NADAL Homar, MIQUEL SOLER Sarasols, Alejandro CAMPANO Hernando (70 Alvaro NOVO Ramírez), Vicente ENGONGA Maté, MARCOS Martín de la Fuente (86 Albert RIERA Ortega), Veljko PAUNOVIC, Alberto LUQUE Martos (60 CARLOS Domínguez Domínguez), Samuel ETO'O Fils. Trainer: Bernd Krauss

Goals: Vlaović (25), Konstantinou (28)

PANATHINAIKOS FC ATHINA v ARSENAL FC LONDON 1-0 (1-0)

OAKA Spiros Louis, Athina 26.09.2001

Referee: Vitor Manuel MELO PEREIRA (POR) Att: 15,012

PANATHINAIKOS: Antonis Nikopolidis, Leonidas Vokolos, René Henriksen, Panagiotis Fissas, Jan Michaelsen, PAULO Manuel SOUSA Carvalho, Aggelos Basinas, Giorgos Karagounis (85 Daniel Sarić), Sotiris Kyrgiakos, Goran Vlaovic (65 Mihalis Konstantinou), Emmanuel Olisadebe (70 Joonas Einari Kolkka). Trainer: Giannis Kirastas

ARSENAL: David Seaman, LAUREN Bisan Etame-Mayer, Martin Keown, Matthew Upson, Ashley Cole, Fredrik Ljungberg (68 Nwankwo Kanu), Patrick Vieira, Ray Parlour (53 Giovanni Van Bronckhorst), Robert Pires, Sylvain Wiltord (68 Francis Jeffers), Thierry Henry. Trainer: Arsène Wenger

Goal: Karagounis (25)

SCHALKE 04 GELSENKIRCHEN v RCD MALLORCA 0-1 (0-0)

Parkstadion, Gelsenkirchen 26.09.2001

Referee: Nikolai Levnikov (RUS) Attendance: 51,860

SCHALKE 04: Oliver Reck, Tomasz Hajto, Tomasz Waldoch (70 Gerald Kwabena Asamoah), Nico van Kerckhoven, Jiří Nemec (82 Youri Mulder), Marco van Hoogdalem, Niels Oude Kamphuis, Andreas Möller, Jörg Böhme (67 Michael Büskens), Victor Agali, Emile Mpenza.
Trainer: Hubertus Joseph Stevens

RCD MALLORCA: Carlos Angel ROA, Javíer OLAIZOLA Rodríguez, Miguel Angel NADAL Homar, MIQUEL SOLER Sarasols, Alvaro NOVO Ramírez, Vicente ENGONGA Maté, MARCOS Martín de la Fuente, VICENTE Fernández Pujante (45 FATIH Akyel), Cristian DÍAZ (86 Francisco SOLER Atencia), Alberto LUQUE Martos (72 Veljko PAUNOVIC), Samuel ETO'O Fils. Trainer: Bernd Krauss

Goal: Eto'o (66)

ARSENAL FC LONDON v PANATHINAIKOS FC ATHINA 2-1 (1-0)

Highbury, London 16.10.2001

Referee: Urs Meier (SWI) Attendance: 35,432

ARSENAL: Richard Wright, LAUREN Bisan Etame-Mayer, Sol Campbell, Matthew Upson, Ashley Cole, Fredrik Ljungberg, Patrick Vieira, Giovanni van Bronckhorst, Robert Pires (71 Ray Parlour), Sylvain Wiltord (71 Dennis Bergkamp), Thierry Henry (90 Gilles Grimandi).
Trainer: Arsène Wenger

PANATHINAIKOS: Antonis Nikopolidis, Sotiris Kyrgiakos, René Henriksen, Leonidas Vokolos, Panagiotis Fissas, Jan Michaelsen, PAULO Manuel SOUSA Carvalho (78 Giorgos Seitaridis), Aggelos Basinas, Giorgos Karagounis (78 Joonas Einari Kolkka), Emmanuel Olisadebe, Mihalis Konstantinou (78 Goran Vlaovic). Trainer: Giannis Kirastas

Goals: Henry (23, 52 pen), Olisadebe (50)

RCD MALLORCA v SCHALKE 04 GELSENKIRCHEN 0-4 (0-2)

Son Moix, Palma de Mallorca 16.10.2001

Referee: Jan W. Wegereef (HOL) Attendance: 28,000

RCD MALLORCA: Carlos Angel ROA, Javíer OLAIZOLA Rodríguez, Fernando NIÑO Bejarano, Miguel Angel NADAL Homar (26 FATIH Akyel), MIQUEL SOLER Sarasols, Alejandro CAMPANO Hernando (46 Alvaro NOVO Ramírez), MARCOS Martín de la Fuente, Veljko PAUNOVIC, Cristian DÍAZ (56 CARLOS Dominguez Dominguez), Alberto LUQUE Martos, Samuel ETO'O Fils. Trainer: Bernd Krauss

SCHALKE 04: Oliver Reck, Tomasz Hajto, Tomasz Waldoch, Aníbal Samuel Matellán, Nico van Kerckhoven, Gerald Kwabena Asamoah, Marco van Hoogdalem (79 Sven Kmetsch), Sven Vermant, Olaf Thon (80 Jiří Nemec), Marc Wilmots (74 Michael Büskens), Ebbe Sand.
Trainer: Hubertus Joseph Stevens

Sent off: Eto'o (26)

Goals: van Hoogdalem (12), Hajto (22 pen), Asamoah (77), Sand (84)

ARSENAL FC v RCD MALLORCA 3-1 (0-0)

Highbury, London 24.10.2001

Referee: Dick Z.G. Jol (HOL) Attendance: 34,764

ARSENAL: Richard Wright, LAUREN Bisan Etame-Mayer, Sol Campbell, Martin Keown, Giovanni Van Bronckhorst, Fredrik Ljungberg (79 Nwankwo Kanu), Patrick Vieira, Gilles Grimandi (84 Ray Parlour), Robert PIRES, Dennis Bergkamp (72 Sylvain Wiltord), Thierry Henry. Trainer: Arsène Wenger

RCD MALLORCA: Leonardo "LEO" FRANCO, FATIH Akyel (64 Leonardo Angel BIAGINI Bruzzese), Javíer OLAIZOLA Rodríguez, Miguel Angel NADAL Homar, MIQUEL SOLER Sarasols, Alejandro CAMPANO Hernando, MARCOS Martín de la Fuente (68 Julián ROBLES García), Alvaro NOVO Ramírez, Cristian DÍAZ, Veljko PAUNOVIC, Alberto LUQUE Martos (79 CARLOS Dominguez Dominguez).
Trainer: Bernd Krauss

Goals: Pires (61), Bergkamp (63), Novo (74), Henry (90)

PANATHINAIKOS FC ATHINA v SCHALKE 04 GELSENKIRCHEN 2-0 (1-0)

OAKA Spiros Louis, Athina 24.10.2001

Referee: Alain Sars (FRA) Attendance: 15,097

PANATHINAIKOS: Antonis Nikopolidis, Giorgos Seitaridis (69 Daniel Sarić), René Henriksen, Leonidas Vokolos, Panagiotis Fissas, Jan Michaelsen, PAULO Manuel SOUSA Carvalho, Giorgos Karagounis, Aggelos Basinas (64 Giannis Goumas), Emmanuel Olisadebe, Mihalis Konstantinou (73 Goran Vlaović). Trainer: Giannis Kirastas

SCHALKE 04: Oliver Reck, Tomasz Hajto, Tomasz Waldoch, Aníbal Samuel Matellán (50 Jörg Böhme), Nico van Kerckhoven, Gerald Kwabena Asamoah, Sven Kmetsch, Andreas Möller, Sven Vermant (79 Olaf Thon), Ebbe Sand, Marc Wilmots (67 Youri Mulder). Trainer: H.J. Stevens

Goals: Olisadebe (31), Konstantinou (60)

RCD MALLORCA v PANATHINAIKOS FC ATHINA 1-0 (0-0)

Son Moix, Palma de Mallorca 30.10.2001

Referee: Karl-Erik Nilsson (SWE) Attendance: 11,174

RCD MALLORCA: Miguel Garró Gomila "MIKI", Javíer OLAIZOLA Rodríguez, Fernando NIÑO Bejarano, Miguel Angel NADAL Homar, MIQUEL SOLER Sarasols, Alejandro CAMPANO Hernando, MARCOS Martín de la Fuente, Alvaro NOVO Ramírez (63 Francisco SOLER Atencia), Veljko PAUNOVIC (70 Julián ROBLES García), Leonardo Angel BIAGINI Bruzzese (78 Alberto LUQUE Martos), Samuel ETO'O Fils. Trainer: Sergei Kresić

PANATHINAIKOS: Antonis Nikopolidis, Giannis Goumas, Leonidas Vokolos, Sotiris Kyrgiakos, Panagiotis Fissas, Daniel Sarić, Giorgos Karagounis (82 Krzysztof Warzycha), Derek Boateng, Nikos Liberopoulos, Joonas Einari Kolkka (73 Fernando Edgar Galetto), Goran Vlaovic (82 Mihalis Konstantinou). Trainer: Giannis Kirastas

Goal: Biagini (57)

SCHALKE 04 GELSENKIRCHEN v ARSENAL FC LONDON 3-1 (1-0)

Parkstadion, Gelsenkirchen 30.10.2001

Referee: Ryszard Wojcik (POL) Attendance: 52,321

SCHALKE 04: Oliver Reck, Tomasz Hajto, Tomasz Waldoch, Aníbal Samuel Matellán, Jiří Nemec (67 Olaf Thon), Marco van Hoogdalem (63 Sven Kmetsch), Sven Vermant (74 Kristijan Djordjević), Andreas Möller, Jörg Böhme, Ebbe Sand, Youri Mulder. Trainer: Hubertus Joseph Stevens

ARSENAL: Richard Wright, Oleg Luzhny, Sol Campbell (68 Martin Keown), Matthew Upson (66 Igors Stepanovs), Ashley Cole, Ray Parlour, Gilles Grimandi, Eduardo Cesar Gaspar "EDU", Robert Pires, Nwankwo Kanu (78 Jermaine Pennant), Sylvain Wiltord. Trainer: Arsène Wenger

Sent off: Luzhny (17)

Goals: Mulder (2), Vermant (60), Moller (64), Wiltord (71)

	P	W	D	L	F	A	Pts
Panathinaikos Athina	6	4	0	2	8	3	12
Arsenal FC London	6	3	0	3	9	9	9
RCD Mallorca	6	3	0	3	4	9	9
Schalke 04	6	2	0	4	9	9	6

FIRST STAGE – GROUP D

GALATASARAY SK ISTANBUL v SS LAZIO ROMA 1-0 (0-0)

Ali Sami Yen, Istanbul 11.09.2001

Referee: Ryszard Wojcik (POL) Attendance: 13,850

GALATASARAY: Ali Faryd Camilo MONDRAGÓN, Emre Asik, Bülent Korkmaz, Carlos Alberto de Oliveira "CAPONE" (72 Sébastien Perez), Hakan Ünsal, Ümit Davala, Suat Kaya (88 Berkant Göktan), Ergün Penbe, HASAN Gökhan ŞAŞ, Arif Erdem (63 Sergen Yalçin), Ümit Karan. Trainer: Mircea Lucescu

LAZIO: Angelo Peruzzi, FERNANDO Manuel Silva COUTO, Alessandro Nesta, Jaap Stam, Giuseppe Pancaro (81 Simone Inzaghi), Gaizka MENDIETA Zabala (52 Dejan Stanković), Stefano Fiore, Diego Pablo Simeone, Giuseppe Favalli (72 Rodríguez CESAR APARECIDO), Claudio Javier López, Hernán Jorge Crespo. Trainer: Dino Zoff

Goal: Ümit Karan (79)

FC NANTES v PSV EINDHOVEN 4-1 (3-0)

Stade de la Beaujoire, Nantes 11.09.2001

Referee: Juan Antonio FERNÁNDEZ MARÍN (SPA) Attendance: 23,481

FC NANTES: Mickaël Landreau, Nicolas Laspalles, Nicolas Gillet, Nestor Fabbri, Salomon Olembé-Olembé, Nicolas Savinaud (79 Mathieu Berson), Olivier Quint, Stéphane Ziani, Sylvain Armand, Pierre-Yves André (71 Marama Vahirua), Wilfried Dalmat (86 Eric Djemba-Djemba). Trainer: Raynald Denoueix

PSV: Ronald Waterreus, Rob Wielaert, Yuri Nikiforov (58 Jürgen Colin), Kevin Hofland, Jan Heintze, Adil Ramzi (53 Dennis Rommedahl), Johann Vogel, John de Jong, Wilfred Bouma (76 Georgi Gakhokidze), Arnold Bruggink, Mateja Kezman. Trainer: Eric Gerets

Goals: André (5), Quint (10 pen), Dalmat (44), Vahirua (75), de Jong (90)

SS LAZIO ROMA v FC NANTES 1-3 (1-1)

Stadio Olimpico, Roma 19.09.2001

Referee: Herbert Fandel (GER) Attendance: 17,798

LAZIO: Angelo Peruzzi, FERNANDO Manuel Silva COUTO, Alessandro Nesta, Jaap Stam (73 Giuseppe Pancaro), Dejan Stanković, Gaizka MENDIETA Zabala (65 Claudio Javier López), Stefano Fiore, Diego Pablo Simeone, Giuseppe Favalli, Hernán Jorge Crespo (77 Darko Kovacević), Simone Inzaghi. Trainer: Dino Zoff

FC NANTES: Mickaël Landreau, Yves Deroff, Nicolas Gillet, Nestor Fabbri, Sylvain Armand, Hassan Ahamada (63 Olivier Quint), Pascal Delhommeau, Mathieu Berson, Eric Djemba-Djemba, Stéphane Ziani, Pierre-Yves André (71 Wilfried Dalmat). Trainer: Raynald Denoueix

Goals: Fabbri (3), Fernando Couto (7), Armand (63), Ziani (86)

PSV EINDHOVEN v GALATASARAY SK ISTANBUL 3-1 (1-0)

Gelredome, Arnhem 19.09.2001

Referee: Manuel Enrique MEJUTO GONZÁLEZ (MAL) Attendance: 22,325

PSV: Ronald Waterreus, Jürgen Colin, Eric Addo, Ernest Faber, Wilfred Bouma, Dennis Rommedahl (79 Theo Lucius), Mark van Bommel, Johann Vogel, Adil Ramzi (85 John de Jong), Arnold Bruggink (75 Jan Vennegoor of Hesselink), Mateja Kezman. Trainer: Eric Gerets

GALATASARAY: Ali Faryd Camilo MONDRAGÓN, Emre Asik, Bülent Korkmaz, Carlos Alberto de Oliveira "CAPONE", Hakan Ünsal (61 Gustavo Andrés VICTORIA), Suat Kaya (59 Bülent Akin), Sergen Yalçin, Ergün Penbe, Berkant Göktan (68 Arif Erdem), HASAN Gökhan ŞAŞ, Ümit Karan. Trainer: Mircea Lucescu

Goals: Bruggink (38), Faber (53), Ümit Karan (68), Kezman (90)

FC NANTES v GALATASARAY SK ISTANBUL 0-1 (0-0)

Stade de la Beaujoire, Nantes 26.09.2001

Referee: Tom Henning Øvrebø (NOR) Attendance: 28,546

FC NANTES: Mickaël Landreau, Yves Deroff, Pascal Delhommeau, Nestor Fabbri, Sylvain Armand, Wilfried Dalmat, Salomon Olembé-Olembé (88 Pierre Aristouy), Mathieu Berson, Olivier Quint, Charles Devineau (73 Eric Djemba-Djemba), Hassan Ahamada (88 Grégory Pujol). Trainer: Raynald Denoueix

GALATASARAY: Ali Faryd Camilo Mondragón, Emre Asik, Sébastien Pérez, Carlos Alberto de Oliveira "CAPONE", Hakan Ünsal, Suat Kaya (67 Andres José Fleurquin), Ergün Penbe, Bülent Akin, Hasan Gökhan Şaş, Arif Erdem (57 Sergen Yalçin), Serkan Aykut (77 Ümit Karan). Trainer: Mircea Lucescu

Goal: Sergen (79)

PSV EINDHOVEN v SS LAZIO ROMA 1-0 (1-0)

Philips, Eindhoven 26.09.2001

Referee: Thomas Michael McCurry (SCO) Att: 30,000

PSV: Ivica Kralj, Ernest Faber, Yuri Nikiforov, Kevin Hofland, Wilfred Bouma, Dennis Rommedahl (73 Georgi Gakhokidze), Mark van Bommel, Johann Vogel (62 Theo Lucius), Adil Ramzi, Arnold Bruggink (89 Jan Vennegoor of Hesselink), Mateja Kezman. Trainer: Eric Gerets

LAZIO: Angelo Peruzzi, Francesco Colonnese, Dino Baggio, FERNANDO Manuel Silva COUTO, Gaizka MENDIETA Zabala (71 Karel Poborsky), Stefano Fiore, Diego Pablo Simeone (38 Dejan Stanković), Giuliano Giannichedda, Giuseppe Pancaro, Claudio Javier LÓPEZ, Darko Kovacević (74 Simone Inzaghi). Trainer: Alberto Zaccheroni

Goal: Hofland (40)

GALATASARAY SK ISTANBUL v FC NANTES 0-0

Ali Sami Yen, Istanbul 16.10.2001

Referee: Hellmut Krug (GER) Attendance: 19,100

GALATASARAY: Ali Faryd Camilo Mondragón, Sébastien Pérez, Ergün Penbe, Emre Asik, Hakan Ünsal, Vedat Inceefe, Sergen Yalçin, Bülent Akin (65 Suat Kaya), Hasan Gökhan Şaş, Arif Erdem (74 Andres José Fleurquin), Serkan Aykut (59 Ümit Karan). Trainer: Mircea Lucescu

FC NANTES: Mickaël Landreau, Pascal Delhommeau, Yves Deroff, Nestor Fabbri, Sylvain Armand, Stéphane Ziani, Olivier Quint, Mathieu Berson, Eric Djemba-Djemba, Pierre-Yves André (70 Marama Vahirua), Hassan Ahamada (65 Frédéric da Rocha). Trainer: Raynald Denoueix

SS LAZIO ROMA v PSV EINDHOVEN 2-1 (1-0)

Stadio Olimpico, Roma 16.10.2001

Referee: Antonio Jesus LÓPEZ NIETO (SPA) Att: 18,417

LAZIO: Angelo Peruzzi, FERNANDO Manuel Silva COUTO, Jaap Stam, Giuseppe Favalli, Karel Poborsky (74 Paolo NEGRO), Gaizka MENDIETA Zabala, Stefano Fiore (82 Dino Baggio), Giuliano Giannichedda, Giuseppe Pancaro, Claudio Javier LÓPEZ, Simone Inzaghi (61 Hernán Jorge Crespo). Trainer: Alberto Zaccheroni

PSV: Patrick Lodewijks, André Ooijer, Yuri Nikiforov (66 Jan Vennegoor of Hesselink), Ernest Faber, Kevin Hofland, Jan Heintze (84 Arnold Bruggink), Dennis Rommedahl, Johann Vogel, John de Jong (46 Theo Lucius), Wilfred Bouma, Mateja Kezman. Trainer: Eric Gerets

Goals: Fiore (39), López (55 pen), Kezman (56)

SS LAZIO ROMA v GALATASARAY SK ISTANBUL 1-0 (0-0)

Stadio Olimpico, Roma 24.10.2001

Referee: Nikolai Levnikov (RUS) Attendance: 20,363

LAZIO: Angelo Peruzzi, Jaap Stam (46 Giuseppe Pancaro), Alessandro Nesta, Giuseppe Favalli, Paolo Negro, Gaizka MENDIETA Zabala, Stefano Fiore (62 Dejan Stanković), Giuliano Giannichedda, Rodríguez CESAR APARECIDO, Claudio Javier López (71 Simone Inzaghi), Hernán Jorge Crespo. Trainer: Alberto Zaccheroni

GALATASARAY: Ali Faryd Camilo MONDRAGÓN, Sébastien Pérez, Vedat Inceefe (16 Suat Kaya), Emre Asik, Gustavo Andrés VICTORIA (81 Serkan Aykut), Andres José Fleurquin, Ergün Penbe, Bülent Akin, HASAN Gökhan ŞAŞ, Sergen Yalçin, Ümit Karan (64 Arif Erdem). Trainer: Mircea Lucescu

Goal: Stankovic (76)

PSV EINDHOVEN v FC NANTES 0-0

Philips, Eindhoven 24.10.2001

Referee: Wolfgang Stark (GER) Attendance: 31,200

PSV: Patrick Lodewijks, André Ooijer, Ernest Faber, Kevin Hofland, Jan Heintze, Dennis Rommedahl (62 Arnold Bruggink), Johann Vogel (80 John DE Jong), Theo Lucius, Wilfred Bouma (84 Georgi Gakhokidze), Mateja Kezman, Jan Vennegoor of Hesselink. Trainer: Eric Gerets

FC NANTES: Mickaël Landreau, Nicolas Laspalles, Nicolas Gillet, Nestor Fabbri, Sylvain Armand, Frédéric da Rocha, Mathieu Berson (46 Nicolas Savinaud), Eric Djemba-Djemba, Olivier Quint (83 Salomon Olembé-Olembé), Pierre-Yves André (83 Yves Deroff), Stéphane Ziani.
Trainer: Raynald Denoueix

GALATASARAY SK ISTANBUL v PSV EINDHOVEN 2-0 (1-0)

Ali Sami Yen, Istanbul 30.10.2001

Referee: Ľuboš Michel (SVK) Attendance: 22,100

GALATASARAY: Ali Faryd Camilo MONDRAGÓN, Sébastien Pérez, Ergün Penbe, Emre Asik, Gustavo Andrés VICTORIA, Andres José Fleurquin, Sergen Yalçin (73 Ayhan Akman), Bülent Akin, HASAN Gökhan ŞAŞ, Arif Erdem (81 Suat Kaya), Ümit Karan (70 Serkan Aykut).
Trainer: Mircea Lucescu

PSV: Patrick Lodewijks, André Ooijer, Ernest Faber, Kevin Hofland, Jan Heintze, Dennis Rommedahl, Theo Lucius (60 Jan Vennegoor of Hesselink), Johann Vogel, Wilfred Bouma (71 Georgi Gakhokidze), John de Jong (82 Kasper Bøgelund), Mateja Kezman. Trainer: Eric Gerets

Goals: Sergen (26), Arif (50)

FC NANTES v SS LAZIO ROMA 1-0 (0-0)

Stade de la Beaujoire, Nantes 30.10.2001

Referee: Terje Hauge (NOR) Attendance: 34,754

FC NANTES: Mickaël Landreau, Nicolas Laspalles, Nicolas Gillet, Pascal Delhommeau, Nestor Fabbri, Sylvain Armand, Eric Djemba-Djemba, Stéphane Ziani, Salomon Olembé-Olembé, Pierre-Yves André (87 Yves Deroff), Hassan Ahamada (66 Frédéric da Rocha). Trainer: Raynald Denoueix

LAZIO: Angelo Peruzzi, Jaap Stam, Alessandro Nesta, Giuseppe Favalli, Paolo Negro, Gaizka MENDIETA Zabala (68 Darko Kovacević), Stefano Fiore (83 Dejan Stanković), Giuliano Giannichedda, Rodríguez Cesar Aparecido, Claudio Javier López (46 Simone Inzaghi), Hernán Jorge Crespo.
Trainer: Alberto Zaccheroni

Goal: André (72)

	P	W	D	L	F	A	Pts
FC Nantes	6	3	2	1	8	3	11
Galatasaray Istanbul	6	3	1	2	5	4	10
PSV Eindhoven	6	2	1	3	6	9	7
SS Lazio Roma	6	2	0	4	4	7	6

FIRST STAGE – GROUP E

JUVENTUS FC TORINO v CELTIC FC GLASGOW 3-2 (1-0)

Delle Alpi, Torino 18.09.2001

Referee: Hellmut Krug (GER) Attendance: 43,017

JUVENTUS: Gianluigi Buffon, Cristian Zenoni, Lilian Thuram, Paolo Montero, Gianluca Pessotto (63 Alessandro Birindelli), Alessio Tacchinardi, Alessandro del Piero (88 Nicola Amoruso), Mark Iuliano, Edgar Davids, José Marcelo SALAS Melinao (69 Fabián O'Neill), David Trezeguet.
Trainer: Marcello Lippi

CELTIC: Robert Douglas, Dianbobo Balde, Joos Valgaeren, Johan Mjällby, Alan Thompson (58 Bobby Alfred Manuel Petta), Didier Agathe, Neil Francis Lennon, Paul Lambert, Stilian Petrov, Christopher Roy Sutton, Henrik Larsson.
Trainer: Martin O'Neill

Sent off: Davids (75)

Goals: Trezeguet (43, 55), Petrov (67), Larsson (85 pen), Amoruso (90 pen)

ROSENBORG BK TRONDHEIM v FC PORTO 1-2 (0-1)

Lerkendal, Trondheim 18.09.2001

Referee: Graham Barber (ENG) Attendance: 20,007

ROSENBORG: Arni Gautur Arason, Christer Basma, Erik Hoftun, Bent Inge Johnsen (29 Hassan el Fakiri), Janne Saarinen, Roar Strand, Bent Andre Skammelsrud, Ørjan Berg, Sigurd Rushfeldt, Harald Martin Brattbakk (84 Dagfinn Enerly), Frode Johnsen. Trainer: Nils Arne Eggen

FC PORTO: Sergei Ovchinnikov, Hugo Benjamin IBARRA, JORGE Paulo COSTA Almeida, JORGE Almeida Gomes de ANDRADE, MARIO Magalhães da SILVA, Anderson Luis de Sousa "DECO", Francisco José Rodrigues da Costa "COSTINHA", RUBENS dos Santos JUNIOR (37 Carlos Humberto PAREDES Monges), RICARDO Alberto CARVALHO, Nuno Fernando Gonçalves da Rocha "CAPUCHO" (90 Dmitriy Alenichev), Renivaldo Pereira des Jesus "PENA" (84 HÉLDER Manuel POSTIGA).
Trainer: Octavio Coelho Machado

Goals: Pena (10), Deco (60), Rushfeldt (90)

CELTIC FC GLASGOW v FC PORTO 1-0 (1-0)

Celtic Park, Glasgow 25.09.2001

Referee: Dick Z.G. Jol (HOL) Attendance: 54,664

CELTIC: Robert Douglas, Joos Valgaeren, Johan Mjällby, Dianbobo Balde, Didier Agathe, Neil Francis Lennon, Paul Lambert, Stilian Petrov (89 Jackie McNamara), Bobby Alfred Manuel Petta (69 Alan Thompson), Christopher Roy Sutton, Henrik Larsson. Trainer: Martin O'Neill

FC PORTO: Sergei Ovchinnikov, Hugo Benjamin IBARRA (76 HÉLDER Manuel POSTIGA), JORGE Paulo COSTA Almeida, RICARDO Alberto CARVALHO, MARIO Magalhães da SILVA (46 Dmitriy Alenichev), Francisco José Rodrigues da Costa "COSTINHA" (46 RUBENS dos Santos JUNIOR), Anderson Luis de Sousa "DECO", JORGE Almeida Gomes de ANDRADE, Carlos Humberto PAREDES Monges, Nuno Fernando Gonçalves da Rocha "CAPUCHO", Renivaldo Pereira des Jesus "PENA". Trainer: Octavio Coelho Machado

Goal: Larsson (36)

ROSENBORG BK TRONDHEIM v JUVENTUS FC TORINO 1-1 (0-0)

Lerkendal, Trondheim 25.09.2001

Referee: Jan W. Wegereef (HOL) Attendance: 20,748

ROSENBORG: Arni Gautur Arason, Christer Basma, Erik Hoftun, Dagfinn Enerly (79 Bent Inge Johnsen), Janne Saarinen (72 Ståle Stensaas), Roar Strand (46 Odd Inge Olsen), Harald Martin Brattbakk, Bent Andre Skammelsrud, Ørjan Berg, Sigurd Rushfeldt, Frode Johnsen.
Trainer: Nils Arne Eggen

JUVENTUS: Gianluigi Buffon, Lilian Thuram, Mark Iuliano, Paolo Montero, Gianluca Pessotto, Cristian Zenoni (78 Enzo Maresca), Alessio Tacchinardi, Fabián O'Neill (59 José Marcelo SALAS Melinao), Gianluca Zambrotta, Alessandro del Piero, David Trezeguet. Trainer: Marcello Lippi

Goals: del Piero (85), Skammelsrud (89 pen)

CELTIC FC GLASGOW v ROSENBORG BK TRONDHEIM 1-0 (1-0)

Celtic Park, Glasgow 10.10.2001

Referee: Alain Sars (FRA) Attendance: 54,000

CELTIC: Robert Douglas, Dianbobo Balde, Joos Valgaeren, Johan Mjällby, Alan Thompson (66 Stephen Andrew Guppy), Didier Agathe, Neil Francis Lennon, Paul Lambert, Stilian Petrov, Christopher Roy Sutton, Henrik Larsson.
Trainer: Martin O'Neill

ROSENBORG: Arni Gautur Arason, Odd Inge Olsen (86 Bent Inge Johnsen), Erik Hoftun, Christer Basma, Janne Saarinen, Roar Strand (82 Fredrik Winsnes), Harald Martin Brattbakk (74 Christer George), Bent Andre Skammelsrud, Ørjan Berg, Sigurd Rushfeldt, Frode Johnsen. Trainer: Nils Arne Eggen

Goal: Thompson (21)

FC PORTO v JUVENTUS FC TORINO 0-0

Estádio das Antas, Porto 10.10.2001

Referee: Manuel Enrique MEJUTO GONZÁLEZ (SPA)
Attendance: 40,228

FC PORTO: Sergei Ovchinnikov, Hugo Benjamin IBARRA, RICARDO Alberto CARVALHO, JORGE Almeida Gomes de ANDRADE, MARIO Magalhães da SILVA, Carlos Humberto PAREDES Monges (71 Sven Fredrick Olof SÖDERSTRÖM), Francisco José Rodrigues da Costa "COSTINHA", CLAYTON Ferreira CRUZ, Anderson Luis de Sousa "DECO", Nuno Fernando Gonçalves da Rocha "CAPUCHO" (77 Dmitriy Alenichev), Renivaldo Pereira des Jesus "PENA" (66 HÉLDER Manuel POSTIGA). Trainer: Octavio Coelho Machado

JUVENTUS: Gianluigi Buffon, Alessandro Birindelli (12 Michele Paramatti), Paolo Montero, Lilian Thuram, Gianluca Pessotto (65 Cristian Zenoni), Gianluca Zambrotta, Alessio Tacchinardi, Igor Tudor, Edgar Davids, Alessandro del Piero, José Marcelo SALAS Melinao (84 Fabián O'Neill).
Trainer: Marcello Lippi

JUVENTUS FC TORINO v ROSENBORG BK TRONDHEIM 1-0 (1-0)

Delle Alpi, Torino 17.10.2001

Referee: Graham Poll (ENG) Attendance: 38,642

JUVENTUS: Gianluigi Buffon, Lilian Thuram, Paolo Montero, Igor Tudor, Gianluca Pessotto, Gianluca Zambrotta, Edgar Davids, Enzo Maresca (62 Mark Iuliano), Pavel Nedved (84 Michele Paramatti), Alessandro del Piero (90 José Marcelo SALAS Melinao), David Trezeguet. Trainer: Marcello Lippi

ROSENBORG: Arni Gautur Arason, Bent Inge Johnsen, Erik Hoftun, Christer Basma, Janne Saarinen, Hasan el Fakiri (46 Dagfinn Enerly), Andre Skammelsrud, Ørjan Berg, Roar Strand, Harald Martin Brattbakk (59 Christer George), Bent Sigurd Rushfeldt (75 Frode Johnsen).
Trainer: Nils Arne Eggen

Goal: Trezeguet (25)

FC PORTO v CELTIC FC GLASGOW 3-0 (2-0)

Estádio das Antas 17.10.2001

Referee: Rene H.J. Temmink (HOL) Attendance: 30,313

FC PORTO: Sergei Ovchinnikov, Hugo Benjamin IBARRA, RICARDO Alberto CARVALHO, JORGE Almeida Gomes de ANDRADE, MARIO Magalhães da SILVA, Carlos Humberto PAREDES Monges, Francisco José Rodrigues da Costa "COSTINHA" (81 Sven Fredrick Olof SÖDERSTRÖM), CLAYTON Ferreira CRUZ (75 RUBENS dos Santos JÚNIOR), Anderson Luis de Sousa "DECO", Nuno Fernando Gonçalves da Rocha "CAPUCHO" (86 PAULO COSTA), Renivaldo Pereira des Jesus "PENA". Trainer: Octavio Coelho Machado

CELTIC: Robert Douglas, Dianbobo Balde, Joos Valgaeren, Johan Mjällby, Alan Thompson (56 Lubomir Moravcik), Didier Agathe, Neil Francis Lennon, Paul Lambert, Stilian Petrov (67 Mohamed "Momo" Sylla), Henrik Larsson, John Hartson (88 Sean Maloney). Trainer: Martin O'Neill

Goals: Clayton (1, 61), Mario Silva (45)

JUVENTUS FC TORINO v FC PORTO 3-1 (1-1)

Delle Alpi, Torino 23.10.2001

Referee: Anders Frisk (SWE) Attendance: 38,328

JUVENTUS: Gianluigi Buffon, Lilian Thuram, Paolo Montero, Mark Iuliano, Michele Paramatti, Gianluca Zambrotta (72 Cristian Zenoni), Alessio Tacchinardi, Edgar Davids (88 Alessandro Birindelli), Pavel Nedved, Alessandro del Piero (76 Enzo Maresca), David Trezeguet. Trainer: Marcello Lippi

FC PORTO: Sergei Ovchinnikov, Hugo Benjamin IBARRA (75 RUBENS dos Santos JÚNIOR), RICARDO Alberto CARVALHO, JORGE Almeida Gomes de ANDRADE, MARIO Magalhães da SILVA, Nuno Fernando Gonçalves da Rocha "CAPUCHO", Sven Fredrick Olof SÖDERSTRÖM, Francisco José Rodrigues da Costa "COSTINHA", Anderson Luis de Sousa "DECO" (67 RAFAEL Gustavo DIAS), Renivaldo Pereira des Jesus "PENA", CLAYTON Ferreira CRUZ (61 HÉLDER Manuel POSTIGA). Trainer: Octavio Coelho Machado

Goals: Clayton (13), del Piero (32), Montero (47), Trezeguet (73)

ROSENBORG BK TRONDHEIM v CELTIC FC GLASGOW 2-0 (2-0)

Lerkendal, Trondheim 23.10.2001

Referee: Juan Antonio FERNANDEZ MARIN (SPA) Attendance: 21,540

ROSENBORG: Arni Gautur Arason, Odd Inge Olsen, Erik Hoftun, Christer Basma, Janne Saarinen, Roar Strand, Andre Skammelsrud, Ørjan Berg (74 Fredrik Winsnes), Christer George (83 Bent Inge Johnsen), Harald Martin Brattbakk, Bent Sigurd Rushfeldt. Trainer: Nils Arne Eggen

CELTIC: Robert Douglas, Dianbobo Balde, Johan Mjällby, Joos Valgaeren, Didier Agathe, Neil Francis Lennon, Paul Lambert, Stilian Petrov (68 Lubomir Moravcik), Alan Thompson (79 John Hartson), Christopher Roy Sutton, Henrik Larsson. Trainer: Martin O'Neill

Goals: Brattbakk (19, 36)

CELTIC FC GLASGOW v JUVENTUS FC TORINO 4-3 (2-1)

Celtic Park, Glasgow 31.10.2001

Referee: Gilles Veissière (FRA) Attendance: 57,717

CELTIC: Robert Douglas, Dianbobo Balde, Johan Mjällby, Joos Valgaeren, Didier Agathe, Neil Francis Lennon, Paul Lambert, Lubomir Moravcik (65 Stilian Petrov), Bobby Alfred Manuel Petta, Christopher Roy Sutton, Henrik Larsson. Trainer: Martin O'Neill

JUVENTUS: Fabián Carini, Alessandro Birindelli, Ciro Ferrara, Mark Iuliano, Michele Paramatti, Cristian Zenoni, Alessio Tacchinardi, Enzo Maresca (81 Alessandro Frara), Pavel Nedved, Alessandro del Piero (46 David Trezeguet), Nicola Amoruso (67 Gianluca Pessotto). Trainer: Marcello Lippi

Goals: del Piero (19), Valgaeren (24), Sutton (45, 64), Trezeguet (51, 77), Larsson (57 pen)

FC PORTO v ROSENBORG BK TRONDHEIM 1-0 (1-0)

Estádio das Antas, Porto 31.10.2001

Referee: Hartmut Strampe (GER) Attendance: 31,429

FC PORTO: PAULO Jorge SANTOS, Hugo Benjamin IBARRA, RICARDO Alberto CARVALHO, JORGE Almeida Gomes de ANDRADE, MARIO Magalhães da SILVA, Nuno Fernando Gonçalves da Rocha "CAPUCHO" (68 Juan Eduardo ESNAIDER), Francisco José Rodrigues da Costa "COSTINHA" (78 RUBENS dos Santos JÚNIOR), Carlos Humberto PAREDES Monges, Anderson Luis de Sousa "DECO", Renivaldo Pereira des Jesus "PENA", CLAYTON Ferreira CRUZ (69 Sven Fredrick Olof SÖDERSTRÖM). Trainer: Octavio Coelho Machado

ROSENBORG: Arni Gautur Arason, Odd Inge Olsen, Erik Hoftun (46 Dagfinn Enerly), Christer Basma, Bent Inge Johnsen, Roar Strand, Ørjan Berg (88 Fredrik Winsnes), Andre Skammelsrud, Ståle Stensaas, Harald Martin Brattbakk (65 Christer George), Frode Johnsen. Trainer: Nils Arne Eggen

Goal: Pena (37)

	P	W	D	L	F	A	Pts
Juventus FC Torino	6	3	2	1	11	8	11
FC Porto	6	3	1	2	7	5	10
Celtic FC Glasgow	6	3	0	3	8	11	9
Rosenborg BK	6	1	1	4	4	6	4

FIRST STAGE – GROUP F

FENERBAHÇE SK ISTANBUL v FC BARCELONA 0-3 (0-2)

Sükrü Saraçoglu, Istanbul 18.09.2001

Referee: Anders Frisk (SWE) Attendance: 23,350

FENERBAHÇE: Rüştü Reçber, Zoran Mirković, Abdullah Ercan, Ogün Temizkanoglu (75 Mert Meric), Mustafa Dogan, Samuel Johnson, Haim Michael Revivo, Ümit Özat, Nikola Lazetic, Milan Rapajc (70 Ceyhun Eris), Niyazi SERHAT Akin (56 Oktay Derelioglu). Trainer: Mustafa Denizli

FC BARCELONA: Roberto Óscar BONANO, Carles PUYOL Saforcada (69 Gabriel García de la Torre "GABRI"), Philippe Christanval, Patrik Andersson, SERGI Barjuán Esclusa, Fábio ROCHEMBACK, Xavier Hernández Creus "XAVI", Philip Cocu, GEOVANNI Deiberson Mauricio (56 Javier Pedro SAVIOLA), Patrick Kluivert, LUIS ENRIQUE Martínez Garcia (60 Frank de Boer). Trainer: Carlos REXACH Cerda

Goals: Kluivert (25), P. Andersson (28), Saviola (66)

OLYMPIQUE LYONNAIS v BAYER 04 LEVERKUSEN 0-1 (0-0)

Gerland, Lyon 18.09.2001

Referee: Graziano Cesari (ITA) Attendance: 37,006

OLYMPIQUE: Grégory Coupet, Eric Deflandre, Patrick Müller, EDMILSON José Gomes de Moraes, Jérémie Bréchet, Eric Carrière (67 Antonio Augusto Ribeiro JUNINHO PERNAMBUCANO), Pierre Laigle (79 Christophe Delmotte), Marc-Vivien Foé, Philippe Violeau, Sidney Govou, Frédéric Née (61 Pegguy Luyindula). Trainer: Jacques Santini

BAYER: Hans-Jörg Butt, Zoltan Sebescen, Jens Nowotny, Lucimar Ferreira da Silva «LUCIO», Diego Rodolfo Placente, Bernd Schneider, Carsten Ramelow, Michael Ballack, Yildiray Bastürk (80 Boris Zivković), Ulf Kirsten (88 Pascal Ojigwe), Oliver Neuville (85 Thomas Brdarić). Trainer: Klaus Toppmöller

Sent off: Juninho (84)

Goal: Kirsten (75)

BAYER 04 LEVERKUSEN v FC BARCELONA 2-1 (0-1)

BayArena, Leverkusen 25.09.2001

Referee: Hugh Dallas (SCO) Attendance: 22,500

BAYER: Hans-Jörg Butt, Lucimar Ferreira da Silva "LUCIO", Jens Nowotny, Diego Rodolfo Placente, Zoltan Sebescen (46 Yildiray Bastürk), Carsten Ramelow, Michael Ballack, Bernd Schneider, José "ZÉ ROBERTO" Da Silva Júnior (83 Boris Zivković), Ulf Kirsten (75 Pascal Ojigwe), Oliver Neuville. Trainer: Klaus Toppmöller

FC BARCELONA: Roberto Óscar BONANO, Carles PUYOL Saforcada (72 Gabriel García de la Torre "GABRI"), Philippe Christanval, Patrik Andersson, SERGI Barjuán Esclusa, Fábio ROCHEMBACK (78 GERARD López Segú), Xavier Hernández Creus "XAVI", Philip Cocu, LUIS ENRIQUE Martínez Garcia, GEOVANNI Deiberson Mauricio (55 Javier Pedro SAVIOLA), Patrick Kluivert. Trainer: Carlos REXACH Cerda

Goals: Luis Enrique (22), Bastürk (52), Neuville (69)

FENERBAHÇE SK ISTANBUL v OLYMPIQUE LYONNAIS 0-1 (0-0)

Sükrü Saraçoglu, Istanbul 25.09.2001

Referee: Frank de Bleeckere (BEL) Attendance: 16,000

FENERBAHÇE: Rüstü Reçber, Zoran Mirkovic, Samuel Johnson, Ogün Temizkanoglu, Mert Meric, Nikola Lazetic (82 Ceyhun Eris), Mustafa Dogan, ALI Mehmet GÜNES (73 Niyazi SERHAT Akin), Abdullah Ercan, Haim Michael Revivo, Milan Rapajc (46 Kennet Andersson). Trainer: Mustafa Denizli

OLYMPIQUE: Grégory Coupet, Eric Deflandre, Patrick Müller, EDMILSON José Gomes de Moraes (63 Claudio Roberto da Silva CAÇAPA), Jérémie Bréchet, Philippe Violeau, Eric Carrière (84 Pierre Laigle), Marc-Vivien Foé, Christophe Delmotte, Pegguy Luyindula (90 David Linarès), Sidney Govou. Trainer: Jacques Santini

Goal: Delmotte (89)

FC BARCELONA v OLYMPIQUE LYONNAIS 2-0 (0-0)

Camp Nou, Barcelona 10.10.2001

Referee: Kim Milton Nielsen (DEN) Attendance: 60,757

FC BARCELONA: Roberto Óscar BONANO, Gabriel García de la Torre «GABRI», Carles PUYOL Saforcada, Frank de Boer, Francesco Coco, LUIS ENRIQUE Martínez Garcia (90 Thiago Motta), Xavier Hernández Creus «XAVI», Philip Cocu, GEOVANNI Deiberson Mauricio (46 Javier Pedro SAVIOLA), Patrick Kluivert, Reinaldo Vítor Borba Ferreira «RIVALDO» (87 Michael Reiziger). Trainer: Carlos REXACH Cerda

OLYMPIQUE: Grégory Coupet, Eric Deflandre, Patrick Müller, Claudio Roberto da Silva CAÇAPA, EDMILSON José Gomes de Moraes, Jérémie Bréchet, David Linarès (83 Christophe Delmotte), Marc-Vivien Foé, Pierre Laigle, Sonny ANDERSON Da Silva (48 Pegguy Luyindula, 84 Frédéric Née), Sidney Govou. Trainer: Jacques Santini

Goals: Kluivert (79), Rivaldo (87 pen)

BAYER 04 LEVERKUSEN v FENERBAHÇE SK ISTANBUL 2-1 (1-1)

BayArena, Leverkusen 10.10.2001

Referee: Alain Hamer (LUX) Attendance: 22,500

BAYER: Hans-Jörg Butt, Bernd Schneider, Jens Nowotny, Lucimar Ferreira da Silva "LUCIO", Diego Rodolfo Placente, Michael Ballack, Carsten Ramelow, Yildiray Bastürk, José "ZÉ ROBERTO" Da Silva Júnior (90 Jurica Vranjes), Ulf Kirsten (86 Zoltan Sebescen), Oliver Neuville (68 Dimitar Berbatov). Trainer: Klaus Toppmöller

FENERBAHÇE: Rüstü Reçber, Zoran Mirković, Samuel Johnson, Ogün Temizkanoglu (79 Niyazi SERHAT Akin), Ümit Özat, Mert Meric, Nikola Lazetic (79 ALI Mehmet GÜNES), Ali Akdeniz, Abdullah Ercan, Haim Michael Revivo (64 Hakan Bayraktar), Milan Rapajc. Trainer: Mustafa Denizli

Sent off: S. Johnson (37)

Goals: Revivo (6), Lucio (36), Ballack (59)

FC BARCELONA v BAYER 04 LEVERKUSEN 2-1 (2-1)

Camp Nou, Barcelona 17.10.2001

Referee: Pierluigi Collina (ITA) Attendance: 60,432

FC BARCELONA: Roberto Óscar BONANO, Carles PUYOL Saforcada, Frank de Boer, Philippe Christanval, Francesco Coco, LUIS ENRIQUE Martínez Garcia, Xavier Hernández Creus «XAVI» (48 GERARD López Segú), Philip Cocu, Javier Pedro SAVIOLA (79 GEOVANNI Deiberson Mauricio), Patrick Kluivert, Reinaldo Vítor Borba Ferreira «RIVALDO» (74 Gabriel García de la Torre "GABRI").

BAYER: Hans-Jörg Butt, Bernd Schneider, Lucimar Ferreira da Silva «LUCIO», Jens Nowotny (46 Boris Zivković), Diego Rodolfo Placente, Carsten Ramelow (76 Thomas Brdarić), Michael Ballack, Yildiray Bastürk, José «ZÉ ROBERTO» Da Silva Júnior, Ulf Kirsten (76 Zoltan Sebescen), Oliver Neuville. Trainer: Klaus Toppmöller

Goals: Kluivert (12), Ramelow (32), Luis Enrique (38)

OLYMPIQUE LYONNAIS
v FENERBAHÇE SK ISTANBUL 3-1 (1-1)

Gerland, Lyon 17.10.2001

Referee: Konrad Plautz (AUS) Attendance: 37,773

OLYMPIQUE: Grégory Coupet, Philippe Violeau, Patrick Müller, EDMILSON José Gomes de Moraes, Jean-Marc Chanelet, Christophe Delmotte, Eric Carrière, Marc-Vivien Foé, Antonio Augusto Ribeiro JUNINHO PERNAMBUCANO (67 Jérémie Bréchet), Pegguy Luyindula (79 Frédéric Née), Sidney Govou (86 David Linarès). Trainer: Jacques Santini

FENERBAHÇE: Rüstü Reçber, Ümit Özat, Ogün Temizkanoglu, Mustafa Dogan (24 Deniz Uygar), Mert Meric, Nikola Lazetic (73 ALI Mehmet GÜNES), Ali Akdeniz, Yusuf Simsek, Abdullah Ercan, Haim Michael Revivo (73 Milan Rapajc), Oktay Derelioglu. Trainer: Mustafa Denizli

Goals: Oktay (35), Govou (45), Carrière (53), Delmotte (68)

FENERBAHÇE SK ISTANBUL
v BAYER 04 LEVERKUSEN 1-2 (1-2)

Sükrü Saraçoglu, Istanbul 23.10.2001

Referee: Terje Hauge (NOR) Attendance: 9,335

FENERBAHÇE: Rüstü Reçber, Mustafa Dogan, Mert Merić, Samuel Johnson, Deniz Uygar, Nikola Lazetić (65 Hakan Bayraktar), Ali Akdeniz (77 Milan Rapajć), Yusuf Simsek (52 Ogün Temizkanoglu), ALI Mehmet GÜNES, Haim Michael Revivo, Oktay Derelioglu. Trainer: Mustafa Denizli

BAYER: Hans-Jörg Butt, Zoltan Sebescen, Jens Nowotny, Boris Zivković, Bernd Schneider, Carsten Ramelow, Michael Ballack, Yildiray Bastürk (89 Jurica Vranjes), José «ZÉ ROBERTO» Da Silva Júnior, Ulf Kirsten (68 Thomas Brdarić), Oliver Neuville (83 Pascal Ojigwe).
Trainer: Klaus Toppmöller

Goals: Schneider (21), Kirsten (34), Oktay (40)

OLYMPIQUE LYONNAIS
v FC BARCELONA 2-3 (0-2)

Gerland, Lyon 23.10.2001

Referee: Graham Poll (ENG) Attendance: 37,800

OLYMPIQUE: Grégory Coupet, Jean-Marc Chanelet (53 Christophe Delmotte), Patrick Müller, EDMILSON José Gomes de Moraes (26 Claudio Roberto da Silva Caçapa), Jérémie Bréchet (78 Pierre Laigle), Antonio Augusto Ribeiro JUNINHO PERNAMBUCANO, Eric Carrière, Marc-Vivien Foé, Philippe Violeau, Pegguy Luyindula, Sidney Govou.
Trainer: Jacques Santini

FC BARCELONA: Roberto Óscar BONANO, Carles PUYOL Saforcada, Frank de Boer, Philippe Christanval, Francesco Coco (58 Michael Reiziger), LUIS ENRIQUE Martínez Garcia (73 GERARD López Segú), Xavier Hernández Creus «XAVI», Gabriel García de la Torre «GABRI», Philip Cocu, Patrick Kluivert, Reinaldo Vítor Borba Ferreira «RIVALDO» (87 GEOVANNI Deiberson Mauricio).
Trainer: Carlos REXACH Cerda

Goals: Kluivert (9), Rivaldo (18), Luyindula (66), Carrière (88), Gerard (90+4)

FC BARCELONA
v FENERBAHÇE SK ISTANBUL 1-0 (0-0)

Camp Nou, Barcelona 31.10.2001

Referee: Stuart Dougal (SCO) Attendance: 35,233

FC BARCELONA: José Manuel REINA Páez, Carles PUYOL Saforcada, Frank de Boer, Michael Reiziger, Gabriel García de la Torre «GABRI», Xavier Hernández Creus «XAVI», Reinaldo Vítor Borba Ferreira «RIVALDO», GERARD López Segú, GEOVANNI Deiberson Mauricio (59 Fabio Rochemback), Javier Pedro SAVIOLA (74 Daniel García Laran «DANI»), Marc Overmars (81 ALFONSO Pérez Muñoz).
Trainer: Carlos REXACH Cerda

FENERBAHÇE: Rüştü Reçber, Mustafa Dogan, Samuel Johnson, Ümit Özat, Mert Meric, Nikola Lazetic, Ali Akdeniz, ALI Mehmet GÜNES (89 Ceyhun Eris), Abdullah Ercan (77 Hakan Bayraktar), Milan Rapajc (79 Yusuf Simsek), Niyazi SERHAT Akin. Trainer: Mustafa Denizli

Goal: Rivaldo (90)

BAYER 04 LEVERKUSEN
v OLYMPIQUE LYONNAIS 2-4 (1-2)

BayArena, Leverkusen 31.10.2001

Referee: Iordan Ivanov (BUL) Attendance: 22,500

BAYER: Hans-Jörg Butt, Boris Zivković, Lucimar Ferreira da Silva «LUCIO», Diego Rodolfo Placente, Bernd Schneider, Pascal Ojigwe (46 Yildiray Bastürk), Zoltan Sebescen, Jurica Vranjes, José «ZÉ ROBERTO» Da Silva Júnior, Oliver Neuville, Dimitar Berbatov (72 Markus Daun).
Trainer: Klaus Toppmöller

OLYMPIQUE: Grégory Coupet, Eric Deflandre, Florent Laville, Christophe Delmotte, Patrick Müller, Jean-Marc Chanelet, David Linarès, Eric Carrière (77 Philippe Violeau), Antonio Augusto Ribeiro JUNINHO PERNAMBUCANO (68 Sidney Govou), Pierre Laigle, Frédéric Née.
Trainer: Jacques Santini

Goals: Carrière (32, 38), Sebescen (45), Berbatov (52), Née (64), Govou (81)

	P	W	D	L	F	A	Pts
FC Barcelona	6	5	0	1	12	5	15
Bayer 04 Leverkusen	6	4	0	2	10	9	12
Olympique Lyonnais	6	3	0	3	10	9	9
Fenerbahçe SK Istanbul	6	0	0	6	3	12	0

FIRST STAGE – GROUP G

RC DEPORTIVO LA CORUÑA v OLYMPIAKOS PEIRAIAS 2-2 (1-0)

Estadio Municipal de Riazor, La Coruña 18.09.2001

Referee: Jan W. Wegereef (HOL) Attendance: 20,873

DEPORTIVO: José Francisco MOLINA Gimenez, MANUEL PABLO García Díaz, Nourredine Naybet, SERGIO González Soriano (84 Juan Carlos VALERÓN Santana), Enrique Fernández ROMERO, VÍCTOR Sánchez del Amo (37 Lionel Sebastián SCALONI), DONATO Gama da Silva, MAURO da SILVA Gomes, Francisco Javier González Pérez "FRAN", DIEGO TRISTÁN Herrera (70 Roy Makaay), Walter Gerardo PANDIANI. Trainer: Javier IRURETAgoyena Amiano

OLYMPIAKOS: Dimitrios Eleftheropoulos, Dimitrios Mavrogenidis (76 Hristos Patsatzoglu), Giorgos Anatolakis, Jorge Hernán BERMÚDEZ Morales, Stylianos Venetidis, Stylianos Giannakopoulos, Christian KAREMBEU, Pär Zetterberg (60 Peter Ofori-Quaye), José Elías Junior M. «ZÉ ELIAS», Predrag Djordjević, GIOVANNI Silva de Oliveira (84 Giorgos Amanatidis). Trainer: Panagiotis Lemonis

Goals: Fran (22), Giannakopoulos (80), Ofori-Quaye (83), Valerón (90)

MANCHESTER UNITED FC v LILLE OLYMPIQUE SC 1-0 (0-0)

Old Trafford, Manchester 18.09.2001

Referee: Rene H.J. Temmink (HOL) Attendance: 64,827

MANCHESTER UNITED: Fabien Barthez, Gary Neville (12 Mikaël Silvestre), Wesley Brown, Laurent Blanc, Denis Irwin, David Beckham, Roy Keane, Paul Scholes, Juan Sebastián Verón, Ryan Giggs (74 Ole Gunnar Solskjaer), Ruud van Nistelrooy. Manager: Alex Ferguson

OLYMPIQUE: Grégory Wimbée, Stéphane Pichot, Pascal Cygan, Abdelilah Fahmi, Johnny Ecker, Grégory Tafforeau (86 Rafaël Schmitz), Fernando Osvaldo D'Amico, Sylvain N'Diaye, Bruno Cheyrou (75 Djezon Boutoille), Dagui Orphie Bakari, Mile Sterjovski (90 Adekanmi Olufadé).
Trainer: Vahid Halilhodzić

Goal: Beckham (90)

RC DEPORTIVO LA CORUÑA v MANCHESTER UNITED FC 2-1 (0-1)

Estadio Municipal de Riazor, La Coruña 25.09.2001

Referee: Stefano Braschi (ITA) Attendance: 33,108

DEPORTIVO: José Francisco MOLINA Gimenez, MANUEL PABLO García Díaz, Nourredine Naybet, DONATO Gama da Silva, Enrique Fernández ROMERO, Roy Makaay (61 Walter Gerardo PANDIANI), MAURO da SILVA Gomes, SERGIO González Soriano (61 Lionel Sebastián SCALONI), EMERSON Moisés Costa (46 Juan Carlos VALERÓN Santana), Francisco Javier González Pérez «FRAN», DIEGO TRISTÁN Herrera.
Trainer: Javier IRURETAgoyena Amiano

MANCHESTER UNITED: Fabien Barthez, Gary Neville, Ronny Johnsen, Laurent Blanc, Denis Irwin, David Beckham (90 Andy Cole), Roy Keane, Paul Scholes, Juan Sebastián Verón, Ryan Giggs, Ruud van Nistelrooy (90 Ole Gunnar Solskjaer). Manager: Alex Ferguson

Goals: Scholes (40), Pandiani (86), Naybet (90)

LILLE OLYMPIQUE SC v OLYMPIAKOS PEIRAIAS 3-1 (2-0)

Grimonprez-Jooris, Lille 25.09.2001

Referee: Stuart Dougal (SCO) Attendance: 35,000

OLYMPIQUE: Grégory Wimbée, Stéphane Pichot, Pascal Cygan, Abdelilah Fahmi, Johnny Ecker, Djezon Boutoille (66 Mathieu Delpierre), Fernando Osvaldo D'Amico, Sylvain N'Diaye, Bruno Cheyrou (76 Grégory Tafforeau), Dagui Orphie Bakari (88 Adekanmi Olufadé), Mile Sterjovski.
Trainer: Vahid Halilhodzić

OLYMPIAKOS: Dimitrios Eleftheropoulos, Dimitrios Mavrogenidis (64 Andreas Niniadis), Giorgos Anatolakis, Jorge Hernán BERMÚDEZ Morales, Stylianos Venetidis, Hristos Patsatzoglu, Christian Karembeu, GIOVANNI Silva de Oliveira, Stylianos Giannakopoulos, Peter Ofori-Quaye, Zizi Roberts (77 Alekos Alexandris).
Trainer: Panagiotis Lemonis

Goals: Bakari (33), Br. Cheyrou (44), Tafforeau (79), Giannakopoulos (90)

LILLE OLYMPIQUE SC v RC DEPORTIVO LA CORUÑA 1-1 (0-0)

Grimonprez-Jooris, Lille 10.10.2001

Referee: Claus Bo Larsen (DEN) Attendance: 37,033

OLYMPIQUE: Grégory Wimbée, Stéphane Pichot, Pascal Cygan, Abdelilah Fahmi, Johnny Ecker, Sylvain N'Diaye, Fernando Osvaldo D'Amico, Mile Sterjovski (74 Adekanmi Olufadé), Christophe Landrin (61 Salaheddine Bassir), Bruno Cheyrou (78 Edwin Murati), Dagui Orphie Bakari.
Trainer: Vahid Halilhodzić

DEPORTIVO: José Francisco MOLINA Gimenez, HÉCTOR Berenguel Del Pino, Nourredine Naybet, DONATO Gama da Silva, Enrique Fernández ROMERO, VÍCTOR Sánchez del Amo (71 Lionel Sebastián SCALONI), Juan Carlos VALERÓN Santana (79 SERGIO González Soriano), EMERSON Moisés Costa, Aldo Pedro DUSCHER, Francisco Javier González Pérez «FRAN» (64 José Emilio AMAVISCA), Walter Gerardo PANDIANI. Trainer: Javier IRURETAgoyena Amiano

Goals: Valerón (49), Olufadé (87)

OLYMPIAKOS PEIRAIAS
v MANCHESTER UNITED FC 0-2 (0-0)

OAKA Spiros Louis, Athina 10.10.2001

Referee: Graziano Cesari (ITA) Attendance: 73,537

OLYMPIAKOS: Dimitrios Eleftheropoulos, Hristos Patsatzoglou, Giorgos Anatolakis, Jorge Hernán BERMÚDEZ Morales, Stylianos Venetidis, Stylianos Giannakopoulos, Christian Karembeu, Pär Zetterberg (66 Andreas Niniadis), Athanasios Kostoulas (70 Peter Ofori-Quaye), Predrag Djordjević (80 Alekos Alexandris), GIOVANNI Silva de Oliveira. Trainer: Panagiotis Lemonis

MANCHESTER UNITED: Fabien Barthez, Gary Neville, Ronny Johnsen, Laurent Blanc, Denis Irwin (89 Mikaël Silvestre), David Beckham, Roy Keane, Paul Scholes, Juan Sebastián Verón (80 Andy Cole), Ryan Giggs, Ruud van Nistelrooy (85 Ole Gunnar Solskjaer).
Manager: Alex Ferguson

Goals: Beckham (66), Cole (82)

MANCHESTER UNITED FC
v RC DEPORTIVO LA CORUÑA 2-3 (2-2)

Old Trafford, Manchester 17.10.2001

Referee: Herbert Fandel (GER) Attendance: 65,585

MANCHESTER UNITED: Fabien Barthez, Gary Neville, Ronny Johnsen (7 Wesley Brown), Laurent Blanc, Denis Irwin (85 Ole Gunnar Solskjaer), David Beckham, Roy Keane, Paul Scholes (63 Andy Cole), Juan Sebastián Verón, Ryan Giggs, Ruud van Nistelrooy. Manager: Alex Ferguson

DEPORTIVO: José Francisco MOLINA Gimenez (46 NUNO Herlandes Simões), HÉCTOR Berenguel Del Pino, Nourredine Naybet, DONATO Gama da Silva, Enrique Fernández ROMERO (79 Joan CAPDEVILA Méndez), VÍCTOR Sánchez del Amo, Juan Carlos VALERÓN Santana, SERGIO González Soriano, Aldo Pedro DUSCHER, José Emilio AMAVISCA, DIEGO TRISTÁN Herrera (82 Walter Gerardo PANDIANI).
Trainer: Javier IRURETAgoyena Amiano

Goals: van Nistelrooy (7, 40), Sergio (37), Diego Tristán (39, 60)

OLYMPIAKOS PEIRAIAS
v LILLE OLYMPIQUE SC 2-1 (0-1)

OAKA, Athina 17.10.2001

Referee: Alfredo Trentalange (ITA) Attendance: 40,000

OLYMPIAKOS: Dimitrios Eleftheropoulos, Hristos Patsatzoglu, Giorgos Anatolakis (62 Andreas Niniadis), Jorge Hernán Bermúdez Morales (46 Giorgos Amanatidis), Stylianos Venetidis, Dimitrios Mavrogenidis, Christian Karembeu, Pär Zetterberg (46 GIOVANNI Silva de Oliveira), Predrag Djordjević, Alekos Alexandris, Peter Ofori-Quaye.
Trainer: Panagiotis Lemonis

OLYMPIQUE: Grégory Wimbée, Pascal Cygan, Abdelilah Fahmi, Mathieu Delpierre, Johnny Ecker, Edwin Murati (84 Mikkel Beck), Benoît Cheyrou, Fernando Osvaldo D'Amico, Christophe Landrin, Dagui Orphie Bakari (5 Salaheddine Bassir), Adekanmi Olufadé (60 Stéphane Pichot).
Trainer: Vahid Halilhodzić

Sent off: Giovanni (88)

Goals: Bassir (38), Alexandris (53), Niniadis (64)

RC DEPORTIVO LA CORUÑA
v LILLE OLYMPIQUE SC 1-1 (1-1)

Estadio Municipal de Riazor, La Coruña 23.10.2001

Referee: L'uboš Michel (SVK) Attendance: 22,983

DEPORTIVO: NUNO Herlandes Simões, HÉCTOR Berenguel Del Pino, DONATO Gama da Silva, HÉLDER Marino Rodríguez Cristavão, Joan CAPDEVILA Méndez, VÍCTOR Sánchez del Amo, Juan Carlos VALERÓN Santana (70 Djalma Feitosa Dias "DJALMINHA"), EMERSON Moisés Costa (60 SERGIO González Soriano), Aldo Pedro DUSCHER, José Emilio AMAVISCA, DIEGO TRISTÁN Herrera (82 Walter Gerardo PANDIANI).
Trainer: Javier IRURETAgoyena Amiano

OLYMPIQUE: Grégory Wimbée, Mathieu Delpierre, Abdelilah Fahmi, Johnny Ecker, Stéphane Pichot, Mile Sterjovski (88 Patrick Collot), Christophe Landrin, Fernando Osvaldo D'Amico, Sylvain N'Diaye (81 Benoît Cheyrou), Bruno Cheyrou, Salaheddine Bassir (90 Mikkel Beck).
Trainer: Vahid Halilhodzić

Goals: Diego Tristán (14 pen), Br. Cheyrou (20 pen)

MANCHESTER UNITED FC
v OLYMPIAKOS PEIRAIAS 3-0 (0-0)

Old Trafford, Manchester 23.10.2001

Referee: Vitor Manuel MELO PEREIRA (POR) Att: 66,769

MANCHESTER UNITED: Fabien Barthez, Gary Neville, Wesley Brown, Laurent Blanc, Denis Irwin, David Beckham, Nicky Butt (73 Ole Gunnar Solskjaer), Paul Scholes, Juan Sebastián Verón, Ryan Giggs, Ruud van Nistelrooy.
Manager: Alex Ferguson

OLYMPIAKOS: Dimitrios Eleftheropoulos, Hristos Patsatzoglou, Giorgos Anatolakis, Giorgos Amanatidis, Hristos Kontis, Dimitrios Mavrogenidis (46 Ilias Poursanidis), Christian Karembeu, Stylianos Giannakopoulos (83 Zizi Roberts), Predrag Djordjević, Alekos Alexandris (63 Jorge Gabriel ALVEZ Fernández), Peter Ofori-Quaye.
Trainer: Panagiotis Lemonis

Goals: Solskjaer (79), Giggs (88), van Nistelrooy (90)

LILLE OLYMPIQUE SC
v MANCHESTER UNITED FC 1-1 (0-1)

Félix Bollaert, Lens 31.10.2001

Referee: Urs Meier (SWI) Attendance: 38,402

OLYMPIQUE: Grégory Wimbée, Stéphane Pichot, Johnny Ecker, Abdelilah Fahmi, Pascal Cygan, Mile Sterjovski, Fernando Osvaldo D'Amico, Sylvain N'Diaye (86 Christophe Landrin), Bruno Cheyrou, Salaheddine Bassir (78 Edwin Murati), Djezon Boutoille (59 Mikkel Beck).
Trainer: Vahid Halilhodzić

MANCHESTER UNITED: Roy Carroll, Denis Irwin, David May (69 John O'Shea), Philip Neville, Mikaël Silvestre, David Beckham, Nicky Butt, Paul Scholes, Quinton Fortune, Andy Cole (76 Dwight Yorke), Ole Gunnar Solskjaer.
Manager: Alex Ferguson

Goals: Solskjaer (6), Br. Cheyrou (65)

OLYMPIAKOS PEIRAIAS
v RC DEPORTIVO LA CORUÑA 1-1 (0-0)

OAKA Spiros Louis, Athina 31.10.2001

Referee: Markus Merk (GER) Attendance: 20,293

OLYMPIAKOS: Aggelos Georgiou, Hristos Patsatzoglou, Giorgos Anatolakis, Giorgos Amanatidis (21 Athanasios Kostoulas), Hristos Kontis, Dimitrios Mavrogenidis (46 Andreas Niniadis), Christian Karembeu, Stylianos Giannakopoulos, Predrag Djordjević, Alekos Alexandris, Peter Ofori-Quaye (66 Ilias Poursanidis).
Trainer: Panagiotis Lemonis

DEPORTIVO: NUNO Herlandes Simões, HÉCTOR Berenguel Del Pino (53 José Emilio AMAVISCA), HÉLDER Marino Rodríguez Cristavão, CÉSAR Martín Villar (40 DONATO Gama da Silva), Joan CAPDEVILA Méndez, EMERSON Moisés Costa, MAURO da SILVA Gomes (63 Walter Gerardo PANDIANI), Djalma Feitosa Dias "DJALMINHA", Lionel Sebastián SCALONI, Roy MAKAAY, JOSÉ MANUEL Colmereno Crespo. Trainer: Javier IRURETAgoyena Amiano

Goals: Alexandris (51), Capdevila (84)

	P	W	D	L	F	A	Pts
Deportivo La Coruña	6	2	4	0	10	8	10
Manchesrer United FC	6	3	1	2	10	6	10
Lille Olympique SC	6	1	3	2	7	7	6
Olympiakos Peiraias	6	1	2	3	6	12	5

FIRST STAGE – GROUP H

FC BAYERN MÜNCHEN v AC SPARTA PRAHA 0-0

Olympiastadion, München 18.09.2001

Referee: Leslie J.R. Irvine (NIR) Attendance: 16,000

BAYERN: Oliver Kahn, Willy Sagnol, Samuel Osei Kuffour, Robert Kovac, Bixente Lizarazu, Nico Kovac (46 PAULO SÉRGIO do Nascimento), Thorsten Fink, Ciriaco Sforza (46 Owen Hargreaves), Hasan Salihamidzić, Giovane Elber (72 Claudio Pizarro), Carsten Jancker. Trainer: Ottmar Hitzfeld

SPARTA: Petr Cech, Zdenek Grygera, Jiri Novotny, Martin Hasek, Vladimir Labant, Libor Sionko, Jiri Jarošik, Lukáš Hartig (57 Peter Babnic, 90 Lukáš Zelenka), Rastislav Michalík (90 Jan Flachbart), Marek Kincl, Tomáš Hübschmann.
Trainer: Jaroslav Hrebík

SPARTAK MOSKVA
v SC FEYENOORD ROTTERDAM 2-2 (0-1)

Luzhniki, Moskva 18.09.2001

Referee: Antonio Jesus LÓPEZ NIETO (SPA) Att: 25,000

SPARTAK: Maxim Kabanov, Jerry Christian Tchuisse (32 Dmitry Ananko), Yuri Kovtun, Igor Mitreski, Dmitry Parfenov, Vasily Baranov, Egor Titov, Viktor Bulatov, Eduard Tsykhmeistruk, Vladimir Beschastnykh, Luis ROBSON Pereira da Silva. Trainer: Oleg Romantsev

FEYENOORD: Edwin Zoetebier, Brett Emerton, Ulrich van Gobbel, Ferry de Haan, Tomasz Rzasa, Paul Bosvelt, Jon Dahl Tomasson, Jean-Paul van Gastel (67 Jan de Visser), Patrick Paauwe, Pierre van Hooijdonk, Bonaventure Kalou (71 Pieter Collen). Trainer: Bert van Marwijk

Goals: Bosvelt (12), Robson (62), Tomasson (59), Beschastnykh (69)

AC SPARTA PRAHA
v SC FEYENOORD ROTTERDAM 4-0 (2-0)

Letná, Praha 25.09.2001

Referee: Fritz Stuchlik (AUS) Attendance: 15,150

SPARTA: Petr Cech, Zdenek Grygera, Jiri Novotny, Tomáš Hübschmann, Vladimir Labant, Libor Sionko (87 Petr Papousek), Jiri Jarošik, Martin Hasek, Rastislav Michalík (80 Lukáš Zelenka), Marek Kincl, Lukáš Hartig (84 Radim Holub).
Trainer: Jaroslav Hrebík

FEYENOORD: Edwin Zoetebier, Brett Emerton, Ulrich van Gobbel, Ferry de Haan, Tomasz Rzasa, Bonaventure Kalou, Paul Bosvelt, Jean-Paul van Gastel (80 LEONARDO de Vitor Santiago), Patrick Paauwe, Pierre van Hooijdonk, Jon Dahl Tomasson. Trainer: Bert van Marwijk

Sent off: Van Gobbel (37)

Goals: Hartig (24), Labant (37 pen), Kincl (71), Michalík (74)

SPARTAK MOSKVA
v FC BAYERN MÜNCHEN 1-3 (0-2)

Luzhniki, Moskva 25.09.2001

Referee: Arturo DAUDEN IBÁÑEZ (SPA) Att: 37,000

SPARTAK: Maxim Kabanov, Dmitry Ananko, Yuri Kovtun, Igor Mitreski, Dmitry Parfenov (46 Jerry Christian Tchuisse), Vasily Baranov, Egor Titov, Viktor Bulatov, Artem Bezrodny (46 Eduard Tsykhmeistruk), Vladimir Beschastnykh, Luis ROBSON Pereira da Silva. Trainer: Oleg Romantsev

BAYERN: Oliver Kahn, Willy Sagnol, Samuel Osei Kuffour, Robert Kovac, Bixente Lizarazu, Nico Kovac, Thorsten Fink (87 Owen Hargreaves), Pablo Thiam, Hasan Salihamidzić (82 PAULO SÉRGIO do Nascimento), Giovane Elber, Roque SANTA CRUZ (79 Claudio Pizarro).
Trainer: Ottmar Hitzfeld

Goals: Salihamidzić (16), Baranov (64), Elber (41, 74)

FC BAYERN MÜNCHEN
v SPARTAK MOSKVA 5-1 (3-0)

Olympiastadion, München 17.10.2001

Referee: Frank de Bleeckere (BEL) Attendance: 19,000

BAYERN: Oliver Kahn, Willy Sagnol, Samuel Osei Kuffour, Robert Kovac (85 Thomas Linke), Bixente Lizarazu, Hasan Salihamidzić, Thorsten Fink, Owen Hargreaves, PAULO SÉRGIO do Nascimento (78 Alexander Zickler), Giovane Elber (65 Roque SANTA CRUZ), Claudio Pizarro.
Trainer: Ottmar Hitzfeld

SPARTAK: Maxym Levitsky, Jerry Christian Tchuisse, Yuri Kovtun, Igor Mitreski, Dmitry Parfenov, Vasily Baranov, Egor Titov, Viktor Bulatov, Eduard Tsykhmeistruk, Vladimir Beschastnykh, Luis ROBSON Pereira da Silva.
Trainer: Oleg Romantsev

Goals: Pizarro (7, 22), Elber (34, 52), Beschastnykh (58), Zickler (90)

FEYENOORD ROTTERDAM
v FC BAYERN MÜNCHEN 2-2 (2-1)

Feyenoord, Rotterdam 10.10.2001

Referee: Gilles Veissrière (FRA) Attendance: 37,500

FEYENOORD: Edwin Zoetebier, Pieter Collen, Kees van Wonderen, Ferry de Haan, Tomasz Rzasa (66 Ramon van Haren), Brett Emerton, Paul Bosvelt, Patrick Paauwe, Bonaventure Kalou (74 Shinji Ono), Jon Dahl Tomasson, Pierre van Hooijdonk. Trainer: Bert van Marwijk

BAYERN: Oliver Kahn, Willy Sagnol, Samuel Osei Kuffour, Robert Kovac, Bixente Lizarazu, Hasan Salihamidzić, Thorsten Fink (84 Ciriaco Sforza), Pablo Thiam (46 Owen Hargreaves), PAULO SÉRGIO do Nascimento, Giovane Elber (78 Roque SANTA CRUZ), Claudio Pizarro. Trainer: Ottmar Hitzfeld

Goals: Elber (13, 50), van Hooijdonk (38), Tomasson (45)

FEYENOORD ROTTERDAM
v AC SPARTA PRAHA 0-2 (0-1)

Feyenoord, Rotterdam 17.10.2001

Referee: Arturo DAUDEN IBAÑEZ (SPA) Att: 37,200

FEYENOORD: Henk Timmer, Pieter Collen (62 Leonardo DOS SANTOS Silva), Kees van Wonderen, Ferry de Haan, Tomasz Rzasa, Brett Emerton, Paul Bosvelt, Patrick Paauwe, LEONARDO de Vitor Santiago (46 Bonaventure Kalou), Pierre van Hooijdonk, Shinji Ono. Trainer: Bert van Marwijk

SPARTA: Petr Cech, Zdenek Grygera, Jiri Novotny, Tomáš Hübschmann, Vladimir Labant, Libor Sionko, Jiri Jarošik, Martin Hasek, Rastislav Michalík (88 Lukáš Zelenka), Marek Kincl, Lukáš Hartig. Trainer: Jaroslav Hrebík

Sent off: Van Hooijdonk (67), de Haan (74)

Goals: Jarošik (43), Novotny (78)

AC SPARTA PRAHA
v SPARTAK MOSKVA 2-0 (0-0)

Letná, Praha 10.10.2001

Referee: Eric Poulat (FRA) Attendance: 17,221

SPARTA: Petr Cech, Zdenek Grygera, Jiri Novotny, Tomáš Hübschmann, Vladimir Labant, Libor Sionko, Jiri Jarošik, Martin Hasek, Rastislav Michalík (60 Lukáš Zelenka), Marek Kincl (90 Petr Papousek), Lukáš Hartig (80 Radim Holub).
Trainer: Jaroslav Hrebík

SPARTAK: Maxym Levitsky, Dmitry Ananko, Yuri Kovtun, Igor Mitreski, Dmitry Parfenov, Vasily Baranov, Egor Titov, Viktor Bulatov, Artem Bezrodny (58 Eduard Tsykhmeistruk), Vladimir Beschastnykh, Luis ROBSON Pereira da Silva (61 German Lovchev). Trainer: Oleg Romantsev

Goals: Kincl (57), Sionko (88)

FC BAYERN MÜNCHEN
v FEYENOORD ROTTERDAM 3-1 (2-1)

Olympiastadion, München 23.10.2001

Referee: Lucilio CARDOSO CORTEZ BATISTA (POR)
Attendance: 40,000

BAYERN: Oliver Kahn, Willy Sagnol, Samuel Osei Kuffour, Robert Kovac, Bixente Lizarazu (46 Michael Tarnat), Hasan Salihamidzić, Thorsten Fink (84 Pablo Thiam), Owen Hargreaves, PAULO SÉRGIO do Nascimento (69 Alexander Zickler), Roque SANTA CRUZ, Claudio Pizarro.
Trainer: Ottmar Hitzfeld

FEYENOORD: Edwin Zoetebier, Pieter Collen, Ulrich van Gobbel (46 Christian Gyan), Kees van Wonderen, Tomasz Rzasa, Brett Emerton, Paul Bosvelt, Jean-Paul van Gastel (80 Ebi Smolarek), Patrick Paauwe, Johan Elmander, Shinji Ono.
Trainer: Bert van Marwijk

Goals: Kuffour (12), Elmander (25), Santa Cruz (30, 90)

SPARTAK MOSKVA v AC SPARTA PRAHA 2-2 (2-1)

Luzhniki, Moskva 23.10.2001

Referee: Graham Barber (ENG) Attendance: 5,300

SPARTAK: Maxym Levitsky, Dmitry Parfenov, Yuri Kovtun, Dmitry Ananko, Baye Kebe, Vasily Baranov, Egor Titov, Viktor Bulatov, Eduard Tsykhmeistruk (46 Igor Mitreski), Vladimir Beschastnykh, Luis ROBSON Pereira da Silva.
Trainer: Oleg Romantsev

SPARTA: Petr Cech, Zdenek Grygera, Jiri Novotny, Tomáš Hübschmann, Vladimir Labant, Libor Sionko (83 Radek Sloncik), Jiri Jarošik, Martin Hasek, Rastislav Michalík (73 Peter Babnic), Radim Holub (57 Lukáš Zelenka), Marek Kincl.
Trainer: Jaroslav Hrebík

Goals: Robson (4), Holub (29), Beschastnykh (34), Babnic (90)

SC FEYENOORD ROTTERDAM v SPARTAK MOSKVA 2-1 (2-1)

De Kuip, Rotterdam 31.10.2001

Referee: Graziano Cesari (ITA) Attendance: 40,000

FEYENOORD: Edwin Zoetebier, Pieter Collen (64 Jean-Paul van Gastel), Christian Gyan, Ferry de Haan, Tomasz Rzasa, Brett Emerton, Paul Bosvelt, Patrick Paauwe, Shinji Ono, Jon Dahl Tomasson, Johan Elmander (88 Ebi Smolarek).
Trainer: Bert van Marwijk

SPARTAK: Maxym Levitsky, Yuri Kovtun, Igor Mitreski, Kakhaber Mzhavanadze (83 Alexandr Pavlenko), Dmitry Parfenov, Vasily Baranov, Egor Titov, Viktor Bulatov, Eduard Tsykhmeistruk, Vladimir Beschastnykh, Luis ROBSON Pereira da Silva (76 Alexandr Danishevski).
Trainer: Oleg Romantsev

Goals: Tomasson (5), Beschastnykh (14), Elmander (18)

AC SPARTA PRAHA v FC BAYERN MÜNCHEN 0-1 (0-1)

Letná, Praha 31.10.2001

Referee: Alain Hamer (LUX) Attendance: 19,396

SPARTA: Petr Cech, Zdenek Grygera, Jiri Novotny, Tomáš Hübschmann, Vladimir Labant, Libor Sionko, Jiri Jarošik, Martin Hasek (70 Radek Sloncik), Rastislav Michalík (80 Radim Holub), Marek Kincl, Peter Babnic (53 Lukáš Zelenka).
Trainer: Jaroslav Hrebík

BAYERN: Stefan Wessels, Thomas Linke, Robert Kovac, Samuel Osei Kuffour, Michael Tarnat, Pablo Thiam, Ciriaco Sforza, Owen Hargreaves (46 PAULO SÉRGIO do Nascimento), Markus Feulner, Alexander Zickler (84 Thorsten Fink), Claudio Pizarro (72 Roque SANTA CRUZ).
Trainer: Ottmar Hitzfeld

Goal: Novotny (41 og)

	P	W	D	L	F	A	Pts
FC Bayern München	6	4	2	0	14	5	14
AC Sparta Praha	6	3	2	1	10	3	11
Feyenoord Rotterdam	6	1	2	3	7	14	5
Spartak Moskva	6	0	2	4	7	16	2

SECOND STAGE – GROUP A

FC BAYERN MÜNCHEN v MANCHESTER UNITED FC 1-1 (0-0)

Olympiastadion, München 20.11.2001

Referee: Anders Frisk (SWE) Attendance: 59,000

BAYERN: Oliver Kahn, Willy Sagnol, Samuel Osei Kuffour, Robert Kovac, Bixente Lizarazu, Hasan Salihamidzić (73 Alexander Zickler), Stefan Effenberg (67 Ciriaco Sforza), Owen Hargreaves, PAULO SÉRGIO do Nascimento, Giovane Elber (67 Carsten Jancker), Claudio Pizarro.
Trainer: Ottmar Hitzfeld

MANCHESTER UNITED: Fabien Barthez, Gary Neville, Wesley Brown, Laurent Blanc, Denis Irwin (46 Mikaël Silvestre), David Beckham, Roy Keane, Paul Scholes, Juan Sebastián Verón, Quinton Fortune, Ruud van Nistelrooy (85 Dwight Yorke). Manager: Alex Ferguson

Goals: van Nistelrooy (74), Paulo Sérgio (87)

BOAVISTA FC PORTO v FC NANTES 1-0 (1-0)

Estádio do Bessa, Porto 20.11.2001

Referee: Jan W. Wegereef (HOL) Attendance: 7,700

BOAVISTA: RICARDO Alexandre Pereira, RUI ÓSCAR Neves de Sousa (20 Joaquim Pereira da Silva "MARTELINHO"), PAULO Cesar TURRA, MÁRIO Jorge Amoro LOJA, ERIVAN Nascimento de Lima, José da Silva BOSINGWA (59 PEDRO J. Santos dos SANTOS), Nuno Miguel FRECHAUT Barreto, Erwin SÁNCHEZ Freking, Carlos Eduardo Ventura "DUDA", Elpidio Pereira da SILVA Filho, ALEXANDRE Luiz GOULART (63 Luis JORGE Pinto da SILVA).
Trainer: Jaime Moreira PACHECO

FC NANTES: Mickaël Landreau, Nicolas Laspalles, Nicolas Gillet, Pascal Delhommeau, Nestor Fabbri, Sylvain Armand, Frédéric da Rocha, Salomon Olembé-Olembé (78 Stéphane Ziani), Mathieu Berson, Pierre-Yves André (67 Marama Vahirua), Hassan Ahamada (67 Wilfried Dalmat).
Trainer: Raynald Denoueix

Goal: Sánchez (24)

MANCHESTER UNITED FC v BOAVISTA FC PORTO 3-0 (1-0)

Old Trafford, Manchester 5.12.2001

Referee: Antonio Jesus LÓPEZ NIETO (SPA) Att: 66,769

MANCHESTER UNITED: Fabien Barthez, Gary Neville (77 John O'Shea), Philip Neville, Laurent Blanc, Mikaël Silvestre, Nicky Butt, Roy Keane, Juan Sebastián Verón, Paul Scholes (85 Quinton Fortune), Ruud van Nistelrooy (88 Ole Gunnar Solskjaer), Dwight Yorke. Manager: Alex Ferguson

BOAVISTA: RICARDO Alexandre Pereira, Luis JORGE Pinto da SILVA (61 Joaquim Pereira da Silva "MARTELINHO"), ERIVAN Nascimento de Lima, PAULO Cesar TURRA, PEDRO EMANUEL dos Santos Silva, Armando Gonçalves Teixeira "PETIT", Nuno Miguel FRECHAUT Barreto, Erwin SÁNCHEZ Freking (69 PEDRO J. Santos dos SANTOS), Carlos Eduardo Ventura "DUDA", Elpidio Pereira da SILVA Filho (58 MARCIO Mandinga dos SANTOS), ALEXANDRE Luiz GOULART.
Trainer: Jaime Moreira PACHECO

Goals: van Nistelrooy (31, 62), Blanc (55)

FC NANTES v FC BAYERN MÜNCHEN 0-1 (0-0)

Stade de la Beaujoire, Nantes 5.12.2001

Referee: Pierluigi Collina (ITA) Attendance: 30,000

FC NANTES: Mickaël Landreau, Nicolas Laspalles, Nicolas Gillet, Nestor Fabbri, Sylvain Armand, Olivier Quint, Charles Devineau (59 Salomon Olembé-Olembé), Stéphane Ziani (77 Pierre-Yves André), Mathieu Berson, Frédéric da Rocha, Hassan Ahamada (63 Viorel Moldovan).
Trainer: Raynald Denoueix

BAYERN: Stefan Wessels, Willy Sagnol, Samuel Osei Kuffour, Robert Kovac, Bixente Lizarazu, Nico Kovac, Thorsten Fink, Owen Hargreaves (68 Ciriaco Sforza), PAULO SÉRGIO do Nascimento, Claudio Pizarro (71 Giovane Elber), Carsten Jancker (83 Alexander Zickler). Trainer: Ottmar Hitzfeld

Goal: Paulo Sérgio (65)

BOAVISTA FC PORTO v FC BAYERN MÜNCHEN 0-0

Estádio Do Bessa, Porto 20.02.2002

Referee: Ľuboš Michel (SVK) Attendance: 13,000

BOAVISTA: RICARDO Alexandre Pereira, Luis JORGE Pinto da SILVA, Fernando AVALOS, PAULO Cesar TURRA, PEDRO EMANUEL dos Santos Silva (Cap), Elisérgio da Silva "SERGINHO" (55 Carlos Eduardo Ventura "DUDA"), MARCIO Mandinga dos SANTOS (57 Elpidio Pereira da SILVA Filho), Joaquim Pereira da Silva "MARTELINHO", MÁRIO Jorge Amoro LOJA, Nuno Miguel FRECHAUT Barreto, Erwin SÁNCHEZ Freking (72 ALEXANDRE Luiz GOULART).
Trainer: Jaime MOREIRA PACHECO

BAYERN: Oliver Kahn, Willy Sagnol, Bixente Lizarazu, Samuel Osei Kuffour, Mehmet Scholl (82 Markus Feulner), Giovane Elber (72 Claudio Pizarro), Stefan Effenberg (Cap), Robert Kovac, Jens Jeremies, Thorsten Fink, Roque SANTA CRUZ (90 Carsten Jancker). Trainer: Ottmar Hitzfeld

FC NANTES v MANCHESTER UNITED FC 1-1 (1-0)

La Beaujoire, Nantes 20.02.2002

Referee: Kyros Vasaras (GRE) Attendance: 35,000

FC NANTES: Mickaël Landreau; Nestor Fabbri, Mario Yepes, Mathieu Berson, Nicolas Savinaud, Marama Vahirua (61 Frédéric da Rocha), Olivier Quint (79 Jean-Hugues BILAYI ATEBA), Sylvain Armand, Stéphane Ziani, Viorel Moldovan (76 Pierre-Yves André), Mauro Cetto.
Trainer: Ángel MARCOS

MANCHESTER UNITED: Fabien Barthez, Gary Neville (78 Diego Forlán), Juan Sebastián Veron (64 Ole Gunnar Solskjaer), Laurent Blanc, David Beckham, Ruud van Nistelrooy, Ryan Giggs, Philip Neville, Roy Keane (C), Paul Scholes, Mikaël Silvestre. Manager: Alex Ferguson

Sent off: Yepes (90+3)

Goals: Moldovan (9), van Nistelrooij (90+4)

FC BAYERN MÜNCHEN v BOAVISTA FC PORTO 1-0 (0-0)

Olympiastadion, München 26.02.2002

Referee: Terje Hauge (NOR) Attendance: 32,000

BAYERN: Oliver Kahn; Willy Sagnol, Samuel Osei Kuffour, Robert Kovac, Bixente Lizarazu, Owen Hargreaves, Stefan Effenberg (Cap), Jens Jeremies (61 Claudio Pizzaro), Mehmet Scholl (76 PAULO SÉRGIO do Nascimento), Roque SANTA CRUZ, Giovane Elber (83 Thorsten Fink).
Trainer: Ottmar Hitzfeld

BOAVISTA: RICARDO Alexandre Pereira; José da Silva BOSINGWA, ERIVAN Nascimento de Lima, PEDRO EMANUEL dos Santos Silva (Cap), MÁRIO Jorge Amoro LOJA, Fernando AVALOS, Luis JORGE Pinto da SILVA, Erwin SÁNCHEZ Freking (78 RUI Manuel Pinto de LIMA), Joaquim Pereira da Silva "MARTELINHO", Elpidio Pereira da SILVA Filho (45 ALEXANDRE Luiz GOULART), JORGE António Pinto do COUTO (66 Carlos Eduardo Ventura "DUDA").
Trainer: Jaime MOREIRA PACHECO

Goal: Santa Cruz (81)

MANCHESTER UNITED FC v FC NANTES 5-1 (3-1)

Old Trafford, Manchester 26.02.2002

Referee: Manuel Enrique MEJUTO GONZALEZ (SPA)
Attendance: 66,492

MANCHESTER UNITED: Fabien Barthez; Gary Neville, Denis Irwin, Laurent Blanc (69 Ronny Johnsen), Mikael Silvestre; David Beckham, Juan Sebastian Veron, Roy Keane (Cap) (75 Nicky Butt), Ryan Giggs; Ruud van Nistelrooy (69 Diego Forlán), Ole Gunnar Solskjaer.
Manager: Alex Ferguson

FC NANTES: Mickael Landreau (Cap), Yves Deroff, Mauro Cetto, Nestor Fabbri, Sylvain Armand, Jean-Hugues BILAYI ATEBA (62 Marama Vahirua), Mathieu Berson, Eric Djemba-Djemba (57 Nicolas Savinaud), Stephane Ziani (78 Olivier Quint), Pierre-Yves André, Frederic da Rocha.
Trainer: Ángel MARCOS

Goals: da Rocha (17), Beckham (18), Solskjaer (31, 78), Silvestre (38), van Nistelrooy (64)

MANCHESTER UNITED FC v FC BAYERN MÜNCHEN 0-0

Old Trafford, Manchester 13.03.2002

Referee: Gilles Veissiere (FRA) Attendance: 66,818

MANCHESTER UNITED: Fabien Barthez; Gary Neville, Laurent Blanc, Ronny Johnsen, Mikael Silvestre; David Beckham, Roy Keane (Cap), Juan Sebastian Veron, Ryan Giggs; Ruud van Nistelrooy, Ole Gunnar Solskjaer (78 Diego Forlán).
Manager: Alexander Ferguson

BAYERN: Oliver Kahn; Samuel Kuffour, Thomas Linke, Robert Kovac, Bixente Lizarazu; Owen Hargreaves, Stefan Effenberg (Cap), Jens Jeremies (73 Thorsten Fink), PAULO SÉRGIO do Nascimento (83 Giovane Elber); Roque Santa Cruz (77 Aleksander Zickler), Claudio Pizarro.
Trainer: Ottmar Hitzfeld

FC NANTES v BOAVISTA FC PORTO 1-1 (1-0)

La Beaujoire, Nantes 13.03.2002

Referee: Hugh Dallas (SCO) Attendance: 28,554

FC NANTES: Mickael Landreau (Cap); Mauro Cetto, Mario Yepes, Nicolas Gillet, Jean-Hugues BILAYI ATEBA; Frederic Da Rocha, Eric Djemba-Djemba, Nicolas Savinaud (53 Nicolas Laspalles), Olivier Quint (61 Charles Devineau); Viorel Moldovan (46 Marama Vahirua), Pierre-Yves André.
Trainer: Ángel MARCOS

BOAVISTA: RICARDO Alexandre Pereira; RUI ÓSCAR Neves de Sousa, PAULO Cesar TURRA (46 Joaquim Pereira da Silva "MARTELINHO"), PEDRO EMANUEL dos Santos Silva (Cap), ERIVAN Nascimento de Lima, Armando Gonçalves Teixeira "PETIT", Luis JORGE Pinto da SILVA, Carlos Eduardo Ventura "DUDA", PEDRO J. Santos dos SANTOS (46 Erwin SÁNCHEZ Freking), RUI Manuel Pinto de LIMA, ALEXANDRE Luiz GOULART (64 MARCIO Mandinga dos SANTOS). Trainer: Jaime Moreira Pacheco

Goals: Moldovan (43), Martelinho (78)

BOAVISTA FC PORTO v MANCHESTER UNITED FC 0-3 (0-2)

Estádio do Bessa, Porto 19.03.2002

Referee: Konrad Plautz (AUS) Attendance: 10,000

BOAVISTA: RICARDO Alexandre Pereira; Nuno Miguel FRECHAUT Barreto, PAULO Cesar TURRA, PEDRO EMANUEL dos Santos Silva (Cap), Erwin SÁNCHEZ Freking, MÁRIO Jorge Amoro LOJA, Armando Gonçalves Teixeira "PETIT", Luis JORGE Pinto da SILVA (33 Joaquim Pereira da Silva "MARTELINHO"), Carlos Eduardo Ventura "DUDA", Elisérgio da Silva "SERGINHO", Elpidio Pereira da SILVA Filho (20 ALEXANDRE Luiz GOULART, 59 MARCIO Mandinga dos SANTOS). Trainer: Jaime Moreira Pacheco

MANCHESTER UNITED: Fabien Barthez; Gary Neville, Ronny Johnsen (72 Phil Neville), Laurent Blanc (72 John O'Shea), Mikael Silvestre, David Beckham, Ryan Giggs (Cap), Nicky Butt, Paul Scholes (59 Michael Stewart), Ole Gunnar Solskjaer, Diego Forlán. Trainer: Alexander Ferguson

Goals: Blanc (14), Solskjaer (29), Beckham (50 pen)

FC BAYERN MÜNCHEN v FC NANTES 2-1 (0-0)

Olympiastadion, München 19.03.2002

Referee: Knud Erik Fisker (DEN) Attendance: 23,000

BAYERN: Oliver Kahn; Samuel Kuffour, Thomas Linke, Owen Hargreaves, Michael Tarnat; Thorsten Fink, Stefan Effenberg (Cap) (46 Hasan Salihamidzic), Jens Jeremies; Roque Santa Cruz (72 Alexander Zickler), Claudio Pizarro, PAULO SÉRGIO do Nascimento (85 Markus Feulner).
Trainer: Ottmar Hitzfeld

FC NANTES: Willy Grondin; Yves Deroff, Nicolas Gillet (Cap), Mauro Cetto, Jean-Hugues BILAYI ATEBA (63 Nicolas Laspalles); Goran Rubil, Loic Pailléres, Sylvain Armand, Charles Devineau (78 Mathieu Berson), Jeremy Toulalan, Hassan Ahamada (63 Chiva Star N'Zigou).
Trainer: Angel MARCOS

Goals: Ahamada (54), Jeremies (58), Pizarro (87)

	P	W	D	L	F	A	Pts
Manchester United FC	6	3	3	0	13	3	12
FC Bayern München	6	3	3	0	5	2	12
Boavista FC Porto	6	1	2	3	2	8	5
FC Nantes	6	0	2	4	4	11	2

SECOND STAGE – GROUP B

GALATASARAY SK ISTANBUL v AS ROMA 1-1 (1-0)

Ali Sami Yen, Istanbul 20.11.2001

Referee: Claude Colombo (FRA) Attendance: 15,750

GALATASARAY: Ali Faryd Camilo MONDRAGÓN, Carlos Alberto de Oliveira "CAPONE", Bülent Korkmaz, Emre Asik, Hakan Ünsal, Sébastien Perez, Bülent Akin (46 Andres José Fleurquin), Ayhan Akman, HASAN Gökhan ŞAŞ, Sergen Yalçin, Ümit Karan (88 Arif Erdem). Trainer: M. Lucescu

AS ROMA: Francesco Antonioli, Jonathan Zebina (81 Diego Fuser), ALDAIR Nascimento dos Santos, Walter Adriano Samuel, Marcos Evangelista de Moraes "CAFU", Damiano Tommasi (46 Antonio Cassano), Francisco Govinho LIMA (75 Marcos ASSUNÇAO Dos Santos), EMERSON Ferreira da Rosa, Vincent Candela, Gabriel Omar Batistuta, Francesco Totti.

Goals: Perez (22), Emerson (90)

LIVERPOOL FC v FC BARCELONA 1-3 (1-1)

Anfield, Liverpool 20.11.2001

Referee: Hellmut Krug (GER) Attendance: 41,521

LIVERPOOL: Jerzy Dudek, Jamie Carragher, Sami Tuomas Hyypiä, Stéphane Henchoz, John Arne Riise, Vladimir Smicer (80 Jari Litmanen), Gary McAllister (69 Patrik Berger), Steven George Gerrard, Danny Ben Murphy, Michael James Owen, Emile William Wanhoe Heskey (66 Robbie Fowler). Trainer: Philip Brian Thompson

FC BARCELONA: Roberto Óscar BONANO, Philippe Christanval, Frank de Boer, Patrik Andersson, Francesco Coco, Gabriel García de la Torre "GABRI" (58 Fabio ROCHEMBACK), Xavier Hernández Creus "XAVI", Philip Cocu, LUIS ENRIQUE Martínez Garcia (17 Marc Overmars), Patrick Kluivert (89 Michael Reiziger), Reinaldo Vítor Borba Ferreira "RIVALDO". Trainer: Carlos REXACH Cerda

Goals: Owen (27), Kluivert (41), Rochemback (65), Overmars (84)

FC BARCELONA v GALATASARAY SK ISTANBUL 2-2 (0-1)

Camp Nou, Barcelona 5.12.2001

Referee: Markus Merk (GER) Attendance: 50,000

FC BARCELONA: Roberto Óscar BONANO, Carles PUYOL Saforcada, Philippe Christanval, Patrik Andersson, Francesco Coco, Fabio Rochemback (46 GERARD López Segú), Xavier Hernández Creus "XAVI" (46 Marc Overmars), Philip Cocu (Cap), Javier Pedro SAVIOLA, Patrick Kluivert, Reinaldo Vítor Borba Ferreira "RIVALDO". Trainer: Carlos REXACH Cerda

GALATASARAY: Ali Faryd Camilo MONDRAGÓN, Carlos Alberto de Oliveira "CAPONE", Bülent Korkmaz (Cap), Emre Asik, Hakan Ünsal, Sébastien Perez, Ergün Penbe, Bülent Akin (85 Sergen Yalçin), Ayhan Akman (51 Suat Kaya), Andres José Fleurquin, Ümit Karan. Trainer: Mircea Lucescu

Sent off: Capone (62) and Hakan Ünsal (90)

Goals: Ümit Karan (5), Saviola (49, 66), Fleurquin (51)

AS ROMA v LIVERPOOL FC 0-0

Stadio Olimpico, Roma 5.12.2001

Referee: Dick Z.G. Jol (HOL) Attendance: 57,819

AS ROMA: Francesco Antonioli, Jonathan Zebina, ALDAIR Nascimento dos Santos, Walter Adriano Samuel, Gianni GUIGOU Martínez (46 Marcos ASSUNÇAO Dos Santos), Damiano Tommasi (78 Diego Fuser), Francisco Govinho LIMA, EMERSON Ferreira da Rosa, Vincent Candela, Gabriel Omar Batistuta, Francesco Totti. Trainer: Fabio Capello

LIVERPOOL: Jerzy Dudek, Jamie Carragher, Sami Tuomas Hyypiä, Stéphane Henchoz, John Arne Riise, Steven George Gerrard (84 Igor Bišcan), Danny Ben Murphy (61 Patrik Berger), Dietmar Hamann, Vladimir Smicer (63 Gary McAllister), Michael James Owen, Emile William Wanhoe Heskey. Trainer: Philip Brian Thompson

FC BARCELONA v AS ROMA 1-1 (0-0)

Camp Nou, Barcelona 20.02.2002

Referee: Gilles Veissiere (FRA) Attendance: 72,000

FC BARCELONA: José Manuel REINA Páez; Frank de Boer, SERGI Barjuán Esclusa (Cap) (74 Xavier Hernández Creus «XAVI»), Philippe Christanval, LUIS ENRIQUE Martínez Garcia, Carles PUYOL Saforcada, Thiago Motta (68 Fabio Rochemback), Philip Cocu, Javier Pedro SAVIOLA (57 Marc Overmars), Patrick Kluivert, Reinaldo Vítor Borba Ferreira "RIVALDO". Trainer: Carlos REXACH Cerda

AS ROMA: Francesco Antonioli; Marcos Evangelista de Moraes "CAFU", Francisco Govinho LIMA (74 Gianni GUIGOU Martínez), Christian Panucci, Jonathan Zébina, Damiano Tommasi, Walter Adriano Samuel, EMERSON Ferreira da Rosa, Vincent Candela, Gabriel Omar Batistuta, Francesco Totti (Cap) (81 Marco Delvecchio). Trainer: Fabio Capello

Goals: Panucci (57), Kluivert (82)

LIVERPOOL FC v GALATASARAY ISTANBUL 0-0

Anfield, Liverpool 20.02.2002

Referee: Vitor Manuel MELO PEREIRA (POR) Att: 36,000

LIVERPOOL: Chris Kirkland; Jamie Carragher (67 Vladimir Smicer), Sami Tuomas Hyypiä (Cap), Stéphane Henchoz, John Arne Riise, Steven George Gerrard (73 Gary McAllister), ABEL Luís da Silva Costa XAVIER, Danny Ben Murphy, Dietmar Hamann, Michael James Owen, Emile William Wanhoe Heskey. Trainer: Philip Brian Thompson

GALATASARAY: Ali Faryd Camilo MONDRAGÓN; Bülent Korkmaz (Cap), Emre Asik, Berkant Göktan, Ümit Karan, HASAN ŞAŞ (80 Murat Sözkesen, 90+4 Radu Niculescu), Bülent Akin, Gustavo Andrés VICTORIA, Sébastien Pérez, Andres José Fleurquin, Ergün Penbe. Trainer: Mircea Lucescu

AS ROMA v FC BARCELONA 3-0 (0-0)

Stadio Olimpico, Roma 26.02.2002

Referee: Kim Milton Nielsen (DEN) Attendance: 69,869

AS ROMA: Francesco Antonioli; Walter Adriano Samuel, Jonathan Zebina, Christian Panucci; Marcos Evangelista de Moraes "CAFU", Francisco Govinho LIMA, EMERSON Ferreira da Rosa, Vincent Candela; Francesco Totti (Cap) (86 Antonio CASSANO), Marco Delvecchio (46 Vincenzo Montella), Gabriel Omar Batistuta (71 Damiano Tommasi). Trainer: Fabio Capello

FC BARCELONA: José Manuel REINA Páez; Frank de Boer, Carles PUYOL Saforcada, Philipe Christanval, SERGI Barjuán Esclusa (Cap) (77 Xavier Hernández Creus «XAVI»), GERARD López Segú, Philip Cocu, Thiago Motta (64 Marc Overmars), LUIS ENRIQUE Martínez Garcia (81 Fabio Rochemback), Patrick Kluivert, Reinaldo Vítor Borba Ferreira "RIVALDO". Trainer: Carlos REXACH Cerda

Goals: Emerson (60), Montella (73), Tommasi (90+1)

GALATASARAY ISTANBUL v LIVERPOOL FC 1-1 (0-0)

Ali Sami Yen 26.02.2002

Referee: Urs Meier (SWI) Attendance: 22,000

GALATASARAY: Ali Faryd Camilo MONDRAGÓN, Bülent Korkmaz (Cap), Gustavo Andres VICTORIA, Andres José Fleurquin, Sébastien Perez, HASAN ŞAŞ, Ayhan Akman, Ergün Penbe, Berkant Göktan, Radu Niculescu (79 Serkan Aykut), Arif Erdem. Trainer: Mircea Lucescu

LIVERPOOL: Chris Kirkland, Stéphane Henchoz, ABEL Luís da Silva Costa XAVIER, Sami Tuomas Hyypiä (Cap), Jamie Carragher, Vladimir Smicer (73 Jari Litmanen), Danny Ben Murphy, Dietmar Hamann, John Arne Riise, Emile William Wanhoe Heskey, Michael James Owen. Trainer: Philip Brian Thompson

Goals: Niculescu (70), Heskey (78)

AS ROMA v GALATASARAY ISTAMBUL 1-1 (0-1)

Stadio Olimpico 13.03.2002

Referee: Anders Frisk (SWE) Attendance: 59,000

AS ROMA: Francesco Antonioli; Walter Adriano Samuel, Jonathan Zébina (46 ALDAIR Nascimento dos Santos), Christian Panucci; Marcos Evangelista de Moraes "CAFU", Vincent Candela, EMERSON Ferreira da Rosa, Francisco Govinho LIMA; Francesco Totti (Cap); Vincenzo Montella (56 Gabriel Omar Batistuta), Marco Delvecchio (81 Marcos ASSUNÇAO Dos Santos). Trainer: Fabio Capello

GALATASARAY: Ali Faryd Camilo MONDRAGÓN; Bülent Korkmaz (Cap), Emre Asik, Sebastien Pérez (82 Carlos Alberto de Oliveira "CAPONE"), Gustavo Andres VICTORIA; Andres José Fleurquin, Ayhan Akman; Ergün Penbe, Berkant Göktan; Ümit Karan (87 Radu Niculescu), HASAN Gökhan ŞAŞ. Trainer: Mircea Lucescu

Goals: Umit Karan (44), Cafu (52)

FC BARCELONA v LIVERPOOL FC 0-0

Camp Nou, Barcelona 13.03.2002

Referee: Kyros Vassaras (GRE) Attendance: 90,000

FC BARCELONA: Roberto Óscar BONANO; Carles PUYOL Saforcada, Frank de Boer, Philippe Christanval, Francesco Coco; Philip Cocu, LUIS ENRIQUE Martínez Garcia (Cap) (77 GERARD López Segú), Thiago Motta; Reinaldo Vítor Borba Ferreira "RIVALDO", Javier Pedro SAVIOLA (87 GEOVANNI Deiberson Mauricio), Patrick Kluivert. Trainer: Carlos REXACH Cerdá

LIVERPOOL: Jerzy Dudek; ABEL Luís da Silva Costa XAVIER, Stéphane Henchoz, Sami Hyypia (Cap), Jamie Carragher; Danny Murphy, Steven Gerrard (80 Nick Barmby), Dietmar Hamann, John Arne Riise; Jari Litmanen (70 Vladimir Smicer), Emile Heskey (75 Milan Baros). Trainer: Philip Brian Thompson

GALATASARAY ISTANBUL v FC BARCELONA 0-1 (0-0)

Ali Sami Yen, Istanbul 19.03.2002

Referee: Rene Temmink (HOL) Attendance: 21,870

GALATASARAY: Ali Faryd Camilo MONDRAGÓN; Bülent Korkmaz (Cap), Emre Asik, Arif Erdem (74 Suat Kaya), Berkant Göktan, Ümit Karan, Hasan Şaş, Sebastien Pérez (79 Carlos Alberto de Oliveira "CAPONE"), Ayhan Akman (62 Radu Niculescu), Andres José Fleurquin, Ergün Penbe. Trainer: Mircea Lucescu

FC BARCELONA: Roberto Óscar BONANO, ABELARDO Fernández Antuña, Xavier Hernández Creus "XAVI", Patrick Kluivert, Marc Overmars (84 Thiago Motta), Fabio ROCHEMBACK, Philippe Christanval, Gabriel García de la Torre "GABRI", LUIS ENRIQUE Martínez Garcia (89 Michael Reiziger), Francesco Coco, Carles PUYOL Saforcada. Trainer: Carlos REXACH Cerdá

Goal: Luis Enrique (58)

LIVERPOOL FC v AS ROMA 2-0 (1-0)

Anfield, Liverpool 19.03.2002

Referee: Rune Pedersen (NOR) Attendance: 41,794

LIVERPOOL: Jerzy Dudek; ABEL Luís da Silva Costa XAVIER, Sami Hyypia (Cap), Stéphane Henchoz, Jamie Carragher, Vladimir Šmicer (90 Gary McAllister), Danny Murphy, Steven Gerrard, John Arne Riise, Emile Heskey, Jari Litmanen (88 Igor Bišcan). Trainer: Philip Brian Thompson

AS ROMA: Franceso Antonioli; Walter Adriano Samuel, ALDAIR Nascimento dos Santos, Marcos ASSUNÇAO Dos Santos (69 Antonio Cassano), Vincent Candela, Christian Panucci, Damiano Tommasi, EMERSON Ferreira da Rosa, Francisco Govinho LIMA (46 Vincenzo Montella), Francesco Totti (Cap), Gabriel Omar Batistuta (46 Marco Delvecchio). Trainer: Fabio Capello

Goals: Litmanen (7 pen), Heskey (64)

	P	W	D	L	F	A	Pts
FC Barcelona	6	2	3	1	7	7	9
Liverpool FC	6	1	4	1	4	4	7
AS Roma	6	1	4	1	6	5	7
Galatasaray Istanbul	6	0	5	1	5	6	5

SECOND STAGE – GROUP C

PANATHINAIKOS FC ATHINA v FC PORTO 0-0

OAKA Spiros Louis, Athina 21.11.2001

Referee: Graham Poll (ENG) Attendance: 15,208

PANATHINAIKOS: Antonis Nikopolidis, Giorgos Seitaridis, René Henriksen, Sotiris Kyrgiakos, Panagiotis Fissas, Jan Michaelsen (70 Nikos Liberopoulos), PAULO Manuel SOUSA Carvalho (80 Joonas Einari Kolkka), Giorgos Karagounis, Aggelos Basinas, Emmanuel Olisadebe (82 Goran Vlaovic), Mihalis Konstantinou. Trainer: Giannis Kirastas

FC PORTO: PAULO Jorge SANTOS, Hugo Benjamin IBARRA, RICARDO Alberto CARVALHO, JORGE Almeida Gomes de ANDRADE, MARIO Magalhães da SILVA, Nuno Fernando Gonçalves da Rocha "CAPUCHO", Francisco José Rodrigues da Costa "COSTINHA" (90 RUBENS dos Santos JÚNIOR), Carlos Humberto PAREDES Monges, Anderson Luis de Sousa "DECO", Renivaldo Pereira des Jesus "PENA" (88 RICARDO Emidio Ramalho da SILVA), CLAYTON Ferreira CRUZ (78 Sven Fredrick Olof SÖDERSTRÖM). Trainer: Octavio Coelho Machado

AC SPARTA PRAHA v REAL MADRID CF 2-3 (1-2)

Letná, Praha 21.11.2001

Referee: Stefano Braschi (ITA) Attendance: 19,156

SPARTA: Petr Cech, Jan Flachbart, Jiri Novotny, Tomáš Hübschmann, Vladimir Labant, Libor Sionko, Jiri Jarošik, Martin Hasek (71 Radek Sloncik), Rastislav Michalík (52 Lukáš Zelenka), Marek Kincl, Lukáš Hartig (78 Petr Papousek). Trainer: Jaroslav Hrebík

REAL: Iker CASILLAS Fernández, Miguel Angel "MICHEL" SALGADO, Fernando Ruíz HIERRO, Francisco PAVÓN Barahona, ROBERTO CARLOS da Silva, Luis Filipe Madeira FIGO (89 José María Gutiérrez "GUTI"), Zinedine Zidane, Claude Makelele, Iván HELGUERA Bujía, RAÚL González Blanco, Fernando MORIENTES Sánchez (85 Steve McManaman). Trainer: Vicente Del BOSQUE Gonzalez

Goals: Zidane (20), Michalík (30), Morientes (36, 74), Sionko (72)

FC PORTO v AC SPARTA PRAHA 0-1 (0-0)

Estadio das Antas, Porto 4.12.2001

Referee: Nikolai Levnikov (RUS) Attendance: 25,000

FC PORTO: PAULO Jorge SANTOS, Hugo Benjamin IBARRA (76 CANDIDO Alveira Moreira da COSTA), RICARDO Alberto CARVALHO, JORGE Almeida Gomes de ANDRADE, MARIO Magalhães da SILVA, Sven Fredrick Olof SÖDERSTRÖM, Anderson Luis de Sousa "DECO", Carlos Humberto PAREDES Monges, CLAYTON Ferreira CRUZ (73 HÉLDER Manuel POSTIGA), Nuno Fernando Gonçalves da Rocha "CAPUCHO", Renivaldo Pereira des Jesus "PENA" (46 PAULO COSTA). Trainer: Octavio Coelho Machado

SPARTA: Petr Cech, Jan Flachbart, Jiri Novotny, Tomáš Hübschmann, Vladimir Labant, Libor Sionko (83 Petr Papousek), Jiri Jarošik, Martin Hasek (90 Lukáš Zelenka), Rastislav Michalík, Marek Kincl, Lukáš Hartig (88 Radim Holub). Trainer: Jaroslav Hrebík

Goal: Sionko (75)

REAL MADRID CF v PANATHINAIKOS FC ATHINA 3-0 (1-0)

Santiago Bernabéu, Madrid 4.12.2001

Referee: Gilles Veissière (FRA) Attendance: 52,320

REAL: Iker CASILLAS Fernández, Miguel Angel "MICHEL" SALGADO, Fernando Ruíz HIERRO (52 Aitor KARANKA De la Hoz), Francisco PAVÓN Barahona, ROBERTO CARLOS da Silva (77 Santiago Hernán SOLARI), Luis Filipe Madeira FIGO, Albert CELADES López, Iván HELGUERA Bujía, Zinedine Zidane, RAÚL González Blanco, Fernando MORIENTES Sánchez (85 Pedro MUNITIS Alvarez). Trainer: Vicente Del BOSQUE Gonzalez

PANATHINAIKOS: Antonis Nikopolidis, Giorgos Seitaridis, René Henriksen, Giannis Goumas, Sotiris Kyrgiakos, Panagiotis Fissas, Jan Michaelsen (46 Giorgos Karagounis), PAULO Manuel SOUSA Carvalho (46 Derek Boateng), Aggelos Basinas, Emmanuel Olisadebe, Mihalis Konstantinou (70 Goran Vlaovic). Trainer: Giannis Kirastas

Goals: Helguera (41), Raúl (66, 72)

REAL MADRID CF v FC PORTO 1-0 (1-0)

Estadio Santiago Bernabéu, Madrid 19.02.2002

Referee: Markus Merk (GER) Attendance: 70,000

REAL: Iker CASILLAS Fernández, Miguel Angel "MICHEL" SALGADO, Fernando Ruíz HIERRO (Cap), ROBERTO CARLOS da Silva, José María Gutiérrez "GUTI" (41 Pedro MUNITIS Alvarez), Aitor KARANKA De la Hoz, Claude MAKELELE, Luis Filipe Madeira FIGO (17 Steve McMANAMAN), Iván HELGUERA Bujía (77 Santiago Hernán SOLARI), Zinedine Zidane, Fernando MORIENTES Sánchez. Trainer: Vicente Del BOSQUE Gonzalez

FC PORTO: VÍTOR Manuel Martins BAÍA (Cap); JORGE Almeida Gomes de ANDRADE, Sven Fredrick Olof SÖDERSTRÖM, Francisco José Rodrigues da Costa "COSTINHA" (85 Dmitri Alenichev), Carlos Alberto Oliveira SECRETÁRIO, Anderson Luis de Sousa "DECO", Carlos Humberto PAREDES Monges, HÉLDER Manuel POSTIGA (66 Renivaldo Pereira des Jesus "PENA"), Nuno Fernando Gonçalves da Rocha "CAPUCHO", MARIO Magalhães da SILVA (84 CANDIDO Alveira Moreira da COSTA), RICARDO Emidio Ramalho da SILVA. Trainer: José MOURINHO

Goal: Solari (83)

AC SPARTA PRAHA v PANATHINAIKOS ATHINA 0-2 (0-1)

Letná, Praha 19.02.2002

Referee: Stuart Dougal (SCO) Attendance: 15,557

SPARTA: Petr Cech, Jan Flachbart, Jiri Novotny (Cap), Libor Sionko, Jiri Jarošik, Rastislav Michalík, Lukáš Hartig (46 Tomáš Cizek), Tomáš Hübschmann, Radek Mynar (53 Lukáš Zelenka), Zavadil, Marek Kincl. Trainer: Jaroslav Hrebík

PANATHINAIKOS: Antonis Nikopolidis, René Henriksen, Daniel Sarić, Giannis Goumas (Cap), Sotiris Kyrgiakos, Minas Pitsos, Nikos Liberopoulos, Fernando Edgar Galetto (66 Robert Jarni), Aggelos Basinas, Mihalis Konstantinou (86 Leonidas Vokolos), Giorgos Karagounis.
Trainer: Sergio Markarian

Sent off: Hübschmannn (86)

Goals: Karagounis (39), Konstantinou (71)

PANATHINAIKOS ATHINA v AC SPARTA PRAHA 2-1 (1-0)

OAKA, Athina 27.02.2002

Referee: Knud Erik Fisker (DEN) Attendance: 17,000

PANATHINAIKOS: Antonis Nikopolidis, René Henriksen, Daniel Sarić, Giannis Goumas (C), Sotiris Kyrgiakos, Minas Pitsos (77 Robert Jarni), Nikos Liberopoulos, Jan Michaelsen (62 Fernando Edgar Galetto), Aggelos Basinas, Mihalis Konstantinou (82 Joonas Einari Kolkka), Giorgos Karagounis. Trainer: Sergio Markarian

SPARTA: Petr Cech, Jan Flachbart, Jiri Novotny (C), Libor Sionko, Jiri Jarošik, Lukáš Zelenka, Rastislav Michalík, Tomáš Cizek, Radek Mynar, Zavadil (38 Martin Klein), Marek Kincl.
Trainer: Jaroslav Hrebík

Goals: Konstantinou (15, 47), Klein (90)

FC PORTO v REAL MADRID CF 1-2 (1-2)

Estádio das Antas, Porto 27.02.2002

Referee: Pierluigi Collina (ITA) Attendance: 37,000

FC PORTO: VÍTOR Manuel Martins BAÍA (Cap); JORGE Almeida Gomes de ANDRADE, Carlos Alberto Oliveira SECRETÁRIO, Miran Pavlin, Anderson Luis de Sousa "DECO", Carlos Humberto PAREDES Monges, HÉLDER Manuel POSTIGA (67 Renivaldo Pereira des Jesus "PENA"), Nuno Fernando Gonçalves da Rocha "CAPUCHO", MARIO Magalhães da SILVA, CANDIDO Alveira Moreira da COSTA (56 CLAYTON Ferreira CRUZ), RICARDO Emidio Ramalho da SILVA (68 Dmitri Alenichev).
Trainer: José Maria dos Santos MOURINHO

REAL: CÉSAR Sánchez Domínguez; Fernando Ruíz HIERRO (Cap), José María Gutiérrez "GUTI", Aitor KARANKA De la Hoz (46 Albert CELADES López), FLÁVIO de CONCEIÇÃO, Steve McManaman (63 Pedro MUNITIS Alvarez), Iván HELGUERA Bujía, Oscar MIÑAMBRES Pascual, Raúl BRAVO Sanfélix (75 Miguel Angel "MICHEL" SALGADO), Francisco PAVÓN Barahona, Santiago Hernán SOLARI.
Trainer: Vicente Del BOSQUE Gonzalez

Goals: Solari (7), Helguera (20), Capucho (28)

FC PORTO v PANATHINAIKOS ATHINA 2-1 (1-0)

Das Antas, Porto 12.03.2002

Referee: L'uboš Michel (SVK) Attendance: 12,835

FC PORTO: PAULO Jorge SANTOS; Carlos Alberto Oliveira SECRETÁRIO (Cap), RICARDO Emidio Ramalho da SILVA, JORGE Almeida Gomes de ANDRADE, Sven Fredrick Olof SÖDERSTRÖM, Carlos Humberto PAREDES Monges, Francisco José Rodrigues da Costa "COSTINHA", Anderson Luis de Sousa "DECO" (89 HÉLDER Manuel POSTIGA), Nuno Fernando Gonçalves da Rocha "CAPUCHO", Renivaldo Pereira des Jesus "PENA" (83 Miran Pavlin), CLAYTON Ferreira CRUZ (67 CANDIDO Alveira Moreira da COSTA).
Trainer: José Mário dos Santos Mourinho

PANATHINAIKOS: Antonis Nikopolidis; Rene Henriksen, Leonidas Vokolos (70 Goran Vlaović), Sotiris Kyrgiakos, Panagiotis Fissas, Daniel Sarić, Aggelos Basinas, Giorgos Karagounis, Robert Jarni (35 Joonas Einari Kolkka), Mihalis Konstantinou (30 Emmanuel Olisadebe), Nikos Liberopoulos (Cap). Trainer: Sergio Markarian

Sent off: Secretario (79)

Goals: Deco Sousa (12), Pena (54), Kolkka (65)

REAL MADRID CF v AC SPARTA PRAHA 3-0 (0-0)

Santiago Bernabéu, Madrid 12.03.2002

Referee: Graham Poll (ENG) Attendance: 40,000

REAL: Iker CASILLAS Fernández; GEREMI Sorele Fotso Ndjitap, Iván HELGUERA Bujía (77 Fernando MORIENTES Sánchez), Francisco PAVÓN Barahona, Raúl BRAVO Sanfélix; FLAVIO de CONCEIÇÃO, Albert CELADES López, Steve McManaman (53 SÁVIO Bortolini Pimentel), Santiago Hernán SOLARI (63 Oscar MIÑAMBRES Pascual); José María Gutiérrez "GUTI" (Cap), Pedro MUNITIS Alvarez.

SPARTA: Petr Cech; Tomáš Cizek, Tomas Hübschmann, Jiri Novotny (Cap), Jan Flachbart; Libor Sionko, Jiri Jarošik, Martin Klein, Rastislav Michalík; Marek Kincl, Patrice Abanda (66 Peter Babnic). Trainer: Jaroslav Hrebík

Goals: Solari (60), Guti (64), Savio (71)

PANATHINAIKOS ATHINA v REAL MADRID CF 2-2 (1-1)

Apostolos Nikolaidis, Athina 20.03.2002

Referee: Domenico Messina (ITA)

PANATHINAIKOS: Antonis Nikopolidis; Rene Henriksen, Giorgos Seitaridis, Goran Vlaović (86 Krzysztof Warzycha), Fernando Edgar Galetto, Giannis Goumas (Cap), Jan Michaelsen, Panagiotis Fissas, Giorgos Karagounis, Mihalis Konstantinou (71 Emmanuel Olisadebe), Nikos Liberopoulos (77 Leonidas Vokolos). Trainer: Sergio Markarian

REAL: Iker CASILLAS Fernández; GEREMI Sorele Fotso Ndjitap, Fernando MORIENTES Sánchez (Cap) (60 Javier García PORTILLO), FLAVIO de CONCEIÇÃO, Steve McManaman (80 Santiago Hernán SOLARI), SÁVIO Bortolini Pimentel (74 Lopéz Rocha Valmiro "VALDO"), Raúl BRAVO Sanfélix, Albert CELADES López, Oscar MIÑAMBRES Pascual, IVÁN CAMPO Ramos, RUBÉN González Rocha. Trainer: Vicente Del BOSQUE Gonzalez

Goals: Liberopoulos (9), Morientes (11), Goumas (64), Garcia Portillo (80)

AC SPARTA PRAHA v FC PORTO 2-0 (0-0)

Letná, Praha 20.03.2002

Referee: Wolfgang Stark (GER) Attendance: 14,621

SPARTA: Petr Cech; Tomáš Cizek, Tomas Hübschmann, Jiri Novotny (Cap), Jan Flachbart; Libor Sionko (90 Martin Klein), Jiri Jarošik, Zdenek Grygera, Lukáš Hartig (78 Peter Babnic); Marek Kincl (46 Pavel Zavadil), Pavel Mareš. Trainer: Jaroslav Hrebík

FC PORTO: PAULO Jorge SANTOS; RICARDO Emidio Ramalho da SILVA, JORGE Almeida Gomes de ANDRADE, Carlos Humberto PAREDES Monges, Francisco José Rodrigues da Costa "COSTINHA" (65 RAFAEL Gustavo DIAS), Anderson Luis de Sousa "DECO" (73 Sven Fredrick Olof SÖDERSTRÖM), Hugo Benjamin IBARRA, HÉLDER Manuel POSTIGA (46 Renivaldo Pereira des Jesus "PENA"), Nuno Fernando Gonçalves da Rocha "CAPUCHO" (Cap), CLAYTON Ferreira CRUZ, MARIO Magalhães da SILVA.

Goal: Sionko (63), Jarošik (71)

	P	W	D	L	F	A	Pts
Real Madrid CF	6	5	1	0	14	5	16
Panathinaikos Athina	6	2	2	2	7	8	8
AC Sparta Praha	6	2	0	4	6	10	6
FC Porto	6	1	1	4	3	7	4

SECOND STAGE – GROUP D

RC DEPORTIVO LA CORUÑA v ARSENAL FC LONDON 2-0 (2-0)

Estadio Municipal de Riazor, La Coruña 21.11.2001

Referee: Terje Hauge (NOR) Attendance: 25,864

DEPORTIVO: José Francisco MOLINA Gimenez, Lionel Sebastián SCALONI, Nourredine Naybet, DONATO Gama da Silva, Enrique Fernández ROMERO, Juan Carlos VALERÓN Santana (73 Djalma Feitosa Dias "DJALMINHA"), MAURO da SILVA Gomes, EMERSON Moisés Costa, VÍCTOR Sánchez del Amo, Roy MAKAAY (49 Walter Gerardo PANDIANI), DIEGO TRISTÁN Herrera (29 José Emilio AMAVISCA). Trainer: Javier IRURETAgoyena Amiano

ARSENAL: Richard Wright (46 Stuart Taylor), LAUREN Bisan Etame-Mayer, Sol Campbell, Matthew Upson, Ashley Cole, Fredrik Ljungberg, Patrick Vieira, Giovanni van Bronckhorst (78 Eduardo Cesar Gaspar "EDU"), Robert Pires, Sylvain Wiltord (73 Nwankwo Kanu), Thierry Henry. Trainer: Arsène Wenger

Goals: Makaay (9), Diego Tristán (25)

JUVENTUS FC TORINO v BAYER 04 LEVERKUSEN 4-0 (3-0)

Delle Alpi, Torino 29.11.2001

Referee: Urs Meier (SWI) Attendance: 4,526

JUVENTUS: Gianluigi Buffon, Alessandro Birindelli, Lilian Thuram, Mark Iuliano, Gianluca Pessotto, Gianluca Zambrotta, Alessio Tacchinardi, Igor Tudor, Pavel Nedved (84 Edgar Davids), Alessandro del Piero (Cap), David Trezeguet (77 Nicola Amoruso). Trainer: Marcello Lippi

BAYER: Hans-Jörg Butt, Zoltan Sebescen, Jens Nowotny (Cap), Lucimar Ferreira da Silva "LUCIO", Diego Rodolfo Placente (66 Boris Zivković), Michael Ballack, Carsten Ramelow, Yildiray Bastürk (52 Bernd Schneider), José "ZÉ ROBERTO" Da Silva Júnior, Ulf Kirsten (75 Jurica Vranjes), Oliver Neuville. Trainer: Klaus Toppmöller

Goals: Trezeguet (8, 60), del Piero (37), Tudor (44)

ARSENAL FC LONDON
v JUVENTUS FC TORINO 3-1 (2-0)

Highbury, London 4.12.2001

Referee: Vitor Manuel MELO PEREIRA (POR) Att: 35,421

ARSENAL: Stuart Taylor, LAUREN Bisan Etame-Mayer, Sol Campbell, Matthew Upson, Ashley Cole (90 Martin Keown), Fredrik Ljungberg, Patrick Vieira, Ray Parlour, Robert Pires, Nwankwo Kanu (69 Dennis Bergkamp), Thierry Henry (84 Gilles Grimandi). Trainer: Arsène Wenger

JUVENTUS: Gianluigi Buffon, Alessandro Birindelli, Paolo Montero, Lilian Thuram, Gianluca Pessotto (78 Michele Paramatti), Gianluca Zambrotta, Alessio Tacchinardi, Igor Tudor (21 Edgar Davids), Pavel Nedved (71 Nicola Amoruso), Alessandro del Piero, David Trezeguet.
Trainer: Marcello Lippi

Goals: Ljungberg (21, 88), Henry (28), Taylor (49 og)

BAYER 04 LEVERKUSEN
v RC DEPORTIVO LA CORUÑA 3-0 (0-0)

BayArena, Leverkusen 4.12.2001

Referee: Kyros Vassaras (GRE) Attendance: 22,500

BAYER: Hans-Jörg Butt, Boris Zivković, Jens Nowotny, Lucimar Ferreira da Silva «LUCIO», Diego Rodolfo Placente, Bernd Schneider, Michael Ballack (87 Jurica VRANJES), Carsten Ramelow, José «ZÉ ROBERTO» Da Silva Júnior, Ulf Kirsten (76 Yildiray Bastürk), Oliver Neuville (86 Dimitar Berbatov). Trainer: Klaus Toppmöller

DEPORTIVO: José Francisco MOLINA Gimenez, HÉCTOR Berenguel Del Pino, Nourredine NAYBET, DONATO Gama da Silva, Enrique Fernández ROMERO, Lionel Sebastián SCALONI (71 Djalma Feitosa Dias "DJALMINHA"), MAURO da SILVA Gomes, Juan Carlos VALERÓN Santana (76 DIEGO TRISTÁN Herrera), EMERSON Moisés Costa, Francisco Javier González Pérez «FRAN» (59 José Emilio AMAVISCA), Roy MAKAAY. Trainer: Javier IRURETAgoyena Amiano

Goals: Zé Roberto (64), Neuville (67), Ballack (79)

BAYER 04 LEVERKUSEN
v ARSENAL FC LONDON 1-1 (0-0)

BayArena, Leverkusen 19.02.2002

Referee: Alain Sars (FRA) Attendance: 22,500

BAYER: Hans-Jörg Butt, Boris Zivković, Jens Nowotny (Cap) (61 Jurica Vranjes), Lucimar Ferreira da Silva «LUCIO», Diego Rodolfo Placente (75 Dimitar Berbatov), Bernd Schneider, Michael Ballack, José «ZÉ ROBERTO» Da Silva Júnior, Ulf Kirsten, Yildiray Bastürk, Oliver Neuville.
Trainer: Klaus Toppmöller

ARSENAL: David Seaman; LAUREN Bisan Etame-Mayer, Sol Campbell, Patrick Vieira (Cap), Ray Parlour, Robert Pires, Nwankwo Kanu (76 Eduardo Cesar Gaspar "EDU"), Sylvain Wiltord (71 Gilles Grimandi), Thierry Henry, Giovanni van Bronckhorst, Igors Stepanovs. Trainer: Arsène Wenger

Sent off: Parlour (68)

Goals: Pires (56), Kirsten (90)

JUVENTUS FC TORINO
v RC DEPORTIVO LA CORUÑA 0-0

Delle Alpi, Torino 19.02.2002

Referee: Hugh Dallas (SCO) Attendance: 25,000

JUVENTUS: Gianluigi Buffon, Ciro Ferrara, Lilian Thuram, Antonio Conte (79 Marcelo Zalayeta), Mark Iuliano, Gianluca Pessotto (79 Cristian Zenoni), Gianluca Zambrotta, Alessio Tacchinardi (61 Enzo Maresca), Edgar Davids, Alessandro del Piero (Cap), David Trezeguet. Trainer: Marcello Lippi

DEPORTIVO: José Francisco MOLINA Gimenez, Lionel Sebastián Scaloni, Nourredine Naybet, CÉSAR Martín Villar, Enrique Fernández Romero, Juan Carlos VALERÓN Santana (68 Aldo Pedro Duscher), Mauro da SILVA Gomes (Cap), SERGIO González Soriano, HÉCTOR Berenguel Del Pino, DIEGO TRISTÁN Herrera (81 Walter Gerardo Pandiani), José Emilio Amavisca (90 Joan CAPDEVILA Méndez).
Trainer: Javier IRURETAgoyena Amiano

ARSENAL FC LONDON
v BAYER 04 LEVERKUSEN 4-1 (2-0)

Arsenal Stadium Highbury, London 27.02.2002

Referee: Alain Hamer (LUX) Attendance: 35,000

ARSENAL: David Seaman; Lee Dixon, LAUREN Bisan Etame-Mayer (84 Junichi Inamoto), Sol Campbell, Patrick Vieira (Cap), Robert Pires, Sylvain Wiltord (90 Jermaine Pennant), Gilles Grimandi (67 Eduardo Cesar Gaspar "EDU"), Thierry Henry, Dennis Bergkamp, Igors Stepanovs.
Trainer: Arsène Wenger

BAYER: Hans-Jörg Butt, Boris Zivković (74 Zoltan Sebescen), Jens Nowotny (C), Lucimar Ferreira da Silva «LUCIO», Diego Rodolfo Placente, Bernd Schneider (46 Yildiray Bastürk), Michael Ballack, José «ZÉ ROBERTO» Da Silva Júnior, Carsten Ramelow, Ulf Kirsten (46 Dimitar Berbatov), Oliver Neuville.
Trainer: Klaus Toppmöller

Goals: Pires (5), Henry (7), Vieira (48), Bergkamp (83), Sebescen (86)

RC DEPORTIVO LA CORUÑA
v JUVENTUS FC TORINO 2-0 (1-0)

Riazor, La Coruña 27.02.2002

Referee: Andres Frisk (SWE) Attendance: 33,000

DEPORTIVO: José Francisco MOLINA Gimenez, Lionel Sebastián Scaloni, Nourredine Naybet, CÉSAR Martín Villar (86 Joan CAPDEVILA Méndez), Enrique Fernández Romero, Juan Carlos VALERÓN Santana (70 Djalma Feitosa Dias "DJALMINHA"), VÍCTOR SÁNCHEZ (61 Aldo Pedro Duscher), MAURO da SILVA Gomes, SERGIO González Soriano, Francisco Javier González Pérez "FRAN" (Cap), DIEGO TRISTÁN Herrera. Trainer: Javier IRURETA

JUVENTUS: Gianluigi Buffon, Ciro Ferrara, Paolo Montero (46 Edgar Davids), Mark Iuliano, Gianluca Pessotto, Alessio Tacchinardi (68 Marcelo Zalayeta), Enzo Maresca (46 Antonio Conte), Alessandro Birindelli, Pavel Nedved, Alessandro del Piero (Cap), David Trezeguet. Trainer: Marcello Lippi

Sent off: Davids (74)

Goals: Diego Tristán (8), Djalminha (77)

BAYER 04 LEVERKUSEN
v JUVENTUS FC TORINO 3-1 (1-0)

BayArena, Leverkusen 12.03.2002

Referee: Kim Milton Nielsen (DEN) Attendance: 22,500

BAYER: Hans-Jörg Butt; Zoltan Sebescen, Lucimar Ferreira da Silva "LUCIO", Jens Nowotny (Cap) (12 Jurica Vranjes), Diego Placente; Bernd Schneider, Carsten Ramelow, Yildiray Bastürk (90 Thomas Kleine), José "ZÉ ROBERTO" Da Silva Júnior; Dimitar Berbatov (81 Marko Babić), Thomas Brdarić.

JUVENTUS: Gianluigi Buffon; Gianluca Pessoto (46 Igor Tudor), Ciro Ferrara, Alessandro Birindelli, Cristian Zenoni; Antonio Conte (Cap) (46 Enzo Maresca), Pavel Nedved, Gianluca Zambrotta, Alessio Tacchinardi; David Trezeguet, Nicola Amoruso (61 Marcelo Zalayeta). Trainer: M. Lippi

Goals: Butt (24 pen), Tudor (61), Brdarić (71), Babić (88)

ARSENAL FC LONDON
v RC DEPORTIVO LA CORUÑA 0-2 (0-2)

Highbury, London 12.03.2002

Referee: Urs Meier (SWI) Attendance: 35,392

ARSENAL: David Seaman; Oleg Luzhny, Igors Stepanovs, Sol Campbell, LAUREN Bisan Etame-Mayer; Robert Pires, Dennis Bergkamp, Patrick Vieira (Cap), Gilles Grimandi (64 Fredrik Ljungberg); Thierry Henry, Sylvain Wiltord (64 Nwankwo Kanu). Trainer: Arséne Wenger

DEPORTIVO: José Francisco MOLINA Gimenez; Lionel Sebastián SCALONI, CÉSAR Martín Villar, Nourredine Naybet, Enrique Fernández ROMERO; SERGIO González Soriano, MAURO da SILVA Gomes, Víctor Sánchez, Francisco Javier González Pérez "FRAN" (Cap) (72 Joan CAPDEVILA Méndez), Juan Carlos VALERÓN Santana (80 Aldo Pedro DUSCHER); DIEGO TRISTÁN Herrera (85 Roy Makaay). Trainer: Javier IRURETAgoyena Amiano

Goals: Valerón (30), Naybet (40)

RC DEPORTIVO LA CORUNA
v BAYER 04 LEVERKUSEN 1-3 (0-1)

Riazor, La Coruña 20.03.2002

Referee: Iordan Ivanov (BUL) Attendance: 23 000

DEPORTIVO: NUNO Herlandes Simões; HÉCTOR Berenguel Del Pino (67 DIEGO TRISTÁN Herrera), CÉSAR Martín Villar, Nourredine Naybet, Joan CAPDEVILA Méndez; Aldo Pedro DUSCHER (60 Juan Carlos VALERÓN Santana), MAURO da SILVA Gomes (Cap); Djalma Feitosa Dias "DJALMINHA", Jose Emilio Amasvica; Roy Makaay, Walter Gerardo PANDIANI (60 SERGIO González Soriano). Trainer: Javier IRURETAgoyena Amiano

BAYER: Hans-Jörg Butt; Zoltan Sebescen, Lucimar Ferreira da Silva "LUCIO", Jens Nowotny (Cap), Diego Placente; Bernd Schneider (90 Boris Zivković), Yildiray Bastürk (88 Jurica Vranjes), Michael Ballack; Thomas Brdarić (64 Oliver Neuville), Carsten Ramelow, José "ZÉ ROBERTO" Da Silva Júnior. Trainer: Klaus Toppmöller

Goals: Ballack (34), Schneider (54), Diego Tristan (75), Neuville (86)

JUVENTUS FC TORINO
v ARSENAL FC LONDON 1-0 (0-0)

Delle Alpi, Torino 20.03.2002

Referee: Karl-Erik Nilsson (SWI) Attendance: 6 500

JUVENTUS: Fabian Carini; Cristian Zenoni, Alessandro Birindelli, Mark Iuliano, Michele Paramatti (24 Gianluca Pessotto); Gianluca Zambrotta (70 Nicola Amoruso), Antonio Conte (Cap), Edgar Davids; Enzo Maresca; Tomas Guzmán (61 Vincent Pericard), Marcelo Zalayeta.
Trainer: Marcello Lippi

ARSENAL: David Seaman; Lee Dixon, Oleg Luzhny, Sol Campbell, LAUREN Bisan Etame-Mayer (82 Ashley Cole); Fredrik Ljungberg, Patrick Vieira (Cap), Eduardo Cesar Gaspar "EDU" (79 Sylvain Wiltord), Robert Pires; Thierry Henry, Nwankwo Kanu. Trainer: Arséne Wenger

Goal: Zalayeta (76)

	P	W	D	L	F	A	Pts
Bayer 04 Leverkusen	6	3	1	2	11	11	10
Deportivo La Coruña	6	3	1	2	7	6	10
Arsenal FC London	6	2	1	3	8	8	7
Juventus FC Torino	6	2	1	3	7	8	7

QUARTER-FINALS

FC BAYERN MÜNCHEN
v REAL MADRID CF 2-1 (0-1)

Olympiastadion, München 2.04.2002

Referee: Hugh Dallas (SCO) Attendance: 60,000

BAYERN: Oliver Kahn; Samuel Kuffour, Bixente Lizarazu, Willy Sagnol (62 Hasan Salihamidzic); Owen Hargreaves, Jens Jeremies (83 Nico Kovac), Robert Kovac, Stefan Effenberg (Cap); Roque Santa Cruz, PAULO SÉRGIO do Nascimento (52 Claudio Pizarro), Giovane Elber. Trainer: Ottmar Hitzfeld

REAL: CÉSAR Sánchez Domínguez; Miguel Angel "MICHEL" SALGADO, Fernando Ruíz HIERRO (Cap), Francisco PAVÓN Barahona, ROBERTO CARLOS da Silva; Iván HELGUERA Bujía, Claude Makelele, GEREMI Sorele Fotso Ndjitap (83 FLÁVIO de CONCEIÇÃO), Zinedine Zidane, RAÚL González Blanco; Santiago Hernán SOLARI (75 Steve McManaman). Trainer: Vicente DEL BOSQUE González

Goals: Geremi (11), Effenberg (81), Pizarro (87)

REAL MADRID CF
v FC BAYERN MÜNCHEN 2-0 (0-0)

Santiago Bernabéu 10.04.2002

Referee: Stefano Braschi (ITA) Attendance: 75,328

REAL: CÉSAR Sánchez Domínguez; Miguel Angel "MICHEL" SALGADO, Fernando Ruíz HIERRO (Cap), Iván HELGUERA Bujía, ROBERTO CARLOS da Silva; Luis Filipe Madeira FIGO (86 GEREMI Sorele Fotso Ndjitap), Claude Makelele, Zinedine Zidane, Santiago Hernán SOLARI; RAÚL González Blanco, Fernando MORIENTES Sánchez (77 José María Gutiérrez "GUTI"). Trainer: Vicente DEL BOSQUE González

BAYERN: Oliver Kahn; Samuel Kuffour (72 Claudio Pizarro), Thomas Linke, Robert Kovac, Bixente Lizarazu; Owen Hargreaves, Stefan Effenberg (Cap), Jens Jeremies (80 Thorsten Fink); Hasan Salihamidzić, Giovane Elber, Roque Santa Cruz. Trainer: Ottmar Hitzfeld

Sent off: Salihamidzić (90)

Goals: Helguera (67), Guti (81)

RC DEPORTIVO LA CORUÑA
v MANCHESTER UNITED FC 0-2 (0-2)

Riazor, La Coruña 2.04.2002

Referee: Kyros Vassaras (GRE) Attendance: 31,000

DEPORTIVO: José Francisco MOLINA Gimenez; Lionel Sebastián SCALONI, Nourredine Naybet, CÉSAR Martín Villar, Enrique Fernández ROMERO; MAURO da SILVA Gomes, SERGIO González Soriano; Víctor Sánchez (82 Aldo Pedro DUSCHER), Juan Carlos VALERÓN Santana (68 Djalma Feitosa Dias "DJALMINHA"), Francisco Javier González Pérez "FRAN" (60 Roy Makaay), DIEGO TRISTÁN Herrera.
Trainer: Javier IRURETAgoyena Amiano

MANCHESTER UNITED: Fabien Barthez; Gary Neville, Ronny Johnsen, Laurent Blanc, Mikael Silvestre; David Beckham (Phil Neville 90), Nicky Butt, Roy Keane (Cap) (45 Quinton Fortune), Paul Scholes; Ryan Giggs; Ruud van Nistelrooy (72 Ole Gunnar Solskjaer).
Trainer: Alexander Chapman Ferguson

Goals: Beckham (15), van Nistelrooy (41)

MANCHESTER UNITED FC
v RC DEPORTIVO LA CORUNA 3-2 (1-1)

Old Trafford, Manchester 10.04.2002

Referee: Markus Merk (GER) Attendance: 65,875

MANCHESTER UNITED: Fabien Barthez; Gary Neville, Ronny Johnsen (36 Wes Brown), Laurent Blanc, Mikael Silvestre; David Beckham (22 Ole Gunnar Solskjaer), Nicky Butt, Juan Sebastian Veron (73 Phil Neville), Ryan Giggs (Cap), Quinton Fortune; Ruud van Nistelrooy.
Trainer: Alexander Chapman Ferguson

DEPORTIVO: José Francisco MOLINA Gimenez; Enrique Fernández ROMERO, Noureddine Naybet, HÉCTOR Berenguel Del Pino, Lionel Sebastián SCALONI; Djalma Feitosa Dias "DJALMINHA", Francisco Javier González Pérez "FRAN" (63 Joan CAPDEVILA Méndez), Juan Carlos VALERÓN Santana, Víctor Sánchez (51 Roy Makaay), Aldo Pedro DUSCHER; DIEGO TRISTÁN Herrera (71 Walter Gerardo PANDIANI).
Trainer: Javier IRURETAgoyena Amiano

Sent off: Scaloni (60), Duscher (75)

Goals: Solskjaer (23, 56), Blanc (45 og), Giggs (68), Djalminha (90)

PANATHINAIKOS ATHINA
v FC BARCELONA 1-0 (0-0)

Apostolos Nikolaidis, Athina 3.04.2002

Referee: Terje Hauge (NOR) Attendance: 15,800

PANATHINAIKOS: Antonis Nikopolidis, Rene Henriksen, Giannis Goumas (Cap), Daniel Sarić, Sotiris Kyrgiakos, Joonas Einari Kolkka, Aggelos Basinas, Goran Vlaovic (74 Emmanuel Olisadebe), Mihalis Konstantinou (90 Leonidas Vokolos), Nikos Liberopoulos (59 Derek Boateng), Panagiotis Fissas.
Trainer: Sergio Markarian

FC BARCELONA: Roberto Oscar BONANO; Francesco Coco (68 Michael Reiziger), Frank De Boer, ABELARDO Fernández Antuña, Carles PUYOL Saforcada; Fabio ROCHEMBACK (72 Reinaldo Vítor Borba Ferreira "RIVALDO"), Gabriel García de la Torre "GABRI", Thiago Motta, Philip Cocu (53 Xavier Hernández Creus "XAVI"), Patrick Kluivert, Marc Overmars.
Trainer: Carlos REXACH Cerdá

Goal: Basinas (79 pen)

FC BARCELONA
v PANATHINAIKOS ATHINA 3-1 (1-1)

Camp Nou, Barcelona 9.04.2002

Referee: Urs Maier (SWI) Attendance: 90,000

FC BARCELONA: Roberto Óscar BONANO (84 Jose Manuel REINA); Carles PUYOL Saforcada, Frank de Boer, ABELARDO Fernández Antuña (Cap), Francesco Coco (45 Patrick Kluivert), Xavier Hernández Creus "XAVI", LUIS ENRIQUE Martínez Garcia, Philip Cocu, Reinaldo Vítor Borba Ferreira "RIVALDO", Marc Overmars (76 Gabriel García de la Torre "GABRI"), Javier Pedro SAVIOLA.
Trainer: Carlos REXACH Cerdá

PANATHINAIKOS: Antonis Nikopolidis; Daniel Sarić, Sotiris Kyrgiakos, Rene Henriksen, Giannis Goumas (Cap), Panagiotis Fissas, Giorgos Karagounis (44 Jan Michaelsen), Aggelos Basinas, Joonas Einari Kolkka (76 Goran Vlaovic), Nikos Liberopoulos (46 Emmanuel Olisadebe), Mihalis Konstantinou. Trainer: Sergio Markarian

Goals: Konstantinou (8), Luis Enrique (23, 49), Saviola (61)

LIVERPOOL FC v BAYER 04 LEVERKUSEN 1-0 (1-0)

Anfield, Liverpool 3.04.2002

Referee: Anders Frisk (SWE) Attendance: 42,454

LIVERPOOL: Jerzy Dudek; Stéphane Henchoz, Sami Hyypia, John Arne Riise, Jamie Carragher; Vladimir Smicer (75 Patrik Berger), Danny Murphy, Steven Gerrard, Dietmar Hamann; Michael Owen (70 Jari Litmanen), Emile Heskey. Trainer: Gérard Houllier

BAYER: Hans-Jörg Butt; Diego Placente, Lucimar Ferreira da Silva "LUCIO", Bernd Schneider, José "ZÉ ROBERTO" Da Silva Júnior; Yildiray Bastürk, Michael Ballack, Zoltan Sebescen, Carsten Ramelow; Oliver Neuville (74 Ulf Kirsten), Dimitar Berbatow (66 Boris Zivković). Trainer: Klaus Toppmöller

Goal: Hyypia (44)

BAYER 04 LEVERKUSEN v LIVERPOOL FC 4-2 (1-1)

BayArena, Leverkusen 9.04.2002

Referee: Vitor Manuel MELO PEREIRA (POR) Att: 22,500

BAYER: Hans-Jörg Butt; Zoltan Sebescen (46 Oliver Neuville), Lucimar Ferreira da Silva "LUCIO", Jens Nowotny (Cap), Diego Placente; Bernd Schneider, Michael Ballack, Yildiray Bastürk, José "ZÉ ROBERTO" Da Silva Júnior; Ulf Kirsten (46 Dimitar Berbatov), Thomas Brdarić (70 Boris Zivković). Trainer: Klaus Toppmöller

LIVERPOOL: Jerzy Dudek; John Arne Riise, Sami Hyypia (Cap), Stéphane Henchoz, Jamie Carragher, ABEL Luís da Silva Costa XAVIER (75 Patrik Berger); Danny Murphy, Dietmar Hamann (61 Vladimir Šmicer), Steven Gerrard; Emile Heskey (41 Jari Litmanen), Michael Owen. Trainer: Gérard Houllier

Goals: Ballack (16, 63), Abel Xavier (42), Berbatov (68), Litmanen (79), Lucio (84)

SEMI-FINALS

FC BARCELONA v REAL MADRID CF 0-2 (0-0)

Camp Nou, Barcelona 23.04.2002

Referee: Anders Frisk (SWE) Attendance: 85,000

FC BARCELONA: Roberto Oscar BONANO; Michael Reiziger (59 GEOVANNI Deiberson Mauricio), Frank De Boer, ABELARDO Fernández Antuña (Cap) (73 Philippe Christanval), Thiago Motta (82 Gabriel García de la Torre "GABRI"); LUIS ENRIQUE Martínez Garcia, Fabio Rochemback, Philip Cocu, Marc Overmars; Javier Pedro SAVIOLA, Patrick Kluivert. Trainer: Carlos REXACH Cerdá

REAL: CÉSAR Sánchez Domínguez; Miguel Angel "MICHEL" SALGADO, Fernando Ruíz HIERRO (Cap), Francisco PAVÓN Barahona, ROBERTO CARLOS da Silva; Claude Makelele, Iván HELGUERA Bujía, Santiago Hernán SOLARI (89 FLÁVIO de CONCEIÇÃO), Zinedine Zidane; RAÚL González Blanco, José María Gutiérrez "GUTI" (80 Steve McManaman). Trainer: Vicente DEL BOSQUE González

Goals: Zidane (54), McManaman (90)

REAL MADRID CF v FC BARCELONA 1-1 (1-0)

Santiago Bernabéu, Madrid 1.05.2002

Referee: Pierluigi Collina (ITA) Attendance: 80,000

REAL: CÉSAR Sánchez Domínguez; Miguel Angel "MICHEL" SALGADO, Fernando Ruíz HIERRO (Cap), Iván HELGUERA Bujía, ROBERTO CARLOS da Silva; Luis Filipe Madeira FIGO (68 Steve McManaman), Claude Makelele, Santiago Hernán SOLARI, Zinedine Zidane (46 FLÁVIO de CONCEIÇÃO); RAÚL González Blanco, José María Gutiérrez "GUTI" (87 Francisco PAVÓN Barahona).
Trainer: Vicente DEL BOSQUE González

FC BARCELONA: Roberto Oscar BONANO; Carles PUYOL Saforcada, ABELARDO Fernández Antuña (Cap), Frank De Boer, Francesco Coco (46 Marc Overmars); LUIS ENRIQUE Martínez Garcia, Xavier Hernández Creus "XAVI", Fabio Rochemback (67 GEOVANNI Deiberson Mauricio), Philip Cocu (75 SERGI Barjuán Esclusa); Javier Pedro SAVIOLA, Patrick Kluivert. Trainer: Carlos REXACH Cerdá

Goals: Raúl (43), Helguera (49 og)

MANCHESTER UNITED FC v BAYER 04 LEVERKUSEN 2-2 (1-0)

Old Trafford, Manchester 24.04.2002

Referee: L'uboš Michel (SVK) Attendance: 65,000

MANCHESTER UNITED: Fabien Barthez; Gary Neville (18 Phil Neville, 87 Denis Irwin), Wesley Brown, Laurent Blanc, Mikael Silvestre; Nicky Butt, Juan Sebastian Veron, Paul Scholes (82 Roy Keane), Ryan Giggs (Cap); Ole Gunnar Solskjaer, Ruud van Nistelrooy.
Trainer: Alexander Chapman Ferguson

BAYER: Hans-Jörg Butt; Boris Zivković, Lucimar Ferreira da Silva "LUCIO", Jens Nowotny (Cap) (46 Zoltan Sebescen), Diego Placente; Bernd Schneider, Carsten Ramelow, Michael Ballack, José "ZÉ ROBERTO" Da Silva Júnior; Yildiray Bastürk (77 Jurica Vranjes), Dimitar Berbatov (72 Oliver Neuville).
Trainer: Klaus Toppmöller

Goals: Solskjaer (29), Ballack (62), van Nistelrooy (67), Neuville (75)

BAYER 04 LEVERKUSEN v MANCHESTER UNITED FC 1-1 (1-1)

BayArena, Leverkusen 30.04.2002

Referee: Kim Milton Nielsen (DEN) Attendance: 22,500

BAYER: Hans-Jörg Butt, Boris Zivković, Jens Nowotny (Cap) (8 Zoltan Sebescen), Lucimar Ferreira da Silva "LUCIO", Diego Placente, Yildiray Bastürk (79 Jurica Vranjes), Bernd Schneider, Carsten Ramelow, Michael Ballack, José "ZÉ ROBERTO" Da Silva Júnior, Oliver Neuville (85 Dimitar Berbatov). Trainer: Klaus Toppmöller

MANCHESTER UNITED: Fabien Barthez, Wesley Brown (81 Diego Forlán), Laurent Blanc, Ronny Johnsen (60 Denis Irwin), Mikael Silvestre, Paul Scholes, Roy Keane (Cap), Juan Sebastian Veron, Nicky Butt (61 Ole Gunnar Solskjaer), Ryan Giggs, Ruud Van Nistelrooy. Trainer: Alex Ferguson

Goals: Keane (28), Neuville (45)

FINAL

REAL MADRID CF
v BAYER 04 LEVERKUSEN 2-1 (2-1)

Hampden Park, Glasgow 15.05.2002

Referee: Urs Meier (SWI) Attendance: 51,567

REAL: CÉSAR Sánchez Domínguez (68 Iker CASILLAS Fernández); Miguel Angel "MICHEL" SALGADO, Fernando Ruíz HIERRO (Cap), Iván HELGUERA Bujía, ROBERTO CARLOS da Silva; Luis Filipe Madeira FIGO (61 Steve McManaman), Claude Makelele (73 FLÁVIO de CONCEIÇÃO), Santiago Hernán SOLARI, Zinedine Zidane; RAÚL González Blanco, Fernando MORIENTES Sánchez.
Trainer: Vicente DEL BOSQUE González

BAYER: Hans-Jörg Butt, Zoltan Sebescen (64 Ulf Kirsten), Boris Zivković, Diego Placente, Carsten Ramelow (Cap), Lucimar Ferreira da Silva "LUCIO" (90 Marko Babic), Bernd Schneider, Michael Ballack, Yildiray Bastürk, Thomas Brdarić (39 Dimitar Berbatov), Oliver Neuville.
Trainer: Klaus Toppmöller

Goals: Raúl (9), Lucio (14), Zidane (45)

European Cup Goalscorers 2001-02:

10 goals: Ruud van Nistelrooij (Manchester United)

8 goals: Ole Gunnar Solskjaer (Manchester United), David Trezeguet (Juventus Torino)

7 goals: Thierry Henry (Arsenal London), Patrick Kluivert (FC Barcelona), Ümit Karan (Galatasaray Istanbul), Oliver Neuville (Bayer Leverkusen), Renivaldo Pereira "PENA" (FC Porto), RAÚL González Blanco (Real Madrid)

6 goals: Michael Ballack (Bayer Leverkusen), Giovane Élber (Bayern München), Diego Tristán (Deportivo La Coruña), Luis Enrique (FC Barcelona), Anderson de Sousa "DECO" (FC Porto), Mihalis Konstantinou (Panathinaikos Athina), Vitor Barbosa RIVALDO (FC Barcelona)

5 goals: David Beckham (Manchester United), Michael Owen (Liverpool FC)

4 goals: Glen de Boeck (Anderlecht), Ulf Kirsten (Bayer Leverkusen), Claudio Pizarro (Bayern München), Elpidio SILVA (Boavista Porto), Jan Koller (Borussia Dortmund), Olexandr Melashchenko (Dinamo Kyiv), Javier Pedro Saviola (FC Barcelona), CLAYTON Ferreira (FC Porto), Péter Kovács (Haka Valkeakoski), Alessandro del Piero (Juventus Torino), Georgi Ivanov (Levski Sofia), Emile Heskey (Liverpool FC), Eric Carrière (Olympique Lyonnais), Santiago Hernan Solari (Real Madrid), Libor Sionko (Sparta Praha), Vladimir Beschastnykh (Spartak Moskva)

3 goals: Ljungberg, Pires (Arsenal), Totti (AS Roma), Santa Cruz (Bayern München), Sánchez (Boavista Porto), Lembakoali (Inter Bratislava), Lucio (Bayer Leverkusen), Crowe (Bohemians Dublin), Amoroso (Borussia Dortmund), Larsson, Sutton (Celtic Glasgow), Valerón (Deportivo La Coruña), Zuma (FC København), Tomasson (Feyenoord), Flo (Glasgow Rangers), Jönsson, Selaković (Halmstads BK), Crespo (Lazio Roma), Br. Cheyrou (Lille OSC), Litmanen (Liverpool FC), Buznikin (Lokomotiv Moskva), Basinas, Karagounis (Panathinaikos), Figo, Guti, Iván Helguera, Morientes, Zidane (Real Madrid), Brattbakk, Skammelsrud (Rosenborg), Stripeikis (Slaviya Mozyr), Răducanu, Trică (Steaua Bucureşti)

2 goals: Crasson, Mornar (Anderlecht), Bergkamp (Arsenal), Cafu, Émerson (AS Roma), Phillips (Barry Town), Berbatov, Schneider, Sebescen (Bayer Leverkusen), Paulo Sergio (Bayern München), Ricken (Borussia Dortmund), Djalminha, Naybet (Deportivo La Coruña), Belkevich, Ghioane, Lucky Idahor (Dinamo Kyiv), Cicchirillo (F91 Dudelange), Fernandez (FC København), André, Moldovan (FC Nantes), Capucho (FC Porto), Oktay, Revivo (Fenerbahçe), Elmander (Feyenoord), Serkan Aykut, Arif Erdem, Ali Riza Yalçin (Galatasaray), Caniggia (Glasgow Rangers), Petrić (Grasshopper), Tudor (Juventus), Fiore, López (Lazio Roma), Bassir (Lille OSC), Hyypiä, Murphy (Liverpool FC), Izmailov (Lokomotiv Moskva), Blanc, Giggs (Manchester United), Alexandris, Giannakopoulos (Olympiakos Peiraias), Delmotte, Govou (Olympique Lyonnais), Liberopoulos, Olisadebe, Vlaović (Panathinaikos), Kezman (PSV Eindhoven), Eto'o (RCD Mallorca), McManaman, Sávio (Real Madrid), Rushfeldt (Rosenborg), van Hoogdalem (Schalke 04), Aghahowa (Shakhtar Donetsk), Kolesnichenko, Mikholap (Skonto Riga), Arben Nuhiji (Sloga Skopje), Jarošik, Kincl, Michalík (Sparta Praha), Robson (Spartak Moskva), Ashvetia (Torpedo Kutaisi), Duro (Vllaznia Shkodër), Pater, Zurawski (Wisla Kraków)

1 goal: Arveladze, Wamberto (Ajax Amsterdam), Dindane, Hasi, Hendrikx, Ilić, Seol, Yashchuk (Anderlecht Brussel), Vieira, Wiltord (Arsenal London), Delvecchio, Montella, Panucci, Tommasi (AS Roma), York (Barry Town), Drobnak, Kunzo (Inter Bratislava), Flynn, French, Lloyd (Barry Town), Babić, Bastürk, Brdarić, Ramelow, Zé Roberto (Bayer Leverkusen), Effenberg, Jeremies, Kuffour, Salihamidzić, Zickler (Bayern München), Alexandre Goulart, Duda, Martelinho (Boavista Porto), Maher (Bohemians Dublin), Oliseh, Rosicky (Borussia Dortmund), Walltin (Brann Bergen), Agathe, Petrov, Petta, Thompson, Valgaeren (Celtic Glasgow), Aćimović, Lerinc, Pjanović (Crvena Zvezda Beograd), Capdevila, Fran, Makaay, Pandiani, Sergio (Deportivo La Coruña), Papeckys (FBK Kaunas), Andersson, Gerard, Overmars, Rochemback (FC Barcelona), Laursen, Lønstrup (FC København), Gaspoz, Rossi (FC Lugano), Ahamada, Armand, da Rocha, Dalmat, Fabbri, Quint, Vahirua, Ziani (FC Nantes), Hélder Postiga, Mário Silva, Paredes, Rafael, Söserström (FC Porto), Brzeczek, Kirchler (FC Tirol Innsbruck), Serhat Akin (Fenerbahçe), Bosvelt, van Hooijdonck (Feyenoord), Ümit Davala, Fleurquin, Suat Kaya, Niculescu, Pérez, Hasan Şaş (Galatasaray), Chapuisat, Nuñez (Grasshopper), Bilić (Hajduk Split), Marco, Torkkeli (Haka Valkeakoski), Svensson (Halmstads BK),

Amoruso, Montero, Zalayeta (Juventus Torino), Benediktsson, Olafsson (KR Reykjavík), Fernando Couto, Stanković (Lazio Roma), Markov, Pantelić, Terziev (Levski Sofia), Bakari, Ecker, Olufadé, Tafforeau (Lille OSC), Abel Xavier, Fowler, Gerrard, Redknapp, Smicer, Wright (Liverpool FC), Cherevchenko, Ignashevich, Lekcetho, Maminov, Obradović, Pimenov (Lokomotiv Moskva), Zano (Maccabi Haifa), Cole, Keane, Scholes, Silvestre (Manchester United), Starcević (NK Maribor), Luyindula, Née (Olympique Lyonnais), Niniadis, Ofori-Quaye (Olympiakos Peiraias), Kaiafas, Thiebaut (Omonia Nicosia), Goumas, Kolkka (Panathinaikos), Sensini (Parma), Bruggink, de Jong, Faber, Hofland (PSV Eindhoven), Biagini, Engonga, Luque, Novo (RCD Mallorca), Celades, Geremi, Munitis, Portillo, Roberto Carlos (Real Madrid), Johnsen, Strand (Rosenborg), Asamoah, Hajto, Möller, Mpenza, Mulder, Sand, Vermant (Schalke 04), Bakharev, Tymoshchuk, Vorobei (Shakhtar Donetsk), Barburoş, Boreţ, Comlionoc, Dadu (Sheriff Tiraspol), Korgalidze, Verpakovskis, Zemlinsky (Skonto Riga), Rybakov (Slaviya Mozyr), Kuka (Slavia Praha), Babnic, Hartig, Holub, Klein, Labant, Novotný (Sparta Praha), Baranov (Spartak Moskva), Falemi, Neaga (Steaua Bucureşti), Kutateladze (Torpedo Kutaisi), Sinani (Vllaznia Shkodër), Frankowski, Glowacki (Wisla Kraków)

Own goals: Helguera (Real Madrid) for FC Barcelona, Blanc (Manchester United) for Deportivo La Coruña, Jacobsen (VB Vagur) for Slavia Mozyr), Wilson (Haka Valkeakoski) for Liverpool FC), Chugainov (Lokomotiv Moskva) for AS Roma, Novotný (Sparta Praha) for Bayern München, Taylor (Arsenal London) for Juventus Torino, Kunzo (Inter Bratislava) for Rosenborg

UEFA CHAMPIONS LEAGUE 2002-2003

FIRST QUALIFYING ROUND

FBK KAUNAS v KS DINAMO TIRANË 2-3 (2-0)

"S. Darius & S. Girenas Sport C", Kaunas 17.07.2002

Referee: Oleg Chikun (BLS)

FBK KAUNAS: Eduardas Kurskis, Darius Sanajevas (46 Irmantas Zelmikas), Tomas Kancelskis, Darius Regelskis, Gytis Gelgota, Gintaras Juodeikis, Marius Bezykornovas, Tadas Papeckys (72 Andrius Puotkalis), Tomas Miklinevicius, Audrius Slekys, Andrius Velicka (62 Remigijus Pocius). Trainer: Saulius Širmelis

DINAMO: Ilion Lika, Alpin Gallo, Luan Pinari, Julian Ahmataj, Arian Pisha, Artian Poci, Ergert Bakalli, Ilir Qorri, Klodian Asllani, Serhiy Romanishin, Daniel Xhafaj (46 Rigels Qosa). Trainer: Faruk Sejdini

Goals: Velicka (38, 42 pen), Ahmataj (55), Pisha (56), Qorri (76)

KS DINAMO TIRANË v FBK KAUNAS 0-0

Qemal Stafa, Tirana 24.07.2002

Referee: Roland Beck (LIE)

DINAMO: Ilion Lika, Alpin Gallo, Luan Pinari, Julian Ahmataj, Arian Pisha, Artian Poci (85 Ligor Tiko), Ergert Bakalli, Ilir Qorri, Klodian Asllani (71 Daniel Xhafaj), Serhiy Romanishin (90 Artim Polozani), Rigels Qosa. Trainer: Faruk Sejdini

FBK KAUNAS: Eduardas Kurskis, Darius Sanajevas, Tomas Kancelskis, Darius Regelskis, Gytis Gelgota, Gintaras Juodeikis (67 Andrius Puotkalis), Marius Bezykornovas, Tadas Papeckys, Tomas Miklinevicius (46 Vitalijus Danilicevas), Audrius Slekys, Andrius Velicka. Trainer: Saulius Širmelis

TAMPERE UNITED FC v FC PYUNIK YEREVAN 0-4 (0-1)

Tammela, Tampere 17.07.2002

Referee: Marian Mircea Salomir (ROM)

TAMPERE UNITED: Mikko Juhani Kaven, Pasi Salmela, Mikko Salo, Jussi Kuoppala, Heikko Aho (46 Lee Jones), Janne Räsänen, Jari Niemi (72 Matti Santahuhta), Sakori Saarinen (72 Toni Hevonkorpi), Tero Koskela, Ville Lehtinen, Mika Nenonen. Trainer: Ari Hjelm

FC PYUNIK: Andronik Karaguezian, Artur Mkrchyan, Jose Andres Bilibio, Aleksandar Stevanovic, Alou Traoré, Vardan Minasyan (88 Arsen Meloyan), Artavazd Karamyan, Hovhannes Antonyan (81 Arkadi Chilingaryan), Miguel Cisterna, Mamadou Diawara (75 Aghvan Mkrtchyan), Arman Karamyan. Trainer: Oskar Lopez

Goals: Arman Karamyan (32, 67), Artavazd Karamyan (48), Artur Mkrchyan (72)

FC PYUNIK EREVAN v TAMPERE UNITED FC 2-0 (0-0)

Republican, Erevan 24.07.2002

Referee: Yuri Kliuchnikov (RUS) Attendance: 22,000

FC PYUNIK: Andronik Karaguezian (80 Edel APOULA EDIMA BETE), Artur Mkrchyan, Jose Andres Bilibio, Aleksandar Stevanovic, Alou Traoré, Vardan Minasyan, Artavazd Karamyan, Hovhannes Antonyan (67 Fernando Zagharian), Miguel Cisterna, Mamadou Diawara (75 Aghvan Mkrtchyan), Arman Karamyan. Trainer: Oskar Lopez

TAMPERE UNITED: Petri Viljanen, Mikko Salo, Lee Jones, Jussi Kuoppala, Heikko Aho (46 Sakori Saarinen), Janne Räsänen, Kari Sainio, Tero Koskela, Toni Hevonkorpi, Matti Santahuhta (56 Mika Nenonen), Matti Hiukka.
Trainer: Ari Hjelm

Goals: Diawara (53), Cisterna (90)

PORTADOWN FC v FC BELSHINA BOBRUISK 0-0

Shamrock Park, Portadown 17.07.2002

Referee: Drazenko Kovačić (CRO)

PORTADOWN: Michael Keenan, Keith O'Hara, Neil Ogden, Philip Craig, Dean Fitzgerald, Richard Clarke, Paul McAreavey, Peter McCann, Gary Hamilton, Vinny Arkins, Kyle Neill.
Trainer: Ronald Joseph Mcfall

FC BELSHINA: Sergei Sinitsyn, Alexandr Sednev, Mikhail Garbachov (46 Alexandr Shagoiko), Vladimir Klimovich, Viktor Kukar, Vyacheslav Gormash, Igor Trukhov, Valeriy Stripeikis, Denis Korolik, Viktor Malyavko (72 Eduard Gradoboyev), Eduard Boltrushevich.
Trainer: Viachaslau Akshayeu

FC SKONTO RIGA v BARRY TOWN FC 5-0 (1-0)

Skonto, Riga 17.07.2002

Referee: Lubomir Pucek (CZE)

FC SKONTO: Andrey Pavlov, Aleksander Isakov, Mikhail Zemlinsky, Mantas Samusevas, Victor Moroz, Oleg Blagonadezhdin, Ignas Dedura, Zurab Menteshashvili (46 Levan Korgalidze), Maris Verpakovsky (78 Audrius Ksanavicius), Vladimir Kolesnichenko, Mikhail Mikholap (66 Alexander Eliseyev). Trainer: Aleksandrs Starkovs

BARRY TOWN: Simon Christopher Rayner, Gary Lloyd, Kenneth Brown (82 Lee Jarman), Scott Morgan, Lee Phillips, Richard Kennedy, Andrew York (66 David Alan Toomey), Jonathan French, Thomas Ramasut (74 Nathan Cotterrall), Ian William Bishop, Jamie Moralee.

Goals: Kolesnichenko (13), Zemlinsky (61), Korgalidze (65), Ksanavicius (86), Eliseyev (90)

FC BELSHINA BOBRUISK v PORTADOWN FC 3-2 (2-1)

City, Borisov 24.07.2002

Referee: Jouni Hyytiä (FIN)

FC BELSHINA: Sergei Sinitsyn, Alexandr Sednev, Mikhail Garbachov, Vladimir Klimovich, Viktor Kukar, Vyacheslav Gormash (46 Eduard Gradoboyev), Igor Trukhov, Valeriy Stripeikis (72 Vladimir Ostrikov), Denis Korolik, Alexandr Shagoiko (74 Viktor Malyavko), Eduard Boltrushevich.
Trainer: Viachaslau Akshayeu

PORTADOWN: Michael Keenan, Keith O'Hara, Neil Ogden, Philip Craig, Weil Alderdice (76 Andrew Hamilton), Dean Fitzgerald, Paul McAreavey, Peter McCann, Gary Hamilton, Vinny Arkins, Kyle Neill. Trainer: Ronald Joseph Mcfall

Goals: Stripeikis (6), Korolik (22, 59), G. Hamilton (39), Fitzgerald (74)

BARRY TOWN FC v FC SKONTO RIGA 0-1 (0-0)

Jenner Park, Barry 24.07.2002

Referee: Gylfi Thor Orrason (ICE) Attendance: 1,507

BARRY TOWN: Simon Christopher Rayner, Lee Jarman, Gary Lloyd, Richard Kennedy (68 Thomas Ramasut), Lee Phillips, David Alan Toomey (74 Andrew York), Jonathan French, Nathan Cotterrall, Leigh Michael Pratt, Ian William Bishop, Jamie Moralee (63 Nicholas Padraig Burke).
Trainer: Kenneth James Brown

FC SKONTO: Andrey Pavlov, Aleksander Isakov, Mikhail Zemlinsky, Mantas Samusevas, Ignas Dedura, Oleg Blagonadezhdin, Victor Moroz, Zurab Menteshashvili (46 Levan Korgalidze), Maris Verpakovsky (57 Audrius Ksanavicius), Vladimir Kolesnichenko, Mikhail Mikholap (68 Alexander Eliseyev). Trainer: Aleksandrs Starkovs

Goal: Kolesnichenko (52)

HIBERNIANS PAOLA v SHELBOURNE FC 2-2 (2-1)

National, Ta'Qali 17.07.2002

Referee: Eric Blareau (BEL)

HIBERNIANS: Mario Muscat, Kevin Cassar (74 Antoine Zahra), Branko Nisevic, Silvio Vella, Adrian Ciantar, Essien Mbong, Adrian Mifsud, Ndubisi Chukunyere, Peter Pullicino, Adrian Pulis, Roderick Baldacchino (79 Miguel Mifsud).
Trainer: Robert Gatt

SHELBOURNE: Steve Williams, Owen Heary, David Crawley, Tony McCarthy, Kevin Doherty (62 Barry Prenderville), James Gannon, Oliver Cahill, Stuart Byrne, Trevor Molloy, Richard Baker, Mark Roberts. Trainer: John Mcdonnell

Goals: Byrne (6), Chukunyere (7), Pulis (37), Gannon (66)

SHELBOURNE FC v HIBERNIANS FC PAOLA 0-1 (0-0)

Tolka Park, Dublin 24.07.2002

Referee: Vitaliy Godulyan (UKR)

SHELBOURNE: Steve Williams, Owen Heary, David Crawley (90 Wesley Houlihan), Tony McCarthy, James Gannon, Oliver Cahill, Stuart Byrne, Trevor Molloy, Richard Baker, Barry Prenderville, Mark Roberts. Trainer: John Mcdonnell

HIBERNIANS: Mario Muscat, Branko Nisevic, Silvio Vella, Aaron Xuereb, Adrian Ciantar, Essien Mbong, Adrian Mifsud, Ndubisi Chukunyere, Peter Pullicino (67 Antoine Zahra), Adrian Pulis, Roderick Baldacchino. Trainer: Robert Gatt

Goal: Chukunyere (90)

F91 DUDELANGE v FK VARDAR SKOPJE 1-1 (0-0)

Josy Barthel, Luxembourg 17.07.2002

Referee: Kostadin Kostadinov (BUL)

F91 DUDELANGE: Albert Polo, Roger Lutz, Frank Deville, Rainer Hauck, Cosimo Barnabo, Joaquim Machado (71 Christophe Boulard), Stéphane Martine, Evariste Kabongo, Gordon Braun (81 José Llamas), Sébastien Remy, Thomas Gruszczynski (90 Rudy Marchal). Trainer: Carlo Weis

VARDAR: Muarem Zekir (56 Gogo Jovcev), Dragan Veselinovski, Nikola Doševski, Aleksandar Vasovski, Saso Janev, Mile Dimov, Ilir Elmazovski (79 Vojislav Simonovski), Srdjan Zaharievski, Aguinaldo De Jesús BRAGA (67 Slavco Georgievski), Dejan Ristovski, Rogerio DA COSTA Oliveira. Trainer: Dokica Hadzievski

Goals: Remy (54), Georgievski (68)

FK VARDAR SKOPJE v F91 DUDELANGE 3-0 (0-0)

City, Skopje 24.07.2002

Referee: Attila Juhos (HUN)

VARDAR: Muarem Zekir, Dragan Veselinovski, Nikola Doševski (67 Marian Petkov), Aleksandar Vasovski, Saso Janev, Mile Dimov, Ilir Elmazovski (65 Slavco Georgievski), Srdjan Zaharievski, Aguinaldo De Jesús BRAGA, Dimitar Spasovski, Rogerio DA COSTA Oliveira (78 Vojislav Simonovski). Trainer: Dokica Hadzievski

F91 DUDELANGE: Albert Polo, Roger Lutz, Frank Deville (74 Frédéric Cicchirillo), Christophe Boulard, Rainer Hauck, Joaquim Machado, Stéphane Martine (90 Rudy Marchal), Evaristc Kabongo, Sébastien Remy, Gordon Braun (83 José Llamas), Thomas Gruszczynski. Trainer: Carlo Weis

Goals: Spasovski (70, 75), Petkov (85)

FC TORPEDO KUTAISI v B36 TÓRSHAVN 5-2 (2-0)

David Kiladze, Kutaisi 17.07.2002

Referee: Ceri Richards (WAL)

FC TORPEDO: Zviadi Sturua, Mikheil Makhviladze, Lasha Chelidze, Vakhtang Akofian, Revaz Kemoklidze, Kakha Kvetenadze, Shota Babunashvili (66 David Janashia), Walter Guchua (46 David Gamezardashvili), Malkhaz Asatiani, Zuradzi Ionanidze, Zviad Kutateladze (53 Andriy Poroshyn). Trainer: Olexander Shtelin

B36 TÓRSHAVN: René Tórgard, Arn Björn Danielsen, Iulian Florescu, Fródi Clementsen (90 Steffan í Skorini), Julian Jónsson, Jákup á Borg, John Petersen, Magni á Lakjuni (89 Ragnar Poulsen), Bárdur Mortensson, Egil Zachariasen, Klæmint Matras (68 Kenneth Jacobsen). Trainer: Piotr Krakowski

Goals: Asatiani (15, 46), Ionanidze (33), á Lakjuni (53), Kvetenadze (67), Poroshyn (71), Mortensson (74)

B36 TÓRSHAVN v FC TORPEDO KUTAISI 0-1 (0-0)

Tørsvøllur, Tórshavn 24.07.2002

Referee: Paul McKeon (IRE)

B36 TÓRSHAVN: René Tórgard, Arn Björn Danielsen, Iulian Florescu (85 Kenneth Jacobsen), Fródi Clementsen, Julian Jónsson, Jákup á Borg, John Petersen, Magni á Lakjuni (85 Ragnar Poulsen), Bárdur Mortensson (85 Tóralvur Poulsen), Egil Zachariasen, Klæmint Matras. Trainer: Piotr Krakowski

FC TORPEDO: Giorgi Chanturia, Mikheil Makhviladze, Givi Didava, Lasha Chelidze, Revaz Kemoklidze, Kakha Kvetenadze, Walter Guchua, Malkhaz Asatiani, Roman Akhaikatsi, David Janashia, Zuradzi Ionanidze (46 Andriy Poroshyn). Trainer: Olexander Shtelin

Goal: Janashia (76)

FK ZELJEZNICAR SARAJEVO v ÍA AKRANES 3-0 (2-0)

Olimpijski, Sarajevo 17.07.2002

Referee: Dietmar Drabek (AUS)

FK ZELJEZNICAR: Miroslav Kruzik, Bulend Biscević, Edis Mulalić, Haris Alihodzić, Adin Mulaosmanović, Sergej Tica (83 Sanel Jahić), Almir Gredić, Dalibor Silić, Sead Seferović, Jure Guvo (79 Senad Zerić), Almir Cosić (70 Denis Karić). Trainer: Amar Osim

ÍA AKRANES: Ólafur Thór Gunnarsson, Sturlaugur Haraldsson, Gunnlaugur Jonsson, Reynir Leósson, Pálmi Haraldsson, Gudjón H. Sveinsson, Ellert Björnsson (71 Sturla Gudlaugsson), Grétar Rafn Steinsson, Hjörtur Julius Hjartarson (80 Gardar Gunnlaugsson), Jóhannes Gíslason, Kári Steinn Reynisson (89 Hermann Geir Thorsson). Trainer: Olafur Thordarson

Goals: Guvo (4, 56), Gredic (38)

ÍA AKRANES
v FK ZELJEZNICAR SARAJEVO 0-1 (0-1)

Akranesvöllur 24.07.2002

Referee: Romans Lajuks (LAT)

ÍA AKRANES: Ólafur Thór Gunnarsson, Sturlaugur Haraldsson (55 Gudjón H. Sveinsson), Andri Karvelsson, Gunnlaugur Jonsson, Ellert Björnsson, Reynir Leósson, Grétar Rafn Steinsson, Pálmi Haraldsson (66 Jon Thor Hauksson), Hjörtur Julius Hjartarson, Gardar Gunnlaugsson (46 Bjarki Gunnlaugsson), Kári Steinn Reynisson.
Trainer: Olafur Thordarson

FK ZELJEZNICAR: Miroslav Kruzik, Bulend Biscević (81 Sanjin Mesić), Edis Mulalić, Haris Alihodzić, Adin Mulaosmanović, Sergej Tica (64 Dalibor Silić), Denis Karić, Almir Gredić, Sead Seferović, Jure Guvo, Almir Cosić (76 Emir Hadzić). Trainer: Amar Osim

Goal: Gredic (33)

FC SHERIFF TIRASPOL
v FC ZHENIS ASTANA 2-1 (0-1)

Sheriff, Tiraspol 17.07.2002

Referee: Bülent Uzun (TUR)

FC SHERIFF: Alexandru Chirilov, Chidi Odiah, Vaja Tarhnishvili, Sorin Botiş, Alberto Blanco (32 Ruslan Barburoş), Stanislav Ivanov, Iuriy Priganiuc, Victor Comlionoc, Vadim Boreţ (71 Roberto Brown), Evgheny Patula, Cristian Dorin Tudor (57 Andriy Nesteruk).
Trainer: Gavril Pele Balint

FC ZHENIS: David Loria, Sergey Kozulin, Maxim Zabelin, Goran Dragicevic, Andrei Travin, Artur Martens, Igor Avdeev (71 Sergey Kirov), Evgeniy Lovchev, Alexey Klishin (81 Martin Bielik), Arsen Tlekhougov, Nilton Mendes (64 Askhat Kadyrkulov). Trainer: Vladimir Fomichyov

Goals: Lovchev (8), Priganiuc (57), Tarhnishvili (85 pen)

FC ZHENIS ASTANA
v FC SHERIFF TIRASPOL 3-2 (2-0)

Khadzhimukan Munaitpasov, Astana 24.07.2002

Referee: Hermann Albrecht (GER) Attendance: 12,000

FC ZHENIS: David Loria, Sergey Kozulin, Maxim Zabelin, Goran Dragicevic, Andrei Travin, Artur Martens, Evgeniy Lovchev, Alexey Klishin, Arsen Tlekhougov (86 Sergey Kirov), Nilton Mendes (66 Martin Bielik), Askhat Kadyrkulov (59 Dmitriy Kichshenko). Trainer: Vladimir Fomichyov

FC SHERIFF: Sebastian Huţan (14 Alexandru Chirilov), Dmytro Parhomenko (59 Victor Comlionoc), Chidi Odiah, Vaja Tarhnishvili, Sorin Botiş, Marius Ciubăncan, Iuriy Priganiuc, Stanislav Ivanov, Vadim Boreţ, Ruslan Barburoş (46 Evgheny Patula), Andriy Nesteruk.
Trainer: Gavril Pele Balint

Goals: Tlekhougov (32), Lovchev (41), Klishin (52), Boreţ (58), Nesteruk (59)

FC FLORA TALLINN v APOEL NICOSIA FC 0-0

A Le Coq Arena, Tallinn 17.07.2002

Referee: Tommy Skjerven (NOR)

FC FLORA: Martin Kaalma, Teet Allas, Taavi Rähn, Raio Piiroja, Erko Saviauk (53 Kert Haavistu), Martin Reim, Meelis Rooba, Marko Kristal, Aleksandr Kulik, Tor Henning Hamre (83 Aleksander Saharov), Joel Lindpere.
Trainer: Arno Pijpers

APOEL: Mihalis Morfis, Dimitris Daskalakis, Zaharin Sirakov, Stavros Georgiou, Marinos Ouzounidis, Marinos Satsias, Romik Khachatryan, Barnabas Sztipanovics, Costas Malekkos, Costas Haralambides (78 Marios Ilia), Marios Agathocleous (65 Orosco Anonam). Trainer: Euge Gerards

APOEL NICOSIA FC
v FC FLORA TALLINN 1-0 (0-0)

GSP, Nicosia 24.07.2002

Referee: Miroslav Radoman (YUG)

APOEL: Mihalis Morfis, Dimitris Daskalakis, Zaharin Sirakov, Stavros Georgiou, Marinos Ouzounidis, Stelios Okkarides, Romik Khachatryan, Barnabas Sztipanovics (16 Marios Agathocleous, 87 Nektarios Alexandrou), Costas Malekkos, Costas Haralambides, Orosco Anonam (46 Marios Ilia). Trainer: Euge Gerards

FC FLORA: Martin Kaalma, Teet Allas, Taavi Rähn, Raio Piiroja, Andrei Sidorenkov, Martin Reim, Meelis Rooba (76 Aleksander Saharov), Ray Gian Carlo Frankel (76 Kert Haavistu), Tor Henning Hamre (67 Aleksandr Kulik), Marko Kristal, Joel Lindpere. Trainer: Arno Pijpers

Sent off: Piiroja (86)

Goal: Georgiou (51)

SECOND QUALIFYING ROUND

AC SPARTA PRAHA
v FC TORPEDO KUTAISI 3-0 (2-0)

Letná, Praha 31.07.2002

Referee: Karl-Erik Nilsson (SWE) Attendance: 9,650

SPARTA: Michal Spit, Zdenek Grygera, Pavel Mares, Jiri Novotny, Tomáš Hubschman, Karel Poborsky (60 Rastislav Michalik), Lukáš Zelenka, Jiri Jarosik, Libor Sionko, Tomáš Jun (67 Michal Pospisil), Miroslav Baranek (81 Peter Babnic).
Trainer: Jozef Jarabinský

FC TORPEDO: Zviadi Sturua, Givi Didava, Sevast Todua, Vakhtang Khvadagiani, Lasha Chelidze, Malkhaz Asatiani, Kakha Kvetenadze (39 Revaz Kemoklidze), Roman Akhaikatsi (76 Zuradzi Ionanidze), Walter Guchua, David Janashia (46 Shota Babunashvili), Andriy Poroshyn.
Trainer: Olexander Shtelin

Goals: Baranek (7, 20), Pospisil (75)

FC TORPEDO KUTAISI v AC SPARTA PRAHA 1-2 (1-1)

David Kiladze, Kutaisi 7.08.2002

Referee: Kenneth William Clark (SCO)

FC TORPEDO: Giorgi Chanturia, Lasha Chelidze (70 Vakhtang Khvadagiani), Mikheil Makhviladze, Malkhaz Asatiani, Revaz Kemoklidze, Kakha Kvetenadze, Shota Babunashvili (64 Roman Akhaikatsi), Walter Guchua, Zuradzi Ionanidze (79 Gaga Chkhetiani), David Janashia, Andriy Poroshyn. Trainer: Olexander Shtelin

SPARTA: Michal Spit, Zdenek Grygera (76 Jan Flachbart), Tomáš Hubschman, Jiri Novotny, Pavel Mares, Karel Poborsky, Lukáš Zelenka, Jiri Jarosik (64 Tomáš Sivok), Libor Sionko (58 Rastislav Michalik), Peter Babnic, Tomáš Jun. Trainer: Jozef Jarabinský

Goals: Ionanidze (32), Zelenka (41), Jun (56)

MSK ZILINA v FC BASEL 1-1 (1-1)

Mestsky Sportovy, Zilina 31.07.2002

Referee: Laurent Duhamel (FRA) Attendance: 6,258

MSK ZILINA: Marek Cech, Jaroslav Trhancik, Branislav Labant, Mario Klago, Radoslav Zabavnik, Daniel Kosmel (59 Marek Bazík), Dušan Sninský, Marek Mintal, Martin Durica, Miroslav Barcík, Miroslav Nemec (59 Richard Varadin). Trainer: Leon Kalvoda

FC BASEL: Pascal Zuberbühler, Alexandre Quennoz, Grégory Duruz, Marco Zwyssig, Antonio Esposito, Ivan Ergic (76 Carlos Varela), Mario Cantaluppi, Scott Chipperfield, Sébastien Barberis, Hervé Tum, Julio Hernán Rossi (64 Hakan Yakin). Trainer: Christian Gross

Goals: Barcík (30), Klago (39 og)

FC BASEL v MSK ZILINA 3-0 (2-0)

Saint Jakob, Basel 7.08.2002

Referee: Darko Ceferin (SVN) Attendance: 16,562

FC BASEL: Pascal Zuberbühler, Grégory Duruz, Marco Zwyssig, Antonio Esposito (72 Carlos Varela), Murat Yakin (77 Alexandre Quennoz), Ivan Ergic, Christian Gimenez, Mario Cantaluppi, Sébastien Barberis, Julio Hernán Rossi (82 Hervé Tum), Hakan Yakin. Trainer: Christian Gross

MSK ZILINA: Marek Cech, Jaroslav Trhancik, Branislav Labant, Mario Klago (46 Cyril Spendla), Radoslav Zabavnik, Daniel Kosmel, Dušan Sninský (46 Vladimir Stas), Marek Mintal, Martin Durica, Miroslav Barcík, Miroslav Nemec (76 Michal Gottwald). Trainer: Leon Kalvoda

Goals: Gimenez (12, 50), H. Yakin (23)

FC SKONTO RIGA v FC LEVSKI SOFIA 0-0

Skonto, Riga 31.07.2002

Referee: Philippe Leuba (SWI)

FC SKONTO: Andrey Pavlov, Aleksander Isakov, Mikhail Zemlinsky, Mantas Samusevas, Oleg Blagonadezhdin, Ignas Dedura, Victor Moroz, Zurab Menteshashvili (61 Orestas Buitkus), Maris Verpakovsky, Vladimir Kolesnichenko (89 Alexander Eliseyev), Mikhail Mikholap (69 Levan Korgalidze). Trainer: Aleksandrs Starkovs

FC LEVSKI: Dimitar Ivankov, Stanislav Angelov (46 Garba Lawal), Danail Bachkov, Georgi Markov, Saša Simonovic, Stanimir Stoilov, Konstantin Golovskoy, Dimitar Telkiyski (72 Elin Topuzakov), Ilian Stoianov, Georgi Chilikov (69 Todor Kolev), Miodrag Pantelic. Trainer: Slavoljub Muslin

FC LEVSKI SOFIA v FC SKONTO RIGA 2-0 (2-0)

Georgi Asparuhov, Sofia 7.08.2002

Referee: Mikko Vuorela (FIN)

FC LEVSKI: Dimitar Ivankov, Garba Lawal, Danail Bachkov (78 Dimitar Telkiyski), Saša Simonovic, Stanimir Stoilov, Biser Ivanov, Konstantin Golovskoy (81 Justice Christopher), Elin Topuzakov, Ilian Stoianov (66 Georgi Markov), Georgi Chilikov, Miodrag Pantelic. Trainer: Slavoljub Muslin

FC SKONTO: Andrey Pavlov, Aleksander Isakov, Mikhail Zemlinsky, Mantas Samusevas, Oleg Blagonadezhdin, Ignas Dedura, Victor Moroz, Orestas Buitkus (78 Levan Korgalidze), Maris Verpakovsky (71 Alexander Eliseyev), Vladimir Kolesnichenko, Mikhail Mikholap (65 Audrius Ksanavicius). Trainer: Aleksandrs Starkovs

Goals: Chilikov (12), Simonovic (31)

HAMMARBY IF v FK PARTIZAN BEOGRAD 1-1 (1-1)

Råsunda, Solna 31.07.2002

Referee: Lutz Michael Fröhlich (GER) Attendance: 19,417

HAMMARBY IF: Ante Covic, Mikael Hellström, Jonas Stark, Johan Andersson, Trym Bergman, Christer Fursth, Fredrik Winsnes, Mikael Andersson, Kennedy Bakircioglü (85 Pablo Piñones-Arce), Andreas Hermansson (74 Antti Pohja), Peter Markstedt. Trainer: Anders Linderoth

FK PARTIZAN: Radovan Radakovic, Dragoljub Jeremic, Branko Savic, Branimir Bajic, Milivoje Cirkovic, Igor Duljaj, Vladimir Ivic (85 Damir Cakar), Saša Ilic, Zvonimir Vukic, Danko Lazovic (90 Dejan Rusmir), Ivica Iliev. Trainer: Ljubiša Tumbaković

Goals: Winsnes (17), Lazović (37)

FK PARTIZAN BEOGRAD
v HAMMARBY IF 4-0 (0-0)

FK Partizan, Beograd 7.08.2002

Referee: Stefano Farina (ITA) Attendance: 13,914

FK PARTIZAN: Radovan Radakovic, Milivoje Cirkovic, Dragoljub Jeremic (29 Nenad Miskovic), Branko Savic, Branimir Bajic, Igor Duljaj, Zvonimir Vukic, Vladimir Ivic (78 Damir Cakar), Saša Ilic, Ivica Iliev (68 Goran Trobok), Danko Lazović. Trainer: Ljubiša Tumbaković

HAMMARBY IF: Ante Covic, Mikael Hellström, Jonas Stark, Johan Andersson, Suleyman Sleyman, Christer Fursth (61 Andreas Hermansson), Fredrik Winsnes (78 Jonas Andersson), Mikael Andersson (74 Max Von Schlebrügge), Kennedy Bakircioglü, Antti Pohja, Peter Markstedt. Trainer: Anders Linderoth

Goals: Ivic (49), Lazovic (54), Iliev (64), Ilić (75)

LILLESTRØM SK
v FK ZELJEZNICAR SARAJEVO 0-1 (0-0)

Åråsen, Lillestrøm 31.07.2002

Referee: Alon Yefet (ISR)

LILLESTRØM SK: Emille Baron, Peter Werni, Torgeir Bjarmann, Torjus Hansén, Frode Kippe, Magnus Kihlberg, Gylfi Einarsson, Gunnar Halle, Pål Strand (77 Stian Berget), Rikhardur Dadason (77 Arild Sundgot), Uwe Rösler. Trainer: Arne Erlandsen

FK ZELJEZNICAR: Kennan Hasagic, Bulend Biscevic, Edis Mulalic, Haris Alihodzic, Adin Mulaosmanovic, Denis Karic, Almir Gredic, Dalibor Silic (87 Denis Mudrinic), Sead Seferovic, Jure Guvo, Almir Cosic (74 Sanel Jahic). Trainer: Amar Osim

Goal: Gredić (49)

FK ZELJEZNICAR SARAJEVO
v LILLESTRØM SK 1-0 (0-0)

Kosevo, Sarajevo 7.08.2002

Referee: Attila Hanacsek (HUN)

FK ZELJEZNICAR: Kennan Hasagic, Bulend Biscevic, Edis Mulalic, Haris Alihodzic, Adin Mulaosmanovic, Denis Karic, Almir Gredic, Dalibor Silic (84 Sanjin Radonja), Sanel Jahic, Jure Guvo, Almir Cosic. Trainer: Amar Osim

LILLESTRØM SK: Emille Baron, Peter Werni, Torgeir Bjarmann (83 Espen Søgård), Torjus Hansén, Frode Kippe, Magnus Kihlberg, Gylfi Einarsson, Stian Berget, Pål Strand (39 Gunnar Halle), Rikhardur Dadason, Uwe Rösler (27 Arild Sundgot). Trainer: Arne Erlandsen

Goal: Biscević (90+2)

FC DYNAMO KYIV
v FC PYUNIK YEREVAN 4-0 (1-0)

"Valeri Lobanovski", Kyiv 31.07.2002

Referee: Bernhard Brugger (AUS)

DYNAMO: Vitaliy Reva, Yuriy Dmytrulin, László Bodnár, Andriy Nesmachnyi, Goran Gavrancic, Florin Lucian Cernat (81 Aleksandr Khatskevich), Georgi Ivanov Peev (60 Vasyl Kardash), Andriy Husin, Tiberiu Ghioane, Maksim Shatskikh, Olexandr Melashchenko (70 LEANDRO Machado). Trainer: Olekseiy Mykhaylychenko

FC PYUNIK: Andronik Karaguezian, Aghvan Mkrtchyan, Jose Andres Bilibio, Aleksandar Stevanovic, Alou Traoré, Vardan Minasyan (70 Arsen Meloyan), Artavazd Karamyan, Hovhannes Antonyan (46 Arkadi Chilingaryan), Miguel Cisterna, Mamadou Diawara (59 Artur Mkrchyan), Arman Karamyan. Trainer: Oskar Lopez

Sent off: Bilibio (64)

Goals: Cernat (15), Shatskikh (65), Leandro (84), Bodnár (90)

FC PYUNIK YEREVAN
v FC DYNAMO KYIV 2-2 (1-2)

Republican, Erevan 7.08.2002

Referee: Stephen Graham Bennett (ENG)

FC PYUNIK: Andronik Karaguezian, Aghvan Mkrtchyan, Alou Traoré, Arkadi Chilingaryan, Hovhannes Antonyan (90 Fernando Zagharian), Artur Mkrchyan, Vardan Minasyan, Aleksandar Stevanovic (46 Arsen Meloyan), Miguel Cisterna, Artavazd Karamyan, Arman Karamyan. Trainer: Oskar Lopez

DYNAMO: Olexandr Shovkovskyi, Goran Gavrancic (53 Olexandr Radchenko), László Bodnár, Andriy Husin, Andriy Nesmachnyi, Yuriy Dmytrulin, Olexandr Melashchenko (46 LEANDRO Machado), Tiberiu Ghioane, Maksim Shatskikh, Florin Lucian Cernat, Georgi Ivanov Peev (63 Vasyl Kardash). Trainer: Olekseiy Mykhaylychenko

Goals: Shatskikh (8), Melashchenko (28), Artavazd Karamyan (31), Arman Karamyan (57)

MACCABI HAIFA FC
v FC BELSHINA BOBRUISK 4-0 (3-0)

GSP, Nicosia 31.07.2002

Referee: Anton Stredak (SVK)

MACCABI: Nir Davidovich, Alon Harazi, Arik Benado, Adoram Keissy, Avishay Zano, Raimondas Zutautas (70 Eyal Almoshnino), Giovanni Rosso, Eric Ejiofor, Nenad Pralija, Rafi Cohen (86 Guillermo Israilevich), Yaniv Katan (76 Oluwasegun Abiodun). Trainer: Itzhak Shum

FC BELSHINA: Sergei Sinitsyn, Alexandr Sednev, Mikhail Garbachov, Viktor Kukar, Vladimir Ostrikov (46 Andrei Khrypach), Vyacheslav Gormash (46 Eduard Gradoboyev), Igor Trukhov, Valeriy Stripeikis, Denis Korolik, Alexandr Shagoiko (76 Vitali Semerykov), Viktor Malyavko. Trainer: Viachaslau Akshayeu

Goals: Cohen (19, 22), Rosso (45), Abiodun (86)

FC BELSHINA BOBRUISK
v MACCABI HAIFA FC 0-1 (0-1)

City, Borisov 7.08.2002

Referee: Emil Božinovski (MAC)

FC BELSHINA: Sergei Sinitsyn, Alexandr Sednev, Vladimir Klimovich, Eduard Boltrushevich, Viktor Kukar, Vyacheslav Gormash (46 Mikhail Garbachov), Igor Trukhov, Valeriy Stripeikis, Denis Korolik, Alexandr Shagoiko (73 Vitali Semerykov), Viktor Malyavko (65 Eduard Gradoboyev). Trainer: Viachaslau Akshayeu

MACCABI: Nir Davidovich, Raimondas Zutautas, Alon Harazi, Arik Benado, Adoram Keissy, Rafi Cohen (63 Guillermo Israilevich), Giovanni Rosso, Eric Ejiofor, Yaniv Katan, Nenad Pralija (85 Eran Levy), Walid Badier (70 Avishay Zano). Trainer: Itzhak Shum

Goal: Pralija (7 pen)

FK VARDAR SKOPJE
v WKS LEGIA WARSZAWA 1-3 (0-2)

City, Skopje 31.07.2002

Referee: Kostas Kapitanis (CYP) Attendance: 10,000

FK VARDAR: Muarem Zekir, Dragan Veselinovski, Nikola Doševski (63 Ilir Elmazovski), Aleksandar Vasovski, Saso Janev, Mile Dimov, Aguinaldo De Jesús BRAGA, Srdjan Zaharievski, Slavco Georgievski (46 Dejan Ristovski), Dimitar Spasovski, Rogerio DA COSTA Oliveira (73 Marian Petkov). Trainer: Dokica Hadzievski

WKS LEGIA: Radostin Stanev, Dariusz Dudek, Sergei Omelyanchuk, Marek Jozwiak, Wojciech Szala, Jacek Magiera, Adam Majewski (89 Sebastian Nowak), Tomasz Kielbowicz, Aleksandar Vukovic (70 Marek Citko), Cezary Kucharski, Moussa Yahaya (73 Stanko Svitlica). Trainer: Dragomir Okuka

Goals: Kucharski (3), Yahaya (37), Ristovski (63), Svitlica (89)

WKS LEGIA WARSZAWA
v FK VARDAR SKOPJE 1-1 (1-0)

Wojska Polskiego, Warszawa 7.08.2002

Referee: Dick J.H. van Egmond (HOL) Attendance: 5,600

WKS LEGIA: Radostin Stanev, Dariusz Dudek, Sergei Omelyanchuk, Wojciech Szala, Marek Jozwiak, Adam Majewski, Tomasz Kielbowicz (68 Radoslaw Wroblewski), Jacek Magiera (83 Mariusz Zganiacz), Aleksandar Vukovic, Moussa Yahaya (46 Stanko Svitlica), Cezary Kucharski. Trainer: Dragomir Okuka

FK VARDAR: Gogo Jovcev, Dragan Veselinovski, Ilir Elmazovski (83 Aleksander Radovic), Aleksandar Vasovski, Saso Janev (71 Slavco Georgievski), Mile Dimov, Srdjan Zaharievski, Dejan Ristovski, Rogerio DA COSTA Oliveira, Dragan Nacevski, Vojislav Simonovski. Trainer: Dokica Hadzievski

Goals: Kucharski (33), Da Costa (51)

CLUB BRUGGE KV
v FC DINAMO BUCUREŞTI 3-1 (2-1)

Jan Breydelstadion, Brugge 31.07.2002

Referee: Yuri Baskakov (RUS) Attendance: 10,837

CLUB BRUGGE: Dany Verlinden, Birger Maertens, Marek Spilar, Timmy Simons, Peter Van Der Heyden, Philippe Clement (72 Olivier De Cock), Gaëtan Englebert, Sergiy Serebrennikov (59 Tim Smolders), José DUARTE FILHO (84 Sandy Martens), Andrés MENDOZA Acevedo, Rune Lange. Trainer: Trond Sollied

DINAMO: Cristian Marian Munteanu, Giani Stelian Kiriţă, Bogdan Mihai Onuţ, Cornel Dănuţ Frăsineanu, Flavius Vladimir Stoican (78 Ştefan Costel Grigorie), Cristian Bolohan, Dan Alexa, Florin Pârvu, Ciprian Danciu, Claudiu Niculescu (72 Ionel Dănciulescu), Claudiu Drăgan (83 Cosmin Bărcăuan). Trainer: Cornel Dinu

Sent off: Danciu (84)

Goals: Lange (24), Alexa (43), Mendoza (44, 85)

FC DINAMO BUCUREŞTI
v CLUB BRUGGE KV 0-1 (0-1)

Cotroceni, Bucureşti 7.08.2002

Referee: Leif Sundell (SWE) Attendance: 10,000

DINAMO: Cristian Marian Munteanu, Giani Stelian Kiriţă, Bogdan Mihai Onuţ, Angelo Dumitru Alistar, Cornel Dănuţ Frăsineanu, Ştefan Costel Grigorie (55 Cosmin Bărcăuan), Cristian Bolohan, Dan Alexa, Iulian Tameş, Claudiu Niculescu (46 Florentin Petre), Claudiu Drăgan (25 Ionel Dănciulescu). Trainer: Cornel Dinu

CLUB BRUGGE: Dany Verlinden, Birger Maertens, Marek Spilar, Timmy Simons, Peter Van Der Heyden (88 Bratislav Ristic), Philippe Clement, Gaëtan Englebert, Sergiy Serebrennikov, José DUARTE FILHO (70 Ebrima Sillah), Andrés MENDOZA Acevedo (55 Olivier De Cock), Rune Lange. Trainer: Trond Sollied

Goal: Lange (20)

NK MARIBOR BRANIK
v APOEL NICOSIA FC 2-1 (1-0)

Ljudski vrt, Maribor 31.07.2002

Referee: Grzegorz Gilewski (POL)

NK MARIBOR: Tomasz Murko, Fabijan Cipot, Muamer Vugdalic, Suad Filekovic, Miha Pitamic, Stipe Balajic, Samir Duro, Dejan Djuranovic, Danijel Brezic (63 Djordje Indjic), Ermin Rakovic (77 Damir Pekic), Nemanja Corovic. Trainer: Bojan Prašnikar

APOEL: Mihalis Morfis, Dimitris Daskalakis, Zaharin Sirakov, Stavros Georgiou, Marinos Ouzounidis, Stelios Okkarides, Romik Khachatryan, Marinos Satsias (73 Marios Ilia), Marios Agathocleous, Costas Malekkos (79 Zaharias Haralambous), Costas Haralambides. Trainer: Euge Gerards

Goals: Corovic (45, 64), Sirakov (90)

APOEL NICOSIA FC v NK MARIBOR BRANIK **4-2** (2-1)

GSP, Nicosia 7.08.2002

Referee: Olegario Manuel BARTOLO F. BENQUERENÇA (POR)
Attendance: 10,564

APOEL: Mihalis Morfis, Marios Ilia, Stelios Okkarides, Marinos Ouzounidis, Romik Khachatryan, Kostas Malekkos (90 Nektarios Alexandrou), Marios Agathocleous, Stavros Georgiou (68 Barnabas Sztipanovics), Marinos Satsias, Dimitris Daskalakis, Costas Haralambides (86 Petros Petrou). Trainer: Euge Gerards

NK MARIBOR: Tomasz Murko, Stipe Balajic, Marinko Sarkezi (65 Damir Pekic), Fabijan Cipot, Samir Duro, Dalibor Teinovic, Suad Filekovic, Dejan Djuranovic (56 Djordje Indjic), Danijel Brezic (76 Miha Pitamic), Ermin Rakovic, Nemanja Corovic. Trainer: Bojan Prašnikar

Sent off: Agathocleous (38)

Goals: Duro (31 pen, 81), Malekkos (33 pen), Ilia (44), Haralambides (56), Daskalakis (69)

BRØNDBY IF v KS DINAMO TIRANË **1-0** (0-0)

Brøndby Stadion, København 31.07.2002

Referee: Alexandru Dan Tudor (ROM)

BRØNDBY IF: Mogens Krogh, Allan Arenfeldt Olesen (77 Dan Anton Johansen), Aurelius Skarbalijus, Morten Weighorst, Per Nielsen, Kim Daugaard, Thomas Kallenberg (67 Mads Jørgensen), Thomas Lindrup, Peter Madsen, Mattias Jonsson (62 Ruben Bagger), Kasper Dalgas.
Trainer: Michael Laudrup

DINAMO: Ilion Lika, Alpin Gallo, Luan Pinari, Julian Ahmataj, Arian Pisha, Ligor Tiko (46 Daniel Xhafaj), Ergert Bakalli, Ilir Qorri (83 Klodian Asllani), Serhiy Romanishin, Rigels Qosa, Redi Jupi (90+6 Artian Poci).
Trainer: Faruk Sejdini

Goal: Bagger (90+6)

SK DINAMO TIRANË v BRØNDBY IF **0-4** (0-0)

Qemal Stafa, Tirana 7.08.2002

Referee: Giorgos Kaznaferis (GRE)

DINAMO: Ilion Lika, Alpin Gallo, Luan Pinari (74 Artian Poci), Julian Ahmataj, Arian Pisha, Klodian Asllani, Ergert Bakalli, Ilir Qorri (46 Daniel Xhafaj), Serhiy Romanishin (85 Artim Polozani), Rigels Qosa, Redi Jupi.
Trainer: Faruk Sejdini

BRØNDBY IF: Mogens Krogh, Allan Arenfeldt Olesen, Aurelius Skarbalijus, Morten Weighorst (60 Kim Daugaard), Allan Ravn Jensen, Per Nielsen, Thomas Kallenberg, Peter Madsen (70 Rafal Niznik), Mattias Jonsson, Ruben Bagger, Kasper Dalgas (60 Mads Jørgensen).
Trainer: Michael Laudrup

Goals: Madsen (47), Bagger (50, 87), Skarbalijus (89 pen)

FC SHERIFF TIRASPOL v GRAZER AK **1-4** (0-2)

Sheriff, Tiraspol 31.07.2002

Referee: Nicolai Vollquartz (DEN)

FC SHERIFF: Alexandru Chirilov, Vaja Tarhnishvili, Chidi Odiah, Iuriy Priganiuc (46 Cristian Dorin Tudor), Marius Ciubăncan, Ion Testimiţanu, Stanislav Ivanov, Sorin Botiş, Victor Comlionoc, Evgheny Patula, Andriy Nesteruk (81 Roberto Brown). Trainer: Gavril Pele Balint

GRAZER AK: Franz Almer, Gregor Pötscher, Richard Hastings, Mario Tokic, Dieter Ramusch, Ales Ceh (90 Peter Halmosi), Boban Dmitrovic, René Aufhauser, Jones Kusi-Asare (62 Roland Kollmann), Ronald Brunmayr, Mario Bazina (86 Gernot Sick). Trainer: Thijs Libregts

Goals: Bazina (3, 50), Aufhauser (45), Tarhnishvili (51 pen), Hastings (71)

GRAZER AK v FC SHERIFF TIRASPOL **2-0** (0-0)

Arnold Schwarzenegger, Graz 7.08.2002

Referee: Edo Trivković (CRO)

GRAZER AK: Franz Almer, Gregor Pötscher, Mario Tokic, Dieter Ramusch, Ales Ceh, Boban Dmitrovic (50 Jürgen Hartmann), Jones Kusi-Asare, Ronald Brunmayr (65 Ilco Naumoski), René Aufhauser (58 Stefán Gíslason), Mario Bazina, Peter Halmosi. Trainer: Thijs Libregts

FC SHERIFF: Alexandru Chirilov, Chidi Odiah, Vaja Tarhnishvili, Ion Testimiţanu, Stanislav Ivanov, Iuriy Priganiuc, Victor Comlionoc, Marius Ciubăncan, Cristian Dorin Tudor (66 Ruslan Barburoş), Evgheny Patula, Andriy Nesteruk (84 Alberto Blanco). Trainer: Gavril Pele Balint

Goals: Pötscher (58), Bazina (88)

ZALAEGERSZEGI TE v NK ZAGREB **1-0** (1-0)

Ferencváros, Budapest 31.07.2002

Referee: Paul Allaerts (BEL)

ZALAEGERSZEGI TE: Saša Ilic, Gergely Kocsardi, Tamás Szamosi, Flórián Úrban, Zsolt Csóka, Radoslav Kral, Ferenc Babati, Darko Ljubojevic (83 Béla Koplárovics), Ottó Vincze, Gábor Egressy (64 Csaba Balog), Krisztián Kenesei (78 Radu Sabo). Trainer: Péter Bozsik

NK ZAGREB: Vladimir Vasilj, Marijo Osibov, Vedran Jese, Darko Vukic (55 Emir Spahic), Damir Milinovic, Ibrahim Duro (53 Dalibor Poldrugac), Admir Hasancic (69 Krunoslav Lovrek), Predrag Simic, Ivan Milas, Jasmin Samardzic, Petar Krpan. Trainer: Ivan Katalinić

Goal: Ljubojević (17)

NK ZAGREB v ZALAEGERSZEGI TE 2-1 (2-0)

Maksimir, Zagreb 7.08.2002

Referee: Alfonso PÉREZ BURRULL (SPA)

NK ZAGREB: Vladimir Vasilj, Dalibor Poldrugac, Marijo Osibov, Vedran Jese, Damir Milinovic, Domagoj Verhas, Admir Hasancic (68 Hrvoje Strok), Krunoslav Lovrek, Ivan Milas, Jasmin Samardzic (59 Darko Vukic), Petar Krpan (83 Radomir Dalovic). Trainer: Ivan Katalinić

ZALAEGERSZEGI TE: Saša Ilic, Gergely Kocsardi, Tamás Szamosi, Flórián Úrban, Zsolt Csóka, Ferenc Babati (66 Radu Sabo), Darko Ljubojevic, Ottó Vincze, Gábor Egressy, Csaba Balog (86 Igor Budisa), Krisztián Kenesei.
Trainer: Péter Bozsik **Sent off**: Kocsardi (81)

Goals: Milinovic (2), Lovrek (28), Úrban (88 pen)

BOAVISTA FC PORTO v HIBERNIANS FC PAOLA 4-0 (3-0)

Do Bessa, Porto 31.07.2002

Referee: Tomasz Mikulski (POL)

BOAVISTA: RICARDO Alexandre Martins Soares Pereira, RUI OSCAR Neves de Sousa Viana, Fernando Horácio ÁVALOS, ÉDER Guterres Silveira, Luís JORGE Pinto da SILVA, Carlos Alberto Eduardo Ventura "DUDA", Elpidio Pereira da SILVA Filho (59 LUIZ CLAUDIO Soares de Barros), MÁRIO Jorge Amora LOJA, JOCIVALTER Liberato (81 PEDRO Jorge SANTOS dos Santos), Arlindo Gomes Semedo "CAFU" (62 José BOSINGWA Silva), ALEXANDRE Luís GOULART.
Trainer: Jaime MOREIRA PACHECO

HIBERNIANS: Mario Muscat, Branko Nisevic, Silvio Vella, Aaron Xuereb, Adrian Ciantar, Essien Mbong, Adrian Mifsud (52 Antoine Zahra), Ndubisi Chukunyere, Peter Pullicino (46 Kevin Cassar), Adrian Pulis, Roderick Baldacchino (81 Miguel Mifsud). Trainer: Robert Gatt

Goals: Silva (16 pen, 29), Alexandre Goulart (17), Ávalos (89)

HIBERNIANS FC PAOLA v BOAVISTA FC PORTO 3-3 (1-3)

National, Ta'Qali 7.08.2002

Referee: Kristinn Jakobsson (ICE)

HIBERNIANS: Mario Muscat, Adrian Mifsud (90 Terence Scerri), Branko Nisevic, Silvio Vella (65 Kevin Cassar), Aaron Xuereb, Adrian Ciantar, Essien Mbong, Ndubisi Chukunyere, Antoine Zahra (86 Peter Pullicino), Adrian Pulis, Roderick Baldacchino. Trainer: Robert Gatt

BOAVISTA: RICARDO Alexandre Martins Soares Pereira, RUI OSCAR Neves de Sousa Viana, Fernando Horácio ÁVALOS, PAOLO César TURRA, ÉDER Guterres Silveira, Carlos Alberto Eduardo Ventura "DUDA" (66 Joaquim Pereira da Silva "MARTELINHO"), Elisérgio da Silva "SERGINHO", MÁRIO Jorge Amora LOJA, JOCIVALTER Liberato (57 José BOSINGWA Silva), LUIZ CLAUDIO Soares de Barros (57 Arlindo Gomes Semedo "CAFU"), ALEXANDRE Luís GOULART. Trainer: Jaime MOREIRA PACHECO

Goals: Jocivalter (29), Mifsud (32, 55 pen), Luiz Claudio (38), Turra (40), Chukunyere (52)

THIRD QUALIFYING ROUND

MACCABI HAIFA FC v SK STURM GRAZ 2-0 (1-0)

Balgarska Armia, Sofia 13.08.2002

Referee: Graham Barber (ENG)

MACCABI: Dudu Awat, Raimondas Zutautas, Alon Harazi, Arik Benado, Adoram Keissy, Giovanni Rosso, Eric Ejiofor, Yaniv Katan (73 Rafi Cohen), Nenad Pralija, Walid Badier (76 Avishay Zano), Yakubu Ayegbeni. Trainer: Itzhak Shum

SK STURM: Richard Wemmer, Günther Neukirchner, Francisco Ulise Rojas, Anto Petrovic, Gerald Strafner, Alain Masudi, Ekrem Dag, Jerzy Brzeczek, Arnold Wetl (66 Roman Mählich), Mario Haas, Charles Amoah (73 Imre Szabics).
Trainer: Ivan Osim

Goals: Ayegbeni (17, 90+3)

SK STURM GRAZ v MACCABI HAIFA FC 3-3 (1-1)

Arnold Schwarzenegger, Graz 28.08.2002

Referee: Alain Hamer (LUX)

SK STURM: Heinz Weber, Didier Angan, Eddy Bosnar, Günther Neukirchner, Francisco Ulise Rojas (46 Arnold Wetl), Gerald Strafner, Alain Masudi, Ekrem Dag, Roman Mählich (60 Horst Heldt), Charles Amoah (46 Martin Pregelj), Imre Szabics. Trainer: Ivan Osim

MACCABI: Dudu Awat, Raimondas Zutautas, Alon Harazi, Arik Benado, Adoram Keissy, Giovanni Rosso, Eric Ejiofor, Yaniv Katan (59 Avishay Zano), Nenad Pralija, Walid Badier, Yakubu Ayegbeni. Trainer: Itzhak Shum

Sent off: Pregelj (90+2), Bosnar (90) and Ayegbeni (69)

Goals: Bosnar (11), Rosso (26), Szabics (58), Neukirchner (71), Keissy (78), Badier (90)

KRC GENK v AC SPARTA PRAHA 2-0 (2-0)

Fenix, Genk 13.08.2002

Referee: Kim Milton Nielsen (DEN) Attendance: 9,969

KRC GENK: Jan Moons, Soley Seyfo, Didier Zokora, Akram Roumani, Kevin Vanbeuren, Koen Daerden, Josip Skoko, Bernd Thijs, Mirsad Beslija (75 Takayuri Suzuki), Wesley Sonck, Beli-Moumouni Dagano (90+1 Marco Ingrao).
Trainer: Sef Vergoosen

SPARTA: Michal Spit, Zdenek Grygera, Jan Flachbart, Tomáš Hubschman, Jiri Novotny, Karel Poborsky, Lukáš Zelenka, Jiri Jarosik, Libor Sionko (82 Rastislav Michalik), Michal Pospisil (65 Tomáš Jun), Miroslav Baranek (46 Peter Babnic).
Trainer: Jozef Jarabinský

Goals: Thijs (33), Beslija (40)

AC SPARTA PRAHA v KRC GENK 4-2 (0-1)

Letná, Praha 27.08.2002

Referee: Kyros Vassaras (GRE) Attendance: 12,856

SPARTA: Michal Spit, Zdenek Grygera, Pavel Mares, Tomáš Hubschman, Jiri Novotny, Karel Poborsky, Lukáš Zelenka, Jiri Jarosik, Libor Sionko, Michal Pospisil (83 Peter Babnic), Miroslav Baranek (46 Marek Kincl).
Trainer: Jozef Jarabinský

KRC GENK: Jan Moons, Soley Seyfo, Didier Zokora, Akram Roumani, Kevin Vanbeuren (63 Justice Wamfor), Koen Daerden, Josip Skoko, Bernd Thijs, Mirsad Beslija (81 Takayuri Suzuki), Wesley Sonck, Beli-Moumouni Dagano (70 Igor Tomasic). Trainer: Sef Vergoosen

Goals: Dagano (25), Poborsky (56), Sonck (57), Jarosik (58, 64), Mares (84)

APOEL NICOSIA FC v AEK FC ATHINA 2-3 (1-1)

GSP, Nicosia 13.08.2002

Referee: Eric Poulat (FRA) Attendance: 16,192

APOEL: Mihalis Morfis, Marios Ilia, Stelios Okkarides, Marinos Ouzounidis, Romik Khachatryan (82 Petros Petrou), Costas Malekkos, Stavros Georgiou, Marinos Satsias, Dimitris Daskalakis, Costas Haralambides (57 Barnabas Sztipanovics), Petros Petrou (70 Nektarios Alexandrou).
Trainer: Euge Gerards

AEK: Dionisis Hiotis, Vasilis Borbokis, Mihalis Kasapis, Mauricio Wright, Vasilis Lakis (70 Nikos Kostenoglou), Theodoros Zagorakis, Hristos Maladenis, Michel Kreek, Vasilis Tsartas (86 Walter Centeno), Themistoklis Nikolaidis, Grigoris Georgatos (72 Konstantinos Katsouranis).
Trainer: Dusko Bajević

Goals: Ouzounidis (23), Borbikis (44, 47), Malekkos (90 pen), Nikolaidis (90+3)

FEYENOORD ROTTERDAM v FENERBAHÇE SK ISTANBUL 1-0 (0-0)

Feyenoord, Rotterdam 13.08.2002

Referee: Stéphane Bré (FRA) Attendance: 28,500

FEYENOORD: Edwin Zoetebier, Christian Gyan, Kees Van Wonderen, Patrick Paauwe, Tomasz Rzasa (46 Ramon Van Haaren), Brett Emerton, Paul Bosvelt, Shinji Ono, Bonaventure Kalou, Pierre Van Hooijdonk, Anthony Lurling (59 LEONARDO dos Santos Silva). Trainer: Bert van Marwyk

FENERBAHÇE: Rüstü Reçber, Zoran Mirkovic, Fatih Akyel, Ümit Özat, Mustafa Dogan, Milan Rapaic (74 Ariel Ortega), Miroslav Stevic, Ogün Temizkanoglu, Samuel Johnson (86 Abdullah Ercan), Michael Haim Revivo, WASHINGTON Stecanela Cerqueira (71 Serhat Akin).
Trainer: Werner Lorant

Goal: Ono (64)

AEK FC ATHINA v APOEL NICOSIA FC 1-0 (0-0)

Nikos Gkoumas, Athina 28.08.2002

Referee: Claus Bo Larsen (DEN) Attendance: 9,204

AEK: Dionisis Hiotis, Mihalis Kasapis, Mauricio Wright, Mihalis Kapsis, Vasilis Lakis (82 Milen Petkov), Theodoros Zagorakis, Konstantinos Katsouranis, Vasilis Tsartas, Themistoklis Nikolaidis, Grigoris Georgatos, Sotiris Konstantinidis (54 Ilija Ivic). Trainer: Dusko Bajević

APOEL: Mihalis Morfis, Zaharin Sirakov (46 Nektarios Alexandrou), Marios Ilia (72 Zaharias Haralambous), Stelios Okkarides, Romik Khachatryan, Costas Malekkos, Stavros Georgiou, Marinos Satsias, Dimitris Daskalakis, Costas Haralambides, Marios Agathocleous (59 Orosco Anonam).
Trainer: Euge Gerards

Goal: Wright (58)

FENERBAHÇE SK ISTANBUL v FEYENOORD ROTTERDAM 0-2 (0-0)

Şükrü Saraçoglu, Istanbul 27.08.2002

Referee: Markus Merk (GER) Attendance: 39,705

FENERBAHÇE: Rüstü Reçber, Fatih Akyel, Ogün Temizkanoglu, Mustafa Dogan, Abdullah Ercan, Ariel Ortega, Zoran Mirkovic (53 Oktay Derelioglu), Michael Haim Revivo, Miroslav Stevic, WASHINGTON Stecanela Cerqueira (63 Milan Rapaic), Serhat Akin. Trainer: Werner Lorant

FEYENOORD: Edwin Zoetebier, Christian Gyan, Kees Van Wonderen, Patrick Paauwe, Tomasz Rzasa, Brett Emerton, Paul Bosvelt, Shinji Ono, Anthony Lurling (77 Thomas Buffel), Pierre Van Hooijdonk, Bonaventure Kalou.
Trainer: Bert van Marwyk

Goals: Ono (48), Buffel (88)

BOAVISTA FC PORTO v AJ AUXERRE 0-1 (0-0)

Do Bessa, Porto 13.08.2002

Referee: Valentin Ivanov (RUS) Attendance: 8,000

BOAVISTA: RICARDO Alexandre Martins Soares Pereira, PAOLO César TURRA, ÉDER Guterres Silveira, Luís JORGE Pinto da SILVA, Elpidio Pereira da SILVA Filho (63 LUIZ CLAUDIO Soares de Barros), António Dioclécio Alves da Silva "ICO", Joaquim Pereira da Silva "MARTELINHO" (69 Elisérgio da Silva "SERGINHO"), José BOSINGWA Silva, MÁRIO Jorge Amora LOJA, ALEXANDRE Luís GOULART, Erwin SÁNCHEZ Freking (46 Carlos Alberto Eduardo Ventura "DUDA"). Trainer: Jaime MOREIRA PACHECO

AUXERRE: Fabien Cool, Johan Radet, Jean-Sébastien Jaures, Jean-Alain BOUMSONG Somko, Philippe Mexes, Yann Lachuer, Djibril Cissé (79 BENJAMIN Mwaruwari), Teemu Tainio (72 Amdy Mustapha Faye), Khalilou Fadiga, Lionel Mathis, Aranud Gonzalez. Trainer: Guy Roux

Goal: Cissé (71)

AJ AUXERRE v BOAVISTA FC PORTO 0-0

Abbé Deschamps, Auxerre 28.08.2002

Referee: Pierluigi Collina (ITA) Attendance: 14,500

AUXERRE: Fabien Cool, Johan Radet, Jean-Sébastien Jaures, Jean-Alain BOUMSONG Somko, Philippe Mexes, Amdy Mustapha Faye, Yann Lachuer, Djibril Cissé, Khalilou Fadiga, Lionel Mathis (78 Teemu Tainio), Narcisse Olivier KAPO Obou. Trainer: Guy Roux

BOAVISTA: RICARDO Alexandre Martins Soares Pereira, PAOLO César TURRA (72 SANÃ Fadeira), ÉDER Guterres Silveira, Luís JORGE Pinto da SILVA, MÁRIO Jorge Amora LOJA, António Dioclécio Alves da Silva «ICO», José BOSINGWA Silva, PEDRO Jorge SANTOS dos Santos (57 ALEXANDRE Luís GOULART), Carlos Alberto Eduardo Ventura «DUDA», JORGE António Pinto do COUTO (46 Joaquim Pereira da Silva «MARTELINHO»), LUIZ CLAUDIO Soares de Barros. Trainer: Jaime MOREIRA PACHECO

FC SHAKHTAR DONETSK v CLUB BRUGGE KV 1-1 (0-0)

Shakhtyor, Donetsk 14.08.2002

Referee: Herbert Fandel (GER) Attendance: 27,982

FC SHAKHTAR: Wojciech Kowalewski, Mykhailo Starostyak, Anatoliy Tymoshchuk, Serhiy Popov (76 Mariusz Lewandowski), Assane Ndiaye (59 Oscar DAMIÁN Rodríguez), Hennadiy Zubov (84 BRANDÃO), Olexiy Gay, Isaak Okoronkwo, Daniel Florea, Andriy Vorobei, Julius Aghahowa. Trainer: Nevio Scala

CLUB BRUGGE: Dany Verlinden, Birger Maertens, Marek Spilar, Timmy Simons, Peter Van Der Heyden, Philippe Clement (67 Olivier De Cock), Gaëtan Englebert, Sergiy Serebrennikov, José DUARTE FILHO (81 Sandy Martens), Andrés MENDOZA Acevedo, Rune Lange (81 Bratislav Ristic). Trainer: Trond Sollied **Sent off**: van der Heyden (79)

Goals: Aghahowa (47), Simons (86 pen)

CLUB BRUGGE KV v FC SHAKHTAR DONETSK 1-1 (0-1, 1-1) (AET)

Jan Breydelstadion, Brugge 28.08.2002

Referee: Terje Hauge (NOR) Attendance: 17,463

CLUB BRUGGE: Dany Verlinden, Birger Maertens, Marek Spilar, Timmy Simons, Olivier De Cock, Gaëtan Englebert, Gert Verheyen (63 Tim Smolders), Sergiy Serebrennikov (69 Nastja Ceh), Andrés MENDOZA Acevedo (109 Sandy Martens), Rune Lange, Bratislav Ristic.
Trainer: Trond Sollied

FC SHAKHTAR: Wojciech Kowalewski, Mykhailo Starostyak, Anatoliy Tymoshchuk, Serhiy Popov (46 Mariusz Lewandowski), Assane Ndiaye, Olexiy Gay (91 Hennadiy Zubov), Isaak Okoronkwo, Daniel Florea, Andriy Vorobei, Julius Aghahowa, Olexiy Bielik (71 Oleg Pestriakov).
Trainer: Nevio Scala

Goals: Vorobei (13), Ceh (75)

Penalties: 1-0 Maertens, Pestriakov (miss), 2-0 De Cock, Vorobei (miss), 3-0 Simons, 3-1 Lewandowski, 4-1 Lange

CELTIC FC GLASGOW v FC BASEL 3-1 (1-1)

Celtic Park, Glasgow 14.08.2002

Referee: Manuel Enrique MEJUTO GONZALEZ (SPA)
Attendance: 49,200

CELTIC: Robert Douglas, Joos Valgaeren, Dianbobo Balde, Johan Mjällby, Paul Lambert (77 Jackie Mcnamara), Bobby Petta (56 Steve Guppy), Stilian Petrov, Mohamed Sylla, Henrik Larsson, Chris Sutton, Neil Lennon. Trainer: Martin O'Neill

FC BASEL: Pascal Zuberbühler, Grégory Duruz, Marco Zwyssig (41 Alexandre Quennoz), Antonio Esposito, Murat Yakin, Ivan Ergic (59 Carlos Varela), Christian Gimenez, Mario Cantaluppi, Sébastien Barberis, Julio Hernán Rossi (67 Hervé Tum), Hakan Yakin. Trainer: Christian Gross

Goals: Gimenez (2), Larsson (3 pen), Sutton (52), Sylla (88)

FC BASEL v CELTIC FC GLASGOW 2-0 (2-0)

Saint Jakob, Basel 28.08.2002

Referee: Anders Frisk (SWE) Attendance: 30,510

FC BASEL: Pascal Zuberbühler, Grégory Duruz, Alexandre Quennoz, Murat Yakin, Ivan Ergic, Carlos Varela (60 Philipp Degen), Christian Gimenez (85 George Koumantarakis), Mario Cantaluppi, Sébastien Barberis, Julio Hernán Rossi (70 Hervé Tum), Hakan Yakin. Trainer: Christian Gross

CELTIC: Robert Douglas, Joos Valgaeren, Dianbobo Balde, Ulrik Laursen (46 Steve Guppy), Johan Mjällby, Paul Lambert (46 Didier Agathé), Stilian Petrov, Mohamed Sylla (70 John Hartson), Henrik Larsson, Chris Sutton, Neil Lennon.
Trainer: Martin O'Neill

Goals: Gimenez (9), M. Yakin (22)

FK ZELJEZNICAR SARAJEVO v NEWCASTLE UNITED FC 0-1 (0-0)

Kosevo, Sarajevo 14.08.2002

Referee: L'uboš Michel (SVK) Attendance: 28,500

FK ZELJEZNICAR: Kennan Hasagić, Edis Mulalić, Haris Alihodzić, Adin Mulaosmanović, Denis Karić, Almir Gredić, Sead Seferović, Sanjin Mesić (81 Denis Mudrinić), Sanel Jahić (71 Mirzet Alagić), Jure Guvo, Almir Cosić (88 Sanjin Radonja). Trainer: Amar Osim

NEWCASTLE UNITED: Shay Given, Aaron Hughes, Titus Bramble, Nikos Dabizas (88 Robbie Elliott), Olivier Bernard, HUGO Miguel Ferreira VIANA (88 Wayne Quinn), Norberto Solano, Jermaine Jenas, Kieron Dyer, Alan Shearer, Lomana Tresor LUA v LUA (81 Shola Ameobi).
Trainer: Robert Robson

Goal: Dyer (56)

NEWCASTLE UNITED FC v FK ZELJEZNICAR SARAJEVO 4-0 (2-0)

Saint James' Park, Newcastle 28.08.2002

Referee: Frank de Bleeckere (BEL) Attendance: 34,067

NEWCASTLE UNITED: Shay Given, Aaron Hughes, Titus Bramble, Nikos Dabizas (71 Andy O'Brien), Olivier Bernard, HUGO Miguel Ferreira VIANA, Norberto Solano (75 Brian Kerr), Gary Speed, Kieron Dyer, Alan Shearer, Lomana Tresor LUA v LUA (51 Shola Ameobi). Trainer: Robert Robson

FK ZELJEZNICAR: Kennan Hasagić, Bulend Biscević, Edis Mulalić, Haris Alihodzić, Adin Mulaosmanović, Denis Karić (63 Sergej Tica), Sanjin Radonja, Sead Seferović, Sanel Jahić, Jure Guvo (46 Mirzet Alagić), Almir Cosić (75 Denis Mudrinić). Trainer: Amar Osim

Sent off: Jahić (69)

Goals: Dyer (23), Lua-Lua (37), Hugo Viana (74), Shearer (80)

FK PARTIZAN BEOGRAD v FC BAYERN MÜNCHEN 0-3 (0-1)

FK Partizan, Beograd 14.08.2002

Referee: Stuart Dougal (SCO) Attendance: 29,000

FK PARTIZAN: Radovan Radakovic, Dragoljub Jeremic, Branko Savic, Branimir Bajic, Igor Duljaj, Goran Trobok, Zvonimir Vukic, Vladimir Ivic (79 Dejan Rusmir), Saša Ilic (71 Damir Cakar), Danko Lazovic, Ivica Iliev. Trainer: Ljubiša Tumbaković

BAYERN: Oliver Kahn, Willy Sagnol, Robert Kovac, Thomas Linke, Michael Tarnat, Mehmet Scholl, Michael Ballack (79 Pablo Thiam), Jens Jeremies, Owen Hargreaves (82 Markus Feulner), Giovane Élber (71 ZÉ ROBERTO da Silva), Claudio Pizarro. Trainer: Ottmar Hitzfeld

Sent off: Duljaj (75)

Goals: Tarnat (21), Jeremies (70), Pizarro (77)

FC BAYERN MÜNCHEN v FK PARTIZAN BEOGRAD 3-1 (1-0)

Olympiastadion, München 27.08.2002

Referee: Claude Colombo (FRA) Attendance: 66,814

BAYERN: Oliver Kahn, Bixente Lizarazu (76 Michael Tarnat), Samuel Osei Kuffour, Thomas Linke, Hasan Salihamidzic (79 Markus Feulner), Michael Ballack, Jens Jeremies (76 Thorsten Fink), Owen Hargreaves, ZÉ ROBERTO da Silva, Giovane Élber, Claudio Pizarro. Trainer: Ottmar Hitzfeld

FK PARTIZAN: Radovan Radakovic, Branko Savic, Branimir Bajic), Milivoje Cirkovic, Nenad Miskovic, Goran Trobok, Zvonimir Vukic (63 Damir Cakar), Vladimir Ivic (73 Dejan Rusmir), Saša Ilic, Danko Lazovic, Ivica Iliev (76 Andrija Delibasic). Trainer: Ljubiša Tumbaković

Goals: Ballack (26), Élber (71), Cakar (72), Salihamidzic (73 pen)

AC MILAN v FC SLOVAN LIBEREC 1-0 (0-0)

Giuseppe Meazza, Milano 14.08.2002

Referee: Konrad Plautz (AUS) Attendance: 30,064

AC MILAN: Christian Abbiati (46 Nélson de Jesus Silva "DIDA"), Cosmin Contra, José Vitor ROQUE JUNIOR (25 Martin Laursen), Paolo Maldini, Kakha Kaladze, Gennaro Gattuso, Massimo Ambrosini, RUI Manuel César COSTA, Sérgio Cláudio dos Santos "SERGINHO" (60 Clarence Seedorf), Andriy Shevchenko, Filippo Inzaghi. Trainer: Carlo Ancelotti

FC SLOVAN: Zbynek Hauzr, Bohuslav Pilny, Petr Johana, Miroslav Holenák, Tomáš Janu, Pavel Capek (69 Petr Papousek), David Langer, Ivan Hodúr, Miroslav Slepicka (90 Juraj Ancic), Martin Zboncák, Jan Nezmar (83 Lubomir Blaha). Trainer: Ladislav Škorpil

Goal: Inzaghi (68)

FC SLOVAN LIBEREC v AC MILAN 2-1 (0-1)

FC Slovan, Liberec 28.08.2002

Referee: Arturo DAUDEN IBAÑEZ (SPA) Att: 8,740

FC SLOVAN: Antonin Kinsky, Bohuslav Pilny, Petr Johana, Miroslav Holenák, Tomáš Janu, Petr Papousek, David Langer, Ivan Hodúr (77 Lubomir Blaha), Miroslav Slepicka, Martin Zboncák (65 Juraj Ancic), Jan Nezmar (46 Baffour Gyan). Trainer: Ladislav Škorpil

AC MILAN: Nélson de Jesus Silva "DIDA", Dario Simic, Martin Laursen, Paolo Maldini, Kakha Kaladze, Andrea Pirlo (82 Samuele Dalla Bona), Gennaro Gattuso, RUI Manuel César COSTA (70 "RIVALDO" Vítor Barbosa Ferreira), Clarence Seedorf, Jon Dahl Tomasson (60 Massimo Ambrosini), Filippo Inzaghi. Trainer: Carlo Ancelotti

Sent off: Langer (90+2)

Goals: Inzaghi (20), Slepicka (47), Langer (87)

FC LEVSKI SOFIA v FC DYNAMO KYIV 0-1 (0-0)

Georgi Asparuhov, Sofia 14.08.2002

Referee: Massimo de Santis (ITA) Attendance: 18,000

FC LEVSKI: Dimitar Ivankov, Garba Lawal, Danail Bachkov, Saša Simonovic, Stanimir Stoilov, Biser Ivanov (64 Marcelo Vieira), Konstantin Golovskoy, Elin Topuzakov (36 Dalibor Dragic), Ilian Stoianov, Georgi Chilikov, Miodrag Pantelic (78 Todor Kolev). Trainer: Slavoljub Muslin

DYNAMO: Vitaliy Reva, Yuriy Dmytrulin, Olexandr Radchenko, László Bodnár, Goran Gavrancic, Aleksandr Khatskevich, Florin Lucian Cernat, Tiberiu Ghioane, Olexandr Melashchenko, Georgi Ivanov Peev (76 Igor Skoba), Maksim Shatskikh. Trainer: Oleksеiy Mykhaylychenko

Goal: Cernat (60)

FC DYNAMO KYIV v FC LEVSKI SOFIA 1-0 (1-0)

Valeri Lobanovskiy, Kyiv 28.08.2002

Referee: Graham Poll (ENG) Attendance: 16,863

DYNAMO: Vitaliy Reva, Andriy Nesmachnyi, Goran Sablic, Yuriy Dmytrulin, Olexandr Radchenko, Aleksandr Khatskevich, Badr El Kaddouri, Florin Lucian Cernat (90 Olexandr Melashchenko), Tiberiu Ghioane, Georgi Ivanov Peev (72 Andriy Husin), Maksim Shatskikh.
Trainer: Olekseiy Mykhaylychenko

FC LEVSKI: Dimitar Ivankov, Ilian Stoianov, Georgi Markov, Stanislav Angelov (76 Todor Kolev), Garba Lawal, Saša Simonovic, Stanimir Stoilov, Konstantin Golovskoy, Marcelo Vieira, Georgi Chilikov, Miodrag Pantelic (72 Dimitar Telkiyski). Trainer: Slavoljub Muslin

Goal: Cernat (42)

GRAZER AK v FC LOKOMOTIV MOSKVA 0-2 (0-2)

Arnold Schwarzenegger, Graz 14.08.2002

Referee: Alain Sars (FRA) Attendance: 5,271

GRAZER AK: Andreas Schranz (46 Franz Almer), Gregor Pötscher, Mario Tokic, Dieter Ramusch, Nikola Milinkovic, Martin Amerhauser (69 Peter Halmosi), Jürgen Hartmann, Ronald Brunmayr, René Aufhauser, Mario Bazina, Roland Kollmann (76 Ilco Naumoski). Trainer: Thijs Libregts

LOKOMOTIV: Sergey Ovchinnikov, Gennady Nizhegorodov, Yuri Drozdov, Jacob Lekcetho, Sergey Ignashevich, Vladimir Maminov, Dmitry Loskov, Oleg Pashinin, Maksim Buznikin (75 Nemanja Vucicevic), Vadim Evseyev (54 Dmitri Sennikov), Ruslan Pimenov (80 JULIO CESAR da Silva e Souza).
Trainer: Yuri Semin

Goals: Lekcetho (6), Loskov (42)

FC LOKOMOTIV MOSKVA v GRAZER AK 3-3 (3-1)

Lokomotiv, Moskva 28.08.2002

Referee: Jan W. Wegereef (HOL) Attendance: 13,400

LOKOMOTIV: Sergey Ovchinnikov, Gennady Nizhegorodov, Jacob Lekcetho, Sergey Ignashevich, Vladimir Maminov, Dmitriy Loskov (46 Nemanja Vucicevic, 65 Yuri Drozdov), Oleg Pashinin, Maksim Buznikin, Vadim Evseyev, JULIO CESAR da Silva e Souza, Narvik Sirkhayev.
Trainer: Yuri Semin

GRAZER AK: Franz Almer, Anton Ehmann, Mario Tokic, René Aufhauser, Ales Ceh, Boban Dmitrovic, Dieter Ramusch, Jürgen Hartmann (52 Peter Halmosi), Ronald Brunmayr, Mario Bazina, Ilco Naumoski. Trainer: Thijs Libregts

Goals: Ignashevich (6), Evseyev (32), Naumoski (38), Julio Cesar (45), Bazina (48), Aufhauser (63)

ZALAEGERSZEGI TE v MANCHESTER UNITED FC 1-0 (0-0)

"Ferénc Puskas", Budapest 14.08.2002

Referee: Wolfgang Stark (GER) Attendance: 28,500

ZALAEGERSZEGI TE: Saša Ilic, Tamás Szamosi, Igor Budisa, Flórián Úrban, Zsolt Csóka, Ferenc Babati, Darko Ljubojevic, Ottó Vincze, István Farago (75 Csaba Balog), Gábor Egressy (65 Balazs Molnar), Krisztián Kenesei (83 Béla Koplárovics). Trainer: Péter Bozsik

MANCHESTER UNITED: Roy Carroll, Wesley Brown (6 Philip Neville), Laurent Blanc, John O'Shea, Mikael Silvestre, David Beckham, Juan Sebastián Veron, Roy Keane, Ryan Giggs, Ole Gunnar Solskjær (80 Diego FORLÁN Corazo), Ruud Van Nistelrooy.
Trainer: Alexander Chapman Ferguson

Goal: Koplárovics (90)

MANCHESTER UNITED FC v ZALAEGERSZEGI TE 5-0 (3-0)

Old Trafford, Manchester 27.08.2002

Referee: Lucilio CARDOSO CORTEZ BATISTA (POR)
Attendance: 66,814

MANCHESTER UNITED: Roy Carroll, Philip Neville, Rio Ferdinand (68 John O'Shea), Laurent Blanc, Mikael Silvestre, David Beckham (72 Diego FORLÁN Corazo), Juan Sebastián Veron, Roy Keane, Paul Scholes (50 Ole Gunnar Solskjær), Ryan Giggs, Ruud Van Nistelrooy.
Trainer: Alexander Chapman Ferguson

ZALAEGERSZEGI TE: Saša Ilić, Igor Budisa, Tamás Szamosi, Flórián Úrban, Zsolt Csóka, Ferenc Babati (75 Géza Turi), Darko Ljubojevic (59 István Farago), Ottó Vincze (63 Csaba Balog), Gábor Egressy, Balazs Molnar, Krisztián Kenesei. Trainer: Péter Bozsik

Sent off: Ilić (74)

Goals: Van Nistelrooy (5, 75 pen), Beckham (14), Scholes (20), Solskjær (83)

ROSENBORG BK TRONDHEIM v BRØNDBY IF 1-0 (0-0)

Lerkendal, Trondheim 14.08.2002

Referee: Domenico Messina (ITA) Attendance: 18,800

ROSENBORG: Arni Gautur Arason, Erik Hoftun, Ole Christer Basma, Janne Saarinen, Azar Karadas (50 Odd Inge Olsen), Roar Strand, Ørjan Berg, Bent Skammelsrud, Dagfinn Enerly (77 Trond Fredrik Ludvigsen), Frode Johnsen, Harald Martin Brattbakk. Trainer: Nils Arne Eggen

BRØNDBY IF: Mogens Krogh, Allan Arenfeldt Olesen, Aurelius Skarbalijus, Morten Weighorst, Kim Daugaard, Per Nielsen, Thomas Kallenberg (67 Allan Ravn Jensen), Peter Madsen, Mattias Jonsson (83 Thomas Lindrup), Ruben Bagger, Mads Jørgensen (74 Rafal Niznik).
Trainer: Michael Laudrup

Goal: Brattbakk (53)

BRØNDBY IF
v ROSENBORG BK TRONDHEIM 2-3 (0-1)

Brøndby Stadion, København 28.08.2002

Referee: Antonio Jesus LOPEZ NIETO (SPA) Att: 20,935

BRØNDBY IF: Mogens Krogh, Allan Arenfeldt Olesen, Aurelius Skarbalijus, Morten Weighorst (56 Mads Jørgensen), Kim Daugaard, Per Nielsen, Thomas Kallenberg, Peter Madsen, Mattias Jonsson, Ruben Bagger (72 Thomas Lindrup), Kasper Dalgas (81 Jonas Kamper). Trainer: Michael Laudrup

ROSENBORG: Arni Gautur Arason, Erik Hoftun, Ole Christer Basma, Janne Saarinen (88 Ståle Stensaas), Azar Karadas (71 Dagfinn Enerly), Odd Inge Olsen, Roar Strand, Ørjan Berg (79 Macbeth Sibaya), Bent Skammelsrud, Frode Johnsen, Harald Martin Brattbakk. Trainer: Nils Arne Eggen

Goals: Johnsen (9, 72), Brattbakk (78), Jonsson (81), Jørgensen (83)

SPORTING CLUBE DE PORTUGAL LISBOA
v FC INTERNAZIONALE MILANO 0-0

José Alvalade, Lisboa 14.08.2002

Referee: Rune Pedersen (NOR) Attendance: 25,421

SPORTING: TIAGO Alexandre Baptista Ferreira, Facundo Hernan QUIROGA, CÉSAR Luís PRATES, Roberto Luís Gaspar Deus Severo "BETO", RUI JORGE de Sousa Dias Macedo de Oliveira, RUI Fernando da Silva Calapez Pereira BENTO, Pablo CONTRERAS Fica (76 RICARDO Ribeiro FERNANDES), António Jesus Garcia González "TOÑITO" (58 CHRISTIANO RONALDO Santos Aveiro), PEDRO Alexandre Santos BARBOSA, Ricardo Andrade QUARESMA Bernardo (70 Vitaliy KUTUZOV), Marius Constantin NICULAE. Trainer: Ladislau Bölöni

INTERNAZIONALE: Francesco Toldo, Iván Ramiro Cordoba, Marco Materazzi, Francesco Coco, Javier Zanetti, Domenico Morfeo, SERGIO Paulo Merceneiro CONCEIÇÃO (79 Andrés "GULY" GUGLIELMINPIETRO), Luigi Di Biagio (65 Matías Jesús Almeyda), Stéphane Dalmat, Mohamed Kallon (67 Alvaro Recoba), Christian Vieri. Trainer: Hector Raúl Cúper

FC INTERNAZIONALE MILANO v SPORTING CLUBE DE PORTUGAL LISBOA 2-0 (2-0)

Giuseppe Meazza, Milano 27.08.2002

Referee: Rene H.J. Temmink (HOL) Attendance: 51,405

INTERNAZIONALE: Francesco Toldo, Iván Ramiro Cordoba, Marco Materazzi, Francesco Coco, Javier Zanetti, Domenico Morfeo, Andrés "GULY" GUGLIELMINPIETRO (60 Fabio Cannavaro), Luigi Di Biagio (80 Matías Jesús Almeyda), Stéphane Dalmat, Alvaro Recoba, Christian Vieri (86 Bernardo Corradi). Trainer: Hector Raúl Cúper

SPORTING: TIAGO Alexandre Baptista Ferreira, Facundo Hernan QUIROGA, CÉSAR Luís PRATES, Roberto Luís Gaspar Deus Severo "BETO", RUI JORGE de Sousa Dias Macedo de Oliveira (85 RICARDO Ribeiro FERNANDES), RUI Fernando da Silva Calapez Pereira BENTO, Pablo CONTRERAS Fica, Antonio Jesus Garcia González "TOÑITO" (60 Vitaliy KUTUZOV), PEDRO Alexandre Santos BARBOSA, Ricardo Andrade QUARESMA Bernardo (75 DANNY Miguel Alves Gomes), Marius Constantin NICULAE. Trainer: Ladislau Bölöni

Goals: Di Biagio (31), Recoba (44)

FC BARCELONA
v WKS LEGIA WARSZAWA 3-0 (1-0)

Camp Nou, Barcelona 14.08.2002

Referee: Michal Benes (CZE) Attendance: 67,078

FC BARCELONA: VÍCTOR VALDÉS Arribas, Frank De Boer, Carlos PUYOL Saforcada (83 Philippe Christanval), FERNANDO NAVARRO Corbacho, Xavier Hernández Creus "XAVI", Javier Pedro SAVIOLA, Philip Cocu, Patrick Kluivert, Gaizka MENDIETA Zabala, LUIS ENRIQUE Martínez García (58 Juan Román RIQUELME), Thiago Motta. Trainer: Louis van Gaal

WKS LEGIA: Radostin Stanev, Dariusz Dudek, Sergei Omelyanchuk, Wojciech Szala, Jacek Magiera, Marek Jozwiak, Adam Majewski, Tomasz Kielbowicz, Aleksandar Vukovic (88 Stanko Svitlica), Cezary Kucharski, Moussa Yahaya (61 Radoslaw Wroblewski). Trainer: Dragomir Okuka

Goals: De Boer (8), Riquelme (80), Cocu (90+3)

WKS LEGIA WARSZAWA
v FC BARCELONA 0-1 (0-0)

Wojska Polskiego, Warszawa 28.08.2002

Referee: Alfredo Trentalange (ITA) Attendance: 11,500

WKS LEGIA: Radostin Stanev, Sergei Omelyanchuk, Wojciech Szala (82 Dariusz Dudek), Jacek Zielinski, Jacek Magiera, Marek Jozwiak, Adam Majewski, Tomasz Kielbowicz, Aleksandar Vukovic (62 Radoslaw Wroblewski), Stanko Svitlica, Cezary Kucharski (77 Mariusz Zganiacz). Trainer: Dragomir Okuka

FC BARCELONA: VÍCTOR VALDÉS Arribas, Frank De Boer, Carlos PUYOL Saforcada, Philippe Christanval, FERNANDO NAVARRO Corbacho, Xavier Hernández Creus "XAVI", Javier Pedro SAVIOLA, Philip Cocu, Patrick Kluivert (70 GEOVANNI Deiberson Mauricio), Gaizka MENDIETA Zabala, LUIS ENRIQUE Martínez García (73 Daniel García Lara "DANI"). Trainer: Louis van Gaal

Sent off: Magiera (86)

Goal: Mendieta (68 pen)

FIRST STAGE – GROUP A

ARSENAL FC LONDON v BV BORUSSIA DORTMUND 2-0 (0-0)

Arsenal Stadium, London 17.09.2002

Referee: Anders Frisk (SWE) Attendance: 34,907

ARSENAL: David Seaman, Oleg Luzhny (74 LAUREN Etame-Mayer), Sol Campbell, Martin Keown, Ashley Cole, Fredrik Ljungberg (85 Pascal Cygan), Patrick Vieira, GILBERTO Aparecido da Silva, Sylvain Wiltord (90 Kolo Abib Touré), Dennis Bergkamp, Thierry Henry. Manager: Arsène Wenger

BV BORUSSIA: Jens Lehmann, EVANILSON Aparecido Ferreira, Christoph Metzelder, Juan Ramón Fernández (72 Heiko Herrlich), Torsten Frings, Leonardo de Deus Santos "DEDE", Sebastian Kehl, Ahmed Reda Madouni, Jörg Heinrich, Jan KolLER, EWERTHON Henrique de Souza (72 Giuseppe Reina). Trainer: Matthias Sammer

Goals: Bergkamp (62), Ljungberg (77)

AJ AUXERRE v PSV EINDHOVEN 0-0

Abbé Deschamps, Auxerre 17.09.2002

Referee: Alfredo Trentalange (ITA) Attendance: 11,902

AUXERRE: Fabien Cool, Johan Radet, Jean-Alain BOUMSONG Somko, Philippe Mexes, Jean-Sébastien Jaures, Teemu Tainio, Amdy Mustapha Faye, Yann Lachuer, Khalilou Fadiga, Narcisse Olivier KAPO Obou, BENJAMIN Mwaruwari (84 Arnaud Gonzalez). Trainer: Guy Roux

PSV: Jelle Ten Rouwelaar, Kasper Bøgelund, André Ooijer, Kevin Hofland, Jan Heintze, Dennis Rommedahl, Remco Van Der Schaaf (40 Theo Lucius), Johann Vogel, Wilfred Bouma, Arnold Bruggink (86 LEANDRO do Bomfim), Mateja Kezman. Trainer: Guus Hiddink

BV BORUSSIA DORTMUND v AJ AUXERRE 2-1 (1-0)

Westfalenstadion, Dortmund 25.09.2002

Referee: Terje Hauge (NOR) Attendance: 46,500

BV BORUSSIA: Jens Lehmann, EVANILSON Aparecido Ferreira, Christian Wörns, Christoph Metzelder, Jörg Heinrich, Stefan Reuter, Sebastian Kehl, Torsten Frings (74 Lars Ricken), Tomáš Rosicky (66 Marcio AMOROSO dos Santos, EWERTHON Henrique de Souza (84 Leonardo de Deus Santos "DEDE"), Jan Koller. Trainer: Matthias Sammer

AUXERRE: Fabien Cool, Johan Radet, Jean-Alain BOUMSONG Somko, Philippe Mexes, Jean-Sébastien Jaures, Yann Lachuer, Teemu Tainio, Amdy Mustapha Faye, Khalilou Fadiga, Narcisse Olivier KAPO Obou, BENJAMIN Mwaruwari. Trainer: Guy Roux

Goals: Koller (6), Amoroso (78), Benjamin (83)

PSV EINDHOVEN v ARSENAL FC LONDON 0-4 (0-1)

Philips, Eindhoven 25.09.2002

Referee: Ľuboš Michel (SVK) Attendance: 29,500

PSV: Ronald Waterreus, Kasper Bøgelund, André Ooijer, Kevin Hofland (46 Jan Vennegoor Of Hesselink), Jan Heintze (62 Theo Lucius), Mark Van Bommel, Johann Vogel (27 LEANDRO do Bomfim), Dennis Rommedahl, Wilfred Bouma, Arnold Bruggink, Mateja Kezman. Trainer: Guus Hiddink

ARSENAL: David Seaman, Martin Keown (10 Pascal Cygan), Sol Campbell, Ashley Cole, LAUREN Etame-Mayer, GILBERTO Aparecido da Silva, Patrick Vieira, Fredrik Ljungberg (86 Kolo Abib Touré), Sylvain Wiltord, Thierry Henry, Dennis Bergkamp (80 Nwankwo Kanu). Manager: Arsène Wenger

Goals: Gilberto (1), Ljungberg (66), Henry (81, 90+2)

AJ AUXERRE v ARSENAL FC LONDON 0-1 (0-0)

Abbé Deschamps, Auxerre 2.10.2002

Referee: Frank de Bleeckere (BEL) Attendance: 19,454

AUXERRE: Fabien Cool, Johan Radet, Jean-Alain BOUMSONG Somko, Philippe Mexes, Jean-Sébastien Jaures, Yann Lachuer (73 Arnaud Gonzalez), Teemu Tainio (90+1 Pantxi Sirieix), Amdy Mustapha Faye, Khalilou Fadiga, Narcisse Olivier KAPO Obou, BENJAMIN Mwaruwari. Trainer: Guy Roux

ARSENAL: David Seaman, LAUREN Etame-Mayer, Sol Campbell, Pascal Cygan, Ashley Cole, Sylvain Wiltord (84 Oleg Luzhny), Patrick Vieira, GILBERTO Aparecido da Silva, Kolo Abib Touré (60 Eduardo Edu), Thierry Henry (58 Jermaine Pennant), Nwankwo Kanu. Manager: Arsène Wenger

Goal: Gilberto (48)

PSV EINDHOVEN v BV BORUSSIA DORTMUND 1-3 (0-1)

Philips, Eindhoven 2.10.2002

Referee: Pierluigi Collina (ITA) Attendance: 26,100

PSV: Ronald Waterreus, Kasper Bøgelund, André Ooijer, Ernest Faber, Wilfred Bouma, Mark Van Bommel, Johann Vogel, Dennis Rommedahl, LEANDRO do Bomfim (55 Arjen Robben), Remco Van Der Schaaf, Mateja Kezman (75 Jan Vennegoor Of Hesselink). Trainer: Guus Hiddink

BV BORUSSIA: Jens Lehmann, Ahmed Reda Madouni, Christian Wörns, Christoph Metzelder, Leonardo de Deus Santos "DEDE", Stefan Reuter (90+1 Lars Ricken), Torsten Frings, Jörg Heinrich, Tomáš Rosicky (79 Sebastian Kehl), EWERTHON Henrique de Souza (65 Marcio AMOROSO dos Santos), Jan Koller. Trainer: Matthias Sammer

Goals: Koller (21), Rosicky (69), Amoroso (90+2), van der Schaaf (74)

ARSENAL FC LONDON v AJ AUXERRE 1-2 (0-2)

Arsenal Stadium, London 22.10.2002

Referee: Domenico Messina (ITA) Attendance: 35,206

ARSENAL: David Seaman, LAUREN Etame-Mayer (77 Kolo Abib Touré), Sol Campbell, Pascal Cygan, Ashley Cole, Fredrik Ljungberg, Patrick Vieira, GILBERTO Aparecido da Silva (72 Robert Pires), Sylvain Wiltord, Nwankwo Kanu, Thierry Henry. Manager: Arsène Wenger

AUXERRE: Fabien Cool, Johan Radet, Jean-Alain BOUMSONG Somko, Jean-Sébastien Jaures, Philippe Mexes, Yann Lachuer, Teemu Tainio, Amdy Mustapha Faye, Khalilou Fadiga, Narcisse Olivier KAPO Obou, BENJAMIN Mwaruwari. Trainer: Guy Roux

Goals: Kapo (8), Fadiga (27), Kanu (53)

BV BORUSSIA DORTMUND v PSV EINDHOVEN 1-1 (1-0)

Westfalenstadion, Dortmund 22.10.2002

Referee: Lucilio CARDOSO CORTEZ BATISTA (POR) Attendance: 47,000

BV BORUSSIA: Jens Lehmann, EVANILSON Aparecido Ferreira, Christian Wörns, Ahmed Reda Madouni, Leonardo de Deus Santos "DEDE", Stefan Reuter (78 Torsten Frings), Tomáš Rosicky, Sebastian Kehl, EWERTHON Henrique de Souza, Lars Ricken (72 Marcio AMOROSO dos Santos), Jan Koller. Trainer: Matthias Sammer

PSV: Ronald Waterreus, Kasper Bøgelund, Ernest Faber, André Ooijer, Jan Heintze (46 Arjen Robben), Dennis Rommedahl, Johann Vogel, Mark Van Bommel, Wilfred Bouma, Arnold Bruggink (80 Adil Ramzi), Mateja Kezman (85 Jan Vennegoor Of Hesselink). Trainer: Guus Hiddink

Goals: Koller (10), Bruggink (47)

BV BORUSSIA DORTMUND v ARSENAL FC LONDON 2-1 (1-1)

Westfalenstadion, Dortmund 30.10.2002

Referee: Manuel Enrique MEJUTO GONZALEZ (SPA) Attendance: 51,200

BV BORUSSIA: Jens Lehmann, EVANILSON Aparecido Ferreira, Christian Wörns, Christoph Metzelder, Leonardo de Deus Santos "DEDE", Lars Ricken (84 Jörg Heinrich), Tomáš Rosicky (90 Ahmed Reda Madouni), Sebastian Kehl (69 Stefan Reuter), Torsten Frings, Jan Koller, EWERTHON Henrique de Souza. Trainer: Matthias Sammer

ARSENAL: David Seaman, LAUREN Etame-Mayer, Sol Campbell, Pascal Cygan, Ashley Cole, Fredrik Ljungberg, Patrick Vieira, GILBERTO Aparecido da Silva (80 Eduardo EDU), Robert Pires (67 Kolo Abib Touré), Sylvain Wiltord (79 Nwankwo Kanu), Thierry Henry. Manager: Arsène Wenger

Goals: Henry (18), Gilberto (38 og), Rosicky (62 pen)

PSV EINDHOVEN v AJ AUXERRE 3-0 (1-0)

Philips, Eindhoven 30.10.2002

Referee: Knud Erik Fisker (DEN) Attendance: 24,500

PSV: Ronald Waterreus, Kasper Bøgelund, Ernest Faber, Kevin Hofland, Wilfred Bouma, Dennis Rommedahl, Mark Van Bommel (65 Remco Van Der Schaaf), Johann Vogel (78 Theo Lucius), Arjen Robben (70 Adil Ramzi), Arnold Bruggink, Mateja Kezman. Trainer: Guus Hiddink

AUXERRE: Fabien Cool, Johan Radet, Jean-Alain Boumsong Somko, Philippe Mexes, Jean-Sébastien Jaures, Yann Lachuer (81 Pantxi Sirieix), Amdy Mustapha Faye, Lionel Mathis, Khalilou Fadiga (87 Arnaud Gonzalez), Narcisse Olivier KAPO Obou, BENJAMIN Mwaruwari (27 Stéphane Grichting). Trainer: Guy Roux

Sent off: Mexes (26), Kapo (51)

Goals: Bruggink (34), Rommedahl (48), Robben (64)

AJ AUXERRE v BV BORUSSIA DORTMUND 1-0 (0-0)

Abbé Deschamps, Auxerre 12.11.2002

Referee: Sorin Corpodean (ROM) Attendance: 16,959

AUXERRE: Fabien Cool, Johan Radet, Stéphane Grichting, Jean-Alain BOUMSONG Somko, Jean-Sébastien Jaures, Yann Lachuer, Teemu Tainio (46 BENJAMIN Mwaruwari), Amdy Mustapha Faye, Khalilou Fadiga, Lionel Mathis, Djibril Cissé. Trainer: Guy Roux

BV BORUSSIA: Jens Lehmann, Jörg Heinrich (26 Guy Demel), Sebastian Kehl, Ahmed Reda Madouni, Leonardo de Deus Santos "DEDE", Torsten Frings, Stefan Reuter, Lars Ricken, EWERTHON Henrique de Souza (65 Marcio AMOROSO dos Santos), Jan Koller, LEANDRO De Deus Santos (81 Giuseppe Reina). Trainer: Matthias Sammer

Goal: Benjamin (76)

ARSENAL FC LONDON v PSV EINDHOVEN 0-0

Arsenal Stadium, London 12.11.2002

Referee: Tom Henning Ovrebo (NOR) Attendance: 35,274

ARSENAL: Rami Shaaban, Oleg Luzhny, Igor N.Stepanov (LAT), Pascal Cygan, Giovanni Van Bronckhorst, Kolo Abib Touré, Patrick Vieira (78 GILBERTO Aparecido da Silva), Eduardo Edu, Robert Pires, Francis Jeffers (70 Sylvain Wiltord), Thierry Henry (64 Dennis Bergkamp). Manager: Arsène Wenger

PSV: Ronald Waterreus, Kasper Bøgelund, André Ooijer (80 Jan Vennegoor Of Hesselink), Kevin Hofland, Wilfred Bouma, Dennis Rommedahl, Johann Vogel (42 Theo Lucius), Mark Van Bommel, Arjen Robben, Arnold Bruggink (71 Remco Van Der Schaaf), Mateja Kezman. Trainer: Guus Hiddink

Sent off: Touré (35)

Arsenal FC and BV Borussia Dortmund qualified for the Second Group Stage. AJ Auxerre qualified for the UEFA Cup.

	P	W	D	L	F	A	Pts
Arsenal FC London	6	3	1	2	9	4	10
Borussia Dortmund	6	3	1	2	8	7	10
AJ Auxerre	6	2	1	3	4	7	7
PSV Eindhoven	6	1	3	2	5	8	6

FIRST STAGE – GROUP B

FC BASEL v FC SPARTAK MOSKVA 2-0 (0-0)

St Jakob, Basel 17.09.2002

Referee: Claus Bo Larsen (DEN) Attendance: 29,500

FC BASEL: Pascal Zuberbühler, Bernt Haas, Murat Yakin, Alexandre Quennoz, Antonio Esposito, Sébastien Barberis, Hakan Yakin (87 Nenad Savic), Mario Cantaluppi, Thimothée Atouba, Christian Gimenez, Julio Hernán Rossi (75 Hervé Tum). Trainer: Christian Gross

SPARTAK: Stanislav Cherchessov, Maksym Kalynychenko (72 Igor Mitreski), Yuri Kovtun, Jerry-Christian Tchuisse, MOISÉS Moura Pinheiro, Vasily Baranov (56 MARCELO José Da SILVA), Dmitry Khlestov, Dmitri Kudryashov, Baye Aly Ibra Kebe, Vladimir Beschastnykh, Alexander Danishevskiy (46 Flo ESSIEN Okon). Trainer: Oleg Romantsev

Goals: H. Yakin (50), Rossi (55)

VALENCIA CF v LIVERPOOL FC 2-0 (2-0)

Mestalla, Valencia 17.09.2002

Referee: Herbert Fandel (GER) Attendance: 35,333

VALENCIA: José Santiago CAÑIZARES Ruiz, Cristobal Emilio Torres Ruiz "CURRO TORRES", Roberto Fabián AYALA, Mauricio Pellegrino, Amedeo Carboni, David ALBELDA Aliques (84 Gonzalo DE LOS SANTOS da Rosa), Rubén BARAJA Vegas, Francisco Joaquín Pérez "RUFETE" (75 Miguel Ángel ANGULO Valderrey), VICENTE Rodríguez Guillén, John Carew, Pablo César Aimar (71 Miguel Ángel Ferrer Martínez "MISTA").
Trainer: Rafael BENÍTEZ MAUDES

LIVERPOOL: Jerzy Dudek, Jamie Carragher, Sami Hyypiä, Salif Diao (46 Bruno Cheyrou), Djimi Traore, Danny Murphy (76 Milan Baros), Dietmar Hamann, Steven Gerrard, John Arne Riise, Emile Heskey, El Hadji Diouf (46 Michael Owen).
Trainer: Gérard Houllier

Sent off: Hamann (77)

Goals: Aimar (20), Baraja (38)

LIVERPOOL FC v FC BASEL 1-1 (1-1)

Anfield, Liverpool 25.09.2002

Referee: Dick J.H. van Egmond (HOL) Attendance: 37,634

LIVERPOOL: Jerzy Dudek, Jamie Carragher, Stéphane Henchoz, Sami Hyypiä, John Arne Riise, Danny Murphy, Steven Gerrard, Bruno Cheyrou, Emile Heskey (71 El Hadji Diouf), Milan Baros, Michael Owen (79 Patrik Berger).
Trainer: Gérard Houllier

FC BASEL: Pascal Zuberbühler, Bernt Haas, Murat Yakin, Alexandre Quennoz, Thimothée Atouba, Sébastien Barberis, Mario Cantaluppi, Antonio Esposito, Hakan Yakin (67 Grégory Duruz), Christian Gimenez, Julio Hernán Rossi (74 Hervé Tum). Trainer: Christian Gross

Goals: Baros (34), Rossi (43)

FC SPARTAK MOSKVA v VALENCIA CF 0-3 (0-1)

Dinamo, Moskva 25.09.2002

Referee: Stéphane Bré (FRA) Attendance: 10,500

SPARTAK: Stanislav Cherchessov, Igor Mitreski, Jerry-Christian Tchuisse, MOISÉS Moura Pinheiro, Yuri Kovtun (46 Vasily Baranov), Baye Aly Ibra Kebe, Dmitri Kudryashov, Dmitry Khlestov, Maksym Kalynychenko, Vladimir Beschastnykh, Alexander Danishevskiy (54 Flo ESSIEN Okon).
Trainer: Oleg Romantsev

VALENCIA: José Santiago CAÑIZARES Ruiz, Cristobal Emilio Torres Ruiz "CURRO TORRES", Roberto Fabián AYALA, Mauricio Pellegrino, Amedeo CARBONI, Miguel Ángel ANGULO Valderrey (74 JUAN Ginés SÁNCHEZ Moreno), David ALBELDA Aliques, Rubén BARAJA Vegas, VICENTE Rodríguez Guillén (67 Francisco Joaquín Pérez "RUFETE"), Pablo César AIMAR, John CAREW (58 Miguel Ángel Ferrer Martínez "MISTA").
Trainer: Rafael BENÍTEZ MAUDES

Goals: Angulo (6), Mista (71), Sánchez (85)

LIVERPOOL FC v FC SPARTAK MOSKVA 5-0 (3-0)

Anfield, Liverpool 2.10.2002

Referee: Alain Hamer (LUX) Attendance: 40,812

LIVERPOOL: Jerzy Dudek, Jamie Carragher, Stéphane Henchoz (67 Djimi Traore), Sami Hyypiä, John Arne Riise, Danny Murphy, Steven Gerrard (76 Salif Diao), Dietmar Hamann, Bruno Cheyrou (82 El Hadji Diouf), Michael Owen, Emile Heskey. Trainer: Gérard Houllier

SPARTAK: Stanislav Cherchessov, Baye Aly Ibra Kebe, MOISÉS Moura Pinheiro, Igor Mitreski, Yuri Kovtun (63 Valeri Abramidze), Dmitry Khlestov (26 Artem Bezrodny), Dmitri Kudryashov (50 MARCELO José da SILVA), Alexander Pavlenko, Maksym Kalynychenko, Vladimir Beschastnykh, Alexander Danishevskiy. Trainer: Oleg Romantsev

Goals: Heskey (7, 89), Cheyrou (15), Hyypiä (28), Diao (81)

VALENCIA CF v FC BASEL 6-2 (4-0)

Mestalla, Valencia 2.10.2002

Referee: Cosimo Bolognino (ITA) Attendance: 27,394

VALENCIA: José Santiago CAÑIZARES Ruiz, Cristobal Emilio Torres Ruiz "CURRO TORRES", Mauricio PELLEGRINO, Roberto Fabián AYALA, FÁBIO AURÉLIO Rodrigues, Miguel Ángel ANGULO Valderrey, David ALBELDA Aliques, Rubén BARAJA Vegas (46 Miguel Ángel Ferrer Martínez "MISTA"), VICENTE Rodríguez Guillén (60 Javier GARRIDO Ramírez), Pablo César AIMAR (71 JUAN Ginés SÁNCHEZ Moreno), John CAREW.
Trainer: Rafael BENÍTEZ MAUDES

FC BASEL: Pascal Zuberbühler, Bernt Haas, Murat Yakin, Alexandre Quennoz (62 Ivan Ergic), Thimothée Atouba, Sébastien Barberis, Mario Cantaluppi, Antonio Esposito (79 Grégory Duruz), Hakan Yakin, Julio Hernán Rossi, Christian Gimenez (46 Carlos Varela). Trainer: Christian Gross

Goals: Carew (10, 13), Fábio Aurélio (17), Baraja (28), Rossi (46), Aimar (58), Mista (60), H. Yakin (90)

FC BASEL v VALENCIA CF 2-2 (1-1)

"Saint Jakob", Basel 22.10.2002

Referee: Helmut Fleischer (GER) Attendance: 29,603

FC BASEL: Pascal Zuberbühler, Bernt Haas, Murat Yakin, Marco Zwyssig, Grégory Duruz, Carlos Varela (65 Julio Hernán Rossi), Mario Cantaluppi, Ivan Ergic, Antonio Esposito (85 George Koumantarakis), Hakan Yakin, Christian Gimenez (60 Hervé Tum). Trainer: Christian Gross

VALENCIA: José Santiago CAÑIZARES Ruiz, Cristobal Emilio Torres Ruiz «CURRO TORRES», Roberto Fabián AYALA, Mauricio PELLEGRINO, FÁBIO AURÉLIO Rodrigues, Francisco Joaquín Pérez «RUFETE» (71 Miguel Ángel ANGULO Valderrey), Rubén BARAJA Vegas (76 Carlos MARCHENA López), Gonzalo DE LOS SANTOS da Rosa, Cristian Alberto «KILY» GONZÁLEZ, Miguel Ángel Ferrer Martínez «MISTA», JUAN Ginés SÁNCHEZ Moreno (80 John Carew). Trainer: Rafael BENÍTEZ MAUDES

Sent off: Ayala (88)

Goals: Ergic (32, 90), Baraja (36), Curro Torres (72)

FC SPARTAK MOSKVA v LIVERPOOL FC 1-3 (1-1)

Dinamo, Moskva 22.10.2002

Referee: Konrad Plautz (AUS) Attendance: 10,000

SPARTAK: Maxym Levitsky, Dmitry Khlestov, Alexander Pavlenko, Valeri Abramidze, Yuri Kovtun (36 Baye Aly Ibra Kebe), Igor Mitreski (82 Dmitri Kudryashov), Maksym Kalynychenko, Alexander Sonin (60 Dmitry Torbinskiy), Artem Bezrodny, Vladimir Beschastnykh, Alexander Danishevskiy. Trainer: Oleg Romantsev

LIVERPOOL: Jerzy Dudek, Jamie Carragher, Sami Hyypiä, Djimi Traore, John Arne Riise, Danny Murphy, Dietmar Hamann, Salif Diao, Emile Heskey (56 Grégory Vignal, 76 Igor Biscan), Michael Owen, Milan Baros (70 El Hadji Diouf).
Trainer: Gérard Houllier

Goals: Danishevskiy (23), Owen (29, 70, 90+1)

LIVERPOOL FC v VALENCIA CF 0-1 (0-1)

Anfield, Liverpool 30.10.2002

Referee: Terje Hauge (NOR) Attendance: 41,831

LIVERPOOL: Jerzy Dudek, Jamie Carragher (82 Bruno Cheyrou), Sami Hyypiä, Djimi Traore, John Arne Riise, Steven Gerrard, Dietmar Hamann, Salif Diao, Danny Murphy (61 Vladimir Smicer), Michael Owen, Emile Heskey (61 Milan Baros). Trainer: Gérard Houllier

VALENCIA: José Santiago CAÑIZARES Ruiz, Cristobal Emilio Torres Ruiz "CURRO TORRES", Carlos MARCHENA López, Mauricio PELLEGRINO, Amedeo CARBONI, Francisco Joaquín Pérez "RUFETE", David ALBELDA Aliques, Rubén BARAJA Vegas, Cristian Alberto "KILY" GONZÁLEZ (88 VICENTE Rodríguez Guillén), John CAREW (79 Miguel Ángel Ferrer Martínez "MISTA"), Pablo César AIMAR (68 Miguel Ángel ANGULO Valderrey).
Trainer: Rafael BENÍTEZ MAUDES

Goal: Rufete (34)

FC SPARTAK MOSKVA v FC BASEL 0-2 (0-1)

Dinamo, Moskva 5.11.2002

Referee: Stuart Dougal (SCO) Attendance: 5,500

SPARTAK: Maxym Levitsky, Dmitry Khlestov, Baye Aly Ibra Kebe (77 Igor Mitreski), MOISÉS Moura Pinheiro, Alexander Pavlenko, Valeri Abramidze, Yuri Kovtun, Maksym Kalynychenko (71 Dmitry Torbinskiy), Artem Bezrodny (46 Dmitri Kudryashov), Vladimir Beschastnykh, Alexander Danishevskiy. Trainer: Oleg Romantsev

FC BASEL: Pascal Zuberbühler, Bernt Haas, Murat Yakin, Marco Zwyssig, Grégory Duruz, Mario Cantaluppi, Ivan Ergic, Antonio Esposito (16 Thimothée Atouba), Hakan Yakin, Julio Hernán Rossi (67 Christian Gimenez), Hervé Tum.
Trainer: Christian Gross

Goals: Rossi (18), Gimenez (89)

FC BASEL v LIVERPOOL FC 3-3 (3-0)

"Saint Jakob", Basel 12.11.2002

Referee: Claude Colombo (FRA) Attendance: 29,534

FC BASEL: Pascal Zuberbühler, Bernt Haas, Murat Yakin, Marco Zwyssig, Thimothée Atouba, Ivan Ergic, Hakan Yakin (90 George Koumantarakis), Mario Cantaluppi, Antonio Esposito, Christian Gimenez (66 Sébastien Barberis), Julio Hernán Rossi (76 Hervé Tum). Trainer: Christian Gross

LIVERPOOL: Jerzy Dudek, Jamie Carragher (79 El Hadji Diouf), Sami Hyypiä, Djimi Traore, John Arne Riise, Danny Murphy, Dietmar Hamann, Steven Gerrard (46 Salif Diao), Vladimir Smicer, Michael Owen, Emile Heskey (61 Milan Baros). Trainer: Gérard Houllier

Goals: Rossi (2), Gimenez (22), Atouba (29), Murphy (61), Smicer (64), Owen (85)

VALENCIA CF v FC SPARTAK MOSKVA 3-0 (1-0)

Mestalla, Valencia 12.11.2002

Referee: Georgios Kasnaferis (GRE) Attendance: 27,000

VALENCIA: Andrés PALOP Cervera, Javier GARRIDO Ramírez, Miroslav Djukic, Carlos MARCHENA López, FÁBIO AURÉLIO Rodrigues, Miguel Ángel ANGULO Valderrey, Miguel Ángel Ferrer Martínez "MISTA", Gonzalo DE LOS SANTOS da Rosa (87 DAVID SÁNCHEZ Ridaura), Cristian Alberto "KILY" GONZÁLEZ, Salvador Ballesta Vialcho "SALVA BALLESTA" (71 Miguel ALBIOL Tortajada), JUAN Ginés SÁNCHEZ Moreno (88 DAVID NAVARRO Pedrós). Trainer: Rafael BENÍTEZ MAUDES

SPARTAK: Maxym Levitsky, Igor Mitreski (77 Samuel Ogunsanya), MOISÉS Moura Pinheiro, Valeri Abramidze, Yuri Kovtun, Alexander Pavlenko, Maksym Kalynychenko, Dmitri Kudryashov (62 Alexander Sonin), Artem Bezrodny (46 MARCELO José da Silva), Vladimir Beschastnykh, Alexander Danishevskiy. Trainer: Oleg Romantsev

Goals: Sánchez (38, 46), Fábio Aurélio (78)

Valencia CF and FC Basel qualified for the Second Group Stage. Liverpool FC qualified for the UEFA Cup.

	P	W	D	L	F	A	Pts
Valencia CF	6	5	1	0	17	4	16
FC Basel	6	2	3	1	12	12	9
Liverpool FC	6	2	2	2	12	8	8
Spartak Moskva	6	0	0	6	1	18	0

FIRST STAGE – GROUP C

KRC GENK v AEK FC ATHINA 0-0

Fenix, Genk 17.09.2002

Referee: Konrad Plautz (AUS) Attendance: 22,000

KRC GENK: Jan Moons, Kevin Vanbeuren, Igor Tomasic, Didier Zokora, Marco Ingrao, Mirsad Beslija, Bernd Thijs, Josip Skoko, Koen Daerden, Wesley Sonck, Beli-Moumouni Dagano. Trainer: Sef Vergoosen

AEK: Dionisis Hiotis, Vasilis Borbokis (53 Milen Petkov), Nikos Kostenoglou, Mauricio Wright, Mihalis Kasapis, Konstantinos Katsouranis, Theodoros Zagorakis, Mihalis Kapsis, Dimitris Nalitzis (64 Vasilis Lakis), Themistoklis Nikolaidis, Vasilis Tsartas (90+1 Hristos Maladenis). Trainer: Dusko Bajević

AS ROMA v REAL MADRID CF 0-3 (0-1)

Stadio Olimpico, Roma 17.09.2002

Referee: Markus Merk (GER) Attendance: 71,130

AS ROMA: Francesco Antonioli, Traianos Dellas, Walter Adriano Samuel, Leandro Damián Cufré (46 Josep GUARDIOLA Sala), Christian Panucci, Marcos Evangelista de Moraes "CAFÚ", Damiano Tommasi, ÉMERSON Ferreira da Rosa, Vincent Candela, Vincenzo Montella, Antonio Cassano (64 Marco Delvecchio). Trainer: Italo Galbiati

REAL MADRID: Iker CASILLAS Fernández, Miguel Ángel "MICHEL" SALGADO, Fernando Ruíz HIERRO, Iván HELGUERA Bujía, ROBERTO CARLOS da Silva, Luís Felipe Madeira Caeiro "FIGO", Zinédine Zidane (70 Santiago Hernán SOLARI), Claude MAKELELE (78 Steve McManaman), Esteban CAMBIASSO Deleau, RAÚL González Blanco, José María Gutiérrez "GUTI".
Trainer: Vicente DEL BOSQUE González

Goals: Guti (41, 74), Raúl (56)

AEK FC ATHINA v AS ROMA 0-0

Nea Philadelphia, Athina 25.09.2002

Referee: Graham Barber (ENG) Attendance: 9,444

AEK: Dionisis Hiotis, Nikos Kostenoglou, Mauricio Wright, Mihalis Kapsis, Theodoros Zagorakis, Konstantinos Katsouranis, Mihalis Kasapis (46 Grigoris Georgatos), Vasilis Lakis, Vasilis Tsartas (85 Milen Petkov), Themistoklis Nikolaidis, Ilija Ivic (63 Dimitris Nalitzis).
Trainer: Dusko Bajević

AS ROMA: Francesco Antonioli, Christian Panucci, Walter Adriano Samuel, Leandro Damián Cufré, Marcos Evangelista de Moraes "CAFÚ", Vincent Candela, Damiano Tommasi, Francisco Govinho Lima, ÉMERSON Ferreira da Rosa, Gabriel Omar Batistuta (90 Antonio Cassano), Vincenzo Montella.
Trainer: Fabio Capello

REAL MADRID CF v KRC GENK 6-0 (2-0)

Santiago Bernabéu 25.09.2002

Referee: Knud Erik Fisker (DEN) Attendance: 65,700

REAL MADRID: Iker CASILLAS Fernández, Miguel Ángel "MICHEL" SALGADO, Fernando Ruíz HIERRO, Iván HELGUERA Bujía, ROBERTO CARLOS da Silva (70 RAÚL BRAVO Sanfelix), Luís Felipe Madeira Caeiro "FIGO", Esteban CAMBIASSO Deleau (67 Fernando MORIENTES Sánchez), Albert CELADES López, Santiago Hernán SOLARI, RAÚL González Blanco (76 Javier García PORTILLO), José María Gutiérrez "GUTI". Trainer: Vicente DEL BOSQUE González

KRC GENK: Jan Moons, Kevin Vanbeuren (61 Soley Seyfo), Igor Tomasic, Didier Zokora, Akram Roumani, Mirsad Beslija (83 Takayuri Suzuki), Josip Skoko, Justice Wamfor, Koen Daerden, Wesley Sonck, Beli-Moumouni Dagano (79 Igor-Alberto-Rinck De Camargo). Trainer: Sef Vergoosen

Goals: Zokora (44 og), Michel Salgado (45+1), Figo (55 pen), Guti (64), Celades (74), Raúl (76)

AEK FC ATHINA v REAL MADRID CF 3-3 (3-2)

Nea Philadelphia, Athina 2.10.2002

Referee: Iordan Ivanov (BUL) Attendance: 9,444

AEK: Dionisis Hiotis, Nikos Kostenoglou, Mauricio Wright, Mihalis Kapsis, Theodoros Zagorakis (84 Walter Centeno), Konstantinos Katsouranis, Mihalis Kasapis, Vasilis Lakis, Milen Petkov (15 Hristos Maladenis), Vasilis Tsartas (84 Ilija Ivic), Themistoklis Nikolaidis. Trainer: Dusko Bajević

REAL MADRID: Iker CASILLAS Fernández, Miguel Ángel "MICHEL" SALGADO, Iván HELGUERA Bujía, Francisco PAVÓN Barahona, ROBERTO CARLOS da Silva, Luís Felipe Madeira Caeiro "FIGO", Claude Makelele, Esteban CAMBIASSO Deleau, Zinédine Zidane (84 Javier García PORTILLO), RAÚL González Blanco (81 Fernando MORIENTES Sánchez), José María Gutiérrez "GUTI" (87 Steve McMANAMAN). Trainer: Vicente DEL BOSQUE González

Goals: Tsartas (6), Zidane (15, 39), Maladenis (25), Nikolaidis (28), Guti (60)

KRC GENK v AS ROMA 0-1 (0-0)

Fenix, Genk 2.10.2002

Referee: Alain Sars (FRA) Attendance: 22,260

KRC GENK: Jan Moons, Justice Wamfor, Didier Zokora, Igor Tomasic, Akram Roumani (85 Marco Ingrao), Mirsad Beslija (11 Davy Schollen), Josip Skoko, Bernd Thijs, Koen Daerden (68 Soley Seyfo), Beli-Moumouni Dagano, Wesley Sonck. Trainer: Sef Vergoosen

AS ROMA: Francesco Antonioli, Jonathan Zebina, Walter Adriano Samuel, Christian Panucci, Marcos Evangelista de Moraes "CAFÚ" (46 Antonio Cassano), Vincent Candela, Damiano Tommasi (53 Ivan Tomic), Francisco Govinho Lima, EMERSON Ferreira da Rosa, Gabriel Omar Batistuta (68 Vincenzo Montella), Francesco Totti. Trainer: Fabio Capello

Sent off: Moons (10)

Goal: Cassano (81)

REAL MADRID CF v AEK FC ATHINA 2-2 (2-0)

Santiago Bernabéu, Madrid 22.10.2002

Referee: Herbert Fandel (GER) Attendance: 58,343

REAL MADRID: Iker CASILLAS Fernández, Miguel Ángel "MICHEL" SALGADO, Fernando Ruíz HIERRO, Iván HELGUERA Bujía, ROBERTO CARLOS da Silva (75 RAÚL BRAVO Sanfelix), Steve McManaman (82 Óscar MIÑAMBRES Pascual), Albert CELADES López, Esteban CAMBIASSO Deleau, Zinédine Zidane (61 Santiago Hernán SOLARI), RONALDO Luis Nazario de Lima, José María Gutiérrez "GUTI". Trainer: Vicente DEL BOSQUE González

AEK: Dionisis Hiotis, Nikos Kostenoglou, Mihalis Kapsis, Mauricio Wright, Grigoris Georgatos (69 Walter Centeno), Vasilis Lakis, Theodoros Zagorakis, Konstantinos Katsouranis, Mihalis Kasapis, Themistoklis Nikolaidis (54 Ilija Ivic), Vassili Tsartas (54 Hristos Maladenis). Trainer: Dusko Bajević

Goals: McManaman (24, 43), Katsouranis (74), Centeno (86)

AS ROMA v KRC GENK 0-0

Olimpico, Roma 22.10.2002

Referee: Zeljko Sirić (CRO) Attendance: 25,592

AS ROMA: Francesco Antonioli, Jonathan Zebina, Walter Adriano Samuel, Christian Panucci, Marcos Evangelista de Moraes "CAFÚ" (84 Davide Bombardini), Damiano Tommasi (60 Gianni GUIGOU Martínez), Francisco Govinho LIMA, EMERSON Ferreira da Rosa, Vincent Candela, Gabriel Omar Batistuta, Antonio Cassano (46 Vincenzo Montella). Trainer: Fabio Capello

KRC GENK: Davy Schollen, Justice Wamfor, Igor Tomasic, Didier Zokora, Akram Roumani, Mirsad Beslija, Bernd Thijs, Josip Skoko, Koen Daerden (77 Takayuri Suzuki), Wesley Sonck, Beli-Moumouni Dagano. Trainer: Sef Vergoosen

AEK FC ATHINA v KRC GENK 1-1 (1-1)

Nea Philadelphia, Athina 30.10.2002

Referee: Massimo Busacca (SWI) Attendance: 19,775

AEK: Dionisis Hiotis, Nikos Kostenoglou, Mihalis Kapsis, Mauricio Wright, Grigoris Georgatos (78 Hristos Maladenis), Vasilis Lakis, Vasilis Borbokis (66 Walter Centeno), Konstantinos Katsouranis, Mihalis Kasapis, Themistoklis Nikolaidis, Vasilis Tsartas (66 Ilija Ivic). Trainer: Dusko Bajević

KRC GENK: Jan Moons, Justice Wamfor, Igor Tomasic, Didier Zokora, Akram Roumani, Mirsad Beslija (90+1 Thomas Chatelle), Bernd Thijs, Josip Skoko, Koen Daerden, Wesley Sonck, Takayuri Suzuki (90+4 Soley Seyfo). Trainer: Sef Vergoosen

Goals: Sonck (22), Lakis (30)

REAL MADRID CF v AS ROMA 0-1 (0-1)

Santiago Bernabéu, Madrid 30.10.2002

Referee: Hugh Dallas (SCO) Attendance: 72,035

REAL MADRID: Iker CASILLAS Fernández, Miguel Ángel "MICHEL" SALGADO, Fernando Ruíz HIERRO, Iván HELGUERA Bujía, ROBERTO CARLOS da Silva, Luís Felipe Madeira Caeiro "FIGO", Claude MAKELELE, Esteban CAMBIASSO Deleau (86 José María Gutiérrez "GUTI"), Zinédine ZIDANE (78 Santiago Hernán SOLARI), RONALDO Luis Nazario de Lima (79 Fernando MORIENTES Sánchez), RAÚL González Blanco. Trainer: Vicente DEL BOSQUE González

AS ROMA: Francesco Antonioli, Christian Panucci, ALDAIR Nascimento dos Santos (90+2 Jonathan Zebina), Walter Adriano Samuel, Marcos Evangelista de Moraes "CAFÚ", Damiano Tommasi, Francesco Totti, EMERSON Ferreira da Rosa, Vincent Candela, Marco Delvecchio (88 Francisco Govinho Lima), Vincenzo Montella (72 Gabriel Omar Batistuta). Trainer: Fabio Capello

Goal: Totti (27)

KRC GENK v REAL MADRID CF 1-1 (0-1)

Fenix, Genk 12.11.2002

Referee: Jacek Granat (POL) Attendance: 22,260

KRC GENK: Jan Moons, Igor Tomasic, Didier Zokora, Soley Seyfo, Akram Roumani, Mirsad Beslija, Bernd Thijs, Josip Skoko, Marco Ingrao (60 Takayuri Suzuki), Wesley Sonck, Kevin Vandenbergh (69 Thomas Chatelle).
Trainer: Sef Vergoosen

REAL MADRID: CÉSAR Sánchez Domínguez, Óscar MIÑAMBRES Pascual, Fernando Ruíz HIERRO (30 Iván HELGUERA Bujía), Francisco PAVÓN Barahona, ROBERTO CARLOS da Silva, Luís Felipe Madeira Caeiro "FIGO" (67 Steve McManaman), Albert CELADES López, FLÁVIO da CONCEICÃO, Jorge López Marco "TOTE", José María Gutiérrez "GUTI", Fernando MORIENTES Sánchez (77 Santiago Hernán SOLARI).
Trainer: Vicente DEL BOSQUE González

Goals: Tote (21), Sonck (86)

AS ROMA v AEK FC ATHINA 1-1 (1-0)

Olimpico, Roma 12.11.2002

Referee: Stéphane Bré (FRA) Attendance: 32,734

AS ROMA: Francesco Antonioli, Jonathan Zebina, Walter Adriano Samuel, Christian Panucci, Marcos Evangelista de Moraes "CAFÚ" (90 Davide Bombardini), Damiano Tommasi, EMERSON Ferreira da Rosa, Francisco Govinho Lima (81 Gianni GUIGOU Martínez), Antonio Cassano (65 Leandro Damián Cufré), Vincenzo Montella, Marco Delvecchio.
Trainer: Fabio Capello

AEK: Dionisis Hiotis, Vasilis Borbokis, Mihalis Kapsis (46 Nikos Kostenoglou), Mauricio Wright, Grigoris Georgatos, Vasilis Lakis (61 Vasilis Tsartas), Theodoros Zagorakis, Konstantinos Katsouranis, Walter Centeno, Themistoklis Nikolaidis, Dimitris Nalitzis (46 Ilija Ivic).
Trainer: Dusko Bajević

Goals: Delvecchio (40), Centeno (90)

Real Madrid CF and AS Roma qualified for the Second Group Stage. AEK Athina qualified for the UEFA Cup.

	P	W	D	L	F	A	Pts
Real Madrid CF	6	2	3	1	15	7	9
AS Roma	6	2	3	1	3	4	9
AEK Athina	6	0	6	0	7	7	6
KRC Genk	6	0	4	2	2	9	4

FIRST STAGE – GROUP D

AFC AJAX AMSTERDAM v OLYMPIQUE LYONNAIS 2-1 (2-0)

Amsterdam ArenA 17.09.2002

Referee: Michael Riley (ENG) Attendance: 37,104

AJAX: Maarten Stekelenburg, Hatem Trabelsi, Cristian Chivu, Abubakari Yakubu, John O'Brien, Tomáš Galásek (57 Jan Van Halst), Jari Litmanen, MAXWELL Scherer Cabelino Andrade, Victor Sikora (68 Steven Pienaar), Zlatan Ibrahimovic (81 André Bergdølmo), Andy Van Der Meyde.
Trainer: Ronald Koeman **Sent off**: Yakubu (85)

OLYMPIQUE: Grégory Coupet, Jean-Marc Chanelet (79 Mahamadou Diarra), Claudio Roberto Da Silva CAÇAPA, José EDMILSON Gomes de Moraes, Jérémie Bréchet, Vikash Dhorasoo, Eric Carrière, Philippe Violeau (46 Florent Laville), Antiono Augusto Ribeiro JUNINHO PERNAMBUCANO, Sonny ANDERSON da Silva, Sidney Govou (41 Tony Vairelles).

Goals: Ibrahimovic (11, 34), Anderson (84)

ROSENBORG BK TRONDHEIM v FC INTERNAZIONALE MILANO 2-2 (0-1)

Lerkendal, Trondheim 17.09.2002

Referee: Juan Antonio FERNANDEZ MARIN (SPA)
Attendance: 21,040

ROSENBORG: Arni Gautur Arason, Roar Strand (75 Ståle Stensaas), Erik Hoftun, Ole Christer Basma, Janne Saarinen, Odd Inge Olsen, Bent Skammelsrud, Ørjan Berg, Azar Karadas, Harald Martin Brattbakk, Frode Johnsen.
Trainer: Nils Arne Eggen

INTERNAZIONALE: Francesco Toldo, Fabio Cannavaro, Marco Materazzi, Iván Ramiro Cordoba, Francesco Coco, Stéphane Dalmat (63 Emre Belözoglu), Matías Jesús Almeyda, Javier Zanetti, Domenico Morfeo (77 Alvaro Recoba), Hernán Jorge Crespo (88 Daniele Adani), Christian Vieri.
Trainer: Hector Raúl Cúper **Sent off**: Cannavaro (69)

Goals: Crespo (33, 79), Karadas (52, 65)

FC INTERNAZIONALE MILANO v AFC AJAX AMSTERDAM 1-0 (0-0)

Giuseppe Meazza, Milano 25.09.2002

Referee: Stuart Dougal (SCO) Attendance: 45,784

INTERNAZIONALE: Francesco Toldo, Javier Zanetti, Marco Materazzi, Iván Ramiro Cordoba, Giovanni Pasquale, Okan Buruk (69 SÉRGIO Paulo Marceneiro CONCEIÇÃO), Luigi Di Biagio (65 Matías Jesús Almeyda), Emre Belözoglu (52 Alvaro Recoba), Stéphane Dalmat, Christian Vieri, Hernán Jorge Crespo. Trainer: Hector Raúl Cúper

AJAX: Maarten Stekelenburg (23 Henk Timmer), Hatem Trabelsi, Petri Pasanen (80 Ahmed HOSSAM «MIDO»), Cristian Chivu, Jelle Van Damme, Tomáš Galásek, Jari Litmanen, MAXWELL Scherer Cabelino Andrade, Andy Van Der Meyde (76 Steven Pienaar), Zlatan Ibrahimovic, Victor Sikora. Trainer: Ronald Koeman

Goal: Crespo (75)

OLYMPIQUE LYONNAIS v ROSENBORG BK TRONDHEIM 5-0 (4-0)

Gerland, Lyon 25.09.2002

Referee: Franz-Xaver Wack (GER) Attendance: 37,505

OLYMPIQUE: Grégory Coupet, Eric Deflandre, Patrick Müller, Claudio Roberto Da Silva CAÇAPA, Jérémie Bréchet, Philippe Violeau, Mahamadou Diarra, Vikash Dhorasoo (78 Christophe Delmotte), Eric Carrière, Sonny ANDERSON da Silva (67 Antiono Augusto Ribeiro JUNINHO PERNAMBUCANO), Tony Vairelles (72 Pegguy Luyindula). Trainer: Paul Le Guen

ROSENBORG: Arni Gautur Arason, Janne Saarinen (83 Lars Blixt), Ole Christer Basma, Erik Hoftun, Ståle Stensaas (72 Trond Fredrik Ludvigsen), Bent Skammelsrud, Odd Inge Olsen (65 Macbeth Sibaya), Ørjan Berg, Azar Karadas, Frode Johnsen, Harald Martin Brattbakk. Trainer: Nils Arne Eggen

Goals: Carrière (6), Vairelles (26, 45), Anderson (34), Luyindula (75)

FC INTERNAZIONALE MILANO v OLYMPIQUE LYONNAIS 1-2 (0-1)

Giuseppe Meazza, Milano 2.10.2002

Referee: Manuel Enrique MEJUTO GONZALEZ (SPA) Attendance: 31,448

INTERNAZIONALE: Francesco Toldo, Javier Zanetti, Marco Materazzi, Fabio Cannavaro, Francesco Coco (86 Giovanni Pasquale), Iván Ramiro Cordoba, Luigi Di Biagio (69 SÉRGIO Paulo Marceneiro CONCEIÇÃO), Matías Jesús Almeyda, Stéphane Dalmat (61 Domenico Morfeo), Alvaro Recoba, Hernán Jorge Crespo. Trainer: Hector Raúl Cúper

OLYMPIQUE: Grégory Coupet, Patrick Müller, Vikash Dhorasoo, Claudio Roberto Da Silva CAÇAPA, José EDMILSON Gomes de Moraes, Jérémie Bréchet, Philippe Violeau, Mahamadou Diarra, Eric Carrière (88 Antiono Augusto Ribeiro JUNINHO PERNAMBUCANO), Sonny ANDERSON da Silva (77 Florent Laville), Sidney Govou (90+1 Tony Vairelles). Trainer: Paul Le Guen

Goals: Govou (21), Anderson (60), Cannavaro (73)

ROSENBORG BK TRONDHEIM v AFC AJAX AMSTERDAM 0-0

Lerkendal, Trondheim 2.10.2002

Referee: Michal Benes (CZE) Attendance: 20,948

ROSENBORG: Arni Gautur Arason, Roar Strand, Ole Christer Basma, Erik Hoftun, Janne Saarinen, Odd Inge Olsen, Bent Skammelsrud, Ørjan Berg, Azar Karadas, Frode Johnsen (35 Dagfinn Enerly), Harald Martin Brattbakk (40 Christer George). Trainer: Nils Arne Eggen

AJAX: Joey Didulica, Hatem Trabelsi, André Bergdølmo, Cristian Chivu, Jelle Van Damme, Jan Van Halst (69 Aron Winter), Tomáš Galásek, Richard Witschge (79 MAXWELL Scherer Cabelino Andrade), WAMBERTO de Jesus Sousa Campos, Zlatan Ibrahimovic (69 Andy Van Der Meyde), Ahmed HOSSAM "MIDO". Trainer: Ronald Koeman

AFC AJAX AMSTERDAM v ROSENBORG BK TRONDHEIM 1-1 (1-0)

Amsterdam ArenA 22.10.2002

Referee: Arturo DAUDEN IBAÑEZ (SPA) Att: 42,026

AJAX: Henk Timmer, Hatem Trabelsi, André Bergdølmo, Cristian Chivu, Jelle Van Damme, Tomáš Galásek, Jari Litmanen, Richard Witschge (83 Nigel De Jong), Andy Van Der Meyde, Zlatan Ibrahimovic (71 Ahmed HOSSAM "MIDO"), Nourdin Boukhari. Trainer: Ronald Koeman

ROSENBORG: Arni Gautur Arason, Roar Strand, Erik Hoftun, Ole Christer Basma, Janne Saarinen, Ørjan Berg, Bent Skammelsrud (39 Odd Inge Olsen), Harald Martin Brattbakk (74 Trond Fredrik Ludvigsen), Frode Johnsen, Azar Karadas, Dagfinn Enerly. Trainer: Nils Arne Eggen

Sent off: van Damme (84)

Goals: Ibrahimovic (41), Enerly (85 pen)

OLYMPIQUE LYONNAIS v FC INTERNAZIONALE MILANO 3-3 (2-1)

Gerland, Lyon 22.10.2002

Referee: Kim Milton Nielsen (DEN) Attendance: 37,770

OLYMPIQUE: Grégory Coupet, Patrick Müller, Claudio Roberto Da Silva CAÇAPA, José EDMILSON Gomes de Moraes , Jérémie Bréchet, Antiono Augusto Ribeiro JUNINHO PERNAMBUCANO (58 Florent Laville), Eric Carrière, Philippe Violeau (69 Tony Vairelles), Mahamadou Diarra, Vikash Dhorasoo, Sonny ANDERSON da Silva. Trainer: Paul Le Guen

INTERNAZIONALE: Francesco Toldo, Javier Zanetti, Marco Materazzi, Iván Ramiro Cordoba, Francesco Coco, SÉRGIO Paulo Marceneiro CONCEIÇÃO (72 Daniele Adani), Luigi Di Biagio (24 Matías Jesús Almeyda), Emre Belözoglu, Domenico Morfeo, Hernán Jorge Crespo (78 Alvaro Recoba), Christian Vieri. Trainer: Hector Raúl Cúper

Goals: Anderson (21, 75), Caçapa (31 og), Carrière (44), Crespo (56, 66)

FC INTERNAZIONALE MILANO v ROSENBORG BK TRONDHEIM 3-0 (1-0)

Giuseppe Meazza, Milano 30.10.2002

Referee: Frank de Bleeckere (BEL) Attendance: 33,500

INTERNAZIONALE: Francesco Toldo, Javier Zanetti, Fabio Cannavaro, Marco Materazzi, Francesco Coco (87 Giovanni Pasquale), SÉRGIO Paulo Marceneiro CONCEIÇÃO, Luigi di Biagio, Emre Belözoglu, Alvaro Recoba, Hernán Jorge Crespo (75 Matías Jesús Almeyda), Christian Vieri. Trainer: Hector Raúl Cúper

ROSENBORG: Arni Gautur Arason, Roar Strand, Erik Hoftun, Ole Christer Basma, Janne Saarinen, Ørjan Berg, Bent Skammelsrud, Harald Martin Brattbakk (57 Odd Inge Olsen), Frode Johnsen, Azar Karadas, Dagfinn Enerly (80 Trond Fredrik Ludvigsen). Trainer: Nils Arne Eggen

Goals: Recoba (31), Saarinen (52 og), Crespo (72)

OLYMPIQUE LYONNAIS
v AFC AJAX AMSTERDAM 0-2 (0-1)

Gerland, Lyon 30.10.2002

Referee: Kyros Vassaras (GRE) Attendance: 38,134

OLYMPIQUE: Grégory Coupet, Patrick Müller, Claudio Roberto Da Silva CAÇAPA, José EDMILSON Gomes de Moraes, Jérémie Bréchet, Antiono Augusto Ribeiro JUNINHO PERNAMBUCANO, Eric Carrière (80 Pegguy Luyindula), Vikash Dhorasoo, Philippe Violeau (59 Tony Vairelles), Sonny ANDERSON da Silva, Sidney Govou. Trainer: Paul Le Guen

AJAX: Joey Didulica, Hatem Trabelsi, Cristian Chivu, André Bergdølmo, Nigel De Jong, MAXWELL Scherer Cabelino Andrade, Tomáš Galásek, Steven Pienaar, Victor Sikora (65 Abubakari Yakubu), Zlatan Ibrahimovic (77 Andy Van Der Meyde), Ahmed HOSSAM "MIDO" (55 Rafael Van Der Vaart). Trainer: Ronald Koeman

Sent off: Chivu (62)

Goals: Pienaar (7), Van Der Vaart (90+3)

AFC AJAX AMSTERDAM
v FC INTERNAZIONALE MILANO 1-2 (0-0)

Amsterdam ArenA 12.11.2002

Referee: Urs Meier (SWI) Attendance: 50,272

AJAX: Joey Didulica, Hatem Trabelsi, André Bergdølmo, Nigel De Jong, Jelle Van Damme (58 Richard Witschge), Steven Pienaar (58 WAMBERTO de Jesus Sousa Campos), Tomáš Galásek (71 Abubakari Yakubu), MAXWELL Scherer Cabelino Andrade, Andy Van Der Meyde, Rafael Van Der Vaart, Ahmed HOSSAM «MIDO». Trainer: Ronald Koeman

INTERNAZIONALE: Francesco Toldo, Javier Zanetti, Marco Materazzi, Iván Ramiro Cordoba, Francesco Coco, SÉRGIO Paulo Marceneiro CONCEIÇÃO (72 Daniele Adani), Matías Jesús Almeyda, Luigi Di Biagio, Domenico Morfeo (90+3 Emre Belözoglu), Hernán Jorge Crespo (65 Alvaro Recoba), Christian Vieri. Trainer: Hector Raúl Cúper

Goals: Crespo (50, 52), Van Der Vaart (90+4)

ROSENBORG BK TRONDHEIM
v OLYMPIQUE LYONNAIS 1-1 (0-0)

Lerkendal, Trondheim 12.11.2002

Referee: Hugh Dallas (SCO) Attendance: 21,008

ROSENBORG: Arni Gautur Arason, Roar Strand, Erik Hoftun, Ole Christer Basma, Janne Saarinen, Frode Johnsen, Bent Skammelsrud, Ørjan Berg, Dagfinn Enerly (79 Trond Fredrik Ludvigsen), Azar Karadas, Harald Martin Brattbakk. Trainer: Nils Arne Eggen

OLYMPIQUE: Grégory Coupet, Patrick Müller, Claudio Roberto Da Silva CAÇAPA, José EDMILSON Gomes de Moraes , Jérémie Bréchet, Vikash Dhorasoo (72 Christophe Delmotte), Philippe Violeau (66 Antiono Augusto Ribeiro JUNINHO PERNAMBUCANO), Mahamadou Diarra, Eric Carrière (72 Pegguy Luyindula), Sonny ANDERSON da Silva, Sidney Govou. Trainer: Paul Le Guen

Goals: Brattbakk (69), Govou (84)

Internazionale FC and AFC Ajax qualified for ythe Second Group Stage. Olympique Lyonnais qualified for the UEFA Cup.

	P	W	D	L	F	A	Pts
Internazionale FC	6	3	2	1	12	8	11
AFC Ajax Amsterdam	6	2	2	2	6	5	8
Olympique Lyonnais	6	2	2	2	12	9	8
Rosenborg BK	6	0	4	2	4	12	4

FIRST STAGE – GROUP E

FC DYNAMO KYIV
v NEWCASTLE UNITED FC 2-0 (1-0)

"Valeri Lobanovskiy", Kyiv 18.09.2002

Referee: Eduardo ITURRALDE GONZALEZ (SPA)
Attendance: 48,000

DYNAMO: Vitaliy Reva, Goran Sablic, Andriy Nesmachnyi, Tiberiu Ghioane, Georgi Ivanov Peev, Florin Lucian Cernat, Aleksandr Khatskevich (75 Goran Gavrancic), Andriy Husin, Jerko Leko, Maksim Shatskikh, LEANDRO Machado (56 Olexandr Melashchenko).
Trainer: Olekseiy Mykhaylychenko

NEWCASTLE UNITED: Shay Given, Andy Griffin, Nikos Dabizas, Andy O'Brien, Olivier Bernard, Kieron Dyer, Aaron Hughes (69 Norberto Solano), Gary Speed, HUGO Miguel Ferreira VIANA (69 Laurent Robert), Alan Shearer (79 Shola Ameobi), Craig Bellamy. Trainer: Robert Robson

Goals: Shatskikh (17), Khatskevich (62)

FEYENOORD ROTTERDAM
v JUVENTUS FC TORINO 1-1 (0-1)

Feyenoord, Rotterdam 18.09.2002

Referee: Antonio Jesus LOPEZ NIETO (SPA) Att: 40,751

FEYENOORD: Edwin Zoetebier, Christian Gyan (70 Mariano Bombarda), Kees Van Wonderen, Patrick Paauwe, Ramon Van Haaren, Chong-Gug Song, Brett Emerton, Shinji Ono, Sebastián Pardo (55 Bonaventure Kalou), Thomas Buffel, Pierre Van Hooijdonk. Trainer: Bert van Marwyk

JUVENTUS: Gianluigi Buffon, Lilian Thuram, Paolo MONTERO Iglesias, Ciro Ferrara, Alessandro Birindelli, Mauro Camoranesi (81 Davide Baiocco), Alessio Tacchinardi, Edgar Davids (65 Salvatore Fresi), Pavel Nedved, Alessandro Del Piero (76 José Marcelo Salas Melinao), Marco Di Vaio. Trainer: Marcello Lippi

Goals: Camoranesi (32), van Hooijdonk (75)

JUVENTUS FC TORINO v FC DYNAMO KYIV 5-0 (2-0)

Delle Alpi, Torino 24.09.2002

Referee: Wolfgang Stark (GER) Attendance: 26,876

JUVENTUS: Gianluigi Buffon, Lilian Thuram, Ciro Ferrara, Paolo MONTERO Iglesias (76 Davide Baiocco), Emiliano Moretti, Mauro Camoranesi, Alessio Tacchinardi (68 Igor Tudor), Edgar Davids, Pavel Nedved, Marco Di Vaio (72 David Trezeguet), Alessandro Del Piero. Trainer: Marcello Lippi

DYNAMO: Vitaliy Reva, Tiberiu Ghioane, Georgi Ivanov Peev, Andriy Husin, Goran Sablic, Andriy Nesmachnyi, Jerko Leko, Goran Gavrancic, Florin Lucian Cernat, Aleksandr Khatskevich (71 Olexandr Melashchenko), Maksim Shatskikh. Trainer: Olekseiy Mykhaylychenko

Goals: Di Vaio (14, 52), Del Piero (22), Davids (67), Nedved (79)

NEWCASTLE UNITED FC v FEYENOORD ROTTERDAM 0-1 (0-1)

Saint James' Park, Newcastle 24.09.2002

Referee: Claude Colombo (FRA) Attendance: 40,540

NEWCASTLE UNITED: Shay Given, Andy Griffin, Andy O'Brien, Nikos Dabizas, Aaron Hughes, Norberto Solano, Kieron Dyer, Gary Speed, Laurent Robert, Craig Bellamy (77 Lomana Tresor Lua-Lua), Alan Shearer.
Trainer: Robert Robson

FEYENOORD: Edwin Zoetebier, Brett Emerton, Kees Van Wonderen, Patrick Paauwe, Tomasz Rzasa, Chong-Gug Song, Paul Bosvelt, Shinji Ono, Sebastián Pardo (82 Anthony Lurling), Thomas Buffel, Pierre Van Hooijdonk.
Trainer: Bert van Marwyk

Goal: Pardo (4)

FEYENOORD ROTTERDAM v FC DYNAMO KYIV 0-0

Feyenoord, Rotterdam 1.10.2002

Referee: Tom Henning Ovrebo (NOR) Attendance: 41,200

FEYENOORD: Edwin Zoetebier, Brett Emerton, Ferry De Haan, Patrick Paauwe, Tomasz Rzasa, Chong-Gug Song, Paul Bosvelt, Shinji Ono, Sebastián Pardo (55 Robin Van Persie), Thomas Buffel (66 Bonaventure Kalou), Pierre Van Hooijdonk.
Trainer: Bert Van Marwyk

DYNAMO: Vitaliy Reva, László Bodnár, Tiberiu Ghioane, Andriy Nesmachnyi, Andriy Husin, Goran Gavrancic, Georgi Ivanov Peev, Florin Lucian Cernat (84 DIOGO de Fontoura "RINCÓN"), Aleksandr Khatskevich (63 Jerko Leko), Olexandr Melashchenko, Maksim Shatskikh.
Trainer: Olekseiy Mykhaylychenko

JUVENTUS FC TORINO v NEWCASTLE UNITED FC 2-0 (0-0)

Delle Alpi, Torino 1.10.2002

Referee: René H.J. Temmink (HOL) Attendance: 41,424

JUVENTUS: Gianluigi Buffon, Lilian Thuram, Mark Iuliano, Paolo MONTERO Iglesias, Emiliano Moretti, Davide Baiocco (86 Salvatore Fresi), Igor Tudor (84 Alessandro Birindelli), Edgar Davids, Pavel Nedved, Marco Di Vaio (17 David Trezeguet), Alessandro Del Piero. Trainer: Marcello Lippi

NEWCASTLE UNITED: Shay Given, Andy Griffin (79 Shola Ameobi), Andy O'Brien, Nikos Dabizas, Aaron Hughes, Norberto Solano (70 HUGO Miguel Ferreira VIANA), Gary Speed, Jermaine Jenas (80 Lomana Tresor Lua-Lua), Laurent Robert, Kieron Dyer, Alan Shearer. Trainer: Robert Robson

Goals: Del Piero (66, 81)

FC DYNAMO KYIV v FEYENOORD ROTTERDAM 2-0 (1-0)

"Valeri Lobanovskiy", Kyiv 23.10.2002

Referee: Markus Merk (GER) Attendance: 60,800

DYNAMO: Vitaliy Reva, Georgi Ivanov Peev, Goran Gavrancic, Tiberiu Ghioane, Yuriy Dmytrulin (77 Goran Sablic), Andriy Husin, Aleksandr Khatskevich, Valentin Belkevich, Badr El Kaddouri, DIOGO de Fontoura "RINCÓN" (57 Andriy Nesmachnyi), Maksim Shatskikh.
Trainer: Olekseiy Mykhaylychenko

FEYENOORD: Edwin Zoetebier, Chong-Gug Song, Glenn Loovens, Patrick Paauwe, Ramon Van Haaren (56 Tomasz Rzasa), Brett Emerton (62 Mariano Bombarda), Kees Van Wonderen, Shinji Ono, Robin Van Persie (39 Anthony Lurling), Thomas Buffel, Bonaventure Kalou.
Trainer: Bert van Marwyk

Goals: Khatskevich (16), Belkevich (47)

NEWCASTLE UNITED FC v JUVENTUS FC TORINO 1-0 (0-0)

Saint James' Park, Newcastle 23.10.2002

Referee: Rune Pedersen (NOR) Attendance: 48,370

NEWCASTLE UNITED: Steve Harper, Aaron Hughes, Andy O'Brien, Titus Bramble, Andy Griffin, Norberto Solano, Gary Speed, Jermaine Jenas, Laurent Robert (85 HUGO Miguel Ferreira VIANA), Alan Shearer, Lomana Tresor Lua-Lua (86 Shola Ameobi). Trainer: Robert Robson

JUVENTUS: Gianluigi Buffon, Lilian Thuram, Ciro Ferrara, Mark Iuliano, Alessandro Birindelli, Mauro Camoranesi (69 Gianluca Zambrotta), Alessio Tacchinardi, Pavel Nedved, Edgar Davids (46 Antonio Conte), Alessandro Del Piero, Marco Di Vaio (57 Marcelo Danubio Zalayeta).
Trainer: Marcello Lippi

Goal: Griffin (62)

JUVENTUS FC TORINO
v FEYENOORD ROTTERDAM 2-0 (1-0)

Delle Alpi, Torino 29.10.2002

Referee: Gilles Veissière (FRA) Attendance: 35,789

JUVENTUS: Gianluigi Buffon, Lilian Thuram (71 Mark Iuliano), Igor Tudor (89 Gianluca Zambrotta), Ciro Ferrara, Alessandro Birindelli, Mauro Camoranesi, Alessio Tacchinardi, Pavel Nedved (82 Emiliano Moretti), Edgar Davids, Alessandro Del Piero, Marco Di Vaio.
Trainer: Marcello Lippi

FEYENOORD: Edwin Zoetebier (46 Patrick Lodewijks), Chong-Gug Song, Kees Van Wonderen, Patrick Paauwe, Tomasz Rzasa, Brett Emerton, Paul Bosvelt, Shinji Ono, Anthony Lurling, Mariano Bombarda, Thomas Buffel.
Trainer: Bert Van Marwyk

Goals: di Vaio (4, 69)

FEYENOORD ROTTERDAM
v NEWCASTLE UNITED FC 2-3 (0-1)

Feyenoord, Rotterdam 13.11.2002

Referee: Franz-Xaver Wack (GER) Attendance: 45,000

FEYENOORD: Patrick Lodewijks, Christian Gyan, Kees Van Wonderen, Patrick Paauwe, Tomasz Rzasa, Chong-Gug Song (52 Mariano Bombarda), Paul Bosvelt, Brett Emerton, Anthony Lurling, Thomas Buffel, Bonaventure Kalou.
Trainer: Bert Van Marwyk

NEWCASTLE UNITED: Shay Given, Andy Griffin, Nikos Dabizas, Andy O'Brien, Aaron Hughes, Kieron Dyer, Gary Speed, Jermaine Jenas, HUGO Miguel Ferreira VIANA (83 Olivier Bernard), Alan Shearer, Craig Bellamy.
Trainer: Robert Robson

Goals: Bellamy (45+1, 90+1), Hugo Viana (49), Mombarda (65), Lurling (71)

NEWCASTLE UNITED FC
v FC DYNAMO KYIV 2-1 (0-0)

Saint James' Park, Newcastle 29.10.2002

Referee: Juan Antonio FERNANDEZ MARIN (46 José Javier LOSANTOS OMAR) (SPA) Attendance: 40,185

NEWCASTLE UNITED: Steve Harper, Andy Griffin, Andy O'Brien (46 Olivier Bernard), Titus Bramble (27 Nikos Dabizas), Aaron Hughes, Norberto Solano (82 Kieron Dyer), Gary Speed, Jermaine Jenas, Laurent Robert, Alan Shearer, Shola Ameobi. Trainer: Robert Robson

DYNAMO: Vitaliy Reva, Andriy Nesmachnyi, Goran Gavrancic, Tiberiu Ghioane, Yuriy Dmytrulin, Georgi Ivanov Peev, Andriy Husin, Valentin Belkevich, Jerko Leko (71 DIOGO de Fontoura "RINCÓN"), Badr El Kaddouri (77 Florin Lucian Cernat), Maksim Shatskikh.
Trainer: Olekseiy Mykhaylychenko

Goals: Shatskikh (47), Speed (58), Shearer (69 pen)

Juventus FC and Newcastle United FC qualified for the Second Group Stage. FC Dynamo Kyiv qualified for the UEFA Cup.

	P	W	D	L	F	A	Pts
Juventus FC Torino	6	4	1	1	12	3	13
Newcastle United FC	6	3	0	3	6	8	9
Dynamo Kyiv	6	2	1	3	6	9	7
Feyenoord Rotterdam	6	1	2	3	4	8	5

FC DYNAMO KYIV
v JUVENTUS FC TORINO 1-2 (0-0)

"Valeri Lobanovskiy", Kyiv 13.11.2002

Referee: Claus Bo Larsen (DEN) Attendance: 76,000

DYNAMO: Vitaliy Reva, Andriy Nesmachnyi, Goran Gavrancic, Tiberiu Ghioane, Yuriy Dmytrulin, László Bodnár, Andriy Husin, Valentin Belkevich, Aleksandr Khatskevich (59 Jerko Leko), Maksim Shatskikh, DIOGO de Fontoura "RINCÓN" (67 Florin Lucian Cernat).
Trainer: Olekseiy Mykhaylychenko

JUVENTUS: Antonio Chimenti, Alessandro Birindelli, Salvatore Fresi, Mark Iuliano, Gianluca Pessotto, Antonio Conte (27 Matteo Paro), Davide Baiocco, Ruben Olivera (76 Edgar Davids), Gianluca Zambrotta, Marcelo Danubio Zalayeta, José Marcelo SALAS Melinao (90+3 Mattia Cassani).
Trainer: Marcello Lippi

Goals: Shatskikh (50), Salas (53), Zalayeta (61)

FIRST STAGE – GROUP F

MANCHESTER UNITED FC
v MACCABI HAIFA FC 5-2 (2-1)

Old Trafford, Manchester 18.09.2002

Referee: Paul Allaerts (BEL) Attendance: 63,439

MANCHESTER UNITED: Fabian Barthez (67 RICARDO López Felipe), John O'Shea, Rio Ferdinand, Laurent Blanc, Mikael Silvestre, David Beckham, Philip Neville, Juan Sebastián Veron, Ryan Giggs (56 Diego FORLÁN Corazo), Ole Gunnar Solskjær, Ruud Van Nistelrooy (75 Danny Pugh).
Trainer: Alexander Chapman Ferguson

MACCABI: Dudu Awat, Adoram Keissy, Arik Benado, Eyal Almoshnino (56 Avishay Zano), Alon Harazi (74 Rafi Cohen), Yaniv Katan, Walid Badier, Eric Ejiofor, Nenad Pralija, Giovanni Rosso, Michael Zandberg (65 Guillermo Israilevich).
Trainer: Itzhak Shum

Goals: Katan (8), Giggs (10), Solskjær (35), Veron (46), van Nistelrooy (54), Cohen (85), Forlán (89 pen)

OLYMPIAKOS PEIRAIAS v BAYER 04 LEVERKUSEN 6-2 (3-1)

Rizoupoli, Athina 18.09.2002

Referee: Arturo DAUDEN IBAÑEZ (SPA) Att: 12,909

OLYMPIAKOS: Dimitris Eleutheropoulos, Hristos Patsatzoglou, Giorgos Anatolakis, Paraskevas Antzas, Stelios Venetidis, Stelios Giannakopoulos (83 Peter Ofori-Quaye), Christian Karembeu, José Elias Moedim "ZÉ ELIAS", Pär Zetterberg, Predrag Djordjević (90 Eduardo Luis Abonizio De Souza "EDU DRACENA"), GIOVANNI Silva de Oliveira (86 Alexis Alexandris). Trainer: Panagiotis Lemonis

BAYER: Frank Juric, Hanno Balitsch (71 Pascal Ojigwe), Lucimar Ferreira da Silva "LÚCIO", Thomas Kleine (51 Thomas Brdaric), Boris Zivkovic, Bernd Schneider, Carsten Ramelow, Yildiray Bastürk, Jan Simák, Jurica Vranjes, Oliver Neuville. Trainer: Klaus Toppmöller

Goals: Schneider (22, 78 pen), Kleine (27 og), Giannakopoulos (38), Djordjević (44, 64 pen, 73), Zetterberg (87)

BAYER 04 LEVERKUSEN v MANCHESTER UNITED FC 1-2 (0-2)

BayArena, Leverkusen 24.09.2002

Referee: Jan W. Wegereef (HOL) Attendance: 22,500

BAYER: Frank Juric, Boris Zivkovic, Carsten Ramelow, Lucimar Ferreira da Silva "LÚCIO", Hanno Balitsch (81 Françoaldo Sena de Souza "FRANÇA"), Marco Babic, Pascal Ojigwe (64 Jan Simák), Bernd Schneider, Yildiray Bastürk, Thomas Brdaric, Oliver Neuville (22 Dimitar Berbatov). Trainer: Klaus Toppmöller

MANCHESTER UNITED: Fabian Barthez, John O'Shea (46 Gary Neville), Rio Ferdinand, Laurent Blanc, Mikael Silvestre, David Beckham, Philip Neville, Nicky Butt, Juan Sebastián Veron (88 Ole Gunnar Solskjær), Ryan Giggs, Ruud Van Nistelrooy (46 Diego FORLÁN Corazo).
Trainer: Alexander Chapman Ferguson

Goals: Van Nistelrooy (31, 44), Berbatov (52)

MACCABI HAIFA FC v OLYMPIAKOS PEIRAIAS 3-0 (1-0)

GSP, Nicosia 24.09.2002

Referee: Massimo de Santis (ITA) Attendance: 14,893

MACCABI: Dudu Awat, Alon Harazi (52 Avishay Zano), Eric Ejiofor, Arik Benado, Adoram Keissy, Walid Badier, Raimondas Zutautas, Nenad Pralija (87 Guillermo Israilevich), Giovanni Rosso, Yakubu Ayegbeni, Yaniv Katan (79 Michael Zandberg).
Trainer: Itzhak Shum

OLYMPIAKOS: Dimitris Eleutheropoulos, Hristos Patsatzoglou, Paraskevas Antzas, Giorgos Anatolakis, Stelios Venetidis, Christian Karembeu, José Elias Moedim «ZÉ ELIAS» (55 Alexis Alexandris), Pär Zetterberg (71 Andreas Niniadis), Stelios Giannakopoulos (80 Peter Ofori-Quaye), Predrag Djordjević, GIOVANNI Silva de Oliveira.
Trainer: Panagiotis Lemonis

Goals: Ayegbeni (27 pen, 60, 86)

MACCABI HAIFA FC v BAYER 04 LEVERKUSEN 0-2 (0-1)

GSP, Nicosia 1.10.2002

Referee: Jacek Granat (POL) Attendance: 6,320

MACCABI: Dudu Awat, Avishay Zano, Eric Ejiofor, Arik Benado, Adoram Keissy, Walid Badier (60 Michael Zandberg), Raimondas Zutautas, Nenad Pralija (70 Guillermo Israilevich), Giovanni Rosso, Yaniv Katan (60 Rafi Cohen), Yakubu Ayegbeni. Trainer: Itzhak Shum

BAYER: Hans-Jörg Butt, Boris Zivkovic, Carsten Ramelow, Lucimar Ferreira da Silva «LÚCIO», Hanno Balitsch, Pascal Ojigwe, Bernd Schneider (85 Daniel Bierofka), Yildiray Bastürk, Marco Babic (77 Jurica Vranjes), Oliver Neuville, Thomas Brdaric (70 Dimitar Berbatov).
Trainer: Klaus Toppmöller

Goals: Babic (31, 64)

MANCHESTER UNITED FC v OLYMPIAKOS PEIRAIAS 4-0 (2-0)

Old Trafford, Manchester 1.10.2002

Referee: Gilles Veissière (FRA) Attendance: 66,902

MANCHESTER UNITED: Fabian Barthez, Gary Neville, Rio Ferdinand, Laurent Blanc (69 John O'Shea), Mikael Silvestre, David Beckham, Nicky Butt, Juan Sebastián Veron, Ryan Giggs (69 Quinton Fortune), Paul Scholes (77 Diego FORLÁN Corazo), Ole Gunnar Solskjær.
Trainer: Alexander Chapman Ferguson

OLYMPIAKOS: Dimitris Eleutheropoulos, Giorgos Amanatidis (73 Hristos Patsatzoglou), Giorgos Anatolakis, Paraskevas Antzas, Stelios Venetidis, Stelios Giannakopoulos (46 Eduardo Luis Abonizio De Souza "EDU DRACENA"), Christian Karembeu, José Elias Moedim "ZÉ ELIAS", Predrag Djordjević, Pär Zetterberg, Peter Ofori-Quaye (59 Alexis Alexandris). Trainer: Panagiotis Lemonis

Sent off: Zé Elias (45+1)

Goals: Giggs (19, 66), Veron (26), Solskjær (77).

BAYER 04 LEVERKUSEN v MACCABI HAIFA FC 2-1 (1-0)

BayArena, Leverkusen 23.10.2002

Referee: Eric Poulat (FRA) Attendance: 22,500

BAYER: Hans-Jörg Butt, Zoltán Sebescen, Lucimar Ferreira da Silva "LÚCIO", Juan Silviera dos Santos "JUAN", Diego Rodolfo Placente, Bernd Schneider, Carsten Ramelow, Yildiray Bastürk, Marco Babic, Thomas Brdaric (46 Oliver Neuville), Françoaldo Sena de Souza "FRANÇA" (60 Jan Simak).
Trainer: Klaus Toppmöller

MACCABI: Dudu Awat, Adoram Keissy, Arik Benado, Raimondas Zutautas, Avishay Zano (80 Nir Sivilia), Michael Zandberg (74 Yaniv Katan), Alon Harazi, Walid Badier, Nenad Pralija (74 Guillermo Israilevich), Giovanni Rosso, Yakubu Ayegbeni. Trainer: Itzhak Shum

Goals: Babic (45), Pralija (53), Juan (67)

OLYMPIAKOS PEIRAIAS v MANCHESTER UNITED FC 2-3 (0-1)

Rizoupoli, Athina 23.10.2002

Referee: Pierluigi Collina (ITA) Attendance: 13,220

OLYMPIAKOS: Dimitris Eleutheropoulos, Hristos Patsatzoglou, Giorgos Anatolakis, Paraskevas Antzas, Stelios Venetidis, Stelios Giannakopoulos (87 Dimitris Mavrogenidis), Christian Karembeu, Eduardo Luis Abonizio De Souza "EDU DRACENA", Predrag Djordjević, Pär Zetterberg (71 Peter Ofori-Quaye), GIOVANNI Silva de Oliveira (46 Lampros Houtos). Trainer: Giannis Kollias

MANCHESTER UNITED: Fabian Barthez, Gary Neville, Laurent Blanc, John O'Shea, Mikael Silvestre, David Beckham (63 Luke Chadwick), Philip Neville, Juan Sebastián Veron (87 Kieran Edward Richardson), Ryan Giggs (63 Quinton Fortune), Paul Scholes, Diego FORLÁN Corazo. Trainer: Alexander Chapman Ferguson

Goals: Blanc (21), Veron (59), Houtos (70), Djordjević (74), Scholes (84)

BAYER 04 LEVERKUSEN v OLYMPIAKOS PEIRAIAS 2-0 (1-0)

BayArena, Leverkusen 29.10.2002

Referee: Alfredo Trentalange (ITA) Attendance: 22,500

BAYER: Hans-Jörg Butt, Boris Zivkovic, Lucimar Ferreira da Silva "LÚCIO", Juan Silviera dos Santos "JUAN" (45+2 Pascal Ojigwe), Diego Rodolfo Placente, Bernd Schneider, Yildiray Bastürk, Hanno Balitsch, Marco Babic, Oliver Neuville (62 Jan Simak), Dimitar Berbatov (90 Thomas Brdarić). Trainer: Klaus Toppmöller

OLYMPIAKOS: Dimitris Eleutheropoulos, Dimitris Mavrogenidis, Giorgos Anatolakis (46 Pär Zetterberg), Paraskevas Antzas (63 Peter Ofori-Quaye), Hristos Patsatzoglou, Stelios Venetidis, Stelios Giannakopoulos, Christian Karembeu, Eduardo Luis Abonizio De Souza "EDU DRACENA", Predrag Djordjević, Lampros Houtos (24 GIOVANNI Silva de Oliveira). Trainer: Giannis Kollias

Goals: Juan (14), Schneider (90 pen)

MACCABI HAIFA FC v MANCHESTER UNITED FC 3-0 (1-0)

GSP, Nicosia 29.10.2002

Referee: Antonio Jesus LOPEZ NIETO (SPA) Att: 16,653

MACCABI: Dudu Awat, Avishay Zano, Alon Harazi, Arik Benado, Raimondas Zutautas (81 Michael Zandberg), Adoram Keissy, Walid Badier, Yaniv Katan, Nenad Pralija, Giovanni Rosso, Yakubu Ayegbeni (84 Eyal Almoshnino). Trainer: Itzhak Shum

MANCHESTER UNITED: RICARDO López Felipe, Gary Neville, Rio Ferdinand, John O'Shea, Mikael Silvestre, Philip Neville, Paul Scholes, Kieran Edward Richardson (61 Daniel Nardiello), Quinton Fortune, Ole Gunnar Solskjær, Diego Forlán Corazo (79 Mads Timm). Trainer: Alexander Chapman Ferguson

Goals: Katan (40), Zutautas (56), Ayegbeni (77 pen)

MANCHESTER UNITED FC v BAYER 04 LEVERKUSEN 2-0 (1-0)

Old Trafford, Manchester 13.11.2002

Referee: Vladimir Hrinak (SVK) Attendance: 66,185

MANCHESTER UNITED: RICARDO López Felipe, John O'Shea, Laurent Blanc (77 Gary Neville), Rio Ferdinand, Mikael Silvestre, David Beckham (78 Ole Gunnar Solskjær), Ryan Giggs (81 Luke Chadwick), Juan Sebastián Veron, Quinton Fortune, Paul Scholes, Ruud Van Nistelrooy. Trainer: Alexander Chapman Ferguson

BAYER: Hans-Jörg Butt, Zoltán Sebescen, Carsten Ramelow, Thomas Kleine, Boris Zivkovic, Daniel Bierofka (78 Hüzeyfe Dogan), Hanno Balitsch (81 Christoph Preuss), Jan Simak, Marco Babic, Thomas Brdaric, Dimitar Berbatov (62 Françoaldo Sena de Souza "FRANÇA"). Trainer: Klaus Toppmöller

Goals: Veron (42), Van Nistelrooy (69)

OLYMPIAKOS PEIRAIAS v MACCABI HAIFA FC 3-3 (1-3)

Rizoupoli, Athina 13.11.2002

Referee: Rene H.J. Temmink (HOL) Attendance: 29,000

OLYMPIAKOS: Dimitris Eleutheropoulos, Hristos Patsatzoglou, Christian Karembeu, Paraskevas Antzas, Stelios Venetidis, Stelios Giannakopoulos, Pär Zetterberg (46 Andreas Niniadis), Eduardo Luis Abonizio De Souza "EDU DRACENA", Predrag Djordjevic, Alexis Alexandris, GIOVANNI Silva de Oliveira (71 Peter OFORI-QUAYE). Trainer: Srecko Katanec

MACCABI: Dudu Awat, Avishay Zano, Alon Harazi, Arik Benado, Adoram Keissy, Walid Badier, Yaniv Katan (68 Michael Zandberg), Eric Ejiofor, Nenad Pralija (79 Eyal Almoshnino), Giovanni Rosso, Yakubu Ayegbeni. Trainer: Itzhak Shum

Goals: Badier (9), Ayegbeni (10), Alexandris (37), Katan (41), Niniadis (51), Antzas (79)

Manchester United FC and Bayer 04 Leverkusen qualified for the Second Group Stage. Maccabi Haifa FC qualified for the UEFA Cup.

	P	W	D	L	F	A	Pts
Manchester United FC	6	5	0	1	16	8	15
Bayer 04 Leverkusen	6	3	0	3	9	11	9
Maccabi Haifa FC	6	2	1	3	12	12	7
Olympiakos Peiraias	6	1	1	4	11	17	4

FIRST STAGE – GROUP G

FC BAYERN MÜNCHEN v RC DEPORTIVO LA CORUÑA 2-3 (0-2)

Olympiastadion, München 18.09.2002

Referee: Graham Poll (ENG) Attendance: 35,000

BAYERN: Oliver Kahn, Willy Sagnol (46 Owen Hargreaves), Samuel Osei Kuffour, Thomas Linke, Michael Tarnat, Hasan Salihamidzic, Jens Jeremies (78 Niko Kovac), Michael Ballack, ZÉ ROBERTO da Silva (81 Alexander Zickler), Giovane Élber, Claudio Pizarro. Trainer: Ottmar Hitzfeld

DEPORTIVO: Juan Miguel García Inglés "JUANMÍ", HÉCTOR Berenguel Del Pino, Nourredine NAYBET, DONATO Gama da Silva, Enrique Fernández ROMERO, VÍCTOR Sánchez del Amo (71 Roberto Miguel ACUÑA), MAURO da SILVA Gomes, Juan Carlos VALERÓN Santana, SERGIO González Soriano, Francisco J.González Pérez "FRAN" (67 Joan CAPDEVILA Méndez), Roy MAKAAY (86 Alberto LUQUE Martos). Trainer: Javier IRURETAGOYENA

Goals: Makaay (12, 45+1, 77), Salihamidzić (57), Élber (64)

AC MILAN v RACING CLUB DE LENS 2-1 (0-0)

Giuseppe Meazza, Milano 18.09.2002

Referee: Kyros Vassaras (GRE) Attendance: 70,459

AC MILAN: Nélson de Jesus Silva "DIDA", Dario Simic, Paolo Maldini, Alessandro Nesta, Kakha Kaladze, Gennaro Gattuso, Andrea Pirlo, RUI Manuel César COSTA (82 Jon Dahl Tomasson), Clarence Seedorf, Filippo Inzaghi (85 Martin Laursen), "RIVALDO" Vítor Barbosa Ferreira (77 Massimo Ambrosini). Trainer: Carlo Ancelotti

RC LENS: Guillaume Warmuz, Adama Coulibaly, Abdoulaye Diagne-Faye (64 Seydou Keita), Jacek Bak, Ferdinand Coly, Bahanag Rigobert Song, Jocelyn Blanchard (84 Dagui Bakari), Pape Bouba Diop, Antoine Sibierski, Olivier Thomert (64 John Chukwudi Utaka), Daniel Moreira. Trainer: Joël Muller

Goals: Inzaghi (57, 61), Moreira (75)

DEPORTIVO LA CORUÑA v AC MILAN 0-4 (0-2)

Riazor, La Coruña 24.09.2002

Referee: Kom Milton Nielsen (DEN) Attendance: 27,614

DEPORTIVO: Juan Miguel García Inglés "JUANMÍ", Lionel Sebastián SCALONI, CÉSAR Martín Víllar, Nourredine NAYBET, Enrique Fernández ROMERO, VÍCTOR Sánchez del Amo, Roberto Miguel ACUÑA (62 Aldo Pedro DUSCHER), MAURO da SILVA Gomes (79 DONATO Gama da Silva), Francisco J. González Pérez "FRAN" (62 DIEGO TRISTAN Herrera), SERGIO González Soriano, Roy MAKAAY. Trainer: Javier IRURETAGOYENA AMIANO

AC MILAN: Nélson de Jesus Silva «DIDA», Dario Simic, Alessandro Nesta, Paolo Maldini, Kakha Kaladze, Andrea Pirlo (64 Massimo Ambrosini), Gennaro Gattuso, RUI Manuel César COSTA (83 Samuele Dalla Bona), Clarence Seedorf, «RIVALDO» Vítor Barbosa Ferreira, Filippo Inzaghi (80 Jon Dahl Tomasson). Trainer: Carlo Ancelotti

Goals: Seedorf (17), Inzaghi (33, 55, 62)

RACING CLUB DE LENS v FC BAYERN MÜNCHEN 1-1 (0-1)

Félix Bollaert, Lens 24.09.2002

Referee: Lucilio CARDOSO CORTEZ BATISTA (POR)
Attendance: 39,567

RC LENS: Guillaume Warmuz, Ferdinand Coly, Bahanag Rigobert Song, Jacek Bak, Cyril Rool, Seydou Keita, Jocelyn Blanchard (68 Dagui Bakari), Pape Bouba Diop, John Chukwudi Utaka, Daniel Moreira, Antoine Sibierski. Trainer: Joël Muller

BAYERN: Oliver Kahn, Owen Hargreaves, Robert Kovac, Thomas Linke, Michael Tarnat (77 Samuel Osei Kuffour), Hasan Salihamidzic, Jens Jeremies, Michael Ballack, ZÉ ROBERTO da Silva, Claudio Pizarro, Giovane Élber (73 Alexander Zickler). Trainer: Ottmar Hitzfeld

Goals: Linke (23), Utaka (76)

FC BAYERN MÜNCHEN v AC MILAN 1-2 (0-0)

Olympiastadion, München 1.10.2002

Referee: Hugh Dallas (SCO) Attendance: 59,000

BAYERN: Oliver Kahn, Robert Kovac, Thomas Linke, Owen Hargreaves, Jens Jeremies, Michael Tarnat (87 Alexander Zickler), Hasan Salihamidzic, Michael Ballack, ZÉ ROBERTO da Silva, Claudio Pizarro, Giovane Élber. Trainer: Ottmar Hitzfeld

AC MILAN: Nélson de Jesus Silva "DIDA", Dario Simic, Alessandro Nesta, Paolo Maldini, Kakha Kaladze, Andrea Pirlo (77 Sérgio Cláudio dos Santos "SERGINHO"), Gennaro Gattuso, RUI Manuel César COSTA (87 Martin Laursen), Clarence Seedorf, "RIVALDO" Vítor Barbosa Ferreira (66 Massimo Ambrosini), Filippo Inzaghi. Trainer: Carlo Ancelotti

Goals: Inzaghi (52, 84), Pizarro (54)

RC DEPORTIVO LA CORUÑA v RACING CLUB DE LENS 3-1 (0-1)

Riazor, La Coruña 1.10.2002

Referee: Rune Pedersen (NOR) Attendance: 24,734

DEPORTIVO: José Francisco MOLINA Giménez, HÉCTOR Berenguel Del Pino (46 SERGIO González Soriano), Nourredine NAYBET, CÉSAR Martín Víllar, Enrique Fernández ROMERO, MAURO da SILVA Gomes, Aldo Pedro DUSCHER (70 Joan CAPDEVILA Méndez), Lionel Sebastián SCALONI, Francisco J.González Pérez "FRAN", DIEGO TRISTAN Herrera (76 Alberto LUQUE Martos), Roy MAKAAY. Trainer: Javier IRURETAGOYENA AMIANO

RC LENS: Guillaume Warmuz, Ferdinand Coly, Jacek Bak (65 Adama Coulibaly), Bahanag Rigobert Song, Cyril Rool, Jocelyn Blanchard, Antoine Sibierski (84 Dagui Bakari), Charles-Edouard Coridon, Stéphane Pedron (76 Abdoulaye Diagne-Faye), John Chukwudi Utaka, Daniel Moreira. Trainer: Joël Muller

Goals: Moreira (10), Makaay (49), Capdevila (79), César (84)

RACING CLUB DE LENS v RC DEPORTIVO LA CORUÑA 3-1 (0-1)

Félix Bollaert, Lens 23.10.2002

Referee: Iordan Ivanov (BUL) Attendance: 37,982

RC LENS: Guillaume Warmuz, Adama Coulibaly, Bahanag Rigobert Song, Jacek Bak, Cyril Rool, Antoine Sibierski (73 Dagui Bakari), Seydou Keita, Pape Bouba Diop (73 Charles-Edouard Coridon), Olivier Thomert (86 Rod Fanni), John Chukwudi Utaka, Daniel Moreira. Trainer: Joël Muller

DEPORTIVO: Juan Miguel García Inglés «JUANMÍ», HÉCTOR Berenguel Del Pino, DONATO Gama da Silva, Nourredine NAYBET, Enrique Fernández ROMERO, VÍCTOR Sánchez del Amo (65 Lionel Sebastián SCALONI), SERGIO González Soriano, Francisco J.González Pérez «FRAN», MAURO da SILVA Gomes, Joan CAPDEVILA Méndez (84 Alberto LUQUE Martos), Roy MAKAAY (70 DIEGO TRISTAN Herrera). Trainer: Javier IRURETAGOYENA AMIANO

Goals: Makaay (15), Coulibaly (61), Moreira (79), Thomert (84)

AC MILAN v FC BAYERN MÜNCHEN 2-1 (1-1)

Giuseppe Meazza, Milano 23.10.2002

Referee: Ľuboš Michel (SVK) Attendance: 75,611

AC MILAN: Nélson de Jesus Silva "DIDA", Dario Simic, Paolo Maldini, Alessandro Nesta, Kakha Kaladze, Clarence Seedorf, Massimo Ambrosini (46 Gennaro Gattuso), RUI Manuel César COSTA (85 Martin Laursen), Sérgio Cláudio dos Santos "SERGINHO" (79 Samuele Dalla Bona), Andrea Pirlo, Filippo Inzaghi. Trainer: Carlo Ancelotti

BAYERN: Oliver Kahn (51 Stefan Wessels), Willy Sagnol, Samuel Osei Kuffour, Robert Kovac, Michael Tarnat, Hasan Salihamidzic (70 Mehmet Scholl), Jens Jeremies, Michael Ballack, ZÉ ROBERTO da Silva, Giovane Élber, Claudio Pizarro (72 Roque Santa Cruz). Trainer: Ottmar Hitzfeld

Goals: Serginho (11), Tarnat (23), Inzaghi (64)

RC DEPORTIVO LA CORUÑA v FC BAYERN MÜNCHEN 2-1 (0-0)

Riazor, La Coruña 29.10.2002

Referee: Anders Frisk (SWE) Attendance: 26,948

DEPORTIVO: Juan Miguel García Inglés "JUANMÍ", Lionel Sebastián SCALONI, Nourredine NAYBET, CÉSAR Martín Víllar, Enrique Fernández ROMERO, VÍCTOR Sánchez del Amo (84 DIEGO TRISTAN Herrera), Francisco J.González Pérez "FRAN" (66 Roberto Miguel ACUÑA), MAURO da SILVA Gomes, SERGIO González Soriano, Joan CAPDEVILA Méndez, Roy MAKAAY (90+2 DONATO Gama da Silva). Trainer: Javier IRURETAGOYENA AMIANO

BAYERN: Stefan Wessels, Willy Sagnol, Samuel Osei Kuffour, Robert Kovac, Michael Tarnat (60 Bixente Lizarazu), Hasan Salihamidzic (46 Roque Santa Cruz), Jens Jeremies, Michael Ballack (52 Thorsten Fink), ZÉ ROBERTO da Silva, Giovane Élber, Mehmet Scholl. Trainer: Ottmar Hitzfeld

Goals: Víctor (54), Santa Cruz (77), Makaay (89)

RACING CLUB DE LENS v AC MILAN 2-1 (1-1)

Félix Bollaert, Lens 29.10.2002

Referee: Graham Barber (ENG) Attendance: 39,474

RC LENS: Guillaume Warmuz, Adama Coulibaly, Bahanag Rigobert Song, Jacek Bak, Cyril Rool, Charles-Edouard Coridon, Antoine Sibierski (87 Abdoulaye Diagne-Faye), Pape Bouba Diop (57 Ferdinand Coly), Seydou Keita, Daniel Moreira (90 Olivier Thomert), John Chukwudi Utaka. Trainer: Joël Muller

AC MILAN: Christian Abbiati, Thomas Helveg, Alessandro Costacurta, Martin Laursen, Paolo Maldini (65 Kakha Kaladze), Samuele Dalla Bona, Andrea Pirlo, Massimo Ambrosini, Sérgio Cláudio dos Santos "SERGINHO" (65 Clarence Seedorf), Jon Dahl Tomasson, Andriy Shevchenko (46 Carlo Borriello). Trainer: Carlo Ancelotti

Goals: Shevchenko (31), Moreira (41), Utaka (49)

AC MILAN v RC DEPORTIVO LA CORUÑA 1-2 (1-0)

Giuseppe Meazza, Milano 13.11.2002

Referee: Michael Riley (ENG) Attendance: 56,294

AC MILAN: Christian Abbiati, Thomas Helveg, Paolo Maldini, Dario Simic, Kakha Kaladze (85 Catilina AUBAMEYANG "AUBAME"), RUI Manuel César COSTA (75 Filippo Inzaghi), Andrea Pirlo, Samuele Dalla Bona, Sérgio Cláudio dos Santos "SERGINHO", Jon Dahl Tomasson, Andriy Shevchenko. Trainer: Carlo Ancelotti

DEPORTIVO: Juan Miguel García Inglés "JUANMÍ", Lionel Sebastián SCALONI, HÉCTOR Berenguel Del Pino, Enrique Fernández ROMERO, Joan CAPDEVILA Méndez, MAURO da SILVA Gomes, SERGIO González Soriano, Francisco J.González Pérez "FRAN" (65 Roberto Miguel ACUÑA), Roy MAKAAY (78 Aldo Pedro DUSCHER), DIEGO TRISTAN Herrera, Alberto LUQUE Martos (56 José Emilio AMAVISCA Gárate). Trainer: Javier IRURETAGOYENA AMIANO

Goals: Tomasson (34), Diego Tristan (58), Makaay (70)

FC BAYERN MÜNCHEN v RACING CLUB DE LENS 3-3 (2-1)

Olympiastadion, München 13.11.2002

Referee: Paul Allaerts (BEL) Attendance: 22,000

BAYERN: Stefan Wessels, Robert Kovac, Thomas Linke, Bixente Lizarazu, Hasan Salihamidzic, Thorsten Fink, Niko Kovac, Markus Feulner (90+2 Philipp Lahm), Mehmet Scholl (76 Bastian Schweinsteiger), Alexander Zickler, Claudio Pizarro (46 Giovane Élber). Trainer: Ottmar Hitzfeld

RC LENS: Guillaume Warmuz, Adama Coulibaly, Bahanag Rigobert Song, Jacek Bak, Cyril Rool (69 Seydou Keita), Antoine Sibierski, Jocelyn Blanchard, Charles-Edouard Coridon (29 Abdoulaye Diagne-Faye), John Chukwudi Utaka, Daniel Moreira, Dagui Bakari (76 Olivier Thomert). Trainer: Joël Muller

Goals: Kovac (6), Salihamidzic (19), Fink (20 og), Bakari (54), Feulner (87), Blanchard (90)

Milan AC and RC Deportivo La Coruña qualified for the Second Group Stage. Racing Club de Lens qualified for the UEFA Cup

	P	W	D	L	F	A	Pts
AC Milan	6	4	0	2	12	7	12
Deportivo La Coruña	6	4	0	2	11	12	12
RC Lens	6	2	2	2	11	11	8
FC Bayern München	6	0	2	4	9	13	2

FIRST STAGE – GROUP H

FC BARCELONA v CLUB BRUGGE KV 3-2 (3-1)

Camp Nou, Barcelona 18.09.2002

Referee: Helmut Fleischer (GER) Attendance: 83,000

FC BARCELONA: VÍCTOR VALDÉS Arribas, Carlos PUYOL Saforcada, Frank DE BOER, FERNANDO NAVARRO Corbacho, Gaizka MENDIETA Zabala (76 Fabio ROCHEMBACK), Xavier Hernández Creus "XAVI", Philip COCU, Thiago MOTTA, Javier Pedro SAVIOLA, LUIS ENRIQUE Martínez García (73 Juan Román RIQUELME), Patrick KLUIVERT. Trainer: Louis van Gaal

CLUB BRUGGE: Dany Verlinden, Olivier De Cock, Marek Spilar, Birger Maertens, Peter Van Der Heyden (56 Alin Stoica), Gaëtan Englebert, Sergiy Serebrennikov (46 Milan Lesnjak), Timmy Simons, Sandy Martens (71 Nastja Ceh), Gert Verheyen, Andrés MENDOZA Acevedo. Trainer: Trond Sollied

Goals: Luis Enrique (5), Simons (22 pen), Mendieta (40), Saviola (44), Englebert (85)

FC LOKOMOTIV MOSKVA v GALATASARAY SK ISTANBUL 0-2 (0-0)

Lokomotiv, Moskva 18.09.2002

Referee: Massimo Busacca (SWI) Attendance: 24,000

LOKOMOTIV: Sergey Ovchinnikov, Gennady Nizhegorodov, Sergey Ignashevich, Oleg Pashinin (60 Dmitri Sennikov), Jacob Lekcetho, Vladimir Maminov, Yuri Drozdov, Dmitry Loskov, Vadim Evseyev, Maksim Buznikin (46 Ruslan Pimenov), JULIO CESAR da Silva e Souza (74 Amando BABA ADAMU). Trainer: Yuri Semin

GALATASARAY: Ali Faryd Camilo Mondragon, Ümit Davala, Bülent Korkmaz, Trevino Sergio Almaguer, Hakan Ünsal, Jorge FELIPE Loreiro, Ayhan Akman (46 FABIO PINTO), João Batista, Ergün Penbe, Arif Erdem (84 Emre Asik), HASAN Gökhan SAS (70 Mohammed Sarr). Trainer: Fatih Terim

Goals: Sarr (72), Arif Erdem (81)

CLUB BRUGGE KV v FC LOKOMOTIV MOSKVA 0-0

Jan Breydelstadion, Brugge 24.09.2002

Referee: Paulo Manuel GOMES COSTA (POR) Att: 25,878

CLUB BRUGGE: Dany Verlinden, Olivier De Cock, Marek Spilar (61 Philippe Clement), Birger Maertens, Peter Van Der Heyden, Gaëtan Englebert, Sergiy Serebrennikov, Timmy Simons, Gert Verheyen, Rune Lange, Andrés MENDOZA Acevedo (66 Alin Stoica). Trainer: Trond Sollied

LOKOMOTIV: Sergey Ovchinnikov, Gennady Nizhegorodov, Sergey Ignashevich, Dmitri Sennikov, Jacob Lekcetho, Vladimir Maminov (46 Milan Obradovic), Dmitry Loskov, Vadim Evseyev, Maksim Buznikin (46 Narvik Sirkhayev), Ruslan Pimenov, JULIO CESAR da Silva e Souza (74 James Obiorah). Trainer: Yuri Semin

Sent off: Obiorah (84)

GALATASARAY SK ISTANBUL v FC BARCELONA 0-2 (0-1)

Ali Sami Yen, Istanbul 24.09.2002

Referee: Domenico Messina (ITA) Attendance: 20,327

GALATASARAY: Ali Faryd Camilo MONDRAGON, Mohammed Sarr (46 HASAN Gökhan SAS), Bülent Korkmaz, Trevino Sergio Almaguer, Hakan Ünsal, Ümit Davala, João Batista, Jorge FELIPE Loreiro, Ergün Penbe (80 Ümit Karan), Arif Erdem, CHRISTIAN Correia Dionisio (70 Suat Kaya). Trainer: Fatih Terim

FC BARCELONA: VÍCTOR VALDÉS Arribas, Carlos PUYOL Saforcada, Frank DE BOER, FERNANDO NAVARRO Corbacho, Gaizka MENDIETA Zabala, Xavier Hernández Creus "XAVI" (74 Gabriel García de la Torre "GABRI"), Philip COCU, Thiago MOTTA, Javier Pedro SAVIOLA (83 GEOVANNI Deiberson Mauricio), LUIS ENRIQUE Martínez García, Patrick KLUIVERT (90+1 GERARD López Segú). Trainer: Louis van Gaal

Goals: Kluivert (27), Luis Enrique (59)

GALATASARAY SK ISTANBUL v CLUB BRUGGE KV 0-0

Ali Sami Yen, Istanbul 1.10.2002

Referee: Eric Poulat (FRA) Attendance: 19,163

GALATASARAY: Ali Faryd Camilo MONDRAGON, Ümit Davala, Emre Asik, Bülent Korkmaz (83 Vedat Inceefe), Hakan Ünsal, João Batista, Suat Kaya, Jorge FELIPE Loreiro (70 Ayhan Akman), HASAN Gökhan SAS (46 Elvir Baljic), Arif Erdem, Ümit Karan. Trainer: Fatih Terim

CLUB BRUGGE: Dany Verlinden, Birger Maertens, Timmy Simons, Philippe Clement, Olivier De Cock, Peter Van Der Heyden, Sergiy Serebrennikov, Alin Stoica (87 Nastja Ceh), Gaëtan Englebert, Gert Verheyen (90+1 Sandy Martens), Rune Lange (54 Andrés MENDOZA Acevedo). Trainer: Trond Sollied

FC LOKOMOTIV MOSKVA
v FC BARCELONA 1-3 (0-2)

Lokomotiv, Moskva 1.10.2002

Referee: Thomas Michael McCurry (SCO) Att: 21,000

LOKOMOTIV: Sergey Ovchinnikov, Gennady Nizhegorodov, Sergey Ignashevich, Dmitri Sennikov, Milan Obradovic, Yuri Drozdov, Jacob Lekcetho, Vadim Evseyev, Vladimir Maminov, James Obiorah (66 Maksim Buznikin), Ruslan Pimenov. Trainer: Yuri Semin

FC BARCELONA: VÍCTOR VALDÉS Arribas, Carlos PUYOL Saforcada, Frank DE BOER, FERNANDO NAVARRO Corbacho, Gaizka MENDIETA Zabala, Xavier Hernández Creus "XAVI", Philip COCU, Thiago MOTTA, Javier Pedro SAVIOLA (86 Fabio ROCHEMBACK), LUIS ENRIQUE Martínez García (61 GEOVANNI Deiberson Mauricio), Patrick KLUIVERT (75 GERARD López Segú). Trainer: Louis van Gaal

Goals: Kluivert (29), Saviola (32, 49), Obiorah (56)

FC BARCELONA
v FC LOKOMOTIV MOSKVA 1-0 (0-0)

Camp Nou, Barcelona 23.10.2002

Referee: Alain Hamer (LUX) Attendance: 62,426

FC BARCELONA: Roberto Óscar BONANO, Carlos PUYOL Saforcada, Frank de Boer, FERNANDO NAVARRO Corbacho, Gaizka MENDIETA Zabala (66 Fabio Rochemback), Xavier Hernández Creus "XAVI", Philip COCU, Gabriel García de la Torre "GABRI", Patrick KLUIVERT, Juan Román Riquelme, Javier Pedro SAVIOLA. Trainer: Louis van Gaal

LOKOMOTIV: Sergey Ovchinnikov, Dmitri Sennikov, Dmitry Loskov, Sergey Ignashevich, Oleg Pashinin, Milan Obradovic, Vadim Evseyev, Vladimir Maminov, JULIO CESAR da Silva e Souza (84 Maksim Buznikin), James Obiorah, Ruslan Pimenov. Trainer: Yuri Semin

Goal: de Boer (76)

CLUB BRUGGE KV
v GALATASARAY SK ISTANBUL 3-1 (1-0)

Jan Breydelstadion, Brugge 23.10.2002

Referee: Antonio de Santis (ITA) Attendance: 27,500

CLUB BRUGGE: Dany Verlinden, Olivier De Cock, Philippe Clement, Birger Maertens, Peter Van Der Heyden, Gaëtan Englebert, Alin Stoica (84 Marek Spilár), Timmy Simons, Nastja Ceh (64 Bengt Sæternes), Gert Verheyen (90 Tim Smolders), Sandy Martens. Trainer: Trond Sollied

GALATASARAY: Ali Faryd Camilo MONDRAGON, Mehmet Polat (46 Jorge FELIPE Loreiro), Bülent Korkmaz, Emre Asik (82 CHRISTIAN Correia Dionisio), Hakan Ünsal, Ümit Davala, Ergün Penbe, Cihan Haspolatli, FABIO PINTO, Arif Erdem (55 Ayhan Akman), Elvir Baljić. Trainer: Fatih Terim

Goals: Martens (45+1), Fabio Pinto (56), Verheyen (72), Sæternes (90+1)

CLUB BRUGGE KV v FC BARCELONA 0-1 (0-0)

Jan Breydelstadion, Brugge 20.10.2002

Referee: Graham Poll (ENG) Attendance: 27,334

CLUB BRUGGE: Dany Verlinden, Olivier De Cock, Philippe Clement (68 Marek Spilár), Birger Maertens, Peter Van Der Heyden (68 Bratislav Ristic), Gaëtan Englebert, Alin Stoica, Timmy Simons, Milan Lesnjak (80 Bengt Sæternes), Gert Verheyen, Sandy Martens. Trainer: Trond Sollied

FC BARCELONA: Robert ENKE, Carlos PUYOL Saforcada, Daniel "DANI" TORTOLERO Núñez, FERNANDO NAVARRO Corbacho, Fabio ROCHEMBACK, GERARD López Segú, Juan Román RIQUELME, Andrés INIESTA Lujan, Gabriel García de la Torre "GABRI" (89 DAVID SÁNCHEZ Rodríguez), Daniel García Lara "DANI", GEOVANNI Deiberson Mauricio (62 SERGIO GARCÍA de la Fuente). Trainer: Louis van Gaal

Goal: Riquelme (64)

GALATASARAY SK ISTANBUL
v FC LOKOMOTIV MOSKVA 1-2 (0-0)

Ali Sami Yen, Istanbul 29.10.2002

Referee: Wolfgang Stark (GER) Attendance: 19,789

GALATASARAY: Ali Faryd Camilo MONDRAGON, Ümit Davala, Bülent Korkmaz, Emre Asik, Hakan Ünsal, FABIO PINTO, Ergün Penbe, Cihan Haspolatli (70 Jorge FELIPE Loreiro), Elvir Baljic (46 HASAN Gökhan ŞAŞ), CHRISTIAN Correia Dionisio, Arif Erdem (46 João BATISTA). Trainer: Fatih Terim

LOKOMOTIV: Sergey Ovchinnikov, Gennady Nizhegorodov, Sergey Ignashevich, Oleg Pashinin, Dmitri Sennikov, Vadim Evseyev, Vladimir Maminov, Dmitry Loskov, Jacob Lekcetho, James Obiorah (78 JULIO CESAR da Silva e Souza), Ruslan Pimenov. Trainer: Yuri Semin

Goals: Loskov (70), Hasan Şaş (73), Evseyev (75)

FC BARCELONA
v GALATASARAY SK ISTANBUL 3-1 (2-1)

Camp Nou, Barcelona 13.11.2002

Referee: Dick J.H. van Egmond (HOL) Attendance: 42,928

FC BARCELONA: Robert ENKE, Michael REIZIGER, Carlos PUYOL Saforcada (61 Daniel "DANI" TORTOLERO Núñez), Frank de Boer (86 OLEGUER Preses Renom), FERNANDO NAVARRO Corbacho, Gaizka MENDIETA Zabala, GERARD López Segú, Thiago Motta, GEOVANNI Deiberson Mauricio (79 Patrick Kluivert), Daniel García Lara "DANI", Javier Pedro SAVIOLA. Trainer: Louis van Gaal

GALATASARAY: Ali Faryd Camilo MONDRAGON, Mohammed Sarr, Bülent Korkmaz, Trevino Sergio ALMAGUER, Hakan Ünsal, FABIO PINTO, Ergün Penbe, Cihan Haspolatli (46 Suat Kaya), João BATISTA (61 Ayhan Akman), HASAN Gökhan ŞAŞ, Elvir Baljić (75 CHRISTIAN Correia Dionisio). Trainer: Fatih Terim

Goals: Dani (10), Cihan (20), Gerard (44), Geovanni (56)

FC LOKOMOTIV MOSKVA
v CLUB BRUGGE KV 2-0 (1-0)

Lokomotiv, Moskva 13.11.2002

Referee: Alain Sars (FRA) Attendance: 17,000

LOKOMOTIV: Sergey Ovchinnikov, Oleg Pashinin, Sergey Ignashevich, Gennady Nizhegorodov, Dmitri Sennikov, Vadim Evseyev, Vladimir Maminov, Dmitry Loskov, Jacob Lekcetho, Maksim Buznikin (66 James Obiorah), JULIO CESAR da Silva e Souza (90+1 Amando BABA ADAMU).
Trainer: Yuri Semin

CLUB BRUGGE: Dany Verlinden, Olivier De Cock, Philippe Clement, Birger Maertens, Peter Van Der Heyden, Gert Verheyen, Gaëtan Englebert, Timmy Simons, Alin Stoica (84 Nastja Ceh), Sandy Martens, Andrés MENDOZA Acevedo (72 Milan Lesnjak). Trainer: Trond Sollied

Goals: Julio Cesar (44), Loskov (90+2)

FC Barcelona and FC Lokomotiv Moskva qualified for the Second Group Stage. Club Brugge KV qualified for the UEFA Cup.

	P	W	D	L	F	A	Pts
FC Barcelona	6	6	0	0	13	4	18
FC Lokomotiv Moskva	6	2	1	3	5	7	7
Club Brugge KV	6	1	2	3	5	7	5
Galatasaray Istanbul	6	1	1	4	5	10	4

SECOND STAGE – GROUP A

BAYER 04 LEVERKUSEN
v FC BARCELONA 1-2 (1-0)

BayArena, Leverkusen 27.11.2002

Referee: Kyros Vassaras (GRE) Attendance: 22,500

BAYER: Hans-Jörg Butt, Boris Zivkovic, Carsten Ramelow, Lucimar Ferreira da Silva "LÚCIO", Diego Rodolfo Placente, Bernd Schneider, Yildiray Bastürk, Hanno Balitsch, Marco Babic (66 Daniel Bierofka), Thomas Brdaric (55 Oliver Neuville), Dimitar Berbatov (83 Jan Simak).
Trainer: Klaus Toppmöller

FC BARCELONA: Roberto Óscar BONANO, Carlos PUYOL Saforcada, Michael Reiziger, Philip Cocu, FERNANDO NAVARRO Corbacho, Gaizka MENDIETA Zabala (46 Javier Pedro SAVIOLA), Xavier Hernández Creus "XAVI", Gabriel García de la Torre "GABRI" (46 Juan Roman Riquelme), Fabio Rochemback, Thiago Motta (75 Marc Overmars), Patrick Kluivert. Trainer: Louis van Gaal

Goals: Berbatov (39), Saviola (48), Overmars (88)

NEWCASTLE UNITED FC
v FC INTERNAZIONALE MILANO 1-4 (0-3)

Saint James' Park, Newcastle 27.11.2002

Referee: Stéphane Bré (FRA) Attendance: 50,108

NEWCASTLE UNITED: Shay Given, Andy Griffin, Nikos Dabizas, Andy O'Brien, Aaron Hughes (86 Stephen Caldwell), Norberto Solano, Gary Speed, Kieron Dyer, HUGO Miguel Ferreira VIANA (46 Laurent Robert), Alan Shearer, Craig Bellamy. Trainer: Robert Robson

INTERNAZIONALE: Francesco Toldo, Javier Zanetti, Fabio Cannavaro, Marco Materazzi (15 Iván Ramiro Cordoba), Giovanni Pasquale, Okan Buruk (66 Stéphane Dalmat), Matías Jesús Almeyda, Emre Belözoglu, Domenico Morfeo, Hernán Jorge Crespo (81 Alvaro Recoba), Christian Vieri.
Trainer: Hector Raúl Cúper

Sent off: Bellamy (5)

Goals: Morfeo (2), Almeyda (35), Crespo (45+1), Solano (72), Recoba (81)

FC INTERNAZIONALE MILANO
v BAYER 04 LEVERKUSEN 3-2 (2-0)

Giuseppe Meazza, Milano 10.12.2002

Referee: Hugh Dallas (SCO) Attendance: 36,342

INTERNAZIONALE: Francesco Toldo, Javier Zanetti, Iván Ramiro Cordoba, Carlos Alberto Gamarra, Giovanni Pasquale, Matías Jesús Almeyda, Luigi Di Biaggo (71 Nicola Beati), Emre Belözoglu, Alvaro Recoba, Hernán Jorge Crespo (88 Mohamed Kallon), Christian Vieri (74 SÉRGIO Paulo Marceneiro CONCEIÇÃO). Trainer: Hector Raúl Cúper

BAYER: Hans-Jörg Butt, Boris Zivkovic, Carsten Ramelow, Thomas Kleine, Juan Silveira dos Santos "JUAN", Bernd Schneider, Yildiray Bastürk (83 Jan Simak), Hanno Balitsch (78 Daniel Bierofka), Diego Rodolfo Placente, Oliver Neuville, Dimitar Berbatov (75 Françoaldo Sena de Souza "FRANÇA").
Trainer: Klaus Toppmöller

Goals: di Biaggo (15, 27), Zivkovic (63), Butt (80 og), França (90+1)

FC BARCELONA
v NEWCASTLE UNITED FC 3-1 (2-1)

Camp Nou, Barcelona 11.12.2002

Referee: Frank de Bleeckere (BEL) Attendance: 45,100

FC BARCELONA: Roberto Óscar Bonano, Michael Reiziger (14 Philippe Christanval), Carlos PUYOL Saforcada, Frank de Boer, Thiago Motta, Xavier Hernández Creus "XAVI", Philip Cocu (16 Gaizka MENDIETA Zabala), Juan Román Riquelme, Marc Overmars, Patrick Kluivert, Daniel García Lara "DANI" (78 Javier Pedro Saviola). Trainer: Louis van Gaal

NEWCASTLE UNITED: Shay Given, Andy Griffin, Aaron Hughes, Andy O'Brien, Olivier Bernard, Norberto Solano, Kieron Dyer, Gary Speed, Laurent Robert, Shola Ameobi, Lomano Tresor Lua Lua (84 Michael Chopra).
Trainer: Robert Robson

Goals: Dani (7), Ameobi (24), Kluivert (35), Motta (58)

FC BARCELONA
v FC INTERNAZIONALE MILANO 3-0 (2-0)

Camp Nou Barcelona 18.02.2003

Referee: Anders Frisk (SWE) Attendance: 45,100

FC BARCELONA: Roberto Óscar Bonano, Michael Reiziger, Frank de Boer, Carlos PUYOL Saforcada, Gabriel García de la Torre "GABRI", Marc Overmars (71 Fabio Rochemback), Xavier Hernández Creus "XAVI", Philip Cocu, Thiago Motta (73 Gaizka MENDIETA Zabala), Patrick Kluivert, Javier Pedro Saviola (81 LUIS ENRIQUE Martínez García). Trainer: Radomir Antić

INTERNAZIONALE: Francesco Toldo, Javier Zanetti, Fabio Cannavaro, Carlos Alberto Gamarra, Iván Ramiro Cordoba, Stéphane Dalmat, Luigi Di Biaggo (59 Okan Buruk), Cristiano Zanetti, Domenico Morfeo (66 Mohamed Kallon), Alvaro Recoba, Christian Vieri. Trainer: Hector Raúl Cúper

Sent off: Recoba (80)

Goals: Saviola (7), Cocu (29), Kluivert (67)

BAYER 04 LEVERKUSEN
v NEWCASTLE UNITED FC 1-3 (1-3)

BayArena, Leverkusen 18.02.2003

Referee: Terje Hauge (NOR) Attendance: 22,500

BAYER: Hans-Jörg Butt, Christoph Preuss (46 Bernd Schneider), Thomas Kleine, Cristiano Marques Gomes "CRIS" (72 Jan-Ingwer Callsen Braker), Pascal Ojigwe, Oliver Neuville, Yildiray Bastürk, Hanno Balitsch (79 Radoslaw Kaluzny), Jan Simak, Thomas Brdaric, Françoaldo Sena de Souza "FRANÇA". Trainer: Thomas Hörster

NEWCASTLE UNITED: Shay Given, Aaron Hughes, Andy O'Brien, Titus Bramble, Olivier Bernard, Jermaine Jenas, Gary Speed, Kieron Dyer, Laurent Robert, Shola Ameobi (84 Carl Cort), Lomano Tresor Lua Lua (84 Michael Chopra). Trainer: Robert Robson

Goals: Ameobi (5, 16), França (26), Lua Lua (32)

FC INTERNAZIONALE MILANO
v FC BARCELONA 0-0

Giuseppe Meazza, Milano 26.02.2003

Referee: Urs Meier (SWI) Attendance: 75,000

INTERNAZIONALE: Francesco Toldo, Javier Zanetti, Fabio Cannavaro, Carlos Alberto Gamarra, Giovanni Pasquale, Domenico Morfeo, Stéphane Dalmat (61 Akinwunmi MARTINS Obafemi), Cristiano Zanetti, Andrés "GULY" GUGLIELMINPIETRO (78 SÉRGIO Paulo Marceneiro CONCEIÇÃO), Mohamed Kallon (34 Luigi Di Biaggo), Christian Vieri. Trainer: Hector Raúl Cúper

FC BARCELONA: Roberto Óscar BONANO, Gabriel García de la Torre «GABRI», Carlos PUYOL Saforcada (78 Patrik Andersson), Frank de Boer, Michael Reiziger, Fabio Rochemback (67 Juan Román Riquelme), Xavier Hernández Creus «XAVI», Philip Cocu (59 Gaizka MENDIETA Zabala), Thiago Motta, Patrick Kluivert, Javier Pedro Saviola. Trainer: Radomir Antić

NEWCASTLE UNITED FC
v BAYER 04 LEVERKUSEN 3-1 (3-0)

Saint James' Park, Newcastle 26.02.2003

Referee: Claus Bo Larsen (DEN) Attendance: 51,000

NEWCASTLE UNITED: Shay Given, Andy Griffin, Titus Bramble, Stephen Caldwell, Olivier Bernard, Brian Kerr (82 HUGO Miguel Ferreira VIANA), Gary Speed, Kieron Dyer (70 Norberto Solano), Laurent Robert, Alan Shearer (81 Lomano Tresor Lua Lua), Shola Ameobi. Trainer: Robert Robson

BAYER: Hans-Jörg Butt, Christoph Preuss, Thomas Kleine, Cristiano Marques Gomes "CRIS" (29 Boris Zivkovic), Diego Rodolfo Placente, Carsten Ramelow (46 Marko Babic), Yildiray Bastürk, Radoslaw Kaluzny, Jan Simak, Oliver Neuville (61 Thomas Brdaric), Françoaldo Sena de Souza "FRANÇA". Trainer: Thomas Hörster

Goals: Shearer (5, 11, 36 pen), Babić (73)

FC BARCELONA
v BAYER 04 LEVERKUSEN 2-0 (1-0)

Camp Nou, Barcelona 11.03.2003

Referee: Stéphane Bré (FRA) Attendance: 75,000

FC BARCELONA: Roberto Óscar Bonano, Gabriel García de la Torre «GABRI», Frank de Boer (62 OLEGUER Preses Renom), Patrik Andersson, Michael Reiziger, Marc Overmars (68 Andrés INIESTA Lujan), Gaizka MENDIETA Zabala, Juan Román Riquelme, Xavier Hernández Creus «XAVI», Patrick Kluivert, Javier Pedro Saviola (46 Thiago Motta). Trainer: Radomir Antić

BAYER: Hans-Jörg Butt, Pascal Ojigwe, Thomas Kleine, Cristiano Marques Gomes «CRIS», Radoslaw Kaluzny, Jan Simak, Yildiray Bastürk (74 Bernd Schneider), Hanno Balitsch, Marko Babic (33 Hüzeyfe Dogan), Dimitar Berbatov (58 Thomas Brdaric), Françoaldo Sena de Souza «FRANÇA». Trainer: Thomas Hörster

Goals: Saviola (17), de Boer (49)

FC INTERNAZIONALE MILANO
v NEWCASTLE UNITED FC 2-2 (0-1)

Giuseppe Meazza, Milano 11.03.2003

Referee: Lucilio CARDOSO CORTEZ BATISTA (POR) Attendance: 55,000

INTERNAZIONALE: Francesco Toldo, Javier Zanetti, Fabio Cannavaro, Iván Ramiro Cordoba, Francesco Coco, SÉRGIO Paulo Marceneiro CONCEIÇÃO, Luigi Di Biaggo, Emre Belözoglu (77 Giovanni Pasquale), Okan Buruk, Andrés "GULY" GUGLIELMINPIETRO (46 Akinwunmi MARTINS Obafemi), Christian Vieri. Trainer: Hector Raúl Cúper

NEWCASTLE UNITED: Shay Given, Olivier Bernard, Andy Griffin, Titus Bramble, Andy O'Brien (59 Aaron Hughes), Norberto Solano (83 Lomano Tresor Lua Lua), Gary Speed, Jermaine Jenas, Laurent Robert (83 HUGO Miguel Ferreira VIANA), Alan Shearer, Craig Bellamy. Trainer: Robert Robson

Goals: Shearer (42, 49), Vieri (47), Cordoba (61)

BAYER 04 LEVERKUSEN v FC INTERNAZIONALE MILANO 0-2 (0-1)

BayArena, Leverkusen 19.03.2003

Referee: Valentin Ivanov (RUS) Attendance: 22,500

BAYER: Hans-Jörg Butt, Pascal Ojigwe, Radoslaw Kaluzny, Thomas Kleine, Diego Rodolfo Placente, Thomas Brdaric (46 Oliver Neuville), Carsten Ramelow, Jan Simak (62 Cristiano Marques Gomes "CRIS"), Yildiray Bastürk (46 Bernd Schneider), Daniel Bierofka, Françoaldo Sena de Souza "FRANÇA". Trainer: Thomas Hörster

INTERNAZIONALE: Francesco Toldo, Javier Zanetti, Fabio Cannavaro, Iván Ramiro Cordoba, Francesco Coco, SÉRGIO Paulo Marceneiro CONCEIÇÃO (83 Andrés "GULY" GUGLIELMINPIETRO), Luigi Di Biaggo, Okan Buruk (19 Cristiano Zanetti), Emre Belözoglu, Domenico Morfeo (75 Giovanni Pasquale), Akinwunmi MARTINS Obafemi. Trainer: Hector Raúl Cúper

Goals: Martins (36), Emre Belözoglu (90)

NEWCASTLE UNITED FC v FC BARCELONA 0-2 (0-0)

Saint James' Park, Newcastle 19.03.2003

Referee: Jan W. Wegereef (HOL) Attendance: 52,000

NEWCASTLE UNITED: Shay Given, Andy Griffin, Andy O'Brien, Titus Bramble, Olivier Bernard, Norberto Solano (67 Shola Ameobi), Kieron Dyer, Jermaine Jenas, Laurent Robert (67 HUGO Miguel Ferreira VIANA), Alan Shearer, Craig Bellamy. Trainer: Robert Robson

FC BARCELONA: VÍCTOR VALDÉS Arribas, Gabriel García de la Torre "GABRI", Patrik Andersson, Frank De Boer, Michael Reiziger, Fabio Rochemback, Gaizka MENDIETA Zabala (66 Andrés INIESTA Lujan), Xavier Hernández Creus "XAVI" (46 GERARD López Segú), Thiago Motta, Patrick Kluivert (70 SERGIO GARCÍA de la Fuente), Juan Román Riquelme. Trainer: Radomir Antić

Goals: Kluivert (60), Motta (74)

FC Barcelona and Internazionale Milano FC qualified for the quarter finals.

	P	W	D	L	F	A	Pts
FC Barcelona	6	5	1	0	12	2	16
Internazionale FC	6	3	2	1	11	8	11
Newcastle United FC	6	2	1	3	10	13	7
Bayer 04 Leverkusen	6	0	0	5	5	15	0

SECOND STAGE – GROUP B

AS ROMA v ARSENAL FC LONDON 1-3 (1-1)

Olimpico, Roma 27.11.2002

Referee: L'uboš Michel (SVK) Attendance: 49,860

AS ROMA: Francesco Antonioli, Jonathan Zebina, Walter Adriano Samuel, Christian Panucci, Marcos Evangelista de Moraes "CAFÚ", Francisco Govinho Lima (73 Gabriel Omar Batistuta), Francesco Totti, EMERSON Ferreira da Rosa, Vincent Candela, Marco Delvecchio (57 Gianni GUIGOU Martínez), Antonio Cassano (65 Vincenzo Montella).

ARSENAL: Rami Shaaban, Oleg Luzhny, Sol Campbell, Pascal Cygan, Ashley Cole, Fredrik Ljungberg (90+2 Eduardo Edu), Patrick Vieira, GILBERTO Aparecido da Silva, Robert Pires (79 Giovanni Van Bronckhorst), Sylvain Wiltord (85 Martin Keown), Thierry Henry. Manager: Arsène Wenger

Goals: Cassano (4), Henry (6, 70, 75)

VALENCIA CF v AFC AJAX AMSTERDAM 1-1 (0-0)

Mestalla, Valencia 27.11.2002

Referee: Gilles Veissière (FRA) Attendance: 40,000

VALENCIA: José Santiago CAÑIZARES Ruiz, Cristobal Emilio Torres Ruiz «CURRO TORRES», Roberto Fabián AYALA, Mauricio PELLEGRINO, Amedeo CARBONI (74 FÁBIO AURÉLIO Rodrigues), Miguel Ángel ANGULO Valderrey, David ALBELDA Aliques (84 Gonzalo DE LOS SANTOS da Rosa), Rubén BARAJA Vegas, VICENTE Rodríguez Guillén, Miguel Ángel Ferrer Martínez «MISTA» (67 JUAN Ginés SÁNCHEZ Moreno), John CAREW. Trainer: Rafael BENÍTEZ MAUDES

AJAX: Joey Didulica, Hatem Trabelsi, André Bergdølmo, Cristian Chivu, MAXWELL Scherer Cabelino Andrade, Steven Pienaar (71 Nigel De Jong), Tomáš Galásek, Rafael Van Der Vaart, Andy Van Der Meyde, Jari Litmanen (59 Zlatan Ibrahimovic), Ahmed HOSSAM «MIDO» (85 Nourdin Boukhari). Trainer: Ronald Koeman

Goals: Ibrahimovic (88), Angulo (90+2)

AFC AJAX AMSTERDAM v AS ROMA 2-1 (1-0)

Amsterdam ArenA 10.12.2002

Referee: Markus Merk (GER) Attendance: 51,148

AJAX: Maarten Stekelenburg, Hatem Trabelsi (33 Abubakari Yakubu), André Bergdølmo, Petri Pasanen, MAXWELL Scherer Cabelino Andrade, Andy Van Der Meyde (80 Nourdin Boukhari), Steven Pienaar, Nigel De Jong, Richard Witschge, Zlatan Ibrahimovic, Ahmed HOSSAM "MIDO" (57 Jari Litmanen). Trainer: Ronald Koeman

AS ROMA: Francesco Antonioli, Jonathan Zebina, Walter Adriano Samuel, Traianos Dellas (61 Vincenzo Montella), Christian Panucci, Marcos Evangelista de Moraes «CAFÚ», Francisco Govinho LIMA, EMERSON Ferreira da Rosa, Vincent Candela, Francesco Totti, Antonio Cassano (72 Gabriel Omar Batistuta). Trainer: Fabio Capello

Goals: Ibrahimovic (11), Litmanen (66), Batistuta (89)

ARSENAL FC LONDON v VALENCIA CF 0-0

Arsenal Stadium, London 10.12.2002

Referee: Kim Milton Nielsen (DEN) Attendance: 34,793

ARSENAL: David Seaman, LAUREN Etame-Mayer, Martin Keown, Pascal Cygan, Ashley Cole, Robert Pires (83 Nwankwo Kanu), Patrick Vieira (38 Ray Parlour), GILBERTO Aparecido da Silva, Fredrik Ljungberg (79 Sylvain Wiltord), Dennis Bergkamp, Thierry Henry. Manager: Arsène Wenger

VALENCIA: Andrés PALOP Cervera, Cristobal Emilio Torres Ruiz "CURRO TORRES", Roberto Fabián Ayala, Mauricio Pellegrino, Amedeo Carboni, Miguel Ángel ANGULO Valderrey, David ALBELDA Aliques, Rubén BARAJA Vegas (87 FÁBIO AURÉLIO Rodrigues), VICENTE Rodríguez Guillén (68 Francisco Joaquim Pérez RUFETE), John Carew, Pablo César Aimar (80 Carlos MARCHENA López). Trainer: Rafael BENÍTEZ MAUDES

Sent off: Angulo (72)

ARSENAL FC LONDON v AFC AJAX AMSTERDAM 1-1 (1-1)

Arsenal Stadium, London 18.02.2003

Referee: Lucilio CARDOSO CORTEZ BATISTA (POR) Attendance: 35,427

ARSENAL: David Seaman (46 Stuart Taylor), LAUREN Etame-Mayer, Sol Campbell, Pascal Cygan, Ashley Cole, Sylvain Wiltord, Patrick Vieira, GILBERTO Aparecido da Silva (72 Francis Jeffers), Robert Pires, Dennis Bergkamp (85 Nwankwo Kanu), Thierry Henry. Manager: Arsène Wenger

AJAX: Bogdan Lobonţ, Hatem Trabelsi, Cristian Chivu, Petri Pasanen, Jelle Van Damme (76 Richard Witschge), Nigel De Jong, Tomáš Galásek, Steven Pienaar (90+2 Abubakari Yakubu), MAXWELL Scherer Cabelino Andrade, Andy van der Meyde, Zlatan Ibrahimovic (79 Nourdin Boukhari). Trainer: Ronald Koeman

Goals: Wiltord (5), De Jong (17)

AS ROMA v VALENCIA CF 0-1 (0-0)

Olimpico, Roma 18.02.2003

Referee: Wolfgang Stark (GER) Attendance: 40,000

AS ROMA: Ivan Pelizzoli, Jonathan Zebina, ALDAIR Nascimento dos Santos, Traianos Dellas (54 Leandro Damián Cufré), Christian Panucci, Marcos Evangelista de Moraes "CAFÚ", Damiano Tommasi, Francisco Govinho Lima, Gianni GUIGOU Martínez, Marco Delvecchio (54 Davide Bombardini), Vincenzo Montella (46 Antonio Cassano). Trainer: Fabio Capello

VALENCIA: José Santiago CAÑIZARES Ruiz, Anthony RÉVEILLÈRE, Miroslav Djukić, Mauricio Pellegrino, Amedeo Carboni, Francisco Joaquim Pérez RUFETE (73 Miguel Ángel Ferrer Martínez "MISTA"), David ALBELDA Aliques, Rubén BARAJA Vegas, VICENTE Rodríguez Guillén (63 Cristian Alberto "KILY" GONZÁLEZ), John Carew, Pablo César Aimar (89 Carlos MARCHENA López). Trainer: Rafael BENÍTEZ MAUDES

Goal: Carew (78)

AFC AJAX AMSTERDAM v ARSENAL FC LONDON 0-0

Amsterdam ArenA 26.02.2003

Referee: Valentin Ivanov (RUS) Attendance: 51,025

AJAX: Bogdan Lobonţ, Hatem Trabelsi, Petri Pasanen, Cristian Chivu, MAXWELL Scherer Cabelino Andrade, Nigel De Jong, Tomáš Galásek (71 Abubakari Yakubu), Steven Pienaar (90 +1 Wesley Sneijder), Richard Witschge, Andy Van Der Meyde, Zlatan Ibrahimovic (84 Ahmed HOSSAM "MIDO"). Trainer: Ronald Koeman

ARSENAL: David Seaman, LAUREN Etame-Mayer, Sol Campbell, Martin Keown, Ashley Cole, Sylvain Wiltord (79 Francis Jeffers), GILBERTO Aparecido da Silva, Patrick Vieira, Robert Pires (87 Giovanni Van Bronckhorst), Dennis Bergkamp (79 Ray Parlour), Thierry Henry. Manager: Arsène Wenger

VALENCIA CF v AS ROMA 0-3 (0-3)

Mestalla, Valencia 26.02.2003

Referee: Frank de Bleeckere (BEL) Attendance: 55,000

VALENCIA: José Santiago CAÑIZARES Ruiz, Anthony RÉVEILLÈRE, Roberto Fabián AYALA, Mauricio PELLEGRINO (77 Amedeo CARBONI), FÁBIO AURÉLIO Rodrigues, Francisco Joaquim Pérez RUFETE (64 Pablo César AIMAR), David ALBELDA Aliques, Rubén BARAJA Vegas, VICENTE Rodríguez Guillén (52 Cristian Alberto "KILY" GONZÁLEZ), JUAN Ginés SÁNCHEZ Moreno, John Carew. Trainer: Rafael BENÍTEZ MAUDES

AS ROMA: Francesco Antonioli, Jonathan Zebina (63 Leandro Damián Cufré), ALDAIR Nascimento dos Santos, Walter Adriano Samuel, Vincent Candela, Marcos Evangelista de Moraes "CAFÚ", Damiano Tommasi, EMERSON Ferreira da Rosa, Francisco Govinho Lima, Francesco Totti (88 Diego Fuser), Antonio Cassano (90+1 Gianni GUIGOU Martínez). Trainer: Fabio Capello

Goals: Totti (23, 30), Emerson (36)

AFC AJAX AMSTERDAM v VALENCIA CF 1-1 (0-1)

Amsterdam ArenA 11.03.2003

Referee: Ľuboš Michel (SVK) Attendance: 49,500

AJAX: Bogdan Lobonţ, Hatem Trabelsi, Petri Pasanen, Cristian Chivu, John O'Brien, Nigel De Jong (46 Andy Van Der Meyde), Tomáš Galásek, Steven Pienaar, MAXWELL Scherer Cabelino Andrade, Rafael Van Der Vaart, Zlatan Ibrahimovic. Trainer: Ronald Koeman

VALENCIA: José Santiago CAÑIZARES Ruiz, Anthony Réveillère, Roberto Fabián Ayala (88 Carlos MARCHENA López), Mauricio Pellegrino, Amedeo Carboni, Francisco Joaquim Pérez Rufete, David ALBELDA Aliques, Pablo César AIMAR (84 JUAN Ginés SÁNCHEZ Moreno), Rubén BARAJA Vegas, Cristian Alberto "KILY" GONZÁLEZ, John Carew (64 Miguel Ángel Ferrer Martínez "MISTA"). Trainer: Rafael BENÍTEZ MAUDES

Goals: Kily González (28 pen), Pasanen (57)

ARSENAL FC LONDON v AS ROMA 1-1 (1-1)

Arsenal Stadium, London 11.03.2003

Referee: Urs Meier (SWI) Attendance: 38,500

ARSENAL: David Seaman, LAUREN Etame-Mayer (88 Nwankwo Kanu), Martin Keown, Pascal Cygan, Giovanni Van Bronckhorst, Sylvain Wiltord (73 Fredrik Ljungberg), Patrick Vieira, Gilberto Aparecido Da Silva, Robert Pires, Dennis Bergkamp (73 Francis Jeffers), Thierry Henry. Manager: Arsène Wenger

AS ROMA: Ivan Pelizzoli, Christian Panucci, ALDAIR Nascimento dos Santos, Walter Adriano Samuel, Vincent Candela, Marcos Evangelista de Moraes "CAFÚ", Damiano Tommasi, EMERSON Ferreira da Rosa, Francisco Govinho Lima, Francesco Totti, Antonio Cassano (62 Vincenzo Montella). Trainer: Fabio Capello

Sent off: Totti (22)

Goals: Vieira (12), Cassano (45+2)

AS ROMA v AFC AJAX AMSTERDAM 1-1 (1-1)

Olimpico, Roma 19.03.2003

Referee: Herbert Fandel (GER) Attendance: 54,000

AS ROMA: Ivan Pelizzoli, Leandro Damián Cufré, Christian Panucci, ALDAIR Nascimento dos Santos, Vincent Candela, Marcos Evangelista de Moraes "CAFÚ" (80 Diego Fuser), Damiano Tommasi (80 Gianni GUIGOU Martínez), EMERSON Ferreira da Rosa, Francisco Govinho Lima (66 Vincenzo Montella), Marco Delvecchio, Antonio Cassano. Trainer: Fabio Capello

AJAX: Bogdan Lobonț, Hatem Trabelsi, Petri Pasanen, Cristian Chivu, John O'Brien (90+5 Jelle Van Damme), Steven Pienaar, Tomáš Galásek, Rafael Van Der Vaart, MAXWELL Scherer Cabelino Andrade, Andy Van Der Meyde (72 Victor Sikora), Zlatan Ibrahimovic (90+1 Richard Witschge). Trainer: Ronald Koeman

Goals: van der Meyde (1), Cassano (24)

VALENCIA CF v ARSENAL FC LONDON 2-1 (1-0)

Mestalla, Valencia 19.03.2003

Referee: Kyros Vassaras (GRE) Attendance: 50,000

VALENCIA: José Santiago CAÑIZARES Ruiz (71 Andrés PALOP Cervera), Anthony RÉVEILLÈRE, Roberto Fabián AYALA, Mauricio Pellegrino, Amedeo Carboni, Francisco Joaquim Pérez RUFETE, David ALBELDA Aliques, Pablo César AIMAR, VICENTE Rodríguez Guillén, JUAN Ginés SÁNCHEZ Moreno (68 Miguel Ángel ANGULO Valderrey), John Carew (89 Carlos MARCHENA López). Trainer: Rafael BENÍTEZ MAUDES

ARSENAL: Stuart Taylor, LAUREN Etame-Mayer, Sol Campbell, Pascal Cygan, Kolo Abib Touré (86 Nwankwo Kanu), Fredrik Ljungberg, Patrick Vieira, GILBERTO Aparecido da Silva, Robert Pires, Sylvain Wiltord (76 Francis Jeffers), Thierry Henry. Trainer: Arsène Wenger

Goals: Carew (34, 56), Henry (48)

Valencia CF and AFC Ajax qualified for the quarter finals.

	P	W	D	L	F	A	Pts
Valencia CF	6	2	3	1	5	6	9
AFC Ajax Amsterdam	6	1	5	0	6	5	8
Arsenal FC London	6	1	4	1	6	5	7
AS Roma	6	1	2	3	7	8	5

SECOND STAGE – GROUP C

FC LOKOMOTIV MOSKVA v BV BORUSSIA DORTMUND 1-2 (1-2)

Lokomotiv, Moskva 26.11.2002

Referee: Rene H.J. Temmink (HOL) Attendance: 17,000

LOKOMOTIV: Sergey Ovchinnikov, Gennady Nizhegorodov, Sergey Ignashevich, Oleg Pashinin, Dmitri Sennikov, Vadim Evseyev, Vladimir Maminov (46 Milan Obradovic), Dmitry Loskov, Jacob Lekcetho, James Obiorah (65 Maksim Buznikin), Ruslan Pimenov (74 Amando BABA ADAMU). Trainer: Yuri Semin

BV BORUSSIA: Jens Lehmann, Torsten Frings, Christian Wörns, Christoph Metzelder, Jörg Heinrich, Stefan Reuter, Tomáš Rosicky (90+2 Giuseppe Reina), Sebastian Kehl (89 Ahmed Reda Madouni), Leonardo de Deus Santos "DEDE", Jan Koller, EWERTHON Henrique de Souza (82 Lars Ricken). Trainer: Matthias Sammer

Goals: Ignashevich (31), Frings (33), Koller (43)

AC MILAN v REAL MADRID CF 1-0 (1-0)

Giuseppe Meazza, Milano 26.11.2002

Referee: Urs Meier (SWI) Attendance: 75,777

AC MILAN: Nélson de Jesus Silva "DIDA", Dario Simic (89 José Antonio Chamot), Alessandro Costacurta, Paolo Maldini, Kakha Kaladze, Gennaro Gattuso, Massimo Ambrosini, RUI Manuel César COSTA (76 Sérgio Cláudio dos Santos "SERGINHO"), Clarence Seedorf, Andriy Shevchenko (82 Jon Dahl Tomasson), "RIVALDO" Vítor Barbosa Ferreira. Trainer: Carlo Ancelotti

REAL MADRID: Iker CASILLAS Fernández, Miguel Ángel "MICHEL" SALGADO, Iván HELGUERA Bujía, Francisco PAVÓN Barahona, ROBERTO CARLOS da Silva, Luís Felipe Madeira Caeiro "FIGO", Albert CELADES López, Esteban CAMBIASSO Deleau (76 Santiago Hernán SOLARI), Zinédine ZIDANE, RAÚL González Blanco, Fernando MORIENTES Sánchez (61 Javier García PORTILLO). Trainer: Vicente DEL BOSQUE González

Goal: Shevchenko (40)

BORUSSIA DORTMUND v AC MILAN 0-1 (0-0)

Westfalenstadion, Dortmund 11.12.2002

Referee: Anders Frisk (SWE) Attendance: 68,300

BV BORUSSIA: Jens Lehmann, Jörg Heinrich (73 Aparecido Ferreira Evanilson), Christian Wörns, Christoph Metzelder, Leonardo de Deus Santos "DEDE", EWERTHON Henrique de Souza (64 Lars Ricken), Tomáš Rosicky, Sebastian Kehl (83 Giuseppe Reina), Torsten Frings, Marcio AMOROSO dos Santos, Jan Koller. Trainer: Matthias Sammer

AC MILAN: Nélson de Jesus Silva "DIDA", Dario Simic, Paolo Maldini, Alessandro Nesta, Kakha Kaladze, Clarence Seedorf, Andrea Pirlo, RUI Manuel César COSTA (78 Sérgio Cláudio dos Santos "SERGINHO"), Massimo Ambrosini, Filippo Inzaghi (86 "RIVALDO" Vítor Barbosa Ferreira), Andriy Shevchenko (90+2 Martin Laursen). Trainer: C. Ancelotti

Goal: Inzaghi (49)

REAL MADRID CF v FC LOKOMOTIV MOSKVA 2-2 (1-0)

Santiago Bernabéu, Madrid 11.12.2002

Referee: Graham Barber (ENG) Attendance: 75,000

REAL MADRID: Iker CASILLAS Fernández, Miguel Ángel "MICHEL" SALGADO, Fernando Ruíz HIERRO, Francisco PAVÓN Barahona, ROBERTO CARLOS da Silva, Luís Felipe Madeira Caeiro "FIGO", Zinédine Zidane, Claude Makélélé (32 FLÁVIO da CONCEICÃO), Esteban CAMBIASSO Deleau (77 Fernando MORIENTES Sánchez), RONALDO Luis Nazario de Lima (46 José María Gutiérrez "GUTI"), RAÚL González Blanco. Trainer: Vicente DEL BOSQUE González

LOKOMOTIV: Sergey Ovchinnikov, Vadim Evseyev, Sergey Ignashevich, Oleg Pashinin, Gennady Nizhegorodov, Jacob Lekcetho, Vladimir Maminov, Bennett Mnguni, Dmitry Loskov, Ruslan Pimenov (81 Yuri Drozdov), JULIO CESAR da Silva e Souza (46 James Obiorah). Trainer: Yuri Semin

Goals: Raúl (21, 76), Obiorah (47), Mnguni (74)

REAL MADRID CF v BV BORUSSIA DORTMUND 2-1 (1-1)

Santiago Bernabéu, Madrid 19.02.2003

Referee: Ľuboš Michel (SVK) Attendance: 70,000

REAL MADRID: Iker CASILLAS Fernández, Miguel Ángel "MICHEL" SALGADO, Iván HELGUERA Bujía, Francisco PAVÓN Barahona, ROBERTO CARLOS da Silva, Luís Felipe Madeira Caeiro "FIGO", FLÁVIO da CONCEICÃO, Claude Makélélé, Zinédine Zidane (81 Santiago Hernán SOLARI), RONALDO Luis Nazario de Lima (74 José María Gutiérrez "GUTI"), RAÚL González Blanco.
Trainer: Vicente DEL BOSQUE González

BV BORUSSIA: Jens Lehmann, Aparecido Ferreira Evanilson (83 Lars Ricken), Christian Wörns, Christoph Metzelder, Leonardo de Deus Santos "DEDE", EWERTHON Henrique de Souza, Stefan Reuter (76 Sebastian Kehl), Tomáš Rosicky, Torsten Frings, Marcio AMOROSO dos Santos (67 Giuseppe Reina), Jan Koller. Trainer: Matthias Sammer

Goals: Koller (30), Raúl (43), Ronaldo (56)

AC MILAN v FC LOKOMOTIV MOSKVA 1-0 (0-0)

Giuseppe Meazza, Milano 19.02.2003

Referee: Gilles Veissière (FRA) Attendance: 55,000

AC MILAN: Nélson de Jesus Silva "DIDA", Cristian Brocchi (79 Dario Simic), Alessandro Costacurta, Alessandro Nesta, Paolo Maldini, Gennaro Gattuso, Andrea Pirlo, RUI Manuel César COSTA (63 Sérgio Cláudio dos Santos "SERGINHO"), "RIVALDO" Vítor Barbosa Ferreira, Jon Dahl Tomasson (68 Clarence Seedorf), Filippo Inzaghi. Trainer: Carlo Ancelotti

LOKOMOTIV: Sergey Ovchinnikov, Gennady Nizhegorodov, Sergey Ignashevich (83 Winston Parks), Oleg Pashinin, Dmitri Sennikov, Milan Obradovic, Vladimir Maminov, Dmitry Loskov, Jacob Lekcetho, Maksim Buznikin (46 Marat Izmailov), Ruslan Pimenov. Trainer: Yuri Semin

Goal: Tomasson (62)

BV BORUSSIA DORTMUND v REAL MADRID CF 1-1 (1-0)

Westfalenstadion, Dortmund 25.02.2003

Referee: Graham Poll (ENG) Attendance: 52,000

BV BORUSSIA: Jens Lehmann, Christoph Metzelder, Christian Wörns, Ahmed Reda Madouni, Leonardo de Deus Santos "DEDE" (90 Marcio AMOROSO dos Santos), Aparecido Ferreira Evanilson (80 Lars Ricken), Stefan Reuter, Sebastian Kehl, Torsten Frings, Jan Koller, EWERTHON Henrique de Souza (87 Giuseppe Reina). Trainer: Matthias Sammer

REAL MADRID: Iker CASILLAS Fernández, Miguel Ángel "MICHEL" SALGADO, Iván HELGUERA Bujía, Francisco PAVÓN Barahona (90 Javier García PORTILLO), ROBERTO CARLOS da Silva, Luís Felipe Madeira Caeiro "FIGO" (72 Óscar MIÑAMBRES Pascual), FLÁVIO da CONCEICÃO (68 José María Gutiérrez "GUTI"), Claude Makélélé, Zinédine Zidane, RONALDO Luis Nazario de Lima, RAÚL González Blanco. Trainer: Vicente DEL BOSQUE González

Goals: Koller (23), Portillo (90+2)

FC LOKOMOTIV MOSKVA v AC MILAN 0-1 (0-1)

Lokomotiv, Moskva 25.02.2003

Referee: Kyros Vassaras (GRE) Attendance: 20,000

LOKOMOTIV: Sergey Ovchinnikov, Dmitri Sennikov, Sergey Ignashevich, Gennady Nizhegorodov, Vadim Evseyev), Marat Izmailov, Vladimir Maminov, Bennett Mnguni, Narvik Sirkhayev (58 Ruslan Pimenov), Dmitry Loskov, JULIO CESAR da Silva e Souza (82 Winston Parks).
Trainer: Yuri Semin

AC MILAN: Nélson de Jesus Silva "DIDA", Alessandro Costacurta, Paolo Maldini, Alessandro Nesta, Kakha Kaladze, Gennaro Gattuso, Fernando Carlos Redondo (76 Cristian Brocchi), Clarence Seedorf, Sérgio Cláudio dos Santos "SERGINHO" (87 RUI Manuel César COSTA), Filippo Inzaghi (84 Jon Dahl Tomasson), "RIVALDO" Vítor Barbosa Ferreira.
Trainer: Carlo Ancelotti

Goal: Rivaldo (34 pen)

BV BORUSSIA DORTMUND v FC LOKOMOTIV MOSKVA 3-0 (1-0)

Westfalenstadion, Dortmund 12.03.2003

Referee: Frank de Bleeckere (BEL) Attendance: 48,000

BV BORUSSIA: Jens Lehmann, Aparecido Ferreira Evanilson, Christian Wörns, Christoph Metzelder, Leonardo de Deus Santos "DEDE" (20 Ahmed Reda Madouni), Stefan Reuter, Torsten Frings, Sebastian Kehl, EWERTHON Henrique de Souza, Jan Koller (70 Lars Ricken), Marcio AMOROSO dos Santos (83 Heiko Herrlich). Trainer: Matthias Sammer

LOKOMOTIV: Sergey Ovchinnikov, Milan Obradovic (46 JULIO CESAR da Silva e Souza), Sergey Ignashevich, Oleg Pashinin, Dmitri Sennikov, Bennett Mnguni, Vadim Evseyev, Vladimir Maminov, Jacob Lekcetho, Ruslan Pimenov, Marat Izmailov. Trainer: Yuri Semin

Goals: Frings (39), Koller (58), Amoroso (66)

REAL MADRID CF v AC MILAN 3-1 (1-0)

Santiago Bernabéu, Madrid 12.03.2003

Referee: Kim Milton Nielsen (DEN) Attendance: 75,000

REAL MADRID: Iker CASILLAS Fernández, Miguel Ángel "MICHEL" SALGADO, Iván HELGUERA Bujía, Francisco PAVÓN Barahona, ROBERTO CARLOS da Silva, Luís Felipe Madeira Caeiro "FIGO", FLÁVIO da CONCEICÃO, Claude Makélélé, Zinédine Zidane (88 Santiago Hernán SOLARI), RONALDO Luis Nazario de Lima (67 José María Gutiérrez "GUTI"), RAÚL González Blanco (90 Javier García PORTILLO). Trainer: Vicente DEL BOSQUE González

AC MILAN: Christian Abbiati, Dario Simic (62 Alessandro Nesta), Alessandro Costacurta, Martin Laursen, Paolo Maldini, Cristian Brocchi, Fernando Carlos Redondo (79 Andrea Pirlo), Clarence Seedorf, Samuele Dalla Bona (46 RUI Manuel César COSTA), Andriy Shevchenko, "RIVALDO" Vítor Barbosa Ferreira. Trainer: Carlo Ancelotti

Goals: Raúl (12, 57), Rivaldo (81), Guti (86)

FC LOKOMOTIV MOSKVA v REAL MADRID CF 0-1 (0-1)

Lokomotiv, Moskva 18.03.2003

Referee: Claude Colombo (FRA) Attendance: 28,000

LOKOMOTIV: Sergey Ovchinnikov, Oleg Pashinin, Sergey Ignashevich, Gennady Nizhegorodov, Vadim Evseyev, Vladimir Maminov (81 Narvik Sirkhayev), Dmitry Loskov, Bennett Mnguni (72 JULIO CESAR da Silva e Souza), Dmitri Sennikov, Ruslan Pimenov, Marat Izmailov. Trainer: Yuri Semin

REAL MADRID: Iker CASILLAS Fernández, Miguel Ángel "MICHEL" SALGADO, Iván HELGUERA Bujía, Francisco PAVÓN Barahona, Santiago Hernán SOLARI, Luís Felipe Madeira Caeiro "FIGO", FLÁVIO da CONCEICÃO, Claude Makélélé, Zinédine Zidane (90 Esteban CAMBIASSO Deleau), RONALDO Luis Nazario de Lima (81 José María Gutiérrez "GUTI"), RAÚL González Blanco.
Trainer: Vicente DEL BOSQUE González

Goal: Ronaldo (35)

AC MILAN v BV BORUSSIA DORTMUND 0-1 (0-0)

Giuseppe Meazza, Milano 18.03.2003

Referee: Graham Barber (ENG) Attendance: 40,000

AC MILAN: Christian Abbiati, Dario Simic, Alessandro Nesta, Martin Laursen, Paolo Maldini (46 Alessandro Costacurta), Gennaro Gattuso, Fernando Carlos Redondo, RUI Manuel César COSTA (62 Filippo Inzaghi), Cristian Brocchi (82 Andrea Pirlo), Jon Dahl Tomasson, "RIVALDO" Vítor Barbosa Ferreira. Trainer: Carlo Ancelotti

BV BORUSSIA: Jens Lehmann, Aparecido Ferreira Evanilson, Christian Wörns, Christoph Metzelder, Leonardo de Deus Santos "DEDE" (83 Ahmed Reda Madouni), Sebastian Kehl, Stefan Reuter (50 Lars Ricken), Torsten Frings, EWERTHON Henrique de Souza (74 David Odonkor), Jan Koller, Marcio AMOROSO dos Santos.
Trainer: Matthias Sammer

Goal: Koller (80)

Milan AC and Real Madrid CF qualified for the quarter finals.

	P	W	D	L	F	A	Pts
AC Milan	6	4	0	2	5	4	12
Real Madrid CF	6	3	2	1	9	6	11
Borussia Dortmund	6	3	1	2	8	5	10
FC Lokomotiv Moskva	6	0	1	5	3	10	1

SECOND STAGE – GROUP D

FC BASEL v MANCHESTER UNITED FC 1-3 (1-0)

Saint Jakob, Basel 26.11.2002

Referee: Iordan Ivanov (BUL) Attendance: 29,501

FC BASEL: Pascal Zuberbühler, Bernt Haas, Murat Yakin, Marco Zwyssig, Thimothée Atouba, Ivan Ergic (84 Sébastien Barberis), Hakan Yakin, Mario Cantaluppi, Scott Chipperfield (73 Hervé Tum), Christian Gimenez, Julio Hernán Rossi (84 Grégory Duruz). Trainer: Christian Gross

MANCHESTER UNITED: Fabian Barthez, Philip Neville, Wesley Brown (90+3 David May), John O'Shea, Mikael Silvestre, Paul Scholes, Quinton Fortune, Juan Sebastián Veron, Ryan Giggs, Ole Gunnar Solskjær (90 Luke Chadwick), Ruud Van Nistelrooy (73 Diego FORLÁN Corazo).
Trainer: Alexander Chapman Ferguson

Goals: Gimenez (1), Van Nistelrooy (62, 63), Solskjær (68)

RC DEPORTIVO LA CORUÑA v JUVENTUS FC TORINO 2-2 (2-1)

Riazor, La Coruña 26.11.2002

Referee: Herbert Fandel (GER) Attendance: 32,000

DEPORTIVO: Juan Miguel García Inglés "JUANMÍ", Lionel Sebastián SCALONI, Enrique Fernández ROMERO, CÉSAR Martín Villar, Joan CAPDEVILA Méndez, SERGIO González Soriano, Francisco J.González Pérez "FRAN" (77 José Emilio AMAVISCA Gárate), MAURO da SILVA Gomes, Aldo Pedro DUSCHER, Roy MAKAAY (62 VÍCTOR Sánchez del Amo), DIEGO TRISTAN Herrera (64 Alberto LUQUE Martos). Trainer: Javier IRURETAGOYENA AMIANO

JUVENTUS: Gianluigi Buffon, Lilian Thuram, Paolo MONTERO Iglesias, Mark Iuliano, Alessandro Birindelli, Mauro Camoranesi (75 Gianluca Zambrotta), Alessio Tacchinardi, Pavel Nedved, Edgar Davids, Alessandro Del Piero, Marco Di Vaio (75 Marcelo Danubio Zalayeta). Trainer: Marcello Lippi

Goals: Diego Tristan (9), Makaay (11), Birindelli (38), Nedved (57)

JUVENTUS FC TORINO v FC BASEL 4-0 (3-0)

Delle Alpi, Torino 11.12.2002

Referee: Lucilio CARDOSO CORTEZ BATISTA (POR) Attendance: 42,000

JUVENTUS: Gianluigi Buffon, Lilian Thuram (59 Ciro Ferrara), Paolo Montero Iglesias, Mark Iuliano, Alessandro Birindelli, Gianluca Zambrotta, Alessio Tacchinardi, Pavel Nedved, Edgar Davids, Alessandro del Piero (72 Antonio Conte), David Trezeguet (64 Marcelo Danubio Zalayeta). Trainer: Marcello Lippi

FC BASEL: Pascal Zuberbühler, Sébastien Barberis, Murat Yakin, Marco Zwyssig, Thimothée Atouba, Antonio Esposito, Hakan Yakin (77 Hervé Tum), Mario Cantaluppi, Scott Chipperfield (65 Grégory Duruz), Christian Gimenez (46 Carlos Varela), Julio Hernán Rossi. Trainer: Christian Gross

Goals: Trezeguet (3), Montero (34), Tacchinardi (43), del Piero (51 pen)

MANCHESTER UNITED FC v RC DEPORTIVO LA CORUÑA 2-0 (1-0)

Old Trafford, Manchester 11.12.2002

Referee: Terje Hauge; Ole Hermann Borgan, Steinar Holvik (NOR) Attendance: 67,014

MANCHESTER UNITED: Fabian Barthez, Gary Neville, Wesley Brown, Mikael Silvestre, John O'Shea (81 David Backham), Ole Gunnar Solskjær, Philip Neville (81 Diego FORLÁN Corazo), Paul Scholes, Juan Sebastián Veron, Ryan Giggs, Ruud Van Nistelrooy (89 Kieran Edward Richardson). Trainer: Alexander Chapman Ferguson

DEPORTIVO: Juan Miguel García Inglés "JUANMÍ", Lionel Sebastián SCALONI, Enrique Fernández ROMERO, CÉSAR Martín Villar, Joan CAPDEVILA Méndez, VÍCTOR Sánchez del Amo (76 Alberto LUQUE Martos), MAURO da SILVA Gomes, Juan Carlos VALERÓN Santana (65 Roberto Miguel ACUÑA), SERGIO González Soriano, José Emilio AMAVISCA Gárate (46 DIEGO TRISTAN Herrera), Roy MAKAAY. Trainer: Javier IRURETAGOYENA AMIANO

Goals: van Nistelrooy (7, 55)

FC BASEL v RC DEPORTIVO LA CORUÑA 1-0 (1-0)

Saint Jakob, Basel 19.02.2003

Referee: René H.J. Temmink (HOL) Attendance: 23,000

FC BASEL: Pascal Zuberbühler, Bernt Haas, Murat Yakin, Marco Zwyssig, Thimothée Atouba, Sébastien Barberis, Hakan Yakin (85 Carlos Varela), Mario Cantaluppi, Scott Chipperfield (70 Grégory Duruz), Christian Gimenez, Julio Hernán Rossi (51 Benjamin Huggel). Trainer: Christian Gross

DEPORTIVO: Juan Miguel García Inglés «JUANMÍ», HÉCTOR Berenguel Del Pino, Nourredine Naybet, JORGE Manuel A. Gomes ANDRADE, Enrique Fernández ROMERO, Lionel Sebastián SCALONI, DONATO Gama da Silva (46 DIEGO TRISTAN Herrera), Aldo Pedro DUSCHER, SERGIO González Soriano (82 Roberto Miguel ACUÑA), Alberto LUQUE Martos (64 José Emilio AMAVISCA Gárate), Roy Makaay. Trainer: Javier IRURETAGOYENA AMIANO

Goal: H. Yakin (30)

MANCHESTER UNITED FC v JUVENTUS FC TORINO 2-1 (1-0)

Old Trafford, Manchester 19.02.2003

Referee: Kim Milton Nielsen (DEN) Attendance: 68,500

MANCHESTER UNITED: Fabian Barthez, Gary Neville, Rio Ferdinand, Wesley Brown, Mikael Silvestre (52 John O'Shea), David Backham, Roy Keane, Nicky Butt, Ryan Giggs (90+1 Diego FORLÁN Corazo), Paul Scholes (80 Ole Gunnar Solskjær), Ruud Van Nistelrooy. Manager: Alexander Chapman Ferguson

JUVENTUS: Antonio Chimenti, Cristian Zenoni, Paolo MONTERO Iglesias, Ciro Ferrara, Gianluca Pessotto, Mauro Germán Camoranesi, Alessio Tacchinardi, Edgar Davids, Pavel Nedved, Marcelo Danubio Zalayeta, David Trezeguet (66 Ruben Olivera). Trainer: Marcello Lippi

Goals: Brown (4), Van Nistelrooy (85), Nedved (90+2)

RC DEPORTIVO LA CORUÑA v FC BASEL 1-0 (1-0)

Riazor, La Coruña 25.02.2003

Referee: Stéphane Bré (FRA) Attendance: 34,000

DEPORTIVO: Juan Miguel García Inglés "JUANMÍ", HÉCTOR Berenguel Del Pino, Nourredine NAYBET, JORGE Manuel A. Gomes ANDRADE, Enrique Fernández Romero, Lionel Sebastián Scaloni, SERGIO González Soriano, Aldo Pedro DUSCHER, Francisco J.González Pérez «FRAN» (59 José Emilio AMAVISCA Gárate), Roy Makaay (79 Alberto LUQUE Martos), DIEGO TRISTAN Herrera (69 Juan Carlos VALERÓN Santana).
Trainer: Javier IRURETAGOYENA AMIANO

FC BASEL: Pascal Zuberbühler, Bernt Haas, Marco Zwyssig, Alexandre Quennoz, Thimothée Atouba, Carlos Varela (57 Julio Hernán Rossi), Sébastien Barberis (73 Hervé Tum), Hakan Yakin, Benjamin Huggel, Scott Chipperfield, Christian Gimenez. Trainer: Christian Gross

Goal: Diego Tristan (4)

JUVENTUS FC TORINO v MANCHESTER UNITED FC 0-3 (0-2)

Delle Alpi, Torino 25.02.2003

Referee: Markus Merk (GER) Attendance: 60,000

JUVENTUS: Gianluigi Buffon, Lilian Thuram, Paolo MONTERO Iglesias, Ciro Ferrara, Gianluca Zambrotta (67 Gianluca Pessotto), Mauro Germán Camoranesi, Antonio Conte (46 Igor Tudor), Edgar Davids, Pavel Nedved, David Trezeguet, Marco Di Vaio (46 José Marcelo SALAS Melinao).
Trainer: Marcello Lippi

MANCHESTER UNITED: Fabian Barthez, Gary Neville, Rio Ferdinand, Roy Keane, John O'Shea (60 Daniel Pugh), David Backham, Philip Neville, Nicky Butt, Juan Sebastián Veron, Ole Gunnar Solskjær, Diego FORLÁN Corazo (8 Ryan Giggs, 49 Ruud Van Nistelrooy).
Manager: Alexander Chapman Ferguson

Goals: Giggs (15, 41), Van Nistelrooy (63)

JUVENTUS FC TORINO v RC DEPORTIVO LA CORUÑA 3-2 (1-1)

Delle Alpi, Torino 12.03.2003

Referee: Anders Frisk (SWE) Attendance: 35,000

JUVENTUS: Gianluigi Buffon, Lilian Thuram, Paolo MONTERO Iglesias, Ciro Ferrara, Gianluca Zambrotta, Mauro Germán Camoranesi (46 Gianluca Pessotto), Alessio Tacchinardi (77 Igor Tudor), Edgar Davids, Pavel Nedved, David Trezeguet, Marco Di Vaio (46 Marcelo Danubio Zalayeta). Trainer: Marcello Lippi

DEPORTIVO: Juan Miguel García Inglés «JUANMÍ», HÉCTOR Berenguel Del Pino, Nourredine Naybet, CÉSAR Martín Víllar (71 JORGE Manuel A. Gomes ANDRADE), Enrique Fernández Romero, Lionel Sebastián Scaloni, MAURO da SILVA Gomes, Aldo Pedro DUSCHER, Francisco J.González Pérez «FRAN» (46 Joan CAPDEVILA Méndez), Roy Makaay, DIEGO TRISTAN Herrera (66 Juan Carlos VALERÓN Santana).
Trainer: Javier IRURETAGOYENA AMIANO

Goals: Ferrara (12), Diego Tristan (34), Makaay (52), Trezeguet (63), Tudor (90+3)

MANCHESTER UNITED FC v FC BASEL 1-1 (0-1)

Old Trafford, Manchester 12.03.2003

Referee: Claus Bo Larsen (DEN) Attendance: 66,870

MANCHESTER UNITED: Roy Carroll, Gary Neville, Rio Ferdinand, Laurent Blanc (74 Paul Scholes), John O'Shea, Darren Fletcher (74 David Backham), Philip Neville, Nicky Butt, Kieran Edward Richardson (46 Ryan Giggs), Ole Gunnar Solskjær, Diego FORLÁN Corazo.
Manager: Alexander Chapman Ferguson

FC BASEL: Pascal Zuberbühler, Bernt Haas, Murat Yakin, Marco Zwyssig, Thimothée Atouba, Sébastien Barberis, Hakan Yakin, Mario Cantaluppi, Scott Chipperfield, Christian Gimenez (77 Hervé Tum), Julio Hernán Rossi (63 Benjamin Huggel). Trainer: Christian Gross

Goals: Gimenez (14), G. Neville (53)

FC BASEL v JUVENTUS FC TORINO 2-1 (1-1)

Saint Jakob, Basel 18.03.2003

Referee: Wolfgang Stark (GER) Attendance: 30,500

FC BASEL: Pascal Zuberbühler, Bernt Haas, Murat Yakin, Marco Zwyssig, Thimothée Atouba, Sébastien Barberis (56 Benjamin Huggel), Hakan Yakin (79 Carlos Varela), Mario Cantaluppi, Scott Chipperfield, Christian Gimenez, Julio Hernán Rossi (72 Hervé Tum). Trainer: Christian Gross

JUVENTUS: Gianluigi Buffon, Lilian Thuram (70 Alessandro Del Piero), Paolo MONTERO Iglesias, Mark Iuliano, Alessandro Birindelli, Cristian Zenoni, Alessio Tacchinardi, Igor Tudor (46 Gianluca Pessotto), Gianluca Zambrotta, Pavel Nedved, David Trezeguet (30 José Marcelo SALAS Melinao).
Trainer: Marcello Lippi

Goals: Tacchinardi (10), Cantaluppi (38), Gimenez (90+2)

RC DEPORTIVO LA CORUÑA v MANCHESTER UNITED FC 2-0 (1-0)

Riazor, La Coruña 18.03.2003

Referee: Vladimir Hrinak (SVK) Attendance: 20,000

DEPORTIVO: Daniel DANI MALLO Castro, MANUEL PABLO Garcia Diaz, CÉSAR Martín Víllar, JORGE Manuel A. Gomes ANDRADE (64 Goran Djorovic), Joan CAPDEVILA Méndez, VÍCTOR Sánchez del Amo (78 HÉCTOR Berenguel Del Pino), Roberto Miguel ACUÑA, Aldo Pedro Duscher, Francisco J.González Pérez «FRAN» (52 Lionel Sebastián SCALONI), Juan Carlos VALERÓN Santana, Alberto LUQUE Martos. Trainer: Javier IRURETAGOYENA AMIANO

MANCHESTER UNITED: RICARDO López Felipe, Lee Roche (46 Michael Stewart), Laurent Blanc, John O'Shea, Mark Lynch, Nicky Butt, Philip Neville, Daniel Pugh, Darren Fletcher, Ryan Giggs (72 Kieran Edward Richardson), Diego Forlán Corazo (72 Danny Webber).
Manager: Alexander Chapman Ferguson

Goals: Víctor (32), Lynch (47 og)

Manchester United FC and Juventus FC qualified for the quarter finals.

	P	W	D	L	F	A	Pts
Manchester United FC	6	4	1	1	11	5	13
Juventus FC Torino	6	2	1	3	11	11	7
FC Basel	6	2	1	3	5	10	7
Deportivo La Coruña	6	2	1	3	7	8	7

QUARTER-FINALS

AFC AJAX AMSTERDAMv AC MILAN 0-0

Amsterdam ArenA 8.04.2003

Referee: Terje Hauge (NOR) Attendance: 50,000

AJAX: Bogdan Lobonţ, Hatem Trabelsi, Cristian Chivu, Petri Pasanen (74 Nigel De Jong), John O'Brien, Steven Pienaar, Tomáš Galásek (67 Wesley Sneijder), Abubakari Yakubu, MAXWELL Scherer Cabelino Andrade, Rafael Van Der Vaart, Zlatan Ibrahimovic (73 Jari Litmanen).
Trainer: Ronald Koeman

AC MILAN: Nélson de Jesus Silva "DIDA", Dario Simić, Paolo Maldini, Alessandro Nesta, Alessandro Costacurta, Gennaro Gattuso, Massimo Ambrosini, RUI Manuel César COSTA, Clarence Seedorf (26 Sérgio Cláudio dos Santos "SERGINHO"), Filippo Inzaghi (73 Jon Dahl Tomasson), Andriy Shevchenko (79 "RIVALDO" Vítor Barbosa Ferreira). Trainer: Carlo Ancelotti

AC MILAN v AFC AJAX AMSTERDAM 3-2 (1-0)

Giuseppe Meazza, Milano 23.04.2003

Referee: Manuel Enrique MEJUTO GONZÁLEZ (SPA)
Attendance: 76,079

AC MILAN: Nélson de Jesus Silva "DIDA", Dario Simić (84 Jon Dahl Tomasson), Alessandro Nesta, Paolo Maldini, Alessandro Costacurta; Cristian Brocchi, Massimo Ambrosini, Kakha Kaladze (80 "RIVALDO" Vítor Barbosa Ferreira), RUI Manuel César COSTA (85 Fernando Carlos Redondo); Andriy Shevchenko, Filippo Inzaghi. Trainer: Carlo Ancelotti

AJAX: Bogdan Lobonţ; Hatem Trabelsi, Petri Pasanen, Cristian Chivu, Jelle van Damme (46 Jari Litmanen); Abubakari Yakubu, Wesley Sneijder, John O'Brien; Steven Pienaar (84 Nigel De Jong), Zlatan Ibrahimovic, Andy van der Meyde (89 André Bergdølmo). Trainer: Ronald Koeman

Goals: Inzaghi (30), Litmanen (63), Shevchenko (65), Pienaar (78), Tomasson (90+1)

REAL MADRID CF v MANCHESTER UNITED FC 3-1 (2-0)

Santiago Bernabéu, Madrid 8.04.2003

Referee: Anders Frisk (SWE) Attendance: 80,000

REAL MADRID: Iker CASILLAS Fernández, Miguel Angel "MICHEL" SALGADO, Fernando Ruíz HIERRO, Iván HELGUERA Bujía, ROBERTO CARLOS da Silva, Luís Felipe Madeira Caeiro "FIGO", FLÁVIO da CONCEICÃO, Claude MAKÉLÉLÉ, Zinédine ZIDANE, RONALDO Luis Nazario de Lima (84 José María Gutiérrez "GUTI"), RAÚL González Blanco. Trainer: Vicente DEL BOSQUE González

MANCHESTER UNITED: Fabian Barthez, Gary Neville (86 Ole Gunnar Solskjær), Rio Ferdinand, Wesley Brown, Mikael Silvestre (58 John O'Shea), David Beckham, Roy Keane, Nicky Butt, Paul Scholes, Ryan Giggs, Ruud Van Nistelrooy.
Manager: Alexander Chapman Ferguson

Goals: Figo (12), Raúl (28, 49), van Nistelrooy (52)

MANCHESTER UNITED FC v REAL MADRID CF 4-3 (1-1)

Old Trafford, Manchester 23.04.2003

Referee: Pierluigi Collina (ITA) Attendance: 67,000

MANCHESTER UNITED: Fabian Barthez; Wesley Brown, Rio Ferdinand, Mikael Silvestre (79 Philip Neville), John O'Shea; Nicky Butt, Roy Keane (80 Quinton Fortune), Juan Sebastián Veron (63 David Beckham), Ole Gunnar Solskjær, Ryan Giggs; Ruud Van Nistelrooy. Manager: Alex Ferguson

REAL MADRID: Iker CASILLAS Fernández; Miguel Angel "MICHEL" SALGADO, Fernando Ruíz HIERRO, Iván HELGUERA Bujía, ROBERTO CARLOS da Silva; Claude MAKÉLÉLÉ, Luís Felipe Madeira Caeiro "FIGO" (88 Francisco PAVÓN Barahona), Zinédine ZIDANE, Steve McManaman (69 Javier García PORTILLO); RONALDO Luis Nazario de Lima (67 Santiago Hernán SOLARI), José María Gutiérrez "GUTI".
Trainer: Vicente DEL BOSQUE González

Goals: Ronaldo (12, 50, 59), van Nistelrooij (43), Iván Helguera (52 og), Beckham (71, 85)

JUVENTUS FC TORINO v FC BARCELONA 1-1 (1-0)

Delle Apli, Torino 9.04.2003

Referee: Ľuboš Michel (SVK) Attendance: 50,000

JUVENTUS: Gianluigi Buffon, Lilian Thuram, Paolo Montero Iglesias, Ciro Ferrara, Gianluca Zambrotta (67 Marcelo Danubio Zalayeta), Mauro Germán Camoranesi, Alessio Tacchinardi, Igor Tudor (61 Alessandro Birindelli), Pavel Nedved, Edgar Davids, Alessandro Del Piero (82 Marco Di Vaio). Trainer: Marcello Lippi

FC BARCELONA: Roberto Oscar BONANO, Gabriel García de la Torre "GABRI", Frank de Boer, Carlos PUYOL Saforcada, Michael Reiziger, Marc Overmars (83 LUIS ENRIQUE Martínez García), Xavier Hernández Creus "XAVI" (74 GERARD López Segú), Thiago MOTTA, Juan Román RIQUELME (63 Gaizka MENDIETA Zabala), Patrick Kluivert, Javier Pedro Saviola. Trainer: Radomir Antić

Goals: Montero (16), Saviola (78)

FC BARCELONA v JUVENTUS FC TORINO 1-2 (0-0, 1-1) (AET)

Camp Nou, Barcelona 22.04.2003

Referee: Graham Poll (ENG) Attendance: 95,000

FC BARCELONA: Roberto Oscar BONANO, Michael Reiziger (91 GERARD López Segú), Frank de Boer, Patrik Andersson (61 Gaizka MENDIETA Zabala), Carlos PUYOL Saforcada, Xavier Hernández Creus "XAVI", Javier Pedro Saviola, Patrick Kluivert, Marc Overmars (85 Juan Román RIQUELME), LUIS ENRIQUE Martínez García, Thiago MOTTA. Trainer: Radomir Antić

JUVENTUS: Gianluigi Buffon, Ciro Ferrara, Alessio Tacchinardi, Paolo MONTERO Iglesias, Alessandro Del Piero (83 Igor Tudor), Pavel Nedved, Mauro Germán Camoranesi (46 Alessandro Birindelli), Marco Di Vaio (46 Marcelo Danubio Zalayeta), Gianluca Zambrotta, Lilian Thuram, Edgar Davids. Trainer: Marcello Lippi

Sent off: Davids (79)

Goals: Nedved (53), Xavi (66), Zalayeta (114)

FC INTERNAZIONALE MILANO v VALENCIA CF 1-0 (1-0)

Giuseppe Meazza, Milano 9.04.2003

Referee: Markus Merk (GER) Attendance: 55,000

INTERNAZIONALE: Francesco Toldo, Javier Zanetti, Marco Materazzi, Iván Ramiro Cordoba, Francesco Coco (31 Giovanni Pasquale), SÉRGIO Paulo Marceneiro CONCEIÇÃO (65 Okan Buruk), Luigi Di Biagio, Cristiano Zanetti, Emre Belözoglu, Hernán Jorge Crespo (83 Fabio Cannavaro), Christian Vieri. Trainer: Hector Raúl Cúper

VALENCIA: José Santiago CAÑIZARES Ruiz, Anthony RÉVEILLÈRE, Roberto Fabián AYALA, Carlos MARCHENA López, Amedeo CARBONI, Francisco Joaquim Pérez RUFETE (80 Miguel Angel Ferrer Martínez «MISTA»), David ALBELDA Aliques, Rubén BARAJA Vegas, VICENTE Rodríguez Guillén (85 FÁBIO AURÉLIO Rodrigues), John CAREW (66 Miguel Angel ANGULO Valderrey), Pablo César AIMAR. Trainer: Rafael BENÍTEZ MAUDES

Sent off: Emre (57) and Albelda (57)

Goal: Vieri (14)

VALENCIA CF v FC INTERNAZIONALE MILANO 2-1 (1-1)

Mestalla, Valencia 22.04.2003

Referee: Kim Milton Nielsen (DEN) Attendance: 50,000

VALENCIA: José Santiago CAÑIZARES Ruiz, Roberto Fabián AYALA, John CAREW (73 Francisco Joaquim Pérez RUFETE), Rubén BARAJA Vegas, Miguel Angel ANGULO Valderrey, JUAN Ginés SÁNCHEZ Moreno, Carlos MARCHENA López, VICENTE Rodríguez Guillén, Amedeo CARBONI (80 FÁBIO AURÉLIO Rodrigues), Pablo César AIMAR (84 Miguel Angel Ferrer Martínez «MISTA»), Anthony RÉVEILLÈRE. Trainer: Rafael BENÍTEZ MAUDES

INTERNAZIONALE: Francesco Toldo, Iván Ramiro Cordoba, Javier Zanetti, Cristiano Zanetti, Hernán Jorge Crespo, Luigi Di Biagio (75 Okan Buruk), Stéphane Dalmat, Marco Materazzi, Carlos Alberto Gamarra, Giovanni Pasquale (46 Daniele Adani), Christian Vieri (32 Alvaro Recoba). Trainer: Hector Raúl Cúper

Goals: Vieri (5), Aimar (7), Baraja (51)

SEMI-FINALS

REAL MADRID CF v JUVENTUS FC TORINO 2-1 (1-1)

Santiago Bernabéu, Madrid 6.05.2003

Referee: Terje Hauge (NOR) Attendance: 70,000

REAL MADRID: Iker CASILLAS Fernández; Miguel Angel "MICHEL" SALGADO, Fernando Ruíz HIERRO, Iván HELGUERA Bujía, ROBERTO CARLOS da Silva; Claude MAKÉLÉLÉ, Luís Felipe Madeira Caeiro "FIGO", José María Gutiérrez "GUTI", Zinédine ZIDANE; Fernando MORIENTES Sánchez (79 Santiago Hernán SOLARI), RONALDO Luis Nazario de Lima (50 Javier García PORTILLO). Trainer: Vicente DEL BOSQUE González

JUVENTUS: Gianluigi Buffon, Alessandro Birindelli, Lilian Thuram, Ciro Ferrara, Mark Iuliano (46 Gianluca Pessotto); Antonio Conte, Igor Tudor (80 Mauro Germán Camoranesi), Pavel Nedved (82 Marco di Vaio), Gianluca Zambrotta; Alessandro Del Piero, David Trezeguet. Trainer: Marcello Lippi

Goals: Ronaldo (23), Trezeguet (45), Roberto Carlos (73)

JUVENTUS FC v REAL MADRID CF 3-1 (2-0)

Delle Alpi, Torino 14.05.2003

Referee: Urs Meier (SWI) Attendance: 67299

JUVENTUS: Gianluigi Buffon, Alessio Tacchinardi, Paolo MONTERO Iglesias, Igor Tudor, Pavel Nedved, Alessandro Birindelli (60 Gianluca Pessotto), David Trezeguet (77 Mauro Germán Camoranesi), Gianluca Zambrotta, Lilian Thuram; Alessandro Del Piero, Edgar Davids (89 Antonio Conte). Trainer: Marcello Lippi

REAL MADRID: Iker CASILLAS Fernández; Miguel Angel «MICHEL» SALGADO, Fernando Ruíz HIERRO, Iván HELGUERA Bujía, ROBERTO CARLOS da Silva; RAÚL González Blanco, Luís Felipe Madeira Caeiro "FIGO", José María Gutiérrez "GUTI", Zinédine ZIDANE; FLÁVIO da Conceição (52 RONALDO Luis Nazario de Lima), Esteban Matías CAMBIASSO Deleau (76 Steve McManaman). Trainer: Vicente DEL BOSQUE González

Goals: Trezeguet (12), Del Piero (43), Nedved (73), Zidane (89)

AC MILAN v FC INTERNAZIONALE MILANO 0-0

Giuseppe Meazza, Milano 7.05.2003

Referee: Valentin Ivanov (RUS) Attendance: 78,000

AC MILAN: Nélson de Jesus Silva "DIDA", Alessandro Costacurta, Alessandro Nesta, Paolo Maldini, Kakha Kaladze; Cristian Brocchi (73 Sérgio Cláudio dos Santos "SERGINHO"), Gennaro Gattuso (78 Fernando Carlos Redondo), RUI Manuel César COSTA, Clarence Seedorf; Andriy Shevchenko (81 "RIVALDO" Vítor Barbosa Ferreira), Filippo Inzaghi. Trainer: Carlo Ancelotti

INTERNAZIONALE: Francesco Toldo, Iván Ramiro Cordoba, Fabio Cannavaro, Marco Materazzi, Francesco Coco (84 Giovanni Pasquale); Javier Zanetti, SÉRGIO Paulo Marceneiro CONCEIÇÃO (66 Andrés «GULY» GUGLIELMINPIETRO), Luigi Di Biagio, Emre Belözoglu; Hernán Jorge Crespo, Alvaro Recoba (72 Mohamed Kallon). Trainer: Hector Raúl Cúper

FC INTERNAZIONALE MILANO v AC MILAN 1-1 (0-1)

Giuseppe Meazza, Milano 13.05.2003

Referee: Gilles Veissière (FRA) Attendance: 76,000

INTERNAZIONALE: Francesco Toldo, Iván Ramiro Cordoba (46 Akinwunmi MARTINS Obafemi), Javier Zanetti, Emre Belözoglu, Cristiano Zanetti, SÉRGIO Paulo Marceneiro CONCEIÇÃO, Hernán Jorge Crespo (71 Mohamed Kallon), Fabio Cannavaro, Luigi Di Biagio (46 Stéphane Dalmat),Alvaro Recoba, Marco Materazzi. Trainer: Hector Raúl Cúper

AC MILAN: Christian Abbiati, Paolo Maldini, Kakha Kaladze, Andriy Shevchenko, Gennaro Gattuso, Filippo Inzaghi (73 Sérgio Cláudio dos Santos "SERGINHO"), RUI Manuel César COSTA (64 Massimo Ambrosini), Alessandro Costacurta, Alessandro Nesta, Clarence Seedorf, Andrea Pirlo (89 Cristian Brocchi). Trainer: Carlo Ancelotti

Goals: Shevchenko (45+1), Martins (84)

FINAL

AC MILAN v JUVENTUS FC TORINO 0-0 (AET)

Old Trafford, Manchester 28.05.2003

Referee: Markus Merk (GER) Attendance: 62,300

JUVENTUS: Gianluigi Buffon; Lilian Thuram, Ciro Ferrara, Igor Tudor (42 Alessandro Birindelli), Paolo MONTERO Iglesias, Mauro Germán Camoranesi (46 Antonio Conte), Alessio Tacchinardi, Edgar Davids (65 Marcelo Danubio Zalayeta), Gianluca Zambrotta, David Trezeguet, Alessandro del Piero. Trainer: Marcello Lippi

AC MILAN: Nélson de Jesus Silva "DIDA"; Alessandro Costacurta (65 José Vitor ROQUE JUNIOR), Alessandro Nesta, Paolo Maldini, Kakha Kaladze, Gennaro Gattuso, Andrea Pirlo (70 Sérgio Cláudio dos Santos "SERGINHO"), Clarence Seedorf, RUI Manuel César COSTA (86 Massimo Ambrosini), Andriy Shevchenko, Filippo Inzaghi. Trainer: Carlo Ancelotti

Penalties: Trezeguet (miss), 1-0 Serginho, 1-1 Birindelli, Seedorf (miss), Zalayeta (miss), Kaladze (miss), Montero (miss), 1-2 Nesta, 2-2 del Piero, 2-3 Shevchenko

European Cup Goalscorers 2002-03:

14 goals: Ruud van Nistelrooy (Manchester United)

12 goals: Filippo Inzaghi (Milan AC)

9 goals: Christian Gimenez (FC Basel), Roy Makaay (Deportivo La Coruña), RAÚL González Blanco (Real Madrid)

8 goals: Jan Koller (Borussia Dortmund)

7 goals: Javier Pedro SAVIOLA (FC Barcelona), Alan Shearer (Newcastle United), Thierry Henry (Arsenal London), Yakubu Ayegbeni (Maccabi Haifa)

6 goals: RONALDO Nazario de Lima (Real Madrid)

5 goals: Zlatan Ibrahimovic (Ajax Amsterdam), Patrick Kluivert (FC Barcelona), Julio Rossi (FC Basel), Maksim Shatskikh (Dinamo Kyiv), Ryan Giggs (Manchester United), Sonny Andersson (Olympique Lyonnais), John Carew (Valencia CF), Guti (Real Madrid), Pavel Nedved, Alessandro del Piero (Juventus Torino)

4 goals: Antonio Cassano (AS Roma), Marko Babić (Bayer Leverkusen), Diego Tristan (Deportivo La Coruña), Hakan Yakin (FC Basel), Bazina (Grazer AK), Michael Owen (Liverpool FC), Ole Gunnar Solskjaer, Juan Sebastián Veron (Manchester United), Daniel Moreira (RC Lens), Djordjević (Olympiakos Peiraias), Baraja (Valencia CF), Shevchenko (Milan AC), Marco di Vaio, David Trezeguet (Juventus Torino)

3 goals: Totti (AS Roma), Schneider (Bayer Leverkusen), Salihamidzić (Bayern München), Amoroso (Borussia Dortmund), Bagger (Brøndby IF), Cernat (Dinamo Kyiv), F. De Boer (FC Barcelona), Chukunyere (Hibernians Paola), Loskov (Lokomotiv Moskva), Cohen, Katan (Maccabi Haifa), Sonck (KRC Genk), Beckham (Manchester United), Ameobi (Newcastle United), Karamyan (Pyunik Erevan), Brattbakk (Rosenborg), Aimar, Juan Sánchez (Valencia CF), Gredić (Zeljeznicar Sarajevo), Recoba, Vieri (Internazionale Milano), Zidane (Real Madrid), Tomasson (Milan AC)

2 goals: Borbokis, Centeno, Nikolaidis (AEK Athina), Benjamin (AJ Auxerre), Litmanen, Pienaar, van der Vaart (Ajax Amsterdam), Malekkos (Apoel Nicosia), Gilberto, Ljungberg (Arsenal London), Berbatov, Franca, Juan (Bayer Leverkusen), Élber, Pizarro, Tarnat (Bayern München), Korolik (Belshina Bobruisk), Silva (Boavista Porto), Frings, Rosicky (Borussia Dortmund), Lange, Mendoza, Simons (Club Brugge), Víctor (Deportivo La Coruña), Khatskevich (Dinamo Kyiv), Velicka (FBK Kaunas), Cocu, Dani, Luis Enrique, Mendieta, Motta, Riquelme (FC Barcelona), Ergic (FC Basel), Ono (Feyenoord), Aufhauser (Grazer AK), Mifsud (Hibernians Paola), Kucharski (Legia Warszawa), Heskey (Liverpool FC), Evseyev, Ignashevich, Julio Cesar, Obiorah (Lokomotiv Moskva), Badier, Pralija, Rosso (Maccabi Haifa), Scholes (Manchester United), Bellamy, Dyer, Hugo Viana, Lua-Lua (Newcastle United), Corović, Duro (NK Maribor), Carrière, Govou, Vairelles (Olympique Lyonnais), Lazović (Partizan Beograd), Bruggink (PSV Eindhoven), Karamyan (Pyunik Erevan), Utaka (RC Lens), Johnsen, Karadas (Rosenborg), Tarhnishvili (Sheriff Tiraspol), Kolesnichenko (Skonto Riga), Baranek, Jarošik (Sparta Praha), Asatiani, Ionanidze (Torpedo Kutaisi), Angulo, Fábio Aurélio, Mista (Valencia CF), Spasovski (Vardar Skopje), Guvo (Zeljeznicar Sarajevo), Lovchev (Zhenis Astana), Martins (Internazionale Milano), Figo, McManaman (Real Madrid), Rivaldo (Milan AC), Montero, Tacchinardi, Zalayeta (Juventus Torino)

1 goal: Katsouranis, Lakis, Maladenis, Tsartas, Wright (AEK Athina), Cissé, Fadiga, Kapo (AJ Auxerre), de Jong, Pasanen, van der Meyde (Ajax Amsterdam), Daskalakis, Georgiou, Haralambides, Ilia, Ouzounidis, Sirakov (Apoel Nicosia), Bergkamp, Kanu, Vieira, Wiltord (Arsenal London), Batistuta, Delvecchio, Emerson (AS Roma), Ballack, Feulner, Jeremies, Kovac, Linke (Bayern München), Alexandre Goulart, Ávalos, Jocivalter, Luiz Cláudio (Boavista Porto), á Lakjuni, Mortensson (B 36 Tórshavn), Zivković (Bayer Leverkusen), Santa Cruz (Bayern München), Stripeikis (Belshina Bobruisk), Paulo Turra (Boavista Porto), M. Jonson, M. Jørgensen, P. Madsen, Skarbalijus (Brøndby IF), Larsson, Sutton, Sylla (Celtic Glasgow), Ceh, Englebert, Martens, Saetrens, Verheyen (Club Brugge), Capdevila, César (Deportivo La Coruña), Alexa (Dinamo Bucureşti), Belkevich, Bodnár, Leandro, Melashchenko (Dinamo Kyiv), Ahmataj, Pisha, Qorri (Dinamo Tirana), Remy (F91 Dudelange), Geovanni, Gerard, Overmars, Xavi (FC Barcelona), Atouba, Cantaluppi, Yakin (FC Basel), Bombarda, Buffel, Lurling, Pardo, van Hooijdonk (Feyenoord), Arif Erdem, Fabio Pinto, Hasan Şaş, Cihan Aspolatli, Sarr (Galatasaray Istanbul), Hastings, Naumoski, Pötscher (Grazer AK), Winsnes (Hammarby IF), Pulis (Hibernians Paola), Beslija, Dagano, Thijs (KRC Genk), Svitlica, Yahaya (Legia Warszawa), Chilikov, Simonović (Levski Sofia), Baros, Cheyrou, Salif Diao, Hyypiä, Murphy, Šmicer (Liverpool FC), Lekcetho, Mnguni (Lokomotiv Moskva), Abiodun, Keissy, Zutautas (Maccabi Haifa), Blanc, Brown, Forlán, G. Neville (Manchester United), Barcík (MSK Zilina), Griffin, Solano, Speed (Newcastle United), Lovrek, Milinović (NK Zagreb), Alexandris, Antzas, Giannakopoulos, Houtos, Luyindula (Olympique Lyonnais), Niniadis, Zetterberg (Olympiakos Peiraias), Cakar, Ilić, Iliev, Ivić (Partizan Beograd), Fitzgerald, Hamilton (Portadown FC), Robben, Rommedahl, van der Schaaf (PSV Eindhoven), Cisterna, Diawara, Mkrchyan (Pyunik Erevan), Bakari, Blanchard, Coulibaly, Thomert (RC Lens), Enerly (Rosenborg), Aghahowa, Vorobey (Shakhtar Donetsk), Byrne, Gannon (Shelbourne FC), Boreţ, Nesteruk, Priganiuc (Sheriff Tiraspol), Eliseyev, Korgalidze, Ksanavicius, Zemlinsky (Skonto Riga), Langer, Slepicka (Slovan Liberec), Jun, Mareš, Poborský, Pospíšil, Zelenka (Sparta Praha), Danishevskiy (Spartak Moskva), Bosnar, Neukirchner, Szabics (Sturm Graz), Janashia, Kvetenadze, Poroshyn (Torpedo Kutaisi), Almeyda, Emre, Cannavaro, Cordoba, Morfeo (Internazionale Milano), Curro Torres, Kily González, Rufete (Valencia CF), da Costa, Georgievski, Petkov, Ristovski (Vardar Skopje), Koplárovics, Ljubojević, Urbán (Zalaegerszegi TE), Bišcević (Zeljeznicar), Klishin, Tlekhougov (Zhenis Ashtana), Celades, Míchel, Portillo, Roberto Carlos, Tote (Real Madrid), Seedorf, Serginho (Milan AC), Birindelli, Camoranesi, Davids, Ferrara, Salas, Tudor (Juventus Torino)

Own goals: Kleine (Bayer Leverkusen) for Olympiakos Peiraias, Fink (Bayern München) for RC Lens, Lynch (Manchester United) for Deportivo La Coruña, Gilberto (Arsenal London) for Borussia Dortmund, Klago (MSK Zilina) for FC Basel, Zokora (KRC Genk) for Real Madrid, Caçapa (Olympique Lyonnais), Saarinen (Rosenborg) & Butt (Bayer Leverkusen) for Inter Milano, Helguera (Real Madrid) for Manchester United

UEFA CHAMPIONS LEAGUE 2003-04

FIRST QUALIFYING ROUND

SLIEMA WANDERERS FC v FC SKONTO RIGA 2-0 (0-0)

Hibernians Ground, Corradino 16.07.2003

Referee: Dejan Stanisić (SER) Attendance: 1,200

SLIEMA WANDERERS: Murphy Akanji, Kristian Laferla, Brian Said, Jeffrey Chetcuti, Noel Turner, Stefan Giglio, Joe Brincat, Carlo Mamo, Orosco Anonam, Danilo Doncic, Daniel Bogdanovic (90 Nenad Veselji). Trainer: Edward Aquilina

SKONTO: Andrejs Piedels, Aleksandr Isakov, Mikhail Zemlinsky, Valentin Lobanyov, Ignas Dedura, Aaron Nguimbat, Victor Moroz, Oresta Buitkus, Igor Semyonov, Maris Verpakovsky (88 Gatis Kalnips), Kristap Blank (69 Levan Korgalidze). Trainer: Aleksandrs Starkovs

Sent off: Isakov (66)

Goals: Bogdanovic (62), Doncic (67 pen)

FC SKONTO RIGA v SLIEMA WANDERERS FC 3-1 (1-0)

Skonto, Riga 23.07.2003

Referee: Mustafa Culcu (TUR) Attendance: 1,500

SKONTO: Andrejs Piedels, Mikhail Zemlinsky, Valentin Lobanyov (90 Levan Korgalidze), Ignas Dedura, Aaron Nguimbat, Victor Moroz, Oresta Buitkus, Igor Semyonov, Maris Verpakovsky, Kristap Blank (46 Audrius Ksanavicius), Gatis Kalnips (77 Krzysztof Lagiewka).
Trainer: Aleksandrs Starkovs **Sent off**: Moroz (67)

SLIEMA WANDERERS: Murphy Akanji (38 Matthew Farrugia), Brian Said, Carlo Mamo (74 Nenad Veselji), Stefan Giglio, Jeffrey Chetcuti, Noel Turner, Jamie Pace (55 Kristian Laferla), Joe Brincat, Orosco Anonam, Danilo Doncic, Daniel Bogdanovic. Trainer: Edward Aquilina

Goals: Buitkus (14), Verpakovsky (64), Dedura (72), Brincat (90)

FC BATE BORISOV v BOHEMIANS FC DUBLIN 1-0 (1-0)

City, Borisov 16.07.2003

Referee: Jaroslav Jara (CZE) Attendance: 4,500

BATE: Yuriy Zhevnov, Dmitry Likhtarovich, Alexei Baga, Gennadiy Mardas, Valery Tarasenka, Dmitriy Molosh, Yevgeniy Loshankov, Oleg Shkabara (78 Dmitriy Rovneika), Pavel Shmigero, Valeriy Stripeikis (46 Igor Chumachenko), Pavel Beganskiy (68 Alexandr Kobets). Trainer: Yury Puntus

BOHEMIANS: Matthew Gregg, Damien Lynch, Simon Webb, Kevin Hunt, Thomas Heary, Colin Hawkins, Barry Ryan (78 Fergal Harkin), Stephen Caffrey, Robert Doyle (80 Paul Keegan), Glen Crowe, Mark Rutherford.
Trainer: Stephen Kenny

Goal: Loshankov (25)

BOHEMIANS FC DUBLIN v FC BATE BORISOV 3-0 (2-0)

Dalymount Park, Dublin 23.07.2003

Referee: Ivan Dobrinov (BUL) Attendance: 5,500

BOHEMIANS: Seamus Kelly, Damien Lynch, Simon Webb, Kevin Hunt, Thomas Heary, Colin Hawkins, Barry Ryan (73 Fergal Harkin), Stephen Caffrey, Robert Doyle, Glen Crowe (90 Andrei Pereplyothin), Mark Rutherford (89 David Morrison).
Trainer: Stephen Kenny

BATE: Yuriy Zhevnov, Dmitry Likhtarovich, Alexei Baga, Gennadiy Mardas, Igor Chumachenko (78 Dmitriy Shchahrykovich), Yevgeniy Loshankov, Oleg Shkabara (69 Dmitriy Rovneika), Valery Tarasenka, Pavel Shmigero (61 Alexandr Kobets), Dmitriy Klimovich, Valeriy Stripeikis.
Trainer: Yury Puntus

Goals: Caffrey (38), Ryan (45), Crowe (58)

HB TÓRSHAVN v FBK KAUNAS 0-1 (0-0)

Tórsvøllur, Tórshavn 16.07.2003

Referee: Igor Ishchenko (UKR) Attendance: 1,200

HB TÓRSHAVN: Bárdur Johannesen, Hans Á Lag, Simun Eliasen, Jan C. Dam, Hallur Danielsen, Rógvi Jacobsen, Rúni Nolsøe, Martin Christensen, Nicu Dogaru (87 Pall M. Joensen), Andrew Av Fløtum, Karsten From (76 Tór-Ingar Akselsen). Trainer: Frank Skytte

FBK KAUNAS: Gytis Padimanskas, Darius Gvildys, Tomas Kancelskis, Darius Regelskis, Irmantas Zelmikas, Milan Pastva (80 Andrius Puotkalis), Marius Bezykornovas (84 Andrius Velicka), Andrius Gedgaudas, Gintas Širmelis, Giedrius Barevicius, Martynas Karalius (71 Martin Opic).
Trainer: Siarhei Barouski

Sent off: Gedgaudas (85)

Goal: Opic (75)

FBK KAUNAS v HB TÓRSHAVN 4-1 (3-1)

S. Darius & S. Girenas, Kaunas 23.07.2003

Referee: Alojzije Supraha (CRO) Attendance: 1,000

FBK KAUNAS: Gytis Padimanskas, Darius Gvildys, Tomas Kancelskis, Darius Regelskis, Irmantas Zelmikas, Marius Bezykornovas (53 Milan Pastva), Tadas Papeckys, Gintas Širmelis (77 Andrius Velicka), Giedrius Barevicius, Martin Opic, Ricardas Beniusis (80 Martynas Karalius).
Trainer: Siarhei Barouski

HB TÓRSHAVN: Bárdur Johannesen, Hans Á Lag (58 Janus M.Joensen), Simun Eliasen, Jan C.Dam, Hallur Danielsen (79 Bjarni Jørgensen), Rógvi Jacobsen, Rúni Nolsøe, Martin Christensen, Nicu Dogaru, Andrew Av Fløtum, Tór-Ingar Akselsen (68 Karsten From). Trainer: Frank Skytte

Sent off: Jacobsen (79)

Goals: Beniusis (5, 77), Jacobsen (9), Kancelskis (36), Opic (40)

GLENTORAN FC BELFAST v HJK HELSINKI 0-0

The Oval, Belfast 16.07.2003

Referee: Darius Miezelis (LIT)

GLENTORAN: Elliott Morris, Colin Nixon, Mark Glendinning, Chris Walker (27 Darren Armour), Paul Leeman, Gary Smyth, Kevin Keegan, Scott Young (73 Michael O'Neill), Andy Smith, Darren Lockhart, Tim McCann (73 Tim McCann). Trainer: Robert Coyle

HJK: András Vilnrotter, Mike Peltola, Aarno Turpeinen, Joakim Jensen, Iiro Aalto, Antti Heinola, Alexei Yeremenko Sr (69 László Fekete), Rami Hakanpää, Mika Kottila, Toni Kallio, Juho Mäkelä (60 Alexei Yeremenko Jr.). Trainer: Keith Armstrong

HJK HELSINKI v GLENTORAN FC BELFAST 1-0 (0-0)

Pohjola, Vantaa 23.07.2003

Referee: Miroslaw Ryszka (POL) Attendance: 4,270

HJK: András Vilnrotter, Aarno Turpeinen, Ville Nylund, Joakim Jensen, Iiro Aalto, Antti Heinola, Alexei Yeremenko Jr. (19 Mike Peltola), Rami Hakanpää, Mika Kottila, Toni Kallio (66 Christian Sund), Juho Mäkelä (89 Vili Savolainen). Trainer: Keith Armstrong

GLENTORAN: Elliott Morris, Colin Nixon, Mark Glendinning, Paul Leeman, Scott Young (85 Andrew Kilmartin), Gary Smyth, Tim McCann, Michael O'Neill, Andy Smith, Darren Lockhart (85 Tim McCann), Kevin Keegan (76 Darren Armour). Trainer: Robert Coyle

Sent off: Turpeinen (82)

Goal: Mäkelä (72)

FC DINAMO TBILISI v KS TIRANA 3-0 (2-0)

Boris Paichadze, Tbilisi 16.07.2003

Referee: David Malcolm (NIR)
Attendance: Played behind closed doors

DINAMO: Irakli Zoidze (81 David Gvaramadze), Georgi Shashiashvili, Aleksandr Amisulashvili, Otar Khizaneishvili, Vitali Daraselia (86 KARLOS Da Rosha), Aleksandre Gogoberishvili, Vladimer Burduli, George Anchabadze, Dato Kvirkvelia, Lado Akhalaia, Levan Melkadze (66 Ilia Kandelaki). Trainer: Ivan Šušak

KS TIRANA: Ndubuisi Egbo, Elvis Sina, Rezart Dabulla, Nevil Dede, Luan Pinari, Ervin Bulku (46 Gentian Hajdari), Devis Mukaj, Suad Liçi (72 Eldorado Merkoçi), Indrit Fortuzi, Mahir Halili (46 Saimir Patushi), Fjodor Xhafa. Trainer: Sulejman Mema

Goals: Melkadze (6), Anchabadze (45), Daraselia (50 pen)

KS TIRANA v FC DINAMO TBILISI 3-0 (1-0, 3-0) (AET)

Qemal Stafa, Tiranë 23.07.2003

Referee: Alan Kelly (IRE) Attendance: 6,000

KS TIRANA: Ndubuisi Egbo, Elvis Sina (84 Eldorado Merkoçi), Nevil Dede, Gentian Hajdari, Luan Pinari, Ervin Bulku (64 Sokol Bulku), Devis Mukaj, Suad Liçi, Saimir Patushi, Indrit Fortuzi, Fjodor Xhafa (64 Mahir Halili). Trainer: Sulejman Mema

DINAMO: Irakli Zoidze, Georgi Shashiashvili, Dato Kvirkvelia, Aleksandr Amisulashvili, Otar Khizaneishvili, Vitali Daraselia (64 KARLOS Da Rosha), Aleksandre Gogoberishvili, Vladimer Burduli, George Anchabadze (22 Ilia Kandelaki), Levan Melkadze (58 Irakli Samkharadze), Lado Akhalaia. Trainer: Ivan Šušak

Goals: Liçi (11), Fortuzi (64), Halili (77)

Penalties: 1-0 Patushi, Gogoberishvili (miss), 2-0 Liçi, 2-1 Samkharadze, 3-1 Dede, 3-2 Khizaneishvili, 4-2 Halili, Akhalaia (miss)

CS GREVENMACHER v FK LEOTAR TREBINJE 0-0

Josy Barthel, Luxembourg 16.07.2003

Referee: Janos Megyebiro (HUN) Attendance: 900

CS GREVENMACHER: Jonathan Joubert, Stephan Kordian, Christian Albrecht, Jérôme Henrot, Luc Thimmesch (50 Daniel Huss), Karim Groune (65 Frank Buschmann), Steve Birtz, Kevin Martin, Ahmed El Aouad, MARCIO Rodrigues da Cruz, Marco Toppmöller. Trainer: Herbert Herres

FK LEOTAR: Vladimir Stojkovic, Bojan Jucinic, Bojan Simic, Sejmon Miloševic, Ninoslan Milenkovic, Zdravko Šaraba, Marko Popovic, Dušan Kerkez (66 Boban Stojanovic, 90 Palo Jankovic), Sinisa Mulina, Branislav Krunic, Pavle Delibasic (73 Aleksandar Jovanovic). Trainer: Mile Jovin

FK LEOTAR TREBINJE v CS GREVENMACHER 2-0 (1-0)

FK Leotar, Trebinije 23.07.2003

Referee: Anton Heleşteanu (ROM) Attendance: 3,000

FK LEOTAR: Vladimir Stojkovic, Zdravko Šaraba, Sejmon Miloševic, Ninoslan Milenkovic, Bojan Jucinic (76 Gavrilo Corlija), Sinisa Mulina, Branislav Krunic, Dušan Kerkez, Marko Popovic, Pavle Delibasic (46 Bojan Simic), Boban Stojanovic (76 Aleksandar Jovanovic). Trainer: Mile Jovin

CS GREVENMACHER: Jonathan Joubert, Pierre MANZANGALA KANDU, Stephan Kordian, Jérôme Henrot, Christian Albrecht, Steve Birtz, Kevin Martin, Luc Thimmesch (65 Manuel Morocutti), Daniel Huss (46 Marco Toppmöller), MARCIO Rodrigues da Cruz, Ahmed El Aouad. Trainer: Herbert Herres

Sent off: Milenkovic (34)

Goals: Kerkez (23, 83)

OMONOIA FC NICOSIA v FC IRTYSH PAVLODAR 0-0

GSP, Nicosia 16.07.2003

Referee: Sinisa Zrnic (BOS) Attendance: 15,000

OMONOIA: Nikolaos Mihopoulos, Georgos Theodotou (84 Zoran Stjepanovic), Akis Ioakim, Marios Nicolaou (78 Vesko Mihailovic), Gábor Korolovszky, Marco Haber, Nicolaos Georgiou (76 Efstathios Aloneftis), Haris Nicolaou, Rainer Rauffmann, Kostas Kaiafas, Jozef Kozlej. Trainer: Toni Savevski

FC IRTYSH: Yuriy Novikov, Serguei Timofeev, Tomas Schastka, Fevzi Davletov, Aidar Kumisbekov, Alexei Zakharov, Kairat Nurdauletov, Farkhadbek Irismetov, Andrey Kucheryavykh, Muslim Agayev (85 Bagdad Dostayev), Murat Tleshev (46 Sergei Ivanov, 80 Egidijus Juska). Trainer: Dmitriy Ogai

Sent off: Haber (90)

FC IRTYSH PAVLODAR v OMONOIA FC NICOSIA 1-2 (1-0)

Centralnyi, Pavlodar 23.07.2003

Referee: Petteri Kari (FIN) Attendance: 12,000

FC IRTYSH: Yuriy Novikov, Serguei Timofeev, Tomas Schastka, Fevzi Davletov, Andrey Kucheryavykh, Alexei Zakharov (46 Aidar Kumisbekov), Kairat Nurdauletov, Farkhadbek Irismetov, Serik Zheylitbayev, Muslim Agayev (73 Sergey Skorykh), Rustam Usmanov (70 Murat Tleshev). Trainer: Dmitriy Ogai

OMONOIA: Nikolaos Mihopoulos, Georgos Theodotou, Akis Ioakim, Gábor Korolovszky, Marios Nicolaou, Nicolaos Georgiou, Jozef Kozlej (85 Panagiotis Panagiotou), Haris Nicolaou (90 Elias Haralambous), Rainer Rauffmann, Vesko Mihailovic (46 Zoran Stjepanovic), Kostas Kaiafas. Trainer: Toni Savevski

Goals: Agayev (21), Rauffmann (61), Georgiou (90)

FC SHERIFF TIRASPOL v FC FLORA TALLINN 1-0 (0-0)

Sheriff, Tiraspol 16.07.2003

Referee: Imankhan Sultani (AZE) Attendance: 8,000

FC SHERIFF: Sebastian Huțan, Ivan Testimițanu, Vaja Tarkhnishvili, Oleg Gumenyuk (62 Leandro Farias), Florin Dan Lăcustă, Iuriy Priganiuc, Stanislav Ivanov, Vadim Boreț, Eduard Bandi (31 Victor Barîşev), Cristian Tudor, Sergei Dadu (75 Andrei Nesteruk). Trainer: Igor Nakonechnyy

FC FLORA: Martin Kaalma, Teet Allas, Andrei Stepanov, Enar Jääger, Erko Saviauk, Ott Reinumäe, Meelis Rooba, Marko Kristal, Kristan Viikmäe, Vjatseslav Zahovaiko, Joel Lindpere (90 Ragnar Klavan). Trainer: Jelle Goes

Goal: Tudor (88)

FC FLORA TALLINN v FC SHERIFF TIRASPOL 1-1 (0-0)

A Le Coq Arena, Tallinn 23.07.2003

Referee: Michael Leslie Dean (ENG) Attendance: 2,500

FC FLORA: Martin Kaalma, Teet Allas (80 Taavi Rähn), Andrei Stepanov, Enar Jääger, Erko Saviauk (66 Ragnar Klavan), Ott Reinumäe, Kristan Viikmäe, Marko Kristal, Tor Henning Hamre (74 Aleksander Saharov), Joel Lindpere, Vjatseslav Zahovaiko. Trainer: Arnoldus Dick Pijpers

FC SHERIFF: Sebastian Huțan, Ivan Testimițanu, Vaja Tarkhnishvili, Odiah Chidi, Florin Dan Lăcustă, Iuriy Priganiuc, Stanislav Ivanov (85 Valentin Gini Necşulescu), Vadim Boreț, Victor Barîşev, Cristian Tudor (84 Leandro Farias), Sergei Dadu (72 Andrei Nesteruk). Trainer: Igor Nakonechnyy

Goals: Nesteruk (80), Viikmáe (88)

FK VARDAR SKOPJE v BARRY TOWN FC 3-0 (1-0)

Gradski, Skopje 16.07.2003

Referee: Asaf Kenan (ISR) Attendance: 5,000

VARDAR: Muarem Zekir, Dragan Veselinovski, Nikola Djosevski, Blessing Chinedu Anyanviu, Vlatko Grozdanovski (78 Darko Taševski), Mario Petkov (65 ROGERIO da Costa Oliviera), Srdan Zaharievski, Dejan Ristovski, Slavco Georgievski, Dejan Brankovic, Oliveira WANDEIR dos Santos (81 Dragan Nacevski). Trainer: Zoran Stratev

BARRY TOWN: Mark Ovendale, Lee Jarman, Gary Lloyd (67 Nathan Cotterrall), Jamie Jenkins, Scott Morgan, Lee Phillips, Mark Molloy (75 Richard Kennedy), Jon French, Jamie Moralee, Tom Ramasut, Adebayo Akinfenwa (63 Danny Ocquaye). Trainer: Kenneth James Brown

Goals: Wandeir (38, 70), Ristovski (49)

BARRY TOWN FC v FK VARDAR SKOPJE 2-1 (1-0)

Jenner Park, Barry 23.07.2003

Referee: Sergey Kapanin (KAZ) Attendance: 1,400

BARRY TOWN: Mark Ovendale, Lee Jarman, Lee Phillips, Richard Kennedy, Scott Morgan, Jon French, Tom Ramasut (85 Jamie Jenkins), Jamie Moralee, Adebayo Akinfenwa, Nathan Cotterrall (76 Mark Molloy), Danny Ocquaye (76 David Moss). Trainer: Kenneth James Brown

FK VARDAR: Muarem Zekir, Dragan Veselinovski, Nikola Djosevski, Blessing Chinedu Anyanviu, Dejan Brankovic, Jovica Trajcev, Slavco Georgievski (83 Bobi Božinovski), Mario Petkov (46 ROGERIO da Costa Oliviera), Srdan Zaharievski, Dejan Ristovski, Oliveira WANDEIR dos Santos (90 Igor Milevski). Trainer: Zoran Stratev

Goals: Jarman (1), Rogerio (60), Moralee (63)

FC PYUNIK EREVAN v KR REYKJAVIK 1-0 (0-0)

Republika, Erevan 16.07.2003

Referee: Johny Ver Eecke (BEL) Attendance: 14,000

FC PYUNIK: Edel Apoula Edima BETE, Artur Mkrtchyan, Tudor Marian Zeciu, Khose Bilibio, Rafael Nazaryan (84 Ndoumbouk BALEP BA)), Edouard Partsikian, Carl Lombe, Agvan Mkrtchyan (79 Edgar Manucharyan), Juan Pablo Peralta, Levon Pachajyan (89 Zhdra Hovhannisyan), Miguel Cisterna. Trainer: Mihai Stoichiţă

KR REYKJAVIK: Kristján Finnbogason, Jókuli I. Elisabetarson, Gunnar Einarsson, Kristján Örn Sigurdsson, Sigursteinn Gíslason (61 Sverrir Bergsteinsson), Kristinn Johannes Magnússon, Jón Skaftason, Arnar Jón Sigurgeirsson, Veigar Páll Gunnarsson, Einar Thór Danielsson (82 Sölvi Davidsson), Sigurdur Ragnar Eyjolfsson (58 Gardar Johannsson). Trainer: Willum Thor Thorsson

Goal: Pachajyan (61)

KR REYKJAVIK v FC PYUNIK YEREVAN 1-1 (0-0)

Laugardalsvöllur, Reykjavik 23.07.2003

Referee: Andrejs Sipailo (LAT) Attendance: 2,069

KR REYKJAVIK: Kristján Finnbogason, Jókuli I. Elisabetarson, Gunnar Einarsson, Kristján Örn Sigurdsson, Sigursteinn Gíslason (82 Sigurdur Ragnar Eyjolfsson), Kristinn Johannes Magnússon (68 Sigurvin Olafsson), Veigar Páll Gunnarsson, Bjarki Gunnlaugsson, Einar Thór Danielsson (46 Arnar Bergmann Gunnlaugsson), Sölvi Davidsson, Gardar Johannsson. Trainer: Willum Thor Thorsson

FC PYUNIK: Edel Apoula Edima BETE, Artur Mkrtchyan, Tudor Marian Zeciu, Khose Bilibio, Ndoumbouk BALEP BA (84 Vardan Minasyan), Edouard Partsikian, Carl Lombe, Agvan Mkrtchyan, Juan Pablo Peralta (62 Edgar Manucharyan), Levon Pachajyan (89 Rafael Nazaryan), Miguel Cisterna. Trainer: Mihai Stoichiţă

Goals: Agvan Mkrtchyan (73), Davidsson (82 pen)

SK SLAVIA PRAHA v FK LEOTAR TREBINJE 2-0 (1-0)

Evzena Rošického, Praha 6.08.2003

Referee: Mikko Vuorela (FIN) Attendance: 6,141

SLAVIA: Radek Černý, Milan Zachariáš, Adam Petrouš, Tomáš Hrdlička, Lukáš Došek (46 Martin Müller), Patrick Gedeon, Richard Dostálek, Rudolf Skácel, Tomáš Došek (61 Karel Piták), Pavel Kuka, Adauto Evandro Da Silva (78 Pavel Fort). Trainer: Miroslav Beranek

LEOTAR: Vladimir Stojkovic, Sejmon Miloševic, Goran Jerinic, Gavrilo Corlija, Bojan Simic (90 Saša Miljanovic), Marko Popovic, Dušan Kerkez, Sinisa Mulina, Branislav Krunic, Pavle Delibasic (52 Aleksandar Jovanovic), Boban Stojanovic. Trainer: Mile Jovin

Goals: Kuka (42), Skácel (73)

KS TIRANA v GRAZER AK 1-5 (1-3)

Qemal Stafa, Tiranë 30.07.2003

Referee: Georgios Douros (GRE) Attendance: 9,000

KS TIRANA: Ndubuisi Egbo, Elvis Sina, Rezart Dabulla (46 Sokol Bulku), Nevil Dede, Gentian Hajdari, Luan Pinari (57 Mahir Halili), Devis Mukaj, Suad Liçi, Saimir Patushi, Indrit Fortuzi (72 Eldorado Merkoçi), Fjodor Xhafa. Trainer: Sulejman Mema

GRAZER AK: Andreas Schranz, Mario Tokic, Anton Ehmann, Joachim Standfest, Emanuel Pogatetz, Dieter Ramusch (70 Gregor Pötscher), Nikola Milinkovic, René Aufhauser (58 Enrico Kulovits), Mario Bazina, Ilco Naumoski, Matthias Dollinger (75 Martin Amerhauser). Trainer: Walter Schachner

Goals: Xhafa (5), Bazina (14), Aufhauser (32), Naumoski (41, 82), Standfest (56)

SECOND QUALIFYING ROUND

FK LEOTAR TREBINJE v SK SLAVIA PRAHA 1-2 (1-1)

FK Leotar, Trebinje 30.07.2003

Referee: Sergey Shebek (UKR) Attendance: 4,256

LEOTAR: Vladimir Stojkovic, Sejmon Miloševic, Goran Jerinic, Zdravko Šaraba (78 Gavrilo Corlija), Bojan Jucinic (61 Aleksandar Jovanovic), Dušan Kerkez, Sinisa Mulina, Branislav Krunic (80 Palo Jankovic), Marko Popovic, Pavle Delibasic, Boban Stojanovic. Trainer: Mile Jovin

SLAVIA: Radek Černý, Lukáš Došek, Radek Bejbl (46 Martin Müller), Adam Petrouš, Tomáš Hrdlička, Karel Piták, Patrick Gedeon, Richard Dostálek (90 Milan Zachariáš), Rudolf Skácel, Pavel Kuka, ADAUTO Evandro da Silva (77 Tomáš Došek). Trainer: Miroslav Beranek

Goals: Adauto (16), Delibasic (42 pen), Dostálek (48)

GRAZER AK v KS TIRANA 2-1 (1-0)

Arnold Schwarzenegger, Graz 6.08.2003

Referee: Kristinn Jakobsson (ICE) Attendance: 7,500

GRAZER AK: Andreas Schranz, Gregor Pötscher, Mario Tokic, Emanuel Pogatetz (75 Joachim Standfest), Dieter Ramusch, Nikola Milinkovic (57 Mario Bazina), Enrico Kulovits, Gernot Sick, Michaël Goossens, Matthias Dollinger (66 Martin Amerhauser), Roland Kollmann. Trainer: Walter Schachner

KS TIRANA: Ndubuisi Egbo, Elvis Sina, Rezart Dabulla, Nevil Dede, Luan Pinari, Sokol Bulku (87 Sokol Prenga), Devis Mukaj, Ansi Agolli, Saimir Patushi (59 Suad Liçi), Mahir Halili, Fjodor Xhafa (42 Indrit Fortuzi). Trainer: Sulejman Mema

Goals: Sick (16), Kollmann (75), Agolli (90)

GTS WISLA KRAKÓW v OMONOIA FC NICOSIA 5-2 (3-0)

Wisly, Kraków 30.07.2003

Referee: Ceri Richards (WAL) Attendance: 9,000

WISLA: Adam Piekutowski, Maciej Stolarczyk, Lukasz Nawotczynski, Mariusz Jop, Marcin Baszczynski, Cristiano Pereira De Souza BRASILIA, Miroslaw Szymkowiak, Pawel Strak, Grzegorz Pater, Tomasz Frankowski (63 Daniel Dubicki), Maciej Zurawski (71 Damian Gorawski). Trainer: Henryk Ksperczak

OMONOIA: Nikolaos Mihopoulos, Georgos Theodotou (69 Elias Haralambous), Akis Ioakim, Panagiotis Panagiotou (81 Marios Nicolaou), Gábor Korolovszky, Zoran Stjepanovic (46 Efstathios Aloneftis), Haris Nicolaou, Kostas Kaiafas, Nicolaos Georgiou, Jozef Kozlej, Rainer Rauffmann. Trainer: Toni Savevski

Goals: Zurawski (11, 49), Frankowski (19), Baszczynski (44), Dubicki (70), Rauffmann (74 pen, 86 pen)

ROSENBORG BK TRONDHEIM v BOHEMIANS FC DUBLIN 4-0 (1-0)

Lerkendal, Trondheim 6.08.2003

Referee: Ruud Bossen (HOL) Attendance: 15,911

ROSENBORG: Espen Johnsen, Erik Hoftun, Christer Basma, Vidar Riseth, Ståle Stensaas, Fredrik Winsnes (80 Dagfinn Enerly), Roar Strand (69 Jan Gunnar Solli), Ørjan Berg, Frode Johnsen, Azar Karadas (85 Christer George), Harald Martin Brattbakk. Trainer: Åge Hareide

BOHEMIANS: Seamus Kelly, Damien Lynch, Simon Webb, Kevin Hunt, Thomas Heary, Colin Hawkins, Barry Ryan (65 David Morrison), Stephen Caffrey, Robert Doyle, Glen Crowe (76 Paul Keegan), Mark Rutherford (56 Fergal Harkin). Trainer: Stephen Kenny

Goals: Karadas (43), Brattbakk (51), Strand (68), F. Johnsen (76)

OMONOIA FC NICOSIA v GTS WISLA KRAKÓW 2-2 (1-1)

GSP, Nicosia 6.08.2003

Referee: Philippe Leuba (SWI) Attendance: 13,000

OMONOIA: Nikolaos Mihopoulos, Georgos Theodotou (37 Efstathios Aloneftis), Akis Ioakim, Nicolaos Georgiou, Gábor Korolovszky, Marco Haber (64 Zoran Stjepanovic), Elias Haralambous, Haris Nicolaou, Rainer Rauffmann, Kostas Kaiafas (79 Vesko Mihailovic), Jozef Kozlej. Trainer: Toni Savevski

WISLA: Adam Piekutowski, Marcin Baszczynski, Mariusz Jop, Lukasz Nawotczynski, Maciej Stolarczyk, Damian Gorawski (51 Kamil Kuzera), Pawel Strak, Miroslaw Szymkowiak, CRISTIANO Pereira De Souza BRASILIA (84 Pawel Brozek), Daniel Dubicki, Maciej Zurawski. Trainer: Henryk Ksperczak

Sent off: Stolarczyk (25)

Goals: Zurawski (6, 72), Rauffmann (16), Haralambous (51)

MTK HUNGÁRIA FC BUDAPEST v HJK HELSINKI 3-1 (2-0)

Hidegkuti Nándor, Budapest 30.07.2003

Referee: Darko Ceferin (SVN) Attendance: 4,000

MTK HUNGÁRIA: Zoltán Vegh, Oliver Pusztai (61 Gábor Halmai), Roland Juhász, Adam Komlósi, Goran Jezdimirovic, Ákos Füzi, Gábor Zavadszky, István Pisont (61 Péter Czvitkovics), WELTON Carlos da Silva, Sandor Torghelle, Otto Szabo (78 Daniel Eugen Rednic). Trainer: Sándor Egervári

HJK: András Vilnrotter, Mike Peltola, Ville Nylund, Joakim Jensen, Iiro Aalto, Antti Heinola, Christian Sund (79 László Fekete), Rami Hakanpää, Mika Kottila, Ridvan Zeneli (64 Juho Mäkelä), Toni Kallio. Trainer: Keith Armstrong

Goals: Welton (37, 42), Kottila (53), Rednic (90 pen)

BOHEMIANS FC DUBLIN v ROSENBORG BK TRONDHEIM 0-1 (0-1)

Dalymount Park, Dublin 30.07.2003

Referee: Bernhard Brugger (AUS) Attendance: 8,500

BOHEMIANS: Seamus Kelly, Damien Lynch, Simon Webb, Kevin Hunt, Thomas Heary, Colin Hawkins, Barry Ryan (83 Fergal Harkin), Stephen Caffrey, Robert Doyle (60 Paul Keegan), Glen Crowe, Mark Rutherford (70 Andrei Pereplyothin). Trainer: Stephen Kenny

ROSENBORG: Espen Johnsen, Erik Hoftun, Christer Basma, Vidar Riseth, Ståle Stensaas, Fredrik Winsnes (83 Roar Strand), Ørjan Berg, Frode Johnsen, Christer George (70 Jan Gunnar Solli), Azar Karadas, Harald Martin Brattbakk. Trainer: Åge Hareide

Goal: Karadas (35)

HJK HELSINKI v MTK HUNGÁRIA FC BUDAPEST 1-0 (0-0)

Pohjola, Vantaa 6.08.2003

Referee: Dejan Delevic (SER) Attendance: 2,650

HJK: András Vilnrotter, Mike Peltola (64 Iiro Aalto), Ville Nylund, Joakim Jensen, Antti Heinola, Christian Sund, Rami Hakanpää, Ridvan Zeneli (62 László Fekete), Toni Kallio (81 Jon Poulsen), Juho Mäkelä, Mika Kottila. Trainer: Keith Armstrong

MTK HUNGÁRIA: Zoltán Vegh, Oliver Pusztai, Roland Juhász, Adam Komlósi, Ákos Füzi, Gábor Zavadszky, Goran Jezdimirovic, Gábor Halmai, Sandor Torghelle (70 István Pisont), WELTON Carlos da Silva (90 Attila Zabos), Otto Szabo (73 Daniel Eugen Rednic). Trainer: Sándor Egervári

Goal: Mäkelä (63)

FC SHERIFF TIRASPOL v FC SHAKHTAR DONETSK 0-0

Sheriff, Tiraspol 30.07.2003

Referee: Karel Vidlak (CZE) Attendance: 13,000

SHERIFF: Sebastian Huţan, Ivan Testimiţanu, Vaja Tarkhnishvili, Odiah Chidi, Iuriy Priganiuc, Stanislav Ivanov, Vadim Boreţ, Leandro Farias (60 Sergei Dadu), Alberto Blanco, Victor Barîşev, Cristian Tudor (71 Andrei Nesteruk). Trainer: Igor Nakonechnyy

SHAKHTAR: Stipe Pletikosa, Anatoliy Tymoshchuk, Serhiy Popov, Predrag Pazhin, Răzvan Raţ, Zvonimir Vukic (82 Adrian Pukanych), Mariusz Lewandowski, Olexiy Gay, Serhiy Zakarliuka, Andriy Vorobey (75 Darijo Srna), Olexiy Bielik (61 Evaeverson da Silva "BRANDÃO"). Trainer: Bernd Schuster

FC SHAKHTAR DONETSK v FC SHERIFF TIRASPOL 2-0 (0-0)

Centralny, Donetsk 6.08.2003

Referee: Bertrand Layec (FRA) Attendance: 31,600

SHAKHTAR: Stipe Pletikosa, Anatoliy Tymoshchuk, Serhiy Popov, Predrag Pazhin, Răzvan Raţ, Zvonimir Vukic (89 Adrian Pukanych), Aleksei Bakharev (56 Darijo Srna), Mariusz Lewandowski, Olexiy Gay, Andriy Vorobey, Olexiy Bielik (70 Evaeverson da Silva "BRANDÃO"). Trainer: Bernd Schuster

SHERIFF: Sebastian Huţan, Ivan Testimiţanu, Vaja Tarkhnishvili, Odiah Chidi, Iuriy Priganiuc, Stanislav Ivanov, Vadim Boreţ, Sergei Dadu (70 Andrei Nesteruk), Alberto Blanco, Victor Barîşev (81 Victor Comleonoc), Cristian Tudor (24 Leandro Farias). Trainer: Igor Nakonechnyy

Sent off: Tarkhnishvili (84)

Goals: Vukic (59), Brandão (89)

CSKA MOSKVA v FK VARDAR SKOPJE 1-2 (0-0)

Dinamo, Moskva 30.07.2003

Referee: Stefano Farina (ITA) Attendance: 12,000

CSKA: Igor Akinfeev, Deividas Semberas, Denis Evsikov, Bohdan Shershun, Igor Yanovski, Rolan Gusev, Jurijs Laizans (58 Alan Kusov), Jiri Jarosik, Elvir Rahimic, Spartak Gogniev (34 Dmitri Kirichenko), Denis Popov (77 Sergei Samodin). Trainer: Valeriy Gazzaev

VARDAR: Muarem Zekir, Dragan Veselinovski, Nikola Djosevski, Blessing Chinedu Anyanviu, Dejan Brankovic, Vlatko Grozdanovski (86 Igor Milevski), Jovica Trajcev, Slavco Georgievski (77 Bobi Božinovski), Srdan Zaharievski, Dejan Ristovski, Oliveira WANDEIR dos Santos (79 ROGERIO da Costa Oliviera). Trainer: Zoran Stratev

Goals: Grozdanovski (54), Wandeir (64), Samodin (89)

FK VARDAR SKOPJE v CSKA MOSKVA 1-1 (0-1)

Gradski, Skopje 6.08.2003

Referee: Victor José ESQUINAS TORRES (SPA) Att: 14,000

VARDAR: Muarem Zekir, Dragan Veselinovski, Nikola Djosevski, Blessing Chinedu Anyanviu, Dejan Brankovic, Vlatko Grozdanovski (55 ROGERIO da Costa Oliviera), Jovica Trajcev, Slavco Georgievski, Srdan Zaharievski, Dejan Ristovski (74 AGUINALDO Braga de Jesus), Oliveira WANDEIR dos Santos (71 Mario Petkov). Trainer: Zoran Stratev

CSKA: Veniamin Mandrikin, Alexei Berezoutski, Denis Evsikov, Vassili Berezoutski, Bohdan Shershun (62 Jurijs Laizans), Igor Yanovski (46 Dmitri Kirichenko, 71 Sergei Samodin), Rolan Gusev, Jiri Jarosik, Elvir Rahimic, Spartak Gogniev, Denis Popov. Trainer: Valeriy Gazzaev

Goals: Gogniev (30), Wandeir (64)

FK PARTIZAN BEOGRAD v DJURGÅRDENS IF STOCKHOLM 1-1 (0-0)

FK Partizan, Beograd 30.07.2003

Referee: Attila Hanacsek (HUN) Attendance: 23,400

FK PARTIZAN: Radovan Radakovic, Milivoje Cirkovic, Nenad Djordjevic, Taribo West, Nebojsa Malbasa, Milan Stojanoski (63 Bojan Brnovic), Igor Duljaj, Albert Nadj, Damir Cakar (82 Ljubinko Drulovic), Saša Ilic, Ivica Iliev. Trainer: Lothar Matthäus

DJURGÅRDENS IF: Andreas Isaksson, Fredrik Stenman (85 Stefan Bergtoft), Toni Kuivasto, Markus Karlsson, Niklas Rasck, Johan Arneng, Andreas Johansson, Kim Källström, Geert Den Ouden (57 Samuel Wowoah), Aziz Corr Nyang (68 Henrik Daniel Sjölund), René Makonoele. Trainer: Sören Åkeby

Goals: Ilic (59), Makonoele (72)

DJURGÅRDENS IF STOCKHOLM v FK PARTIZAN BEOGRAD 2-2 (1-0)

Råsunda, Solna 6.08.2003

Referee: Yuri Baskakov (RUS) Attendance: 28,287

DJURGÅRDENS IF: Andreas Isaksson, Fredrik Stenman, Toni Kuivasto, Markus Karlsson, Niklas Rasck, Johan Arneng (27 Yanick BAPUPA v NGABU), Andreas Johansson, Kim Källström, Geert Den Ouden (70 Samuel Wowoah), Babis Stefanidis (68 Lars Jesper Blomqvist), René Makonoele. Trainer: Sören Åkeby

FK PARTIZAN: Ivica Kralj, Nenad Djordjevic, Milivoje Cirkovic, Nebojsa Malbasa, Taribo West, Albert Nadj, Igor Duljaj, Damir Cakar (46 Ljubinko Drulovic), Saša Ilic, Milan Stojanoski (76 Branimir Bajic), Ivica Iliev (90 Dzenan Radoncic). Trainer: Lothar Matthäus

Goals: Johansson (10), Ilic (61), Malbasa (66 pen), Wowoah (77)

FC KØBENHAVN v SLIEMA WANDERERS FC 4-1 (3-0)

Parken, København 30.07.2003

Referee: Alexandru Dan Tudor (ROM) Attendance: 14,197

FC KØBENHAVN: Balasz Raboczki, Ole Tobiasen, Martin Albrechtsen, Bo Svensson, Urmas Rooba, Hjalte Bo Nørregaard, Peter Nielsen, Erik Mykland (76 Christian Lønstrup), Thomas Røll Larsen, Todi Jónsson (72 Peter Møller), Sibusiso Zuma (88 Bora Zivkovic). Trainer: Hans Backe

SLIEMA WANDERERS: Murphy Akanji, Brian Said, Carlo Mamo, Kristian Laferla, Jeffrey Chetcuti, Stefan Giglio, Noel Turner (81 Massimo Grima), Joe Brincat, Orosco Anonam, Danilo Doncic (90+4 Kevin Sammut), Daniel Bogdanovic (54 Nenad Veselji). Trainer: Edward Aquilina

Goals: Zuma (24), Røll Larsen (26 pen, 66), Jónsson (45), Doncic (51)

SLIEMA WANDERERS FC v FC KØBENHAVN 0-6 (0-3)

National, TaQali 6.08.2003

Referee: Andrew Paul D'Urso (ENG) Attendance: 1,400

SLIEMA WANDERERS: Murphy Akanji, Carlo Mamo, Brian Said (56 Lee Lombardi, 69 Massimo Grima), Noel Turner, Danilo Doncic, Daniel Bogdanovic, Nenad Veselji (46 Jamie Pace), Jeffrey Chetcuti, Orosco Anonam, Joe Brincat, Kristian Laferla. Trainer: Edward Aquilina

FC KØBENHAVN: Balasz Raboczki, Ole Tobiasen, Martin Albrechtsen, Bo Svensson, Urmas Rooba, Hjalte Bo Nørregaard, Peter Nielsen (68 Christian Lønstrup), Erik Mykland, Thomas Røll Larsen, Todi Jónsson (46 Peter Møller), Sibusiso Zuma (64 Jörgen Pettersson). Trainer: Hans Backe

Goals: Jónsson (18, 41), Nørregaard (36), Chetcuti (47 og), Zuma (49), Røll Larsen (69)

MSK ZILINA v MACCABI TEL AVIV FC 1-0 (0-0)

Metsky Sportovy, Zilina 30.07.2003

Referee: Tonny Kolbech Poulsen (DEN) Attendance: 5,988

MSK ZILINA: Ivan Trabalik, Martin Konecny, Branislav Labant, Radoslav Zábavnik, Vladimír Staš (66 Michal Drahno), Martin Durica, Zdeno Štrba, Miroslav Barcík, Dušan Sninský, Pavel Putík (76 Marek Bazík), Martin Fabuš (68 Michal Gottwald). Trainer: Milan Lešický

MACCABI: Liran Strauber, Gadi Brumer, Salem ABU SIAM, John Pantsil, Tal BEN HAIM, Tal Banin (66 Assaf Crispis), Avi Nimny, BRUNO REIS, Eli Biton (79 Liran Cohen), Andrejs Prohorenkovs, Tamir Cohen. Trainer: Nir Klinger

Goal: Bazík (86)

MACCABI TEL AVIV FC v MSK ZILINA 1-1 (1-1)

Megyeri út, Budapest (HUN) 6.08.2003

Referee: Hermann Albrecht (GER) Attendance: 350

MACCABI: Liran Strauber, Avi Strool, Salem ABU SIAM, Tal BEN HAIM, John Pantsil, Tal Banin, Avi Nimny, Andrejs Prohorenkovs (61 Eli Biton), Liran Cohen (75 Koby Moosa), Reuven Oved, BRUNO REIS (61 Rodrigo Goldberg). Trainer: Nir Klinger

MSK ZILINA: Ivan Trabalik, Martin Konecny, Branislav Labant, Radoslav Zábavnik, Vladimír Staš (78 Michal Drahno), Martin Durica, Zdeno Štrba, Miroslav Barcík, Marek Bazík, Dušan Sninský, Ľuboš Cervenec (32 Pavel Putík, 90 Marián Klago). Trainer: Milan Lešický

Goals: Sninský (16), Pantsil (25)

NK MARIBOR BRANIK v NK DINAMO ZAGREB 1-1 (1-1)

Ljudski vrt, Maribor 30.07.2003

Referee: Eric Blareau (BEL) Attendance: 9,000

NK MARIBOR: Stanislav Kuzma, Miha Golob (60 Igor Mostarlic), Miha Pitamic, Stipe Balajic, Zikica Vuksanovic, Ales Ceh, Dalibor Teinovic, Peter Franci, Amir Karic, Suad Filekovic, Damir Pekic. Trainer: Matjaz Kek

DINAMO: Mario Jozic, Goce Sedloski, Andre Mijatovic, Dino Drpic, Jasmin Agic, Edin Mujcin, Mihael Mikic (46 Bostjan Cesar), Ante Tomic, Niko Kranjcar, Dumitru Mitu (88 Dario Zahora), Mladen Bartolovic (44 EDUARDO da Silva). Trainer: Nikola Jurcevic

Goals: Kranjcar (33), Pekic (36)

NK DINAMO ZAGREB v NK MARIBOR BRANIK 2-1 (0-1)

Maksimir, Zagreb 6.08.2003

Referee: Kostas Kapitanis (CYP) Attendance: 12,000

DINAMO: Mario Jozic, Goce Sedloski, Andre Mijatovic, Dino Drpic, Jasmin Agic, Edin Mujcin, Mihael Mikic, Ante Tomic (56 Hrvoje Strok), Niko Kranjcar (87 Bostjan Cesar), Dumitru Mitu, EDUARDO da Silva (90 Dario Zahora). Trainer: Nikola Jurcevic

NK MARIBOR: Stanislav Kuzma, Miha Golob, Miha Pitamic, Stipe Balajic, Zikica Vuksanovic (73 Peter Franci), Ales Ceh (83 Dejan Komljenovic), Dalibor Teinovic, Amir Karic, Suad Filekovic (64 Danijel Brezic), Ermin Rakovic, Damir Pekic. Trainer: Matjaz Kek

Sent off: Mitu (67)

Goals: Balajic (10), Mijatovic (59), Drpic (63)

FC PYUNIK EREVAN v FC CSKA SOFIA 0-2 (0-1)

Republika, Erevan 30.07.2003

Referee: Martin Ingvarsson (SWE) Attendance: 14,000

FC PYUNIK: Edel Apoula Edima BETE, Artur Mkrtchyan (78 Rafael Nazaryan), Tudor Marian Zeciu, Khose Bilibio, Carl Lombe, Edouard Partsikian, Miguel Cisterna, Agvan Mkrtchyan, Vardan Minasyan (70 Edgar Manucharyan), Levon Pachajyan, Juan Pablo Peralta (53 Mamadou Diawara). Trainer: Mihai Stoichiță

CSKA: Stoian Kolov, Georgi Antonov, Ibrahima Gueye, JOÃO CARLOS, Alexandar Tomash, Svetoslav Petrov, Todor Yanchev, Altin Haxhi, Emil Gargorov (89 Hristo Yanev), João Paulo BRITO (63 Evgeni Iordanov), Macdonald Mukasi (71 Iordan Todorov). Trainer: Stoicho Mladenov

Sent off: Antonov (87)

Goals: Yanchev (20), Mukasi (48)

CELTIC FC GLASGOW v FBK KAUNAS 1-0 (1-0)

Celtic Park, Glasgow 6.08.2003

Referee: Jacek Granat (POL) Attendance: 40,104

CELTIC: Robert Douglas, Joos Valgaeren, Dianbobo Balde, Johan Mjällby, Mohamed Sylla (57 Neil Francis Lennon), Liam Miller, Paul Lambert, Alan Thompson (80 Ross Wallace), Jamie Smith, Shaun Maloney (57 Craig Beattie), Chris Sutton. Trainer: Steven Joseph Walford

FBK KAUNAS: Gytis Padimanskas, Tomas Kancelskis, Irmantas Zelmikas, Darius Gvildys, Darius Regelskis, Andrius Gedgaudas, Vadim Petrenko, Giedrius Barevicius, Tadas Papeckys (77 Andrius Puotkalis), Ricardas Beniusis (35 Martynas Karalius), Martin Opic (87 Darius Sanajevas). Trainer: Siarhei Barouski

Goal: Gvildys (21 og)

CSKA SOFIA v FC PYUNIK YEREVAN 1-0 (0-0)

Balgarska Armia, Sofia 6.08.2003

Referee: Douglas McDonald (SCO) Attendance: 10,000

CSKA: Stoian Kolov, Iordan Todorov, Ibrahima Gueye, JOÃO CARLOS (80 Iordan Varbanov), Altin Haxhi, Todor Yanchev, Svetoslav Petrov, LEONARDO Lima da Silva, João Paulo BRITO (65 Hristo Yanev), Emil Gargorov, MacDonald Mukasi (71 Evgeni Iordanov). Trainer: Stoicho Mladenov

FC PYUNIK: Edel Apoula Edima BETE, Valeri Aleksanyan, Tudor Marian Zeciu, Khose Bilibio, Edouard Partsikian, Miguel Cisterna, Carl Lombe (89 Ndoumbouk BALEP BA), Agvan Mkrtchyan, Levon Pachajyan, Mamadou Diawara (82 Edgar Manucharyan), Galust Petrosyan (86 Zhdra Hovhannisyan). Trainer: Mihai Stoichiță

Goal: Leonardo (90 pen)

RAPID BUCUREŞTI v RSC ANDERLECHT BRUSSEL 0-0

Național, Bucureşti 30.07.2003

Referee: Anton Stredak (SVK) Attendance: 12,000

RAPID: Ibrahim Dossey, Mihai Adrian Iencsi, Vasile Maftei, Danut Perjă, Valentin Emanoil Bădoi, Robert Ilyes (79 Henri Olufosoye Makinwa), Nouredine Ziyati, Emmanuel Godfroid, Florin Costin Şoavă, Florin Daniel Bratu (89 Robert Ionel Niță), Daniel George Niculae (58 Ion Ionut Luțu). Trainer: Mircea Rednic

ANDERLECHT: Daniel Zitka, Olivier Doll, Hannu Tihinen, Vincent Kompany, Olivier Deschacht, Goran Lovre, Besnik Hasi, Walter Baseggio, Ki-Hyeon Seol, Nenad Jestrovic (75 Ivica Mornar), Aruna Dindane. Trainer: Hugo Broos

FBK KAUNAS v CELTIC FC GLASGOW 0-4 (0-2)

S. Darius & S. Girenas, Kaunas 30.07.2003

Referee: Joaquim Paulo PARATY DA SILVA (POR) Attendance: 2,500

FBK KAUNAS: Gytis Padimanskas, Darius Gvildys, Tomas Kancelskis, Darius Regelskis, Irmantas Zelmikas, Vadim Petrenko, Tadas Papeckys (66 Martin Opic), Andrius Gedgaudas, Gintas Širmelis (75 Milan Pastva), Giedrius Barevicius, Ricardas Beniusis (80 Martynas Karalius). Trainer: Siarhei Barouski

CELTIC: Robert Douglas, Didier Agathe, Joos Valgaeren, Johan Mjällby, Stanislav Varga, Stilian Petrov, Neil Francis Lennon (46 Shaun Maloney), Paul Lambert, Alan Thompson (70 James Smith), Henrik Larsson, Chris Sutton (72 Liam Miller). Trainer: Martin O'Neill

Goals: Larsson (12), Sutton (28), Maloney (54), Miller (86)

RSC ANDERLECHT BRUSSEL v RAPID BUCUREŞTI 3-2 (0-2)

Constant van den Stock, Brussel 6.08.2003

Referee: Emil Božinovski (MAC) Attendance: 22,432

ANDERLECHT: Daniel Zitka, Olivier Doll, Hannu Tihinen, Vincent Kompany, Olivier Deschacht, Besnik Hasi (46 Christian Wilhelmsson), Pär Zetterberg, Walter Baseggio, Ki-Hyeon Seol, Nenad Jestrovic (86 Marc Hendrikx), Aruna Dindane. Trainer: Hugo Broos

RAPID: Emilian Dolha, Dănuț Perjă, Mihai Adrian Iencsi, Vasile Maftei, Florin Costin Şoavă, Nouredine Ziyati (77 Ion Ionuț Luțu), Robert Ilyes (88 Henri Olufosoye Makinwa), Emmanuel Godfroid, Valentin Emanoil Bădoi, Florin Daniel Bratu (70 Robert Ionel Niță), Daniel George Niculae. Trainer: Mircea Rednic

Goals: Ilyes (42), Bratu (45), Jestrovic (50), Zetterberg (52), Seol (75)

THIRD QUALIFYING ROUND

FC DYNAMO KYIV v NK DINAMO ZAGREB 3-1 (2-1)

Valeri Lobanovskiy, Kyiv 12.08.2003

Referee: Stuart Dougal (SCO) Attendance: 8,200

FC DYNAMO: Olexandr Shovkovskiy, Andriy Nesmachniy, Serhiy Fedorov, Goran Gavrancic, ALESSANDRO Mori Nunes (68 Oleh Husev), Aleksandr Khatskevich (60 Yuriy Dmytrulin), Andriy Husin, DIOGO "RINCÓN" Augusto Pacheco da Fontoura (76 Florin Lucian Cernat), Jerko Leko, Valentin Belkevich, Maksim Shatskikh.
Trainer: Oleksiy Mykhaylychenko

NK DINAMO: Mario Jozic, Goce Sedloski, Andre Mijatovic, Dino Drpic, Jasmin Agic, Edin Mujcin (87 Damir Krznar), Mihael Mikic, Ante Tomic, Niko Kranjcar, Mladen Bartolovic (60 Hrvoje Strok), EDUARDO da Silva (74 Dario Zahora).
Trainer: Nikola Jurcevic

Goals: Fedorov (32), Leko (39), Kranjcar (42), Husev (82)

NK DINAMO ZAGREB v FC DYNAMO KYIV 0-2 (0-0)

Maksimir, Zagreb 27.08.2003

Referee: Claus Bo Larsen (DEN) Attendance: 22,000

NK DINAMO: Mario Jozic, Goce Sedloski, Andre Mijatovic, Dino Drpic, Jasmin Agic, Mihael Mikic, Ante Tomic (58 Dalibor Poldrugac), Edin Mujcin, Niko Kranjcar, EDUARDO da Silva (83 Dario Zahora), Mladen Bartolovic (71 Hrvoje Strok). Trainer: Nikola Jurcevic

FC DYNAMO: Olexandr Shovkovskiy, Yuriy Dmytrulin, Goran Gavrancic (83 Denys Onyschenko), Serhiy Fedorov, Andriy Nesmachniy, Oleh Husev, Tiberiu Ghioane, Jerko Leko (86 Goran Sablic), Valentin Belkevich, DIOGO "RINCÓN" Augusto Pacheco da Fontoura (71 Aleksandr Khatskevich), Maksim Shatskikh. Trainer: Oleksiy Mykhaylychenko

Goals: Shatskikh (47), Diogo "Rincón" (70)

GRAZER AK v AFC AJAX AMSTERDAM 1-1 (0-0)

Arnold Schwarzenegger, Graz 12.08.2003

Referee: Massimo De Santis (ITA) Attendance: 12,382

GRAZER AK: Andreas Schranz, Gregor Pötscher, Anton Ehmann, Mario Tokic, Emanuel Pogatetz, Dieter Ramusch, Nikola Milinkovic (60 Enrico Kulovits), René Aufhauser, Matthias Dollinger (69 Martin Amerhauser), Roland Kollmann, Ilco Naumoski (77 Michaël Goossens).
Trainer: Walter Schachner

AJAX: Maarten Stekelenburg, Hatem Trabelsi, Zdenek Grygera, Julien Escudé, MAXWELL Scherer Cabelino Andrade, Steven Pienaar (69 Victor Sikora), Abubakari Yakubu, Rafael Van Der Vaart, Wesley Sneijder (88 Jelle Van Damme), Wesley Sonck (64 Zlatan Ibrahimovic), WAMBERTO de Jesus Sousa Campos. Trainer: Ronald Koeman

Goals: Pogatetz (56), Sneijder (79)

AFC AJAX AMSTERDAM v GRAZER AK 2-1 (1-1, 1-1) (AET)

Amsterdam, ArenA 27.08.2003

Referee: Valentin Ivanov (RUS) Attendance: 48,470

AJAX: Bogdan Lobonţ, Zdenek Grygera, Petri Pasanen, Julien Escudé, Jelle Van Damme (56 Wesley Sneijder), Steven Pienaar (93 Wesley Sonck), Tomáš Galásek, Rafael Van Der Vaart, MAXWELL Scherer Cabelino Andrade, Zlatan Ibrahimovic, Victor Sikora (68 WAMBERTO de Jesus Sousa Campos).
Trainer: Ronald Koeman

GRAZER AK: Andreas Schranz, Gregor Pötscher, Anton Ehmann, Mario Tokic, Emanuel Pogatetz, Dieter Ramusch (74 Joachim Standfest), Nikola Milinkovic, René Aufhauser, Matthias Dollinger, Roland Kollmann, Ilco Naumoski (100 Mario Bazina). Trainer: Walter Schachner

Sent off: Pötscher (97), Ehmann (102)

Goals: Ibrahimovic (15), Kollmann (40), Galásek (104 pen)

RC CELTA DE VIGO v SK SLAVIA PRAHA 3-0 (1-0)

Balaídos, Vigo 12.08.2003

Referee: Gilles Veissière (FRA) Attendance: 13,500

RC CELTA: Pablo Oscar CAVALLERO Rodríguez, Juan VELASCO Damas, Pablo Andres CONTRERAS Fica, Fernando Gabriel CÁCERES Zaya, Sílvio «SYLVINHO» Mendes de Campos Junior, JOSÉ IGNACIO Sáenz Marín, Everton GIOVANELLA, Luis Eduardo Schmidt «EDÚ» (68 ÁNGEL Domingo López Ruano), Alexandre Vladimirovich MOSTOVOI, Jesús Antonio Mora Nieto «JESULI» (82 Alejandro «JANDRO» Castro Fernández), Savo MILOSEVIC (64 Henrique Guedes da Silva «CATANHA»).
Trainer: Miguel Ángel LOTINA ORUECHEBARRÍA

SLAVIA: Radek Černý, Lukáš Došek (87 Martin Latka), Adam Petrouš, Milan Zachariáš, Tomáš Hrdlička (65 Martin Lukeš), Karel Piták, Patrick Gedeon, Richard Dostálek, Rudolf Skácel, Pavel Kuka, ADAUTO Evandro da Silva (57 Tomáš Došek). Trainer: Miroslav Beranek

Goals: Mostovoi (17), Jesuli (49), Edú (55)

SK SLAVIA PRAHA v CELTA DE VIGO 2-0 (2-0)

Evzena Rošického, Praha 27.08.2003

Referee: Frank De Bleeckere (BEL) Attendance: 8,091

SLAVIA: Matúš Kozáčik, Lukáš Došek, Radek Bejbl, Adam Petrouš, Tomáš Hrdlička (72 Martin Latka), Karel Piták (82 Pavel Fort), Richard Dostálek, Milan Zachariáš, Rudolf Skácel, Tomáš Došek, Pavel Kuka (61 ADAUTO Evandro da Silva). Trainer: Miroslav Beranek

RC CELTA: Pablo Oscar CAVALLERO Rodríguez, Juan VELASCO Damas, SERGIO Fernández González, Fernando Gabriel CÁCERES Zaya, Sílvio «SYLVINHO» Mendes Campos Junior, JOSÉ IGNACIO Sáenz Marín, Everton GIOVANELLA (59 GUSTAVO Adrián LÓPEZ, 84 Pablo Andres CONTRERAS Fíca), Luis Eduardo Schmidt «EDÚ», Alexandre Vladimirovich MOSTOVOI, Jesús Antonio Mora Nieto «JESULI», Savo MILOSEVIC (89 Henrique Guedes da Silva «CATANHA»). Trainer: Miguel Ángel LOTINA ORUECHEBARRÍA

Sent off: Mostovoi (81)

Goals: Dostálek (17), Hrdlička (30)

SHAKHTAR DONETSK v FC LOKOMOTIV MOSKVA 1-0 (0-0)

Centralny, Donetsk 13.08.2003

Referee: Massimo Busacca (SWI) Attendance: 31,700

SHAKHTAR: Stipe Pletikosa, Anatoliy Tymoshchuk, Serhiy Popov, Predrag Pazhin, Răzvan Raț, Zvonimir Vukic, Aleksei Bakharev (80 Darijo Srna), Mariusz Lewandowski, Olexiy Gay, Andriy Vorobey, Olexiy Bielik (59 Julius Aghahowa). Trainer: Bernd Schuster

LOKOMOTIV: Sergei I.Ovchinnikov, Gennadiy Nizhegorodov, Jacob Lekcetho, Sergei Ignashevich, Oleg Pashinin, Dmitriy Sennikov, Vladimir Maminov, Dmitriy Loskov (67 Maxim Buznikin, 74 Jorge WAGNER Gomes Conceição), Dmitri Khokhlov, Winston Parks, Mikheil Ashvetia (41 Marat Izmailov). Trainer: Yuri Semin

Sent off: Pashinin (87)

Goal: Vukic (56 pen)

LOKOMOTIV MOSKVA v FC SHAKHTAR DONETSK 3-1 (2-0)

Lokomotiv, Moskva 27.08.2003

Referee: Alain Hamer (LUX) Attendance: 28,000

LOKOMOTIV: Sergei I. Ovchinnikov, Gennadiy Nizhegorodov, Vadim Yevseyev, Sergei Ignashevich, Jacob Lekcetho, Vladimir Maminov, Dmitriy Khokhlov, Dmitriy Loskov, Marat Izmailov (88 Dmitriy Sennikov), Maxim Buznikin (66 LEANDRO Lessa Azevedo), Mikheil Ashvetia (85 Ruslan Pimenov). Trainer: Yuri Semin

SHAKHTAR: Stipe Pletikosa, Anatoliy Tymoshchuk, Serhiy Popov, Predrag Pazhin (90+2 Olexiy Bielik), Răzvan Raț, Zvonimir Vukic (76 Darijo Srna), Aleksei Bakharev, Mariusz Lewandowski, Olexiy Gay, Andriy Vorobey, Evaeverson da Silva "BRANDÃO" (69 Julius Aghahowa). Trainer: B. Schuster

Goals: Ashvetia (21, 45+2), Lewandowski (71), Ignashevich (86 pen)

GLASGOW RANGERS FC v FC KØBENHAVN 1-1 (1-0)

Ibrox, Glasgow 13.08.2003

Referee: Manuel Enrique MEJUTO GONZÁLEZ (SPA) Attendance: 47,401

RANGERS: Stefan Klos, Fernando Ricksen, Craig Moore, Mikel ARTETA Amatriain, Zurab Khizanishvili, Michael Ball, Maurice Ross (59 Nuno Fernando Gonçalves da Rocha "CAPUCHO"), Barry Ferguson, Ronald De Boer (69 Steven Thompson), Michael Mols, Peter Løvenkrands. Trainer: Alexander McLeish

FC KØBENHAVN: Balasz Raboczki, Ole Tobiasen, Martin Albrechtsen, Bo Svensson, Urmas Rooba, Hjalte Bo Nørregaard, Peter Nielsen, Erik Mykland, Thomas Røll Larsen, Todi Jónsson (75 Peter Møller), Sibusiso Zuma. Trainer: Hans Backe

Goals: Løvenkrands (8), Jónsson (50)

FC KØBENHAVN v GLASGOW RANGERS FC 1-2 (0-0)

Parken, København 27.08.2003

Referee: Zeljko Siric (CRO) Attendance: 35,319

FC KØBENHAVN: Balasz Raboczki, Ole Tobiasen (77 Peter Møller), Martin Albrechtsen, Bo Svensson, Urmas Rooba, Hjalte Bo Nørregaard, Peter Nielsen, Erik Mykland (64 ÁLVARO Santos), Thomas Røll Larsen, Todi Jónsson (64 Jörgen Pettersson), Sibusiso Zuma. Trainer: Hans Backe

RANGERS: Stefan Klos, Fernando Ricksen, Zurab Khizanishvili, Mikel Arteta Amatriain, Michael Ball, Henning Berg (72 Robert Malcolm), Barry Ferguson, Christian Nerlinger, Ronald De Boer (75 Paolo Vanoli), Shota Arveladze, Michael Mols (61 Steven Thompson). Trainer: Alex McLeish

Goals: Arteta (52 pen), Álvaro (83), Arveladze (87)

FK VARDAR SKOPJE v AC SPARTA PRAHA 2-3 (0-2)

Gradski, Skopje 13.08.2003

Referee: Terje Hauge (NOR) Attendance: 23,000

VARDAR: Muarem Zekir, Blessing Chinedu Anyanviu, Dragan Veselinovski, Slavco Georgievski, Dejan Brankovic, Vlatko Grozdanovski (67 Darko Taševski), Dragan Nacevski (61 AGUINALDO Braga de Jesus), Dejan Ristovski, Srdan Zaharievski, ROGERIO da Costa Oliviera, Oliveira WANDEIR dos Santos (61 Mario Petkov). Trainer: Zoran Stratev

SPARTA: Jaromir Blazek, Martin Petras, Tomáš Hübschman, Petr Johana, Mirko Poledica, Karel Poborský, Radoslav Kovác, Jirí Nemec, Patrik Jezek (69 Rastivlav Michalik), Libor Sionko (62 Tomáš Jun), Igor Gluscevic (74 Jan Flachbart). Trainer: Jirí Kotrba

Sent off: Poledica (72)

Goals: Poborský (37, 89), Gluscevic (41), Rogerio (61), Georgievski (74)

AC SPARTA PRAHA v FK VARDAR SKOPJE **2-2** (1-1)

Toyota Arena, Praha 26.08.2003

Referee: Stéphane Bré (FRA) Attendance: 12,345

SPARTA: Jaromir Blazek, Martin Petras, Tomáš Hübschman, Petr Johana, Martin Zboncák, Karel Poborský, Radoslav Kovác, Jirí Nemec, Patrik Jezek (59 Rastivlav Michalik), Tomáš Jun (90 Marek Kincl), Igor Gluscevic (69 Libor Sionko). Trainer: Jirí Kotrba

FK VARDAR: Gogo Jovcev, Blessing Chinedu Anyanviu, Dragan Veselinovski, Slavco Georgievski, AGUINALDO Braga de Jesus, Dejan Brankovic, Vlatko Grozdanovski (64 Mario Petkov), Dejan Ristovski, Srdan Zaharievski, ROGERIO da Costa Oliviera, Oliveira WANDEIR dos Santos (82 Zoran Miserdovski). Trainer: Zoran Stratev

Goals: Georgievski (31), Poborský (33), Anyanviu (66), Sionko (85)

MSK ZILINA v CHELSEA FC LONDON **0-2** (0-1)

Mestsky Sportovy, Zilina 13.08.2003

Referee: Rene H.J. Temmink (HOL) Attendance: 6,211

MSK ZILINA: Ivan Trabalik, Martin Konecny, Branislav Labant, Radoslav Zábavnik, Vladimír Staš (66 Michal Drahno), Martin Durica (66 Pavel Putík), Zdeno Štrba, Miroslav Barcík, Marek Bazík, Dušan Sninský, Richard Varadin (82 Martin Fabuš). Trainer: Milan Lešický

CHELSEA: Carlo Cudicini, Glen Johnson, Marcel Desailly, Wayne Bridge, John George Terry, Frank Lampard, Damien Duff (69 Joe Cole), GEREMI Sorele Fotso Ndjitap, Juan Sebastián Verón, Eidur Gudjohnsen, Mikael Forssell (57 Jesper Grønkjær). Trainer: Claudio Ranieri

Goals: Gudjohnsen (42), Drahno (76 og)

MTK HUNGÁRIA FC BUDAPEST v CELTIC FC GLASGOW **0-4** (0-2)

Ferénc Puskas, Budapest 13.08.2003

Referee: Kim Milton Nielsen (DEN) Attendance: 4,773

MTK HUNGÁRIA: Zoltán Vegh, Zoltán Molnar (72 István Pisont), Roland Juhász, Oliver Pusztai, Ákos Füzi, Gábor Zavadszky, Gábor Halmai, Goran Jezdimirovic (24 Sandor Torghelle), WELTON Carlos da Silva, Béla Illés, Daniel Eugen Rednic (64 Otto Szabo). Trainer: Sándor Egervári

CELTIC: Robert Douglas, Joos Valgaeren, Dianbobo Balde (81 Stephen Crainey), Stanislav Varga, Alan Thompson, Paul Lambert, Neil Francis Lennon, Stilian Petrov (78 Liam Miller), Henrik Larsson, Chris Sutton, Didier Agathe (78 Mohamed Sylla). Trainer: Martin O'Neill

Goals: Larsson (17), Agathe (36), Petrov (70), Sutton (90)

CHELSEA FC LONDON v MSK ZILINA **3-0** (1-0)

Stamford Bridge, London 26.08.2003

Referee: Kyros Vassaras (GRE) Attendance: 23,408

CHELSEA: Carlo Cudicini, Glen Johnson, Celestine Babayaro, Marcel Desailly (64 Robert Huth), John George Terry, Frank Lampard (46 Emmanuel Petit), Joe Cole, GEREMI Sorele Fotso Ndjitap, Jimmy Floyd Hasselbaink, Eidur Gudjohnsen, Jesper Grønkjær (68 Mario Stanic). Trainer: Claudio Ranieri

MSK ZILINA: Branislav Rzeszoto, Martin Konecny, Branislav Labant, Radoslav Zábavnik, Vladimír Staš, Daniel Kosmel (89 Marián Klago), Martin Durica (83 Pavel Putík), Miroslav Barcík, Marek Bazík, Dušan Sninský, Richard Varadin (71 Martin Fabuš). Trainer: Milan Lešický

Goals: Johnson (32), Huth (67), Hasselbaink (79)

CELTIC FC GLASGOW v MTK HUNGÁRIA FC BUDAPEST **1-0** (1-0)

Celtic Park, Glasgow 27.08.2003

Referee: Wolfgang Stark (GER) Attendance: 43,008

CELTIC: Magnus Hedman, Dianbobo Balde (46 John Kennedy), Stanislav Varga, Stephen Crainey, Alan Thompson, Paul Lambert, Stilian Petrov (46 Bobby Petta), Liam Miller, Henrik Larsson (59 John Hartson), Chris Sutton, Didier Agathe. Trainer: Martin O'Neill

MTK HUNGÁRIA: Zoltán Vegh, Zoltán Molnar, Adam Komlósi, Roland Juhász, Gábor Halmai, Goran Jezdimirovic, Gábor Zavadszky, István Pisont (46 Péter Czvitkovics), Sandor Torghelle (80 WELTON Carlos da Silva), Béla Illés (70 Attila Zabos), Ákos Füzi. Trainer: Sándor Egervári

Goal: Sutton (14)

GRASSHOPPER CLUB ZÜRICH v AEK FC ATHINA **1-0** (0-0)

Hardturm, Zürich 13.08.2003

Referee: Eric Poulat (FRA) Attendance: 12,400

GRASSHOPPER: Fabrice Borer, Fernando Andrés Gamboa, Pascal Castillo, Stephan Lichtsteiner, Mihai Tararache, Christoph Spycher, José María Chatruc, Aleksandar Mitreski, Ribeiro Eduardo (84 Feliciano Magro), Mladen Petric, Richard Darío Núñez. Trainer: Marcel Koller

AEK: Dionisios Hiotis, Vassilios Borbokis, Nikolaos Kostenoglou (66 Grigorios Georgatos), Nikolaos Georgeas, Mihalis Kasapis, Mihalis Kapsis, Theodoros Zagorakis, Christos Maladenis (87 Evangelos Moras), Vassilios Tsiartas, Kostas Katsouranis, Ilija Ivic (66 Giannis Okkas). Trainer: Dusko Bajević

Goal: Núñez (83)

AEK FC ATHINA
v GRASSHOPPER-CLUB ZÜRICH 3-1 (3-0)

Apostolos Nikolaidis, Athina 27.08.2003

Referee: Lucilio CARDOSO CORTEZ BATISTA (POR)
Attendance: 16,045

AEK: Dionisios Hiotis, Kofi Amponsah, Vassilios Borbokis, Grigorios Georgatos (61 Dimitrios Nalitzis), Nikolaos Georgeas, Mihalis Kapsis, Theodoros Zagorakis, Vassilios Tsiartas (53 Hristos Maladenis), Kostas Katsouranis, Giannis Okkas, Nikolaos Lyberopoulos (80 Nikolaos Kostenoglou).
Trainer: Dusko Bajević

GRASSHOPPER: Fabrice Borer, Fernando Andrés Gamboa, Pascal Castillo, Stephan Lichtsteiner (79 Ionel Gane), Mihai Tararache, Christoph Spycher, Ribeiro Eduardo (46 Alfred Embefe), Feliciano Magro (55 José María Chatruc), Aleksandar Mitreski, Mladen Petric, Richard Darío Núñez.
Trainer: Marcel Koller **Sent off**: Castillo (75), Gamboa (90)

Goals: Katsouranis (20), Lyberopoulos (25), Castillo (39 og), Núñez (68)

RSC ANDERLECHT BRUSSEL
v GTS WISLA KRAKÓW 3-1 (2-0)

Constant van den Stock, Brussel 13.08.2003

Referee: Arturo DAUDÉN IBÁÑEZ (SPA) Att: 17,630

ANDERLECHT: Daniel Zitka, Olivier Doll, Hannu Tihinen, Vincent Kompany, Olivier Deschacht, Besnik Hasi, Walter Baseggio, Ki-Hyeon Seol, Goran Lovre (86 Pär Zetterberg), Aruna Dindane, Nenad Jestrovic (39 Christian Wilhelmsson).
Trainer: Hugo Broos

GTS WISLA: Adam Piekutowski, Marcin Baszczynski, Lukasz Nawotczynski, Mariusz Jop, Jacek Paszulewicz, Grzegorz Pater (46 Lantame Ouadja), Pawel Strak, CRISTIANO Pereira de Souza "BRASILIA", Miroslaw Szymkowiak, Maciej Zurawski, Tomasz Frankowski (46 Daniel Dubicki).
Trainer: Henryk Kasperczak

Goals: Jestrovic (13), Lovré (38), Dindane (59), Zurawski (77 pen)

FK PARTIZAN BEOGRAD
v NEWCASTLE UNITED FC 0-1 (0-1)

FK Partizan, Beograd 13.08.2003

Referee: Vladimir Hrinak (SVK) Attendance: 30,000

FK PARTIZAN: Ivica Kralj, Branimir Bajic, Nenad Djordjevic, Taribo West, Milivoje Cirkovic, Igor Duljaj (46 Ljubinko Drulovic), Albert Nadj, Nebojsa Malbasa, Saša Ilic, Andrija Delibasic (60 Milan Stojanoski), Ivica Iliev.
Trainer: Lothar Matthäus

NEWCASTLE UNITED: Shay Given, Andy Griffin, Andy O'Brien, Jonathan Woodgate, Olivier Bernard, Nolberto Solano (84 Jermaine Jenas), Kieron Dyer, Gary Speed, Laurent Robert (65 Shola Ameobi), Alan Shearer, Craig Bellamy.
Trainer: Robert Robson

Goal: Solano (39)

NEWCASTLE UNITED FC
v FK PARTIZAN BEOGRAD 0-1 (0-0, 0-1) (AET)

St James Park, Newcastle 27.08.2003

Referee: Jan W. Wegereef (HOL) Attendance: 37,239

NEWCASTLE UNITED: Shay Given, Andy O'Brien, Aaron Hughes, Jonathan Woodgate, Olivier Bernard, Nolberto Solano (106 Lomano Tresor Lualua), Kieron Dyer, Gary Speed (91 Jermaine Jenas), HUGO Miguel Ferreira VIANA (85 Laurent Robert), Alan Shearer, Shola Ameobi.
Trainer: Robert Robson

FK PARTIZAN: Ivica Kralj, Nenad Djordjevic, Taribo West, Nebojsa Malbasa, Milivoje Cirkovic, Igor Duljaj, Albert Nadj, Saša Ilic, Andrija Delibasic (116 Damir Cakar), Ivica Iliev, Milan Stojanoski. Trainer: Lothar Matthäus

Goal: Iliev (50)

Penalties: Shearer (miss), Malbasa (miss), Dyer (miss), 0-1 Nadj, Woodgate (miss), Stojanoski (miss), 1-1 Ameobi, 1-2 Cakar (miss), 2-2 Lualua, Iliev (miss), 3-2 Jenas, 3-3 Ilic, Hughes (miss), 3-4 Cirkovic

GTS WISLA KRAKÓW
v RSC ANDERLECHT BRUSSEL 0-1 (0-0)

Wisly, Kraków 26.08.2003

Referee: Konrad Plautz (AUS) Attendance: 8,200

GTS WISLA: Adam Piekutowski, Marcin Baszczynski, Mariusz Jop, Maciej Stolarczyk (65 Daniel Dubicki), Jacek Paszulewicz (71 Lukasz Nawotczynski), Damian Gorawski, Miroslaw Szymkowiak (76 Grzegorz Pater), Cristiano Pereira de Souza BRASILIA, Pawel Strak, Maciej Zurawski, Tomasz Frankowski. Trainer: Henryk Kasperczak

ANDERLECHT: Daniel Zitka, Olivier Doll, Hannu Tihinen, Vincent Kompany, Olivier Deschacht, Besnik Hasi, Walter Baseggio, Ki-Hyeon Seol, Goran Lovre (72 Christian Wilhelmsson), Aruna Dindane (87 Ivica Mornar), Pär Zetterberg (87 Marc Hendrikx). Trainer: Hugo Broos

Goal: Dindane (85)

FK AUSTRIA WIEN
v OLYMPIQUE de MARSEILLE 0-1 (0-1)

Ernst Happel, Wien 13.08.2003

Referee: Luis MEDINA CANTALEJO (SPA) Att: 28,300

FK AUSTRIA: Thomas Mandl, Rabiu Afolabi, Ernst Dospel, Frank Verlaat, Krzysztof Ratajczyk (50 Paul Scharner), Petter Rudi, Michael Wagner, Ivica Vastic, Vladimir Janocko (59 Richard Kitzbichler), Sean Dundee, Radoslaw Gilewicz (76 Sigurd Rushfeldt). Trainer: Joachim Löw

OLYMPIQUE: Vedran Runje, Daniel Van Buyten, Abdoulaye Méïté, Habib Bèye, Brahim Hemdani, Stepan Vachousek, Pascal Johansen, Fabio Celestini, Ahmed Hossam «Mido» (67 Tébily-Didier Drogba), FERNANDÃO Lúcio da Costa (67 Sylvain NDiaye), Dmitri Sytchev (82 Salomon Olembé).
Trainer: Alain Perrin

Goal: Sytchev (4)

OLYMPIQUE de MARSEILLE v FK AUSTRIA WIEN 0-0

Vélodrome, Marseille 27.08.2003

Referee: Anders Frisk (SWE) Attendance: 41,253

OLYMPIQUE: Vedran Runje, Daniel Van Buyten, Abdoulaye Méïté, Johnny Ecker (74 Sylvain Ndiaye), Habib Bèye, Brahim Hemdani, Pascal Johansen (86 Sébastien Pérez), Fabio Celestini, Tébily-Didier Drogba, FERNANDÃO Lúcio da Costa (58 Stepan Vachousek), Dmitri Sytchev.
Trainer: Alain Perrin

FK AUSTRIA: Thomas Mandl, Fernando Troyansky (71 Jocelyn Blanchard), Rabiu Afolabi, Ernst Dospel, Frank Verlaat, Krzysztof Ratajczyk, Paul Scharner, Thomas Flögel (71 Radoslaw Gilewicz), Ivica Vastic, Vladimir Janocko (81 Sean Dundee), Sigurd Rushfeldt. Trainer: Joachim Löw

CLUB BRUGGE KV v BV BORUSSIA DORTMUND 2-1 (2-0)

Jan Breydelstadion, Brugge 13.08.2003

Referee: Pierluigi Collina (ITA) Attendance: 19,364

CLUB BRUGGE: Dany Verlinden, Olivier De Cock, Philippe Clement, David Rozehnal, Peter Van Der Heyden, Timmy Simons, Alin Stoica (86 Ivan Gvozdonovic), Nastja Ceh, Gert Verheyen, Sandy Martens (73 Bengt Sæternes), Andrés MENDOZA Acevedo (86 Tim Smolders).
Trainer: Trond Sollied

BV BORUSSIA: Roman Weidenfeller, Stefan Reuter, Christian Wörns, Ahmed Madouni, André Bergdølmo (46 Otto Addo), Tomáš Rosický (86 Lars Ricken), FLAVIO da CONCEIÇÃO, Sebastian Kehl, Leonardo de Deus Santos "DEDÉ", Jan Koller, Márcio AMOROSO dos Santos (71 EWERTHON Henrique de Sousa). Trainer: M. Sammer

Goals: Ceh (33), Verheyen (44), Amoroso (53)

BV BORUSSIA DORTMUND v CLUB BRUGGE KV 2-1 (1-1, 2-1) (AET)

Westfalenstadion, Dortmund 27.08.2003

Referee: Michael Riley (ENG) Attendance: 62,000

BV BORUSSIA: Roman Weidenfeller, André Bergdølmo, Christian Wörns, Ahmed Madouni (75 EWERTHON Henrique de Sousa), Leonardo de Deus Santos "DEDÉ", Stefan Reuter (86 Juan Ramón Fernández), Sebastian Kehl, Tomáš Rosický, Otto Addo, Jan Koller, Márcio AMOROSO dos Santos.
Trainer: Matthias Sammer

CLUB BRUGGE: Tomislav Butina, Olivier De Cock, Philippe Clement, David Rozehnal, Peter Van Der Heyden, Timmy Simons, Gaëtan Englebert, Alin Stoica (46 Nastja Ceh), Gert Verheyen (114 Birger Maertens), Sandy Martens (82 Bengt Sæternes), Andrés MENDOZA Acevedo.
Trainer: Trond Sollied

Sent off: Rozenhal (112)

Goals: Amoroso (3), Mendoza (26), Ewerthon (86)

Penalties: Amoroso (miss), 0-1 Simons, André Bergdølmo (miss), 0-2 Ceh, 1-2 Koller, 1-3 De Cock, 2-3 Fernández, 2-4 Mendoza

ROSENBORG BK TRONDHEIM v RC DEPORTIVO LA CORUÑA 0-0

Lerkendal, Trondheim 13.08.2003

Referee: Graham Poll (ENG) Attendance: 21,167

ROSENBORG: Espen Johnsen, Christer Basma, Vidar Riseth, Erik Hoftun, Ståle Stensaas, Roar Strand, Ørjan Berg, Dagfinn Enerly (46 Christer George), Frode Johnsen, Harald Martin Brattbakk, Azar Karadas (71 Jan Gunnar Solli).
Trainer: Åge Hareide

DEPORTIVO: Francisco José MOLINA Jiménez, HÉCTOR Berenguel del Rio, Jorge Manuel Almeida Gomes ANDRADE, Nourredine NAYBET, Enrique Fernández ROMERO (78 Joan CAPDEVILA Méndez), VÍCTOR Sánchez del Amo (74 Lionel Sebastian SCALONI), MAURO da SILVA Gomes, SERGIO González Soriano, Juan Carlos VALERÓN Santana, José Emilio AMAVISCA Gárate, DIEGO TRISTÁN Herrera (65 Walter Gerardo PANDIANI Urquiza).
Trainer: Javier IRURETAGOYENA AMIANO

RC DEPORTIVO LA CORUÑA v ROSENBORG BK TRONDHEIM 1-0 (1-0)

Riazor, La Coruña 26.08.2003

Referee: Ľuboš Michel (SVK) Attendance: 22,153

DEPORTIVO: Francisco José MOLINA Jiménez, HÉCTOR Berenguel del Rio, Jorge Manuel Almeida Gomes ANDRADE, Nourredine NAYBET, Enrique Fernández ROMERO, VÍCTOR Sánchez del Amo (81 Lionel Sebastian SCALONI), MAURO da SILVA Gomes, SERGIO González Soriano, Juan Carlos VALERÓN Santana, Alberto LUQUE Martos (73 Francisco «FRAN» Javier González Pérez), DIEGO TRISTÁN Herrera (46 Walter Gerardo PANDIANI Urquiza).
Trainer: Javier IRURETAGOYENA AMIANO

ROSENBORG: Espen Johnsen, Christer Basma, Vidar Riseth, Erik Hoftun, Ståle Stensaas (86 Morten Knutsen), Roar Strand, Ørjan Berg, Fredrik Winsnes (75 Jan Gunnar Solli), Azar Karadas (66 Øyvind Storflor), Frode Johnsen, Harald Martin Brattbakk. Trainer: Åge Hareide

Goal: Luque (16)

SS LAZIO ROMA
v SPORT LISBOA E BENFICA 3-1 (1-0)

Olimpico, Roma 13.08.2003

Referee: Herbert Fandel (GER) Attendance: 57,926

LAZIO: Angelo Peruzzi, Luciano Zauri, Sinisa Mihajlovic, Guiseppe Favalli (74 Fabio Liverani), Massimo Oddo, Jaap Stam, Demetrio Albertini (74 SÉRGIO Paulo Marcenero CONCEIÇÃO), Dejan Stankovic, Stefano Fiore, Claudio Javier López (87 Giuliano Giannichedda), Bernardo Corradi.
Trainer: Roberto Mancini

BENFICA: José Filipe da Silva MOREIRA, Argélico Fucks "ARGEL", CRISTIANO Rocha Canedo Roland, RICARDO Sergio ROCHA Azevedo, Armando Gonçalves Teixeira "PETIT", Zlatko Zahovic (55 ROGER Galera Flores), FERNANDO João Lobo AGUILAR (55 Per Anders ANDERSSON), GEOVANNI Deiberson Mauricio (85 Miklós FEHÉR), SIMÃO Pedro Fonseca Sabrosa, Luis MIGUEL Brito Garcia Monteiro, Tomislav Šokota.
Trainer: José Antonio CAMACHO ALFARO

Goals: Corradi (16), Fiore (54), Mihajlovic (80), Simão (65)

SPORT LISBOA E BENFICA
v SS LAZIO ROMA 0-1 (0-1)

Do Bessa, Porto 27.08.2003

Referee: Urs Meier (SWI) Attendance: 16,974

BENFICA: José Filipe da Silva MOREIRA, Argélico Fucks "ARGEL", RICARDO Sergio ROCHA Azevedo (73 CRISTIANO Rocha Canedo Roland), Armando Gonçalves Teixeira "PETIT", HÉLDER Marinho Rodrigues Cristóvão, Zlatko Zahovic (33 ROGER Galera Flores), TIAGO Cardoso Mendes (69 Per Anders ANDERSSON), GEOVANNI Deiberson Mauricio, Miklós FEHÉR, SIMÃO Pedro Fonseca Sabrosa, Luis MIGUEL Brito Garcia Monteiro.
Trainer: José Antonio CAMACHO ALFARO

LAZIO: Angelo Peruzzi, Rodríguez CÉSAR Aparecido, Sinisa Mihajlovic, Guiseppe Favalli, Massimo Oddo, Jaap Stam (57 FERNANDO Manuel Silva COUTO), Demetrio Albertini, Dejan Stankovic, Stefano Fiore (84 SÉRGIO Paulo Marcenero CONCEIÇÃO), Claudio Javier López (78 Giuliano Giannichedda), Bernardo Corradi.
Trainer: Roberto Mancini

Goal: César (28)

GALATASARAY SK ISTANBUL
v FC CSKA SOFIA 3-0 (3-0)

Atatürk Olimpiyat, Istanbul 13.08.2003

Referee: Markus Merk (GER) Attendance: 66,300

GALATASARAY: Aly Faryd Camilo Mondragon, Bülent Korkmaz, Frank De Boer, CÉSAR Luís PRATES, Hakan Ünsal, JOÃO Casemir BATISTA Marqués, Volkan Arslan (73 Ayhan Akman), Ergün Penbe, Ümit Karan (30 Arif Erdem), Hakan Sükür (90 Ömer Erdoga), HASAN Gökhan SAS.
Trainer: Fatih Terim

CSKA: Stoian Kolov, Iordan Todorov (57 LEONARDO Lima da Silva), Ibrahima Gueye, Iordan Varbanov, Alexandar Tomash, Altin Haxhi, Svetoslav Petrov, Todor Yanchev, Emil Gargorov, Velizar Dimitrov (79 RODRIGO de Souza Cardoso), MacDonald Mukasi (46 Evgeni Iordanov).
Trainer: Stoicho Mladenov

Sent off: Iordanov (59)

Goals: Hasan Sas (3), Hakan Şükür (6), Arif (37)

FC CSKA SOFIA
v GALATASARAY SK ISTANBUL 0-3 (0-1)

Balgarska Armia, Sofia 27.08.2003

Referee: Domenico Messina (ITA) Attendance: 9,600

CSKA: Stoian Kolov, Iordan Todorov, Ibrahima Gueye (75 Iordan Varbanov), JOÃO CARLOS, Marcos Charras (55 João Paulo BRITO), Todor Yanchev, Altin Haxhi, Velizar Dimitrov, RODRIGO de Souza Cardoso, LEONARDO Lima da Silva (61 MacDonald Mukasi), Emil Gargorov.
Trainer: Stoicho Mladenov

GALATASARAY: Aly Faryd Camilo Mondragon, Bülent Korkmaz, Frank De Boer, Gabriel Sebastian Tamas (68 Berkant Göktan), CÉSAR Luís PRATES, Hakan Ünsal (79 Orhan Ak), Sabri Sarioglu, JOÃO Casemir BATISTA Marqués, Ergün Penbe, Hakan Sükür, Hasan Gökhan Sas (74 Arif Erdem). Trainer: Fatih Terim

Goals: César Prates (28), Sabri (53), Arif (86)

GROUP STAGE

GROUP A

FC BAYERN MÜNCHEN
v CELTIC FC GLASGOW 2-1 (0-0)

Olympiastadion, München 17.09.2003

Referee: Massimo de Santis (ITA) Attendance: 48,000

BAYERN: Oliver Kahn, Willy Sagnol, Robert Kovac, Thomas Linke, Bixente Lizarazu (73 Tobias Rau), Owen Hargreaves, Michael Ballack, Hasan Salihamidzic (73 Roque Santa Cruz), ZÉ ROBERTO da Silva, Claudio Pizarro, Roy Makaay.
Trainer: Ottmar Hitzfeld

CELTIC: Robert Hedman, Stanislav Varga, Bobo Balde, Jackie McNamara, Didier Agathe, Stilian Petrov, Neil Francis Lennon, Alan Thompson, Chris Sutton, John Hartson (66 Liam Miller), Henrik Larsson. Trainer: Martin O'Neill

Goals: Thompson (57), Makaay (73, 86)

OLYMPIQUE LYONNAIS
v RSC ANDERLECHT BRUSSEL 1-0 (1-0)

Gerland, Lyon 17.09.2003

Referee: Paulo Manuel GOMES COSTA (POR) Att: 37,002

OLYMPIQUE: Grégory Coupet, Eric Deflandre, José EDMILSON Gomes de Moraes, Patrick Müller, Anthony Réveillière, Mahamadou Diarra, Mickaël Essien, Vikash Dhorasoo, Antonio Augusto Ribeiro Reis «JUNINHO PERNAMBUCANO» (69 Eric Carrière), Sidney Govou (72 Florent Malouda), Giovane De Souza Elber (88 Péguy Luyindula). Trainer: Paul Le Guen

ANDERLECHT: Daniel Zitka, Michal Zewlakow, Glen De Boeck, Hannu Tihinen, Olivier Deschacht, Besnik Hasi (64 Ivica Mornar), Walter Baseggio, Christian Wilhelmsson, Pär Zetterberg, Ki-Hyeon Seol, Aruna Dindane.
Trainer: Hugo Broos

Goal: Juninho Pernambucano (26 pen)

RSC ANDERLECHT BRUSSEL
v FC BAYERN MÜNCHEN 1-1 (0-0)

Constant van den Stock, Brussel 30.09.2003

Referee: Luis MEDINA CANTALEJO (SPA) Att: 21,788

ANDERLECHT: Daniel Zitka, Michal Zewlakow, Vincent Kompany, Hannu Tihinen, Olivier Deschacht, Marc Hendrikx (83 Martin Kolar), Besnik Hasi, Ki-Hyeon Seol, Walter Baseggio, Ivica Mornar (87 Pär Zetterberg), Aruna Dindane.
Trainer: Hugo Broos

BAYERN: Oliver Kahn, Samuel Osei Kuffour (73 Hasan Salihamidzic), Robert Kovac, Thomas Linke, Bixente Lizarazu, Martín Demichelis, Michael Ballack, Owen Hargreaves (63 Bastian Schweinsteiger), ZÉ ROBERTO da Silva (63 Roque SANTA CRUZ), Claudio Pizarro, Roy Makaay.
Trainer: Ottmar Hitzfeld

Sent off: Pizarro (36)

Goals: Mornar (53), Santa Cruz (74)

CELTIC FC GLASGOW
v OLYMPIQUE LYONNAIS 2-0 (0-0)

Celtic Park, Glasgow 30.09.2003

Referee: Eduardo ITURRALDE GONZALEZ (SPA)
Attendance: 58,027

CELTIC: Robert Hedman, Stanislav Varga, Bobo Balde, Jackie Mcnamara, Didier Agathe, Neil Francis Lennon, Chris Sutton, Stilian Petrov, Alan Thompson, Henrik Larsson, John Hartson (64 Liam Miller). Trainer: Martin O'Neill

OLYMPIQUE: Grégory Coupet, Eric Deflandre, Patrick Müller, José EDMILSON Gomes de Moraes, Anthony Réveillière, Mahamadou Diarra, Vikash Dhorasoo (74 Péguy Luyindula), Sidney Govou (79 Florent Malouda), Antonio Augusto Ribeiro Reis "JUNINHO PERNAMBUCANO", Eric Carrière (63 Mickaël Essien), Giovane De Souza Elber.
Trainer: Paul Le Guen

Goals: Miller (70), Sutton (78)

RSC ADERLECHT BRUSSEL
v CELTIC FC GLASGOW 1-0 (0-0)

Constant van den Stock, Brussel 21.10.2003

Referee: Fritz Stuchlik (AUS) Attendance: 21,835

ANDERLECHT: Daniel Zitka, Michal Zewlakow, Vincent Kompany, Glen De Boeck, Olivier Deschacht, Martin Kolar (90+1 Hannu Tihinen), Besnik Hasi, Christian Wilhelmsson (88 Marc Hendrikx), Walter Baseggio, Ivica Mornar, Aruna Dindane. Trainer: Hugo Broos

CELTIC: Robert Hedman, Stanislav Varga, Bobo Balde, Jackie McNamara (46 Joos Valgaeren), Didier Agathe, Neil Francis Lennon (80 Liam Miller), Chris Sutton, Stilian Petrov, Alan Thompson, Henrik Larsson, John Hartson.
Trainer: Martin O'Neill

Sent off: de Boeck (26)

Goal: Dindane (72)

OLYMPIQUE LYONNAIS
v FC BAYERN MÜNCHEN 1-1 (0-1)

Gerland, Lyon 21.10.2003

Referee: Ľuboš Michel (SVK) Attendance: 37,658

OLYMPIQUE: Grégory Coupet, Eric Deflandre (46 Florent Malouda), Patrick Müller, José EDMILSON Gomes de Moraes, Anthony Réveillière, Mickaël Essien, Vikash Dhorasoo (71 Eric Carrière), Mahamadou Diarra, Antonio Augusto Ribeiro Reis "JUNINHO PERNAMBUCANO", Sidney Govou (67 Péguy Luyindula), Giovane De Souza Elber. Trainer: Paul Le Guen

BAYERN: Oliver Kahn, Samuel Osei Kuffour, Robert Kovac, Thomas Linke, Bixente Lizarazu, Sebastian Deisler, Martín Demichelis (46 Jens Jeremies), Michael Ballack, ZÉ ROBERTO da Silva (90+1 Hasan Salihamidzic), Roque SANTA CRUZ, Roy Makaay. Trainer: Ottmar Hitzfeld

Goals: Makaay (25), Luyindula (88)

CELTIC FC GLASGOW
v RSC ANDERLECHT BRUSSEL 3-1 (3-0)

Celtic Park, Glasgow 5.11.2003

Referee: Kyros Vassaras (GRE) Attendance: 59,201

CELTIC: Robert Hedman, Stanislav Varga, Bobo Balde, Jackie McNamara, Didier Agathe, Neil Francis Lennon, Chris Sutton, Stilian Petrov, Liam Miller (76 Michael Gray), Henrik Larsson, John Hartson (83 Shaun Maloney, 90+2 Mohamed Sylla).
Trainer: Martin O'Neill

ANDERLECHT: Daniel Zitka, Michal Zewlakow, Vincent Kompany, Hannu Tihinen, Olivier Deschacht, Marc Hendrikx (63 Martin Kolar), Besnik Hasi, Christian Wilhelmsson, Walter Baseggio, Ivica Mornar, Aruna Dindane.
Trainer: Hugo Broos

Goals: Larsson (12), Miller (17), Sutton (29), Dindane (77)

FC BAYERN MÜNCHEN v OLYMPIQUE LYONNAIS 1-2 (1-1)

Olympiastadion, München 5.11.2003

Referee: Graham Barber (ENG) Attendance: 59,000

BAYERN: Oliver Kahn, Willy Sagnol (72 Mehmet Scholl), Samuel Osei Kuffour, Robert Kovac, Bixente Lizarazu, Hasan Salihamidzic, Martín Demichelis (72 Jens Jeremies), ZÉ ROBERTO da Silva, Michael Ballack, Claudio Pizarro (67 Roque SANTA CRUZ), Roy Makaay.
Trainer: Ottmar Hitzfeld

OLYMPIQUE: Grégory Coupet, Jérémie Berthod, Patrick Müller, José EDMILSON Gomes de Moraes, Anthony Réveillière, Mickaël Essien (77 Sidney Govou), Florent Malouda, Mahamadou Diarra, Antonio Augusto Ribeiro Reis "JUNINHO PERNAMBUCANO" (90 Eric Carrière), Péguy Luyindula, Giovane De Souza Elber (78 CLAUDIO Roberto de Silva "CAÇAPA"). Trainer: Paul Le Guen

Goals: Juninho Pernambucano (6), Makaay (14), Elber (53).

FC BAYERN MÜNCHEN v RSC ANDERLECHT BRUSSEL 1-0 (1-0)

Olympiastadion, München 10.12.2003

Referee: Kim Milton Nielsen (DEN) Attendance: 52,000

BAYERN: Oliver Kahn, Hasan Salihamidzic (79 Bastian Schweinsteiger), Samuel Osei Kuffour, Thomas Linke, Bixente Lizarazu, Owen Hargreaves, Michael Ballack, ZÉ ROBERTO da Silva (67 Willy Sagnol), Roque SANTA CRUZ, Roy Makaay, Claudio Pizarro. Trainer: Ottmar Hitzfeld

ANDERLECHT: Daniel Zitka, Michal Zewlakow (63 Christian Wilhelmsson), Vincent Kompany, Hannu Tihinen, Olivier Deschacht, Besnik Hasi (79 Oleh Yashchuk), Pär Zetterberg, Walter Baseggio, Marc Hendrikx (86 Martin Kolar), Ivica Mornar, Aruna Dindane. Trainer: Hugo Broos

Goal: Makaay (42 pen)

RSC ANDERLECHT BRUSSEL v OLYMPIQUE LYONNAIS 1-0 (0-0)

Constant van den Stock, Brussel 25.11.2003

Referee: Domenico Messina (ITA) Attendance: 20,779

ANDERLECHT: Daniel Zitka, Michal Zewlakow (67 Marc Hendrikx), Vincent Kompany, Hannu Tihinen, Olivier Deschacht, Pär Zetterberg (87 Yves Vanderhaeghe), Besnik Hasi, Christian Wilhelmsson, Walter Baseggio, Ivica Mornar, Martin Kolar (89 Oleh Yashchuk). Trainer: Hugo Broos

OLYMPIQUE: Nicolas Puydebois, Jérémie Berthod (81 CLAUDIO Roberto de Silva "CAÇAPA"), Patrick Müller, José EDMILSON Gomes de Moraes, Anthony Réveillière, Sidney Govou, Florent Malouda, Mahamadou Diarra (74 Eric Carrière), Antonio Augusto Ribeiro Reis "JUNINHO PERNAMBUCANO", Péguy Luyindula, Giovane De Souza Elber. Trainer: Paul Le Guen

Goal: Tihinen (71)

OLYMPIQUE LYONNAIS v CELTIC FC GLASGOW 3-2 (1-1)

Gerland, Lyon 10.12.2003

Referee: Urs Meier (SWI) Attendance: 38,659

OLYMPIQUE: Grégory Coupet, Anthony Réveillière, Jérémie Berthod (77 Eric Carrière), José EDMILSON Gomes de Moraes, CLAUDIO Roberto de Silva «CAÇAPA», Florent Malouda, Mahamadou Diarra, Antonio Augusto Ribeiro Reis «JUNINHO PERNAMBUCANO» (89 Patrick Müller), Péguy Luyindula, Giovane De Souza Elber (87 Vikash Dhorasoo), Sidney Govou. Trainer: Paul Le Guen

CELTIC: Robert Hedman, Bobo Balde, Johan Mjällby, Michael Gray (68 Mohamed Sylla), Stanislav Varga, Neil Francis Lennon, Stilian Petrov, Liam Miller, Chris Sutton (80 John Kennedy), Henrik Larsson, John Hartson (68 Ross Wallace). Trainer: Martin O'Neill

Goals: Elber (6), Hartson (24),
Juninho Pernambucano (52, 86 pen), Sutton (75)

CELTIC FC GLASGOW v FC BAYERN MÜNCHEN 0-0

Celtic Park, Glasgow 25.11.2003

Referee: Rene H.J. Temmink (HOL) Attendance: 60,506

CELTIC: Robert Hedman, Bobo Balde, Stanislav Varga, Jackie Mcnamara, Didier Agathe (63 Liam Miller), Alan Thompson, Stilian Petrov, Neil Francis Lennon, Chris Sutton, Henrik Larsson, John Hartson (86 Mohamed Sylla).
Trainer: Martin O'Neill

BAYERN: Oliver Kahn, Willy Sagnol, Samuel Osei Kuffour, Robert Kovac, Bixente Lizarazu, Owen Hargreaves, Jens Jeremies, Michael Ballack, Roque SANTA CRUZ (73 Claudio Pizarro), Hasan Salihamidzic, Roy Makaay.
Trainer: Ottmar Hitzfeld

	P	W	D	L	F	A	Pts
Olympique Lyonnais	6	3	1	2	7	7	10
FC Bayern München	6	2	3	1	6	5	9
Celtic FC Glasgow	6	2	1	3	8	7	7
RSC Anderlecht Brussel	6	2	1	3	4	6	7

GROUP B

ARSENAL FC LONDON v FC INTERNAZIONALE MILANO **0-3** (0-3)

Highbury, London 17.09.2003

Referee: Manuel Enrique MEJUTO GONZALEZ (SPA)
Attendance: 34,393

ARSENAL: Jens Lehmann, LAUREN Etame-Mayer, Sol Campbell, Kolo Abib Touré, Robert Pires (64 Dennis Bergkamp), Ashley Cole, Patrick Vieira, GILBERTO Aparecido da Silva (64 Nwankwo Kanu), Fredrik Ljungberg, Thierry Henry, Sylvain Wiltord (79 Ray Parlour). Trainer: A. Wenger

INTER: Francesco Toldo, Javier Zanetti, Fabio Cannavaro, Marco Materazzi, Iván Ramiro Cordoba, Andy Van Der Meyde (70 Thomas Helveg), Cristiano Zanetti, Emre Belözoglu (66 Sabri Lamouchi), Cristian Alberto "KILY" GONZÁLEZ, Julio Ricardo CRUZ (84 Mohamed Kallon), Obafemi Martins. Trainer: Hector Raúl Cúper

Goals: Cruz (22), Van Der Meyde (24), Martins (41)

FC DYNAMO KYIV v FC LOKOMOTIV MOSKVA **2-0** (0-0)

Valeri Lobanovskiy, Kyiv 17.09.2003,

Referee: Peter Fröjdfeldt (SWE) Attendance: 72,500

DYNAMO: Olexandr Shovkovskiy, Serhiy Fedorov, Yuriy Dmytrulin (46 Aleksandr Khatskevich), Goran Gavrancic, Andriy Nesmachniy, Valentin Belkevich, Tiberiu Ghioane (79 Florin Lucian Cernat), Georgi Ivanov Peev, Oleh Husev (62 DIOGO «RINCÓN» Augusto Pacheco da Fontoura), Jerko Leko, Maksim Shatskikh. Trainer: Oleksiy Mykhaylychenko

LOKOMOTIV: Sergei I. Ovchinnikov, Gennadiy Nizhegorodov, Sergei Ignashevich, Oleg Pashinin, Dmitriy Sennikov, Jacob Lekcetho, Vladimir Maminov, Marat Izmailov (87 LEANDRO Lessa Azevedo), Dmitriy Loskov, Dmitriy Khokhlov, Mikheil Ashvetia (88 Ruslan Pimenov). Trainer: Yuri Semin

Goals: Diogo «Rincón» (83, 90+1).

FC INTERNAZIONALE MILANO v FC DYNAMO KYIV **2-1** (1-1)

Stadio Giuseppe Meazza, Milano 30.09.2003

Referee: Stéphane Bré (FRA) Attendance: 24,326

INTER: Francesco Toldo, Javier Zanetti, Daniele Adani, Fabio Cannavaro, Iván Ramiro Cordoba, Andy Van Der Meyde (61 Thomas Helveg), Cristiano Zanetti, Emre Belözoglu, Cristian Alberto "KILY" GONZÁLEZ, Julio Ricardo CRUZ (78 Mohamed Kallon), Obafemi Martins (59 Christian Vieri). Trainer: Hector Raúl Cúper

DYNAMO: Olexandr Shovkovskiy, Yuriy Dmytrulin (68 Aleksandr Khatskevich), Georgi Ivanov Peev, Serhiy Fedorov, Goran Sablic, Andriy Nesmachniy, Tiberiu Ghioane, DIOGO "RINCÓN" Augusto Pacheco da Fontoura, Jerko Leko, Valentin Belkevich, Maksim Shatskikh (86 Olexandr Melashchenko). Trainer: Oleksiy Mykhaylychenko

Goals: Adani (23), Fedorov (34), Vieri (90)

FC LOKOMOTIV MOSKVA v ARSENAL FC LONDON **0-0**

Lokomotiv, Moskva 30.09.2003

Referee: Jan W. Wegereef (HOL) Attendance: 30,000

LOKOMOTIV: Sergei Ovchinnikov, Dmitriy Sennikov, Oleg Pashinin, Sergei Gurenko, Sergei Ignashevich, Vadim Yevseyev (73 Gennadiy Nizhegorodov), Vladimir Maminov, Dmitriy Loskov, Dmitriy Khokhlov, Marat Izmailov, Mikheil Ashvetia (65 Ruslan Pimenov). Trainer: Yuri Semin

ARSENAL: Jens Lehmann, LAUREN Etame-Mayer, Martin Keown, Kolo Abib Touré, Ashley Cole, Robert Pires, Eduard Cesar Daud Gasper "EDU", GILBERTO Aparecido da Silva, Ray Parlour, Thierry Henry, Sylvain Wiltord. Trainer: Arsène Wenger

FC DYNAMO KYIV v ARSENAL FC LONDON **2-1** (1-0)

Valeri Lobanovskiy, Kyiv 21.10.2003

Referee: Konrad Plautz (AUS) Attendance: 82,750

DYNAMO: Olexandr Shovkovskiy, Yuriy Dmytrulin (33 Goran Sablic), Georgi Ivanov Peev, Goran Gavrancic, Serhiy Fedorov, Andriy Nesmachniy, Tiberiu Ghioane (79 Aleksandr Khatskevich), Oleh Husev (65 DIOGO "RINCÓN" Augusto Pacheco da Fontoura), Jerko Leko, Valentin Belkevich, Maksim Shatskikh. Trainer: Oleksiy Mykhaylychenko

ARSENAL: Jens Lehmann, LAUREN Etame-Mayer, Sol Campbell, Kolo Abib Touré, Ashley Cole, Robert Pires, Eduard Cesar Daud Gasper "EDU" (61 Patrick Vieira), GILBERTO Aparecido da Silva (74 Nwankwo Kanu), Ray Parlour (74 Fredrik Ljungberg), Thierry Henry, Sylvain Wiltord. Trainer: Arsène Wenger

Goals: Shatskikh (27), Belkevich (64), Henry (80)

FC LOKOMOTIV MOSKVA v FC INTERNAZIONALE MILANO **3-0** (1-0)

Lokomotiv, Moskva 21.10.2003

Referee: Franz-Xaver Wack (GER) Attendance: 26,000

LOKOMOTIV: Sergei Ovchinnikov, Dmitriy Sennikov, Jacob Lekcetho, Maxim Buznikin (46 Oleg Pashinin), Sergei Ignashevich, Vadim Yevseyev (75 Sergei Gurenko), Vladimir Maminov, Dmitriy Loskov, Dmitriy Khokhlov, Marat Izmailov, Mikheil Ashvetia. Trainer: Yuri Semin

INTER: Francesco Toldo, Javier Zanetti, Jérémie Bréchet (72 Francesco Coco), Fabio Cannavaro, Iván Ramiro Cordoba, Matías Jesús Almeyda, Cristiano Zanetti, Alvaro Recoba, Marco Materazzi (61 Emre Belözoglu), Julio Ricardo Cruz (61 Obafemi Martins), Christian Vieri. Trainer: Corrado Verdelli

Goals: Loskov (2), Ashvetia (50), Khokhlov (57)

ARSENAL FC LONDON
v FC DYNAMO KYIV 1-0 (0-0)

Highbury, London 5.11.2003

Referee: Lucilio CARDOSO CORTEZ BATISTA (POR)
Attendance: 34,419

ARSENAL: Jens Lehmann, LAUREN Etame-Mayer, Sol Campbell, Kolo Abib Touré, Ashley Cole, Robert Pires, Fredrik Ljungberg (69 Sylvain Wiltord), GILBERTO Aparecido da Silva, Ray Parlour (76 Nwankwo Kanu), Thierry Henry, Dennis Bergkamp (90+1 Eduard Cesar Daud Gasper "EDU"). Trainer: Arsène Wenger

DYNAMO: Olexandr Shovkovskiy, Georgi Ivanov Peev, Goran Gavrancic, Serhiy Fedorov, Andriy Nesmachniy, Denys Onyshchenko (22 Goran Sablic), Tiberiu Ghioane, Oleh Husev (60 DIOGO "RINCÓN" Augusto Pacheco da Fontoura), Jerko Leko, Valentin Belkevich, Maksim Shatskikh (71 Roberto Antonio Nanni). Trainer: Oleksiy Mykhaylychenko

Goal: Cole (89)

FC INTERNAZIONALE MILANO
v FC LOKOMOTIV MOSKVA 1-1 (1-0)

Stadio Giuseppe Meazza, Milano 5.11.2003

Referee: Frank De Bleeckere (BEL) Attendance: 22,822

INTER: Francesco Toldo, Javier Zanetti, Thomas Helveg, Fabio Cannavaro, Daniele Adani, Matías Jesús Almeyda, Cristiano Zanetti (68 Sabri Lamouchi), Marco Materazzi, Cristian Alberto "KILY" GONZÁLEZ (90 Giorgios Karagounis), Christian Vieri, Alvaro Recoba (77 Julio Ricardo Cruz). Trainer: Alberto Zaccheroni

LOKOMOTIV: Sergei Ovchinnikov, Dmitriy Sennikov, Jacob Lekcetho, Oleg Pashinin, Sergei Ignashevich, Vadim Yevseyev, Vladimir Maminov, Dmitriy Loskov, Dmitriy Khokhlov, Marat Izmailov (90 Gennadiy Nizhegorodov), Mikheil Ashvetia (77 Maxim Buznikin). Trainer: Yuri Semin

Goals: Recoba (14), Loskov (54)

FC INTERNAZIONALE MILANO
v ARSENAL FC LONDON 1-5 (1-1)

Stadio Giuseppe Meazza, Milano 25.11.2003

Referee: Wolfgang Stark (GER) Attendance: 44,884

INTER: Francesco Toldo, Javier Zanetti, Iván Ramiro Cordoba, Fabio Cannavaro (59 Giovanni Pasquale), Jérémie Bréchet, Sabri Lamouchi (57 Matías Jesús Almeyda), Cristiano Zanetti, Marco Materazzi, Andy Van Der Meyde (69 Julio Ricardo Cruz), Christian Vieri, Obafemi Martins. Trainer: Alberto Zaccheroni

ARSENAL: Jens Lehmann, Pascal Cygan, Sol Campbell, Kolo Abib Touré, Ashley Cole, Robert Pires, Fredrik Ljungberg, Eduard Cesar Daud Gasper «EDU», Ray Parlour, Thierry Henry (89 Jeremie Aliadière), Nwankwo Kanu (73 GILBERTO Aparecido da Silva). Trainer: Arsène Wenger

Goals: Henry (25, 85), Vieri (33), Ljungberg (49), Edu (88), Pires (89)

FC LOKOMOTIV MOSKVA
v FC DYNAMO KYIV 3-2 (2-1)

Lokomotiv, Moskva 25.11.2003

Referee: Arturo DAUDÉN IBÁÑEZ (SPA) Att: 23,000

LOKOMOTIV: Sergei Ovchinnikov, Dmitriy Sennikov, Jacob Lekcetho, Oleg Pashinin, Sergei Ignashevich, Vadim Yevseyev, Vladimir Maminov, Dmitriy Loskov, Dmitriy Khokhlov, Maxim Buznikin (83 Winston Parks, 90+2 Gennadiy Nizhegorodov), Mikheil Ashvetia. Trainer: Yuri Semin

DYNAMO: Olexandr Shovkovskiy, Denys Onyshchenko (66 Georgi Ivanov Peev), Goran Gavrancic, Goran Sablic, Andriy Nesmachniy, Tiberiu Ghioane (57 Aleksandr Khatskevich), Oleh Husev, Yuriy Dmytrulin, Valentin Belkevich, DIOGO "RINCÓN" Augusto Pacheco da Fontoura, Maksim Shatskikh. Trainer: Oleksiy Mykhaylychenko

Goals: Buznikin (28), Belkevich (37), Ignashevich (45+1 pen), Shatskikh (65), Parks (89)

ARSENAL FC LONDON
v FC LOKOMOTIV MOSKVA 2-0 (1-0)

Highbury, London 10.12.2003

Referee: L'uboš Michel (SVK) Attendance: 35,343

ARSENAL: Jens Lehmann, Pascal Cygan, Sol Campbell, Kolo Abib Touré, Ashley Cole, Robert Pires, Patrick Vieira, GILBERTO Aparecido da Silva, Dennis Bergkamp (76 Nwankwo Kanu), Thierry Henry, Fredrik Ljungberg. Trainer: Arsène Wenger

LOKOMOTIV: Sergei Ovchinnikov, Dmitriy Sennikov, Jacob Lekcetho, Oleg Pashinin, Sergei Ignashevich, Vadim Yevseyev, Vladimir Maminov, Dmitriy Loskov, Dmitriy Khokhlov, Maxim Buznikin (46 Sergei Gurenko), Mikheil Ashvetia (46 Winston Parks). Trainer: Yuri Semin

Sent off: Lekcetho (45)

Goals: Pires (12), Ljungberg (67)

FC DYNAMO KYIV
v FC INTERNAZIONALE MILANO 1-1 (0-0)

Valeri Lobanovskiy, Kyiv 10.12.2003

Referee: GillesVeissièrre (FRA) Attendance: 82,893

DYNAMO: Olexandr Shovkovskiy, Goran Gavrancic, Goran Sablic, Andriy Nesmachniy, Jerko Leko, Tiberiu Ghioane (74 Oleh Husev), Georgi Ivanov Peev (84 Artem Milevskiy), Yuriy Dmytrulin (78 Florin Lucian Cernat), Valentin Belkevich, DIOGO "RINCÓN" Augusto Pacheco da Fontoura, Maksim Shatskikh. Trainer: Oleksiy Mykhaylychenko

INTER: Francesco Toldo, Javier Zanetti, Iván Ramiro Cordoba, Fabio Cannavaro, Daniele Adani, Emre Belözoglu (88 Alvaro Recoba), Matías Jesús Almeyda, Giovanni Pasquale, Andy Van Der Meyde (49 Obafemi Martins), Christian Vieri, Julio Ricardo Cruz (83 Sabri Lamouchi). Trainer: Alberto Zaccheroni

Goals: Adani (69), Diogo "Rincón" (85)

	P	W	D	L	F	A	Pts
Arsenal FC London	6	3	1	2	9	6	10
FC Lokomotiv Moskva	6	2	2	2	7	7	8
Internazionale FC	6	2	2	2	8	11	8
Dynamo Kyiv	6	2	1	3	8	8	7

GROUP C

AEK FC ATHINA v RC DEPORTIVO LA CORUÑA 1-1 (0-1)

Apostolos Nikolaidis, Athina 17.09.2003

Referee: Thomas Michael McCurry (SCO) Att: 14,583

AEK: Dionisios Hiotis, Vassilios Borbokis, Mihalis Kapsis (21 Evangelos Moras), Nikolaos Kostenoglou, Nikolaos Georgeas, Theodoros Zagorakis, Kostas Katsouranis, Michel Kreek (81 Dimitrios Nalitzis), Vassilios Tsartas, Giannis Okkas, Nikolaos Lyberopoulos (64 Ilija Ivic). Trainer: Dusko Bajević

DEPORTIVO: Francisco José MOLINA Jiménez, Enrique Fernández ROMERO, Nourredine NAYBET, MAURO da SILVA Gomes, Jorge Manuel Almeida Gomes ANDRADE, Juan Carlos VALERÓN Santana, HÉCTOR Berenguel del Rio, SERGIO González Soriano (66 Aldo Pedro DUSCHER), Alberto LUQUE Martos (71 DIEGO TRISTÁN Herrera), Walter Gerardo PANDIANI Urquiza (78 Lionel Sebastian SCALONI), VÍCTOR Sánchez del Amo.
Trainer: Javier IRURETAGOYENA AMIANO

Goals: Pandiani (12), Tsartas (86)

PSV EINDHOVEN v AS MONACO 1-2 (0-1)

Philips, Eindhoven 17.09.2003

Referee: Stephen Graham Bennett (ENG) Att: 24,500

PSV: Ronald Waterreus, Jürgen Colin, Wilfred Bouma, André Ooijer, Young-Pyo Lee, Remco Van Der Schaaf (46 Jan Vennegoor Of Hesselink), Mark Van Bommel, Dennis Rommedahl, Arjen Robben (83 John De Jong), Mateja Kezman, Ji-Sung Park. Trainer: Guus Hiddink

AS MONACO: Flavio Roma, Julien Rodriguez, Sébastien Squillaci, Patrice Evra, Gaël Givet, Edouard Cissé (73 Jaroslav Plasil), Ludovic Giuly (86 Emmanuel Adebayor), Jérôme Rothen (89 Dado Prso), Lucas Ademar Bernardi, Fernando Morientes Sanchéz, Andreas Zikos.
Trainer: Didier Claude Deschamps

Goals: Morientes (31), Cissé (56), Bouma (65)

RC DEPORTIVO LA CORUÑA v PSV EINDHOVEN 2-0 (1-0)

Riazor, La Coruña 30.09.2003

Referee: Claus Bo Larsen (DEN) Attendance: 24,300

DEPORTIVO: Francisco José MOLINA Jiménez, MANUEL PABLO García Díaz, Jorge Manuel Almeida Gomes ANDRADE, Nourredine NAYBET, Joan CAPDEVILA Méndez, SERGIO González Soriano, MAURO da SILVA Gomes, VÍCTOR Sánchez del Amo, Juan Carlos VALERÓN Santana (81 Pedro Manuel MUNITIS Alvarez), Alberto LUQUE Martos (46 Francisco «FRAN» Javier Gonzalez Perez), Walter Gerardo PANDIANI Urquiza (58 DIEGO TRISTÁN Herrera).
Trainer: Javier IRURETAGOYENA AMIANO

PSV: Ronald Waterreus, André Ooijer, Kevin Hofland, Wilfred Bouma, Young-Pyo Lee, Mark Van Bommel, Johann Vogel (78 Jan Vennegoor Of Hesselink), Dennis Rommedahl, Ji-Sung Park, Remco Van Der Schaaf (54 Arjen Robben), Mateja Kezman. Trainer: Guus Hiddink

Goals: Sergio (20), Pandiani (52 pen)

AS MONACO v AEK FC ATHINA 4-0 (2-0)

Louis II, Monaco 30.09.2003

Referee: Stefano Farina (ITA) Attendance: 11,790

AS MONACO: Flavio Roma, Gaël Givet, Sébastien Squillaci, Julien Rodriguez, Patrice Evra, Andreas Zikos, Lucas Ademar Bernardi, Ludovic Giuly, Jérôme Rothen (85 Jaroslav Plasil), Fernando MORIENTES Sanchéz (76 Dado Prso), Emmanuel Adebayor (69 Edouard Cissé).
Trainer: Didier Claude Deschamps

AEK: Dionisios Hiotis, Kofi Amponsah, Michel Kreek (15 Nikolaos Kostenoglou), Evangelos Moras (61 Vasilis Tsartas), Nikolaos Georgeas, Theodoros Zagorakis (76 Mihalis Kapsis), Kostas Katsouranis, Grigorios Georgatos, Christos Maladenis, Giannis Okkas, Nikolaos Lyberopoulos.
Trainer: Dusko Bajević

Goals: Giuly (23), Morientes (27, 56), Prso (86)

AEK FC ATHINA v PSV EINDHOVEN 0-1 (0-1)

Apostolos Nikolaidis, Athina 21.10.2003

Referee: Leslie Irvine (NIR) Attendance: 10,530

AEK: Hrisostomos Mihailidis, Kofi Amponsah, Mihalis Kasapis (78 Vassilio Borkokis), Mihalis Kapsis, Nikolaos Georgeas, Theodoros Zagorakis, Kostas Katsouranis, Vasilis Tsartas, Ivan Rusev (61 Vasilis Lakis), Giannis Okkas, Nikolaos Lyberopoulos (61 Ilija Ivic). Trainer: Dusko Bajević

PSV: Ronald Waterreus, André Ooijer, Kevin Hofland (63 Jürgen Colin), Wilfred Bouma, Young-Pyo Lee, Theo Lucius, Johann Vogel, Dennis Rommedahl, John De Jong, Mateja Kezman, Arjen Robben. Trainer: Guus Hiddink

Sent off: Amponsah (65)

Goal: Lucius (37)

RC DEPORTIVO LA CORUÑA v AS MONACO 1-0 (0-0)

Riazor, La Coruña 21.10.2003

Referee: Frank De Bleeckere (BEL) Attendance: 21,507

DEPORTIVO: Francisco José MOLINA Jiménez, MANUEL PABLO García Díaz, Jorge Manuel Almeida Gomes ANDRADE, Nourredine NAYBET, Enrique Fernández ROMERO, SERGIO González Soriano, VÍCTOR Sánchez del Amo (81 Lionel Sebastian SCALONI), Juan Carlos VALERÓN Santana (65 Walter Gerardo PANDIANI Urquiza), Alberto LUQUE Martos (57 Francisco «FRAN» Javier Gonzalez Perez), Aldo Pedro DUSCHER, DIEGO TRISTÁN Herrera.
Trainer: Javier IRURETAGOYENA AMIANO

AS MONACO: Flavio Roma, Gaël Givet, Sébastien Squillaci, Julien Rodriguez, Patrice Evra, Jaroslav Plasil (87 Dado Prso), Lucas Ademar Bernardi, Ludovic Giuly, Jérôme Rothen, Edouard Cissé, Fernando MORIENTES Sanchéz (78 Emmanuel Adebayor). Trainer: Didier Claude Deschamps

Goal: Diego Tristán (83)

AS MONACO v RC DEPORTIVO LA CORUÑA 8-3 (5-2)

Louis II, Monaco 5.11.2003

Referee: Terje Hauge (NOR) Attendance: 15,882

AS MONACO: Flavio Roma, Gaël Givet, Sébastien Squillaci, Julien Rodriguez, Patrice Evra (83 Hugo Ibarra), Jaroslav Plasil (66 Andreas Zikos), Lucas Ademar Bernardi, Ludovic Giuly, Jérôme Rothen, Edouard Cissé, Dado Prso (75 Emmanuel Adebayor). Trainer: Didier Claude Deschamps

DEPORTIVO: Francisco José MOLINA Jiménez (46 Gustavo Adolfo MUNÚA Vera), MANUEL PABLO García Díaz (46 Pedro Manuel MUNITIS Alvarez), Jorge Manuel Almeida Gomes ANDRADE, Nourredine NAYBET, Enrique Fernández ROMERO, MAURO da SILVA Gomes, Lionel Sebastian SCALONI, Juan Carlos VALERÓN Santana, SERGIO González Soriano (60 Walter Gerardo PANDIANI Urquiza), José Emilio AMAVISCA Garate, DIEGO TRISTÁN Herrera.
Trainer: Javier IRURETAGOYENA AMIANO

Goals: Rothen (2), Giuly (11), Prso (26, 29, 45+2, 49), Diego Tristán (39, 52), Scaloni (45), Plasil (47), Cissé (67)

PSV EINDHOVEN v AEK FC ATHINA 2-0 (0-0)

Philips, Eindhoven 5.11.2003

Referee: Konrad Plautz (AUS) Attendance: 28,000

PSV: Ronald Waterreus, André Ooijer, Kevin Hofland, Wilfred Bouma, Young-Pyo Lee, Theo Lucius, Jürgen Colin, Ji-Sung Park, John De Jong, Mateja Kezman, Arjen Robben.
Trainer: Guus Hiddink

AEK: Hrisostomos Mihailidis, Nikolaos Kostenoglou, Mihalis Kasapis, Evangelos Moras, Nikolaos Georgeas, Theodoros Zagorakis, Kostas Katsouranis, Vassilios Lakis (69 Sotirios Konstantinidis), Ivan Rusev (33 Vassilios Tsartas), Giannis Okkas (78 Ilija Ivic), Nikolaos Lyberopoulos.
Trainer: Dusko Bajević

Goals: Bouma (51), Robben (63)

RC DEPORTIVO LA CORUÑA v AEK FC ATHINA 3-0 (1-0)

Riazor, La Coruña 25.11.2003

Referee: Michael Riley (ENG) Attendance: 17,205

DEPORTIVO: Francisco José MOLINA Jiménez, HÉCTOR Berenguel del Rio, Jorge Manuel Almeida Gomes ANDRADE, Joan CAPDEVILA Méndez, CÉSAR Martín Villar (72 Enrique Fernández ROMERO), Francisco «FRAN» Javier Gonzalez Perez, VÍCTOR Sánchez del Amo (69 Lionel Sebastian SCALONI), Juan Carlos VALERÓN Santana (59 Alberto LUQUE Martos), SERGIO González Soriano, Aldo Pedro DUSCHER, Walter Gerardo PANDIANI Urquiza.
Trainer: Javier IRURETAGOYENA AMIANO

AEK: Hrisostomos Mihailidis, Vassilio Borkokis, Mihalis Kapsis, Mihalis Kasapis (44 Nikolaos Kostenoglou), Kofi Amponsah, Theodoros Zagorakis, Kostas Katsouranis, Vassilios Tsartas, Vassilios Lakis (73 Milen Petkov), Giannis Okkas (77 Sotirios Konstantinidis), Dimitrios Nalitzis.
Trainer: Dusko Bajević

Goals: Héctor (22), Valerón (51), Luque (71)

AS MONACO v PSV EINDHOVEN 1-1 (1-0)

Louis II, Monaco 25.11.2003

Referee: Zeljko Sirić (CRO) Attendance: 14,587

AS MONACO: Flavio Roma, Gaël Givet, Sébastien Squillaci, Julien Rodriguez, Patrice Evra (75 Hugo Ibarra), Andreas Zikos, Lucas Ademar Bernardi, Ludovic Giuly, Jérôme Rothen, Fernando MORIENTES Sanchéz (81 Emmanuel Adebayor), Dado Prso (59 Edouard Cissé).
Trainer: Didier Claude Deschamps

PSV: Ronald Waterreus, Kasper Bøgelund (72 Jürgen Colin), Ernest Faber, Wilfred Bouma, Young-Pyo Lee (78 John De Jong), Theo Lucius, Johann Vonlanthen (64 Jan Vennegoor Of Hesselink), Ji-Sung Park, Johann Vogel, Mateja Kezman, Arjen Robben. Trainer: Guus Hiddink

Sent off: Zikos (83), Giuly (88), Lucius (49)

Goals: Morientes (34), Vennegoor Of Hesselink (84)

AEK FC ATHINA v AS MONACO 0-0

Apostolos Nikolaidis, Athina 10.12.2003

Referee: Wolfgang Stark (GER) Attendance: 5,000

AEK: Hrisostomos Mihailidis, Vassilio Borkokis, Michel Kreek, Evangelos Moras, Mihalis Kapsis, Theodoros Zagorakis, Vassilios Tsartas, Kostas Katsouranis, Vassilios Lakis (56 Dimitrios Nalitzis), Nikolaos Lyberopoulos (67 Christos Maladenis), Giannis Okkas (83 Sotirios Konstantinidis).
Trainer: Dusko Bajević

AS MONACO: Tony Mario Sylva, Julien Rodriguez, Hugo Ibarra (73 Sébastien Carole), Sébastien Squillaci, Patrice Evra, Gaël Givet, Edouard Cissé, Lucas Ademar Bernardi, Jaroslav Plasil, Fernando MORIENTES Sanchéz, Emmanuel Adebayor (62 Souleymane Camara).
Trainer: Didier Claude Deschamps

PSV EINDHOVEN
v RC DEPORTIVO LA CORUÑA 3-2 (1-0)

Philips, Eindhoven 10.12.2003

Referee: Pierluigi Collina (ITA) Attendance: 28,000

PSV: Ronald Waterreus, Kasper Bøgelund, Wilfred Bouma, Young-Pyo Lee, André Ooijer, John De Jong, Jan Vennegoor Of Hesselink, Ji-Sung Park (46 Dennis Rommedahl), Johann Vogel, Mateja Kezman, Arjen Robben.
Trainer: Guus Hiddink

DEPORTIVO: Francisco José MOLINA Jiménez, HÉCTOR Berenguel del Rio, Jorge Manuel Almeida Gomes ANDRADE, Joan CAPDEVILA Méndez, Lionel Sebastian SCALONI (84 CÉSAR Martín Villar), Francisco "FRAN" Javier Gonzalez Perez, Nourredine NAYBET, Aldo Pedro DUSCHER, Juan Carlos VALERÓN Santana, SERGIO González Soriano (57 Alberto LUQUE Martos), DIEGO TRISTÁN Herrera (63 Walter Gerardo PANDIANI Urquiza).
Trainer: Javier IRURETAGOYENA AMIANO

Goals: De Jong (14, 90+4), Robben (48), Luque (59), Pandiani (83)

	P	W	D	L	F	A	Pts
AS Monaco	6	3	2	1	15	6	11
Deportivo La Coruña	6	3	1	2	12	12	10
PSV Eindhoven	6	3	1	2	8	7	10
AEK FC Athina	6	0	2	4	1	11	2

GROUP D

JUVENTUS FC TORINO
v GALATASARAY SK ISTANBUL 2-1 (1-1)

Delle Alpi, Torino 17.09.2003

Referee: Valentin Ivanov (RUS) Attendance: 14,420

JUVENTUS: Gianluigi Buffon, Lilian Thuram, Ciro Ferrara, Paolo MONTERO IGLESIAS, Alessio Tacchinardi (46 Edgar Davids), Gianluca Zambrotta, Stephen Appiah, Mauro German Camoranesi (65 Igor Tudor), Pavel Nedved, Alessandro Del Piero, David Trezeguet (78 Marco Di Vaio).
Trainer: Marcello Lippi

GALATASARAY: Aly Faryd Camilo Mondragon, Bülent Korkmaz, Frank De Boer, Hakan Ünsal, CÉSAR Luís PRATES, HASAN Gökhan SAS (66 Cihan Haspolatli), Ergün Penbe, JOÃO Casemir BATISTA Marqués, Sabri Sarioglu, Fabio PINTO (80 Arif Erdem), Hakan Sükür (84 Gabriel Sebastian Tamaş). Trainer: Fatih Terim

Goals: Del Piero (5), Hakan Şükür (19), Ferrara (73)

REAL SOCIEDAD DE FÚTBAL SAN SEBASTIAN
v OLYMPIAKOS PEIRAIAS 1-0 (0-0)

Anoeta, San Sebastian 17.09.2003

Referee: Knud Erik Fisker (DEN) Attendance: 29,091

REAL SOCIEDAD: Sander WESTERVELD, Aitor LOPEZ REKARTE, Igor JAUREGUI Iraola, Gabriel Francisco SCHÜRRER Peralta, Agustin ARANZÁBAL Alkorta, Valery KARPIN, José Javier BARKERO Saludes (61 LEE CHUN Soo), Mikel ARANBURU Eizaguirre, Xabier ALONSO Olano, Darko KOVACEVIC, Oscar DE PAULA Gamero (61 NIHAT Kahveci).
Trainer: Raynald Denoueix

OLYMPIAKOS: Theofanis Katergiannakis, Hristian Karembeu, Athanasios Kostoulas, Dimitrios Mavrogenidis (75 Anastasios Pantos), Georgios Anatolakis, Stylianos Venetidis, Pantelis Kafes (83 Panagiotis Gonias), Ieroklis Stoltidis, Georgios Georgiadis, Predrag Djordjevic, GIOVANNI Silva de Oliveira (64 Labros Houtos). Trainer: Oleg Protasov

Goal: Kovacevic (80 pen)

GALATASARAY SK ISTANBUL v REAL SOCIEDAD DE FÚTBAL SAN SEBASTIÁN 1-2 (0-1)

Ali Sami Yen, Istanbul 30.09.2003

Referee: Herbert Fandel (GER) Attendance: 58,617

GALATASARAY: Ly Faryd Camilo Mondragon, CÉSAR Luís PRATES (40 JOÃO Casemir BATISTA Marqués), Bülent Korkmaz, Frank De Boer, Gabriel Sebastian Tamas (46 Arif Erdem), Sabri Sarioglu, Ayhan Akman, Cihan Haspolatli (84 Elvir Baljic), Ergün Penbe, Hasan Gökhan Şaş, Hakan Sükür.
Trainer: Fatih Terim **Sent off**: Hasan Şaş (82)

REAL SOCIEDAD: Sander WESTERVELD, Lionel PORTILLON, Igor JAUREGUI Iraola, Bjorn Tore KVARME, Agustin ARANZÁBAL Alkorta, Valery KARPIN, Igor GABILONDO del Campo (67 LEE CHUN Soo), Mikel ARANBURU Eizaguirre, Xabier ALONSO Olano, NIHAT Kahveci (65 Bittor ALKIZA Fernández), Darko KOVACEVIC (78 Oscar DE PAULA Gamero). Trainer: Raynald Denoueix

Goals: Kovacevic (3), Hakan Şükür (61), Alonso (72)

OLYMPIAKOS PEIRAIAS
v JUVENTUS FC TORINO 1-2 (1-1)

Giorgos Kamaras, Athina 30.09.2003

Referee: Eric Poulat (FRA) Attendance: 12,921

OLYMPIAKOS: Theofanis Katergiannakis, Anastasios Pantos, Paraskevas Antzas, Athanasios Kostoulas, Stylianos Venetidis, Dimitrios Mavrogenidis (66 Panagiotis Gonias), Christian Karembeu, Ieroklis Stoltidis, Predrag Djordjevic, Nery Alberto CASTILLO (74 Alexandros Tatsis), GIOVANNI Silva de Oliveira (66 Georgios Georgiadis). Trainer: Oleg Protasov

JUVENTUS: Gianluigi Buffon, Lilian Thuram, Nicola Legrottaglie, Paolo MONTERO IGLESIAS, Gianluca Zambrotta, Stephen Appiah, Edgar Davids, Alessio Tacchinardi, Pavel Nedved (89 Alessandro Birindelli), David Trezeguet, Marco Di Vaio (56 Fabrizio Miccoli).
Trainer: Marcello Lippi

Goals: Stoltidis (11), Nedved (21, 79)

GALATASARAY SK ISTANBUL v OLYMPIAKOS PEIRAIAS 1-0 (1-0)

Atatürk Olimpiyat, Istanbul 21.10.2003

Referee: Urs Meier (SWI) Attendance: 41,125

GALATASARAY: Aly Faryd Camilo Mondragon, CÉSAR Luís PRATES (69 Hakan Ünsal), Bülent Korkmaz, Frank De Boer, Sabri Sarioglu (90+1 Suat Usta), JOÃO Casemir BATISTA Marqués, Ayhan Akman, Cihan Haspolatli, Ergün Penbe, Arif Erdem (76 Ovidiu Petre), Hakan Şükür. Trainer: Fatih Terim

OLYMPIAKOS: Jurai Bucek, Anastasios Pantos, Paraskevas Antzas, Georgios Anatolakis, Stylianos Venetidis, Dimitrios Mavrogenidis (85 Alexandros Tatsis), Christian Karembeu, Ieroklis Stoltidis (62 Pantelis Kafes), Predrag Djordjevic, Nery Alberto Castillo (77 Georgios Georgiadis), GIOVANNI Silva de Oliveira. Trainer: Oleg Protasov

Goal: Cihan (9)

JUVENTUS FC TORINO v REAL SOCIEDAD DE FÚTBAL SAN SEBASTIÁN 4-2 (3-0)

Delle Alpi, Torino 21.10.2003

Referee: Graham Poll (ENG) Attendance: 17,246

JUVENTUS: Gianluigi Buffon, Lilian Thuram, Igor Tudor (75 Paolo MONTERO IGLESIAS), Mark Iuliano, Gianluca Zambrotta, Stephen Appiah, Mauro German Camoranesi (66 Edgar Davids), Alessio Tacchinardi, Pavel Nedved, David Trezeguet, Marco Di Vaio (84 Alessandro Birindelli). Trainer: Marcello Lippi

REAL SOCIEDAD: Sander WESTERVELD, Lionel PORTILLON, Igor JAUREGUI Iraola, Gabriel Francisco SCHÜRRER Peralta, Agustin ARANZÁBAL Alkorta, Valery KARPIN, Igor GABILONDO del Campo, Bittor ALKIZA Fernández, Xabier ALONSO Olano (81 Mikel ARANBURU Eizaguirre), LEE CHUN Soo (66 Francisco Javier DE PEDRO Falque), Darko KOVACEVIC (74 NIHAT Kahveci). Trainer: Raynald Denoueix

Goals: Trezeguet (3, 63), Di Vaio (7, 45+1), Tudor (67 og), de Pedro (80)

REAL SOCIEDAD DE FÚTBAL SAN SEBASTIAN v JUVENTUS FC TORINO 0-0

Anoeta, San Sebastian 5.11.2003

Referee: Stéphane Bré (FRA) Attendance: 29,500

REAL SOCIEDAD: Sander WESTERVELD, Aitor LÓPEZ REKARTE, Igor JAUREGUI Iraola, Gabriel Francisco SCHÜRRER Peralta, Agustin ARANZÁBAL Alkorta, Valery KARPIN, Francisco Javier DE PEDRO Falque (75 LEE CHUN Soo), Bittor ALKIZA Fernández, Xabier ALONSO Olano, NIHAT Kahveci, Darko KOVACEVIC.
Trainer: Raynald Denoueix

JUVENTUS: Gianluigi Buffon, Ciro Ferrara, Igor Tudor, Mark Iuliano, Alessandro Birindelli, Edgar Davids, Antonio Conte (82 Alessio Tacchinardi), Gianluca Pessotto (69 Stephen Appiah), Pavel Nedved, Fabrizio Miccoli, Marco Di Vaio (76 Marcelo Danubio Zalayeta). Trainer: Marcello Lippi

OLYMPIAKOS PEIRAIAS v GALATASARAY SK ISTANBUL 3-0 (2-0)

Giorgos Kamaras, Athina 5.11.2003

Referee: L'uboš Michel (SVK) Attendance: 12,145

OLYMPIAKOS: Theofanis Katergiannakis, Georgios Georgiadis (89 Andreas Niniadis), Paraskevas Antzas, Georgios Anatolakis, Stylianos Venetidis, Dimitrios Mavrogenidis (90+1 Athanasios Kostoulas), Christian Karembeu, Ieroklis Stoltidis, Predrag Djordjevic, Nery Alberto Castillo (65 Pantelis Kafes), GIOVANNI Silva de Oliveira.

GALATASARAY: Aly Faryd Camilo Mondragon, CÉSAR Luís PRATES (81 Sabri Sarioglu), Bülent Korkmaz, Frank De Boer, Orhan Ak, Ovidiu Petre, Ayhan Akman, Cihan Haspolatli (40 Elvir Baljic), Ergün Penbe (66 Mabula Lukunku), Hasan Gökhan Sas, Hakan Sükür. Trainer: Fatih Terim

Sent off: Djordjević (90+4) and Ayhan Akman (88)

Goals: Mavrogenidis (6), Castillo (34), Giovanni (90+6).

OLYMPIAKOS PEIRAIAS v REAL SOCIEDAD DE FÚTBAL SAN SEBASTIÁN 2-2 (0-1)

Giorgos Kamaras, Athina 25.11.2003

Referee: Alain Hamer (LUX) Attendance: 13,948

OLYMPIAKOS: Theofanis Katergiannakis, Georgios Georgiadis, Paraskevas Antzas (46 Pantelis Kafes), Georgios Anatolakis, Stylianos Venetidis (86 Alexandros Tatsis), Dimitrios Mavrogenidis (57 Andreas Niniadis), Christian Karembeu, Ieroklis Stoltidis, Anastasios Pantos, Nery Alberto Castillo, GIOVANNI Silva de Oliveira. Trainer: Oleg Protasov

REAL SOCIEDAD: Sander WESTERVELD, Aitor LÓPEZ REKARTE, Igor JAUREGUI Iraola, Gabriel Francisco SCHÜRRER Peralta, Agustin ARANZÁBAL Alkorta, Valeryi KARPIN (82 Mikel ARANBURU Eizaguirre), Igor GABILONDO del Campo, Bittor ALKIZA Fernández, Xabier ALONSO Olano (89 Sergio BORIS González Monteagudo), NIHAT Kahveci (76 LEE CHUN Soo), Darko KOVACEVIC. Trainer: Raynald Denoueix

Sent off: Kovacevic (68)

Goals: Gabilondo (31), Stoltidis (59), Castillo (71), Schürrer (74)

GALATASARAY SK ISTANBUL v JUVENTUS FC TORINO 2-0 (0-0)

Westfalenstadion, Dortmund (GER) 2.12.2003

Referee: Kim Milton Nielsen (DEN) Attendance: 44,045

GALATASARAY: Aly Faryd Camilo Mondragon, CÉSAR Luís PRATES (45 Hasan Gökhan Şaş), Frank De Boer (84 Bülent Korkmaz), Orhan Ak, Ovidiu Petre, Berkant Göktan, Gabriel Sebastian Tamaş, Sabri Sarioglu, Ergün Penbe, Hakan Ünsal, Hakan Sükür (90+7 Cihan Haspolatli). Trainer: Fatih Terim

JUVENTUS: Antonio Chimenti, Ciro Ferrara, Igor Tudor, Mark Iuliano (75 Stephen Appiah), Gianluca Pessotto, Edgar Davids, Antonio Conte (86 Mauro German Camoranesi), Enzo Maresca, Marcelo Danubio Zalayeta, Fabrizio Miccoli, Marco Di Vaio. Trainer: Marcello Lippi

Goals: Hakan Şükür (47, 90+4)

JUVENTUS FC TORINO
v OLYMPIAKOS PEIRAIAS 7-0 (4-0)

Delle Alpi, Torino 10.12.2003

Referee: Konrad Plautz (AUS) Attendance: 12,578

JUVENTUS: Antonio Chimenti, Paolo MONTERO IGLESIAS, Igor Tudor, Mark Iuliano (84 Gianluca Zambrotta), Gianluca Pessotto, Alessandro Birindelli, Antonio Conte, Enzo Maresca, Marcelo Danubio Zalayeta, Fabrizio Miccoli (66 Alessandro Del Piero), David Trezeguet (58 Marco Di Vaio). Trainer: Marcello Lippi

OLYMPIAKOS: Dimitrios Eleftheropoulos, Athanasios Kostoulas, Dimitrios Mavrogenidis, Georgios Anatolakis (68 Georgios Georgiadis), Stylianos Venetidis, Christian Karembeu, Pantelis Kafes (61 Panagiotis Gonias), Anastasios Pantos, GIOVANNI Silva de Oliveira (77 Andreas Niniadis), Predrag Djordjevic, Nery Alberto Castillo. Trainer: Oleg Protasov

Goals: Trezeguet (14, 25), Miccoli (19), Maresca (28), Di Vaio (62), Del Piero (67), Zalayeta (79)

REAL SOCIEDAD DE FÚTBAL SAN SEBASTIAN
v GALATASARAY SK ISTANBUL 1-1 (0-1)

Anoeta, San Sebastian 10.12.2003

Referee: Terje Hauge (NOR) Attendance: 29,000

REAL SOCIEDAD: ALBERTO López Fernández, Bjorn Töre KVARME, Aitor LÓPEZ REKARTE, Gabriel Francisco SCHÜRRER Peralta, Agustin ARANZÁBAL Alkorta, Valeryi KARPIN, Igor GABILONDO del Campo, Bittor ALKIZA Fernández (87 Sergio BORIS González Monteagudo), Xabier ALONSO Olano, NIHAT Kahveci (90 Igor JAUREGUI Iraola), Óscar DE PAULA Gamero (72 Mikel ARANBURU Eizaguirre). Trainer: Raynald Denoueix

GALATASARAY: Aly Faryd Camilo Mondragon, Bülent Korkmaz, Frank De Boer (86 Ümit Karan), Gabriel Sebastian Tamas, Ovidiu Petre, Berkant Göktan, Sabri Sarioglu, Ergün Penbe, Hakan Ünsal (76 Cihan Haspolatli), Hakan Sükür, Hasan Gökhan Sas (66 Arif Erdem). Trainer: Fatih Terim

Goals: Hakan Şükür (27), De Paula (51)

	P	W	D	L	F	A	Pts
Juventus FC Torino	6	4	1	1	15	6	13
Real Sociedad	6	2	3	1	8	8	9
Galatasaray Istanbul	6	2	1	3	6	8	7
Olympiakos Peiraias	6	1	1	4	6	13	4

GROUP E

MANCHESTER UNITED FC
v PANATHINAIKOS FC ATHINA 5-0 (4-0)

Old Trafford, Manchester 16.09.2003

Referee: Alain Sars (FRA) Attendance: 66,520

MANCHESTER UNITED: Tim Howard, Gary Neville, Rio Ferdinand, John O'Shea (58 Darren Fletcher), Mikaël Silvestre, Phil Neville, Nicky Butt (58 Eric Djemba-Djemba), Quinton Fortune, Ryan Giggs, Ole Gunnar Solskjær (45 David Bellion), Ruud Van Nistelrooy. Trainer: Alex Ferguson

PANATHINAIKOS: Antonis Nikopolidis (46 Konstantinos Halkias), Yourkas Seitaridis, René Henriksen, Sotiris Kyrgiakos, Panagiotis Fyssas, Raimondas Zutautas, Silvio Maric, Giannis Goumas (46 Joël Dieudonne Epallé), Lucian Iulian Sanmartean, Dimitrios Papadopoulos (62 Emmanuel Olisadebe), Mihalis Konstantinou. Trainer: Itzhak Shum

Goals: Silvestre (13), Fortune (14), Solskjær (33), Butt (40), Djemba-Djemba (83)

GLASGOW RANGERS FC
v VfB STUTTGART 2-1 (0-1)

Ibrox, Glasgow 16.09.2003

Referee: Gilles Veissièrre (FRA) Attendance: 47,957

RANGERS: Stefan Klos, Henning Berg, Zurab Khizanishvili, Michael Ball, Christian Nerlinger, Fernando Ricksen (34 Maurice Ross), EMERSON Moisés Costa (66 Nuno Fernando Gonçalves da Rocha "CAPUCHO"), Paolo Vanoli (46 Peter Løvenkrands), Mikel ARTETA Amatriain, Michael Mols, Shota Arveladze. Trainer: Alexander McLeish

VfB: Timo Hildebrand, Andreas Hinkel, FERNANDO José da Silva Freitas MEIRA, Marcelo José Bordon, Heiko Gerber (81 Imre Szabics), Zvonimir Soldo, Christian Tiffert, Aleksandr Hleb, Horst Heldt (70 Silvio Meissner), Kevin Kuranyi, Jeronimo Barreto "CACAU" (46 Giannis Amanatidis). Trainer: Felix Magath

Goals: Kuranyi (45+34), Nerlinger (74), Løvenkrands (79)

PANATHINAIKOS FC ATHINA
v GLASGOW RANGERS FC 1-1 (0-1)

Apostolos Nikolaidis, Athina 1.10.2003

Referee: Arturo DAUDEN IBAÑEZ (SPA) Att: 13,718

PANATHINAIKOS: Konstantinos Halkias, Yourkas Seitaridis, Nasief Magammat Morris, Sotiris Kyrgiakos (46 Giannis Goumas), Panagiotis Fyssas, Jan Michaelsen, Raimondas Zutautas, Joël Dieudonne Epallé (79 Pantelis Konstantinidis), Silvio Maric, Mihalis Konstantinou, Goran Vlaovic (64 Dimitrios Papadopoulos). Trainer: Itzhak Shum

RANGERS: Stefan Klos, Zurab Khizanishvili, Craig Moore, Henning Berg, Michael Ball, Nuno Fernando Gonçalves da Rocha "CAPUCHO", EMERSON Moisés Costa, Mikel ARTETA Amatriain, Peter Løvenkrands (77 Paolo Vanoli), Shota Arveladze (85 Christian Nerlinger), Michael Mols.

Sent off: Goumas (57)

Goals: Emerson (35), Konstantinidis (88)

VfB STUTTGART
v MANCHESTER UNITED FC 2-1 (0-0)

Gottlieb-Daimler, Stuttgart 1.10.2003

Referee: Cosimo Bolognino (ITA) Attendance: 48,684

VfB: Timo Hildebrand, Andreas Hinkel, FERNANDO José da Silva Freitas MEIRA, Marcelo José Bordon, Philipp Lahm (71 Heiko Gerber), Zvonimir Soldo, Jurica Vranjes (73 Christian Tiffert), Aleksandr Hleb (87 Silvio Meissner), Horst Heldt, Kevin Kuranyi, Imre Szabics. Trainer: Felix Magath

MANCHESTER UNITED: Tim Howard, Gary Neville, Rio Ferdinand (82 Diego FORLÁN Corazo), Mikaël Silvestre, John O'Shea (65 Quinton Fortune), Roy Keane, Paul Scholes, Phil Neville, Ryan Giggs, CRISTIANO RONALDO Santos Aveiro (90+2 Darren Fletcher), Ruud Van Nistelrooy. Trainer: Alexander Chapman Ferguson

Goals: Szabics (50), Kuranyi (52), Van Nistelrooy (67 pen)

MANCHESTER UNITED FC
v GLASGOW RANGERS FC 3-0 (2-0)

Old Trafford, Manchester 4.11.2003

Referee: Pierluigi Collina (ITA) Attendance: 66,707

MANCHESTER UNITED: Tim Howard, Gary Neville, Rio Ferdinand, Mikaël Silvestre, Quinton Fortune, CRISTIANO RONALDO Santos Aveiro, Roy Keane, Phil Neville, Ryan Giggs (67 David Bellion), Diego FORLÁN Corazo (67 José KLÉBERSON Pereira), Ruud Van Nistelrooy (77 Darren Fletcher). Trainer: Alexander Chapman Ferguson

RANGERS: Stefan Klos, Zurab Khizanishvili, Henning Berg, Craig Moore (68 Maurice Ross), Michael Ball, Peter Løvenkrands, Mikel ARTETA Amatriain, Stephen Hughes, Paolo Vanoli (82 Chris Burke), Shota Arveladze, Michael Mols (57 Nuno Fernando Gonçalves da Rocha "CAPUCHO"). Trainer: Alexander McLeish

Goals: Forlán (6), Van Nistelrooy (44, 60)

GLASGOW RANGERS FC
v MANCHESTER UNITED FC 0-1 (0-1)

Ibrox, Glasgow 22.10.2003

Referee: Anders Frisk (SWE) Attendance: 48,730

RANGERS: Stefan Klos, Zurab Khizanishvili (86 Maurice Ross), Craig Moore, Henning Berg, Michael Ball, Fernando Ricksen, Mikel ARTETA Amatriain, Paolo Vanoli (67 Christian Nerlinger), Peter Løvenkrands, Shota Arveladze, Michael Mols. Trainer: Alexander McLeish

MANCHESTER UNITED: Tim Howard, Gary Neville, Rio Ferdinand, Mikaël Silvestre, John O'Shea, Roy Keane, Paul Scholes, Phil Neville (86 Nicky Butt), Quinton Fortune (90+4 Eric Djemba-Djemba), Ryan Giggs, Ruud Van Nistelrooy. Trainer: Alexander Chapman Ferguson

Goal: P. Neville (5)

PANATHINAIKOS FC ATHINA
v VfB STUTTGART 1-3 (0-0)

Apostolos Nikolaidis, Athina 4.11.2003

Referee: Massimo De Santis (ITA) Attendance: 6,018

PANATHINAIKOS: Antonis Nikopolidis, Giannis Goumas, René Henriksen, Yourkas Seitaridis, Panagiotis Fyssas, Raimondas Zutautas, Angelos Basinas, Jan Michaelsen (72 Lucian Iulian Sanmartean), Silvio Maric (79 Pantelis Konstantinidis), Michalis Konstantinou, Dimitrios Papadopoulos. Trainer: Itzhak Shum

VfB: Timo Hildebrand, Andreas Hinkel, FERNANDO José da Silva Freitas MEIRA, Timo Wenzel, Philipp Lahm, Zvonimir Soldo, Jurica Vranjes (46 Horst Heldt), Christian Tiffert, Giannis Amanatidis (46 Aleksandr Hleb), Kevin Kuranyi, Imre Szabics (79 Silvio Meissner). Trainer: Felix Magath

Goals: Konstantinou (60), Fyssas (67 Og), Kuranyi (75), Hinkel (77)

VfB STUTTGART
v PANATHINAIKOS FC ATHINA 2-0 (2-0)

Gottlieb-Daimler, Stuttgart 22.10.2003

Referee: Paul Allaerts (BEL) Attendance: 48,645

VfB: Timo Hildebrand, Andreas Hinkel, FERNANDO José da Silva Freitas MEIRA, Marcelo José Bordon, Philipp Lahm, Zvonimir Soldo, Jurica Vranjes (77 Silvio Meissner), Aleksandr Hleb, Horst Heldt (62 Christian Tiffert), Imre Szabics (84 Giannis Amanatidis), Kevin Kuranyi. Trainer: Felix Magath

PANATHINAIKOS: Antonis Nikopolidis, Yourkas Seitaridis, René Henriksen, Nasief Magammat Morris, Jan Michaelsen, Raimondas Zutautas, Panagiotis Fyssas, Angelos Basinas, Markus Münch (69 Pantelis Konstantinidis), Silvio Maric, Dimitrios Papadopoulos (46 Michalis Konstantinou). Trainer: Itzhak Shum

Goals: Szabics (13), Soldo (25)

PANATHINAIKOS FC ATHINA
v MANCHESTER UNITED FC 0-1 (0-0)

Apostolos Nikolaidis, Athina 26.11.2003

Referee: Jan W. Wegereef (HOL) Attendance: 6,890

PANATHINAIKOS: Antonis Nikopolidis, Giannis Goumas, René Henriksen, Yourkas Seitaridis, Markus Münch, Raimondas Zutautas, Angelos Basinas, Lucian Iulian Sanmartean (46 Joël Dieudonne Epallé), Silvio Maric, Michalis Konstantinou (75 Goran Vlaovic), Dimitrios Papadopoulos (83 Miltiadis Sapanis). Trainer: Itzhak Shum

MANCHESTER UNITED: Tim Howard, John O'Shea, Rio Ferdinand, Mikaël Silvestre, Quinton Fortune, CRISTIANO RONALDO Santos Aveiro, Nicky Butt, José KLÉBERSON Pereira, Ryan Giggs, Darren Fletcher (75 David Bellion), Diego FORLÁN Corazo. Trainer: Alexander Chapman Ferguson

Goal: Forlán (85)

VfB STUTTGART v GLASGOW RANGERS FC 1-0 (1-0)

Gottlieb-Daimler, Stuttgart 26.11.2003

Referee: Manuel Enrique MEJUTO GONZÁLEZ (SPA)
Attendance: 48,348

VfB: Timo Hildebrand, Andreas Hinkel, FERNANDO José da Silva Freitas MEIRA, Timo Wenzel, Philipp Lahm, Zvonimir Soldo, Silvio Meissner, Horst Heldt (49 Christian Tiffert), Aleksandr Hleb (72 Emanuel Adrián Centurión), Kevin Kuranyi, Imre Szabics (89 Serge Branco).
Trainer: Felix Magath

RANGERS: Stefan Klos, Maurice Ross (70 Egil John Østenstad), Henning Berg, Zurab Khizanishvili, Michael Ball, Fernando Ricksen, Stephen Hughes, Nuno Fernando Gonçalves da Rocha "CAPUCHO", Paolo Vanoli (54 Michael Mols), Shota Arveladze, Peter Løvenkrands (80 Chris Burke).
Trainer: Alexander McLeish

Goal: Wenzel (45+2)

MANCHESTER UNITED FC v VfB STUTTGART 2-0 (1-0)

Old Trafford, Manchester 9.12.2003

Referee: Eric Poulat (FRA) Attendance: 67,141

MANCHESTER UNITED: Roy Carroll, Gary Neville, Rio Ferdinand, Mikaël Silvestre, John O'Shea, Darren Fletcher, Philip Neville, Paul Scholes (79 Eric Djemba-Djemba), Quinton Fortune, Ryan Giggs (71 David Bellion), Ruud Van Nistelrooy (71 Diego FORLÁN Corazo).
Trainer: Alexander Chapman Ferguson

VfB: Timo Hildebrand, Andreas Hinkel, FERNANDO José da Silva Freitas MEIRA, Timo Wenzel, Philipp Lahm, Zvonimir Soldo, Jurica Vranjes (46 Christian Tiffert), Aleksandr Hleb (76 Emanuel Adrián Centurión), Horst Heldt, Kevin Kuranyi, Imre Szabics (46 Jeronimo Barreto "CACAU").
Trainer: Felix Magath

Goals: Van Nistelrooy (45+2), Giggs (58)

GLASGOW RANGERS FC v PANATHINAIKOS FC ATHINA 1-3 (1-1)

Ibrox, Glasgow 9.12.2003

Referee: Herbert Fandel (GER) Attendance: 48,588

RANGERS: Stefan Klos, Maurice Ross (84 Darryl Duffy), Henning Berg, Zurab Khizanishvili (66 Paolo Vanoli), Michael Ball, Fernando Ricksen, Stephen Hughes, Nuno Fernando Gonçalves da Rocha "CAPUCHO", Chris Burke (70 Egil John Østenstad), Michael Mols, Peter Løvenkrands.
Trainer: Alexander McLeish

PANATHINAIKOS: Antonis Nikopolidis, Giannis Goumas, René Henriksen, Yourkas Seitaridis, Nasief Magammat Morris, Raimondas Zutautas, Angelos Basinas, Lucian Iulian Sanmartean (46 Joël Dieudonne Epallé), Markus Münch, Michalis Konstantinou, Miltiadis Sapanis (78 Goran Vlaovic).
Trainer: Itzhak Shum

Goals: Mols (28), Zutautas (32), Basinas (62), Konstantinou (80)

	P	W	D	L	F	A	Pts
Manchester United FC	6	5	0	1	13	2	15
VfB Stuttgart	6	4	0	2	9	6	12
Panathinaikos FC	6	1	1	4	5	13	4
Glasgow Rangers FC	6	1	1	4	4	10	4

GROUP F

FK PARTIZAN BEOGRAD v FC PORTO 1-1 (0-1)

FK Partizan, Beograd 16.09.2003

Referee: Michal Benes (CZE) Attendance: 29,968

FK PARTIZAN: Radovan Radakovic, Nenad Djordjevic, Milan Stojanoski (46 Branko Savic), Taribo West, Milivoje Cirkovic (46 Ljubinko Drulovic), Albert Nadj, Igor Duljaj, Tomasz Rzasa, Saša Ilic, Ivica Iliev (84 Bojan Brnovic), Andrija Delibasic. Trainer: Lothar Matthäus

FC PORTO: VÍTOR Manuel Martins BAÍA, PAULO Renato Rebocho FERREIRA, JORGE Paulo COSTA Almeida, RICARDO Alberto Silveira CARVALHO, NUNO Jorge Pereira Silva VALENTE, Francisco José da Costa "COSTINHA", PEDRO Miguel da Silva MENDES, Nuno Ricardo Oliveira Ribeiro "MANICHE" (79 José BOSINGWA da Silva), Anderson Luis de Souza "DECO" (89 RICARDO Ribeiro FERNANDES), Benni McCARTHY (70 Edgaras JANKAUSKAS), Vanderlei F. da Silva "DERLEI".
Trainer: José Mário DOS SANTOS MOURINHO FÉLIX

Goals: Costinha (22), Delibasic (54)

REAL MADRID CF v OLYMPIQUE de MARSEILLE 4-2 (2-1)

Santiago Bernabéu, Madrid 16.09.2003

Referee: Wolfgang Stark (GER) Attendance: 60,433

REAL MADRID: Iker CASILLAS Fernández, Miguel Angel «MICHEL» SALGADO Fernández, Francisco PAVON Barahona, RAÚL BRAVO Sanfélix, ROBERTO CARLOS da Silva, Luis Filipe Madeira Caeiro «FIGO», David BECKHAM, Esteban Matías CAMBIASSO Deleau (73 José María Gutiérrez Hernández «GUTI»), RAÚL González Blanco, Zinedine ZIDANE (86 Santiago Hernán SOLARI), RONALDO Luis Nazario da Lima (86 Javier García PORTILLO).
Trainer: Carlos Manuel BRITO LEAL DE QUEIROZ

OLYMPIQUE: Vedran Runje, Daniel Van Buyten, Johnny Ecker, Abdoulaye Méïté, Habib Bèye, Brahim Hemdani (62 Stepan Vachousek), Camel Meriem, Fabio Celestini, Steve Marlet (38 Pascal Johansen), Ahmed Hossam «MIDO», Tébily-Didier Drogba (66 Sylvain NDiaye). Trainer: Alain Perrin

Goals: Drogba (26), Roberto Carlos (29), Ronaldo (34, 57), Figo (61 pen), Van Buyten (83)

OLYMPIQUE de MARSEILLE v FK PARTIZAN BEOGRAD 3-0 (0-0)

Vélodrome, Marseille 1.10.2003

Referee: Domenico Messina (ITA) Attendance: 56,825

OLYMPIQUE: Vedran Runje, Daniel Van Buyten, Johnny Ecker, Abdoulaye Méïté, Sébastien Pérez, Stepan Vachousek, Camel Meriem (73 Brahim Hemdani), Fabio Celestini, Steve Marlet (61 Lucio da Costa FERNANDÃO), Ahmed Hossam «MIDO» (77 Dmitri Sychev), Tébily-Didier Drogba.
Trainer: Alain Perrin

FK PARTIZAN: Radovan Radakovic, Nenad Djordjevic, Milan Stojanoski, Taribo West, Nikola Malbasa, Milivoje Cirkovic (87 Branko Savic), Albert Nadj, Igor Duljaj, Saša Ilic (81 Ljubinko Drulovic), Ivica Iliev (81 Bojan Brnovic), Andrija Delibasic. Trainer: Lothar Matthäus

Sent off: Delibasic (45+1)

Goals: Drogba (62, 68, 85)

FC PORTO v REAL MADRID CF 1-3 (1-2)

Das Antas, Porto 1.10.2003

Referee: Pierluigi Collina (ITA) Attendance: 37,506

FC PORTO: VÍTOR Manuel Martins BAÍA, PAULO Renato Rebocho FERREIRA, PEDRO EMANUEL dos Santos Martins da Silva (70 Edgaras JANKAUSKAS), RICARDO Alberto Silveira CARVALHO, NUNO Jorge Pereira Silva VALENTE, Francisco José da Costa "COSTINHA", PEDRO Miguel da Silva MENDES (46 Benni McCARTHY), Nuno Ricardo Oliveira Ribeiro "MANICHE", Anderson Luis de Souza "DECO", RICARDO Ribeiro FERNANDES (46 José BOSINGWA da Silva), Vanderlei F. da Silva "DERLEI".
Trainer: José Mário DOS SANTOS MOURINHO FÉLIX

REAL MADRID: Iker CASILLAS Fernández, Miguel Angel "MICHEL" SALGADO Fernández, Francisco PAVON Barahona, RAÚL BRAVO Sanfélix, ROBERTO CARLOS da Silva, Iván HELGUERA Bujía, José María Gutiérrez Hernández "GUTI", Luis Filipe Madeira Caeiro "FIGO", Zinedine ZIDANE, Santiago Hernán SOLARI (90+2 Esteban Matías CAMBIASSO Deleau), RONALDO Luis Nazario da Lima (83 RAÚL González Blanco).
Trainer: Carlos Manuel BRITO LEAL DE QUEIROZ

Goals: Costinha (7), Helguera (28), Solari (37), Zidane (67)

OLYMPIQUE de MARSEILLE v FC PORTO 2-3 (1-2)

Vélodrome, Marseille 22.10.2003

Referee: Kyros Vassaras (GRE) Attendance: 55,209

OLYMPIQUE: Vedran Runje, Daniel Van Buyten, Johnny Ecker, Abdoulaye Méïté, Sébastien Pérez (66 Dmitri Sychev), Brahim Hemdani, Camel Meriem, Fabio Celestini, Steve Marlet, Ahmed Hossam «MIDO» (67 Stepan Vachousek), Tébily-Didier Drogba. Trainer: Alain Perrin

FC PORTO: VÍTOR Manuel Martins BAÍA, PAULO Renato Rebocho FERREIRA (73 Dimitri ALENICHEV), JORGE Paulo COSTA Almeida, RICARDO Alberto Silveira CARVALHO, NUNO Jorge Pereira Silva VALENTE, Francisco José da Costa «COSTINHA», Nuno Ricardo Oliveira Ribeiro «MANICHE», Anderson Luis de Souza «DECO», MARCO Júlio Castanheiro Alfonso Alves FERREIRA, Paulo CÉSAR Silva PEIXOTO (65 José BOSINGWA da Silva), Vanderlei F. da Silva «DERLEI» (88 Edgaras JANKAUSKAS).
Trainer: José Mário DOS SANTOS MOURINHO FÉLIX

Goals: Drogba (24), Maniche (31), Derlei (35), Alenichev (81), Marlet (84)

REAL MADRID CF v FK PARTIZAN BEOGRAD 1-0 (1-0)

Santiago Bernabéu, Madrid 22.10.2003

Referee: Massimo Busacca (SWI) Attendance: 63,711

REAL MADRID: Iker CASILLAS Fernández, Miguel Angel "MICHEL" SALGADO Fernández, Francisco PAVON Barahona (46 José María Gutiérrez Hernández "GUTI"), RAÚL BRAVO Sanfélix, ROBERTO CARLOS da Silva, David BECKHAM, Iván HELGUERA Bujía, Luis Filipe Madeira Caeiro "FIGO", Zinedine ZIDANE (79 Santiago Hernán SOLARI), RAÚL González Blanco, RONALDO Luis Nazario da Lima (79 Javier García PORTILLO).
Trainer: Carlos Manuel BRITO LEAL DE QUEIROZ

FK PARTIZAN: Djordje Pantic, Nenad Djordjevic (90 Bojan Brnovic), Dejan Ognjanovic, Tomasz Rzasa (46 Milan Stojanoski), Nikola Malbasa, Branko Savic, Albert Nadj (90+2 Damir Cakar), Igor Duljaj, Ljubinko Drulovic, Saša Ilic, Ivica Iliev. Trainer: Lothar Matthäus

Goal: Raúl (38)

FK PARTIZAN BEOGRAD v REAL MADRID CF 0-0

FK Partizan, Beograd 4.11.2003

Referee: Cosimo Bolognino (ITA) Attendance: 29,355

FK PARTIZAN: Djordje Pantic, Nenad Djordjevic, Branimir Bajic, Taribo West, Branko Savic, Albert Nadj (67 Ljubinko Drulovic), Nikola Malbasa (19 Tomasz Rzasa), Igor Duljaj, Saša Ilic, Andrija Delibasic (46 Milan Stojanoski), Ivica Iliev.
Trainer: Lothar Matthäus

REAL MADRID: Iker CASILLAS Fernández, Miguel Angel "MICHEL" SALGADO Fernández, Francisco PAVON Barahona, RAÚL BRAVO Sanfélix, ROBERTO CARLOS da Silva (12 José María Gutiérrez Hernández "GUTI"), Luis Filipe Madeira Caeiro "FIGO", David BECKHAM, Iván HELGUERA Bujía, Zinedine ZIDANE, RAÚL González Blanco, RONALDO Luis Nazario da Lima.
Trainer: Carlos Manuel BRITO LEAL DE QUEIROZ

FC PORTO v OLYMPIQUE de MARSEILLE 1-0 (1-0)

Das Antas, Porto 4.11.2003

Referee: Graham Poll (ENG) Attendance: 33,215

FC PORTO: VÍTOR Manuel Martins BAÍA, PAULO Renato Rebocho FERREIRA, JORGE Paulo COSTA Almeida, RICARDO Alberto Silveira CARVALHO, NUNO Jorge Pereira Silva VALENTE (61 RICARDO Miguel Moreira COSTA), Dimitri ALENICHEV, Francisco José da Costa «COSTINHA», Nuno Ricardo Oliveira Ribeiro «MANICHE», José BOSINGWA da Silva (82 PEDRO Miguel da Silva MENDES), Benni McCARTHY (62 MARCO Júlio Castanheiro Alfonso Alves FERREIRA), Vanderlei F. da Silva «DERLEI».
Trainer: José Mário DOS SANTOS MOURINHO FÉLIX

OLYMPIQUE: Vedran Runje, Abdoulaye Méïté, Daniel Van Buyten, Philippe Christanval, Johnny Ecker, Sébastien Pérez (53 Ahmed Hossam «MIDO»), Camel Meriem, Brahim Hemdani, Stepan Vachousek (79 Pascal Johansen), Steve Marlet (80 Dmitri Sychev), Tébily-Didier Drogba.
Trainer: Alain Perrin

Goal: McCarthy (21)

OLYMPIQUE de MARSEILLE v REAL MADRID CF 1-2 (0-1)

Vélodrome, Marseille 26.11.2003

Referee: Anders Frisk (SWE) Attendance: 54,745

OLYMPIQUE: Vedran Runje, Abdoulaye Méïté, Daniel Van Buyten, Philippe Christanval, Johnny Ecker, Fabio Celestini, Camel Meriem, Brahim Hemdani, Stepan Vachousek (72 Dmitri Sychev), Ahmed Hossam «MIDO» (82 Lucio da Costa FERNANDÃO), Tébily-Didier Drogba. Trainer: Alain Perrin

REAL MADRID: Iker CASILLAS Fernández, Miguel Angel «MICHEL» SALGADO Fernández, Iván HELGUERA Bujía, RAÚL BRAVO Sanfélix, ROBERTO CARLOS da Silva (82 Santiago Hernán SOLARI), Luis Filipe Madeira Caeiro «FIGO», David BECKHAM, Esteban Matías CAMBIASSO Deleau, Zinedine ZIDANE (87 José María Gutiérrez Hernández «GUTI»), RAÚL González Blanco, RONALDO Luis Nazario da Lima (90+4 RUBÉN González Rocha).
Trainer: Carlos Manuel BRITO LEAL DE QUEIROZ

Goals: Beckham (36), Mido (63), Ronaldo (74)

FC PORTO v FK PARTIZAN BEOGRAD 2-1 (1-0)

Das Antas, Porto 26.11.2003

Referee: Paul Allaerts (BEL) Attendance: 21,177

FC PORTO: VÍTOR Manuel Martins BAÍA, PAULO Renato Rebocho FERREIRA, JORGE Paulo COSTA Almeida, RICARDO Alberto Silveira CARVALHO, MÁRIO Fernando Magalhães da SILVA, Anderson Luis de Souza "DECO", Francisco José da Costa "COSTINHA", Nuno Ricardo Oliveira Ribeiro "MANICHE", José BOSINGWA da Silva (46 PEDRO Miguel da Silva MENDES), Benni McCARTHY (67 HUGO Miguel Pereira de ALMEIDA), Vanderlei F. da Silva "DERLEI" (80 Edgaras JANKAUSKAS). Trainer: José MOURINHO

FK PARTIZAN: Djordje Pantic, Nenad Djordjevic, Milivoje Cirkovic (38 Miroslav Radovic), Milan Stojanoski (78 Ljubinko Drulovic), Branko Savic, Vladimir Ivic, Nikola Malbasa, Igor Duljaj, Saša Ilic (58 Damir Cacak), Andrija Delibasic, Ivica Iliev. Trainer: Lothar Matthäus

Goals: McCarthy (25, 50), Delibasic (90+2)

FK PARTIZAN BEOGRAD v OLYMPIQUE de MARSEILLE 1-1 (0-0)

FC Partizan, Beograd 9.12.2003

Referee: Manuel Enrique MEJUTO GONZÁLEZ (SPA)
Attendance: 28,000

FK PARTIZAN: Djordje Pantic, Nikola Malbasa, Milivoje Cirkovic, Dejan Ognjanovic, Branko Savic, Saša Ilic (88 Dzenan Radoncic), Tomasz Rzasa (66 Ljubinko Drulovic), Vladimir Ivic, Igor Duljaj, Ivica Iliev (88 Damir Cacak), Andrija Delibasic. Trainer: Lothar Matthäus

OLYMPIQUE: Jérémy Gavanon, Philippe Christanval (16 Habib Beye), Johnny Ecker, Abdoulaye Méïté, Daniel Van Buyten, Sylvain Ndiaye, Brahim Hemdani, Pascal Johansen, Stepan Vachousek, Tébily-Didier Drogba, Ahmed Hossam «MIDO». Trainer: Alain Perrin

Goals: Mido (61), Delibasic (80)

REAL MADRID CF v FC PORTO 1-1 (1-1)

Santiago Bernabéu, Madrid 9.12.2003

Referee: Stephen Graham Bennett (ENG) Att: 25,000

REAL MADRID: CESAR Sánchez Dominguez, Miguel Angel "MICHEL" SALGADO Fernández, BORJA Fernández Fernández (89 JORDI López Felpeto), RAÚL BRAVO Sanfélix, ROBERTO CARLOS da Silva, Luis Filipe Madeira Caeiro "FIGO" (46 Oscar MIÑAMBRES Pascual), Santiago Hernán SOLARI, Esteban Matías CAMBIASSO Deleau, Zinedine ZIDANE, RONALDO Luis Nazario da Lima (46 Javier García PORTILLO), Francisco PAVÓN Barahona.
Trainer: Carlos Manuel BRITO LEAL DE QUEIROZ

FC PORTO: VÍTOR Manuel Martins BAÍA, PAULO Renato Rebocho FERREIRA, JORGE Paulo COSTA Almeida, PEDRO EMANUEL dos Santos Martins da Silva, RICARDO Alberto Silveira CARVALHO, PEDRO Miguel da Silva MENDES, Dimitri A.ALENICHEV (81 José BOSINGWA da Silva), Anderson Luis de Souza "DECO", Francisco José da Costa "COSTINHA", Edgaras JANKAUSKAS (73 HUGO Miguel Pereira de ALMEIDA), Vanderlei F. da Silva "DERLEI" (90+3 BRUNO Santos MORAES).
Trainer: José Mário DOS SANTOS MOURINHO FÉLIX

Goals: Solari (9), Derlei (35 pen)

	P	W	D	L	F	A	Pts
Real Madrid CF	6	4	2	0	11	5	14
FC Porto	6	3	2	1	9	8	11
Olympique de Marseille	6	1	1	4	9	11	4
FK Partizan Beograd	6	0	3	3	3	8	3

GROUP G

BEŞIKTAŞ JK ISTANBUL v SS LAZIO ROMA 0-2 (0-1)

Inönü, Istanbul 16.09.2003

Referee: Kim Milton Nielsen (DEN) Attendance: 20,787

BEŞIKTAŞ: Óscar Eduardo CORDOBA Arce, Tayfur Havutçu, Antonio Carlos Zago, Kaan Dobra, RONALDO Guiaro, Tümer Metin (56 Ahmed HASSAN Kamel), Federico Giunti (72 Sinan Kaloglu), Ahmet Yildirim, Ibrahim Üzülmez, Daniel Gabriel Pancu, Ilhan Mansiz (56 Sergen Yalçin). Trainer: Mircea Lucescu

LAZIO: Angelo Peruzzi, Massimo Oddo, Jaap Stam, FERNANDO Manuel Silva COUTO, Guiseppe Favalli, Stefano Fiore, Demetrio Albertini, Dejan Stankovic, SÉRGIO Paulo Marcenero CONCEIÇÃO (60 Giuliano Giannichedda), Bernardo Corradi (83 Fabio Liverani), Claudio Javier López (70 Roberto Muzzi). Trainer: Roberto Mancini

Goals: Stam (37), Fiore (77)

AC SPARTA PRAHA v CHELSEA FC LONDON 0-1 (0-0)

Toyota Arena, Praha 16.09.2003

Referee: Helmut Fleischer (GER) Attendance: 18,597

SPARTA: Jaromir Blazek, Martin Petras (46 Libor Sionko), Petr Johana, Tomáš Hübschman, Vladimir Labant (87 Patrik Jezek), Karel Poborský, Jirí Nemec, Radoslav Kovác, Rastivlav Michalik (56 Martin Zboncák), Igor Gluscevic, Tomáš Jun. Trainer: Jirí Kotrba

CHELSEA: Carlo Cudicini, Glen Johnson, Marcel Desailly, Wayne Bridge, William Gallas, Emmanuel Petit (46 Frank Lampard), GEREMI Sorele Fotso Ndjitap, Claude Makelele, Juan Sebastián Verón, Hernán Jorge Crespo (72 Jimmy Floyd Hasselbaink), Adrian Mutu (46 Damien Duff). Trainer: Claudio Ranieri

Goal: Gallas (85)

CHELSEA FC LONDON v BEŞIKTAŞ JK ISTANBUL 0-2 (0-2)

Stamford Bridge, London 1.10.2003

Referee: Lucilio CARDOSO CORTEZ BATISTA (POR) Attendance: 32,957

CHELSEA: Carlo Cudicini, John George Terry, Marcel Desailly, William Gallas, Celestine Babayaro (24 Wayne Bridge), Frank Lampard, GEREMI Sorele Fotso Ndjitap, Claude Makelele, Juan Sebastián Verón, Hernán Jorge Crespo (46 Jimmy Floyd Hasselbaink), Adrian Mutu (46 Damien Duff). Trainer: Claudio Ranieri

BEŞIKTAŞ: Óscar Eduardo CORDOBA Arce, Tayfur Havutçu, Antonio Carlos Zago, RONALDO Guiaro, Emre Asik, Okan Koç (58 Kaan Dobra), Federico Giunti (68 Yasin Sülün), Sergen Yalçin (82 Ahmed HASSAN Kamel), Ibrahim Üzülmez, Daniel Gabriel Pancu, Ilhan Mansiz.
Trainer: Mircea Lucescu **Sent off**: Ilhan Mansiz (50)

Goals: Sergen Yalçin (24, 29)

SS LAZIO ROMA v AC SPARTA PRAHA 2-2 (0-2)

Olimpico, Roma 1.10.2003

Referee: Claude Colombo (FRA) Attendance: 25,405

LAZIO: Angelo Peruzzi, Massimo Oddo, Jaap Stam, Sinisa Mihajlovic, Guiseppe Favalli, Stefano Fiore, Demetrio Albertini (46 Fabio Liverani), Dejan Stankovic, SÉRGIO Paulo Marcenero CONCEIÇÃO (61 Roberto Muzzi), Bernardo Corradi, Simone Inzaghi (82 Ousmane Dabo). Trainer: Roberto Mancini

SPARTA: Jaromir Blazek, Jan Flachbart, Petr Johana, Tomáš Hübschman, Vladimir Labant, Karel Poborský, Pavel Pergl, Radoslav Kovác, Lukáš Zelenka (90+2 Pavel Krmas), Marek Kincl (82 Igor Gluscevic), Libor Sionko (87 Rastivlav Michalik). Trainer: Jirí Kotrba

Goals: Sionko (27), Poborsky (36), Inzaghi (47, 61 pen)

CHELSEA FC LONDON v SS LAZIO ROMA 2-1 (0-1)

Stamford Bridge, London 22.10.2003

Referee: Terje Hauge (NOR) Attendance: 40,405

CHELSEA: Carlo Cudicini, John George Terry, Glen Johnson, William Gallas, Wayne Bridge, Frank Lampard, Claude Makelele, Juan Sebastián Verón (64 Jesper Grønkjær), Adrian Mutu (87 Joe Cole), Hernán Jorge Crespo, Damien Duff (78 GEREMI Sorele Fotso Ndjitap). Trainer: Claudio Ranieri

LAZIO: Angelo Peruzzi, Massimo Oddo, Jaap Stam, Sinisa Mihajlovic, Guiseppe Favalli, Luciano Zauri (75 Stefano Fiore), Demetrio Albertini, Dejan Stankovic (84 Fabio Liverani), SÉRGIO Paulo Marcenero CONCEIÇÃO, Bernardo Corradi, Simone Inzaghi (68 Roberto Muzzi). Trainer: Roberto Mancini

Goals: Inzaghi (38), Lampard (57), Mutu (65)

AC SPARTA PRAHA v BEŞIKTAŞ JK ISTANBUL 2-1 (0-0)

Toyota Arena, Praha 22.10.2003

Referee: Manuel Enrique MEJUTO GONZÁLEZ (SPA) Attendance: 14,512

SPARTA: Jaromir Blazek, Pavel Pergl, Tomáš Hübschman, Petr Johana, Vladimir Labant, Libor Sionko (88 Tomáš Jun), Lukáš Zelenka (90+1 Rastivlav Michalik), Jirí Nemec, Radoslav Kovác, Karel Poborský, Marek Kincl (86 Igor Gluscevic). Trainer: Jirí Kotrba

BEŞIKTAŞ: Óscar Eduardo CORDOBA Arce, Emre Asik, RONALDO Guiaro, Antonio Carlos Zago, Kaan Dobra, Tayfur Havutçu, Sergen Yalçin (81 Ahmed HASSAN Kamel), Federico Giunti, Ibrahim Üzülmez, Daniel Gabriel Pancu, Ahmet Dursun (65 Sinan Kaloglu). Trainer: Mircea Lucescu

Goals: Zelenka (58), Pancu (60 pen), Poborský (84)

SS LAZIO ROMA v CHELSEA FC LONDON 0-4 (0-1)

Olimpico, Roma 4.11.2003

Referee: Valentin Ivanov (RUS) Attendance: 48,485

LAZIO: Matteo Sereni, Luciano Zauri, FERNANDO Manuel Silva COUTO, Sinisa Mihajlovic, Guiseppe Favalli, Stefano Fiore (59 Paolo Negro), Demetrio Albertini (71 Roberto Muzzi), Fabio Liverani, Dejan Stankovic, Bernardo Corradi, Simone Inzaghi (71 Claudio Javier López). Trainer: Roberto Mancini

CHELSEA: Carlo Cudicini, Glen Johnson, John George Terry, William Gallas, Wayne Bridge, Claude Makelele, Frank Lampard, Damien Duff, Juan Sebastián Verón (77 Joe Cole), Hernán Jorge Crespo (67 Eidur Gudjohnsen), Adrian Mutu (57 Jesper Grønkjær). Trainer: Claudio Ranieri

Sent off: Mihajlovic (52) and Johnson (90)

Goals: Crespo (15), Gudjohnsen (70), Duff (75), Lampard (80)

BEŞIKTAŞ JK ISTANBUL v AC SPARTA PRAHA 1-0 (0-0)

Inönü, Istanbul 4.11.2003

Referee: Massimo Busacca (SWI) Attendance: 18,000

BEŞIKTAŞ: Óscar Eduardo CORDOBA Arce, Tayfur Havutçu, Antonio Carlos Zago, RONALDO Guiaro, Ahmet Yildirim, Kaan Dobra (62 Ahmed HASSAN Kamel), Federico Giunti, Sergen Yalçin (90+2 Ahmet Dursun), Ibrahim Üzülmez (72 Tümer Metin), Daniel Gabriel Pancu, Ilhan Mansiz. Trainer: Mircea Lucescu

SPARTA: Jaromir Blazek, Radoslav Kovác, Petr Johana, Tomáš Hübschman, Vladimir Labant, Karel Poborský, Pavel Krmas (84 Igor Gluscevic), Pavel Pergl, Lukáš Zelenka, Marek Kincl (77 Rastivlav Michalik), Libor Sionko (60 Tomáš Jun). Trainer: Jirí Kotrba

Goal: Ronaldo (81)

CHELSEA FC LONDON v AC SPARTA PRAHA 0-0

Stamford Bridge, London 26.11.2003

Referee: Claus Bo Larsen (DEN) Attendance: 40,152

CHELSEA: Carlo Cudicini, Mario Melchiot, John George Terry, William Gallas, Wayne Bridge, Claude Makelele, Frank Lampard, Damien Duff, Joe Cole (74 GEREMI Sorele Fotso Ndjitap), Hernán Jorge Crespo (74 Eidur Gudjohnsen), Adrian Mutu. Trainer: Claudio Ranieri

SPARTA: Jaromir Blazek, Pavel Pergl, Jirí Homola, Tomáš Hübschman, Vladimir Labant, Karel Poborský, Radoslav Kovác, Pavel Krmas, Lukáš Zelenka (88 Jan Flachbart), Rastivlav Michalik (73 Igor Gluscevic), Libor Sionko (90+3 Patrik Jezek). Trainer: Jirí Kotrba

SS LAZIO ROMA v BEŞIKTAŞ JK 1-1 (0-1)

Olimpico, Roma 26.11.2003

Referee: Markus Merk (GER) Attendance: 24,120

LAZIO: Angelo Peruzzi, Massimo Oddo, Jaap Stam, Paolo Negro, Guiseppe Favalli (53 Luciano Zauri), SÉRGIO Paulo Marcenero CONCEIÇÃO (46 Roberto Muzzi), Demetrio Albertini, Giuliano Giannichedda (46 Stefano Fiore), Dejan Stankovic, Bernardo Corradi, Simone Inzaghi. Trainer: Fernando Orsi

BEŞIKTAŞ: Óscar Eduardo CORDOBA Arce, Tayfur Havutçu, Antonio Carlos Zago, RONALDO Guiaro, Emre Asik, Okan Koç, Federico Giunti (90 Ahmet Yildirim), Sergen Yalçin (81 Tümer Metin), Ibrahim Üzülmez, Daniel Gabriel Pancu, Ilhan Mansiz. Trainer: Mircea Lucescu

Goals: Pancu (45+2 pen), Muzzi (56)

BEŞIKTAŞ JK ISTANBUL v CHELSEA FC LONDON 0-2 (0-0)

Arena Aufschalke, Gelsenkirchen (GER) 9.12.2003

Referee: Anders Frisk (SWE) Attendance: 55,350

BEŞIKTAŞ: Óscar Eduardo CORDOBA Arce, Antonio Carlos Zago, RONALDO Guiaro, Emre Asik, Tayfur Havutçu, Yasin Sülün (81 Ahmet Hassan Kamel), Kaan Dobra (70 Okan Koç), Sergen Yalçin (75 Tümer Metin), Ibrahim Üzülmez, Daniel Gabriel Pancu, Ilhan Mansiz. Trainer: Mircea Lucescu

CHELSEA: Carlo Cudicini, Glen Johnson, Celestine Babayaro (83 Wayne Bridge), Marcel Desailly, William Gallas, Claude Makelele, Frank Lampard, John George Terry, GEREMI Sorele Fotso Ndjitap, Jesper Grønkjær (72 Damien Duff), Jimmy Floyd Hasselbaink. Trainer: Claudio Ranieri

Goals: Hasselbaink (77), Bridge (85)

AC SPARTA PRAHA v SS LAZIO ROMA 1-0 (0-0)

AC Sparta Praha 9.12.2003

Referee: Lucilio CARDOSO CORTEZ BATISTA (POR) Attendance: 17,825

SPARTA: Jaromir Blazek, Radoslav Kovác, Petr Johana, Tomáš Hübschman, Vladimir Labant, Karel Poborský, Igor Gluscevic (85 Patrik Jezek), Pavel Pergl, Lukáš Zelenka, Rastivlav Michalik (73 Marek Kincl), Libor Sionko (89 Tomáš Jun). Trainer: Jirí Kotrba

LAZIO: Angelo Peruzzi, FERNANDO Manuel Silva COUTO, Jaap Stam, Paolo Negro, Guiseppe Favalli (89 SÉRGIO Paulo Marcenero CONCEIÇÃO), Guerino Gottardi (53 Fabio Liverani), Demetrio Albertini, Stefano Fiore, Dejan Stankovic, Bernardo Corradi, Roberto Muzzi (73 Simone Inzaghi). Trainer: Roberto Mancini

Goal: Kincl (90+3)

	P	W	D	L	F	A	Pts
Chelsea FC London	6	4	1	1	9	3	13
AC Sparta Praha	6	2	2	2	5	5	8
Beşiktaş JK Istanbul	6	2	1	3	5	7	7
SS Lazio Roma	6	1	2	3	6	10	5

GROUP H

CLUB BRUGGE KV v RC CELTA DE VIGO 1-1 (0-0)

Jan Breydelstadion, Brugge 16.09.2003

Referee: Giorgos Kasnaferis (GRE) Attendance: 26,639

CLUB BRUGGE: Tomislav Butina, Olivier De Cock, Philippe Clement, Birger Maertens (69 Ivan Gvozdenovic), Peter Van Der Heyden, Timmy Simons, Alin Stoica (32 Gaëtan Englebert), Nastja Ceh (78 Bengt Sæternes), Gert Verheyen, Sandy Martens, Andrés MENDOZA Acevedo.
Trainer: Trond Sollied

RC CELTA: José Manuel PINTO Colorado, SERGIO Fernández González, Manolo Eduardo BERIZZO, Pablo Andres CONTRERAS Fíca, Juan Francisco García García "JUANFRAN", JOSÉ IGNACIO Sáenz Marín, ÁNGEL López Ruano (78 Juan VELASCO Damas), Jesús Antonio Mora Nieto "JESULI" (82 Sílvio "SYLVINHO" Mendes Campos Junior), VAGNER Rogerio Nunes, GUSTAVO Adrián LÓPEZ (64 Alejandro Castro Fernández "JANDRO"), Savo MILOSEVIC.
Trainer: Miguel Ángel LOTINA ORUECHEBARRÍA

Sent off: Martens (90+1)

Goals: Juanfran (50, 84 og)

AC MILAN v AFC AJAX AMSTERDAM 1-0 (0-0)

Giuseppe Meazza, Milano 16.09.2003

Referee: Ľuboš Michel (SVK) Attendance: 45,931

AC MILAN: "DIDA" Nelson de Jesus Silva, Marcos Evangeliste de Moraes "CAFÚ", Alessandro Nesta, Paolo Maldini, Alessandro Costacurta (33 Martin Laursen), Ivan Gennaro Gattuso, Andrea Pirlo, Clarence Seedorf (64 Sérgio Cláudio dos Santos "SERGINHO"), Ricardo Izecson dos Santos Leite "KAKÁ", Andriy Shevchenko, Filippo Inzaghi (76 Massimo Ambrosini). Trainer: Carlo Ancelotti

AJAX: Bogdan Lobonţ, Hatem Trabelsi, Petri Pasanen, Julien Escudé (70 Tom Soetaerts), Abubakari Yakubu, MAXWELL Scherer Cabelino Andrade, Steven Pienaar (80 Victor Sikora), Tomáš Galásek, Rafael Van Der Vaart, Wesley Sonck (54 Wesley Sneijder), Zlatan Ibrahimovic.
Trainer: Ronald Koeman

Sent off: Gattuso (90+1)

Goal: Inzaghi (67)

AFC AJAX v CLUB BRUGGE KV 2-0 (1-0)

ArenA, Amsterdam 1.10.2003

Referee: Graham Barber (ENG) Attendance: 49,371

AJAX: Bogdan Lobonţ, Petri Pasanen, Tomáš Galásek, MAXWELL Scherer Cabelino Andrade, Tom Soetaerts (46 Wesley Sneijder), Hatem Trabelsi, Julien Escudé, Steven Pienaar (60 Nigel De Jong), Rafael Van Der Vaart (77 Jelle Van Damme), Wesley Sonck, Zlatan Ibrahimovic.

CLUB BRUGGE: Tomislav Butina, Olivier De Cock, Hans Cornelis, David Rozehnal, Peter Van Der Heyden, Timmy Simons, Philippe Clement, Gaëtan Englebert (66 Nastja Ceh), Ivan Gvozdenovic (79 Josip Simic), Gert Verheyen, Bengt Sæternes (87 Rune Lange). Trainer: Trond Sollied

Goals: Sonck (11, 54)

RC CELTA DE VIGO v AC MILAN 0-0

Balaídos, Vigo 1.10.2003

Referee: Michael Riley (ENG) Attendance: 28,000

RC CELTA: José Manuel PINTO Colorado, Juan VELASCO Damas, Fernando Gabriel CÁCERES Zaya, Pablo Andres CONTRERAS Fíca (45+3 SERGIO Fernández González), Juan Francisco García García «JUANFRAN», Everton GIOVANELLA, ÁNGEL López Ruano, Jesús Antonio Mora Nieto «JESULI» (86 Alejandro Castro Fernández «JANDRO»), VAGNER Rogerio Nunes, Alexandre Vladimirovich MOSTOVOI, GUSTAVO Adrián LÓPEZ (58 Savo MILOSEVIC). Trainer: Ramón Carnero

AC MILAN: «DIDA» Nelson de Jesus Silva, Marcos Evangeliste de Moraes «CAFÚ», Alessandro Nesta, Paolo Maldini, Alessandro Costacurta, RUI Manuel César COSTA, Andrea Pirlo, Massimo Ambrosini, Ricardo Izecson dos Santos Leite «KAKÁ» (64 «RIVALDO» Vítor Barbosa Ferreira), Andriy Shevchenko (73 Cristian Brocchi), Sérgio Cláudio dos Santos «SERGINHO» (62 Filippo Inzaghi).
Trainer: Carlo Ancelotti

AFC AJAX AMSTERDAM v RC CELTA DE VIGO 1-0 (0-0)

ArenA, Amsterdam 22.10.2003

Referee: Markus Merk (GER) Attendance: 48,514

AJAX: Bogdan Lobonţ, Petri Pasanen, Tomáš Galásek, MAXWELL Scherer Cabelino Andrade, Jelle Van Damme, Hatem Trabelsi (64 Nigel De Jong), Wesley Sneijder, Steven Pienaar, Rafael Van Der Vaart (39 Nicolae Mitea), Wesley Sonck (79 Abubakari Yakubu), Zlatan Ibrahimovic.
Trainer: Ronald Koeman

RC CELTA: José Manuel PINTO Colorado, Juan VELASCO Damas, Fernando Gabriel CÁCERES Zaya (85 ÁNGEL López Ruano), Sílvio "SYLVINHO" Mendes Campos Junior, Juan Francisco García García "JUANFRAN", Everton GIOVANELLA (81 Henrique Guedes da Silva "CATANHA"), Manolo Eduardo BERIZZO, Jesús Antonio Mora Nieto "JESULI", Peter Bernard LUCCIN, Alexandre Vladimirovich MOSTOVOI, Savo MILOSEVIC.
Trainer: Miguel Ángel LOTINA ORUECHEBARRÍA

Goal: Ibrahimovic (53)

AC MILAN v CLUB BRUGGE KV 0-1 (0-1)

Giuseppe Meazza, Milano 22.10.2003

Referee: Tom Henning Ovrebo (NOR) Attendance: 43,823

AC MILAN: "DIDA" Nelson de Jesus Silva, Marcos Evangeliste de Moraes "CAFÚ", Alessandro Nesta, Paolo Maldini, Giuseppe Pancaro, Clarence Seedorf (62 Sérgio Cláudio dos Santos "SERGINHO"), Andrea Pirlo, Cristian Brocchi, Ricardo Izecson dos Santos Leite "KAKÁ" (62 RUI Manuel César COSTA), Andriy Shevchenko (76 Jon Dahl Tomasson), Filippo Inzaghi. Trainer: Carlo Ancelotti

CLUB BRUGGE: Dany Verlinden, Olivier De Cock, David Rozehnal, Peter Van Der Heyden, Birger Maertens, Timmy Simons, Philippe Clement, Ivan Gvozdenovic, Sandy Martens (78 Gert Verheyen), Nastja Ceh (90+2 Alin Stoica), Andrés MENDOZA Acevedo (79 Bengt Sæternes). Trainer: Trond Sollied

Goal: Mendoza (33)

RC CELTA DE VIGO v AFC AJAX 3-2 (2-0)

Balaídos, Vigo 4.11.2003

Referee: Gilles Veissièrre (FRA) Attendance: 18,700

RC CELTA: José Manuel PINTO Colorado, SERGIO Fernández González, Fernando Gabriel CÁCERES Zaya, Sílvio «SYLVINHO» Mendes Campos Junior, Juan Francisco García García «JUANFRAN», VAGNER Rogerio Nunes (86 Pablo Andres CONTRERAS Fíca), ÁNGEL López Ruano, Jesús Antonio Mora Nieto «JESULI» (82 GUSTAVO Adrián LÓPEZ), Peter Bernard LUCCIN, Alexandre Vladimirovich MOSTOVOI (90+3 Borja OUBIÑA Meléndez), Savo MILOSEVIC. Trainer: Miguel Ángel LOTINA ORUECHEBARRÍA

AJAX: Bogdan Lobont, Abubakari Yakubu (65 John Heitinga), Tomáš Galásek (78 WAMBERTO de Jesus Sousa Campos), Nigel De Jong, Zdenek Grygera, Julien Escudé, Nicolae Mitea, MAXWELL Scherer Cabelino Andrade, Rafael Van Der Vaart, Wesley Sonck, Zlatan Ibrahimovic (69 Jari Litmanen). Trainer: Ronald Koeman **Sent off**: Grygera (90)

Goals: Luccin (25 pen), Milosevic (39), Sonck (53), Vagner (63), Van Der Vaart (81)

CLUB BRUGGE KV v AC MILAN 0-1 (0-0)

Jan Breydelstadion, Brugge 4.11.2003

Referee: Herbert Fandel (GER) Attendance: 27,834

CLUB BRUGGE: Dany Verlinden, Olivier De Cock, David Rozehnal, Birger Maertens, Peter Van Der Heyden, Ivan Gvozdenovic, Philippe Clement (77 Bengt Sæternes), Timmy Simons, Gert Verheyen, Nastja Ceh (62 Alin Stoica), Andrés MENDOZA Acevedo. Trainer: Trond Sollied

AC MILAN: «DIDA» Nelson de Jesus Silva, Marcos Evangeliste de Moraes «CAFÚ», Alessandro Nesta, Paolo Maldini (35 Alessandro Costacurta), Giuseppe Pancaro, Ivan Gennaro Gattuso, Andrea Pirlo, Clarence Seedorf, Ricardo Izecson dos Santos Leite «KAKÁ» (87 Massimo Ambrosini), Andriy Shevchenko, Jon Dahl Tomasson (42 Dario Simic). Trainer: Carlo Ancelotti **Sent off**: Nesta (37)

Goal: Kaká (86)

AFC AJAX AMSTERDAM v AC MILAN 0-1 (0-0)

ArenA, Amsterdam 26.11.2003

Referee: Urs Meier (SWI) Attendance: 50,210

AJAX: Bogdan Lobonţ, Abubakari Yakubu, Tomáš Galásek, Nigel De Jong, John Heitinga, Julien Escudé, Nicolae Mitea (77 Victor Sikora), MAXWELL Scherer Cabelino Andrade, Wesley Sneijder, Anthony Obodai (54 WAMBERTO de Jesus Sousa Campos), Zlatan Ibrahimovic (40 Jari Litmanen). Trainer: Ronald Koeman

AC MILAN: "DIDA" Nelson de Jesus Silva, Marcos Evangeliste de Moraes "CAFÚ", Alessandro Costacurta, Paolo Maldini, Martin Laursen (46 Giuseppe Pancaro), Ivan Gennaro Gattuso, Andrea Pirlo, Clarence Seedorf, Ricardo Izecson dos Santos Leite "KAKÁ" (77 RUI Manuel César COSTA), Andriy Shevchenko, Filippo Inzaghi (71 Massimo Ambrosini). Trainer: Carlo Ancelotti

Goal: Shevchenko (52)

RC CELTA DE VIGO v CLUB BRUGGE KV 1-1 (0-0)

Balaídos, Vigo 26.11.2003

Referee: Eric Poulat (FRA) Attendance: 18,173

RC CELTA: Pablo Oscar CAVALLERO Rodríguez (63 José Manuel PINTO Colorado), SERGIO Fernández González, Manolo Eduardo BERIZZO, Sílvio "SYLVINHO" Mendes Campos Junior (46 GUSTAVO Adrián LÓPEZ), Juan Francisco García García "JUANFRAN", JOSÉ IGNACIO Sáenz Marín, ÁNGEL López Ruano, Jesús Antonio Mora Nieto "JESULI", Peter Bernard LUCCIN, Alexandre Vladimirovich MOSTOVOI (77 Alejandro Castro Fernández "JANDRO"), Savo MILOSEVIC. Trainer: Miguel Ángel LOTINA ORUECHEBARRÍA

CLUB BRUGGE: Dany Verlinden, Olivier De Cock, David Rozehnal, Gaëtan Englebert, Sandy Martens, Ivan Gvozdenovic (81 Rune Lange), Philippe Clement, Timmy Simons, Gert Verheyen, Nastja Ceh (85 Kevin Roelandts), Bengt Sæternes. Trainer: Trond Sollied

Goals: Mostovoi (74), Lange (90+2)

CLUB BRUGGE KV v AFC AJAX AMSTERDAM 2-1 (1-1)

Jan Breydelstadion, Brugge 9.12.2003

Referee: Domenico Messina (ITA) Attendance: 28,041

CLUB BRUGGE: Dany Verlinden, Olivier De Cock, David Rozehnal (79 Tim Smolders), Gaëtan Englebert, Sandy Martens (89 Hans Cornelis), Peter Van Der Heyden, Philippe Clement, Timmy Simons, Gert Verheyen, Nastja Ceh, Rune Lange (66 Bengt Sæternes). Trainer: Trond Sollied

AJAX: Bogdan Lobont, Zdenek Grygera (85 Jelle Vandamme), John Heitinga, Julien Escudé, MAXWELL Scherer Cabelino Andrade, Nigel De Jong, Rafael Van Der Vaart, Wesley Sneijder, Wesley Sonck, Zlatan Ibrahimovic (72 Jari Litmanen), Nicolae Mitea (79 Tom Soetaers). Trainer: Ronald Koeman

Goals: Lange (27), Sonck (42 pen), Sæternes (84)

AC MILAN v RC CELTA DE VIGO 1-2 (1-1)

Giuseppe Meazza, Milano 9.12.2003

Referee: Kyros Vassaras (GRE) Attendance: 36,107

AC MILAN: Christian Abbiati, Kakha Kaladze, Alessandro Costacurta (69 Ignazio Abate), Dario Simic, Martin Laursen, Fernando Redondo, Clarence Seedorf (46 RUI Manuel César COSTA), Sérgio Cláudio dos Santos «SERGINHO», Ricardo Izecson dos Santos Leite «KAKÁ» (46 Jon Dahl Tomasson), Marco Borriello, Christian Brocchi. Trainer: Carlo Ancelotti

RC CELTA: Pablo Oscar CAVALLERO Rodríguez, Fernando Gabriel CÁCERES Zaya, Manolo Eduardo BERIZZO, Sílvio «SYLVINHO» Mendes Campos Junior, Juan Francisco García García «JUANFRAN», JOSÉ IGNACIO Sáenz Marín (80 Everton GIOVANELLA), ÁNGEL López Ruano, Jesús Antonio Mora Nieto «JESULI», Peter Bernard LUCCIN, GUSTAVO Adrián LÓPEZ (90 Pablo Andres CONTRERAS Fíca), Savo MILOSEVIC (84 Henrique Guedes da Silva «CATANHA»). Trainer: Miguel Ángel LOTINA ORUECHEBARRÍA

Goals: Kaká (40), Jesuli (42), José Ignacio (71)

	P	W	D	L	F	A	Pts
AC Milan	6	3	1	2	4	3	10
RC Celta de Vigo	6	2	3	1	7	6	9
Club Brugge KV	6	2	2	2	5	6	8
AFC Ajax Amsterdam	6	2	0	4	6	7	6

SECOND ROUND

FC BAYERN MÜNCHEN v REAL MADRID CF 1-1 (0-0)

Olympiastadion, München 24.02.2004

Referee: Terje Hauge (NOR) Attendance: 59,000

BAYERN: Oliver Kahn, Willy Sagnol, Bixente Lizarazu (46 Hasan Salihamidzic), Samuel Osei Kuffour, Robert Kovac, Martín Demichelis (90+2 Jens Jeremies), Roy Makaay, ZÉ ROBERTO da Silva, Michael Ballack, Claudio Pizarro (76 Roque SANTA CRUZ), Owen Hargreaves. Trainer: Ottmar Hitzfeld

REAL: Iker CASILLAS Fernández; Miguel Angel «MICHEL» SALGADO Fernández, ROBERTO CARLOS da Silva, Zinedine Zidane, Iván HELGUERA Bujía, RAÚL González Blanco, RONALDO Luis Nazario da Lima (90+1 Santiago Hernán SOLARI), Luis Filipe Madeira Caeiro «FIGO», José María Gutiérrez Hernández «GUTI», RAÚL BRAVO Sanfélix, David Beckham. Trainer: Carlos Queiroz

Goals: Makaay (75), Roberto Carlos (83)

REAL MADRID CF v FC BAYERN MÜNCHEN 1-0 (1-0)

Santiago Bernabéu, Madrid 10.03.2004

Referee: Urs Meier (SWI) Attendance: 71,000

REAL: Iker CASILLAS Fernández; Miguel Angel «MICHEL» SALGADO Fernández, Zinedine Zidane, Iván HELGUERA Bujía, RAÚL González Blanco, Luis Filipe Madeira Caeiro «FIGO», José María Gutiérrez Hernández «GUTI» (90+6 BORJA Fernández Fernández), RAÚL BRAVO Sanfélix, Santiago Hernán SOLARI (90+3 Esteban Matías CAMBIASSO Deleau), David Beckham, Alvaro MEJÍA Pérez. Trainer: Carlos Queiroz

BAYERN: Oliver Kahn, Willy Sagnol (67 Hasan Salihamidzic), Bixente Lizarazu, Samuel Osei Kuffour, Robert Kovac, Martín Demichelis, Roy Makaay, ZÉ ROBERTO da Silva, Michael Ballack, Claudio Pizarro (68 Roque SANTA CRUZ), Owen Hargreaves (46 Bastian Schweinsteiger). Trainer: Ottmar Hitzfeld

Goal: Zidane (32)

RC CELTA DE VIGO v ARSENAL FC LONDON 2-3 (1-1)

Balaídos, Vigo 24.02.2004

Referee: Anders Frisk (SWE) Attendance: 19,500

CELTA: Pablo Oscar CAVALLERO Rodríguez; Juan VELASCO Damas, Sílvio "SYLVINHO" Mendes Campos Junior, Manolo Eduardo BERIZZO, ÁNGEL López Ruano (64 VAGNER Rogerio Nunes), Savo Milosevic, Alexandre Vladimirovich Mostovoi, JOSÉ IGNACIO Sáenz Marín, Luis Eduardo Schmidt "EDÚ" (75 Mauricio Ricardo Pinilla), Peter Bernard LUCCIN, SERGIO Fernández González. Trainer: Radomir Antic

ARSENAL: Jens Lehmann, Patrick Vieira, Robert Pires, Fredrik Ljungberg (89 David Bentley), José Antonio Reyes (78 Nwankwo Kanu), LAUREN Etame-Mayer, Thierry Henry, Eduard Cesar Daud Gasper "EDU", Gaël Clichy (89 Pascal Cygan), Sol Campbell, Kolo Abib Touré. Trainer: Arsène Wenger

Goals: Edu (Arsenal-18, 58), Edu (Celta-27), José Ignacio (64), Pires (80)

ARSENAL FC LONDON v RC CELTA DE VIGO 2-0 (2-0)

Highbury, London 10.03.2004

Referee: Pierluigi Collina (ITA) Attendance: 35,402

ARSENAL: Jens Lehmann, Ashley Cole, Patrick Vieira, Robert Pires (69 José Antonio Reyes), Fredrik Ljungberg, Dennis Bergkamp (77 Nwankwo Kanu), LAUREN Etame-Mayer, Thierry Henry, Eduard Cesar Daud Gasper "EDU" (69 GILBERTO Aparecido da Silva), Sol Campbell, Kolo Abib Touré. Trainer: Arsène Wenger

CELTA: Pablo Oscar CAVALLERO Rodríguez; Juan VELASCO Damas, Sílvio "SYLVINHO" Mendes Campos Junior (21 Pablo Andres CONTRERAS Fíca), Fernando Gabriel CÁCERES Zaya, Alexandre Vladimirovich Mostovoi, GUSTAVO Adrián LÓPEZ (70 VAGNER Rogerio Nunes), JOSÉ IGNACIO Sáenz Marín, Mauricio Ricardo Pinilla, Peter Bernard LUCCIN (29 Jesús Antonio Mora Nieto "JESULI"), SERGIO Fernández González, Borja OUBIÑA Meléndez. Trainer: Radomir Antic

Sent off: Contreras (74)

Goals: Henry (14, 34)

AC SPARTA PRAHA v AC MILAN 0-0

Toyota Arena, Praha 24.02.2004

Referee: Graham Poll (ENG) Attendance: 20,640

SPARTA: Jaromir Blazek; Vladimir Labant, Pavel Pergl, Lukáš Zelenka (90+2 Tomáš Sivok), Karel Poborský, Rastivlav Michalik, Radoslav Kovác, Tomáš Hübschman, Petr Johana, Jirí Štajner (85 Vladimir Glušcevic), Igor Glušcevic (73 Miroslav Baranek). Trainer: Jirí Kotrba

AC MILAN: Nelson de Jesus Silva "DIDA"; Marcos Evangeliste de Moraes «CAFÚ», Paolo Maldini, Andriy Shevchenko, Ivan Gennaro Gattuso, Filippo Inzaghi (85 Sérgio Cláudio dos Santos "SERGINHO"), Alessandro Costacurta, Clarence Seedorf, Andrea Pirlo, Ricardo Izecson dos Santos Leite «KAKÁ», Giuseppe Pancaro. Trainer: Carlo Ancelotti

LOKOMOTIV MOSKVA v AS MONACO 2-1 (1-0)

Lokomotiv, Moskva 24.02.2004

Referee: Manuel Enrique MEJUTO GONZÁLEZ (SPA) Attendance: 21,500

LOKOMOTIV: Sergei Ovchinnikov; Marat Izmailov (79 Winston Parks), Vladimir Maminov, Dmitriy Loskov, Oleg Pashinin, Vadim Evseyev, Dmitriy Sennikov, Dmitriy Khokhlov (83 Gennadiy Nizhegorodov), Malkhaz Asatiani, Mikheil Ashvetia (46 James Obiorah), Sergei Gurenko. Trainer: Yuri Senin

AS MONACO: Flavio Roma, Hugo Benjamin Ibarra, Julien Rodriguez, Gaël Givet, Patrice Evra, Edouard Cissé, Andreas Zikos, Lucas Ademar Bernardi, Jérôme Rothen, Fernando MORIENTES Sanchéz, Dado Prso (64 Emmanuel Adebayor). Trainer: Didier Deschamps

Goals: Izmailov (32), Maminov (59), Morientes (69)

AC MILAN v AC SPARTA PRAHA 4-1 (1-0)

Giuseppe Meazza, Milano 10.03.2003

Referee: Markus Merk (GER) Attendance: 49,364

AC MILAN: Nelson de Jesus Silva «DIDA»; Marcos Evangeliste de Moraes «CAFÚ» (88 Alessandro Costacurta), Paolo Maldini, Andriy Shevchenko (86 RUI Manuel César COSTA), Ivan Gennaro Gattuso, Filippo Inzaghi (76 Jon Dahl Tomasson), Alessandro Nesta, Andrea Pirlo, Ricardo Izecson dos Santos Leite «KAKÁ», Massimo Ambrosini, Giuseppe Pancaro. Trainer: Carlo Ancelotti

SPARTA: Jaromir Blazek; Tomáš Sivok, Vladimir Labant, Pavel Pergl, Lukáš Zelenka (57 Tomáš Jun), Karel Poborský, Rastivlav Michalik (71 Vladimir Glušcevic), Radoslav Kovác, Tomáš Hübschman, Petr Johana, Jirí Štajner (88 Mirko Poledica). Trainer: Jirí Kotrba

Goals: Inzaghi (45+2), Jun (59), Shevchenko (66, 79), Gattuso (85)

AS MONACO v LOKOMOTIV MOSKVA 1-0 (0-0)

Louis II, Monaco 10.03.2004

Referee: Lucilio Cardoso CORTEZ BATISTA (POR) Attendance: 16700

AS MONACO: Flavio Roma; Patrice Evra, Hugo Benjamin Ibarra, Lucas Ademar Bernardi, Dado Pršo (90 Jaroslav Plasil), Fernando MORIENTES Sanchéz, Andreas Zikos, Emmanuel Adebayor (77 Edouard Cissé), Jérôme Rothen, Julien Rodriguez, Gaël Givet. Trainer: Didier Deschamps

LOKOMOTIV: Sergei Ovchinnikov; Gennadiy Nizhegorodov, Marat Izmailov, Vladimir Maminov, Dmitriy Loskov, Oleg Pashinin, Vadim Evseyev, Dmitriy Sennikov (65 Sergei Gurenko), Malkhaz Asatiani, Mikheil Ashvetia (67 Winston Parks), James Obiorah. Trainer: Yuri Senin

Sent off: Loskov (22)

Goal: Pršo (60)

RC DEPORTIVO LA CORUÑA v JUVENTUS FC TORINO 1-0 (1-0)

Riazor, La Coruña 25.02.2004

Referee: Gilles Veissière (FRA) Attendance: 22,266

DEPORTIVO: Francisco José MOLINA Jiménez; Enrique Fernández ROMERO, Nourredine Naybet, MAURO da SILVA Gomes, SERGIO González Soriano, DIEGO TRISTÁN Herrera (69 Walter Gerardo PANDIANI Urquiza), Lionel Sebastian SCALONI, Jorge Manuel Almeida Gomes ANDRADE, VÍCTOR Sánchez del Amo (85 MANUEL PABLO García Díaz), Alberto LUQUE Martos (81 Francisco «FRAN» Javier Gonzalez Perez), Juan Carlos VALERÓN Santana. Trainer: Javier IRURETAGOYENA AMIANO

JUVENTUS: Gianluigi Buffon, Alessio Tacchinardi, Paolo MONTERO IGLESIAS (56 Alessandro Birindelli), Gianluca Pessotto (63 Antonio Conte), Alessandro Del Piero, Pavel Nedved, David Trezeguet (46 Fabrizio Miccoli), Stephen Appiah, Gianluca Zambrotta, Lilian Thuram, Nicola Legrottaglie. Trainer: Marcello Lippi

Goal: Luque (37)

JUVENTUS FC TORINO v RC DEPORTIVO LA CORUÑA 0-1 (0-1)

Delle Alpi, Torino 9.03.2004

Referee: Ľuboš Michel (SVK) Attendance: 24,680

JUVENTUS: Gianluigi Buffon, Ciro Ferrara, Alessio Tacchinardi, Paolo MONTERO IGLESIAS, Alessandro Del Piero (8 Fabrizio Miccoli), Pavel Nedved, Mauro German Camoranesi (70 Davide Chiumento), Stephen Appiah, Marco di Vaio, Lilian Thuram, Nicola Legrottaglie (46 Gianluca Pessotto). Trainer: Marcello Lippi

DEPORTIVO: Francisco José MOLINA Jiménez; Nourredine Naybet, MAURO da SILVA Gomes, Walter Gerardo PANDIANI Urquiza (82 DIEGO TRISTÁN Herrera), SERGIO González Soriano, Lionel Sebastian SCALONI, Jorge Manuel Almeida Gomes ANDRADE, Joan CAPDEVILA Méndez, VÍCTOR Sánchez del Amo, Alberto LUQUE Martos (62 Francisco «FRAN» Javier Gonzalez Perez), Juan Carlos VALERÓN Santana (77 Aldo Pedro DUSCHER).
Trainer: Javier IRURETAGOYENA AMIANO

Goal: Pandiani (12)

FC PORTO v MANCHESTER UNITED FC 2-1 (1-1)

O Dragão, Porto 25.02.2004

Referee: Herbert Fandel (GER) Attendance: 49,977

FC PORTO: VÍTOR Manuel Martins BAÍA; JORGE Paulo COSTA Almeida, RICARDO Alberto Silveira CARVALHO, NUNO Jorge Pereira Silva VALENTE, Anderson Luis de Souza «DECO», Dimitri Alenichev (63 Edgaras Jankauskas), Nuno Ricardo Oliveira Ribeiro «MANICHE», CARLOS ALBERTO Gomes de Jesus (75 RICARDO Ribeiro FERNANDES), PAULO Renato Rebocho FERREIRA, PEDRO Miguel da Silva MENDES, Benni McCarthy (83 BRUNO Santos MORAES).
Trainer: José Mário DOS SANTOS MOURINHO FÉLIX

MANCHESTER UNITED: Tim Howard ; Gary Neville, Philip Neville (70 John O'Shea), Wesley Brown, Nicky Butt, Louis Laurent Saha (76 CRISTIANO RONALDO Santos Aveiro), Ruud van Nistelrooij, Ryan Giggs, Roy Keane, Paul Scholes, Quinton Fortune. Trainer: Alex Ferguson

Sent off: Keane (87)

Goals: Fortune (14), McCarthy (29, 78)

MANCHESTER UNITED FC v FC PORTO 1-1 (1-0)

Old Trafford, Manchester 9.03.2004

Referee: Valentin Ivanov (RUS) Attendance: 67,029

MANCHESTER: Tim Howard; Gary Neville, Philip Neville, Wesley Brown, Nicky Butt, Ruud van Nistelrooij, Ryan Giggs, Paul Scholes, Eric Djemba-Djemba (46 Louis Laurent Saha), John O'Shea, Darren Fletcher (75 CRISTIANO RONALDO Santos Aveiro (83 Ole Gunnar Solskjaer)).
Trainer: Alex Ferguson

FC PORTO: VÍTOR Manuel Martins BAÍA; JORGE Paulo COSTA Almeida (37 PEDRO EMANUEL dos Santos Martins da Silva), RICARDO Alberto Silveira CARVALHO, Francisco José da Costa «COSTINHA», NUNO Jorge Pereira Silva VALENTE, Anderson Luis de Souza «DECO», Dimitri Alenichev (81 RICARDO Ribeiro FERNANDES), Nuno Ricardo Oliveira Ribeiro «MANICHE», CARLOS ALBERTO Gomes de Jesus (61 Edgaras Jankauskas), PAULO Renato Rebocho FERREIRA, Benni McCarthy.
Trainer: José Mário DOS SANTOS MOURINHO FÉLIX

Goals: Scholes (32), Costinha (90)

REAL SOCIEDAD DE FÚTBAL SAN SEBASTIAN v OLYMPIQUE LYONNAIS 0-1 (0-1)

Anoeta, San Sebastian 25.02.2004

Referee: Massimo De Santis (ITA) Attendance: 29,000

REAL SOCIEDAD: Sander Westerveld, Bjorn Töre Kvarme, Agustin ARANZÁBAL Alkorta, XABIer ALONSO Olano (74 Mikel ARANBURU Eizaguirre), Gabriel Francisco SCHÜRRER Peralta, Valeryi Karpin, Darko Kovacevic, Aitor LÓPEZ REKARTE, Nihat Kahveci (80 Óscar DE PAULA Gamero), Igor GABILONDO del Campo (64 LEE CHUN Soo), Bittor ALKIZA Fernández. Trainer: Raynald Denoueix

OLYMPIQUE: Grégory Coupet; Eric Deflandre, José EDMILSON Gomes de Moraes, Mickaël Essien, Mahamadou Diarra, Antonio Augusto Ribeiro Reis «JUNINHO PERNAMBUCANO», Florent Malouda, Sidney Govou (80 Vikash Dhorasoo), Péguy Luyindula, Patrick Müller, Romain Sartre (66 Jérémie Berthod). Trainer: Paul Le Guen

Goal: Schürrer (18 og)

OLYMPIQUE LYONNAIS v REAL SOCIEDAD DE FÚTBAL SAN SEBASTIAN 1-0 (0-0)

Gerland, Lyon 9.03.2004

Referee: Michael Riley (ENG) Attendance: 38,914

OLYMPIQUE: Grégory Coupet (16 Rémy Vercoutre); Eric Deflandre, José EDMILSON Gomes de Moraes, Mickaël Essien, Mahamadou Diarra, Antonio Augusto Ribeiro Reis «JUNINHO PERNAMBUCANO», Florent Malouda, Sidney Govou, Péguy Luyindula (83 Giovane De Souza ELBER), Patrick Müller, Vikash Dhorasoo (87 Jérémie Berthod).
Trainer: Paul Le Guen

REAL SOCIEDAD: ALBERTO López Fernández, XABIer ALONSO Olano, Gabriel Francisco SCHÜRRER Peralta (85 Óscar DE PAULA Gamero), Igor JAUREGUI Iraola, Valeryi Karpin, Darko Kovacevic, Mikel ARANBURU Eizaguirre (60 Nihat Kahveci), Aitor LÓPEZ REKARTE, Igor GABILONDO del Campo (60 Francisco Javier DE PEDRO Falque), Bittor ALKIZA Fernández, Lionel Potillon.
Trainer: Raynald Denoueix

Goal: Juninho (77)

VfB STUTTGART
v CHELSEA FC LONDON 0-1 (0-1)

Gottlieb-Daimler, Stuttgart 25.02.2004

Referee: Kyros Vassaras (GRE) Attendance: 42,000

VfB: Timo Hildebrand; Andreas Hinkel, Marcelo José BORDON, FERNANDO José da Silva Freitas MEIRA, Silvio Meissner (46 Christian Tiffert), Aleksandr Hleb, Horst Heldt (66 Jeronimo Barreto "CACAU"), Imre Szabics, Zvonimir Soldo, Philipp Lahm, Kevin Kuranyi. Trainer: Felix Magath

CHELSEA: Carlo Cudicini; Glen Johnson, Claude Makelele, Frank Lampard, William Gallas, GEREMI Sorele Fotso Ndjitap, Wayne Bridge, Hernán Jorge Crespo (89 Joe Cole), Eidur Gudjohnsen (73 Jimmy Floyd Hasselbaink), John George Terry, Jesper Grønkjaer (66 Damien Duff). Trainer: Claudio Ranieri

Goal: Fernando Meira (12 og)

CHELSEA FC LONDON v VfB STUTTGART 0-0

Stamford Bridge, London 9.03.2004

Referee: Kim Milton Nielsen (DEN) Attendance: 36,657

CHELSEA: Carlo Cudicini; Glen Johnson (31 Marcel Desailly), Claude Makelele, Frank Lampard, Damien Duff (82 Adrian Mutu), William Gallas, Wayne Bridge, Scott Mathew Parker (61 GEREMI Sorele Fotso Ndjitap), Hernán Jorge Crespo, John George Terry, Jesper Grønkjaer. Trainer: Claudio Ranieri

VfB: Timo Hildebrand; Andreas Hinkel (81 Mario Gomez), Boris Zivkovic, Marcelo José BORDON, FERNANDO José da Silva Freitas MEIRA, Silvio Meissner (63 Christian Tiffert), Aleksandr Hleb, Jeronimo Barreto "CACAU" (40 Imre Szabics), Zvonimir Soldo, Philipp Lahm, Kevin Kuranyi. Trainer: Felix Magath

QUARTER-FINALS

FC PORTO v OLYMPIQUE LYONNAIS 2-0 (1-0)

O Dragão, Porto 23.03.2004

Referee: Terje Hauge (NOR) Attendance: 46,910

FC PORTO: VÍTOR Manuel Martins BAÍA, PAULO Renato Rebocho FERREIRA, PEDRO EMANUEL dos Santos Martins Silva, RICARDO Alberto Silveira CARVALHO, NUNO Jorge Pereira Silva VALENTE, Francisco José da Costa "COSTINHA" (78 José BOSINGWA da Silva), Nuno Ricardo Oliveira Ribeiro "MANICHE", Dimitri Alenichev (82 RICARDO Ribeiro FERNANDES), Anderson Luis de Souza «DECO», Benni McCARTHY, CARLOS ALBERTO Gomes de Jesus (58 Edgaras JANKAUSKAS). Trainer: José Mário DOS SANTOS MOURINHO FÉLIX

OLYMPIQUE: Grégory Coupet, Mahamadou Diarra, Eric Deflandre (73 Anthony Réveillière), José EDMILSON Gomes de Moraes, Mickaël Essien, Florent Malouda, Antonio Augusto Ribeiro Reis "JUNINHO PERNAMBUCANO" (46 Vikash Dhorasoo), Sidney Govou, Péguy Luyindula, Giovane de Souza ELBER, Patrick Müller. Trainer: Paul Le Guen

Goals: Deco (44), Ricardo Carvalho (71).

OLYMPIQUE LYONNAIS v FC PORTO 2-2 (1-1)

Gerland, Lyon 7.04.2004

Referee: Anders Frisk (SWE) Attendance: 41,000

OLYMPIQUE: Grégory Coupet, Jérémie Berthod, Patrick Müller, José EDMILSON Gomes de Moraes, Vikash Dhorasoo (77 Eric Deflandre), Florent Malouda, Mahamadou Diarra, Mickaël Essien (60 Anthony Réveillière), Antonio Augusto Ribeiro Reis "JUNINHO PERNAMBUCANO" (60 Bryan Bergougnoux), Péguy Luyindula, Giovane de Souza ELBER. Trainer: Paul Le Guen

FC PORTO: VÍTOR Manuel Martins BAÍA, NUNO Jorge Pereira Silva VALENTE, JORGE Paulo COSTA Almeida, RICARDO Alberto Silveira CARVALHO, PAULO Renato Rebocho FERREIRA, Francisco José da Costa «COSTINHA», Dimitri ALENICHEV, Anderson Luis de Souza «DECO» (76 PEDRO Miguel da Silva MENDES), Nuno Ricardo Oliveira Ribeiro "MANICHE", Benni McCarthy (56 Edgaras Jankauskas), CARLOS ALBERTO Gomes de Jesus (48 PEDRO EMANUEL dos Santos Martins Silva). Trainer: José Mário DOS SANTOS MOURINHO FÉLIX

Sent off: Edmilson (73)

Goals: Maniche (6, 47), Luyindula (14), Elber (90).

AC MILAN
v RC DEPORTIVO LA CORUÑA 4-1 (1-1)

Giuseppe Meazza, Milano 23.03.2004

Referee: Valentin Ivanov (RUS) Attendance: 60,335

AC MILAN: Nelson de Jesus Silva "DIDA", Marcos Evangeliste de Moraes "CAFÚ", Alessandro Costacurta, Paolo Maldini, Giuseppe Pancaro (73 Sérgio Cláudio dos Santos «SERGINHO»), Ivan Gennaro Gattuso, Andrea Pirlo, Clarence Seedorf, Ricardo Izecson dos Santos Leite "KAKÁ", Filippo Inzaghi (79 Massimo Ambrosini), Andriy Shevchenko (84 Jon Dahl Tomasson). Trainer: Carlo Ancelotti

DEPORTIVO: Francisco José MOLINA Jiménez, Joan CAPDEVILA Méndez, Nourredine NAYBET, Jorge Manuel Almeida Gomes ANDRADE, Lionel Sebastian SCALONI, MAURO da SILVA Gomes, Juan Carlos VALERÓN Santana, Aldo Pedro DUSCHER (66 Francisco «FRAN» Javier Gonzalez Perez), SERGIO González Soriano (81 MANUEL PABLO García Díaz), Walter Gerardo PANDIANI Urquiza, Alberto LUQUE Martos (83 DIEGO TRISTÁN Herrera). Trainer: Javier IRURETAGOYENA AMIANO

Goals: Pandiani (11), Kaka (45, 49), Shevchenko (46), Pirlo (53)

RC DEPORTIVO LA CORUÑA v AC MILAN 4-0 (3-0)

Riazor, La Coruña 7.04.2001

Referee: Urs Meier (SWI) Attendance: 29,000

DEPORTIVO: Francisco José MOLINA Jiménez, Jorge Manuel Almeida Gomes ANDRADE, Nourredine NAYBET, Enrique Fernández ROMERO, MANUEL PABLO García Díaz, VÍCTOR Sánchez del Amo, Juan Carlos VALERÓN Santana (90+1 DJALMINHA Feitisa Dias), MAURO da SILVA Gomes, SERGIO González Soriano (87 Aldo Pedro DUSCHER), Alberto LUQUE Martos (66 Francisco «FRAN» Javier Gonzalez Perez), Walter Gerardo PANDIANI Urquiza. Trainer: Javier IRURETAGOYENA AMIANO

AC MILAN: Nelson de Jesus Silva "DIDA", Paolo Maldini, Alessandro Nesta, Giuseppe Pancaro (77 RUI Manuel César COSTA), Marcos Evangeliste de Moraes "CAFÚ", Clarence Seedorf, Andrea Pirlo (59 Sérgio Cláudio dos Santos "SERGINHO"), Ivan Gennaro Gattuso, Ricardo Izecson dos Santos Leite "KAKÁ", Jon Dahl Tomasson (67 Filippo Inzaghi), Andriy Shevchenko. Trainer: Carlo Ancelotti

Goals: Pandiani (5), Valerón (35), Luque (44), Fran (76)

CHELSEA FC LONDON v ARSENAL FC LONDON 1-1 (0-0)

Stamford Bridge, London 24.03.2004

Referee: Manuel Enrique MEJUTO GONZÁLEZ (SPA) Attendance: 40,778

CHELSEA: Marco Ambrosio, Marcel Desailly, John George Terry, William Gallas, Wayne Bridge, Scott Mathew Parker (72 Joe Cole), Claude Makelele, Frank Lampard, Damien Duff, Adrian Mutu (72 Hernán Jorge Crespo), Eidur Gudjohnsen (86 Mario Melchiot). Trainer: Claudio Ranieri

ARSENAL: Jens Lehmann, LAUREN Etame-Mayer, Kolo Abib Touré, Sol Campbell, Ashley Cole, Fredrik Ljungberg (78 José Antonio Reyes), Patrick Vieira, Eduard Cesar Daud Gasper "EDU", Robert Pires, Dennis Bergkamp (72 GILBERTO Aparecido da Silva), Thierry Henry. Trainer: Arsène Wenger

Sent off: Desailly (83)

Goals: Gudjohnsen (53), Pires (59)

ARSENAL FC LONDON v CHELSEA FC LONDON 1-2 (1-0)

Highbury, London 6.04.2004

Referee: Markus Merk (GER) Attendance: 35,486

ARSENAL: Jens Lehmann, Sol Campbell, LAUREN Etame-Mayer, Ashley Cole, Kolo Abib Touré, Robert Pires, Patrick Vieira, Fredrik Ljungberg, Eduard Cesar Daud Gasper "EDU", Thierry Henry (82 Dennis Bergkamp), José Antonio Reyes. Trainer: Arsène Wenger

CHELSEA: Marco Ambrosio, William Gallas, Mario Melchiot, John George Terry, Wayne Bridge, Claude Makelele, Damien Duff (83 Joe Cole), Frank Lampard, Scott Mathew Parker (46 Jesper Grønkjær), Jimmy Floyd Hasselbaink (83 Hernán Jorge Crespo), Eidur Gudjohnsen. Trainer: Claudio Ranieri

Goals: Reyes (45+1), Lampard (51), Bridge (87)

REAL MADRID CF v AS MONACO 4-2 (0-1)

Santiago Bernabéu, Madrid 24.03.2004

Referee: L'uboš Michel (SVK) Attendance: 69,327

REAL: Iker CASILLAS Fernández, Miguel Angel «MICHEL» SALGADO Fernández , Alvaro MEJÍA Pérez, Iván HELGUERA Bujía, RAÚL BRAVO Sanfélix (28 Francisco PAVÓN Barahona), David BECKHAM, José María Gutiérrez Hernández "GUTI" (77 BORJA Fernández Fernández), Luis Filipe Madeira Caeiro «FIGO», Zinedine ZIDANE, RONALDO Luis Nazario da Lima (82 Santiago Hernán SOLARI), RAÚL González Blanco. Trainer: Carlos Queiroz

AS MONACO: Flavio Roma, Julien Rodriguez, Patrice Evra (89 Hassan El Fakiri), Gaël Givet (83 Hugo Benjamin Ibarra), Sébastien Squillaci, Jérôme Rothen, Lucas Ademar Bernardi, Ludovic Giuly, Andreas Zikos, Fernando MORIENTES Sanchéz, Edouard Cissé (66 Jaroslav Plasil). Trainer: Didier Deschamps

Goals: Squillaci (43), Helguera (51), Zidane (70), Figo (77), Ronaldo (81), Morientes (83)

AS MONACO v REAL MADRID CF 3-1 (1-1)

Louis II, Monaco 6.04.2004

Referee: Pierluigi Collina (ITA) Attendance: 18,000

AS MONACO: Flavio Roma, Julien Rodriguez, Hugo Benjamin Ibarra, Patrice Evra, Gaël Givet, Edouard Cissé, Ludovic Giuly (82 Hassan El Fakiri), Jérôme Rothen, Jaroslav Plasil, Dado Prso (61 Shabani Nonda), Fernando MORIENTES Sanchéz (85 Emmanuel Adebayor). Trainer: Didier Deschamps

REAL: Iker CASILLAS Fernández, ROBERTO CARLOS da Silva, Miguel Angel "MICHEL" SALGADO Fernández (85 RAÚL BRAVO Sanfélix), BORJA Fernández Fernández (72 Santiago Hernán SOLARI), Alvaro MEJÍA Pérez, Luis Filipe Madeira Caeiro "FIGO", Zinedine ZIDANE, Iván HELGUERA Bujía, José María Gutiérrez Hernández "GUTI" (88 Javier García PORTILLO), RAÚL González Blanco, RONALDO Luis Nazario da Lima. Trainer: Carlos Queiroz

Goals: Raul (36), Giuly (45+1, 66), Morientes (48)

SEMI-FINALS

AS MONACO v CHELSEA FC LONDON 3-1 (1-1)

Louis II, Monaco 20.04.2004

Referee: Urs Meier (SWI) Attendance: 18,500

AS MONACO: Flavio Roma, Julien Rodriguez, Hugo Benjamin Ibarra, Patrice Evra, Gaël Givet, Ludovic Giuly (82 Shabani Nonda), Jérôme Rothen (89 Jaroslav Plasil), Lucas Ademar Bernardi, Andreas Zikos, Dado Prso (57 Edouard Cissé), Fernando MORIENTES Sanchéz. Trainer: Didier Deschamps

CHELSEA: Marco Ambrosio, Mario Melchiot (62 Jimmy Floyd Hasselbaink), Marcel Desailly, John George Terry, Wayne Bridge, Jesper Grønkjær (46 Juan Sebastián Verón), Claude Makelele, Frank Lampard, Scott Mathew Parker (68 Robert Huth), Hernán Jorge Crespo, Eidur Gudjohnsen. Trainer: Claudio Ranieri

Sent off: Zikos (53)

Goals: Prso (17), Crespo (22) Morientes (78), Nonda (83)

CHELSEA FC LONDON v AS MONACO 2-2 (2-1)

Stamford Bridge, London 5.05.2004

Referee: Anders Frisk (SWE) Attendance: 37,132

CHELSEA: Carlo Cudicini, William Gallas, Mario Melchiot (64 Glen Johnson), John George Terry, Wayne Bridge, Jesper Grønkjær, Frank Lampard, Joe Cole, GEREMI Sorele Fotso Ndjitap (69 Scott Mathew Parker), Jimmy Floyd Hasselbaink (69 Hernán Jorge Crespo), Eidur Gudjohnsen. Trainer: Claudio Ranieri

AS MONACO: Flavio Roma, Julien Rodriguez, Hugo Benjamin Ibarra, Sébastien Squillaci (46 Jaroslav Plasil), Patrice Evra, Gaël Givet, Edouard Cissé, Ludovic Giuly (67 Dado Prso), Jérôme Rothen, Lucas Ademar Bernardi, Fernando MORIENTES Sanchéz (81 Shabani NONDA). Trainer: Didier Deschamps

Goals: Grønkjær (23), Lampard (44), Ibarra (45+2), Morientes (61)

FC PORTO v RC DEPORTIVO LA CORUÑA 0-0

O Dragão, Porto 21.04.2004

Referee: Markus Merk (GER) Attendance: 52,000

FC PORTO: VÍTOR Manuel Martins BAÍA, NUNO Jorge Pereira Silva VALENTE, JORGE Paulo COSTA Almeida, RICARDO Alberto Silveira CARVALHO, PAULO Renato Rebocho FERREIRA, Francisco José da Costa "COSTINHA" (46 Edgaras JANKAUSKAS), Dimitri ALENICHEV (46 PEDRO Miguel da Silva MENDES), Anderson Luis de Souza "DECO", Nuno Ricardo Oliveira Ribeiro "MANICHE", Benni McCARTHY (70 MARCO Júlio Castanheiro Alfonso Alves FERREIRA), CARLOS ALBERTO Gomes de Jesus. Trainer: José Mário DOS SANTOS MOURINHO FÉLIX

DEPORTIVO: Francisco José MOLINA Jiménez, Jorge Manuel Almeida Gomes ANDRADE, Nourredine NAYBET, Enrique Fernández ROMERO, MANUEL PABLO García Díaz, VÍCTOR Sánchez del Amo (89 CÉSAR Martín Villar), Juan Carlos VALERÓN Santana, MAURO da SILVA Gomes, SERGIO González Soriano (79 Aldo Pedro DUSCHER), Alberto LUQUE Martos (45 Francisco "FRAN" Javier Gonzalez Perez), Walter Gerardo PANDIANI Urquiza. Trainer: Javier IRURETAGOYENA AMIANO

Sent off: Andrade (86)

RC DEPORTIVO LA CORUÑA v FC PORTO 0-1 (0-0)

Riazor, La Coruña 4.05.2004

Referee: Pierluigi Collina (ITA) Attendance: 35,000

DEPORTIVO: Francisco José MOLINA Jiménez, CÉSAR Martín Villar, Nourredine NAYBET, Enrique Fernández ROMERO, MANUEL PABLO García Díaz, VÍCTOR Sánchez del Amo (55 Lionel Sebastian SCALONI), Juan Carlos VALERÓN Santana, SERGIO González Soriano (67 DIEGO TRISTÁN Herrera), Aldo Pedro DUSCHER, Alberto LUQUE Martos (73 Francisco "FRAN" Javier Gonzalez Perez), Walter Gerardo PANDIANI Urquiza. Trainer: Javier IRURETAGOYENA AMIANO

FC PORTO: VÍTOR Manuel Martins BAÍA, NUNO Jorge Pereira Silva VALENTE, JORGE Paulo COSTA Almeida, RICARDO Alberto Silveira CARVALHO, PAULO Renato Rebocho FERREIRA, Francisco José da Costa "COSTINHA", Anderson Luis de Souza "DECO", Nuno Ricardo Oliveira Ribeiro "MANICHE", PEDRO Miguel da Silva MENDES (87 José BOSINGWA da Silva), Vanderlei F. da Silva "DERLEI" (90+3 Benni McCARTHY), CARLOS ALBERTO Gomes de Jesus (68 PEDRO EMANUEL dos Santos Martins da Silva). Trainer: José Mário DOS SANTOS MOURINHO FÉLIX

Sent off: Naybet (70)

Goal: Derlei (59 pen)

FINAL

FC PORTO v AS MONACO 3-0 (1-0)

AufSchalke, Gelsenkirchen 26.05.2004

Referee: Kim Milton Nielsen (DEN) Attendance: 52,000

FC PORTO: VÍTOR Manuel Martins BAÍA, JORGE Paulo COSTA Almeida, RICARDO Alberto Silveira CARVALHO, Francisco José da Costa "COSTINHA", NUNO Jorge Pereira Silva VALENTE, Anderson Luis de Souza "DECO" (85 PEDRO EMANUEL dos Santos Martins da Silva), Vanderlei F. da Silva "DERLEI" (78 Benni McCarthy), Nuno Ricardo Oliveira Ribeiro "MANICHE", CARLOS ALBERTO Gomes de Jesus (60 Dimitri Alenichev), PAULO Renato Rebocho FERREIRA, PEDRO Miguel da Silva MENDES. Trainer: José Mário DOS SANTOS MOURINHO FÉLIX

AS MONACO: Flavio Roma, Patrice Evra, Hugo Benjamin Ibarra, Lucas Ademar Bernardi, Ludovic Giuly (23 Dado Prso), Fernando MORIENTES Sanchéz, Edouard Cissé (64 Shabani Nonda), Andreas Zikos, Jérôme Rothen, Julien Rodriguez, Gaël Givet (72 Sébastien Squillaci). Trainer: Didier Deschamps

Goals: Carlos Alberto (39), Deco (71), Alenichev (75)

European Cup Goalscorers 2002-03:

9 goals: Morientes (AS Monaco)

7 goals: Pršo (AS Monaco)

6 goals: Sutton (Celtic FC), Pandiani (RC Deportivo La Coruña), Makaay (FC Bayern München), Hakan Şükür (Galatasaray SK)

5 goals: Zurawski (GTS Wisla Kraków), Poborský (AC Sparta Praha), Drogba (Olympique de Marseille), Juninho Pernambucano (Olympique Lyonnais), Henry (Arsenal FC), Luque (RC Deportivo La Coruña), McCarthy (FC Porto)

4 goals: Rauffmann (Omonoia FC), Jónsson (FC København), Dindane (RSC Anderlecht), Diogo "Rincón" (FC Dynamo Kyiv), Sonck (AFC Ajax), Lampard (Chelsea FC), Pires (Arsenal FC), Giuly (AS Monaco), Trezeguet (Juventus FC), Van Nistelrooy (Manchester United), Ronaldo (Real Madrid CF), Kaká, Shevchenko (AC Milan), Wandeir (FK Vardar Skopje)

3 goals: Georgievski, Rogerio (FK Vardar Skopje), Delibasic (FK Partizan Beograd), Røll Larsen (FC København), Miller, Larsson (Celtic FC), Shatskikh (FC Dynamo Kyiv), Ashvetia (FC Lokomotiv Moskva), Gudjohnsen (Chelsea FC), Edu (Arsenal FC), Diego Tristán (RC Deportivo La Coruña), Di Vaio (Juventus FC), Kuranyi (VfB Stuttgart), Costinha, Derlei, Maniche (FC Porto), Zidane (Real Madrid CF), Simone Inzaghi (SS Lazio)

2 goals: Doncic (Sliema Wanderers), Beniusis, Opic (HB Tórshavn), Mäkelä (HJK Helsinki), Kerkez (FK Leotar Trebinje), Dostálek (SK Slavia Praha), Kollmann, Naumoski (Grazer AK), Karadas (Rosenborg BK), Welton (MTK Hungária FC), Vukic (FC Shakhtar Donetsk), Ilic (FK Partizan Beograd), Zuma (FC København), Kranjcar (NK Dinamo Zagreb), Jestrovic (RSC Anderlecht), Belkevich, Fedorov (FC Dynamo Kyiv), Ibrahimovic (AFC Ajax), Jesuli, Edú, Mostovoi, José Ignacio (RC Celta de Vigo), Ignashevich, Loskov (FC Lokomotiv Moskva), Løvenkrands (Glasgow Rangers FC), Sionko (AC Sparta Praha), Crespo, Hasselbaink, Bridge (Chelsea FC), Núñez (Grasshopper-Club Zürich), Mido (Olympique de Marseille), Mendoza, Lange (Club Brugge KV), Amoroso (BV Borussia Dortmund), Luyindula (Olympique Lyonnais), Adani, Vieri (FC Internazionale), Ljungberg (Arsenal FC), Valerón (RC Deportivo La Coruña), Bouma, Robben, De Jong (PSV Eindhoven), Cissé (AS Monaco), Arif (Galatasaray SK), Del Piero, Nedved (Juventus FC), Kovacevic (Real Sociedad), Stoltidis, Castillo (Olympiakos), Fortune, Forlán (Manchester United FC), Szabics (VfB Stuttgart), Konstantinou (Panathinaikos FC), Alenichev, Deco (FC Porto), Roberto Carlos, Figo, Helguera, Solari, Raúl (Real Madrid CF), Fiore (SS Lazio), Sergen Yalçin, Pancu (Beşiktaş JK), Filippo Inzaghi (AC Milan)

1 goal: Buitkus, Dedura, Verpakovsky (Skonto Riga), Bogdanovic, Brincat (Sliema Wanderers), Loshankov (Bate Borisov), Caffrey, Crowe, Ryan (Bohemians FC), Jacobsen (HB Tórshavn), Kancelskis (FBK Kaunas), Kottila (HJK Helsinki), Melkadze, Anchabadze, Daraselia (Dinamo Tbilisi), Agolli, Liçi, Fortuzi, Halili, Xhafa (KS Tirana), Delibasic (FK Leotar Trebinje), Georgiou, Haralambous (Omonoia FC), Agayev (FC Irtysh), Tudor, Nesteruk (FC Sheriff), Viikmáe (FC Flora), Jarman, Moralee (Barry Town FC), Agvan Mkrtchyan, Pachajyan (FC Pyunik Erevan), Davidsson (KR Reykjavik), Adauto, Kuka, Skácel, Hrdlička (SK Slavia Praha), Bazina, Aufhauser, Pogatetz, Standfest, Sick (Grazer AK), Frankowski, Baszczynski, Dubicki, Brattbakk, Strand, F. Johnsen (Rosenborg BK), Rednic (MTK Hungária FC), Lewandowski, Brandão (FC Shakhtar Donetsk), Samodin, Gogniev (CSKA Moskva), Grozdanovski, Ristovski, Anyanviu (FK Vardar Skopje), Makonoele, Johansson, Wowoah (Djurgårdens IF), Malbasa, Iliev (FK Partizan Beograd), Nørregaard, Álvaro (FC København), Bazík, Sninský (MSK Zilina), Pantsil (Maccabi Tel Aviv), Balajic, Pekic (NK Maribor Branik), Mijatovic, Drpic (NK Dinamo Zagreb), Yanchev, Leonardo, Mukasi (CSKA Sofia), Maloney, Agathe, Petrov, Thompson, Hartson (Celtic FC), Seol, Zetterberg, Lovré, Mornar, Tihinen (RSC Anderlecht), Ilyes, Bratu (Rapid Bucureşti), Leko, Husev (FC Dynamo Kyiv), Galásek, Sneijder, Van Der Vaart (AFC Ajax), Juanfran, Luccin, Milosevic, Vagner (RC Celta de Vigo), Khokhlov, Buznikin, Parks, Izmailov, Maminov (FC Lokomotiv Moskva), Arteta, Arveladze, Emerson, Mols (Glasgow Rangers FC), Gluscevic, Zelenka, Kincl, Jun (AC Sparta Praha), Johnson, Huth, Gallas, Mutu, Duff, Grønkjær (Chelsea FC), Katsouranis, Lyberopoulos, Tsartas (AEK FC Athina), Solano (Newcastle United FC), Sytchev, Van Buyten, Marlet (Olympique de Marseille), Verheyen, Sæternes (Club Brugge KV), Ceh, Ewerthon (BV Borussia Dortmund), Simão (Sport Lisboa e Benfica), Elber, Santa Cruz (FC Bayern München), Elber (Olympique Lyonnais), Cruz, Van Der Meyde, Martins, Recoba (FC Internazionale), Cole, Reyes (Arsenal FC), Sergio, Scaloni, Héctor, Fran (RC Deportivo La Coruña), Lucius, Vennegoor Of Hesselink (PSV Eindhoven), Rothen, Plasil, Squillaci, Nonda, Ibarra (AS Monaco), Cihan, Hasan Sas, César Prates, Sabri (Galatasaray SK), Ferrara, Miccoli, Maresca, Zalayeta (Juventus FC), Alonso, de Pedro, Gabilondo, Schürrer, De Paula (Real Sociedad), Mavrogenidis, Giovanni (Olympiakos), Silvestre, Solskjær, Butt, Djemba-Djemba, P. Neville, Giggs, Scholes (Manchester United), Nerlinger, Soldo, Hinkel, Wenzel (VfB Stuttgart), Konstantinidis, Zutautas, Basinas (Panathinaikos FC), Ricardo Carvalho, Carlos Alberto (FC Porto), Beckham (Real Madrid CF), Stam, Muzzi, Corradi, Mihajlovic, César (SS Lazio), Ronaldo Guiaro (Beşiktaş JK), Gattuso, Pirlo (AC Milan)

Own goals: Gvildys (FBK Kaunas) for Celtic FC, Chetcuti (Sliema Wanderers FC) for FC København, Drahno (MSK Zilina) for Chelsea FC, Castillo (Grasshopper-Club Zürich) for AEK FC Athina, Tudor (Juventus FC) for Real Sociedad, Fyssas (Panathinaikos FC) for VfB Stuttgart, Juanfran (RC Celta de Vigo) for Club Brugge KV, Schürrer (Real Sociedad) for Olympique Lyonnais, Fernando Meira (VfB Stuttgart) for Chelsea FC